OXFORD HISTORY OF
EARLY MODERN EUROPE

General Editor: R. J. W. Evans

The Dutch Republic

THE
DUTCH REPUBLIC

Its Rise, Greatness, and Fall
1477–1806

❖

Jonathan Israel

CLARENDON PRESS · OXFORD

OXFORD
UNIVERSITY PRESS

Great Clarendon Street, Oxford OX2 6DP

Oxford University Press is a department of the University of Oxford.
It furthers the University's objective of excellence in research, scholarship,
and education by publishing worldwide in

Oxford New York

Auckland Bangkok Buenos Aires
Cape Town Chennai Dar es Salaam Delhi Hong Kong Istanbul
Karachi Kolkata Kuala Lumpur Madrid Melbourne Mexico City Mumbai
Nairobi São Paulo Shanghai Taipei Tokyo Toronto

Oxford is a registered trade mark of Oxford University Press
in the UK and in certain other countries

Published in the United States
by Oxford University Press Inc., New York

First published 1995
Reprinted 1996, 1997
Paperback with corrections 1998

British Library Cataloguing in Publication Data

Data available

Library of Congress Cataloging in Publication Data

Data applied for

ISBN 0-19-873072-1 (hb)
ISBN 0-19-820734-4 (pb)

7 9 10 8 6

Printed in Great Britain
on acid-free paper by
The Bath Press, Bath

PREFACE

AT the outset of such a large work it seems appropriate to provide a few words of explanation of the approach employed and the interpretative framework.

My aim has been to set the Dutch Revolt and the Golden Age in their wider context, which means the whole of the early modern period. As I have laboured on this work I have more and more become convinced that both the Revolt, and the Golden Age, only begin to make sense if we place them in their full setting. This means going back to the Burgundian period, on the one hand, and forward to Napoleonic times, on the other. The Union of Utrecht of 1579, the founding contract of the United Provinces, as the Dutch Republic was officially called between 1579 and 1795, is often seen as an abrupt break with the past; it assumes a quite different significance, however, when looked at against the backcloth of the fourteenth and fifteenth centuries.

One of the main interpretative problems one encounters on approaching a task such as this is that of how to present the relationship between the northern Netherlands, roughly the area which developed into the modern kingdom of the Netherlands, and the south, roughly the area which later became modern Belgium and Luxemburg. When I began writing, back in 1982, I was as convinced as any colleague that, before the Revolt, there was no meaningful separation of north and south in the Low Countries, that there was just one Habsburg Netherlands in which the then seventeen provinces (despite wide differences between them) were more or less united under the rule of the Habsburg court in Brussels. It seemed clear that the centre of political, economic, and cultural gravity lay in the south and that the north was in many ways an appendage and subsidiary of the south. Looked at in this light, the separation of north and south which resulted from the Revolt of 1572, and which was confirmed by the events of 1579–85, appeared to be an artificial, unnatural rupture which had no basis in previous history. Pieter Geyl, the first historian to see clearly that there was no such thing as a 'specifically Northern consciousness', or Dutch national awareness, separate from that of the south, before the Revolt, was incontestably right on that point, but seemed to be correct also in the further conclusion he drew—that the outcome of the Revolt was an accident, with no roots in the past, which destroyed a greater unity. It would, I think, be fair to say that the conviction of a greater Netherlands entity, artificially torn asunder in the 1570s, subsequently developed into a firm consensus. But, as I worked on, I came to believe that only the first part of Geyl's revisionism is correct. There was certainly no 'Dutch', or specifically north Netherlands identity before 1572, nor any specifically southern Netherlands awareness. Indeed, it is questionable whether either of these existed in any meaningful sense before the late eighteenth century. Yet, despite this, political, economic, and geographical factors had rendered north and south separate entities long before the great 'Revolt of 1572'. Seen against the backcloth of the later Middle Ages, and early sixteenth century, there is an important sense in which 1572, and the final separation of north and south, merely completed—were the logical outgrowth of—a duality which had, in reality, existed for centuries.

During most of the history of the United Provinces, allegiance and identity were based on provincial, civic, and sometimes also local rural sentiment rather than attachment to the Republic as a whole. In this respect, the loose federal structure which evolved was well suited to the disposition, and attitudes, of its population. In particular, politics frequently revolved around the tension between the dominant province of Holland, and the rest of the provinces, which continually strove to protect their local interests and avoid being dominated. But, to my mind, it is precisely this tension which also for centuries before the Revolt formed the framework of politics north of the Scheldt estuary and the Maas.

But if north and south formed two largely separate arenas politically and economically before, as well as after, 1572, it is true that in religion, ideas, art, and to a large extent (as far as the Dutch-speaking southern provinces of Flanders, Brabant, and Limburg are concerned) also in language and literature, they formed, before the Revolt, one single culture. In this respect, the Revolt did constitute an unprecedented and decisive break. By introducing a Calvinist Reformation in the north whilst, in the south, the Catholic Counter-Reformation triumphed, the Revolt severed what had been one culture and replaced it with two warring, antagonistic cultures. In this respect, the Revolt can be said to have widened, and reinforced, a duality which had long existed in politics and economic life.

My subject is the Dutch Republic. But I have not wanted to adopt a narrow approach either chronologically or geographically. To understand the Republic, and appreciate the full significance of its achievements in art, science, and intellectual life, as well as commerce, shipping, social welfare, and technology, it is, I would argue, not only necessary to begin the story long before 1572 (as well as glance at the Batavian Republic which replaced it in the years 1795–1806) but also to employ a wider frame than that merely of the north Netherlands. While focusing primarily on the north, I have tried to elucidate the relationship between north and south, bringing out the contrasts, and similarities, so that even though the south receives less attention, it remains an integral part of the picture. But besides this, I have taken the view that there was no hard and fast boundary between the Netherlands and Germany until the eighteenth century and that the over-lapping of jurisdictions, disputes over border areas, and above all the religious and cultural interaction between the Netherlands and adjoining German states forms both an integral, and highly significant, part of the story which is all too often neglected. I have therefore not only made frequent mention of East Friesland, Bentheim, Lingen, the Münsterland, Geldern, Mark, and Jülich-Cleves but have sought to encompass these areas to some extent within the general purview of the work.

Finally, I should perhaps explain that I have been intentionally very brief in my account of the last part of the eighteenth century. It was not, of course, feasible to end in 1780, the point at which E. H. Kossmann's *The Low Countries, 1780–1940* (Oxford, 1978) begins. For then the reader would have been left in mid-air without any notion as to how the story ended. But neither did it seem necessary or desirable to enter into an extensive discussion of the final years of the Republic comparable to the treatment I have given to the rest of the story. Consequently, my only objective in the final two chapters of this work has been to provide a concise denouement for the themes developed in the main body of the book.

ACKNOWLEDGEMENTS

IN writing a hefty volume such as this, covering such a large span of history, one is likely to accumulate a great many debts and certainly I have, both of the sort which are strictly academic and those which come under the heading of 'support and encouragement'. The former include the testing, in discussion, of ideas and approaches, as well as assistance with bibliographical queries, elusive information, and much else. Particularly extensive have been the suggestions and help of the late K. W. Swart, Richard H. Popkin, Jan de Vries, Simon Groenveld, Henk (H. K. F.) van Nierop, Wijnand Mijnhardt, Ernestine van der Wall, Jan van den Berg, H. P. H. Nusteling, Alastair Duke, and Graham Gibbs. But much the largest academic debt is that which I owe to the general editor of the series, Robert Evans, whose masterly grasp, and wonderfully scholarly eye, have provided me with acres of the best constructive criticism and improved the shape of many parts of the book. As regards more general assistance, I would, first of all, like to thank my family not least for having put up, with the best grace possible, with my having been for so long preoccupied with this task. Indeed I would like Danny and Naomi to regard the book as partly theirs. Others whose assistance with particular aspects is much appreciated are Robert Oresko, Christopher Brown, Saskia Lepelaar, and Elizabeth Edwards.

I would also like to take the opportunity to express my gratitude to the British Academy and Twenty-Seven Foundation for providing research grants which greatly assisted my work in Dutch archives and libraries and, above all, among institutions, to the Netherlands Institute for Advanced Study in the Humanities and Social Sciences (NIAS), at Wassenaar, where I was fortunate enough to spend the academic year 1991–2 and which provides the most ideal circumstances imaginable for a scholar in the humanities to bring a large work to fruition.

Finally, for providing many of the illustrations, I would like to thank the Prentenkabinet of the University of Leiden, the Rijksmuseum Het Catharijneconvent in Utrecht, the University of Amsterdam Library, and also Fred Bachrach.

CONTENTS

LIST OF PLATES

(Between pp. 562–563)

EXPLANATORY NOTES TO THE PLATES

PLATE 1.   Charles V combats heresy. A woodcut published at Antwerp in 1531 representing the Emperor Charles V kneeling, holding the Imperial orb in his left hand and with his crown and sceptre on the ground before him. The arm of the Almighty presents him with the sword with which to combat heresy, surrounded by words from 2 Maccabees 15. Charles responds with the words 'Lord Give me prowess against your enemies.'

PLATE 2.   *The Ship of the Church*, an anonymous Dutch painting (late 16th or early 17th century), satirizing the many heretical doctrines abounding in the Netherlands. In the water, wielding swords, are, on the left, a bald Luther and, to the right, Jan Hus and Arius. Between Luther and Hus, without a sword, is Menno Simons.

PLATE 3.   The iconoclastic fury in Antwerp, on 20 August 1566, continued after dark by torchlight. Engraving by Frans Hogenberg, executed in 1583. The images in the city's churches were systematically destroyed.

PLATE 4.   *The Lamentation of the Devastated Netherlands*, engraving by Hendrik Collaert, *c.*1570. The print shows the Dutch Maid seated before a ruined edifice with four rapacious Spanish soldiers tearing out her heart. The proceedings are presided over by *Ambitio*, to the left, and *Avaritia*, to the right. Above, *Invidia* and *Dissidentia* are pulling the Netherlands provinces apart while *Fiducia* (trust in God) holds together the cord on which hang the coats of arms of the seventeen provinces.

PLATE 5.   The Revolt as religious strife. Print published by Coornhert in 1573, presenting *Seditio* (the Revolt) as division of the body politic against itself. On the left, the Revolt drives out monks and priests. On the right, the Revolt provokes iconoclastic attacks on images.

PLATE 6.   Hendrik Goltzius' masterly engraving of 1581 portrayed the prematurely ageing William the Silent at the age of 48, almost certainly from life, and was the source for many subsequent engravings. It shows the Prince in armour, gripping a staff of command against his side. The chain and emblem of the Order of the Golden Fleece, seen in the earlier portraits, has now been removed. The oval portrait is surrounded by an elaborate allegorical framework representing scenes of Moses leading the Children of Israel in the wilderness— the pillars of Fire and Smoke which guided them by night and day and Moses receiving the tablets of stone bearing the Ten Commandments. The implication is that, through the Prince, the Almighty has guided the new Israelites, the Dutch people, through a new wilderness, that of Spanish and papal oppression.

PLATE 7.   The Dutch defensive Ring. The town of Sluis, in States Flanders, was one of the most strategic of the heavily fortified garrison towns at the south-western end of the defensive Ring. This engraving, from Nicolaus Visscher, *Speculum Zelandiae* (Amsterdam, 1662), was executed about 1655.

PLATE 8.   The arms of the States and cities of Zeeland (1604). Last of the series of tapestries, commissioned by the States of Zeeland between 1591 and 1604, this splendid tapestry, woven to a design by Karel van Mander, has at its centre the arms of Zeeland with the motto *Luctor et Emergo* (I struggle and rise up), first adopted in 1586. The arms are flanked by Neptune and Mars, indicating that the struggle was in large part by sea. Above the arms is a count's crown surmounted by a portrait of William the Silent with his own arms to his right. The border is decorated with the civic coats of arms of Middelburg (golden tower), Goes (silver goose against black background), Flushing (silver flask, alluding to St Willibrord's flask), Veere (two towers with a ship between), Tholen (hull with a mast flasked by lions), and Zierikzee (black lion against red background). The tapestries were hung in the former Abbey of Middelburg which, after the Revolt, served as the home of the States of Zeeland.

PLATE 9.   *Vreemden handel* (Strange Business), an anti-Oldenbarnevelt print of 1614. The dragon represents Spain trampling on Wesel and other German Calvinist cities bordering the Netherlands, assisted by two creatures to the right, standing for gullibility and wilful neglect. The tower with water pouring out (a play on Aquisgranum) represents Aachen. The Dutch Lion meanwhile, with seven arrows for the seven provinces on its shield, arises in arms to deal with the dragon, directed by Prince Maurits, who is labelled 'Loyal Sentry'. In the background, the Dutch Maid, in her garden, has been tricked by a monk, offering a peace palm while endeavouring to trap her in his net.

PLATE 10.   *The Power of Peace* (1609). Engraving proclaiming the wisdom and benefits of the Truce, depicting all manner of weaponry being smelted into implements of crafts and agriculture. 'Violence' is chained to the furnace which he is obliged to help operate. The rendering is eloquent but also remarkably non-partisan, avoiding all reference to Spain or the 'rebels', to Catholicism or Protestantism. Only the discreet escutcheon on the furnace indicates that the engraving was produced in the south, presumably Antwerp.

PLATE 11.   Print showing various incidents at the 'Arminian Redoubt', the barricaded area in front of the Leiden town hall, notably the disturbances of 3 October 1617, with (in the background) *waardgelders* attempting to disperse the demonstrators and being pelted with stones. In the foreground is carried the coffin of the demonstrator killed in the riot. In June 1618, the barricades were strengthened, the iron spikes, added then, being dubbed by the people 'Olden-barnevelt's teeth'. Though the *waardgelders* wore the red and white colours of the city, the protesters insisted these were 'Spanish' colours.

PLATE 12. Maurits's military occupation of the city of Utrecht and the disbandment of the *waardgelders* on 31 July 1618.

PLATE 13. The opening of the National Synod of Dordrecht in November 1618. The 'president', Johannes Bogerman, sits with the secretaries at the small table immediately in front of the fireplace. The foreign colleges, with the symbolic empty bench for the absent Huguenots, are seated to the right, the Dutch colleges to the left and in front. Episcopius and the Remonstrant participants are seated at the table in the middle.

PLATE 14. The residence built in the 1630s by Frederik Hendrik at Rijswijk (also known as the Huis ter Nieuwburg), close to The Hague, was intended especially for official and state receptions. William III continued this tradition when he assigned it as the venue for the Rijswijk peace negotiations of 1697. The gardens, yielding a view of The Hague in the distance, were among the finest laid out by Frederik Hendrik. House and gardens formed an integrated, symmetrical whole, reflecting the strong French influence. Nothing remains of either residence or gardens today.

PLATE 15. The inauguration of the new university of the rebel state, at Leiden, on 8 February 1575, was nominally held in the name of Philip II, but in fact all allusion to the Spanish Crown and Habsburg dynasty was absent from the published representation. The two banners held aloft show the Netherlands Lion and arms of Leiden (crossed keys). Similarly, the Church is represented only by Holy Scripture sitting on a triumphal car being drawn by the Four Evangelists. The festive boat on Rapenburg Canal contains Neptune, Apollo, and the Nine Muses. Significant also are the personifications of academic disciplines and great writers in the procession, Theology, Law, and Medicine being followed by Aristotle, Plato, Cicero, and Virgil.

PLATE 16. Allegory by Govaert Flinck representing the birth of William III and renewal of the House of Orange in 1650. The infant is flanked by the goddesses Juno (crowned) and Pallas (in armour). The angels hold aloft his coat of arms and one of them also a phoenix rising from the ashes, alluding to the premature death of William II. In the background are represented the government buildings at the centre of The Hague.

PLATE 17. The title-page of a book on Dutch shipbuilding published at Amsterdam in 1697.

PLATE 18. *Only in a Republic are True Peace and Happiness to be Experienced* (1669). Dutch Republican ideology. The engraving shows the four columns on which the vitality and prosperity of Holland rest: Industry, Fisheries, Shipping, and Trade adorned with various republican slogans such as 'Pax optima rerum'. Beneath are the States of Holland in session. The engraving was used as the frontispiece for Pieter de la Court's *Aanwysing* of 1669, a strongly republican book banned by the States of Holland for criticizing the Reformed Church and advocating general religious freedom.

PLATE 19. *The Great Assembly at The Hague* (1651). The States General of the United Provinces meeting in the Great Assembly of 1651. Above are the coats of arms of the Seven Provinces grouped around the Netherlands Lion holding the Liberty Hat aloft. This engraving was used as the frontispiece to Lieuwe van Aitzema's *Herstelde Leeuw* (The Hague, 1652), a detailed account of the proceedings of the Great Assembly which was banned by the Hof of Holland in April 1652.

PLATE 20. The Battle of Portland Bill (February 1653). One of the heavy Dutch defeats of that year. The Dutch fleet is shown in the foreground, the English to the rear. Tromp's flagship is marked 'A', De Ruyter's vessel is marked 'D'. On the horizon to the left is Calais, to the right, Dover and Margate.

PLATE 21. *Pax Una Triumphis Innumeris Potior*. Print of 1667 representing the peace of Breda. The figures shaking hands, marked 2 and 3, stand for England and the Republic. They are flanked by four maidens with coats of arms representing France, Sweden, Denmark, and East Friesland. In the top right-hand corner, Neptune and Mercury, followed by seamen and fishermen, prepare to resume business. To the right the plenipotentiaries swear to uphold the treaty. The burning of pitch barrels to celebrate the conclusion of the peace was ordered by the States General.

PLATE 22. The Republican Triumph of Cornelis de Witt (1670). Print derived from the painting by Jan de Baen, hung in the Justice Chamber of Dordrecht town hall in 1670 and destroyed in 1672, depicting the raid on Chatham in 1667. It shows Cornelis de Witt dressed in official robes over armour, with English warships burning in the background. Beside De Witt is *Victoria* pouring forth the Horn of Plenty, symbolizing the fruits of trade and industry. Above are the arms of Dordrecht, below the arms of the De Witt family flanked by cherubs holding Liberty Hats on poles.

PLATE 23. *A Night-Scene in which is Shown a Pressed Cow*. A political print of 1672 accusing the brothers De Witt of subverting the Fatherland and colluding with the French. The print shows the Dutch Cow caught in a press being operated by two evil spirits representing Johan and Cornelis de Witt. Meanwhile, a cock (France), perched on the press, tears the Cow's side open, assisting the press to squeeze money out of the Cow. In the foreground on the left are a merchant and peasant weeping in despair. To the right is the Dutch

Lion holding an orange, representing the Orange party-faction preparing to drive the evil spirits away.

PLATE 24. This print, published in July 1672, one of the first proclaiming William III Stadholder, well illustrates the techniques of political representation in the Dutch Golden Age. The engraving is basically that used to present a portrait bust of Prince Maurits in 1624, which was used again, to present the bust of Frederik Hendrik, in 1628. In each case, the portrait of the Stadholder is flanked by *Religio* and *Libertas*, the latter holding aloft the pole with a Liberty Hat. The text beneath stresses William III's virtues, insisting that it is the Almighty who has raised him to the stadholderate. Beneath him are the figures of *Prudentia, Victoria, Politia*, and *Negotiatio*, flanked by Neptune. These, as well as the curious figures of American Indians and Asians, appear in all three prints. Above the Stadholder's head is a wreath with the coats of arms of the Seven Provinces with Holland, Zeeland, and Utrecht to the left, Groningen, Overijssel, and Friesland to the right, and Gelderland in pride of place above. Below are the arms of William III (compare with those shown in Flinck's allegory of 1650 in Plate 16).

PLATE 25. *Utrecht Restored*, engraving by Romeyn de Hooghe of 1674 representing the readmittance of the province of Utrecht to the Union. In the foreground is the Dutch Lion bearing the coat of arms of the province surrounded by those of the five voting towns—Utrecht (first on the left), Amersfoort, Rhenen, Wijk-bij-Duurstede, and Montfoort. Above the Lion, the province is depicted as a maid while the Generality, an armed warrior bearing the coats of arms of the four fighting provinces, takes her hand. Behind them stands Unity, her foot on a stone which is the Union, adding a fifth shaft (Utrecht) to the four already in her left hand. William III looks down from his triumphal car while to the left sits True Religion, with the States Bible in her hand, over the debris of the Catholic Church. Above her, the arms of Orange are being hoisted over Utrecht.

PLATE 26. Print showing the Amsterdam militia drawn up on parade on the Dam, in the centre of the city, in front of the Town Hall, in 1686. Note how the Town Hall, built in the 1650s to designs by Jacob van Campen, visually dominated the city centre, including the New Church (where the De Ruyter tomb was, and is, housed) behind it. Above are the arms of Amsterdam.

PLATE 27. William III, the States General, and their allies thwart Louis XIV. A Dutch print depicting the situation of Europe in 1689, immediately after the Glorious Revolution. It suggests that Louis XIV and James II are fighting a godless war 'tegens God ist quaat te vegten'. James gives a nervous hand to Louis (who is engrossed in fighting Leopold, for domination of the Empire), attempting to draw his attention to William III, and the Dutch army and fleet, who, having secured England, are turning towards the Continent. William remarks, 'nunc est delenda Carthago'. To the right is Father Edward Petre holding the infant James (the Old Pretender), while a monk reassures Mary of Modena who reclines with her breasts exposed, alluding to her allegedly having prostituted herself (at the instigation of the Catholic Church) to produce an heir to the British thrones.

PLATE 28. *The Chief Occurrences of the Year 1692.* A symbolic representation of the episodes of war by land and sea in 1692, engraved by Jan van Vianen. Most emphasized are the Anglo-Dutch victory over the French at sea, at La Hogue, in May, and the hard-fought, inconclusive battle of Steenkerken, between Brussels and Mons, at which Marshal Luxembourg repulsed the attack of the allied army commanded by William III in person.

PLATE 29. Print by Petrus Schenk showing the VOC storehouse (built 1660) and wharves at Amsterdam at the beginning of the eighteenth century.

PLATE 30. *William IV, Prince of Orange, Rescues the Dutch Maid.* A political print of the spring of 1747, showing the Dutch Maid in her Garden seriously under threat from without, being defended by a distracted Dutch Lion. She turns to Pallas (William IV), defender of her Freedom and Religion, bearing in her right hand the Liberty banner, proclaiming that Pallas will right grievances and repel the oppressor. Behind Pallas are banners proclaiming 'Vivat Oranje!' In front of the Maid stands an altar with a States Bible on it, flanked by a column of cloud representing the true doctrine of the Trinity which is being threatened in vain by the Dragon of false doctrine. The Cock represents the French attempting to break their way in. In the background, the French bombard Sluis.

PLATE 31. An engraving depicting the rioting in Amsterdam in June 1748, featuring the sacking of a wine merchant's house on the Singel. Note the quantity of fine furniture hurled into the canal.

PLATE 32. Stadholder William V being welcomed by the States of Zeeland on 29 June 1786. Engraving by M. D. Sallieth of 1787 from *Zelandia Illustrata*, iii. 256.

LIST OF MAPS

LIST OF TABLES

ABBREVIATIONS

AAG *Bijdragen*	*Bijdragen* of the Afdeling Agrarische Geschiedenis of the Landbouwuniversiteit at Wageningen
AGKN	*Archief voor de Geschiedenis van de Katholieke kerk in Nederland*
AGS	Archivo General de Simancas, Valladolid
AHN	Archivo Histórico Nacional, Madrid
ARB SEG	Archives Générales du Royaume, Brussels, section 'Secrétairerie d'État et de Guerre'
arch.	archives
ARH	Algemeen Rijksarchief, The Hague
ARH PR	Algemeen Rijksarchief, The Hague, section 'Provincial Resolutions' in the archives of the States General
ARH SG	Algemeen Rijksarchief, The Hague, archives of the States General
ARH SH	Algemeen Rijksarchief, The Hague, archives of the States of Holland
ARH WIC	Algemeen Rijksarchief, The Hague, archives of the West India Company
BGN	*Bijdragen voor de geschiedenis der Nederlanden*
BL MS	British Library, London, department of manuscripts
BMGN	*Bijdragen en mededelingen betreffende de geschiedenis der Nederlanden*
BMHG	*Bijdragen en mededelingen van het Historisch Genootschap gevestigt te Utrecht*
BN	*Britain and the Netherlands*
BOX MS Rawl.	Bodleian Library, Oxford, Rawlinson Papers
BRB	Bibliothèque Royale, Brussels, section des manuscrits
BVGO	*Bijdragen voor vaderlandsche geschiedenis en oudheidkunde*
Cal. St. Papers	Calendar of State Papers
CODOIN	*Colección de documentos inéditos para la historia de España*
EHJ	*Economisch-Historisch Jaarboek*
GA Amsterdam	Amsterdam City Archives

GA Amsterdam PJG	Amsterdam City Archives, archives of the Portuguese Jewish Community
GA Breda	Breda City Archives
GA Delft	Delft City Archives
GA Dordrecht	Dordrecht City Archives
GA Gouda	Gouda City Archives
GA Groningen	Groningen City Archives
GA Haarlem	Haarlem City Archives
GA Kampen	Kampen City Archives
GA Leiden Sec. Arch.	Leiden City Archives, archives of the Secrétairerie
GA Nijmegen	Nijmegen City Archives
GA Rotterdam	Rotterdam City Archives
GA Utrecht	Utrecht City Archives
GA Zutphen	Zutphen City Archives
Gesch.	Geschiedenis (history)
JGA	*Jaarboek van het Genootschap Amstelodamum*
KBH	Koninklijke Bibliotheek, The Hague
Kn.	W. P. C. Knuttel, *Catalogus van de Pamfletten-verzameling berustende in de Koninklijke Bibliotheek*
KHG	*Kroniek van het Historisch Genootschap te Utrecht*
leg.	legajo (bundle)
LIAS	*LIAS: Sources and Documents relating to the Early Modern History of Ideas*
NAK	*Nederlands Archief voor kerkgeschiedenis*
NAGN	*(Nieuw) Algemene Geschiedenis der Nederlanden* (15 vols.; Haarlem, 1977–83)
NHB	*Nederlandse Historische Bronnen*
PER	*Parliaments, Estates and Representation*
PRO SP	Public Record Office, London, State Papers
RAF M	Rijksarchief in Friesland, Leeuwarden, archives of the Mindergetal
RAF SF	Rijksarchief in Friesland, Leeuwarden, archives of the States of Friesland
RAF stadhoud. arch.	Rijksarchief in Friesland, archives of the Frisian Stadholders
RAGr SGr	Rijksarchief in Groningen, archives of the States of Groningen (Stad en Lande)
RAU SU	Rijksarchief in Utrecht, archives of the States of Utrecht
RAZ SZ	Rijksarchief in Zeeland, Middelburg, archives of the States of Zeeland
res.	resolution

Res. Holl.	Resolutions of the States of Holland, especially as recorded in *Resolutien van de Staten van Holland* (289 vols.; Amsterdam, 1789–1814)
RvS	Raad van State
sec. res.	secret resolution
SF	States of Friesland
SG	States General
S.Geld.	States of Gelderland
S.Gr.	States of Groningen (Stad en Lande)
SH	States of Holland
SO	States of Overijssel
SU	States of Utrecht
SZ	States of Zeeland
TvG	*Tijdschrift voor Geschiedenis*
TvSG	*Tijdschrift voor Sociale Geschiedenis*
VOC	Verenigde Oostindische Compagnie (United East India Company)
vroed.	vroedschap
WHG	*Werken van het Historisch Genootschap te Utrecht*
WIC	Westindische Compagnie (West India Company)

1

Introduction

❖

What has aptly been called the 'New World of the Dutch Republic'[1] made a deep impression on both Europeans and non-European peoples during the seventeenth and eighteenth centuries, whether they came in contact with this other 'New World' at first hand or indirectly through its shipping and trade, or prints and books. It was a society, and culture, which regularly fascinated contemporary diplomats, scholars, merchants, churchmen, soldiers, tourists, sailors, and connoisseurs of art from many lands and which retains today a special significance in the history of modern western civilization. Early modern observers were especially struck by the innumerable 'novelties' and innovations which one encountered there in virtually every field of activity. Visitors continually marvelled at the prodigious extent of Dutch shipping and commerce, the technical sophistication of industry and finance, the beauty and orderliness, as well as cleanliness, of the cities, the degree of religious and intellectual toleration to be found there, the excellence of the orphanages and hospitals, the limited character of ecclesiastical power, the subordination of military to civilian authority, and the remarkable achievements of Dutch art, philosophy, and science.

Needless to say, the wonder foreigners expressed was rarely unmixed with criticism, resentment, disdain, and sometimes outright hostility. Numerous features of Dutch society under the Republic seemed aberrant or abhorrent to outsiders. Until the late seventeenth century many were appalled by the diversity of churches which the authorities permitted and the relative freedom with which religious and intellectual issues were discussed. Others disapproved of the excessive liberty, as it seemed to them, accorded to specific groups, especially women, servants, and Jews, who were invariably confined, in other European countries, to a lowlier, more restricted existence. Foreign noblemen were apt to scoff at the bourgeois flavour of Dutch life and politics and the lack of a proper social hierarchy. Many a foreign

---

[1] Swart, *Miracle*, 3.

gentleman travelling on the Dutch passenger barges—a routine conveyance found nowhere else in seventeenth-century Europe—was disconcerted to find the most ordinary folk casually engaging him in conversation as if he were just anyone, without the least regard for his rank.[2] A German observer noted, in 1694, that servant girls in Holland behaved and dressed so much like their mistresses that it was hard to tell which was which.[3] The United Provinces—to give the Republic its official name—were widely perceived in Europe as a seedbed of theological, intellectual, and social promiscuity which subverted the usual, and proper, relations between men and women, Christians and non-Christians, masters and servants, nobles and non-nobles, soldiers and civilians, perversely refusing to accord the noble, the soldier, and even the husband the honour and status which were their due. Meanwhile, the political institutions of the Republic, according to most foreign observers, were worthier of contempt than admiration.

Consequently, it was practically never the integrated reality of the 'New World' of the Dutch Republic which outsiders wished to emulate. As a rule, far more interest was shown in adopting this or that innovation from among the profusion of novelties in every field. Those eager for economic success studied Dutch methods of commerce and finance and borrowed much that they found. From the 1590s down to around 1740, for roughly a century and a half, the Republic exercised a general primacy in world shipping and trade and was the central reservoir of goods of every conceivable type. It was the central storehouse not only of commodities from all parts of the globe but also of information about them, techniques for storing and processing them, methods for classifying and testing them, and ways of advertising and negotiating them. During the seventeenth century, even the greatest enemies of Dutch commercial prosperity, such as Louis XIV's minister, Colbert, or the English ambassador, Sir George Downing—after whom Downing Street is named—assiduously imitated Dutch methods and sought to attract Dutch skills. Inseparably entwined with Dutch primacy in world trade, the Republic, from the end of the sixteenth down to the early eighteenth century, was also the technological leader of Europe and many visitors—among them Peter the Great of Russia, who visited Holland in 1697–8 and again in 1716–17—concentrated on the technical inventions, from new practices in shipbuilding to improved sluices, harbour cranes, timber-saws, textile looms, windmills, clocks, and street lamps.[4] Relatively few foreigners showed interest in agricultural innovation. But those who did

[2] De Vries, *Barges and Capitalism*, 114–16.
[3] Benthem, *Holländischer Kirch- und Schulen-Staat*, i. 9.
[4] Davids, 'Technische ontwikkeling', 13–17.

encountered much in Dutch drainage, horticulture, fodder crops, and methods of soil replenishment which could, with profit, be applied elsewhere. A large part of the agricultural revolution in England, in the eighteenth century, was based on techniques and innovations borrowed from the United Provinces. Other observers were struck by the orderliness of Dutch civic life, the effectiveness of the welfare system, prisons, and penal practice, and the remarkably low levels of crime which characterized Dutch society. Military men took a keen interest, especially in the period down to 1648, in the military revolution carried through in the United Provinces, since the 1590s, by the Stadholders Maurits and Frederik Hendrik, a revolution characterized not only by innovations in artillery, tactics, fortification, siege techniques, and military transportation, but by a vast improvement in the discipline and orderliness of the military. Together, the north and south Netherlands were the principal school of warfare of both Protestant and Catholic Europe from the 1580s down to the middle of the seventeenth century and were again one of the main schools of warfare, for Europe, from 1672 down to 1713, a period in which the Low Countries were the strategic hub of the great struggle between Louis XIV and the European coalition ranged against him. Finally, there was a constant stream of visitors more inclined to scholarly and artistic pursuits—among them several of the greatest philosophers of early modern times, Descartes, Locke, and Bayle—who were attracted by the abundance of libraries, scientific collections, and publishers in the United Provinces and, above all, the intellectual and religious freedom to be found there. There was no other country, averred Descartes, 'où l'on puisse jouir d'une liberté si entière'.[5]

During the seventeenth and eighteenth centuries, outsiders thought of the Republic as giving its citizens, and foreign residents, greater 'freedom' than other European societies of the time and it is true that the politics and culture of the Golden Age laid a special stress on 'freedom'. Thus, the only one of the many plays of Vondel, the greatest writer of the Dutch Golden Age, to deal with a specifically Dutch theme—his *Batavische Gebroeders* (1663)—dramatizes the struggle of the ancient Batavians (whom the seventeenth-century Dutch regarded as their ancestors) to win their 'freedom' from the Romans.[6] 'The inhabitants', asserted the same German writer who commented on the servant girls, 'love nothing so much as they do their freedom.'[7] This celebrated 'freedom' of the Dutch Republic was based on freedom of conscience. But as the English ambassador Sir William Temple

---

[5] Quoted in Cohen, *Séjour de Saint-Évremond*, 2.
[6] Smit, *Van Pascha tot Noah*, iii. 233–77.
[7] Bientjes, *Holland und die Holländer*, 22.

wrote, around 1672, it extended much further, creating a 'general liberty and ease, not only in point of conscience, but all others that serve to the commodiousness and quiet of life, every man following his own way, minding his own business, and little enquiring into other men's.'[8] The Italian Protestant writer Gregorio Leti, who settled in Amsterdam in 1683, having lived in Italy, Geneva, and England, was delighted with what he found, contrasting the genuine 'freedom' encountered in Holland with the corruption, institutionalized despotism, and lack of respect for the individual, which, in his opinion, characterized the decayed Italian republics of Venice and Genoa.[9]

'Freedom' was adopted by William the Silent and his propagandists as the central justifying principle of the Revolt against Spain. In his manifestos of 1568, explaining his taking up arms against the legitimate ruler of the Netherlands, William referred, on the one hand, to the Spanish king's violation of the 'freedoms and privileges' of the provinces, using 'freedom' in this restricted sense; but he also claimed to be the defender of 'freedom' in the abstract, in the modern sense. He maintained that the people had 'enjoyed freedom in former times' but were now being reduced to 'unbearable slavery' by the king of Spain.[10] After the Revolt, 'freedom' remained a key element in defining the respective positions of the rival ideological blocs. Characteristically, one of the most famous placards published by the States of Holland, under the Republic, the so-called Perpetual Edict, of 1667, suppressing the stadholderate in Holland, justified the step as necessary for safeguarding and advancing *Vryheid* (Freedom).[11] In 1706 Romeyn de Hooghe, one of the great artists of the late seventeenth century, and an active propagandist for William III of Orange, published a two-volume description of the United Provinces styling the Republic the 'freest and safest state' in which to live 'of all those known in the world'.[12]

Yet many of the most creative and innovative geniuses active in the Republic during the Golden Age were disappointed, finding that this celebrated freedom did not, in reality, stretch far enough. Descartes, initially enthusiastic, was by the 1640s worried by its limitations. Spinoza was continually anxious. Ericus Walten, one of the principal seventeenth-century Dutch republican writers, who reverenced 'freedom', and abhorred 'despotism', died in gaol in The Hague under investigation for blasphemy. De Hooghe was obliged to move from Amsterdam to Haarlem to avoid trial

---

[8] Temple, *Observations*, 134.
[9] Leti, *Raguagli politici*, 2, ii. 408–10.
[10] Kossmann and Mellink, *Texts*, 86.
[11] *Perpetual Edict, en Eeuwigh-durende Wet*, p. A2.
[12] De Hooghe, *Spiegel van staat*, i. 57.

for distributing erotic pictures. And, besides these, Grotius, Episcopius, and many other famous men had cause to complain. Yet in the eyes of all of these its comparative freedom was one, if not the most precious, of the amenities and advantages which the Republic offered.

The Republic was indeed, in the context of its time, peculiarly well suited to assist intellect, imagination, and talent, offering the scholar books, the scientist research collections, the artist materials, and the theologian different points of view, with a profusion found nowhere else. The north Netherlands produced, or were the adopted home of, a remarkably large number of the greatest minds and cultural figures of early modern Europe, among them Erasmus, Lipsius, Scaliger, Grotius, Rembrandt, Vondel, Descartes, Huygens, Vermeer, Spinoza, and Bayle. This astounding concentration, in such a small space, not only coincided with, but was linked to, Dutch pre-eminence in commerce, shipping, and finance, as well as in agriculture and technology. Furthermore, none of this could have occurred, or been sustained, had the United Provinces not become one of Europe's military great powers for over a century and one of the world's principal naval powers for longer. All this was accomplished by a society considerably smaller than its main rivals, the Dutch population scarcely touching two million even at the height of the Republic's greatness.

Moments of heightened creativity and achievement in numerous fields, in a single region, are undoubtedly rather rare in history. When they do occur, as with classical Athens or Renaissance Florence, it is often striking that the sustained creativity is confined to a remarkably small geographical space. Also, precisely because of their rarity and creative intensity, such golden ages are not easy to appraise in terms of normal historical criteria. To present a comprehensive picture of the Dutch Golden Age is difficult and, inevitably, much remains elusive. For historians it is thus tempting, indeed usual, to fasten on just one aspect, or another, of Dutch achievement—art, agriculture, or shipping—and then compare developments in that sphere with those elsewhere in Europe and the world. Looking at the whole of such an immensely rich tableau is less usual as well as more arduous. Yet how worthwhile it is to make the effort! For everyone who has appreciated any particular aspect of the Dutch Republic, striving to grasp the total picture unfailingly serves to deepen and enrich perceptions of each and every particular dimension, as well as of the whole.

PART I

The Making of the Republic, 1477–1588

❖

2

On the Threshold of the Modern Era

❖

THE RISE OF HOLLAND

The political, economic, and cultural core of the Dutch Republic after 1572 was the province of Holland, and it is logical that our story should begin with the rise of Holland to prominence in the Low Countries during the thirteenth century. The thirteenth century was indeed a crucial period in the shaping of the Dutch context. Much of the foundation for the later emergence of the north Netherlands in ways which were to astound Europe, and the wider world, was laid at that time. Earlier there had been some primitive construction of dikes and dams to control the movement of water and some digging of drainage channels. But, until around 1200, such work had been on a limited scale and insufficient to allow regular cultivation of the low-lying western regions of the Netherlands. For even much of the area which was not normally under water remained subject to frequent flooding. Twelfth-century Holland, like Zeeland, much of Friesland, Groningen, and Utrecht, and the part of Flanders adjoining the Scheldt estuary, was a waterlogged marshy land, dangerous, thinly populated, and marginal to the life of the Low Countries as a whole. Most agricultural and commercial activity was carried out on the higher ground, safe from flooding, to the south and also to the east. At that time, north of the great rivers, Utrecht, Kampen, Deventer, Zwolle, Nijmegen, and Zutphen were the principal towns. Only after 1200 did construction of dikes and land reclamation proceed systematically and on a large scale throughout the low-lying regions from the Scheldt estuary to the estuary of the Ems. During the thirteenth century, extensive areas were diked, drained, made cultivable, and intensively colonized. From this resulted an internal shift, especially within the northern Netherlands, with the populousness and vitality of the low-lying areas, above all Holland, steadily increasing relative to the higher ground to the south and east.

The building of huge sea-dikes of earth and rubble, commencing in the thirteenth century, however rudimentary in design, was to have vast consequences for the future. For this development marked the onset of a new stage in the epic contest between man and the sea in much of the Netherlands which has continued uninterrupted down to the present day. From the thirteenth century onwards large areas were reclaimed, made productive, and up to a point rendered secure. But the degree of security achieved tended to fluctuate with circumstances. The dikes and embankments required constant maintenance and could readily deteriorate as well as improve, leading intermittently to setbacks and, on occasion, huge catastrophes. Nevertheless, there was a gradual improvement in techniques, and build-up in the pace and capacity of poldering and drainage, culminating in the early part of the Golden Age (1590–1648). This was followed by a marked slackening, and after 1672 stagnation, which persisted until the middle of the eighteenth century. Only after 1850 was the pre-1650 momentum in Dutch drainage and land reclamation resumed.

But even compared with the remarkable advances made in the period between 1590 and 1672, the achievements in drainage and land reclamation of the thirteenth century were imposing. Moreover, that century not only witnessed the start of this vast drama, one of the most impressive of all examples of man's cumulative impact on his physical environment, but was the period in which evolved the institutional and juridical apparatus needed to sustain it. To build and maintain dikes, dams, and drainage channels, and find the necessary resources, local drainage and polder boards arose, which in Holland were called *heemraadschappen*, committees on which villages, towns, and local nobles had their representatives, and which provided a mechanism for co-operation between them. Though they were essentially local and spontaneous in origin, by the early thirteenth century the count of Holland, and neighbouring princes, exerted a growing influence on this emerging, and already vital, framework of dike, drainage, and waterway control, especially by setting up larger regional jurisdictions to oversee the work of the drainage boards, called *hoogheemraadschappen*. These were again 'colleges' of representatives of towns, rural localities, and the nobility but with their procedures fixed by the count and presided over by a *dijkgraaf* (dike count) who, in Zeeland as in Holland, was usually a nominee of the count and often one of his district officials and who then combined his role in dike maintenance and flood control with a wide range of fiscal, policing, and judicial responsibilities.

Holland, Zeeland, and appreciable slices of Utrecht, Flanders, Friesland, and Groningen constituted, by 1300, what was virtually a new country, protected and rendered productive by dikes, dams, polders, and huge river

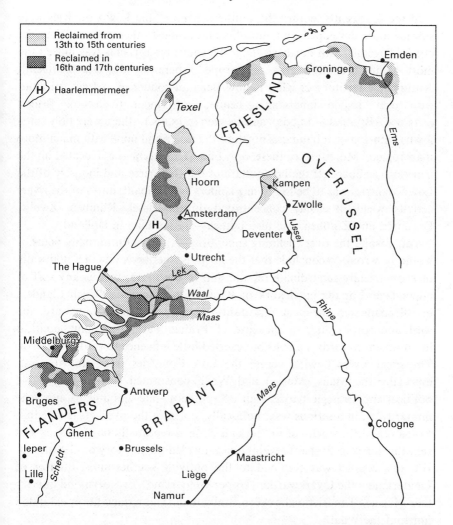

MAP 1. The Low Countries, showing main rivers and areas reclaimed from the sea, river estuaries, and lakes in medieval and early modern times

embankments and providing much greater scope than in the past for settlements, agriculture, navigation, and trade. Furthermore, the shift in population and activity changed the political and cultural balance. Still marginal in 1200, by the 1290s Holland had carved a dominant position for herself amongst the patchwork of small states evolving north of the great rivers and, as a power, was beginning to compare with Flanders and Brabant.

In the fourteenth century the southern parts of the Low Countries were still far more developed economically, and in most other respects, than the north. Together with northern Italy, the south Netherlands was indeed the most highly urbanized area of Europe. Where, by the late fourteenth century, the territory of what is now Belgium contained at least ten cities with over 10,000 inhabitants—headed by Ghent (*c.*60,000), Bruges (*c.*35,000), Brussels (*c.*17,000), and Leuven (*c.*15,000)—there were only three towns with 10,000 inhabitants north of the rivers and none with much more than 10,000.[1] Moreover, of these, only one—Dordrecht—was located on the maritime seaboard. If the lion's share of the commerce and industry of the Low Countries was to be found in Flanders and Brabant, north of the rivers activity was still chiefly concentrated on the IJssel—Kampen, Zwolle, Deventer, and Zutphen, and also Utrecht—rather than in Holland.

Yet, despite the overwhelming superiority of the south in many fields, it would be wrong to conclude that the north Netherlands was in a politically or economically subordinate relationship to the south, or was any sort of appendage. For the patchwork of states in the south—of which Flanders and Brabant were the most important—were chiefly orientated towards the west and south (and, in the case of Brabant, also had some political involvement towards the east) but exerted little influence towards the north. The great rivers flowing across the Low Countries from east to west, especially the Maas (Meuse) and Waal, constituted such a formidable political and strategic barrier that no southern state was able to intervene militarily or, in a serious way, politically, north of the rivers. It is true that Brabant and the duchy of Gelderland clashed repeatedly on the Maas and that the dukes of Brabant several times invaded the territory of Gelderland. But this conflict was confined to the outlying southernmost quarter of Gelderland—the Overkwartier (Upper Gelderland), or Roermond quarter (see Map 4).[2] The friction between Brabant and Gelderland never extended north of the Waal.

The rivers forming an effective barrier, there was little interference from Flanders or Brabant with the efforts of the counts of Holland to achieve a broad hegemony over the complex of principalities in the north. During the later Middle Ages down to the fifteenth century, the Netherlands formed two essentially separate political arenas—as, in many respects, they were to continue to do later. In the north, the small states on the higher ground tried to resist the encroachment of Holland and defend their trade and shipping.

[1] Visser, 'Dichtheid', 16; Van Uytven, 'Oudheid en middeleeuwen', 23; Klep, 'Urban Decline', 266–7.

[2] Jappe Alberts, *Gesch. van de beide Limburgen*, i. 76, 93.

But while there was no lack of antagonism to the Hollanders, these territories and cities were not well placed to oppose Holland's rise. Once protected from the sea and cultivable, the heavy clay soil region to the west was considerably more fertile than the mostly rather poor, sandy soils of the inland areas.[3] Thus, rural population density in the north-east was, and remained, relatively low. Utrecht and the eastern states, for the time being, had most of the main towns but lacked a political framework capable of defending and prolonging the commercial ascendancy of their towns. Politically, all the states to the east and north of Holland were inherently weak. The prince-bishop of Utrecht, unable to control his unruly nobility, or the citizenry of the city, was only sporadically a rival to the count of Holland. From the early fourteenth century onwards he was, at times, reduced to being a virtual protégé of the increasingly ambitious count.

Holland's expansion towards the north began with the successful annexation by Count Floris V (1256–96), in the 1280s, of the area known as West Friesland (see Map 2), thereby acquiring a land bridge reaching towards Friesland proper. Soon Holland began to extend her sway further north and across the Zuider Zee. Assuredly, there were reverses. After repeated attempts to subjugate Friesland, Count William IV was killed fighting the Frisians in 1345. But Holland's efforts resumed and, by the mid-fourteenth century, enjoyed substantial support within Friesland, especially from towns willing to submit for the sake of the more orderly conditions that would result. The Holland towns, and especially Amsterdam, backed their count's policy, anxious to curb the depredations of Frisian pirates against their ships sailing to the north, and, in 1396, helped finance a large expedition which succeeded in conquering most of Friesland and the Ommelands in alliance with the Frisian faction known as the *Vetkopers*. The count of Holland, eager to expand his power and territory, and thwart the then prince-bishop of Utrecht who had designs on Groningen and Drenthe, was also impelled by the potentially disruptive impact of the growing tensions among the Holland nobles. He needed to reunify them and divert their restless energies from the domestic scene, by steering them into external conquest.[4] Temporarily he succeeded. But the anti-Holland faction in Friesland and the Ommelands, the *Schieringers*, fought on and by 1414 Holland, distracted by difficulties elsewhere, had lost her grip over Friesland.

More conclusive was the extension of Holland's sway over Zeeland. As we have seen, Flanders and Brabant exercised little influence north of the rivers. But Zeeland was a special case—culturally and economically as well

[3] De Vries, *Dutch Rural Economy*, 24, 33.
[4] Janse, *Grenzen aan de macht*, 45–53, 88–98, 371.

as politically—wedged between north and south, an intermediary zone long contested by the counts of Holland and Flanders. This struggle commenced in the twelfth century with Flanders initially having the upper hand. But with the growth of Holland's power and resources, in the thirteenth century, the balance shifted.[5] In 1253, Count William II (1234–56) defeated a Flemish army on Walcheren, the principal island of Zeeland, and under the treaty of Brussels (1256) effective control over Zeeland passed to Holland. Nevertheless, the count of Flanders continued to challenge this result until he was defeated by the French and Hollanders in a sea-battle, off Zierikzee, in 1304. Under the treaty of Paris (1323), Count Louis of Flanders surrendered all Flemish claims to the province and recognized the count of Holland as count also of Zeeland. Holland was not yet as strong as Flanders or Brabant. But the struggle for Zeeland showed not just that Holland was unrivalled north of the rivers but that she surpassed Flanders and Brabant along, and between, the rivers. After 1323, the subordination of Zeeland to Holland was never again disputed.

After the Black Death of 1348 most of Europe suffered demographic and economic contraction, and shrinkage of towns, which lasted a century. Although the Low Countries as a whole escaped relatively lightly, the great Flemish and Brabantine cities did decline somewhat in population and activity.[6] Holland and Zeeland, however, uniquely in Europe, experienced a continuous expansion of urban life throughout the long depression elsewhere. Consequently, the balance between, on the one hand, Holland and the rest of the north and, on the other, that between Holland and the principal states in the south, continually shifted in favour of Holland.[7] Where, in 1300, a mere 8,000 people dwelt in townships of over 2,500 in Holland, a total minute compared with the north-east let alone Flanders and Brabant, by 1400, some 42,000 people lived in towns of over 2,500 in Holland. By 1514, some 120,000 people, or 44 per cent of Holland's population, was town-dwelling and the four leading Holland towns had overtaken the chief towns of the north-east except Utrecht, which in the early and mid-sixteenth century was still the largest city in the north Netherlands. It is true that the great cities of the south were still far larger and more important than those of the north. Ghent and Antwerp, in 1500, had populations of over 40,000, and Bruges and Brussels of over 30,000, whereas Holland's four principal towns—Leiden, Amsterdam, Haarlem,

---

[5] Kokken, *Steden en Staten*, 32–3.
[6] Van der Wee, 'Overgang', 18.
[7] Visser, 'Dichtheid', 19–20; Van der Woude, 'Demografische ontwikkeling', 136–7; Van Houtte, *Economische en sociale gesch.* 129–31.

and Delft—were still all in the ten to fifteen thousand range. But in terms of both total population and levels of urbanization, Holland was now heavily preponderant in the north and of growing weight in relation to the south (see Tables 1 and 2).

By the late fifteenth century Flanders and Brabant were still the two most populous and economically developed provinces. But Holland was now unquestionably the third province in order of importance and, while she still had no large cities, she was remarkable also for having a uniquely high percentage of her population living in towns. There were no other Dutch-speaking provinces remotely comparable with Flanders, Brabant, and Holland in importance or population. Of the other provinces of the Low Countries, only the French-speaking province of Artois had a population even half as large as that of Holland (see Table 1).

TABLE 1. *The population of the main provinces of the Low Countries in 1477*

Province	Population			Province Total as % of Netherlands total
	in Total	% rural	% urban	
Flanders	660,000	64	36	26.0
Brabant	413,000	69	31	16.0
Holland	275,000	55	45	10.5
Artois	140,000	78	22	5.5
Hainault	130,000	70	30	5.0
Liège	120,000	–	–	4.5
Gelderland	98,000	56	44	3.8
Walloon Flanders	73,000	64	36	2.8
Friesland	71,000	78	22	2.7
Luxemburg	68,000	85	15	2.6
Overijssel	53,000	52	48	2.0

Sources: Van Houtte, *Economische en sociale gesch.* 130–1; Blockmans and Prevenier, *Bourgondische Nederlanden*, 392.

But if Holland was gaining ground in terms of population and urbanization, with regard to commerce, industry, wealth, and fiscal weight she continued to be dwarfed by both Flanders and Brabant. Admittedly, by the fifteenth century Holland boasted far more ships, and seamen, than both these provinces combined. But Holland's maritime strength was confined to the bulk-carrying traffic—the freightage of bulky goods of low value, especially grain, timber, salt, and fish—and the fisheries, and this meant that she possessed hardly any major merchants, little commercial wealth, and far less export-orientated industry than Flanders or Brabant.[8] The Habsburg government in the sixteenth century accordingly fixed Holland's fiscal liability at only half that of Brabant, Brabant being assessed at one-sixth less than Flanders.[9] Holland's inferiority was most marked in the sphere of high-value commerce and industry. Industrial output in Holland was valued for fiscal purposes, as late as the mid-sixteenth century, at less than one-fifth of that of Flanders and only one-twentieth of that of the south Netherlands as a whole.[10]

A crucially important feature, a key contrast between Holland and the other two large provinces of the Low Countries, was the much greater concentration in the south of population, activity, wealth, and influence in a small number of very large cities which were thus overwhelmingly dominant in the affairs of the provinces. Ghent, Bruges, Antwerp, Brussels, Leuven and 's-Hertogenbosch were all larger than any town in Holland. But in Flanders three, and in Brabant four, cities were preponderant each in its own quarter. Thus, in Flanders, the three principal cities—Ghent, Bruges, and Ieper—together paid 35 per cent of the total quota for the whole province while no other Flemish town paid a significant proportion, the next largest, Dunkirk, contributing a mere 1.2 per cent.[11] By contrast, in Holland there were no dominant towns in the Flemish sense but rather six or seven towns, all of about the same size, with populations of around ten to twelve thousand—Leiden, Haarlem, Dordrecht, Delft, Amsterdam, Gouda, and Rotterdam—none of which could preside over the province, or a part of it. The preponderance of a few great cities in Flanders and Brabant aggravated the disunity of those provinces, and vulnerability to civic particularism, whereas the more even dispersal of urban population in Holland encouraged the tendency noticeable there from early on towards provincial cohesion.

Decisive for the rise of Holland was the first half of the fifteenth century. It was then that the Hollanders first developed the full-rigged seagoing ships which formed the basis of the subsequently burgeoning bulk-carrying traffic.[12] From around 1400, Holland's ships began to sail in impressive numbers both to the Baltic, for grain and timber, and western France and Portugal, for salt. It was also in the early fifteenth century that the Dutch full-rigged herring buss evolved, the vessel which ensured the dominance of Holland and Zeeland over the North Sea herring grounds for over three

---

[8] Israel, *Dutch Primacy*, 9–10, 18–27.
[9] Grapperhaus, *Alva en de Tiende Penning*, 27.
[10] Ibid. 119.
[11] Maddens, *Beden in het graafschap Vlaanderen*, 15.
[12] Unger, *Dutch Shipbuilding*, 33–4; Unger, 'Dutch herring', 256–9.

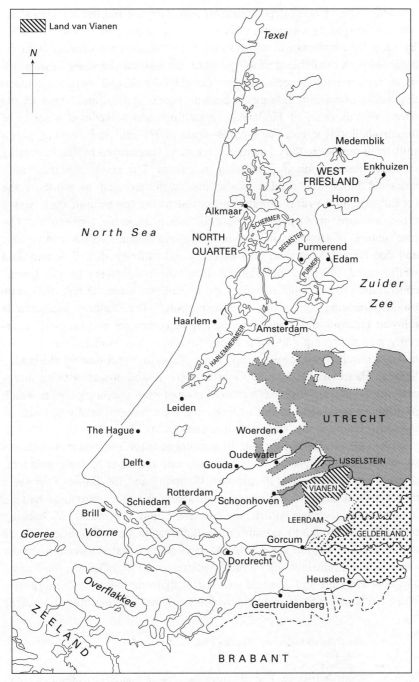

MAP 2.　Holland in the fifteenth and sixteenth centuries

centuries. This growing dependence on bulk-carrying and the herring fishery was encouraged by mounting difficulties in agriculture and water control.[13] By 1400, land reclamation was slowing down, as the limits of what could be achieved with available technology were reached. At the same time, much of the land previously reclaimed continued to shrink, and therefore sink, so that areas previously safe again became prone to flooding.[14] One of the effects of this crisis in Holland's agriculture, which included a series of disastrous floods inundating sizeable areas of Holland and Zeeland, was a shift from arable to dairy farming, a recourse encouraged by the importing of cheap Baltic grain in increasing quantities. The result was that more imported grain was needed, fewer men were required to work in the countryside, more rural population moved to the towns, and there was a rapid increase in surplus cheese and butter available for export. The combination of growing difficulty in agriculture during the fifteenth century, and floods, with success in bulk-carrying and fisheries, shifted activity and vitality (and therefore population) from the countryside to the towns, contributing to the rapid urbanization in Holland when the rest of Europe was experiencing contraction and stagnation.[15] The southern Netherlands eclipsed Holland and Zeeland in high-value commerce and industry, especially manufacturing goods for export overseas. Yet Holland's was by no means a purely maritime economy. Four of the six 'big towns' of Holland—Leiden, Haarlem, Delft, and Gouda—were inland towns without bulk-carrying or herring fleets. These were modest manufacturing towns which produced a good deal of beer, mostly for consumption locally but also in the south Netherlands, and some medium-quality cloth.[16]

In the face of Holland's expanding seaborne trade and power, the inland states of the north Netherlands had only one recourse: to form alliances, directed against Holland, in northern Germany and the Baltic. There was no point in looking to Flanders and Brabant: for these provinces had no influence, or leverage, north of the rivers and no means of backing opposition to Holland's expansion. In their economic and political life, as in their culture, Flanders and Brabant remained orientated towards the west and south and relied wholly on intermediaries—the IJssel towns, the Hansa, and also Holland and Zeeland—to carry their commerce with the north. Thus, Holland's expansion heightened not only her own orientation towards

---

[13] Van Zanden, 'Op zoek naar de "Missing Link" ', 372.
[14] Van Zanden, *Rise and Decline*, 30–3.
[15] Visser, 'Dichtheid', 16–17.
[16] Jappe Alberts and Jansen, *Welvaart in wording*, 139–42; Van Houtte, 'Zestiende eeuw', 56–60.

northern Germany and the Baltic but also that of the rest of the northern Netherlands. In 1441 for example, Kampen joined the Hanseatic League, as a full member, while Deventer and Zwolle, already members, tightened their links with Lübeck and other Hansa ports. For their part, the North German Hansa towns willingly concerned themselves with the Low Countries, needing allies, and expedients, with which to check the growing influence of the Hollanders in the Baltic. For as the Hollanders' share of the bulk-carrying traffic grew, as it did steadily through the fifteenth century, the friction between them and their German Hanseatic competitors inexorably mounted. Lübeck, which headed the Hanseatic League, was anxious to maintain the exclusion of the Hollanders from the 'rich trades' in textiles and other high-value commodities by collaborating closely with the great commercial and industrial centres of Flanders and Brabant.[17] In the north Netherlands, the Hansa backed the Hollanders' competitors, especially Kampen and Deventer.

Thus Holland grew more powerful and to a degree affluent, and acquired incomparable numbers of ships and seamen, without acquiring a wealthy merchant élite.[18] At the same time, the rise of Holland generated political and economic tensions not only between her and her neighbours, but also within the province. For as Holland expanded, territorially and in terms of population and ships, she also acquired the rudiments of a more integrated administration while, at the same time, the influence of the towns increased at the expense of the countryside. To finance their administration and wars, the counts of Holland imposed a growing fiscal pressure and this, in turn, meant extending their administrative apparatus. The result was a widening rift between those nobles and urban patricians, on the one hand, who backed the count and were favoured at his court and, on the other, those excluded from favour and position, and consequently resentful.[19] At the same time, the efforts of the count to regulate commerce and shipping, and administer the waterways, dikes, dams, and sluices, created patterns of control, and privilege, which generated stresses among the towns. Especially contentious were the staple rights affecting shipping sailing along the lower Maas, sold by William IV to Dordrecht, in 1334, which thoroughly antagonized Delft and Rotterdam.

These internal tensions erupted in 1350, when the leading group of noble families—the Wassenaar, Van Polanen, Brederode, Kralingen, and Raephorst—currently monopolizing favour and office, were thrust aside by

[17] Dollinger, *The German Hansa*, 298–302.
[18] Jappe Alberts and Jansen, *Welvaart in wording*, 259–60, 281–3.
[19] Jansen, *Hoekse en Kabeljauwse twisten*, 18–22.

their rivals, leading to an outbreak of bitter civil war. The newly dominant grouping received the backing of all the main towns, except Dordrecht, and came to be known (for reasons which remain a mystery) as the 'Cod-Fish' or *Cabeljauwen*.[20] Their opponents then came to be called the *Hoeks* (Hooks), those who opposed the 'Cod-Fish'.

The strife between *Hoeks* and *Cabeljauwen* in Holland and Zeeland persisted for a century and a half and became as deeply embedded in Dutch life and culture as the comparable feud between Guelphs and Ghibellines in late medieval Italy. After a time, the *Cabeljauwen*, originally the party of opposition, became firmly identified as the party of the 'ins', of the regime, and the ruling block of nobles, and the *Hoeks* as the party of the 'outs', of opposition nobles and patricians. For this reason, several principal noble families, such as the Wassenaar, originally figuring among the *Hoeks*, defected and joined the *Cabeljauwen*. On the other hand, those lower down in society, who had reason for discontent, tended to sympathize with the *Hoeks*.

Despite being deserted by most leading nobles and patriciates, the *Hoeks* remained formidable, and became more so as the count's administration and taxation pressed harder. By the middle of the fifteenth century, the *Hoek* party was deeply entrenched among the guilds and militias of the towns so that the conflict assumed a local civic, as well as a broader provincial, and inter-provincial, character.[21] At Leiden and Gouda, where the woollen cloth industry attained some importance, the weavers sided with the *Hoeks*, expressing their allegiance in ballads and songs, as well as sporadic outbursts of violence, while the cloth dealers backed the *Cabeljauwen*. At Amsterdam, there was a similar division between artisans, on the one side, and the commercial community on the other.

Before long, the struggle in Holland and Zeeland became entangled with parallel factional feuds festering in the rest of the north Netherlands.[22] In the later Middle Ages all the north Netherlands principalities were unstable both socially and politically. In Utrecht, the conflict between noble and patrician parties became inextricably entwined with that in Holland so that the factions eventually adopted the names *Hoeks* and *Cabeljauwen*. But traditional local names were retained in Friesland, where the rival blocks continued to be called *Vetkopers* and *Schieringers*, and in the Ommelands, Overijssel, and in Gelderland, where the antagonists were called *Bronkhorsten* and *Hekerens*, after leading noble families on either side.

[20] Brokken, *Ontstaan van de Hoekse en Kabeljauwse twisten*, 254, 289.
[21] Carasso-Kok, 'Schutters', 65–6.
[22] Jansen, *Hoekse en Kabeljauwse twisten*, 84, 92.

UNDER THE BURGUNDIANS

Until 1425, the Low Countries formed two separate political theatres, with little linkage between what went on north of the rivers, where the story revolved around Holland's drive for hegemony, and what went on in the south, where there were not one but two main power centres—in Flanders and Brabant. Both the latter were deeply divided not only in terms of towns versus nobles, but also quarter versus quarter, and patricians versus guilds. Furthermore, whereas neither France nor England influenced what went on north of the rivers, in the south French and English involvement was decisive in shaping—and further fragmenting—the play of forces.

This almost complete separation of north and south ended in 1425 with the death of the last independent count of Holland. By 1428 the new lord of Holland and Zeeland was Duke Philip the Good of Burgundy (1419–67), which meant that for the first time since the Carolingian era part of the north was incorporated into a large European state with its main power base south of the rivers. The Burgundian state in the Low Countries had begun with the death of Louis de Mâle, the last independent count of Flanders, in 1384, when his lands were inherited by his daughter, Margaret, and her husband, Philip the Bold, duke of Burgundy, younger brother of the French king, Charles V (1364–80). Originally, the Burgundian dynasty possessed Flanders plus Walloon Flanders, and Mechelen, and had close ties with Artois and the Franche-Comté, as well as the duchy of Burgundy. But the state grew steadily in both the Low Countries and north-eastern France. The acquisition of Brabant and Limburg, both in 1404–6, confirmed the Burgundians as overwhelmingly the dominant power in the Low Countries. Subsequently, they annexed Namur (1421), Hainault (1428), Holland and Zeeland (1425–8), Luxemburg (1451), and eventually also Gelderland (1473).

After a fresh bout of *Hoek–Cabeljauw* strife between 1425 and 1428, with the *Hoeks* opposing the Burgundians, Holland and Zeeland entered a more tranquil period, taking their place within the rapidly evolving Burgundian state. In the 1430s, Duke Philip embarked on a programme of administrative reorganization and state-building intended to weld the Burgundian Netherlands into a more coherent entity. Among the new central institutions established in this period were the States General, a gathering of representatives from the various provincial States of the Burgundian Netherlands, a central Chamber of Accounts with a treasurer and receiver-general, and the celebrated noble order of the Golden Fleece.[23] But whilst the Burgundian Netherlands was the first state in the Low Countries since

---

[23] Blockmans, 'Corruptie', 241; De Schepper, *Belgium Nostrum*, 4–7.

Carolingian times extending both south and north of the rivers, it was undeniably a state based on the south.[24] After 1451, and the building of the ducal palace in Brussels, the court resided chiefly in that city, with spells in Lille, Bruges, and Mechelen, and occasionally Dijon.[25] Brussels was the capital. Decision-making, high office, ducal favour and rewards were reserved for great magnates whose lands and dependants were located overwhelmingly to the south of the rivers, with a sprinkling of jurists and churchmen who were also usually southerners. Likewise French, and not Dutch, was the language of the central administration and court under the Burgundians. This suited the magnates, who mostly belonged to French-speaking Walloon dynasties, in any case, and posed no problem for the patrician élites of Flanders and Brabant, both of which were Dutch-speaking provinces but where there was a long tradition—especially in the former case—of using French. North of the rivers, though, French was in some degree an alienating factor since local élites there were unaccustomed to its use.

Similarly, the impetus given to cultural and artistic activity by the ducal court, courts of the magnates, and senior ecclesiastics, was chiefly confined to the south. The founding of the first, and only, university of the Burgundian Netherlands at Leuven in 1425 did, to an extent, work as a unifying factor for the whole Low Countries but also placed the academic centre of gravity firmly in central Brabant, near where the court was to settle a quarter of a century later. After around 1430 there was an impressive increase in production of tapestries, paintings, fine furniture, sculptures, silk furnishings, jewellery, painted glass, and courtly music. But it is striking that this output, and the specialization and refinement of techniques which made possible the unprecedentedly high level of art and décor in the Burgundian Netherlands, were concentrated in Brussels, Ghent, Bruges, Leuven, Mechelen, and Antwerp. This refined splendour, which had no parallel elsewhere in fifteenth-century Europe north of the Alps, was the result less of any general rise in affluence in Burgundian society than of the concentration of wealth in the hands of the court, high magnates, and leading churchmen.[26] Art and décor became one of the principal activities of the towns of Brabant and Flanders. Talented artists and craftsmen were drawn into these towns, near the court, from a wide surrounding area. Rogier van der Weyden (c.1399–1464) was a Walloon who trained in Tournai but painted his masterpieces chiefly in Brussels. Dieric Bouts (d. 1475) seems to

[24] Gosses and Japikse, *Handboek*, p. ccxlviii.
[25] Blockmans and Prevenier, *Bourgondische Nederlanden*, 211.
[26] Van Uytven, 'Splendour or Wealth', 104–6.

have come from Haarlem but worked principally in Leuven. Hans Memling (d. 1494), born and trained in the Rhineland, became the foremost painter of Bruges. Tapestry-weaving during the Burgundian period was concentrated in Brussels, Leuven, and Ghent.[27]

Politically and culturally Holland was thus in some respects subordinated to the needs and interests of southern élites and a Burgundian court residing in Brussels. Under Philip the Good, Holland and Zeeland were placed under the duke's lords lieutenant or 'Stadholders', as provincial governors were called in the Low Countries, and these were nearly always chosen from among the southern magnates. The duke himself only rarely paid a visit north of the rivers and, when he did, stayed only briefly. Still more important, few Holland or Zeeland nobles, in contrast to Walloons and Brabanters, were assigned places at the ducal court.[28]

The southern orientation of the Burgundian state in the Netherlands was reflected in the functioning of its central institutions. The States General always gathered in Brussels or another city in the south. The Order of the Golden Fleece, established in 1430, as a means of binding leading nobles more closely to the court, and person, of the Burgundian duke, was from the outset composed almost exclusively of southern noblemen. Of the original twenty-five nobles accepted into the order, not a single one was a north Netherlander.[29] Later in the century, two or three northerners were admitted but by that time the total had risen to around forty. The Order of the Golden Fleece gathered twenty-three times between 1430 and 1559, on all but two occasions south of the rivers.

In practice, Duke Philip's only interest in his northern provinces was that they should remain quiescent and meet his tax requirements. His policy towards the noble and patrician factions in those provinces was geared to this end. For *baljuws*—as the main rural judicial officers were called—and other major office-holders, he mainly chose *Cabeljauwen* but with a sprinkling of *Hoeks* so as not to alienate them altogether. In the town councils, he deliberately selected men from either side, balancing the parties, so as to make both dependent on his favour and reduce party hatred.[30] It was also a means of preventing whole towns from obstructing his rule or deciding to rebel.

The interests of Holland and Zeeland, as such, were of less concern to the Burgundians. There was little point in the Hollanders, increasingly locked

[27] Ibid. 110.
[28] Paravacini, 'Expansion et intégration', 301–6.
[29] Baelde, 'Het Gulden Vlies', 220–1.
[30] Jansen, *Hoekse en Kabeljauwse twisten*, 83–4.

in conflict with the Hanseatic League for maritime and commercial hegemony in the north, looking to the duke to champion their interests, since he
was absorbed in the Hundred Years War in France, and in relations with
England, and had neither time, nor resources, to spare for Germany and the
Baltic.[31] Neither did Flanders and Brabant have much sympathy for
Holland's complaints about the Hansa, since Holland's endeavours, if
successful, would enhance not only her commerce but also her textile
production, which was in direct competition with that of Flanders. Consequently, as the conflict in the north intensified, the States of Holland—
while always acting in the name of the duke—proceeded virtually as if they
were a separate government. As war between Holland and the Hansa
loomed, Flanders and Brabant sought to prevent it. In the war which ensued
(1438–41), the States of Holland fought Lübeck and the latter's North
German allies raising the large sums needed from the whole province,
equipping war fleets, and becoming deeply entangled in the politics of
Denmark-Norway, as well as of northern Germany. What is especially
noteworthy is the ability of the States of Holland to act as a cohesive and
more or less efficient government, with no prince, or only a very distant
prince,[32] the six towns which dominated the States working together, the
inland towns supporting the maritime towns.

In most of the provinces of the Low Countries not only was the nobility
deeply divided but urban particularism was stronger than provincial cohesion. In this latter respect, Holland was peculiar and there is little doubt that
the reasons for this were the same as explain the peculiarity of her economy
and social structure. Two aspects deserve special emphasis. The late colonization of large areas, combined with the agricultural crisis of the fifteenth
century, and accompanying acceleration of the urban economy, had left
Holland and Zeeland top-heavy with towns. Towns now dominated the
countryside to a greater extent than in the rest of the Low Countries. As a
result, urban patriciates increasingly came to preside over the provincial
assembly, the States of Holland. But, even more important than this, was the
fact that the two main economic assets of Holland—the bulk-carrying fleet
and herring fishery—were neither located in, nor directly managed by, the
six 'big towns'—Dordrecht, Haarlem, Leiden, Amsterdam, Delft, and
Gouda—which dominated the States. Nor were the dikes and sluices which
protected both towns and countryside. The consequence, in contrast to
northern Italy and the southern Netherlands, was the curtailment of urban
particularism and autonomy. There was no point in individual towns going

[31] Bonenfant, *Philippe-le-Bon*, 28.   [32] Jansma, 'Philippe-le-Bon', 14–17.

their own way if, in doing so, they had no control over their most vital assets. Bulk-carrying and the herring fleets were mainly concentrated in a string of outports to the north—Enkhuizen, Hoorn, Medemblik, and Edam—and in and around Rotterdam and the Maas estuary. The only way that the six 'large towns' could control and defend these assets, the basis of their collective economy and prosperity, was by acting together. This was true even of Dordrecht, which in the past had frequently clashed with the other towns, had links with the Hansa, and quarrelled with Delft and Rotterdam over her staple privileges. For in the fifteenth century, Dordrecht's flourishing Rhine trade was increasingly interfered with by the Gelderlanders and her patriciate decided that the best way to defend her trade was to drop the Hansa and close ranks with the other Holland towns.[33]

The Burgundian duke kept aloof from Holland's Baltic war and politics. He sought neither to direct, nor to restrain, the States.[34] For it was only by allowing Holland to go her own way, even when clashing with the interests of Flanders and Brabant, that Holland could be successfully accommodated within the Burgundian state. The Burgundian Netherlands of the fifteenth century was thus essentially a duality, with north and south scarcely less fundamentally divided politically and economically than in the past.

Duke Philip's strategy of balancing the parties in the Holland town councils and *ridderschap* (nobility) broke down in the late 1440s, when there was a new eruption of *Hoek* insurgency, led by disaffected nobles. The towns were now the chief element in the administration of Holland and Zeeland. But the nobles were still of great importance and many were intensely hostile to the existing distribution of offices and patronage. At the same time, while the patriciates of the Holland towns co-operated with each other, most experienced difficulty with their guilds and disaffected artisans. In 1445, the duke came in person to Holland—his first visit since 1433—to restore order and effect changes to the provincial administration. He purged the *Hoeks* from the city councils, again banned the use of the labels 'Hoeks' and 'Cabeljauwen', and remodelled civic government so as to strengthen the patrician element, which was the chief force for stability in both Holland and Zeeland.[35] To curtail the influence of the guilds and militias, he drastically reduced the *vroedschappen* (town councils) in size—that of Haarlem, for example, from eighty to forty members—making them more manageable and less representative of the populace.[36] Most of the Holland

[33] Van Dalen, *Gesch. van Dordrecht*, i. 313–14.
[34] Jansma, 'Philippe-le-Bon', 16–18.
[35] Gouthoeven, *D'Oude Chronijcke*, 463–4.
[36] Jansen, 'Bredase Nassaus', 30–2.

town councils now consisted of forty, thirty-six (as at Amsterdam), or twenty-four members. At first, the burgomasters—usually four in each town—were still chosen by broadly based colleges of electors, from the guilds and town quarters. But soon this democratic element was suppressed and the burgomasters, the chief office-holders in the towns, came to be chosen by the *vroedschap* itself. In this way, in Holland and Zeeland during the mid-fifteenth century, was created that politically and economically privileged regent patriciate, sharply differentiated from the mass of the citizenry, who were to dominate civic life in the north Netherlands down to the Napoleonic era. This suited the Burgundian duke, who in return for his favour could expect them to provide stability, administer justice, and collect his taxes, and also suited the patricians who thereby gained in power and yet needed him to preserve and defend their privileged position.

In forging his state, even when reorganizing Holland and Zeeland, Duke Philip was advised by a small circle of great noblemen whose lands and influence were mainly in the south. Prominent among these was Count Johan IV of Nassau, whose family—modest princes in Germany—had joined the front rank of the high nobility of the Burgundian state, since the marriage, in 1403, of Engelbrecht I of Nassau to Jeanne van Polanen, one of the richest heiresses of the Netherlands. The core of the Nassau domains in the Netherlands lay in northern Brabant, where the family resided in their town, and castle, of Breda. Other leading magnates belonged to the Walloon houses of Croy, Lalaing, and Lannoy, and also to the house of Egmond, which originated in Holland, and possessed land in North Holland, but which through intermarriage with the Walloon nobility, and the favour of the Burgundian court, became as much a southern as a northern family.

While the Burgundian dukes ignored Holland's concerns in the Baltic, they by no means neglected the historic claims to supremacy over other parts of the north Netherlands, inherited from the former counts of Holland.[37] To expand and integrate their new state, the dukes needed to neutralize the trouble-making potential especially of Gelderland and Friesland. Thus there is a sense in which the pre-Burgundian rise of Holland to dominance north of the rivers continued unabated after the advent of the Burgundians. For it was logical, even unavoidable, that Philip the Good and his successor should chiefly employ Holland's resources for the purpose of subduing parts of the north outside their control since the men and money of Flanders and Brabant were (as always) engaged to the south and west.

---

[37] Gosses and Japikse, *Handboek*, pp. ccxlii–ccxlvi.

Duke Philip revived Holland's claims to Friesland and in the 1450s there was, briefly, a possibility that both Friesland and the Ommelands would be forcibly annexed to the Burgundian Netherlands. At the same time the duke extended his influence in Utrecht and Gelderland. Utrecht, seething (as usual) with internal tensions, erupted in armed conflict in 1455, when the ecclesiastical chapters—encouraged by the duke of Gelderland—elected an anti-Burgundian candidate as the new prince-bishop. This was a brother of Reinoud, lord of Brederode, leader of the *Hoeks*, the traditionally anti-Burgundian element, in Holland. The Brederode prince-bishop enjoyed the support of the Utrecht guilds and the *Lichtenbergers*, the Utrecht nobles allied with the Holland *Hoeks*, as well as of his brother, whose town, and castle, of Vianen lay on the Holland–Utrecht border. Duke Philip promptly raised an army in Holland, with Holland's money, and invaded Utrecht. The Brederode prince-bishop was ejected and the duke's illegitimate son, David of Burgundy, made prince-bishop in his stead, a change the Pope swiftly endorsed. Holland's troops also entered Overijssel, the other part of the prince-bishop's territory, quelled support for the Brederodes, and reduced Deventer, after a five-week siege.

The Burgundian state reached its zenith under Duke Charles the Bold (1467–77). A harsh, authoritarian ruler, with pronounced monarchical tendencies, Charles lost no opportunity to show the provincial States of the Netherlands who was master and how he saw their role. His policy was straightforward: to expand his army, conquer more territory, advance administrative centralization, and raise more taxation. His methods were heavy-handed and unpopular. In 1468, the duke toured Zeeland and Holland, putting new men into positions in the provincial administration, and also into the town councils, to ensure that those with power were subservient to his wishes and fiscal needs.[38] For the first time, the Hof, or provincial high court of Holland and Zeeland—they shared the same high court—was brought under central supervision. Charles's most resounding success in the north was his acquisition of Gelderland, in 1473, on the death of the childless Duke Arnold. The duchy was seized by force in the face of considerable opposition, and with the local nobility deeply divided.

The sensational news, in January 1477, of Charles the Bold's death in battle, against the Swiss near Nancy, instantly transformed the situation throughout the Netherlands. Everywhere deep grievances had accumulated against the duke's policies and methods, against the centralization process, and, not least, the concentration of influence and wealth in the hands of the

---

[38] Gouthoeven, *D'Oude Chronijcke*, 499–500.

duke's principal supporters and officials. Consequently, his death, and the loss of his army, precipitated a thoroughgoing crisis of the Burgundian state, a reaction against both centralization and the pervasive corruption associated with the duke's rule. Charles was succeeded by his daughter, Mary of Burgundy (1477–82), who found herself facing opposition and revolt on every side, without money or troops, and with the armies of the king of France invading the French provinces of her state.

The main thrust of the revolt against Burgundian supremacy was in the south Netherlands and especially Flanders, where the city of Ghent took the lead. Three weeks after her father's death, Mary was forced to concede, under Flemish pressure, the celebrated *Grand Privilège* of 1477, a charter which gave the States General of the Burgundian Netherlands the right to gather on their own initiative whenever they saw fit and drastically curbed the power of the ruler to levy taxes, or gather troops, without the consent of the provinces.[39] Constitutionally, there were definite affinities between the revolt of 1477 and the later great Revolt against Spain.[40] As in the later revolt there was a marked tension between the general movement and attempts of the provinces to combine, through the States General—and the particularism of individual provinces. Flanders both took the lead on behalf of the common cause and yet sought to reinforce her own provincial autonomy and, within her borders, the ascendancy of the principal 'members', especially the two leading cities of Ghent and Bruges.[41] At the same time, Holland and Zeeland showed no desire to co-operate with Flanders and were only marginally involved in the dealings surrounding the *Grand Privilège*. In fact, Holland's revolt in 1477 against Burgundian rule was simultaneously a reaction against Flanders and Brabant. Holland and Zeeland shared Flanders' desire to curb the authority of the Burgundian ruler, but showed no interest in a general charter, enhancing the role of the States General, in the south, and the leadership of Flanders. What they wanted was a separate charter for Holland and Zeeland in particular.[42] Mary complied, in March 1477, issuing another 'Great Privilege' specific to Holland and Zeeland, one of its principal provisions being the exclusion of 'strangers'—by which was chiefly meant Flemings and Brabanters—from administrative and judicial posts in Holland and Zeeland.[43] The Flemish noble Lodewijk van Gruuthuse, who had been Stadholder of Holland and

[39] Koenigsberger, 'Fürst und Generalstaaten', 561–2.
[40] Blockmans and Van Peteghem, 'Pacificatie van Gent', 330.
[41] Blockmans, 'Breuk of continuiteit?', 109, 114.
[42] Hugenholz, 'The 1477 Crisis', 37–8.
[43] Jansen, *Hoekse en Kabeljauwse twisten*, 89.

Zeeland for fourteen years, was replaced with the Zeelander Wolfert van Borselen. It is noteworthy that Holland's reaction against Burgundian rule in 1477 was tinged also with language particularism, the States of Holland and Zeeland insisting on using only Dutch rather than the French employed by the Burgundians and, subsequently, the Habsburgs as the language of central administration.[44]

THE EARLY HABSBURG NETHERLANDS

Mary married Maximilian of Habsburg (1459–1519) who, from the outset, strove to claw back the constitutional concessions yielded in 1477 to the States General and the provinces, including those conceded to Holland and Zeeland.[45] In this endeavour he enjoyed the backing of the great magnates, who continued to play as vital a role in the government of the Low Countries under the Habsburgs as they had under the Burgundians. After Mary's death in 1482, they supported Maximilian's regency, on behalf of his and Mary's son, Philip I of Habsburg, against the opposition of Flanders. Also against the wishes of Flanders, they backed his policy of unrelenting conflict with France. When Maximilian temporarily returned to Austria in 1486, he left the government of the Habsburg Netherlands in the hands of his trusted military commander, Albrecht of Saxony, and a council of state consisting of great magnates noted for their loyalty to the Burgundian state and now to the Habsburgs. These consisted of leading Walloon nobles plus Engelbrecht II van Nassau (1451–1504), head of the House of Nassau in the Netherlands.

After his return, Maximilian suffered reverses at the hands of the French king, Charles VIII, followed, in 1487, by a massive resumption of the revolt in Flanders. Instigated by Ghent, this new bout of rebellion won the backing of the guilds of Bruges, whose insurrection trapped Maximilian himself in their city. But even within Flanders, the revolt continued to pull in divergent directions, with the leading cities, Ghent and Bruges, each unwilling to submit to the leadership of the other. In contrast to Bruges, Ghent did not hesitate to conclude a formal alliance with France and admit a French garrison.[46]

Maximilian's father, the Holy Roman Emperor Frederick III, sent in German troops to punish Ghent and Bruges, which initially served only to widen the revolt, rousing Brabant and the *Hoek* allies of the Flemish rebels

---

[44] Boone and Brand, 'Ondermijning van het Groot Privilege', 6.
[45] Ibid. 19–21.
[46] Van Uytven, 'Crisis als cesuur', 430.

in Holland. In Holland, the *Hoek* insurgents captured Rotterdam, Woerden, and Geertruidenberg. But by 1489, this wider revolt in the Netherlands against the Habsburgs had begun to falter. The assistance provided by the French proved half-hearted and inadequate. Co-operation between the main towns of Flanders and Brabant was minimal. One of Maximilian's chief supporters, Jan, count of Egmond, who served as Stadholder of Holland and Zeeland for thirty years (1484–1515), starved Rotterdam into surrender in June 1489. Yet the rebellion dragged on for three years more, Ghent finally surrendering to Albrecht of Saxony in July 1492. All resistance ended at Sluis in October, except in Gelderland where Maximilian's rival pretender to the duchy, Karel van Egmond—or Karel van Gelre, as he became known—led an anti-Habsburg rebellion in 1491, with French backing, which proved successful. The Gelderland towns and lower nobility rallied behind 'Duke' Karel.[47] Maximilian, enraged, but with his hands tied by his difficulties elsewhere, could only threaten the duchy with the 'totale destruction dudict pays'. Later, in 1504, his son Philip I launched a full-scale invasion of Gelderland, but failed to bring the duchy back under Habsburg sway.

This great revolt, and the profound political crisis engulfing the Habsburg Netherlands in the years 1477–92, inevitably invite comparison with the more celebrated revolt against Habsburg rule in the Low Countries during the reign of Philip II.[48] There are some striking parallels. In both great upheavals, Habsburg rulers, locked in rivalry with France and pursuing a wide-ranging European policy, employed foreign troops and authoritarian methods in the Netherlands and, stepping up fiscal pressure, faced widespread opposition from towns and sections of the nobility. In both cases, heavy taxation, alleged violation of privileges, use of foreign troops, and bureaucratic centralization figured among the chief causes of the rebellion. Also, the point of rebelling, in both cases, was to curb the power of the Habsburg ruler and compel him to acknowledge constitutional constraints designed to enhance the role of the States General and the provincial States. In both cases, there were also elements which aspired to break away from Habsburg rule altogether.[49]

Yet there were also striking differences and it is these, undoubtedly, which explain why the Revolt of 1477–92 failed where the Revolt of 1572–90 partially succeeded—despite the increased power of the Habsburg state. Four major differences are evident. Of course, there was no Reformation in

---

[47] Struick, *Gelre en Habsburg*, 23–6.
[48] Blockmans and Prevenier, *Bourgondische Nederlanden*, 255.
[49] Koenigsberger, 'Fürst und Generalstaaten', 574–6.

progress in the late fifteenth century and it was perhaps this, more than any other factor, which hardened attitudes, and prevented compromise, during the struggle of the 1570s and 1580s. But, besides this, it is important to notice that there was no coherent political leadership, on the rebel side, in the Revolt of 1477–92, Flanders and Brabant both lacking internal unity, with their constituent cities and quarters often working at cross purposes. By contrast, in the Revolt of 1572, until 1576, and again from 1584 onwards, Holland, owing to the special circumstances of the past, was able to offer—and frequently impose—much more coherent leadership. Thirdly, in the revolt of 1477–92 the magnates were solidly behind the Habsburgs. Even in Gelderland, the titled lords, or *bannerheren*, as they were called, dissociated themselves from the support lent to Duke Karel by the towns and lower nobility.[50] By contrast, in 1572 part of the higher nobility joined the revolt against the Habsburg ruler. Finally, in the earlier revolt the ruler, Maximilian, was an active participant in the struggle, determined from the outset to negate the privileges and powers conceded to the States General and provinces in 1477.[51] In the later revolt, the Habsburg ruler, Maximilian's great-grandson Philip II, resided far away and was prone, intermittently, to give higher priority to other concerns.

The obstacles to achieving political co-ordination within the States of Flanders, or of Brabant, the two dominant provinces in the south, need to be emphasized. For these, more than any other factor, made it not only difficult but seemingly impossible for provinces south of the rivers to build on the constitutionalism of 1477. Flanders, the richest and most populous province of the Habsburg Netherlands, was, in reality, three separate entities; the chief cities—Ghent, Bruges and Ieper, each heading its own quarter and exercising an unchallenged and unchallengeable supremacy within it—formed largely separate political and administrative blocks.[52] The towns dominated in the States of both Flanders and Brabant. Nevertheless, the growth of the Burgundian, and then the Habsburg, state had revived the power of the nobility, and to a lesser extent the great abbeys, especially in Brabant where nobility and clergy were sufficiently influential in the States to oppose the sway of the four 'head towns'—Antwerp, Brussels, Leuven, and 's-Hertogenbosch—on the rare occasions when these co-operated.[53] The result was that the States of Brabant were an unwieldy body, almost permanently deadlocked.[54] It was, thus, not so much provincial as quarter,

[50] Heiningen, *Batenburg*, 33.
[51] Wellens, *États Généraux*, 286.
[52] Ibid. 298; De Schepper, 'Burgerlijke overheden', 324.
[53] Kokken, *Steden en Staten*, 12.
[54] Verhofstad, *Regering der Nederlanden*, 73–5.

and civic, particularism which pervaded the political, institutional, economic, and cultural life of the southern Netherlands. Even so, it is true that the *Grand Privilège* of 1477, though rapidly negated in practice, developed into a political myth of how things should be, which profoundly influenced the discourse and aspirations of the many opponents of Habsburg rule, especially in the south, throughout the sixteenth century.[55]

Only the higher nobility could be relied on to disdain both quarter and provincial particularism. Consequently, Maximilian assiduously cultivated the magnates, as had his Burgundian predecessors.[56] Nor could it have been otherwise. For in the fifteenth century not only did noblemen fill the great offices of state, and the stadholderates, but their relatives and client lesser nobles held most judicial and administrative posts in the countryside, as well as the office of *schout* (sheriff), charged with maintaining order and policing, in the towns. In addition, the leading nobles commanded the ruler's army and their relatives were well represented among the upper echelons of the Church. In the fifteenth century, there was no other method of state-building but in collaboration with the most powerful and wealthiest nobles. It was only later, in the sixteenth century, with the rise of humanism, that there were enough university-trained bureaucrats, jurists, and functionaries for the ruler to rely chiefly on this sector of society to staff his administrative apparatus. It was especially in the reign of Charles V that the Habsburg state in the Netherlands, while becoming more orderly and efficient, gradually dispensed with the services of the sons and grandsons of the men who were the chief backers of the Burgundians and Maximilian.

Maximilian received the call to return to Austria, to succeed his father as Holy Roman Emperor, in August 1493. The gathering of the States General in that month set the seal on Maximilian's success in the Low Countries. His now 15-year-old son, Philip, was proclaimed ruler of the Habsburg Netherlands. At the same time Maximilian achieved his aim of having the sweeping privileges granted by Mary, in 1477, declared void by the States General.[57] Philip of Habsburg, at his inauguration, swore to uphold only those rights and privileges to which Philip the Good and Charles the Bold had sworn before him.

The accession of Philip was greeted with satisfaction by both nobles and patricians.[58] The magnates had supported Maximilian but had also been troubled by his Imperial commitments, domineering personality, and relent-

[55] Koenigsberger, 'Fürst und Generalstaaten', 561–3, 579.
[56] Jansen, 'Bredase Nassaus', 34–6.
[57] Blockmans and Van Herwaarden, 'De Nederlanden van 1493 tot 1555', 443.
[58] Wellens, *États Généraux*, 237–8.

less rivalry with France, as well as his unabashed use of the resources of the Netherlands for purposes which had little or nothing to do with the provinces' interests. Philip, unlike his father, was a Netherlander. He was also the son of the not unpopular Mary, last of the Burgundians. More important still, in the eyes of the magnates, he was an inexperienced youth with no other recourse but to rule in conjunction with those nobles who had supported his father against Ghent and Bruges.[59] This, together with the fact that the French crown was now so deeply entangled in Italy as to cease to pose a threat to the Netherlands for an entire generation, rendered the regime of Philip I (1493–1506) and the subsequent regency of Margaret of Austria (1506–15) a period of exceptional stability and relative harmony in the history of the Netherlands, especially in the south.

Nevertheless, major stresses persisted. Within the Habsburg Netherlands there was a gradual strengthening of central authority in various spheres. A notable step was taken in 1504 with the re-establishment, at Mechelen, of the Great Council (*Grote Raad*) to serve as the supreme judicial organ of most of the Netherlands. As the necessary corollary of centralization, civic and quarter autonomy was slowly eroded. At the same time in the cities, especially of Flanders, the influence of the guilds, which had formed the backbone of the revolt against Maximilian, was weakened as the patrician élites, with the encouragement of central government, strengthened their grip on civic administration.

But north of the rivers the chief tension was between the Habsburg and non-Habsburg Netherlands. The repulse of Philip's forces from Gelderland, in 1504–5, signalled the start of a reaction against both the Habsburgs and Holland, which was to grow and destabilize the northern Netherlands for several decades.[60] Besides Gelderland, a major focus of conflict was Friesland, where in 1498 Philip named Albrecht of Saxony (as part of his reward for reducing Flanders) his delegate ruler of the province—with the support of the Frisian *Schieringers*. Maximilian made Albrecht a vassal of the Empire in this capacity.

Albrecht subjugated Friesland and, on his death in 1500, was succeeded by his son Georg, who began centralizing the Frisian provincial administration, establishing a provincial high court or Hof, along the lines of that of Holland and Zeeland.[61] But Georg faced fierce *Vetkoper* resistance, encouraged by the city of Groningen. In the years 1505–6, when his master, Philip of Habsburg, failed to subjugate Gelderland, Georg was repulsed from

[59] Jansen, 'Bredase Nassaus', 36.
[60] Formsma, *Historie van Groningen*, 178–9.
[61] Theissen, *Centraal gezag*, 26–8.

Groningen. He was beaten off again in 1514. To defeat him, Groningen turned for help to Duke Karel of Gelderland, who from this point emerged as the leader of the anti-Habsburg reaction in the north. Karel not only backed Groningen but invaded Friesland, in alliance with the *Vetkopers*. Gelderlanders and *Vetkopers* captured Sneek and Bolswaard, effectively ending Habsburg authority in most of Friesland and the Ommelands.[62] Georg retained Leeuwarden but, concluding that his position was hopeless, surrendered his rights over Friesland and Groningen to his new master Charles (whose father Philip had died in Spain), later the Emperor Charles V.

The young Charles of Luxemburg (as he was then known) was proclaimed ruler of the Habsburg Netherlands before the States General, at Brussels, in January 1515. He was inaugurated as duke of Brabant in the traditional manner, at Leuven, and then grandly visited Antwerp, Mechelen, 's-Hertogenbosch, Breda, Bergen-op-Zoom, Namur, Ghent, and Bruges. The new ruler's most urgent initial task was to check the crumbling of Habsburg authority in large areas north of the rivers. Using Holland's resources, an army was assembled to reduce Friesland and Groningen to obedience. Floris van Egmond, count of Buren and Leerdam, was appointed commander and 'Stadholder of Friesland'.[63] The operation resulted in the recapture of parts of Friesland, but the *Vetkopers* and Gelderlanders fought tenaciously, with widespread support, holding the countryside as well as Sneek and Bolsward. The invasion ended in stalemate, to the dismay of Amsterdam and the West Frisian ports. For continued Frisian resistance meant that the Zuider Zee and Holland's sea-lanes would remain unsafe. Over the winter of 1515-16, Holland's shipping was seriously disrupted by armed Frisian vessels.[64]

At the commencement of Charles V's reign the Netherlands was thus at a crucial juncture. The south was relatively stable under the future Emperor, but the north deep in turmoil. The prospect of the union of all the Netherlands above the rivers under Habsburg rule had come closer and it was emphatically in Holland's interest to welcome it.[65] For the anti-Habsburg (and anti-Holland) insurgency in Friesland, Groningen, Gelderland, and soon also Utrecht, was severely disrupting both sea, and inland river, traffic. Yet Charles, distracted by other commitments and (on the death of his maternal grandfather, Ferdinand of Aragon, in 1516) his succession to

[62] Sjoerds, *Algemene Beschryvinge*, i, part 1, 501-2.
[63] Theissen, *Centraal gezag*, 89.
[64] Wagenaar, *Amsterdam*, i. 190.
[65] Tracy, *Holland*, 72-87.

the Spanish throne, could give the north Netherlands neither the attention, nor the resources needed to bring the instability to an early end. In effect, Charles left it to his northern Stadholders, and the States of Holland, to find a solution to the north Netherlands conundrum.

THE INSTITUTIONS OF THE HABSBURG NETHERLANDS

Charles V left via Flushing for Spain, to claim his Spanish inheritance, in September 1517. The Habsburg Netherlands was, for the second time, placed under the regency of his aunt, Philip of Habsburg's sister, Margaret of Austria, a regency which lasted thirteen years (1517–30). The interlude was significant for her style of government which, from this point on, diverged fundamentally from past practice. Her attitude was strongly dynastic, and authoritarian, and showed little inclination to cultivate either the provincial States or the high nobility.[66] Her personal advisers were mainly foreigners, such as Mercurino di Gattinara and Nicholas Perrenot, father of the future Cardinal Granvelle, an official from the Franche-Comté. Ignoring most of the high nobility, including Hendrik III, count of Nassau (1483–1538), the only magnate for whom she showed any regard was Antoine de Lalaing, count of Hoogstraten.

The coolness between Margaret and the high nobility reached such a point that in 1524 a group of them sent a petition to Charles in Spain, complaining that, when they went to see her, she kept them waiting and would not discuss major matters with them. Charles wrote to his aunt from Valladolid, urging her to mend her ways in this respect, show the nobility more regard, and always consult the counts of Nassau and Buren, as well as Lalaing, before taking key decisons.

It was not until he returned in person, and spent most of 1531 in Brussels, that Charles left his own stamp on the government of the Habsburg Netherlands. During that year, he gave most of his attention to reorganizing, and strengthening, the administration of the Low Countries. Margaret having died, he chose as regent his sister, Mary of Hungary (1531–40), deliberately choosing an inexperienced figurehead, with little knowledge of the Netherlands, forbidding her to bring her Viennese favourites with her. Charles intended that she should rely on, and leave the main decisions to, his trusted officials.

The Emperor set up three new central institutions in 1531—a rather grand formal body called the 'Council of State', a reorganized council of finance,

---

[66] Blockmans and Van Herwaarden, 'De Nederlanden van 1493 tot 1555', 452.

MAP 3. The provinces of the Netherlands in the age of Charles V

and a Secret Council. These were the so-called Collateral Councils at Brussels, which were to survive, roughly in the same form, at the head of the administration of the Habsburg Netherlands down to 1788.[67] Officially, the Council of State was the most important of these organs and this was the forum of the principal *seigneurs*. It consisted of twelve members, most of whom were southern magnates, plus its presiding figure, Jean Carondolet,

---

[67] Baelde, 'De Nederlanden', 48.

archbishop of Palermo, a jurist and churchman. The Secret Council, on the other hand, contained no magnates and was staffed by professional bureaucrats and jurists who had risen to the head of the administration.[68] Charles was trying to reconcile the status and aspirations of the great magnates with the new reality that power lay partly in the hands of professional bureaucrats, some of whom were foreigners. By formalizing two chains of authority and patronage, he hoped to accommodate both and minimize friction.[69]

The chief representatives of the Habsburg ruler, in the provinces, were the provincial governors, or Stadholders. Only Brabant and Mechelen, close to the court in Brussels, had no governor. The other provinces were grouped under Stadholders who were invariably chosen from among the leading nobles. Thus, Zeeland, and (from 1528) Utrecht, had the same stadholder as Holland, while Flanders, Walloon Flanders, and Artois tended to be grouped together, as, later, were Friesland, Groningen, Drenthe, and Overijssel. Grandest of Charles' Stadholders was Hendrik of Nassau's son who became known as René de Châlons (1519–44), on inheriting the principality of Orange (in southern France); René succeeded his father in the Nassau possessions in the Netherlands in 1538. Born at Breda, a Knight of the Golden Fleece, from the age of 12, this first of the Nassau line to bear the title 'Prince of Orange', uncle and predecessor in the title to William the Silent, was appointed Stadholder of Holland, Zeeland, and Utrecht, in 1540, to which was added, after its conquest in 1543, the stadholderate of Gelderland. The following year, besieging a town in France, he was killed by a cannon-ball.

Charles saw the danger of alienating the nobility. But his Stadholders were absent from their provinces much of the time and incapable of closely supervising the fiscal and judicial administration, lacking the time, training, and inclination. Thus, pruning the role in administration not only of the Stadholders but of the nobility generally was an inherent process which acquired a logic of its own and continued under Mary, as it had under Margaret.[70] It was inevitable that the Collateral Councils, in Brussels, and the *Grote Raad* (Great Council) at Mechelen, the highest court of the Habsburg Netherlands, should work, in their relations with individual provinces, less with the staff of the Stadholders than through the permanent judicial administration. Thus, increasingly, the key connection in administering the Habsburg Netherlands was that between central councils and provincial high courts, which steadily expanded their political and fiscal as

---

[68] De Schepper, 'Burgerlijke overheden', 331; Tracy, *Holland*, 46.
[69] Baelde, 'De Nederlanden', 49–52.
[70] Baelde, 'Edellieden', 47–51.

well as judicial functions. At the close of the fifteenth century, most of the councillors of these high courts, including those of the Hof of Holland (which also had responsibility for Zeeland), were still noblemen. But, during the first half of the sixteenth century, the role of nobles in provincial administration diminished, as central government found more university-trained jurists to fill these posts and, with the growing complexity of administration, needed their greater expertise, diligence, and regular work habits. In 1520, six of the thirteen councillors of the Hof of Holland were still nobles; by 1572, the number of nobles had fallen to two or three.[71]

In the past, the nobility had predominated also in filling the main offices in the rural districts and 'quarters'. There was much variation as to the names of these officers and the extent of their jurisdictions. But in all the provinces they were a vital element in the administrative process. In the north, where they were mostly called *baljuws* or *drosten*, they were the crucial link between the provincial high courts and countryside, small towns, and villages, and, in the low-lying areas, they also presided over the *hoogheemraadschappen*, the regional dike and drainage boards. They were appointed in Brussels and were, above all, the representatives, at district level, of the Habsburg ruler, charged with publishing, and enforcing, royal placards, maintaining order, and supervising the conduct of civil and criminal justice as well as taxation. In some cases, they were also governors of royal fortresses. In all, there were sixteen *baljuws* and *drosten* in Holland.

While those rural magistrates who also had responsibility for a royal castle continued to be nobles, most of the rest, lacking military responsibilities, including most *baljuws* in Holland and Zeeland, gradually ceased to be nobles. In 1530, non-military district magistrates in Holland were about half and half noble and non-noble.[72] By 1570, nearly all the non-military *baljuws* of Holland were non-nobles. Under the *baljuws*, in the rural districts of Holland and also in the main towns (which were outside the jurisdiction of the *baljuws*), was a lower officer, the *schout*, representing the ruler and in charge of policing activities. Here again, there was a marked tendency, under Charles V, for non-nobles to replace nobles.[73]

The chief element in the administration of the towns was the city council, the *raad*, or *vroedschap* as it was called in Holland and Zeeland, headed by the burgomasters. Civic government and magistracies remained in the hands of patrician regents, just as before. Nevertheless, they too were affected in many ways by the growth of central government and changes in provincial government, finding themselves subjected not only to mounting fiscal

---

[71] Van Nierop, *Van ridders tot regenten*, 162–4.   [72] Ibid. 167.   [73] Ibid. 170.

pressure, especially after 1540, but to progressively closer supervision than in the past both from central councils and, especially, the provincial high courts—whose senior officials were appointed in Brussels.

Finally, there were the provincial States and States General. Despite the progress of bureaucratization and centralization under Charles V, a considerable measure of autonomy remained vested in the provincial States. Indeed, paradoxical though it may seem, centralization proceeded hand in hand with the strengthening of the provincial States.[74] Locked in conflict with France, the Habsburg rulers, especially from 1542 onwards, urgently needed more revenue in the Netherlands, and, lacking direct control over the fiscal machinery at provincial and civic level, found they could best boost taxation by delegating the task to the provincial assemblies and cities, thereby enabling them to expand their administrative functions and financial operations. Seeing the fate of Ghent which rebelled against the Emperor's authority in 1539–40 and was punished by losing its privileges, towns and provinces, on the whole, preferred to co-operate rather than resist. Thus, the States gained in institutional strength but largely by becoming accomplices of the regime in raising more money for the ruler, in both town and countryside. Charles V's revenues in the Netherlands roughly quintupled during his reign, over a period in which prices only slightly more than doubled.

It was otherwise with the States General. Philip the Good's original purpose in creating the States General had been to simplify the process of putting fiscal demands to his subjects, and to further the cohesion of the Netherlands not least by stabilizing, and co-ordinating the provincial currencies.[75] But under the Habsburgs central government found that it was through the provincial States that it could most effectively demand, and increase, revenue and, in Maximilian's case, also manipulate the coinage. Furthermore, Maximilian relentlessly opposed the wider powers conceded to the States General in 1477 (and again in 1488), and especially the principle that they be allowed to gather as of right, each year, in a town of Flanders, Brabant, or Hainault. Between 1488 and 1559 the States General met irregularly but nevertheless relatively frequently, on average twice per year. Often the States General were convened merely as a method of communicating rapidly with all the main provincial States at once. In the matter of the government's financial requirements it was usual to put a 'general proposition' to the States General followed by a 'particular

[74] Grapperhaus, *Alva en de Tiende Penning*, 23; Tracy, *A Financial Revolution*, 45; Tracy, *Holland*, 116–22, 209–12; Koopmans, *Staten van Holland*, 57, 64, 66–71.
[75] Spufford, *Monetary Problems*, 154–7, 164.

proposition' to each of the provincial delegations, as far as possible preventing the States General discussing either the ruler's needs, or the respective contributions of the provinces, in plenary sessions.[76] The privileges granted in 1477 having been annulled, the States General met only when summoned by the ruler.

All considered, the Habsburg Netherlands in the middle of the sixteenth century presented an imposing spectacle in which an assortment of thriving provinces, prosperous, densely populated, crowded with impressive walled cities, and presided over by acquiescent assemblies, were to all appearances being successfully welded into a viable and coherent whole with the support of both the magnates and the new élite of humanist-trained career bureaucrats. The commercial, financial, and industrial heart of northern Europe and, in the conditions of sixteenth-century warfare, an admirable strategic base, the Netherlands seemed a formidable adjunct to Habsburg primacy in Europe and the world more generally.

---

[76] Maddens, 'Invoering', 348–54; Tracy, *A Financial Revolution*, 35.

3

Humanism and the Origins of the Reformation, 1470–1520

❖

The rise of north European Christian humanism, one of the most crucial cultural shifts in western history, began in the Netherlands in the 1470s and 1480s, in the relatively remote north-eastern provinces of Overijssel and Groningen. It may seem odd that a cultural development of such significance for all Europe should have originated in a locality which, at the time, was becoming a backwater both economically and politically. But the ground for this great upheaval in thought and piety had been prepared in precisely this area by devotional and educational developments reaching far back into the medieval past.

This preparation was the achievement of the *Devotio Moderna*, or 'Modern Devotion', an uncontroversial religious and educational movement originating in the teachings of a devout burgher, Geert Groote, at Deventer and its environs during the late fourteenth century.[1] The movement developed in both the civic context and monasteries, and rapidly gained impetus, exerting its greatest influence in the middle of the fifteenth century, under Philip the Good, a time of relative peace and stability when Deventer and the other IJssel cities still exerted a considerable economic and cultural influence over the Rhineland and Westphalia, as well as the north Netherlands. The special emphasis which the *Devotio* placed on the improvement, and spread, of schools, and establishing libraries, flowed from the capacity, created by the thriving trade of the IJssel cities, to provide resources for more teachers, schools, and books. Though the movement permeated much of the Netherlands, as well as Westphalia, it continued to be centred on Deventer, Zwolle, Kampen, and also Groningen.

The key distinguishing feature of the *Devotio Moderna*, as a spiritual movement, was its stress on the inner development of the individual. The *Devotio* did not concern itself much with questions of dogma, or Church

[1] Post, *The Modern Devotion*, 521, 677.

organization, and in the main avoided arousing the disapproval of the Papacy and Church hierarchy,[2] though some of its later luminaries, notably Wessel Gansfort (1419–89), a Dutch theologian whose writings influenced Luther, did eventually come under suspicion of heresy. Much the most famous book produced by the Devotio was the De Imitatione Christi (Imitation of Christ) of Thomas à Kempis (c.1379–1471), a work which circulated widely in the Netherlands first in manuscript and then, following the first edition in 1473, as a printed book. Thomas à Kempis expressed the essential message of the movement, stressing the significance of the inner life of the individual: 'the man who knows how to walk the road of the inward life, and set little store by things outside of himself, has no need of special places, nor set times, to perform his exercises of devotion'.[3] By separating the essentials of the Christian life from what society does, and the doings of the Church, staking all on the individual's inner absorption in Christ, the Devotio helped pave the way for the later philosophia Christi of Agricola and Erasmus, and devotional ideals of the Reformers of the 1520s. Thomas made a lasting impression on the culture of the Netherlands and more than any other figure of the Dutch-speaking lands of the Middle Ages remained an inspiration for the Dutch Reformed Church of the seventeenth and eighteenth centuries, even among its most rigidly Calvinist spokesmen.[4]

But, if the Devotio helped prepare the ground, it was not a forerunner of Christian humanism.[5] Unlike Christian humanism, and the Reformation, the Devotio did not (expressly) reject conventional religious forms, or criticize aspects of the contemporary Church and its theologians. Where Christian humanism rejected scholastic theology, and the Reformation broke new theological ground, the Devotio was almost reverential towards the theology of its time. Where the later movements rejected monasticism, the monastic ideal remained integral to the Devotio's concerns. Yet there can be no denying the profound influence of the Devotio on the developments which came later.[6] The emphasis on literacy, and schooling, and removing the spiritual life of the individual from outward, formal religion, paved the way for the spiritual upheaval which was to follow, the linkage being reflected in the emergence, and early flourishing, of Christian humanism in the north-east Netherlands, the heartland of the former Devotio Moderna.[7] Gansfort, after his return to the Netherlands in 1475, worked successively

[2] Lourdaux, 'Dévots modernes', 279–82; Weiler, 'Betekenis', 41–2.
[3] Thomas à Kempis, Imitation of Christ, 85.
[4] Sjoerds, Algemene Beschrijvinge, ii, part 1, 770–1; Exalto, 'Willem Teellinck', 21.
[5] Lourdaux, 'Dévots modernes', 280, 296; Schoeck, Erasmus, 264–8.
[6] Lourdaux, 'Dévots modernes', 281–91.
[7] Tilmans, Aurelius en de Divisiekroniek, 19–22.

at Zwolle, Deventer, and Groningen, and served as a living bridge between the two movements. Educated by the *Devotio* in Groningen, his native town, and Zwolle, he was a prominent participant in the 'academy' which met in the 1470s and 1480s at the famous Cistercian Abbey of Aduard, north of Groningen, a group which combined intensive Bible study, in the tradition of the *Devotio*, with cultivating the humanist techniques of exegesis introduced by Agricola.[8] He linked the two strands, moreover, in Bible studies where he was a major forerunner of Christian humanism.[9]

Rudolph Agricola, the illegitimate son of the provost of Baflo, one of the six principal churches of the Ommelands, was educated by the *Devotio* at Groningen, and spent many years in the north-east Netherlands before leaving for Italy. On returning to the Netherlands in 1479, he was a famous man, renowned at the Burgundian court in Brussels, in educational circles throughout the Netherlands and Germany, and beyond. Among jobs he was offered was that of rector of the Latin school at Antwerp. But while complaining of the coarseness, and lack of culture, at Groningen, he felt tied to the north-east by family and other bonds and spent his remaining years (when his influence was at its height) mostly in that area.[10] He was the founding father of northern European humanism not only in being the first to master, practise, and spread *bonae litterae*, the methods of Italian humanist exegesis, but also in the sense that he became a key role model, inspiring others to immerse themselves in classical Latin, the new critical philology, and Greek studies.[11] After his death, his renown grew further through the several published accounts of his life which appeared. He was revered not only by the next generation of Dutch and German humanists but also by the third, not least Erasmus, who readily acknowledged Agricola as the *fons et origo* of northern humanism and his own great debt to him. On one occasion, at the Latin school at Deventer in 1484, the young Erasmus heard Agricola lecture. The Abbey of Aduard (Adwert), where the abbot, Hendrik van Rees, convened the circle in which Agricola and his followers—Alexander Hegius, Anthonius Liber (de Vrije), and Rudolph von Langen, as well as Gansfort and other scholars—participated, contributed much to propagating the new scholarly techniques which Agricola had brought back from Italy. But in the early period, before 1490, the prime channel by which Christian humanism pervaded the cultural life of the Low Countries was through the civic, or 'Latin', schools, especially those

---

[8] Waterbolk, *Verspreide opstellen*, 175–6.
[9] Lancée, *Erasmus en het Hollands Humanisme*, 122; Oberman, 'Wessel Gansfort', 113–20.
[10] Akkerman, 'Agricola and Groningen', 11, 17–19.
[11] Ibid. 9; Schoeck, 'Agricola and Erasmus', 181–2, 184.

strongly influenced by the *Devotio*, located in the north-eastern Nether-lands.[12] Agricola's leading disciple, Alexander Hegius, was rector of the Latin school of Deventer in the years 1483–93, the school (attended by Thomas à Kempis back in the 1390s) renowned throughout the north-east-ern Netherlands and Westphalia, which now became the seed-ground of Dutch humanism. Erasmus (*c*.1466–1536) attended this school in the years 1475–84 and was thus still at Deventer when Hegius arrived and introduced the new methods for which he became celebrated, including the Greek studies which he had imbibed from Agricola.[13] Until around 1500 Deventer was also the leading centre of humanist printing in northern Europe, producing more Greek editions than Paris and an imposing series of editions of classical Latin authors.[14]

Dutch humanism arose in the 1470s and 1480s at Deventer, Zwolle, Groningen, Kampen (where Liber became town secretary in 1485) and nearby locations. From the outset it represented a fusion of Italian humanist scholarly methods with Christian spiritual ideals nurtured by the traditions of the *Devotio*. Agricola opened the way for Erasmus, his *De Formando Studio* (1484) already using the term *philosophia Christi*.[15] It was only gradually, after 1490, that the new humanism penetrated Holland, Brabant, and Flanders, with a crucial intermediary role still being played by adherents of the *Devotio*. The young Erasmus carried his optimism that the 'dark ages' were ending from the *Devotio* school where he completed his schooling, at 's-Hertogenbosch, to the monastery where he began his career as a human-ist, at Steyn near Gouda, in 1489. He stayed in Holland until 1493. His chief ally in Holland was Cornelius Aurelius (*c*.1460–1531), a Gouda monk who spent his adult life in Augustinian monasteries steeped in Thomas à Kempis and the non-scholastic, non-speculative spirituality of the *Devotio*; but who, at the same time, helped pioneer the introduction of humanist studies in Holland, and who later was the foremost creator of the myth that the ancient Batavians, eulogized by Tacitus, were the forebears of the Hollan-ders.[16] Like Erasmus, Aurelius venerated the memory of Agricola.

The beginnings were slow. But after 1490 Dutch humanism rapidly gained momentum. Fanning out from the Overijssel towns and Groningen, *bonae litterae* spread during the 1490s into all the leading Latin schools of Holland, Brabant, and Flanders including such key centres as Gouda,

[12] Schoeck, 'Agricola and Erasmus', 181, 184.
[13] Huizinga, *Erasmus of Rotterdam*, 7.
[14] Schoeck, 'Agricola and Erasmus', 182, 187.
[15] Ibid. 186; Schoeck, *Erasmus of Europe*, 112.
[16] Tilmans, 'Cornelius Aurelius', 204–6; Schöffer, 'The Batavian Myth', 65–6.

Alkmaar, 's-Hertogenbosch, Ghent, and Antwerp. A growing band of humanist schoolmasters threw themselves into the task of propagating the new studies, and nurturing classical Latin and Greek, likening themselves to an army storming some detested citadel, vehemently hostile to scholasticism and the teaching methods—as well as barbarous Latin—of the past.[17] In this respect Erasmus, a zealot filled with a vision of Christendom as an arena in which two mutually exclusive worlds of study, and culture, battled for supremacy, was a typical rather than exceptional figure. The towering greatness of Erasmus, as a thinker and innovator, lay less in his mastery of humanist techniques—though certainly in critical exegesis, he surpassed most contemporaries—than in the integrated *Weltanschauung* he forged by combining the new scholarly apparatus with a more systematic articulation of, and stronger commitment to, the moralistic Christian philosophy stemming from the traditions of the *Devotio* as modified by the early humanists.

Christian humanism in its fully-fledged Erasmian form was more than just a revolution in studies and secular culture: it was a revolution in religious thought, piety, philosophy, and art.[18] The distancing of the individual from fixed patterns of devotion, and the self-immersion in Scripture, commenced before Erasmus. But it was Erasmus who brought out the full implications of *philosophia Christi*, propagating a fresh vision of Christian truth infused with a powerful spiritual yearning and iconoclastic zeal which, combined with his personal timidity, produced a refined, intellectualized zealotry at times of startling intensity. In Erasmus' eyes, humanist scholarship lacked validity unless it led to a deepening, and purification, of the scholar's commitment to Christ. *Bonae litterae* in Erasmus' philosophy were merely beguiling, worthless, indeed dangerous, unless infused with a thirst for Christian truth, as defined by humanists such as himself, in non-speculative, moralistic terms. Thus, for Erasmus, the new age dawning with the onset of humanism was simultaneously a time of exhilaration and unprecedented spiritual danger. In Erasmus' world-view, contemporary Christendom was confronted with three great perils which it was the responsibility of scholars to guard society against.[19] First, as his three-year stay in Italy (1506–9) taught him, preoccupation with classical antiquity and literature was capable of degenerating into a modern paganism (by which Erasmus meant a secular spirit inspired by classical pagan ideals), a tendency he viewed with abhorrence as a disastrous diversion from Christ. Secondly, there was 'Judaism', by which he meant something wider and more far-reaching than

[17] IJssewijn, 'The Coming of Humanism', 271, 281; Bots, *Humanisme en onderwijs*, 29–40.
[18] Van Gelder, *The Two Reformations*, 213, 312.
[19] Screech, *Erasmus*, 234–40; Markish, *Erasmus and the Jews*, 16–23.

actual Jews and Judaism. For Erasmus, 'Jewish' influence and 'Judaism' meant the prevalence of ceremony, ritual, and legalism, a subverting of true piety, and diversion from Christ, through outward show and adherence to form. Erasmus' passionate polemic against 'Judaism' was not anti-Semitism in any conventional sense.[20] But he does see actual Jews and Judaism as the core of the wider 'Judaism', religion based on dogma, and ritual, which he condemned and regarded as a more imminent menace to Christendom than paganism. Finally, the third peril was the threat of schism, with all the catastrophic effects that would follow, through disruption of society and civil war.

All of Erasmus' output, including the *Praise of Folly* (1511), is saturated with his philosophy of Christ.[21] But his message is stated with particular directness in the *Enchiridion* (1503) and two explanatory tracts, the *Paracelsis* and the *Methodus*, introducing his scholarly edition of the New Testament published at Basel, in 1516.[22] He urges the individual to model his, or her, life on the example of Christ, and commune directly with Christ, stripping away the whole façade of false piety—images, cult of saints, pilgrimages, fasting, empty recital of prayers in Latin (which most people do not understand), and preoccupation with ceremony and ritual in all guises.[23] No sacrament, status, or condition could confer salvation or sanctity. He denied that the monastic ideal in itself had any value, though he tactfully maintained that he was neutral rather than positively hostile to monasticism.[24] In short, Erasmus set up that stark duality between 'true Christianity' and false religion (assuring his readers that most practice in contemporary Christendom was of the latter variety) which lies at the centre of his religious thought and at the root of the Reformation.

A striking feature of Erasmus' philosophy of Christ is its idealization of the (literate) individual. The individual carries the responsibility of finding Christ and shaping the Christian content of his or her life, a content essentially human, worldly, and moralistic. His philosophy revolves around this. Certainly Erasmus had to make some concessions to the ignorance and illiteracy which were the lot of most inhabitants of Christian lands. With regard to the cult of saints, for example, he was more inclined to view leniently those that venerated saints 'with a simple and childish sort of superstition', even though, according to him, such reverence had little spiritual value, than the monks and priests who encouraged such veneration,

[20] Augustijn, 'Erasmus und die Juden', 32–6; Markish, *Erasmus and the Jews*, 8–13.
[21] Screech, *Erasmus*, 228–40.
[22] Augustijn, *Erasmus en de Reformatie*, 12–13.
[23] Lindeboom, *Het Bijbelsch humanisme*, 16–17.
[24] Schoeck, *Erasmus of Europe*, 127–9.

exploiting superstition for worldly ends, dispensing 'sweet benedictions'.[25] Whether he considered all, or only some, of the clergy to be guilty of gross betrayal of Christ he preferred not to say. The literate individual must immerse himself in the sacred texts and in the Fathers, seeking guidance from those whose knowledge best fitted them to expound these texts. The true theologian must not set himself up over the layman, seeking to blind him with dry dogma and technical jargon which can only divert attention from Christ's truth.[26] One of the main justifications for humanist studies according to Erasmus is that they illumine the Gospel and stimulate the seeker after Christ in that, as he put it at the end of the *Enchiridion*, such erudition 'adorns the Lord's temple with literary richness'.

During the three decades between 1490 and 1520 Christian humanism made great strides in the Low Countries, more so than in any other part of northern Europe. Humanism captured the Latin schools, found many adherents in civic government, and generally exerted an immense influence over education, culture, and religious sensibility. Nevertheless, as Erasmus noted, the defenders of scholastic theology, monasticism, and 'superstition' remained both stubborn and powerful.[27] The cultural and religious edifice of the past, buttressed by power and privilege, was too strong simply to be swept aside. It was shaken; but did not collapse. In historical perspective this is, indeed, scarcely surprising. For the Low Countries of the late fifteenth century, in which humanism made such rapid strides, was, at the same time, a cultural world in which scholastic theology and monasticism still flourished, cults of saints proliferated, religious art emphasized the great sacramental moments, and popular enthusiasm for pilgrimages to Rome and the Holy Land was at its zenith.[28] Passionate absorption in Christ Crucified, the Virgin, and the saints infused both popular piety and religious art. Aside from Hieronymus Bosch, most of the great masters of the later fifteenth century in the Netherlands continued the artistic traditions of Jan van Eyck and Rogier van der Weyden, depicting a world of sacred happenings, pious gestures, angels' wings, and haloes. Like Bouts, Memling, and Hugo van der Goes in Brabant and Flanders, the group of painters led by Geertgen tot Sint Jans who gathered at Haarlem, the first important centre of painting in the north Netherlands, represented a world pervaded with a sensuous sacramental religiosity.[29]

[25] Augustijn, *Erasmus en de Reformatie*, 13–16.
[26] Ibid. 12–13; Augustijn, 'Ecclesiology of Erasmus', 143–4.
[27] *Collected Works of Erasmus*, viii. 44.
[28] Van Gelder, *The Two Reformations*, 213, 312; Herwaarden, 'Geloof en geloofsuitingen', 403–4.
[29] Châtelet, *Early Dutch Painting*, 118–20.

During the early sixteenth century the fundamental duality, the clash of worlds, which characterized learning extended to all religious sensibility and also to art.[30] Some masters such as Gerard David and Quentin Massys persisted with a late Gothic, sacramental style of religious art down to, and beyond, the 1520s. But, by then, a rapid transformation was under way. The three leading painters of the north Netherlands of the early and mid-sixteenth century—Lucas van Leyden (1494–1533), Jan van Scorel (1495–1562), and Maarten van Heemskerck (1498–1574)—all reacted strongly against the styles of the fifteenth century. Sacred scenes of annunciation, crucifixion, resurrection, and the Virgin and Child, scenes basic to the old art, receded to the margins.[31] In their place came an assortment of biblical anecdotes represented in a worldly, moralizing way as if scenes of classical history and mythology.

Conscious of being radical innovators, transforming art, Van Leyden and Van Scorel were as much humanists, albeit humanists of the brush, as were the humanists of the pen. Van Scorel, a canon of Utrecht cathedral, who in his youth made the pilgrimage to Jerusalem, regarded himself as the foremost transmitter of Italian Renaissance techniques and aesthetic ideals to the art studios of the Netherlands.[32] He sought unity of composition, introduced radically new colour schemes, and, like Erasmus in the moral and religious sphere, idealized the individual, transforming the devotional picture into a 'history piece' in the grand manner. Van Leyden's style was influenced more by Dürer and the German Renaissance than the Italian, but otherwise what is true of Van Scorel is true also of him. He was the first Dutch artist to draw frequent inspiration from the Old Testament, which provided him with many stories and anecdotes. Van Leyden's innovations began in the second decade of the century. Van Scorel returned to the Netherlands from Italy in the mid-1520s.

Although, initially, Erasmus tentatively supported the Lutheran Reformation, there was from the first a deep ambivalence in his attitude to Luther.[33] This arose partly from Erasmus' horror of conflict and schism, partly from the fact that, in the years 1516–21 when the Reformation began, Erasmus was residing in the Netherlands where the power of the Emperor Charles V, and the Church, to combat the Lutherans was more formidable than in Germany, and partly from unease at the implications of the uproar, over Luther, for humanist studies. Erasmus always disliked Luther's abrasive

---

[30] Veldman, 'Maarten van Heemskerck's visie', 193.
[31] Van Gelder, *Erasmus, schilders, en rederijkers*, 13, 42–3.
[32] Hoogewerff, *Jan van Scorel*, 57.
[33] Augustijn, *Erasmus en de Reformatie*, 25–9.

tone and combative style.[34] Luther for his part harboured strong reservations about Erasmus, recognizing from the outset that the great humanist's religious thought had more to do with the human and worldly than the divine.[35] Nevertheless, until 1524, both Erasmus and Luther kept their doubts about the other private, Luther and his adherents hoping that Erasmus would come out openly in their support, Erasmus secretly supporting Luther's attack on the Church and its shortcomings, and, in 1521, publicly attacking monasticism.

Erasmus had his reservations about Luther. But still less was he a friend of the contemporary Church. What troubled Erasmus about the Reformation was not the attack on the Church, or the Papacy *per se*, but his fear that Luther's revolt would provide those in the Church who opposed Erasmus with the opportunity to mobilize Church, Papacy, and Europe's rulers against humanist studies. He dreaded being linked to Luther because of the likelihood that Luther would be defeated, dragging himself and humanism down with him. Again and again Erasmus returned to this theme in his letters. In September 1520, he wrote of his fears to Gerard Geldenhauer, chaplain of the bishop of Utrecht, a humanist from Nijmegen: 'I am filled with foreboding about that wretched Luther; the conspiracy against him is strong everywhere and everywhere the ruling princes are being provoked against him'.[36] He predicted, should Luther's enemies win, that 'they will not rest until they have overthrown all study of [ancient] languages and all liberal studies'. In a letter to Nicholas Everaerts, a humanist and senior judicial functionary at The Hague, in February 1521, Erasmus exclaimed, 'What a burden of unpopularity Luther is heaping on humanist studies and on true Christianity!'[37] In another letter to Everaerts, a month later, he accused Luther of provoking 'great hostility to Reuchlin, greater still to me, and what is worse, to liberal studies'.[38] In yet another letter to Everaerts, he sighed that humanism was 'threatened with extinction by the Luther business'.[39]

Erasmus' fears were by no means without justification. Luther's critique of the Church provoked uproar in the Netherlands, especially in Holland, where early support for Luther was strong. After a disturbance at Dordrecht in 1520, a Dominican doctor of divinity who had preached against Luther and been attacked by an angry crowd blamed Erasmus for the outbreak.

[34] Ibid. 29, 45.
[35] Bietenholz, 'Erasmus, Luther und die Stillen', 31–2.
[36] *The Collected Works of Erasmus*, viii. 44.
[37] Ibid. 155.
[38] Ibid. 160.
[39] Ibid. 312.

This friar, Erasmus wrote to the rector magnificus of Leuven university, 'lays the uproar in Holland at my door because, after a most foolish sermon that he preached there, he was nearly stoned by the crowd, while I have never written to any Hollander either for Luther or against him'.[40] Erasmus, now at the peak of his European fame, enjoyed a vast influence with the educated élite of the Netherlands and not least the regents, jurists, and officials of Holland. At The Hague, according to a letter written to Erasmus in November 1519, all important and educated people continually extolled Erasmus and read his work.[41] But by 1520 Erasmus' fame was inextricably linked to the phenomenon of Luther: another letter written at The Hague at this time reported that 'Luther . . . is in high favour here'.[42] The leaders of Erasmian humanism at Delft, in the 1520s, were precisely those most interested in the cause of religious reform.[43]

Erasmus' relations with the University of Leuven, and leading Church spokesmen in the Netherlands, uneasy since the publication of his critical New Testament in 1516, had by 1520 become exceedingly tense.[44] Leuven, a university which then had some 3,000 students and, after Paris, was the second largest, and most important, in Europe, was a flourishing centre of humanist studies and printing. Erasmus had laboured hard to promote the famous *Collegium Trilingue* set up in 1517 as a focus for Greek, Latin, and Hebrew studies. But his biblical exegesis and textual scholarship, and thus the College, were becoming increasingly controversial within the university, and theological circles throughout the Low Countries. By 1519 it was apparent just how far Erasmus had diverged from the Vulgate, how impatient he was of scholarly criticism, and how far-reaching the implications of his biblical commentaries were.[45] The academic tone of the controversy of 1516–19 gave way to something altogether more virulent. The advent of Luther enabled the conservatives to cite the Reformation as proof of the dangers of Erasmus' approach and agitate against him in princely and episcopal courts—and in Rome.

By 1520 the increasingly harsh official onslaught against Luther in the Netherlands was beginning to spill over against Erasmus also.[46] The Dominican theologian attacked by a pro-Luther crowd at Dordrecht remarked: 'Luther is pestilential, but Erasmus more so, for Luther sucked

[40] Ibid. 101.
[41] Ibid. vii. 135.
[42] Ibid. 136.
[43] Grosheide, 'Enige opmerkingen', 78.
[44] Rummel, 'Nameless Critics', 42.
[45] Huizinga, *Erasmus of Rotterdam*, 130–7; Rummel, 'Nameless Critics', 42–5.
[46] Duke, *Reformation and Revolt*, 12, 83, 155–6.

all his poison from Erasmus' teats'.[47] Erasmus' refusal to condemn Luther, given the feverish atmosphere now prevailing in the Netherlands, could only be seen as surreptitious support for him. Indeed, while assuring the university authorities that he was not supporting Luther, Erasmus made no secret of his abhorrence of the methods used to inflame opinion against the German Reformers. As early as May 1519, Erasmus deplored the anti-Luther campaign in the Netherlands as a dangerous stirring up of 'foolish women and the ignorant multitude'.[48] 'I have never approved, and never shall', he wrote to the rector magnificus of Leuven, in October 1520, 'of the suppression of [Luther] in this way by public uproar, before his books have been read and discussed'.[49] Shocked by the 'savage and tyrannous behaviour' with which the university publicly condemned and burnt Luther's works, Erasmus continued to resist demands that he denounce Luther as obdurately as he ignored the appeals of Wolfgang Capito, Ulrich von Hutten, and Philip Melanchthon that he come out in Luther's support.[50] By 1521, when he left the Netherlands for good and settled in Basel, Erasmus' position in the life and culture of the Low Countries had become untenable.

Erasmus removed himself to Switzerland, evading the mounting furore in the Netherlands. But his spiritual legacy, his immense impact on the mind and culture of the Low Countries remained. The country was in a state of spiritual civil war.[51] Erasmus' himself haughtily denied responsibility. Yet however blinkered the denunciations of monks and conservative theologians, there was, all the same, more than a little logic to their claim that it was Erasmus, and the new humanism, which were the cause of the uproar.[52] By insisting that ultimate authority in the exposition of Scripture lay with the humanist scholar, Erasmus had in effect usurped the authority of Papacy, theological faculties, and the Church. By redefining Christian salvation in terms of the individual will and living life by Christ's example, he had debased the Church's teachings and sacraments, even if he had expressly scorned only clergy who were ignorant and corrupt. Nor was it just monks and theologians who considered him the true author of the Reformation. Italian humanists who refrained from mixing humanist scholarship with theology asserted it too. Reporting to the Pope, in February 1521, on the great impact of the Lutheran revolt in the Netherlands, and

---

[47] *The Collected Works of Erasmus*, viii. 403.
[48] Ibid. vi. 297.
[49] Ibid. viii. 71.
[50] Augustijn, *Erasmus en de Reformatie*, 29; Augustijn, 'Ecclesiology of Erasmus', 152–3.
[51] Spruyt, 'Humanisme, Evangelisme en Reformatie', 26–7, 36.
[52] Eckert, *Erasmus von Rotteram*, ii. 344–5; Rummel, 'Nameless Critics', 45.

especially Holland, the papal nuncio Girolamo Aleandro, a humanist who had once shared lodgings with Erasmus in Venice, wrote that Luther's doctrines were being preached publicly in Holland and that 'all this happens because of the Hollander Erasmus'.[53]

Nowhere in Europe was the collision between public authority and the Reformation more evident and explosive than in the Netherlands in the 1520s. This was partly because central government there, directed by the Habsburg court, took a stronger line against the Reformation than did governments elsewhere. But it was also because the impact of Christian humanism on society was deeper and more widespread than in Germany, France, or England. Christian humanism had arisen first in the Netherlands and, in contrast to the Latin schools of cities such as Strasburg, Basel, Frankfurt, and Augsburg, humanism in the Low Countries had captured the civic schools early enough to have shaped an entire generation of the educated élite by 1520. Furthermore, because the theological and propaganda reaction against the Reformation was stronger in the Low Countries by 1520 than elsewhere, there the linkage between Erasmus and Luther became more firmly embedded in the popular mind. As Juan Luis Vives, the great humanist of Bruges, wrote to Erasmus in 1522: 'that you are looked upon as a Lutheran here is certain'.[54]

Erasmus at the time of his departure for Basel was idolized by many influential figures in the Netherlands and perhaps especially in the north Netherlands, where the Christian humanist tradition had arisen. Many of those shaping education and culture in the country were convinced that they owed the exciting new intellectual and spiritual world they inhabited to Erasmus personally. As Gerardus Listrius, humanist rector of the Latin school at Zwolle in the years 1516–22, wrote to Erasmus: 'What could a man like me have achieved, or even attempted, without you? Everything I have, such as it is, I owe to you'.[55] By and large such men were also supporters of the Reformation.[56] Nor did, or could, the open break between Erasmus and Luther over the theology of the human will, in 1524 change this. On the contrary, in an important sense Erasmus' open break with Luther strengthened the linkage between Erasmus and the incipient Reformation in the Low Countries. For the dogmatic, increasingly confessional-minded Luther of the later 1520s was not suited to be a continuing inspiration to a suppressed, clandestine Reformation encountering formi-

---

[53] *The Collected Works of Erasmus*, viii. 382; Eckert, loc. cit.

[54] Huizinga, *Erasmus of Rotterdam*, 161.

[55] *The Collected Works of Erasmus*, iv. 157.

[56] Grosheide, 'Enige opmerkingen', 73–8; Augustijn, 'Gerard Geldenhouwer', 134.

dable governmental counter-pressure. From the early 1520s onwards, the main Netherlands Reformation could, for some decades, develop only as a non-dogmatic pluriform crypto-Protestantism and this, by its nature, could more easily draw on the biblical humanism of Erasmus than the theology of Luther.[57]

The appropriation of Erasmus by Dutch humanists and crypto-Protestants as the central figure in Dutch culture was to have major implications for the subsequent unfolding of Dutch history. It was a process which Erasmus himself viewed with misgivings. He abhorred conflict and schism, and disliked the preoccupation with national identity which humanist studies aroused in Von Hutten and numerous other German, French, and Dutch humanists.[58] The humanist debate about national identity became something of an undercurrent to the wider encounter about theology and scholarship, subtly influencing attitudes to culture and religion as well as nationality. Erasmus had no wish to be labelled a 'German', refused to identify himself with French culture, and joked about the Batavian myth so dear to the hearts of Aurelius and Geldenhauer. Scorning the label 'Batavian', he insisted he belonged to all Christendom.[59] But if Erasmus held aloof from the new Batavian obsession, the Batavian myth by no means held itself aloof from him.[60] For just as all Dutch crypto-Protestant strands, including the Spiritualist movements associated later with Niclaes and Coornhert, drew on and idolized Erasmus, so any exponent of biblical humanism in the Netherlands resisting Habsburg pressure to conform to Catholic orthodoxy was bound to find inspiration in Erasmus' and his works—as well as a useful vehicle for spreading crypto-Protestantism—and derive encouragement from the ancient Batavians' heroic struggle for freedom against the Romans.

Erasmus' works in Dutch translation in fact contributed substantially to the rapid progress of the Reformation in the Low Countries during the crucial 1520s. Some of Erasmus' writings highly prized today were at that time not especially esteemed or thought relevant to the wider public. Thus, the *Praise of Folly* did not figure prominently and no Dutch version appeared until as late as 1560.[61] But Erasmus' *Enchiridion*, commentaries on the New Testament, and version of the New Testament itself, were found

[57] Lindeboom, *Het Bijbelsch humanisme*, 26–7; Bietenholz, 'Erasmus, Luther und die Stillen', 43–6.

[58] Tilmans, *Aurelius en de Divisiekroniek*, 128, 152.

[59] Huizinga, *Verzamelde werken*, vi. 255–60.

[60] Lancée, *Erasmus en het Hollands Humanisme*, 97–100.

[61] Bijl, *Erasmus in het Nederlands*, 245–6.

by crypto-Protestant publicists and printers to be highly effective in spreading pro-Reformation attitudes, and they appeared in Dutch versions from 1523 onwards, at Amsterdam, Leiden, Delft, Antwerp, and Kampen.[62] The *Enchiridion* in particular was often reprinted, despite being quickly identified by the authorities as an obvious vehicle of the Reformation and banned.

[62] Ibid. 30, 49–50, 58–60, 73.

4

Territorial Consolidation, 1516–1559

❖

The unification of the Netherlands north of the rivers under the Habsburgs during the years 1516–49 was a complex political drama replete with implications for the future. It marked the culmination of a process reaching back three centuries whereby the outlying lesser states of the Low Countries were progressively absorbed into a power network dominated by the rulers, and now ruler, of the three big provinces—Flanders, Brabant, and Holland. During the course of these three centuries, the three large provinces had become more and more preponderant in terms of both population and economic influence. By the 1540s, the role of the States of these three in the affairs of the seventeen provinces of the Habsburg Netherlands was so overwhelming that they were providing around 75 per

TABLE 2. *The tax contributions of the highest-contributing provinces in 1540–1548 (% of the total contributed by the Seventeen Provinces under the Habsburgs)*

Province	%	Province	%
Flanders	33.8	Lille, Douai, Orchies	3.29
Brabant	28.76	Gelderland	1.14
Holland	12.69	Tournai and the Tournaisis	0.93
Artois	5.65	Namur	0.90
Hainault	5.47	Friesland	0.59
Zeeland	4.37	Overijssel (with Drenthe)	0.55

Source: Maddens, *Beden in het graafschap Vlaanderen*, 10–11.

cent of the total revenue of the Habsburg Netherlands and the other fourteen provinces together a mere 25 per cent (see Table 2).

But while all three of the large provinces had, since the 1420s, been under the same ruler and while first Burgundian, and now Habsburg, power was centred in Brussels, it was nevertheless chiefly with the men and resources of Holland that the Habsburg regime achieved the unification of the north. Flanders and Brabant contributed large sums to the Emperor's coffers in Brussels throughout the era of the unification struggle between 1516 and 1543. But it was a consequence of the growing reliance of the regime on the provincial States, and the new methods employed by the provincial States (at least in the more developed parts of the Netherlands) of raising money for military expenditure, that the Habsburg ruler had to concede a great deal of leverage to the three large provinces in determining how taxation granted by the provincial States was used. This meant that the persistent refusal of Flanders and Brabant to consider affairs north of the rivers to be any concern of theirs had a decisive influence on the deployment of resources and revenues in the Netherlands. It was a fixed principle of the States of Flanders that the sums the province voted the Emperor towards his military expenses could not be used north of the rivers.[1] It was laid down in every grant that the money of Flanders had to be used to defend Flanders against the French, which meant that, in effect, the only other province in which Flemish funds could be spent was Artois, which Ghent and Bruges regarded as the bulwark of Flanders.

The play of social, economic, and political forces in the north which generated unification and, once achieved, made it last was thus mainly an interaction—both attraction and resistance—with Holland. The resources and armies which subjugated the lesser provinces above the rivers were provided principally by Holland. But while Charles V's claims to overlordship in the north derived from his title of count of Holland and Zeeland, his interests and objectives diverged widely from those of the States of Holland and he took care to receive the submission of the newly acquired provinces as count of Flanders and duke of Brabant, as much as count of Holland. As far as the Habsburg government was concerned, the new territories were being incorporated into a greater Netherlands entity with the seat of power south of the rivers and its capital, and chief fount of patronage, political and ecclesiastical, at Brussels; the chief purpose of the exercise was to strengthen the Habsburgs' Netherlands bastion against France.

The result was an uneasy duality of power structures which held together, inevitably, rather loosely and, as it turned out, just briefly. The break of 1572 was only in a superficial sense a reversal of the unification of 1516–49. In reality, the Revolt against Spain was to confirm the underlying separation of north and south and long-term gradual integration of the north under Holland's hegemony.

[1] Maddens, *Beden in het graafschap Vlaanderen*, 365–9.

Holland's thus far inconclusive striving for preponderance over the lesser provinces of the north had, by 1516, been in progress for centuries and met still with determined resistance. But this opposition to Holland's ascendancy in the north was by no means universal. It was partial and factional. All along, and increasingly so, Holland's interventions had been supported, as well as opposed, by some towns and sections of the nobility and it was this growing dependency, as well as Holland's expanding wealth and power, which rendered the unification of the northern provinces both inherently logical and eventually irreversible.

This element of subordination to Holland colouring the unification process was at once political, economic, and cultural. On their own, as the recent past showed, the north-eastern provinces were irretrievably trapped in instability and turmoil. Provincial government, in so far as this existed, was too fragile in Friesland, Groningen, Overijssel, Drenthe, and Utrecht, and arguably even in Gelderland, to provide a viable basis for resolving the party strife endemic throughout the region and establishing stable adminis-tration. Stability, if it was to come at all, could only derive from the sole potentially dominant power centre—Holland.

Nor could Flanders and Brabant have served as a plausible alternative. The rivers and inland waterways, and thus internal trade generally, flowed from west to east not south to north, so that, for the river towns of Gelderland and Overijssel, what mattered in economic life was the flow of traffic along the Rhine, Maas, and Waal, and across the Zuider Zee—that is their interaction with Holland—rather than their tenuous contact with Flanders and Brabant.

The ambiguous, or double, character of the unification process of 1516–49 in the north, and of the preceding war between Holland and Gelderland in the years 1506–8, was mirrored in the humanist controversies surrounding the birth of the Batavian myth.[2] This myth, the alluring notion that the ancient Batavians described in Tacitus—heroic, virtuous, and freedom-loving who, under their leader, Claudius Civilis, had successfully revolted against the Romans—had lived in the north Netherlands, or part of it, had arisen assuming important political and cultural undertones in Dutch humanist circles in the years around 1500.

From the outset the Batavian myth was a potent factor in building a new, broader sense of patriotic identification with Holland as a political, moral, and cultural entity, as *patria* and 'nation'—words much employed by Aurelius—and for this reason later became an integral part of Dutch

[2] Tilmans, *Aurelius en de Divisiekroniek*, 122–7, 146–56.

cultural identity during the Revolt and the Golden Age.[3] The humanists saw at once what was at stake. For whichever people dwelling in, or near, the Low Countries were descendants of the ancient Batavians would thereby acquire a political and moral status, and potentially an imperial mantle, which would justify pretensions to pre-eminence and set that folk above its neighbours. No one supposed the Batavians had lived south of the rivers, but southern humanists participated by casting doubt on the claim of Cornelis Aurelius set out in his *Defensio Gloriae Batavinae* (1510) that Holland had been the home of the Batavians and that the Hollanders were their descendants. The sharpest challenge to Aurelius' ideas came, however, from another direction. Geldenhauer, a Gelderlander, argued for twenty years, culminating in his *Historia Batavica* (1530), that it was not 'Hollandia' but 'Geldria' which had been the ancient Batavians' home.[4]

Thus, the onset of strife at the beginning of the sixteenth century between Gelderland and the Habsburg Netherlands, and the escalating struggle in Utrecht, Friesland, Groningen, and Drenthe came to be viewed on two distinct levels. On the one hand, it was a dynastic struggle in which the Habsburg ruler, his power centred in Brussels, confronted his opponents, and especially the duke of Gelderland. But, on the other, it appeared to many Hollanders, including Erasmus,[5] and most extensively in Aurelius' great chronicle of Holland, of 1517, as a contest between Holland and her troublesome neighbours over whom Holland had every right to preside. The Holland noble Johan II van Wassenaer, commander of Charles's army in Friesland, who was killed at the siege of Sloten in 1522, was the Emperor's representative but was eulogized by Aurelius as embodying Holland's virtues and freedom and as the epitome of Holland's nobility.

The Holland expedition sent to Friesland, in 1516, failed but was not decisively repulsed. Rather the war dragged on inconclusively with the Habsburg cause slowly gaining ground. The initially firm alliance between the Gelderlanders and the anti-Habsburg faction in Friesland was viewed by the latter as chiefly a means to preserve 'Frisian Freedom' and avoid the detested excise taxes Albrecht and Georg of Saxony had levied and which the victory of the Burgundian-Habsburg state would surely reintroduce.[6] As the strife continued, though, and the often unruly Gelderlanders marauded and plundered, more and more Frisians came to see that, privileges or no

---

[3] Ibid. 127–8.
[4] Schöffer, 'The Batavian Myth', 65–6.
[5] Tracy, *Holland*, 73.
[6] Theissen, *Regeering van Karel V*, 50.

privileges, the only way to end the turmoil was through the triumph of Habsburg arms.[7]

As the Frisian war dragged on, support for the *Schieringers* and Charles V increased. The *Schieringers* strove to salvage as much of 'Frisian Freedom' as they could. Charles had issued vague promises to respect Friesland's ancient privileges. The *Schieringers* pressed for clear guarantees that the Emperor's authority would be minimal and the States of Friesland, not Charles and his advisers, would appoint the key judicial and fiscal officers of the province—the rural magistrates, or *grietmannen*.[8]

The protracted struggle in Friesland was a considerable inconvenience for Charles even though he had to give it lower priority than other and greater concerns. For whilst the Emperor, as he now was, contended with the revolt of the *Comuneros* in Spain (1520), the French challenge in Italy, and the Reformation in Germany, he was fully aware that the anti-Habsburg revolt in the north Netherlands could spread and get out of hand. Before long, Duke Karel placed garrisons in Coevorden and Zwolle and extended his sway over much of Drenthe and Overijssel.[9] But the continuing turmoil in Friesland, and growth of Gelderland's power, was an even greater nuisance for Holland.[10] During their counter-offensive in Friesland in 1517, *Vetkopers* and Gelderlanders stepped up their attacks on shipping in the Zuider Zee while a raiding force, shipped from Friesland, landed in Holland and plundered a swathe of territory stretching from Medemblik to the walls of Amsterdam. The anger which swept Holland was shared by Erasmus, who was then in Brussels; Charles V and his entourage heard the unpalatable news whilst at Middelburg, awaiting favourable winds for their voyage to Spain.

With Charles residing mainly in Spain and Germany in the decade from 1517, the Netherlands was once again under the regency of Margaret. Moreover, following the outbreak of war with France, in 1521, the attention of the court at Brussels, and the great magnates of the Netherlands, was focused mainly on the French border rather than the struggle in the north Netherlands. That the Frisian war, and Frisian independence, ended in 1522–3 was due principally to two factors: first, support for the war, and the Gelderland alliance, in Friesland itself had weakened;[11] secondly, Holland was determined to subdue the Frisians. In 1521–3 the States of Holland voted exceptionally large sums for an expedition to Friesland;[12] and a

[7] Struick, *Gelre en Habsburg*, 282–4.
[8] Woltjer, *Friesland in hervormingstijd*, 6–7.
[9] Heringa, *Gesch. van Drenthe*, i. 282.
[10] Wagenaar, *Amsterdam*, i. 190.
[11] Sjoerds, *Algemene Beschryvinge*, ii, part 1, 819.
[12] Tracy, *Holland*, 75.

powerful army, commanded by Jan van Wassenaer, the last of the senior branch of his house, invaded from Holland. In 1523 the last Frisian resistance collapsed.

Duke Karel and his Gelderlanders had lost their base in Friesland. In the Ommelands his position was weaker still. Here politics revolved around the perennial dispute between the city of Groningen (which had acquired a wider economic ascendancy over its hinterland than probably any other city in the Low Countries) and the Ommelander *jonkers* (gentry), or at least the more powerful and influential of them. Since the city *raad* had thrown in its lot with Duke Karel, the leading *jonkers*—the Van Ewsum, Ripperda, Rengers, and Tamminga—were pro-Habsburg, as, indeed, were the guilds in the city.[13] The city patriciate did, however, gain support among some less prominent Ommelander *jonkers*, who resented being excluded from influence and office.

Thus, there was no possibility of a counter-offensive in Friesland and Duke Karel's grip over Groningen, Drenthe, and Overijssel remained precarious. Nevertheless, the political future of the entire north Netherlands hung in the balance. A critical point in the struggle was reached in 1524 with the death of Philip of Burgundy, prince-bishop of Utrecht, Overijssel, and Drenthe, and a bastion of Habsburg influence. With Utrecht and Overijssel split between pro- and anti-Habsburg parties, and the entire region on the verge of chaos, the divided canons of the Utrecht chapters devised a compromise by electing as their new prince-bishop Henry of Bavaria, a neutral figure, with ties with both the Emperor and Duke Karel. The latter agreed to recognize Henry as prince-bishop and, in return for an indemnity, withdrew from Overijssel and Drenthe.

But the newcomer proved incapable of quelling the seething tensions in Utrecht not least because of the heavy excises he had to levy to pay off Duke Karel. The situation was further aggravated by the intrigues of Francis I, who designed to promote his prospects in Italy by destabilizing Habsburg power in the Netherlands. In 1525, the Utrecht guilds rose in revolt and seized the city, installing a new *raad* strongly tinged with an anticlerical attitude, which curtailed the privileges of the city's numerous and wealthy clergy, notably by ending clerical exemption from the beer and wine excises.[14] The patricians of Utrecht, backed by the clergy and nobility, fought to recover power. After pitched battles in the streets, the popular party was overthrown. At this point, in August 1527, spurred by France,

[13] Formsma *et al.*, *Historie van Groningen*, 174, 178–9.
[14] Post, *Kerkelijke verhoudingen*, 209–10.

Karel intervened to assist the rebels against the prince-bishop and sent in his troops.[15]

Duke Karel was a resourceful opportunist who strove ceaselessly to undo Habsburg hegemony in the north Netherlands. He had the advantage that anti-Habsburg, and anti-Holland, sentiment, and a deeply rooted institutional particularism, were widespread throughout the region. Even so, his position was fragile less because Charles was incomparably the more powerful ruler than because the political élites throughout the north-east Netherlands were irretrievably divided. The particularism he exploited was matched by a longing for peace and stability which only acquiescence in Habsburg supremacy—and Holland's—could bring. Karel confined his struggle against the Habsburgs, moreover, to the political sphere, evincing no desire to espouse the Reformation, or ally with the German Protestant princes.[16] Gerard Geldenhauer's open letter of 1526, calling on him to chase out the monks and confiscate Church property,[17] fell on deaf ears, the duke preferring to combat the spread of Lutheran influence in his lands, appreciating that whilst he eschewed Protestantism, the Emperor would continue to consider him a secondary problem compared with France, Lutheranism, and the Turks, and put up with the uneasy half-war, half-peace situation which best suited Gelderland's limited resources.

Invading Utrecht and Overijssel in 1527 was arguably Karel's greatest error, for it provoked precisely the response it was in his interest to avoid.[18] He now found himself hard-pressed from both the north and the west. He entirely failed in his bid to gain control of Overijssel where the prince-bishop's authority had now collapsed but where the towns and nobles preferred to submit to the Emperor than to Gelderland.[19] Meanwhile, the prince-bishop, seeing no prospect of restoring his authority, was persuaded to abandon his princely rights in both Utrecht and Overijssel to Charles, the States of Overijssel acknowledging the Emperor as their ruler in January 1528. Even so, ejecting the Gelderlanders from Utrecht required considerable resources, resources which only Holland could provide. Holland readily complied. For years inland trade through Gelderland and Overijssel had been hampered by war and disorder. The turmoil in Utrecht was seen as a major nuisance even before the famous raid of 1528 when Karel's commander, Maarten van Rossum, swept across South Holland and plundered The Hague. In the wake of Van Rossum's raid, Holland granted an

---

[15] Struick, *Gelre en Habsburg*, 311.
[16] Wessels, 'Ketterij in de graafschap', 55, 59, 67.
[17] Augustijn, 'Gerard Geldenhouwer', 136.
[18] Struick, *Gelre en Habsburg*, 311.
[19] Slicher van Bath, *Gesch. van Overijssel*, 119.

unprecedentedly large subsidy while 3,500 men were specially raised to form the core of the army to invade Utrecht.[20] This force drove Karel's troops from Utrecht and then captured Hattem, Elburg, and Harderwijk in Gelderland itself. In October 1528 Karel capitulated, recognizing the Emperor as sovereign of Utrecht and Overijssel, but on terms which left him in effective control of Gelderland, Groningen, and Drenthe.

The States of Utrecht acknowledged Charles V at Gorcum, inside Holland, at a moment when the Emperor himself was at Toledo. Utrecht's incorporation into the Habsburg Netherlands, and the administering of the new oath of allegiance to the province's office-holders,[21] was carried out by the Stadholder of Holland and Zeeland, Antoine de Lalaing, count of Hoogstraten (1522–40). The consent of Pope Clement VII—Utrecht and Overijssel were, after all, ecclesiastical territory—was readily obtained, Rome having been sacked by the Emperor's troops the year before, leaving the Pope at the Emperor's mercy.[22]

Charles's authority in the north Netherlands was greatly enhanced by the events of 1528. But it was Holland which had provided the means and the new situation was bound to generate tension between the States of that province and the government of Charles's regent, first Margaret, and then the Emperor's sister, Mary of Hungary (1531–55). The regents and *ridder-schap* of Holland expected a due reward for their support: not only greater security, and better conditions for trade, but also the Emperor's agreeing to settle in Holland's favour the long-standing disputes between Holland and the newly annexed provinces. Amsterdam and the West Frisian ports, for example, demanded annulment of the privilege, claimed by Overijssel, excluding Hollanders from fishing along the Overijssel shore of the Zuider Zee.[23] With regard to Utrecht, Holland hoped for some form of annexation, or at least political subordination, of the province to herself.[24] The States continually reminded the government in Brussels during the 1530s, that Holland had played the main role in 'reducing' Friesland, Utrecht, and Overijssel, and that this should be reflected in the new arrangements for the government of these provinces.

Charles had no intention of allowing Utrecht to be annexed to Holland. But strategic considerations, and the obvious impossibility of holding the new provinces without Holland's help, did result in Utrecht being placed

---

[20] Tracy, *Holland*, 75–6.
[21] Theissen, *Regeering van Karel V*, 92.
[22] Doeleman, *Heerschappij*, 146.
[23] Res. SH 13 Oct. 1538.
[24] Res. SH 22 Nov. 1531, 16 Aug. 1532, and 21 Apr. 1536.

under the same Stadholder as Holland and Zeeland. In 1528, construction began of the Vredenburg, a large citadel built within the walls of the city of Utrecht, with money voted by Holland, to overawe the city's unruly guilds. The new bishop of Utrecht, Georges van Egmond (1535–59), was a scion of a Holland noble house. The Emperor refused, however, to place the judicial administration of Utrecht under the Hof of Holland and Zeeland, preferring, in 1528, to set up a separate provincial high court, or Hof, of Utrecht.[25]

The argument that Holland had played the principal role in acquiring the new provinces was used by the States of Holland during the 1530s not only to claim advantages in relation to those provinces but also to try to deflect the growing pressure, from Brussels, for Holland to contribute more towards the escalating cost of defending the south against France. The States of Holland saw no reason why they should be greatly concerned about the French threat to Flanders and Brabant. In June 1536, the States of Holland, annoyed by demands for money, reminded Mary that for thirty years, since the death of Philip of Habsburg, Holland on her own, 'apart' from the southern provinces, had financed the wars 'against' Gelderland, Friesland, and Utrecht, and protection of her shipping in the Baltic, while at the same time joining 'with the other lands', in paying for defence against France, in which 'they were not concerned but yet had contributed as if they sat right next to the blaze'.[26] The States of Holland argued that the needs and priorities of the Netherlands north of the rivers were fundamentally different from those of the south, as indeed they were.

During the early and mid-1530s the Emperor's attention was focused on Italy, the Mediterranean, and his feud with France. Holland at this time was chiefly concerned with relations with Lübeck and Denmark-Norway, and the need to protect shipping and the North Sea herring fishery. Meanwhile, instability and anti-Habsburg intrigue continued in Gelderland, Groningen, and Drenthe. Duke Karel had several garrisons in the Ommelands but none in the city of Groningen. When, in 1536, the duke tried to move troops into the city to overawe the guilds, the *raad* withdrew their support and resolved to end the civil war in the province by accepting the sovereignty over the city and its dependencies—the Gorecht and Oldambt—of Charles V. The latter's Stadholder of Friesland, Schenck von Tautenburg, invaded, defeating Karel's forces, and his *Vetkoper* allies, at the battle of Heiligerlee, and occupied the province. Also Schenck seized the border territory of Westerwolde, which Charles assigned to him as a personal fief and which now remained part of the Habsburg Netherlands but outside the province of

[25] Fockema Andreae, *Nederlandse staat*, 57.   [26] Res. SH 26 June 1536.

Groningen.[27] Before long Schenck's troops had also captured Coevorden and established Habsburg rule in Drenthe. Under the treaty of Grave (December 1536) Karel ceded overlordship over Groningen, the Ommelands, and Drenthe, to the Emperor.

Duke Karel died in 1538 without an heir and was succeeded as duke of Gelderland by Johan III and, shortly after, in 1539, by Duke Wilhelm von der Marck, of Cleves. Duke Wilhelm was the last prince to oppose unification of the Netherlands under the Habsburgs. Strategically, Charles V's position north of the rivers was much stronger in 1539 than at the outset of his reign. On the other hand, Wilhelm in some respects posed a more dangerous threat to Habsburg hegemony than Duke Karel.[28] By uniting Gelderland with Cleves, Mark, Berg, and Jülich, he possessed a relatively large territory wedged between the Netherlands and Germany. Also, the new duke became a Lutheran in 1541 and, under his rule, Lutheranism made rapid strides in Gelderland as well as adjoining German duchies.[29] Not surprisingly, given this and the duke's alliances with the German Protestant Schmalkaldic League, France, and Denmark, Charles concluded that Gelderland's independence was now too dangerous to tolerate. In 1542, the Gelderlanders, under Maarten van Rossum, launched their last raids into Habsburg territory and briefly occupied Amersfoort. The following year, the Emperor, advancing with a German army down the Rhine from Bonn, defeated his adversary and under the treaty of Venlo (September 1543) compelled him to cede sovereignty over Gelderland.

The unification process was now complete, or almost so, the finishing touch being put in 1548 with the promulgation by the States General, and the Imperial Diet of the Holy Roman Empire, of the so-called Pragmatic Sanction, recognizing the Habsburg Netherlands as a separate, and single, entity and laying down the principle that sovereignty over the whole Habsburg Netherlands would pass to the Emperor's heir, and heirs, in perpetuity, as well as seeking to define the future relationship between the Netherlands and the rest of the Holy Roman Empire.[30] The articles of the Pragmatic Sanction were then endorsed, and sworn to, during 1549 by all the provincial assemblies and high courts of the seventeen provinces.[31]

The consolidation completed in 1548 brought with it substantial changes in the political, economic, and cultural life of the Netherlands. Most

[27] Bannier, *Landgrenzen*, 1, 46.
[28] Wagenaar, *Hervormer van Gelderland*, 11.
[29] Wessels 'Ketterij in de graafschap', 71-3.
[30] Malengreau, *L'Esprit particulariste*, 54, 58.
[31] Gosses and Japikse, *Handboek*, pp. ccciv-cccv.

fundamental was the ending of the political instability and endemic disorder, verging on lawlessness, which had been the lot of the north-eastern provinces for centuries. The old party strife between Frisian *Schieringers* and *Vetkopers*, and their equivalents in the other provinces, ceased during the middle decades of the sixteenth century. Gelderland was last to make the transition, but made it fairly swiftly during the 1540s and 1550s, changing from a notoriously turbulent, unsafe land, where nobles settled their disputes with the sword, to a 'land of justice', to use the contemporary expression, where disputes were settled by courts of law.[32] At the same time, border districts such as Tiel and Zaltbommel in western Gelderland, ravaged by warfare since the 1490s, began to recover. Holland too gained many benefits from unification, including improved security, an uninterrupted flow of traffic along the rivers, and better management of dams and sluices along the border with Utrecht.

While Charles did not deny Holland's special role in pacifying the provinces, and garrisoning them, his main priority, in reorganizing the institutions of the north Netherlands after 1522–3, was to tie the newly annexed regions to Brussels, rather than The Hague, and forge a more integrated Habsburg Netherlands.[33] The States of Friesland failed to retain the right to appoint the rural magistrates (*grietmannen*) in their province. After 1523 it was the regent in Brussels, together with the Stadholder and Hof of Friesland, which exercised this power.[34] Appointing the Stadholder, *grietmannen*, leading magistrates in the towns, and judges of the new Hof of Friesland, which was set up in its definitive form in 1527, the Emperor possessed greater leverage, and more patronage, in the province than had any previous regime.[35] Furthermore, even after annexing Groningen, in 1536, the Emperor retained three garrisoned citadels at Leeuwarden, Harlingen, and Staveren.

From the outset, Groningen posed a thorny administrative problem because it consisted in reality of two separate entities which continually encroached upon each other—the city with its subject districts of Gorecht and Oldambt, conquered in the fifteenth century, and the Ommelands. The Ommelands had their own assembly and were, in turn, divided into three quarters—Hunsingo, Fivelingo, and the Westerkwartier (see Map 8)—each of which also had its own quarter assembly. Although the city had previously been more anti-Habsburg than the Ommelands, the Habsburg

---

[32] Coonen, 'Gelderland', 8–16, 38–40.
[33] Lademacher, *Geschichte der Niederlande*, 32–4; Lademacher, *Die Niederlande*, 46–8.
[34] Woltjer, *Friesland in hervormingstijd*, 9–10.
[35] Theissen, *Centraal gezag*, 146, 181–4.

government, after 1536, sought to control the province by supporting the pretensions of the city.[36] Thus the Emperor confirmed the city's juridical sway over the Gorecht and Oldambt districts, disputed by the Ommelands, and upheld the city's sweeping staple rights so that much economic activity, including brewing and the marketing of some agricultural produce, was reserved for the city and forbidden in the Ommelands. At the same time the Habsburg government confirmed the grip of the leading Ommelander *jonker* families on the rural magistracies and local institutions of the Ommelands. The relationship between city and Ommelands remained an insoluble conundrum, however, and Habsburg power probably weaker than in any other province down to 1572.[37] The bafflement of central government was compounded by the proceedings against the city initiated by the Ommelanders in 1561 before the tribunals of Brussels and Mechelen, employing the noted Frisian jurist Aggaeus de Albada as their spokesman. The legal labyrinth remained unresolved when the troubles of the 1560s engulfed the Habsburg Netherlands.

In Overijssel, the Habsburg government was scarcely any more successful. The three chief towns—Deventer, Zwolle, and Kampen—prided themselves on their links with the Hanseatic League and Imperial Diet, and in 1528 had (unsuccessfully) tried to arrange Overijssel's submission to Charles as Holy Roman Emperor, rather than as count of Flanders and Holland, and duke of Brabant. In contrast to Friesland and Gelderland, it was the towns, rather than nobles, who traditionally dominated political life. But their objective had always been to maximize their civic autonomy rather than the authority of the provincial States. Consequently, Charles and his advisers simultaneously strove to strengthen provincial administration, to weaken the autonomy of the towns, while rendering provincial institutions more dependent on central government. A key change was the detaching of the previous functions of the States as a provincial high court and setting up of a separate Hof along similar lines as in Friesland and Utrecht.[38] This new Hof of Overijssel, with judicial responsibility also for Drenthe and Lingen, and, like that of Utrecht, theoretically subject to the Great Council of Mechelen,[39] was set up at Zwolle, in 1553. But the obstruction of the States was such that it had barely begun to function as late as 1566.[40]

---

[36] Ros, *Rennenberg*, 7–8.
[37] Bergsma, *Aggaeus van Albada*, 6.
[38] Slicher van Bath, *Gesch. van Overijssel*, 119.
[39] De Schepper, 'Grote Raad van Mechelen', 408.
[40] Reitsma, *Centrifugal and Centripetal Forces*, 40, 46–8.

In Utrecht, by contrast, Habsburg reorganization was more effective. Before 1528, the prince-bishop had been a notoriously weak prince, residing at Wijk-bij-Duurstede, his authority constantly challenged by the city with which he was in ceaseless conflict. The States had won the right to gather on their own initiative and set their own agenda, a right now suppressed.[41] After 1528 the States convened only with the permission of the Stadholder and central government, and their agenda was set by the Hof of Utrecht formed in 1529–30. The States of Utrecht met fairly frequently under Charles V, but usually only to vote subsidies for central government, the province's payments being fixed at 10 per cent of those of Holland.[42] While the form of the States was retained, with three 'members'—ecclesiastical chapters, *ridderschap*, and the five towns of the province—with each member having one vote, the influence of the chapters was now much reduced. The city's autonomy was also curtailed, symbolized by the removal, on the Emperor's orders, of the image of St Martin from the civic coat-of-arms. Since 1304, the Utrecht city council had been elected annually by a college of delegates of the city guilds on the 'east Netherlands model', not unlike the method at Groningen, Nijmegen, and other towns in the east. After 1528, however, the role of the guilds was ended and the ruler, through his Stadholder and Hof, nominated members of the council.[43] Utrecht city government thus came to be dominated by an élite of regents and nobles who were clients of the Emperor. In 1534 the States defined the *ridderschap* as the owners of fifty-five recognized manor houses, or *hofsteden*, with drawbridges which, though not bound by formal laws of entail, were supposed to be bought, and sold, only by nobles of the province.

Habsburg policy wrought major changes also in Gelderland. With the possible exception of Groningen, Gelderland—a relatively large territory by Netherlands standards—presented Brussels with its most intractable problem of political and legal integration. One major difficulty was that, to a much greater extent than elsewhere, numerous enclaves had survived in and adjoining Gelderland claiming direct ties with the Holy Roman Empire.[44] The group of titled nobles, or *bannerheren*, of Gelderland had evolved since 1492, almost as independent princelings, either staying neutral, or as outright supporters of the Habsburgs, in defiance of Duke Karel. The counts of Buren, and of Bronckhorst-Batenburg, had been especially active in opposing Karel's authority.[45] When Gelderland came under Charles V, the counts

[41] Fruin, *Gesch. der staatsinstellingen*, 85.
[42] Moore, 'Cathedral Chapter of St Maarten', 241–2.
[43] Vijlbrief, *Van anti-aristocratie tot democratie*, 40, 45.
[44] Jappe Alberts, *Gesch. van de beide Limburgen*, i. 124–6.
[45] Struick, *Gelre en Habsburg*, 25–6.

of Buren, Bronckhorst-Batenburg, Bergh, Culemborg, and Limburg-Stirum, and indeed also the city of Nijmegen, all claimed the right of direct appeal to the Imperial Chancery and the Diet of the Holy Roman Empire, as well as exemption from the authority of the duke of Gelderland.[46] Some lands of these lords, such as the count of Bergh's domains around 's-Heerenberg, or Bredevoort which belonged to the count of Bronckhorst-Batenburg, were along Gelderland's border with the Empire and, arguably, simply parts of the Empire.[47] Also sizeable enclaves belonged to Cleves.

Another obvious difficulty was the highly decentralized character of the province's administration and institutions. Gelderland was divided into four quarters (see Map 4)—those of Arnhem (Veluwe), Nijmegen, Zutphen, and Upper Gelderland or the Overkwartier (Roermond)—each possessing its own quarter assembly. In each of these the *ridderschap* of the quarter and small towns, as well as the 'head town', were represented. The States, or *Landdag*, of Gelderland normally met only once a year, gathering by turn in each of the 'head towns'. Both the judicial and fiscal administration were in a state of considerable disarray when the province came into the Emperor's hands in 1543.

Charles placed Gelderland under a separate Stadholder from the two existing blocks of northern provinces, that of Holland, Zeeland, and Utrecht, on the one hand, and that of Friesland, Groningen, Drenthe, Overijssel, and Lingen, on the other. The pattern thus established of dividing the northern provinces between three stadholders was to persist down to 1589. But the main innovation with which the Emperor sought to impart greater cohesion to Gelderland, and integrate the province into the Netherlands as a whole, was the Hof, or Chancery, set up at Arnhem in 1547.[48] This new body was designed to exercise both legal and political functions like the existing provincial high courts, of Holland (with Zeeland), Friesland, and Utrecht. The Hof became the main link between Brussels and the States of Gelderland as well as the four quarter assemblies. Under its articles the Hof consisted of seven councillors appointed for life, selected by means of double lists of nominees submitted by the quarter assemblies from which the Stadholder made the final choice. To preside over the Hof, Charles placed a 'Chancellor' who, from the 1540s onwards, was exceeded in political importance in the province only by the Stadholder, whose functions he assumed during the latter's absence. Through the Hof, the regime aspired to set the agenda, and control the meetings, of the States, and impose the rule, hotly

[46] Nève, *Rijkskamergerecht*, 167, 183–4.
[47] Heeringa, *De Graafschap*, 39.
[48] Zijp, *Strijd*, 177–8.

contested by the States, that they—and the quarter assemblies—could assemble only when summoned by central government, through the Hof.[49]

The Hof of Gelderland attests the not inconsiderable impact of Habsburg reorganization of the north-east during the mid-sixteenth century. The province became more orderly. Central government gained a measure of leverage. In the towns the influence of the guilds was reduced along with that of their colleges of representatives, or *gemeenslieden*.[50] The power of the patrician oligarchies was correspondingly enhanced. The Brussels regime, and Hof of Gelderland, also whittled away some of the autonomous status of the *bannerheren* (see Map 4). A few of these lordships were partially integrated into the new juridical and fiscal framework established after 1543 and the ties of the *bannerheren* with the Holy Roman Empire were reduced by the Pragmatic Sanction, at least with regard to lands fully enclaved within Gelderland.[51]

Yet the separate status of the enclaves, and *bannerheren*, was far from wholly suppressed, especially not juridically or psychologically, even where the process of Habsburg bureaucratization and centralization was most successful. By a variety of methods the titled lords defended their sovereign, or semi-sovereign, independence. The counts van den Bergh, at their town of 's-Heerenberg, and the lords of Batenburg continued minting their own coinage for several decades after 1543.[52] The situation offered innumerable administrative and judicial anomalies and Habsburg efforts to reduce these generated a resentment which was to have serious consequences for the regime in the future. The Gelderland counts, formerly the chief sponsors of Burgundian-Habsburg influence in the province, became, after 1548, not just the foremost opponents of Habsburg state-building but, down to the 1580s, the main local champions of the Reformation.

The treaty of Venlo, and subsequent Pragmatic Sanction, largely united the Low Countries under Habsburg rule. Yet it has to be recognized that this process of unification was, in several respects, superficial, more apparent than real. Not only did the prince-bishopric of Liège, a large independent principality, together with the attached county of Loon, remain outside the Habsburg Netherlands but, in large part, so did the enclaves in, and adjoining, Gelderland, including the counties of Buren and Culemborg, as well as the lordships of Leerdam, Vianen, and IJsselstein, on the border of Holland and Utrecht. Additionally, there were some thirty small lordships outside the Habsburg Netherlands, juridically under the Holy Roman

[49] Jappe Alberts, *Gesch. van Gelderland*, 91–2.
[50] Frijhoff, *Gesch. van Zutphen*, 78.
[51] Nève, *Rijkskamergerecht*, 167, 183.
[52] Heiningen, *Batenburg*, 63.

MAP 4. The four quarters of Gelderland and attached semi-sovereign lordships in the sixteenth century

Empire, strung out, south of the Overkwartier, in the Maas valley around Maastricht.[53] One of these, Gronsveld, immediately adjoined Maastricht to the south; another, Lanaken, one of the largest, practically adjoined the city to the north. Besides all this, appreciable areas of the Low Countries, today within the borders of the Netherlands, including Ravenstein, Susteren, Gennep, Mook, Sittard, Tegelen, Borculo, Lichtenvoorde, Liemers, and Huissen were acknowledged by Charles V to belong to the neighbouring German states of Jülich, Cleves, and Münster (see Map 5).

[53] Jappe Alberts, *Gesch. van de beide Limburgen*, i. 124–6.

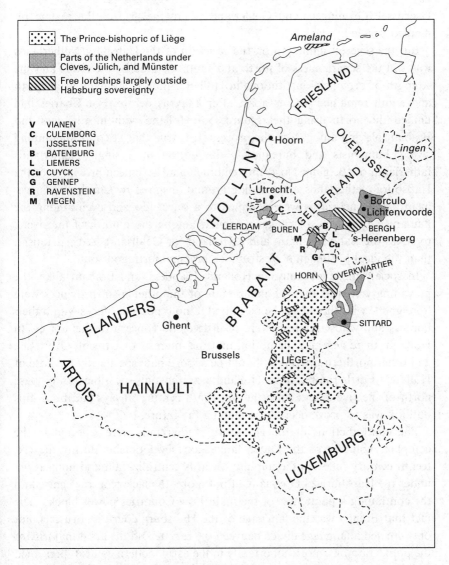

The legend reads:

The Prince-bishopric of Liège

Parts of the Netherlands under Cleves, Jülich, and Münster

Free lordships largely outside Habsburg sovereignty

V VIANEN
C CULEMBORG
I IJSSELSTEIN
B BATENBURG
L LIEMERS
Cu CUYCK
G GENNEP
R RAVENSTEIN
M MEGEN

MAP 5. The separate sovereignties and autonomous lordships of the Netherlands after 1543

The reforms, and advance of bureaucratization, in the middle decades of the sixteenth century equipped Charles with the apparatus to mount the most sustained, and determined, attempt to suppress the Reformation by administrative means seen in sixteenth-century Europe. Yet it proved an apparatus inadequate for the task, most of all in provinces such as

Overijssel, Groningen, and Gelderland where the grip of the regime remained decidedly slack.

But the severest limitation on the cohesion of the Habsburg Netherlands was still the separateness of north and south dictated by the rivers and the strength of provincial institutions in Holland. Indeed, in many ways north and south remained just as apart after 1543 as before. For Charles had unified the north using the resources of Holland without Flanders and Brabant playing any part in the process. It is true that at court and among a few humanists and bureaucrats the notion of a single Netherlands fatherland, or 'Belgium Nostrum', embracing all seventeen provinces of the Habsburg Netherlands, was gaining ground, inspired by Charles's achievement.[54] But such ideas were confined to a select few and even among the humanists there was a stronger tendency, among those north of the rivers, to stress the Batavian myth, and a Holland- or Geldrian-based patriotism, than the ideal of 'Belgium Nostrum' embracing north and south.

In society more generally, in Holland, Flanders, and Brabant alike, the prevailing view was that the inhabitants of the other main provinces were 'foreigners' who should not be permitted to hold posts or offices within their borders and whose interests were of little or no concern to themselves. In Holland, there was also the notion that the interests of Utrecht, Overijssel, and other northern provinces should be subordinate specifically to those of Holland. Furthermore, since Holland was the only possible power base north of the rivers, and since the thirteenth century always had been, this outlook was to prove decisive in shaping the future.

The contradictions of the Habsburg Netherlands were reflected in the complex evolution of the Dutch language. Developments during the sixteenth century reflected the impulse towards centralization and unification, under the Habsburgs, but equally, if not more, the lack of a true centre and the continuing separateness of the main Low Countries power blocks. The fact that French was the language of the Habsburg court, at Brussels, not only created a language divide between the regime and the great majority of the population but, more importantly in the early modern context, prevented the harnessing of court influence to any one version of Dutch. In the later Middle Ages, there were five main variants of the Dutch language—Flemish, Brabants, Hollands, Limburgs, and north-east Dutch or 'Oosters'. The political fragmentation of the Low Countries, before 1543, had served only to confirm the separateness of these various branches.[55] The commercial

---

[54] De Schepper, *Belgium Nostrum*, 5–7.
[55] De Vooys, *Gesch. van de Nederlandse taal*, 34–9, 60–1.

preponderance of Antwerp and the fact that the court, even if French-speaking, resided at Brussels helped the advance of Brabants, but not decisively. In the north it was mainly Hollands which was gaining ground, helped by the early spread of printing to cities such as Amsterdam, Delft, Leiden, Gouda, and Utrecht. But, nourished by links with the *Devotio Moderna*, the vitality of printing at Kampen and Deventer, and anti-Holland attitudes of the IJssel cities, Oosters, for the moment, held its own in the north-east and was extensively used by several of the Dutch Reformers.

In Friesland, a region with its own separate spoken language—Frisian—which was to survive as the spoken tongue of the majority throughout the early modern period and down to the present day, a version of Hollands tinted with Frisian had, over many decades, steadily been displacing Frisian as the language of the Church, culture, learning, and law. Originally, this was probably because many of the regular clergy inhabiting Friesland's cloisters were non-Frisians.[56] But the process accelerated, from the late fifteenth century, with the rise of printing. Most books in early sixteenth-century Frisian libraries not in Latin were printed in a Holland-style version of Dutch.

Undoubtedly printing, the early Reformation, and unification under the Habsburgs, together greatly strengthened the general impulse towards standardizing and unifying the Dutch language. There are innumerable indications of this. A Dutch New Testament published in 1525 professed to render the Gospel not in 'Hollands or Brabants but something between the two', a compromise 'common tongue' comprehensible throughout the Dutch-language area to all.[57] But in the absence of a specific government and Church policy on language, and the exclusive use by the court and high nobility of French, circumstances prevented the completion of this process. Several different variants of Dutch, especially Hollands, Brabants, and Oosters, continued, locally, to be the major vehicles of religion and culture.

---

[56] Hermans, 'Wat lazen Friezen', 20–1.
[57] De Vooys, *Gesch. van de Nederlandse taal*, 60.

5

The Early Dutch Reformation, 1519–1565

❖

THE NETHERLANDS CHURCH
ON THE EVE OF THE REFORMATION

The Reformation in the Low Countries began early, soon pervaded all parts of society, and ran deep. But for decades it was also an abortive Reformation, a process arrested owing to government action which left religious life and, therefore, all thought and culture in a state of profound disorientation and shock. It was a process of Reformation strikingly different from that in Germany, Switzerland, Britain, and Scandinavia in that (especially in its crucial pre-Calvinist phase) it worked essentially from the bottom upwards instead of from government circles downwards.

Dutch Protestantism was, eventually, to be dominated by Calvinism. But Calvinism appeared late on the scene in the Low Countries and played no real role before the 1550s. By that time some of the most profound effects of the Reformation, the spread of Protestant attitudes, and the undermining of the established Church, were already largely evident. By 1559, when Calvinism was only just beginning to have an impact, the Catholic Church in the Low Countries was already so weakened that its very survival in its traditional form was in doubt. King Philip II himself, when pressing the Pope to agree to the setting up of fourteen new bishoprics, assured His Holiness that without radical change 'I cannot see how our religion can be maintained in these states', and that even with such change, saving the Netherlands Church would be difficult.[1]

The most striking feature of the Netherlands Church before Philip II's 'New Bishoprics' scheme was the peripheral nature of ecclesiastical organization both north and south of the rivers. In the whole Netherlands, an area with a population of over three million, there were only five bishoprics—Arras, Cambrai, Tournai, Liège, and Utrecht—and four of these

---

[1] Dierickx, *Documents*, i. 181.

lay in the French-speaking southernmost provinces (see Map 6a).[2] The bulk of the Dutch-speaking Netherlands was comprised within just two bishoprics—Liège and Utrecht—one of which had its seat outside Habsburg territory and both of which fell under the ecclesiastical jurisdiction of the archbishop-elector of Cologne, placing Charles V in the strange position of having his northern possessions largely under the ecclesiastical supervision of a neighbouring minor vassal. To add to this picture of pastoral overlap and marginality, Cambrai came under the archbishop of Rheims, a subject of the Emperor's arch-enemy, the king of France, while parts of the north-east Netherlands lay outside the see of Utrecht, most of Groningen, together with part of Friesland, forming the archdeaconate 'Frisia' of the diocese of Münster. The ancient border between the latter and the see of Utrecht also left much of eastern Gelderland, including Hengelo, Grol, Borculo-Lichtenvoorde, and Bredevoort, under Münster.[3] To add to the patchwork, Nijmegen came under Cologne and Westerwolde, a border enclave between Groningen and the Empire, under Osnabrück.

Such lack of coherence had long worried the Burgundian and Habsburg rulers of the Netherlands. Charles the Bold, Maximilian, Philip I, and Charles V all pondered plans for ecclesiastical reorganization, especially to end the episcopal sway of Liège over large areas under Burgundian, and Habsburg, rule. But their dissatisfaction was of a political rather than spiritual nature and met with little sympathy from the Papacy. In the end, nothing came of these efforts.

The few bishops there mostly belonged to leading noble families and were of a distinctly worldly disposition. Charles de Croy, bishop of Tournai (1525–64), was a scion of one of the great Walloon noble families and took little interest in his ecclesiastical responsibilities, celebrating his first mass in Tournai only in 1540 and being practically always absent.[4] Georges van Egmond, Charles V's bishop of Utrecht (1535–59), similarly stemmed from a leading family and exemplified the old-style, pre-Reformation worldly bishop. To the neglect and disarray arising from an inadequate ecclesiastical structure were added the disparities and imbalance resulting from the population shifts of the later Middle Ages. Distribution of parishes north of the rivers, for example, still reflected the situation prior to the thirteenth century when most of the population, and significant towns, lay in the north-east. Thus, there were over one thousand parishes in the see of Utrecht but with roughly two and a half times as many in the inland

[2] De Meester, *Le Saint-Siège et les troubles*, 3.
[3] Thielen, *Gesch. van de enclave Groenlo*, 25–8.
[4] DuPlessis, *Lille and the Dutch Revolt*, 167.

provinces as in Holland and Zeeland.[5] As a result, parish organization in large Holland towns, such as Amsterdam and Delft, was exceedingly sparse.

There is little doubt that lack of clerical discipline, poor training, and absenteeism, were rife at all levels of ecclesiastical life. A frequent form of criticism directed against the Church, during the early and mid-sixteenth century, targeted the moral shortcomings of the clergy. There was complaint about the failure to live up to vows of celibacy and abstinence.[6] Some scattered statistics are available which show that concubinage among the clergy was indeed fairly widespread. In the countryside around Geertruidenberg, under 20 per cent of the lower clergy kept concubines; in other areas it appears that as many as 25 per cent did so. What was new in these complaints, though, was not the fact itself but the changing attitude towards clerical concubinage among the laity.

Beneath the bishops came the archdeacons and provosts, again often worldly noblemen. But, in many areas, the richest, most powerful part of the Church were the abbeys and monasteries, again frequently headed by indifferently motivated nobles. Monastic establishments were very numerous. In 1517, the diocese of Utrecht included 193 monastic foundations and 284 nunneries. Many were small and unimportant. But the great abbeys profoundly influenced politics, society, and culture, over wide areas. On Walcheren Island, the heart of Zeeland, the pre-eminent ecclesiastic was the abbot of Middelburg, sole representative of the Church in the pre-1572 States of Zeeland, though he sat in the States on the strength of his lands and revenues rather than as a member of the clergy. When the see of Haarlem, one of the fourteen new bishoprics, was created in 1561, much of its revenue came from the great abbey of Egmond, north of Haarlem, the position of abbot being merged with the new dignity of bishop. In Groningen, the famous old abbey of Aduard had long been at the heart of the province's spiritual life.

Despite its worldliness and lack of coherent organization, the Church in the Netherlands in the early and mid-sixteenth century was rich and powerful and exerted, as it had for centuries, an immense influence in society. The largest and most important artistic commissions, before 1572, emanated from the Church, The reason why Utrecht was the leading artistic centre north of the rivers was simply that it was the chief ecclesiastical centre.[7] Like his predecessor, Bishop van Egmond was a munificent patron, installing stained-glass windows in many churches, as well as imposing

---

[5] Post, *Kerkelijke verhoudingen*, 39.
[6] Ibid. 124–5.
[7] Dubbe and Vroom, 'Mecenaat en kunstmarkt', 17.

altarpieces such as that which Maarten van Heemskerck painted for the main church of Alkmaar in 1540–1. The great abbots were likewise major patrons. Jan van Scorel was the herald of change in painting; but his commissions came from Church bodies of one kind or another.

Society's estrangement from the established Church began, as we have seen, with the transformation of education and piety through humanism. It follows that the weakening of the Church began before 1520, as much evidence attests. Outwardly, it is true, the Catholic Church in the Netherlands was still imposing and dynamic in the decades after 1519. Numerous ecclesiastical building projects, often partly funded by lay donations, were completed during the first two-thirds of the century, including the great church spires of Breda, Amersfoort, and Groningen.[8] The principal church at Gouda, the Sint Janskerk, one of the glories of north Netherlands church architecture, was completed early in the century but heavily damaged by fire, in 1552, and then magnificently restored in the last years before the Revolt, its famous stained-glass windows being installed in the years 1555–70 in the midst of growing religious turmoil. Nevertheless, the signs are that lay enthusiasm for new ecclesiastical foundations and building was largely spent by the 1480s. The initiatives, and designs, of the great projects completed in the mid-sixteenth century mostly dated from the fifteenth. Completion of large projects in the decades after 1519 thus reflected the continued wealth and resources of the Church but not necessarily continuance of its former prestige.

The Church was imposing too in terms of numbers of clergy. In the Netherlands north of the Maas, a territory comprising about three-quarters of the area of the future Dutch Republic, there were in the early sixteenth century some 5,200 parish clergy and around 3,000 regulars, monks and friars, as well as several thousand nuns.[9] In all, the ecclesiastical population thus amounted to about 15,000 or between 1 and 2 per cent of the total population, with those directly dependent on the clergy as assistants, housekeepers, concubines, and illegitimate children comprising another 1 per cent. In some localities, the concentration of clergy was particularly high. The city of Utrecht boasted, around 1500, some 360 resident secular clergy, 7 per cent of all parish clergy in the northern Low Countries. The Sint Janskerk at Gouda and main church at Dordrecht were each served by about fifty clergy. In the city of Groningen, in 1522, there were at least fifty seculars besides a substantial number of regular clergy. Even a large village

[8] Post, *Kerkelijke verhoudingen*, 509.
[9] Rogier, *Geschiedenis*, i. 16–17; Post, *Kerkelijke verhoudingen*, 149, 165.

such as Oisterwijk in northern Brabant might have fifteen resident priests, serving as many as twenty chapels.

But, while numbers were impressive, they were steadily declining throughout the region, a process well under way before the Reformation began and even before 1500.[10] When the young Erasmus left the monastery at Steyn, near Gouda, at 25 years of age, in 1493, feeling disillusioned, he was participating in the first stirrings of a great social change which was to have a profound impact throughout the Low Countries. Everywhere monasteries and nunneries were emptying.[11] The monastery of Wateringen, near The Hague, inhabited by thirteen monks after it was founded, in 1485, contained only three by 1538. In the aristocratic nunnery of Rijnsburg, near Leiden, thirty-six sisters resided in 1453, twenty-nine in 1494, and only twenty in 1553. In Friesland and Groningen, monasteries had been traditionally strong and played an exceptionally important part during the Middle Ages. In Friesland, the number of monastic institutions was substantially greater than elsewhere, totalling around fifty. In 1511, the regular clergy alone, male and female, nearly 2,000 strong, amounted to over 2 per cent of the total Frisian population of 75,000.[12] But while the population of the province grew over the next few decades, that of the cloisters steadily declined.

More significant than loss of numbers was the loss of prestige and social standing.[13] Erasmus remarked, in 1525, on the antipathy towards monks of the general population in Holland, Zeeland, and Flanders. In 1567, the count of Aremberg, Stadholder of Friesland, and staunch upholder of the old Church, admitted that in Friesland the regular clergy were 'universally hated'.[14] Several leading Inquisitors admitted this too. Moreover, the devotional practices and attitudes inculcated by the old Church were manifestly losing their hold on the population. Pilgrimages, still immensely popular at the beginning of the century, including the pilgrimage to Jerusalem, had lost much of their former appeal by the 1550s. Traditional religious processions in towns continued to be put on, as before, by town councils and guilds, but there are numerous signs that these were treated less reverently than in the past by much of the population.[15] By the early sixteenth century, outspoken criticism of the clergy was widespread. Hieronymus Bosch (c.1450–1516) may have been an altogether unique phenome-

[10] Rogier, *Geschiedenis*, i. 21; Duke, *Reformation and Revolt*, 9–10.
[11] Post, *Kerkelijke verhoudingen*, 151.
[12] Faber, *Drie Eeuwen Friesland* i. 23–4; Woltjer, *Friesland in hervormingstijd*, 67–8, 75–6.
[13] Duke, *Reformation and Revolt*, 10, 56, 60–1, 77–9.
[14] Woltjer, *Friesland in hervormingstijd*, 75–6, 182.
[15] De Klerk, 'Zestiende-eeuwse processies', 90; Van der Pol, *Reformatie te Kampen*, 133.

non in pre-Reformation Netherlandish culture in many respects but there was nothing unusual about the preoccupation revealed by his pictures with the avariciousness of monks, sins of nuns, and licentiousness of father confessors.

THE IMPACT OF LUTHER

But if the discrediting of the old Church and its loss of moral authority began before 1520, there is no doubt that the process was powerfully accelerated, from 1519, by the impact of Luther. Martin Luther, particularly the early Luther, exerted an enormous influence in the Low Countries with his resounding protest against the moral and religious decadence of the Church and by focusing attention on the Gospels. The latter in itself involved a religious and intellectual revolution; for the elaborate forms of late medieval piety, in the Low Countries as elsewhere, centred on the sacraments, Church, and popular cults, rather than the Gospel, which was generally available only in Latin. Versions of Luther's early writings surfaced in Emden, Dordrecht, Delft, Antwerp, and elsewhere as early as 1518–19.[16] In May 1519, Erasmus wrote to Thomas Wolsey, from Antwerp, that Luther's works were circulating 'everywhere' in the Low Countries.[17] In June 1521, Albrecht Dürer, then in Antwerp, noted that he swapped copies of Lutheran texts with Cornelius Grapheus, pensionary of Antwerp and one of the few office-holders among early open advocates of Luther in the country. By the early 1520s, the Reformation, unopposed in Emden (being adopted by Count Edzard the Great, of East Friesland), and spreading through Luther's texts, was already a major religious and cultural factor in every part of the Low Countries.[18]

The Emperor Charles reacted by condemning Luther and his writings, with public book-burnings, and by setting up the Inquisition. The Emperor's ban of March 1521, published in Flanders, prohibited the 'books, sermons, and writings of the said Luther and of all his followers and adherents', ordering such works to be burnt. This was followed by a stream of local bans both in the Habsburg Netherlands and neighbouring states, particularly the ecclesiastical principalities of Liège, Utrecht, Cologne, and Münster. The public book-burnings provide an insight into the scale of the country's invasion by Lutheran literature. At Leuven, in October 1520, eighty copies of Luther's works were burnt. At Antwerp, in July 1521, in

[16] De Hoop Scheffer, *Gesch. der kerkhervorming*, i. 70–1.
[17] Visser, *Luther's geschriften in de Nederlanden*, 16.
[18] De Hoop Scheffer, *Gesch. der kerkhervorming*, i. 70, 230.

the Emperor's presence, no fewer than 400 Lutheran books—300 of them reportedly seized from booksellers—were destroyed. At Ghent, also in July 1521, another 300 Lutheran volumes were cast into the flames, while more public book-burnings followed, notably at Bruges and twice more at Antwerp, in 1522.[19]

The preponderance of south Netherlands locations should not, however, lead one to suppose that the tide of Lutheran publications was less in the north, though, owing to greater distance from central government and the fact that much of the region was still outside Habsburg territory, the repression was less intense there to begin with. Nevertheless, in May 1522, the Leiden *vroedschap* ordered that all Lutheran texts in the town be surrendered. At Deventer, in September 1524, the magistracy complained that Luther's works were being widely distributed and read amongst both clergy and laity.[20] In August 1525, Erasmus reported that most of the 'Hollanders, Zeelanders, and Flemish knew the doctrines of Luther'.[21] In the Emperor's edict for Holland of September 1525, the spread of Luther's influence was specifically blamed on the fact that many clergy had adopted Luther's views and that unsophisticated folk were reading Luther in translation. The mass burning of Lutheran literature in the north began in the episcopal city of Utrecht in 1521, but it was not until 1526 that the first book-burnings occurred on Habsburg territory, at Amsterdam.[22] The English ambassador in the Habsburg Netherlands, Sir John Hackett, a man with extensive knowledge of the country, and the Dutch language, reported to Cardinal Wolsey, in May 1527, that Luther's influence was spreading 'gretly in this partys specially in Holland, Seland, Brabant and Flandrys' and that the Low Countries 'be all reddy in great danger for yf there be three men that speckes, the tweyn keepis Luther ys openyon'.[23] The latter was somewhat exaggerated perhaps but there is no question that Luther's influence was extremely widespread, except in the French-speaking areas.[24]

That Luther's publications, and extracts from Luther, circulated more profusely in the Dutch-speaking Netherlands than France, England, or Scandinavia, is unsurprising. In the first place, the Netherlands, having a more highly urbanized society than neighbouring lands, boasted higher levels of literacy. Secondly, Christian humanism had begun in the Netherlands and, by the early 1520s, made a greater impact in civic Latin schools,

[19] Kronenberg, *Verboden boeken*, 31–3.
[20] Visser, *Luther's geschriften*, 18.
[21] Te Water, *Kort Verhael*, 5.
[22] Visser, *Luther's geschriften*, 11.
[23] Hackett, *The Letters*, 80–1.
[24] Spruyt, 'Humanisme, evangelisme en Reformatie', 36.

and society generally, than elsewhere. Among the most notable early Protestants in the Netherlands were such leading humanists as Geldenhauer and Gerardus Listrius, rector of the Latin school at Zwolle. Listrius was already an adherent of Luther by 1520 and, in 1521, was expelled by the city council because of the effect he was having on civic life.[25] Thirdly, Antwerp was, with the possible exception of Paris, the chief centre for publishing in the whole of Europe, while the Netherlands, more generally, was noted for the large number of its printers and booksellers. Finally, the intense river and coastal traffic between Germany and the Netherlands rendered the Low Countries the principal outlet for literature being transported from Germany.

In the north great quantities of Lutheran literature emanated from Emden, the Hansa towns, and Antwerp, and also, during the early and mid-1520s, before government persecution became more systematic, was printed locally. The principal printing centres there were Deventer, Zwolle, Amsterdam, and Leiden.[26] No doubt works by Luther himself comprised a comparatively small part of the total volume of publications in the Netherlands. Altogether around fifty of Luther's texts were published in Dutch—in various places, including Overijssel before that province's incorporation into the Habsburg Netherlands—in the period down to 1540, without counting translations of Luther's renderings of Scripture and extracts incorporated into other books. This is modest, given that, between them, the fifty-six printers active at Antwerp in the four decades 1500–40 produced 2,480 books and that this figure comprises no more than 54 per cent of the total published in the Netherlands.[27] But the number of editions of Luther, and frequency of extracts in works which did not bear his name, would have been much less had not total printed output and the number of bookshops and libraries been so great.

Initially, Charles encountered immense difficulty in combating the Reformation in the Netherlands, especially in the north. While Protestantism filtered only slowly down the Rhine, past Cologne, the Reformation triumphed in Bremen and East Friesland as early as 1524. Moreover, much of the north remained outside Habsburg control until many years after Luther's influence began to permeate the region. No measures combated the Reformation in Friesland until Charles's Stadholder published a ban against Luther and his writings in 1526. Nothing could be done in Groningen until the late 1530s.[28] At Utrecht where the Erasmian bishop Philip of Burgundy

[25] Ibid. 45.
[26] Visser, *Luther's geschriften*, 27.
[27] Kronenberg, *Verboden boeken*, 65; Kronenberg, 'Uitgaven van Luther', 5–15.
[28] Meihuizen, *Menno Simons*, 22.

(d. 1524) was himself not unsympathetic, seemingly, to the Lutheran message, no heretic was burnt until 1533. In the Overijssel cities where, again, crypto-Protestantism was widespread from the early 1520s onwards, it is doubtful whether any serious pressure was brought to bear at any stage down to the coming of Alva.[29]

But, despite the difficulties, Charles gradually mobilized a formidable system of repression.[30] In this he showed great determination and was assisted by political developments which extended Habsburg sway across the north-east and by the simultaneous intensification of persecution in the neighbouring prince-bishopric of Liège. Central to his strategy was the Netherlands Inquisition set up with Frans Van der Hulst as inquisitor-general, in 1522, and approved by the Pope the following year. Several deputy inquisitors were appointed, among them the Dominican Jacob van Hoogstraten, a notorious obscurantist loathed by German, as well as Dutch, humanists, and Nicolaas van Egmond, an anti-humanist feared by Erasmus. Initially, the Inquisition concentrated its attention on the friars of Luther's own order, the Augustinians, whose friaries in the Low Countries were suspected of being breeding grounds of Lutheran doctrine.[31] The first two men executed by the Inquisition, Hendrik Voet and Jan van Etten, were Augustinian friars from 's-Hertogenbosch burnt in the great market-place of Brussels, in July 1523. These were the first Protestant martyrs not only in the Netherlands but in western Europe, and the news of their fate caused a sensation throughout Germany, as well as the Low Countries, prompting Luther to send his famous open letter from Wittenberg to 'all beloved brothers in Christ in Holland, Brabant, and Flanders', lamenting the two lost 'pearls of Christ'. More executions followed though it was not until 1525 that the Inquisition burnt its first victim in the north Netherlands.[32]

Executions of Protestants in these years were few in number but great in impact. In September 1526, Jan Jansen, of Woerden, a former priest at The Hague who had espoused Luther's cause and visited Luther at Wittenberg, was burnt in the Binnenhof, the administrative centre of The Hague, in the presence of inquisitors, senior officials, and judges.[33] The first woman executed in Holland, Wendelmoet Claesdochter, of Monnikendam, was burnt at The Hague before three inquisitors, in November 1527. Many people, evidently, felt intense sympathy for these martyrs. Poetic laments

[29] Van der Pol, *Reformatie te Kampen*, 91–2, 128–31.
[30] Duke, *Reformation and Revolt*, 57, 73–4, 153–4.
[31] De Hoop Scheffer, *Gesch. der kerkhervorming*, i. 245, 253.
[32] Valvekens, *Inquisitie in de Nederlanden*, 177, 193.
[33] Ibid. 194–5.

over their fate, composed by members of rhetoric clubs (see p. 122 below), began circulating. There was also official obstruction. Willem Gnapheus, rector of the Latin school in The Hague, was arrested by the Inquisition for heresy in 1523, but released by the States of Holland, re-arrested in 1525, and condemned to death, but helped to escape to Germany before he could be executed.[34]

At the same time the Emperor stepped up the pressure on the authorities in the north Netherlands to act against the Reformation. Persecution began in earnest in Holland in 1525. The same year the new bishop of Utrecht changed his predecessor's lenient policy and began to take repressive measures. In Friesland, the first heretic was burnt in 1530.[35] Karel, duke of Gelderland, instigated the first executions at Nijmegen and Arnhem.[36] It is true that by the time the pressure began to be felt in the mid-1520s pro-Reformation attitudes and literature were so widespread, that there was no possibility of suppressing the Reformation as such. The inquisitors knew that Protestant books were to be found everywhere at least in the towns, that everyone knew and talked about them, and that support for the established Church was generally weak.[37] But this does not mean that the persecution and operations of the Inquisition were pointless. On the contrary, given the limited resources at the Inquisition's disposal, it was remarkably effective in helping the Emperor curb, and partly paralyse, the Reformation in the Low Countries. This it did by targeting the intellectual élite, especially clergy, booksellers, schoolmasters, and officials, and making it impossible for such men to adhere openly to the Reformation without sacrificing their posts, possessions, and lives. The repression did not silence the voice of Protestantism in the Low Countries, and there was never any prospect that it could. But it did compel the country's intellectual élites to draw a veil of concealment over their religious beliefs, discussions, and reading, creating a duality, a gulf between conviction and practice, which shattered and traumatized the spiritual world of the Netherlands. The divorce of appearance from reality, and prevalence of subterfuge, hypocrisy, and pretence, quickly pervaded every corner of Low Countries life. As early as 1522, the rector of the Latin school at Delft remarked that most men kept their Protestant sympathies to themselves and that the town was rife with Nicodemism (dissimulation).[38]

[34] Ibid. 202–3.
[35] Bergsma, 'Uyt Christelijcken yver', 70.
[36] Wagenaar, *Hervormer van Gelderland*, 2–9.
[37] Valvekens, *Inquisitie in de Nederlanden*, 270–3.
[38] Spruyt, 'Humanisme, evangelisme en Reformatie', 35.

Most decisive of all, the Emperor's crack-down rendered it impossible, without taking extreme risks, to set up any overtly Protestant organization or group. By the mid 1520s pro-Reformation sentiment was widespread, at least in the Dutch-speaking provinces where printing, humanism and Lutheranism had had their main impact and there was a correspondingly strong desire for new forms of devotion and spiritual guidance. In 1527, the Stadholder of Holland declared 'that the land of Holland and especially Amsterdam, Delft, and Hoorn are very heavily infected [with heresy, and] that they are full of Lutheranism'.[39] The impulse was there but not the opportunity. There are indications that in some places, notably Leiden, Utrecht, 's-Hertogenbosch, and Veere, organized conventicles with Protestant preaching did emerge for a few years in the late 1520s.[40] But such activity proved ephemeral and was further hindered by Luther's own condemnation of clandestine congregations.[41]

FRAGMENTATION

The situation prevailing by the late 1520s, with the Reformation lacking any kind of institutional structure, was to exert a lasting influence on the subsequent development of Protestantism in the Netherlands. Just when, in Germany, confessional lines hardened, and doctrinal positions were becoming entrenched, in the Low Countries all prospect of imparting a disciplined theological and organizational framework to the Reformation withered, and remained absent for decades. Thus, the parting of ways between Dutch and German Protestantism, and Dutch and German Protestant culture, had already taken place by the late 1520s. This is not to say that the Netherlands crypto-Protestants were sealed off from, or unresponsive to, the disputes over the eucharist and other theological issues escalating in Germany and Switzerland. On the contrary, Zwinglian and, to a lesser extent, Buceran influences were powerfully felt in the Low Countries, including East Friesland, from around 1525 onwards.[42] In July 1525, Bucer himself wrote to Zwingli, from Strasburg, that (as a result especially of the activity of Hinne Rode, former rector of the Hieronymus school at Utrecht, who had spent many months in 1523–4 among Zwingli's circle at Zurich) 'all Holland and Friesland' knew of the growing split between Luther and his Reformed

[39] Mellink, *Wederdopers*, 340.
[40] De Hoop Scheffer, *Gesch. der kerkhervorming*, i. 515, 519; Knappert, *Opkomst*, 119–20.
[41] Pont, *Gesch. van het Lutheranisme*, 41.
[42] Pettegree, *Emden and the Dutch Revolt*, 12, 34.

critics, and were adopting Zwinglian-Buceran views.[43] But in the spiritual climate prevailing in the Low Countries there was no way that doctrinal lines could be drawn up or become rigid. In such conditions Lutheranism in its more structured, dogmatic, post-1525 form, made little headway.[44] By 1530, in outlook and matters of doctrine, the German and Netherlands Reformations were already worlds apart. The distinctive character of early Dutch Protestantism, a spiritual outlook which was to endure and retain its force despite the later onset of Calvinism, and become an integral part of the religious world of the north Netherlands after 1572, was not so much Erasmian and undogmatic—as has often been claimed—as dogmatically pluriform and radically decentralized, a bewildering plethora of doctrines and standpoints with the lines between them continually fluid. In Groningen the term 'Zwinglians' was still being used as a generic term for all the Protestant streams collectively as late as 1580.[45]

Early Dutch Protestantism was so fluid that it was unable to fragment. In the 1530s only one doctrinal rift had any broad significance—that between mainstream Dutch crypto-Protestantism, on the one hand, and Anabaptism, on the other.[46] Before 1530 no Protestants in the Low Countries were Anabaptists and after 1530 only a small minority were. But only the Anabaptists, in their fervour, separated themselves from the rest of the community, refusing to attend church and forming their own prayer-gatherings in defiance of the government.[47] These were the Protestants who accepted the risks and paid the price. Their defiance resulted in terrible persecution which was to last more than three decades. But while their uncompromising stance, and vulnerability, ensured they remained a small minority of those who rejected the established Church, they were the majority of those who unreservedly laboured for a Reformation in the Low Countries, gaining a sense of moral superiority from suffering, and being in the forefront, whilst the rest, to save themselves, held back. This created a paradoxical situation. Although a tiny minority—and doctrinally untypical—they were, nevertheless, the vanguard of the Dutch Reformation during the long period of gestation between 1530 and the 1560s, except in East Friesland,[48] where non-Anabaptist Dutch Protestant exiles, such as

---

[43] Dankbaar, *Martin Bucer's Beziehungen zu den Niederlanden*, 14; De Bruin, 'Hinne Rode', 205.
[44] Visser, *Luther's geschriften*, 130–7.
[45] Trosée, *Verraad van George van Lalaing*, 180.
[46] Duke, *Reformation and Revolt*, 57–8.
[47] Augustijn, 'Anabaptisme', 21.
[48] Pettegree, *Emden and the Dutch Revolt*, 11–12, 29–35.

Hinne Rode, could organize freely, and in Lutheran enclaves, along the Jülich, Cleves, and Gelderland borders.

The Anabaptist movement which arose first in Zurich, in the mid-1520s, subsequently spread rapidly to other parts of Switzerland and Germany but did not reach the Low Countries until June 1530 when Melchior Hoffman arrived in Emden, from Strasburg, and spent several months organizing a community. Emden served as the hub of early Dutch Anabaptism. Entering Habsburg territory, Melchiorite converts, notably the tailor Sikke Freerks, working at Leeuwarden, and Jan Volkertsz. Trijpmaker, at Amsterdam, established the original network of Anabaptist communities in the Netherlands. These early Dutch Anabaptist leaders were soon eliminated: Freerks was beheaded, at Leeuwarden, in March 1531, while Trijpmaker, and eight others of the Amsterdam community, were seized, sent to The Hague, and executed there, later in 1531. But the effect of these executions enhanced rather than lessened the movement's appeal. Communities rapidly took root especially in the northern part of Holland, Friesland, and, also, Groningen, then still outside the Habsburg Netherlands and where, until 1537,[49] Anabaptists were relatively safe.

Melchiorite Anabaptism in the Netherlands, though fervent, was organizationally and doctrinally a chaotic movement prone to fragment.[50] It was radical not so much theologically as emotionally and psychologically. The intensifying repression in the Netherlands generated a frustration and pent-up iconoclastic fury which marked the Dutch Reformation off in yet another respect from the Reformation elsewhere. In the Low Countries, around 1530, those whose anger at having to bottle up their alienation from the old Church boiled over simply had nowhere to turn except the Anabaptists. Those too aroused to keep quiet ended up in their midst, among them David Joris of Delft, one of the most remarkable figures of the Dutch Reformation, whose Lutheran phase (1524–8) already displayed frequent indications of activism, including harsh reproaches against those who knelt before images of the Virgin in the streets, and depositing Protestant texts in churches. Finally, he was forced to go into hiding, after causing an uproar in Delft, shouting out protests against a religious procession in the street. Absorbing the activist impulse gave Anabaptism in the Netherlands a quite different role than in Germany or Switzerland where, on the whole, Anabaptism was socially and theologically a marginal factor. In the Low Countries, from 1530 to the late 1550s, Anabaptism

[49] Doornkaat Koolman, *Dirk Philips*, 17.
[50] Meihuizen, *Menno Simons*, 2–4.

fulfilled a crucial function, acting as the Reformation's arm and mouth-piece.[51] Not a few Lutherans and Zwinglians went over to Anabaptism.[52]

The movement rapidly split into those who expressed their rejection of the old Church, by taking up arms to assist the Almighty in the work of destroying an ungodly order, and those who preached passive defiance in the face of persecution.[53] It was especially the more militant wing which became infused with chiliastic yearnings and apocalyptic notions. Those who preached revolution, Jan Matthijsz, the prophet of Haarlem, and Jan Beuckelsz, the prophet of Leiden, stirred an agitation which they trans-ferred, at the beginning of 1534, to the Westphalian town of Münster.[54] Local Anabaptists together with recent Dutch arrivals took control of the town, expelling everyone who refused to undergo second baptism. From Münster, a summons then went out to the Anabaptist communities in the Low Countries to come with their weapons, and wives, and help build the New Jerusalem. Hundreds of armed Anabaptists, including around 200 from the Leiden area, streamed from Holland, Friesland, and also the Maas valley around Maastricht and Roermond, crossing the IJssel and Rhine on their way to Münster,[55] though many were intercepted by the authorities and dispersed.

Once an organized siege began, Anabaptists from elsewhere could no longer reach the town. But the siege heightened the sense of being on the verge of a great, and violent, apocalyptic change. The ferment at Amster-dam (where, it was estimated, there were some 3,000 Anabaptists) produced an incident, in March 1534, when a small group ran naked through the city brandishing swords and menacing the godless.[56] The civic militia were called out, and a crack-down began. The first batch of executions took place in Haarlem and on the Dam, in Amsterdam, at the end of March. The radicals in Münster held out stubbornly, the siege dragging on for eighteen months, exerting an unsettling influence throughout the Dutch-speaking Nether-lands, including Flanders, as well as Jülich-Cleves and Westphalia.[57] Besides Amsterdam and Haarlem, the ferment seethed with particular force in Delft, where the glass-painter David Joris was increasingly drawn into local Anabaptist gatherings while steering clear of Munsterite militancy. As with

[51] Duke, *Reformation and Revolt*, 58–9, 85–9.
[52] Mellink, *Wederdopers*, 334–6.
[53] Meihuizen, *Menno Simons*, 4, 29.
[54] Mellink, *Wederdopers*, 25–30, 186.
[55] Ibid. 32–8; Jappe Alberts, *Gesch. van de beide Limburgen*, i. 134.
[56] Brugmans, *Gesch. van Amsterdam*, i. 275–81.
[57] Mellink, *Wederdopers*, 25–38; Decavele, *Dageraad*, ii. 301–4, 607.

Menno Simons in Friesland, the Munsterite rising inspired in some a strongly pacifist reaction.[58]

In March 1535, an armed band of some 300 Frisian Anabaptists, including Pieter Simons, an elder brother of Menno, seized, and fortified, the Cistercian abbey of Oldeclooster, near Bolsward.[59] Destroying the images and altars, they set up there their New Jerusalem. The Stadholder, Schenk von Tautenburg, besieged the abbey, using artillery to reduce its defenders. Many were dead when the abbey fell. Of the remainder, twenty-four men were hanged on the spot, or afterwards beheaded, while the women were taken to a nearby river and executed by drowning. Another band, from Groningen, unable to reach Oldeclooster, unsuccessfully attacked the abbey of Warsum. These events, and the continuing Munsterite resistance, led to an intensification of persecution and successive waves of executions at Amsterdam, The Hague, Leiden, Maastricht, Liège, Middelburg, Deventer, and Wesel, in Cleves. On 10 May 1535, armed militants stormed the Amsterdam town hall and were only dislodged by the city authorities after a pitched battle which left dozens of dead and dying. Further executions followed. On 15 May, seven Anabaptist women were executed together, at Amsterdam, by drowning.

The intensifying spiral of violence and repression, followed by the traumatic impact of the fall of Münster, in the summer of 1535, plunged Dutch Anabaptism into its culminating spiritual crisis. The movement responded in different ways to the shock, splitting into warring fragments.[60] In the last phase of the Münster revolution, Jan of Leiden and other leaders had established a new social order, with a hierarchy of authority and a system of polygamous marriage. But the Münster programme, and its violence, proved deeply divisive. In vain, the leaders of the splinter groups tried to reunify their movement, holding gatherings of delegates from all over the Netherlands and Westphalia, at Bocholt, in September 1536, and at Oldenburg in 1538.[61]

After Münster, there were broadly five groups making up the world of Anabaptism in the Netherlands, and north-west Germany.[62] There were the Munsterites who adhered to the programme of Jan of Leiden, retaining his fanatical chiliastic expectations steeped in fierce eschatology and divine vengeance on the godless. Secondly, a still more extreme wing, active

[58] Brandsma, *Menno Simons*, 35–42.
[59] Ibid. 34.
[60] Doornkaat Koolman, *Dirk Philips*, 12–13.
[61] Bainton, *David Joris*, 25.
[62] Kühler, *Gesch. der Ned. Doopsgezinden*, 192–3; Waite, *David Joris*, 113–14; see also Hsia, *Society and Religion in Münster*, 7–8.

terrorists, followed the lead of Jan van Batenburg, an illegitimate son of a Dutch nobleman, in roaming the countryside in bands, raiding villages, monasteries, and churches, in western Westphalia and the north Netherlands. The 'Batenburgers' made a considerable impact even after Batenburg himself was caught, in 1537, and executed. In December 1535, some sixty armed radicals tried to seize the village of Hazerswoude, near Delft; ten were killed in the attempt, others captured, most escaped.

On the pacifist side, there were the original Melchiorites, the Davidites— or followers of David Joris—and, finally, at this stage mainly in Friesland and Groningen, and more rural in character, the followers of Obbe Philips and Menno Simons. An analysis of some seventy known Dutch Anabaptist teachers and leaders active in the years 1536–40 shows that at this time the followers of David Joris were the most important group and the Mennonites a lesser stream.[63] At the Bocholt conference, in 1536, a meeting of some twenty-five delegates from Holland, Friesland, Groningen, Overijssel, Gelderland, Jülich-Cleves, and Westphalia, Joris led the pacifist opposition to the eschatology of godly vengeance on the godless, propounded by the Batenburgers and Munsterites.[64]

Remarkably, Joris survived in hiding, at Delft, with a huge price on his head, through the late 1530s. His movement was fiercely persecuted. A total of twenty-seven David-Jorists—including his mother—were executed, in Delft alone, in 1539; at least another seventy-three of his followers—including thirteen in Haarlem—were executed in Holland in the same year.[65] The strain of the terror, judicial liquidation of his followers, and effects of lying still for long periods in unheated attics made him increasingly prone to visionary experiences. Despite the circumstances, he had some success in extending his influence in Holland, Friesland, and Utrecht, at one point winning over a whole group of former Batenburgers.

Although Joris's message spread, his movement remained predominantly Holland-based and urban in character. Of 219 Davidites identified by scholarly research, some two-thirds lived in the main Holland towns.[66] Typically, though, they were 'outsiders', often migrant artisans from outside Holland. Most of Joris's adherents were artisans, especially cloth workers; a few were wealthy, even noble. The essentially urban character of the David-Jorists helps explain the most striking difference between this movement and the Anabaptism of Menno Simons which, subsequently, became

---

[63] Waite, *David Joris*, 114.
[64] Bainton, *David Joris*, 25.
[65] Ibid. 72–3.
[66] Ibid. 145–7.

the mainstream of Dutch Anabaptism. Where the latter was fully separatist, and sectarian, in character,[67] segregating itself rigidly from the world of non-believers, Joris had little choice but to adapt to an urban environment where insistence on gathering in separate conventicles was tantamount to self-destruction. Joris accordingly allowed his followers to merge with their surroundings and attend Catholic churches, including conventional baptisms.

This tension between Nicodemist compromise and unreserved commitment, leading to martyrdom, often arose in Joris's life and work. What, above all, his movement exemplifies is the hazardous nature of pacifist Anabaptism in the Dutch urban context of the time. Ultimately, the only viable alternative to Joris's partial Nicodemism was the guerrilla warfare of the Batenburgers. Whilst he remained within the Anabaptist camp, Joris was irretrievably trapped in his spiritual dilemma. On the one hand, he shrank from the sacrifice inherent in undisguised defiance; on the other, he rebutted accusations that he urged his flock to conceal their beliefs and avoid martyrdom: 'I advise no one that he should seek to keep his own life here', he wrote, 'or that he should run from death . . . but instead to desire to stand against [his enemy] ready to be delivered up as sheep to the slaughter'.[68]

In 1539 Joris fled Delft, first to Haarlem, then Deventer, and, finally, Antwerp. There he found refuge in a noble household and took stock. From 1540 onwards, Joris's teaching increasingly diverged from its previous Anabaptist course.[69] The Nicodemist tendencies prevailed and he shifted to an essentially Spiritualist stance. At the heart of his new approach was a conviction of the duality of all reality and supremacy of inner truth over outward appearance. All external means, including sacraments and Scripture itself, lost their centrality for Joris. Now, what mattered for him, as for all Spiritualists, was the direct entry of the Spirit of God into the hearts and minds of believers.[70] Although it is not known whether Joris was, at this time, directly influenced by the great German Spiritualists Sebastian Franck and Caspar von Schwenckfeld, it is evident these leaders were becoming known in the Low Countries at this time, and that, in the face of stiffer persecution than was to be encountered anywhere else outside the Iberian peninsula, Spiritualism attained, from this point on, a position of great importance in the Dutch Reformation. Joris finally parted ways with the

---

[67] Kühler, *Gesch. der Ned. doopsgezinden*, 301, 316–18.
[68] Waite, *David Joris*, 79–80.
[69] Ibid. 177–86.
[70] Zijlstra, 'Tgeloove is vrij', 44–5.

Anabaptist movement in 1544 when he moved to Basel, where he spent the remainder of his life.

After 1540, mainstream Dutch Anabaptism followed the lead of the Frisian movement of Obbe and Dirk Philips and Menno Simons. Pacifist Anabaptism was now firmly entrenched in Holland, Utrecht, and Overijssel, as well as further south in Antwerp, Flanders, and, sporadically, in the Walloon area. But it was in Friesland and Groningen that the movement was to consolidate. Menno Simons (c.1496–1561), arguably the greatest figure of the Dutch Reformation, was also in many ways a profoundly representative figure. Privately, as he recorded later, he had been won over by Luther's doctrines, by the early 1520s.[71] Subsequently, like many Dutch crypto-Protestants, he discarded Luther for Zwingli. Finally, around 1531, he rejected the Zwinglian-Buceran approach in favour of Anabaptist teaching.[72] Nevertheless (like many others) he remained outwardly loyal to the old Church and remained the Catholic parish priest at the village of Witmarsum in Friesland. In 1534–5 he preached fervently against the violence of the Munsterites.[73] Only in 1536, after being a crypto-Protestant for more than a decade, did he finally break openly with the Catholic Church. Joining the Anabaptists, he fled to Groningen only to find, a year later, that Habsburg persecution followed him there. He then reverted to a clandestine existence in Friesland. It was here that he wrote his principal work, the *Fondament-Boeck* (1539), known to modern American Mennonites as the *The Foundation of Christian Doctrine*. In the years 1541–3, Menno laboured mainly in Amsterdam, after 1543, chiefly in north-west Germany, carving out a zone of influence extending from Cologne as far east as Lübeck, on the Baltic coast. But Menno continued to visit the north of the Habsburg Netherlands, as well as Emden, intermittently and remained in touch with the Dutch communities by letter.

Menno, assisted by Dirk Philips, stabilized and reinvigorated Dutch Anabaptism. Though it cannot be said that he built a great system of theology, he did set out pacifist Anabaptist teaching in a more orderly manner than had been done before, the *Fondament-Boeck* being for the Anabaptists what Calvin's *Institutes* was for the Calvinists.[74] He was not a great scholar or biblical exegete. His greatness lay chiefly in his personality and ability, through his writing and life-style, to propagate a vision of practical holiness and submission to the congregation, a vision of a

---

[71] *The Complete Writings of Menno Simons*, 8, 11.
[72] Brandsma, *Menno Simons*, 42.
[73] *The Complete Writings of Menno Simons*, 11.
[74] Brandsma, *Menno Simons*, 52–4.

disciplined, sober life-style, based on Scripture.[75] What Menno asked of the believer was humility and the faithful practice of a Christian way of life as he understood Christ to have lived and taught it. Of women, he asked also that they avoid 'all unnecessary adornment and display, making or desiring no other clothes than those which are necessary'.[76] His inspiration has continued to be a force in the Christian world until the present day.

Menno denounced violence. But it cannot be said that he was passive in his attitude to the Habsburg government and the established Church. On the contrary, there is a sense in which he took up the fight of the Munsterites whilst rejecting their weapons. His weapon was the pen. In the late 1530s, in Friesland, Menno completed a series of works (in Dutch), and took a keen interest in their distribution throughout the Netherlands. One of his chief helpers in Amsterdam, Jan Claeszoon, was a bookseller and zealous distributor of his writings, until his arrest and execution in 1544, shortly after Menno's flight to Germany. Menno's writings were addressed to the Habsburg authorities and general public, as well as to the Anabaptist faithful, and were not just an exposition of theology but a form of counter-offensive against the persecution to which he and his followers were being subjected. In his *Fondament-Boeck*, he urges the secular and ecclesiastical authorities to 'humble yourselves in the name of Jesus': 'examine, I say, our doctrine, and you will find, through the grace of God, that it is the pure and unadulterated teaching of Christ, the holy Word, the sword of the Spirit by which all must be judged that dwell upon the earth'.[77] Menno may have been a pacifist but, like the Anabaptist militants and Batenburgers, he urged his followers to acknowledge no government other than that of Christ.[78] Menno's attack was directed not only against secular authorities and the Catholic Church, which he regarded as an abomination, but also against Luther and Bucer, false prophets, as he saw them, who professed to be renewing Christianity on the basis of Scripture, whilst, in fact, disregarding Scripture. He emphasizes this not least in his discussion of infant baptism: Luther and Bucer subscribe to the same doctrine on infant baptism as the Catholic Church and by doing so discredit themselves, 'for we know, by the Grace of God, that there is not one jot of Scripture with which they can support it'.[79]

Dirk Philips (1504–68), like Menno, was a Frisian, pacifist, advocate of discipline and the congregation, and wielder of the pen against the estab-

---

[75] Ibid. 47–54; Meihuizen, *Menno Simons*, 32–4.
[76] *The Complete Writings of Menno Simons*, 381.
[77] Ibid. 28, 117, 105.
[78] Wessel, *Leerstellige strijd*, 268–70.
[79] *The Complete Writings of Menno Simons*, 129.

lished order. An eager scholar, he was better acquainted than Menno with the works of Erasmus and Luther and no less tireless as an organizer and preacher. He was also more authoritarian and placed greater emphasis on the submission of the individual to the congregation and elders. His *Enchiridion*, like the *Fondament-Boeck* a general statement of the pacifist Anabaptist position, is one of the bulkiest as well as most important works of the Dutch Reformation.[80]

The new emphasis on orderliness and discipline gave Menno's Anabaptism durability and a greater capacity to expand than any previous German or Dutch Anabaptist movement. Through Menno's writings, written in a simple Dutch, and their system of employing full-time itinerant preachers, and by establishing a strong hierarchy of authority, Menno and Dirk built a relatively cohesive movement not only in the northern Netherlands but also in the Dutch-speaking south and adjoining parts of Westphalia and East Friesland. In Flanders, the initial Anabaptist upsurge, in the wake of Münster, was virtually extinguished by severe persecution, particularly in 1538. But from around 1550, Flemish Anabaptism revived, inspired by Menno's teachings and the vigorous proselytizing of his deputies, notably Leenaert Bouwens, who was constantly on the move, and Gillis van Aken, who plied ceaselessly between Aachen, Antwerp, Ghent, and Kortrijk.[81]

In Friesland, a peripheral province where persecution was perfunctory, large numbers of ordinary folk flocked to the Mennonites. By the late sixteenth century, the indications are, the Anabaptists accounted for as much as 20 per cent, or even 25 per cent, of the Frisian population.[82] By contrast, in the inner provinces, the Anabaptists' defiance of government and established Church ensured that the Anabaptists supplied most of those who fell victim to the persecution—in the south as in the north. At Antwerp 161 persons were executed for heresy between 1522 and 1565, including six 'Lutherans', a dozen Calvinists, and 139 Anabaptists of various hues. Of fifty-six martyrs executed at Ghent, fifty were Anabaptists, a pattern repeated throughout the county of Flanders.[83] The pattern was the same around Maastricht and Roermond, in the Maas valley, and the Dutch-speaking north of the bishopric of Liège where Anabaptism (like Lutheran-Zwinglian influence) was much stronger than in the French-speaking areas further south. In Friesland the total number of martyrs was a few dozen but

[80] Kühler, *Gesch. der Ned. doopsgezinden*, 301, 321.
[81] Decavele, *Dageraad*, ii. 301–4, 433–6.
[82] Bergsma, 'Uyt Christelijcken yver', 79.
[83] Van der Wiele, 'Inquisitierechtbank', 60; Valvekens, *Inquisitie*, 225.

nearly all were Anabaptists. In Holland, executions were fairly numerous in the 1530s and 1540s;[84] but again mostly of Anabaptists.

But the nature of the religious crisis gripping the Netherlands by the 1540s cannot be grasped by looking at the pattern of executions. Anabaptists constituted a small proportion of the population and included no humanists, office-holders, or regents, and few merchants or educated men. The real crisis, no less frightening to the first Calvinist preachers, in the 1550s, than to the government and Inquisition, was the silent, and pluriform, defection of the highly educated, of the country's élites, and of a great part of the general public, from the old Church. Many of the premisses of the Ana-baptists differed little from those of the mass of those who rejected the exist-ing Church inwardly. The real difference between Anabaptists and the rest was that the former physically separated themselves from the Church, setting up their own organization, while the majority, crypto-Protestants and Ni-codemists, stuck to intermediate solutions, paths passing noncommittally between the Reformation and Catholicism.[85] The first Calvinist preachers, such as Guy de Brès, labouring in Valenciennes and Tournai, were appalled to find, wherever they turned, not only Anabaptists and David- Jorists but great numbers of semi-Lutherans, 'Libertines', 'Epicureans', and, still worse in de Brès's view, Nicodemists and confirmed dissimulators.[86]

It was natural, certainly in the core provinces, that office-holders, regents, nobles, and, not least, nominally Catholic priests should be reluctant to defy the Habsburg regime by openly championing Protestantism. Among the higher nobility, only such nobles as Hendrik van Brederode, at Vianen, or the count of Culemborg, who entertained no hope of winning the ruler's favour, or high offices, and who felt safe in the judicial autonomy of their lordships (eventually) became more or less open about their Protestant sympathies.[87] In general, the broad response of the Netherlands élites was to strive for one or another theological *via media*, enabling them to reject the old Church inwardly, and partake of new theologies, while, at the same time, outwardly conforming to Catholicism. In the northern peripheral provinces where the royal grip on the judicial process was weak, less subtlety was required.[88] A few Anabaptists were executed in the three IJssel cities in the 1530s. But even at Kampen, where persecution lingered longest, it had effectively ceased by 1543. After that, neither 'Lutherans', nor Reformed,

[84] Duke, *Reformation and Revolt*, 99.
[85] Augustijn, 'Anabaptisme', 27.
[86] Braekman, *Guy de Brès*, 95–6.
[87] Brandt, *Historie der Reformatie*, i. 315.
[88] Reitsma, *Centrifugal and Centripetal Forces*, 49–54.

nor Anabaptists were prosecuted in Overijssel until the coming of Alva. The city magistrates almost openly tolerated Protestant activity. An attempt by Catholic clergy to force the removal of a well-known crypto-Lutheran preacher from Kampen, in 1539, provoked a riot and was thwarted by the magistracy. By the 1540s there was practically no further attempt by the *drosten* of Overijssel to enforce the anti-heresy placards. In Gelderland the position was much the same.[89]

Broadly, the religious situation in the Low Countries in the mid-sixteenth century, before the rise of Calvinism, paralleled that prevailing in Westphalia and the North Rhine region of Germany: in (large parts of) both areas the old faith was staunchly upheld by the State, but, in society, Catholic support was generally weak except in the Walloon provinces and French-speaking parts of Liège, areas much less subject to Protestantizing printing and where the early Reformation had had less impact. In the Dutch-speaking Netherlands and adjoining parts of Germany—where forms of Low German were spoken which were close to the *Oosters* of the north-east Low Countries—Protestantism of diverse hues was everywhere widespread. On both sides of the Dutch–German border (which was itself not clearly defined), there were many districts where no significant persecution of Protestants could be enforced. Much of Westphalia, and the North Rhine, were dominated by the ecclesiastical princes of Cologne, Münster, Osnabrück, and Paderborn, rulers who remained firm allies of the Emperor in combating the Reformation. The Reformation, consequently, in Westphalia as in the Netherlands, developed in a fragmented fashion, from below rather than, as in most of Germany and Scandinavia, from above.[90] Though seemingly a special case owing to the Anabaptist revolution of 1534–5, the city of Münster was already predominantly Lutheran before the Anabaptist take-over, and Protestantism of various kinds remained widespread in the Münsterland until the early seventeenth century.[91] Cologne, conscious of its trade links with the Habsburg Netherlands, and host to an arch-conservative, anti-Erasmian university, did remain loyal to the old Church, but nevertheless had to compromise with Protestantism while in the other cities of the region—Aachen, Emden, Bremen, Paderborn, Wesel, and Osnabrück (which was largely Lutheran by the 1540s)—the Protestant upsurge was stronger. Finally, besides East Friesland, there was a smattering of loosely Protestant lordships, including the county of Bentheim (with Steinfurt), which became officially Lutheran in 1544,[92] scattered along the

[89] Wessels, 'Ketterij in de graafschap', 69–73.
[90] Schilling, 'Politische Elite', 245–79; Schilling, 'Bürgerkämpfe', 180.
[91] Hsia, *Society and Religion in Münster*, 3, 45, 93, 201.
[92] Schröer, *Korrespondenz*, 137.

length of the border, from Emden to Aachen, wedged between the ecclesiastical states and the Habsburg Netherlands.

SPIRITUALISM AND THE IMPACT OF PERSECUTION

In the core provinces of the Habsburg Netherlands a variety of spiritual and intellectual strategies were available by which the educated individual could hope to transcend the Catholic–Protestant divide. One recourse favoured by nobles and regents was that of the *politiques*.[93] The arch-*politique* undoubtedly was William the Silent, the greatest nobleman of the Netherlands, who not only believed that forcing the individual conscience was wrong, but, by the early 1560s, was prepared to assert, in the Council of State, in Brussels, that repression of the individual conscience had no place in the proper government of the country and that enforcement of the anti-heresy placards should be halted. Even before he married the Lutheran heiress Anna of Saxony, in 1561, William intimated to the German Protestant princes that he was a 'Lutheran' at heart (as his father had been),[94] though what he meant by this was that his sympathies were broadly Protestant in a loose, non-confessional sense. He met avowed Protestants in secret, at Antwerp, to confer over how to block the religious policy of the Habsburg government. In his own sovereign principality of Orange, in southern France, he introduced a limited toleration of Calvinist Protestantism as early as 1563.

But the *politique* stance of a William of Orange was essentially a political stance tinged with incipient notions of *raison d'état* and toleration. A great many Netherlanders who were office-holders, magistrates, clergymen, or prominent merchants, academics, and artists needed a *via media* which was spiritually more uplifting, theologically more satisfying, than mere non-commitment, evasion, and compromise.[95] It is this that explains the growing appeal in the Low Countries of the irenic, Spiritualist tendencies arising from the German Reformation, in opposition to Luther and Zwingli, claiming a gap between outward reality which is superficial and false, and inner truth, a disjunction of body and spirit.[96] In Germany, the Spiritualist tendency springing from Sebastian Franck and Caspar von Schwenkfeld in the long run proved marginal. But, in the Netherlands, owing to the very different political situation, Spiritualism emerged as one of the major

[93] Mout, 'Intellectuele milieu', 605–10.
[94] Swart, 'Willem de Zwijger', 54.
[95] Van Gelder, *The Two Reformations*, 312–21.
[96] Zijlstra, 'Tgeloove is vrij', 45.

strands of the Reformation. David Joris's *Wonder-Boeck* (1542), saturated with Spiritualist mysticism, transfigured the human body into its spiritual opposite, generating inner force and light, united, in joy, with God, stripping faith of practically the whole of traditional Christian dogma.[97] The later Joris unwaveringly advocated outward conformity with the established Church and seeking spiritual truth only inwardly.[98] Another influential stream was that of the Familists, or *Huys der Liefde* (*Familia Caritatis*, or Family of Love), founded by Hendrik Niclaes (1502–c.1580).[99] Niclaes, who founded his movement at Amsterdam in 1540, chiefly resided, over the next twenty years, at Emden, then, in the 1560s, at Kampen and Rotterdam, and, finally, Cologne. An affluent merchant with followers and contacts all over the Netherlands and Westphalia, he taught outward conformity with whatever established Church prevailed where one lived.[100] He and his followers eschewed confrontation, martyrdom, and proseltyzing, deeming salvation a purely inner, personal process, arising from direct communion with God. Being inwardly separate but concealing this, the movement appealed to leading Spanish New Christian merchants at Antwerp, such as Luis and Marcos Perez, as well as such intellectual luminaries as Christopher Plantin, the great Antwerp printer, the geographer Abraham Ortelius, the celebrated humanist Lipsius, and Benito Arias Montano, the Spanish humanist resident in the Netherlands.[101]

Other Spiritualist, mystical streams flowed from different sources. The Frisian jurist Aggaeus van Albada (c.1525–87), who became a councillor of the Hof of Friesland in 1533, had, as a young man studying in Germany, been inspired by von Schwenkfeld, whose following in towns such as Strasburg and Ulm included a high proportion of patricians and nobles. Albada wanted a church of discreet sophisticates meeting in informal conventicles, dispensing with ritual and clergy, where the New Testament would be imbibed in a tranquil atmosphere.[102] Despite the similarities between his stance and theirs, he stood apart from the Familists and Niclaes. Albada was exceptional in his avowed commitment to toleration and refusal to persecute heretics. By 1559 his unorthodox opinions had become sufficiently conspicuous for him to be dismissed from his post, though he was not otherwise interfered with. But foremost among the Spiritualists was Dirk Volckertsz. Coornhert, one of the outstanding figures of

---

[97] Joris, *Wonder-Boeck*, i. 68–9 and ii. 71–86.
[98] Zijp, 'Spiritualisme in de 16e eeuw', 79.
[99] Ibid. 83–4; Simon, 'Hendrik Niclaes', 434–6.
[100] Hamilton, *Family of Love*, 39.
[101] Ibid. 70–1, 97, 106.
[102] Bergsma, *Aggaeus van Albada*, 4–5.

the Dutch Reformation. The son of a merchant, born at Amsterdam in 1522, he first encountered Protestant ideas in Vianen, in the early 1540s, at the court of Reinoud van Brederode, one of whose mistresses was Coornhert's sister-in-law. At Haarlem, where he settled in the mid-1540s, he was in close contact over many years with Niclaes, who lodged with him several times, as well as with the Spiritualist artist Maarten van Heemskerck. Coornhert played a notable role in 1566, in dissuading the Iconoclasts from attacking Haarlem's churches. He was a fiercely independent spirit (see illustr. 5) who opposed both the Lutheran and Calvinist Reformations, advocating remaining within the Catholic Church whilst adhering to Spiritualist and toleration-ist ideas sharply at variance with Counter-Reformation Catholic teaching but yet supporting the Revolt against Philip II. He was the most fervent Dutch champion of religious toleration of the Revolt period, advocating toleration on religious grounds, as did the other Spiritualist, and Anabaptist, leaders, citing passages from the Bible in its defence.[103] While adhering to a theology with many affinities with that of Niclaes and Albada, Coornhert recoiled from the Family of Love, David-Jorists, and Schwenckfeldians, as too hierarchical and fixated on the personalities of their leaders.[104]

Coornhert's critique of the Family of Love and its bible—Niclaes's *Glass of Righteousness*—culminated in his *Little Glass of Unrighteousness* (1579), accusing Niclaes of presumption in claiming his own words as a new Gospel and his spiritual leadership as indispensable. Niclaes's megalomania indeed undermined the Family of Love, most of his prominent followers defecting in the wake of Hendrik Jansen van Barrefelt, a disciple who broke with Niclaes in 1573. But Coornhert's rejection of the main Spiritualist streams went beyond issues of personality, and leadership. He rejected the quest for 'safe tranquility' and the Familists' reluctance to propagate their teachings widely.[105] Like other Spiritualists, Coornhert distinguished between outer religion of ceremonies and inner religion of truth. But he was truer to the Erasmian roots of the movement in rejecting all necessity for an interpreter of God's Word to mediate between the individual and the Almighty. In contrast to Catholics and Protestants, Coornhert rejected original sin and predestination, seeing man as free and capable of improvement.[106] True religion, for Coornhert, lay in the individual's subjection to God, praise of God, and imitation of God. Where the Family of Love upheld a political philosophy approving the right of the secular authority to impose a single

[103] Güldner, *Toleranz-Problem*, 66–73; Van Gelderen, *Political Thought*, 246.
[104] Van Gelder, *The Two Reformations*, 313.
[105] Hamilton, *Family of Love*, 72, 106–7.
[106] Ibid. 103–4; Lindeboom, *Stiefkinderen*, 271.

religion, exercise censorship, and punish those who rebelled outwardly against the public Church, Coornhert insisted the magistrate possessed no such right and that such doctrines should be combated. On those who saw the path, it was encumbent to work at enlightening their fellow men.

By the late 1540s, Coornhert and his circle were developing a biblically based, non-dogmatic piety, focusing on the individual's spiritual striving, and efforts to gain salvation, dispensing with organized religion.[107] One of the main methods of propagating Coornhert's mystical, Erasmian Christianity was through the many prints he helped to produce and publish,[108] including the notable series executed in 1550, in collaboration with Van Heemskerck (1498–1574), depicting the stages by which the individual strives for, and attains, redemption.

Internalization of the Reformation flourished the more as repression of heresy intensified. In 1545, dissatisfied with the results thus far, the Emperor decided to set up a network of regional tribunals of the Inquisition capable of initiating large numbers of prosecutions, as in Spain. Lack of personnel and resources, together with the reluctance of the provincial and civic authorities to co-operate, meant that this network of tribunals in the Netherlands was installed only slowly, step by step, and by the 1550s it was still only in a few provinces that the Inquisition was actively engaged in the fight against heresy. In April 1550, to clarify the legal position, the Crown issued its 'eternal edict' laying down the death sentence and confiscation of all goods for heresy and distributing heretical literature.[109] Under the decree, men who confessed to heresy were to be beheaded, women buried alive; those who remained obstinate, refusing to confess, were to be burnt alive.

The most active of the tribunals from the late 1540s down to the crisis of 1565–6 was that of Flanders, where Pieter Titelmans (1501–72) was installed as inquisitor in 1545.[110] An ardent foe of heresy, who strove tirelessly with a small staff and limited resources, to step up the repression, he continually toured the province, and districts of Lille, Tournai, and Douai, gathering information, arresting suspects, interrogating witnesses, and arranging trials. His strategy was to target key groups, especially booksellers, rhetoric chambers, and members of Anabaptist congregations. In the decade 1550–59 Titelmans processed 494 trials for heresy and was responsible for over half the total number of executions for heresy, 105 out of 200, carried out in Flanders. He showed what the Inquisition could achieve, but, as Sonnius

[107] Bonger, *Motivering*, 75–83.
[108] Veldman, 'Maarten van Heemskerck's visie', 194–6.
[109] Thomas, 'Mythe van de Spaanse Inquisitie', 335.
[110] Van de Wiele, 'Inquisitierechtbank', 41.

acknowledged, there was little prospect, given the political and legal obstruction, of accomplishing similar things north of the rivers, in provinces such as Holland, Gelderland, and Friesland.[111] The executions greatly disturbed the general public, the 'Inquisition' becoming deeply feared in provinces where it was inactive, such as Friesland and Groningen, as well as where it operated. It was so unpopular that on a number of occasions angry crowds forcibly released prisoners, attacking Inquisition staff and the soldiers escorting them. In addition the Inquisition was widely regarded as infringing the privileges of the provinces and towns. The principle, shocking to regent and general opinion alike, that convicted heretics should lose all their property, thereby punishing the families, as well as the persons, of heretics, had already been introduced by the Crown, through the provincial high courts, in the 1530s. But the Inquisition broke new ground in taking prosecutions out of the hands of the civic magistrates and, indeed, often removing suspects from the towns of which they were burghers.

To those responsible for enforcing Charles V's policies in the Low Countries it was evident that brute repression in itself could neither arrest the advance of Protestant heresy nor save the Catholic Church in the region. In all about 1,300 persons were executed for heresy in the Habsburg Low Countries between 1523 and 1565[112]—slightly more than were executed afterwards, during the years of Alva's repression—but plainly this was merely the tip of the iceberg. The authorities saw that what was needed was a radical reorganization of the Netherlands Church to strengthen it and block the further progress of Protestantism. It was at the council of Trent, during the second sitting, from May 1551 to April 1552, that Franciscus Sonnius, who was with the Netherlands delegation, first presented a comprehensive scheme for a reorganized episcopal structure.[113] The idea was not in itself new. But Sonnius' concept whereby the costs of the new bishoprics, and seminaries to go with them, would be financed from reallocated revenues of monasteries and abbeys involved a far-reaching, structural transformation.[114] Difficulties, however, delayed implementation, not least the bitter quarrel between Charles V and Pope Julius III, and pressures of the war with France. But Philip II proved a more energetic sponsor of the idea than his father and, from 1556, amid great secrecy, plans for implementing Sonnius' scheme were drawn up in Brussels and, in April 1559, these finally met with the Papacy's approval.

[111] Valvekens, *Inquisitie in der Nederlanden*, 270–3.
[112] Bergsma, 'Uyt christelijcken yver', 70.
[113] Postma, 'Nieuw licht op een oude zaak', 14.
[114] Dierickx, *L'Érection des nouveaux diocèses*, 24–9.

The sense of urgency behind the government's new bishoprics proposals arose from the realization, by the late 1550s, that even outwardly the official Church was crumbling. The spiritual crisis gripping the Netherlands was now entering a new phase: a growing boycott of the official Church. There was evidence of a massive falling off in numbers taking holy communion at Amsterdam.[115] A leading inquisitor, Wilhelmus Lindanus, reported in 1559 that the number of congregants who fulfilled their Easter obligations at Leeuwarden that year amounted to thousands less than the equivalent figure of a few years before.[116] At Sneek it was estimated that regular church attendance had fallen off, in a few years, by a quarter. At Dokkum, congregations were reportedly down by a half. The government in Brussels began giving more attention to methods of enforcing church attendance on the population. The States of Holland were appalled to hear a government proposal, in April 1564, whereby offenders reprimanded for absenteeism from church, who then failed to attend mass for four consecutive months, 'should be banned from the land of Holland with confiscation of their goods'.[117] It was an unenforceable proposal but also a sign of Philip's unshakeable resolve.

THE RISE OF CALVINISM

Until the 1550s Calvinism was a minor factor in the Low Countries Reformation except in the case of a few Walloon towns, notably Valenciennes and Tournai, where Calvinism appeared on the scene, and set down deep roots, as early as the mid 1540s.[118] It has long been supposed by historians that the predominantly Calvinist character of the later Dutch Reformation must have derived from these early advances in Wallonia and that, therefore, Calvinism entered the Dutch-speaking area essentially from France. Recent research has shown, however, that this was, in fact, not the case and that intellectual and religious interaction across the language line in the southern Netherlands was comparatively weak. Even in the parts of Dutch-speaking Flanders immediately adjoining the Walloon area, the main impulse behind the rise of the Reformed Church to dominance within the Netherlands Reformation flowed not from the Walloon towns but the Dutch-speaking refugee churches in London and in Germany.[119] In London,

[115] Van Nierop, *Beeldenstorm*, 41.
[116] Woltjer, *Friesland in hervormingstijd*, 98.
[117] Res. SH 17 Apr. 1564.
[118] Steen, *A Chronicle*, 24; DuPlessis, *Lille and the Dutch Revolt*, 174.
[119] Decavele, *Dageraad*, ii. 330–2.

the advance of Calvinism among the Netherlands refugees was interrupted, in 1553, when Mary Tudor came to the throne and a Catholic reaction set in. But this only strengthened the growing Calvinist tendency among the German refugee churches whither the leading exiles from London now went. Calvinism in the Dutch refugee churches in Germany—at Emden, Wesel, Duisburg, Frankfurt, and Frankenthal—was grafted on to an earlier Reformed tradition, a *mélange* of Buceran and Zwinglian influences which remained a vital part of the Dutch, as of the German and Swiss, Reformed traditions. The Reformed movement in the Netherlands was thus by no means purely Calvinist in origin and, in its early stages, had few direct links with Calvin, Geneva, or with French Protestantism.

The men who were to lead the Reformed Church to triumph in a large part of the Netherlands tended to be refugees who spent long periods, especially during the 1550s, in Germany. Thus, for example, Pieter Dathenus (1531–88), one of the principal leaders of the Calvinists in Antwerp in 1566, and of the Calvinist revolution in Ghent in the late 1570s, and who was to become a bitter adversary of the church policy of William the Silent, was a former Carmelite monk who fled Flanders around 1551 and served in the years 1555–62 as a Reformed preacher in the refugee church at Frankfurt, from where he maintained contact with Reformed communities all over Germany as well as with Geneva.[120] Herman Moded, the key figure in fomenting Calvinism at Antwerp, before 1566, was also a refugee, formerly a priest; he learnt his Reformed Protestantism at Emden, perhaps the most crucial of all the refugee churches in Germany.

Emden before the Reformation had been an insignificant town of only around 4,000 inhabitants. Under the rule of Count Enno of East Friesland (1528–40), both the town and East Friesland as a whole had become officially Lutheran. But under Enno's successor, Countess Anna, there had been a change of direction and she had invited the anti-Lutheran Polish Reformer John a Lasco to take charge of the East Frisian Church. Lasco introduced a new blend of Reformation in East Friesland, by turning to the confessions, and church orders, of the Buceran-Zwinglian tradition, discarding the Lutheran model. He took up doctrinal cudgels against the Anabaptists, Catholics, and Lutherans and, after public disputations with the David-Jorists (and, in 1544, with Menno himself), obtained the formal suppression of Anabaptism in East Friesland. In 1544 Lasco established the church council, or *Kirchenrat*, and confession, of Emden, one of the principal sources for the later consistory, and Reformed doctrine, of the Netherlands.[121] The advance of Reformed Protestantism in East Friesland

[120] Ibid. 391.   [121] Pettegree, *Emden and the Dutch Revolt*, 32–4.

was interrupted, however, by Charles V's victory in the Schmalkaldic War of 1546–8, which ended in an accommodation between the Emperor and the Lutherans, at the expense of the rest of the Reformation, and which forced Countess Anna to revert, officially, to Lutheranism. Lasco and other leaders of the East Frisian Reformed tradition then migrated to London where, among the newly formed Dutch refugee church, they helped forge a church order, and confession, based heavily on Genevan practice and the theology of Calvin. Then, after 1552, the church in East Friesland veered back towards the Reformed camp and, after the Catholic reaction began, in England, under Queen Mary, Lasco and his helpers resumed where they had left off, in Emden. During the 1550s, the Dutch refugee congregations in Germany were the bastion of the Reformed movement for the whole of the Dutch-speaking Netherlands.[122] As its confessional stance became more sharply defined, the East Frisian Reformed Church also became more intolerant: the remaining Catholic priests were expelled in 1557, the Spiritualist leader, Niclaes, in 1560. At the same time, the town grew appreciably in population and commercial importance, owing to an influx of large numbers of merchants and seamen, as well as religious refugees, from the Habsburg Low Countries, tightening the already close links between Emden and the Dutch seaboard.

Doctrinally, the strength of Calvinism, which by the 1550s had eclipsed (but also absorbed) the Buceran and Zwinglian strands of the Reformation in northern Europe, sprang from its clear, systematic exposition, above all in Calvin's great work, the *Institutes*, its ability to provide that stable and orderly structure, both in dogma and organization, needed to counter the fragmentation, and proliferation of theological tendencies, so characteristic of the early Netherlands Reformation. Those dismayed by the profusion of Reformations around them found the antidote for which they thirsted in Calvin. Thus Calvinism built on, and absorbed into itself, a large part of the vague, unstructured Protestantism which had for decades pervaded all parts of the Low Countries. By contrast in rural areas untouched by industrial activity, seafaring, and fishing, purely agricultural villages such as one found here and there in Flanders, Brabant, and the Walloon country, and more extensively in Luxemburg, east Overijssel, and Drenthe, localities where humanism and the early Dutch Reformation had had little or no impact, Calvinism too mostly failed to take root.[123]

Nevertheless, the visible triumph of Netherlands Calvinism in the 1550s was still largely confined to the refugee churches abroad. The trend towards

---

[122] Ibid. 37–8.   [123] Decavele, *Dageraad*, ii. 574; Duke, *Reformation and Revolt*, 228–9.

a firm set of teachings, and stable organization, depended heavily on the successful forging of consistories, with elders and ordained preachers, and this, for the moment, was both a dangerous and difficult activity within the borders of the Habsburg Netherlands and prince-bishopric of Liège. In the late 1550s, organized Calvinist congregations, in contact with each other, and the refugee churches in Germany—or with French Protestantism, in the case of the Walloon area—existed in a few Walloon towns, and Antwerp, but hardly anywhere else.

After 1559, Calvinism in the Low Countries gained fresh impetus, from the rapid advance of Calvinism in France, Britain, and Germany, and the weakening of Habsburg authority within the Netherlands. During the early 1560s organized clandestine congregations took shape in Flanders at Ghent, Ostend, Hulst, Oudenaarde, Hondschoote, and Bruges, in Brabant at Brussels, Mechelen, and Breda, at Middelburg and Flushing, and, more tentatively, in Holland, at Amsterdam, Enkhuizen, and Alkmaar.[124] Clearly, the rise of Calvinism, before 1565, was much less pronounced north of the rivers than in Flanders, Antwerp, and the Walloon area. Nevertheless, because so many of the trained preachers, working in, and around, the Dutch language area were now tied doctrinally to the Reformed stream of Protestantism, Calvinism exerted an imminent, or potential, dominance also north of the rivers. As the grip of the Habsburg government loosened during the early 1560s, and Protestant preaching and other activity could come out into the open, as happened in 1566, it was predictable that Calvinism would play the dominant role.

With the proliferation of consistories, Calvinism in the Low Countries began to organize over a wider area, and tighten its doctrinal cohesion further. A series of clandestine synods were convened, mainly at Antwerp, during the early 1560s. A development of particular importance was the drawing up of what became known as the Netherlands Confession of Faith (*Confessio Belgica*) by Guy de Brès, preacher of the Calvinist congregation at Valenciennes, in 1561, and its rapid acceptance as the creed of the Reformed congregations throughout the Netherlands. The text exerted a powerful impact not only during the early rise of Calvinism in the Low Countries but, as a cultural and educational tool, throughout the subsequent history of Dutch Protestantism.[125] The first Dutch edition was printed at Emden, early in 1562, eloquent testimony to the pivotal role of East Friesland in the onset of the Dutch Reformation.

[124] Decavele, *Dageraad*, ii. 433; Pettegree, *Emden and the Dutch Revolt*, 69–80.
[125] Crew, *Calvinist Preaching and Iconoclasm*, 64–5; Pettegree, *Emden and the Dutch Revolt*, 102.

From the late 1550s Calvinism emerged as the strongest force in Netherlands Protestantism. With its clear doctrines and formidable structure it made it possible for Protestantism in the Low Countries to organize into a more powerful movement than had been seen previously. Yet while it partly absorbed, it by no means wholly displaced, the looser, more diffuse tendencies of the past, creating a deep tension between tightly controlled and 'libertine' tendencies which was to remain at the heart of Dutch Protestantism throughout the modern era.

6

Society before the Revolt

❖

THE LAND, RURAL SOCIETY, AND AGRICULTURE

A broad tendency developed, from the twelfth and thirteenth centuries onwards, throughout the Low Countries towards freeing the peasantry from feudal ties and obligations. Land reclamation, and colonization of new areas, in Flanders and Brabant, as well as north of the rivers, together with the high level of urbanization, led the nobility and Church to offer attractive terms, and free status, in order to coax peasant farmers to work newly cultivated areas (and others to remain on older land) as well as counter the attraction of migration to newly colonized regions of Germany.[1] Thus, at a faster rate than in France or England, it became usual, in the greater part of the Netherlands, north and south, to lease lands out to peasant farmers, free from seigneurial control, for plain money rents.

While seigneurial ties dissolved in the south and centre, in the northernmost areas—Friesland, West Friesland, Groningen—feudal forms and institutions had never gained any hold. Consequently, by 1500, the larger part of the Low Countries was a country in which most of the land was held in fee simple and the bulk of the peasantry were free.[2] Everywhere, in the west and north, the tendency was to parcellize the land into small plots, whether it belonged to nobles, the Church, town-dwellers, or to small farmers themselves. In the newly colonized areas of the polders, the countryside became covered with large numbers of medium-sized farmhouses, built according to typical styles in each area, on small parcels of land, of standard size, deemed sufficient to support individual families. It was a trend which minimized both seigneurial influence and the pull of village institutions. Away from the polders, ancient common fields and pastures existed here and there but, except on the Frisian Islands and the sandy-soil Gooi district near Amster-

[1] Van Houtte, *Economische en sociale gesch.* 48–52.
[2] De Vries, *Dutch Rural Economy*, 25, 34.

dam, only as a small remnant of what there had once been. Most of the common land had been parcelled out to small farmers too.

The whole Netherlands was thus a land of comparatively weak seigneurial control of the land, characterized, especially in the highly urbanized provinces, by a prevailing pattern of short-term leases of farms for money rents. In addition, the north, this time in contrast to the south, was marked by a relative absence of large, consolidated blocks of land belonging to great nobles. If the high nobility of the Burgundian and Habsburg Netherlands were orientated chiefly towards the south this was because their lands and influence were more extensive there. It is true that a few of the greatest families had sizeable holdings in both south and north. But this was still with a pronounced tilt towards the south. When the Prince of Orange's lands were confiscated by the Habsburg regime in 1567—and he was by far the richest nobleman in the Low Countries—it was found that his lands in Flanders, Brabant, Luxemburg, and Wallonia produced more than twice as much revenue as his lands north of the rivers.[3] The house of Egmond may have originated in Holland, but by Charles V's time over half the count's income derived from lands in the south, where also most of his residences were located.

The Orange-Nassau dynasty owned a considerable territory in northern Brabant, and along the rivers, which was handsomely expanded by William the Silent's first marriage, in 1551, to Anna of Buren, heiress to the sovereign lordships of Buren, Leerdam, IJsselstein, and Cuyck (see Map 5).[4] But apart from this, the Egmond lands in North Holland, and the extensive domain of Bergh, wedged between Habsburg Gelderland, the Münsterland, Liemers, and the county of Wisch (see Map 4), a sovereign territory around the little town of 's-Heerenberg, there were scarcely any sizeable blocks of land belonging to high nobles in the north.

It is true that inland, in the sandy-soil, more wooded, regions of Overijssel, Gelderland, Drenthe, eastern Utrecht, Limburg, and north-east Brabant, as well as Luxemburg and adjoining parts of Westphalia, one encountered a rural society which approximated more closely to what one found in most of western Europe. Here the pull of the village was stronger, and seigneurial influence greater. But, as recent research has emphasized, here too rural life was less static and self-contained than was once supposed, and the peasantry relatively free.[5] The deep and lasting differences between the character of agriculture in the maritime zone (of both north and south),

[3] Baelde, 'Edellieden en juristen', 40–1.
[4] Veeze, *Raad van de Prinsen van Oranje*, 7–9.
[5] Bieleman, *Boeren op het Drentse zand*, 39–54.

on the one hand, and the eastern, inland areas, on the other, though influenced by contrasts in soil and social structure, were essentially due to the much greater impact of the urban market in the west and relative weakness of the cities in the east.[6] In the east, crop yields were markedly lower than in the maritime zone (both north and south of the rivers) and specialization both in non-arable agriculture and industrial crops much less common. The slower growth and lack of dynamism of towns in the east, compared to the west, also meant that the stimulus to invest and adopt improvements to boost output was decidedly less. Finally, a major factor in Groningen, which in this respect was almost unique in the north, was the subjection of a comparatively large territory to extensive staple privileges, the economic sway of one particular city.[7]

Most noble land in the north belonged to a relatively large number of middling and lesser nobles and was fragmented into scattered and mostly small holdings. In Holland, around 200 families comprising the province's nobility, in 1500, possessed approximately 5 per cent of the total cultivable land, which was undeniably meagre when compared with most of Europe but by no means negligible, especially since their possessions included much of the best land.[8] In Holland the Church too lagged behind, owning under 10 per cent, though here again it tended to be prime land. In other northern provinces, the proportion of noble land was appreciably higher than in Holland though, in most areas, it was still far from preponderant. In Drenthe nobles owned scarcely more land than they did in Holland.[9] In the Ommelands, on the eve of the Revolt, nobles owned about 15 per cent of the cultivable land.[10]

A third of the land in Holland—and in Zeeland and western Utrecht, a probably comparable proportion—was owned by town-dwellers. In the fifteenth and sixteenth centuries, it was common for profits from commerce to filter back into land purchase and reclamation, the land then being leased out to peasant farmers for fixed-term rents. Sometimes there was also a more direct link between urban business and land exploitation. The brewers who dominated the regent élites of Haarlem, Delft, and Gouda in the sixteenth century also owned appreciable tracts of peatbogs, all over Holland, which they worked to provide fuel for their breweries. In Holland and Zeeland, town-dwellers thus surpassed the nobility and Church as

---

[6] Bieleman, 'Dutch Agriculture', 161–2.
[7] Ros, *Rennenberg*, 7–9.
[8] Van Nierop, *Nobility of Holland*, 98.
[9] Feenstra, *Drentse edelen*, 7–8.
[10] Feenstra, *Adel in de Ommelanden*, 80.

owners and exploiters of the land.[11] Nevertheless, the peasantry themselves owned the largest proportion of the land in the maritime west, possessing around 45 per cent of the land in Holland. It has to be borne in mind, though, that they rarely owned the best tracts and that the proportion of land in their hands varied greatly from one part of the province to another. Peasant ownership was more prevalent in the north than the south of the province and in areas remote from towns. As in Drenthe and Overijssel, peasant ownership was often a sign of the poverty of the soil. The proportion of the land attaching to particular villages, owned by peasant farmers, in Holland, ranged from 100 per cent on the North Holland islands of Texel and Wieringen, to proportions as low as 8 per cent on the South Holland Islands.[12] The parcellization of the land into separate farms, with farmhouses on each, tended to mean, even where villagers owned relatively little land, that ownership was rarely concentrated in a few hands or villages subjected to particular families or towns.[13] Typical in West Friesland, for example, was the village of Twisk, where about half the land belonged to town-dwellers but this was evenly divided between inhabitants of the rival shipping towns of Hoorn and Medemblik. In Abbekerk, another village where, in 1514, half the land belonged to town-dwellers, this was evenly divided between burghers of Alkmaar and Hoorn, with some belonging to citizens of other towns.

Although, generally, the buying and selling of land was fluid and free from legal restrictions, for reasons of prestige, tradition, and legal status, the nobility and Church treated land-ownership differently from independent farmers and town-dwellers, being more concerned with the social and seigneurial aspects and less willing to alienate their lands.[14] Consequently, in the inland provinces and Friesland, where nobility and Church owned higher proportions of the land than in Flanders or Holland, rural society was more static and controlled in character, if still relatively fluid compared to other regions of Europe. In Friesland and Groningen, nobles did not form a legally defined separate class, enjoying formal privileges, as they did elsewhere. Nevertheless, in practice, even without defined legal privileges and separate juridical status, nobles in the northernmost provinces were a powerfully entrenched rural élite, deriving their income from land and judicial office, and playing a more dominant part in provincial life than their legally better defined counterparts in Holland, Zeeland, or Flanders.[15] North

[11] Jappe Alberts and Jansen, *Welvaart in wording*, 112–13.
[12] Van Gelder, *Nederlandse dorpen*, 14, 32.
[13] De Vries, *Dutch Rural economy*, 44–7.
[14] Van Houtte, 'De zestiende eeuw', 51–2.
[15] Faber, *Drie eeuwen Friesland*, i. 316–60.

of the rivers, Overijssel and Gelderland were exceptional in having a large proportion of their land owned by nobles. In the late sixteenth century nobles in the Salland quarter of Overijssel owned 35 per cent of the land, and in Twenthe no less than 52 per cent.[16] Gelderland was also remarkable for having a noticeably larger number of nobles than the other northern provinces. In the late sixteenth century, in the three quarters of Gelderland above the rivers there were over 300 acknowledged nobles, the majority owning modest holdings.[17]

Outside Friesland, Groningen, and (until the late sixteenth century) also Drenthe, noble status was legally defined and institutionalized. In 1578, seventy-six noblemen held the right to sit as members of the *ridderschap* in the States of Overijssel, possessing manors recognized as noble seats. In Zeeland, the nobility had once been represented (and claimed still to be represented) through the First Noble. In Holland, Flanders, and Brabant, the nobility was a class defined not in terms of land-ownership, or any particular social function, but legal, political, and social privileges which distinguished them from the rest of the population and provided access to certain kinds of power and influence.[18] Generally, nobles possessed separate judicial status, rights of precedence, hunting rights, the right to be addressed in certain terms, and in most provinces—but no longer in Zeeland—to be separately represented in the provincial States, and quarter assemblies, where these existed. Nobles were also the only element of rural society represented in the provincial States, and quarter assemblies, again except in Friesland, Groningen, and Drenthe, where other landowners were also represented, and Zeeland, where no part of rural society enjoyed representation. Finally, until around 1500, the nobility had always monopolized the higher judicial offices in the countryside—those of *drost* and *baljuw*, and in Friesland that of *grietman*. But, by the middle of the sixteenth century, precisely this crucial asset had been extensively eroded by the Habsburg government.

The areas of greatest seigneurial influence were Gelderland, the outlying parts of Brabant, both to the north and south of the main Brabant towns, and in the French-speaking southernmost provinces, particularly east Hainault, Namur, and Luxemburg. The Church too was strongly represented in these areas as well as in the prince-bishopric of Liège and Utrecht and generally owned appreciably more land in Brabant, Wallonia, and the north-east than in the maritime provinces. In Friesland, the province's forty-three monasteries and convents together possessed about 20 per cent

---

[16] Slicher van Bath, *Samenleving*, 310.
[17] Zijp, *Strijd*, 54.
[18] Van Nierop, *Nobility of Holland*, 35–8.

of the cultivable land; in Groningen, the region's twenty-five monasteries and nunneries owned one-quarter of the land with a further appreciable percentage belonging to church chapters.[19]

But by far the most striking feature of agriculture in Brabant, Flanders, Holland, Zeeland, west Utrecht, Friesland, and Groningen—the highly urbanized maritime seaboard—was its sustained intensity, versatility, and higher crop yields than were to be found elsewhere in Europe. This was the only part of Europe which had, thus far, experienced a true 'agricultural revolution' and it was one which was already largely complete in Flanders and south Brabant by 1500.[20] The impressive changes which had come about in agriculture uniquely in this region—the sophisticated drainage techniques based on dikes, canals, and windmills and the concentrated use of manure made possible by the stalling of cattle and extensive use of fodder crops—resulted from the unique conditions: the threat of flooding, large number of towns, and exceptionally high level of urbanization generating an unparalleled demand for cereals, dairy produce, meat, and beer to supply the urban population. Also contributing to the intensity, and impressive crop yields, was the pressure generated by high rents and division of the land into large numbers of small farms.

As the quantity of Baltic grain imported into the Low Countries increased—and it rose by five times between 1500 and 1560—one might have expected arable farming, at least in the north, to contract, making way for more dairy output. Several dairy products, especially cheese, were valuable export items and there was indeed a considerable growth in production. Yet paradoxically the main shift, even in Friesland, was towards an extension of arable farming, stimulated above all by the growth of the cities and needs of industry in Flanders and Brabant.[21] It is due to this that the rural population of Holland, Friesland, and Utrecht increased more vigorously (down to 1585) than the urban population, the faster rise of wages, and constant shortage of labour in the towns, notwithstanding.[22] This dramatic rise in rural employment in the maritime zone of the north arose from both overall intensification of agricultural activity and increasing specialization. Early in the sixteenth century there was still extensive waste, and uncultivated land, especially in Friesland and Groningen, which was now brought into cultivation. In West Friesland, a predominantly pasture area, the growth in output resulted chiefly from the introduction of larger and more

[19] De Vries, *Dutch Rural Economy*, 41–2.
[20] Vandenbroeke and Vanderpijpen, 'The Problem', 167–8.
[21] Bieleman, 'Dutch Agriculture', 162–3.
[22] Van Zanden, 'Op zoek naar de "Missing Link" ', 385–6.

powerful windmills and the improved possibilities for drainage and reclamation that went with them, extending the area in use for dairy agriculture.[23] Another factor, especially in South Holland and Zeeland, was the switching of land formerly used for cereals to production of labour-intensive industrial crops such as hops for the breweries, hemp, flax, and madder.[24]

But the increasing intensification, and specialization, of agriculture on the maritime seaboard of the north Netherlands provides only part of the explanation for the impressive rise of the rural population of Holland from 148,000, in 1514, to 220,000, in 1575, while the population of the nineteen towns rose from 127,000 to about 180,000. A striking contrast between rural life in the maritime seaboard and in the inland regions was the large and increasing segment of rural society in the former not primarily engaged in agricultural activity, a rural proletariat working principally in the maritime sector and fishing rather than farming.[25] A great many seamen and fishermen dwelt in villages rather than towns. The maritime area abounded also in bargemen, peat-diggers, and shipbuilding workers, as well as villagers employed in dike maintenance. In 1514, in South Holland, landless poor active mainly outside of agriculture already constituted a third of the rural population.[26] Likewise Friesland accommodated an appreciable non-agricultural rural work-force.

Dike, drainage, and water regulation techniques in the low-lying zones markedly improved during the sixteenth century. A major factor here were the new windmills and the more systematic use of windmills for drainage. Although the use of windmills to pump water out of polders encircled by dikes can be traced back to the early fifteenth century, the technique, facilitated by dramatic improvements in windmill construction, became much more widespread during the sixteenth century. But while water control methods improved, and there were no more catastrophes on the scale of the awesome St Elizabeth's Day flood of November 1421, which inundated a large area of South Holland engulfing seventy-two villages, the sea encroaching virtually to the walls of Dordrecht and slicing off segments of West Friesland, there were still periodic disasters through dikes being overwhelmed. Particularly traumatic were the St Felix Day inundation of 1530 which submerged a large part of South Beveland Island, in Zeeland, and the floods of 1551 and 1555 which drowned the Zeeland town of Reimerswaal. The All Saints Day Flood, of November 1570, caused widespread damage in Holland, Zeeland, and Friesland alike.

[23] Lesger, *Hoorn als stedelijk knooppunt*, 71–2.
[24] De Vries, *Dutch Rural Economy*, 72, 153.
[25] Van der Woude, *Het Noorderkwartier*, i. 339–61; Van der Wee, 'Overgang', 31.
[26] De Vries, *Dutch Rural Economy*, 229–34.

URBANIZATION

During the later Middle Ages, Europe possessed two focuses of commercial and industrial development where urbanization proceeded much faster than in the rest of the continent—northern Italy and the Low Countries. By 1300, the south Netherlands was a highly urbanized region which also had a large rural population and which—together with northern Italy, the Paris basin, and southern England—was also, overall, one of the most densely populated parts of Europe. This was still the position in 1500. By contrast, the north Netherlands was a relatively thinly populated region in 1300 but, by 1500, was in the unique position of having a comparatively low overall density of population but an unusually high proportion of its population living in towns.

Altogether, including north Brabant, the territory which later comprised the Dutch Republic had a total population, in 1500, of under one million.[27] Yet this modest total masked a structure which was highly distinctive. Although its foremost towns—Utrecht, Dordrecht, Leiden, and Amsterdam—did not yet compare with the half-dozen largest cities of the south Netherlands, it had, in fact, become the most highly urbanized region in Europe in terms of the ratio of urban to rural inhabitants.[28] By 1560, with Baltic bulk trade near its peak, Amsterdam was beginning to rival Mechelen or Bruges, though still considerably smaller than Antwerp, Brussels or Ghent (see Table 3). Including Middelburg and 's-Hertogenbosch, there were, by 1550, no fewer than twelve cities in the north with more than 10,000 inhabitants, a remarkable number given the comparatively small population of the region overall.[29] These twelve boasted a collective total population of some 182,000. But it is striking that the five located in the province of Holland had a combined population of only 80,000 or still well under half the total for the twelve. Roughly half Holland's population was urban.[30] But the phenomenon of a high ratio of inhabitants living in towns was by no means confined to Holland. Other parts—most parts—of the north Netherlands were also highly urbanized. In the late fifteenth century, the three large cities of Overijssel alone accounted for 38 per cent of the province's population, and together with the smaller towns, about 52 per cent.[31] Apart from Drenthe, no province of the north can be said to have been predominantly rural in the sense that most of Europe then was. Even

---

[27] Van der Woude, 'Demografische ontwikkeling', 134–5.
[28] Nusteling, 'Periods and Caesurae', 92.
[29] Visser, 'Dichtheid', 13, 19; Klep, 'Urban Decline', 266–7.
[30] Faber, Diederiks, and Hart, 'Urbanisering', 255; De Vries, *Dutch Rural Economy*, 87.
[31] Slicher van Bath, *Samenleving*, 60–1.

TABLE 3. *The Population of the Main Cities of the Low Countries, 1300–1560 (estimates)*

	1300	1400	1500	1560
1. Flanders, Brabant, and Limburg				
Antwerp	10,000		45,000	85,000
Brussels		25,000	35,000	50,000
Ghent	50,000		40,000	45,000
Bruges	35,000	20,000	30,000	35,000
Mechelen		12,000		30,000
's-Hertogenbosch		9,000	17,000	17,500
Maastricht	5,000	7,000	10,000	13,500
2. Holland				
Amsterdam	1,000	3,000	12,000	27,000
Haarlem	2,000	7,000	11,500	14,000
Leiden	3,000	5,000	14,000	14,000
Delft	2,000	6,500	10,500	14,000
Dordrecht	5,000	8,000	11,500	10,500
Gouda	1,000	3,000	7,000	9,000
Rotterdam		3,000	5,000	8,000
Enkhuizen		2,000	3,500	8,000
3. North-Eastern Provinces				
Utrecht	5,500	9,000	15,000	26,000
Groningen	4,000	5,000	7,500	12,500
Deventer	4,000	10,000	8,000	10,500
Zwolle		10,000	7,000	10,000
Kampen	3,500	12,000	10,000	8,000
Nijmegen	3,000	6,000	8,000	11,000
4. Wallonia				
Lille	20,000	12,000	20,000	30,000
Liège		20,000	20,000	
Tournai			20,000	

Sources: Van Uytven, 'Oudheid en middeleeuwen', 23; Van der Woude, 'Demografische ontwikkeling', 134–6; Visser, 'Dichtheid', 19–20; Van Houtte, *Economische en sociale gesch.*, 130, 209–11; De Boer, *Leidse facetten*, 7; DuPlessis, *Lille and the Dutch Revolt*, 322–3; Van Houtte, 'De zestiende eeuw', 73.

Friesland, the most rural province, apart from Drenthe, had approximately 20 per cent of its population living in the province's eleven recognized towns.[32]

[32] Faber, *Drie eeuwen Friesland*, ii. 413.

On the other hand, where Flanders and Brabant were densely packed with villages, and had large peasant populations, there was a striking paucity in the north of precisely that living unit—villages devoted to agriculture—which formed the usual environment of European life at the time. Not only was the proportion of the population in the countryside relatively low but much of what there was dwelt in isolated farmhouses or else, as we have seen, in villages but earning their livelihood from shipping, river traffic, fishing, and peat-digging, rather than farming. Thus, it was scarcity of villages, and the uniquely high ratio of towns to villages, rather than the size of the towns as such, which rendered the north more highly urbanized, even before the Revolt, than any other part of Europe.

TABLE 4. *Urbanization in the Low Countries and Britain, 1375–1800*

(*a*) Number of Cities with over 10,000 inhabitants

	1375	1475	1500	1550	1600	1650	1700	1750	1800
North Netherlands[a]	2(0)	9(4)	10(5)	11(6)	19(12)	19(12)	20(12)	18(10)	19(10)
South Netherlands	11	11	11	12	11	12	12	12	18
Britain	1	1	5	4	6	9	13	23	47

(*b*) Total population of cities with over 10,000 inhabitants per territory (in thousands)

	1375	1475	1500	1550	1600	1650	1700	1750	1800
North Netherlands	20	98	120	182	365	600	640	570	580
South Netherlands	210	310	300	360	250	360	380	350	460
Britain	35	70	80	110	250	500	720	1,020	1,870

[a] The number in Holland is given in parentheses.

Sources: as for Table 3, plus De Vries, *European Urbanization*, 29, 271–2; Klep, 'Urban Decline', 266–7; Visser, 'Dichtheid', 16.

Over the next century and a half this peculiarity of Dutch society became more, rather than less, pronounced.[33] In 1500, the north was noticeably but not vastly more highly urbanized than the south. After the Revolt the gap widened, as it did also with respect to England, France, and Italy (see Table 4). By 1600, more than one in four Dutchmen lived in a town of over 10,000 population, whilst in England the comparable figure was then less than one in ten.[34]

The dynamism of the north in the sixteenth century was most obvious from the rapid growth of its maritime cities, and also Utrecht and Groningen,

[33] Nusteling, 'Periods and Caesurae', 92.   [34] De Vries, *European Urbanization*, 39–45.

and of the rural, non-agricultural proletariat.[35] While the speed of urban growth varied from town to town, there was no tendency, as in England, the Paris basin, and central Spain, for urbanization to proceed at a single point, creating a metropolis surrounded by a vast rural and small town hinterland. In this respect the north was again unique, even compared with the south Netherlands, or with north Italy, where there was no single metropolis either but where a few very large towns dominated well-defined regions politically and economically. In the north Netherlands there were many middle-sized rather than a few large towns, none of which, not even Amsterdam or Utrecht, exerted the sort of control which Bruges, Ghent, and Antwerp did in their respective areas. The biggest town in Holland, according to the census of 1514, was then Leiden with some 12,500 inhabitants, by no means an especially large town. But there were four other towns in the province—Amsterdam (12,000), Dordrecht (11,500), Haarlem (11,500), and Delft (10,500)—which were comparable in size.[36] This absence of a real metropolis before the Revolt, and evenness of distribution of urban population, especially in Holland, was a circumstance of overriding import-ance for the subsequent development of Dutch politics and society. For it reflected the wide dispersal of wealth and economic assets inherent in the bulk-carrying trade, river traffic, and herring fishery, and the dependence of main centres on a large number of outports and subsidiary depots.

THE URBAN ECONOMY

During the sixteenth century, the main thrust, the dynamism, of the south Netherlands urban economy sprang both from the 'rich trades'—textiles, spices, metals, and sugar—based, above all at Antwerp, and the connected industries—woollen cloth, linen, tapestries, and sugar-refining—based in the Flemish and Brabant towns, and also metal-working based in Liège and Aachen. In the north, by contrast, the main thrust of the urban economy derived from bulk freightage and the herring fishery. Before 1585, the 'rich trades' played virtually no part north of the rivers, except only for the export—after 1520 unsuccessfully, in the face of English competition—of old-style Leiden cloth.[37]

Towns north of the rivers which grew rapidly during the sixteenth century down to the 1580s were for the most part—and in Holland exclusively—maritime towns. Amsterdam, the fastest-growing, was essentially a depot for

[35] Van Zanden, 'Prijs van de vooruitgang?', 82–3.
[36] Van Houtte, 'De zestiende eeuw', 73.
[37] Ibid. 59–60.

Baltic grain and timber. Having no 'rich trades', or important merchants, at this stage, the commerce of Amsterdam was largely confined to the southern shores of the Baltic, the great grain and timber ports of Danzig, Königsberg, and Riga. Middelburg also specialized, being the acknowledged staple for French wine for the Habsburg Netherlands, since a government privilege of 1523. In 1550, approximately 60 per cent of all the wine imported into the Habsburg Netherlands (including the Rhine wine shipped down to Dordrecht, on river barges) consisted of French wines imported to Middelburg. Like Amsterdam, the West Frisian ports—Hoorn, Enkhuizen, and Medemblik—built up a flourishing Baltic commerce while Hoorn especially also imported great quantities of timber, from Norway, and salt from France and Portugal.

The herring fishery was also of great importance, and, like bulk freightage, expanded steadily, albeit not so rapidly, rising from about 250 herring busses, manned by under 3,000 men, around 1470, to around 500 busses manned by some 7,000 men by 1560.[38] There were three main divisions of the herring fishery in the north—the Zeeland fleet, based on Zierikzee, Veere, and Brouwershaven, the South Holland fleet based in the small ports below Rotterdam, on the Maas estuary, and, largest of all, the North Holland fleet based on Enkhuizen. Before the Revolt, there was also a small herring fleet in the Flemish seaports—Dunkirk, Ostend, and Nieuwpoort. All the herring towns imported, and stored, large quantities of salt for their herring business and several, especially Hoorn and Zierikzee, had important salt-refining industries.

Shipping in all its aspects, including shipbuilding, the equipping, and manning, of ships, rope and sail-making, and the making of barrels, casks, and sacks in which to ship, and store, goods, constituted an immense activity. By the 1560s, Holland alone is estimated to have possessed some 1,800 seagoing ships, around 500 of which were based in Amsterdam.[39] This was far more than were to be found at the time in any other European country. Venice, at the height of her success, around 1450, is estimated to have possessed some 300 seafaring ships. The great majority of Holland's ships were used for voyages to the Baltic, Norway, or western France and Portugal. In the mid-1560s, over 1,000 Dutch vessels—some sailing for the second time within a season—passed annually in and out of the Baltic, which was more than three times the number of north German ships.[40] About four-fifths of Dutch vessels sailing to the Baltic were based in

[38] Lesger, *Hoorn als stedelijk knooppunt*, 83–4; Unger, 'Dutch Herring', 256–9.
[39] Unger, 'Scheepvaart', 112.
[40] Bang, *Tabeller*, i. 30–63.

Amsterdam and the North Holland ports with around 20 per cent based in Friesland.[41]

Lacking 'rich trades', Dutch shipbuilders constructed cheap vessels designed to carry maximum cargo at low cost, with simple designs, a minimum of rigging, no armament, and small crews. They were not ships suitable to carry valuable cargo but bulky low-value goods at a cost that no foreign competitor could match. Building for bulk freightage culminated in the famous *fluit*, a design which originated at Hoorn in the 1590s.

The contrast between south and north in the structure of commerce and industry—'rich trades' versus bulk—was reflected in the difference between the respective merchant fleets. That based on Antwerp was small but included robust, expensive ships designed to carry high-value merchandise over great distances. Much valuable cargo, such as English cloth, arrived in Antwerp on comparable English, or Hanseatic, vessels. The contrast between the two spheres of trade, and shipping fleets, was, in turn, reflected in the difference between the respective business élites and their methods of investing in ships. At Antwerp, there was a stratum of very wealthy merchants rich enough to own their own ships, or ships divided into two, three, and four shares. In the north, by contrast, there were no important merchants before 1585 and, even though the ships were of a much cheaper variety, ownership had to be much more widely dispersed among a mass of modestly affluent brewers, millers, grain and timber buyers, herring dealers, and the like. Thus, ships in the north in the sixteenth century, in contrast also to England and north Germany, were owned in numerous shares, often thirty-second and sixty-fourth parts,[42] making possible ownership of an unprecedentedly large merchant fleet without any significant concentration of capital.

But in the north, inland towns, relying on crafts and manufacturing, were much less flourishing than in the south. Holland's cloth industry had expanded in the fifteenth century but, from the 1520s, declined both at Leiden, the main centre, and Haarlem, Gouda, and other places where cloth was woven.[43] Formerly, Holland cloth had had a modest niche among exports to the Baltic but, by 1550, had dwindled to insignificance. Apart from shipbuilding, herring-packing, and other crafts directly linked to the\ maritime sector, and confined to the maritime towns, industry in sixteenth-century Holland was largely local in character or else geared to consumption in the towns of the south Netherlands. The most important

[41] Faber, *Drie eeuwen Friesland*, i. 272–3.
[42] Brulez, 'Scheepvaart', 126; Hart, 'Rederij', 107–8.
[43] Noordegraaf, 'Nijverheid', 18.

was brewing, both in Holland and at Groningen and several other inland towns.[44] Owing to the large quantities brewed, and consumed, and the beer's proneness to spoil quickly, production was widely dispersed. Nevertheless, three inland towns—Haarlem, Delft, and Gouda—acquired a surpassing reputation for quality, and specialized in brewing and transporting beer, in quantity, via the inland waterways, particularly to the south. Yet even brewing, though it remained a major industry, waned in sixteenth-century Holland while expanding vigorously at Antwerp, Brussels, and Leuven. At Haarlem, brewing, the town's main industry, declined continually, and steeply, after 1520; by the 1560s, production was running at little more than one third of the level of 1519.[45] At Gouda, an even more stagnant town in the sixteenth century, beer production fell from 290,000 vats yearly in the 1480s to 122,000 vats by 1557 and, later, still lower levels.[46] Delft found itself in a slightly healthier state than the others, but all inland Holland towns either stagnated or grew only marginally after 1500, whilst the maritime towns grew vigorously.

Further inland, there were cities which achieved more impressive growth, notably Utrecht and Groningen (see Table 3). But more common was a similar tendency to stagnate. This was especially the case with the IJssel towns—Zwolle, Kampen, Deventer, and Zutphen—which, owing in part to the silting up of the river IJssel, lost their maritime traffic and, by the middle of the sixteenth century, also much of their once flourishing trade with the Rhineland.

INSTITUTIONS OF CIVIC LIFE: GUILDS, MILITIAS, CHAMBERS OF RHETORIC

Economic life in the towns, throughout the Low Countries and north-western Germany, was deeply enmeshed in the guild system. Every town boasted a mass of guilds, in Antwerp well over one hundred, in most large towns, many dozens. The major guilds continued to figure, as they had for centuries, among the most prominent bodies in urban life. They extended right across the economic spectrum with different kinds of merchants and dealers being grouped into guilds, as well as artisans, shopkeepers, professionals, wagoners, and harbour crane operatives. As in the rest of Europe, in the sixteenth century, production in the towns was mostly confined to small workshops, with often a single master craftsman working on his own,

[44] Ibid. 19–20.
[45] Van Loenen, *Haarlemse brouwindustrie*, 20, 47–8.
[46] Hibben, *Gouda in Revolt*, 21–2.

assisted by a few apprentices and journeymen. The guilds, and their statutes, were endorsed, and often encouraged, by the city government and they always exerted a strong influence over economic life, sometimes amounting to a stranglehold.

In all the towns there were guilds of bakers, butchers, fishmongers, grocers, tailors, shoemakers, as well, often, as porters and bargemen, and, where there was any textile activity, of weavers, fullers, dyers, and so forth. The most important function of the guilds was to restrict participation in any trade, or economic activity, to those admitted as members, which meant that they had to be acknowledged citizens of the town and to possess a variety of qualifications, as well as pay their entry fees. Members were then expected to conform to stipulated work-practices, forms of quality con-trol—a point often insisted on by civic government—and sometimes also pricing guidelines. Thus, the basic purpose of the guilds was to restrict competition, regulate production, and above all provide a degree of security for paid-up members while simultaneously protecting the consumer, in some measure, against cheating and shoddy goods.[47] An essential part of their purpose, made more or less stringent from time to time, according to economic and demographic circumstances, was to discriminate against outsiders, in favour of sons of existing members. At Ghent, in the early sixteenth century, the brewers' guild restricted entry almost exclusively to sons of existing masters.[48]

The guilds all had their own insignia, collections of ceremonial objects, and chambers, the major guilds in large towns possessing guild houses which were often among the most imposing buildings in the city. Before the Reformation they all also participated in religious festivals and processions and maintained their own chapels and altars in the parish churches. Out of their fees and subscriptions, they paid their administrative costs and funded the cultural, social, and religious events and celebrations which they put on. They also contributed extensively to the cities' plethora of welfare endow-ments and institutions, especially on behalf of sick, incapacitated, or aged guild members, and their families.

The corporative and regulatory spirit of the guilds entwined with the concerns of civic government at innumerable points. Activity within the towns was everywhere subjected to a very high degree of regulation. Fishmongers, for example, could only sell fish in the civic fish market, abiding by all kinds of rules. Moreover, as the industrial and inland economy of Holland and the other northern provinces more and more

---

[47] Van Houtte, *Economische en sociale gesch.* 98–9.
[48] Blockmans and Prevenier, *Bourgondische Nederlanden,* 164.

stagnated, during the sixteenth century (until the 1580s), the major guilds regulating textiles, brewing, and retailing, tended to extend their grip, and tighten their regulations, in order to afford maximum protection to members and ward off goods and competitors from outside.

Artists too had their guilds of St Luke and, here again, there was an elaborate administration, with fees, qualifications, and statutes, in each town where they existed. Undoubtedly, they did much to impart a corporate spirit to artistic activity in the main centres, and were to continue to do so, extending to additional towns, such as Rotterdam (1609) where they had not previously existed, in later decades. They still played a major role in the life of artists in Holland in the eighteenth century.[49]

The guilds were one network of corporations, forming a major dimension of urban life. But there were several others. Another key entity was formed by the militia companies or *schutterijen*, the chief means of maintaining order and quelling disturbances in the towns, as well as defending them in case of need. The Dutch civic militias have aptly been described as an 'élite of the second rank', higher than mere wage-earners but lower than patricians.[50] Often they were craft masters, shopkeepers, or dairy, herring, or timber dealers. Poor men and wage-earners were excluded by the relatively high cost of buying one's outfit, and arms, and contributing to the militias' costs, especially of food and drink. Research has shown that scarcely 5 per cent of the Leiden militia were drawn from the poorer half of the population. The great majority of the militia came from the ranks of the modestly affluent and propertied. Ever since the late fourteenth century, the tendency in the Dutch towns was to maintain roughly one hundred to one hundred and fifty militiamen for every 5,000 of population.[51] Thus, Leiden and Haarlem in the 1560s both had militias totalling around 400, whilst Amsterdam maintained a militia of around 600. The officers of the militia companies were usually closely related to members of the city government.

In their organization and method of recruiting, the militias closely resembled the guilds and, indeed, were called *schutters'* guilds. Like the guilds, they were not only functional but also cultural, social, and religious bodies. *Schutters* met regularly for shooting practice, and social events, as well as for parades, and patrolling the city gates and walls. Each company had its own building with shooting range attached and, during the summer months, it was usual to hold monthly shooting competitions, ending in elaborate feasts. Like other guilds, each company had its own emblems and

---

[49] Hoogewerff, *Gesch. van de St Lucasgilden*, 119–24, 167.
[50] Grayson, 'Civic Militia', 39–40.
[51] Ibid. 39; Carasso-Kok, 'Schutterijen', 27.

collection of plate and finery. From the 1520s onwards, beginning in Amsterdam, it became the custom to hang up large group portraits of members of contingents. In Amsterdam, since 1522, there were three militia companies, or *schutters'* guilds, each consisting of twelve contingents of seventeen *schutters*. The oldest surviving secular militia group portrait, or *schuttersstuk*, was painted in Amsterdam, in 1529, depicting an entire contingent of seventeen men. The first militia group portrait showing a contingent round a table, feasting (albeit sparsely), dates from 1533.

Also given to feasting, and again a major dimension of urban life in both the north and south, were the Chambers of Rhetoric, or *rederijkerskamers*, an offshoot of the French *rhétoriqueurs* which flourished in the Netherlands from the early fifteenth century onwards.[52] In the fifteenth century, these bodies, amateur poetical and theatrical societies, chiefly performed pious miracle and mystery plays. But, by the 1520s and 1530s, humanism, and its broad cultural influence, had revolutionized the *rederijkers'* activities, just as humanism revolutionized religious art (see p. 48 above). The new outlook changed neither the late medieval corporate organization of these civic literary guilds, nor the form and popular ambience of their performances but did transform the content, bringing in moralistic commentary, allegory based on classical mythology, and often biblical themes with a thinly disguised topical message.[53]

In organization, the Chambers of Rhetoric resembled the guilds and militias. They too had their statutes and chambers, and were administered by deacons and governing bodies. Again their activities were social, civic, and religious as well as specifically theatrical and literary. Before the Reformation, they played a prominent part in laying on religious festivals and celebrations. But, like the rest of society, they became heavily permeated with Protestant ideas, as well as Erasmian sentiments, in the 1520s and 1530s, and their tone quickly became anti-sacramentarian and averse to images and relics.[54] Predictably, this earned them the deep suspicion, if not outright hostility, of both the Church and Habsburg authorities and many performances were censored, or suppressed, by the Hof of Holland and other judicial authorities.[55] The effect was to render the Chambers of Rhetoric bastions of the same kind of non-explicit, subdued Protestantism that permeated society at large. Their speciality was veiled irreverence and rejection of the old Church, an attitude which they did much much to propagate amongst the populace.

[52] Weevers, *Poetry of the Netherlands*, 102–3.
[53] Ibid. 104; Van Gelder, *Erasmus, schilders en rederijkers*, 59–61.
[54] Ibid. Duke, *Reformation and Revolt*, 90–1, 106–7.
[55] Worp, *Drama en toneel*, i. 184–91.

POVERTY AND CIVIC WELFARE

The proportion of the urban population classified, for fiscal purposes, as too poor to pay property taxes oscillated widely, from year to year, being influenced dramatically by economic ups and downs.[56] In Leiden, a city for which some statistics survive, the figure swung from 33 per cent in 1514 to a lower figure, in 1529, to around 40 per cent by the mid-1540s.[57] Proportions would have been similar in the other inland manufacturing towns. Nevertheless, because the north Netherlands towns where poverty pressed most—the inland towns—were also the towns which grew least between 1500 and 1585, the problem of urban poverty, in this region, was not as severe as in the faster-growing cities of the south, or France or Germany. In the north, numbers of poor, in the mid-sixteenth century, were little different from in 1500, a situation quite unlike that in neighbouring countries. This was, undoubtedly, the main reason why in the north there was less pressure on city governments to introduce radical changes to the system of urban poor relief than in the south.

The later Middle Ages had bequeathed, to all the cities of western Europe, a tangled mass of charitable foundations and endowments set up by individuals, guilds, and clergy, and administered by a wide range of bodies, albeit frequently staffed by members of religious orders. Numerous charitable houses and institutions, as well as friaries and monasteries, distributed alms and dispensed sick care, food, and fuel. Large towns also had a general hostel, in Haarlem called the *St Elisabethgasthuis*, where (especially) the sick poor could stay, as well as lesser hospices, orphanages, and often also *hofjes*, blocks of small cottages provided free for certain categories of house-bound poor, often elder disabled guild brothers or widows of guild members. The *hofjes* and most other charitable endowments had elaborate statutes confining charity to particular groups, linked by family, locality, or occupation, to the founder or founding body. The whole system was effectively directed towards excluding outsiders and newcomers, though alms and short-term accommodation were available to pilgrims and vagrants.

During the first half of the sixteenth century, western Europe, both Protestant and Catholic, was swept by new attitudes, and a new approach, to the problem of poor relief. There were several factors behind this change. Partly, it was a response to humanist criticism of monks and friars and the principle of unrestricted giving of alms, and charity, to beggars. Partly, it was an inherent result of the Reformation which, by sweeping away the

[56] Blockmans and Prevenier, 'Armoede', 516.
[57] Ligtenberg, *Armenzorg te Leiden*, 13–14.

Catholic clergy, and confiscating Church property and revenues, left a large gap in urban welfare which civic government had no choice but to fill. But partly also, the change resulted from population growth, the rapid expansion of the largest cities in most of Europe, and burgeoning of the problem of poverty.

Fundamental reorganization was unavoidable and it was only the city governments which could undertake it. Both the administration and the aims of welfare changed. Late medieval religiosity accorded a sacred value to poverty, begging, and giving alms, which the new humanist philosophy of poor relief was unwilling to share. Priority was now assigned to checking the growth of poverty, vagrancy, and idleness, so the new approach tended to be much more questioning, if not outright hostile, to begging and alms-giving. Ambitious programmes reorganized civic welfare in many German, Italian, and French cities and also in the cities of the south Netherlands.[58] In the 1520s, several Flemish cities forbade begging, except by certain groups, cracked down on vagrancy, and centralized their welfare systems under welfare boards, or colleges, set up by the municipality. In 1527, Lille followed Bruges and Ieper, adopting a new 'Order for the Poor', suppressing begging except for categories such as pilgrims and orphans, condemning idleness, confining charity to those who had lived in Lille for two years or more, and setting up a civic college to administer the welfare system, keeping a register of those eligible to receive relief and to what extent.[59] A key step in bringing 'discipline and order' to poor relief was the transfer of existing endowments and funds into a central poor relief chest controlled by the new civic college.

These fundamental changes in Flanders and the Walloon cities did not go unnoticed in the north Netherlands. In 1527, the States of Holland took steps to gather information about the measures adopted by Bruges and Ieper. But, despite this, no major initiative in poor relief was undertaken north of the rivers before the Revolt.[60] Consequently, in the north unlike the south, civic poor relief was transformed only after, and as an inherent part of, the Revolt which swept away the monasteries, religious functions of the guilds, and the old Church itself. It was not until the 1570s and 1580s that towns such as Leiden and Haarlem took measures to rationalize, standardize, and centralize poor and sick relief under the control of civic government.

---

[58] Blockmans and Prevenier, *Bourgondische Nederlanden*, 187.
[59] DuPlessis, *Lille and the Dutch Revolt*, 140–3.
[60] Spaans, *Haarlem na de Reformatie*, 171–4.

THE REGENTS

At the forefront of civic society and, later, a class of paramount significance in the history of the Republic, were the regents. Broadly, the regents were those who participated in civic government as members of the *vroedschappen*, as the town councils were called, in Holland, or *raad* in the north-east, or *magistraat* or *wet* in Brabant. The regents were never an oligarchy defined by birth or social status, even though, as far as they could, they became a closed patrician oligarchy, with a characteristic life-style of their own, especially after around 1650, and tended to marry exclusively amongst each other. What defined them as a group, and always formed the basis of their influence in civic society, was holding office in city government.[61] Thus, young people, and women, could belong to regent families but no one could be a regent without holding civic office. Moreover, even though being co-opted, or appointed, to membership of a town *vroedschap* in principle meant membership for life, there were situations in which *vroedschap* members were removed, never to return, and thus ceased to be regents. Thus, even after becoming a regent, one did not automatically remain one until death.

The Burgundian dukes, from the mid-fifteenth century onwards, had deliberately encouraged the development of closed regent oligarchies, reducing access to civic government and confining it to the hands of the richest segment of urban society.[62] Wealth was explicitly part of the rationale of the regent class in the late fifteenth and sixteenth centuries: as its foremost members the regents were supposed to represent the propertied sector of the urban population. Wealth was also assumed to provide the necessary freedom, time, and means if one was to devote oneself seriously to public affairs. But wealth alone was never a sufficient qualification for entry into the *vroedschap*. In the first place, it was taken for granted that *vroedschap* members should be natives of the province, and preferably the town, in which they were regents and that their families should long have been linked to the town. Secondly, persons considered unsuitable, by the Burgundian dukes and their Habsburg successors, or their Stadholders, could be removed, or debarred, from the *vroedschap*. Also unwanted candidates including former regents could be prevented from by-passing the current *vroedschap* and being elected *schepenen* (town magistrates, or eschevins) and in many towns also as burgomasters, by means of the selection made by the Stadholders from double lists of nominees for these offices which the town

[61] Van Dijk and Roorda, *Patriciaat in Zierikzee*, 11–15; Price, *Holland*, 32–56.
[62] Tracy, *Holland*, 14.

governments were obliged to submit. Furthermore, even though the regents may have been the richest segment in a town originally, with the passage of time, and changes in circumstances, others became as wealthy or wealthier, and disparities of wealth among regents widened, so that neither in the sixteenth century, nor later, can the regents be equated purely and simply with the richest stratum of the urban population. On the contrary, their place within, and relationship to, the richest stratum of urban society was always complex and frequently fraught with tensions, sometimes leading to a bitter rivalry of élites within a town.

Although one became a *vroedschap* member, in principle, for life, membership could be temporary. The *schepenen*, by contrast, were elected for one year only and did not have to be members of the *vroedschap*, though, if they were not, this was usually because a close relative was already a sitting member. Seldom was someone appointed *schepen* who did not, sooner or later, enter the *vroedschap*. However, the chief salaried official in each town, the town secretary or 'pensionary', was not necessarily considered a regent, since what was needed for this important post was a competent official with legal training who might well be hired, and often was, from outside.[63] But, equally, he might belong to a regent family, in the town where he served as pensionary, or in another town, as was later the case with Grotius, who came from a Delft regent family but became pensionary of Rotterdam, and would then clearly count as a 'regent'.

The cohesion and homogeneity imparted to the regent group by their exclusive control of civic government, and the influence this gave over patronage in the towns and administration of the charitable houses and welfare was, to an extent, compromised by the variety of backgrounds and economic origins of the regent class. In Rotterdam, for example, in the middle of the sixteenth century, it is possible to distinguish between a tightly-knit core who had been part of the Rotterdam patriciate for decades, since Burgundian or early Habsburg days, and who were mostly brewers, or else cloth, herring, or dairy dealers, from a group of relative newcomers, largely unconnected with the older patriciate, whose families had come in from outside, often but a few decades before, and often of only recent wealth, though in some cases members of regent families in other towns.[64]

In Amsterdam, in the early sixteenth century, the regent élite consisted largely of Baltic traders who had been filling *vroedschap* vacancies, since 1477, with members drawn from their own circle. But the continuity broke owing to the spread of Protestant influence in the city. Like so much of civic

---

[63] De Jongste, 'Hollandse stadspensionarissen', 86–7, 90.
[64] Ten Boom, 'Patriciaat te Rotterdam', 174–6.

society, the Amsterdam regent group became permeated with Protestant ideas and sympathies and after the Anabaptist rising of 1535, most were purged by the Habsburg authorities and replaced with 'sincere Catholycken'. These new men, often belonging to families only recently arrived in Amsterdam, or become wealthy,[65] formed a close-knit oligarchy which lasted forty years (1538–78); they were mostly brewers, cloth, dairy, or herring dealers, or soap-boilers, rather than participants in overseas trade.[66] One of the dairy dealers, Jan Vechtersz (1520–91), was born in Hoorn; another of the new men, the lawyer Arent Sandelijn (d. 1607), later a staunch royalist who, after the Revolt, left Holland and became a member of the royalist Hof of Gelderland, was born at The Hague, as also was the brewer Jan Michiel Loeffsz. Two key members of the 'sincere Catholycke' oligarchy of 1538–78 were Joost Buyck (1505–88), burgomaster of Amsterdam seventeen times between 1549 and 1577, who was the son of a brewer, and himself a cloth dealer, and Sijbrant Occo (1514–87), much the most cosmopolitan figure among them, who had studied at Ingolstadt, Leuven, Bourges, Orléans, and Bologna and who, like his father before him, was the Amsterdam factor of the great German banking house of Fugger.

In the inland provinces, a regent patriciate had also evolved but along somewhat different lines, less fully, and with less external regulation. As against the north-west Netherlands model of civic government—burgomasters, *schepenen* and ordinary *vroedschap* members exercising exclusive control and subject to intervention only from above—in Utrecht, and the cities of the north-east Netherlands, the guilds traditionally exercised greater influence and there was generally a second council, in addition to the *raad*, a wider consultative body, intended as a supplementary authority and counter-weight. In Utrecht, guilds had been dominant in civic politics before 1528, but incorporation into the Habsburg Netherlands resulted in the city's government being reshaped along the lines of the Holland model and the influence of the guilds being ended. Elsewhere, a situation developed in which the second council, usually called the Sworn Council (*Gezworen Gemeente*), as in Groningen and Deventer, or the *Gemeenslieden*, as in Nijmegen and other Gelderland towns, which was larger than the *raad*, and supposed to represent the guilds and the community, elected the burgomasters and *schepenen* each year.[67] In practice, the *raad* tended to extend its influence over the Sworn Council, absorbing it into the regent oligarchy by ensuring that it filled vacancies by co-opting patricians who then kept their

[65] Dudok van Heel, 'Een kooplieden-patriciaat kijkt ons aan', 31.
[66] Dudok van Heel, 'Waar waren de Amsterdamse katholieken', 14–27.
[67] Te Brake, *Regents and Rebels*, 24–5; Van den Bergh, *Life and Work of Gerard Noodt*, 12–14.

seats for life and were closely related to members of the *raad*. But the influence of the guilds was never wholly extinguished and at times of agitation or tension among the community tended to become stronger. Thus, the situation in the north-east tended towards greater dispersal of power in civic politics. The *raad*, in the east, was generally smaller than the *vroedschap*, in the west, in Groningen, for example, comprising sixteen persons, including four burgomasters, while the Sworn Council consisted of twenty-four. On taking major decisions, the practice was for the *raad* to consult the Sworn Council and act in its name, as well as its own.

In the cities of Flanders and Brabant, the patrician oligarchies had generally been locked in protracted and often bitter conflict with the major textile guilds during the later Middle Ages and been forced to make many more concessions to guild participation in city government than had those of the north. Although Antwerp (from 1486) and some others had subsequently eliminated this guild involvement, or drastically curtailed it, in other cases, such as at Ghent (until 1540) and Mechelen, 'deacons' and 'sworn' representatives of the guilds still constituted a large and important part of the city council. In contrast to the cities of the north where there were usually four burgomasters (except Zeeland where Middelburg, Zierikzee, and Flushing all had two), the Flemish and Brabantine cities normally had two burgomasters. As in the north, the number of magistrates varied, Leuven and Brussels each having seven, Ghent thirteen, and Antwerp, from 1556, no fewer than eighteen. In the south, no less than the north, the court at Brussels, under Charles V, was forceful and systematic in exercising its power, usually through the Stadholders, to choose burgomasters and magistrates each year from double and treble lists of nominations presented by the city councils. Only Antwerp enjoyed virtual autonomy. Ghent after 1540 was brought especially firmly under the ruler's thumb (see p. 132 below).

Throughout the Habsburg Netherlands, then, the cities were governed by a patrician élite drawn from amongst each city's wealthiest and most prominent citizens. But the leverage of the court in Brussels, and the Stadholders, over the selection of burgomasters and magistrates, combined with the fact that civic administration greatly restricted time for one's private business and also the tendency of regent élites (as far as they could) to become self-perpetuating, meant that there was generally a growing gap between the regent élites, on the one hand, and the cities' active business élites, which might well include immigrants from elsewhere or men of recent wealth, on the other. The tensions this created tended to be exacerbated from the 1520s onwards, moreover, by differences of attitude on religion and towards the regime.

7

The Breakdown of the Habsburg Regime, 1549–1566

❖

THE SEEDS OF REVOLT

Since 1492 the Habsburg Netherlands had been generally quiescent. With the unification process north of the rivers accelerating after 1522, the Low Countries were, to all appearances, being successfully welded into a single, increasingly integrated state serviced by a growing, university-trained bureaucracy.[1] Admittedly, this transition towards a more orderly, cohesive, Habsburg Netherlands was not proceeding smoothly in all respects. The processes of unification, centralization, and bureaucratization were bound to generate serious stresses, especially where the changes were most extensive—in the north. The recently annexed provinces showed considerable reluctance to accept the new provincial high courts and other innovations introduced by the Habsburg authorities. In Holland the regime's policy of turning the Hof into an instrument of central government, staffed by university-trained lawyers, discontinuing the Burgundian practice of drawing the Hof's judges from the Holland and Zeeland nobility, as well as the general (and growing) reliance on non-noble administrators, had planted seeds of discord between regime and nobility which was to have serious consequences in the future.[2] Holland nobles also resented the assigning of posts in their province to Brabanters, persons who 'do not use the Dutch language', and others who are 'not subjects of the Emperor's lands over on this side'—that is the Low Countries.[3]

A further cause of disgruntlement among the nobilities of all three large provinces was the deliberate placing of officials from lesser provinces, whom the regime particularly trusted in influential positions, thereby diverting,

[1] De Schepper, 'Vorstelijke ambtenarij', 358, 375–6; Baelde, 'De Nederlanden', 59; Jongste, 'Hollandse stadspensionarissen', 86–7.
[2] Vermij, 'Staten van Holland en de adel', 221–3.
[3] Res. Holl. 9 Apr., 20 Apr., 28 May, and 10 Oct. 1554.

into the hands of such men, patronage which had formerly been exercised by leading nobles. One example of this was the appointment of the Frisian jurist Viglius van Aytta (1507–77), a man proud of his Frisian background (who became one of the leading figures of central government in Brussels, under Philip II), as keeper of the charters of Holland, in 1550.[4] At the same time the anti-heresy campaign was generating stress between central government and local authorities fearful of loss of jurisdiction and violation of 'privileges' in all the provinces.

But, until the 1550s, these tensions, though considerable, seemed manageable. It appeared that the Habsburg government was succeeding in uniting the Netherlands, expanding and refining the apparatus of central government, and containing, if not eliminating, Protestantism without simultaneously provoking more opposition than it could cope with. But the relative smoothness of the transition, until the 1540s, resulted partly from absence of the pressures associated with waging war. Whilst there was no major military threat the Crown had no need to heap fresh exactions on the populace.

This relative tranquillity ended in the 1540s. After 1540, the Habsburg Netherlands was once again drawn into prolonged confrontation, and war, with France. As a consequence, all provinces were subjected to heavy new burdens of taxation, recruiting, billeting, provisioning, and movement of troops.[5] Up to a point, Charles V and his successor, Philip II of Spain, were fortunate in the timing of this escalation of pressure. Antwerp's progress as the hub of Europe's rich trades' was stimulating industrial activity, and creating new wealth in the south while, simultaneously, the expansion of Holland's bulk-carrying and fisheries increased the affluence and population of the maritime zone in the north.[6] But the very success of the economy posed dangers for the regime. The growing prosperity of the Habsburg Netherlands compared with Spain, or Habsburg Italy, and the sophistication of the Antwerp money market, were bound to tempt a government, straining every nerve to expand its military establishment, to rely excessively on these resources. The ease of communications, readiness with which money could borrowed or raised, and availability of everything that might be needed was all too apt to encourage an unhealthy financial, logistical, and strategic dependence of the Habsburg Crown on its Netherlands provinces.[7]

---

[4] Waterbolk, *Vigliana*, 8.
[5] Tracy, *A Financial Revolution*, 75.
[6] Van Houtte, 'De zestiende eeuw', 65–71.
[7] Israel, 'Spanje en de Nederlandse Opstand', 51–3.

The fundamental change in the 1540s, resulted from a shift in the focus of Habsburg–Valois conflict in Europe. Until around 1540 rivalry between Spain and France for hegemony of Europe had focused primarily on Italy. Western Europe's two great powers had contended for control of Naples and southern Italy and later for Milan. For decades Italy was Europe's *école de guerre*, the strategic arena where new types of fortification and military techniques evolved, the general *place d'armes* where the leading powers paraded their might and grappled for supremacy.

By the late 1530s, however, France had been effectively shut out of Italy and François I was seeking ways to both widen the conflict and more effectively challenge Habsburg dominance. As he began to shift troops and resources to the Netherlands frontier and construct a string of the new Italian-style fortresses, resistant to artillery, posing a strategic threat to Flanders and the Walloon provinces, Charles V had little alternative but to follow suit.[8] A network of major new fortresses, such as those at Mons and Gravelines, took shape. The regime in Brussels began to make sharply escalating demands on the Netherlands for funds, men, and supplies.

As the build-up on both sides of the French–Netherlands frontier continued, it became apparent that the shift of focus in Habsburg–Valois rivalry in Europe in fact favoured the Habsburgs rather than France. During the 1540s, and still more in the 1550s, it became obvious that the Netherlands was, from many points of view, the ideal strategic base for Habsburg power in Europe.[9] Not only were transportation, and the logistics of war, more easily and efficiently handled in the Low Countries than Italy, not only was it easier to feed, and supply, troops there, and obtain cash at short notice, but the geography of the Low Countries—in the conditions of warfare of the time—was peculiarly favourable. While it was difficult for François to construct enough fortresses to seal France off effectively, so that the terrain on the French side lay invitingly open, the dense clustering of fortresses, walled towns, dikes, canals, and rivers on the Netherlands side rendered the Habsburg Low Countries a virtually impenetrable defensive network. Moreover, Paris itself was not far from the then Netherlands frontier. Merely by crossing the border in strength one could sow panic in France. Pressure could thus be more effectively exerted on France from the Netherlands than from Italy or Spain, Charles knowing (from experience) how frustratingly inconclusive it could be invading southern, or eastern, France.[10] In short, once armed and primed, the Netherlands was the strategic base of Europe *par excellence*. If she based her military might there, Spain had a permanent,

---

[8] Ibid. 52. [9] Ibid. [10] Ibid.

built-in advantage, being able to penetrate into France almost at will, while the French could effect little against the Netherlands. Thus the Netherlands came to be seen, as Spanish ministers later expressed it, as the 'bridle' of France.[11]

But if the Netherlands was to fulfil its potential as the 'bridle' of France, an adequate flow of funds was needed and Charles had to persuade the seventeen provinces to co-operate, or at least acquiesce. There was bound to be some obstruction. But at first this seemed to pose no great difficulty. Only Ghent directly opposed the Emperor's demands, rebelling against his regent, Mary of Hungary, in 1539–40. Charles came in person to suppress the revolt, harshly punishing the city—and warning others of the consequences of disobedience—by cancelling its privileges.[12] During the 1540s, the Habsburg regime appeared to be achieving all its strategic, fiscal, administrative, and political objectives in the Low Countries. Between 1542 and 1544, the provinces met the Crown's demands by levying direct taxes on wealth and through packages of excises, especially on beer, wine, salt, and herring, which came to be known as the *nieuwe middelen*—or 'new means'.[13] The Brussels regime achieved a major breakthrough by inducing the provincial States to adopt the method (which in the past individual cities had experimented with) of issuing interest-bearing annuities, or bonds, known as *renten*. In Holland, where the States were eager to co-operate whilst the war was directed against Gelderland, the transition to organizing the province's contributions to central government on the basis of a long-term funded debt, based on issues of bonds administered by the States themselves, took place precisely during the conquest of Gelderland, in 1542–3.

By means of these interest-yielding *renten*, issued to the public, large sums could be raised with which to fund the central government's military expenditure by provincial States which had the local connections, and status, to inspire confidence that the interest on the annuities would be regularly paid.[14] Although, at first, a proportion were compulsorily imposed on civic and ecclesiastical bodies of various sorts, there was, also from the outset, genuine interest among the public. States of Holland *renten* were often purchased as family investments by officials and especially civic magistrates and regents in Holland itself.[15]

[11] BL MS Add. 14005, fo. 85v. 'Discurso' of the duke of Osuna.
[12] Tracy, *A Financial Revolution*, 72.
[13] Ibid. 87–91.
[14] Ibid. 75, 90–1.
[15] Tracy, *Holland*, 130–2.

To begin with, the new province-based system of funding the government's war expenses proved an efficient means of coping with the burden, and mitigating the disruptive effect of rising fiscal pressure. But as the years passed, and there was no let up in government's demands, it became apparent that the Emperor was routinely using the Netherlands as his chief strategic bulwark and resource, in pursuit of goals which were vital to him but had little to do with the Netherlands.[16] This feeling was particularly strong north of the rivers, the States of Holland having traditionally taken the view that conflict with France was no concern of theirs. With the onset of the Habsburg–Valois war of 1552–9, disaffection rapidly mounted. The scale of military operations was now much greater than in the 1540s, as was the escalation in demands on the provinces for money, men, and supplies. Military expenditure in the Netherlands during this war rose to twice the level of 1542–4 when government spending had already reached unprecedented heights. Moreover, this time the emergency lasted considerably longer. Besides more excises, the provinces had to impose frequent levies on assessed wealth. With the funded debt overstretched, an unsecured deficit accumulated which, by 1557, had reached seven times the level of 1544.[17]

Different provinces responded to the financial crisis in different ways. Many simply knuckled under and issued unprecedented quantities of interest-bearing bonds. By exploiting this avenue to the limit, some provincial and town governments paid for a period of continued tranquillity at the price of severe financial dislocation later. Until 1562 Lille, for example, was able to keep up interest payments on the huge quantity of bonds issued by the city in the 1550s, but then found itself in chronic financial difficulty.[18] As long as the system functioned smoothly, the most affluent sections of society were happy enough to co-operate with Brussels. The public were paying the interest on the annuities, through indirect taxation, so that the bonds themselves proved increasingly attractive as an investment among the rich and influential. After 1550, it was no longer necessary for the States to arrange compulsory sales. In Holland the chief problem was that government demands eventually involved sums too large to be raised through the bonds system without pushing excises up to impossible levels with the result that the proceeds had increasingly to be supplemented with additional taxation.

The position was quite different, however, in the newly acquired provinces. Here the exactions of central government encountered less developed

[16] Rodríguez-Salgado, *Changing Face of Empire*, 354–5.
[17] Tracy, *A Financial Revolution*, 92–7.
[18] DuPlessis, *Lille and the Dutch Revolt*, 44.

financial systems and raised all kinds of constitutional and political, as well as fiscal, issues. The nobles and regents of the recently subdued provinces insisted that both the heavy taxation and other government initiatives violated their constitutions and the terms on which they had accepted Charles V as their sovereign.[19] Friesland, Overijssel, and Gelderland drew inspiration from the mounting obstreperousness which they perceived in each other, insisting that they would only vote money for the Crown if their grievances were addressed. The Stadholder of Friesland managed to fob off the States of that province in 1554, with a promise to attend to complaints after a subsidy was agreed. But this did not work again and by the time of its gathering in 1558 the Frisian assembly was refusing to vote any money at all.

In the newly won provinces, the escalation in fiscal pressure had the effect of exacerbating deep-seated political resentments over the way the Crown had sought to integrate them into the rest of Habsburg Netherlands and the powers which central government, had arrogated to itself. In Overijssel and Gelderland it was especially the Emperor's efforts to set up provincial high courts, and to subordinate provincial government to central government, which was the bone of contention.[20] In Friesland, besides dislike of the new Hof the nobles resented the Crown's appropriation of the power to appoint the rural magistrates, or *grietmannen*. Habsburg policy in Friesland since the 1520s had had the effect of reducing the proportion of the *grietmannen* who were Frisian nobles to a minority, through assigning many of these key posts to non-noble Frisians or non-Frisians.[21]

In several provinces tension between the provincial States and the provincial high courts, backed by central government, was aggravated by the way the financial emergency led to an expansion of the functions of the States. A central objective of the Habsburg regime was to subordinate the provincial administrations to central government. But under the pressure of war, and pressing need for more funds, the regime had little alternative but to assign a larger and larger role to the States in the collection of taxation and management of finance. The basic principle of the funded debt, that the bonds were issued by the provincial States,[22] who guaranteed them and who alone could inspire confidence among the public, made this inevitable. The result was a political contradiction which lay at the root of the mounting friction evident throughout the Netherlands in the 1550s.[23]

---

[19] Jappe Alberts, *Gesch. van Gelderland*, 92; Woltjer, *Friesland in hervormingstijd*, 38–9.
[20] Zijp, *Strijd*, 177.
[21] Waterbolk, *Vigliana*, 9.
[22] Koopmans, *Staten van Holland*, 55–8.
[23] Tracy, *Holland*, 180–5.

Everywhere, the States began to meet more frequently than before and discharge more business. Between 1542 and 1562, the States of Holland convened no fewer than 285 times, an average of 13.5 times per year.[24] The then secretary or 'Advocate' of the States of Holland, Adriaen van der Goes (1543–60), presided over a rapid extension of the tasks and scope of his office. A direct consequence in various provinces was a growing tussle over whether the provincial States had the right to gather of their own accord, and determine their agenda, or could meet only when summoned by the ruler, or his Stadholder, or Hof, under an agenda set by central government. For the moment the issue remained unresolved.

The situation in the mid 1550s was not helped by the sudden disarray at court. The transfer of power from Charles V who, weary of his wars and responsibilities, had decided to abdicate to his son Philip, proved a complicated procedure. Philip arrived from Spain in the Netherlands, where he was to spend the next four years, in September 1555. On 22 October he was proclaimed Master of the Order of the Golden Fleece. Three days later, before a full gathering of the States General in Brussels, in the presence of delegations from all the provinces except Overijssel, the aged Emperor, leaning on the shoulder of the young Prince of Orange, read out his abdication speech, proclaiming Philip the new ruler of the seventeen provinces.

But the Netherlands was the first of the Emperor's territories to be transferred to Philip and, at that point, Charles seems not to have intended a full transfer of his power. He marked his pending but, it was widely presumed, only partial departure from the scene by making numerous appointments to high administrative, ecclesiastical, and military office which Philip then had little choice but to confirm.[25] The temporary lack of a clear focus of power was compounded in that in recent years, with Philip in Spain, father and son had disagreed over a range of strategic issues facing their empire, besides which it was expected that Philip would shortly be leaving the Netherlands. It was for this reason that Charles chose (in consultation with Philip) Emanuele Filiberto, duke of Savoy (1528–80), one of his trusted commanders whom he had admitted into the Order of the Golden Fleece in 1546 (at the same time as the duke of Alva), to come to Brussels to act as 'lieutenant-governor' and, in practice, regent in the Netherlands. Charles was the main influence not only in installing Savoy but also in determining the composition of his Council of State, which included

---

[24] Tracy, *A Financial Revolution*, 124.
[25] Rodríguez-Salgado, *Changing Face of Empire*, 127–9.

the young Prince of Orange, Granvelle, Lalaing, and Viglius.[26] The fact that Philip, contrary to expectation, then stayed at Brussels, despite being proclaimed king of Spain and the Americas, in January 1556, and being (since 1553) consort of Queen Mary of England, and exercised power without reference to this Council of State, created a context of extraordinary overlap in no way eased by the fact that Charles (still with the title of Holy Roman Emperor) also remained in the Netherlands until September 1556.

Philip put his first package of financial demands to the States General in March 1556. The Crown's financial exigency was now such that the king demanded the unheard of sum of 3 million guilders to be raised through direct levies on assessed wealth including a 100th Penny, or 1 per cent, levy on fixed property and 2 per cent of liquid assets.[27] The provinces, headed by Brabant, refused. An exasperated Savoy then reconvened the States General at Valenciennes, in August, insisting the war was now at a critical juncture and that the money was urgently required. Convinced that the Netherlands was paying too much, compared with Spain and Spanish Italy, and that the war was being fought more in the interest of Spain and Italy than the Low Countries, the delegations spent their time airing their grievances. The king was mightily displeased. Not until 1558 did the States General belatedly concede most of the money and even then only on their own terms. The subsidy they offered, and which Philip had no alternative but to accept, the so-called Novennial Aid of 1558, was to run over nine years with the funds being collected, managed, and accounted by the States General. The assembly of 1558, strained though the occasion was, was the last on which Crown, provinces, and States General could find any basis on which they could work together.

Meanwhile, Philip clinched victory in his war with France. In 1557, exploiting to the full the strategic advantages offered by the Netherlands, his forces shattered the French army at Saint-Quentin (across the border from Cambrai), capturing the town and surrounding area. As a result of this great victory the prestige of the Spanish Crown was vastly enhanced throughout Europe even though the original intention to project the king as a conqueror had been somewhat marred by the fact that Savoy had been forced to start the battle whilst Philip was still some distance away at Cambrai. Nevertheless, it was a triumph both strategically and psychologically, Saint-Quentin being half-way on the main route between Brussels and Paris. It sowed panic in Paris and compelled Henri II to come to terms. The battle was fought on St Lawrence's day, 10 August, a fact which figured prominently sub-

[26] Ibid. 128.   [27] Grapperhaus, *Alva en de Tiende Penning*, 53.

sequently in the iconography of the great palace of the Escorial which Philip dedicated to 'San Lorenzo' and work on which began in 1563. The Escorial and its décor were intended, in part, to be a monument not just to Philip II's victory in the Netherlands but to his striving for a hegemony in Europe which would be religious as well as political.[28] The frescos of the battle of Saint-Quentin in the hall of battles, at the Escorial, painted in the late 1580s, deliberately pair Saint-Quentin with the victory of Christian Castile over the Muslims of Granada, at Higueruela, in 1431. One of the main effects of Saint-Quentin was that it freed Philip to resume his struggle against both Protestantism and Islam.

CRISIS, 1559–1566

Philip's decision to return to Spain after making peace with France at Cateau-Cambrésis (April 1559) was rightly perceived at the time as a key event. The war with France had ended. But the grave problems in the Low Countries which that war had given rise to, or aggravated, had not. The king's advisers in Brussels, especially his new right-hand-man, Antoine Perrenot de Granvelle (1517–86), a bureaucrat of non-noble background from the Franche-Comté, urged him to remain in the troubled Netherlands rather than return to Spain. Philip, as well as they, was deeply worried. The immense debt which the Crown had accumulated, the fiasco of the States General gatherings of 1556 and 1558, the obstreperousness of the newly acquired provinces, the desperate need for cash with which to pay off the army (most of which now had to be disbanded), the restlessness of the nobility, and the inexorable advance of Protestantism, represented each in itself a formidable difficulty. Together, all this constituted a challenge to the regime, and Catholic faith, of frightening proportions, not eased by Savoy's refusal to continue as regent in Philip's absence.[29]

Philip's return to Spain was neither a sign of his undervaluing the Netherlands, nor underestimating the crisis which now engulfed the northern part of his world-monarchy. On the contrary, he was convinced the situation in the Low Countries, above all regarding religion, was extremely grave.[30] But he also believed, with some justification, that the whole of the Spanish monarchy was in the midst of a crisis. He had defeated France— just. But France still appeared strong and likely to continue to challenge Spain's supremacy and be a vast drain on Philip's resources. Besides this,

[28] Osten Sacken, *El Escorial*, 86–9.
[29] Rodríguez-Salgado, *Changing Face of Empire*, 347–53.
[30] Dierickx, *Documents*, i. 181, 184.

he had to confront the growing Ottoman offensive in the Mediterranean, hampered by decades of neglect of Spain's defences in the south, and innumerable financial and administrative problems in Spain itself. Philip returned to Castile not only set on reviving his galley fleets in the Mediterranean, and organizing a counter-offensive against the advance of Islam, but convinced that only by reasserting royal authority, and husbanding resources, in Spain, would he be able to rescue his empire as a whole, including the Netherlands, from imminent disintegration.

In one respect the outlook brightened unexpectedly. France's strong king, Henri II, died in a jousting accident shortly after the conclusion of the Franco-Spanish peace. As a consequence France was neutralized, indeed soon sank into a state of internal disarray which led, in 1562, to the onset of decades of civil war, and international weakness. An enormous pressure was thus lifted from the Low Countries. Yet this was to have none of the beneficial effects which diversion of French attention from the Netherlands after 1492 had had. This time there was no easy transition to harmonious relations between ruler and ruled following the lapsing of the external threat. For unlike his father and grandfather, Philip had no intention of delegating his power to the great magnates, or permitting their clienteles to monopolize the proceeds of political, administrative, and ecclesiastical patronage. After 1492, Maximilian and Philip I had largely accepted the ascendancy of the magnates. There was (then) no other plausible course. But, for Philip, there was an alternative political strategy which his ingrained suspiciousness of powerful men, and his religious convictions, encouraged him to follow.[31] The rise in the Netherlands, as in all western Europe, of a university-trained non-noble bureaucracy, staffing much of the judicial and fiscal administration, had driven a wedge between Crown and nobles which had scarcely existed before 1500 and which could not be removed without reversing the growth in the power of central administration and the state, which had taken place since Maximilian's time.[32] Nor was it possible to abandon the processes of centralization and bureaucratization in the Low Countries without also abandoning the drive to combat heresy and reinvigorate the Church.

To preside over central government in the Low Countries in his absence, Philip chose as regent his illegitimate half-sister, Margaret of Parma, a Habsburg lady who he knew lacked experience and political skill and would require extensive advice and guidance. At the same time, he avowed his confidence in the great magnates, appointing William of Orange Stadholder

[31] Vermij, 'Staten van Holland en de adel', 217–23.
[32] De Schepper, *Belgium Nostrum*, 7–16.

of Holland, Zeeland, and Utrecht, and Lamoraal, count of Egmond, Stadholder of Flanders and Artois. Nominally, the magnates were again to form the heart of the government as members of the Council of State, in Brussels, where they sat alongside the heads of the royal bureaucracy— Granvelle and Viglius van Aytta, president of the Council.[33] But, from the outset, despite Philip's formal instructions to Margaret, effective control over decision-making, and administrative and ecclesiastical patronage, lay with Granvelle and Viglius.[34] Before leaving, Philip did what he could to make the arrangement a stable one and secure the co-operation of the *grands seigneurs*. But, partly owing to his deficiency in languages and reserved personality, he lacked that ease of manner with the great lords characteristic of his father. Convening the Order of the Golden Fleece, on the eve of his departure, he admonished the magnates to combat heresy, champion the Church, and attend mass daily. His remarks were interpreted as implying they had thus far been negligent in this respect and were ill-received.[35]

The split between the magnates and Granvelle which rapidly developed, after Philip's departure, reflected the wider rift in Netherlands society between power structures and patronage systems. Granvelle enjoyed a solid base of support in the judicial administration, in sections of the Church, and from one or two great magnates—notably Philippe de Croy, duke of Aerschot, and Jean de Ligne, count of Aremberg—who opposed Orange.[36] But the disaffected great lords possessed, as Granvelle and Philip well knew, immense influence at many levels throughout the seventeen provinces. Crucial was the role of William of Orange, wealthiest, as well as cleverest and most eloquent of the magnates—his later sobriquet 'the Silent' referred not to any taciturn inclination (he was in fact loquacious) but to his not saying what he thought. This outstandingly adroit politician soon emerged as Granvelle's chief rival for power. Head of the Nassau dynasty since the death of René of Châlons in 1544, when he had moved from Dillenburg to the ancestral palace of the Nassaus at Breda,[37] William had long been a pre-eminent figure at Brussels and in Brabant. Moreover, hitherto, he had been an energetic supporter of royal policy;[38] and had been much in favour with the Emperor. After Philip's accession, Orange had made a considerable contribution to organizing the war against France. Philip's appointing him

---

[33] Koopmans, *Staten van Holland*, 54–64.
[34] Grapperhaus, *Alva en de Tiende Penning*, 69–70; Koenigsberger, 'Orange, Granvelle and Philip II', 577.
[35] Rodríguez-Salgado, *Changing Face of Empire*, 350.
[36] Van Durme, *Antoon Perrenot*, 178.
[37] Rachfahl, *Wilhelm von Oranien*, i. 140–5.
[38] Swart, 'Willem de Zwijger', 48–9.

Stadholder of Holland, Zeeland, and Utrecht was not just an acknowledgment of his power and wealth but an indication the Crown expected him
to be as supportive in the future as he had been in the past.

There were hints of discord between William and the king even before
Philip departed for Spain, notably concerning the latter's wish that some
Spanish troops should remain in the country.[39] Probably there was also
already an element of personal antipathy between the reserved and pious
monarch and the extrovert *grand seigneur*. But both before, and for two
years after, Philip's departure, there was no suggestion that William would
soon cease to be a central pillar of royal authority and the regime. It was not
until 1561, the year of William's second marriage, to Anna of Saxony, that
the tension between the Prince and Granvelle became an open split. The
early motivation for Orange's opposition to royal policy in the Netherlands
was probably just the usual one amongst great noblemen of the sixteenth
century—the ambitious pursuit of power and prestige. Especially after the
outbreak of civil war in France, in which the main role was played by the
great nobles, Granvelle was convinced that the underlying disaffection, and
progress of Protestantism, in the Netherlands might well tempt a leading
seigneur, such as Orange, to put himself at the head of the growing forces of
opposition and exploit them for his own ends.[40] But while there was a strong
dose of self-seeking ambition in William's break with Granvelle, there was
also, from the outset, a deeper commitment to the cause of freedom of
conscience, and religious compromise, than was to be found amongst the
other great lords of the Netherlands.[41] No doubt this had much to do with
his early background and family's German Protestant connections. His
father, William the Rich, had exhibited strong Lutheran tendencies.

In any case, by 1561, the year the split between Orange and Granvelle
became irrevocable, he nailed his colours inextricably to the mast of
religious compromise by marrying Anna of Saxony, niece of the leading
Lutheran prince of Germany. The marriage was bound to heighten Philip's
suspicions and encourage the public to see him as a champion of policies of
religious compromise. A *politique* to his fingertips, lacking strong commitment to any confessional stance, William showed great dexterity in position-
ing himself between the irresistible force of advancing Protestantism in the
Netherlands and immovable object of Philip's Catholic zeal. Well versed in
saying different things to different correspondents, he still professed unswerving loyalty to the Catholic Church in letters to Philip. But his basic

[39] Ibid. 49.
[40] Koenigsberger, 'Orange, Granvelle and Philip II', 581.
[41] Swart, 'Wat bewoog Willem van Oranje', 555–6; Mout, 'Intellectuele milieu', 605–10.

aim remained consistent: to broker a negotiated religious compromise in the Habsburg Netherlands of which the magnates, led by himself, would be the arbiters and political beneficiaries.[42]

Since the royal administration, headed by Granvelle and Viglius, was striving to intensify the anti-heresy campaign, and simultaneously strengthen central government's administrative and judicial grip over the provinces and towns, it was natural that magnates opposing Granvelle should work against the anti-heresy drive. By the early 1560s some nobles, especially north of the rivers, were beginning to reveal their Protestant sympathies and openly tolerate Protestant activism in emulation, in part, of what was happening in France. In the Brederode lordship of Vianen, wedged between Holland and Utrecht, there was more or less open Protestantizing activity by the early 1560s.[43] In the enclaves of the *banner-heren* of Gelderland, such as Culemborg, Borculo-Lichtenvoorde, and Batenburg, a similar Protestantizing atmosphere prevailed.[44] William too, in his town of Breda, conspicuously intervened, if not actively to promote Protestant worship, then certainly to shield Protestants from official persecution.[45] Philippe de Montmorency, count of Horn (1524–68), did likewise in his autonomous county of Horn.

Philip himself knew that the position of the Catholic Church in the Habsburg Netherlands was now critical.[46] Protestantism, open, semi-concealed, or Nicodemist, saturated the entire country. Furthermore, the edifice of royal authority and administrative centralization which formed the sole basis on which the anti-heresy campaign in the Habsburg Netherlands could proceed, or even survive, had now been seriously undermined by both the split in the Council of State and the fact that the king, under pressure from the States and nobility, had had to recall the last Spanish troops from the country, in January 1561. The grip of the royal administration had clearly been weakened. Yet the king judged, despite the evident dangers, that he had no choice, unless he was willing to see the Catholic Church in the Low Countries collapse completely within a few years, but to press on with reforming the Netherlands Church and enforcing his measures against heresy.

The plans for reorganizing the Netherlands Church and setting up the new archbishoprics and bishoprics to provide a firm organizational structure had

[42] Swart, 'Wat bewoog Willem van Oranje', 556.
[43] Fontaine Verwey, 'Rôle d'Henri de Brederode', 297–300.
[44] Van Beuningen, *Wilhelmus Lindanus*, 252; De Jong, *Reformatie in Culemborg*, 83, 133.
[45] Beenakker, *Breda in de eerste storm*, 45.
[46] Dierickx, *Documents*, i. 181, 184.

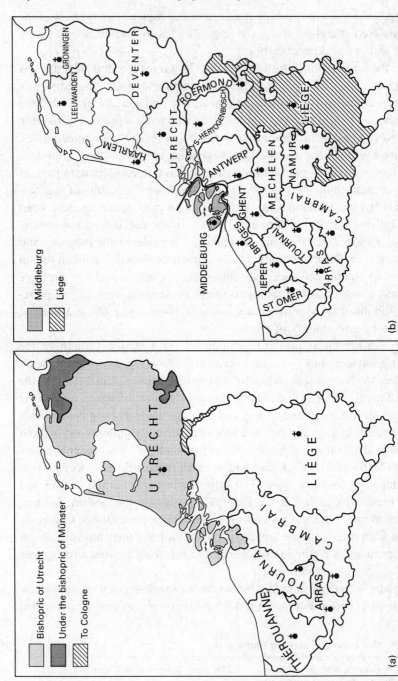

MAP 6. The bishoprics of the Netherlands, before (*a*) and after (*b*) the introduction of the New Bishoprics in the years 1559–1570

been published in the papal bull *super universas*, in 1559.[47] It was not until 1561, however, that the preliminary work of planning the new bishoprics and their boundaries, and earmarking abbey lands and other ecclesiastical revenues, for transfer to the new episcopal seats (see Map 6*b*), was completed, and the harder task of implementation could begin. Philip and Granvelle were hoping to entrust the new bishoprics to efficient, reliable churchmen, selected by virtue of education, and zeal, rather than aristocratic connections. To oversee the process Granvelle himself was appointed primate of the Netherlands Church as first archbishop of Mechelen. But if the intention was to create a bench of bishops who would be the ecclesiastical counterparts of the new class of jurists and bureaucrats staffing the king's judicial administration, in practice the king was forced to compromise with local patronage networks, and the views of the magnates, including William the Silent, and of the senior canons, who were often not the clergy most committed to suppressing heresy.[48] Thus, the first archbishop of Utrecht, the indolent nobleman Schenck von Tautenburg, the younger, possessed neither the ability, nor inclination, to discipline the clergy of Utrecht.[49] On the other hand, some of the new bishops were men from modest backgrounds chosen for their zeal, anti-Protestant credentials, and administrative efficiency. The new bishop of Middelburg, Nicholas de Castro, a man of humble origins, Sonnius, the new bishop of 's-Hertogenbosch and author of the new bishoprics scheme, and Wilhelmus Lindanus, designated for Roermond, were all professional inquisitors, zealots who could be relied on to pursue the goals set by the king with energy. The new bishop of Haarlem, Nicholas van Nieuwland, also a professional inquisitor, was less suitable, being a notorious drunkard.

The disaffected magnates had little difficulty in mobilizing opposition to the new bishoprics programme, especially in the north. Here the newly acquired provinces, or rather their towns and nobilities, viewed the new dioceses as a political and administrative device to erode their influence, regarding them with implacable suspicion.[50] There was also firm opposition from influential elements among the clergy, wherever the projected transfer of revenues and benefices threatened to upset established patronage networks. At 's-Hertogenbosch, the installing of Bishop Sonnius was obstructed by the abbots of the Meierij, as well as the States of Brabant, and, behind the scenes, William of Orange, who owned much land in the

[47] Dierickx, *L'Érection des nouveaux diocèses*, 18–19, 29.
[48] More, 'Cathedral Chapter of St Maarten', 223.
[49] Rogier, *Gesch. van het katholicisme*, i. 260–1.
[50] Slicher van Bath, *Gesch. van Overijssel*.

environs.[51] Lindanus, a university graduate and son of a Dordrecht burgo-master, was consecrated bishop of Roermond by Granvelle, at Mechelen, in April 1562. But after the *raad* of Roermond protested to the States of Gelderland, Margaret of Parma, fearing major complications should she proceed without the consent of the States, postponed his instalment indefin-itely. Yet, as Sonnius had predicted, writing to Philip from Rome in 1559, the most obdurate opposition stemmed from the States of Overijssel, Friesland, and Groningen.[52] In Overijssel, Deventer, Zwolle, and Kampen led a determined campaign denouncing the new bishops as 'heretic-hunters and inquisitors'. In none of these provinces was any progress made before the coming of Alva, in 1567.

The unpopularity of the clergy was now palpable. Sonnius entered 's-Hertogenbosch in November 1562, to find the city heavy with tension. In defiance of a placard of 1559 forbidding songs, plays, and pasquinades deriding Church or clergy, irreverent verses circulated freely.[53] The Francis-cans of Gelderland complained they dwelt in acute poverty, receiving no alms, since the people, moved by hatred of the Church of Rome, refused to give them any.[54] There were sporadic outbreaks of violence. In March 1563, a Cistercian nunnery near Leiden was plundered by a hostile mob.[55]

Such was the opposition to Granvelle that Philip was forced to dismiss him, in December 1563. With this it appeared that Orange had achieved his goal: Philip, it seemed, would soon also be compelled to suspend the anti-heresy placards, the Inquisition, and the executions. The Prince spoke more forcefully than ever in the Council of State, criticizing rulers who sought to force the consciences of their subjects, and impose religious uniformity by coercion.[56] Orange, Horn, and Egmond deliberately fomented opposition to the anti-heresy measures and new bishoprics, aiming to extend their own influence but not to challenge the sovereignty, or authority, of Philip II as such, or stir up the States to try to set up a new form of state. Orange's attitude during his disagreement with Holland in 1564–5 over whether or not the States had the right to meet on their own initiative, in which he resolutely opposed their view, is not a little ironic in view of later events.[57] At that stage neither William, nor the other magnates, were endeavouring to alter the government of the country other than substitute

[51] Rogier, *Gesch. van het katholicisme*, i. 360–2.
[52] Ibid., 314–15, 360–2.
[53] Worp, *Gesch. van het drama*, i. 191.
[54] Wagenaar, *Hervormer van Gelderland*, 13.
[55] Knappert, *Opkomst*, 218.
[56] Rachfahl, *Wilhelm von Oranien*, ii. 474–5.
[57] Res. SH. 13 Dec. 1564 and 26 Sept. 1565.

their own preponderance for that of the bureaucrats, Granvelle and Viglius.[58] The prolonged period of royal silence after the dismissal of Granvelle, and marked weakening of royal authority in the Netherlands in the years 1564–5, seemed to vindicate William's judgement, and his skill in handling the situation in the country.

Consequently, Philip's famous letters sent from the woods of Segovia, of October 1565, rejecting the Council's advice to relax the anti-heresy measures, and insisting on continuing the campaign against heresy, had a sensational effect. To those determined to halt the oppression, the endeavours of Orange and the magnates suddenly appeared both spineless and fruitless. A wave of protest pamphlets and handwritten pasquinades swept the land, causing mounting anxiety to the Brussels regime and not least Viglius.[59] Those nobles, mostly in the north, who had been espousing Protestantism privately over the last few years,[60] now took matters into their own hands. Hendrik van Brederode, scion of the family which had led the *Hoek* rebellions of the fifteenth century, with his base in his juridically autonomous lordship of Vianen, took the lead, together with Floris, count of Culemborg (who, like Brederode and Orange, had a German Lutheran wife),[61] and Orange's younger brother, Count Louis of Nassau (1538–74), in harnessing the mounting agitation amongst the middling, and lower, nobility and setting up, in November 1565, the famous League of Compromise.[62] This was a movement of Protestant and crypto-Protestant nobles intended to attract the support of all who desired a religious peace along the lines the Huguenots were striving for in France. On 5 April 1566, some two hundred noblemen from various parts of the Low Countries, led by Brederode, forced their way into the presence of Margaret of Parma in Brussels, and presented her with the Petition of Compromise, a vehement denunciation of the Inquisition and demand for its dismantlement, published in Dutch and German as well as French versions, which included a scarcely veiled threat to resort to armed rebellion should it be rejected. It was on this occasion that the sobriquet *Gueux* (beggars) was first pinned on the dissidents, a name which stuck and which they now proudly adopted as a badge of revolt.

The Petition of Compromise denounced only the Inquisition, not the king, royal administration, or Church.[63] By focusing exclusively on the Inquisi-

---

[58] Rosenfeld, 'Provincial Governors', 53–9.
[59] Geurts, *Nederlandse Opstand in de pamfletten*, 4–6.
[60] Pont, *Gesch. van het Lutheranisme*, 158.
[61] De Jong, *Reformatie in Culemborg*, 83–4.
[62] Bor, *Oorspronck*, i. 38–40v.
[63] Kossmann and Mellink, *Texts*, 60.

tion, the challengers to royal authority could claim that they were not rebelling against king or Church, and that their sole concern was to dismantle an institution universally hated in the Low Countries. But, at the same time, the petitioners made clear that in their eyes the Inquisition was not only evil but subversive of law and society, in conflict with both the rights and well-being of the country. The Inquisition, they asserted, 'would deprive the States of this country of all freedom to express their opinions, do away with all ancient privileges, franchises, and immunities, and not just make the burghers and inhabitants of this country miserable and perpetual slaves of the Inquisitors, who are worthless people, but even subject magistrates, office-holders, and all nobles to the mercy of their investigations'.[64] Over the Inquisition there could be no compromise, whoever sought to authorize or champion it.

Margaret had no alternative but to give way. She agreed that the anti-heresy placards should be suspended for the interim whilst a delegation from the States General travelled to Spain to petition the king.[65] Royal authority in the Habsburg Netherlands was now visibly disintegrating; Brederode triumphantly moved from town to town canvassing support and gathering noble signatures for his Compromise.[66] Large numbers of nobles signed in Flanders, Brabant, and especially Holland. There were also popular demonstrations at Haarlem, Amsterdam, and other towns with the mob yelling their support for the 'Beggars'.

With royal authority breaking down, and the Inquisition bridled, it was inevitable that there should be an immediate and vast upsurge of Protestant activity, including the forming of Calvinist consistories, throughout the Netherlands. A substantial number of Calvinist preachers, often former friars, who had been living in exile abroad, streamed back and joined in the work of forming organized congregations. Protestant sympathizers among the nobility who had thus far held back now cast off all inhibition. Especially blatant was the Protestantizing in the autonomous lordships, particularly Horn, Batenburg, Culemborg, and Brederode's town of Vianen. Viglius afterwards described Vianen as the 'hydra of the Revolt' and the 'receptacle of all heretics'.[67]

Mass Calvinist preaching in the open air, the so-called hedge-preaching of 1566, began the month after Brederode's coup in Brussels, in west Flanders. The movement spread rapidly. By June, mass Calvinist gather-

[64] Ibid.
[65] Lademacher, *Geschichte der Niederlande*, 57.
[66] Brandt, *Historie der Reformatie*, i. 319.
[67] Fontaine Verwey, 'Rôle d'Henri de Brederode', 300.

ings, attended by crowds numbering hundreds, and not infrequently thousands, took place in the fields outside Antwerp, Breda, and 's-Hertogenbosch.[68] In Holland, the mass preaching began in mid-July, outside Hoorn, and then spread rapidly to Enkhuizen, Haarlem, Amsterdam, and, during August, the towns of South Holland, except Dordrecht and Gouda.[69] Also in August, mass preaching began outside Utrecht. In Friesland, commencing at Leeuwarden, the Protestants came out into the open during September, as elsewhere, with huge crowds listening to the Reformed preachers.[70]

The surge of hedge-preaching released an accumulation of tension which had built up over four decades. An intoxicating expectation of spiritual renewal swept the Low Countries, creating a feverish mood which pervaded every niche of culture and social awareness, though outwardly restraint continued for the moment in the towns—where the town councils ruled—even while obedience to the king was disintegrating without. Within the town walls, there were as yet no open attacks on the Church in word, deed, prints, or woodcuts. Nevertheless, there are many indications of the spiritual ferment of these months of an indirect kind, not least in art. Commencing in 1565, Maarten van Heemskerk published a series of prints, showing the destruction of idolatrous temples and statues by enraged men wielding hammers and axes. It was at this time that Pieter Breughel (d. 1569) at Brussels, a famous man and favourite of Granvelle (who kept several of his paintings in his archiepiscopal palace in Mechelen), painted his imposing *Sermon of St John the Baptist* showing a large crowd, gathered under trees, intently listening to a sermon outside a city, in effect eulogizing the hedge-preaching, just as his later scenes of snow-carpeted Brabant villages, invaded by soldiers, captured the trauma of the events of the winter of 1566–7 and suppression of the Protestant upsurge by the Habsburg government.

The massive scale of the hedge-preaching, spreading across the Low Countries from Flanders to Friesland, in five months, convinced even the most timid that central government and the Church were now powerless to arrest the advance of Protestant activity. With the government's authority paralysed, it was probably inevitable that the frustration of previous decades would erupt in a wave of popular violence against the old Church and its images. It was not long before the iconoclastic frenzy began, even though the Calvinist preachers, the most militant among the Protestants, were divided as to the legitimacy of using force to attain God's ends, most

---

[68] Beenakker, *Breda in de eerste storm*, 61; Duke, *Reformation and Revolt*, 129.
[69] Brandt, *Historie der Reformatie*, i. 315–18; Smit, 'Hagepreeken', 212.
[70] Schotanus, *Geschiedenissen*, 728.

disapproving of the violence which now erupted.[71] On 10 August, after a sermon near Steenvoorde, in west Flanders, crowds attacked a convent and smashed the images. From there, the iconoclastic fury spread, both spontaneously and with the help of roving, organized bands, all over Flanders, Hainault, Brabant, Zeeland, Holland, Utrecht, Gelderland, and finally also Friesland and Groningen.

Decades of iconoclastic indoctrination by Erasmian humanists and crypto-Protestants in the schools, rhetoric chambers, and taverns of the Low Countries—even in the churches—had done its work. A deep estrangement from the traditional forms of piety had set in decades before, and advanced so far by this point that the country's vast and ancient fabric of faith, resplendent with images, paintings, vestments, altars, and church plate, was looked on without veneration by most and with hostility by many.[72] Alienation of a society from its own religious culture, on such a scale, was a phenomenon without precedent or parallel. Historians sometimes seek to explain the iconoclastic fury, or *beeldenstorm* as it was known in the Netherlands—at least in part—in terms of the economic dislocation of the mid-1560s caused by war in the Baltic and a suspension of imports of English unfinished cloth. These developments did depress employment and drive up food prices.[73] Economic distress and insecurity probably played some part in kindling the iconoclastic fury. Yet the iconoclastic outbreaks of 1566 involved no assaults on government officials or town halls, or against tax-farmers, and no plundering of shops and food-stores. In form the *beeldenstorm* was purely and simply an attack on the Church and not anything else.

The frenzy swept across the south Netherlands reaching Antwerp on 21–2 August. There, the image-breakers proceeded, watched by large crowds yelling 'Vivent les Gueux!'[74] No one opposed them. All forty-two churches in the city were ransacked, the images, paintings, and other objects hauled out into the streets, smashed, and the plate pilfered, the work continuing at night under the light of torches. Two days after Antwerp, the mob struck in Middelburg and Flushing, pillaging the great abbey-church of Middelburg and many village churches across Walcheren Island. On the same day, image-breaking erupted at Breda; the day after youths attacked one of the main churches in Amsterdam.

[71] Van der Linde, *Jean Taffin*, 52.

[72] Van Gelder, *Erasmus, schilders en rederijkers*, 45–6, 59; Van Gelder, *The Two Reformations*, 213.

[73] Res. Holl. 1565, pp. 10–12. SH to Margaret of Parma, 20 May 1565; Nusteling, *Welvaart en werkgelegenheid*, 260.

[74] Bor, *Oorspronck*, i. 59.

Initially, the iconoclastic fury in the north had the same fleeting, spontaneous quality as in the south. But, from late August onwards, as the *beeldenstorm* north of the rivers developed, it assumed a more systematic, organized character, with nobles and some prominent citizens intervening to direct the violence.[75] At 's-Hertogenbosch the image-breaking began after the Protestants had seized several churches in the city and sung psalms in front of the cathedral. In the outbreaks at Utrecht, in which great heaps of art treasures and vestments, including the entire library of the Friars Minor, were put to the torch, local Protestant nobles took the lead.[76] During September, by which time the violence was over south of the rivers, it continued to spread in the north, displaying an increasingly controlled and directed character. The outbreaks at The Hague and Leiden, on 25 September, took place under the protection of groups of armed nobles. The counts of Culemborg and Batenburg ordered the stripping of the altars and images from the churches on their lands in mid-September.[77] Both in the town of Brill and the surrounding countryside, the churches were systematically stripped, partly on the initiative of local nobles such as Willem Blois de Treslong.[78]

In those parts of the Habsburg Netherlands where there was substantial Catholic support amongst the populace, the town governments mobilized the civic militias, and rapidly suppressed, or altogether prevented, both iconoclastic outbreaks and the setting up of Protestant congregations. The presence, or absence, of sufficient Catholic allegiance to confront Protestant zeal was decisive not only in determining the outcome of the religious clashes in the Low Countries in 1566 but in shaping much of what was to follow. Where there was appreciable Catholic support among the people, Protestants, even if relatively numerous, had little chance of making headway, given that central government and the town governments were solidly against them. As was seen also in northern France in the 1560s and 1570s, what mattered was often less the number and resolve of the Protestants than the extent to which, with government backing, it was possible to mobilize a Catholic backlash.

What is most remarkable about the *beeldenstorm* in the Netherlands in 1566, consequently, is not the eruption of Protestant violence, spectacular though it was, but the mostly weak response of the Catholics, particularly north of the rivers. Indeed, the Catholic reaction to the systematic assaults

---

[75] Freedberg, 'Art and Iconoclasm', 74; Duke, *Reformation and Revolt*, 132.
[76] Bor, *Oorspronck*, i. 64–5; Kleijntjens and Van Kampen, 'Bescheiden', 66–9.
[77] De Jong, *Reformatie in Culemborg*, 133, 156–7; Scheerder, *Beeldenstorm*, 77–9.
[78] Troost and Woltjer, 'Brielle in hervormingstijd', 330–9.

on the old Church and its images and altars was largely confined to the southern provinces plus Gelderland. In Walloon towns, such as Lille, Liège, Namur, and Douai, Catholics resisted the Protestant challenge with a vigour comparable to that shown in northern France. In Lille the Catholics were more energetic and violent than the Protestants.[79] There was no question of Protestant congregations being set up. On the contrary, Catholics assaulted Protestant gatherings, ransacked Protestant homes, and forcibly rebaptized Protestant children. In Antwerp Catholic support was weak, but in some Brabant towns much stronger. In Gelderland, the iconoclastic fury erupted in the Roermond quarter and more sporadically further north.[80] But here too there was a forceful Catholic response. While the *bannerheren* had, for the moment, mostly veered towards Protestantism, many of the lower nobility were ready to take up arms for the old Church. The hedge-preaching reached Nijmegen in late August and the Protestants briefly seized the city. But the Catholic *jonkers* of the Nijmegen quarter staged a counter-coup and regained the city, purging the *raad* of Protestants and crypto-Protestants.[81] By contrast, the Calvinist upsurge met with no Catholic response in the small towns of Harderwijk and Elburg, on the Zuider Zee. Arnhem and Zutphen, where the Stadholder of Gelderland, the count of Megen, placed troops, remained quiescent.

Apart from Gelderland, most localities where Protestant action provoked vigorous Catholic counteraction were south of the rivers. It may be true that in the south there were marked variations, from town to town, and that this may be related to differences in local economic conditions and civic welfare policy.[82] In Lille, Catholic allegiance was much firmer than in Tournai or Valenciennes, in Mechelen, stronger than in Antwerp or Breda. But what is remarkable about the north Netherlands, in 1566, is that (except in Gelderland) there was practically no popular Catholic response to Protestant action at all. No doubt only a minority of the populace were committed Protestants. But committed Catholics, in the sense of people willing to go into the streets and demonstrate, or fight, to defend the old Church and its symbols and clergy, must have been far fewer. So few, indeed, that they were powerless to intervene.

At Amsterdam the citizenry were divided into a (small) activist, iconoclast element, drawn mostly from the lower strata of the population, a main body of Protestant citizenry, led by the new Calvinist consistory, presided over by

---

[79] Duplessis, *Lille and the Dutch Revolt*, 225–6.
[80] Jappe Alberts, *Gesch. van Gelderland*, 98–9.
[81] Coonan, 'Gelderland', 188–9; Kolman, *Reductie van Nijmegen*, 19.
[82] DuPlessis, *Lille and the Dutch Revolt*, 309–16; Steen, *A Chronicle*, 85–8.

the merchant Laurens Jacobsz. Reael, who disapproved of the violence, and finally, a more or less passive majority, non-confessionalized and inactive on either side.[83] A crucial factor at Amsterdam, as elsewhere, was the conduct of the town militias. For the civic militia was the basic instrument of law and order in the towns. If the militias refused to move against, or open fire on, iconoclastic mobs, the town regents were powerless to act.[84] In practically every case the militias did indeed refuse to confront the mobs and by this refusal, and attitude of support for Brederode and the Compromise, engineered the shift from the initial, spontaneous outbreaks of iconoclastic fury to a more orderly and systematic attack on the Church. At Delft, where (as everywhere else) the regents tried to prevent the establishment of Protestant worship, the militia not only refused to suppress a fresh icono-clastic outbreak, on 5 October, but helped force the *vroedschap* to hand over the Franciscan priory to the Calvinists.[85] In Haarlem, the town council, warned by the civic militia that they would act neither against the image-breakers nor Protestant preaching, were left with no option but to suspend Catholic worship—except in the monasteries—and authorize the forming of a Calvinist consistory.[86] In some towns it needed a second outbreak of iconoclastic violence, or the clear threat of violence, before the city council permitted Protestant worship within the city walls, but nearly everywhere Protestant congregations were established, against the wishes of the town councils, under pressure from influential citizens and the militias.

South of Antwerp, the only major outbreak of iconoclasm after August was at Maastricht. But in the north the *beeldenstorm* spread during the autumn wherever Protestant worship was not formally established, as a means of forcing the pace. At Leeuwarden, in September, it was the town council itself, under pressure from the militia, which stripped the parish churches of images and established Protestant preaching. Most Catholic priests in the city either fled or joined the Protestants. Over the next months Reformed consistories were established all over Friesland.[87] Except for the Stadholder and the Hof, there was virtually no resistance. In the Frisian countryside a hard core of thirty or forty Protestant nobles presided over the setting up of the new congregations and stripping of the churches.[88] In Ommelander villages such as Middelstum, Winsum, Ten Post, Garsthuizen, and others, it was the local farmers, spurred on by the *jonkers*, who attacked

---

[83] Van Nierop, *Beeldenstorm*, 32.
[84] Woltjer, 'Dutch Privileges', 28–9; Grayson, 'Civic Militia', 44–9.
[85] Woltjer, 'Dutch Privileges', 28–9; Grayson, 'Civic Militia', 47–9.
[86] Spaans, *Haarlem na de Reformatie*, 34–5.
[87] Schotanus, *Geschiedenissen*, 728.
[88] Woltjer, *Friesland in hervormingstijd*, 163–7.

the parish churches and images.[89] At Winsum it was the brothers Ripperda, and at Garsthuizen the Starckenborch family, who led the *beeldenstorm*.

The iconoclastic fury cast the nobility of the Netherlands into mounting disarray. They were already split three ways with some supporting those magnates, like Aerschot, Aremberg, and Megen, who remained loyal to the king's policy, while others backed Orange and the advocates of a 'religious peace', and still others the more militant course advocated by Brederode and the instigators of the Compromise. With the *beeldenstorm* many who had followed William's lead, or supported the Compromise, took fright. Even Brederode was, initially, taken aback. In August and early September, like most magnates, Brederode tried to restrain the violence, extending his protection, for example, to the abbey of Egmond.[90] But as more of the nobility reverted to supporting the regime in Brussels, he and his supporters veered towards greater militancy. Most magnates, deeply shaken, sought to regain control of events by offering Margaret their support in restoring order, if she would agree to permit Protestant worship in those places were it was already being practised. With this 'Accord' (23 August 1566), the League of Compromise dissolved. For Brederode this agreement came as a profound shock.[91] For a time, it appeared that Orange and the middle grouping would succeed in dismantling the king's policy peacefully, building on the Accord to achieve their 'religious peace'. For several months, Orange strove tirelessly in Antwerp, Breda, and afterwards in Amsterdam, Haarlem, and other Holland towns, mediating between Protestants and city councils, negotiating local religious settlements, and allocating churches both to Catholics and Calvinists—and here and there, as at Antwerp, also Lutherans.[92] But although effective locally—notably in Antwerp, in September 1566—in restoring order and defusing tension, against the wider canvas of the Habsburg Netherlands, Orange's policy was riven with contradictions and unsustainable. On the one hand he tried to retain his links with those nobles, in the south, who refused to countenance armed revolt against the king and opposed the Protestant agitation, while, on the other, cultivating Brederode and those unfurling the banner of armed rebellion. By the end of 1566 the middle ground had become untenable: the choice was armed revolt or submission.

Government troops, recruited by Margaret and those magnates now assisting her, began to suppress the Protestants in the Walloon provinces,

[89] *It aade Friesche Terp*, 170; Van Gelder, 'Nederlandsche adel', 10.
[90] Duke, *Reformation and Revolt*, 146.
[91] Ibid.
[92] Beenakker, *Breda in de eerste storm*, 114–15; Spaans, *Haarlem na de Reformatie*, 35–6; Ramsay, *The Queen's Merchants*, 43–5.

in December. Nobles willing to fight, mainly north of the rivers, began to gather money and men and pressed the towns to support them. At this point Orange probably considered putting himself at the head of the revolt. But the disintegration of his middle position, and the determination of those magnates who had been his allies, Egmond, Horn, and Hoogstraten, not to fight the king, persuaded him that the rebels' position was hopeless.[93] Initially, Brederode rallied appreciable support for an armed Protestant rebellion, particularly in Amsterdam, Utrecht, and adjoining areas.[94] But the defeat of a rebel force near Antwerp, in March 1567, and capitulation of Valenciennes, the bastion of Calvinism in the Walloon area, after a long and terrible siege, a few days later, took the heart out of the revolt.[95] By late April Brederode too had become discouraged. Long before the arrival of the Spanish army, under Alva, with which the king hoped to bring the Low Countries to heel, the armed rebellion had disintegrated. With it, open adherence to Protestantism collapsed also.[96] As early as January 1567, Protestant preaching ceased in the Walloon countryside, hundreds of Calvinists reconverting to Catholicism. In the north many towns had escaped an iconoclastic fury because there had been little resistance to the establishment of Protestant worship; this had flourished since September 1566 at Sneek and Franeker, in Friesland, for example, Hoorn in West Friesland, and the Overijssel towns. But in all these places, as well as towns where there had been violent outbreaks, Protestant preachers fled during the spring of 1567, Protestant churches were closed, and the consistories suppressed. The Amsterdam *vroedschap* ordered Protestant preaching in the city to cease on 17 April 1567.[97] Brederode fled shortly after. Orange judged it would be prudent to reside for a time outside the Netherlands and, in May, moved to his family's castle at Dillenburg. Hoogstraten, Culemborg, and other prominent nobles likewise migrated to Germany.

The rebellion seemed dead, the Netherlands cowed and submissive. There was throughout the land an unmistakable air of fear and demoralization. Yet a resolute opposition continued through the establishment of Dutch Protestant communities abroad as well as a spreading, and increasingly sophisticated, campaign of political propaganda. One leading apologist of the rebellion of 1566–7 who sought to keep its spirit alive was the Flemish noble Philip Marnix of St Aldegonde (1540–98), who subsequently became

---

[93] Swart, 'Willem de Zwijger', 55.
[94] Van Nierop, *Beeldenstorm*, 53–6.
[95] Rachfahl, *Wilhelm von Oranien*, ii. part 2, 891–2.
[96] Duke, *Reformation and Revolt*, 149.
[97] Evenhuis, *Ook dat was Amsterdam*, i. 68.

William of Orange's secretary and chief publicist. In 1567, Marnix published his *Vraye Narration et apologie*, claiming that the king had violated the privileges and 'freedom' of the Netherlands provinces. This theme was further developed by Jacob van Wesembeeke (1524–75), pensionary of Antwerp in the years 1556–67, who had assisted in negotiating the accommodation between the city's Calvinists, Lutherans, and Catholics, and followed Orange into exile. In a series of tracts published in 1568–9, Van Wesembeeke proclaimed that 'natural ingrained freedom, which man above all esteems and will not allow to be taken away'.[98] For Van Wesembeeke, as in subsequent rebel ideology, 'freedom' in the abstract and singular was the heart of the matter, albeit inextricably entwined with the privileges of the towns and provinces, and their prosperity. In his view, and many were inclined to agree, the king of Spain's violation of Netherlanders' 'freedom' in general, and privileges in particular, was sufficient reason to justify armed resistance to his authority.

[98] Van Gelderen, *Political Thought*, 115–19.

8

Repression under Alva, 1567–1572

❖

With the collapse of the revolt of 1566–7, the reaction against Protestants gathered momentum. After its victory, in March, the government in Brussels felt strong enough to disperse its forces, sending garrisons to numerous towns and localities.[1] Aremberg introduced garrisons into Leeuwarden, Sneek, and Sloten, and suppressed Protestant worship in Friesland. Many towns such as Haarlem, Venlo, and Roermond, which were still unoccupied, expelled their Calvinist preachers and terminated Protestant services both inside and outside their walls; during April, the exodus of Protestants began.

Alva arrived, in August, at the head of 10,000 Spanish and Neapolitan troops, supplemented by German auxiliaries. By then, not only had all visible sign of Protestant activity ceased but many of those linked to Brederode's rebellion or the freedom of conscience agitation had fled, or been driven underground. But neither Alva, nor the king, was satisfied with this. Philip had felt driven to send an army to the Netherlands at a time of difficulty and danger for the Spanish empire in the Mediterranean. The drain on Spain's resources was such that there was little prospect, with the war against the Ottomans continuing, that the strain of keeping an army in the Low Countries could be sustained for long. Whilst a powerful force was available, the Crown was determined to use it to such effect that subversion and conspiracy would be—if not eradicated—at least crushed sufficiently to render the Netherlands quiescent, secure, and reliably Catholic for the foreseeable future.[2]

Don Fernando Alvarez de Toledo, third duke of Alva (1507–82), was one of the principal nobles of Castile and unswerving, even fanatical, in his detestation of Protestant heresy. His reputation was of a man of iron and he was certainly coldly austere and rigidly authoritarian with a streak of harsh irritability in his make-up. Sixty years old when he arrived, the

---

[1] Steen, *A Chronicle*, 11; Maltby, *Alba*, 143.   [2] Verheyden, *Conseil des Troubles*, 508.

advance of gout, and other bodily afflictions, rendered his temper worse with the passage of time. Capable of great cruelty but always out of calculation, his outlook was a strange mixture of humanist cosmopolitanism and xenophobic bigotry. A grandee well versed in Latin, French, and Italian, who also spoke some German, he was, nevertheless, narrowly Castilian in his attitudes and unusually puritanical in sexual matters. His deeply suspicious attitude towards the Netherlands nobility and population was tinged with scarcely veiled contempt.[3] Though, initially, it was Philip's intention that Margaret should remain as regent and Alva's authority be confined to the military sphere, and maintaining order, it quickly became apparent that it was Alva, not Margaret, who wielded power in Brussels. Margaret, utterly dismayed by Alva's harsh proceedings, resigned her regency in September, and left for Italy in December. Alva was now in name, as well as fact, governor-general of the Spanish Netherlands. Philip's ablest general, he had also, for many years, been the leading advocate at the Spanish court of draconian measures as the best way to secure the king's authority, and the Catholic faith, in the Netherlands. He now had his chance to show what severity could do.

Margaret had been especially outraged by Alva's arrest of two of the country's leading magnates, Egmond and Horn, after a banquet, in Brussels, on 9 September. The two men had remained loyal to the old Church and, latterly, having assisted Margaret, assumed they had nothing to fear from the king; but they now found themselves greatly mistaken. Their papers were seized and scrutinized and they were tried for treason. Ten months after Alva's arrival in the Low Countries, the two counts were beheaded in the Grand-Place at Brussels before an appalled crowd, many of whom wept openly. Their execution, four days after that of eighteen rebel nobles, including the brothers Carel, Dirk, and Gijsbert van Bronckhorst van Batenburg, and others of Brederode's lieutenants, caught before they could escape, became a stock feature of subsequent anti-Spanish propaganda in both text and prints.

Even before the arrest of the counts, and Margaret's resignation, Alva had set up, in accordance with plans formed previously in Spain, the soon notorious *Conseil des Troubles*, the commission which was to be his chief instrument for investigating the disturbances of the previous two years and punishing the guilty. By sixteenth-century standards, this organ, which by 1569 had a prosecuting staff of 170, proved highly effective. Altogether, under the Alva regime, some 8,950 persons, from all levels of society, were

[3] Maltby, *Alba*, 146–7, 256.

investigated and sentenced for treason or heresy, or both, more than one thousand being executed.[4] Predictably, after the seizure of Egmond and Horn, there was a renewed rush of horrified nobles to flee the country. More noble residences were searched and papers confiscated. Culemborg was ransacked. Alva placed a garrison in Orange's palace at Breda, shipping off most of the weapons and other contents (in seven barges) to Ghent.

William the Silent had been warier than Egmond and Horn, and, like Hoogstraten, ignored Alva's summons to return to Brussels, remaining in Germany. Yet he too had failed to grasp the extent of the crack-down the king had ordered. Thus, he had left his eldest son, Philips Willem (1554–1618), a boy of 13, at Leuven, studying at the university; he was never to see him again. The boy was seized, the king, on the advice of Granvelle (who gladly availed himself of this chance to strike back at his old rival),[5] having resolved that he should be brought to Spain, partly as a hostage, but especially to be raised as a good Catholic and loyal subject, who could, should Philip so decide, be made Prince of Orange in place of his ousted and dispossessed father. Philips Willem was sent to Spain in February 1568, resuming his education at the university of Alcalá de Henares.

Though some were caught, most nobles active in the upheavals of 1565–7 escaped, in many cases returning later to participate in the main Revolt. In contrast to the south, a large section of the nobility in the north had openly participated in stirring up agitation against Church and royal authority. This was especially true of Holland, where more nobles—over fifty, including six of the eleven sitting members of the Holland *ridderschap*—had signed the Compromise of 1565 than in any other Netherlands province.[6] Also in Utrecht, Friesland, and the Ommelands large sections of the nobility had opted for rebellion.[7] Over a quarter of the nobility of Holland were directly implicated in heresy and opposition and many more had scant sympathy for Philip II's policies. Even in Overijssel (where there was no iconoclastic violence in 1566), it is clear that most of the nobility were opposed to the anti-heresy campaign, except for the *ridderschap* of Twenthe, which did support firm Catholic policies.

Among prominent nobles who fled to join those plotting in Germany were the *schout* of Breda, Godfried van Haestrecht, lord of Drunen, Willem de Treslong, an iconoclast of 1566, who was to distinguish himself in the capture of Brill in 1572, Gijsbrecht van Duivenvoorde, lord of Obdam

---

[4] Ibid., p. xiii; Dierickx, 'Lijst der veroordeelden', 415–22; Maltby, *Alba*, 140.

[5] Scherft, 'Philips Willem', 28.

[6] Van Nierop, *Van ridders tot regenten*, 195; Van Gelder, 'Nederlandsche adel', 3, 18–19.

[7] *It aade Friesche Terp*, 170.

(1540–80), later eminent in the defence of Haarlem, Jacob van Duivenvoorde (1509–77), lord of Warmond, prominent in the capture of Brill, and
the defence of Leiden in 1574, Jacob Oem van Wijngaerden, Floris van den
Boetzelaer, lord of Langerak (who had licensed Mennonites as well as
Calvinists to worship on his lands), and Willem van Zuylen van Nyevelt, a
dissident noble and iconoclast of Utrecht.

It is true the repression in the northern peripheral provinces was often
perfunctory.[8] Nevertheless, there were executions in Deventer, Groningen,
and other outlying cities and steps were taken to ensure greater compliance
with orders emanating from Brussels than had been the case in the past. On
Alva's instructions, a citadel was constructed within the walls of Groningen
and German troops in royal service stationed in the city to overawe the
populace.[9] A garrison was also stationed at Deventer and plans drawn up
to construct a citadel there.

A number of regents and civic magistrates were condemned by the *Conseil
des Troubles*, the most prominent of whom was the Advocate of the States
of Holland, Jacob van den Eynde (c.1515–69), who was imprisoned near
Brussels and died there soon afterwards. But these were strikingly few
compared to the number who had, in one way or another, been accomplices
to the spread of Protestant worship in 1566. In many towns of Holland, as
in Antwerp, even burgomasters—such as Nicolaas van der Laan, at Haarlem—who had authorized the handing over of churches to Protestants were
left unmolested.[10] The situation in Leeuwarden, where two burgomasters
and four of the six magistrates fled, and were condemned, was untypical. At
Haarlem, Dirk Volckertsz. Coornhert, secretary of the town, later to emerge
as the northern Netherlands' greatest writer on toleration, was almost alone
amongst civic officials arrested. But even he escaped and fled to the
Rhineland.

The brunt of Alva's condemnations and confiscations was borne by those
upper middle-class strata immediately below the level of the regents,
magistrates, and pensionaries. A large number of affluent citizens were the
victims of the regime's repression. At Haarlem, the thirteen citizens condemned as the ringleaders of the Protestant movement in the city included
several wealthy brewers.[11] At Amsterdam, those who headed the exodus of
1567, the men who had taken the lead in establishing Protestant worship in
the city the previous year, were the stratum of businessmen immediately

---

[8] Formsma *et al.*, *Historie van Groningen*, 223; Reitsma, *Centrifugal and Centripetal Forces*,
189.
[9] Ros, *Rennenberg*, 10.
[10] Spaans, *Haarlem na de Reformatie*, 36–7.
[11] Ibid.

below the regents—the group who were to take over the government of the city in 1578. Among them were the personalities from whom sprang the great Amsterdam regent dynasties of the Golden Age such as Laurens Jacobsz. Reael (founder of the Amsterdam Reformed consistory, in 1566), Jan Jacobz. Huydecooper (1541–1624), Dirck Jansz. de Graeff (1529–89), Adriaen Pauw (1516–78), and Pieter Cornelisz. Hooft, father of the great writer.[12] Adriaen Pauw, a prosperous grain merchant, had, during the troubles of 1566, been a militia captain and used his influence amongst the citizenry to favour the Protestants.

Similarly, in the case of Zeeland, the refugees included many prominent citizens who later founded some of the leading regent dynasties of the province.[13] Among these were Pieter Boreel, Jan van der Perre, Gaspar van Vosbergen, and Salvador de la Palma. Pieter Boreel, of Middelburg, fled to Norwich, where he died in 1568. His eldest son, Jacob, who went with him to England, was later, after 1574, many times burgomaster of his native city and eventually Dutch ambassador in England, where he was knighted by James I. Jan van Reigersberg, an apothecary of Veere, who fled in 1567, was to become a leading figure in his home town in 1575, when he was installed in the *vroedschap* by William of Orange.

In much of the periphery of the north Netherlands, very small numbers of suspects were condemned. At Kampen, where two Protestant preachers had been active for about half a year and there were hundreds of Calvinists, only four persons were sentenced.[14] At Zwolle the total was twelve; in Franeker sixteen, and at Harlingen eleven.[15] Elsewhere in the outlying provinces, more substantial totals were registered but without in any way eliminating the Protestant presence. In Deventer seventy-eight persons were condemned, all during 1571. But Protestant influence in the town was undoubtedly far more widespread than this figure would suggest. It would be inadvisable to read too much significance into the wide variations in the numbers of condemned in different localities often within the same province. Nevertheless, it is worth noting that if one excepts a few southern towns such as Tournai (1,063), Antwerp (525), Valenciennes (425), and Ieper (478), the *Conseil des Troubles* on the whole condemned relatively small numbers in the towns of the south, uncovering more evidence of organized sedition and propagation of heresy further north. Most southern cities, including Ghent (248), Brussels (157), Bruges (149), Hondschoote (116), Kortrijk (84),

[12] Elias, *Vroedschap van Amsterdam*, i. 47–52, 61–2, 92–6.
[13] Water, *Kort Verhael*, 107–10.
[14] Reitsma, *Centrifugal and Centripetal Forces*, 97–8.
[15] Verheyden, *Conseil des Troubles*, 486, 488, 505.

Mechelen (83), Lille (68), Namur (21), Leuven (20), and Douai (4) registered only modest numbers of condemned. Further north, particularly given the smaller size of the towns, the numbers registered in places such as 's-Hertogenbosch (360), Utrecht (288), Amsterdam (242), Groningen (209), Nijmegen (187), Breda (140), Middelburg (140), Leeuwarden (105), Brill (88), and Leiden (83) tended to be higher, even though there were also northern towns, such as Haarlem (35) or Gouda (6), with strikingly low totals.[16]

It was the greater complicity of the noble and civic élites of the north in the sedition of 1566, and the relatively large number of prominent exiles from north of the rivers, rather than any basic difference between north and south in religion, which caused the leadership of the refugees in exile, and of the movement of resistance to Alva's regime and to Spain, to be concentrated increasingly in the hands of northerners. The noblemen who rallied to William of Orange, once he unfurled the banner of revolt in 1568, derived more from the north than the south. Among the officers of the Sea-Beggars, the maritime force which the rebels established in 1568, there were a few southern noblemen but the bulk were Hollanders and Frisians.[17]

The exodus from the Low Countries proceeded in two main waves—in the spring of 1567 and then again, following the first wave of arrests, over the winter of 1567–8, helped by the freezing-over of the Zuider Zee. From Enkhuizen alone, reportedly, some 350 refugees fled over the ice to East Friesland. Those fleeing the Netherlands moved in three main directions. From Amsterdam, the West Frisian towns, Friesland, and Groningen, the flow was towards the north-western corner of Germany, especially Emden. From Flanders and Zeeland, emigration was chiefly by sea to England. From Brabant, southern Holland, and Utrecht, the exiles gravitated mainly to Cleves and the Rhineland. The total exodus has been estimated at around, or approaching, 60,000.[18]

Many emigrated. Yet the repression did not and could not eradicate Protestant activity (let alone belief) from the Netherlands. Estrangement from the Catholic Church was so widespread, and deeply rooted, that that was not possible. Not only in the outlying provinces but also in Holland, Brabant, and Flanders, many of those who had participated in the setting up of Protestant congregations, in 1566–7, escaped detection and remained unmolested in their home towns.[19] In some towns such as Delft, Haarlem,

[16] Ibid. 477–505.
[17] De Meij, *Watergeuzen*, 149–50, 154.
[18] Parker, *Dutch Revolt*, 119.
[19] Troost and Woltjer, 'Brielle in hervormingstijd', 336.

Enkhuizen, and Leeuwarden whole Reformed congregations, complete with consistories, survived until 1572, in clandestine circumstances.[20] The Mennonites too, who had also gained many new converts during the early and mid-1560s, survived, not only in Friesland and the Ommelands but also in South Holland and many other parts. On the surface the country was re-Catholicized. At the time of Alva's arrival, in 1567, many Netherlanders who had not attended Catholic mass for years resumed attendance.[21] But it does not appear that such outward submission was kept up for long. By the beginning of the 1570s the same reports of disaffection and low levels of attendance at mass at Easter time were heard as in the 1550s and early 1560s.[22] There was even the occasional anti-Catholic demonstration. A monk who preached at the main church in Hoorn in 1570 was interrupted by protesting townsmen singing psalms.[23]

During the opening months of the Alva regime, the outlook for armed opposition to Habsburg rule in the Low Countries looked bleak. Brederode, *le grand Gueux*, having failed to win Orange over to the cause of armed revolt, on his visit to Dillenburg, in June 1567, died dispirited a few months later, having deleted the Prince from the beneficiaries to his will. Both Orange's reputation and popularity slumped severely during 1567 and early 1568.[24] Nevertheless, it was apparently not until William learnt, early in 1568, of his condemnation, and the confiscation of all his property in the Netherlands, by the *Conseil des Troubles*, that he concluded, seeing his lands gone and reputation with both king and rebels wrecked, that the only option left, however unpromising, was to take Brederode's place and unfurl the banner of revolt.[25]

As a leader of rebellion, William of Orange disposed of much greater resources than had *le grand Gueux*. With help from German Protestant princely neighbours, especially the Reformed Elector of the Palatinate, he raised impressive sums of money.[26] He surrounded himself with a sizeable retinue of exiled Netherlands noblemen, including members of his former household at Breda. He negotiated with other German princes, and European rulers, as one sovereign to another, as a German (Protestant) prince himself and sovereign of Orange, in southern France. He brought to his

---

[20] Jaanus, *Hervormd Delft*, 24–7; Duke, *Reformation and Revolt*, 201–2.

[21] Brandt, *Historie den Reformatie*, i. 461.

[22] Beenakker, *Breda*, 150; Woltjer, *Friesland in hervormingstijd*, 213; Van der Pol, *Reformatie te Kampen*, 191–4.

[23] Velius, *Chronyk van Hoorn*, 321.

[24] Rachfahl, *Wilhelm von Oranien*, ii. 226–8.

[25] Swart, 'Wat bewoog Willem van Oranje', 561–2.

[26] Glawischnig, *Niederlande, Kalvinismus und Reichsgrafenstand*, 82.

assistance highly skilled propagandists, most notably his talented secretary, Marnix of St Aldegonde. From Nassau-Dillenburg he generated a stream of propaganda, elaborating on 'Spanish cruelty', vilifying Alva, and assuring the populace of the Netherlands that his resort to arms was the only means to save the country from 'unbearable slavery'.

Orange denied that he was rebelling against the king as such, and acknowledged Philip his rightful sovereign. His rebellion was against evil policies and especially the tyranny of Alva. Nor, as yet, did he become a Calvinist. A true *politique*, he avoided commitment to a particular confessional stance, not wanting to burn all bridges with Philip, or alienate the German Lutheran princes.[27] Furthermore, his propaganda deliberately played down the religious aspect of the struggle. The emphasis in his manifestos of 1568 was on the need to save 'worthy inhabitants who enjoyed freedom in former times' from cruel tyranny.[28]

It was thus during this dark period, the year after the coming of Alva, that William of Orange became the main focus of the hopes of those in the Netherlands who continued to oppose the Habsburg regime in their hearts. It is no accident that it was also in 1568, or soon after, that the famous heroic song, the 'Wilhelmus', was composed by an unknown poet, extolling the godliness and heroism of William of Orange, seeking to comfort a frightened, demoralized people with the promise that he will return. The 'Wilhelmus' is often called the oldest of all modern national anthems. In a sense this is true. But though the ballad became the best-known of a whole canon of Beggar war-songs, spreading first in Dutch and, then, after 1572, in Wallonia and the Rhineland, also in French, German, and Yiddish versions, in the seventeenth and eighteenth centuries it was specifically an anthem of adherents of the House of Orange, frowned on by opponents as excessively glorifying the Prince as 'Father of the Fatherland'. Only at the end of the nineteenth century was the song adopted as the Dutch national anthem.

Initially, the summons to arms, and stirring propaganda, had a considerable impact within the Netherlands, as well as among the 60,000 Netherlands Protestant exiles living in north-west Germany and south-east England. Even before Louis of Nassau's victory over the count of Aremberg at the battle of Heiligerlee, of May 1568, the first (and for many long years, the only) triumph the rebels were to win, hundreds of supporters streamed to his banner from all over Friesland and Groningen. It was also during the brief time that he occupied the north-east corner of Groningen that Count Louis established the rebel naval force, the Sea-Beggars, in the Ems estuary,

[27] Swart, *William the Silent*, 16.   [28] Kossmann and Mellink, *Texts*, 86.

using many of the men who flocked to him there. At the subsequent débâcle, at Jemminghen, in July 1568, where Alva crushed the rebel army, slaughtering most of them on the banks of the Ems, near Emden, on the German side of the border, a larger number of north Netherlanders, as well as hired German mercenaries, perished.

Orange was no match for Alva as a military commander, and his own subsequent thrust into Brabant was a failure. From 1568 down to 1572, he was unable to mount another large-scale invasion and circumstances left him with no choice but to settle down to a war of attrition. This consisted of sporadic pinprick attacks from Germany and later, in alliance with the Huguenots, also from the south. More effective, though, was the raiding of the Sea-Beggar fleet. Operating out of Emden and, intermittently, the English Channel ports, this force amounted, by the spring of 1571, to some thirty ships carrying letters of marque signed by Orange.[29] They not only disrupted maritime traffic around the coasts of the Netherlands but effected a series of landings, plundering monasteries and pillaging supplies. In 1570 they raided Hindeloopen and Workum.

Most noble exiles served with Orange or else travelled. The Utrecht nobleman Willem van Zuylen van Nyevelt, who settled at Emmerich, in Cleves, earning his living as a bookbinder and participating in Calvinist community politics, was an exception.[30] But the majority of non-noble exiles had to work, engaging in trade and the crafts, to feed themselves and their families. Reformed communities of exiled Netherlanders proliferated all over north-west Germany, as far south as Frankfurt am Main, and in south-east England. At the head of these congregations were a growing body of several dozen Calvinist pastors from the Netherlands, some of whom had been Catholic priests and monks until 1566, when they had made the break and helped shape the newly formed Reformed communities within the Netherlands.

The congregations in exile needed to co-ordinate their efforts and integrate their theological and political stance. But almost as soon as they began to organize, differences and tensions arose. The first gathering of delegates, meeting at Wesel, in Cleves, in November 1568, experienced difficulty over doctrine in a way pregnant with implications for the future.[31] With few prominent men among them, there was a tendency for the refugees from south Netherlands, who were usually from a lower middle-class background, to adhere to a rigid hardline Calvinist orthodoxy, and to distrust

[29] De Meij, *Watergeuzen*, 60–1.
[30] De Jong, *Voorbereiding*, 138.
[31] Ibid. 49–52; Nauta, *Opera minora*, 37–8.

those who had held positions of influence in civic government.[32] By contrast, exiles from Holland, often of a higher social status, tended towards a more latitudinarian stance and greater respect for civil authority. This incipient rift was confirmed at the first full Synod of the Netherlands Reformed Church which convened at Emden in 1571. The lay leader of the Amsterdam exiles at Emden, Laurens Jacobsz. Reael, accused his more doctrinaire opponents of trying to subject the congregations in exile to a 'new popery' of rigid dogma.[33] But, for the moment, it was the strict Calvinists, led by Herman Moded and Pieter Dathenus, who triumphed. The acts of the Synod of Emden made the consistories alone responsible for appointing future ministers of the Netherlands Reformed Church, without assigning any role to civil authority.[34] Neither did the acts make any conciliatory gesture towards the Lutherans, as Reael's adherents wanted, or make any reference to the armed struggle, or declare support for Orange. This was perhaps partly due to the traditional hesitation of the Protestant churches regarding armed revolt against legitimate authority, however tyrannical. But this lack of explicit support for Orange was probably also influenced by distaste for Orange's political propaganda, which was secular in tone and directed at Calvinists and non-Calvinists (including Catholics) alike. Orange's ideology was aimed at overthrowing Alva's tyranny and the Inquisition, and restoring 'freedom'—not at bringing the whole country over to God's truth and the one 'true faith'.[35] Orange's Revolt was not one of which the likes of Moded and Dathenus could approve.

While most Protestant exiles divided into Calvinists and liberal Reformed, both anxious to build a comprehensive Netherlands Reformed Church, there were other elements amongst the émigré population which can be fitted into neither category. The Sea-Beggars were certainly ferociously anti-Catholic, and capable of killing monks in the most brutal manner, but many Reformed émigrés regarded them as an ill-disciplined, godless crew whose piratical conduct, and carousing with prostitutes, put them beyond the pale of decent society.[36] Then, less unruly but scarcely more palatable to Reformed ministers, were an assortment of intellectuals, often professional scholars or lawyers, who, as humanists and Spiritualists, equally rejected the Catholic Church and dogmas (and discipline) of the Reformed. Prominent amongst these 'libertines' were the great humanist scholar Justus Lipsius

---

[32] Nauta, *Opera minora*, 37–8; Van 't Spijker, 'Stromingen', 52, 59.
[33] Nauta, *Opera minora*, 37–8; Fruin, *Verspreide geschriften*, ii. 238–40.
[34] Nijenhuis, 'De publieke kerk', 336.
[35] Woltjer, 'Politieke betekenis', 43–4, 47.
[36] De Meij, *Watergeuzen*, 166–8.

who, anxious to escape the turbulence of the Low Countries, went to study at the Lutheran university of Jena; Dirk Volckertsz. Coornhert (a future adversary of Lipsius as well as of the Calvinists), who developed his own intensely private spirituality in the Rhineland; the *politique* Adriaen van der Mijle, member of a leading Dordrecht regent family, and former senior judicial official at The Hague, who fled in 1567 and then travelled, and studied, in Italy; and the young lawyer Jan van Oldenbarnevelt, who became a token Calvinist at Heidelberg in 1568, but who from the outset nurtured serious reservations about Calvin's teaching. Having toured several Continental universities, Oldenbarnevelt returned to The Hague in 1570, to live, like so many others, as a crypto-Protestant in outward submission to the Catholic Church.[37]

Philip and Alva strove to suppress heresy and sedition through the *Conseil des Troubles* and its commissions in each province. In addition, the country had to be made secure against internal, and external, enemies without heaping too much of the financial burden on Castile. Thus, a sizeable standing army had to be maintained for the time being and, to pay for it, the king deemed it essential that more revenue be raised in the Netherlands. The military strategy adopted by Alva and approved by the king—splitting the army into small contingents, billeting troops on towns, and building citadels to overawe towns throughout the Netherlands—only intensified the need to step up fiscal pressure.[38] But most vital of all in Philip's eyes, the key ingredient, was the programme to revive the Catholic Church in the Netherlands and assist it in winning back the hearts and minds of the populace. The intimidation of the country was just a means to an end.

With Alva's coming, resistance to the new bishops and promulgation of the decrees of the Council of Trent, rapidly ceased.[39] Sonnius was installed at 's-Hertogenbosch, followed by the adoption of the first bishop of Groningen. Lindanus was installed at Roermond in March 1569, and Cunerus Petri, a Zeelander, as first bishop of Friesland in February 1570. The last of the new bishops was installed at Deventer in October 1570. In each new diocese, the decrees of the Council of Trent were published and reforming diocesan councils convened.[40] The Catholic Reformation in the Low Countries commenced its work. But the task of strengthening and revitalizing the Church proved difficult. The whole fabric of Church organization, local politics, and education in the country was unconductive

[37] Den Tex, *Oldenbarnevelt* (English), i. 9.
[38] Verheyden, *Conseil des Troubles*, 508; Maltby, *Alba*, 151–2.
[39] Dierickx, *L'Érection des nouveaux diocèses*, 125.
[40] Sjoerds, *Algemene Beschrijvinge*, ii, part 1, 700.

to such reform. The town councils, in most cases, remained uncooperative, and this had far-reaching consequences in many spheres, not least control of the schools. A major objective of the new bishops was to purge unreliable rectors and schoolmasters, especially from the civic Latin schools, and, as far as possible, all schools, substituting zealous Catholics. But control over teaching posts in civic schools had long been a jealously guarded prerogative of the town councils. Even under Alva, as Lindanus discovered in imposing his nominee as rector of the Latin school at Nijmegen, overcoming the obstruction of town councils could be an exasperatingly slow business.[41]

Ultimately, Philip hoped to transform the Netherlands into a secure bastion of Spanish power which would simultaneously serve as a bulwark against the spread of heresy. He held no illusions that he could eradicate Protestantism completely. But the repression proved it was possible, not just to hold the country by force, but to drive Protestant activity underground and curtail, if not stop, publication and distribution of heretical literature. A combination of severity and energetic government support for reform and reorganization of the Church, could, perhaps, in time, lead to the effective re-Catholicization of Netherlands society.

Crucial to the agenda was the imposition of new taxes. Sixteenth-century European monarchies were at their weakest in managing their finances. But they were not so weak that they could not, where they had sufficient political leverage, implement far-reaching fiscal measures in a short space of time. On returning to Spain, Philip had succeeded in pushing up revenues substantially, thereby generating the resources needed to combat the Ottomans. Now that he had a second major military commitment on his hands, in the Low Countries, he sought to solve the attendant financial problem as he had in Spain.

Work on new tax measures proceeded unremittingly. In March 1569, Alva convened the States General, for the first time since 1559, presenting the provincial delegations with demands for huge new sums to be raised by means of three separate fiscal, measures.[42] The first, and least controversial, was for a 100th Penny, or 1 per cent levy on assessed wealth. The second was a 5 per cent impost on sales intended as a permanent tax. The third, the famous Tenth Penny, was to be a fixed 10 per cent tax on sales, loosely modelled on the Castilian *alcabala*. The demands were of far-reaching political and constitutional, as well as fiscal, significance, not only because, by securing these taxes, the regime would possess the means to maintain the

---

[41] Van Beuningen, *Wilhelmus Lindanus*, 237, 255.
[42] Grapperhaus, *Alva en de Tiende Penning*, 106–10; Parker, *Dutch Revolt*, 114–17.

standing army with which to hold the country in subjection, but because, by acquiescing in permanent taxes, the provincial States, and States General, would be surrendering their leverage over government revenues. Had he succeeded, Philip would have been freed from the constitutional constraints which had previously limited Burgundian and Habsburg power in the Netherlands.

The provincial States, and town governments, were cowed by the events of the last two years but not so intimidated that they were willing to capitulate on the constitutional front. Most of the newly annexed provinces were let off the Tenth Penny, in exchange for agreeing to vote annual subsidies for the Crown. Only Utrecht, a province which had particularly aroused the duke's wrath, was subjected, together with the patrimonial core of the Habsburg Netherlands, to the campaign of pressure, and punitive billeting of troops, on which Alva now embarked.[43] He made it clear that he intended to obtain a great deal of new revenue and without obstruction or delay.

The States General had in 1569 agreed to a form of words which Alva construed as consent in principle to the three measures which, however, the provincial assemblies and town councils denied. As a stopgap measure Alva accepted the provinces' assent to temporary subsidies. But the assemblies (unlike the duke) understood these to have been voted in exchange for Alva agreeing to drop the Tenth Penny and 5 per cent tax.[44] When the term of the temporary subsidies expired in 1571 and Alva renewed his insistence on the Tenth and Twentieth Penny taxes, unilaterally imposing them, by decree of 31 July 1571, a wave of bitter frustration swept the country. But what caused the greatest resentment were the methods Alva used to coerce the town governments into putting his new taxes into effect. Count Bossu, the new Stadholder of Holland, Zeeland, and Utrecht, assigned officials of the Hof of Holland to ensure implementation in his provinces by menacing civic officials with fines—in Gouda, for example, of 1,000 guilders per burgomaster and 500 guilders per magistrate—if tax-collectors were not appointed and the machinery for collecting the taxes not set in motion.[45] Even Amsterdam eventually submitted albeit holding out longer than the rest, caving in shortly before the arrival of the Sea-Beggars at Brill.

Popular loathing of the new taxes, especially in Flanders, Brabant, and Holland, was such that collaboration with officials of the provincial courts, delegated to supervise collection, involved appreciable personal risk to the

[43] Geyl, *Revolt of the Netherlands*, 109.
[44] Craeybeckx, 'Alva's Tiende Penning', 185.
[45] Hibben, *Gouda in Revolt*, 42–4; Grapperhaus, *Alva en de tiende penning*, 218–19.

regents concerned. At Brussels, where there were repeated signs of pending unrest, the burgomasters preferred to brave Alva rather than the populace. But even where there was no disturbance, tension was acute. At Gouda the burgomasters provided themselves with bodyguards. The magistracies nervously consulted their militia captains, enquiring if they could count on them to suppress disorder should implementation proceed. At Gouda, the militia contingents answered that they would do nothing to enforce the Tenth Penny—even if the king himself demanded it. By March 1572, many militia units were seriously alienated against their own town governments.[46] Thus, even though the two new permanent taxes had been considerably diluted, and were never actually collected, they had the consequence of opening a breach between central government and the provincial assemblies, and damaging irreparably the standing of the town governments, in the eyes of the citizenry and militias.

That the political storm over the Tenth Penny was in practice not strengthening, but seriously damaging, the position of the Crown, and playing into Orange's hands by stoking up popular discontent, was plain to Viglius and the king's other most loyal supporters in the government of the Low Countries. Viglius suspected that Alva with his irascible insistence on the Tenth Penny was not so much representing the expressed will of the king—he doubted whether Philip was sufficiently aware of the actual situation—as his own unconquerable obduracy.[47] Even Alva's closest adherent amongst the Netherlands nobility, Charles, comte de Berlaymont, wrote behind his back to Madrid, warning the king that persisting with the Tenth Penny would seriously impair the loyalty of his Netherlands subjects. The Flemish bishops, and other ultra-loyalists, also tried to have the Tenth Penny suspended. But Alva stubbornly refused to change course until the summer of 1572, by when it was too late.

---

[46] Grayson, 'Civic Militia', 55–7.   [47] Waterbolk, *Rond Viglius van Aytta*, 51–2.

9

The Revolt Begins

❖

A revolution, a truly great revolt of a kind which fundamentally trans-
forms the course of history, can arise only where there has been a long
gestation creating unbridgeable constitutional, social, ideological, and spiritual rifts. All kinds of revolts can arise out of short-term grievances. But
repression and exploitation, even had Alva's regime been more brutal and
rapacious than it was, cannot themselves generate a far-reaching rejection
of the political and religious foundations of a society such as occurred in
1572 in the Netherlands. For that to happen there must be a preparatory
period of polarization of attitudes, ideologies, and constitutional views
lasting decades. The economic and military circumstances which precipitated the outbreak of rebellion in 1572, though not unimportant, are thus
essentially secondary.

It is certainly true that the Tenth Penny furore greatly aggravated the
tensions besetting the Netherlands in 1571 and early 1572, when Alva
resorted to unilateral imposition of the tax. But this was because the Tenth
Penny had become a symbol of unbridled central authority riding rough-
shod over venerated constitutional procedures, a symbol of government
illegality and the ruthless coercion of the towns.

There was no difference in response to the Tenth Penny as between the
north and south of the Netherlands.[1] Similarly, the resented burden of
military occupation, construction of citadels in major towns, the new
dioceses, religious repression, and the *Conseil des Troubles* affected the entire
Habsburg Netherlands without difference between north and south. Nevertheless, the insurrection of 1572, rapidly produced an entirely different
situation in the north than in the south and this sharp, and fundamental,
contrast was subsequently decisive in shaping not only the development of
the Revolt but also the growing divergence between north and south.[2] That
the response to the Revolt of 1572 was so different in the north from the

---

[1] Craeybeckx, 'Alva's tiende penning', 183–4.   [2] Woltjer, *Kleine Oorzaken*, 9.

south resulted from basic differences in social structure, the religious situation, and economic life reaching back not just years or decades, but centuries. Three basic differences proved fundamental: in the north there was only one power block whereas in the south there were several; in the north a large part of the nobility and patriciate were behind the Revolt whereas in the south this was not the case; and finally, militant Catholicism was a significant force in Wallonia and parts of Brabant whereas there was virtually no firm Catholic support amongst the populace north of the rivers. To this may be added the strategic factor: it was unquestionably more difficult for the Spanish army to operate effectively in the low-lying areas, particularly Holland and Zeeland, than below the rivers.

The contrast in constitutional structures was a legacy of the distant past: Flanders and Brabant both lacked internal cohesion; Holland, by contrast, its States accustomed to acting as a provincial government to protect the province's bulk-carrying fleet and herring fishery—neither of which was mainly based in any of the six 'large towns'—was the only province in the Habsburg Netherlands with a measure of real institutional cohesion. No less important, Flanders and Brabant had always lacked the capacity to intervene in, or exert any political or military influence over, the north. Consequently, there was no way of challenging Holland's potential dominance, should Habsburg power falter, over the rest of the north. The contrast with regard to social élites was also, in part, a legacy of the distant past. Above the rivers the magnates had less influence than below while the urban artisanate was smaller and also less inured to confrontation with patricians, so that there was less chance of paralysing splits within society. But the social factor was also shaped by the outcome of the rebellion of 1566–7. Because the *beeldenstorm*, and establishment of Protestant worship in the north, had been more organized, with a greater participation by élites, than in the south, many more nobles and influential men had been driven into exile from the north than the south, facing permanent loss of their influence and wealth. This means that in 1572 there were more men of substance from the north with an interest in overthrowing the existing regime, and replacing it with something different, than was the case in the south.

The great Revolt was triggered by the Sea-Beggars. On 1 April 1572, six hundred *Gueux*, recently expelled from the English Channel ports, on Queen Elizabeth's orders, under the command of Count Lumey de la Marck, a Liègeois nobleman whom Orange now made his representative in South Holland, seized the small port of Brill which had been temporarily left without a Spanish garrison, owing to Alva's concentration of his forces along the French border to guard against an expected incursion from

France. Willem Blois de Treslong, his second-in-command, persuaded Lumey not just to raid the town and its churches (which were thoroughly pillaged and stripped of images) but to try to hold Brill, a town inaccessibly placed and surrounded by waterways, against the inevitable counter-attack.

The growing threat from the Sea-Beggars, since 1568, had led Alva to station substantial forces around the Scheldt and Maas estuaries. Some of these had recently been drawn off for service on the French border but on the news of the capture of Brill, reinforcements were dispatched to Bossu, and the new Portuguese Stadholder of Friesland and Groningen, Gaspar de Robles. The regents of Holland and Zeeland, recently bullied into surrender over the Tenth Penny, afraid of disturbances amongst their own citizenry, and professing to be staunchly Catholic, were willing enough to try to keep the Sea-Beggars out in the name of king and Church.[3] But the approach of Spanish and Walloon reinforcements placed them in an almost hopeless position. The civic militias had already intimated they would not back the town councils against popular unrest for the sake of the Tenth Penny. There was no reason to assume the militias would spring to the support of the town councils if it came to letting in Spanish garrisons and closing gates against the Beggars, quite the contrary.[4]

Brill was a small, and relatively unimportant, town. But once the Beggars realized how fragile was the situation in the north-west Netherlands, and how precarious the position of government, Church, and regents, they lost no time in pouncing on bigger prey, riding a wave of popular fury against the town governments and regime. Five days after the capture of Brill, it was the turn of the strategically crucial port of Flushing, at the mouth of the Scheldt. Flushing had been selected by Alva as the site for one of the new citadels designed to overawe the citizenry and hold the Netherlands more securely. But, in contrast to Antwerp, Groningen, and Utrecht, where the citadels were formidable, that at Flushing was still at an embryonic stage, less a fortress than a symbol of oppression. On the approach of Spanish reinforcements, the citizenry seized the town, ejected its Walloon garrison, and called in the Beggars, some 800 of whom were sent from Brill in eight vessels. The town government was changed and an edict issued in the name of the Prince of Orange (and king of Spain) sternly forbidding attacks on the churches under pain of severe penalties. Later in April Veere, followed by the rest of Walcheren Island, except Middelburg, rose against the Spaniards. Veere was seized by its fishermen. So strongly pro-Beggar

[3] Hibben, *Gouda in Revolt*, 33–4, 44; Spaans, *Haarlem na de Reformatie*, 38–41.
[4] Grayson, 'Civic Militia', 55–7.

was sentiment in Zeeland that the Spaniards were greatly hampered in their efforts to react by the refusal of local seamen to serve on the king's ships and supply barges.[5] Flushing, an admirable naval base, assured the rebels control of the Scheldt estuary.[6]

Bossu, having failed to eject the Beggars from Brill, proceeded to seal off the town from the rest of Holland and blockade it. Rotterdam closed its gates on him, the town being divided but predominantly in favour of the Beggars.[7] But Bossu's troops burst in and suppressed the incipient rebellion there. It was at this point, with the situation in Holland and Zeeland in the balance, that Count Louis of Nassau, eager to seize the opportunity, invaded Hainault and captured Mons, one of the principal Habsburg fortress towns on the French border. It was only some weeks later, in August, that the St Bartholomew's Day Massacre, in Paris, removed the threat of a large-scale Huguenot-backed invasion of the Spanish Nether-lands, from France, so that, from April to July, however critical the position in Holland and Zeeland, Alva felt obliged to keep the bulk of his forces further south.[8] With the rebels holding their enclaves in Holland and Zeeland, and Alva's army encamped around Mons, another rebel force under the Gelderland magnate Count Van den Bergh invaded Gelderland, from Germany, and captured Zutphen, bringing most of Gelderland and Overijssel into revolt. Finally, in August (following the massacre in Paris), Orange in person led a largely German mercenary army of 16,000 men into Brabant, aiming to relieve Mons. Significantly, only two southern towns, Mechelen and Oudenaarde, thereupon revolted spontaneously and re-quested garrisons from Orange.

After the fall of Brill, Flushing, and Veere the position of the Spanish forces and royalists, in Holland and Zeeland, seemed briefly to stabilize. There was acute tension inside Middelburg where the regents and officials put in by Alva held firm while the common folk wished to emulate Flushing.[9] But the Spaniards sent in reinforcements and secured the city. After a lengthy pause, the next town to go over, this time in North Holland, was Enkhuizen, like Veere a major fishing port and one which had suffered severely from the disruption caused by the Sea-Beggars but which blamed the Spaniards for the slump. On 21 May, the town militia opted for the Beggars and seized the town.[10] Only afterwards, when the town's royalist

[5] BL MS Add.28387, fos. 77–8. 'Relacion de Gelanda y Flesingas' (April 1572).
[6] Ramsay, *The Queen's Merchants*, 175–6.
[7] Melles, *Ministers aan de Maas*, 42–3.
[8] Geyl, *Revolt of the Netherlands*, 116–22.
[9] BL MS Add 28387, fo. 73v. 'Relacion de lo que ha passado' (8 April 1572).
[10] Brandt, *Historie . . . Enkhuizen*, 155–72.

regents had fled and the rest agreed to join the Revolt, were the Beggars called in. On 2 June the Beggar leader, Diederik Sonoy, Orange's commander in North Holland, established his base in Enkhuizen, which became the nerve-centre of rebel operations throughout North Holland and, initially, also Friesland.

The insurrection at Enkhuizen undermined the position of the pro-government, pro-Catholic city governments throughout North Holland, though it was not for another month that Hoorn and Alkmaar came over, in both cases through internal unrest against the sitting regents rather than Beggar intervention. At Hoorn, a town where (as in Amsterdam) there was a sharp split between the pro-government ruling patriciate and the business community (many of whom were exiles), most of the town council fled and were replaced with prominent Protestants returning from Emden.[11] At Haarlem, which remained ostensibly loyal until early July, after most of the other main Holland towns had gone over, the *vroedschap* prevaricated for as long as possible; then, having sensed the mood and consulted the civic militia, the regents refused the garrison offered by Bossu and instead admitted Orange's emissaries, agreeing to recognize Orange as rightful Stadholder of Holland, which was tantamount to joining the Revolt of their own accord.[12] The Haarlem regents acted thus because feeling in the town was strongly on the side of Orange and the Beggars, and support for king and Church minimal. Opening the city gates to Orange's envoys also meant accepting his 'Religious Peace' and consequently the introduction of Protestant worship, though the regents knew full well that, should Alva regain control of the city, this would have extremely serious consequences for themselves. A fortnight after opening their gates, the Haarlem city authorities permitted the first Reformed service to be held in a church inside the city.[13]

With the fall of Haarlem, all North Holland except Amsterdam was in rebel hands. As the Revolt spread it produced sporadic mob demonstrations, unruliness against unpopular regents, a creeping *beeldenstorm*, and expulsion of Catholic priests and the closing of Catholic churches despite Orange's efforts to prevent this. In South Holland, the government was militarily in a stronger position; for here Bossu had the bulk of his force and could call on assistance from the Spanish garrison at Utrecht. Yet, in South Holland the civic patriciates were in as precarious a situation, just as vulnerable to popular anger, as further north. Ironically, Gouda—one of

---

[11] Velius, *Chronyk van Hoorn*, 331–8; Grayson, 'Civic Militia', 56–7.
[12] Wijn, *Beleg van Haarlem*, 9–10.
[13] Spaans, *Haarlem na de Reformatie*, 41.

the towns least affected by the ferment of 1565–7—was the first of the main South Holland towns to go over to the Revolt. On 21 June, a band of Beggars under the command of a local noble, Adriaen van Swieten, having captured Oudewater, appeared before Gouda, calling on the regents to submit to the authority of the Prince of Orange. The *vroedschap*, seeing there was no support for king or Church in Gouda, gave in with great reluctance but equally great promptness.[14] In Leiden, the staunch loyalists of the city council were rapidly overwhelmed by internal pressure.[15] Not only the populace and militia officers (who flatly refused to suppress the popular disturbances in the town) but part of the town council itself, led by the pensionary, Paulus Buys, the man soon to emerge as the leading figure amongst the pro-Orange regents in the province, supported the Revolt. Two burgomasters and a few loyalist councillors fled. Leiden joined the Revolt entirely through internal pressure: it was only ten days later that Beggar troops entered the town. But they certainly served to radicalize the revolution. Following the entry of the Beggars, the city's Catholic churches were pillaged, stripped of images, and closed.[16] Orange's efforts to prevent the sacking of the churches were proving increasingly ineffective.

After Leiden it was the turn of Dordrecht. Of all the Holland towns Dordrecht was reputedly the most conservative and pro-Habsburg in sentiment. In 1566, Dordrecht had been exceptional for the loyal attitude of the civic militia in preventing Protestant preaching and image-breaking. But while most Dordrecht regents were pro-Habsburg, a small core, notably Cornelis van Beveren, Adriaen Bleyenburg, and Jacob Muys van Holy, were Orangists and crypto-Protestants, and swiftly gained the upper hand in the tussle for control, owing to lack of support—both in the militia and town as a whole—for a royalist or Catholic stance.[17] When the people began to demonstrate, the militia joined them, the loyalist regents panicked, and power shifted to the Orangists. As the Beggars streamed in, the town's prominent loyalists departed. Over the next few weeks the churches of Dordrecht were pillaged and stripped. A few were reopened for Protestant worship; most were closed.

Striving to reverse the tide, Bossu issued a summons to the town patriciates of Holland, calling them to an emergency gathering of the States of Holland, at The Hague, where there were Spanish troops and the town authorities remained loyal to the king, until late July.[18] But, by the time his

[14] Hibben, *Gouda in Revolt*, 29–30, 53–5.
[15] Boogman, 'De overgang', 26.
[16] Ibid.; Van Gelder, *Revolutionnaire Reformatie*, 26.
[17] Boogman, 'De overgang', 94–7.
[18] Bakhuizen van den Brink, 'Eerste vergadering', 205–9.

summons went out, only Amsterdam, Rotterdam, Delft, and The Hague, of the larger towns, were still loyal, along with a few small towns such as Schiedam, Schoonhoven, and Heusden. In defiance of Bossu's summons, a majority of the Holland towns, being now Orangist, assembled as a rival States of Holland, on 19 July, in Dordrecht, instead of The Hague.[19]

This, the first gathering of the States of Holland under the aegis of the Revolt against Philip II, deserves attention as it marks a radical break with the past in several respects and exerted a not inconsiderable influence over the subsequent evolution of the Revolt and formation of the Republic.[20] Of the six 'large towns' normally represented, two—Amsterdam and Delft—refused to participate, remaining loyal to the king. On the other hand, a number of small towns—Alkmaar, Hoorn, Enkhuizen, Medemblik, Edam, Monnikendam, Oudewater, and Gorcum—having only exceptionally attended in the past were represented.[21] Rotterdam too sent delegates a few days after the rest, on the withdrawal of the Spanish troops. Particularly striking is the fact that nearly all the delegates sent to the rebel States, at Dordrecht, were either regents who were newcomers to the States or persons who were newcomers to the patriciates.[22]

William the Silent sent his secretary, Marnix, as his representative, furnished with instructions as to provisional arrangements to make with the States.[23] Both the Prince's proposals, and the terms eventually agreed, were a bizarre mix of conservatism and revolution. Prince and States were anxious to preserve as much of a veneer of legality, and constitutional propriety, as possible. In flagrant defiance of Philip's having appointed Bossu his successor as Stadholder, Orange proclaimed that he was still 'governor-general and Stadholder of the king in Holland, Zeeland, and Utrecht', since he had not been 'dismissed in the manner required by the customs and privileges of the country'.[24] The States of Holland accepted this, acknowledging him as Stadholder and captain-general of all three provinces. Furthermore, they recognized Orange 'in the absence of His Royal Majesty' as 'Protector' of the Netherlands as a whole, an astounding step negating totally the authority, and commission, of Alva.[25] The States further accepted Orange's authority to appoint lieutenant-governors, ackowledging Lumey in South Holland, and Sonoy in North Holland, as local military commanders.

[19] Bremmer, *Reformatie en rebellie*, 32.
[20] Kluit, *Historie der Hollandsche staatsregering*, i. 17–19, 27–30.
[21] Koopmans, *Staten van Holland*, 27.
[22] Ibid.
[23] Kossmann and Mellink, *Texts*, 98–100.
[24] Bakhuizen van den Brink, 'Eerste vergadering', 217–21.
[25] Lademacher, *Stellung des Prinzen von Oranien*, 42–3.

The Prince (who was then far away at Venlo) urged the States to abandon the 'cause of the Spaniards' and fight together with the rest of the 'Fatherland', meaning the whole of the Netherlands, to secure the historic 'rights and privileges' of the provinces. The States agreed, undertaking to shoulder a considerable part of the cost, allocating 600,000 guilders for payment of troops, to be paid over three months, with the expectation of raising much of this by selling off confiscated Church property.[26] In addition, the States took measures to exert pressure on Delft, Amsterdam, and Utrecht to come over to the Revolt. Orange made demands on the States; and he sought agreement for a wider Revolt. But he also entered into undertakings. He promised that, in future, he would not govern Holland without the consent of the States 'or at least the majority of them and without consulting the States . . . if and when they desire this'.[27] In addition, Prince and States solemnly agreed not to enter into negotiations with Philip, or any representative of the king, except conjointly and by mutual consent, nor to 'decide anything else concerning the whole province' other than jointly and by mutual consent.

The States proceeded as if adhering to legality. Yet, in all of this, the speciousness of the fiction that the king's authority, rights, and wishes were being respected was transparent. The States pretended that the authority and military responsibilities of the Stadholder derived from, and only from, the Crown. But they not only assembled in open defiance of the king's Stadholder, but acknowledged someone else in his place and proceeded to make major decisions concerning not only taxation, and payment of troops, but military matters, naval organization, church and foreign affairs, spheres which were primarily the business of the sovereign.[28] It was wholly unconvincing to seek to justify this by claiming, as the States of Holland had long claimed, that it was an established privilege of theirs to assemble on their own without a royal summons and to determine their own agenda.[29] Still other revolutionary aspects of the assembly of July 1572 were less immediately obvious. As a consequence of assuming executive and administrative functions they had never exercised before, the frequency and duration of the States' gatherings, from this point on, were much greater than in the past.[30] Although the change would not be fully evident until later, the States of Holland had transformed themselves from being an occasional, chiefly

[26] Muller, *Staat der Vereenigde Nederlanden*, 49.

[27] Kossmann and Mellink, *Texts*, 100.

[28] Berkelbach van der Sprenkel, *Oranje*, 110–12; Koenigsberger, 'Why did the States General of the Netherlands Become Revolutionary?', 106–7.

[29] Bakhuizen van den Brink, 'Eerste vergadering', 214–15.

[30] Koopmans, *Staten van Holland*, 180, 186–7, 284.

advisory body into an embryonic government endeavouring to organize and finance a war while maintaining order and justice and taking over the reins of administration.

As 1572 wore on the cause of the Revolt first prospered, then wilted. The first strategic enterprise of the rebel States of Holland was to blockade Delft. The town's loyalist regents prepared to resist, hired special troops, closed the taverns, and positioned artillery around the town hall. They were soon forced to yield though less to external than internal pressure.[31] Anti-Spanish, anti-Catholic, and anti-royalist sentiment was intense. As the town fell, all four burgomasters fled, leaving their homes and the churches and monasteries of Delft, to be pillaged behind them.[32] Initially, the rebellion gained ground in the north-east too, Van den Bergh consolidating his hold on Gelderland and Overijssel. The Revolt spread also to Friesland despite the success of the Stadholder, Gaspar de Robles, in repulsing several Beggar landings during August. His situation deteriorated when, attempting to extend his grip by introducing troops into more towns, he provoked a rising at Sneek, which closed its gates on his Walloons.[33] After Sneek, Bolsward opened its gates to a detachment sent by Van den Bergh, under an officer designated the 'Prince of Orange's governor' of Friesland, the Protestant Gelderland nobleman Diederik van Bronkhorst van Batenburg. Next Franeker, the second town of Friesland, rose, while the inhabitants of Dokkum, in a spontaneous display of fury, attacked Robles' troops in the open countryside. But in Friesland the Revolt had got ahead of itself. Dokkum was brutally sacked by Robles's troops and many of its citizens massacred. Reinforced from Groningen, Robles secured Leeuwarden and other key locations. There was also political disarray among the insurgents. For while Van den Bergh had designated Bronkhorst 'Stadholder' of Friesland, Orange had meanwhile appointed another noble to that office, the latter's arrival in Friesland, in September, causing considerable confusion.

In the north or at any rate Holland, Zeeland, and Friesland, there was plenty of spontaneous local opposition to the authority of Alva and the king. In the south Netherlands, however, with Alva closer by, this was not the case. Orange himself, though hampered by lack of money, and the distaste of the German Lutheran princes and clergy for his increasingly Calvinist connections,[34] appealed to the cities of Brabant and Flanders to

---

[31] Kernkamp, *Handel op den vijand*, i. 20–1.
[32] Van Dijk, 'Bedreigd Delft', 179–82; Boogman, 'De overgang', 108–10.
[33] Woltjer, *Friesland in hervormingstijd*, 221–2.
[34] Glawischnig, *Niederlande, Kalvinismus und Reichsgrafenstand*, 91.

declare their support, aiming to precipitate a general insurrection that would force Alva to give up the siege of Mons. However, there was little response and, on 19 September, just as the tide was turning in Friesland, Mons surrendered to Alva. One southern town which had opened its gates to Orange was Mechelen and Alva now marched, determined to punish its disloyalty severely. On his approach local Orangists fled and the town gates were thrown open.[35] But Alva nevertheless allowed his men to sack the city, perpetrating a massacre; he also abolished the city's privileges. The lesson instantly induced the other southern insurgent towns to submit, these— Leuven, Oudenaarde and Diest—escaping with heavy fines. Antwerp, Brussels, and the Flemish towns, meanwhile, had not stirred. Orange had no alternative to withdrawing ignominiously, to Gelderland, only to find that, there too, the terrifying news from Mechelen had sapped morale. In mid-October, with Alva advancing on Gelderland, the Prince began to despair. He knew the position in the north-east was untenable and did not believe Holland and Zeeland alone could long resist. In sombre mood he resolved to withdraw to Holland 'ayant deliberé de faire illecq ma sépulture'.[36]

Bolstered by the disintegration of the Revolt in Brabant, Alva aimed to precipitate an equally prompt submission of the north. A fresh massacre ensued, on 14 November, at Zutphen, where hundreds of the town's 7,500 or so population perished. Just as Alva had calculated, the city's fate soon persuaded the other rebel-held towns in Gelderland and Overijssel to capitulate.[37] The insurgents also lost heart in Friesland, Bolsward, Sneek, and Franeker all surrendering after the Zutphen massacre and accepting Walloon garrisons.

This left only Holland and Zeeland without Amsterdam and Middelburg. Despite the lateness of the season and his financial difficulties, Alva hastened to finish the business, not wishing to give the rebels the winter in which to consolidate. Again he sought to engineer a general collapse by means of a deliberate massacre.[38] Finding Naarden, which lay in his path, slow to submit, he authorized the killing of every man, woman, and child in the town. The slaughter at Naarden, on 2 December 1572, in which almost the entire population perished, only a handful escaping in the dark across the snow, had a sensational effect on the popular imagination in the Low Countries, becoming a byword for atrocity and cruelty. A few days later, the Spanish army took up position around Haarlem.

[35] Marnef, *Calvinistisch bewind te Mechelen*, 80–1.
[36] *Archives ou correspondance*, iv. 3–4.
[37] Maltby, *Alba*, 241–2.
[38] Ibid. 243–5.

10

The Revolt and the Emergence of a new State

❖

THE REVOLT SURVIVES, 1573–1575

The massacre at Naarden did not, however, produce the same result in Holland as those of Mechelen and Zutphen had in Brabant and the north-east. The question why goes to the heart of the Dutch Revolt. In Brabant and Flanders, where there had been no extensive spontaneous rising, morale had disintegrated and Orangist regents and militia officers fled on Alva's approach. In Holland, by contrast, the key towns, including Haarlem, which was now about to undergo a terrible siege, had not been conquered by Beggars or occupied by hired soldiery, but spontaneously risen against regime and Church.[1] Here Alva's approach had the opposite effect to that in Brabant and the north-east. Resistance stiffened despite the grim prospect. Opinion further polarized; but it was the loyalists who were overwhelmed, gagged, and marginalized. At Delft the militia pressed the Prince to take ever harsher measures against Catholic worship and property.[2] On the approach of Alva's army, the civic militia of Haarlem, aware that part of the *vroedschap* wanted to surrender, staged a coup together with the town's military governor, Wigbolt Ripperda. The Haarlem town pensionary, Adriaan van Assendelft, accused of plotting with Bossu, was sent to Delft and beheaded on the Prince's orders. It was at this point that the great church of Haarlem, the St Bavo's Church, was stripped of images and converted to Protestant worship.[3] Under pressure from the militia, the town council was purged, a substantial number of new men, as well as existing regents of known Protestant and Orangist sympathies, being chosen.[4]

The decisive factor was that in Holland, Zeeland, and Friesland, the Revolt of 1572 had now been in progress for many months and incipient

[1] Verwer, *Memoriaelbouck*, 4, 195; Overmeer, *Hervorming te Haarlem*, 54–5.
[2] Van Dijk, 'Bedreigd Delft', 185.
[3] Overmeer, *Hervorming te Haarlem*, 54–5.
[4] Spaans, *Haarlem na de Reformatie*, 44.

Protestantization and the institutional formalization of the rebellion against the Spanish Crown had placed the local rebel leadership in a quite different position from their counterparts in the southern and eastern provinces. Returning exiles and Sea-Beggars had already drastically changed the civic political and religious framework in the Holland and Zeeland towns, whereas in the south and east there had been neither enough prominent returning exiles nor enough time, for Protestantism and institutionalization of the Revolt to widen the rift between rebels and Crown.[5] Consequently, by the autumn of 1572, if prompt surrender made sense for towns in the south and east, it made no sense in Holland and Zeeland, where the involvement of leading citizens and returning exiles in the purging of civic government, revolutionary initiatives of the States, pillaging and closing of the Catholic churches, and re-emergence of Protestant worship meant that they could hope to survive only by holding out militarily.

The fact that in the north-west the Revolt had gone further and deeper, and had much more time, from July to December, to consolidate than in the south and east generated a revolutionary fervour and tenacity, a determination to fight to the end, which simply did not exist in other parts of the country. Haarlem's defences were far from formidable. But with such tenacity did the garrison and militia resist, constructing new fortifications inside the old, and harassing the Spanish troops in their trenches, that the besiegers were caught in the bitter cold of winter for many months, suffering heavy losses, as well as incurring huge expense. After a long and terrible siege Haarlem was forced to capitulate. But this did not happen until July 1573, more than a year after the town had gone over to the Revolt, and by the time it fell Haarlem had wrought so much damage on Spain's forces and prestige, and given the rest of the rebel towns so long a respite in which to organize their defence, the entire picture was transformed. If the fall of Haarlem nevertheless gravely weakened the strategic position of the rebels by cutting rebel-held Holland into two parts, Alva's son, Don Fadrique de Toledo, in command of the forces in Holland, diluted the impact of this by turning northwards to try to capture Alkmaar: for the resistance of the rest of North Holland, and the small towns there, was a secondary issue. The fate of the Revolt hung on the outcome in South Holland.

The climax of the struggle for the north-west came during the next eighteen months with the great sieges of Middelburg and Leiden. The insurgents on Walcheren had tightly blockaded the former from the outset. But the city was strongly garrisoned and held out grimly for twenty months.

---

[5] Wijn, *Beleg van Haarlem*, 16–18; Marnef, Calvinistisch bewind te Mechelen, 79–82.

Finally, despite strenuous efforts to relieve the city, several massive river convoys, sent from Antwerp and Bergen-op-Zoom, being repulsed by the Zeelanders' warships, the starving Spanish garrison were forced to surrender in February 1574. At Leiden, it was the turn of the rebels to starve. The siege of Leiden, if not quite the longest—that of Middelburg was longer—was the costliest, hardest fought, and most decisive, as well as the most epic of the great sieges of the Revolt. There were relatively few professional troops in the town. The backbone of the defence were the citizens' militia (*schutters*).[6] The Spanish besiegers came close to succeeding and, had Leiden fallen, The Hague and Delft would have been untenable and the Revolt as a whole might well have collapsed.[7] The first phase of the siege during which the Spaniards occupied much of the countryside of South Holland ended, in March 1574, when the Spanish troops pulled back, to face the army, raised by William's brothers in Germany, seeking to ease the pressure on Holland from the east. The rebel force was crushed at Mook and Count Louis killed. In May the siege resumed. By this stage, Orange had created a rudimentary military administration in Holland and increased his troop strength to perhaps 15,000 men. But in numbers the Dutch army was still less than half the size of the king's and was qualitatively far inferior.[8]

By August 1574 Leiden's supplies had run out and her defenders were in a pitiable state. With the entire Revolt in the balance, Orange staked everything on trying to save the seemingly doomed town. He promised the starving citizenry, by pigeon, that if they could hold on just a little longer he would save them. Boats, supplies, and thousands of seamen were brought up, under Admiral Boisot's command, from Zeeland. Despite opposition in the States of Holland, the dikeᴜ along the Maas were cut so as to inundate the area further north. But the water failed to rise sufficiently to force the Spaniards back, or convey the relief fleet further than midway between Delft and the dying city. Their approach blocked, but within earshot, the relief fleet thundered their guns, to bolster the morale of the besieged; but for weeks could advance no nearer. For the third time in the saga of his struggle against Spain, the Prince, by late September, had given way to despair, convinced that all was lost. Finally, the wind changed and heavy rain fell or, as Protestant contemporaries put it, the Almighty intervened. For days rain fell, the waters rose. The Spaniards were forced to pull back and Boisot was through. So weakened were the defenders that scarcely anyone in the town could stand.

[6] Bremmer, 'Beleg en ontzet van Leiden', 172–3.
[7] Woltjer, *Kleine oorzaken*, 11.
[8] Swart, *Willem van Oranje*, 69.

The relief of Leiden was a crucial event. The Spanish soldiery subsequently evacuated all South Holland, withdrawing on Utrecht and Haarlem.[9] The Revolt was now fairly secure in South Holland and Zeeland and in North Holland, beyond Amsterdam and Haarlem. Since the fierce battle on the Zuider Zee, of 11 October 1573, in which the royalist Amsterdammers and Spaniards had been beaten, and Bossu captured, the rebels also enjoyed naval superiority throughout the war zone from the Scheldt estuary to Friesland. Royalist Amsterdam and Haarlem suffered severely during the mid-1570s, being cut off from their normal markets.

While Amsterdam, Haarlem, and Utrecht remained in loyalist hands the war in the north-west had something of the character of a civil war. But support for king and Church was so limited that it was a civil war only in a marginal sense. If there was any Catholic militancy to be stirred up against the image-breakers who had shut down the Catholic churches of Holland, it was scarcely noticeable. The royalist, and pro-Catholic, element was strongly represented only among the regents and was essentially political in character. Royalist, Catholic regents were relatively numerous but unrepresentative of feeling in their towns, and amongst the civic militias, and by 1573 most had fled, or been removed.[10] This does not mean, of course, that most regents who remained, and continued in civic government, were solidly committed to Orange and the Revolt. On the contrary, while most regents had preferred to stay put rather than flee, those who acquiesced, as was seen during the sieges of Haarlem and Leiden, showed little appetite for fighting to the last and had to be coerced by civic militia, committed Protestant regents, and Orangist newcomers to civic government.[11] The story was the same during the siege of Zierikzee in 1575. It was the seamen, fishermen, and the middling sort who formed the backbone of the Revolt. Only a minority of the town council showed any firm resolve.[12] The rest had had to be coerced into holding out.

Alva's Netherlandish subordinates and allies were much less uncompromising than he.[13] In this situation there was scope, or so it seemed, for negotiation and compromise. Nor was there any lack of would-be intermediaries and peacemakers. As early as the siege of Haarlem, during the spring of 1573, various German Protestant princes approached Orange's younger brothers with proposals for negotiations and settlement. As a consequence,

[9] Geyl, *Revolt of the Netherlands*, 138.
[10] Van Gelder, *Revolutionnaire Reformatie*, 26–33; Hibben, *Gouda in Revolt*, 46–53; Spaans, *Haarlem na de Reformatie*, 41.
[11] Ibid. 137; Wijn, *Beleg van Haarlem*, 11, 72, 19.
[12] Pot, *Beleg van Zierikzee*, 15–16.
[13] Waterbolk, *Rond Viglius van Aytta*, 53–4.

the Prince found himself under some pressure, as time passed, to define more precisely the aims of the Revolt which he led. Orange and his adherents (however hypocritically) claimed to be loyal subjects of the king of Spain, so there was no obstacle in principle to negotiation. It is true that the changes in the government of Holland and Zeeland, introduced in July 1572, were revolutionary in their implications. But they could also be treated as emergency measures of a temporary nature that might be superseded by a negotiated return to an agreed status quo ante. It is worth noting that William the Silent in commenting on his aims during the course of 1573 did not assert that he was striving to set up a separate state, or claim to be fighting for the Protestant faith.[14] He claimed to be seeking the 'liberté du pays tant au fait de la conscience comme de la police', that is for liberty of conscience and civic autonomy in matters of justice and law and order.[15] In order to secure and safeguard these objectives the rebels would need to extract two main concessions from the king in any forthcoming negotiations: first, Philip must withdraw all Spanish and other foreign troops from the Netherlands; secondly the king must formally concede toleration of the public practice of the Reformed and Lutheran faiths.

Philip, contemplating his deteriorating financial situation, strategic difficulties, and the risks to Spain's overall position, and repeatedly urged to compromise by the Emperor, authorized his new governor-general of the Netherlands, Don Luis de Requesens, who took over from Alva, in November 1573, to explore the possibility of ending the Revolt by negotiation.[16] Talks commenced following the relief of Leiden which, for the Spaniards, ended any hope of speedy suppression of the Revolt. In December 1574, a leading academic and humanist, Elbertus Leoninus, a Leuven law professor from Gelderland, friend of Viglius and confidant of many of the Netherlands nobility, was sent to confer with Orange and the States of Holland. Leoninus was a typical representative of the Erasmian and *politique* humanist tradition. Being himself willing to live outwardly as a Catholic, he tried to persuade the rebel leadership that the king of Spain would never permit formal freedom of Protestant worship in his lands and that to insist on this was to condemn the Netherlands to endless strife and disruption. Here then, fully evident in 1575, as it had been in 1565, was the stumbling-block precluding a negotiated solution to the Dutch Revolt. If Orange had been a less skilful, and tenacious, leader, the Revolt might well

[14] *Archives ou correspondance*, iv. 50, 237: Orange to Louis and Jan van Nassau, Delft, 5 Feb. and 13 Nov. 1573.
[15] Ibid.
[16] De Vrankrijker, *Motiveering*, 99–103; Parker, *Dutch Revolt*, 166–7.

have been overwhelmed militarily. But the ideological framework prevailing in the Holland and Zeeland towns, from the very outset, in 1572, based on rejection of Catholicism and insistence on Protestant worship—with Catholic support too weak to mount any real political challenge—meant that no negotiated settlement, even if Orange had been more pliant, was possible.[17]

Requesens nevertheless went ahead with formal talks which were held at Breda in the spring of 1575. The rebel position was jointly formulated by Orange and the States.[18] They had no wish, they declared, to 'separate' themselves from His Majesty, or be anything other than his loyal subjects. But the king, as well as allowing Protestantism, would in future have to rule in the Netherlands in conformity with his oath to uphold the provinces' 'rights and privileges'. The rebels insisted on limited monarchy, with the States General and provincial assemblies sharing in government.[19] This went well beyond what Philip was willing to concede on the political as well as the religious front. Thus the Breda negotiations of 1575 revealed for all to see the fundamental irreconcilability of king and rebels on both essential points—religion and form of government.[20] Effectively, prospects for compromise were so remote as to be negligible.

FROM THE PACIFICATION OF GHENT (1576) TO THE UNION OF UTRECHT (1579)

The combined burden of paying for the war against the rebels in the Netherlands and that against the Ottomans in the Mediterranean had, by the autumn of 1575, stretched Philip II's finances to the point that he could no longer service his mounting debt to his Genoese bankers. He was compelled to suspend interest payments on the royal debt. With this, the entire financial machinery of the Spanish monarchy was thrown into chaos. Requesens, who enjoyed good relations with the bankers of Antwerp, managed nevertheless to go on borrowing, on the strength of future remittances from Spain, partly using his own credit, over the winter of 1575–6. But lack of fresh remittances from Spain, over that winter, and Requesens's death, in March 1576, completely paralysed the royal finances in the Low Countries. The result from the Spanish, Catholic, and loyalist point of view was catastrophic.

The army did not disintegrate immediately. Unpaid and unsupplied, the Spanish soldiery continued the siege of Zierikzee until the town surrendered

---

[17] Bremmer, *Reformatie en rebellie*, 101–2.
[18] Fruin, *Verspreide geschriften*, ii. 377–9.
[19] Geurts, *Nederlandse Opstand in de pamfletten*, 207–9.
[20] Van Gelder, *Van Beeldenstorm tot Pacificatie*, 217–19; Parker, *Dutch Revolt*, 166–7.

on 2 July 1576. But only hours later, the starving veterans mutinied and abandoned the town they had fought so hard to capture. The mutiny rapidly spread. Three weeks after the fall of Zierikzee, mutineers sacked Aalst only a few miles from Brussels. The royal Council of State saw no alternative but to give permission to the States of Brabant to raise their own troops with which to protect Brussels, and neighbouring towns, from the marauding horde of Spanish soldiers. In the power vacuum which developed, following the death of Requesens, the States of Brabant attempted to assume control through the States General which convened, without having been summoned by the ruler (for the first time since 1477), in September 1576.[21] Holland and Zeeland did not participate in this States General, the main aim of which was to end the war with the rebels.[22] On 30 October, the States General's commissioners finalized an armistice with the States of Holland and Zeeland, the two sides agreeing to co-operate to drive the mutinous Spanish contingents out of the country and confer on the subject of religion.

At the beginning of November, the main body of mutineers attacked Antwerp, overwhelming the troops of the States of Brabant trying to protect it. For several days Europe's greatest commercial and financial centre was subjected to slaughter, pillage, and rape. Although probably only a few hundred people were actually murdered,[23] Orange and his propagandists exploited to the full the shock and revulsion the terrifying news from Antwerp spread throughout the Netherlands and beyond. According to some reports as many as 18,000 citizens of Antwerp were slaughtered. The 'Spanish Fury' at Antwerp had important political and religious consequences. It served to give further currency to the 'Black Legend' of Spanish cruelty, further blackened the name of the Spanish regime and soldiery, and reinforced the rebel claim that there was no way out of the impasse in the Low Countries except by armed revolt. The 'Spanish Fury' also gave added urgency to the negotiations over religion between the 'Protestant' provinces, Holland and Zeeland, and Brabant and the rest which were still nominally Catholic.[24] A few days after the 'Spanish Fury', the two sides' commissioners signed the major agreement known as the 'Pacification of Ghent'. There were now two power centres in the Netherlands—Brabant and Holland— neither of which was for the moment under Spanish control and both of which claimed to recognize the sovereignty of the Spanish king. Under the terms of the agreement, the southern provinces, and also Utrecht, agreed to

[21] Kossmann and Mellink, *Texts*, 128.
[22] Van Gelder, *Revolutionnaire Reformatie*, 34–5.
[23] Voet, *Antwerp*, 202–3.
[24] De Vrankrijker, *Motiveering*, 106.

join with the Prince of Orange and the States of Holland and Zeeland in driving out the Spaniards and setting up a provisional government under a single States General, which would continue to meet at Brussels.[25] Whilst the States General sought a final settlement of the religious question, an interim arrangement was to apply whereby the public practice of Protestant-ism would be allowed only in Holland and Zeeland, the rest officially remaining exclusively Catholic.[26] Outside Holland and Zeeland neither nobles nor regents had any wish to land themselves in an endless war with Spain by introducing Protestant worship on a formal basis, in open defiance of the king. All royal edicts concerned with the suppression of heresy were suspended so that private Protestant practice, and possession of Protestant books, were now everywhere allowed. Only Namur, Luxemburg, and part of Limburg rejected the agreement, staying loyal to Spain.

The States General also agreed to recognize the Prince of Orange as Stadholder of those parts of Holland and Zeeland currently under his leadership; but suspended his authority in Utrecht and those parts of Holland where his authority was, at that point, not recognized (that is Haarlem and Amsterdam) until the States negotiated religious settlements satisfactory to the town councils concerned.[27] The provinces also agreed to align their currencies in the interests of monetary stability, demolish the public monuments and inscriptions put up by Alva, and share, on an agreed quota basis, the cost of defending the Netherlands as a whole. In Holland, as at other decisive moments in the early stages of the Revolt, the town councils, to ensure that they had the public support they needed, consulted their civic militias on the terms of the Pacification before ratifying the agreement.[28]

The southern provinces and States General were now, in effect, in revolt alongside Holland and Zeeland, against the Spanish Crown. But there was nevertheless still an immense gap between the two movements of revolt.[29] The one had burnt its bridges with Philip; the other, centring partly on Brabant but also partly on Flanders, remained officially Catholic, for the moment, and kept open the door to swift reconciliation. The States General in Brussels were willing to recognize Philip II's new governor-general, Don Juan of Austria, provided he sent away the Spanish troops, swore to uphold the Pacification of Ghent, and agreed to govern together with the States

[25] Blockmans and Van Peteghem, 'Pacificatie', 323–4.
[26] Baelde, 'Pacificatie van Gent', 379–80.
[27] Ibid. 80.
[28] Woltjer, 'Dutch Privileges', 28–9.
[29] Blockmans and Van Peteghem, 'Pacificatie', 327, 329.

General. Lacking the money and troops to do otherwise, Don Juan acquiesced, signing the so-called Eternal Edict with the States General, in February 1577. But Holland and Zeeland, encouraged by Orange, wanted no part of this agreement, since it provided no guarantees for the Reformed Church and would have stripped Holland and Zeeland of all control over the military.[30] At the same time there were increasing tensions within the southern provinces between rival blocs and social groupings. Orange, who was still in Holland but had adherents and representatives in Brussels, sought to radicalize the Revolt in the south by allying with the main block of burgher opinion, including the guilds and militias, against the nobility and patriciates, who mostly opposed Orange's leadership, and policies, and had adopted a firmly Catholic stance.[31] The Spanish troops departed in April.

A three-cornered contest now ensued between Don Juan seeking to rebuild royal authority, and minimize that of the States General, the States General, dominated by nobles and patricians anxious to settle with the king and uphold the Catholic Church—provided Philip would make some political concessions and keep the Spanish soldiery out—and Orange, Holland, and the southern radicals, intent on going further.[32] Tripartite negotiations were arranged, at Geertruidenberg, but soon collapsed as it became apparent that Holland and Zeeland would neither end the public practice of the Reformed faith on their territory, nor surrender the new powers of their States, nor even recognize Don Juan as governor-general. With his hand becoming steadily weaker, and frustrated by the growing split between moderates and radicals in the south, Don Juan broke with the States General in July, fled Brussels, and set up his new headquarters at Namur, recalling the Spanish soldiery soon afterwards. The rupture between Don Juan and the States General instantly narrowed the gap between the States General and States of Holland and Zeeland.[33] The southern provinces (other than Namur and Luxemburg) now had no alternative to fighting hand in hand with the Protestants against the king. In September William the Silent, for the moment at one with the States General, entered Brussels in triumph.

From September 1577 until the summer of 1583, William the Silent resided in Brabant, first in Brussels and then Antwerp, trying to place the Revolt in the south on a viable basis in collaboration with Holland. The

---

[30] Koopmans, *Staten van Holland*, 124.
[31] Swart, *Willem van Oranje*, 122–4.
[32] Geurts, *Nederlandse Opstand in de pamfletten*, 63–4.
[33] Parker, *Dutch Revolt*, 180–3.

Prince strove to combat the particularism of the provinces and promote cohesion within the Revolt.[34] And yet it cannot be said that he took any effective steps to draw Holland and Zeeland into the new framework he was endeavouring to set up in the south. On the contrary, William in effect simply accepted the fundamental duality of power and structures within the Netherlands, from the moment he arrived in Brussels, rejecting out of hand the States General's proposal that the public practice of Catholicism should now again be tolerated in Holland and Zeeland.[35] William the Silent, with his possessions and family traditions in many parts of the Netherlands, but especially in Brabant, had a strong interest in counteracting the separateness of north and south. But, in terms of power structures, he never even began to tackle it; and indeed had no means of doing so. In this sense the Revolt was based on an underlying dichotomy which remained unchanged and an inherent contradiction which was bound to lead to a parting of ways. When William later strenuously opposed the suppression of Catholic worship by the Ghent Calvinists, it was with considerable justification that they accused him of pursuing one statecraft north of the rivers and a totally different one to the south. William deplored the growing tendency, from 1577 onwards, for Holland and Zeeland to go their own way in fiscal and military matters and show scant respect for the States General in Antwerp. But there was nothing he could do to change matters.[36]

Thus, whilst they now stood closer, and fought together, there were still two incompatible revolutions in progress in the Netherlands battling for the upper hand. Indeed, at grass-roots level, the rift between the two blocs was becoming wider rather than narrower, despite Orange's tireless efforts to preserve some semblance of unity.[37] It was a struggle of faiths more in a political than religious sense: at bottom it was a struggle for local supremacy between warring élites, embittered by the fact that the nobles at the helm of the new anti-Habsburg revolution, emanating from Brussels, had previously mostly fought for the royal regime against the rebels since 1566–8, and in several cases were implacable foes of the House of Orange. The ablest soldier amongst the Netherlands nobles who backed the authority of the States General in Brussels, for the time being, was Gilles de Berlaymont, baron de Hierges, who had been the king's Stadholder of Holland, Zeeland, and Utrecht, in succession to Bossu, since 1574 (see Table 9) and latterly also Gelderland and Overijssel. Hierges was now technically in revolt

[34] *Apologie, ofte Verantwoordinghe*, 48–52.
[35] Decavele, 'Willem van Oranje', 79.
[36] Malengreau, *L'Esprit particulariste*, 138, 143, 146.
[37] Woltjer, 'De Vrede-makers', 312.

against the king alongside Orange. But besides having helped reduce Valenciennes in 1567, played a prominent part, under Alva, in crushing the rebel army at Jemmingen, in 1568, distinguished himself on the royalist side at the siege of Haarlem and in the battle of Mook (in which William the Silent's brothers had perished), he had been responsible for the sack of Oudewater perpetrated in the king's name in June 1575. He was also one of those most keen to restore royal authority by reaching agreement with Don Juan.

Hierges was again in the thick of things where these two irreconcilable revolutions clashed head on in 1577—the province of Utrecht. The States General in Brussels had decreed that Utrecht was not part of the stadhold-erate of William of Orange, recognizing Hierges's authority there. Hierges put himself at the head of the citizenry and German troops in the city and besieged the remaining Spaniards in the great fortress of the Vredenburg, which surrendered in February 1577. But as soon as the Spaniards were removed, Hierges's authority was rapidly impaired as an open rift developed between those few Utrecht regents, led by Floris Thin, and those nobles, who supported Orange and wanted the formal practice of Protestanism permitted, and the conservatives, backed by all the clergy, who continued to recognize Hierges as Stadholder.[38] Moreover, if most regents backed Hierges, the city's guilds and the urban populace were for Orange.[39] To complicate matters further, there was also substantial support for a third contender for the stadholderate—Bossu. Finally, the Orangists gained the upper hand and Hierges defected to Don Juan. On 9 October 1577, the States of Utrecht recognized Orange as Stadholder (albeit against the wishes of Amersfoort) and accepted terms of religious compromise, nominally leaving the Catholic Church supreme, similar to those just agreed for Haarlem and also, in the spring of 1577, for the Zeeland towns of Goes and Tholen, which had been in Spanish hands since 1572.[40] The Vredenburg fortress in Utrecht was demolished.

The struggle between the Revolt Holland style and the Revolt Brabant style, meanwhile, had spread to the northernmost provinces, since the autumn of 1576, when mutinous Walloon troops had seized Caspar de Robles, at Groningen, and a tussle began between pro- and anti-Orange factions for control of Groningen and Friesland. What remained clear in this dauntingly complex situation was that the only way a basically Catholic Revolt rooted in allegiance to the House of Habsburg could be consolidated

---

[38] Woltjer, 'Wisselende gestalten', 90.
[39] Muller, *Staat der Vereenigde Nederlanden*, 163.
[40] Den Tex, 'Staten in Oldenbarnevelt's tijd', 52.

was by enhancing the authority of the States General in Brussels and curtailing the influence of Orange and the States of Holland. The anti-Orange faction in the States General, led by Philippe de Croy, duke of Aerschot (1526–95) (a long-standing rival of the Prince), Philip of Egmond, son of the executed count, and Bossu,[41] scored a major success in October 1577 when they brought to the Netherlands and installed as 'governor-general' (amid much pomp and the issuing of propaganda medals by the States General) a Habsburg prince, the Austrian Archduke Matthias (1557–1619). Matthias, young, inexperienced, and weak, was, from the first, little more than a figurehead. He swore to abide faithfully by the Pacification of Ghent, acquiesce in the restricted powers assigned to him, and govern only in conjunction with the States General.[42] One of the first moves of Matthias and the Brussels States General, in their efforts to extend their authority over the north, was to appoint a conservative Catholic nobleman, Georges de Lalaing, count of Rennenberg, as Stadholder of Friesland, Groningen, Drenthe, Overijssel (and Lingen) in the name of Philip II. Rennenberg stood for the status quo, had instructions from the States General, in Antwerp, to allow the public practice only of the Catholic religion,[43] and sought to prevent the radicals purging Hof of Friesland jurists, royalist regents, and other previous supporters of the Spanish regime from positions of power and influence. In Friesland, pressure for removing conservatives and royalists, not least from the rural magistracies, the *grietenijen*, came mainly from the nobles of the Oostergo and Westergo quarters and from the citizenry in the towns. 'Since the Spaniards in the last years have dismissed many persons from their offices', the Frisian gentry were determined that Rennenberg should restore 'each to his office' and remove the *grietmannen* put in by the Spaniards.[44] Prominent amongst gentry pressing for change in Friesland were those who belonged to families which had formerly been *Vetkopers* and had a tradition of hostility to Burgundian and Habsburg centralizing policies.[45]

Reluctantly, Rennenberg was forced to comply. First the town council of Leeuwarden and then, in February 1578, those of Franeker, Sneek, Bolsward, and Harlingen, were purged of royalists. Also in February, Rennenberg arrested the bishop of Leeuwarden, imprisoning him at Harlingen, though he was later allowed to retire to Cologne.[46] In March, the

[41] Decavele, 'Willem van Oranje', 72.
[42] Swart, 'Willem de Zwijger', 72.
[43] Ros, *Rennenberg*, 72.
[44] ARH PR 362, pp. 215–16. Proposals of Frisian rural deputies, 13 Nov. 1577.
[45] Faber, *Drie eeuwen Friesland*, i. 338–9.
[46] Sjoerds, *Algemene Beschrijvinge*, ii, part 1, 707.

Hof was purged of royalists. Finally, most of the *grietmannen* were changed according to the wishes of the States.[47] But no more than in Holland, Utrecht, or Brabant could the tussle of élites for control in Friesland be separated from the struggle of faiths. For practically the only committed defenders of the Catholic Church were those who, as magistrates, burgo-masters, or jurists, were strong advocates of royal authority. Remove the office-holders whom Alva had installed and the collapse of the Catholic Church in Friesland followed automatically. During the summer of 1578 there was a resurgence of open Protestant activity in Friesland and during the autumn a new *beeldenstorm* commenced with the stripping of the churches of Leeuwarden.

Nowhere was the contest between the two revolts, conservative and radical, and, from July 1577, the triangular contest also with Don Juan, more intense than in Gelderland. The struggle began, following the defec-tion of Hierges with the contest to elect a new Stadholder. The States of Gelderland, at their meetings of November 1577 and January 1578, con-sidered several candidates. The loyalists (headed by the Hof) wanted Hierges's friend Bossu; anti-Holland moderates pressed for the resolutely Catholic and anti-Orange Philip of Egmond; the radicals demanded Orange. Once again, office-holders and regents installed by Alva, especially the regents of Nijmegen and Zutphen, were the main proponents of a Catholic candidate.[48] But so weak was the position of the Gelderland Catholics the only way they could block Orange was to back an alternative who they assumed was a Lutheran—Orange's younger brother, Count Johann von Nassau. In Nijmegen, the militia and citizenry forced the regents to agree to Nassau's appointment. The States of Gelderland finalized their choice of Nassau in March 1578.[49]

Both conservatives and moderates were soon shocked to find that their new Stadholder had recently discarded his Lutheranism and become a Calvinist. While willing to swear oaths of allegiance to the States General and States of Gelderland, he refused to swear allegiance to the king of Spain. Furthermore, despite the protests of the Gelderland regents, Leoni-nus and Matthias himself, he took every opportunity to promote the cause of the Reformed in Gelderland.[50] The civic patriciates endeavoured to defend the Catholic Church, but lacked popular support. The Gelderland patriciates, having closely collaborated with Alva, were deeply unpopular

---

[47] Sickenga, *Hof van Friesland*, 3, 7.
[48] Lenting, 'Benoeming van Graaf Johan van Nassau', 86–9.
[49] Kolman, *Reductie van Nijmegen*, 23.
[50] *Archives ou correspondance*, vi. 450, 502–4.

and, in all the towns, there was a growing agitation against them. There were, it is true, relatively few committed Calvinists; but there were fewer still committed Catholics. In each of the main towns first the so-called *bons patriotes* would insist that a church should be handed over for Protestant worship. Street disturbances would then compel the regents, however reluctantly, to agree. Next there would be demands for the closing of the Catholic churches and the handing over of the chief church for Protestant worship. Finally, image-breaking violence would erupt, as at Nijmegen in February 1579, the 'patriots' storming the churches and destroying the images and paintings.[51] Practically nowhere were there Catholic counter-demonstrations. In some cases Protestant soldiery played a leading part, encouraged by the Stadholder; in others it was just the townsmen who were involved. By January 1579, the town councils had been purged and Protestantized, and Catholic worship effectively suppressed in Harderwijk, Elburg, and other small towns, as well as Arnhem and Nijmegen. Last to go was Zutphen, where the town council was a pillar of conservatism and Catholicism. The arrival of a garrison of Protestant troops from Holland, in April 1579, precipitated a local insurrection against the regents, who fled, leaving the churches to be sacked behind them.

During 1578, the Dutch Revolt Holland style gained the upper hand throughout the north. The States General at Brussels tried to intervene to stem the tide in Friesland, Gelderland, and elsewhere, but without success. Everywhere the Catholic Church was collapsing, including in Utrecht, the only seat of an archbishopric in the north and the Dutch city with the largest number of Catholic clergy. Once the States of Utrecht accepted Orange as Stadholder it was a foregone conclusion that the 'Religious Peace', with formal toleration of Protestant worship, would be imposed on the city. As far as Orange was concerned this sufficed. But it failed to satisfy the burghers of Utrecht, who seethed with resentment against the regents and clergy. On 10 June 1578 there was a popular rising in the city in which the mob pillaged and sacked the churches.[52] Soon after the city council was purged.

The town government of Amsterdam, the last bulwark of conservatism in Holland, was also overwhelmed during 1578. First, in February, a treaty of 'satisfaction' was drawn up with the States of Holland whereby formal Protestant worship was allowed but the Catholic Church retained a nominal supremacy. But this stood no more chance of being respected by the populace than the previous treaties of 'satisfaction' at Haarlem and Utrecht.

---

[51] Van Veen, 'De overgang', 172–6.   [52] Brandt, *Historie der Reformatie*, i. 621.

Next began the popular demonstrations against the Catholic clergy and churches. Then, recently returned prominent citizens were restored to positions of command in the city militia—which now opposed the regents and Catholic Church. Finally, there ensued the '*alteratie*', the coup which removed the old Amsterdam regent class, deporting thirty of them from the city[53] and replacing them mainly with prominent returned exiles who were Protestants.[54] The militia was reorganized and purged of committed Catholics. The remaining Catholic churches in the city were closed. From the autumn of 1578 onwards, Amsterdam was a Protestant city controlled by a new body of regents, modest merchants who had been residing in Germany during the Alva years. Their descendants were to continue to govern Amsterdam through the seventeenth and eighteenth centuries (see p. 159 above).[55] Most of the expelled Catholic regents settled in Haarlem or Leiden; a few migrated to Germany.[56]

As the danger of an irreparable rift between Holland and the Revolt in the south increased, Orange, seriously alarmed, endeavoured to prevent the further crumbling of the conservative and Catholic position. In the north, those who hoped to rescue the Catholic Church were in an increasingly weak position and their crushing defeat could only enhance Orange's hand. To begin with, Orange may well have imagined that the spread of militant Protestantism in the south would meet with the same sweeping success, and that he had only to sit back and watch the conservative Revolt of the southern nobles and patricians collapse before his eyes. But conditions in the south were fundamentally different from in the north, where there were very few examples of Catholic crowds taking the streets resolved to fight Protestantism. Moreover, in the south unlike the north, the nobility were mostly loyal (albeit for political reasons) to the old Church so that the Catholic patricians and clergy were in a generally stronger position. In October 1577, Calvinist citizenry took over the city of Ghent. But, for the time being, in most of Flanders and especially in Brabant and the Walloon areas adhering to the Brussels States General, a predominantly conservative and Catholic regime, dominated by nobles and backed by old patrician families, supporting Matthias and the States General, and distrustful of Orange and his popular supporters,[57] remained in control. Orange, who now resided, alongside Matthias and the States General, as *ruwaard*, or

[53] Dudok van Heel, 'Waar waren de Amsterdamse katholieken?', 13–19.
[54] Ibid.; Pontanus, *Historische Beschijvinghe*, 340.
[55] Elias, *Vroedschap van Amsterdam*, i, pp. l, xlii.
[56] Dudok van Heel, 'Waar waren de Amsterdamse katholieken?', 15–19.
[57] Lademacher, *Stellung des Prinzen von Oranien*, 97–102; Van Gelderen, *Political Thought*, 48.

Stadholder, of Brabant, did indeed exert a growing influence over the conduct of the regime, and not least the archduke, but only by promising that it was not his intention to undermine the Catholic patriciates in the southern towns or the position of the old Church.[58]

After the crushing defeat of the States' army by Don Juan at Gembloux, in January 1578, Brussels became unsafe and Matthias, Orange, and the States General removed to Antwerp, which now became the headquarters of the southern or Brabant Revolt. The growing revival of Spanish power in the southern part of the south Netherlands, already evident from late 1577, precipitated a process of political and social polarization throughout the south which further widened the growing gap between the two parts of the Netherlands.[59] The great nobles of the south, jealous of Orange and painfully aware of Spain's reviving power, saw no sense in a Revolt which risked not only their lands but their very necks and would make any kind of settlement with Philip impossible. At best they were willing to fight on provisionally, as Catholics, to extract political concessions from Philip.[60] But they would not persist if the States were to suffer reverses. In February 1578, the Spaniards captured Leuven, only fifteen miles from Brussels. Spanish and loyalist retribution was literally at their door. Added to this, the coup at Ghent had been engineered by artisans, guildsmen traditionally at odds with the southern patriciates, raising the spectre of combined social and confessional strife in the southern towns, a prospect regarded with horror by patricians, nobles, and clergy.

The revival of Spanish power, and its encroachment into southern Brabant, simultaneously strengthened the aversion of the ruling élites in the south for a Holland-style Protestant revolution and the militancy of southern Calvinists.[61] In February 1578, as the Spaniards advanced from the south, the Calvinists of Ghent marched on Oudenaarde, expelled its Catholic magistrates, and replaced them with a Calvinist 'Committee of Eighteen' on the model of the committee of guildsmen which now ruled Ghent. In March, Calvinist burghers took over Kortrijk, Arras, Ieper, and Bruges. In all these places, the churches and cloisters were attacked and thoroughly stripped of images. Before long the Catholic clergy were expelled. With the proclamation of Orange's 'Religious Peace', of August 1578, the Calvinists (and also Lutherans and Anabaptists) began to make rapid gains in Antwerp.[62]

[58] Berkelbach van der Sprenkel, *Oranje*, 171–5.
[59] Parker, *Dutch Revolt*, 186–9.
[60] De Schepper, *Belgium Nostrum*, 34.
[61] Decavele, 'Willem van Oranje', 72–5; Decavele, 'Brugse en Gentse mendicanten', 78, 92.
[62] Marnef, 'Brabants Calvinisme', 10.

In the south Netherlands the Revolt was thus deeply, even hopelessly, divided between its moderate (Catholic) and radical (Protestant) wings. As both Spaniards and Calvinists gained ground, southern nobles and patricians began to insist on their Catholicism. In the summer of 1578 the States of Hainault and Walloon Flanders, reacting against Orange's policy of 'Religious Peace', declared that they would on no account tolerate the public practice of Protestantism.[63] But if Orange was to succeed, as he hoped, in salvaging a combined north–south Netherlands Revolt against Spain, with its political centre in Brabant, he had to accommodate both Protestantism and Catholicism on a stable basis and achieve a *modus vivendi* between the churches.

Consequently, he saw no alternative but to persevere with his policy of 'Religious Peace', allowing freedom of practice to both Catholicism and Protestantism. Orange's 'Religious Peace' was proclaimed in Brussels in September 1578, and in Mechelen in October. He imposed the same policy on Breda, keeping the town's main church in Catholic hands until as late as June 1581.[64] But the success of his religious policy in Brabant, if feasible at all, depended on repressing the popular agitation against the Catholic Church and defending Catholic churches, clergy, and processions. This was bound to aggravate Orange's already tense relationship with the militant Calvinists. In May 1579, there was a major outbreak of anti-Catholic rioting in Antwerp from which Orange was only able to rescue 180 trapped Catholic clergy, and the archduke Matthias himself, with some difficulty.[65]

If in Antwerp, Breda, and 's-Hertogenbosch, Orange's problem was to restrain the Protestants, nearer the Spanish front line the problem was to persuade nobles and patricians to accept the principle of 'Religious Peace'. With great reluctance, the solidly Catholic patriciate of Mechelen accepted it, in October 1578. But Mechelen, like Lille, was a town where Catholicism enjoyed substantial popular support and, on the news of the anti-Catholic rising at Antwerp of May 1579, the Catholics of Mechelen rose and attacked the Protestants. To calm the city, the regime in Antwerp had to withdraw all Protestant troops. With them fled some 600 Calvinist burghers. The Catholic patriciate ruling Mechelen continued to assure Matthias and the States that they were loyal to the States regime. But little confidence could be placed in such assurances. In the circumstances of 1579, in the south, adherence to Catholicism meant, above all, a willingness to negotiate with the Spaniards and seek an early settlement of the war. Within weeks of

---

[63] DuPlessis, *Lille and the Dutch Revolt*, 277.
[64] *Geschiedenis van Breda*, 166, 214.
[65] Voet, *Antwerp*, 215.

expelling the Protestants, the Mechelen city council entered negotiations with Don Juan, and then his successor as governor-general, Alexander Farnese, duke of Parma.[66]

By contrast, in Ghent, Bruges, Brussels, and the other now radical Calvinist cities of Flanders and Brabant there was no lack of firm commitment to the Revolt and to overthrowing everything connected with the Spanish king and his adherents. But what was the political vision which underlay the policies and decisions of this radical Flemish and Brabantine Revolt of the late 1570s and early 1580s? At its heart was the impulse to abandon the provincial framework built up since the early fifteenth century by the Burgundians and Habsburgs and revert to what has been termed the 'city-state system' characteristic of medieval Flanders and Brabant.[67] The whole tendency of the Revolt in Flanders, after the Calvinist coup of November 1577 in Ghent, pulled away from the emerging institutional framework—based on provinces and, above all, the unique cohesion of Holland—which underlay and buttressed the Revolt north of the rivers and which was to form the basis of the republic which was already taking shape there. Politically, the three great Flemish cities, under their new Calvinist regimes, were seeking to revive their ancient power and autonomy, indeed civic sovereignty, each in its own quarter utterly dominating the small towns and rural districts.

THE TWO NETHERLANDS

The events of 1576–8 did not so much engineer a deep rift between north and south in the Netherlands as reveal, and widen further, a profound rift which had already long existed. It may be true that the non-maritime northern provinces, and Friesland, felt little attraction to being drawn into the orbit of Holland. But the iron logic of the situation was that they were being inexorably sucked into Holland's sphere of control whilst every attempt by the States General, in Brabant, to extend their influence north of the great rivers signally failed.[68]

Structurally, the differences in society, economic life, and religion between north and south were numerous and far-reaching. But the crucial difference in the late 1570s was that the south revolved only very loosely round its political centre, Brabant, and was internally in deep disarray, whilst the north formed a more cohesive entity, a relatively compact block split by no

[66] Marnef, *Calvinistisch bewind te Mechelen*, 120–5.
[67] Blockmans, 'Alternatives', 145, 153.
[68] Malengreau, *L'Esprit particulariste*, 138, 141, 155.

major internecine rift. Partly the difference was a matter of existing institutions: in the south there were two major provinces, and both lacked cohesion,[69] whilst in the north there was only one which could give a lead, Holland, and it was more compact not only, as in the past, in financial and maritime matters, but now also, conspicuously, in the matter of religious policy. Partly, it was a matter of religion with Catholic allegiance considerably stronger in the south, especially (but by no means only) in the Walloon provinces. Partly also it was a matter of social structure: the south, more a society of estates than the north, had a more powerful nobility, clergy, and urban patriciate, a complex of ruling élites which was distinct from the large and wealthy middle stratum and better able to withstand popular pressure than was the case in the north. Orange's alliance with the urban oligarchies of Brabant and Flanders alienated both the nobility, on the one side, and the guilds, on the other.[70]

In the past, the Netherlands south of the great rivers had always carried greater weight politically than the north. But the situation in the rebel Netherlands in 1576–8 increasingly threatened to overturn this traditional balance and, as some Brabanters put it in 1579, 'mettre le pays de Brabant, et mesmes Anvers, pour ung boullevart de ceulx de Hollande et Zeelande' along with Gelderland.[71] For one thing the relentless advance of the Spanish forces into southern Brabant and Limburg, during 1578, significantly reduced the area in the south still in rebel hands. Furthermore, the regime of Matthias, Orange, and the States General, in Antwerp, proved less and less able to cope with the disparate political and religious tendencies of the towns and localities nominally under its sway. Holland, by contrast, had not only enhanced her cohesion through the fighting on her soil in 1572–4 but was effectively consolidating her dominance over the rest of the north.

An important step in this process was the 'Union' of Holland and Zeeland signed in June 1575.[72] This agreement for the first time created a joint (as well as exclusively Protestant) political, military, financial, and religious framework, an entity which was, in embryo, the state which was to be set up subsequently in 1579.[73] This incipient northern state adopted a partially common tax and administrative structure, a single military command, placing Orange unequivocally at the head of affairs, charging His Excellency to 'maintain the practice of the Reformed evangelical religion, suppressing,

---

[69] Verhofstad, *Regering der Nederlanden*, 73–4.
[70] Decavele, 'Mislukking', 626–7.
[71] *Archives ou correspondance*, vii. 92.
[72] Fruin, *Geschiedenis der staatsinstellingen*, 156.
[73] 'Articulen vande Verbondt' (Apr. 1575) in Res. Holl. 20 Apr., 18 and 19 May 1575.

and putting an end to, the exercise of the Romish religion' but, at the same time, guaranteeing that no individual would be investigated, prosecuted, or punished for his, or her, private beliefs and religious practices.[74] It was at this point that individual freedom of conscience was first guaranteed by the embryonic Dutch state. Closely bound up with the establishment of the union of Holland and Zeeland—the foundation of the later Dutch Republic—was the setting up, shortly after the 'Union', of a new university at Leiden to serve as the university of Holland and Zeeland.[75] The University of Leiden was consciously created by its progenitors, headed by Orange, as the intellectual training-ground of a new state and new 'public' Church: its purpose was to train officials, churchmen, and other professionals to staff the institutions of the new entity. It was also consciously intended that the new university should be an intellectual bulwark against 'tyranny' and religious oppression.[76] Of course, there were points of overlap between the union of Holland and Zeeland and the wider Netherlands framework presided over by the States General in Brabant. But, on the main issues, Holland and Zeeland went their own way, ignoring the States General. The States of Zeeland rejected demands for subsidies from Brabant, asserting that, in the raising of money and troops for the war, Zeeland would proceed, under the terms of its union with Holland, solely in conjunction with that province.[77]

In September 1578, the already chronic political disarray in the south became still worse with the mutiny of unpaid military contingents of the States General and some Catholic nobles against the States regime. These 'Malcontents', without yet moving over to reconciliation with the king of Spain, brought much of the Walloon area still in revolt into simultaneous rebellion against the States General. Meanwhile, the Spanish forces continued their inexorable advance northwards, overrunning Limburg during the summer of 1578 and penetrating parts of the Roermond quarter in the south of Gelderland. This acted as a spur to proposals for the formation of a 'closer union' amongst the northern provinces in revolt against Spain, and more effective military and political organization, for with the Spaniards in Upper Gelderland they were now beginning to threaten the north-eastern, as well as the southern, Netherlands.

Faced by a double crisis, in the Walloon country to the south-west, and in the east, the States General, in Antwerp, had little choice but to

[74] Ibid., p. 297 clause XVII.
[75] Res. Holl. 2 June 1575.
[76] Woltjer, *Leidse universiteit*, 2.
[77] *Notulen SZ* 18–21 Sept. 1578.

concentrate such political and military energy as it could muster on what was happening in the south and ignore the threat to Gelderland and Overijssel.[78] At the same time, the emergency in the Walloon area, however distressing for Brabant and Orange, seemed remote to the northern provinces. What worried Holland and Utrecht, as well as Overijssel, was precisely the developing threat to Gelderland. In a way, the strategic dilemma of 1578 was merely a distillation, in harsher form, of the age-old divergence of strategic concerns dividing the southern from the northern Netherlands. Flanders and Brabant had always looked to the south and west and did so again now. Holland, by contrast, found that her vital interests were threatened not in the south and west but to the east and north. Whether the Gelderlanders liked it or not, the unavoidable fact was that the States General in Brabant could provide 'no help for Roermond, Deventer, and Kampen',[79] as a Gelderse petition of January 1579 put it, whilst the States of Holland, Zeeland, and Utrecht, anxious to ensure their own security, rushed men and money to the eastern border, and intervened in the politics of Overijssel, to suppress the remaining loyalist Catholic town governments in Kampen (July 1578) and Deventer (November).[80] The arrival of substantial forces from Holland and Zeeland in Gelderland and Overijssel, and the need to pay for their upkeep, as well as the strengthening of the fortifications along the eastern border, posed the problem of the wider strategic and political relationship between the northern provinces in a new and urgent form.[81] This was the real origin of the famous Union of Utrecht and the formation of a wider north Netherlands state.

An early version of the new 'Union' was drafted by the States of Holland, prompted by Johan van Nassau, Stadholder of Gelderland, together with Floris Thin, Advocate of the States of Utrecht, in the late summer of 1578. It is clear that the original intention was to incorporate all the northern provinces, including Drenthe and the county of Lingen, but not the southern provinces, or the States General, in Antwerp.[82] The purpose was purely and simply to create a northern defensive structure dominated by Holland and excluding the Antwerp States General. There was, from the outset, both powerful support for, and also tenacious opposition to, the concept. In the States of Holland, the most radical and most Protestant towns, led by newly purged Amsterdam, and commanding a sizeable

---

[78] Boogman, 'Union of Utrecht', 380, 383.
[79] *Archives ou correspondance*, vi. 544.
[80] Ibid. 546; Slicher van Bath, *Gesch. van Overijssel*, 122.
[81] Boogman, 'Union of Utrecht', 383–5.
[82] *Notulen SZ* 1578, p. 70; *Archives ou correspondance*, vi. 539.

majority, forced it through over the hesitations of Leiden, Gouda, and Delft. In Zeeland, most towns were in favour but the largest and most influential, Middelburg, demurred, claiming the 'General Union' formed in 1576 and pacification of Ghent were sufficient.[83] The regents of Middelburg, Leiden, and Delft rightly saw the concept as a further step along the road to estrangement from the king, a means of strengthening the Protestant character of the north and building a political framework which could only perpetuate the war. Nothing was said in the draft text about the suppression of Catholic worship. But, in the context, it was clear that closer links with Holland and Zeeland, and joining in their Union, meant ending the policy of 'Religious Peace' upheld by Orange, and the States General in Brabant and, consequently, the final elimination of public Catholic worship in those parts of the provinces of Utrecht, Overijssel, Friesland, and Groningen where it was still permitted. For this reason the proposed Union was vehemently rejected in the States of Utrecht by Amersfoort and the small towns, as well as the clergy. But Thin, supported by the city of Utrecht and the *ridderschap*, forced it through.[84]

In Gelderland, royalists, Catholics, and anti-Holland particularists strove to prevent the Union. The meeting of the States of Gelderland, of September 1578, was pressured by delegations from Holland, Zeeland, and Utrecht. There was no difficulty in winning over the Roermond quarter, and part of the *ridderschap*. But there was determined opposition from some of the *ridderschap* of the Nijmegen quarter, led by Barthold van Gent, lord of Loenen, several of the *bannerheren*, and from Zutphen and Arnhem.[85] Opponents of the Union in the States of Gelderland, as in other provinces, argued that there was no need for a 'Closer Union' as long as the Walloon provinces had not definitely broken with the States General, for the Union would be bound to weaken further the precarious unity of the 'General Union'. They also expressed particularist sentiment, dismissing the arrangement as the 'Hollandsche Union' and criticizing the clause which would prevent Gelderland from negotiating with the king of Spain other than jointly with Holland and the other provinces. Advocates of the Union faced the central issue squarely, arguing that Gelderland was the 'bulwark and parapet' of Holland so that Holland could be relied on to defend Gelderland while Brabant could not.[86]

---

[83] *Notulen SZ* 1578, pp. 70, 170.
[84] Den Tex, 'Staten in Oldenbarnevelt's tijd', 55.
[85] Lenting, 'Gelderland in betrekking tot de Unie', 301–4, 328–9.
[86] *Archives ou correspondance*, vi. 549.

The signing of the final text by delegates of Holland, Zeeland, Utrecht, the Ommelands, and the *ridderschap* of the Arnhem and Zutphen quarters, at Utrecht on 23 January 1579, was no more than a first step in a long and arduous battle to establish the Union.[87] On all sides there was a keen awareness of the great importance of the 'Closer Union' and the arguments in the provincial assemblies and town councils raged for many months. The pro-Brabant, Catholic position in Gelderland was undermined by the crumbling of the Catholic town patriciates. Within days of the anti-Catholic rioting at Nijmegen, in February, the Nijmegen quarter signed the Union.[88] The Arnhem quarter followed suit, in March. Zutphen resisted until the town was occupied by Holland troops in April.

In Friesland too there was opposition to the Union. Initially, the Union was vigorously supported by the new Delegated Council set up, in 1577, on Orange's initiative, on the model of the standing committees of the States of Holland and Zeeland formed in 1572–3. But at that stage, most of the full States of Friesland were against. In March 1579, the conservatives captured control of the Delegated Council but the pro-Union element amongst the nobility, led by Carel Roorda and Witse van Camminga, and the three biggest towns—Leeuwarden, Franeker, and Sneek—refused to accept this, acknowledging only the previous Delegated Council. This radical rump proceeded to sign the Union on behalf of their quarters and towns.[89] Bolsward and other towns became embroiled in bitter local tussles. By June, all the Frisian towns had been brought round in favour of the Union (and closure of the Catholic churches), except Harlingen.[90] At the gathering of the States of Friesland, of August 1579, the Protestants recaptured control of the Delegated Council, and finally signed the Union on behalf of the whole province.

With the adhesion of Gelderland, in March 1579, the battle for the Union of Utrecht was, in essence, won, even though the full States of Friesland did not sign until August, and those of Drenthe not until April 1580, while Overijssel remained too divided to respond and the city of Groningen openly hostile, not out of Catholic sentiment—by 1580 a majority of the *raad* was Protestant—but resentment at Holland's support for the Omme-lander *jonkers* in the local dispute over staple privileges.[91] But, of course, there was opposition to the 'Hollandsche Union' not only in the north but

---

[87] Woltjer, 'Wisselende gestalten van de Unie', 95.
[88] Lenting, 'Gelderland in betrekking tot de Unie', 333.
[89] Schotanus, *Geschiedenissen*, 826–7, 831.
[90] ARH PR 362, pp. 283, 300; Napjus, *Sneek. Historisch Cronyk*, 70–1.
[91] Ros, *Rennenberg*, 75–6, 80.

also the south. The States General at Antwerp and Prince of Orange were profoundly worried by it.[92] For several months, the city of Ghent, bulwark of militant Calvinism in the south, was the only entity to sign. Appreciating the needs of the eastern border, and the success of the initiative, Orange did not openly oppose the Union but his lack of enthusiasm was clear. His chief concern, throughout, was to avoid widening the gulf between north and south. Provided the southern provinces were not excluded, the Prince had no reason to oppose a closer Union as such, but a union generally regarded as anti-Catholic—and certain to suppress Catholic worship—would be bound to drive the Walloon provinces, already teetering on the edge, into the arms of Spain and sow further disunity in Brabant and Flanders, as well as Friesland, Groningen, Overijssel, and Gelderland.[93] To counter this, the Zeeland delegates sent to Antwerp in March 1579, to urge the Prince to approve the Union, pointed out that the delay was encouraging Middelburg in opposing it and sowing dissension in Zeeland.[94]

As late as April 1579 Orange and the States of Brabant were still working on proposals for a different form of Union, one which would assign more power to the States General, at Antwerp, and strengthen central authority, as well as expressly guarantee the toleration of Catholic worship, in the spirit of the Pacification of Ghent. The rival schemes for union represented profoundly different concepts of how to shape the Netherlands future, one based on Holland, the other on the 'south'.[95] But Holland's coolness towards such a 'new closer union', and the decision of the Walloon provinces adhering to the Union of Arras in April, to seek reconciliation with Spain, destroyed this initiative and removed most of Orange's reservations. On 3 May 1579, he finally signed the Union of Utrecht and began encouraging those Brabant and Flemish towns still in a position to sign to do so. Thus, during May and June 1579 Antwerp, Breda, 's-Hertogenbosch, and a few other towns formally joined the Union of Utrecht, even though the States of Brabant and Flanders as a whole, and the nobility and clergy, did not.[96] Orange's efforts to build a common north–south Revolt, accommodating Catholic as well as Protestant worship on the basis of the Pacification of Ghent, and concept of 'Religious Peace', had suffered a further and crippling blow. But by May 1579 he had no realistic alternative to giving in to the burgeoning reality of an uncompromisingly anti-Catholic Revolt based on Holland rather than Brabant, with the Dutch Reformed

[92] Swart, 'Willem de Zwijger', 74.
[93] Woltjer, 'Wisselende gestalten van de Unie', 98–9.
[94] *Notulen SZ* 1578/9, p. 169. Instructions for delegates going to Antwerp, 11 Mar. 1579.
[95] Parker, *Dutch Revolt*, 194.
[96] Christ, *De Brabantsche Saecke*, 17.

Church, as organized in Holland and Zeeland, the official 'public Church' of the Union in practice, even though the text of the Union did not stipulate it as such.[97]

Nevertheless, though he now accepted the inevitability of the Union, and primacy of the Calvinists, William still strove to make Brabant the political centre of the Revolt and refused to accept the elimination of Catholicism as an officially tolerated Church in the new state. For to do so would mean abandoning all hope of winning back those parts of Brabant and Flanders, as well as the Walloon provinces, which had now reverted to Spanish rule, and of eliminating Spanish power from the Netherlands for good. The intolerance and theocratic tendencies of the Calvinist clergy also offended his own personal sensibilities, and he was determined not to concede too much influence, in the new state, to a theology and clergy for which he entertained little personal sympathy. Later, during the Dutch Golden Age, even the most anti-Orangist, republican writers, such as Pieter de la Court, admired the way William the Silent, during the last years of his life, continued to oppose the pretensions of the Reformed clergy to the point of earning their enduring hostility.[98]

In those parts of the north where Catholic worship was still allowed the position, for both Catholics and those *politiques* and liberal Protestants—such as Dirck Volckertsz. Coornhert—who supported Orange's policy of toleration, rapidly deteriorated. After the purge of the town council of Amersfoort, in March 1579, Catholic worship survived at a reduced level, but there was further anti-Catholic rioting in April, and again in June, and it was plainly only a matter of time before popular pressure suppressed Catholic worship in the province of Utrecht completely.[99] In Haarlem, the last town in Holland where Catholic practice was permitted, it was steadily squeezed during 1579, the town's Catholics finding themselves in a more and more precarious position. Only in Overijssel, the northern province most pervaded by war-weariness and a desire to negotiate with Parma, did Catholic worship for the moment prevail. But even there popular Catholic support was generally meagre. For a more robust Catholic reaction one had to look south of the rivers, notably to the Walloon towns, Mechelen and 's-Hertogenbosch, a city now bitterly divided and where, in July 1579, there were pitched battles in the streets.[100]

The strong resistance to the Closer Union in Overijssel and the pressure there for negotiations to settle the war were by no means indications of a

[97] Van der Linde, *Jean Taffin*, 88; Bremmer, *Reformatie en rebellie*, 154–7.
[98] De la Court, *Aanwysing*, 399–400.
[99] Van Kalveen, 'De definitieve vestiging', 31–5.
[100] Pirenne, *'s-Hertogenbosch*, 160, 177, 226.

resurgence of Catholic sentiment in the province. The conservative, Catholic policy of the three town magistracies, on the contrary, conspicuously lacked the support of the populace. In July 1578, the Zwolle magistracy had acknowledged the States General's Stadholder of Overijssel, Rennenberg, provided he guaranteed that the Catholic faith would remain the only religion permitted in Zwolle. But most of the citizenry and militia opposed the *raad* and soon compelled the latter to accept restoration of the citizens' Sworn Council, which had been suppressed in 1573, following Alva's subduing of the northeast. As the guilds and militias took over, the president of the Hof of Overijssel, imposed by Alva, fled fearful of the 'fureur populaire'. In the new *raad*, elected in January 1579, only six of the former pro-Catholic magistracy were retained. Two-thirds of the new Zwolle city council, elected by the Sworn Council, consisted either of the pro-Protestant element, purged in 1573, or new men. Zwolle's principal church, already seized for Calvinist worship in December 1578, was officially assigned to the Reformed Church.

Deventer, garrisoned by royal troops, held out against Rennenberg until November 1578. But though the troops resisted, it was noted that there was scant Catholic support amongst the town's population.[101] Once the town fell, the Protestants immediately gained the upper hand despite Rennenberg's own Catholic stance.[102] At Kampen, the regents pursued a Catholic policy with some tenacity. When Kampen was liberated from the Spanish troops which had occupied the city since 1573, the *raad* promptly subscribed to the 'General Union' and Pacification of Ghent, ordering the newly arrived Protestant preacher to cease preaching, under pain of being punished as a '*perturbateur*' of the common peace under the Pacification.[103] When the Reformed in Kampen then appealed to the Archduke Matthias, at Antwerp, to intercede, the *raad* brusquely rebuffed the latter's plea for toleration, reiterating the States of Overijssel's view that the Pacification authorized each province to decide its own religious policy.[104] But though the Catholic party dominated the *raad*, it lacked support in the town. The Catholic leadership in Kampen was arrested in April 1580.

Yet, despite the weakness of loyalist and Catholic allegiance in Overijssel, opposition to the Union of Utrecht was stronger there than in any other northern province. In May 1579 the States of Overijssel overwhelmingly rejected the Union of Utrecht, Kampen strongly reaffirming its preference

[101]   *Archief . . . aartsbisdom Utrecht*, liv, 257–8.
[102]   Koch, 'Reformation in Deventer', 36–8.
[103]   GA Kampen Oud-archief, 22, pp. 132–3, res. raad. 14 Aug. 1578.
[104]   Ibid. 136–6, res. raad 7 Oct. 1578.

for the General Union and Pacification, and supporting the Archduke Matthias's efforts to negotiate a compromise peace with Spain, under the auspices of the Emperor, at Cologne.[105] The Walloon provinces' defection from the Revolt and reconciliation with Spain, in May, lent added urgency to Overijssel's hopes for the Cologne talks. But while Overijssel longed for peace, and disliked the Closer Union, and not least the hegemony of Holland, the States were also determined to resist the return of the Spanish soldiery or any garrisons, and also restoration of the bishopric of Deventer, reintroduction of the Hof, and resumption of persecution of Protestants.[106] Overijssel, in other words, was caught in a dilemma to which there was no solution. In the end, the States had no alternative but opting for either Spain or Holland.

THE HABSBURG RECONQUEST OF THE SOUTH, 1579–1585

With the advent of the Union of Utrecht, the outlook for Catholic nobles and office-holders still adhering to the cause of the Revolt, and nominal Catholics who had kept their Protestantism private in the hope of an early compromise settlement between rebels and king, seemed increasingly bleak. Briefly they pinned their hopes on the peace talks, held at Cologne under the auspices of the Emperor Rudolph II. But these rapidly broke down, revealing, for all to see, the untenability of the middle ground and hopelessness of attempts at compromise. For middle-of-the-road men there seemed no way out:[107] they must either defect to the king or go over to the Calvinists. Many key figures of the time suffered inner agonies, fighting the great struggle of the Dutch Revolt within themselves as well as participating in the conflict outwardly. Aggaeus de Albada, the representative of Friesland at the Cologne talks (of which he left a Latin account), had no difficulty in accepting the legitimacy of revolt against tyranny, but was as appalled by the religious intolerance of the Calvinists as he had been by that of the Habsburg authorities. Ultimately, he refused to choose, preferring to settle permanently in Cologne. Elbertus Leoninus, the Erasmian scholar-politician cited a century later by Bayle as the very embodiment of the new *politique* spirit, subordinating religion to considerations of state,[108] had been a leading advocate of the General Union, content to remain a nominal Catholic hoping to avoid a definitive break with Spain. On realizing that a General

---

[105] Ibid. 161, res. raad 23 May 1579.
[106] Reitsma, *Centrifugal and Centripetal Forces*, 187–9.
[107] Bremmer, *Reformatie en rebellie*, 201–6.
[108] Bayle, *Dictionnaire*, ii. 1962–3.

Union, based on Brabant, could not succeed, he followed Orange and became a nominal Calvinist. In June 1581, he was appointed Chancellor of the Hof of Gelderland, recently purged of all but firm supporters of the Revolt, and became the leading figure in Gelderland politics, steering the States of Gelderland from the Hof's quarters at Arnhem.

Most dramatic of all was the case of Georges de Lalaing, count of Rennenberg, Stadholder of Friesland, Groningen, Drenthe, Lingen, and Overijssel on behalf of the General Union and the last remaining Catholic magnate on the rebel side. For months he wavered between the General Union and the Union of Utrecht.[109] Eventually, as the General Union crumbled, he made up his mind to break with the Revolt and go over to Spain. Organizing his conspiracy in the city of Groningen, Rennenberg secretly prepared his Catholic revolt against the Union.[110] In March 1580, he broke with Orange, and Holland, and declared his loyalty to the king, calling on Catholics throughout the region under his stadholderate to rise, restore their Church, and acknowledge their legitimate sovereign. Parma promptly confirmed the city's staple rights in the Ommelands.[111]

The Rennenberg revolt against the embryonic Dutch state was the first major emergency to face the new Union. For the Catholics of the north-east it was *the* great opportunity to show their allegiance, overthrow Protestantism, and restore the faith of their fathers. Rennenberg secured Groningen without difficulty and dispatched letters in all directions calling on the citizenry to rise against the tyranny of Holland and the Protestants. The cause of Catholic reaction was helped by the fact that there were relatively few troops present, at the time, loyal to the 'Closer Union' in the provinces under Rennenberg's command.

The Catholics of the north-east had their chance and they rose. But, except at Groningen—and even there the insurrection seems to have been motivated less by Catholic sentiment than zeal for the city's staple privileges and hostility to the Ommelanders[112]—Catholic support was so meagre that the rising was overwhelmed almost immediately. In most places the response amounted to hardly anything. There was no overt support for Catholic insurgency in Kampen, amongst the Ommelanders, or in Drenthe.[113] At Zwolle, the Catholics did take to the streets, sword in hand, but the town's Protestants, without help from outside, swiftly overwhelmed them.[114] As the

[109] Ros, *Rennenberg*, 108–11.
[110] Trosée, *Verraad van George van Lalaing*, 102, 166.
[111] Emmius, *De Agro Frisiae*, 171–2.
[112] Ros, *Rennenberg*, 197–8.
[113] Ibid. 199–204; Van der Pol, *Reformatie te Kampen*, 290–4.
[114] Hattum, *Gesch. der stad Zwolle*, iv. 38–40.

Catholic patricians of Zwolle fled, iconoclastic riots erupted behind them, devastating the city's Catholic churches. At Deventer, the mob, incensed against the Catholics, sacked all the city's churches, destroying the images and vestments. Most of the Catholic clergy fled. Catholic worship was then suppressed by popular and militia pressure. The Catholics asked the *raad* if they could at least have one church; but the civic militia opposed this, insisting that in the interests of civic peace and unity only the religion of 'the majority' of the citizens, the Reformed, should be permitted.[115] By the end of March 1580 the Catholics of Overijssel had lost practically all their churches.

The anti-Catholic backlash in the provinces under Rennenberg's stad-holderate was immediate, and devastating. In Friesland there were sporadic attempts to rise, notably at Bolsward; but in general the Catholics were easily disarmed.[116] Leeuwarden erupted in a new *beeldenstorm*. At Sneek, the citizenry stripped the images from all the city's churches and drove out the clergy.[117] Also in many small places throughout Friesland, as well as in the Ommelands and Drenthe, churches were attacked and stripped. Finally the Calvinist Delegated States of Friesland closed all remaining Catholic churches and cloisters in the province, expelled the Catholic clergy, and prohibited the mass.[118]

The anti-Catholic backlash extended also outside the provinces which had been under Rennenberg's command, with outbreaks of violence in many places in Gelderland, northern Brabant, Holland, and especially Utrecht. At Amersfoort the populace were so enraged the *vroedschap* suspended Catholic worship provisionally to forestall further disorder.[119] Once banned, Catholic services were not again allowed in any of the city's churches. In the city of Utrecht, there was an eruption of anti-Catholic violence, all the churches and cloisters being stripped and pillaged.

Orange, who had still not abandoned his efforts to accommodate Catholic worship in the provinces of the Closer Union, tried to secure two of the city's churches for the Catholics, but without success. By June 1580 the *vroedschap* had closed most of the city's thirty churches, banned Catholic worship throughout the city, and forbidden Catholic priests and monks to appear in their habits.[120] Catholic worship was formally banned by the

---

[115] Koch, 'Reformation in Deventer', 38–40.
[116] Schotanus, *Geschiedenissen*, 830–1.
[117] Napjus, *Sneek*, 71.
[118] Kalma *et al., Gesch. van Friesland*, 298.
[119] Van Kalveen, 'Definitieve vestiging', 41.
[120] Van Gelder, *Revolutionnaire Reformatie*, 147–8.

States of Gelderland, in January 1582, and suppressed in Culemborg at about the same time.[121]

Apart from the guilds of Groningen, the only support for Rennenberg's revolt in the north-east came from some of the nobility of Overijssel and Gelderland, including the count of Limburg Stirum.[122] In Overijssel and Drenthe there was also a peasant revolt against the incoming troops, sent from Holland, which local Catholic nobles were accused of stirring up. But except in the easternmost Twenthe quarter of Overijssel, most of the Overijssel and Gelderse *ridderschap* (though not the *bannerheren*) held firm for the Revolt.[123] At the emergency gathering of the States of Overijssel which Orange attended in person, in March 1580, the States confirmed their support for the 'common cause', though they still held back from signing the Union of Utrecht.

By and large, then, the effect of Rennenberg's 'betrayal' was to strengthen the Revolt and Dutch Protestantism. Nevertheless, Rennenberg's defection posed a major strategic threat to the Union. Groningen was the largest city in the north-east and dominated a considerable area, in the rear of the main Dutch defences. The royalists' grip was consolidated with the arrival of troops, sent by Parma, in June. In July, Rennenberg captured Delfzijl, commanding the Ems estuary. Before long, his forces were ranging beyond the confines of the Ommelands and, in September, he captured Oldenzaal, chief town of the Twenthe quarter of Overijssel. At this point, the Hof of Overijssel, expelled from Zwolle as incorrigibly royalist and Catholic, resumed its functions at Oldenzaal. There were now two competing administrations in the province.[124] Meanwhile, Parma continued to gain ground in the south. Having taken Maastricht, after a bitter four-month siege in June 1579, he seized the west Flemish town of Kortrijk in February 1580. Spanish troops were now advancing on three fronts: in the north-east, south-east, and south-west. To set against this the States General's forces in Brabant recaptured Mechelen, in April, the English soldiery involved subjecting this predominantly Catholic town to what became known as the 'English Fury'.

The territory under the General Union and Closer Union combined was steadily shrinking. Orange was now more than ever convinced that the only way to prevent total defeat was to regain the support of those moderates alienated by Calvinist radicalism and—by making the northern provinces more accommodating to Catholicism (and Lutheranism)—reassure Catho-

[121] De Jong, *Reformatie in Culemborg*, 212.
[122] Van Reyd, *Historie*, 49–50.
[123] Reitsma, *Centrifugal and Centripetal Forces*, 210–13.
[124] Slicher van Bath, *Gesch. van Overijssel*, 123.

lics in the south, as well as gain the confidence of the king of France and Lutheran princes of Germany. It was in the hope both of making the Revolt more accommodating religiously, and securing help from abroad, especially France, that the Prince urged the States General that sovereignty over the Netherlands should be offered to the younger brother of the French king, the duke of Anjou.[125] Needless to say, the offer was to be tightly hedged around with constitutional safeguards.[126] Orange's policy was adopted by the States of Brabant and Flanders, and a treaty signed between Anjou and the States General's representatives, in September 1580. Official pro-Anjou propaganda stressed the links between the French royal house and the former Burgundian rulers under whom the Netherlands had allegedly been vastly better off than under Spain.[127]

Anjou reached Antwerp in January 1581, took his oath to abide by the privileges, before the States, and was proclaimed 'prince and lord of the Netherlands'. Matthias whose position was now both irrelevant and untenable left the country in March. Logically speaking, before the provinces could adopt a new sovereign they had to discard the old one. However, it was not until July 1581 that the States General finally agreed on the text of an Act of Abjuration (*Plakkaat van Verlatinge*), repudiating Philip II and his heirs in perpetuity. The act renounced the king of Spain, decreed the removal of his portrait from coins minted in the provinces of the General Union, and from official seals, and the erasure of the Habsburg coat of arms from public buildings and documents. There was to be no further reference to the king of Spain, or any of his titles, in courts of law, town halls, or any official body. Furthermore, the Act of Abjuration required new oaths of allegiance to be taken from all office-holders and magistrates, as well as the civic militias, whereby holders of office had to swear that they no longer held themselves to be bound by their former oaths of loyalty to the Spanish king and 'swear further to be true and obedient to the States against the king of Spain and his followers'.[128]

While the articles of the Union of Utrecht marked the real beginning of the Dutch Republic as a federal state encompassing the whole of the northern Netherlands, the Act of Abjuration, though framed in Antwerp, by the States General, did more to alter the appearance of things in the rebel Netherlands. In Holland and Zeeland recognition of the sovereignty of Philip since 1572 had had less and less real meaning. The official oaths

---

[125] Swart, 'Willem de Zwijger', 75.
[126] De Vrankrijker, *Motiveering*, 121–2.
[127] Geurts, *Nederlandse Opstand in de pamfletten*, 294–6.
[128] Kossmann and Mellink, *Texts*, 227; Bremmer, *Reformatie en Rebellie*, 218–19.

drawn up for the Pensionary and Delegated Council of Zeeland in 1578, for example, obliged them to swear to uphold the 'Particular Union' of Holland and Zeeland but make no mention of the king of Spain.[129] The text of the articles of the Union of Utrecht, of 1579, does mention 'His Majesty' but only once and *en passant*. But in other provinces, especially those such as Overijssel, Gelderland, Drenthe, and Groningen partly in the hands of royal troops, there was a great deal of difference between administering justice, in the name of Philip, or under oath to resist Philip. Officials had been appointed to their offices, and sworn their oaths of allegiance, in the name of the king of Spain; to renounce that oath was a momentous step, confirming unequivocal allegiance to the Revolt. Not surprisingly, many reacted with alarm, both ideological and practical.[130] Until 1581 everyone had paid lip-service to Philip II. Suddenly, his portrait disappeared from all coins minted in the rebel Netherlands,[131] and his name from buildings and documents. The Revolt against the king of Spain was now enshrined in every transaction no matter how large or small.

The Act of Abjuration also caused the propaganda war raging on all sides to boil over.[132] Particularly effective in portraying Spanish rule in the Low Countries as 'tyranny' and 'barbarous crueltie' and blackening the names of Philip and Alva, was the *Apology* (1581) of William of Orange published in reply to the king's ban, of June 1580, outlawing him and promising a reward for whoever assassinated him. Parma had opposed the edict, issued at the king's insistence (inspired by Granvelle), seeing it was likely to be counter-productive in propaganda terms, and it was. William's *Apology*, penned by a panel which included the famous Huguenot political writer, Philippe du Plessis-Mornay, stooped to the usual propaganda devices, attributing un-speakable depravity to the king of Spain and his advisers and openly inciting hispanophobia. Nevertheless, it is a remarkable text full of high-sounding phrases, extolling toleration, 'freedom', and the privileges of the land. Also Orange insisted that it was no fault of his that Catholicism had been suppressed in Holland and Zeeland, that at first he and the States had agreed that 'both the one and the other religion should be tollerated', but that the States had been compelled by the 'insolencies, attemptes and treasons' of their enemies within to ban the Roman faith.[133] Another key publication of 1581 was the account of the Cologne peace talks of 1579 by

---

[129]　*Notulen* SZ 1578/9, pp. 12–13.
[130]　Jappe Alberts, *Gesch. van Gelderland*, 121.
[131]　De Voogt, *Gesch. van het muntwezen*, 84–5.
[132]　Van Gelderen, *Political Thought*, 151–7.
[133]　*The Apologie of Prince William*, 85.

the Spiritualist jurist Aggaeus de Albada. This likewise justified resistance to despotic kings in the most uncompromising terms, citing the famous Huguenot tract *Vindiciae contra Tyrannos* (1579) and maintaining that kings, like magistrates, were subject to laws and ultimately to the people.

In the Low Countries resistance theories were now in vogue. But there were still many who abhorred such doctrines and rejected the Act of Abjuration. Numerous office-holders resigned their positions especially in Gelderland, Overijssel, and Friesland. The States of Overijssel accepted the Act only with great reluctance.[134] If Calvinist preachers were delighted, some Lutheran, as well as Catholic, clergy voiced disapproval.[135] But the Act of Abjuration not only antagonized yet another batch of moderates, it also further widened the split between the General Union and the Closer Union, between Brabant and Holland, between north and south. Part of Orange's purpose in bringing Anjou into the picture had been to tilt the balance back towards more moderate religious policies, towards the States General, and therefore towards Brabant. Anjou's power, such as it was, was based on Brabant.[136] In much of Flanders as well as north of the rivers Anjou's authority never amounted to much, indeed was little more than an empty formality, and in Overijssel, Gelderland, and Utrecht was never acknowledged even in theory. Holland and Zeeland did make perfunctory acknowledgment of Anjou; but the oaths of allegiance which they administered were solely to the Union, the provincial States, and Orange as Stadholder.

By 1580 north and south were drifting further and further apart. Since Rennenberg's defection the division of the war into separate northern and southern theatres had become even more marked than before. Anjou and the States of Brabant and Flanders had more than enough to do trying to stem Parma's advance in the south and south-west. Even if they had wished to, it was impossible for them to pay much attention to, or spare resources for, the struggle to the east and north. The garrisons and troops maintained north of the rivers, and the raising of the necessary resources, were controlled solely by the northern group of provinces headed by Holland. On one level the duality of executive power which manifested itself so plainly during the early 1580s was incidental, arising from the separation of military fronts.[137] But the fragmentation of power in the south—with the Flemish towns going their own way—and the primacy of Holland in the north, deeper down, reflected a profound, inherent, and growing rift in patterns of

---

[134] Hattum, *Gesch. der stad Zwolle*, iv. 215.
[135] Kluit, *Historie*, i. 276–7.
[136] Holt, *Duke of Anjou*, 167–9, 171.
[137] Geyl, *Revolt of the Netherlands*, 187.

power and patronage reaching back not just decades, but centuries.[138] The plain fact was that Flanders and Brabant could not work together and neither was able to exert any significant leverage above the rivers whereas Holland had long regarded the inland provinces of the north as her indispensable hinterland and sphere of influence. Gelderland, Overijssel, and the Ommelands had become Holland's defensive shield. In theory a single Council of State was set up, under Anjou, in 1581, to direct the war. In practice, this council was divided into two distinct bodies, a southern council, located in Brabant, and the so-called Council of the Lands east of the Maas, responsible for conducting the war in Gelderland, Overijssel, Drenthe, and Groningen, which was from the outset entirely dominated by Holland.

Paradoxically, the coming of Anjou, on which Orange had so strenuously insisted, instead of imparting greater cohesion served further to accentuate the growing separation of power. Anjou concentrated his efforts, and his French troops, in the south but nevertheless signally failed to slow the pace of the royalist resurgence.[139] On the contrary, buoyed by the silver of the Spanish Indies, and free now from his war against the Ottoman Turks, Philip's power in the Netherlands recovered rapidly. Parma had 45,435 troops under his command in September 1580. By October 1582, this figure had risen to 61,000.[140] But the improvement was qualitative as well as quantitative. In 1580, the royal army consisted almost entirely of locally recruited Walloon troops and German mercenaries. By 1582 a large portion of the army consisted of high-grade Spanish, Italian, and German troops. The growing separation of north and south was further emphasized by Parma's success, in June 1581, in capturing Orange's own town of Breda, extending Spanish power along the southern side of the rivers, thereby driving a wedge between the rebel zones above and below the rivers.

Prospects for the rebels, on both sides of Parma's wedge, looked increasingly sombre. During 1582, Spanish forces advanced in Gelderland and, in November, Parma took Steenwijk, the fortress town commanding the land routes between Overijssel and Friesland. The great Italian general seemed poised to slice what he called this 'damnable Union d'Utrecht' into helpless strips. As the Spaniards advanced, morale on the rebel side sank, the temptation of office-holders and commanders to enter into secret compacts with Parma increased, and the frustration of Anjou intensified. Weary of the

[138] Blockmans, 'Alternatives', 145–6.
[139] Van Meteren, *Historie*, iv. 47.
[140] Parker, *Army of Flanders*, 271–2.

restraints on his authority, the duke conspired, and, in January 1583, attempted, to take effective power in rebel Brabant and Flanders through a military coup. He seized Dunkirk, Aalst, and several other places in Flanders; but, in Antwerp, the citizenry rushed to arms and set upon Anjou's men, leaving hundreds of French dead in the streets. After this fiasco, Anjou's position became untenable and Orange's own popularity sank to its lowest point since 1572, especially at Antwerp. The rebel Netherlands were in greater disarray than ever. Orange, still believing that the one hope of saving the Revolt, and the Union, lay in securing French help, tried to patch matters up.[141] But both Anjou and the Brabanters had had enough and, in June, the duke left the country.

By the spring of 1583 Orange was close to despair. Both his pro-French strategy and his 'Religious Peace' were in ruins. The fall of Breda, reputedly the work of local Catholics opening the town's gates to the Spaniards, had so enraged the Protestant population of Antwerp as to cause another wave of iconoclastic fury to erupt and the drastic curtailment, despite Orange's efforts to prevent it, of Catholic freedom of worship in both Antwerp and Brussels. As the Spaniards gained ground, the mood amongst the Protestant citizenry of the threatened towns of Flanders and Brabant became increasingly intolerant and antagonistic to Orange's 'Religious Peace'.[142] But, at the same time, morale sagged. During the summer of 1583, in the wake of Anjou's departure, the Spaniards captured the predominantly Protestant Flemish towns of Dunkirk and Nieuwpoort almost without firing a shot. The Revolt in the south seemed doomed. Finally, in July, in a mood of deepening pessimism, the Prince abandoned his efforts to place the Revolt in the south on a viable basis and left Brabant for good. He transferred his headquarters to Holland, establishing himself in a former convent in Delft which now became known as the 'Prinsenhof' and where he was to remain for the last eighteen months of his life. Orange was now again the head of the rebel state based on Holland. But both his prestige, and the powers which the States of Holland and Zeeland accorded him, were appreciably less than in the years 1572-6.[143] During the years of Orange's absence, the States of Holland had greatly consolidated their position as an embryonic government.

With Orange's removal to Delft and new agreement with Holland, his vision of a Netherlands united, north and south, in revolt against Spain under joint Protestant–Catholic leadership subscribing to a 'Religious

---

[141] Holt, *Duke of Anjou*, 185–92.
[142] Van Gelder, *Revolutionnaire Reformatie*, 165–8.
[143] Koopmans, *Staten van Holland*, 130.

Peace' was definitively shattered.[144] He was compelled to accept that there was not going to be a Netherlands state based on Brabant and that, if the Revolt was to survive to all, the only possible base was Holland and suppression of Catholic worship. In August 1583, the States General transferred their gathering from Antwerp to Middelburg, and later Delft, before settling finally in The Hague.[145] The Council of State in Brabant dissolved itself in October 1583. There was now only one power centre—Holland.

But if Orange abandoned much of what he had previously sought to achieve, his argument that the rebel state of the United Provinces was too weak, on its own, to resist the might of Spain and that the only plausible source of help was France, had lost none of its cogency. Holland's dominance within the United Provinces was now unchallengeable. But how was Holland to stave off creeping defeat? The overwhelming superiority, and relentless advance, of the Spanish army of Flanders, fashioned by Parma into a highly disciplined instrument of war, gathered momentum month by month. The Spaniards captured Ieper in April 1584, Bruges in May, and Ghent, the bastion of radical Calvinism, in September. A swelling stream of defeated, frightened Protestants began to flow from Flanders and Brabant into Holland and Zeeland.

During the last months of his life Orange was more convinced than ever that the 'patriots' of the Netherlands had no other practicable recourse but to throw themselves at the feet of the king of France. Whatever his own, and others', reservations about the French Crown, and the French, he did not doubt that it was better for the Netherlands to be under France rather than Spain.[146] He changed his mind about the proposal, originally put forward by the States of Holland and Zeeland, at the prompting of the Advocate of the States of Holland, Paulus Buys, in 1581, that the title of 'count of Holland and Zeeland', with sovereign rights over the two provinces, should be conferred on his own person.[147] Earlier the proposal had been essentially a manœuvre to prevent Anjou being accorded sovereignty over the two provinces and Orange had rejected it precisely because he had no wish to weaken Anjou's position.[148] But now, with Anjou gone, and most Holland and Zeeland towns agreed, Orange responded more favourably to the idea.

[144] Decavele, 'Willem van Oranje', 83.
[145] Delfos, *Anfänge der Utrechter Union*, 249.
[146] *Archives ou correspondance*, viii. 341, 358, 361.
[147] Rowen, *Princes of Orange*, 28–31.
[148] Swart, *William the Silent*, 35.

But just at this point enthusiasm for the proposal, in at least some town councils, waned. Especially three cities—Amsterdam, Gouda, and Middelburg—turned against conferring the title of 'count' on Orange. The Prince still enjoyed considerable popularity in the north. No other figure in the rebel state had remotely the same status. Nevertheless, his prestige had diminished and militant Calvinists were more wary of him than ever. Also many moderates, particularly those lukewarm towards the Revolt and Calvinist Reformation—a category well represented in the Gouda *vroedschap*—disliked the idea because such a step would make eventual reconciliation with Philip even more remote than it was already.[149] But while most doubts flowed from considerations such as these, in the minds of at least a few Holland, regents there was also a strain of nascent republicanism, or a commitment to the idea of the States of Holland, rather than any sovereign head, providing the political leadership of the provinces united in the Union of Utrecht.

This tendency is strongly evident in the discourse delivered by Cornelis Hooft, the regent father of the playwright and historian Pieter Cornelisz. Hooft, before the Amsterdam *vroedschap* in June 1584.[150] Hooft argued, firstly, that the Union of Utrecht had forged an indissoluble union of the provinces 'as if they were but one province', and that this precluded two provinces choosing their own separate sovereign head. Secondly, he maintained that the authority of the regents derived from support of the substantial citizenry, militias, and seamen and that in such a fundamental matter it was essential that the regents should not proceed without the backing of these groups, urging his fellow regents to consult 'not only the captains and lieutenants of the militia and civic quarters, but all the burghers and also the seafaring folk . . . who are our greatest strength'.[151] Hooft insisted that the ordinary populace of Amsterdam were willing to continue the fight against Spain but were against conferring sovereignty on the Prince of Orange and that the regents should respect this.

The question how far the Holland regents should consult the citizenry, and specifically the militias and guilds, before reaching major decisions had been controversial ever since the regent consultations with the militias about allowing Protestant worship, in 1566. Since 1572, the militias and guilds of Holland had on occasions, such as ratification of the Pacification of Ghent and of the Union of Utrecht, played an influential part in

---

[149] Hibben, *Gouda in Revolt*, 178–82.
[150] Van Gelder, *Levensbeschouwing*, 163–4.
[151] Hooft, *Memorien*, ii. 8.

decision-making.[152] Orange himself had sometimes urged the town councils to consult the militias and citizenry, knowing they were more resolutely opposed to Philip, and more anti-Spanish, than the regents. But, precisely for this reason, many regents had become restive at the way their more radical colleagues mobilized popular pressure against them by appealing to citizen bodies. In March 1581, when the debates about Anjou and Abjuration were at their height, worries of this sort had induced the States of Holland to resolve that, henceforth, no town councils of the province should consult 'militias, guilds, or other' bodies about matters of state, as had been done in recent years 'by some towns'.[153] But it was a resolution that by no means everyone, even among the regents, regarded as appropriate or legitimate.

A month after Hooft delivered his discourse, the whole business of Orange's elevation was rendered obsolete by the pistol shots of a Catholic fanatic on a staircase of the Prince's quarters, in Delft. The Prince died of his wounds, his last recorded words, according to the States of Holland, being 'Mon Dieu, mon Dieu, ayez pitié de moy et de ce pauvre peuple.'[154]

Virtually the first action of the States of Holland, on hearing the sombre news, was to dispatch a letter to Brabant, where the Spanish troops were now encircling Antwerp, urging the States there not to give up the struggle but fight on 'for the defence and liberation of the country against Spanish tyranny'.[155] For the first time Holland now had to contemplate not only leading the Revolt, without Orange at their head, but also shouldering the bulk of the cost. So much of Flanders and Brabant had been overrun by Parma, by July 1584, that the now skeletal States of those provinces could no longer contribute much. Henceforth, the burden was to be Holland's. After some wrangling as to how to allocate the burden within the province, Holland voted an emergency subsidy for the defence of Antwerp, still assigning a relatively low share to Leiden and Haarlem, on account of their poor economic shape, following the great sieges, and heavy shares to Delft, and also the West Frisian ports where bulk-carrying and the fisheries were flourishing (see Table 5).

But Holland's contributing more to the war in the south, and the increasing desperation of the rebel remnants of Flanders and Brabant, did nothing to bring Holland and the Reformed provinces in the south together.[156] As was explained to the English secretary of state, Walsingham,

[152] Woltjer, 'Dutch Privileges', 28–9.
[153] Res. Holl. 23 Mar. 1581; Kluit, *Historie*, i. 263–4.
[154] Res. Holl. 11 July 1584.
[155] Ibid.
[156] Decavele, 'Willem van Oranje', 80.

the Flemish and Brabanters 'have little affection for the Hollanders, seeing themselves despised by them'.[157]

Holland now had to find resources in ever mounting quantities and also to streamline her own executive machinery and the political leadership of the rebel state generally. In the ensuing deliberations, much stress was placed on the Particular Union of Holland and Zeeland, of the year 1576, as the constitutional embryo of the larger confederacy which had since come into being, and as being still the only solid precedent for the close collaboration of another province with Holland in financial, judicial, and ecclesiastical administration, as well as in military and naval matters.[158] Priority was also given to negotiating with Utrecht as part of what we might term the inner confederal bloc of three to which the outlying provinces would then have no choice but to subordinate themselves.[159] The most important decision concerning the government of the confederacy as a whole was the setting up of the *Raad van State* (Council of State) to function as a general executive, under agreed rules, to replace Orange and the informal executive body which had advised him.[160] The *Raad* was entrusted with conducting the war and administering the army and navy. Places on the *Raad* were assigned to Flanders and Brabant as well as to Holland, Zeeland, Utrecht, and Friesland but initially not to Overijssel, Gelderland, and Groningen.

TABLE 5. *The quota for the States of Holland's emergency subsidy for Antwerp in 1584*

City	%	City	%
Amsterdam	16.5	Rotterdam	6
Delft	13.5	Enkhuizen	6
Dordrecht	10	Hoorn	6
Haarlem	7	Alkmaar	5
Leiden	6	Gouda	4.5
The Hague	6	(seven small towns)	13.5
TOTAL	59	TOTAL	41

Source: SH Resolutions for 1584, p. 544.

Between 1576 and 1583 there had been two theatres of war, and two separate centres of command, in the rebel Netherlands. From 1583, and still

[157] *Cal. St. Papers*. Elizabeth, XVIII, 354, 24 Feb. 1584.
[158] Res. Holl. 17 July 1584.
[159] Res. Holl. 23 July 1584.
[160] Res. Holl. 30 Aug. 1584; Fockema Andreae, *Nederlandse staat*, 19.

more so after Orange's death, Holland alone provided the leadership and
resources which kept the rebel Netherlands in being. Even so, the States of
Brabant, at this point, took one last major initiative in the making of the
rebel state. Support for Orange's policy of tying the fate of the Netherlands
to France, as the only possible counterweight to Spain, had in the past
derived more from Brabant than from north of the rivers. With most of
Brabant and Flanders now under the enemy, the remnants of the two
provinces saw no other recourse than to revert to Orange's pro-French
strategy. On 3 September 1584, the States of Brabant, through their agent
at The Hague, the merchant Daniel van der Meulen, proposed that the only
way to save the rebel state, and its 'freedom', was to accede to the popular
clamour (which Brabant claimed to detect) for 'one head', reminding
Holland that the greatness of the Netherlands had begun with the commencement of the Burgundian regime in the time of Philip the Good.[161]
Furthermore, the States of Brabant reminded the Hollanders, the king of
France, Henri III, unlike the Spanish king, tolerated Protestant as well as
Catholic worship.

The Brabanters' proposal led to intensive debate in Holland and Zeeland.
Holland fell into momentary disarray, the Amsterdam *vroedschap* in particular being deeply divided. The desperation in Brabant and Flanders was
beginning to seep through into Holland, and especially Zeeland, and by
October most of the States had come round to the view that sovereignty
over the Netherlands should be offered to Henri III. Only Amsterdam,
Gouda, and Medemblik still dragged their feet, Gouda more out of
defeatism and a desire to end the war than antipathy to the idea of coming
under the French Crown as such.[162] But the incipient republicanism which
had reared its head in the last months of Orange's life also played a role in
the discussions about offering sovereignty to Henri III. Again Hooft
submitted a discourse, which, though not containing any republican principles as such, argued that the towns of Holland and their allies in the other
provinces should trust in their own leadership and resources and not throw
themselves on the mercy of the king of France.[163] Hooft's main objection
was that the French king was not trustworthy, an allusion, among other
things, to his alleged complicity in the St Bartholomew's Day Massacre in
Paris. But the continuing deterioration in the general situation led to
Amsterdam's doubts being swept aside.

[161] Jongbloet-van Houtte, 'Belegering', 29, 35–6.
[162] Res. Holl. 6 Oct. 1584; Hibben, *Gouda in Revolt*, 190–1.
[163] Hooft, *Memorien*, 13–212.

A Dutch embassy, sent to Paris, offered the French king sovereignty over the Netherlands in February 1585. Henri III, his own land torn by civil war and domestic authority in tatters, fearful of not only Spain but the militant French Catholic League, judged it prudent to decline the offer. During the winter of 1584–5, Antwerp's 80,000 inhabitants, closely besieged, since Parma had completed his famous floating bridge of barges and gun-platforms, linking Spanish-held forts either side of the river, began to starve. A deepening gloom settled over the rebel state despite the unremitting efforts of the Reformed preachers to raise morale. Brussels surrendered to the Spanish army in March. The major amphibious attempt mounted by the States of Holland and Zeeland to break the siege of Antwerp, in April 1585, was repulsed. Antwerp, the commercial metropolis of the world, finally capitulated to Parma in August. There was no retribution. Parma and his troops behaved impeccably. But the city was strongly garrisoned with crack Castilian troops;[164] and Protestants who refused to reconvert to Catholicism were ordered to sell their homes and immoveable possessions and depart. Around half of Antwerp's population, some 38,000 people, emigrated to the north over the next four years.[165]

With all other options exhausted, the States General, at The Hague, turned in May 1585 to England. But Queen Elizabeth, on being offered sovereignty over the Netherlands, responded as had the king of France. She was a cautious monarch who on principle disapproved of rebellion and who had no wish to become embroiled in endless strife with Spain. To accept sovereignty over the Netherlands would mean turning the king of Spain, ruler of the most powerful monarchy in Christendom, into an irreconcilable enemy. Nevertheless, Elizabeth and her ministers feared lest Parma's triumphs lead to the collapse of the rebel state and restoration of Spanish power throughout the Low Countries. For this would place Philip in a much stronger strategic position with respect to England, as well as France, and enable him to exert greater pressure on Elizabeth to halt the expeditions to the New World which were causing such exasperation in Spain. The triumph of Parma in the Netherlands would also lift the morale of Catholics throughout Britain and Ireland and weaken the Protestant position in Europe generally.

Elizabeth, consequently, agreed to assist the States General, and rebel provinces, provided she be given a say in strategy and decision-making befitting her investment in Dutch defence.[166] If she was to take the United

---

[164] O'Donnell, *Fuerza de desembarco*, 71–2.
[165] Briels, *Zuid-Nederlanders*, 80; Thijs, *Van Geuzenstad tot katholiek bolwerk*, 37–8.
[166] Wilson, *Queen Elizabeth and the Revolt*, 81–6.

Provinces under her protection, and provide military assistance, she wanted to nominate the Republic's military and political head and be allocated seats in the *Raad van State*. The States General had no option but to agree and signed the terms which turned the United Provinces into a protectorate of England. On the Dutch side, Paulus Buys was a major influence in the making of the treaty.[167]

The treaty of Nonsuch (20 August 1585) was the United Provinces' first treaty with another European state. The queen of England undertook to send an expeditionary force of 6,350 foot and 1,000 horse, and to share the cost, together with the States.[168] To command this force, as well as the States' army, and to be political leader of the rebel state under the title 'governor-general', Elizabeth nominated the earl of Leicester. He was to supervise the collective affairs of the rebel provinces as head of the *Raad van State*, in which college the queen was also given the right to nominate two additional English representatives. Not the least advantageous aspect of the treaty, from the queen's point of view, was that it was one from which she could extricate herself quickly should she need to.

THE NORTH NETHERLANDS UNDER LEICESTER, 1585–1587

The English interlude (1585–7), though brief, was, in many ways, a formative episode in the history of the Dutch Republic. The basis of the Revolt of 1572, and its subsequent evolution in the northern Netherlands, had been the hegemony of Holland—even during the years, after 1576, when Orange had tried to focus the political leadership for the whole of the Netherlands, in Brabant. Holland's predominance had, as we have seen, been long in the making, reaching back not just decades but centuries. But, in much of the northern Netherlands, it had also been long resented, and resisted. The importance of the Leicester episode lay in its providing the forces of particularism, and opposition to Holland's hegemony, with an opportunity to remodel the infant republic along radically different lines.[169] On their own, the lesser provinces, even if Groningen, Overijssel, and Gelderland had not been partly under Spanish occupation at this time, lacked the power and resources to subordinate the Holland regents to some form of collective leadership. But the forces of anti-Holland particularism in the north plus the English influence created a new situation. Under

---

[167] Rogier, *Paulus Buys en Leicester*, 5.
[168] Wernham, 'English Policy and the Revolt', 36–8.
[169] Vijlbrief, *Van anti-aristocratie tot democratie*, 59.

English sponsorship, efforts to subordinate Holland to a different type of federal framework acquired greater plausibility.[170]

The Leicester episode was a time of profound crisis in the Dutch body politic. The leading figures of the States of Holland, among them Johan van Oldenbarnevelt, who already before Orange's death had for some time been at the helm of Holland's financial management, were from the outset determined to limit both Leicester's authority and the influence of his political allies in the north Netherlands. It was a question of control and power, but also of principles and purpose. The Holland regents had come to see their ascendancy in the affairs of the United Provinces as embodying the goals of the Revolt. Hooft had opposed offering sovereignty to the king of France on the grounds that this was incompatible with the basic purpose of the Revolt which, according to him, was to 'defend the privileges and our freedom'. For the Holland regents, the upholding of the privileges of the provinces, as they understood them, and of 'freedom', religious and political, stood or fell with the supremacy of the States of Holland.

But the issue was not simply one of how much, or how little, power the English Crown and Dutch opponents of the Holland regents, through Leicester and the English army in the Netherlands, would possess. Religion was also involved. The hardline Calvinists within the Dutch Reformed Church, strengthened by the stream of zealous Calvinists migrating from Flanders and Brabant, disliked the comparatively tolerant policy of the Holland regents.[171] Neither Orange, nor the Holland regents, had been willing to allow the Reformed Church to set its stamp on the Revolt to the extent the Calvinist clergy deemed appropriate. Ever since the Synod of Emden, in 1571, a tussle had been developing within the Church, as to how rigorously Calvinist uniformity should be imposed.[172] Since 1573, the regents had suppressed Catholic services in public churches, but been generally tolerant of private gatherings, or conventicles, for Catholic, Anabaptist, Lutheran, and other forms of worship. The strict Reformed had three basic objectives: to strengthen Calvinist orthodoxy within the public Church, curb toleration of other forms of religious practice, and increase the influence of the public Church in state and society. But they knew that while the Holland regents remained in the saddle their goals were unachievable. Their support for Leicester, a known patron of the Calvinists in England, was thus assured.

[170] Rogier, *Paulus Buys en Leicester*, 10–11; Oosterhoff, *Leicester and the Netherlands*, 71–2.
[171] Nijenhuis, *Adrianus Saravia*, 93–100.
[172] Woltjer, 'Politieke betekenis van de Emdense synode', 44–7.

Finally, festering in the background, there was the frustration of segments of the nobility.[173] The Holland regents were town representatives, the wealthiest stratum of the native-born population of the Holland towns. Since 1572, the Holland regents had led the Revolt. But in many areas of the north it was still the nobility who were the dominant class. The new governor-general, the earl of Leicester, was not only English, a patron of Calvinists, and friendly towards patricians who had fled Flanders and Brabant and resented their exclusion from influence in the north Netherlands, but also a great aristocrat who despised the upstart merchants and brewers—shopkeepers as he thought of them—who presumed to control the state. Once ensconced in the Netherlands, Leicester and his entourage naturally developed links with both the émigré nobles who had fled from the south and those elements among the nobility of the north who were disgruntled with the rule of the regents, Floris, count of Culemborg, being one of his close allies.

Robert Dudley, earl of Leicester (c.1530–88), was a colourful, somewhat baffling personality. His father, duke of Northumberland and a leading champion of the Reformation in the England of Edward VI, had been executed for master-minding the plot to put Lady Jane Grey on the throne, on Edward's death. His own rise followed Elizabeth's accession. She was strongly attached to him and held him in high favour. He became the patron of the Puritan party in English life and politics, and at the same time a noted patron of literature and scholarship. Despite his flamboyance, cosmopolitan interests, and disorderly personal life, his siding with the strict Calvinists in Dutch politics was a natural outgrowth of his family's traditions and his personal links. In matters of religion and foreign policy he was entirely consistent. He had long advocated a more vigorously anti-Spanish policy than the queen herself was inclined to pursue. Yet, at the same time, he was impulsive, as well as tactless, and overly fond of his grandeur as a great noble. There was much in his personality which sat uneasily both with his Calvinist convictions and high administrative responsibilities.[174]

Very different were the background and personality of Johan van Oldenbarnevelt (1547–1619), the man who rapidly emerged as his foremost Dutch adversary. Oldenbarnevelt was born at Amersfoort, in the province of Utrecht, to a regent family purged from the *raad* in 1543, (ironically) by René, Prince of Orange, for their anti-Habsburg sympathies. His mother's

---

[173] De Jong, *Reformatie in Culemborg*, 212–14; Oosterhoff, *Leicester and the Netherlands*, 76–82.
[174] Wilson, *Queen Elizabeth and the Revolt*, 97, 101–3.

family, the Weedes, had formerly evinced anti-Burgundian tendencies. With his homeland in uproar, the young Oldenbarnevelt spent four years (1566–70) studying at various universities abroad. On the outbreak of the Revolt, he was prompt to support the Prince of Orange and soon attracted his attention. One of his specialities being the law of dikes and drainage, he was one of the States of Holland's commissioners sent to supervise the breaking of the dikes during the siege of Leiden. In 1576, he was appointed pensionary of Rotterdam and soon became a prominent figure of the States of Holland. He rose through sheer competence and hard work, totally lacking the charm and tact of his political master. He was greatly attached to the Prince, and evidently admired him, his own strong commitment to the cause of toleration and his later pro-French policy owing not a little to William the Silent's example. It is one of the piquant ironies of the Republic's history that Oldenbarnevelt was a principal mover in the States of Holland, during the last year of the Prince's life, of the proposal to elevate him to the sovereign status of 'Count of Holland'.[175] He was also one of the delegation sent to England which, in August 1585, negotiated the treaty of Nonsuch. Shortly after Leicester's arrival, in March 1586, this experienced but not yet 40-year-old regent, despite being pensionary of a relatively minor town, and a native of Utrecht, not Holland, was appointed by the States of Holland to succeed Paulus Buys as their 'Advocate', a post which went back to Burgundian times but had gained greatly in importance since 1572. As 'Advocate', Oldenbarnevelt was the principal figure in the States of Holland as well as their spokesman in the States General.

Almost from the moment Leicester arrived, and entered into negotiations over the precise form of his power, the Dutch scene was one of confrontation and polarization. The delegation chosen to negotiate with Leicester, in January 1586, consisted of two Hollanders, Zeeland's Caspar van Vosbergen, a committed Calvinist, the *politique* Chancellor Leoninus of Gelderland, Floris Thin, a religious 'Libertine' for Utrecht, and Hessel Aysma, president of the Hof of Friesland.[176] Though the Overijssel *ridderschap*, and Kampen, supported Nonsuch, the States of Overijssel, owing to the refusal of Deventer, had not signed and, consequently, had no representation.[177]

The first issue was to resolve the matter of Stadholders. The treaty stipulated that henceforth Stadholders were to be appointed by the *Raad van State*, including its English members. In other words, no one was to be appointed Stadholder of a province without the English Crown having a say

[175] Den Tex, *Oldenbarnevelt* (English), i. 29.
[176] Brugmans, *Correspondentie*, i. 31–40.
[177] Reitsma, *Centrifugal and Centripetal Forces*, 238–9.

in the matter. Leicester and his entourage were also expecting that the Stadholders would be subordinate to the governor-general and the *Raad van State*, the institutions through which the English Crown sought to exercise its protectorate over the United Provinces. The Stadholder of Gelderland, Overijssel, and Utrecht, Count Adolf von Neuenahr, a hardline German Calvinist, and Willem Lodewijk van Nassau, Stadholder of Friesland and the Ommelands, both appointed after Orange's assassination, had received their commissions from the States General. In Holland and Zeeland, by contrast, no one had been appointed direct successor to Orange, since his eldest Protestant son, Maurits, who had lived on the Nassau lands in Germany, until 1577, was regarded as still too young and inexperienced for the office.[178] The States had, however, designated Maurits their future Stadholder by appointing him head of the newly set-up *Raad van State*, in August 1584.[179] Only in November 1585, after the signing of the treaty of Nonsuch but before the arrival of Leicester in the Netherlands, in December, had the States of Holland and Zeeland proceeded to appoint the now 17-year-old their Stadholder. They had done so, without consulting the English Crown, in an obvious manœuvre to place a check on Leicester's authority before he appeared on the scene. Furthermore, in the negotiations of January 1586, Holland and Zeeland insisted that not just Maurits but also the other two Stadholders, indeed all Stadholders in the Netherlands, derived their authority from the provinces of which they were Stadholder, arguing that Leicester could neither challenge, nor alter, their commissions, since, in the past, the Habsburg governors-general, and latterly Matthias, Leicester's predecessors, had not had the authority to appoint Stadholders.[180] This power had been reserved for the sovereign, and since sovereignty had now devolved upon the provincial States, and the States General, the very body which had offered sovereignty to Elizabeth, and proclaimed Leicester 'governor-general', it was for those bodies to appoint the Stadholders. Leicester could only grumble, remarking that the house of Orange-Nassau, since Orange's assassination, was much diminished, being 'mervellous poor, and little regarded by the States'.[181]

Another thorny issue was that of the representation of the States of Flanders and Brabant in the States General and *Raad van State*. Although only small remnants of the two provinces were still in rebel hands, Leicester was eager to retain the two provinces' representation in the federal colleges

---

[178] Van Deursen, 'Maurits', 87.
[179] Koopmans, *Staten van Holland*, 132.
[180] Brugmans, *Correspondentie*, i. 48.
[181] Van Deursen, 'Maurits', 88.

of the Republic as a further means of offsetting the primacy of Holland. He insisted on keeping their delegates in the *Raad van State*, which mostly convened, during the Leicester years, not at The Hague but in Utrecht, where the new governor-general established his headquarters. The Flemish representative on the *Raad*, Van Meetkerke, was indeed one of the earl's closest advisers. It proved harder, though, to retain Flemish and Brabant representatives in the States General. With Antwerp lost, all the towns which had possessed a vote in the States of Brabant were now again under Spanish control. Those towns of northern Brabant still in Dutch hands— Bergen-op-Zoom and Grave—historically possessed no votes in the provincial States. On these grounds, Holland and Zeeland refused to allow representatives of Brabant and Flanders to participate further in the proceedings of the States General.[182] Leicester tried to assist Bergen-op-Zoom, Grave, and a group of Brabant nobles, to obtain representation in the States General as 'the States of Brabant', but without success.[183]

A third problem was how to organize the finances of the state. By this stage only four provinces—Holland, Zeeland, Friesland, and Utrecht—were furnishing regular contributions to the States General, agreeing collectively to pay 2,400,000 guilders yearly towards the war. In principle, they also accepted that some sort of central treasury was needed.[184] But Leicester's peremptory manner of setting up his central 'Chamber of Finances', and his placing it under the enterprising Brabanter Jacques Reingauld—who had previously served several Spanish governors, as well as Anjou and Orange, as financial adviser—caused considerable irritation.[185] Reingauld was a grasping personality, fluent in French which, under Leicester, had become the official language of the *Raad van State*. But what was chiefly held against him were his efforts to extend his influence into the sphere of provincial administration and take over administration of the proceeds from confiscated Church and noble lands.[186] In the North Quarter of Holland, administration of confiscated Church property was transferred from the towns and assigned to one of Reingauld's underlings, another Brabanter, called Guillaume Mostert.

Another source of friction was Leicester's general embargo on trade with regions under the control of the enemy.[187] From a strategic point of view, Leicester had considerable justification for insisting on this embargo. Over

---

[182] Res. Holl. 1586, p. 188.
[183] Brugmans, *Correspondentie*, i. 47.
[184] Oosterhoff, *Leicester and the Netherlands*, 93–4.
[185] Bor, *Oorspronck*, iii. 31.
[186] Ibid. 57.
[187] Den Tex, 'De Staten in Oldenbarnevelt's tijd', 58.

the winter of 1585–6, there were acute shortages of food in Parma's garrisons, and the southern Netherlands generally. The Dutch Republic possessed the naval power to block the Flemish coast and Ems estuary, and guard the inland waterways and, by this means, hinder the flow of foodstuffs, as well as of munitions, both to the south Netherlands and Spanish-held zones of Gelderland, Overijssel, Drenthe, and Groningen. Leicester's embargo was imposed in April 1586, and extended, in August, so as to ban trade also with Emden, Calais, and all French ports east of the Somme estuary.

Like the ambitious river embargoes imposed by the States General later, in the 1620s and 1630s, Leicester's embargo had a considerable impact.[188] A great part of the usual barge traffic along the Dutch inland waterways was paralysed or diverted.[189] Food prices within the Republic, especially of cheese and butter, fell, bolstering Leicester's popularity amongst the urban population but depressing trade and rural rents. As Dutch merchants were no longer allowed to export grain to the Spanish Netherlands, Spain, or Portugal, the importing of grain from the Baltic in Dutch ships was also adversely affected, much of the normal traffic being diverted to England, France, and even Scotland.[190]

The confrontation between Leicester and Holland, perceptible from the outset, came to pervade every dimension of Dutch life. Practically every new development added to the irritation on either side. From Holland's point of view, not the least annoying of the earl's initiatives were his negotiations, in May 1586, with the States of Overijssel. These States still held aloof from the Union of Utrecht and, over the previous three years, had only perfunctorily participated in the States General. Leicester's method of dealing with Overijssel was through personal envoys and secret messages, instead of the formal machinery of the States General. This gave rise to the suspicion (largely justified) that in return for Overijssel's adherence to the treaty of Nonsuch, and the English alliance, the governor-general was prepared to acknowledge the special links which Overijssel persisted in claiming with the Holy Roman Empire, and respect Overijssel's desire to evade full participation in the Union of Utrecht.[191]

A fundamental aspect of the growing confrontation was that of church affairs. For years a majority of preachers of the Dutch Reformed Church had been calling for a national synod to resolve the many disputes about

---

[188] Israel, *Empire and Entrepots*, 102–3.
[189] Velius, *Chronyk van Hoorn*, 470; Kernkamp, *Handel op den vijand*, i. 185–8.
[190] Hagedorn, *Ostfrieslands Handel*, 173.
[191] De Pater, 'Leicester en Overijssel', 245–6.

doctrine and organization that had arisen since 1572. Leicester supported the call and a national synod was duly convened at The Hague. The Hague Synod drew up a strictly Calvinist Church order and rejected the claims of the provincial States to supervise the annual meetings of the provincial synods, as well as civil control over the appointment of preachers. But Leicester's National Synod remained a dead letter. Though Zeeland, Gelderland, and Overijssel accepted it, the States of Holland simply refused to adopt the new Church order.[192] Nevertheless, there was strong support for Leicester's ecclesiastical policy in church circles in Holland, as well as one or two of the Holland towns, notably Dordrecht, which adopted a consistently pro-Leicester stance during his period as governor-general.

The political crisis in the Dutch Republic took on a sharper edge in June 1586, when the militia of Utrecht, opposed to the tolerant religious policy of the Utrecht regents, began organizing meetings in the city to agitate for a more Calvinist stance and for sovereignty over the United Provinces to be offered again to Queen Elizabeth.[193] In August, some sixty Utrecht regents and nobles, opposed to Leicester and associated with the liberal Reformed Christianity which flourished in Utrecht in the congregation of the preacher Hubert Duifhuis, were driven from the city, and province, and forced to take refuge in Holland. In October, Leicester purged the city council with the backing of the militia captains, and the city's militantly Calvinist popular party, who had long been agitating for tougher measures against Catholicism.[194] A new *vroedschap* was installed which was fiercely Calvinist, anti-Catholic, and pro-English, headed by Burgomaster Gerard Prouninck, an exile from Brabant, who had been one of the main movers of 's-Hertogenbosch's brief adherence to the Union of Utrecht, in 1579.

The Holland regents were incensed by the unceremonious treatment meted out by Leicester, Neuenahr, and their supporters, to the pro-Holland regents and nobles of Utrecht. Holland refused to allow Prouninck to be admitted to the States General, as a representative for Utrecht, claiming he was a Brabanter whose election as burgomaster was illegal, and in violation of the city of Utrecht's privileges. But Holland could not prevent the new Utrecht city council taking over the leadership of the States of Utrecht, and suppressing the vote of the five ecclesiastical chapters which, since 1578, had served as a prop of noble and patrician power.[195] Once in control of the States of Utrecht, the city council, under Prouninck, became the most active

---

[192] Bor, *Oorspronck*, iii. 82v–105; Brandt, *Historie*, i. 715.
[193] Bor, *Oorspronck*, iii. 31.
[194] Oosterhoff, *Leicester and the Netherlands*, 116.
[195] Brugmans, *Correspondentie*, i. 320.

instrument of Calvinist militancy and pro-English sentiment in the Republic. The Utrecht city council also became the spokesman of the popular party in Dutch civic politics—the voice of the strongly anti-Catholic militias and guilds.

In all the provinces, Leicester, Prouninck, and their friends had plenty of matter on which to work. Like Utrecht, Friesland was racked by internal tensions. The Frisian Stadholder, Willem Lodewijk, found himself opposed by a group of fiercely particularist nobles, led by Carel Roorda; the States were locked in constant bickering with the Hof, and the towns with the three rural quarters.[196] Most Reformed preachers in Friesland were militant Calvinists, eager to confer sovereignty over the United Provinces on the queen of England.[197] Leicester and the *Raad van State* had the support of the Hof, Oostergo quarter, towns (except for Franeker), and Reformed clergy. The towns were mainly motivated by hostility to the Delegated States of Friesland, which had acquired the authority to supervise town council elections which, under the Habsburgs, had been exercised by the Hof. Since, in Friesland, the towns possessed only one-quarter of the voting power, and the rural quarters three-quarters, the former preferred to keep the States of their province as weak as possible. The Delegated States aligned with Holland.

By the time Leicester returned to England, temporarily, in December 1586, the Republic was in a state of considerable internal tension. Leicester was accused of endangering the stability of the Republic and having 'put in hazard divers provinces'. On top of everything else, the friction between the English soldiery and the local populace was causing concern. The years 1585–7, when the influx of Protestant refugees from the south Netherlands into Holland and Zeeland was at its height, was a time of exceptionally high rents and acute shortage of accommodation in the Dutch Republic.[198] As a rule, the English troops, both in the 'cautionary towns' of Flushing, Brill, and Rammekens, consigned to English control under the terms of the treaty of Nonsuch, and in other towns where English troops, were stationed, were poorly accommodated and supplied, and tended to take out their frustrations on the local populace, with predictable results. 'So great is the lack of discipline among the garrisons, especially of our nation', wrote Thomas Wilkes, one of the English members of the *Raad*, 'that I am ashamed to hear the continual complaintes which come to the councell-bord against them'.[199]

[196] Van Reyd, *Historie*, 113–14, 118.
[197] Brandt, *Historie*, i. 722.
[198] Van Meteren, *Historie*, iv. 43–4.
[199] Brugmans, *Correspondentie*, i. 46.

'We beginne to grow as hatefull to the people', he added, 'as the Spaniard himself who governeth his townes of conquest with a milder hand than we doe our frends and allyes.'

The States of Holland, under Oldenbarnevelt's leadership, lost no time in taking advantage of Leicester's absence to gain political ground. Over the objections of Dordrecht and Gorcum (which argued that major changes should not be introduced without Leicester's agreement), new regulations were adopted whereby every army officer serving in Holland and Zeeland was obliged to accept his commission from the Stadholder and swear an oath of allegiance to the provincial States. Troop movements within the provinces were no longer deemed legal unless authorized by patents signed by the Stadholder. Leicester's trade embargo was modified to dilute its impact, which so annoyed the English governor of Brill that he refused to allow the changes to be promulgated in the town.[200]

The popular reaction against the English presence strengthened the hand of the States of Holland at this critical juncture, weakening the efforts of Prouninck and Hessel Aysma (who led the pro-Leicester coalition in Friesland) to persuade the States General to offer Elizabeth sovereignty over the United Provinces on the same basis 'as Charles V did hold it'. On his return, Leicester found the 'English party' outmanoeuvred and so weakened that he came to the conclusion, over the next months, that he would either have to give up his efforts or else attempt some form of *coup d'état*—as Anjou had done in 1583. In January 1587, the English garrisons at Deventer, and in the forts around Zutphen, tired of the Dutch, defected to the Spaniards, handing over some of the Republic's key defences to Parma. The resulting 'extreame hatred' of the populace for the English soldiery in turn provoked further mutinies and defections, at Zwolle, Arnhem, and Ostend, thereby generating even greater hostility towards Leicester, and England. At the meeting of the States of Friesland in May 1587, the anti-Leicester faction dominant in Zevenwolden and Westergo gained the upper hand, shutting their leading Oostergo and town opponents out of the assembly.[201]

But there was still an appreciable residue of support for Leicester not only in Utrecht, Zeeland, and Friesland but also in Holland. All three West Frisian towns backed Leicester, being restive under the sway of the States, preferring the virtual autonomy which they had enjoyed in the early years of the Revolt when they had been cut off from the rest of Holland by the

[200] Ibid. ii. 148.   [201] Broersma and Busken Huet, *Brieven*, 66, 71.

Spanish garrisons in Haarlem and Amsterdam. Further south there were only two Holland towns which acted 'against the States', Dordrecht and Gorcum, but, in the other cities, not least Amsterdam and Leiden, Leicester enjoyed strong support among the militantly Calvinist sections of the militias.[202] Some of the Holland nobility (who were not aligned with the clique who led the *ridderschap* in the States of Holland) also, it seems, backed Leicester. According to one report, of February 1587, 'Mylord Brederode and his lady, and the eldest sister of Egmond, and the rest of the nobility of this country, and most of the people but specially all the ministers are for your Excellency'.[203] In Holland, as in Utrecht, some nobles felt antagonistic, on class grounds, to the Holland regents.[204]

During the summer of 1587, Leicester prepared his coup, fomenting opposition to the Holland *vroedschappen* amongst the citizenry and militias, in concert with Dierik Sonoy, military governor of the West Frisian district, who had declined to take the new oath of allegiance to the Stadholder and the States. In September, Leicester moved fresh troops into Holland, occupying Gouda, Schoonhoven, and other places. He entered The Hague with a strong escort in what was probably a mishandled attempt to arrest Maurits and Oldenbarnevelt. When this failed he tried to engineer subversion against the regent town governments, particularly where his popular backing was strongest, in Leiden and Amsterdam. The pro-Leicester movement in Leiden seems to have been chiefly a form of reaction among the immigrant Flemish and Brabant population—which by 1587 totalled over 10,000[205]—against native-born regents whose authority they resented and Protestant commitment they considered lukewarm.[206] A principal conspirator at Leiden was the hardline Calvinist professor of theology, Adrianus Saravia, who denied the States of Holland were sovereign in the province.[207] When the plot collapsed, Saravia and some others escaped but three Flemish conspirators were seized, tried, and beheaded. Leicester made a final try, going in person to Amsterdam, but when this failed, gave up in disgust and returned to England. Thus, the last and most broadly supported attempt to bring the rebel provinces under the benign protection and control of a foreign ruler ended in failure.

[202] Van Reyd, *Historie*, 237–42.
[203] Broersma and Busken Huet, *Brieven*, 168.
[204] Ibid. 105.
[205] Briels, *Zuid-Nederlanders*, 131.
[206] Van Reyd, *Historie*, 237–8.
[207] Nijenhuis, *Adrianus Saravia*, 107.

PART II

The Early Golden Age
1588–1647

❖

11

Consolidation of the Republic, 1588–1590

❖

During the tense and difficult years 1585–7, the United Provinces were the scene of a sustained attempt to challenge the political and military ascendancy gained by Holland over the embryonic state emerging from the Revolt. By backing Leicester, and the moves to confer sovereignty over the rebel Netherlands on the queen of England, a coalition of disaffected groups—by no means only in the lesser provinces—sought to overthrow the hegemony of the Holland regents and replace it with a very different framework, one that was monarchical, more aristocratic, and also more supportive of the concept of a state Church to which all, or most, of the population would be obliged to conform. The contending parties produced no sophisticated political thought. But they certainly argued in terms of monarchies and republics, and those who backed the States of Holland understood, in rudimentary fashion, that they were espousing republican forms and views. Fending off Leicester strengthened the notion perceptible earlier, which Hooft had expressed in his discourse of 1584, that the 'freedom' of the Netherlands would be best preserved by dispensing with the protection of any monarch. Noting the change in mood, in July 1590 Thomas Wilkes commented: 'they hate to be subject not only to a Spaniard but, tasting the sweetness of their liberty, to any kingly government'.[1]

Yet, inevitably, at least in the short term, the struggle within further weakened the Republic and its prospects of survival.[2] If Leicester's regime failed to halt the creeping Spanish reconquest of the Low Countries, his humiliation did nothing to stop it either. Despite diversion of Spanish strength for the Armada campaign against England, in 1588, Parma's troops kept up their steady encroachment from the south, east, and north-east.[3] The garrisons at Groningen, Steenwijk, and Coevorden mounted incursions into Friesland. Parma failed to capture Bergen-op-Zoom in his 1588 offensive,

[1] Wernham, 'Mission of Thomas Wilkes', 452.
[2] Oosterhoff, *Leicester and the Netherlands*, 186–8.
[3] Wilson, *Queen Elizabeth and the Revolt*, 107–9.

but only just. In 1589, he was compensated by the betrayal—by its English garrison—of Geertruidenberg, on the southern fringe of Holland.

In 1588, the United Provinces' strategic situation seemed as precarious as ever. Yet, over the three years 1588–90, the outlook improved dramatically, a crucial transition for Dutch, and all European, history. From being a divided, enfeebled state, incapable of defending its territory, the Republic was transformed into a viable confederacy in which the particularist pressures of the Leicester years were still evident but accommodated, within an orderly and stable framework. The contrast with the immediate past was striking. Writing in April 1589, Thomas Bodley considered the Dutch state 'weaker at this present than it hath been these many years; and unless by Her majesty's extraordinary assistance, and counsel, it be presently holpen, there is little appearance that they can hold it out long'.[4] Little more than a year later, Wilkes was greatly struck by the subsiding of opposition to the States of Holland: 'the mislike of the States, bred in the people heretofore by faction is now removed and the government so quieted and settled (as the States themselves avow) that since the beginning of their troubles the like was never seen'.[5]

This remarkable change was partly the result of external factors, especially shifts in strategy, and foreign policy, on the part of two key monarchs—Elizabeth and Philip II. But it was also the result of internal changes, the growing power of the States of Holland, and, not least, the skilful statecraft of Oldenbarnevelt. It may be that if Elizabeth had not decided, in 1588, to drop her support for Oldenbarnevelt's opponents, and Philip not resolved, in 1590, to concentrate on France, rather than his rebels, for the foreseeable future, developments would have taken a very different course. But it is also true that even had Elizabeth and Philip made the decisions they did but no effective framework been found for resolving the tensions between, and within, the provinces of the Republic, cohesion and stability would have continued to elude the rebel state.

Leicester left a land seething with internecine strife, resentment, and betrayal. The English troops, ill-lodged and ill-paid, and often hungry, were as disgruntled after his departure as before, and as liable to back militant Calvinists against the States of Holland—or intrigue with the Spaniards.[6] Oldenbarnevelt's opponents remained formidable in Friesland, Zeeland, and Overijssel and dominant in Utrecht.[7] Supported by the city militia and

---

[4] Wernham, 'Mission of Thomas Wilkes', 450.
[5] Ibid. 452.
[6] Bor, *Oorspronck*, ii, part 2, 55.
[7] Den Tex, 'Staten in Oldenbarnevelt's tijd', 64.

Calvinist preachers, Burgomaster Prouninck denounced the States of Holland for prizing their own power and authority above all else and striving to dominate other provinces, at the expense of the security, well-being, and spiritual salvation of the population.[8] The States of Utrecht, controlled by the city, and Calvinist faction of the *ridderschap*, continued during the spring of 1588 loudly and uncompromisingly to oppose Holland's leadership. Considering the States General merely the mouthpiece of Holland, the States of Utrecht wanted the federal assembly to have as little authority as possible,[9] preferring to regard the *Raad van State* (where England's, rather than Holland's, influence predominated) as the right body to direct the state and supervise the provinces. Citing Nonsuch, and appealing to London, Utrecht strove to bolster the *Raad van State* and weaken the States General.[10] If this enhanced the queen of England's influence in the Dutch body politic, so much the better. 'Monarchy is best,' insisted the States of Utrecht, in April 1588, 'indeed the only means to overcome all confusion and disorder, and preserve these lands.'[11] The States brusquely rejected Holland's strictures that individual provinces, under the terms of the Union of Utrecht, had no right to appeal to, or negotiate with, the queen, or any ruler, separately from the States General.

In Friesland too the bitter dissension and chronic disarray continued. Leicester had abandoned his plan to go in person to Friesland and 'redress all stryfes that weare amongst them'.[12] But the Frisian Stadholder, Willem Lodewijk, and the Frisian Delegated States, having switched from supporting Leicester to opposing him, had also been unable to consolidate their grip and faced widespread opposition, despite the backing, for the moment, of the strongly particularist faction of Carel Roorda and his adherents who had been outraged by Leicester's efforts to impose the taxes and excises of the 'General Means' (see pp. 285–8 below) 'in lyke manner as in Holland and Zeeland which never was before'.[13] Willem Lodewijk and his supporters were opposed by most of the towns, the Reformed clergy, and the pro-English Oostergo quarter, which vehemently complained of the 'cruelty and tyranny done unto them by the deputies of the States of that province [i.e. the new Delegated States]'. The brother of the president of the Hof of Friesland, a leading *grietman* in Oostergo, was sent by the gentry of his

[8] Kossmann and Mellink, *Texts*, 269–72.
[9] RAU SU 231/4, fos. 12, 28–9. res. 6 Feb. and 9 Apr. 1588.
[10] Bannatyne, 'Utrecht in Crisis', 42–3.
[11] RAU SU 231/4, fo. 26. res. 9 Apr. 1588.
[12] PRO SP 84/30, fo. 9. 'The government in Freeslande at this present' (1588).
[13] Ibid., fos. 9v–10.

quarter to London in May 1588, to appeal directly to Elizabeth against their Stadholder and the Roordists.

Overcoming the centrifugal forces at work in the lesser provinces, as well as the disintegrative tendencies within them—and the Calvinist challenge— was not easy. That the situation could be stabilized so quickly was, in no small measure, due to the energy and skill, during this early part of his career, of Oldenbarnevelt. He was not exactly adroit. Bodley found Olden- barnevelt, at this time, 'very stiffe' and uncooperative, 'his ordinarie phrase' being 'somewhat violent, imperious and bitter'.[14] But he was effective. Oldenbarnevelt, it has been justly said, 'was never so great as in the year [1588] in which he laid the foundation of Netherlands independence'.[15]

One development which Oldenbarnevelt cleverly exploited was the grow- ing rift in Utrecht—since late 1586—between the Stadholder, Count Neue- nahr, on the one hand, and Prouninck, the hardline Reformed preachers, and militia, on the other.[16] The count's brushes with his erstwhile allies, especially Herman Moded, the city's leading Reformed preacher, led him to abandon the 'English faction' and ally with the pro-Holland Utrecht patricians, headed by Floris Thin, former Advocate of the States of Utrecht.[17] Preceding *vroedschap* elections in October 1588, there were disturbances in Utrecht which Neuenahr used as a pretext to arrest Prouninck and orchestrate a coup in the city council, removing Prouninck's, and restoring Thin's, followers. With this, the ascendancy in Utrecht of the 'English faction', and their Calvinist allies, was over. Thin resumed control of the States. The suppressed first (ecclesiastical) estate of the States of Utrecht was revived. The liberal (non-Calvinist) Reformed congregation of Hubert Duifhuis resumed services.

Another threat overcome in a way which strengthened Holland's position was the particularism of the West Frisian towns. Sonoy, having barricaded himself in at Medemblik, openly defied the States of Holland, supported by the strong pro-English faction in the area, particularly the city of Enk- huizen.[18] The obstreperousness of the West Frisian towns was aggravated by the States of Holland's decision to back Amsterdam, against them, in a dispute over the Republic's admiralty administration, which everyone agreed had to be reorganized, Leicester having placed naval and maritime affairs under a single college designed to minimize Holland's influence. The

[14] PRO SP 84/30, fo. 187. Bodley to Walsingham, 30 Jan. 1589.
[15] Den Tex, *Oldenbarnevelt* (English), i. 125.
[16] Broersma and Busken Huet, *Brieven*, 94–5.
[17] Bannatyne, 'Utrecht in Crisis', 44–5.
[18] Brandt, *Historie . . . Enkhuizen*, 183.

danger posed by West Frisian particularism at this point was skilfully removed by a combination of restrained threat of force and negotiation. Medemblik was blockaded by States of Holland troops, under Maurits. The inland towns of the North Quarter—Alkmaar, Edam, Purmerend, and Monnikendam—were encouraged to oppose the pretensions of the three West Frisian ports, splitting the *Gecommitteerde Raden* of the North Quarter. Finally, Oldenbarnevelt brokered a solution, accepted by all parties, in October 1589, whereby Amsterdam and West Frisia each acquired its own admiralty college, and separate zone of jurisdiction, under supervision of the States General, while the North Quarter, as a whole, retained its separate college of *Gecommitteerde Raden* but now with the West Frisian towns as an acknowledged entity within the North Quarter, their three votes in the college to be counted as equal in weight to those of the four inland towns.[19] The college continued to gather chiefly at Hoorn.

Over the winter of 1587–8, the English soldiery were in a mutinous mood in not only West Frisia and Geertruidenberg, but also Naarden, Veere, and several other places.[20] But the presence of the English army posed less of a political threat to Holland than one might suppose. Though present in small numbers in numerous places, the bulk were concentrated in four garrisons tucked away in and around Zeeland, or beyond—in Ostend, in such a way as to pose no real threat to Holland or the most volatile provinces—Friesland and Utrecht (see Table 6). Furthermore, the risk of English intervention evaporated early in 1588, as the menace of the Invincible Armada loomed larger. Once convinced the Armada was in earnest, Elizabeth appreciated that she needed Dutch naval co-operation and was not going to get it whilst her officers, in the Republic, continued obstructing the States on her orders. In April 1588, Elizabeth withdrew her support for the anti-Holland factions, issuing instructions that her commanders henceforth co-operate with Maurits, as captain-general, and the States of Holland. Thus, ironically, Philip II's Armada played an appreciable role, in the months after Leicester's departure, in easing tensions within the Dutch body politic and furthering its consolidation.

The death of Neuenahr at Arnhem, when a gunpowder store he was inspecting exploded, in October 1589—the month of the marriage of Rembrandt's parents, at Leiden, gave Oldenbarnevelt the opportunity to extend Holland's ascendancy further by arranging Maurits's succession as Stadholder of Gelderland, Utrecht, and Overijssel. After some delay the

---

[19] Ibid. 188–9; Fockema Andreae, *Nederlandse staat*, 45.
[20] Bor, *Oorspronck*, ii, part 2, 55.

young head of the house of Orange-Nassau thus became Stadholder also of these provinces, eliminating what had been a separate focus of military command and patronage, and enhancing Holland's role in making strategic decisions, and regulating frontier fortresses, on the eastern side of the Republic.[21]

TABLE 6. *The English garrisons in the Netherlands, August 1588*

Garrison	Strength		Garrison	Strength	
	Nominal	Actual		Nominal	Actual
Flushing	2,100	1,445	Wageningen	900	606
Ostend	1,650	1,245	Utrecht	350	315
Bergen-op-Zoom	1,750	1,068	Amersfoort	77	52
Brill	950	852	Bergh	90	77

Source: PRO SP 84/26, fos. 101–2.

But the key breakthrough was Oldenbarnevelt's success in wresting military and strategic decisions away from the *Raad van State*, nominally to the States General but, in practice, to the States of Holland. English ministers, and commanders in the Republic, tried to resist this process but, having been ordered by their queen to assist Oldenbarnevelt in much else, found it difficult to prevent the 'moste mightie and riche of all the provinces', Holland, from becoming the body to which the 'rest doe alwaies incline'.[22] All that the English members of the *Raad* could do was protest, impotently, to London, at Holland's proceeding 'so premptorily and so flatt against the treaty and against the good liking of the Council of State'. The *Raad* continued to discharge great quantities of business (as it was to do throughout the history of the Dutch Republic). 'The Council of State', in 1590, 'doth never fail to sit twice every daie unless there be some extraordinary lett, in the morning, from nine of the clock till twelve, and from four to seven, in the afternoone':[23] Several of the Dutch members of the *Raad*, including the two Zeelanders, Jacob Valck and Burgomaster Teellinck, of Zierikzee, and the two Frisians, were key members of the provincial States. But, precisely for this reason, they were willing to help the three Hollanders on the board nullify the English presence and turn the *Raad* from being the executive of the United Provinces into a mere administrative organ of the States General.

[21] Van Deursen, 'Maurits', 90.
[22] PRO SP 84/38, fo. 155. Wilkes to Burghley, 7 Aug. 1590.
[23] Ibid., fo. 18.

With Leicester gone, and the *Raad van State* reduced, the activity of the States General steadily expanded. Overijssel, having boycotted the Generality for three years, resumed participation, from December 1587.[24] Of the northern provinces, only Groningen and Drenthe (which never gained a seat) were still missing. By 1590, the States General was a hive of activity, convening practically every day, often morning and afternoon. Officially, Oldenbarnevelt, as Advocate of the States of Holland and pensionary of the Holland *Ridderschap*, had no formal function in the States General. But as he was Holland's main spokesman, and controlled the flow of diplomatic correspondence in and out of the States General's offices, he enjoyed an unchallengeable ascendancy over what went on in the federal assembly. The States General had its own secretary, or *griffier*, to handle incoming diplomatic correspondence. But the holder of this office, the Brabanter Cornelis van Aerssen, became more and more subservient to Oldenbarnevelt.

By 1590, the only avenue by which English ministers in the Netherlands could hope to check Holland, and uphold a degree of English influence, was by encouraging the lesser provinces to play a more independent role in the States General. But, to do this, they needed to strengthen the influence of Oldenbarnevelt's opponents in the lesser provinces. When Floris Thin died, in 1590, the 'English' party for a time hoped that Paulus Buys (who was the son of an Amersfoort miller) would succeed him as Advocate of the States of Utrecht.[25] Buys, despite his resigning as Advocate of Holland in October 1584, had helped shape the United Provinces' pro-English strategy, in 1585, and been held in high esteem in England ever since. After his break with the States of Holland he had also become a leading proponent of a more centralized federal system, and building up the *Raad van State*, at the expense of Holland. He had become estranged from Leicester, however, disliking the populist Calvinism of the Utrecht guilds, the theocratic ideas of Moded, and Leicester's partiality for south Netherlanders.[26] But, like Thin and Leoninus, he remained a pillar of the Generality idea, wanting the States General to be led by a revived *Raad van State* rather than the States of Holland. He was also as brusque and imperious as Oldenbarnevelt. But Holland's Advocate deftly thwarted the campaign for Buys, securing the election of his own protégé, Gillis van Ledenberg. From 1590, down until the overthrow of Oldenbarnevelt, in 1618, the States of Utrecht were little

---

[24] Slicher van Bath, *Gesch. van Overijssel*, 125.
[25] PRO SP 84/39, fos. 32v, 12lv. Bodley to Burghley, 28 Sept. and 7 Oct. 1590.
[26] Rogier, *Paulus Buys en Leicester*, 11.

more than an appendage of Holland. Oldenbarnevelt, in effect, now presided over Utrecht, as well as Holland.[27]

Despite the military setbacks of the late 1580s, the Dutch Republic conquered its internal difficulties, forging an orderly, efficient federal state, organized and directed from the Hague, by Oldenbarnevelt and the States of Holland. All disruptive internal pressures were, if not eliminated, then neutralized in a way which enabled the Holland-dominated Dutch federal state to seize fully the opportunity which the new strategic situation arising in 1590 offered. The result was a series of dazzling successes in almost every sphere.

[27] Den Tex, 'Staten in Oldenbarnevelt's tijd', 66–7.

12

The Republic Becomes a Great Power,
1590–1609

❖

TERRITORIAL EXPANSION

By the late 1580s, the Republic resembled a compressed spring taut with pent-up impetus. After the loss of Zutphen and Deventer virtually the whole eastern side of the north Netherlands, from Nijmegen to the Ems estuary, was again under Spanish control, the States General's troops retreating west of the IJssel. During 1589, the Spaniards took Geertruidenberg and Rheinberg, and besieged Heusden, squeezing the Dutch also along the rivers, to the south. But within this contracting territory, besieged by Spanish armies to the south, east, and north-east, a restructuring of institutions, military organization, and the economy was in progress which, as events were to prove, immeasurably enhanced the prospects of the surviving core of the rebel state.[1]

Successful state-building on the scale achieved in the 1590s, by the Republic, occurs only rarely in history and only when internal changes combine with exceptionally favourable circumstances without. It was Philip II's decision to switch the bulk of the Spanish army of Flanders away from the north Netherlands, and intervene in the French civil war, in the hope of preventing the Protestant Henri IV from securing himself as king of France, which transformed the strategic balance and gave the Dutch their opportunity. But the impetus of the Republic's rise in the 1590s, to become one of the principal military and naval powers of Europe, and the leading commercial power, was possible only because of the far-reaching developments in the Republic's core during the years of retreat and reverses.

From 1590, there was a dramatic improvement in the Republic's economic circumstances (see pp. 307–21 below). Commerce and shipping expanded enormously, as did the towns. As a result, the financial power of

[1] Fruin, *Tien jaren*, 94.

the state rapidly grew;[2] and it was possible to improve the army vastly, both qualitatively, and quantitatively, within a short space of time. The army increased from 20,000 men in 1588 to 32,000 by 1595, and its artillery, methods of transportation, and training were transformed.[3] During the offensive of the 1590s, the army, commanded by Maurits, captured large parts of five Dutch provinces—Gelderland, Overijssel, Drenthe, Groningen, and north Brabant—taking in all forty-three towns (including a number of strongholds in adjacent German lands) and fifty-five forts (see Map 7).

Many of these towns had impressive fortifications and these, and the profusion of forts, attest to the strenuous efforts made by Parma, since recapturing Antwerp in 1585, to create a network of strongholds in the newly reconquered areas, both to hold them and to serve as a springboard for further Spanish advances. This fortified network, achieved at massive expense, became still more vital to Spain, and the Catholic cause, in the Low Countries when Philip ordered the army of Flanders to combine with the Armada in the projected invasion of England, in 1587–8, and during the army's interventions in France, in the 1590s. For Parma's forts and refortified towns were now the chief barrier between north and south. The Castilian troops in the Spanish Netherlands were not only the spearhead of the army but served to secure the most vital garrisons—Antwerp, Ghent, and Dendermonde, as well as Dunkirk and Nieuwpoort commanding the Flemish coast, and Sluis and Sas van Ghent, the fortress towns facing the Dutch enclaves on the Scheldt estuary.[4] Neapolitan troops held Breda. Parma was not so unwilling to trust the 'Walloon' infantry with holding towns exposed to the Dutch as his senior Spanish officers. Nevertheless, in both Brussels and Madrid the Spaniards and Italians continued to be considered vital for securing the south Netherlands for Spain and holding the front separating north and south.

The Dutch break-out began in 1590 with the surprise capture of Breda. Initially, despite the prodding of the Frisian Stadholder (who was the first fully to realize the opportunity which the Republic now enjoyed), Oldenbarnevelt, Maurits, and the *Raad van State* were slow to organize a major offensive. But, by the spring of 1591, the United Provinces were ready. Extra money had been raised, and forces amassed, and the States of Friesland persuaded to allow their contingents to operate far from their province, on the IJssel front. Provided with an army of quality, of 26,000 men—the first large field army the Republic deployed—Maurits and Willem Lodewijk

[2] 't Hart, *Making of a Bourgeois State*, 59–61.
[3] Ten Raa and De Bas, *Staatsche leger*, ii. 346–9.
[4] O'Donnell, *Fuerza de desembarco*, 72–4, 171.

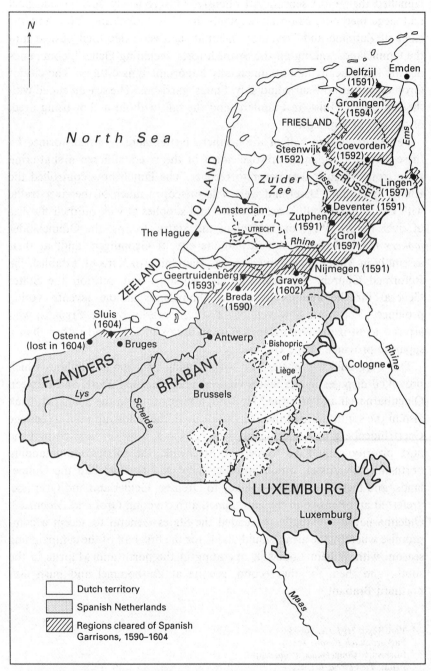

N

North Sea

Delfzijl
(1591)

Emden

Groningen
(1594)

FRIESLAND

Steenwijk
(1592)

Coevorden
(1592)

OVERIJSSEL

Ems

Zuider
Zee

HOLLAND

Lingen
(1597)

Deventer (1591)

Amsterdam

Zutphen
(1591)

The Hague

UTRECHT

Grol
(1597)

Rhine

Nijmegen (1591)

ZEELAND

Geertruidenberg
(1593)

Grave
(1602)

Breda
(1590)

Sluis
(1604)

Ostend
(lost in 1604)

Bruges

Antwerp

Bishopric
of
Liège

Rhine

Cologne

FLANDERS

BRABANT

Lys

Schelde

Brussels

LUXEMBURG

Luxemburg

Maas

	Dutch territory
	Spanish Netherlands
	Regions cleared of Spanish Garrisons, 1590–1604

MAP 7. Dutch recovery of territory from the Spanish Netherlands (1590–1604)

launched their most sensational offensive.[5] Using newly devised transport and siege methods, Maurits swept up the IJssel, capturing forts, and the cities of Zutphen and Deventer, in rapid succession. He then pushed into the Ommelands, taking all the Spanish forts, including Delfzijl, commanding the strategically and commercially important Ems estuary. The city of Groningen was now surrounded by States' garrisons. The season ended with the capture of Hulst, in Flanders, and the fall, without a shot being fired, of the city of Nijmegen.

The entire eastern half of the northern Netherlands was transformed by these victories.[6] Spanish prestige north of the rivers suffered a shattering blow from which it was never to recover. The Dutch now controlled the Rhine, Waal, and IJssel and were able to reopen much of the river traffic with Germany as well as move troops and supplies at will, on their flotillas of river barges. With the arrival of the States' troops, the Ommelander *jonkers* revolted against Spain and the city of Groningen, and, at their assembly in March 1592, voted to sign the Union of Utrecht, establish the Reformed Church, suppress Catholic worship—and petition the States General for the admittance of the Ommelands as the seventh voting province.[7] This was, however, blocked temporarily by the Frisians, who aspired to turn the Ommelands into an annex of Friesland rather than a separate province of the Generality.

The 1591 offensive opened up wide-ranging strategic possibilities which provoked disputes in the States General and *Raad van State*, and between Oldenbarnevelt and Maurits.[8] Holland, aspiring to push the Spaniards back also in the south, wanted the army to be used, the following year, to besiege Geertruidenberg or 's-Hertogenbosch. Friesland, however, argued that the next priority should be to besiege Steenwijk, the fortress commanding north-west Overijssel, which posed a threat to Friesland and the Ommelands, and then Coevorden—the key to Drenthe. Gelderland and Overijssel preferred an offensive in the east, aimed at recovering Grol and Oldenzaal. Oldenbarnevelt eventually persuaded the States General to accept a compromise whereby the army would divide for the first half of the campaigning season, with Willem Lodewijk operating in the north and Maurits in the south, and then, for the second, reunite at Zaltbommel and push into northern Brabant.[9]

[5] Van Reyd, *Historie*, 296–8.
[6] Parker, *Dutch Revolt*, 228–9.
[7] Formsma, *Ommelander strijd*, 140–1.
[8] Fruin, *Tien jaren*, 121–2.
[9] PRO SP 84/45, fo. 77v. Bodley to Burghley, 4 July 1592.

But Maurits ignored all this and joined his cousin in besieging Steenwijk. The siege of this formidable fortress town, defended by 1,060 crack Spanish troops, was seen as one of Maurits's most remarkable exploits. Traditional methods would have involved the town being sealed off and slowly starved into surrender. But it was well supplied and, besieged in this manner, could have resisted for months. Maurits abbreviated matters by cudgelling the garrison with unheard-of quantities of artillery. Fifty artillery pieces fired a total of 29,000 shots. The Stadholder also employed novel methods of advancing his trenches, and mine shafts, devised by his chief engineers, Joost Matthieu, a south Netherlands refugee, and Jacob Kemp of Gorcum. Another new feature was that the Dutch soldiery, instead of disdaining pick and shovel, as was usual among sixteenth-century armies, were made to emulate the ancient Romans and do their own digging without relying on local peasants to assist. Some years before the Stadholder had specially consulted the great humanist scholar Justus Lipsius as to how the Romans had organized their digging. The stronghold surrendered after forty-four days.

After Steenwijk the Stadholders proceeded to besiege Coevorden, one of the three remaining major Spanish fortresses in the north-east, despite grumbling in the States of Holland 'for that Count Maurice in this siege', as Bodley explained, 'hath taken contrary courses to their special directions'.[10] Coevorden, relentlessly bombarded, surrendered after six weeks, bringing all Drenthe under the control of the States General. Immediately, Friesland and Overijssel began to quarrel over which province should garrison Coevorden and be responsible for defending Drenthe. Friesland, like Holland, eagerly used the fixed garrisons on her provincial allocation or *répartition*, and in her pay, as an instrument for extending her influence. A strongly particularist element in the States of Friesland, headed by Carel Roorda, nurtured the ambition of extending Frisian hegemony over not only the Ommelands but also Drenthe, north-west Overijssel, and more.[11] Willem Lodewijk, who preferred co-operation with Maurits and Holland to pursuing narrowly Frisian aims, clashed repeatedly with the Roordists, who accused their Stadholder of proceeding contrary to Friesland's interests and designing to enslave Friesland to 'neighbouring provinces', meaning Holland and Overijssel.[12] Meanwhile, the States of Overijssel complained incessantly in the States General of Friesland's arrogant violations of her

[10] PRO SP 84/45, fo. 213. Bodley to Burghley, 31 Aug. 1592.
[11] Van Reyd, *Historie*, 324, 398.
[12] Ibid. 350.

provincial sovereignty by keeping garrisons in Hasselt and Steenwijk which the Generality had asked Friesland to remove.[13]

The following year Holland insisted on the main campaign being launched in the south, selecting Geertruidenberg as the target. This siege became one of the most celebrated of Maurits's feats. For the town was strongly fortified and located on soft ground near a wide river within easy reach of the main centres of Spanish power further south. Only a few years before the States General would never have dared contemplate such a venture and the regime in Brussels had supposed it safe. To hasten completion of his entrenchments Maurits again ordered his men to dig, inducing them to work rapidly and methodically by paying them an extra wage of ten stuivers daily—equivalent to a labourer's wage—separately from their normal pay, with extra bonuses for those working in especially exposed positions.[14] The work proceeded at such speed that by the time the Spanish relief army appeared it was already too late to break the siege. To prevent his guns sinking into the mud, Maurits's engineers devised special wooden mats. The novelty of the siege works and discipline of the soldiery was such that his camp became thronged with local folk who, seeing there was no molestation or pilfering, came to sell their produce to the soldiers. It also became a tourist attraction for fine ladies, including Louise de Coligny, William the Silent's fourth and last wife, who with her companions rode out from The Hague to visit the scene. Geertruidenberg capitulated, after a four-month siege, in June 1593.

Meanwhile the wrangling between the provinces continued unabated. Roorda opposed domination of Friesland by Holland.[15] But the truth was that there was no alternative to Holland's leadership and ascendancy. For the lesser provinces were not only at odds with each other but also lacked the internal cohesion, and stability, without which no state can long survive. If the United Provinces were to function as a viable political entity the necessary cohesion could only derive from Holland. In this lay the central paradox of the Republic, throughout its history, to 1795: it was perennially a cross between the confederacy of sovereign provinces which it was in theory and the federal entity which, in most respects, it was in reality. 'The warp of the federal elements in the system of government' was, indeed, as one Dutch historian has expressed it, 'interwoven with an unmistakably confederal woof'.[16] The predominance, and unparalleled internal cohesion,

[13] Res. SG 1 Sept. 1592 and 10 Aug. 1593.
[14] Van Meteren, *Historie*, vi. 11–12.
[15] Kalma *et al., Gesch. van Friesland*, 281.
[16] Boogman, 'Union of Utrecht', 396.

of Holland were the twin pillars on which the viability and durability of the United Provinces rested. Without these the entire edifice was unsustainable, perhaps even without outside pressure, through the weight of its own internal contradictions and weakness.

But, even with Holland's strength and Oldenbarnevelt's dexterity, the seething conflicts among, and within, the lesser provinces were not easily settled. The Frisians were irreconcilably split, the Ommelander *jonkers* fearful, on the one side, of Friesland and, on the other, of the city of Groningen, while Hasselt and Steenwijk resisted the States of Overijssel, which, in turn, claimed Coevorden and historic rights over Drenthe, aspirations vigorously opposed by Friesland, the Ommelands, and Groningen.[17]

Oldenbarnevelt unfastened the knot, helped by the two Stadholders, who both saw (whatever their private thoughts about Oldenbarnevelt) that collaboration with Holland was the only way to make the infant republic viable politically and militarily. Either they helped enforce Holland's predominance over the rest, or the entire edifice disintegrated. There was no other possibility. Thus, eventually, a package was worked out at The Hague, and imposed by Holland through the States General.[18] The Frisians were required to evacuate north-west Overijssel and Hasselt and Steenwijk to submit to the States of Overijssel; Coevorden was to continue to be garrisoned by Friesland, temporarily, while neither Friesland nor Overijssel were to have proprietary rights over Drenthe, the future of which would be decided by the Generality—that is Holland.

Spanish forces blockaded Coevorden late in 1593 but failed to recapture the town. With their withdrawal, the capitulation of Groningen, and elimination of Spanish power from the north-east, was just a matter of time. The States General had made no declaration, as yet, about the future of the city, but shortly before the siege began, in April 1594, did vote, by five provinces to one (over the objections of Friesland), to admit the Ommelands—whose territory surrounded the city—as the seventh voting province of the Union.[19] Oldenbarnevelt, and the Holland regents, aware the city was large, well-fortified, resolutely anti-States and pro-Spanish, and hoping to avoid the disruption and expense of a lengthy siege, tried various ploys to induce an early capitulation. Initially, until May 1594, Oldenbarnevelt encouraged the Groningen *raad* to believe they might escape the horrors of a long siege and retain the exercise of the Catholic faith and right to garrison their outlying forts, and even be acknowledged, by the United Provinces, a

---

[17] Heringa, *Gesch. van Drenthe*, 283–4.
[18] Bor, *Oorspronck*, iv. 23–4.
[19] Formsma, *Ommelander strijd*, 146.

city of the Holy Roman Empire under the protection of the Emperor, if they laid down their arms and renounced Philip II.[20] Subsequently, one of the States' commanders, count von Hohenlohe, lieutenant-general of Holland, negotiated secretly with the *raad* about a possible transfer of lordship over the city from Philip II to the Lutheran duke of Brunswick, though this was possibly only a device to sow discord in the city. In any case, the negotiations came to nothing. The siege lasted two months and cost the lives of 400 States' troops and 300 defenders, and consumed ten thousand Dutch cannon-balls. As the city weakened, the magistracy tried to arrange for Catholics to retain one church in the city, but this was refused. On Groningen's capitulation, the whole body of friars and priests that since 1591 had taken refuge within the walls marched out, together with the soldiery and camp women, on their long trek to the Catholic south Netherlands. The city *raad* was purged and the practice of the Catholic faith officially banned.

It was stipulated in the capitulation that Groningen would now enter the Union and that the States General would determine how this should be accomplished.[21] Historically, city and Ommelands had never formed a single entity and their mutual antagonism remained as acute as ever. Conquered by the States General, in effect Holland, Groningen was now bracketed with the Ommelands to make a seventh voting province, which was essentially artificial, a concoction of the Generality.[22] The States General set up a committee comprising Willem Lodewijk, who (to the displeasure of the Roordists) had been designated Stadholder of the new province, Chancellor Leoninus of Gelderland, a Kampen burgomaster, and a delegate from Holland to draft recommendations as to how the new province should function.

What emerged was a States of 'City and Ommelands'—as the states of Groningen were officially entitled—comprising two 'members'—the city and the Ommelands—with approximately half of the population of the province each. The Ommelands continued to be divided into three quarters—Hunsingo, Fivelingo, and Westerkwartier—each with its own quarter assembly, while the city continued to speak also for its subject territories of 't Gorecht and Oldambt (see Map 8). The city was given precedence in signing documents and voting first,[23] but otherwise the two votes carried equal weight. Since this implied perpetual deadlock, a casting vote was assigned

[20] Formsma, 'Aanbieding', 1.
[21] *Journaal van Anthonis Duyck*, i. 460.
[22] Wiersum, *Gedwongen vereeniging*, 20–3.
[23] Emmius, *De Agro Frisiae*, 171–5.

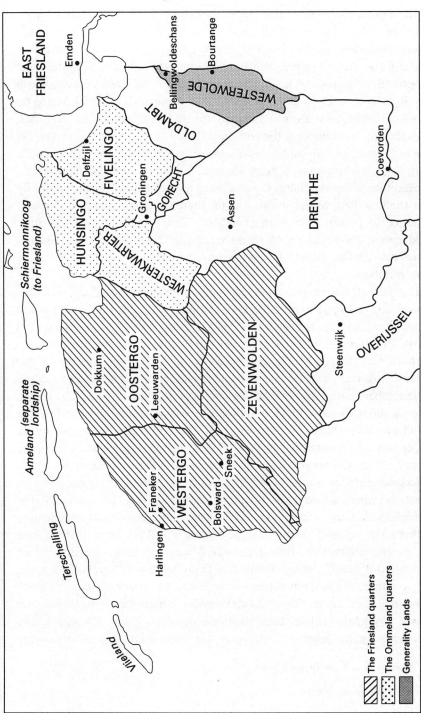

MAP 8. The quarters of Friesland and the Ommelands, under the Republic, with Groningen, Westerwolde, and Drenthe.

to the Stadholder. The Ommelander *jonkers*, displeased at finding themselves placed no higher, if not lower, than the city, were incensed by the
recommendation that Groningen's staple rights be confirmed. Oldenbarnevelt and the States General had not forgotten that the Ommelanders had
supported the Revolt, while Groningen opposed it, but decided not to strip
the city of privileges the Spanish Crown had confirmed, realizing that to do
so would make Groningen's antipathy to the Union permanent and that,
with the city unreconciled, the entire north-east would remain insecure. As
it was Groningen was being forcibly incorporated, stripped of its Catholic
faith, and made to pay a large share of the 6 per cent of Generality's
expenditure which the States General fixed as the new province's quota. By
constructing the province in this way the States General—that is Holland—
expected to preside over both 'members'. The 'instructions' of the Stadholder were drawn up not by the new province but by the States General,
which also devised a coat of arms by combining the existing emblems of the
two 'members'.

The fall of Groningen rendered the Ommelands secure and Drenthe
almost so. Unlike 'City and Lands', Drenthe did constitute a recognized
province with its own provincial States, representing the *ridderschap* and
substantial farmers. Moreover, this assembly now petitioned for Drenthe's
admission as the eighth voting province of the Union with a place on the
Raad van State.[24] But though strategically important and large enough to
form a separate voting province, the land was poor and it had a population
of only about 20,000. The Holland regents wished neither to make Drenthe
a full province, further diluting Holland's vote in federal colleges, nor an
appendage of Friesland or Overijssel.[25] Consideration was given to merging
Drenthe with Groningen, thereby creating an effective counter-weight to
Friesland, but this was opposed by the city of Groningen, mindful that a
third 'member' would end its preponderance in the provincial States.
Drenthe was, thus, refused admission to the States General and Generality
colleges but, in most other respects, deemed a full province, with its own
States and Stadholder. It is true that it was the States General which
appointed Willem Lodewijk the first of Drenthe's eleven Stadholders under
the Republic, in 1596; but subsequently, it was the States of Drenthe which
appointed their Stadholder.[26] Also Drenthe, unlike the Generality Lands
(see p. 300 below), administered its own tax system, albeit within guidelines
laid down by the Generality. However, the *drost* of Drenthe (who was also

[24] Heringa, *Gesch. van Drenthe*, 290–1.
[25] Ibid.
[26] Smit, *Bestuursinstellingen*, 24, 71.

governor of Coevorden), the most powerful judicial and military officer in the province, continued to be appointed by the States General.

Securing Groningen led, in turn, to a shift in the balance in East Friesland. In that principality, the city of Emden, stiffened by a growing Calvinist influence, was at loggerheads with the now militantly Lutheran (and pro-Spanish) count. But with Spain eliminated from Groningen and Drenthe, Count Edzard's efforts to subjugate Emden could more readily be thwarted. Indeed, in 1595 occurred one of the decisive events in the history of East Friesland.[27] The Emden Calvinist consistory, led by Menso Alting— a native of Drenthe who had trained at Heidelberg and been a preacher in Emden for twenty years—seized the city, ejected the count's officials, proclaimed the Reformed the public Church in Emden, and suppressed Lutheran worship, appealing to the States General for help. The Holland regents who considered Edzard and his pro-Spanish attitude a menace to the Republic were not unwilling to collude in this simultaneous check to Spain, princely pretensions, and Lutheranism. Dutch troops were shipped into Emden, leaving the count with little option but to come to terms arbitrated in The Hague. Under the resulting treaty of Delfzijl (1595), the count was obliged to recognize the United Provinces as a legitimate state, acknowledge the Reformed Church as the public Church in Emden and the Republic as protector of the Reformed faith in East Friesland, and agree to the Dutch garrisoning Emden (and Leerort) indefinitely. In effect, he was made to accept Dutch hegemony in East Friesland. At The Hague and Emden there was even talk at this time of incorporating East Friesland into the Union as an eighth voting province.[28]

Nowhere else in Germany did Calvinism become so closely linked to civic autonomy and the defence of local privileges against princely authority as in East Friesland. Indeed, the political ideology, and church politics, of the Emden revolution of 1595 neatly complemented the larger ideological framework of the Dutch Revolt itself.[29] It was in the mid-1590s that Ubbo Emmius, Calvinist divine, friend of Alting, and zealous supporter of both the Revolt against Spain and that against the count of East Friesland, wrote his famous history of Frisian 'freedom', the *Rerum Friscarum Historia* (1596), linking East Friesland with Friesland and Groningen rather than with Germany. It was also the Emden Calvinists who, in 1604, brought Althusius, the pre-eminent German Calvinist political writer, and arch-defender of civic rights and local privileges against princely absolutism, to

---

[27] Pettegree, *Emden and the Dutch Revolt*, 222–3.
[28] Van Winter, 'De Zeven Provincien', 17, 35.
[29] Antholz, *Politische Wirksamkeit des Johannes Althusius*, 28–35.

be Emden's town secretary. Johannes Althusius (1557–1638), Calvinist and anti-absolutist ideologue, never lost sight of the fact that the United Provinces were vital to the survival of East Frisian Calvinism, describing the Dutch garrison in Emden as the 'fundamentum et conservatio' of the city's 'freedom'.[30] It was in the years following the Dutch intervention in East Friesland in 1595 that the balance between Lutheranism and Calvinism in the principality became relatively stable with the Calvinists constituting slightly over 20 per cent of the population (see Table 52). Dutch became the official language of municipal government, law, and the Church in Emden and remained so down to the end of the Napoleonic era.

By 1595, Holland had established a strong Generality presence in the north-east and on the Ems, and quashed efforts to create a Frisian condominium in the area. The Roordists, who resented the affront to Frisian pride as well as the growing tax burden imposed from The Hague, repaid Oldenbarnevelt (whom they held responsible for this outcome) with the most virulent hostility.[31] But the Roordists had not yet abandoned hope of Frisian hegemony in the north. Frisian troops continued to garrison Coevorden and the key fortresses of Bourtange and Bellingwolde, controlling the frontier lordships of Wedde, and Westerwolde, Generality Lands on the eastern frontier beyond the jurisdiction of the new province of Groningen (see Map 8). But there was also much antipathy to Frisian aspirations in Groningen, Drenthe, and Overijssel. In the States General these provinces jointly challenged Friesland's right to garrison Coevorden, and Wedde-Westerwolde. At the same time, Overijssel and Drenthe quarrelled over Coevorden.[32]

Oldenbarnevelt's solution to this conundrum marked a new stage in the formation of the Republic. In November 1596, the States General laid down that all frontier fortresses garrisoned on behalf of the Generality and lying outside Holland, Zeeland, Friesland, and Groningen should henceforth, while remaining on the *répartitions* of particular provinces, no longer be controlled and administered by those provinces but by the *Raad van State*, on behalf of the States General.[33] This was a crucial step towards creating a genuinely federal army, and defence policy, for most major fortresses were situated outside the four provinces, in States Flanders, Brabant, Gelderland, Overijssel, Drenthe, and Wedde-Westerwolde, forming a great arc shielding the Republic on the landward side. This now became a federally controlled

---

[30] Ibid. 121–2.
[31] 'Gedenkschrift van Joris de Bye', 445.
[32] Res. SG 16 Aug and 1 Nov. 1596.
[33] Res. SG 1 Nov. 1596; Bor, *Oorspronck*, v. 59.

cordon, administered and supplied by the *Raad van State* rather than a string of segments pertaining to particular provinces. As part of this change, Willem Lodewijk was made Stadholder also of Wedde and Westerwolde.

The Republic's second great offensive took place in 1597 with the Spanish army of Flanders still tied down on the French frontier. Maurits advanced first along the Rhine, capturing Rheinberg, the 'whore of war' which served the Spaniards as their main crossing-point on the great river. With this, the remaining Spanish strongholds north of the Rhine—Grol, Oldenzaal, Enschedé, Bredevoort, Ootmarsum, and Lingen—were cut off. Maurits next took Grol, Oldenzaal, and Enschedé, and then crossed into the German Empire, sending troops north and south to occupy the counties of Lingen and Moers. The capture of the great fortress of Lingen, after the arrival of artillery (which Maurits shipped round by sea, past the Wadden Islands and Emden), extended Dutch hegemony further up the Ems valley.[34] Possession of Grol completed the elimination of Spanish power from eastern Gelderland, and of Oldenzaal and Enschedé, from Overijssel. Again the campaign was notable for the efficiency of Maurits's transportation—with whole armies being moved swiftly on fleets of river barges—his sophisticated siege techniques, and the use of large quantities of artillery to reduce strongholds quickly.[35] Grol, though well supplied and garrisoned, surrendered after a fortnight.

After a quarter of a century what initially had been a precarious strip of rebel territory had become one of the great powers of Europe. By 1597, the Dutch standing army was the most proficient technically of any in Europe and the second largest after the Spanish. The navy too gained greatly in power and size during the 1590s, tightening the Dutch grip on the Scheldt and Ems estuaries and the States General's blockade of the Flemish sea ports. Consideration also began to be given to using Dutch sea power further afield. Yet it cannot be denied that the spectacular military achievements of the Republic between 1590 and 1597 were possible only because Spain was distracted by the struggle in France. Could the United Provinces stand their ground should the Spanish monarch extricate himself from that entanglement?

Over the winter of 1597–8 Oldenbarnevelt anxiously watched the progress of the Franco-Spanish peace talks which led to the conclusion of the treaty of Vervins (May 1598). Shortly before the peace, Oldenbarnevelt decided to head a States General extraordinary embassy to the French court in person to secure what he could for Dutch interests in what for the Republic was a

[34] Ter Kuile, 'Graafschap Lingen', 17.   [35] Van Meteren, *Historie*, vi. 462–4.

worrying new situation.[36] The party, which among others included the young Hugo Grotius (who was already gaining renown as a brilliant young scholar), and François van Aerssen, the formidable son of the *griffier* of the States General, joined the French court at Angers. Oldenbarnevelt, pre-occupied with Dutch concerns, avoided interfering (as the Huguenots wished him to) in the negotiations between the French Reformed Churches and the king, which were to result in the Edict of Nantes. Holland's Advocate preferred to use such leverage as he possessed to gain maximum assistance for the Republic rather than added concessions for French Protestants. Nor was he eager to risk inviting French pressure on behalf of Catholic worship in the United Provinces. Seeing that he could not prevent the pending Franco-Spanish peace, Oldenbarnevelt concentrated on obtaining as large a package of financial aid as possible.[37] At their final meeting, on 28 April 1598, Henri promised to continue subsidizing the Dutch war effort to the tune of a million écus over the next four years.

Philip II, meanwhile, old and close to death, seeing no prospect of regaining his rebellious provinces in the foreseeable future, by force of arms, sought to create a new political framework in the Low Countries which would enable the Spanish Crown to extricate itself from the struggle without excessive loss of prestige or abandoning its military base in the south. Under his will, the king assigned the 'obedient provinces' to his daughter Isabella and her Austrian Habsburg husband, the Archduke Albert. These were to be joint rulers in Brussels and became known as the 'Archdukes'. However, the sovereignty Philip assigned them was largely nominal. The Spanish army of Flanders, paid for mainly from the Spanish revenues, was to remain; and its commanders and soldiery, including the governors of the fortress towns, continued to swear their oaths of allegiance to the new king Philip III (1598–1621), who paid and controlled them.[38] Armed and subsidized by Madrid, the south Netherlands of Albert and Isabella continued to be generally perceived as a dependency of Spain. Moreover, should the 'Archdukes' produce no legitimate heir, as already seemed likely, Philip's will stipulated that the southern provinces would, on Albert's death, revert to direct rule by the king of Spain.

Nevertheless, ceding the south to the 'Archdukes' made it easier to search for a compromise intended to end the war in the Low Countries.[39] Besides this, the new king and his favourite, the duke of Lerma, faced formidable

[36] Barendrecht, *François van Aerssen*, 24–6.
[37] Den Tex, *Oldenbarnevelt*, iii. 301–3.
[38] Parker, *Army of Flanders*, 247–51.
[39] Geyl, *Revolt of the Netherlands*, 239–41.

financial difficulties and were less inflexible in their attitude to the religious and political rebellion in the north Netherlands than Philip had been. The peace initiative launched by the Archdukes, and Lerma, in 1599 amazed Europe. Spain and the Archdukes showed that they were ready to go quite far towards accepting what had occurred since 1572 in order to end the conflict. Albert offered to accept most of the political and religious changes which had taken place and recognize Maurits as Stadholder of Holland, Zeeland, Utrecht, Gelderland, and Overijssel.[40] Yet, despite this, there was probably never much likelihood that the peace talks which now commenced would succeed. Given Spain's position in Europe, and role as principal protector of the Catholic Church, it was impossible for Lerma and the Archdukes to settle without substantial face-saving concessions from the Dutch. In particular the *de jure* sovereignty of the Archdukes (and thus ultimately of Spain) over the north would have to be acknowledged,[41] and something conceded to the Catholic Church. But, from the outset, Oldenbarnevelt and Maurits were adamant that they would, and could, not compromise the sovereign independence of the United Provinces or make any concession to Catholic worship.[42] The Dutch side nevertheless responded to the peace-feelers from Brussels so as to coax the other side as far as they would go. The main significance of the negotiations of 1598–9 is that they fostered the illusion that peace was around the corner, reducing the likelihood of an imminent Spanish offensive.

At the commencement of the new reign, the Spanish monarchy found itself at a critical turning-point. But the Republic also faced a harsh dilemma. If the war continued, with France and Spain at peace and the English war effort slackening, the United Provinces' future would be increasingly uncertain and dangerous.[43] Spain was now free to shift the full weight of her might against the Republic. Even if the Spaniards failed to make serious inroads into Dutch territory, the Republic would be forced to increase spending on its army and defences, just to keep the enemy at bay. Under increased pressure, the newly won cohesion and prosperity of the Republic might both turn out to be more illusory rather than real. Yet precisely because Oldenbarnevelt and Maurits knew the dangers, and the Republic's underlying fragility, they felt that they could not risk the unsettling effects of compromise with Spain and the Catholic Church. The Republic's leaders, like those of any small country under siege, had

---

[40] CODOIN xliii. 27–30.
[41] Deventer, *Gedenkstukken*, ii. 283–4.
[42] *Lettres de Buzanval*, 289–90.
[43] Barendrecht, *François van Aerssen*, 18–19.

developed a siege mentality steeped in suspicion of anything apt to weaken barriers, lessen vigilance, and blur dividing-lines.

The secret negotiations between the two sides were accompanied by a flurry of rumour and counter-rumour and an elaborate propaganda encounter in both print and engravings, though the latter appeared only in the north, which suggests that there was greater interest in reaching unsophisticated folk there than was the case in the south. The encounter began in the spring of 1598 with a pamphlet published in the south addressed to 'Holland', calling on the Hollanders to return to obedience to their king and enable the Netherlands to resume being one country again.[44] This touched off an exchange which continued for months. Holland's various replies to the 'subjugated provinces' were accompanied by illustrations using the familiar symbols of the visual propaganda developed since 1572: the Dutch lion, the metal collar of subjugation, a deceitful king encased in armour, and a Pope presented as the real power behind the Spanish throne. A constant objective of this publicity was to identify the south in the popular mind with the Pope, Catholicism, and intolerance. Holland's first rejoinder included a depiction of the execution of Anneke Utenhoven, an Anabaptist woman buried alive at Brussels in July 1597, who was in fact the last person ever executed for heresy in the south Netherlands though no one could know that in 1598.[45] But the principal theme of the Dutch propaganda was that the olive-branch offered by the 'subjugated provinces' was merely a deceitful stratagem designed to put the collar of slavery back on the Dutch lion through stealth.

This certainly echoed the prevailing sentiment among the leadership in the north. The English members of the *Raad van State* assured Queen Elizabeth that, at The Hague, the Archduke's peace proposals were 'altogether distrusted as pernicious, and helde full of practice to bring upon them here the inconveniences which they feare as apparent to fall out upon the least treatie or conference of accord, holdinge the very notion thereof dangerous, so as there is no doubt to be had that they will not hearken to any such offers be they never so glorious and smoothe'.[46]

This was correct. Dutch intransigence stemmed not from lack of imagination, or desire to prolong the war for its own sake, or acquire more territory. It was, rather, a typical symptom of a hard-won domestic stability which remained complex and fragile. Catholic allegiance in Holland and Utrecht was now slowly reviving. Internecine tensions among the provinces were

[44] Simoni, '1598: An Exchange', 131–3, 150–1.
[45] Ibid. 132.
[46] PRO SP 84/56, fo. 50. Gilpin to Burghley, 5 Feb. 1599.

acute. Much of the Republic had only recently been conquered and there is no doubt that areas such as Twenthe, Grol, and the city of Groningen were of dubious loyalty and could be kept quiescent only by force. Worse still, there were alarming splits within provinces, especially Friesland, Groningen, and Overijssel. For the moment it seemed less risky for the Republic to face the full might of the Spanish empire on her own than agree to compromise, and interaction, with the south Netherlands, and all the dangers that would entail.

With the Franco-Spanish war at an end, the Spanish army in the Low Countries was, for a time, unsettled by chronic shortage of cash, recurrent mutinies, and the rumours of peace. The Dutch army, by contrast, buoyed by its recent successes, was at a peak of readiness. Consequently, Oldenbarnevelt and the regents decided on a major thrust into Flanders to exploit the situation before Albert managed to restore discipline. This ambitious but risky undertaking originated in the States of Zeeland, where it was felt that something ought to be done to disrupt the building of a network of Spanish forts facing Cadzand. At the same time both Zeeland and Holland were worried by the increase in privateering attacks on their shipping, launched from Dunkirk. Oldenbarnevelt approved a plan to strike deep, along the Flemish coast. Willem Lodewijk objected that such a thrust into enemy territory meant needlessly risking the army.[47] Maurits seems initially to have been in two minds about the scheme.

The decision to invade Flanders also stemmed partly from the Dutch leadership's anxieties over the precarious situation in the north-east. There had not yet been time to repair, and strengthen, the strongholds captured by Maurits so as to form a viable defensive barrier. The continuing political difficulties in Groningen were clearly dangerous. The States General, having failed to end the bickering between the Ommelands and city, in March 1599 set up another commission to review the city's staple rights, which recommended curtailing the city's privileges in favour of the Ommelands. At this point the city ceased all co-operation with the Generality, provincial States, and Stadholder.[48] Alarmed lest Groningen might again, as in 1580, act as a 'bridge' for the restoration of Spanish power in the north-east, the States General, prompted by Holland (and with the approval of the Ommelands), sent troops into the city in the spring of 1600, to disarm the citizenry and construct a citadel within the walls to overawe the populace.[49] Ironically, this citadel, manned by 800 troops under the Ommelander *jonker* Caspar

[47] Fruin, *Verspreide geschriften*, iii. 235–6.
[48] Emmius, *De Agro Frisiae*, 178–83.
[49] Wiersum, *Gedwongen vereeniging*, 11–12.

van Ewsum, *drost* of Drenthe, was constructed on the very site of the fortress Alva had built thirty years before, for the same purpose.

Meanwhile, the rift in Friesland festered also. The two richer quarters, Oostergo and Westergo, Roordist in sentiment, were bitterly at odds with Zevenwolden and the eleven towns, which backed the Stadholder. Zevenwolden and the towns resented the dominance of the other quarters, which they feared would be used (among other things) to heap an unfair proportion of the province's tax quota on them.[50] In 1600, the States of Friesland split in two. One faction, meeting at Leeuwarden, supported Willem Lodewijk, accusing the Frisian nobles of trying to enslave the towns, while the other, opposed to the Stadholder, met at Franeker, accusing the towns of seeking to enslave the countryside. So bitter was the quarrel that Albert and his advisers, in Brussels, became hopeful that Friesland was about to plunge into civil war. At the same time, conflict ensued in Drenthe between Willem Lodewijk and the province's nobles on one side, and the *drost*, Caspar van Ewsum, and non-noble substantial farmers, on the other.[51] Besides all this, the States General were alarmed by the attitude of the new count of East Friesland, Enno III (1599–1625), who was even more militantly Lutheran, anti-Calvinist, and pro-Spanish than his father.[52]

Against this background, the Republic hurled its forces into Flanders. Shipping his troops across the Scheldt, opposite Flushing, Maurits advanced along the coast towards Dunkirk. But no sooner did he invade than the mutinies paralysing the army of Flanders ceased, enabling the Archduke to muster 10,000 crack troops and march towards the Dutch with an *élan* which shook their nerve. Maurits was caught in a situation to which he was totally unaccustomed. His officers lapsed into a state of near panic. If forced to fight a pitched battle in the open, which now seemed likely, they knew their troops lacked the cutting edge and flair of the Spaniards. It became transparent what a momentous risk Oldenbarnevelt had taken, gambling the army, and with it the survival of the Republic, for rewards which now seemed unobtainable.

During the campaign, Oldenbarnevelt and a committee of the States General took up residence at Ostend, the last remaining rebel enclave west of Cadzand. Their purpose was to supervise the army and Maurits's tactics. Throughout its history, the Republic was to insist that key military decisions, affecting the Republic's most vital interests, were too important to be left to the military command alone. But, as the full gravity of the

[50] Van Reyd, *Historie*, 418–19.
[51] Heringa, *Gesch. van Drente*, 294–5.
[52] Ten Raa and De Bas, *Staatsche leger*, ii. 323–4.

situation emerged, tempers frayed and a bitter row erupted between Maurits and Oldenbarnevelt, their first open clash. The Flanders campaign of 1600 was not the only occasion in the history of the Republic when the Holland regents, against their normal habits, took stupendous risks. They were to do so again in 1688. But since 1574 never did the Republic lurch closer to disaster than during the summer of 1600.

Worsted in skirmishes and cornered, Maurits was forced on 2 July 1600 to stake all on a pitched battle on the beaches near Nieuwpoort. The Spanish infantry, still the finest in Europe, pushed their enemy relentlessly back along the dunes. Their military prowess was such that the Dutch would surely have broken but for the years of methodical drill, inculcating the difficult manœuvre of falling back slowly without breaking formation or hindering the fighting effectiveness of the front lines. Hour after hour the Dutch fell slowly back until the Spaniards tired. Two further features of the military reforms helped save the Republic's army:[53] the wooden mats enabling the Dutch gunners (unlike the Spaniards) to keep moving their artillery, and firing, without the guns sinking into the sand, and the principle of keeping part of the army uncommitted in reserve until the decisive moment. Maurits waited until the Spaniards faltered, with the setting sun in their eyes, and then hit them with his cavalry head on, scattering them in all directions. The unthinkable had happened: the proud Spanish veterans had been routed by their confessed inferiors, in a pitched battle. It was the supreme vindication of method over force.

But Nieuwpoort was a hollow victory.[54] It left the Dutch on the wrong side of the main Spanish army, dangerously exposed. Also the battle confirmed that the Spaniards, once organized, were still basically the stronger side. Maurits failed to take Nieuwpoort and, despite Oldenbarnevelt's insistence that the army had to capture something, to justify the scale, and expense, of the invasion, deemed prudence the better part of valour and ordered a humiliating withdrawal. To add to Dutch dismay, a fleet of twelve royal warships and privateers slipped out of Dunkirk and ravaged the North Sea herring grounds during August, destroying thirty-six herring busses or over 10 per cent of the roughly 300 busses of the South Holland herring fleet.

Over the next four years the situation was one of stalemate. The Dutch held the Spaniards at bay. But, to do so, they had to expand their army, undertake costly new fortifications, and step up military expenditure dramatically. Albert and the Spanish commanders, for their part, decided, before attempting to penetrate north of the rivers, to remove the thorn in

---

[53] Van Deursen, 'Maurits', 98.   [54] Fruin, *Verspreide geschriften*, iii. 247–8.

their side and reduce Ostend. Both sides committed men and resources to the siege of Ostend in such profusion that before long it became an enduring symbol of the Low Countries struggle and, for reasons of prestige, it became impossible to withdraw. By March 1602, the Anglo-Dutch garrison had risen to 5,675 men. Ambrosio Spínola, the brilliant new commander of the army of Flanders, neglected his other fronts, staking all on what became known as the new siege of Troy. Noblemen converged from all over Europe to imbibe the new military techniques in this windswept university of war. The siege lasted three years and eighty days.

By expanding their forces, the Dutch could profit from Spínola's absorption in Ostend, while simultaneously holding Count Enno in check. The Dutch army grew from 35,000 men, in 1599, to 51,000, by 1607.[55] In 1602 Enno, backed by Spain and the Emperor Rudolph, besieged Emden. The Dutch sent in more troops and forced the count back. Under a new treaty, signed in 1603, he was again obliged to accept indefinite Dutch occupation of Emden and the primacy of the Reformed Church in the town. Meanwhile, Maurits captured the fortress town of Grave, in northern Brabant, in September 1602. His attempt on 's-Hertogenbosch, at Holland's prompting, in 1603 failed, but the following year, before the fall of Ostend, he scored a major success on the Scheldt estuary, taking Sluis before Spínola could relieve it, with the forts the Spaniards had erected around the town, as well as IJzendijk and Aardenburg.

Ostend capitulated on 22 September 1604. Even though Spain's victory had been deprived of much of its glitter by the recent Dutch successes, elaborate celebrations were mounted throughout the south, Spínola's triumph being presented as a sign of the Catholic Church resurgent. The States of Zeeland replied with commemorative medals proclaiming Ostend a divine instrument for delivering Sluis, Grave, and Aardenburg to the Dutch.[56] One effect of the fall of Ostend was a substantial displacement of Protestant population. For the town comprised the last sizeable Protestant community in Flanders and no one was allowed to remain unless willing to reconvert to the Catholic faith. Most departed with the soldiers, many settling in Sluis and Aardenburg, which were now strongly garrisoned, as the shield of the Scheldt, and chief Reformed foothold in Flanders.[57]

The Spanish revival materialized above the rivers only in 1605. But the consequences of the developments of 1605–6 were dramatic strategically, politically, religiously, and for economic life. Spínola began by pretending

---

[55] Zwitzer, '*Militie van den staat*', 175.
[56] Van Meteren, *Historie*, viii. 369.
[57] Ibid. vii, 367.

to besiege Sluis. Then, breaking camp on 24 July 1605, he swept across north Brabant, leaving Maurits and the States army far in his rear. Crossing the Rhine, and then the Münsterland, via Coesfeld, he appeared on 8 August with 15,000 men before Oldenzaal, an astonishing feat. Pro-Catholic and lightly defended, the town promptly opened its gates. Next Spínola's vanguard appeared before Lingen. Ten days later both fortress town and county were in his hands. In under a fortnight Spínola had seriously dented the States General's previously (since 1597) unchallenged sway over the Dutch–German borderlands. With strong Spanish garrisons ensconced at Lingen and Oldenzaal, the States General's forces were obliged to abandon the whole Twenthe quarter and pull back on the IJssel.[58]

Dutch worries turned to virtual panic the following year. Sallying forth in July 1606 (the month of Rembrandt's birth), Spínola reappeared north of the Rhine, as he advanced gathering reinforcements sent by the new Habsburg governor of Lingen, Philippe de Croy, and the count of East Friesland. This time he invaded the Zutphen quarter of Gelderland, capturing the fortress towns of Grol and Bredevoort while at the same time securing Rheinberg on the Rhine. He then advanced towards the IJssel, capturing Lochem and threatening both Zutphen and Deventer, plunging the entire Republic in turmoil. Fast-days and special services for the saving of the United Provinces were recited in the public churches throughout the Republic. For, by reaching the IJssel, Spínola showed that not just the Zutphen quarter but the interior of the Republic, the Veluwe and beyond, was still vulnerable to Spanish attack.[59] Troops were rushed to the IJssel from distant garrisons in Brabant along with bands of civic militia, 200 Amsterdammers arriving in Zwolle, 200 Utrechters in Deventer, and 100 men of Enkhuizen in Steenwijk. But Spínola, satisfied with the shock he had administered to the entire Dutch state, did not cross the IJssel and, after a while, withdrew.

Maurits and Oldenbarnevelt next resolved on a highly unusual autumn campaign to try to plug the yawning gap in their defences. The Stadholder retook Lochem but failed in his siege of Grol (November 1606), which had been strongly garrisoned and filled with supplies sent from Lingen, a major gathering-point, being on the River Ems, not just for recruits, horses, and foodstuffs but wagons and munitions.

The result of the Spanish gains in 1605–6 was that the whole of the Twenthe and Zutphen quarters, and some adjoining areas, were now once again brought under the Spanish 'contribution' system whereby undefended

---

[58] Ten Raa and De Bas, *Het Staatsche leger*, ii. 397.   [59] Wijn, *Krijgswezen*, 461–5.

villages and small towns paid a tribute in return for exemption from pillage and disruption. With Spanish cavalry patrolling the entire region, 'contribution' money was regularly paid from 1606 right down to 1633, when the Spaniards lost Rheinberg, their last major base on the lower Rhine. Twenthe was assessed at a slightly higher rate than the Zutphen quarter. Count Hendrik van Bergh (whom Spínola left in charge at Grol, in 1606) found himself, as a leading Gelderland titled lord, in the curious position of exacting 'contribution' from the county of Bergh—'s-Heerenberg being in the hands of States' troops—which was his own family's ancient possession. The county of Bergh contributed about one-eighth of the 2,000 guilders paid by the Zutphen quarter to the Spaniards every six months.[60] Borculo-Lichtenvoorde, which Spain deemed to belong to Münster, was initially exempted but 'contribution' was levied from the villages there too, from 1616, when the States General ejected the Munsterites and occupied the towns (see p. 387 below).

Maurits's unsuccessful attempt to recover Grol was the last land campaign of the first part of the Eighty Years War. A stalemate had been reached which was consolidated by the Dutch–Spanish armistice signed the following spring and which opened the way to the more formal negotiations which led to the signing of the Twelve Years Truce in 1609. The borders of the Republic temporarily froze in 1606 and were not again to change until after the war resumed in 1621, giving Spain and the Catholic Church a respite in which to build on their support around the Republic's eastern fringes.

THE FIXED GARRISON SYSTEM

Spínola's chief purpose, in his campaigns of 1605–6, was to wage psychological warfare, making the whole eastern frontier of the Republic insecure. To consolidate his conquests, the Archdukes, and Spanish Crown, spent a good deal refurbishing and manning the captured strongholds. Rheinberg, placed under a Spanish governor, was garrisoned with over 2,000 troops. In 1608, the Spanish garrison at Oldenzaal, controlling Twenthe, comprised 2,500 men. With comparably large Spanish garrisons at Grol and Lingen, and the count of East Friesland openly hostile, the States General had no alternative to embarking on a vast and costly programme of new fortifications along the entire eastern, as well as southern, border of the Republic, creating a huge defensive ring extending from Delfzijl, on the Ems estuary, to Cadzand, at the mouth of the Scheldt (see Map 9).

[60] Tops, *Groll*, 58.

MAP 9. The Dutch defensive ring during the Twelve Years Truce

During the years 1605–8, the States General's top military engineers, including Stevin, surveyed the whole frontier, taking measurements and devising the most sophisticated bastions, ravelines, and horn-works Europe had yet seen. The new fortifications were designed not only to make the Dutch strongholds more secure but also accommodate much larger garrisons than in the past. Between 1588 and 1607, the Dutch standing army nearly trebled in size, [61] to over 50,000 men (see Table 7), which meant the new structures became home to much greater numbers of troops than

[61] 't Hart, *Making of a Bourgeois State*, 43.

before. In 1607 Holland alone paid for 30,000 infantry and 4,000 cavalry, Zeeland for 7,500 men and Friesland for 6,600. By 1608, with the military emergency over and the Truce negotiations under way, the army was reduced to 47,000, and once the Truce took effect, to 29,000.[62] But it was clear that should the war resume the army would have to be expanded again to at least 50,000 men and possibly considerably more.

TABLE 7. *The major Dutch garrisons in 1607*

Garrison	No. of companies stationed in winter	Approx. garrison strength	Province paying for garrison
Breda (Brabant)	26	3,000	Holland
Grave (Brabant)	23	2,700	Utrecht
Doesburg (Gelderland)	22	2,600	Holland
Nijmegen (Gelderland)	21	2,500	Holland
Bergen-op-Zoom (Brabant)	19	2,300	?
Zutphen (Gelderland)	16	2,000	Gelderland
Sluis (Flanders)	16	2,000	Zeeland
Bredevoort (Gelderland)	14	1,700	?
Coevorden (Drenthe)	12	1,600	Friesland/Groningen
Aardenburg (Flanders)	12	1,500	Zeeland
Deventer (Overijssel)	?	?	
Heusden (Holland)	8	1,000	Holland
Willemstad (Brabant)	7	900	Holland
Geertruidenberg (Holland)	7	800	Holland
Bourtange (Wedde)	6	800	Friesland/Groningen
Schenkenschans (Cleves)	4	550	Holland
Steenwijk (Overijssel)	4	550	?
Lillo (Brabant)	4	550	?
Moers (Moers)	3	400	
Bellingwolde (Wedde)	3	400	Friesland/Groningen
Delfzijl (Groningen)	?	?	?

Source: Ten Raa and De Bas, *Staatsche leger*, ii. 396–401.

Some strongholds in the defensive ring, such as Delfzijl, had acquired formidable fortifications in the years following the 1591 offensive. But between 1597 and 1605 there was less urgency and the pace had slackened. Also, where new fortifications were built in the early 1590s these were now

[62] Zwitzer, '*Militie van den staat*', 175.

too small and had to be extended, as at Bourtange, a key stronghold on the north-east border, where elaborate and stronger bastions, encompassing a much larger area, were constructed in 1606–7. Several fortresses—Grol, Grave, Sluis, and Aardenburg—had only been captured recently so that repairs and construction of new bastions and ravelines had in any case only just begun.[63] Elsewhere, as at Zutphen, reconstruction began in 1591 and then continued through the early seventeenth century.[64] At Coevorden the *Raad van State* had been drawing up plans to extend the fortifications since the early 1590s but only commenced work in response to Spínola's offensive of 1605.

Most of the cost of the new fortifications and expanded garrisons was borne by Holland, Zeeland, Friesland, and Utrecht, which were also the provinces geographically distant from the defensive ring. Five-sixths of the resources which made possible the refurbishment of the strongholds and enlargement of the army were thus transferred from the inner core of the Republic to the periphery, where the fortresses were located, troops accommodated, and artillery and munitions stored. In many garrison towns, including Sluis, Aardenburg, IJzendijk, Bergen-op-Zoom, Steenbergen, Breda, Geertruidenberg, Willemstad, Grave, Coevorden, Bourtange, and Doesburg, the garrison was the main, or only, economic activity in the town, so that the enormous expansion of garrisons between 1591 and 1609 profoundly affected every aspect of society and culture throughout the outer defensive ring. The size of the population and general vitality of all the towns was to a very large degree dependent on the size of the fixed garrison.[65]

In the outer periphery of the Republic, fixed garrisons evolved during the period 1591–1609 into one of the chief factors shaping social, economic, and cultural conditions. Garrisons and their commanders spent the money transferred from the core provinces not only on construction, food, munitions, boots, and saddles, but wine, and elegant attire, for officers and great quantities of beer for the men. Even in small garrison towns, taverns, gambling, and prostitution proliferated. Of course, the men also had spiritual needs—and some had families, so that a whole generation of fortress churches were constructed, often of a rather makeshift character but, in some cases, of significance in architectural development. The church at Willemstad built in the years 1597–1607 is considered the first large, purpose-built Protestant church in the Netherlands. Soldiers in taverns and

[63] Tops, *Groll*, 109.
[64] Frijhoff, *Gesch. van Zutphen*, 237.
[65] Wijn, Het *Krijgswezen*, 125–7; De Munck, *Heusden*, 46.

guardrooms became as familiar, and fundamental, in the Dutch periphery as ships and seamen on the maritime seaboard. If the seascape came first, by the 1620s Dutch painters were also regularly painting soldiers in inns and brothels and, by the 1640s, frequently in guardrooms. Pieter de Hoogh concentrated in the early part of his career, in the 1640s, on painting guardroom scenes.

One of the social effects of the fixed garrison system was the creation of a new type of military aristocracy, consisting of men, usually of lesser noble origin, who through long service, ability, and loyalty to the Republic rose to the powerful position of governor, or deputy governor, of a garrison town. These had to be reliable, experienced men in whom the Stadholder had confidence. Though rarely wealthy to begin with, responsibility for large sums of money, and quantities of stores, enabled them to become rich as military governors. The governor's residence was not only a principal house in these towns but usually the centre of social life and refined culture as well. Whereas most of the troops of the Dutch standing army were German, French, English, or Scots, rather than Dutch, the military governors tended to be either Dutch nobles or refugee noblemen from the south Netherlands driven north, with William the Silent, in the early 1580s. They remained in charge of the towns to which they were appointed for long periods and developed strong links with citizenry with which they might well have a prior connection. Justinus van Nassau, governor of Breda for a quarter of a century (1601–25), who appears in Velázquez's famous painting of the surrender of Breda, in 1625, was an illegitimate son of William the Silent by the daughter of a Breda burgher. Marcelis Bacx, governor of Bergen-op-Zoom for eleven years (1606–17), was himself a North Brabanter, his father, son of a high official of the States of Brabant, having supported the Revolt and become governor of Heusden (1578–87). Caspar van Ewsum, the Ommelander *jonker* appointed *drost* of Drenthe by the States General, was governor of Coevorden for nearly half a century until his death in 1639.[66]

Most garrisons stood on the *répartition* of one or another province, and inevitably close ties evolved between garrison towns and the provinces which financed them. Thus, Sluis was garrisoned by Zeeland, and Breda by Holland, while Grave was allocated to Utrecht. The garrisons on the lower Rhine were also mainly paid for by Holland. However, the situation was somewhat different on the north-eastern border where the potential ascendancy of Friesland, and opposition to this of Groningen and Overijssel, enabled Holland to impose mixed garrisoning, notably at Bourtange and Bellingwolde where the garrisons were the joint responsibility of Friesland

[66] Smit, *Bestuursinstellingen*, 101.

and Groningen.[67] In the case of strongholds located on the territory of one of the seven voting provinces, such as Arnhem, Zutphen, and Nijmegen in Gelderland, or Heusden or Geertruidenberg in Holland, it was automatically the right of that province to appoint the garrison commander.[68]

THE DUTCH MILITARY REFORMS AND
THEIR EUROPEAN SIGNIFICANCE

The army reforms undertaken in the 1590s by Maurits, Willem Lodewijk, and the *Raad van State*, backed by Holland and the States General, are rightly held to be a turning-point in the history of soldiering and military organization. The so-called Military Revolution of the sixteenth and seventeenth centuries was a broad phenomenon encompassing new types of fortification, larger and better disciplined armies, greater resources, and more complex logistics, a process which began in Italy in the fifteenth century and culminated with a further phase of rationalization, including the adoption of uniforms, in the age of Louis XIV. But within this larger process, the Dutch military reforms of the 1590s were pivotal, introducing basic changes which were then widely adopted all over Europe.

While part of the wider 'military Revolution', the Dutch reforms must also be seen as a product of the specific circumstances of the Low Countries Wars. Because the struggle in the Netherlands was exceptionally static after 1585, society had to adjust, as it never had previously in Europe, to maintaining large numbers of soldiers stationed among the civilian population, in garrison towns and densely populated districts. Furthermore, these concentrations were frequently close to busy trade routes and waterways, including two of the Republic's most vital estuaries. All this posed unprecedented problems of organization and logistics. At the same time it created a new sedentary military life-style with infrequent bouts of fighting, necessitating a drastic revision of many traditional features of soldiering, and placed a premium on the prompt payment of troops at regular intervals.[69]

Certain aspects of the Dutch military reforms were so specific to the Low Countries context that they did not subsequently have any wider European application. For behind the Dutch reforms was not simply an impulse to improve military efficiency but also, and no less important, to protect civil society from disruption by soldiers. Burgomasters and regents insisted that the soldiery be subordinated to civilian priorities and requirements and that

---

[67] Overdiep, *Groninger schansenkrijg*, 107.
[68] Zwitzer, '*Militie van den staat*', 33.
[69] Ibid. 85.

the citizenry be effectively protected. Thus, from the outset, the Dutch military reforms, in their relation to civil society, differed fundamentally from, for example, the later militarism of Brandenburg-Prussia even though, superficially, the latter was heavily indebted to Dutch example and methods. It is true that under Maurits and his successor Frederik Hendrik (1625–47), soldiers who committed offences against civilians, in towns, were still subject to military courts and discipline. But this was designed to meet civilian requirements and, in 1651, even this was reversed and soldiers' misdemeanours against civilians committed in the towns brought under the jurisdiction of the civilian authorities.

At the heart of the Dutch reforms was the need to protect civil society through tighter discipline and regular payment of the troops at relatively short intervals. The States General's frequently reprinted code of military conduct was first published in 1590.[70] The articles of discipline were read out to all recruits and read out anew, each year, at the outset of the campaigning season. Special military judicial officials were posted in the garrisons to ensure enforcement. For lesser breaches of discipline such as rowdyism, stealing, and engaging in economic activities reserved to members of civic guilds, soldiers were locked up or fined. For more serious breaches, including abduction and rape, they faced the death sentence. Both Maurits and Frederik Hendrik regularly hanged soldiers for rape. Curbing sexual assault was indeed as essential as the new concept of frequent payment if there were to be smooth and orderly relations between military and civil society. The Venetian ambassador noted with surprise, in 1620, that Dutch towns, unlike most others, actually applied to have garrisons quartered in them since the economic benefits outweighed any disruption and the citizenry were unperturbed at seeing their wives and daughters in close proximity to large numbers of soldiers.[71] One result of the regularization of relations between the military and civil society was the discreet prostitution that flourished even in small garrison towns.

This concern with preventing disorder, pilfering, and rape by soldiers manifested itself in many contexts. When Groningen capitulated, in 1594, only a few contingents were allowed into the city and were quartered in specially assigned confiscated cloisters. No pillage or retribution of any sort was tolerated. Even the stripping of the images and altars from the churches by the troops was carried out methodically, under the supervision of the Stadholder.[72]

[70] Wijn, Het *Krijgswezen*, 102–26; Schulten and Schulten, *Het leger*, 57–8.
[71] Oestreich, *Neostoicism*, 79.
[72] Duyck, *Journal*, i. 463–7.

The orderliness, and discipline, which became the hallmarks of Dutch military practice, derived as much from the social and cultural circumstances of the fixed garrisons as any specifically military innovations. Troops in fixed garrisons, on interminable guard duty, needed a set repertoire of military exercises and duties to replace the marauding, foraging, and raiding of old. They also needed to demonstrate their discipline, and rigorous code, to the civilians to whom they were constantly on view. But, equally, the growing complexity of warfare, and advent of more sophisticated tactics, necessitated new forms of drill. A pre-eminent example is the introduction of the 'countermarch' system of deploying infantry armed with arquebuses and muskets.[73] In 1594 Willem Lodewijk first proposed the 'volley' technique, with successive lines of infantry moving through each other's ranks, firing volleys in turn, remarking that he derived the idea from studying the ancient Roman method of hurling javelin volleys. As with the Romans, the key to success with this method, which was to revolutionize battlefield tactics throughout Europe, was to train troops to exacting standards with constant drill. For without it, attempting such complex manœuvres in combat was bound to degenerate into chaos.

The emphasis on discipline necessitated by fixed garrisons, 'countermarch', and volley-firing in turn created a need for standardization of weaponry and ammunition, the gains in efficiency from which the Dutch were quick to appreciate. Standardization, and the volley concept, also generated the requirement for troops to be taught to load, position themselves and fire in a synchronized fashion, leading to intensive loading and weapons drill. To inculcate these new disciplines the army was reorganized into smaller formations so that junior officers could continually put manageable groups through exercises, using illustrated instructions drawn up by the high command.[74] The pictures were published in a finalized version, showing forty-two positions for using arquebuses, and muskets, in the famous manual of Jacob de Gheyn (1607), a work rapidly translated into other European languages.

The preoccupation with order, and method, infusing the Dutch military reforms of the 1590s, arising as it did from social and cultural pressures, was intellectually reinforced by the Neostoic ethics and politics of Lipsius and other late humanists.[75] The conviction that tight military discipline constituted a benefit for society and a strengthening of the State and its capacity successfully to regulate relations between military and civil society, minimizing

---

[73] Parker, *Military Revolution*, 18–20.
[74] Schulten and Schulten, *Het leger*, 92; Parker, *Military Revolution*, 20.
[75] Oestreich, *Neostoicism*, 76–9.

disruption, pervaded the thought-world of the age and clearly appealed to Maurits, Willem Lodewijk, and Oldenbarnevelt. Maurits had studied with Lipsius, in 1583–4, and both he and the Frisian Stadholder showed a keen interest in Roman, Greek, and humanist discourses on warfare, though ironically, Lipsius' principal work on Roman practice, the *De Militia Romana* (1595–6), appeared first in the Spanish Netherlands, after his return to Leuven, and was dedicated to the future Philip III of Spain.

Lipsius, the leading intellectual figure of his day, resided in both the north and south Netherlands and his ideas were influential in both. This underlines the fact that the emphasis on military discipline, though most developed, and innovative, in the north, was nevertheless a product of common circumstances in the Low Countries, and also characterized, from the time of Farnese onwards, and still more under Spínola, the army of Flanders. The 1590s were, indeed, a decade of notable military reforms also in the south. The regime in Brussels introduced improved procedures for feeding the army at that time and, in 1590, adopted a general code of military practice which regulated many aspects of garrison life.[76] After 1598, the Archduke Albert's ambitious programme of building barracks in 's-Hertogenbosch, Geldern, Grol, and other towns was similarly inspired by the need to regularize relations between the military and civil society and minimize disruption to civilians.

Maurits's military reforms, Dutch military science, and Lipsius' ideas were avidly studied, and widely adopted, in Protestant lands and, more fragmentarily, also in southern Europe. In 1616, Count Johann of Nassau, Maurits's cousin, opened a *schola militaris*, or military academy, for gentlemen at Siegen, where intensive courses were given in the art of war.[77] Maurice of Hesse, a leading figure of the German Protestant Union, was an enthusiast and the Union itself promoted the imitation of Dutch methods and drill. Various German princes published their own military exercise manuals in the early seventeenth century, almost all in some degree influenced by the Dutch example. The Great Elector, Friedrich Wilhelm of Brandenburg-Prussia (1640–88), the real founder of the Prussian military tradition, throughout his life maintained close personal and cultural ties with the court of the Dutch Stadholders and originally learnt his soldiering in Dutch army camps.

But, as is well known, the greatest impact of the Dutch military reforms was in Sweden, where tight discipline, extended infantry lines, the 'countermarch' and mobile field artillery were brought to new heights by Gustavus

---

[76] Parker, *Army of Flanders*, 172, 175–6.   [77] Parker, *The Thirty Years' War*, 206.

Adolphus and used with devastating effect in the 1630s and 1640s on the battlefields of Germany.

THE DUTCH IN EUROPE:
SKILLS, TECHNOLOGY, AND ENGINEERING

The centrality of Antwerp's commercial and financial activity in European life before the Revolt, and sophistication of the skills and industries of the south Netherlands, gave rise not only to a diaspora of merchant colonies strung out from Lisbon and Seville to the Baltic but an even more widespread diaspora of engineers, experts, and the technically skilled. Netherlanders with sophisticated expertise of many kinds eventually came to exert an immense impact on European culture and perhaps especially in central Europe, Scandinavia, Spain, and, later, Russia. After the emergence of a powerful and economically highly successful rebel state in the north Netherlands by the 1590s, this extensive diaspora of Netherlanders, like the merchant communities, tended to split along religious and cultural lines. Much of it, not only in Spain, Portugal, and Italy, but also Cologne, Prague, and Vienna, assumed a firmly Catholic character and became chiefly orientated towards, and culturally linked to, Antwerp and the reviving south Netherlands. But much also became integrated into a Reformed (and occasionally, as at Frankfurt and Hamburg, also a Lutheran) context orientated more towards Holland and the Republic.

This growing rift can be discerned in the making amongst some of these groups. The coterie of scholars, artists, and specialist craftsmen from the Low Countries which gathered at Prague and Vienna during the reign of the Emperor Maximilian II (1564–76) and later, was conspicuously, and deeply, divided by the dramatic news from their homeland.[78] Among them were the Hollander Hugo Blotius (1534–1608), who became Imperial court librarian to Maximilian in 1575, and who, though outwardly a Catholic, showed much affinity with the spiritualism of the House of Love; the Walloon botanist Clusius, who later became a professor at Leiden (see p. 572 below); and the miniaturist Jacob Hoefnagel, who became a Calvinist in Bohemia and later threw in his lot with the Czech revolt against the Habsburgs in 1618.

A particularly bizarre case of a Netherlander caught between the opposing pressures was that of the famous mining entrepreneur, industrialist, and financier Hans de Witte. De Witte was a Calvinist from Antwerp who

[78] Mout, *Bohemen*, 99–117.

remained loyal to his Protestant faith but who, employing technicians from the Low Countries (some of whom were also Protestant), took charge of the mines and ironworks on Wallenstein's estates in Bohemia, and generally helped organize the great generalissimo's resources, thereby becoming a crucial cog in the Habsburg military machine during the early stages of the Thirty Years War. He ended, after Wallenstein's assassination, by drowning himself in his garden.

In Spain and Portugal, countries which were relatively backward technically in early modern times, Catholic Netherlanders had been welcomed since the time of Charles V, or earlier, and rapidly achieved prominence in not just the burgeoning commercial world of Seville and Lisbon but many spheres where advanced skills were needed, especially printing, drainage, and mining, a phenomenon which also soon spread to the Spanish New World. Pre-eminent among these Catholic Netherlanders in Spanish America was the engineer Adriaen Boot, sent out by the Council of the Indies, in Madrid, early in the new century to assist with Mexico City's severe drainage problems. Responsible for New Spain's most ambitious drainage schemes, Boot also designed for the Spanish Crown (and in 1615–16 constructed) the Pacific fortress of San Diego at Acapulco, an edifice intended specifically to counter the Dutch maritime threat.

Expertise in drainage and land reclamation acquired in the Netherlands was in strong demand in many parts of Europe during the seventeenth century. After helping drain the Wormer lake in Holland, in the years 1624–6, Jan Adriaensz. Leeghwater was commissioned, in 1628, by the duc d'Epernon to draw up a plan for draining the marshes near Cadillac, south of Bordeaux. Dutch experts were recruited to work on various drainage projects in Tuscany and the Papal States. A prominent figure in this field, in Protestant Europe, was Cornelius Vermuyden (*c*.1595–*c*.1683), who came from Tholen and used skills acquired in Zeeland, together with numerous foremen and engineers whom he recruited there and in Holland, to great effect in England. From 1621, when he was employed to repair a break in the Thames embankment to the east of London, he found himself in charge of a whole array of ambitious projects, especially for reclaiming the Fens in eastern England. Although he had some success and was knighted by Charles I in 1628, his methods and results were widely disputed and by no means all the marshes he tackled were effectively drained.

Two other key strands of the Dutch technological impact on Europe were fortifications and harbour construction, spheres which were not infrequently linked. Dutch renown in planning and constructing fortifications began in the 1570s and 1580s, the period of the Revolt when it was most vital to strengthen the walls of Dutch towns as fast as possible. The most celebrated of the Dutch designers of fortifications was Adriaen Anthonisz (1541–1620) of Alkmaar.[79] Anthonisz, significantly, acquired his pre-1572 technical expertise supervising construction of dikes and working on land reclamation projects. After designing Alkmaar's new fortifications, he experienced the siege of the city in 1573. Subsequently, he was involved in many projects for reconstructing town walls, including the rebuilding of Amsterdam's defences, after 1578, and the designs for the great fortress of Heusden constructed between 1579 and 1586. He became Prince Maurits's most trusted expert in fortifications, as he had been of William the Silent, but at the same time continued working on dikes and drainage. In 1591 he supervised the construction of new dikes on Texel—and also planned town extensions, for example for Enkhuizen in 1590.

But it was especially after 1590, with the great expansion of the Dutch fortification-building programme, that the Dutch established their reputation as Europe's leaders in constructing town walls, fortresses, and harbours. The number of trained military engineers employed by the *Raad van State* increased from thirteen in 1590 to twenty-five by 1598, by which date the Republic's corps of engineers had become an instrument of its growing international influence.[80] When the Elector of the Palatinate wrote to Maurits and Willem Lodewijk in 1599, requesting that they send a skilled military engineer to help design a major new fortress in his territory, he remarked that the greatest sophistication and skill in fortress construction available in Europe was now to be found in the United Provinces.[81] Simon Stevin, who first became heavily involved in fortifications in the 1590s and published his treatise on the subject, *De Sterctenbouwing*, in 1594, was one of those who introduced the new techniques abroad, but again, like most of the others, combining expertise in fortifications with other engineering skills. Thus, in 1591, he visited Danzig, at the request of the burgomasters, and drew up plans for deepening the harbour there. On a subsequent expedition to Calais, he devised plans for improvements to both harbour and fortifications.

Another key fortifications expert was Johan van Rijswijck, whom William the Silent had put in charge of refurbishing the walls of Grave whilst this town was in rebel hands between 1579 and 1586, and who later worked for the States of Zeeland at Bergen-op-Zoom and elsewhere. Later after devising the new bastions the States General erected at Lingen between 1597 and 1605, he travelled to Bremen, Lübeck, and other north German cities,

---

[79] Westra, *Nederlandse ingenieurs*, 36–44.   [80] Ibid. 75.   [81] Ibid. 66, 76.

taking up commissions to design improved town walls. Another of the best-known Dutch engineers was Nicolaes van Kemp, who worked, for a time, for the Elector of Brandenburg in East Prussia. In 1607, he was invited to Sweden, where he remained for three years and helped design the harbour and fortifications of the new town of Göteborg which the Swedish Crown was then striving to develop.

One of the most notable advances in harbour-engineering during this period was the 'mud mill'. This was a device for dredging mud and silt from harbour floors, a mill churning bags fixed on poles worked by horsepower. It was introduced first at Amsterdam around 1590, using human labour, horsepower being adopted in the 1620s.[82] By 1677, four of these engines were continuously operative, each driven principally by two or three horses. Many harbours in Europe suffered, like Amsterdam, with problems from mud, sand, and silting-up, so there was widespread interest in such machines. Hence in 1674, for example, the Venetian senate accepted the plans of the Amsterdam Lutheran engineer, Cornelis Jansz. Meijer, to install Dutch 'mud mills' to dredge the harbour at Venice, though the scheme was never actually put into effect.

The impact of Dutch technology was evident across much of Europe, indeed the world, but nowhere more so than in the rapidly developing kingdom of Sweden. Here circumstances, the lack of native capital and commercial organization, the availability of extensive mineral resources, especially iron and copper, and the ambitious plans of the Swedish Crown enabled the combination of Dutch skills and capital to work to maximum effect. Many Dutchmen moved to Sweden in the early seventeenth century, indeed the new town of Göteborg, in its early years, was virtually a Dutch colony; but it was less their numbers than skills which helped shape Sweden's rapid emergence as a European great power. Amongst the immigrants from the Low Countries was Willem Usselinx (see p. 326 below), who arrived disillusioned with the Dutch West India Company and was encouraged by the Swedish court to form his Swedish-based 'General Company for Commerce with Africa, Asia, and America', which caused a stir though it met with little success. But the presiding figure among the Netherlanders in Sweden was Louis de Geer (1587–1652) who belonged to a Calvinist family originally from Liège which established itself (like many Liège refugees) at Dordrecht. At that stage the family's business was chiefly in the barge traffic in salt, grain, and iron, the last imported from Liège. In 1627, Louis de Geer, a wealthy merchant and specialist in iron products, settled in

---

[82] Davids, 'Technological Change', 88.

Stockholm and rapidly built up the largest business empire in the country, comprising iron mines and works, brass foundries, shipbuilding, rope-making, and much else. De Geer also became the largest producer of cannon and cannon-balls not only in Scandinavia but possibly the whole of Europe. The experts, often Protestant Walloons who had migrated to Holland, whom he and his partner, Willem de Besche (also originally from Liège), brought from the United Provinces to Sweden to take charge of the technical side of their metal processes introduced a range of forging and smelting techniques which were then entirely new to Scandinavia.

13

The Institutions of the Republic

❖

The institutional framework of the Dutch Republic first took shape between 1572 and 1588 and assumed definitive form in the period from the departure of Leicester down to 1609. From the Twelve Years Truce onwards, Dutch institutions remained essentially unchanged, until the fall of the Republic in 1795. The Republic's institutions, it needs to be stressed, differed markedly from those of the Habsburg Netherlands before 1572, and also from what was envisaged in 1579, in the terms of the Union of Utrecht, even though, officially, the Union remained the founding charter of the United Provinces and was continually cited, and venerated, throughout the seventeenth and eighteenth centuries.

The Union of Utrecht had envisaged a league of several (not necessarily seven) sovereign 'provinces' which agreed to give up their sovereign rights in a few limited areas, chiefly defence, taxation for defence, and foreign policy. It was intended that this league should function not as a federal state—for the provinces were supposed to take important decisions in the States General only unanimously—but as a confederacy of states. But what actually emerged, after 1579, was rather different from what had been intended. In the first place, the rule about unanimity turned out to be largely academic. In fact, hardly any major decisions of the United Provinces in the seventeenth century were taken unanimously—the decision to back William III in invading England, in 1688, being a notable, and almost unique, exception—and it frequently happened that principal decisions were taken over the opposition of more than one province. Secondly, not only were key resolutions, on foreign policy, and questions of war and peace, taken by majority vote, but States General decisions came to apply, in practice, to a wider sphere of government than provided for under the terms of the Union. Particularly after 1590, the federal principle was extended to areas such as regulation of shipping, administration of conquered districts, church affairs, and promotion of colonial expansion, in ways the original Union had not foreseen. Yet, despite this, it cannot be said that the United Provinces fully constituted a federal republic. In theory, and matters of form and ceremonial, the seven voting provinces retained the trappings of sovereignty. The best way to describe the political entity created by the Revolt is as a cross between federal state and confederacy,[1] with more of the confederacy in form and theory, and more of the federal state in substance and practice.

In theory, forging the Republic's institutions was a collective undertaking to which all the provinces consented. In reality, the institutional framework was built—and to a large extent imposed—by Holland in the face of obstruction, and objections, by the other provinces. Holland's preponderance was never greater than during the twenty years following Leicester's departure, a time when no foreign power had any real leverage in the Republic.[2] Consequently, the institutionally most formative era in the history of the United Provinces, a time when Holland's hegemony over the lesser provinces was unchallengeable, was in a way a culmination of trends reaching back, through the later Middle Ages, to the thirteenth century: Holland had gradually asserted her ascendancy over the whole northern Netherlands. Powerful counter-weights had held Holland in check, from the early fifteenth century down to Leicester. But, with Leicester's departure, there was no longer any counter-weight at hand—not even the power of Spain. Thus, Holland forged the United Provinces on a basis of allegedly sovereign provincial rights which only Holland could fully utilize, preserving her own historic cohesion, and identity, while employing the lesser provinces' resources and territory to enhance her defences, strategic weight, and economic hinterland.

After Leicester's departure, the States of Holland were the most important decision-making body in the United Provinces. Between 1572 and 1587, the States of Holland were in a transition phase, but had already changed dramatically, in form and functions, since before 1572. It would be entirely wrong to suppose that the Revolt preserved the provinces, and provincial institutions, as they had been under the Burgundians or Habsburgs. Before 1572, the States of Holland, like the other provincial assemblies, were an occasional, advisory body meeting (usually) only when summoned by the ruler, chiefly (though not exclusively) to discuss the ruler's tax needs.[3] Religion, military affairs, and foreign policy (when not directly linked to Holland's North Sea and Baltic interests) were out of bounds. Between 1572

[1] Boogman, 'Union of Utrecht', 390–1.
[2] Boogman, 'Holländische Tradition', 90.
[3] Kluit, *Historie*, i. 17–19.

and 1576, William the Silent was at the centre of decision-making but consulted continuously and extensively with the States of Holland. After 1576, Holland's role in government increased, but it remained shared rule until Leicester's departure. After 1572, the States met both more regularly and for lengthier sessions than in the past. It was also essential, if the Revolt was to survive, that the States of Holland should assume both executive and legislative power, as well as responsibility for implementing decisions.

Instead of the numerous short meetings of the past it became the practice of the States of Holland to meet for four long sessions each year and more often as required.[4] An idea of the change can be gathered from the fact that, before 1572, it was unusual for the States of Holland to meet for as many as sixty days in a year. After 1572, they invariably gathered for over 200 days per year.[5] Under the Habsburgs, the assembly was small with usually only the six 'large towns'—Dordrecht, Haarlem, Delft, Leiden, Gouda, and Amsterdam—attending, together with the *ridderschap*, representing the small towns and countryside.[6] After 1572, many more towns participated. In 1581, the number of voting towns was fixed at fourteen—Rotterdam, Alkmaar, Enkhuizen, Hoorn, Schoonhoven, Gorcum, Brill, and Schiedam being added to the original six. By the 1590s, this had risen to eighteen, with Edam, Purmerend, Medemblik, and Monnikendam being added, as permanent members. But, for a time, particularly during the 1580s, other towns which, by 1600, had finally been excluded—Oudewater, Woerden, Naarden, Heusden, and Geertruidenberg—were still occasionally summoned to the States, for especially important meetings.

A major institutional change, introduced in 1585, was that, except in emergencies, the States could only discuss issues previously set out on an agenda by the States' standing committee, or *Gecommitteerde Raden*, and circulated beforehand among the voting town governments.[7] This meant the towns' participation in the States became more direct, and continuous, delegates to the States, being unable to settle anything until after referral back, for instructions, to their 'principals', as the expression was. Everything of importance was, thus, debated in the town halls, as well as the States, and decisions were the result of a consultative process in the eighteen town councils, as well as the *ridderschap*, *Gecommitteerde Raden*, and full States. The States of Holland were now, more than ever, a gathering of town agents, running the government and administration in consultation with,

  [4] Res. Holl. 16 Mar. 1581.
  [5] Koopmans, *Staten van Holland*, 180.
  [6] Kluit, *Historie*, i. 27–30.
  [7] Koopmans, *Staten van Holland*, 185–6.

and taking orders from, the town governments. In reality, the States of Holland were thus something larger than the assembly meeting in The Hague. They were, in effect, the collectivity of the eighteen town governments and *ridderschap*, steered by the *Gecommitteerde Raden* and the province's Advocate, Oldenbarnevelt.

After 1572, towns were more dominant in the States of Holland than before. But the influence of the *ridderschap* was still appreciable.[8] The nobles were now no longer deemed to speak for the small towns; but they still represented the countryside. Before 1572, all recognized Holland nobles were entitled to attend the assembly of the *ridderschap*, and the States, by virtue of being nobles. After 1572, it became the practice to exclude nobles considered unsuitable, on account of Catholic, or royalist, sympathies, and there was never again an automatic right of access for Holland nobles.[9] One had to be co-opted to the assembly by the *ridderschap*, and this remained a significant political procedure throughout the history of the Republic.

The two most influential delegations in the States of Holland were generally the *ridderschap* and Amsterdam, most of the rest then aligning behind one or other of these. *The ridderschap* came first, in precedence, among the nineteen voting members of the States, and always gave its opinion, and voted, first. This was part of a rigidly adhered to procedural ritual whereby delegations declared their views in a fixed order, Dordrecht speaking, and voting, after the *ridderschap*, followed by Haarlem, Delft, Leiden, and Amsterdam, 'without anyone interrupting any other'.[10] The order of precedence, with the *ridderschap* first, was also always adhered to in ceremonies and seating arrangements in the States.

Central to the political revolution which took place in the northern Netherlands after 1572 were the *Gecommitteerde Raden* set up in Holland and Zeeland and, later, their equivalents, the colleges of Delegated States, set up in the remaining provinces. These were small, hand-picked, standing committees of the States, composed of experienced nobles and regents strongly committed to the Revolt, bound by formal instructions drawn up by the full States, which supervised the routine administration of each province. It was these standing committees which, in the long run, enabled the provincial States to evolve into genuine provincial governments. However, it took time for these 'colleges' to develop into effective administrative organs and to assume their definitive shape. Originally, in the years 1572–7, Holland's *Gecommitteerde Raden* were just a group of members of the States

---

[8] Van Nierop, *Van ridders tot regenten*, 218–19.
[9] ARH SH Ridderschap, viii. 16–17.
[10] Res. Holl. 16 Mar. 1581.

chosen to act as an advisory committee to assist the Stadholder, Orange himself being the real head of the administration.[11] The States of Holland, at this time, acknowledged the Prince as the presiding figure in the government and saw the principle of having a single illustrious personage at the head of the administration as indispensable. After Orange transferred to Brussels, in 1577, the college assumed a more independent character. But it was only after the Prince's assassination, in 1584, that it developed into a fixed commission with clear procedures, and a closely defined relationship to the full States.[12] Even then, it was not until 1590 that Holland's *Gecommitteerde Raden* received their definitive form and instructions. A basic principle, in Holland, as in the other provinces, was that the standing committee of the States should reflect the balance of influence within the full States. Thus the *Gecommitteerde Raden* of Holland—or rather of the South Quarter of Holland (including Amsterdam and Haarlem), for the North Quarter had its own separate college—always included a representative of the *ridderschap* and each of the large towns as well as additional members, representing the small towns, chosen by rota.[13] The college of the *Gecommitteerde Raden* of the North Quarter, set up after the Spaniards cut Holland in two, in 1573, met usually at Hoorn and comprised delegates of the seven voting towns of the region—Alkmaar, Edam, Purmerend, Monnikendam, Hoorn, Enkhuizen, and Medemblik—but with no delegate for the *ridderschap*, the nobility owning little land in the North Quarter.

The other six provinces of the Union were all less cohesive than Holland, under the Republic, but nevertheless also developed, after 1572, into genuine provincial governments. The States of Zeeland changed from being an occasional, advisory body, consisting of three 'members'—Abbot, First Noble, and towns—into a body meeting frequently, in which there was no longer an ecclesiastical vote. As before, the *ridderschap* of Zeeland were represented only by the so-called First Noble of the province, the Prince of Orange, who participated through a permanent proxy.[14] In 1585, Maurits chose for this influential post a Flemish nobleman, Jacob van Malderé, who had long served in the entourage of William the Silent. The Zeeland nobility, led by Maximilian van Cruiningen, requested readmittance, arguing that the Prince of Orange, as First Noble, had previously merely been representing the Zeeland *ridderschap*. But the States of Zeeland rejected this.[15] Until 1572,

[11] Swart, *Willem van Oranje*, 55.
[12] Koopmans, *Staten van Holland*, 194.
[13] Fockema Andreae, *Nederlandse staat*, 45.
[14] Fruin, *Gesch. der staatsinstellingen*, 81.
[15] *Notulen SZ* 1596, pp. 157–60.

there had been seven votes in the States of Zeeland—Abbot, First Noble, and five towns—Middelburg, Goes, Tholen, Zierikzee, and Reimerswaal, the last of which had largely disappeared under the sea in the floods of 1530 and 1532. Flushing and Veere had not been represented. Following the capture of Middelburg in 1574, the States of Zeeland were reconstituted but now with the Abbot and Reimerswaal dropped and Flushing and Veere, the bastions of the Revolt in Zeeland, taking their places, so that the total number of votes was still seven.

Under the Particular Union of Holland and Zeeland, of 1576, Zeeland was closely aligned with Holland. This political linkage, overriding connections with Flanders and Brabant, was reflected in the commission of the *Gecommitteerde Raden* which the States of Zeeland, following Holland's example, set up, in 1576, to administer their province. The States of Zeeland finalized their standing committee's instructions in 1578. These bound the college to protect and promote the Reformed Church as the public Church in the province, suppress Catholic worship throughout Zeeland, and co-operate with the States of Holland, not with the States General in Brussels.[16]

The States of Friesland also changed radically. As in Zeeland, the Church had been represented until 1572. Also, the eleven Frisian towns had possessed no separate representation, being subsumed into the (then) three quarters—Oostergo, Westergo, and Zevenwolden. The States of Friesland, moreover, had been even more of an occasional body than those of Holland and Zeeland, meeting very infrequently, often with gaps of several years. Thus, the States of Friesland had had relatively little influence over the provincial administration before the Revolt.[17] The thirty *grietmannen*, the key rural magistrates in Friesland, had since the 1520s been appointed by the Habsburg ruler, through the Hof.[18] After the Revolt, until 1795, there were four voting members of the States of Friesland in place of the previous three—the three rural quarters plus the eleven towns, which after 1578 were grouped together to form a separate 'quarter', so that the eleven towns collectively now wielded the same voting power as each of the three rural quarters. As the authority of the Hof was cut back, the States took over the administration and, in 1577, on the advice of the Prince of Orange, set up a college of Delegated States, following the example of Holland and Zeeland.[19] It was the Frisian Delegated States, rather than the unwieldy full States, which from this point on were the real organ of government in the

[16] Ibid. 1578/9, pp. 12–13.
[17] Theissen, *Centraal gezag*, 181–4.
[18] Sjoerds, *Algemene Beschryvinge*, i, part 2, 900.
[19] Ibid. ii, part 1, 204–7.

province.[20] The Frisian Delegated States were dominated by Calvinist, pro-Revolt nobles from the three rural quarters, the towns originally having only two of the eight seats in the college. Under an agreement brokered by Orange, in February 1584, the college was increased to nine, giving the towns one-third of the votes—reflecting their share of the province's population. But this then necessitated the formation of a second steering committee to convene the States, and formulate the latter's agenda and resolutions; for this body had to reflect the balance of votes in the full States. This second committee always had eight members, two from each quarter, and was called the *Mindergetal*.[21] The definitive instructions of the Delegated States were drawn up, in 1591, in thirty-three articles, the first of which bound the college to uphold the Reformed religion and suppress Catholic worship.

In Utrecht, too, the changes were fundamental. Under the Habsburgs the Hof had headed the province's administration, under supervision of the Stadholder, the Hof's members being appointed in Brussels. The States met only when summoned by the Hof or Stadholder. After 1577, by contrast, the States of Utrecht took over the province's administration, appointing a full-time 'Advocate', or secretary of the States, on the model of Holland. The States still consisted of three estates—Church chapters, nobles, and towns—but the Church now carried less weight than previously. In 1583, the States forbade the Hof of Utrecht to question any measure of the States and stripped it of jurisdiction in political and fiscal matters.[22] Utrecht too set up a college of Delegated States to head the administrative apparatus.

When the Union of Utrecht was formed in 1579, there were thus already four new-style provincial administrations, headed by provincial States with standing committees. In the eastern provinces, a war zone and partly still in Spanish hands during the 1580s, the setting up of the new provincial governments, and fiscal apparatus, was delayed by the disruption and continued fighting for many years. It was not until June 1593 that the States of Overijssel formally established a college of Delegated States for the province and not for several more years that it was able to operate effectively.[23]

In Gelderland, as in all other provinces which broke away from the Spanish Crown, the provincial Hof, the chief instrument of executive power and patronage under the Habsburgs, was stripped of its main political

[20] Sickenga, *Hof van Friesland*, 8–9.
[21] Guibal, *Democratie en oligarchie*, 20.
[22] Van de Water, *Groot Placaat-Boek . . . Utrecht*, ii. 984–6.
[23] Reitsma, *Centrifugal and Centripetal Forces*, 268–9.

functions. But its powers were not transferred to the States in quite the same sense as in the other provinces. For in Gelderland, owing to the entrenched particularism of the (now three) separate quarters, it proved impossible to set up a standing committee of the States or an integrated fiscal administration for the province as a whole. There was a brief attempt to set up a college of Delegated States in the 1590s, but it quickly foundered. Instead, each quarter acquired its own separate standing committee which resided in the chief town of the quarter, each consisting of six delegates, three for the *ridderschap* and three for the towns, creating a formal equivalence of influence, though in fact the voice of the nobles tended to predominate. There were thus three separate executives and fiscal systems in the province, and three authorities administering confiscated Church property, and it was the quarter assemblies rather than the full States which were the real legislatures of the province. In their procedures, these assemblies observed a formal equality between *ridderschap* and towns, permanently excluding the titled lords or *bannerheren* (who had chosen the side of Spain in the 1580s) despite their important part in the pre-1572 regime in Gelderland and the efforts of the lords of Bronkhorst-Batenburg to recover their lost right to participate in 1596, and again in 1627 and 1644. In each quarter, the votes of the lesser towns—in the Arnhem quarter these were Harderwijk, Wageningen, Hattem, and Elburg—were counted as collectively equal in weight to the voice of the 'chief town'. Broadly, the three quarters contributed to their province's quota of the Generality's income on a fixed basis, with Nijmegen paying 47 per cent, Arnhem 31 per cent, and the Zutphen quarter, the least populous, 22 per cent.[24]

While the Hof of Gelderland still convened the full States, it was not allowed to continue setting the agenda, as it had before 1572, or to mediate between the quarters or participate in formulating resolutions. These crucial tasks were now transferred to a steering committee of the full States, called the *landschapstafel*, a body which consisted of eighteen delegates, six from each quarter, half nobles and half town representatives. Nevertheless, the absence of a provincial Delegated States, and existence of the *landschapstafel* only when the full States were in session, meant that the Hof, unlike in other provinces, retained some elements of its pre-1572 political role, being the only entity representing the sovereignty of Gelderland when the States were not sitting, authorized to receive correspondence from the Generality or other provinces, or German neighbours.

With the partial exception of Gelderland, then, the provincial high courts were deprived of their previous political functions and influence in appoint-

---

[24] Fruin, *Gesch. der staatsinstellingen*, 224.

ments to major administrative and judicial posts outside the towns. Previously, the provincial high courts, acting in conjunction with the court at
Brussels, had selected the *baljuws* and *drosts* and these, even in Holland and
Zeeland, had held sway in the smaller towns as well as the countryside. After
the Revolt, the power to choose the *baljuws* devolved upon the States—or,
after 1618, when there was a strong Stadholder, on the Stadholder;[25] but at
the same time their influence in the towns was eliminated and, certainly
where towns predominated in the States, in Holland and Zeeland, reduced—
to the advantage of the towns—also in the countryside.

The States now also took charge of supervising the flood defences and
drainage boards as well as assuming the sovereign power to grant charters
for new land reclamation projects. As far as the main sea dikes and river
embankments were concerned, there was little for the States to do, and these
continued to be maintained chiefly by the regional drainage boards, reflecting the essentially regional nature of the main flood defences. Above all in
Zeeland each main island—Walcheren, Schouwen, Tholen, etc.—required a
highly integrated flood defence system, a well-maintained perimeter which,
however, did not form part of any wider framework. Consequently what
mattered was that the dike and drainage colleges, albeit presided over by a
high 'dike count' appointed now by the States, or Stadholder, should
effectively represent and promote collaboration between the main interested
parties, the towns, villages, and nobles of the island or district. But in the
case of new drainage projects, where there were often rival schemes and
contending interests, the supervisory role of the States was fundamental.
Thus, for instance, before the States of Holland empowered Alkmaar to
drain the Schermer lake, in September 1631, prolonged negotiations took
place with the States mediating between Alkmaar, a group of investors in
Amsterdam, and the local drainage boards. The most ambitious single
drainage scheme debated during the Golden Age, proposed in its most
sophisticated form by the famous drainage engineer Jan Adriaensz. Leeghwater (1575–1650), in 1630, the plan to drain the Haarlemmermeer, the
largest lake in Holland (covering some 40,000 acres), and create 1,000 new
farms at a cost of 3.6 million guilders, took it for granted that the States of
Holland would not only charter and supervise the plan but actively assist
and subsidize its execution.[26] In the end, the Haarlemmermeer project was
not attempted in early modern times and was finally implemented only in
the mid-nineteenth century.

[25] Koopmans, *Staten van Holland*, 170–1.
[26] de Vries, *Dutch Rural Economy*, 194–5.

TAXATION AND THE TAX SYSTEM

As with any state, a basic aspect of the Republic was the organizing of taxation and the running of the state's finances. Article Five of the Union of Utrecht had envisaged that the provinces would collect 'uniformly and on the same footing, for the general defence of these provinces' imposts on wine, beer, cloth, cattle, and cultivated fields 'by common advice and consent'.[27] In fact, no comprehensive federal system of taxation was ever devised. The provinces retained some autonomy in fiscal matters. Nevertheless, the overall levels of expenditure and taxation were centrally fixed, as was the quota allocated to each province, so that, in practice, the seven provinces were not sovereign bodies in the fiscal sphere but shared a collective system of finance and taxation with built-in provincial variations.

From the outset, the Generality had some revenues of its own, separate from what was raised by the provincial governments. But this was always a relatively small proportion of the total expenditure, and revenue, of the Dutch state. In the years around 1640, approximately 19 per cent of total States General income derived from Generality sources and 81 per cent from the provinces.[28] Generality revenue, separate from that supplied by the provincial governments consisted (in order of importance) of the customs revenues (making up about two-thirds of this income), taxation raised by the Generality in the Generality Lands (about 5 per cent of total States General revenue), forced contributions exacted from enemy districts around the borders, and, lastly, the proceeds of Generality stamp duty.[29]

Thus, some four-fifths of total Dutch revenue was raised in the provinces by means of the separate provincial tax systems. Each province collected its own taxes in its own way or—in the case of Gelderland where each quarter administered its own fiscal system—in three different ways. Yet, the autonomy which this bestowed was more apparent than real. General levels of expenditure, and therefore of taxation, were fixed by the *Raad van State*, and States General, and this meant in practice that Holland had the main say in how much money was needed and how much each province should pay. A quota system evolved which bound each province to pay a fixed proportion of the Generality's annual expenditure and, in this too, Holland had the principal word. As far as taxation and state finance were concerned, provincial sovereignty, in practice, amounted only to the power to determine the shape of the tax package in each province, and sometimes not even that.

[27] Kossmann and Mellink, *Texts*, 168.
[28] 't Hart, *Making of a Bourgeois State*, 86.
[29] Zwitzer, 'Het quotenstelsel', 6.

The Republic's system of provincial quotas evolved from the Habsburg system of the pre-Revolt period. The formula used in 1558, for example, was that Holland should pay one-half of the quota of Brabant, and Zeeland one-quarter of Holland's.[30] This was the starting-point for a quota system which, after 1585, no longer included allocations for Brabant, or other southern provinces, but which, under the 1586 list, still fixed Zeeland's quota at (almost) one-quarter of that of Holland and Utrecht's at (just over) 10 per cent of Holland's (see Table 8). At first, the eastern provinces, partly under Spanish occupation and ravaged by war, remained outside the system,

TABLE 8. *The Dutch provincial quota system for financing the Generality, 1586–1792*

Province	1586/94	1595/1604	1604/9	1609/10	1610/16	1616/58	1658	1792
Holland	64.2	59.75	55.75	57.4	57.14	58.3	58.25	62
Zeeland	15.8	14.6	13.6	12.5	9.1[a]	9.1	9.25	3.9
Friesland	13.3	12.4	11.5	11.6	11.5	11.6	11.6	9.3
Utrecht	6.6	6.4	5.75	5.75	5.75	5.75	5.75	4.5
Groningen	—	7.8	6.4	5.75	5.75	5.75	5.75	5.4
Gelderland	—	—	4.6	4.5	5.5	5.6	5.6	6.0
Overijssel	—	—	2.5	2.75	3.5	3.5	3.1	3.5
Drenthe	—	—	—	—	—	—	0.95	0.95

[a] This large reduction in Zeeland's contribution was negotiated in 1612

Sources: De Wit, *Public Gebedt*, i. 200; Basnage, *Annales*, 26; Zwitzer, 'Het quotenstelsel', 12, 17–18; 't Hart, *In Quest of Funds*, 77 (This table was compiled in consultation with Jan de Vries.)

and did not have provincial tax administrations, special levies being raised in districts under States' control.[31] After 1586 most changes in the quotas came about as a result of inland provinces being incorporated, one by one, into the quota system, thereby reducing the quotas of those provinces already on the list. But some adjustments were made for other reasons. The large reduction in Zeeland's quota, negotiated in 1612, was mainly due to the collapse of Zeeland's prosperity as a result of the truncating of the transit traffic, via Zeeland, along the Scheldt, with the onset of the Truce in 1609 (see p. 313 below).[32] The deliberations between the provinces over this adjustment resulted initially in deadlock and offer a good example of the intermediary role of the Stadholders, who took the lead in breaking the

[30] Grapperhaus, *Alva en de Tiende Penning*, 27.
[31] A. Th. van Deursen, 'Tussen eenheid en zelfstandigheid', in S. Groenveld and H. L. P. Leeuwenberg (eds.), *De Unie van Utrecht* (The Hague, 1979), 147.
[32] GA Amsterdam vroed. res. 8 May 1612.

impasse. The States of Friesland continued obstructing their solution—
reducing Zeeland's quota without increasing the rest—into 1613. The matter
was finally settled after a delegation representing the States General,
Stadholders, and *Raad van State* journeyed to Friesland and gave firm
assurances that Friesland's quota would not rise.[33]

After being raised—by a majority of the States General—in 1616, the
quotas for Gelderland and Overijssel were lowered again, provisionally, on
the expiry of the Truce in 1621, to take account of the disruption (and
enemy tribute) arising from renewal of the war. These quotas later reverted
to their level of 1616, after the last of the Spanish garrisons north of the
Rhine were eliminated in 1633.[34] Drenthe's quota was eventually fixed as
equivalent to 1 per cent of the total for the Seven Provinces but was not
brought on to the list until later, the percentages allocated to the Seven
Provinces continuing to make up the formal total.[35] Thus, Drenthe's 1 per
cent did not count as part of the 100 per cent paid, under fixed quotas, by
the Seven Provinces.

It is often suggested that Holland contributed a disproportionate share of
the burden as, from 1616 onwards, she paid 58 per cent (without counting
the contributions of Drenthe and the Generality Lands) of the total. But
when distribution of population is considered together with the fact that
Holland possessed the bulk of the Republic's commerce, shipping, and
industry and that her soil was more fertile than that of most lesser provinces,
it is apparent that Holland was actually under-, rather than over-assessed
and taxed. Friesland's quota, for example, remained fixed, after 1604, at 11
per cent, which was superficially proportionate given that Friesland's
population indeed amounted to nearly one fifth of Holland's. But given that
Friesland was predominantly rural, and her urban resources and wealth
incomparably smaller, it can hardly be maintained that Friesland was being
fairly treated. The States General's 1792 reform of the quotas belatedly
acknowledged that Holland had (long) been contributing too little and
Zeeland, Friesland, and Utrecht, in particular, too much.

Holland initially tried to compel the rest to raise the great sums needed
for the army and navy by pressing her own tax system on them. The text of
the Particular Union of Holland and Zeeland of 1576—still deemed effective
after the Union of Utrecht—stipulates that 'during the present war, and
until resolved otherwise' all war expenses would be 'levied, raised, and
collected on an equal and common footing as if from one purse'.[36] Zeeland's

[33] ARH SG 8869, fos. 6, 9.
[34] 't Hart, *Making of a Bourgeois State*, 79.
[35] Zwitzer, '*Militie van den staat*', 70–1.
[36] Res. Holl. 15, 17, and 19 Mar. 1576.

tax system (though the excises were mostly lower) subsequently continued to resemble that of Holland, as did that of Utrecht, a province made to adopt the 'General Means', on a basis close to that of Holland, following Leicester's arrival in March 1586. The Leicester regime also forced Friesland to adopt the 'General Means'. But extensive modifications had to be made to overcome the obstruction of the Frisian towns and Roorda's faction, preventing anything like the full package of excises as practised in Holland, Zeeland, and Utrecht taking effect. Consequently, Friesland lagged behind in her payments, which led eventually, in 1635, to direct Generality intervention—that is, intervention by Holland—to force Friesland to pay more by introducing special property taxes.[37]

In the inland provinces too the 'General Means'—which in Holland accounted for 64 per cent of provincial taxation in 1600, rising to 71 per cent by 1640[38]—were adopted only very grudgingly and at lower rates. After Maurits's victorious offensive of 1591, Holland's pressure on these provinces to enter the quota system and, consequently, pay more of the Generality's costs, rapidly built up. Bodley reported to London, in February 1592, that the States General were no longer prepared to listen to Gelderland's pleas of 'inabilitie' to pay the 'general means for the maintenance of these warres'.[39] At the meeting of the States of Gelderland the following year, Chancellor Leoninus read out a letter from the Stadholder admonishing that 'the other provinces' were becoming impatient and that Gelderland must now adopt the 'General Means'. But it proved impossible to secure agreement among the quarters and none was willing to accept the full Holland rates. The States General warned that the idea that each province could go its own way would have 'very bad consequences for the state of the provinces in general, as well as for Gelderland in particular', urging Gelderland to impose a tax system common to all three quarters, on the basis of Holland's, 'to satisfy the other provinces'.[40]

It was the same in Overijssel, where there was great reluctance to adopt the 'General Means', above all at Zwolle. Zwolle insisted that it was not only a question of Overijssel paying more to the Generality's coffers than before. The 'General Means' also meant the end of the political and financial independence of the Overijssel towns.[41] Zwolle pointed out (quite rightly) that there had never been a provincial system of taxation in

[37] 't Hart, *Making of a Bourgeois State*, 135–6.
[38] 't Hart, *In Quest of Funds*, 82.
[39] PRO SP 84/44, fo. 124. Bodley to Burghley, 25 Feb. 1592.
[40] Japikse and Rijperman, *Resolutiën*, viii. 92–3.
[41] Dumbar, *Hedendaagsche historie*, ii. 356–7.

Overijssel, with the same taxes collected, in the same way, throughout the province. In effect, what incorporation into the Generality's quota system, and adoption of the 'General Means', meant was a double suppression of Overijssel's historic privileges and traditions: subordination of the province to a collective system controlled from The Hague, and subordination of the towns and quarters to a provincial government which would have to be created to administer the new provincial tax system. A college of Delegated States was set up in Overijssel in 1593, and a start was made on forging a common provincial system of taxation. But vigorous opposition continued. In March 1597, the Stadholder, accompanied by a Generality delegation, attended the meeting of the States of Overijssel in person. He insisted that Overijssel must now pay much more and should adopt the 'General Means of consumption as practised in Holland, or nearly so'.[42] Most of the province acquiesced but still Zwolle held out, raising the question of whether one of the three chief towns could be overruled, in the States, on such a fundamental issue.[43] It was not until 1600 that the Delegated States of Overijssel finally succeeded in imposing a single, integrated tax structure, based on the 'General Means', on the whole province.

In Groningen and Drenthe opposition to Holland's demands for the 'General Means', Delegated States to collect them, and incorporation into the quota system, to fix the levels, took a different form. With the city just conquered by the Generality's troops, and the new States of 'City and Lands' created by the Generality, the States of Groningen could not formally oppose the setting up of Delegated States or the principle that the newly created province should introduce the 'General Means', 'as they are practised, levied, and received in Holland and Zeeland'.[44] In 1595, the new Delegated States—consisting (from 1601) of six delegates, three from the city and one each from the three Ommelander quarters—were established. On their admittance to the States General, the new Groningen delegation were dismayed to find that the other provinces were pressing Groningen to pay two-thirds of Friesland's quota while Friesland wanted Groningen to contribute even more.[45] Eventually, the quota was fixed at slightly under two-thirds. But if the States of Groningen were unable to resist the pressure to adopt 'General Means', Delegated States, and a substantial quota, the citizenry of Groningen expressed their displeasure by simply not paying the excises. Incorporation into the Generality quota system remained largely

[42] Dumbar, *Verhandeling*, 6–7, 87–8.
[43] Reitsma, *Centrifugal and Centripetal Forces*, 268–9.
[44] Japikse and Rijperman, *Resolutien*, viii. 305.
[45] Duyck, *Journal*, i. 600.

theoretical until, in 1599, the States General, goaded by Holland, dispatched troops to occupy the city and compel compliance.

In Drenthe, the imposing of the 'General Means' by the States General, in 1600, precipitated a bitter struggle between the *ridderschap*—which in Drenthe numbered some twenty families—and the non-noble large farmers, for control of the province.[46] To collect the new taxes the States General set up a college of Delegated States consisting of the *drost* and four delegates— two each from the *ridderschap* and non-noble large farmers. Since this new body would be paramount in the fiscal and judicial administration of the province, as well as in administering the confiscated property of the Catholic Church, much depended on its composition and disputed procedures. To settle matters the States General, in September 1603, imposed a general constitution, or *regeringsreglement*, on the province, defining the procedures of both States and Delegated States. This confirmed that the *ridderschap* possessed merely one out of three votes in the States but had precedence in speaking, voting, and signing, and equal representation to the rest of the States on the Delegated States. After 1603, the province's administration settled into its new pattern. In 1610, the States General fixed Drenthe's quota at 1 per cent of the total for the Seven Provinces.[47] All in all for Drenthe, the 'General Means' meant higher taxation, more administration, and an increased role for the nobility.

It proved impossible to impose the same tax system on all seven provinces. In the Generality Lands too, the States General had little alternative but to impose the 'General Means' at lower rates than applied in Holland. But given the disparities in social structure, prosperity, degree of urbanization, and agricultural productivity, this is scarcely surprising.[48] Had Holland's tax system been more rigidly imposed on the rest, the result would have been grotesquely unfair and, to a large extent, unworkable. By setting up seven provincial governments, and separate tax regimes, but within a common framework, what the Dutch Revolt accomplished was a provincially vari- able confederate tax system which was in reality more efficient, and better adapted to circumstances, than any single, centralized system of taxation could then have been. In Holland, Zeeland, and to an extent also Utrecht, provinces highly urbanized, commercialized, and prosperous, it made sense to collect the bulk of taxation through excises on consumption, of which the two most important were the excises on beer and milled grain, but in which a wide range of excises on other consumables, not least wine, spirits, and

[46] Smit, *Bestuursinstellingen*, 15, 19.
[47] Zwitzer, 'Het quotenstelsel', 19.
[48] Kappelhof, *Belastingheffing*, 102–8.

tobacco, played an appreciable part. In the predominantly rural provinces, on the other hand, and in the Generality Lands, including Wedde and Westerwolde (where the Generality's tax regime served as the model for Drenthe), it was impossible to administer excises as efficiently as in the urban context, and also to collect much, by means of excises, in a rural setting in which most consumption was of locally produced products.[49] In these provinces, and States Brabant, the beer, wine, and other excises yielded comparatively little. Consequently, there it made sense to concentrate on the agricultural taxes encompassed within the 'General Means', on cattle and ploughed fields, and to make up for the overall smaller yield from the 'General Means' by collecting a higher proportion of taxation than in the maritime provinces from traditional direct taxes on land and houses.

Besides colleges of Delegated States, to administer the new provincial tax regimes, additional colleges were needed to handle the accounts. Unlike most of the others, Holland already had a chamber of accounts, or *Rekenkamer*, before the Revolt which was then shared with Zeeland. But Zeeland decided, in 1594, that she needed her own provincial office of accounts. Utrecht too had been placed, since 1528, under Holland's *Rekenkamer*, in The Hague but, from the 1590s on, developed her own. Groningen acquired a provincial chamber of accounts in 1595.

THE GENERALITY

The new type of provincial government set up between 1572 and 1600 bore little resemblance to patterns of provincial government in Habsburg times. In effect, the Revolt not only created a new confederate state and central institutions but also shaped the provinces, as coherent administrative entities, as well. The Revolt made Dutch provincial government stronger, and more efficient, but only because the provinces were now the organs of a partially federal state which required greater collaboration, and heavier taxation, than could be conceived of before 1572. Holland was the driving force behind the new Union. But the Generality provided the machinery, and procedures, which enabled Holland to prod the other provinces to collaborate in the common venture of federal statehood. Troops were sent to Groningen in 1599, at Holland's insistence, to garrison the city and force it to pay. But it was in the name of the Generality that this was done and

---

[49] Ibid.; 't Hart, *In Quest of Funds*, 92–5.

the Generality which provided the framework within which intermittent pressure—usually short of sending troops—was exerted.[50]

Like the provincial States, the Dutch States General of the post-Revolt period bore little resemblance to the States General of the Burgundian and Habsburg Netherlands.[51] Before the Revolt, the States General convened only when summoned by the ruler, not of their own accord. If in 1477 the States General won the right to gather where, when, and as often as the provinces deemed necessary, this change was never achieved in practice. Down to 1572, the States General still met infrequently, usually with intervals of several years, and had no power to set their agenda, or make decisions, as distinct from submit requests. After the rebel States General transferred north of the great rivers, in 1583, they convened initially at Middelburg and then Dordrecht and Delft until the decision, of January 1585, to convene (as long as it remained safe) at The Hague. In 1587, the States of Utrecht, then dominated by Prouninck, backed by Leicester and Neuenahr, tried to move the States General to Utrecht, where the Union of 1579 had been forged.[52] Gelderland and Overijssel, offered closer proximity to the Generality, and a lessening of Holland's influence, agreed to move, but Holland, Zeeland, and Friesland refused. After this, the residence of the States General at The Hague was never again challenged.

From 1583, the States General met increasingly frequently and, from 1593, remained in permanent, unbroken session, for long stretches meeting daily. The States General, in the early seventeenth century, rarely gathered on fewer than sixteen or seventeen days in any month and often met for as many as twenty-eight days in the month, including Sundays.

Only the (since 1594) seven voting provinces were 'members' of the States General. Representation, declarations of view, voting, signing treaties, everything went by provinces and, as in the provincial assemblies, a fixed order of rank was invariably observed. The delegates of Gelderland, as the only duchy, always spoke and voted first and when the States General signed an alliance or agreement with a foreign power, the signature of Gelderland's representatives always preceded those of the other six. Next came Holland, followed by Zeeland, Utrecht, Friesland, Overijssel, and Groningen in fixed sequence, though Friesland disputed Utrecht's precedence over herself.

Each province could send as many delegates to the States General as it wished, but always had only one vote. Also, since the assembly hall, in the

[50] Van Deursen, 'Tussen eenheid en zelfstandigheid', 149.
[51] Fruin, *Gesch. der staatsinstellingen*, 100–4.
[52] Den Tex, 'Staten in Oldenbarnevelt's tijd', 62–3.

Binnenhof, was deliberately kept small, the maximum number of seats for any province was six and the smallest had only two or three. In a typical early seventeenth-century session there would be ten to twenty delegates present, not infrequently with one or two provinces missing. But on important occasions additional delegates attended, the less senior of which would have to stand. Apart from Holland, the provinces each maintained a provincial house, or *logement*, where its delegates could stay and work. While Zeeland chose her delegates for life, the others adhered to three- or six-year terms. The 'chair', or 'presidency', revolved on a weekly basis among the leading figures of the provincial delegations, following the same order as the general ranking of the provinces.

After the move north of the rivers, the States General held both spoken and written proceedings exclusively in Dutch except when addressing foreign powers and their envoys when it was usual to use French, or Latin, though some Central and eastern European princes employed local interpreters to conduct their negotiations in Dutch. The English ambassadors almost invariably addressed the States General in French, though James I's envoy, Henry Wotton, in 1614, addressed them in Italian on the grounds that he knew that language better than French.

To assist the States General in their functions, there were several supplementary Generality institutions. Of these, the most important was the Council of State, or *Raad van State*. Between 1585 and 1587, this had been the principal organ of government in the United Provinces, as stipulated under the Anglo-Dutch treaty of Nonsuch. After Leicester's departure, Oldenbarnevelt and Holland forced new instructions for the *Raad*, through the States General, despite the hesitation of several provinces and determined opposition from Utrecht.[53] These 'instructions' of May 1588 drastically curtailed the power of the *Raad*, stripping it of its previous role in foreign affairs and strategic decisions. In effect, the *Raad* became an arm of the States General, administering the army, fortresses, and Generality lands, with little independent authority even in the collecting of forced tribute from enemy-held border districts.[54] But while its political role lapsed, the *Raad*'s administrative functions expanded, so that it became, and remained, one of the most important institutions of the United Provinces.

The *Raad* convened next to the States General, within the Binnenhof, in The Hague. It thus sat close to the States of Holland but far from other provincial assemblies. There were twelve ordinary provincial delegates— three for Holland (one representing the Holland *ridderschap*) two each for

---

[53] Fontaine, *Raad van State*, 22–7.   [54] Van Deursen, 'Staat van oorlog', 48.

Friesland, Zeeland, and Gelderland, and one each for the other three.[55] Though Gelderland paid less to the federal budget than Utrecht or Groningen, the duchy was given double representation because it had more Generality fortresses on its soil than any other province. The two permanent English members of the *Raad*, stipulated at Nonsuch, continued for many years, their presence ending only with the departure of Sir Dudley Carleton, in 1627. The two Stadholders were members *ex officio* but, evidently, rarely attended its twice daily meetings. When the young Frederik Hendrik, Maurits's brother, was assigned a seat in the *Raad* in 1600, one member noted, in his journal, that the college was less than enthusiastic since they could no longer speak freely about the Stadholders.[56] *Raad* members drew their salaries from their respective provinces but swore their oath of allegiance to the States General.[57]

The proliferation of financial business led the States General, in 1602, to establish a separate Generality accounting office, or *Generaliteits Rekenkamer*. This college computed Generality revenue, and outgoings, drew up estimates, and supplied statements when required by the States General or *Raad*. The provinces' ordinary contributions to the Generality's military costs were decided each year, in the States General, on the basis of an annual forecast of military expenditure known as the *staat van oorlog*. The *Rekenkamer* received, and recorded, these ordinary contributions from the provinces, as well as extraordinary payments, and the lesser revenues raised by the Generality, directly, in the Generality Lands and border zones. The Generality's *Rekenkamer* received its definitive commission in 1607. This college, also housed in the Binnenhof, consisted of fourteen regular delegates—two from each province—plus a permanent administration of six secretaries and clerks.[58] In addition, there were two senior Generality officials in charge of receipts, payments, and accounts, a treasurer-general and receiver-general. The former post was held by Joris de Bye (like most senior Generality officials in this period not a Hollander but a south Netherlands refugee) for forty years (1587–1628).

Another Generality institution, this time expressly under the supervision of the *Raad van State*, was the *Hoge Krijgsraad*, at The Hague. This body developed between 1590 and 1597 at the prompting of Maurits but confirmed by the provinces and States General. There was never a time, after 1572, when the army was essentially an assortment of separate provincial armies, even though it was, and remained, the case that regiments were on

[55] Fockema Andreae, *Nederlandse staat*, 20.
[56] Van Deursen, 'Raad van State', 3.
[57] Fontaine, *Raad van State*, 45–7.
[58] Smit, 'Ambtenaren', 384.

the payroll of one, or another, province. But before 1590, there was no comprehensive code of military discipline, and punishment for offences committed by soldiers, and officers, was sporadic and uncoordinated, a high military court existing only when part of the army was in the field.[59] By contrast, during the 1590s, a permanent high court for the army evolved, consisting of from ten to twenty senior officers and meeting either at The Hague or on campaign. By more methodically reviewing sentences, and appeals, in all the garrisons and units of the army, it gave greater coherence and uniformity to the enforcement of military justice and discipline.

Another federal function was the supervision of the Republic's coinage. The power to issue coinage has always been regarded as one of the basic attributes of sovereignty. Under the terms of the Union of Utrecht, the provinces administered the mints and issued the coinage and in this sphere they were, formally, sovereign.[60] But the Union assigned to the Generality responsibility for regulating the values, weights, and content of the seven coinages so that they formed in effect a single currency. In this way, the Union divided sovereignty in coinage as in so much else. Initially, Generality control was largely nominal. With the States General's placard of 1606 on coinage, however, guidelines on weights and equivalence were laid down which stabilized the Republic's money and remained in effect, with only minor modifications, down to 1795.[61] To handle the technical aspects of this aligning of provincial currencies, the States General set up a Generality Mint Chamber (*Generaliteits Muntkamer*).

Finally, there were the admiralty colleges, one of the principal administrative arms of the Generality. These colleges were responsible for administering the navy, collecting customs, maintaining guard boats on rivers and estuaries, building warships, recruiting naval seamen, and enforcing (and advising on) the States General's regulation of shipping and fisheries. The rudimentary admiralty administration organized by William of Orange was changed several times during the 1580s but serious disagreements continued and it took years of laborious negotiation before a definitive system of five admiralty colleges' was set up in 1597.[62] Zeeland's fears that the new system would enhance the Generality, at the expense of provincial sovereignty, were assuaged by allowing Zeeland's college to retain a more provincial character than the others.

The five colleges resided in Amsterdam, South Holland (Rotterdam), the North Quarter (jointly at Hoorn and Enkhuizen), Zeeland (Middelburg),

[59] Wijn, *Krijgswezen*, 90–1.
[60] Kossmann and Mellink, *Texts*, 169.
[61] Voogt, *Gesch. van het muntwezen*, 100–1.
[62] *Notulen SZ* res. SZ 7 and 16 Jan. 1597.

and Friesland (Dokkum). All estuaries, entry-points by land as well as water, and routes within the Republic were under the jurisdiction of one or other of the five colleges, which maintained customs posts, and river gunboats, on the inland borders as well as the coast. Placing naval, and customs, administration under five colleges meant that, in some respects, the Republic was saddled with five separate navies and customs administrations. Each appointed its own admirals and captains and recruited its own seamen. Each maintained its own shipyards, arsenals, and stores, and kept its own accounts. Each had its own flags and coats of arms, though the flags clearly indicated that the colleges were Generality and not provincial bodies.

Provincial and local particularism influenced the functioning of the admiralty colleges, and sometimes there were serious discrepancies in practice between them. Nevertheless, in the main these were authentic Generality and not provincial, or local, bodies. It was the Generality which fixed the tariffs, and naval policy, and supervised the work of the colleges.[63] To reinforce their federal character, the 1597 arrangements rigidly regulated the colleges' composition. The most important, Amsterdam, had twelve delegates—half non-Hollanders and half Hollanders, the latter consisting of one delegate each from Amsterdam, the *ridderschap*, Haarlem, Leiden, Gouda, and Edam. The Rotterdam college also consisted of twelve delegates, this time seven Hollanders and five non-Hollanders, the latter one each from Zeeland, Gelderland, Utrecht, Friesland, and Overijssel; the Hollanders, one each from Rotterdam, the *ridderschap*, Dordrecht, Delft, Schiedam, Gorcum, and Brill—thus all South Hollanders. The North Quarter college consisted of eleven delegates, six Hollanders and five from outside, the latter one each from Zeeland, Utrecht, Friesland, Gelderland, and Overijssel. The Zeeland college, which alone had an essentially provincial character, comprised nine Zeelanders and only three non-Zeelanders— one each from Amsterdam, South Holland, and Utrecht. The Frisian college, by contrast, consisted of four Frisians and six non-Frisians, comprising two from Groningen (one from the Ommelands and one from the city) and one each from Holland, Utrecht, Gelderland, and Overijssel.

Besides the regent councillors each admiralty college comprised a substantial administrative staff employed by the Generality, including a receiver, secretary, clerks, an Auction Master for prizes and seized merchandise, store and equipment masters, a senior judicial officer and his assistants, messengers, and ushers.[64] Apart from these, each of the customs posts, under each

---

[63] Sjoerds, *Algemene Beschryvinge*, ii, part 1, 72–3; Fruin, *Gesch. der staatsinstellingen*, 199–204.
[64] 't Hart, *Making of a Bourgeois State*, 41.

admiralty college, had a director, or Convoy Master, and a staff of officials for checking ships, river barges, and wagons. In 1600 the Republic had sixty-seven of these customs posts, a number which grew to ninety-one by 1650 and 127 by 1700.

THE GENERALITY LANDS

One of the principal functions of the Generality was the administration of the so-called Generality Lands. These areas, which by 1648 were to comprise almost a third of the Republic, consisted of four entities—States Flanders, States Brabant, Maastricht and the Overmaas (captured in 1632), and Wedde-Westerwolde—to which a fifth, States Upper Gelderland (Roermond and Venlo), was added in 1713. But until the capture of 's-Hertogenbosch in 1629 (see Map 10) the Generality Lands were still a comparatively small area with only fragments of post-1648 States Brabant yet included in the Republic. To set against this, though, in the years 1597–1605, the county of Lingen was counted among the Generality Lands.[65]

In these areas it was not the individual provinces but the Generality which was the formal sovereign in place of the dispossessed Spanish king.[66] Initially, though, the authority of the Generality, as distinct from that of individual provinces administering districts on behalf of the Generality, was more theoretical than real. The absence of any effective check on the influence of whichever province lay nearest enabled Zeeland to dominate States Flanders and, to an extent, the marquisate of Bergen-op-Zoom, in States Brabant, Holland to hold sway over the northern fringes of States Brabant, and Friesland over Wedde and Westerwolde. Only gradually, during the 1590s, did Oldenbarnevelt and the States of Holland succeed in welding together a real Generality administration, run by the *Raad van State* in The Hague, able to curb the influence of the lesser provinces in their respective spheres of influence. A key step was bringing the fortresses of Wedde and Westerwolde under the direct administration of the *Raad van State*, in 1596.

Nevertheless, the Generality was not fully successful throughout the Generality Lands and various disparities, and vestiges of the pre-1590 situation, persisted down to the end of the United Provinces in 1795. In States Flanders, for example, the substitution of the authority of the States General and *Raad van State* for that of the States of Zeeland advanced

---

[65] Van Winter, *Westerwolde*, 27; Van Winter, 'De Zeven Provincien', 14–15.
[66] Van Slingelandt, *Staatkundige geschriften*, ii. 244–5.

further in the main body of States Flanders than in the five garrisons of the so-called *committimus*—Axel, Terneuzen, Biervliet, and the two river fortresses of Lillo and Liefkenshoek, on the Scheldt below Antwerp. In most of States Flanders, not only were the burgomasters and magistrates of towns such as Sluis, Aardenburg, IJzendijke and Hulst (in the years 1591–6 and again after 1645) confirmed or changed each year by delegates from the States General but all aspects of the administration were supervised and checked from The Hague. The various *baljuws* of the region, including the 'high *baljuw*' of the jurisdiction known as the 'Vrije van Sluis', which included the island of Cadzand, were appointed for life by the States General. At the head of the judicial administration of States Flanders stood the so-called *Raad van Vlaanderen* (Council of Flanders), which resided in Middelburg. This was a high court, of initially six magistrates, which dealt with major cases, disputes, and appeals arising in States Flanders. The salaries of these councillors were paid by the Generality out of taxes raised in States Flanders. In most of States Flanders, as in most of the Generality Lands, taxes were not only collected in the name of the States General but by Generality officials employed by the *Raad van State*. The garrisons too were administered and paid by the *Raad van State*, as were the Reformed preachers and schoolmasters.

By contrast, in the five places of the *committimus*, the States of Zeeland, on the grounds of a provisional authorization by the *Raad van State* of 1588 and the plea that these places formed the 'bulwark of Zeeland', insisted on administering the garrisons directly and taking charge of tax collection, albeit in the name of the States General. The other provinces disputed this outcome a number of times during the seventeenth century, but it remained essentially unchanged. Nevertheless, the *baljuw* (at Terneuzen) was appointed by the States General and the magistracies of the towns were confirmed, or changed, each year by representatives of the States General. The Reformed preachers too were paid by the Generality.

In States Brabant, initially, the position was far from clear. For not only were the States of Zeeland, Holland, and Gelderland all striving to extend their leverage in various localities but there were additional contending influences at work in the shape of the Stadholder, Maurits, on the one hand, and his older Catholic half-brother, Philips Willem (1554–1618), on the other. For although the latter remained in Spain until 1596 (when he returned to the south Netherlands), it could not be denied that he was the legitimate Prince of Orange—the English members of the *Raad van State* always referred to the Stadholder as 'Count Maurice' until the death of Philips Willem in 1618—and his interests in the Republic were vigorously defended by his sister, William the Silent's other surviving child by his first marriage (see Table 25), Maria van Nassau. But despite the complexities, Oldenbarnevelt and the States of Holland broadly succeeded during the 1590s in advancing the authority of the Generality, in particular by bringing the fixed garrisons and the fiscal regime under the control of the *Raad van State*. In 1591, they also transferred the power to nominate the magistrates of the high court of States Brabant, the *Raad van Brabant*, from the Stadholder to the States General.[67] But the seigneurial rights of the House of Orange remained formidable, not least in the barony and city of Breda, and the continuing dispute between Maurits and his older half-brother and sister, though it weakened Maurits's position in some respects, also added to the States General's difficulties. For Oldenbarnevelt and the Holland regents were caught on the one hand by their need not to offend Maurits and, on the other, by their anxiety to prevent his extending his seigneurial sway at the expense of the Generality.

Attempting to steer between these pitfalls, the States General recognized Maurits as 'administrator' of the legacy of William the Silent and 'First Noble' of States Brabant but, at the same time, by no means quashed the claims of Philips Willem and Maria.[68] Nor were the Holland regents willing to acquiesce in Maurits's wish that States Brabant should be given representation as a full voting province in the States General. For this would, at a stroke, have greatly diminished the sway of the Generality and enhanced that of the House of Orange. Thus the petition requesting this change in the status of States Brabant, submitted by Bergen-op-Zoom in 1587–8, by Bergen-op-Zoom together with Breda in 1596, and by both these towns, together with Grave and Willemstad, in 1607–8—all three initiatives warmly sponsored by Maurits—was firmly rejected by the Holland regents.[69] The States General did not dispute, though, that it was Orange's right to appoint the burgomasters and magistrates of the towns of which he was lord, as well as the *drost* of Breda. For many years, from 1590 when he captured Breda and Steenbergen, Maurits appointed these officers. However, in 1606 Philips Willem was recognized in the Republic as lord of Breda and Steenbergen, and his right to make these appointments acknowledged, provided, as Oldenbarnevelt stressed, he did so maintaining the 'Union and the Reformed religion'. Philips Willem duly made his ceremonial entry into his town of Breda in July 1610 and, from then until his death, regularly appointed the magistrates in his lordships. Though he restored Catholic

---

[67] Christ, *Brabantsche Saecke*, 55–6.
[68] *Geschiedenis van Breda*, ii. 52–3.
[69] Christ, *Brabantsche Saecke*, 55, 65–6, 104.

services in the castle of Breda, he did not try to challenge the ascendancy of the Reformed Church in the city.[70] On the death of the *drost*, though, in 1613, he did attempt to appoint a Catholic, a move which the States General flatly refused to accept. William the Silent's Catholic successor as Prince of Orange was obliged by the Generality to nominate a member of the public Church as his *drost*.

Such episodes demonstrated that the Generality was the highest authority in the barony of Breda and all States Brabant, despite the extensive rights and powers of the House of Orange, exercising its authority through its garrisons and military governors. The military governor of Breda, Justinus van Nassau, a bastard half-brother of both Philips Willem and Maurits, never ceased to give his primary loyalty to the States General. The position was the same at Bergen-op-Zoom, Grave, and Willemstad. While there were powerful conflicting interests at work in States Brabant, and the solutions were not always clear-cut, during the 1590s the ascendancy of the States General and its administrative organ, the *Raad van State*, became unchallengeable; this meant that the driving force behind them—Oldenbarnevelt and the States of Holland—was ultimately in control.

In theory, the States General, by supplanting the king of Spain as sovereign in States Brabant and Flanders, were obliged to observe the same limits on their power as the Habsburg monarch had sworn to uphold. Among other things, this implied that the Generality had no right to levy taxes not consented to by the States of Brabant and Flanders. The States General circumvented this obstacle by pointing out that these provinces, whilst participating in the General Union, had approved the principle of the 'General Means' in 1583. The towns of States Brabant objected that the consent of 1583 did not stretch to approving the hefty increases introduced by the Generality since that date; but such objections were routinely ignored.

THE STADHOLDERATE

Charles V established the precedent, on acquiring Gelderland in 1543, of grouping the Netherlands provinces north of the rivers under three Stadholders. In this way the northern Netherlands was intentionally divided into three separate blocks regarding military command, patronage, and law and order. By installing three Stadholders in the north, the Emperor prevented any one becoming excessively powerful.

---

[70] *Geschiedenis van Breda*, ii. 53.

After 1572, the role of the provincial States was greatly strengthened, but this did not mean that the Stadholders lost their earlier importance. Between 1572 and 1576 there was just one Stadholder in the rebel Netherlands, William the Silent, but he was overwhelmingly the dominant figure in the regime. Later the States General, in Brabant, appointed Rennenberg Stadholder of Friesland, Groningen, and Overijssel, while Jan van Nassau became Stadholder of Gelderland, so that there were again three Stadholders in the northern provinces. In one respect, indeed, the Union of Utrecht extended the powers of the Stadholders. As there was now no king to mediate between provinces, the provinces agreed that 'their differences must provisionally be referred and submitted to the present stadholders of the provinces who will bring about a settlement or, at their own discretion, give their judgment on the differences'.[71]

After Rennenberg's defection, William the Silent was made Stadholder in the northernmost provinces but, after his assassination, the provinces resumed the tradition of having three different Stadholders. Willem Lodewijk, William the Silent's lieutenant-stadholder in Friesland, was proclaimed full Stadholder of Friesland and the Ommelands, Maurits became Stadholder of Holland and Zeeland, while Utrecht, Gelderland, and Overijssel were placed under the German Calvinist Count Adolf von Neuenahr (1583–9). The importance of the Stadholders was acknowledged in the treaty of Nonsuch, which stipulated that the 'gouverneurs' were to be appointed by the *Raad van State*, then the executive of the Generality. The English queen recognized neither the Generality, nor the provinces, as sovereigns in the northern Netherlands, continuing to see Philip II as rightful sovereign; but she did choose to regard the Generality as a sort of proxy for the king and, since her leverage was chiefly exerted through the States General, desired that the appointment of Stadholders should remain a function of the Generality. Holland, however, argued that since 'Count Maurice and other governors had received their commissions from the States' of the provinces of which they were Stadholder, and since the provinces were the heirs to the king of Spain, as sovereigns, Maurits's commission should stand and the provinces should in future make the appointments.[72]

Though Leicester did not contest Maurits's appointment as Stadholder of Holland and Zeeland, neither did he abandon the principle that Stadholders were appointed by the Generality rather than individual provinces. Like

[71] Kossmann and Mellink, *Texts*, 169.
[72] Wernham, 'English Policy and the Revolt', 36–8.

Rennenberg and Neuenahr, in their provinces, Willem Lodewijk had received his commission as Stadholder of Friesland from the States General, not the provincial States.[73] Leicester confirmed this commission too, though Carel Roorda and his adherents argued that Friesland was no less sovereign than Holland and that Willem Lodewijk's commission from the Generality should be reissued in the name of the provincial States.

TABLE 9. *The Stadholders of Holland, Zeeland, and Utrecht and (from 1590) Gelderland and Overijssel*

Habsburg Stadholders	Dates
Antoine de Lalaing, Count of Hoogstraten	1522–40 (Utrecht from 1527)
René de Châlons, Prince of Orange	1540–4
Lodewijk of Flanders, Lord of Praat	1544–7
Maximilian of Burgundy, Marquis of Veere	1547–58
William I, Prince of Orange	1559–67
Maximilien de Henin, Count of Bossu[a]	1567–73(4)
Gilles de Berlaymont, Baron de Hierges[b]	1574–7
States Stadholders	
William I, Prince of Orange	1572–84
Maurits, Count of Nassau	1585–1625 (Utrecht from 1590)
Frederik Hendrik, Prince of Orange	1625–47
William II, Prince of Orange	1647–50
William III, Prince of Orange	1672–1702
William IV, Prince of Orange	1747–51 (Gelderland from 1729)
William V, Prince Orange	1751–95

[a] Bossu was captured by the rebels in the crushing defeat suffered by the royalist fleet on the Zuider Zee in October 1573 but, in theory, remained the king's Stadholder until the following year.

[b] Hierges was effectively Stadholder of the province of Utrecht plus Amsterdam, Haarlem, and the South Holland towns of Heusden and Geertruidenberg and also Oudewater and Schoonhoven (which he retook in 1575) and the Zeeland towns of Goes and Tholen.

After Leicester's departure, there were, thus, still three Stadholders. But it remained unclear whether the sovereign power of appointing future Stadholders rested with the Generality or the States provincial. Moreover, the continuance of the system of three Stadholders was undeniably fragmenting military command, and patronage, as Charles V had intended but as was scarcely relevant to the existing situation. The death of Neuenahr, in

[73] Bor, *Oorspronck*, v. 62v.

October 1589, provided the opportunity to advance the cohesion of the Republic, and Holland's influence, by bringing Neunahr's three provinces—Utrecht, Overijssel, and Gelderland—under the same Stadholder as Holland and Zeeland. But the States of Friesland saw this too and dispatched a delegation to Overijssel to try to persuade the States there to renew the tradition observed in Habsburg times and under Rennenberg, and choose Friesland's Stadholder rather than Holland's.[74] Overijssel, however, was more interested in securing Holland's help to eject the Frisians, from Hasselt and Steenwijk, than in joining Friesland to oppose Holland. Consequently, Overijssel, like Utrecht, appointed Maurits. However, in both cases, the choice was approved and proclaimed, by the Generality, leaving the constitutional question unresolved.[75]

Maurits was formally appointed Stadholder of Overijssel, by the States General, in February 1590. The States of Gelderland also decided to appoint Maurits. But they proceeded without reference to the Generality. The English members on the *Raad van State* protested, with the result, as was later reported, that the 'Council of State, and likewise the Count [Maurits] himself lett them understand that the forme of their election was against the 24th Article of the Treaty with her Majesty by which it is provided that in every suche vacation of a governor, the province itself shall nominate two or three persons, of which the Council of State shall make election of one'.[76]

Oldenbarnevelt and Maurits persuaded the States General to confirm the appointment, asking the *Raad* to do likewise. The *Raad* would have done so, had the English members not blocked it, in order to uphold the treaty and the queen's prestige. After several months' delay Gelderland agreed to start again and stick to the prescribed procedure. The name of the Calvinist Count Johann, of East Friesland, was placed beside that of Maurits and the double nomination submitted to the *Raad van State*.[77] As Bodley admitted, all this was done only 'for the forme' and once the stipulation in the treaty was complied with, the *Raad* itself chose 'Count Maurice'.

But this still left the question of who appointed the Stadholders unresolved. In 1595, Willem Lodewijk was proclaimed Stadholder of the new province of Groningen by the States General, not the province. Similarly, in 1596, the States General chose Willem Lodewijk Stadholder of Drenthe, and also of Wedde and Westerwolde, though the States of Drenthe drew up

---

[74] Van Reyd, *Historie*, 199.
[75] Overdiep, *Groninger schansenkrijg*, 15.
[76] PRO SP 84/41, fos. 339–40. Bodley to Burghley, 17 Apr. 1591.
[77] De Meester, *Gesch. van de Staten van Gelderland*, 198–9.

their Stadholder's 'instructions'.[78] After 1596, there were no further vacancies for Stadholder until the death of Willem Lodewijk, in 1620. Remarkably enough, it was then, after the victory of the Generality in its contest with the States of Holland, in 1618, that, for the first time, a province chose its Stadholder without any intervention by the *Raad van State* or States

TABLE 10. *The Stadholders of Friesland and (from 1536) Groningen*

Habsburg Stadholders	Dates
Floris van Egmond, Count of Buren	1515–17
Georg Schenck von Tautenburg	1521–40
Maximilian van Egmond, Count of Buren	1540–48
Jean de Ligne, Count of Aremberg	1548–68
Charles de Brimeu, Count of Megen	1568–72
Gilles de Berlaymont, Baron de Hierges	1572–3
Don Caspar de Robles	1573–6
States Stadholders	
Georges de Lalaing, Count of Rennenberg	1576–80 (1580–1 for Philip II)
William the Silent, Prince of Orange	1580–4
Willem Lodewijk, Count of Nassau-Dillenburg	1584–1620 (of Groningen from 1595)
Ernst Casimir, Count of Nassau	1620–32 (but not of Groningen)
Hendrik Casimir I, Count of Nassau	1632–40
Willem Frederik, Count of Nassau	1640–64 (of Groningen, from 1650)
Hendrik Casimir II, Count of Nassau	1664–96
Johan Willem Friso, Count of Nassau and (from 1702) Prince of Orange	1696–1711
William IV, Prince of Orange	1711–51
William V, Prince of Orange	1751–95

General.[79] The Frisians chose Ernst Casimir (see Table 10). Groningen and Drenthe chose Maurits, again without their choices requiring the approval of the States General. After 1620, it was accepted that the provinces alone selected their Stadholders.

The stadholderate in each province was coupled with the captaincy-general, that is, command of the army. In practice, Maurits was also

---

[78] Heringa, *Gesch. van Drente*, i. 290–1.   [79] Fruin, *Gesch. der staatsinsellingen*, 215.

captain-general of the Union as a whole, with the Frisian Stadholder as his deputy, though, in contrast to later Stadholders, this was not formally proclaimed, albeit he was appointed admiral of the Union, overall commander of the navy. But while the stadholderate was coupled with the captaincy-general, it was not identical with it. For the stadholderate, as such, was essentially a non-military office, carrying powers and responsibilities relating to the political process and administration of justice. The Stadholder, no longer appointed by the king but by the provinces, was the highest-ranking office-holder and dignitary in each province. He was not a member of the provincial States, or the colleges of *Gecommitteerde Raden* and Delegated States, but could appear in their midst whenever he chose and address them and, under various rubrics, was charged with resolving conflicts and deadlock within these bodies. In the case of the new province of Groningen, the Stadholder was assigned the casting vote in both the full and Delegated States, under the 'instructions' of 1595; but an argument then ensued in the States of Groningen, which dragged on until 1620, over whether this power did in fact apply in the Delegated States and how it applied in the full States.[80]

In all provinces, the Stadholders were charged with overseeing the administration of justice. The Stadholder, in varying degrees in different provinces, exercised significant powers of appointment and patronage of judicial officials, and although formally it was the States provincial—and, in the case of Drenthe, the States General[81]—who appointed *drosts*, the Stadholders frequently exerted a decisive influence over their selection, as they did also in the case of the *baljuws* in the Holland and Zeeland countryside. In Holland, and comparably in other provinces, it was the Stadholder who selected the magistrates (*schepenen*) in the towns, from nominations submitted by the town councils, and who exercised a general right to supervise *vroedschap* elections and intervene in cases of irregularity. In some towns (but not Amsterdam), the Stadholder also retained the pre-1572 right of the ruler to select the burgomasters from nominations submitted by the *vroedschap*. However, Maurits's powers to decide appointments in the towns were more theoretical than real, down to 1618, when they were vigorously revived. Finally, the Stadholder was charged in each province with a general responsibility for maintaining the Reformed Church.

A key feature of the Dutch scene at the close of the sixteenth century and outset of the seventeenth was the close co-operation between the remaining

---

[80] Wiersum, *Gedwongen vereeniging*, 23–8.   [81] Smit, *Bestuursinstellingen*, 99–101.

Stadholders.[82] Maurits and Willem Lodewijk collaborated not only in the military sphere but also politically, working together, with Oldenbarnevelt and the *Raad van State*, to strengthen the Generality and the federal principle, so as to increase the effectiveness of the Republic. Maurits had his rows with Oldenbarnevelt, notably during the Nieuwpoort campaign of 1600. But in the eyes of the Frisian Roordists, and other particularists in the lesser provinces, both Stadholders worked hand in hand with the Holland regents to subordinate the lesser provinces to the Generality and to Holland.[83]

Under the Habsburgs, the Stadholders had been great nobles whose entourages reflected the splendour and hierarchical world of courtly culture. Despite the fact that, after 1572, the United Provinces were a republic, and had no royal master, the courtly culture and aristocratic outlook surrounding the Stadholders continued as before and, indeed, took hold even more strongly, being used by the new Stadholders to enhance their prestige, authority, and dynastic pretensions. At dinner, in his quarters at the Binnenhof in The Hague, Maurits was surrounded by 'persons of quality', including French and German nobles who held senior commissions in the States General's army, as well as prominent Dutch nobles.[84] Non-nobles occupied a subordinate position at the Stadholder's court, which was comparatively modest before the coup of 1618 but subsequently gained considerably in splendour, especially after the arrival of the 'Winter' king and queen of Bohemia, and their entourage, in The Hague, in 1621 and under Frederik Hendrik, in the 1630s.

---

[82] Van Deursen, 'Maurits', 92, 97.
[83] Ibid.; Rowen, *Princes of Orange*, 40.
[84] Mörke, 'Hofcultuur', 45–6.

14

The Commencement of
Dutch World Trade Primacy

❖

REVOLT, COMMERCE, AND MIGRATION FROM THE SOUTH

The 1590s, the years of transition from the harsh circumstances of the Revolt to the onset of the Golden Age, witnessed a dramatic transformation of Dutch urban society and the economy. At the heart of this process, one of the most crucial shifts in Dutch history, was the rise of the 'rich trades' and the processing industries which accompanied them. This economic 'miracle' of the 1590s resulted from the convergence of many factors: the internal stabilization of the Republic after 1588, improvement in the strategic situation, the reopening of the rivers and waterways linking Holland and Germany, influx of capital and skills from Antwerp after 1585, the lifting of Philip II's embargo on Dutch ships and cargoes in the Iberian peninsula in 1590 (whilst retaining his embargo on England), and the Republic's tightening grip on the Scheldt and Ems estuaries and naval blockade of the Flemish coast. The explosive expansion of its commerce which followed transformed the Republic into Europe's chief emporium and bestowed a general primacy in world commerce which was to endure for a century and a half.[1] The impact of this on a small country was overwhelming, even unparalleled in history, in terms of the pace, and scope, of the socio-economic transformation, the galvanization of an urban civilization which followed in its wake. Dutch dominance of the 'rich trades' made possible not only a rapid increase in prosperity and resources but a massive, sustained expansion of the cities and proliferation of new skills and industries.

Admittedly, the maritime towns of Holland and Zeeland grew also before 1572. In Amsterdam, the number of houses doubled between 1514 and 1562

---

[1] Israel, *Dutch Primacy*, 38–79; Israel, *Empires and Entrepots*, 135–41, 190–202; Israel, 'The "New History" ', 474–80.

and the population almost trebled from 11,000 to around 30,000.[2] But this was still modest compared to Antwerp, which had a population of around 85,000, in 1560, or Ghent with around 45,000, or larger cities, in neighbouring lands, such as London, Rouen, or Lyons. Meanwhile, the non-maritime towns of the north Netherlands stagnated, for an entire century, down to 1590, not just in the case of the IJssel towns—Kampen, Deventer, Zwolle, and Zutphen—and also Utrecht, Groningen, and 's-Hertogenbosch, but the inland towns of Holland—Leiden, Haarlem, Gouda, Delft, and Dordrecht—as well. All these declined, stagnated, or else, in the case of Delft, grew only slightly. Dordrecht lost around 10 per cent of its population between 1514 and 1585, shrinking to around 10,500. When the Spaniards laid siege to Leiden, in 1573, the city's population, around 12,500, was no larger than it had been in 1514.[3] For, until the 1580s, Leiden's cloth industry was contracting and there was no new industrial activity with which to replace it. The Dutch entrepôt of the mid-sixteenth century simply provided no basis for either success or growth in inland manufactures.

The situation began to change, during the mid 1580s, with the great influx of émigré population, and skills, from the south Netherlands. This was one of the four great west European migrations of early modern times with the expulsion of the Jews from Spain (1492), the Protestant exodus from the Habsburg Netherlands in the 1560s, and the flight of the Huguenots from France culminating in the late 1680s. The transfer of population within the Netherlands from south to north, at its peak in 1585–7, may well have been the largest of these, amounting to over 100,000 refugees and, possibly, as many as 150,000. By no means all the émigrés remained in the north Netherlands. Substantial numbers migrated to Germany, others to England. But most settled in the towns of Holland and Zeeland. All the main cities of the south suffered a catastrophic haemorrhage of inhabitants in the late 1580s (see Table 4).[4] Antwerp, where the population stood at 84,000, in 1583, and 55,000, after the siege, in 1585, had dwindled to 42,000, by 1589. Ghent lost about half its population. Mechelen, a city of around 30,000 inhabitants, in 1550, was down to only about 11,000 by 1590. Bruges lost about half its inhabitants.

The large numbers migrating to the north settled mainly in a few cities in one part of the country. The city of Utrecht, with numerous empty cloisters to offer as premises, tried to attract textile workers but few came. After Maurits's capture of Groningen in 1594, the new Protestant *raad* did

[2] Nusteling, *Welvaart en werkgelengenheid*, 234.
[3] See tables 3 and 12.
[4] Briels, *Zuid-Nederlanders*, 28, 47, 69–70; Voet, *Antwerp*, 238.

likewise but again with scant success. The refugees settled extensively only in the towns of Holland and Zeeland. Middelburg trebled in size, to around 30,000, during the half-century, from 1570, mainly owing to immigration from the south Netherlands.[5] Leiden, having stagnated for a century, grew spectacularly from 13,000 in 1581 to over 26,000 by 1600, almost entirely through immigration from the south.[6] Meanwhile, Amsterdam attracted the largest number of immigrants, approximately 30,000; by 1600, they amounted to a third of the city's population. Large numbers settled also in Haarlem, boosting the city's population from 14,000 in 1570 to 39,000 by 1622. Smaller numbers settled in other Holland and Zeeland towns but still with an appreciable impact. At Delft, the immigrants amounted to some 17 per cent of the population by 1600. Flushing, with 4,425 inhabitants, in 885 houses, in 1577,[7] had grown by one-third by the late 1580s. Bodley was amazed to find 5,000 people in Bergen-op-Zoom, in 1589, a large proportion recent immigrants,[8] though many of these subsequently moved on to Holland.

Absorbing a massive influx of immigrants is a complex, and difficult, process in any human context, imposing great strains. The degree of success achieved depends, partly, on the absorptive capacity of the host society and, partly, on the adaptability of the skills of the immigrants. What is most remarkable about the exodus to the north after 1585 is the speed and comparative ease with which the newcomers were integrated into Dutch society and economic life. Some more specialized skills of the immigrants could not be absorbed, initially, because in 1585 the north had no 'rich trades'. The Antwerp sugar-refiners who arrived in Holland, in the late 1580s, for example, moved on to Hamburg, because Holland, as yet, had no share in the international sugar trade. The great merchants who left Antwerp originally preferred north-west Germany[9] to the north Netherlands, because, in the late 1580s, Holland was not suitable for high-value, and long-distance, trade owing (especially) to Philip II's embargo against Dutch shipping and goods (1585–90), excluding the Dutch from the Iberian peninsula, and thus access to the products of the Spanish and Portuguese Indies; also Spanish advances in the north-east Netherlands blocked the routes between Holland and Germany. But Holland and Zeeland were well placed to accommodate the bulk of the immigration and, once absorbed, it

[5] Briels, *Zuid-Nederlanders*, 184–90.
[6] Van Maanen, 'Vermogensopbouw', 11.
[7] Poort, 'English Garrisons', 72.
[8] PRO SP 84/32, fo. 264v. Bodley to Walsingham, Bergen-op-Zoom, 31 May 1589.
[9] Kellenbenz, 'Pfeffermarkt', 33–6.

provided much of what was needed for the subsequent penetration of the
'rich trades'. Baltic grain and herring, combined with Leicester's ban on
exports to the south, ensured that, just when the refugees poured in, the
United Provinces were awash with cheap provisions.[10] There was nowhere
the refugees could have found cheaper, or more plentiful, food. The Holland
and Zeeland towns abounded in confiscated monastic and convent buildings, which the town councils hastened to offer on easy terms, as workshops
and habitations.[11] Housing was a problem and urban rents rose to exorbitant levels. But, at the same time, the Republic, with its inland waterways,
fleets of river vessels, and timber depots, was well equipped to mount a
massive construction boom. At Leiden, the *vroedschap* needed the best
monastic buildings for the university and civic institutions, but there were
plenty more for use for textile workshops and conversion into habitations
for weavers.[12]

Immigrants from the south amounted to approximately 10 per cent of the
total population of the United Provinces in the 1590s, and a far higher
proportion of the population of the large towns of Holland and Zeeland.
The urban labour force had been vastly expanded. Yet there was little
friction in the labour market, for the new labour force hardly anywhere
overlapped, or competed, with the existing Dutch proletariat. The United
Provinces, at the end of the sixteenth century, was a land of two proleta-
riats—the native and the immigrant—which performed largely separate
tasks. The pre-1585 Dutch economy, based on shipping, bulk-carrying,
fisheries, and agriculture, had generated few export-orientated industries
and none of the skills or trained operatives needed to process high-value
commodities. Activities such as printing and art where there were now two
competing groups of trained men were rare. By and large the previous
Dutch proletariat of seamen, fishermen, bargemen, shipyard workers, and
peat-diggers felt little adverse effect from the influx of newcomers.

But the broadening of the economy, and acceleration of urban growth,
resulting from the immigration, could not have proceeded had not massive
penetration of the 'rich trades' followed directly, in the 1590s. For successful
absorption of the émigrés and their skills, and sustaining the expansion of
the Holland towns, depended on transferring a great deal of new commerce
and industrial activity to the Dutch seaboard, and before 1590, immigrants
or no immigrants, it was simply not possible for the Dutch overseas trading
system to grow dramatically in this way, given that the besieged rump of the

[10] Velius, *Chronyk van Hoorn*, 470; Baasch, *Holländische Wirtschaftsgeschichte*, 256–7.
[11] Geselschap, *Gouda. Zeven eeuwen stad*, 136–7.
[12] Orlers, *Beschrijvinge*, 118–20.

Republic was tightly surrounded on three sides by Spanish armies, communications with Germany disrupted, and Dutch shipping and goods under ban in Spain and Portugal. Admittedly, Philip II's embargo was less than watertight. The Dutch carried on some trade, whilst the embargoes were in force, with the Iberian lands. But the Spanish measures cut out most of it and made what remained riskier, more expensive and difficult, severely handicapping the Dutch (and English) to the advantage of the Hanseatics.

The rise of the 'rich trades' in the 1590s, including (from 1598) long-distance colonial commerce, was thus of paramount importance not only for the history of Dutch trade and shipping, but for society, industry, the cities, the entire fabric and culture of the Dutch Golden Age. In the 1580s, the Republic was in retreat on every front. The outlook was decidedly one of gloom for the present and future. Without the fundamental restructuring of the Dutch overseas trading system, in the 1590s, the recent influx of immigrants and skills could not have been absorbed, the cities could not have rapidly expanded, and there could not have been a subsequent Golden Age.

Thus, while it is true that the exodus from the south was a crucial factor it was by no means a sufficient one, on its own, to generate the economic 'miracle' of the 1590s. No less vital was the changed political and strategic context.[13] Philip II's decision to intervene in France in 1590, the drastic weakening of the Spanish pressure on the north which resulted, Maurits's great offensives of 1591, 1593–4, and 1597, clearing the Spaniards from the IJssel, Waal, and other main river routes, the securing of the Republic's territory, and Philip II's lifting of his embargo against Dutch commerce with Spain and Portugal, combined with the tightening of the Dutch naval blockade of the south, created, within a few years, an entirely new framework and altogether more favourable conditions. The 1590s created confidence that the Republic had a secure future and that Holland was a viable base for large-scale investment in commerce and manufacturing processes. This, in turn, began attracting, especially to Amsterdam, many of the élite merchants from Antwerp who had migrated in the 1580s to Hamburg, Bremen, Emden, Stade, Cologne, and Frankfurt in preference to what was then a besieged, gloom-ridden, and economically depressed Republic.

These changes generated massive investment during the 1590s, above all at Amsterdam but also in Middelburg, Rotterdam, Delft, Haarlem, and the West Frisian ports, in a whole range of 'rich trades', commencing with the

[13] Israel, *Dutch Primacy*, 38–43; Israel, *Empires and Entrepots*, 137–45, 189–202.

traffic now reviving with Spain, Portugal, and the Mediterranean. Armed with the spices, sugar, silks, dyestuffs, Mediterranean fruit and wine, and Spanish American silver, obtained in the south, merchants based in Holland and Zeeland then rapidly outstripped merchants operating from Hamburg, Lübeck, and London in supplying these commodities to the north.[14] In this way the Dutch, whose Baltic commerce had previously been confined to a small number of bulky commodities of relatively low value, mainly grain, timber, salt, herring, and wine, and restricted to the grain and timber ports on the southern and eastern shores of the Baltic, embarked on what has been called the 'second Dutch conquest' of the Baltic trade—their penetration of the high-value traffic formerly dominated by the Hanseatics and English. As an extension of this process, Dutch ships began sailing regularly also around the top of Scandinavia to the White Sea port of Archangel, at that time Russia's window on the west. In 1590 this Muscovy traffic was solidly in the hands of the English. But in a situation in which the Dutch now had better access to the Iberian market, and colonial goods, than London there was little chance that the English could long resist the Dutch challenge—for spices and silver were the key. By 1600 merchants based in Amsterdam, mostly Antwerp émigrés, had already outstripped the English Muscovy trade.[15]

Quite soon, Spanish ministers realized that Dutch access to Spain and Portugal, and the control this gave over the distribution of spices, sugar, and other colonial commodities, and Mediterranean products, throughout northern Europe, was fuelling the sensational expansion of Dutch power and wealth, and of the Dutch cities, now in progress. Clearly this access was also nourishing the rise of the new Dutch textile industries based on the techniques brought by the immigrants of 1585 for it was with linen and new draperies, manufactured by southern immigrants at Haarlem and Leiden, as well as with capital transferred from the south Netherlands, that the new merchant élite of Holland and Zeeland were buying up the colonial and high-value commodities of southern Europe.

Consequently, it was decided at the commencement of Philip III's reign, in 1598, to reimpose the embargoes in Spain and Portugal on Dutch ships, goods, and merchants. But this Spanish attempt to reverse what had happened served only further to strengthen the burgeoning Dutch overseas trading system by forcing the élite merchants of Holland and Zeeland—if they were not to lose the newly won 'rich trades' in Europe—to invest

[14] Israel, *Dutch Primacy*, 49–52.
[15] Hart, *Geschrift en getal*, 305–7; Bushkovitch, *Merchants of Moscow*, 45, 61.

immediately, and heavily, in a new direct traffic to the Indies east and west (see pp. 320–1 below).

Dutch world trade primacy, based on the Dutch entrepôt's role, after 1590, as a general reservoir of commodities of all types, and from all parts of the world, both high-value and bulk, and an incomparable mass of shipping with which to bring the goods in and out, lasted almost a century and a half. But during this long period there were a number of basic shifts in the rhythm and general direction of the Dutch entrepôt and it is, consequently, necessary to divide the phenomenon into several phases. Phase One (1590–1609) saw the establishment of the Dutch 'rich trades' and the rise of the new long-distance traffic to the East Indies, Africa, and the Americas. Phase Two (1609–21), shaped by the Twelve Years Truce (1609–21), was characterized by a certain loss of momentum in colonial trade, particularly marked in the Caribbean and Brazil but even greater success than before in European waters. The lifting of the Spanish embargoes, in 1609, combined with the suspension of Spanish and Flemish privateering against Dutch shipping, reduced Dutch freight and marine insurance charges, enhancing further the competitive edge the Dutch enjoyed over the English and Hanseatics through their lower freight rates.[16] This, together with improved access to the Mediterranean as well as Spain and Portugal, greatly strengthened Dutch Mediterranean trade (for the time being), temporarily enabled the Dutch to eclipse the English in the direct seaborne trade to the Levant,[17] and also brought the Dutch to the peak of their ascendancy in Baltic commerce. Phase Two was likewise much more favourable than Phase One for the fisheries.

However, during Phase Two Zeeland failed to share in the prosperity of Holland, for the Truce also involved the temporary lifting of the Dutch naval blockade of the Flemish coast (though not the restrictions on the Scheldt). As a result, merchants in the South Netherlands could resume importing cargoes direct from the Baltic and southern Europe to the Flemish seaports, and then on to Bruges, Ghent, and Antwerp, bypassing the Zeeland entrepôt. Thus, as the States of Zeeland observed, in October 1614, the importing of salt from Portugal and France to the south Netherlands, for refining at Ghent, was totally diverted from Zeeland and the Scheldt to Ostend and Dunkirk.[18] Indeed, much of the Zeeland transit traffic to the south collapsed (until 1621). Since this was Zeeland's principal commerce, the shift was a severe blow to the whole province. It was in

[16] Israel, *Dutch Primacy*, 80–120.
[17] Israel, *Empires and Entrepots*, 139–47.
[18] *Notulen* SZ 1614, 241. 'Advys' of the *Gecommitteerde Raden*, 17 Oct. 1614.

recognition of this that the States General agreed in 1612 to the reduction of Zeeland's quota to the Generality budget, the Amsterdam city council commenting that this was only just, given the 'decadence' into which Zeeland had lapsed.[19]

Phase Three (1621–47) was shaped principally by the resumption of the Dutch–Spanish conflict, reimposition of the embargoes, and the Dutch naval blockade of the Flemish coast. During this phase, Zeeland recovered and colonial commerce gained in momentum, but Dutch European trade was adversely affected, contracting in absolute terms until after 1630, despite the success of re-exports of colonial goods to northern Europe and the supply of provisions, via the North German ports and estuaries, to the armies operating in the devastated interior of Germany. A particular problem, from the late 1620s, was the rapid growth of the Flemish privateering fleet, at Dunkirk and Ostend, and its mounting impact on Dutch shipping. The loss of many hundreds of ships and cargoes in the North Sea and English Channel drove up Dutch freight and marine insurance rates to drastically higher levels than pertained during Phase Two.[20] Especially hard-hit during this period was Dutch commerce with southern Europe, not only Spain and Portugal but also Italy and the Levant. The recently flourishing Dutch Levant trade collapsed almost completely in the early 1620s, and did not recover until the years around 1647. Another difficulty during Phase Three was chronic shortage of salt suitable for the fisheries. The Spaniards not only succeeded in preventing the Dutch obtaining Portuguese salt for twenty years from 1621 to the Portuguese secession of 1640–1, but also, by building forts at the main salt-pans in the Caribbean, deprived the Dutch of the alternative supply to which they had resorted in 1598–1607.

These problems, compounded by the disruption of the Baltic trade in the late 1620s, caused a serious slump in Holland from 1621, the most protracted of the seventeenth century though it was less traumatic than the depression of the 1670s. This recession in the Dutch maritime economy, from 1621 until the early 1630s also adversely affected many industries. Shipbuilding, salt-refining, sugar-refining, and printing[21] all contracted significantly during these years. Recovery began in the early 1630s and by the late 1630s had become a feverish boom in some sectors, especially agriculture, textiles, colonial trade, and financial speculation. But Dutch European

[19] GA Amsterdam vroed. res. 8 May 1612.
[20] Schreiner, 'Niederländer und die norwegische Holzausfuhr', 324.
[21] I am grateful to A. M. van der Woude for showing me his statistics detailing the recession in Dutch printing beginning around 1621.

commerce remained sluggish down to the late 1640s. Full recovery, and further expansion, in European commerce and the fisheries, had to await the onset of Phase Four (1647–72; see pp. 611–12 below).

The slump of the 1620s was severe but the Republic was spared the full impact of the recession by several developments which partly offset the contraction of shipping and trade. In contrast to other industries, the woollen and linen industries of Leiden and Haarlem benefited from the new situation, partly because the naval blockade of the Flemish coast—and high wartime tariffs on Flemish imports via the inland waterways—reduced exports of manufactures (often of directly competing products) from the south Netherlands towns and hampered their imports of wool. At the same time the Thirty Years War devastated the textile towns of Germany. Consequently, while Dutch Baltic trade as a whole slumped disastrously in the 1620s, exports of Dutch textiles to the Baltic went from strength to strength.[22]

But what above all offset the negative consequences of the recession in large areas of trade and industry was the simultaneous vigorous boom in agriculture. The prosperity of Dutch agriculture during Phase Three, together with the connected growth in the river traffic to the Rhineland, Liège, and the Spanish Netherlands, was also essentially a consequence of the resumed Dutch–Spanish conflict and the Thirty Years War. Demand for Dutch provisions of every kind—dairy produce, beer, fish and meat, and (in as far as any was available) grain and salt, as well as French wine for the officers, and tobacco—was never greater, in either Germany or the south Netherlands. The high tolls which applied on the river traffic to Germany and the south Netherlands also enabled the five Dutch admiralty colleges to cream off large sums in customs (*convoyen en licenten*) with which to assist the financing of Dutch naval expansion.

THE CHANGING BALANCE BETWEEN 'BULK-CARRYING' AND THE 'RICH TRADES'

The maritime slump of the 1620s was one of the harshest of the seventeenth century, second only to the trauma of 1672, its effects not being fully overcome until the 1640s. But, in the wider perspective of Dutch history, its real significance lies in the further shift it precipitated, within the Dutch maritime economy, from bulk freightage to the new high-value commerce.

[22] Bang, *Tabeller*, ii. 196–325; Federowicz, *England's Baltic Trade*, 92–6.

The bulk-carrying traffic in grain, timber, salt, and fish originally came to be dominated by the Dutch, as we have seen, in the fifteenth century. It then expanded impressively during the sixteenth century, culminating in the 1590s and first two decades of the seventeenth century, with the introduction of the famous *fluit*, a specialized seagoing vessel, designed to carry maximum cargo at minimum cost. The rise of the *fluit* was also part of a shift towards using larger vessels for bulk-carrying than had been the practice previously.[23]

Bulk-carrying, especially of Baltic grain and timber, was undoubtedly of fundamental importance in laying the foundations of the Golden Age. Holland's resilience, and resourcefulness, during the Revolt owed much to the widely diffused profits, as well as the ships and seamen, of the Baltic trade. The high level of urbanization, and urban vitality, of Holland and Zeeland on the eve of the Golden Age stemmed largely from the carrying traffic. Also, after 1600, bulk-carrying nourished Holland and Zeeland with a more abundant stock of ships, seamen, and naval stores than could be found anywhere else. Yet, if we define the Golden Age as an enriching, and expansion, well beyond the point reached by the 1580s, it is plainly the 'rich trades', and not bulk freightage, which subsequently contributed most to shaping the economic and social context. Bulk-carrying was already close to the limit of its expansion by the 1590s when the Golden Age began. Its subsequent expansion until 1620 was marginal in character. By contrast, the 'rich trades' grew spectacularly after 1590, generating much larger profits and a much greater accumulation of wealth than bulk trade. Baltic grain, for example, was worth about three million guilders yearly, on the Dutch market, in the middle of the seventeenth century, while the combined value of the three largest 'rich trades'—the East India, Spanish, and Levant trades—in the 1650s and 1660s was approximately seven times as great, over 20 million guilders.[24] Moreover, whilst commerce with Mediterranean and colonial markets, and also high-value commerce with the Baltic and Russia, provided the raw materials for the main export industries of the later seventeenth century—Leiden fine cloth (made from Spanish wool), camlets (Turkish mohair), silks, cottons, fine linen, copper, processed sugar, and tobacco—bulk freightage was of less relevance to industry, except for the case of shipbuilding.[25] Finally, there is the cultural dimension. For it was not bulk-carrying but the new high-value commerce which provided the wealth and, no less important, the rare materials and skills which made

---

[23] Klein, 'De zeventiende eeuw', 103.
[24] Israel, 'The "New History" ', 476.
[25] Israel, *Dutch Primacy*, 8, 35, 114–20, 259–69.

possible the astounding variety and sophistication of the Golden Age. Highly specialized techniques were required to produce dyes, glazes, ceramics, diamonds, fine furniture, patterned linens and silks, and such specialities as 'gold leather', tapestry, and wood marquetry.

Moreover, the contribution of the 'rich trades' increased in the first two-thirds of the seventeenth century, while the relative importance of bulk freightage steadily diminished until by the last quarter of the century it was dwarfed by high-value commerce and industry geared to the 'rich trades'. In absolute terms, bulk-carrying expanded until 1620 but then began to contract—especially in Holland.

Both the timing and reasons for the long-term decline of the West Frisian ports, the heart of the bulk-carrying traffic, are clear. The Sound toll statistics show that Hoorn, Enkhuizen, and Medemblik were especially badly affected by the slump of the 1620s and that these towns never recovered. The initial cause was the sudden contraction of supplies of good salt and herring and, from 1621, a marked drop in Enkhuizen's exports of herring to the Baltic.[26] Thus, the West Frisian ports began to decay owing to the Spanish embargoes, and Spain's (rather effective) measures to cut the flow of high-grade salt to the Republic and attacks on the North Sea herring fishery, though later additional factors came into play which prevented recovery.

While the total number of Dutch ships entering the Baltic recovered to pre-1621 levels temporarily in the 1630s, the number of *fluits* sailing from Holland to the Baltic did not. The reason for this was that there was now a shift from using large *fluits* based in the West Frisian ports of North Holland to using smaller craft, based in Friesland and the Wadden Islands. As a result West Friesland's share of the total Dutch Baltic traffic, which stood at over 30 per cent in 1620, fell to 26 per cent by the late 1620s, and only 18 per cent by 1640.[27] Furthermore, while the other main Holland towns continued to grow vigorously down to 1672, the West Frisian ports, the home of the *fluit* fleets, began to shrink in the 1620s, a process of de-urbanization commencing more than half a century before that in the rest of the Republic. At Enkhuizen, the annual number of baptisms into the Dutch Reformed Church reached its peak, of 854, precisely in the year 1621.[28] After 1621, baptisms at Enkhuizen began slowly, but quite definitely, to diminish. Around that year, Enkhuizen thus reached its absolute peak of

---

[26] Lesger, *Hoorn als stedelijk knooppunt*, 61–2, 85.
[27] Ibid. 85–6, 172.
[28] Ibid. 73; De Vries, *Enkhuizen, 1650–1850*, 72.

22,000 inhabitants (see Table 12), and the population and vitality of Hoorn too began to decline from that point.

THE BEGINNINGS OF THE DUTCH COLONIAL EMPIRE

The years around 1590 form a watershed in Dutch history marking the transition from the sombre, difficult conditions of the 1570s and 1580s to the commencement of the Golden Age. That the beginnings of Dutch long-distance navigation, and the colonial empire, also lie in the 1590s is obviously no accident. Rather, these complex phenomena were the direct consequence of the new opportunities, resources, and dynamism generated by the general restructuring, political, strategic, and economic, which took place in the years around 1590.

Many ingredients were necessary to make possible a vigorous, successful, and enduring maritime expansion in Asian, African, and American seas and all the more so at a time when the Republic was engaged in a full-scale struggle, by land and sea, with Spain. These preconditions were a secure home base for long-term investments, a large accumulation of merchant capital, political support at both civic and provincial level, detailed know-ledge about routes and conditions in the Indies, a transferable surplus of naval and military power at home, and, finally, favourable circumstances for breaking into the hotly contested European pepper, spice, and sugar market. Before 1590 not a single one of these conditions applied and there was little or no prospect that the bulk-carrying traditions of Holland and Zeeland could have translated, in pre-1590 circumstances, into a flourishing long-distance traffic or the founding of a colonial empire.

The internal strengthening of the Republic, and its institutions, in the years 1588–90, strategic improvement of the early 1590s, and influx of merchants, and capital, from Antwerp after 1585 were thus all vital factors in the rise of the Dutch long-distance traffic outside of Europe. But most vital of all was the onset of the 'rich trades', a successful Dutch commerce in high-value commodities within Europe.[29] This phenomenon occurred specifically in the early and mid-1590s. The emergence of Amsterdam as the main rival of Hamburg (which had taken over from Antwerp, after 1585) for control of the distribution of pepper, spices, and sugar in northern Europe, the upsurge of imports of colonial products to Holland, from Spain and Portugal, following the lifting of Philip II's embargo against the Dutch in 1590, and the rapid Dutch penetration of the high-value Muscovy trade

---

[29] Israel, *Dutch Primacy*, 50–67.

in the early 1590s, were all immediate precursors of the rise of Dutch navigation to the Indies east and west in the late 1590s. Commercially, Dutch colonial trade stemmed from the breakthrough in European trade.[30]

The first step in the establishment of the Dutch empire of trade in the Indies was the setting up of the private Compagnie van Verre (Long-Distance Company), at Amsterdam in March 1594. This was a consortium of nine élite merchants, two of whom, Reinier Pauw (1564–1636) and Hendrik Hudde, were influential regents who stood close to the heart of civic government, as well as commerce.[31] Several were immigrants, including two south Netherlanders and Jan Poppen (c.1545–1616), a Protestant from Holstein who founded one of the wealthiest merchant dynasties of Amsterdam. The company gathered a starting capital of 290,000 guilders and fitted out a fleet of four ships manned by 249 men, armed with 100 cannon supplied by the States of Holland. The States also allowed the company exemption from Generality customs on its imports from the East Indies. The fleet sailed from Texel in April 1595, three of the ships returning safely in 1597, albeit with only eighty-nine of the men still alive.

The profits of this first expedition were meagre but the merchants remained undaunted. Indeed, so rapid in the years 1594–7 was the rise of Amsterdam's re-exports of (Portuguese) pepper and spices to Germany, the Baltic, and Russia, at the expense of rival trading powers,[32] that it was obvious to every élite merchant, by 1597, that the Republic had now captured control of the distribution of colonial goods in northern Europe, and that (with London still paralysed, as far as colonial products were concerned, by the effects of the Spanish embargoes against England of 1585–1604) heavy investment in a direct East India traffic, bypassing the Lisbon and Seville entrepôts, was likely to result in massive profits and a tightening of the newly won Dutch grip over the 'rich trades' of northern Europe.

At the same time knowledge about commerce in the East Indies, as well as of the commodities of Asia, was being widely disseminated in the Dutch mercantile towns. This stemmed partly from the resumption of trade with Portugal, following the lifting of Philip II's embargo against the Dutch in 1590, partly from the newly arrived Portuguese crypto-Jewish community in Amsterdam, which initially, in the late 1590s, specialized in importing East India commodities from Lisbon, and, finally, partly from the publication of several books. Pre-eminent among the latter was the *Itinerario* (1596) of Jan

---

[30] Ibid. 67–73.
[31] Van Dillen, *Oudste aandeelhoudersregister*, 6.
[32] Kellenbenz, 'Pfeffermarkt', 33–49.

Huigen van Linschoten, who had gone out to Goa in 1584 as an employee
of the House of Fugger and returned to Europe in 1592. His book was a
veritable merchants' manual of routes, commodities, and conditions in the
East Indies.

Stimulated by the highly favourable circumstances created by the breakthrough in the European 'rich trades' after 1590, there arose a frenetic
interest, and involvement, in the East India traffic during the second half of
the 1590s throughout the Dutch seaboard.[33] The original company was
expanded into a larger consortium with eighteen directors and a starting
capital of 768,466 guilders. A second fleet was prepared, this time consisting
of eight vessels and placed under the command of Jacob Cornelisz. van
Neck, a knowledgeable, competent man who later became a burgomaster of
Amsterdam. Yet, at the same time, two more companies, and fleets, took
shape in Zeeland, the three fleets departing almost simultaneously, in the
spring of 1598. Van Neck returned with four richly laden vessels fourteen
months later, to an ecstatic reception from the Amsterdam business community. After deduction of costs, the Compagnie van Verre made a profit
of 400 per cent.

It was doubtless because the Dutch long-distance traffic had already
begun that the reimposition in 1598 of the embargoes on Dutch ships,
goods, and merchants in Spain and Portugal had such a sensational effect.
By cutting off the flow of colonial and Mediterranean products from Iberia
to the Dutch entrepôt, Spanish ministers hoped to abort the massive
expansion of the Dutch 'rich trades' in Europe.[34] But, precisely by threatening the continuance of their commercial success in Europe, as Grotius and
other seventeenth-century Dutch historians later pointed out, the embargoes
compelled the newly arisen merchant élite of the Dutch maritime towns to
invest massively, and without delay, in the traffic of the Indies. Unless they
were willing to see their European commerce evaporate before their eyes,
and see themselves supplanted by the Hanseatics and English (who were
readmitted to Iberian ports in 1604), the Dutch had to sail to the Indies and
obtain the commodities they needed at source. Moreover, it was vital from
the very outset that this new traffic should be on a sufficiently grand scale
to bring in enough pepper and spices to service a distribution system which
now extended from France to Russia. By 1599, there were no fewer than
eight different companies participating in the East India traffic in Holland
and Zeeland, based at Amsterdam, Rotterdam, Middelburg, Hoorn, and

      [33] Van Dillen, *Oudste aandeelhoudersregister*, 6–11.
      [34] Brulez, 'Zoutinvoer', 184–5; Stols, *Spaanse Brabanders*, i. 8–9; Echevarría Bacigalupe,
'Episodio', 58–85.

Enkhuizen. By the autumn of 1601 no fewer than fourteen Dutch fleets, totalling sixty-five ships, had sailed from the United Provinces to the East Indies,[35] a level which far outstripped the East India trade of both Portugal and England.

But such frantic activity inevitably caused chaotic oscillations in the market, in both the Spice Islands (the Moluccas and Amboina) and Java, and at the European end. By 1601 both prices and profits were falling steeply. It was this that led the merchants participating in the various companies to ask the States of Holland and Zeeland to intervene to impose order on the traffic, warning that if this were not done the newly burgeoning Dutch East India traffic would suffer severe difficulties and perhaps collapse.[36] In this way merchants and States commenced consultations as to how to federate the Dutch traffic so as to place it on a stable, orderly, and enduring basis, deliberations in which Oldenbarnevelt himself played a major role.

The unique federal structure of the Dutch state, and powerful influence of civic autonomy within the Republic, made it possible to devise a totally new kind of commercial organization, a chartered, joint-stock monopoly strongly backed by the state which was, at the same time, federated into chambers which kept their capital, and commercial operations, separate from each other, while observing general guidelines, and policies, set by a federal board of directors. The precise form of the new organization resulted from a lengthy process of negotiation. At their conference at The Hague, in December 1601, the directors proposed that the Amsterdam Chamber of the new company should receive half the seats on the projected new federal board of directors since together the Amsterdam companies were contributing (slightly over) half the total starting capital. But Oldenbarnevelt—whose power base lay outside Amsterdam—and the States of Holland and Zeeland were anxious that Amsterdam should have less than half the votes on the federal board. Thus, Amsterdam ended up with eight, out of a total of seventeen, seats in this gathering which became known as the *Heren XVII*. Of the remainder, four were allocated to Zeeland and two each to the North Quarter and the South Holland towns. The latter two chambers were each divided in turn into two sub-chambers, respectively Hoorn and Enkhuizen, and Delft and Rotterdam, each of which nominated one director to the federal board. The seventeenth director was nominated by the three smaller chambers in rotation.[37] Although, from the first, non-regent, élite merchants

---

[35] Van Dillen, *Oudste aandeelhoudersregister*, 11.
[36] Van Deventer, *Gedenkstukken*, ii. 300, 311.
[37] Gaastra, *Bewind en beleid*, 23.

played a large part in running the Amsterdam Chamber, it was inevitable that regents should be preponderant in administering the new organization and heavily so in the case of the smaller chambers.[38] Moreover, in the course of time, the influence of regents over the running of the Amsterdam Chamber tended to increase.

The States of Holland and Zeeland negotiated the arrangements with the merchants. Nevertheless, formally speaking, it was the States General which chartered and set up the new United East India Company (Verenigde Oostindische Compagnie, or VOC). For only the States General could confer upon it the delegated, sovereign, rights to maintain troops and garrisons, fit out warships, impose governors upon Asian populations, and conduct diplomacy with eastern potentates, as well as sign treaties and make alliances. Once the charter was assigned, in 1602, the VOC enjoyed a great deal of freedom of action. Nevertheless, an element of Generality supervision remained.[39] Treaties, alliances, and instructions to VOC governors in Asia had to be approved by the States General and the VOC was required to submit periodic reports on the general state of its affairs in the East Indies. Also the original charter was subject to review, and renewal, by the States General, after twenty-one years. VOC military and naval commanders in Asia, and the Company's diplomatic agents, were required to swear double oaths of allegiance to their employer, the Company, and the States General of the United Provinces.

From the outset the new organization was heavily armed and intent on carving for itself a dominant position in the commerce of the East Indies. The Company achieved its first conquests in 1605 when its forces captured the Indonesian 'Spice Islands' of Ternate, Tidore, and Amboina from the Portuguese. But it was not until the commencement of the Twelve Years Truce, in 1609, that the *Heren XVII* decided to appoint a governor-general and *raad* (council) to administer their trade factories and conquests in Asia. Originally, the headquarters of the Dutch empire of trade in the east was established in Bantam, at the western tip of Java. The first governor-general, Pieter Both (see Table 11), was neither a Hollander nor a Zeelander but came from Amersfoort, which was possibly one reason for his appointment since none could regard him as aligned with any of the regional chambers. He was the first of a long line of governors-general of the Dutch East Indies under the VOC, presiding over a colonial empire, and zone of maritime activity, stretching from the Cape of Good Hope to the shores of Japan and

---

[38] Ibid. 34; Gaastra, *Geschiedenis van de VOC*, 31–2.
[39] Ibid. 21–3.

the Philippines. Though Both was occasionally referred to in Dutch sources as a 'viceroy', with the example in mind of the viceroys in the colonial empires of Spain and Portugal, he was by no means a viceroy in the true sense of the term,[40] being neither the proxy for a ruler, nor at the head of a quasi-monarchical court, nor indeed even a nobleman of any sort, let alone a grandee. In other ways too, his status and functions reflected the fact that the United Provinces were a republic, whose political forms did not correspond to those of Europe's monarchies. Thus, he was bound by his instructions to take important decisions, and sign decrees, treaties, and reports, only in conjunction with his council, the *raad* of the Indies, comprising his principal military, naval, and commercial subordinates. Officially, he possessed authority only in so far as he worked in consultation with his council. Furthermore, the *raad* was far from a rubber stamp and while some future governors-general did exhibit authoritarian tendencies, and there were clashes between governors-general and *raad*, by and large the system of collective responsibility and government worked. It was inherent in this situation that the *Heren XVII* at home showed little inclination to choose relatives of the Princes of Orange, or leading nobles, as their governors-general in the Indies. Both came from a regent background and his early successors were likewise chosen from élite merchant families among the regents. Later, it became usual to select the governors-general from among long-standing senior employees of the Company. The *Heren XVII* looked for competence, experience, and knowledge of the Indies, not social status. Consequently, the list of governors-general of the Dutch East Indies in the seventeenth century (see Table 11) was unique in being the only set of senior governors of a European colonial empire of the time which did not consist of nobles.

The principal Dutch factories when Both reached the East Indies, in 1610, were those of Ternate, Tidore, Amboina, the Banda Islands, and Bantam. In 1619, however, the fourth governor-general and one of the most famous, Jan Pietersz. Coen (1587–1629), seized Jakarta and transferred the VOC's headquarters in Asia there. Coen wanted to name his new conquest 'New Hoorn' after his birthplace, but the *Heren XVII* preferred a name with unifying connotations for the entire Republic and instead chose 'Batavia'.[41] Batavia rapidly developed into the foremost European military, naval, and commercial base in Asia, far outstripping Goa and Malacca, and remained such until the late eighteenth century. The Dutch rebuilt the town and

---

[40] Rietbergen, *Eerste landvoogd Pieter Both*, i. 47–8.
[41] Gaastra, *Geschiedenis van de VOC*, 40.

provided it with formidable fortifications. Though it was not until the late seventeenth century that the town developed much landward interaction with other parts of Java, from the first it served as the general rendezvous for Dutch ships and cargoes converging from the outlying parts of the Indonesian archipelago, India, the China Sea, and Japan. It was also the

TABLE 11. *The governors-general of the Dutch East Indies during the first century of the VOC*

Governor-general	Dates	Place of origin	Social origin
Pieter Both	1609–14	Amersfoort	regent
Gerard Reynst	1614–15	Amsterdam	regent
Laurens Reael	1616–19	Amsterdam	regent
Jan Pietersz. Coen	1619–23	Hoorn	mercantile
Pieter de Carpentier	1623–7	Antwerp	southern refugee
Jan Pietersz. Coen	1627–9	Hoorn	mercantile
Jacques Specx	1629–32	Dordrecht	southern refugee
Hendrik Brouwer	1632–6		
Antonio van Diemen	1636–45	Kuilenburg	mercantile
Cornelis van der Lijn	1645–50	Alkmaar	
Carel Reniersz.	1650–3	Amsterdam	mercantile
Joan Maetsuycker	1653–78	Amsterdam	Catholic professional
Rijcklof van Goens	1678–81	Rees	army
Cornelis Jansz. Speelman	1681–4	Rotterdam	mercantile
Joannes Camphuys	1684–91	Haarlem	skilled artisanate
Willem van Oudthoorn	1691–1704	Amboina	VOC officialdom
Joan van Hoorn	1704–9	Amsterdam	mercantile
Abraham van Riebeek	1709–13	Cape Town	VOC officialdom

principal Dutch military garrison in the East Indies and in the seventeenth, and much of the eighteenth, centuries constituted the largest concentration of Europeans anywhere in Asia. The town acquired a *vroedschap*, consistory, orphanage, and the other usual civic institutions of Dutch towns of the time. By 1700, there were about 6,000 Europeans at Batavia, almost as many as were then to be found in Dutch South Africa. However, the vast majority of the men were soldiers, seamen, or other employees of the VOC, and Batavia never developed an economically independent Dutch burgher class.[42] The total size of Batavia grew from about 8,000, in 1624, to around 70,000 by 1700. The non-European population, untypical of the rest of Java, was extremely mixed, the largest community being the Chinese. There were

[42] Ibid. 71, 74.

also sizeable groups from others parts of Indonesia and of Malays. The consistory of Batavia, which after a few years organized services in Malay and Portuguese, as well as Dutch, employed four Dutch Reformed preachers as early as 1632.

By comparison with the Dutch factories and bases in Asia, their forts and settlements on African and American shores, in the early decades, were distinctly modest. The most important before 1630 was Fort Nassau (Mourée) on the Gold Coast, which the States General (sending a naval contingent) established in 1611, to neutralize Portuguese power in the area and serve as a general rendezvous for Dutch ships and trade on the coasts of western Africa. Since 1598 the Dutch had superseded the Portuguese as the dominant power in West African waters and largely controlled the Guinea gold and ivory traffic.[43] However, before 1634, the Dutch made no effort to enter the slave trade between Africa and the Americas, being content to leave this to the Portuguese, who enjoyed the access to the Spanish American colonies which the Dutch themselves lacked. Most of the Dutch goods shipped to Africa were stockpiled at Fort Nassau, where the bulk of the gold and ivory were stored awaiting shipment to the Republic.

It was also from 1598, and the reimposition of the Spanish embargoes, that Dutch ships began to appear in large numbers in the Caribbean and along the coasts of northern South America.[44] Most of these ships came to fetch high-grade salt, to replace the supplies normally procured in Portugal. Others came to load hides, tobacco, dye-woods, sugar, and silver bought from the Spanish settlers in places remote from the main centres of Spanish authority—notably Venezuela and western Santo Domingo—and from the Indians of the Guyanas and Amazonia.

The private companies trading with Guinea and the Americas in the period down to 1621 soon felt the need for state backing—provision of arms and warships, exemption from customs, help with building forts, and a degree of regulation, to prevent competition between companies undermining profits. By 1606 there was strong support, especially at Amsterdam and in Zeeland, among the directors of the various companies for setting up a state-chartered, joint-stock monopoly organization, on the model of the VOC, to manage the whole of Dutch commerce with the Americas together with West Africa (East Africa and the Cape of Good Hope having been assigned to the VOC). The plans which came before the States of Holland and Zeeland at that time were supported by a publicity fanfare which trumpeted both the riches to be won by breaking into the colonial empires

---

[43] Van den Boogaart, 'Trade', 373–5. [44] Sluiter, 'Dutch–Spanish Rivalry', 173–8.

of Spain and Portugal, and acquiring their colonies, and the benefits of sending out settlers to colonize areas not presently held by the Iberians, notably in the Guyanas and present-day Argentina and Chile. The latter concept was stressed especially by Willem Usselincx (1567–1647), an Antwerp émigré who became the most notable Dutch economic writer of the early seventeenth century. Usselincx held that the best way to strengthen the Republic's commerce and shipping would be to establish colonies which could be populated from the Fatherland and would eventually provide the metropolis with a growing market for its manufactures.[45] But despite the widespread backing for a Dutch West India Company by 1606–7, the scheme was aborted in that year by Oldenbarnevelt who was then in the midst of his truce negotiations with Spain and knew that erecting such an organization would so antagonize the Spanish Crown as to destroy all possibility of a negotiated settlement.

Consequently, the setting up of a Dutch West India Company chartered by the States General was delayed until June 1621, after the expiry of the Twelve Years Truce, and then it took another three years to gather the necessary starting capital. The original monopoly was for twenty-four years and empowered the new Company, the WIC (Westindische Compagnie), just as the VOC had been authorized, to maintain garrisons and warships, appoint governors, and sign alliances with native peoples, under the general supervision of the States General, with the State to assist with procurement of weapons, munitions, troops, and warships. As with the VOC, WIC commanders and governors swore a double oath of allegiance to the Company and the States General.

The WIC was divided into five regional chambers, those of Amsterdam, Zeeland, the Maas (Rotterdam), Groningen, and the North Quarter. As with the chambers of the VOC, each of these kept its own separate capital, and accounts, and overall policy was determined by a federal board of management, in this case called the *Heren XIX*. Again Amsterdam was not allowed to assume a majority share in the Company, being assigned four-ninths of both the seats on the board and weighting in relation to the other chambers. Zeeland was deemed to account for two-ninths of the Company's operations and the other three chambers for one-ninth each. Although non-regent élite merchants were prominent among the directors of the Amsterdam Chamber, in the case of the WIC, as with the VOC, regents were extremely influential in all the chambers and on the federal board.

---

[45] Boxer, *Dutch in Brazil*, 2.

The WIC's initial undertakings in the 1620s all ended in failure, however, and it was not until the capture of Recife, in northern Brazil, in 1630, that the new organization succeeded in acquiring and holding a major base in Ibero-America. Even then, it was not until the mid-1630s that the Company controlled a large share of Brazil's sugar exports to Europe and seemed to offer good prospects of becoming a fully viable commercial operation. Until the mid-1630s, the WIC's profits—from privateering against Spanish and Portuguese shipping in the Atlantic, the Guinea gold trade, and New Netherland fur trade—were wholly insufficient to finance the Company's substantial war fleet, and organization, so that the WIC remained considerably more dependent on States General subsidies and assistance than its more profitable eastern counterpart. The Dutch established a permanent base, with a splendid harbour, in the Caribbean when the WIC captured Curaçao from the Spaniards in 1634.

15

Society after the Revolt

❖

URBANIZATION

Dutch society was transformed after 1572 first by conflict and disruption, during the early stages of the Revolt, and later, in the 1590s and after, by the breakthrough into the 'rich trades', the rise of new industries, and the successful establishment of the long-distance traffic with the Indies. Every aspect of Dutch society was profoundly affected by both the disruption and then the economic 'miracle'. But much the most dramatic manifestation of the restructuring of the Dutch trading system after 1590 was, indubitably, the explosive growth of the cities of the Dutch maritime zone.

TABLE 12. *Urban expansion in Holland and Zeeland, 1570–1647 (estimates)*

City	1570	1600	1622	1632	1647
Amsterdam	30,000	60,000	105,000	116,000	140,000
Leiden	15,000	26,000	44,500	54,000	60,000
Haarlem	16,000	30,000	39,500	42,000	45,000
Middelburg	10,000	20,000	25,000	28,000	30,000
Rotterdam	7,000	12,000	19,500	20,000	30,000
Delft	14,000	17,500	22,750	21,000	21,000
Enkhuizen	7,500	17,000	22,000	19,000	18,000
Dordrecht	10,000	15,000	18,250	18,000	20,000
The Hague	5,000	10,000	15,750	16,000	18,000
Hoorn	7,000	12,000	16,000	15,000	14,000
Gouda	9,000	13,000	14,500	14,500	15,000

Sources: Posthumus, *Geschiedenis*, iii. 882; Hart, *Geschrift en getal*, 118; Briels, *Zuid-Nederlanders*, 188–9, 214; Nusteling, *Welvaart en werkgelegenheid*, 234–5; Wijsenbeek-Olthuis, *Achter de gevels*, 27; Schmal, 'Patterns of De-Urbanization', 291; Willemsen, *Enkhuizen*, 100; Visser, 'Dichtheid', 19–20.

In early modern times, urban growth, even to a modest extent, let alone the kind of spectacular expansion which occurred in Holland and Zeeland between 1585 and 1650, was possible only through high levels of immigration. This could be from rural areas within the country or from abroad, or both, but there had to be a consistently heavy influx from outside for urban growth to take place. For in all early modern cities, including those of the Dutch Golden Age, the death rate appreciably exceeded the birth rate, even when the latter was exceptionally high.[1] Heavy infant mortality, combined with epidemics, especially of plague (until the 1660s), ensured a built-in excess of deaths over births. Epidemics struck everywhere but tended to be most virulent in the overcrowded, unsanitary conditions prevailing in the poorer neighbourhoods of large towns. Consequently, rapid urban growth in early modern times, especially when epidemics were frequent, was a more impressive and astounding phenomenon than it would be in a more recent context. Leiden suffered severely from epidemics during the period, notably in 1599, 1604, 1624, and 1636. Yet, this did not prevent a rate of growth almost as impressive as that of Amsterdam. Amsterdam too experienced serious outbreaks of sickness, that of 1602, for example, reportedly causing 10,000 deaths, which, if accurate, would have amounted to some 15 per cent of the city's population, carrying off many poor, as well as some prominent men.

The exceptionally rapid growth of Holland's cities, after 1590, was assisted by some easing of guild restrictions, certainly in Amsterdam,[2] and better conditions and welfare. Rising prosperity led to improvements in sick-care, diet, housing, and poor relief. Some curtailment of the death rate also resulted from measures to improve sanitation, and the quality of the water in the canals, for example by the civic garbage and waste disposal service set up in Amsterdam, by the municipality, in the 1590s.[3] But undoubtedly the decisive factor was the high level of immigration from both outside the north Netherlands and rural areas within the Republic, rather than natural increase or migration from nearby localities.

The main source of immigration from outside, until around 1620, continued to be the south Netherlands.[4] After around 1590 only part of this would have been motivated to any great extent by religious considerations, though crypto-Protestantism was still an active force in the south at least until the 1620s. But the major motive, after 1590, was simply the better employment prospects, and higher wages, available in Holland and Zeeland.[5] After 1600, especially, the wage-gap between north and south was

[1] Klein, 'Zeventiende eeuw', 88.
[2] Van Zanden, *Rise and Decline*, 51, 62–3.
[3] Faber, Diederiks, and Hart, 'Urbanisering', 267.
[4] Briels, *Zuid-Nederlanders*, 213.
[5] Scholliers, 'Eerste schade', 49–50.

substantial and continued to grow. After 1621, when immigration from the south ceased to be of more than marginal significance for Amsterdam, there was still a substantial flow of immigration from Flanders, and especially the Walloon provinces, to Leiden and Middelburg (see Table 13).

After around 1620, however, the principal source of foreign immigration was Germany. During the 1590s, immigrants had began arriving in the Dutch provinces, from Germany; but, at that stage, these were chiefly south Netherlands refugees who had migrated to north-west Germany in the 1580s—among them the infant Vondel, born in Cologne, in 1587—transferring to the Republic after it became secure in the early 1590s. After the outbreak of the Thirty Years War in central Europe, however, a substantial immigration from Lutheran, as well as Calvinist, areas of Germany began which, from then on, provided the majority of foreign immigrants settling in Amsterdam,[6] Leiden, and other rapidly expanding cities.

TABLE 13. *Provenance of new citizens at Amsterdam, Leiden, and Middelburg, 1590–1659*

Provenance	Amsterdam	Leiden	Middelburg
(a) 1590/4			
Dutch Provinces	422 (51%)	85 (15%)	179 (18%)
Southern Netherlands	300 (36%)	445 (80%)	778 (78%)
Germany	93 (11%)	17 (3%)	19 (2%)
England	8 (1%)	8 (1.5%)	19 (2%)
(b) 1655/59			
Dutch Provinces	1,032 (55.5%)	314 (41%)	242 (44%)
Southern Netherlands	162 (9%)	255 (33%)	243 (44%)
Germany	535 (29%)	164 (21.5%)	18 (3%)
England	129 (7%)	22 (3%)	41 (7%)

Source: Posthumus, *Geschiedenis*, ii. 75 and iii. 892.

A few of the German immigrants were merchants or professional men and some were skilled artisans. But the bulk of the influx from Germany, including most of the German Jews who began arriving in the 1620s in Amsterdam, were from among the poorest strata of German society. A high proportion ended up doing the most menial jobs in Holland,[7] as unskilled labourers, the lowliest seamen, and, in the case of women, servants, tavern-maids, and prostitutes.

[6] Nusteling, *Welvaart en werkgelegenheid*, 44.   [7] Van Deursen, *Het kopergeld*, i. 55.

Immigration from abroad was the most conspicuous part of the flow to the Dutch urban milieu. But immigration from the inland provinces was also fundamental to the process of urban expansion. In the early 1590s, approximately half of newly inscribed burghers at Amsterdam came from the eastern provinces,[8] though at that stage much smaller numbers from these areas settled in Leiden and Middelburg. But, by the 1650s, immigration from the eastern provinces was the largest element in immigration also in these cities. Abel Tasman, the discoverer of Tasmania and New Zealand, was early in life one of many who migrated to Amsterdam from the Ommelands.

Immigration from the three main sources—the south Netherlands, Protestant Germany, and the eastern provinces of the Republic—flowed to the cities of Holland and Zeeland. In the other five provinces, urban growth, from the end of the sixteenth century to the middle of the seventeenth, was altogether slower and more hesitant.[9] Utrecht and Groningen grew much more slowly than the towns in the west. The IJssel towns, particularly Deventer and Zutphen, which were under Spanish occupation for much of the 1580s, and suffered severe dislocation, lost population between 1572 and the 1590s, and were slow to recover thereafter. Deventer had around 10,500 inhabitants in 1578, roughly the same as a century before, but by 1591, when the town was recovered from the Spaniards, this had dwindled to 7,500.[10] The regents controlling the affairs of the IJssel towns after 1591 strove to attract immigrants, especially skilled immigrants in the face of competition from the Holland towns. Kampen announced, in 1592, that for eighteen months the city was offering free (and immediate) citizenship to newcomers 'of whatever nation they may be', without any proviso as to religion.[11] The *raad* of Zutphen offered both tax and guild-entry incentives.[12] But, as with Utrecht earlier, and Groningen subsequently, such measures produced little result. As late as 1607, Zutphen was still severely depopulated and decayed,[13] with a population of only around 4,000 (see Table 14).

The rapid growth in the maritime provinces, from 1585 onwards, turned the Republic into a land with two economies, that of the west expanding, dynamic, and prosperous, and that of the inland provinces largely stagnant and much poorer. The gap between the two Dutch economies was reflected in the wide disparity in wage rates between the towns of the eastern

---

[8] Hart, *Geschrift en getal*, 145.
[9] Schmal, 'Patterns of De-Urbanization', 291–2.
[10] Koch, 'Reformation in Deventer', 29.
[11] GA Kampen Oud-Archief 23, fo. 16. res. raad 5 Dec. 1592.
[12] GA Zutphen 1st afd. no. 2 res. raad 28 Apr. 1592.
[13] Broek Roelofs, *Wilhelmus Baudartius*, 38.

provinces and those of the western seaboard. Wages in the eastern towns during the seventeenth century were generally as much as 50 per cent lower than comparable wages in the west. Moreover, such growth as the eastern towns did achieve, from the 1590s onwards, tended to result from the expansion of the fixed garrisons, military construction, and provisioning, rather than commerce and industry.

TABLE 14. *Urban expansion in the United Provinces outside Holland and Zeeland, 1572–1647 (estimates)*

City	1572	1590	1610	1635	1647
Utrecht	25,000	25,000	25,000	30,000	30,000
Groningen	19,500	19,000	20,000	20,000	20,000
Leeuwarden	8,000	10,000	12,000	14,000	15,000
Maastricht	16,000	10,000	12,000	16,000	15,000
's-Hertogenbosch	17,000	—	18,000	—	15,000
Nijmegen	11,500	7,000	12,000	13,500	12,000
Zwolle	11,000	7,500	10,000	—	9,000
Deventer	11,000	7,500	9,000	—	7,000
Kampen	10,000	7,500	9,000	—	7,000
Zutphen	6,000	3,000	4,000	8,000	7,000

Sources: Holthuis, 'Deventer in oorlog', 35–7; Engelen, *Nijmegen*, 12; Philips, 'Aanduidingen', 32–3; Schmal, 'Patterns of De-Urbanization', 291; Visser, 'Dichtheid', 19–20; Reitsma, *Centrifugal and Centripetal Forces*, 15–17; Frijhoff, *Gesch. van Zutphen*, 93; Jansen, 'Crisis', 152.

RURAL SOCIETY

Dutch agriculture, both in the maritime west and in the rest of the Republic, enjoyed its most thriving and prosperous period from the 1590s down to the end of the Thirty Years and Eighty Years wars, in 1648. In the west, agriculture throve on the rapid growth of the towns and the escalating demand for food and industrial crops such as hops and flax. In the east, agriculture flourished, stimulated by the need for supplies for the garrisons. Maurits's triumphant offensive of 1597 did not finally eliminate the Spanish presence from the eastern fringes of the United Provinces. During their 1605–6 offensive, the Spaniards recovered the Twenthe quarter of Overijssel, the eastern part of the county of Zutphen, and Lingen, and were to hold these areas down to the late 1620s. Even so, the eastern provinces were much less disrupted by warfare, after 1597, than between 1572 and 1597. There were still some major Spanish thrusts into Dutch territory, notably in 1624 and 1629, but the Spanish garrisons, based at Oldenzaal, Grol, Lingen,

Wesel, 's-Hertogenbosch and (in the years 1625–37) also Breda, no longer sacked villages and destroyed crops, as they once had. This was under reciprocal arrangements whereby the Dutch garrisons similarly refrained from ravaging villages and crops on the Spanish side. The episode in 1624, when Spaniards, invading from Lingen, burnt several villages, including Winschoten, Slochteren, and Heiligerlee, was reportedly an error caused by failure to convey orders on this point, in time, to the troops.[14]

The Thirty Years War, in Germany, also exerted a major influence on Dutch agriculture, as it did in Switzerland and the islands of Denmark. As the German countryside was devastated and the size of the armies operating in Germany increased, armies and garrisons on both sides were increasingly compelled to supplement their supplies with provisions imported from outside. The Dutch Republic, moreover, was exceptionally well placed to supply Germany because river craft were the most efficient means of transporting supplies into the interior and the chief rivers all flowed down either to the Republic itself or to estuaries on the north coast, frequented by Dutch shipping.[15] Thus, prodigious quantities of meat, herring, cheese, butter, fruit, and also beer, wine, and tobacco, were shipped, especially from the West Frisian ports and Harlingen, Dokkum, and Groningen, round to Emden, Bremen, Hamburg, and Stettin, and then up the Ems, Weser, Elbe, and Oder, to the waiting armies and garrisons. Victuals were also shipped up the Rhine to Cleves, Cologne, and beyond, and transported into Westphalia and Brunswick via Deventer. In the year 1633 no fewer than 994 of the 1,121 ships which docked in the port of Hamburg were Dutch, the majority bringing fish, meat, and other agricultural produce, and often also horses, munitions, tobacco, beer, and wine.[16]

Nor was it only Germany which suffered chronic shortages. The Spaniards experienced difficulty in supplying their garrisons, in the south Netherlands and Jülich-Cleves, both between 1585 and 1609, and again after the Twelve Years Truce. In some years, particularly in the 1620s, the States General, at the request of the Stadholder, imposed river blockades on the south Netherlands, and Spanish-occupied areas of north-west Germany, to hamper the Spaniards and aggravate the shortages in their towns, during particular campaigns.[17] These stoppages caused huge swings in prices of grain, salt, meat, fish, and cheese throughout the south, including Liège, and

[14] ARB SEG 190, fo. 103. Isabella to Philip V, Brussels, 14 Mar. 1624.
[15] Beutin and Entholt, *Bremen und die Niederlande*, 9–10, 36–7; Gutmann, *War and Rural Life*, 116.
[16] Baasch, 'Hamburg und Holland', 94.
[17] Israel, *Empires and Entrepots*, 107–31.

north-west Germany. But otherwise—apart from during the Spanish river blockade of 1625–9—supplies of every kind except munitions were allowed through, usually southwards from Rotterdam or Dordrecht, or eastwards along the Rhine into Spanish-held Cleves.[18] The last of the stoppages on the rivers was in 1636. After that year, there was an uninterrupted traffic along the Zwin, Scheldt, and Maas.

Some of the supplies in demand could not be provided in increasing quantity. The flow of Baltic grain was impeded during the 1620s by Swedish operations along the Polish coast. The size of the Dutch herring catch fell substantially, from 1625 down to the end of the war in 1648, owing to Spanish attacks on the herring fleets and measures to hinder the flow of high-grade salt to the Republic. Consequently, it was Dutch agriculture itself, rather than the fisheries, or Baltic grain depots, which met the enormous escalation in demand for provisions. It was an exceptional situation but one of sufficient duration for it to make sound sense to invest heavily in land reclamation and expanding output. So profitable was Dutch agriculture, during this period, that many leading merchants, nobles, and high officials eagerly participated in the grander projects. The capital to drain the North Holland Beemster polder, commencing in 1608, amounting to one and a half million guilders—equivalent to nearly one-quarter of the starting capital of the VOC—was put up by 123 prominent investors, including Oldenbarnevelt and Johan van Duivenvoorde. The project involved constructing forty-three windmills, of the newest and largest type, and eventually reclaimed over 7,000 hectares. The neighbouring Schermer polder drainage scheme, which commenced in 1635, was funded by a capital of one million guilders. The last of the big drainage projects in Holland was completed (with remarkably precise timing) in 1647, the last year of fighting in Germany and the south Netherlands. However, though the boom was over, Dutch agriculture held up for a few more years yet, whilst neighbouring war-ravaged regions were recovering, and, down to the 1660s, some smaller-scale land reclamation continued along the coastal dunes of Holland. Even so, the statistics clearly show the marked slackening of investment in agriculture which took place at the end of Phase Three (1621–47) of Dutch world trade primacy, in and around 1647 (see Table 15).

During the first three phases of Dutch world trade primacy, from 1590 to 1647, the six biggest drainage projects in progress in North Holland added no fewer than 1,400 farms to the region.[19] Although on a smaller scale, parallel bursts of land reclamation, beginning in the 1590s and continuing

---

[18] Ibid. 107, 128; Gutmann, *War and Rural Life*, 113.
[19] De Vries, *Dutch Rural Economy*, 160.

down to the 1660s, occurred also in Friesland and Groningen.[20] But fast
though new agricultural land came on to the market, farm rents climbed
faster. In North Holland, farm rents rose by 70 per cent between 1580 and
1600, more than twice the rate of inflation.[21] They climbed by another 50
per cent during the first third of the seventeenth century. After about 1635,
the rise in Dutch farm rents slackened, but it nevertheless continued down
to the 1650s. Rents were then static for a few years before commencing the
sharp fall which began in the late 1660s. In Friesland and Groningen, the
pattern closely followed that in Holland. Farm rents in the Ommelands rose
by 50 per cent between 1596 and 1632.[22]

TABLE 15. *Land reclamation in the United Provinces,*
1565–1714

Period	Hectares	Period	Hectares
1565–89	317	1640–64	1,150
1590–1614	1,431	1665–89	487
1615–39	1,762	1690–1714	495

Source: De Vries, *Dutch Rural Economy*, 194.

If rapid urban growth was the most striking feature of the Dutch scene in
the period 1590–1647, the rural population also increased, albeit more
slowly. Over the longer time-span from 1514 to 1622, total urban population
in Holland grew from 140,000 to 400,000, most of this occurring after 1585.
In the same period rural population in Holland roughly doubled, rising
from 135,000 to 275,000.[23] Even though urban population constituted a
much smaller proportion of the total in Friesland than in Holland, the town
population there increased in relation to the rural population at approximately
the same rate as in Holland. The total population of Friesland
doubled between 1511 and 1660, rising to around 150,000, staying at about
8 per cent of the total population of the Republic. But the Frisian urban
population increased during the same period by more than two and a half
times.[24] The provincial capital, Leeuwarden, more than trebled in size, for
the first time outstripping, Nijmegen, Maastricht, and the IJssel towns (see
Table 14).

[20] Ibid. 188; Faber, *Drie eeuwen Friesland*, i. 149.
[21] Van der Woude, *Het Noorderkwartier*, ii. 530.
[22] De Vries, *Dutch Rural Economy*, 86.
[23] Ibid.
[24] Faber, *Drie eeuwen Friesland*, ii. 405, 413.

Where agricultural investment and expansion took place on a large scale, in the regions of fertile clay soils, roughly corresponding to Holland, Zeeland, Friesland, Groningen, and the western part of Utrecht, the expansion of the rural population was faster than in the inland areas, with growth of urban population faster still. By contrast, in the inland regions of relatively poor, sandy soils where agricultural investment was on a small scale, and expansion modest, the rural population grew slowly but the expansion of the towns was more languid still. Moreover, the growth of urban population, in northern Brabant and Gelderland especially, was closely linked to the size of the fixed military garrisons, which meant, since the military establishment reached its peak in the early 1630s and then began to shrink, that urban growth lasted for a much shorter period than in the west, only from the early 1590s to the mid-1630s. Owing to this difference between east and west, the predominantly urban character of the west (where most agricultural expansion took place) increased while the predominantly rural character of the east, despite the more static, traditional character of rural life, and slower agricultural expansion, was reinforced. In other words, the duality of Dutch society, and the Dutch economy, became more marked than before, with urbanization continuing uninterruptedly in the west, accompanied by de-urbanization in the east. In this respect, the position in Overijssel resembled that in north Brabant and Gelderland, the combined population of the province's three main towns—Zwolle, Deventer, and Kampen—continuing to shrink as a proportion of the total population of the province.[25]

Even the poorest part of Dutch rural society, the peasantry of Drenthe, experienced increased prosperity and agricultural expansion during the first half of the seventeenth century.[26] But the rural prosperity of the inland regions was a marginal improvement of conditions which left traditional patterns of land-holding, and social structure, largely intact. By and large peasants owned relatively little land in the east of the Republic, most of what they farmed consisting of small parcels rented out by nobles or other non-peasant proprietors, often town-dwellers. Thus, while rural society in the west became increasingly mobile, commercialized, dependent on wage-labour, and linked to the urban and overseas market, rural society in the east, despite its role in provisioning military garrisons, both on Dutch soil and in Germany, remained largely static and traditional, consisting of a growing mass of small peasant tenant-farmers who lacked the means to pay wage-labour and relied chiefly on their own labour and that of their

[25] Slicher van Bath, *Samenleving*, 54–5, 60.			[26] Bieleman, 'Dutch Agriculture', 171–3.

relatives. In the west, agriculture became progressively more specialized and intensive, characterized by very high crop yields.[27] In the east the rule was for non-specialized, small peasant farms, featuring low, or at any rate much lower, yields.[28] In the west, a new type of commercialized farmer dominated the rural scene. In the east, those who farmed the land lived within a rural context often dominated by nobles, officials, and, to a lesser extent, absentee town-dwellers.

THE NOBILITY

In contrast to Holland and Zeeland, where the towns gained ground relative to the nobility, after the Revolt, in the other provinces the nobility strengthened their position in society after (and to a large extent as a consequence of) the Revolt. This striking difference was due to four main factors: the decline of the inland towns relative to rural society, a phenomenon absent in Friesland but marked in Overijssel, Gelderland, and north Brabant and to a lesser extent in Groningen; secondly, the elimination of Crown, Hof, and royal bureaucracy, as rivals for influence in the countryside; thirdly, the fact that nobles were often better placed than other groups to profit from the confiscation, and sale, of Church lands; and fourthly, the increased importance of fixed garrisons and the military establishment, the higher echelons of the army being a preserve of both foreign, and Dutch, noblemen.

TABLE 16. *Social background of the Frisian grietmannen, 1525–1675*

Date	Frisian nobility	non-noble Frisians	non-Frisians
1525	13	10	5
1574	8	13	8
1623	19	10	0
1675	17	8	5

Source: Faber, *Drie eeuwen Frisland*, ii. 510.

The removal of external influence from the choosing of rural magistrates was a major element in the shift. In Friesland, for example, the thirty *grietmannen* had been appointed in the period from 1520 to 1572 by the

[27] De Vries, *Dutch Rural Economy*, 229–35.
[28] Ibid. 231–2; Van Zanden, 'Prijs van de vooruitgang?', 80–2.

regime in Brussels, on the advice of the Hof of Friesland. As a result, by 1572 most of these key judicial officers in Friesland were either non-noble Frisians or else non-Frisians (see Table 16). By contrast, after the Revolt shattered the power of central government and the Hof, appointing the *grietmannen* devolved upon the States, and Delegated States, of Friesland, bodies dominated by the Frisian nobility. From the 1580s on, consequently, the tendency was to prefer Frisian nobles to others, non-Frisians being completely eliminated by the early seventeenth century. The Frisian nobility itself had split, some branches of noble families having chosen to remain Catholic. But the men who dominated the States, and Delegated States, were those who were Reformed, and committed to the Revolt, and it was exclusively these sections of old Frisian noble families, such as the Aylva, Burmania, Eysinga, and Osinga, who acquired a grip over the rural magistracies, especially in the zone of richer, more fertile, soils, in the northern and north-western parts of the province, where nobles owned a high proportion of the land. Wielding judicial power then, in turn, provided opportunities for enlarging one's holdings, not least by influencing the disposal of former Church property.[29] The sale of a large batch of former Church lands in Friesland in 1638–40 delivered nearly all of it to Frisian noble families. The Ommelander *jonkers* also split; but, again, Catholics were excluded from administrative and judicial posts.

It is true there was no longer a mechanism by which new families could be raised to noble status and that, eventually, this undermined both the numbers and vitality of the nobility. Like nobilities throughout Europe, Dutch provincial nobilities of the seventeenth and eighteenth centuries adhered to exclusive marriage policies, not wishing to step outside their class and dilute their noble credentials. Consequently, the nobility were shrinking steadily as a proportion of the population and, owing to their low birth rate, also in absolute terms. The roughly forty-five acknowledged *jonker* families in the Ommelands, around 1600, had diminished to only ten by 1800.[30] Eventually, this curtailed noble influence in society. But, until around 1650, the impact of this shrinkage was still marginal and outweighed by factors enhancing the position of the nobility. The number of recognized noble families, in Friesland, static at around sixty-five during the first two-thirds of the sixteenth century, was down to forty-six by 1650; but this in no way hindered their increasing dominance of Frisian society.[31] In Overijssel, in 1675, the *ridderschap* still amounted to 1.1 per cent of the total population

[29] Faber, *Drie eeuwen Friesland*, i. 217.
[30] Feenstra, *Adel in de Ommelanden*, 58.
[31] Faber, *Drie eeuwen Friesland*, i. 347.

of the province and were the owners of no less than 41 per cent of the assessed wealth, including most of the property in the town of Vollenhove.

In Holland and Zeeland, the position was certainly different and here the tremendous growth of the cities, and urban wealth, clearly had the effect of making the town regents more dominant than before, further reducing the relative influence of the nobility. Even so, it would be wrong to suppose, even in Holland and Zeeland, that the nobility were entirely eclipsed after the Revolt. In some respects the Holland nobility can be said to have shared in the growing power and wealth of their province and its growing preponderance over the Republic as a whole. The Holland nobles did not intermarry with the regents. Consequently, they too were a shrinking group. Several of the ancient families of Holland still active during the Revolt— among them the Van Swieten and Assendelft—were extinct by the middle of the seventeenth century. Those who remained were also less well placed than their counterparts in Friesland and the inland provinces to expand their land-holdings, facing stiff competition, for prime land, from regents and élite merchants, and being unable to influence disposal of most former Church property. Nevertheless, since they already owned some of the best land in the province, they profited handsomely from the agricultural boom and steep rise in rural rents, and, like the Frisian nobility, invested heavily in land reclamation. Many of them were able to rebuild in some style their castles and country residences, which had practically all been devastated by the Spaniards during the fighting between 1572 and 1576.[32] Among the most prominent Holland nobles of the seventeenth century, were the lords of Wassenaar, who handsomely restored their ruined family seat, House Duivenvoorde, near Wassenaar, and Johan van Duivenvoorde (1547–1610), who spent large sums rebuilding his castle at Warmond, partly using materials from nearby ruined monasteries.[33]

Holland and Zeeland nobles also continued to play a notable role in the army and navy, noble status still carrying appreciable prestige in both down to the end of the Republic. Many Dutch commanders during the Revolt were Holland and Zeeland nobles, and this tradition survived down to the late eighteenth century. The same Johan van Duivenvoorde, a leading figure in the Holland *ridderschap* during the Revolt, and one of the *Gecommitteerde Raden* who moved, with alacrity, to affirm Holland's grip over the Republic after the assassination of William the Silent, was also a principal military and naval officer, becoming lieutenant-admiral of Holland in 1576,

---

[32] Van Nierop, *Van ridders tot regenten*, 149–50.
[33] Van der Steur, 'Johan van Duivenvoirde', 219.

and one of the commanders of the fleet sent to the Flemish coast, in 1588, to help prevent the junction of the Spanish Armada with Parma's army. Among other prominent men, of similar background, was *jonker* Frederik van Dorp (*c.*1547–1612), one of the captains of the Sea-Beggars, who like Duivenvoorde participated in the capture of Brill in 1572. He later became colonel of a Zeeland regiment and rose to become governor of Ostend, facing Spínola, in the years 1602–4. His son, Filips van Dorp (1587–1652), rose to become lieutenant-admiral of Zeeland. He was dismissed by the States of Zeeland, for incompetence, but this did not prevent his subsequently becoming lieutenant-admiral of Holland. His handling of operations against the Dunkirkers in the mid-1630s, however, was so inept that Stadholder and States were forced to remove him, in favour of his incomparably more able social inferior, Tromp, his departure being greeted with a jump in share prices on the Amsterdam Exchange. But Van Dorp's removal by no means ended the prominence of the nobility in the command structure of the navy.[34] A principal reason for appointing the baron van Obdam commanding admiral of the navy, after Tromp's death, was the deeply rooted belief that a senior noble—however lacking in naval experience—would be better able to maintain order, and discipline, among the (mainly non-noble) admirals than someone chosen from among their own more experienced ranks.

As with all European nobilities in early modern times, the Dutch provincial nobilities under the Republic were split by family and political feuds which, in some cases, dragged on for generations and even centuries. In the Dutch context, such inter-noble feuding was sharpened by religious differences, some of the nobility being militantly Reformed, others pro-Arminian, and still others—quite a number of the Holland nobility as well as those of other provinces—remaining Catholic, and by the prominence of the nobility in the inland provinces, and Friesland, in the forming and leading of political and ideological factions in the provincial assemblies.[35] In some cases, feuds between leading noble clans became major elements in the broader confrontation of political blocks in the provincial assemblies. Two notable examples in the middle decades of the seventeenth century were the rivalries between the Aylva and anti-Aylva blocks among the Frisian nobility and, in Overijssel, the epic contest between the Orangist House of Van Haersolte and the anti-Orangist Raesfelt clan.

An additional factor which helped shore up noble influence was the survival through the seventeenth, and much of the eighteenth, centuries (in

[34] Bruijn, *Dutch Navy*, 77, 125.   [35] Feenstra, *Adel in de Ommelanden*, 60–1, 81–2.

most cases) of the judicially autonomous 'free lordships' *(vrije heer-lijkheiden)*. These countries and lordships, such as Vianen, IJsselstein, Leerdam, Buren, Bergh, Wisch, Culemborg, Batenburg, Ravenstein and Lingen, belonged in several cases (Buren, Leerdam, IJsselstein and Lingen) to the House of Orange but, in others, to leading nobles such as the Brederodes at Vianen or the House of Culemborg at Culemborg. These territories were regarded as part of the Republic and loosely under the sovereignty of the States General and neighbouring provinces. They each paid an annual contribution to the Generality. But for most purposes they remained outside the jurisdiction of both Generality and provincial authorities, preserves of noble influence. Vianen was eventually purchased and absorbed by the States of Holland, in 1725. Culemborg was sold by the German heirs to the county to the Nijmegen quarter of Gelderland in 1720 but was still not absorbed into Gelderland proper and, in 1748, was transferred to William IV as a gift to the House of Orange. The lordship of Ravenstein, a sizeable enclave in States Brabant (see Map 5) was attached, after 1630, to Jülich-Berg.

THE REGENTS

After around 1590 some regents, especially at Amsterdam, were also élite merchants, that is, active, prominent, and particularly wealthy merchants; but most, especially in the inland and smaller towns, cannot be so described. Outside Amsterdam, a high proportion continued to be descendants of pre-1572 regent families, their mounting wealth deriving chiefly from the perquisites and opportunities of civic and provincial office and accumulations of investments both of the traditional type, in provincial bonds, and in the new large-scale capital ventures—drainage projects, urban development, and, from the late 1590s, shares in the colonial companies. Most newcomers to the regent class after 1572 were originally of comparatively modest means. A handful were professionals, usually physicians or lawyers. In Holland, very few wealthy immigrants from the south Netherlands or elsewhere succeeded in gaining entry to the regent class down to the mid-seventeenth century.

The Revolt led to the purging of the old pre-1572 élites of Dutch society but without breaking the continuity with the past. Committed Catholics—nobles and regents—associated with government during the Alva years were removed or forced to take a back seat. They were replaced with men whose Reformed credentials, and commitment to the Revolt, were evident. But frequently the latter were relatives, even sons, of the former, so that a considerable measure of continuity was retained. At the same time, a good deal of new blood was brought into the town halls, particularly in the larger cities. The end result was a regent oligarchy which was a mixture of long-established and new families.

Even in the case of the Holland *ridderschap*, the effect of the upheaval of 1572 was drastic. Membership of the *ridderschap* assembly in the States now came to be more closely controlled by the *ridderschap* itself and the men who figured prominently in the *ridderschap* after 1572 were by no means the same men who had done so before. Johan van Duivenvoorde, Adriaen van Swieten, Rutger van den Boetzelaer, and Willem van Zuylen van Nyevelt, four of the most active members after 1572, had not appeared at all in the *ridderschap* during the Alva years, while those who had been regular attenders before either remained completely absent, after the Revolt, or attended irregularly.[36] The purge was extensive and the shift marked. Nevertheless, the new men, too, came from ancient Holland noble lineages and were often younger relatives of those whom they displaced.

Similarly, among the Holland and Zeeland regents: regents active in the States of Holland after 1572 were practically never the same men who attended regularly before the Revolt, but in many cases they were younger relatives. Thus, Dordrecht's delegation to the States, after 1572, consisted almost entirely of new men who had not played any role before. Nevertheless, most bore established regent surnames, among them the younger Adriaen van Blijenburg, who was Reformed and an Orangist, in 1572, but whose father (who now remained absent from the States and died a Catholic, in 1573) had been *schout* of Dordrecht until 1571, albeit a reluctant persecutor of heretics.[37] In the case of Haarlem, the only regent prominent in the States both before and after 1572 was Nicolaes van der Laen. But he had been a crypto-Protestant before 1572, was an Orangist, and continued to support the Revolt whilst his own city was under Spanish occupation.[38]

The most extensive of the purges, in Holland, was the 'Alteratie', which took place at Amsterdam, in 1578. Amsterdam was to some extent a special case because, in contrast to the other Holland towns, she had remained steadfastly loyal to the king, until 1578, and during that time most of the regents in the city comported themselves as 'sincere Catholijcken'. When Amsterdam was brought over to the Revolt, the entire *vroedschap* was

---

[36] Koopmans, *Staten van Holland*, 40.
[37] Ibid. 43.
[38] Spaans, *Haarlem na de Reformatie*, 37, 44.

purged,[39] and new regent families bearing such names as Bicker, Witsen, Pauw, Reael, Huydecoper, and Hooft, came to the fore. There was thus a clear break from one regent group to another. But this was unique in Holland, and unusual in the United Provinces as a whole, though certainly there were other drastic purges, such as at Middelburg, in 1574, and Groningen, in 1594. In other Holland towns, and most towns outside Holland, the transition was both more gradual and more complex. At Rotterdam, for example, seven of the twenty-four members of the *vroedschap* (including both burgomasters) chose for the Spaniards, in July 1572, and two more subsequently defected to the royalists. These were all replaced by William of Orange and played no further part in Rotterdam. Then, in 1580, the *vroedschap* was enlarged, to thirty-two members, to bring in more new men, so that by that date the Rotterdam *vroedschap* was a half-and-half mixture of old regents and men from new families.[40] Several of the old regents who remained in the *vroedschap* at Rotterdam belonged to families which had entered the regent class in Burgundian, or early Habsburg, times and subsequently remained Catholic or crypto-Catholic. These were then removed, however, in the purge of 1618. Thus, it was by stages that the Rotterdam regent group eventually came to consist exclusively of Protestants and predominantly of men from new families. As in the case of the Vroesen and Haller, most of the best-known regent families of Rotterdam of the seventeenth century entered regent circles during the first decade after the Revolt.

As a rule, the purges seem to have had a more lasting effect in larger than in smaller towns. In the smaller and medium-sized towns, it was far from easy to find suitable wealthy men, with sufficient education and leisure, to devote themselves to civic affairs.[41] Consequently, an appreciable proportion of the newcomers installed during the purges proved unsuitable, or lacked the time for civic affairs, and soon disappeared again from view. For the same reason, there was a tendency for members of old regent families which had been dropped to reappear, at a later stage, even if their Protestantism was often less ardent than that of those they replaced. At Gouda, for example, an extensive purge was carried out, on Orange's orders, in July 1573. No fewer than eighteen members of the *vroedschap* were removed on that occasion. But only about one-third of the new men succeeded in remaining in the *vroedschap* and becoming permanently absorbed into the Gouda regent class, and not a few of those purged eventually reappeared,

---

[39] Dudok van Heel, 'Waar waren de Amsterdamse katholieken?', 13–26.
[40] Ten Boom, 'Patriciaat te Rotterdam', 180–2.
[41] Van Dijk and Roorda, *Patriciaat van Zierikzee*, 59.

despite Orange's orders that those removed should take no further part in civic affairs.[42]

In the eastern provinces, fear of Catholics, and royalists, in civic government remained acute for longer than in Holland, since towns such as Deventer, Nijmegen, and Groningen remained close to the front line, and in constant danger of Spanish attack, down to the 1590s. Also the old patrician oligarchy in Overijssel, Gelderland, and Groningen had shown itself to be more resolutely Catholic than the regent class in the west during the first decade of the Revolt. When the towns which came back into Spanish hands in the 1580s—Nijmegen, Zutphen, Deventer, and Groningen—were recovered by the States General in the early 1590s, drastic purges ensued. Yet, here too, there was a considerable measure of continuity, with many old regent families eventually working their way back into the town halls, except now, generally, as zealous members of the Reformed Church.[43] At Zutphen, for example, ten old regent families reappeared sooner or later in the *raad*, among them the Kreyncks and Schimmelpenninck.

THE MERCHANT ÉLITE

One almost entirely new élite in the Republic after the Revolt was the merchant élite. For there was no true merchant élite in the northern Netherlands in the age of bulk freightage. Until the 1590s, the regents were the wealthiest group in towns of the north Netherlands. Although many of these were active businessmen, they were often brewers or retailers rather than merchants, and those who engaged in commerce were of modest means compared to any real merchant élite such as those of Antwerp, Venice, London, or Lübeck. The regent-merchants of the pre-1590 period dealt in grain, timber, salt, herring, and dairy products. Some of the old Amsterdam *vroedschap* were also cloth dealers.

The Dutch merchant élite came into being in the 1590s with the rise of the 'rich trades'. This group was much richer than the old regents and, from the outset, was a mixture of several elements. For the emergence of this élite was not the result of the arrival of any particular immigrant group but of a restructured economy.[44] Thus, it was by no means only the wealthy immigrant merchants of Antwerp and the south Netherlands which supplied the membership of this new class, even though they did constitute a sizeable part. No less important were those native-born regents who, once the

[42] Hibben, *Gouda in Revolt*, 67–76.
[43] Frijhoff, *Gesch. van Zutphen*, 103.
[44] Israel, *Dutch Primacy*, 46–71.

opportunity arose, invested extensively in the burgeoning new 'rich trades'. There also arrived, from around 1600, élite merchant families such as the Poppen and Deutz from Germany. Like the Antwerp émigrés and Holland regents, these were mostly of the Reformed faith. No élite merchants were Catholics.

Certainly, the largest investors in the new commerce with the Caribbean, Brazil, West Africa, northern Russia, and the East Indies during the 1590s were recently arrived south Netherlanders. But if the native-born Holland regent-merchants had less money to invest, to begin with, they made up for this by having more political influence and this, after a few years, translated into a massive expansion of their wealth and participation in 'high-value' trade. Of course, in the case of the chartered joint-stock companies, it was by no means only élite merchants who invested. But it was the élite merchants who supplied a large proportion of the capital and who, together with the regents, monopolized the directorships, and therefore influence, in both the VOC and WIC. In the Zeeland chamber of the VOC, for example, there were 264 investors in 1602. But, of these, a mere thirty-seven, one-seventh of the total, provided over half the capital.[45]

In the Amsterdam Chamber of the VOC, in 1602, there were a total of 1,143 investors, but, of these, the eighty-one 'chief investors' provided nearly half the total capital. Analysis of these investments provides a guide to the composition of the budding Dutch merchant élite. The 'chief investors' were divided almost evenly into south Netherlanders and native-born Hollanders. Among the latter the most prominent investors were regents. In addition, there were three German 'chief investors', one of whom, Jan Poppen, invested 30,000 guilders.

A number of the Antwerp refugees who figure among the 'chief investors' in the VOC in 1602 belonged to families which remained among the merchant élite of Amsterdam, and other Dutch cities, for many decades. Among these were the families de Vogelaer, Coymans, Sautijn, De Scot, Godijn, and Bartholotti. But equally, many of the Amsterdam regent 'chief investors' were also now highly active in long-distance commerce.[46] Particularly prominent were Reinier Pauw, son of a trader in Baltic grain, who invested 30,000 guilders; Gerrit Bicker (1554–1604), son of a brewer, who invested 21,000 guilders (and who, since 1597, was a leading participant in the Caribbean trade); Geurt Dircksz. van Beuningen (1565–1633), a great merchant who was the son of a cheese dealer, and who had himself once

[45] Van Dillen, *Oudste aandeelhoudersregister*, 46.
[46] Elias, *Vroedschap van Amsterdam*, i. 174, 191, 201, 239.

dealt in cheese, investing 15,000 guilders; Gerrit Reynst (d. 1615), son of a soap-boiler, who became a great merchant and eventually governor-general of the Dutch East Indies, who committed 12,000 guilders; and Jonas Witsen (1560–1626), another key merchant of modest origins, who began in Baltic trade but later graduated to become one of the leading traders with the Caribbean, the Guyanas, Muscovy, and Manhattan, who invested 12,000 guilders.[47]

TABLE 17. *Investors in the Amsterdam Chamber of the VOC in 1602*

	All investors		'Chief investors'	
	Number	Amount invested	Number	Amount invested
North Netherlanders	785	2,023,715	40	635,100
South Netherlanders	302	1,418,700	38	871,160
Germans	38	137,900	3	60,000
English	3	6,900	0	0
Portuguese Jews	2	4,800	0	0

Source: Van Dillen, *Oudste aandeelhoudersregister*, 35, 61.

The original directorate of the Amsterdam Chamber of the VOC consisted of both élite immigrant merchants, such as Isaac le Maire, Marcus de Vogelaer, and Jacques de Velaer, and leading figures of the new native élite merchant group, notably Pauw, Bicker, Van Beuningen, and Reynst.[48] Much the same was true also of the Zeeland chamber. During the early seventeenth century, most regent *bewindhebbers*, as the directors were called, of the VOC (and, after 1621, also the WIC), were, in fact, active merchants. Whereas in the past, down to the 1580s, urban wealth in Amsterdam, and other Dutch cities, had been dominated by the modest affluence stemming from retailing, brewing, soap-boiling, salt-refining, and Baltic bulk-trading, after 1590 this traditional wealth was rapidly driven out of the higher echelons of urban society by the grander 'new wealth' generated by the 'rich trades' with Europe, the Levant, and the Indies. Consequently, the brewers, and dealers in herring, salt, dairy produce, and timber, who had once formed the élite of Holland's urban society, disappeared from the upper crust of urban wealth. According to the Amsterdam tax assessment of 1585,

[47] Van Dillen, *Oudste aandeelhoudersregister*, 106, 115–16, 194.
[48] Gaastra, *Gesch. van de VOC*, 30.

a significant proportion of the 346 richest inhabitants of the city were specialist grain, timber, herring, and dairy dealers. By contrast, the 1631 assessment shows that strikingly few grain and timber merchants remained among the 387 richest men of Amsterdam and that there were no longer any herring or dairy dealers at all. Their places had been taken by sugar refiners, silk merchants, and larger numbers (as well as wealthier) merchants trading with overseas markets (see Table 18). The list of the ten highest assessed citizens of Amsterdam, in 1631, confirms that no one engaged in Baltic or

TABLE 18. *Business activities of Amsterdam's citizens of the top tax category in 1585 and 1631*

Business category	1585	1631
Merchants in overseas trade	147	253
Soap manufacturers	17	7
Grain dealers	16	3
Timber dealers	12	7
Dairy produce dealers	11	0
Herring and fish dealers	8	0
Wine merchants	7	12
Brewers	6	5
Specialist brokers	0	2
Sugar refiners	0	12
Silk merchants	0	14

Source: Van Dillen, *Bronnen*, ii, pp. xxxvi–xxxix; Van Dillen, *Amsterdam in 1585*, pp. xxxiv–vi.

bulk freightage activity was any longer amongst the wealthiest. The city's richest men were specialists in the 'rich trades' and also, in several cases, investors in land reclamation. Bartolotti, Coymans, and De Vogelaer were sons of leading Antwerp émigré élite merchants; Jan de Wael, a nephew of the famous Antwerp merchant Jean de la Faille, specialized in trade with Venice, where he had acted as factor for other Antwerp merchants for many years, before settling in Amsterdam in 1592. Antonio Moens (1574–1638) was a native of Ghent and, like Coymans, a leading trader in Haarlem linens. Dirk Alewijn, son of a mintmaster, had a variety of interests and owned a great deal of land in the Beemster polder, where he and his son commenced building the country house Vredenburgh, in the late 1630s, to designs by Pieter Post and Philips Vingboons.

The massive wealth of the Poppen dynasty derived from various 'rich trades' and land reclamation projects. Jacob Poppen's father, Jan, had been one of the first Amsterdam merchants to invest in the East India trade. He also participated in the Muscovy trade. Jacob invested in the draining of the Beemster. He was so rich that, uniquely for the son of an immigrant, he was made a member of the *vroedschap*.

TABLE 19. *The ten wealthiest citizens of Amsterdam in 1631 ('000 guilders)*

	Assessed wealth		Assessed wealth
Jacob Poppen (estate of)	500	Antonio Moens	320
Guillermo Bartolotti	400	Jan Claesz. van Vlooswijck	320
Balthasar Coymans	400	widow of Cornelis van Lockhorst	310
Adriaen Pietersz. Raep	354	widow of Marcus de Vogelaer	300
Dirk Alewijn	325	Jan de Wael	300

Source: Van Dillen, *Bronnen*, ii, pp. xl–xli.

THE ÉLITE OF THE SKILLED

Another élite created by the restructuring of the Dutch trading system in the 1590s were those possessing specialized skills. The conquest of the 'rich trades' transformed Dutch society in a multitude of ways. But none was more fundamental than the forging of an élite of a type rare in European history and which, more than any other, contributed to the sophistication and polish of Dutch Golden Age culture. Here again, much of it was skill diverted from Antwerp.

During the early and mid-sixteenth century, as Antwerp had developed into the first world trade entrepôt, many new, and specialized, techniques became established on the Scheldt, and in the south Netherlands generally, which had no counterpart elsewhere in northern Europe. Some of the new techniques, especially in cloth-dyeing and the so-called new draperies, such as Hondschoote 'says', were local inventions. Others, such as silk-working, sugar-refining, and diamond-cutting, were of southern European, and especially Italian provenance. With the Spanish reconquest of the south, the fall of Antwerp, and blocking of the Scheldt, the new specialized skills, along with a large part of less skilled labour, emigrated. But many of the specialists, in contrast to the less skilled, went first to Germany (where prospects were better during the 1580s), only reverting to the north Netherlands as the dramatic expansion of the maritime economy began. It was the economic restructuring of the north in the 1590s, not emigration from the south, which enabled the Republic to absorb, and build on, these new skills. It was also the rise of the 'rich trades', and the network of export-orientated industries they created, which made it possible to attract additional refined skills later, in the early seventeenth century, which had no connection with the exodus from the south Netherlands. Among these was expertise in copper production transferred from Aachen, Hamburg, and other German cities during the Twelve Years Truce and several chemical processes transferred from Venice.

Because of their specialized nature, many of the new skills had evolved in only a few places in the south Netherlands and were subsequently transferred to just one or two places in the north.[49] Tapestry-weaving developed especially in Antwerp and Brussels and, in the north, chiefly in Delft. Sugar-refining had been confined to Antwerp and, from the 1590s, was heavily concentrated on Amsterdam. Diamond-cutting and polishing, an exclusively Antwerp industry, based on techniques acquired from Italy and Portugal, was transferred only to Amsterdam in the north. A rare technique earlier based exclusively in Kortrijk was the weaving of designs into fine linens, 'linen damask', a craft established solely in Haarlem. Mixed cotton and wool 'fustians', previously confined to Bruges, became, from the 1580s, a speciality of Leiden. Another specialized activity was linen-bleaching. In the 1580s, experts in bleaching fine linens, from Flanders, established their industry in the villages of Overveen and Bloemendaal, along the dunes, on the outskirts of Haarlem, where the water was especially suitable.[50] Linen-bleaching long remained a speciality of Haarlem.

Other new techniques became more widely diffused within the Republic. Jewellers, velvet-workers, printers, and artists from the south Netherlands settled in all the major Dutch towns, at any rate along the western seaboard. In the south production of coloured tiles for kitchens, pantries, and closets, derived from the Italian technique of majolica, had been chiefly an Antwerp speciality. But in the north, after shifting over, during the 1590s, from the brightly coloured tiles typical of Antwerp to the usually blue, simpler designs, characteristic of the Dutch Golden Age, southern entrepreneurs, and northern imitators, set up flourishing tile works in Delft, Rotterdam, Leiden, and Haarlem, and also, from around 1600, at Harlingen, in Friesland. Frisian glazed tiles formed a substantial part of total Dutch production during the Golden Age and early eighteenth century. The new copper-working techniques, imported from Germany at the beginning of the

---

[49] Van der Wee, 'Industrial Dynamics', 352.
[50] GA Haarlem Ell/2178, 'Rekest van de bleker Pieter van Hulle'.

seventeenth century, led to the establishment of copper mills in Utrecht and The Hague, as well as Amsterdam.

Proliferation of skills, their absorption and rapid extension, is a phenomenon closely related to the sudden, unprecedented expansion of artistic activity. Very few noted artists of the Dutch Golden Age were sons of manual labourers, artisans, seamen, fishermen, or peasants.[51] Most, when not themselves the sons of other artists, like Esaias van de Velde, or the younger Willem van de Velde, were sons of highly trained specialists constituting a new civic type—affluent, well-educated, sophisticated, and extremely skilled. Johannes Torrentius was the son of a fur-cutter, Pieter Saenredam of an engraver, and Gerrit Dou of a prosperous glass-painter who owned a glass workshop and several houses. Jan van de Capelle's father was a manufacturer of dyestuffs, Vermeer's a specialist in patterned satins, and Frans van Mieris's a goldsmith. Jacob van Ruisdael's father (untypically of the major artists) was not affluent but he too was a specialist, a designer of hangings and cartoons for tapestries.[52] Carel Fabritius' grandfather had been a Reformed preacher, from Ghent, his father a schoolmaster in a polder-village, at Midden-Beemster; but his father also had additional means—an annual income of 1,200 guilders—and was a painter in his spare time.[53] Fabritius' marriage to the sister of a successful cloth merchant, who owned several houses, in Amsterdam, was by no means untypical of the comfortable circumstances surrounding most of the noted artists. Affluence, in the post-1590 situation, came with skill and, as Van Hoogstraeten remarked, was essential for the peace of mind artists needed if they were to strive for highly refined effects.[54]

After 1590, art in the northern Netherlands, as in Antwerp, was a route to a large house and higher social position. Van Hoogstraeten describes art as both a way of making money and achieving status and 'glory', forming connections with regents and merchants, and, for the most successful, a path to princely favour, and the tables of the great.[55] The onset of Dutch world trade primacy, and the rapid urban expansion which accompanied it, created a situation, with a new merchant élite, and a newly enriched regent class, in which, suddenly, very many artists could have prosperous careers. With regent and merchant town houses and country villas going up on all sides, demand for high-quality pictures was almost insatiable. During his period as a fashionable portrait-painter in Amsterdam, in the 1630s,

[51] Montias, *Artists and Artisans in Delft*, 149–52.
[52] Slive, *Jacob van Ruisdael*, 20.
[53] Brown, *Carel Fabritius*, 14–15.
[54] Van Hoogstraeten, *Inleyding*, 318, 351.
[55] Ibid. 346, 353.

Rembrandt earned over 2,000 guilders yearly, far more than a university professor could expect.[56] But Rembrandt's earnings were paltry compared to the sums earned by his pupils, Dou, Flinck, and Bol. Like numerous others, Govaert Flinck was already wealthy before becoming an artist, being the son of a merchant; but his art enhanced his wealth, enabling him, in 1649, to acquire a large house in Amsterdam, which he crammed with antiquities, rarities, sculptures, and oriental carpets, and where he received his regent friends, including burgomasters Andries and Cornelis de Graeff.[57]

WAGES

The breakthrough to world trade primacy, and industrial expansion that went with it, generated intense demand both for unskilled labour and specialized skills. In this situation, Dutch wages were bound to be higher than were to be found elsewhere in western Europe. But in an economy characterized by explosive growth in numerous sectors, it is not sufficient to offer wages only marginally higher than elsewhere. For if wages had been only slightly higher, it would not have been possible to pull in the required skills and unskilled labour, fast enough, or on a sufficient scale, to service the newly won dominance of the 'rich trades'. Consequently, it was inherent in the post-1590 Dutch situation that wages should have been dramatically higher than in neighbouring countries. From almost the moment that the new industries were established, Dutch manufactures and employers had to contend with a situation—which persisted throughout the Golden Age and after—in which they paid wages often more than twice as high as those in the south Netherlands, or Germany.[58]

During the sixteenth century, the tendency in western Europe, generally, was for wages to rise more slowly than prices, chiefly because output of food and, to a lesser extent, manufactures, failed to keep pace with the increase in population. Consequently, living standards tended to fall. Only in the Low Countries, north and south, did wages rise fast enough, after 1550, to keep pace with rises in food and non-food prices, thereby avoiding a fall in living standards. But after 1585, the upwards wage spiral in the south Netherlands ceased. Wages levelled out and became static.[59] Since prices continued to rise, the effect was a sharp fall in living standards. After 1590, the north Netherlands became the only part of Europe where wages rose

[56] Schwartz, *Rembrandt*, 153.
[57] Von Moltke, *Govaert Flinck*, 9–11.
[58] Usselincx, *Grondich Discours*, 2, 6.
[59] Scholliers, 'Eerste schade', 47–9.

faster than the cost of living.[60] Real wages showed a strong upwards trend throughout the period from the late 1580s down to 1621.[61] There was then a retreat (with the onset of Phase Three in Dutch world trade primacy), especially during the sharp slump of the 1620s, and early 1630s, but there was a recovery in the buoyancy of real wages from the late 1630s.[62]

As a result, where, in 1585, wages in Holland were comparable with wages in the south, by 1609 Willem Usselincx was warning that Dutch industry would no longer be able to compete with industry in Flanders and Brabant, where wages and taxes, as well as house rents, were now much lower.[63] By this date, wages at Leiden were already more than 50 per cent higher than at Ghent or Bruges and other Flemish towns.[64]

Unskilled labour, as well as skilled, profited from the rise of Dutch world trade primacy. At Antwerp, where wages were some 20 per cent higher than in the Flemish towns, municipal labourers and bricklayers during the second quarter of the seventeenth century earned from 12 to 14 stuivers per day. Comparable work at Leiden, Delft, or Alkmaar earned 22 to 24 stuivers per day.[65] Of course, when allowance is made for higher taxes, and house rents, labourers in the Holland towns were not in fact twice as well off as counterparts in Flemish towns. Life for the unskilled, and semi-skilled, in Dutch Golden Age society was neither affluent nor easy. But the dynamism of the Dutch economy, after 1590, and burgeoning demand for skills, meant that there were good prospects for the highly trained to achieve affluence. The wide gap in remuneration for skilled, as against unskilled, work applied in most industries and crafts, and also at sea. Wages for seamen during the second quarter of the century remained low, at 12 guilders monthly.[66] Naval pay was, officially, even lower, at 11 guilders monthly for ordinary seamen, though, in practice, the Dutch commercial recovery of the 1630s pushed naval wages higher, Admiral Tromp remarking, in 1641, that it was hard to recruit naval seamen at less than 14 guilders monthly.[67] But wages for skilled men in merchant shipping were much higher. Ship's cooks, for example, received 25 guilders monthly and ship's carpenters 30, good pay when captains of merchant vessels were rated at 60 guilders monthly.[68] Ordinary soldiers earned 12.5 guilders monthly.

[60] De Vries, 'An Inquiry', 82.
[61] Nusteling, *Welvaart en werkgelegenheid*, 263.
[62] Ibid.; De Vries, 'Labour Market', 63.
[63] Usselincx, *Grondich Discours*, 2.
[64] Scholliers, 'Eerste schade', 49.
[65] De Vries, 'An Inquiry', 83, 94; Noordegraaf, *Daglonen in Alkmaar*, 47, 49.
[66] ARH SG 12575/34, fo. 3v.
[67] Van Deursen, *Het kopergeld*, i. 39.
[68] ARH SG 12575/34, fo. 3v.

But the Republic was a land with not one but several hierarchies of wages and salaries. In Holland, excises, rents, and bread prices were appreciably higher than in inland areas, and this alone ensured a wide gap in wage levels between the maritime west and rural east. Also one must distinguish between Amsterdam and other Holland and Zeeland towns, Amsterdam wages being appreciably higher still. Finally, there was a large gap between wage levels in Holland towns, on the one hand, and the Holland countryside on the other. Where municipal workers, at Leiden or Delft, earned 22 or 24 stuivers daily, in the 1630s, at Groningen they received 15 and, at Arnhem, only 12.[69] Wages at Arnhem were thus comparable with those at Bruges or Ghent. Dutch Reformed Church preachers, a relatively highly paid group, earned widely disparate salaries depending on where they worked.[70] In the villages of Holland, salaries rose from 200 guilders yearly in 1574, to 350 by 1594, and 500 by 1625, rather more than a skilled worker in a Holland town would earn. By that date preachers in the Holland towns could expect 1,000 guilders yearly and, at Amsterdam, considerably more. In the east, the gap between preachers' salaries in the villages and main towns was likewise appreciable. When Frederik Hendrik captured Roermond and Venlo, in 1632, the first Reformed preachers in those towns were appointed at salaries of 700 guilders yearly. In the countryside of the inland provinces, by contrast, there were preachers earning under 400 and, in some cases, even under 300 guilders yearly.

Wages in Holland and Zeeland in the seventeenth century were thus much higher than comparable wages in the Spanish Netherlands. This means that Dutch wages were dramatically higher than in most of the rest of north-western Europe. In England in the early seventeenth century, one earned less than in the south Netherlands let alone Holland.[71] In France and Germany, the gap was wider still.

CIVIC POOR RELIEF AND CHARITABLE INSTITUTIONS

There was much that was impressive about the Dutch Republic, and much that was unusual. But few aspects of the Dutch seventeenth and eighteenth centuries were more striking than the elaborate system of civic poor relief and charitable institutions. So exceptional, in European terms, were the conditions which gave rise to this system of civic charity that there was probably never much likelihood of its being emulated elsewhere. But its

---

[69] De Vries, 'An Inquiry', 94.
[70] Groenhuis, *De predikanten*, 136–9.
[71] Scholliers, 'Eerste schade', 50.

superiority over what one then found in neighbouring countries was sufficiently obvious to be frequently acknowledged by foreign visitors, though Catholic observers, such as the Venetian envoy Girolamo Trevisano, writing in 1620, stressed that it was largely maintained with revenues taken from the Catholic Church.[72]

Having failed to follow the Flemish and Walloon towns, in the early sixteenth century, in reorganizing their welfare institutions along the then modern, humanist-inspired, lines, the Dutch town governments were faced, all at once, in the 1590s and opening years of the new century, with vast new pressures and a wholly unprecedented situation. Along with new attitudes, and a new public religion, they were swept up in a process of explosive urban growth, and escalating numbers of poor and needy, combined with a tremendous expansion of the urban economy and proliferation of new resources and skills. At the same time, in confronting the new pressures, they found themselves with an extraordinary degree of freedom of action. Not only did the institutional organization of the Republic guarantee a high degree of civic autonomy but there was no Crown, or prince, to dispute their use of confiscated buildings, revenues, and other goods of the old Church.

Not the least unusual feature of the Dutch civic welfare system which now took shape was its pluriform and divided confessional structure. Almost everywhere else in Europe at the time, welfare functioned under the auspices of a single Church whether Catholic or Protestant. But in the Dutch context, the town governments not only took overall charge of the system, and funded many charitable institutions, but decided to what extent, and in what ways, the public Church, and also the other tolerated Churches, were to participate. In some towns the city's almoners, poor chest, and boards of charitable foundations exercised overall control. But, at the same time, it was accepted that the consistories of the Reformed Church, with their deaconates, had a substantial contribution to make and, in many towns, these played a preponderant role. But, while the consistories of the public Church were found to be eminently suitable instruments for administering charity, town governments were no less keen to enlist the boards of elders of other Churches which they formally tolerated, which meant, in Holland, Zeeland and Utrecht, principally the Lutherans, Mennonites, and, in Amsterdam—and later also several other cities—the Jews. These confessions all had their own lists of eligible destitute, excluded from other lists, and their own arrangements for orphans, the poor, sick, and elderly. By contrast, the Catholics, during the seventeenth century, were not permitted

---

[72] *Relazione di Girolamo Trevisano*, 417.

to organize in this way. Rather than allow Catholics scope to consolidate, and expand, their confessional following, which they permitted to the tolerated Churches, the town governments preferred to accept an extra burden of expense, forgoing the chance to transfer the cost on to the shoulders of the Catholic affluent. Thus, at Haarlem it was not until 1715 that the town council decided that, from now on, the Catholic community should be responsible for their poor, enabling them to set up their own charitable institutions, while at Leiden it was not until 1737 that this step was taken.[73]

But the key feature was the overall control from the town hall and highly regulated character of civic welfare. Sir William Temple remarked that while 'charity seems to be very national among them', it was not a system of personal and privately organized charity emanating from below, but rather a matter of the 'admirable provisions that are made . . . for all sorts of persons that can want, or ought to be kept'. Writing of the 'many and various hospitals that are in every man's curiosity and talk that travels their country', he describes how moved he was by the extraordinary care lavished on the home for aged seamen which he visited at Enkhuizen, 'a retreat stor'd with all the eases and conveniencies, that old-age is capable of feeling and enjoying', a fitting retirement, for those who had spent their whole lives 'in the hardships and incommodities of the sea'.[74]

That foreigners were regularly amazed by the attention, and resources, expended on creating an orderly, well-equipped, and smooth-functioning system of old-age and sick care, and poor relief, is undeniable. But charity and compassion, it should be noted, were not the sole motives which went into producing this result. In fact, the Dutch civic welfare system was a product of numerous social, economic, religious, and cultural goals and priorities and it is this broad background which made the Dutch system at once incomparable and inimitable.

It has to be recognized that some of the major motives were in fact quite far removed from those of compassion. In the first place, there were economic pressures.[75] Labour was chronically short in the Dutch towns and wages extremely high. Consequently, the work potential of orphans and the idle poor, and even the partly incapacitated, was a valuable commodity. In all the towns, a strict regime applied in the civic and Reformed Church orphanages and workhouses, imposing not only rigid discipline, regular Sunday prayer in the Reformed Church, and uniforms, but also hard work, in the case of the orphans often spinning and preparing yarn for the textile

[73] De Jongste, *Onrust*, 51; Krikke-Frijns, 'Ontstaan', 296.
[74] Temple, *United Provinces*, 104.
[75] De Vries, 'Labour Market', 67.

industries. Typically, day wages paid to the children had to be handed to the resident director of the orphanage, who would then allocate a proportion of their earnings to the children, on a weekly basis. The large home for poor orphans built at Middelburg, in 1602, clothed its inmates in blue stockings, and black uniforms, with the emblem of Middelburg embroidered, in yellow, on their right sleeves; this was not only to prevent the children selling their clothing but to advertise that they were wards and an asset of the city. At Haarlem, the children wore 'blue coats with one sleeve red and the other green'.[76]

Civic pride also contributed to the impulse to build imposing orphanages, hospitals, old people's homes, and workhouses. The towns vied with one another in every sphere and it was natural that in the building of 'God's houses' too a subtle rivalry should prevail, each town wishing to show how caring, responsible, and well-ordered it was and how admirable were its civic institutions. This also reflects, once again, the fundamental importance in the Dutch context of the power of the town councils, within the towns, and their ability to subordinate every dimension of civic life to regulation by the town hall. What the poor and needy gained from the sway of the regents was that there could never be the slightest question as to who was responsible for the general state of civic charitable foundations and poor relief administration. Civic politics was also a major factor in ensuring rigorous regulation of the 'God's houses' in another respect. Charitable foundations were administered on a week-to-week basis by committees of 'regents', prominent citizens, closely connected with town government, and consistories, whose wives often also gathered weekly, and separately, to deal with other aspects of the administration. They gathered in this way to ensure, under the general supervision of town hall and consistory, the maximum possible orderliness, thrift, cleanliness, and godliness of the inmates and institutions in their charge. They did this totally without remuneration for the sake of the status which accrued from it in both civic and Church society. In the case of the Lutheran, Mennonite, and Jewish communities, this was also the principal means by which prominent citizens could aspire to leadership on the boards of elders.

The social prestige derived from administering organized charity was reflected in art, albeit intermittently and chiefly at Amsterdam and Haarlem.[77] The first batch of group-portraits of austerely attired regents of civic charitable foundations, including one of the regents of Amsterdam's hospital of St Peter, were painted in 1617–18. The most famous are the two

---

[76] Van Strien, *British Travellers*, 198.   [77] Schwartz, *Dutch World of Painting*, 67.

group-portraits, painted by Frans Hals near the end of his life, in 1664, of the regents and regentesses of the Haarlem Old Men's Home, complete with such symbols of their administration as account-books, coins, and legal deeds. In 1626, the Amsterdam civic almoners commissioned a series of five paintings showing themselves at work, registering eligible paupers, distributing bread and clothing, inspecting a hemp works which they ran, and visiting a poor family at home. Such paintings adorned the regents' chambers of some charitable foundations. A more common use of art to enhance the civic welfare system, however, were the large allegorical paintings which embellished the interiors of charitable institutions and hospitals, glorifying healing, charity, and work.[78] A hospital embellished with an unusually large number of such paintings was that of St Job, in Utrecht.

The main hospital in each town was considered a major adjunct of civic life and test of the city's standing and status. At Middelburg, the hospital was administered by four 'regents', one of whom was a member of the *vroedschap*. The city paid the salaries of two university-trained physicians and also several assistants who worked full-time in the hospital. As in most big towns, a large room was set aside for anatomy lessons and clinical demonstrations. At Goes, the hospital was administered by three full regents of the *vroedschap*, and their wives, who were entrusted with implementing the decisions of their husbands; again the town employed two city physicians and assistants. Besides strictly civic considerations, there was also a wider interest in the hospitals in such ports as Flushing, Enkhuizen, Rotterdam, and Amsterdam, heavily frequented by the navy, on the part of the admiralty colleges, and ultimately the States of Holland and Zeeland, especially in wartime when these hospitals acquired a national function, caring for large numbers of wounded seamen. Similarly, in the garrison towns, there was a more than purely local interest in ensuring that hospitals were large, well-equipped, and provided with sufficient expertise, for here these institutions doubled as military hospitals. The large hospital built at Breda, equipped with the usual *theatrum anathomicum*, in 1643-4, shortly after the town was regained from the Spaniards, though mainly financed by the town itself, was in large part a military institution.[79]

One of the most striking contrasts between Dutch welfare institutions and what one normally encountered in the seventeenth and eighteenth centuries were the madhouses. Dealing with insanity was no easy test; but it was felt

---

[78] Ibid. 66, 70-1.   [79] *Geschiedenis van Breda*, ii. 274-5.

that the degradation and disorderly conditions resulting from crowding the insane together in dilapidated premises, and neglecting them, would reflect ill on the town as a whole, and it is clear that some effort was made to ensure as much dignity, and order, as possible. The Amsterdam madhouse, rebuilt in 1592, had separate cubicles for the inmates and an interior garden with plants and trees. 'The very Bedlam', commented one English visitor, in 1662, 'is so stately that one would take it to be the house of some lord.'[80] During his visit to the Republic, in 1667, Cosimo de Medici, son of the Grand Duke of Tuscany, visited, among innumerable other sights, the madhouses of Utrecht and Amsterdam, remarking on the 'cleanliness and good order' in which the inmates were kept.[81] At Middelburg, the madhouse, installed after the Revolt in a confiscated monastery, was administered by four 'regents', the 'president' being one of the magistracy.

At bottom, what lay behind it all was a quest for a well-ordered and industrious civic world based on confessional discipline. All considered, both the poor relief system and charitable foundations were rather effective instruments of social control. Through the meticulous upkeep of their registers, the colleges of municipal almoners and church deacons ensured that they were distributing money, food, clothing, and fuel only to what they regarded as the deserving poor, that is persons born in the town, or of long residence in it, who obeyed the rules and conducted themselves in an orderly manner. One of the chief purposes of the system was to keep destitute outsiders, vagrants, and beggars out of the towns. The foreigners who swarmed into the towns of Holland and Zeeland in the seventeenth century were allowed to stay only if they had money or work. By rigorously excluding vagrants and outsiders, the towns sought not only to keep down the cost of welfare but also to curb crime and disorderly conduct. It was, above all, by registering, restricting, and disciplining the destitute and then providing those who qualified with relatively generous support that Dutch cities in the seventeenth and eighteenth centuries achieved that remarkable orderliness, and low levels of crime, for which Leti and others praised them so highly. Sir Dudley Carleton, arriving in Holland in 1616, found 'Haarlem a whole town so neat and cleanly and all things so regular and in that good order as if it had been all but one house'.[82]

Both city almoners and church boards penalized drunkenness, rowdiness, and licentiousness assiduously and methodically. Caring for the needy, in the Dutch towns, was an integral part of an elaborate cultural, social, and

[80] Van Strien, *British Travellers*, 134.
[81] Hoogewerff, *Twee reizen van Cosimo de' Medici*, 37, 71–2.
[82] Carleton, *Letters*, 218: Carleton to John Chamberlain.

religious framework. In their qualifying and disqualifying paupers, need was never the only criterion and often not the most important. Typically, the poor regulations of the Portuguese Jewish community of Amsterdam, drawn up in the 1620s, confined money payments, ranging between 2 and 6 guilders per month—the maximum being about half the wage of an unskilled paid labourer—to the needy of good morals and conduct.[83] Anyone apprehended by the civic authorities for any sort of criminal activity was automatically excluded from further communal support.

But like everything else in the Dutch Republic, civic welfare policy was permeated by party-factional rivalries and confessional tensions. Before 1618, 'Arminian' towns, such as Leiden and Haarlem, preferred a more centrally organized, civic strategy, minimizing the influence of the Reformed consistory. Thus, at Leiden, all income for poor relief—whether proceeding from legacies, monthly house-to-house collections, Sunday collections in the churches, church-boxes, grants by the municipality from the proceeds of confiscated property of the old Church, or allocations from municipal taxation—was brought together in a single fund, under the control of the city's College of Almoners.[84] One consequence of this was that the city welfare system tended to discriminate in favour of the pre-1585 native population rather than give preference to formal adherence to the Reformed Church, which would have tended to favour the poor of the Flemish, Brabantine, and Walloon communities. Doubtless this was one factor in the notorious hostility of the city's immigrant population towards their regent civic regime.

In Haarlem, the *vroedschap* reorganized the city's poor relief system in 1598, putting the city's almoners in charge, imposing stringent curbs on begging, vagrancy, and private alms-giving, and, again, sharply differentiating between native Haarlemmers and outsiders, ordering the expulsion of non-native paupers.[85] The qualified destitute had to register with the almoners, undertaking not to enter taverns or gamble whilst in receipt of civic charity on pain of being struck off the list. Nevertheless, the deaconates continued to participate substantially in dispensing charity to destitute homes. The rule was that a family qualified for the consistory's poor list only if the husband was formally a member of the Reformed Church. If only the wife was, or both were merely informal 'sympathizers'—as were many Protestant poor—or the husband belonged to another Church, the family

---

[83] Swetschinski, 'Portuguese Jewish Merchants', i. 390.
[84] Van Deursen, *Het kopergeld*, i. 98–100.
[85] Spaans, *Haarlem*, 177–9.

could apply only to the almoners—unless the husband was a Lutheran or Mennonite, in which case he applied to their elders.

Typically, the Haarlem *vroedschap*, between 1598 and 1618, allocated only a small part of the funds dispensed from the confiscated revenues of the old Church to the poor relief chest of the public Church, steering the bulk to the college of Almoners. By contrast, after 1618, under the new Counter-Remonstrant regime, there was a hefty increase in the funds assigned by the city to the consistory for welfare.[86] One effect of this was to enhance the public Church's ability to persuade poor folk to join the Reformed Church and adopt a Reformed life-style, though doubtless a contributory factor in the huge increase in the scale of charity dispensed by the Reformed Church in Haarlem in the 1620s was simply the effect of the slump beginning in 1621.

The civic welfare system profoundly affected the lives of large numbers of people. Not many poor relief statistics are available for the seventeenth century and, in any case, the figures oscillated wildly in any given town from year to year, and between winter and summer, when there was more seasonal employment. But, at all times, those in receipt of charity, either living at home or in the 'God's houses', constituted an appreciable proportion of the urban population. In 1616, the Amsterdam civic chest was supporting 2,500 families—roughly 10,000 people—and between them the various tolerated Churches and guilds may have been supporting a comparable figure, which means that well over 10 per cent of the city's population was in receipt of charity.[87] At Haarlem, at the end of the Golden Age, before disintegration of the urban economy set in, the Reformed deaconate was supporting 500 to 600 families, about 5 per cent of the population, which again suggests that, altogether, over 10 per cent of the city's inhabitants were receiving charitable assistance from one source or another.

---

[86] Ibid. 182.   [87] Evenhuis, *Ook dat was Amsterdam*, ii. 74–5.

16

Protestantization, Catholicization, Confessionalization

❖

THE CONFESSIONAL ARENA

On the outbreak of the great Revolt, in 1572, the States of Holland had made no attempt to curb Protestantism but, initially, did try to ensure that both the old Church, and the Reformed, would be tolerated.[1] Among the regent, and noble, élites, a substantial grouping wished to defend the king's faith and its clergy. However, the mood of the militias and populace was strongly anti-Catholic and official efforts to protect Catholic worship, clergy, and images had little chance of succeeding. Just two weeks after Leiden went over to the Revolt, the several hundred clergy in the city were expelled and Catholic services suppressed.[2] The story was the same in Dordrecht, Rotterdam, Delft, and Gouda. Everywhere, principal churches were seized, the mass forbidden, and Catholic clergy driven out, generally without any demonstration, hardly a protest, from the Catholic side. So weak was the Catholic position that even Orange could do nothing to prevent this. Anxious not to alienate opinion in the south, the Prince made a determined attempt to oppose the suppression and even reintroduced the mass at Delft in December 1572, in one of the city's two main churches. But this brief revival of Catholic practice lasted less than three months.[3] Renewed anti-Catholic rioting erupted in February, and again in March 1573, and the Prince was forced to acquiesce in the total suppression of Catholic worship.

By late 1573, Orange's attempts to steer the Revolt towards acceptance of the public practice of both faiths had conclusively failed. What had begun as spontaneous attacks on Catholic images and clergy had, in a few months, evolved into the organized, general suppression of the Catholic faith, and

[1] Van Gelder, 'Nederland geprotestantiseerd?', 450–1.
[2] Van Gelder, *Revolutionnaire Reformatie*, 26.
[3] Swart, MS 'Willem de Zwijger', ch. 'Oranje's "Finest Hour" ', 10.

seizure of the Church's property, by the rebel States of Holland.[4] The position was the same in Zeeland. In all places held by the rebels, churches were seized, the Catholic clergy fled, or were driven off, and within a short time, without significant protest, Catholic worship was forbidden. When Spanish-held Middelburg, after its epic resistance, finally surrendered to the rebels, in 1574, there was no question of Catholic services being allowed to continue. The bishop and remaining clergy—over one hundred priests and friars—trekked out, in defeat, along with the Spanish soldiery.

Nor, with the vicissitudes of the Revolt over the next few years, was there any change, either in the attitude of the populace and militias, or the policy of the regents. A key ingredient of the Particular Union of Holland and Zeeland of 1575, creating the embryo of a rebel state, was the instruction to the Stadholder to maintain 'the practice of the Reformed evangelical religion, ending and prohibiting the exercise of the Roman religion'.[5] When the militia and populace of Amsterdam overthrew the old, pro-Catholic, town council, in May 1578, their coup led automatically to the expulsion of the Catholic clergy, confiscation of the old Church's buildings, destruction of images, and the suppression of Catholic worship.[6] A further wedge was driven between the infant Republic and Catholics who might have initially supported the Revolt, or considered being reconciled to the Revolt, by the Papacy when, in July 1578, Pope Gregory XIII forbade Catholics to collaborate in any way with the rebellion against Philip II, the legitimate ruler of the Netherlands decreed by God, threatening Catholics who supported the rebel regime with excommunication.[7]

But Reformed preachers now faced what, for them, was a frustrating paradox. The people rejected the old Church. Yet, at the same time, there was but a tepid response to the new. To some extent this was attributable to rival Protestant activity. For it was not only the Reformed who emerged, and organized, following the collapse of Spanish power. In many places, other Protestants, especially Mennonites, had survived Alva's persecution alongside the Reformed.[8] But this was a subsidiary factor. The main reason for the weak early response to the Reformed Church was lack of confessional zeal and the widespread noncommittal attitude bred by decades of heavy-handed official insistence on Catholic allegiance.

---

[4] *Apologie of Prince William*, 85.
[5] Res. Holl. 1575, 206–7, 296–7.
[6] Evenhuis, *Ook dat was Amsterdam*, i. 95–6.
[7] Spiertz, 'Katholieke geestelijke leiders', 3.
[8] Brandt, *Histoire der Reformatie*, i. 550–1; Troost and Woltjer, 'Brielle in hervormingstijd', 343–4.

The result was that the vast, plundered edifice of the old Church remained everywhere conspicuous while the profile of the new remained tentative and elusive. Churches and cloisters in the countryside had been pillaged and left derelict. In the towns, most churches stood empty, and boarded up, rather than in use for Protestant worship. It was clear, by the 1580s, that what had happened was less the replacement of one church by its successor than the shattering of the old and its replacement, in large part, with an ecclesiastical vacuum. The newly organized Reformed congregations grew but slowly, at first. In Alkmaar, there were only 156 communicant members as late as 1576.[9] Even where the Reformed were strongest, as at Delft, Dordrecht, Leiden, and Enkhuizen, active membership remained at under 10 per cent of the population even in the late 1570s. As the Revolt spread, after 1576, the position was much the same in the rest of the north Netherlands. The popular mood was anti-Catholic. Catholic worship was suppressed and Catholic churches closed. But Reformed congregations in the early years remained modest in size. Thus, there was a striking contrast of scale between the pre-1572 and post-1572 public Church: the former, with a vast establishment of buildings and clergy in each town, was now suppressed, while its successor employed a tiny number of preachers, only one or two in most towns, during the early years. This meant that most churches remained redundant, and nowhere more conspicuously than in towns which had been major ecclesiastical centres. 'There be thirty churches', remarked Fines Moryson, of Utrecht, in 1593, 'but only three are used for divine service.'[10]

Thus, during the early years of the Republic neither the old Church, nor the new, commanded the allegiance of most of the populace. Nevertheless, the Reformed Church enjoyed two great advantages over its displaced rival. Firstly, it had more, and more militant, support amongst the people than Catholicism, which enabled it to mobilize popular and militia pressure, and demonstrations, against Catholic worship whereas (even in the towns where Catholic support was strongest) it was too weak to mount counter-pressure. Secondly, the Reformed Church was now the public Church, which meant that it had the backing of the State, and civic authorities, under the terms of the Particular Union of Holland and Zeeland, of 1575, and under provincial legislation.

Catholic weakness was manifest even in the Holland city where Catholicism survived most tenaciously—Haarlem. Haarlem was the last Holland town where the mass was officially allowed, continuing until April 1581

[9] Van Gelder, 'Hervorming . . . te Alkmaar', 63-4.
[10] Moryson, *An Itinerary*, 53.

when the *vroedschap*, under heavy pressure from the States of Holland, was finally compelled to suppress it. There are definite indications that, after 1577, Catholicism in Haarlem retained more vitality than elsewhere and that many of the old civic élite remained 'sincere Catholijcken'.[11] Nevertheless, Haarlem's Catholics found themselves in an untenable position. Urged by Coornhert, they petitioned the States of Holland to be allowed to celebrate the Catholic mass in at least one church, pointing out that since the 'Religious Peace' of 1577 there had been no disorder due to religious differences in Haarlem. The States replied that this was true but that the reason was not because Haarlem's Catholics were loyal to the new order but that they were so few and weak they dared not cause any disturbance.[12] The petition was rejected.

   Catholic practice was universally suppressed in the towns of Holland and Zeeland but (at least in Holland) much more patchily in the countryside. Catholicism was suppressed in Heusden, on the southern fringe of Holland, when the States gained control of the town, in 1579; but in the surrounding villages Catholic services continued throughout the period of the Revolt. In North Holland, the countryside between Haarlem, Alkmaar, and Hoorn included entire villages which remained predominantly Catholic, usually under the influence of a resolute priest.[13] Yet, the general picture in the countryside, of Holland and even Utrecht (the province where rural Catholicism survived most extensively), though more mixed than in the towns, was still one of Catholic weakness overall. The reports compiled by a commission of the States of Utrecht, in 1593, on the religious situation in the countryside confirm that the advance of the Reformed faith was slow and sporadic but also that firm Catholic commitment was at best patchy. If there was only a minority of Utrecht villages, in the 1590s, where the churches had been fully 'cleansed' of images and altars, it was also a minority which was resolutely resisting the Reformation.[14] Most typical was a bizarre mixture of compromise, ignorance, and neglect, a chaotic, non-confessionalized, semi-Protestant Christianity coloured by the wavering of the village pastor. The pastor at Doorn was reported to have been a Catholic priest during the 1570s, Reformed after the collapse of Spanish power in 1576 but, 'through fear of the enemy', somewhere in between since the Spanish revival, in the 1580s. The pastor at Werkhoven was reported to be only 'slightly' Reformed but willing to do better. At Odijk, the pastor

[11] Spaans, *Haarlem*, 72–3.
[12] Res. Holl. 10 and 13 June and 3 July 1581.
[13] Van Deursen, *Plain Lives*, 283–6.
[14] 'Visitatie der kerken ten platten lande', 191–219.

had thrown out some images but retained others, and performed Catholic and Reformed baptisms and marriages, according to parishioners' preferences. At Houten, the preacher was simply hopelessly ignorant about the old faith and the new.

All this was deeply distressing to devout Protestants, who regarded the confusion and lack of confessional zeal as shocking. 'Even here, at The Hague,' noted Bodley, in 1592, 'there is not, in the judgment of those who doe observe it, a quarter part of the multitude well affected to religion, which I also meane not only in heart and deede but not so muche as in shewe and in outward profession.'[15] In Lutheran Germany and England, at the outset of the Reformation, it was also the case that Catholic commitment among the people was weak and yet Protestant awareness meagre, but during the later sixteenth century the populace was being successfully Protestantized. In this respect, the United Provinces lagged behind. But the much higher levels of attendance at Protestant churches in Lutheran Germany, and England, were not only due to the earlier start of the official Reformation in those countries but also to coercion—enforced church attendance.

The Holland regents, in 1587, worked on the assumption that about one-tenth of the province's population belonged to the Reformed Church.[16] By German, or English, standards, this might seem sparse. But when it is considered that this had been achieved without coercion, that there were numerous non-Calvinist Protestants, and that the prevailing political and military insecurity was bound to discourage many from joining the public Church, the figure of 10 per cent is really rather impressive. Catholic support, in the sense of persons willing to defend the old Church, or display their allegiance to it in some way, was certainly much weaker than this. The Reformed were not marginally, but overwhelmingly, the preponderant confessional bloc amongst the populace, as had been shown time and again since 1572. Furthermore, in some main towns, such as Delft, Leiden, and Dordrecht, as well as The Hague, the Reformed already constituted around 20 per cent of the population by the end of the 1580s.[17] In Delft, where there had been 200 members of the Reformed Church, representing, with their families, under 10 per cent of the population in 1583, by 1608 there were 1,600 members, comprising with their families around half the population.[18] This was impressive growth.

[15] PRO SP 84/44, fo. 65. Bodley to Burghley, 27 Jan. 1592.
[16] Rogier, *Gesch. van het katholicisme*, i. 439.
[17] Vermaseren, 'Sasbout Vosmeer', 195.
[18] Jaanus, *Hervormd Delft*, 49.

But while Reformed confessionalization proceeded steadily, Catholic allegiance also gained ground—albeit more slowly. When he arrived in 1583, Sasbout Vosmeer, the great Dutch missionary, who led the Catholic revival in Holland, becoming the first Vicar Apostolic, appointed by the Pope, to head the Dutch Mission, confided to his brother that Catholicism in Delft was virtually extinct.[19] A few years later, though, while admitting that libertinism, and non-attendance at church, was still the best supported denomination in the city, and that Catholics were fewer than the Reformed, he no longer believed that the latter vastly outnumbered the Catholics. At Dordrecht and Amsterdam, too, a slow, but noticeable, Catholic revival was under way. By 1600, it was estimated that there were around 500 Catholics in Dordrecht—exceedingly few but growing stronger.[20]

This incipient revival of Catholic support in the Netherlands north of the rivers was part of a more general phenomenon in western and central Europe which was marked in the north-west German lands bordering the Netherlands, particularly in the towns of the prince-bishops of Cologne, Münster, Osnabrück, and Paderborn where the efforts of the rulers succeeded in turning the tide against the Protestant churches from the 1580s onwards. The Catholic revival was also noticeable in Aachen, where a Spanish-backed coup restored a Catholic civic regime in 1598.[21]

In the late sixteenth century, the majority of the Dutch population, like most of the population in neighbouring Westphalia and the northern Rhineland, cannot unequivocally be described as Protestant or Catholic. For the majority constituted a non-confessionalized, or barely confessionalized, bloc, [22] undecided and unformed, attracting the fierce disapproval of committed men on both sides. Bodley was appalled by the widespread addiction 'to all manner of religions' and none. The French envoy, Buzanval, deplored the fact that much of the population 'suit le libertinisme, c'est à dire s'accomode à toute chaussure'.[23] In such a fluid situation the insistence of the Dutch provincial and civic authorities on formally suppressing Catholic as well as Lutheran and Mennonite worship, like the opposite situation in the neighbouring German prince-bishoprics where Protestantism was coming under pressure, exerted a decisive influence on the confessionalization process. Reformed, Catholics, Lutherans, and Mennonites were all striving to confessionalize the uncommitted and, con-

[19] Vermaseren, 'Sasbout Vosmeer', 193.
[20] Tukker, Classis van Dordrecht, 77.
[21] Schilling, 'Bürgerkämpfe in Aachen', 180, 184.
[22] Frijhoff, 'Katholieke toekomstverwachting', 439.
[23] Buzanval, Lettres, 289.

sequently, all the confessions were gaining ground. But in the Dutch provinces, as in Westphalia and the northern Rhineland, it was the confession which enjoyed the backing of the regime which gained ground fastest.

THE ORGANIZATION OF THE DUTCH REFORMED CHURCH

The first synod of the Dutch Reformed Church held within the Netherlands convened at Edam, in August 1572. At this gathering, and the second North Holland Synod, at Alkmaar in March 1573, and the first meeting of the South Holland Synod, later that year, the foundations of the Dutch system of synods, classes, and consistories were laid.[24] The first National Synod of the Dutch Reformed Church was held at Dordrecht, in 1578. Holland subsequently retained separate synods for North and South Holland, but was the only province of the Union to have more than one synod. In the other provinces, synodal jurisdiction corresponded to the borders of the province. Each provincial synod, once established, met yearly to control the affairs of the Church within the province and co-ordinate policy and activity between the provinces. It was intended that this would proceed under the supervision of a National Synod meeting every three years. A second National Synod did convene, at Middelburg, in 1581. Later, however, political complications, especially the reluctance of the States of Holland, forced the abandonment of the principle of regular gatherings of the National Synod.

Under the provincial synods came the regional classes, the gatherings of preachers in each area providing the link between town and country. Preachers in villages were often isolated, and less highly trained, than their better-paid colleagues in the towns and the classes provided a forum through which they could be guided and kept in touch with wider developments. Classes also had responsibility for erecting new consistories and co-ordinating activity in the educational sphere, and welfare, as well as in Church affairs proper.[25] By 1581, there were six classes in North Holland— Haarlem, Amsterdam, Alkmaar, Hoorn, Enkhuizen, and Edam. Eight classes fell under the synod of South Holland and four, including the largest in the Republic—that of Walcheren Island—under that of Zeeland. Several neighbouring consistories, including those in States Flanders and that of Bergen-op-Zoom (the latter under Walcheren), were also placed under one or other of the Zeeland classes. There were three classes under the synod of

[24] De Jong, 'Eerste drie Noord-Hollandse synoden', 194–6.
[25] Groenhuis, *Predikanten*, 22–3.

Utrecht—those of Utrecht, Amersfoort, and Wijk-bij-Duurstede—and originally four in Gelderland, one for each quarter. Friesland was divided into three classes, again one for each (rural) quarter, Oostergo, Westergo, and Zevenwolden. By contrast, the three Overijssel quarters were divided into five classes because each of the province's three 'head towns'—Deventer, Zwolle, and Kampen—had to be the centre of a classis but they were all in Salland, which meant that two more were needed for Vollenhove and Twenthe.[26] Drenthe was divided into three classes—Emmen, Meppel, and Rolde—eventually forming a separate synod.

But the most fundamental institution of the Dutch Reformed Church, as with all Calvinist churches, was the consistory. In the main towns, these church councils (*kerkeraden*) were sizeable bodies which met frequently to regulate the affairs of the Church within the community. Whereas the classes were gatherings only of preachers, the consistories were dominated by lay elders and included lay deacons, concerned with charitable work, as well as the preachers. At Amsterdam, the consistory began, in 1578, by gathering twice weekly but then settled down to once per week plus additional meetings when there were important developments.[27] The consistories closely supervised the life of the congregation, and matters of life-style, as well as Church affairs proper and the work of the preachers. There was no direct, official linkage between town councils and consistories, but it was frequently the case that one, or more, members of the *vroedschap* also belonged to the church council which was, in many respects, its ecclesiastical equivalent. Whenever preachers in a town were dissatisfied with an aspect of civic life they would mobilize the consistory to pressure the burgomasters and *vroedschap*.

This three-tiered—or, with the National Synod, four-tiered—structure was well suited to a federal edifice such as that of the Dutch Republic. As the public, and only, Church protected, and promoted, by the city councils, provinces, and States General—and upheld by all seven provinces—the Dutch Reformed Church was, in some respects, a state Church.[28] The main difference between it and a state Church in other Protestant lands was that it lacked the power to enforce church attendance and had no representation in Generality and provincial colleges and assemblies. Even in Utrecht the college of the first estate represented the province's five 'secularized' chapters, not the public Church.[29]

---

[26] Van 't Spijker, 'Acta', 81.
[27] Evenhuis, *Ook dat was Amsterdam*, i. 145.
[28] Van Gelder, *Getemperde vrijheid*, 4–5.
[29] Fruin, *Gesch. der staatsinstellingen*, 238–9.

From the outset, the relationship between public Church and town governments, particularly in Holland, showed signs of strain. It was the regents of Holland and Zeeland who had overthrown the old Church, confiscated its property, expelled its clergy, and driven out its schoolmasters. It was they who had authorized the stripping of the churches, and transferred them to the new Church, albeit under popular pressure. But there was a wide chasm between the Reformation of the Calvinist preachers and that of the regents, a point later emphasized by Grotius. As Grotius put it, where the preachers followed Calvin, the regents preferred the Reformation of Erasmus.[30] They too abhorred 'superstition', corrupt Church power, priestly abuses, and the like. They too sought to revitalize the spiritual life of the individual. But where the preachers wanted religion, and society, to be closely regulated, rigidly ordered theologically, and ruled by the new Church, the regents adhered, in their majority (as, he pointed out, had William the Silent), to a mild, non-dogmatic Protestantism which accepted that there should be only one protected public Church, but not that society, and the individual, should be rigorously subordinated to its control.

By the 1590s, hardly any regents were still openly Catholic. But only a small minority were zealous Calvinists who supported the aspirations of the Reformed preachers. Most were mild Protestants who outwardly conformed to the public Church without being zealots or else, as in Oldenbarnevelt's case, belonged only nominally. The majority were also reluctant to allow the public Church anything like as much influence over education, publishing, non-members of the public Church, and matters of life-style as preachers considered the public Church ought to have. To some extent they were also more tolerant. They did not agree with Coornhert that freedom of practice should be extended to Catholics, Lutherans, and Mennonites. But neither did they agree with the preachers that drastic methods should be used to suppress private gatherings of Anabaptists, Lutherans, Jews, Spiritualists, and Catholics. In other words, they were more inclined to connive at Catholic and dissenting conventicles. This clash of principles expressed itself also in a clash of interpretations of the Revolt. For the Calvinists it was above all a struggle about religion, for the 'true faith'. For the regents it was a struggle for freedom from oppression and tyranny. The medals issued by the States of Holland in the early years of the Revolt had shown the Liberty Cap, and extolled the fight for 'freedom', but not proclaimed the triumph of the Reformed Church. The emergency coins issued by the Leiden city council, during the great siege, bore the inscriptions *haec libertatis ergo* and

---

[30] Grotius, *Verantwoordingh*, 29.

pugno pro patria, labels frowned on by the preachers, who judged that *haec religionis ergo* would have been more fitting.[31]

At the very least, the public Church wanted the synods and classes to possess the power to ensure doctrinal purity within the Church and curb theological deviation within their own ranks. But this too the Holland regents were unwilling to concede. The early synods had proclaimed the Calvinist Heidelberg catechism the doctrinal basis of the Church and assigned the consistories control over the appointment and disciplining of preachers. But neither the States of Holland, nor Orange, accepted this and, in 1576, the States drafted a more Erastian 'church order', assigning most of the power, in the appointing and dismissing of preachers, to the town councils. The National Synod of Middelburg, of 1581, had then reasserted the public Church's autonomy from the civil authority, in matters of doctrine and appointments, in accordance with the acts of the Synod of Emden, of 1571.[32] The issue was still unresolved when Leicester's arrival, in 1585, led to the temporary eclipse of the States of Holland. Leicester convened a new National Synod, at The Hague, at which a strictly Calvinist 'Church order' was drawn up, designed to strip the town councils of power in Church affairs, while simultaneously strengthening state backing of the public Church. Several pro-Leicester, Calvinist towns in Holland—notably Amsterdam, Dordrecht, and Enkhuizen—accepted the 1586 'Church order', but most Holland towns rejected it. After Leicester's departure, the States negotiated a compromise which Oldenbarnevelt did his best to push through. But this only aggravated the problem, for most of the towns, on one side, and consistories, on the other, refused to accept Oldenbarnevelt's solution. In Church matters, there were now three blocs in the States of Holland—Calvinist towns, the anti-Calvinist, Erastian grouping—Gouda, Hoorn, Delft, and Rotterdam—and the moderates who supported the Advocate, notably Haarlem and Leiden.[33]

There were repeated quarrels between regents and synods in the decades after 1572 over less than orthodox preachers of the public Church. Most noteworthy were the cases of Caspar Coolhaes, Herman Herbertsz, and Hubert Duifhuis, at Leiden, Gouda, and Utrecht respectively. Coolhaes, a former monk of German background, had been a liberal Protestant preacher at Deventer, in 1566, and then a Reformed preacher at Leiden. In 1579, he became embroiled in controversy over whether the city council should participate in the election of elders, for the consistory, adopting a strongly

[31] Brandt, *Historie der Reformatie*, i. 553–4.
[32] Van 't Spijker, 'Acta', 82–9.
[33] Den Tex, *Oldenbarnevelt*, iii. 50–1.

Erastian standpoint. He also had reservations about Calvinist doctrine, including predestination, and promoted friendly dialogue with Anabaptists and Lutherans.[34] Even worse, in the eyes of many Reformed, he befriended Coornhert, approving of his rejection of dogmatic theology and his plea for toleration. The Leiden city council sought to shield him but had to discard him in 1581, when the National Synod at Middelburg formally condemned Coolhaes and his teachings.

Herbertsz was a preacher of similar stamp, dismissed from Dordrecht, in 1582, for unorthodox views. At Gouda, Herbertsz deviated from the teaching of the Heidelberg catechism, rejected predestination, and, like Coolhaes, cultivated friendly dialogue with other Protestants.[35] The South Holland Synod laboured to secure his dismissal but the Gouda *vroedschap* (which much approved of both the man, and his teachings) insisted on keeping him, as their leading minister, until his death in 1607. Meanwhile, at Utrecht relations between Calvinist orthodox and 'libertines' were even more fraught than at Leiden and Gouda. Hubert Duifhuis (1531–81), an inspiring preacher and respected local figure, much favoured by the *vroedschap*, was a former Catholic priest of Protestantizing tendencies, who forged a liberal, non-dogmatic Protestantism influenced by Spiritualism and opposed to Calvinist theology.[36] In politics, Duifhuis supported Orange's policy of toleration and 'Religious Peace'. His congregation, at the Sint Jacobskerk, was patronized by the civic élite but opposed by the Calvinist guilds and militia. With the coming of Leicester, and victory of the Calvinists on the Utrecht city council in 1586, Duifhuis's congregation was dissolved and his spiritual legacy suppressed.[37] After the 'libertine' victory in 1588, however, his memory and influence were officially rehabilitated.

The tension between regents and consistories showed no sign of decreasing with the passage of time. On the contrary, as confessionalization proceeded, and more of the ordinary populace came under the influence of the preachers, Calvinists had more scope for mobilizing popular opinion against the regents. Of particular significance, in this context, was the influx of Protestant refugees from the South Netherlands, after 1585. The immigrants were not the cause of the tension between consistories and regents or between Calvinist orthodoxy and less dogmatic Protestant attitudes. But they certainly aggravated matters, by strengthening Calvinist orthodoxy and adding a social dimension to a tension basically political and theological in

---

[34] Rogge, *Caspar Janszoon Coolhaas*, i. 190–4; Van Gelderen, *Political Thought*, 231–3.

[35] Hibben, *Gouda in Revolt*, 124–8.

[36] Kaplan, 'Hubert Duifhuis', 6–10.

[37] Den Boer, 'Unie van Utrecht', 73–4.

character. In this way, Calvinist orthodoxy became the ideology of those—often guild-members, militiamen, and semi-literate artisans—who opposed the regents.

THE REJECTION OF TOLERATION

At the commencement of the Revolt the regents had proclaimed the principle of religious freedom. The meeting of the States of Holland at Dordrecht, in July 1572, resolved that 'freedom of religion' would be upheld and no one hindered from the 'free exercise' of either the Reformed or Roman religion. But 'freedom of religion' was soon set aside and, in the years after 1573, few among the regents, or in Dutch society more widely, were prepared to espouse it. The great fighter for toleration, the Spiritualist, and controversialist, Dirk Volkertsz. Coornhert, contested this outcome, insisting that the freedom of conscience enshrined in the articles of the Union of Utrecht necessarily entailed freedom of practice also.[38] But the States of Holland disagreed, condemning him, in 1579, as a 'rustverstoorder', or disturber of the public peace.

Fear of freedom of religion, among the regents, was understandable. It was hard to see how the political, social, or moral order could survive if religion was fragmented and in disarray. Apprehension that doubt, Nicodemism, and libertinism were undermining order and morality was universal. A few sought alternative props. The one point on which Coornhert and his adversary, the great scholar Justus Lipsius, were agreed was the urgent need for a new morality, universally valid and based on non-religious foundations. Lipsius strove to construct a secular ethics based on Roman Stoic philosophy.[39] Coornhert's *Zedekunst* (1587), a treatise in Dutch replying to Lipsius' *Constantia*, offered a secularized, non-confessional biblical ethics.[40] Both detached morality from religion, presenting ethics as a social and political matter, an 'art', as Coornhert calls it, enabling the individual to improve his life once he grasps that avoiding excess, and disorderly living, is an avoiding of the harmful and dangerous.

Offering 'philosophical' reasons for cultivating morality, and discipline, had its relevance in a society fragmented in religion, and thirsty for order, but as was hardly to be denied, a relevance of limited scope. Ultimately, there was no alternative to outward conformity to the public Church, as the mathematician Simon Stevin, a Flemish immigrant, and *protégé* of Prince

---

[38] Bonger, *Motivering*, 23–6, 81.
[39] Lipsius, *De Constantia*, 2–4.
[40] Güldner, *Toleranz-Problem*, 87–90.

Maurits, emphasized in his tract *Het Burgherlick Leven* (1590). Stevin scathingly dismissed 'philosophic teaching' as a practicable means of instilling the discipline that was essential to the infant Republic. Stevin was a *politique* in religion, as well as a genius in algebra and geometry, who saw religion as an indispensable prop to the social order. He conceded that most people did not believe in the doctrines of the Dutch Reformed Church but asked them to conform to it even so. 'Philosophic' reasons mean nothing to children, he insisted, or the man in the street, so that if parents—even when they themselves do not believe—fail to instil veneration for the Church and 'fear of God' into their offspring, then morality, and with it the social order, would surely collapse.[41] His book is a dialogue with sceptics and libertines. He opposed freedom of religion and pleaded with those convinced of the truth of religions other than that upheld by the United Provinces to remain Nicodemist rather than express dissent which, he argued, can only divide, and weaken, both society and State. Like Lipsius, Stevin urged people to conform outwardly with a religion that they might not believe in—for Lipsius too championed outward conformity to the public Church—for the sake of society and the State. An individual whose conscience forbids him to conform to the Dutch Reformed Church should, Stevin suggests, move to another land where the public Church does correspond to his beliefs.[42]

Consequently, even in the most liberal towns, such as Haarlem, Leiden, and Gouda, there was no support for the views of Coornhert. Toleration was simply not regarded, by Erasmian regents and *politiques*, as a viable option. It is true that suppression of Catholic worship and education was enforced more stringently in some towns than in others. But even in the most liberal towns, all Catholic churches, cloisters, and other establishments were seized and Catholic education strongly discouraged. The small Catholic school and lodgings for Catholic students run by Willem van Assendelft in Leiden, in the 1580s, led a precarious existence before being closed down in 1591.[43] Many regents were unhappy at the condemnation of Coolhaes, at the National Synod of Middelburg. But Coornhert's magisterial plea for toleration, the *Synod of Freedom of Conscience* (1582), proved equally unappealing.

Thus, 'libertine' regents, like their Calvinist colleagues, and like the famous Westphalian Calvinist political thinker, Johannes Althusius, in his *Politics* (1603),[44] approved of 'freedom of conscience' while rejecting

---

[41] Stevin, *Het Burgherlick Leven*, 49–53.
[42] Ibid. 55–6.
[43] Geurts, *Eerste grote conflict*, 19–20.
[44] Althusius, *Politics*, 165–8.

freedom of practice, for Catholics, dissenters, and Jews. They were also eager to regulate doctrinal disputes within the public Church. After his first clash with Calvinist orthodoxy, in 1591, Jacobus Arminius, then a preacher at Amsterdam, was called before the burgomasters. Several of the most liberal regents in Amsterdam, including Cornelis Pietersz. Hooft and Laurens Reael, were among those who pondered his dispute with the Flemish immigrant preacher Petrus Plancius. They disliked Plancius' zealotry, but feared the unsettling reverberations of the quarrel even more. The burgomasters wanted such theological differences 'consigned to oblivion' and Arminius and Plancius to 'foster fraternal harmony', and prevent their argument spreading among their congregations.[45]

Even the most liberal regents felt disquiet at the progress of Lutheranism. The regents did not wish to prevent Lutheran immigrants, whether from Antwerp or Germany, settling in their towns. But they dreaded the bitter wrangling which had divided Reformed and Lutherans at Antwerp before 1585, weakening the city's resistance to Catholicism, and Spain, and for years remained reluctant to allow the 'Martinists', as they were called, to organize. At Amsterdam, in 1587, and Utrecht, in 1589, the Lutherans petitioned the regents 'to have a church and libertie to preach that doctrine'.[46] The regents responded with a campaign of harassment and pressure, blocking the public practice of the Lutheran faith and allowing only clandestine meetings, in small groups, in private homes.[47]

The anti-Lutheran campaign in the Dutch towns over the next two decades was a general phenomenon rooted (like the only slightly less hostile attitude towards the Mennonites) in the still non-confessionalized state of much of the population and fear of the gains alternative faiths could make if the official grip were relaxed. Lutheranism loomed larger in the Dutch consciousness at the close of the sixteenth century than is often realized. Lutheran refugees from Antwerp had established communities in several north Netherlands towns. There was a substantial refugee 'Dutch' Lutheran community in Hamburg.[48] Lutheranism, it was recalled, had figured prominently in the Protestant agitation in Overijssel and Gelderland in 1566.[49] At the same time, Lutheran–Calvinist antagonism was intensifying in Germany and drawing closer. The city of Hamburg was rigidly intolerant towards Calvinists in the 1570s and 1580s. In 1591, the last Reformed count of East

[45] Bangs, *Arminius*, 145–6.
[46] PRO SP 84/31, fos. 92–4. Gilpin to Burghley, 1 Mar. 1589.
[47] Loosjes, *Gesch. der Luthersche kerk*, 60–90.
[48] Whaley, *Religious Toleration*, 11, 119.
[49] Pont, *Gesch. van het Lutheranisme*, 229, 552–7.

Friesland died and was succeeded by the zealously Lutheran Count Edzard II. An acrimonious Reformed–Lutheran struggle erupted in East Friesland, and especially in Emden, which inevitably spilled over to heighten Reformed–Lutheran antagonism at Amsterdam, Groningen, Middelburg, and Utrecht.[50]

Lutheranism was perceived to be, and perhaps was, a threat to the stability of the new order. During the 1590s the Amsterdam city council continually persecuted the city's Lutherans and, in 1595, imposed an outright ban on Lutheran worship, threatening Lutherans with expulsion if they persisted with their conventicles. Interrupted briefly by the intercession of German Lutheran princes, in 1597, the pressure soon resumed—just as Hamburg was beginning to relax its attitude towards Reformed worship— and was stepped up during the 1602 plague outbreak when Plancius made it his business to incite hostility to Lutherans. Only after 1602 did Amsterdam change course, following Hamburg in accepting Reformed–Lutheran coexistence. From that point on the Lutheran community in Amsterdam grew steadily from seventy-six, in 1600, to 248 by 1617.[51] But owing to being stunted, and kept small, through official pressure, down to 1600, the community lost its original Dutch-speaking character and became increasingly an 'outsiders' congregation of German-speaking immigrants.

At Utrecht, the Lutheran plea for toleration, of 1589, met with the same reaction as at Amsterdam. At Middelburg, Lutherans were treated even more intolerantly than at Amsterdam and Utrecht.[52] In 1589, Lutheran practice in Middelburg was forbidden; the community survived but remained very small. Even in Haarlem and Leiden, cities which (until 1618) were somewhat more liberal than Amsterdam and where they became firmly established, Lutherans were kept under pressure, to restrict their growth. In 1596, the Lutheran preacher was expelled from Leiden and a new preacher was allowed only from 1606. The Lutheran communities established, in the 1580s, at Rotterdam, The Hague, Dordrecht, Gouda, Zwolle, and Kampen all stagnated or grew only very slowly. The one place in the United Provinces where Lutheranism was officially tolerated was Woerden. The States of Holland grudgingly conceded, in 1603, that Lutheran services at Woerden could continue but only as long as Lutherans eschewed all dispute with the Reformed, held their services at different times, and remained inconspicuous, threatening to withdraw their privilege if they were not discreet.

[50] Smid, *Ostfriesische Kirchengeschichte*, 239–45.
[51] Pont, *Gesch. van het Lutheranisme*, 536.
[52] Loosjes, *Gesch. der Luthersche kerk*, 87.

After 1605, when the first Lutheran synod was held at Amsterdam, attended by representatives from Middelburg, Utrecht, and several Holland towns, the pressure eased. In 1613, the pro-Arminian *vroedschap* of Leiden even allowed the Lutherans to build a 'public' church.[53] At Haarlem the city council (having forbidden Lutheran worship, in 1596) allowed the Lutherans to open a 'public' church, in 1615. But this was only in the Remonstrant towns plus Amsterdam. Elsewhere, even in some Holland towns, Lutheranism continued to be suppressed. In Dordrecht, the Lutherans were meeting regularly, in private homes, by 1613; but their petition for a 'public' church, in 1620, was rejected. When the Enkhuizen Lutherans built a church without permission in 1623, the *vroedschap* closed it down. The city of Utrecht was in Remonstrant hands, until 1618, but it was not until the 1620s that the Lutherans there could organize as a Church.

Anabaptists too encountered official intolerance, particularly during the first four decades of the Republic's existence. Especially abrasive was the anti-Mennonite campaign which followed an acrimonious public dispute between the Mennonite preacher Pieter van Ceulen and the Calvinist Johannes Acronius, in 1596. In May 1598, the States of Friesland issued a placard forbidding the public exercise of Anabaptist worship throughout their province. The city of Groningen followed suit in 1601. A series of fiercely anti-Mennonite placards appeared at Leeuwarden, Sneek, Groningen, and neighbouring towns in the years 1599–1601.[54] At Amsterdam, the *vroedschap* split in 1597, over how to react to the large crowds attending the sermons of the 'Young Frisian' Mennonite preacher Lubbert Gerrits. As part of a strategy to secure suppression of Mennonite worship in the city, the Reformed consistory challenged Gerrits to a public disputation, to clarify his theology, supposedly in the interests of 'truth and tranquillity'.[55] The aim was to cause an uproar and compel the city government to take drastic action.

The Jews were in a not dissimilar position to other dissenters. A small Portuguese Jewish community took root, at Amsterdam, in the late 1590s and tiny groups of German Jews had begun to settle, as early as the 1570s, in a few parts of the Ommelands. But nowhere was Jewish worship officially acknowledged, or permitted. In 1604, a group of Portuguese Jews from Amsterdam, who had been living as Jews, some years before, in Venice and Salonika, applied to the Haarlem city council, then more liberal than that of Amsterdam, for permission to establish a 'public' synagogue. This was

[53] Ibid. 88–9.
[54] Rogge, *Caspar Janszoon Coolhaes*, ii. 91, 97.
[55] Brandt, *Historie der Reformatie*, i. 815.

granted but the project failed, in part owing to Reformed opposition.[56] In 1610, the Portuguese Jews tried again, in Rotterdam. Again permission was secured and a congregation formed. But, after a few years, the Rotterdam *vroedschap* changed its mind and the group of seven families living there returned to Amsterdam. In 1612, the Portuguese Jews in Amsterdam, with the support of some members of the *vroedschap*, tried to build a synagogue but (to the relief of Spanish ministers, in Brussels) the Reformed consistory made such a fuss that the *vroedschap* felt obliged to suppress it.

THE CATHOLIC REVIVAL

The success of the Catholic revival, and confessionalization programme, varied greatly from locality to locality. Catholic allegiance in the Republic (excluding the Generality Lands) during the seventeenth and eighteenth centuries was strikingly uneven, reflecting the decisive part played by local political circumstances in shaping the confessionalization process during the crucially formative first half-century after the Revolt, when the population was being gradually coaxed and catechized out of its initial state of spiritual bewilderment. Towns which later boasted large Catholic minorities, such as Utrecht, Haarlem, Hoorn, Alkmaar, Amersfoort, and (at a later stage) Amsterdam and Rotterdam, were those where political conditions permitted a substantial number of Catholic priests to live, and work, unhindered. By contrast, Catholicism remained weak where it proved difficult for priests to reside and tend their flock.

Initially, Vosmeer based his efforts as Vicar-General (1583–1614) at Delft and Utrecht.[57] Later, after the States of Holland, aware of his contacts with Brussels, ordered his arrest for treason, in 1602, he transferred his headquarters to Cologne. Over the next years, Utrecht and Haarlem emerged as the chief centres of reviving Dutch Catholicism, with seven of the roughly seventy priests active in the Dutch Catholic Mission in 1609 residing in Haarlem. Vosmeer's successor Philip Rovenius (1574–1651) worked originally from Oldenzaal, then in Spanish hands. His first attempt to establish himself inside the Republic, at Utrecht, in 1621, failed and he returned to Oldenzaal. Only under the milder religious climate during the stadholderate of Frederik Hendrik (1625–47)—who conceded him a safe pass, in 1627— was the Vicar-General finally able to create a permanent base for Dutch Catholicism, at Utrecht. There, he lived in the home of a Catholic noble lady, Hendrika van Duivenvoorde.

[56] Seeligmann, 'Het Marranen-probleem', 112.
[57] Rogier, *Gesch. van het katholicisme*, ii. 71.

The Truce years were a crucial phase in the consolidation of the *Missio Hollandica*, facilitating as they did travel and circulation between the Republic and neighbouring lands. Vosmeer founded the first college for training future priests of the Holland Mission, that of SS Willibrord and Boniface, at Cologne, in 1613. But, in 1617, Rovenius formed a second college at Leuven which subsequently developed into the main centre. Trainees were encouraged to emphasize the central role of St Willibrord in the original conversion of the north Netherlands to Christianity as a way of reminding those whom they sought to convert, or whose Catholic faith needed bolstering, that Catholicism was the original Christian faith of their country and had for many centuries been the faith of their ancestors.[58]

Rovenius, the real organizer of the revived Dutch Catholic Church, selected Utrecht as his seat for its centrality and the large number of ex-regents and nobles in, and around, the city who supported the old faith; and also because it was historically the ecclesiastical centre of the north Netherlands. The unusual concentration of wealthy Catholic laity meant that many priests could be accommodated in the city and nearby. Between 1609 and the 1630s, Dutch Catholicism, in the north as a whole, experienced its most decisive phase of growth, the number of priests in the *Missio Hollandica* rising from seventy, in the opening years of the century, to 482 by 1638, a ceiling at which it then remained for several decades before declining slightly in the late seventeenth century and throughout the eighteenth.[59] In 1775, there were 420 priests in the *Missio*. However, not all the priests in the *Missio* (which excluded States Brabant and States Flanders) were on Dutch soil, since a substantial proportion worked in Cleves-Mark—where the public practice of Catholicism was tolerated—Lingen, and other nearby German districts which were part of the *Missio*. Moreover, the distribution of those who were on Dutch soil was, and remained, extremely uneven. Particularly striking was the concentration on Utrecht. As early as 1616 there were forty priests residing in the city, over a quarter of the total in the United Provinces.[60] Of 184 priests with fixed residence in Dutch towns in 1629, a quarter, forty-six, still resided in Utrecht (see Table 20). Several towns had merely one or no resident priest at all.

In principle, all seven provinces adhered to the same church policy. The Dutch Reformed Church was the recognized public Church, protected and favoured by the secular authorities, and Catholicism was banned. All alike forbade Catholic worship. But, in practice, the placards were enforced with

---

[58] Spiertz, 'Priest and Layman', 291–3.
[59] Ibid. 291.
[60] *Archief aartsbisdom Utrecht*, i. 209.

divergent degrees of strictness and in different ways. The Catholic population in nearly the whole territory of the Seven Provinces—as distinct from the Generality Lands—was a relatively small minority. The only towns on the territory of the Republic where Catholics were, or became, the majority were those which came back under Spanish control, for at least part of the crucial early phase of confessionalization, before 1621, and to which Catholic missionaries, based in the Spanish Netherlands, or the prince-bishopric of Münster, had access. Thus, the main towns of States Brabant— Breda, Grave, and (after 1629), 's-Hertogenbosch—were solidly Catholic in sentiment, in the seventeenth and eighteenth centuries, and Catholicism was strong in Twenthe and the easternmost fringes of Gelderland, and south of Nijmegen. Nevertheless, except for part of Twenthe, and with the partial exception of rural Utrecht (where there were an exceptional number of predominantly Catholic villages),[61] nowhere was there a largely Catholic region within the borders of the Seven Provinces themselves. The Generality Lands, of course, were quite another matter.

TABLE 20. *Catholic priests residing in Dutch cities in 1629*

Town	Priests	Town	Priests	Town	Priests
Utrecht	46	Rotterdam	7	Groningen	4
Amsterdam	30	Alkmaar	7	Dordrecht	3
Haarlem	20	Amersfoort	6	Zwolle	2
Leiden	8	The Hague	5	Arnhem	2
Hoorn	8	Delft	5	Zutphen	2

Source: *Archief aartsbisdom Utrecht*, i. 209 and xiii. 244, 254–5.

Moreover, while there were districts of Holland and Utrecht where large Catholic minorities were to be found, there were also areas of the Republic all but denuded of Catholics. Hardly any priests were able to establish themselves in Zeeland, and the South Holland islands, at the close of the sixteenth century or first half of the seventeenth, and here the Catholic population dwindled to minute proportions. Middelburg, a sizeable city, with over 30,000 inhabitants, in 1622, was reported, by the Catholic leadership, in 1616 to have a Catholic community of about 150, or less than half of one per cent (see Table 22). Flushing, Veere, Zierikzee, and Tholen were all almost devoid of Catholics. It was reported to Rome, from Utrecht, in 1635 that no Catholic priest was then resident in Flushing or Veere 'quia

---

[61] Abels and Van Booma, 'Tussen Rooms-katholiek en Utrechts-gereformeerd', 200, 224–5.

paucissimi ibi Catholici'.[62] Only Goes and its environs, a locality more accessible than most of Zeeland to Catholic missionaries from Brabant, had a slightly more substantial Catholic minority.

TABLE 21. *Catholic population of the cities of Holland and Utrecht, 1616–1656*

	Estimated total population in 1622	Estimated Catholic population			
		1616	1622	1635	1656
Amsterdam	105,000	—	—	14,000	30,000
Leiden	45,000	—	—	3,000	6,000
Haarlem	39,500	—	4,800	6,000	6,800
Utrecht	25,000	—	4,000	9,000	10,000
Delft	23,000	—	1,000	4,000	5,500
Enkhuizen	21,000	—	500	1,300	800
Rotterdam	20,000	400	1,000	3,000	6,500
Gouda	14,500	2,000	3,000	3,000	6,000
Dordrecht	18,000	600	600	1,200	—

Sources: Archief aartsbisdom Utrecht, xvii. 459–68; xviii. 5–16, 31–2; and xx. 372–7; De Kok, *Nederland op de breuklijn*, 145–6, 194–5; Spaans, *Haarlem*, 299.

The regents of Holland and Utrecht, by and large, were more tolerant than those in other provinces and the tendency in the large Holland towns, and Utrecht and Amersfoort, was for a steady increase in the Catholic population.[63] But there were also Holland towns, mostly smaller towns, such as Oudewater, Schoonhoven, Edam, and Brill, but also Enkhuizen, where intolerant policies, before, and after, 1618, created an opposite tendency, with the Catholic population shrinking. On the whole, it was this tendency to stagnate (or diminish) which was more typical outside Holland and Utrecht.

The crucial factor in determining Catholic prospects was whether or not priests could reside in a locality, or had ready access to it.[64] Where this was difficult, or impossible, it invariably happened that Catholic support not only failed to hold up but rapidly ebbed away. Despite the fact that Groningen, for example, had been the chief bastion of the royal cause and Catholic allegiance in the north, and a haven for refugee clergy fleeing from all over the northern provinces, until 1594, Catholicism in the town slumped under the harshly intolerant policy of the new *raad*, which strove to prevent

[62] *Archief aartsbisdom Utrecht*, xviii. 16.
[63] Van Deursen, *Het kopergeld*, iv. 74.
[64] Ibid. xx. 374.

Catholic gatherings, as they did those of the Mennonites and Lutherans. The 1601 placard banning Anabaptist worship also stipulated imprisonment and banishment for Catholic priests and fines for laity participating in Catholic services. During the early seventeenth century, priests in Groningen were constantly harassed and, as late as 1629, only four were stationed in the city.[65] Even much later, the *raad* would not tolerate more than a handful of priests within their walls. Consequently, in contrast to Utrecht and the main Holland towns, in Groningen the Catholic population rapidly dwindled.

TABLE 22. *Catholic population of cities outside Holland and Utrecht, 1616–1656*

	Estimated total population in 1622	Estimated Catholic population			
		1616	1622	1635/8	1656
Middelburg	35,000	150	150	300	300
Groningen	25,000	—	8,000	4,000	2,000
Deventer	7,000	—	400	1,200	600
Kampen	7,000	—	800	400	500
Arnhem			400	800	—
Zutphen	6,000	—	200	800	400
Harderwijk	—	—	—	1,200	680
Steenwijk	—	—	—	200	—

Sources: *Archief aartsbisdom Utrecht*, xi. 375, 204–1; xviii. 11; and xx. 377; Spiertz, 'Kerkeraad van Zutphen', 190.

Undoubtedly, there were cities such as Utrecht and Amersfoort where there were large Catholic minorities during the early and mid-seventeenth century, amounting to as much as a third or more of the population. But this was decidedly untypical. In most towns and cities the Catholic population amounted to less than 10 per cent and even a Catholic community constituting as much as 15 per cent, such as that of Haarlem, around 1620, has to be considered unusually large.[66] Haarlem was exceptional not only in that it had been back under Spanish rule in the years 1573–7, years of a determined Catholic restoration in the city, but in having, like Utrecht and Amsterdam, a substantial body of prominent citizens, formerly regents, who had chosen to remain within the old faith.[67]

One of the most important factors in determining the outcome of confessional rivalry in early seventeenth century, as Rovenius noted, was the

[65] Pathuis, 'Handschrift', 2–4.
[66] Spaans, *Haarlem*, 89.
[67] *Archief aartsbisdom Utrecht*, i. 221.

impact of the theologico-political rift increasingly dividing the city governments by 1609.[68] Those towns noted for 'libertine' tendencies in the late
sixteenth century allowed Catholic priests to reside, and propagate their
faith, without much hindrance, and these were also the towns which, after
1609, espoused Arminianism in the escalating struggle within State and
Church. Taking the Arminian side meant leaning towards tolerationist
policies. Thus, Utrecht (since 1588), Leiden, Haarlem, Rotterdam, Hoorn,
Alkmaar, and Gouda, the classic 'libertine' towns of the late sixteenth
century, became the champions of Remonstrantism after 1609,[69] and were
noticeably more tolerant towards Catholics, and other religious minorities,
than their rivals. Consequently, these were the towns with substantial
groups of Catholic priests and the places where Catholic numbers increased
steadily. The Catholic population of Gouda, one of the most resolutely
Remonstrant towns, grew from only 500, well under 10 per cent, in the
1580s, to about 3,000, some 20 per cent of the city, by 1622.[70]

By contrast, towns ruled by those whom the Catholic leadership called
'Gomarists', that is, city councils opposed to Oldenbarnevelt and the
Arminians, were less hospitable to priests, disrupted Catholic activity, and
had much smaller Catholic populations. In Holland, these included Dordrecht, Enkhuizen, Edam, and also (until 1622) Amsterdam.[71] Amsterdam
was, to some extent, an exception, being such a large city and possessing a
substantial Catholic minority. As a Catholic report of 1617 expressed it,
'although the Catholics of Amsterdam do not enjoy so much freedom [as
those of Haarlem] there are many of them'.[72] Nevertheless, in proportional
terms, there were substantially fewer Catholics in Amsterdam during the
first quarter of the seventeenth century, whilst the city was under 'Gomarist'
control, than there were at Haarlem, Leiden, Alkmaar, or Gouda. It was
only after the downfall of the Counter-Remonstrant regime at Amsterdam
that the city's Catholic population rose to 10 per cent, and not until the
middle of the century that it reached 15 per cent.[73] Dordrecht was a
staunchly 'Gomarist' town and had a tiny Catholic population, estimated
by the Catholic leadership, in 1617, at around 600, or some 4 per cent of
the population.[74]

[68] Ibid. xvii. 459: 'Nonnihil juvat ad augmentum numeri et libertatem nonnullam Catholico-
rum Calvinistarum inter se discordia'.
[69] Ibid. xvii. 460; Groenveld, *Evidente factiën*, 13–14.
[70] Geselschap, *Gouda*, 297.
[71] Dudok van Heel, 'Amsterdamse schuil of huiskerken?', 3.
[72] *Archief aartsbisdom Utrecht*, xvii. 467.
[73] See Table 21.
[74] *Archief aartsbisdom Utrecht*, xx. 364.

The Catholic minority, in the Holland towns, was not so large as is often supposed. A Catholic population as high as 15 per cent was the exception rather than the rule, in the early decades of the century. Yet, Catholic strength in Holland and Utrecht, in the countryside and towns alike, was much more substantial than in most of the rest of the United Provinces.[75] Holland and Utrecht were the two provinces were Remonstrantism was in the ascendant, in the years 1609–18, and where liberal policies towards Catholic missionizing prevailed, since the 1580s, and to these two provinces the Catholic revival was largely confined. As far as the Catholic–Protestant balance was concerned, Utrecht stood in sharp contrast to the other inland provinces. Only in the case of the Nijmegen quarter do we find an area outside Holland and Utrecht, which did not again, after 1591, revert to Spanish control, where there was a strong Catholic revival. It is no accident that this was also the only district outside of Holland and Utrecht which, until 1618, was heavily Remonstrant.

It is true that there were numerous noblemen, and ex-regents, in the eastern provinces and Friesland, who remained Catholic. In Holland, nobles who remained Catholic, like the lords of Wassenaar, often allowed priests to lodge in their residences. The lords of Rhoon, after 1621, kept a Jesuit permanently based in their castle. Nobles in the other provinces did the same. Catholic priests touring Friesland would stay in the residences of the Catholic branches of the Camminga, Dekema, Herema, Siccama, Tadema, Aylva, Burmania, and Scheltema families.[76] But, in the inland provinces, as Rovenius stressed in reports to Rome, this asset was largely nullified by the stringent anti-Catholic policies of the provincial governments, dominated by colleges of Delegated States, in which Catholic nobles had no influence and which were controlled by nobles who were uncompromisingly Reformed. Even though they were closer to territory controlled by Spain, or the prince-bishop of Münster, it was harder for Catholic priests to live, and work, in the eastern provinces (except for the extreme eastern fringes) than in Holland or Utrecht.

Persecution of Catholicism was most intense, according to Catholic spokesmen, around 1620, in Friesland and Zeeland. 'Status Frisiae satis est miserabilis', lamented one report, of 1616.[77] But Overijssel and Gelderland, from the Catholic point of view, were scarcely better and Groningen was arguably worse. The number of Catholic priests residing in Groningen, Overijssel (minus Twenthe), and Gelderland was probably less than the

[75] De Kok, *Nederland op de breuklijn*, 181–93.
[76] *Archief aartsbisdom Utrecht*, xi. 199.
[77] Ibid. i. 222 and xx. 373.

nineteen lodged at the time in Friesland. This is not to say that Protestantism had put down strong roots in Friesland, and the inland provinces, in
the late sixteenth century, and at the beginning of the seventeenth. On the
contrary, the situation was no less fluid than in Holland and Utrecht. A
Jesuit report, of 1616, divides the populace of Friesland into four blocs:
Reformed, Mennonite, Catholic, and *politici* (libertines), of which the last
was by no means the smallest. The opportunity was there. But Catholic
missionaries found it difficult to work because of the hostility of the
provincial authorities, especially the *grietmannen*, in the countryside. There
was some growth of Catholic population in the Frisian towns. There were
substantial Catholic minorities at Leeuwarden, Dokkum—a town where
Remonstrants as well as Catholics were strong—and Harlingen.[78] Overall,
the Catholic population in Friesland grew, initially, to about 10 per cent of
the province's population in the 1640s, but then began a slow decline.[79]

Catholic support lapsed even lower in the Salland and Vollenhove
quarters of Overijssel and in Drenthe. A report of 1638 states that in the
countryside of Vollenhove there were practically no Catholics and that the
only organized community in the quarter was in Steenwijk, where Catholics
numbered around 200.[80] Catholicism had more support in the three main
towns of Overijssel but Kampen, in 1618, acquired one of the most
intolerant Counter-Remonstrant regimes in the United Provinces, so that,
by 1635, there was no priest and the Catholic community had shrunk to
only 400.[81] Deventer—Rovenius' native town—was less severe than Kampen, after 1618, but, there too, Catholic support was meagre. Of the main
towns of Overijssel only Zwolle had a more substantial Catholic minority.

In most of Gelderland—the Arnhem quarter, the larger part of the
Zutphen quarter, and the Nijmegen quarter north of the Waal—the situation resembled that in the Salland and Vollenhove quarters of Overijssel,
Drenthe, and Groningen: Catholicism showed little resilience amongst the
population and Catholic congregations shrank to tiny proportions. Catholics in the city of Zutphen around 1650 were estimated to number about
400.[82] Rovenius and his colleagues were under no illusions the sparseness of
Catholic support in Gelderland or as to the reason: 'priests are rare,'
explained a report of 1622, 'owing to the harshness of the inhabitants and
the severe persecution'.[83]

---

[78] Ibid., xviii. 14.
[79] Faber, *Drie eeuwen Friesland*, i. 80.
[80] *Archief aartsbisdom Utrecht*, xviii. ll.
[81] Ibid. xviii. 11.
[82] Ibid. xl. 211.
[83] Ibid. xx. 364; Spiertz, 'Kerkeraad van Zutphen', 191–2.

Until around 1630 both urban and rural authorities in the east feared Lutheran as well as Catholic practice, aware most ordinary folk were as yet unconfessionalized in any direction and as apt to be drawn into reviving Catholicism, or Lutheranism, as the Reformed Church. When Maurits recaptured Zutphen from the Spaniards, in 1591, not only were all Catholic churches and property seized and the Reformed faith proclaimed the only permitted religion, Catholic priests were expelled from the area and the new, militantly Calvinist *raad* closed all the schools in the city except for the Latin school and one large 'Dutch' school in order to prevent non-Reformed catechizing of children.[84] The *raad* persisted in breaking up Catholic conventicles, imprisoning and fining priests they caught until the 1640s.[85]

Just as in the Twenthe quarter of Overijssel, however, an entirely different situation prevailed further east in the region known today as the *Achterhoek* of Gelderland, then the eastern part of the county of Zutphen. The fortress towns of this frontier area—Grol, Borculo, Lichtenvoorde, and Brede-voort—lay close to the prince-bishopric of Münster and enjoyed easier communications by road to the south and east, with Bocholt and Münster, than with Arnhem and Zutphen to the west. Indeed, this area did not form part of the 'Gelderland' under the Holland Mission but remained, in the eyes of the Papacy, under the ecclesiastical jurisdiction of Münster.[86] Two factors proved decisive in imparting a totally different religious character to these border districts than was to be found further west: on the one hand, the strong Spanish presence in both the *Achterhoek* and Twenthe down to the late 1620s and, on the other, the fact that the adjoining regions of Westphalia were a patchwork of political jurisdictions which were the scene of a triangular conflict of faiths: the Catholic, Calvinist, and Lutheran.

Not only was there a patchwork of jurisdictions on the German side but also on the Dutch side there were enclaves which had been partly, or entirely, outside the Habsburg Netherlands, the status of which, since the collapse of Spanish power, was disputed.[87] Charles V had acknowledged that the lordships of Grol and Lichtenvoorde, comprising a large slice of the *Achterhoek*, were part of the prince-bishopric—of Münster and belonged to the Empire. The neighbouring lands of the counts of Limburg-Stirum, Van den Bergh, and Bronckhorst-Batenburg—enclaved between Gelderland and the prince-bishopric—though it was often unclear whether they possessed separate status within the Empire or not, certainly retained a large measure of juridical autonomy.

[84] GA Zutphen 1/108. res. raad, 27 Oct. 1591.
[85] GA Zutphen 1/9. res. raad, 26 June and 1/12 res. raad. 23 Feb. 1647.
[86] Thielen, *Gesch. van de enclave Groenlo*, 16–19.
[87] Ibid. 83–5; Schröer, *Korrespondenz*, 53, 137–8.

These regions were the arena of a war of religions long before the outbreak of the Dutch Revolt in 1572. Protestantism had gained the upper hand in the lands of the prince-bishop of Münster, as in East Friesland and Osnabrück, as early as the 1530s among much of the urban population. Count Arnold II of Bentheim—a principality lodged between Twenthe and the prince-bishopric (see Map 11)—became a Lutheran in 1533 and both Bentheim and, further south, his territory of Steinfurt, enclaved within the prince-bishopric, formally adopted Lutheranism in 1544.[88] At the same time, the leading nobles of Gelderland had been at the forefront of the Protestant upsurge in the 1560s, though tending to vacillate between Lutheranism and Calvinism. Count Joost van Bronckhorst-Borculo, who held Borculo as a vassal of the prince-bishop, had converted to Lutheranism in 1550 and, in Borculo and Lichtenvoorde, Lutheranism prevailed down to the 1580s.

The 1580s were a major turning-point in religious history for the whole of north-west Germany as well as the Low Countries. On the one hand, the victory of the Catholic cause in the War of Cologne (1583–8) and the election of the new Wittelsbach Archbishop-Elector of Cologne, Ernst of Bavaria, as prince-bishop of Münster, in 1585, immensely strengthened the political and military position of Catholic princes and nobles throughout Westphalia and the north Rhine region. The simultaneous triumph of Parma in Flanders and Brabant and his success in recovering Nijmegen, Zutphen, and Deventer, and linking up with Groningen, created a double impetus—in the Netherlands and Westphalia—which marks the commencement of the Counter-Reformation throughout this part of Europe. The *bannerheren* of Gelderland, and many of the lesser princes of Westphalia, were now wedged between the Spaniards and the prince-bishop and lost no time in discarding their Protestantism in favour of Catholicism. The counts of Limburg-Stirum, Van den Bergh, and Bronckhorst-Batenburg all returned to the old Church at this time. Lords on the German side who defied the trend tended to discard Lutheranism for Calvinism since the Dutch rebels were now their likeliest source of support. Thus, in 1588, Count Arnold IV of Bentheim and Steinfurt introduced the Reformed faith, along Dutch lines, into his lands.[89]

New dilemmas arose with the Dutch successes of the 1590s. The Van den Bergh (who possessed lands in north Brabant, and the Roermond quarter, as well as their territory around 's-Heerenberg) stayed loyal to Spain until 1632, Count Hendrik van den Bergh becoming Spínola's second-in-

---

command, and the most senior Netherlander, in the army of Flanders.[90] But, by choosing Spain, and Catholicism, the Van den Bergh lost their family seat, House Bergh, at 's-Heerenberg, and their lands in the Zutphen quarter. By contrast, Count Joost van Limburg-Stirum (1560–1621), first Lutheran and then Catholic, in the 1580s, in the 1590s declared himself neutral, in 1604 entered the service of the States General, and eventually announced that he had converted back to Lutheranism. The conversion of Limburg-Stirum to Lutheranism, for the second time, assumed major political importance, during the Twelve Years Truce, when he claimed possession of Borculo-Lichtenvoorde, which the Spaniards (first in the 1580s, and again after Spínola's offensive of 1605) had returned to the prince-bishop of Münster (see Map 4) to bolster the Counter-Reformation in the area. He submitted his claim to the States of Gelderland who, predictably, found that Borculo-Lichtenvoorde belonged not to Münster but Gelderland.[91] The States of Gelderland's ruling in favour of Limburg-Stirum, ignored by Munster, Spain, and the Archdukes, was backed by Holland and the States General, and, in 1616, States General troops entered Borculo and Lichtenvoorde and ejected the Munsterites. As a result, Calvinism also began to gain ground. But while Lutheranism waned, and Borculo itself eventually became predominantly Reformed, Grol, Lichtenvoorde, and other enclaves where the Counter-Reformation had, by this time, sunk deep roots, remained largely Catholic. In this way, the *Achterhoek* became a patchwork of confessional contrasts, from town to town, and village to village, with militantly Catholic enclaves surrounded by Reformed districts.

If priests were severely hampered in most of Gelderland, Overijssel, Drenthe, and Groningen, the position was otherwise in States Brabant. When Maurits recaptured Grave, in 1603, he entered a town won back for Catholicism by the Counter-Reformation, under Spanish rule, in the 1580s and 1590s. Catholicism was banned, as in the rest of the Generality Lands, and there was no priest resident there, even unofficially, until 1633.[92] But it proved impossible to prevent the town's citizens attending mass, across the border of the nearby, independent, lordship of Ravenstein. Similarly, in the case of Breda, the town's predominantly Catholic character was largely due to the Counter-Reformation, under Spanish rule, in the 1580s, and subsequent ease of access, after Maurits recaptured the town in 1590, to nearby villages in Spanish Brabant, where the Archdukes encouraged a strong missionary effort.[92] Until 1609, the States General's soldiery tried to prevent

[90] Poelhekke, *Frederik Hendrik*, 268–70.
[91] Thielen, *Gesch. van de enclave Groenlo*, 68–9.
[92] *Geschiedenis van Breda*, ii. 170–6.

Breda citizens crossing the border to go to church but, during the Twelve Years Truce, could no longer do so. A priest in the neighbouring Spanish Brabant village of Prinsenhage claimed, in 1615, to have administered Easter communion to no fewer than 1,200 Breda Catholics. A major base for the Counter-Reformation in north Brabant was the (until 1629) still Spanish stronghold of 's-Hertogenbosch, where the Archdukes stationed not only one of their largest garrisons, but numerous clergy, investing heavily in a programme of reindoctrination and Catholic education.

In the last two decades of the sixteenth century and first two of the seventeenth, States Brabant became staunchly Catholic. It was not, however, under the jurisdiction of the Holland Mission, but (in deference to the Spanish Crown) left by the Pope in the ecclesiastical charge of the bishops of 's-Hertogenbosch and Antwerp.[93] But, if States Brabant became solidly Catholic, this was not the case with the part of Flanders which remained in, or reverted to, States' hands down to 1609. Most of this region became predominantly Reformed. For while Spain temporarily regained Sluis, the area remained partly in States' hands throughout and—even more important—geography rendered much of it inaccessible to missionaries operating from nearby Bruges and Ghent. Cadzant and the southern lip of the Scheldt estuary, north of the Passageule canal, lay effectively beyond the reach of the Counter-Reformation and remained much more closely linked economically and culturally with Zeeland than Flanders.[94] Also hard to reach and predominantly Protestant in character, were the fortress towns of Sluis and Aardenburg and their immediate environs. It was here that many of the Protestant refugees settled after being expelled from Ostend when the town fell to Spínola in 1604—in the case of Aardenburg including a group of Anabaptists. The bishop of Bruges reported to Rome, in 1628, that there was little prospect of introducing Catholic services in and around Sluis.[95] But while the villages north of the canal were uniformly Reformed, to the east of Sluis, Catholic priests did have access and here the villages were Catholicized.

By the second quarter of the seventeenth century, the confessionalization process throughout the Low Countries and Westphalia had advanced sufficiently for confessional lines amongst both the urban and the rural populace to have stabilized. This was doubtless the most important reason why confessional tensions began to ease, particularly in Holland, from around 1630. After 1650, even the most rigidly intolerant towns, such as

[93] Toeback, 'Kerkekijk-godsdienstige en culturele leven', 124–7.
[94] De Kok, Nederland op de breuklijn, 140–2.
[95] Trimp, Jodocus van Lodensteyn, 46.

Groningen, Kampen, and Zutphen, began to abandon the active harassment of Catholic missionaries, conventicles, and schools. It was now too late for the Counter-Reformation, or Lutheranism, to make more than a marginal impact. Consequently, Dutch civic and provincial authorities set aside their previous anxieties and became more relaxed in their attitude to dissenting Churches. It is a striking feature of Dutch Catholicism that, once fixed, by around 1630—precisely the same point at which the Catholic authorities

TABLE 23. *President Catholic parish priests in the provinces and quarters, 1629–1701 (rough estimates in parentheses)*

	Number of priests	
	1629	1701
United Provinces		
Holland	(100)	163
Utrecht	(50)	57
Friesland	19	31
Twenthe	25	15
Gelderland (minus Borculo-Grol)	(10)	17
Overijssel (minus Twenthe)	(10)	16
Groningen	4	12
Zeeland	4	5
Drenthe	0	0
German borderlands under the Dutch Catholic Church		
Cleves, duchy of	20	22
Lingen, county of	20	14

Sources: Archief aartsbisdom Utrecht, xiii. 254 and xix. 2–5.

declared Protestantism in Antwerp moribund[96]—confessional boundaries became rigid and subsequently displayed great durability. After 1630 there was little change in the religious map anywhere in the Low Countries. Thus, in 1629 practically three-quarters of all the priests of the Holland Mission— if we leave aside Twenthe, Cleves, and Lingen—resided in the provinces of Holland and Utrecht. Yet, if we compare the figures for distribution of Catholic priests in 1629 with those for 1701 (see Table 23) we see that concentration on Holland and Utrecht became still greater, with over three-quarters of the total number (again minus Twenthe, Cleves, and Lingen) residing in Holland and Utrecht.

[96] Thijs, *Van Geuzenstad tot katholiek bolwerk*, 53.

CONFESSIONALIZATION AND THE STATE

In the major towns of Holland and Utrecht, the Catholic population grew appreciably, from the end of the sixteenth century onwards. Most other confessional groups (the Anabaptists being the main exception) were also growing, including the Lutherans and Jews. But the confessional group which grew fastest, and the only one that grew steadily everywhere—in all the provinces, in town and country, in large town and small—was the Reformed Church. The reason is readily evident: the latter enjoyed the support of the secular authorities—Generality, provincial, civic, and rural. Catholics, Lutherans, Mennonites, and Jews (and the Remonstrants when they became a separate Church, after 1619) lacked access to public funds and patronage, possessed no large buildings capable of accommodating sizeable gatherings of people, and had no means of reaching a large audience. They had to be low-key in their proselytizing, could maintain only small, inconspicuous schools, and print little other than prayer-books. They were not allowed to criticize the public Church or rebut its theology, while it was free to assail theirs. Having only a restricted number of clergy and being allowed to gather only in small groups, in private houses, inevitably restricted access to the population. It is remarkable that in Leiden, in 1641, there were some 3,500 Catholics, around 7 per cent of the population, which then amounted to about 50,000,[97] but while the city's Reformed community was then five times as numerous, virtually the whole of the Reformed community congregated each Sunday in the city's two large churches—St Peter's and the Hooglandse—while the far smaller Catholic population were forced to meet in thirty different houses, taxing to the limit the available clergy.[98] In Amsterdam in the late seventeenth century, Catholics worshipped in over eighty houses.[99]

Church allegiance and confessional rivalry were inextricably entwined in early modern times with political life and statecraft. Religion was such a powerful force in society, culture, and education that it was literally impossible for any political or ideological grouping to remain aloof from the world of confessional strife. In a variety of ways, the Dutch political factions, in the Golden Age, were linked with confessional streams, and theological tendencies, and it was impossible that it should be otherwise whether in Dutch or any society of the time.

Allegiance to the old Church certainly had political connotations and not only down to the end of the Eighty Years War, in 1648. The leaders of the

[97] *Archief aartsbisdom Utrecht*, xii. 203.
[98] Van Deursen, *Plain Lives*, 286.
[99] Van Strien, *British Travellers*, 208.

Dutch Catholic Church in the seventeenth century, and those who backed them, came from specifically Dutch noble and ex-regent circles, rather than the south Netherlands, or elsewhere. Sasbout Vosmeer's mother was the daughter of a Delft burgomaster and Rovenius came from a similar background, at Deventer. Their class had lost its power and influence but not its wealth and aspirations. What they had lost they could recover only if the king of Spain overcame his rebels. In addition, their backing, and financial support, derived from the Spanish Netherlands and Münster, enemies and rivals of the United Provinces. Consequently, in its attitudes and prayers the Dutch Catholic Church was, and had to be, opposed to the Republic and its political leadership. Rovenius ordained priests of the Dutch Catholic Mission in the name of the king of Spain, and called the Dutch political regime 'heretics, rebels, and unlawful authorities'.[100] In principle, the Republic, in Catholic eyes, lacked legitimacy.[101]

In north Brabant, and around the eastern fringes, there was also a tendency for Catholic nobles and patricians to liaise, and not infrequently conspire, with Spanish garrison commanders and leading royalist nobles with ties in the north, not least Count Hendrik van den Bergh, royal Stadholder of Spanish-occupied Gelderland and Twenthe between 1605 and the Dutch reconquest of these areas in the late 1620s.[102] But the situation was different in the core of the Republic. For wealthy Catholic ex-regents in Utrecht, Haarlem, Rotterdam, or Amsterdam, it made little sense to plot against the 'rebel' regime. They had much to lose; and it better served their own interests, and their Church's, to forge a *modus vivendi*.[103] Both Vosmeer and Rovenius deliberately avoided inciting opposition to the regime. For their part, the regents rewarded such discretion by tempering their policy of suppression, turning a blind eye to the presence, and activity, of priests whose attitude they deemed acceptable. On one occasion two Delft burgomasters, accompanied by armed *schutters*, breaking up a Catholic gathering, found that they had seized Vosmeer himself. The burgomasters merely glanced at each other and let him go.[104]

More crucial to domestic Dutch politics was the tension between supporters of the wider aspirations of the Reformed synods in society, politics, and culture and those Erastian, liberal, regents and nobles who wished to limit the influence of the public Church. In Holland and Utrecht two rival traditions emerged during the 1570s and 1580s and were sharply at odds

---

[100] *Archief aartsbisdom Utrecht*, xiii. 222–3.
[101] Rogier, *Gesch. van het katholicisme*, iii. 508.
[102] AHN Estado leg. 727, 'voto' of Olivares (Sept. 1629), fos. 10–v.
[103] Van Deursen, *Plain Lives*, 295.
[104] Fruin, *Verspreide geschriften*, iii. 300.

during the Leicester years. Regents and nobles championing the orthodox Calvinist wing of the Church advocated policies of intolerance towards Catholics, Anabaptists, Lutherans, and Jews, and also those within the public Church who were not orthodox Calvinists. They were also more willing than their opponents to allow the Church control over education and culture in general. 'Libertine' regents, by contrast, not only wished to restrain the power of the Church, and uphold more tolerant policies towards those outside, but also wanted it to be theologically flexible, accommodating different points of view within.[105]

In this way 'party-factions' came into being, in Dutch civic and provincial life and politics, which, on the one hand, were built out of patronage networks, and family influence, giving them (in part) the characteristics of clientage systems, competing for influence and office, and, on the other, represented ideological and theological streams, conflicting attitudes to religion, education, culture, and life-style. This linkage of factional and clientage characteristics with political ideology, and theology, was to prove one of the enduring, fundamental features not only of the Golden Age but the entire history of the Republic.

A typical feature of this interaction of faction and ideology was that every episode in the Dutch past was construed in conflicting terms by the rival blocs, thereby assuming ideological significance. An obvious example was the controversy about the nature of the Revolt against Spain. Thus, leading political figures of the past, such as William the Silent, or Leicester, long remained controversial, as did various theologians and scholars including Erasmus. Many influential men revered the memory of Erasmus and his flexible, undogmatic view of Christianity. But precisely this aspect of Erasmus was scorned by stringent Calvinists such as Plancius and Gomarus. In this way, Erasmus not only remained a vital force in Dutch culture but became a badge for one main grouping within the body politic and target for another. A wooden statue of Erasmus erected in Rotterdam, in 1549, at the time of Philip II's visit to the city, was smashed and hurled into a canal, by the Spaniards, in 1572. It was subsequently replaced by a stone statue which was one of the first of a non-royal, non-mythological, and non-saintly figure ever erected in Europe. In 1616, when the influence of the Arminians (and Grotius) in the city was at its height, the *vroedschap* decided it was insufficiently grand, given its significance, and commissioned another from the Amsterdam architect-sculptor Hendrik de Keyser at a cost of several thousand guilders.[106] But, by the time De Keyser's copper statue of Erasmus

---

[105] Grotius, *Verantwoordingh*, 30–2; Grotius, *Oratie*, 50–2.
[106] Unger, 'Standbeelden', 269–70.

was ready, the Arminians had been overthrown and the Counter-Remonstrants, the strict Calvinist party, controlled the city. Not wishing to erect the statue in a public place, the new regents stored it away out of sight. After the pro-Arminian bloc recaptured Rotterdam in 1622, however, the new *vroedschap* brought it back out and set it up in the city's main market-place, much to the disgruntlement of the Reformed consistory, which protested that Erasmus was an 'adherent of the views of the Arminians' and affront to orthodox Reformed.[107]

Most divisive of all was the liberal Reformed theology of Jacobus Arminius (1560–1609). Soon after he was appointed to a chair in theology at Leiden, in 1603, a deep rift opened up between him and his strict Calvinist, Flemish refugee colleague, Franciscus Gomarus (1563–1641). Even before this, Arminius' appointment, urged at The Hague by Johannes Uyttenbogaert (1557–1644), a leading liberal Reformed preacher, and engineered by Oldenbarnevelt, had aroused disquiet in orthodox quarters. Though circumspect in lectures, in private Arminius confided his doubts about the Calvinist doctrine of predestination to his students. Initially, both Gomarus and Arminius endeavoured to confine their differences to their immediate circles. But the extreme sensitivity of Church, and public, to the issues involved brought the feud out into the open. By 1605, the clash was generating acrimonious dispute not only among Leiden's theology students but even the city's Flemish textile workers.[108]

Gomarus adhered to the orthodox Calvinist doctrine of 'absolute predestination' whereby faith is the 'fruit' of predestination and the individual immutably consigned beforehand to salvation, or damnation, the Last Judgement being envisaged as a timeless process rather than an event. Arminius modified this doctrine radically, defining Grace in such a way that the individual retains choice in the matter of faith. At the heart of Arminius' theology was his concern that the Almighty should not be conceived to be the author of human transgression nor freedom of the will of the individual entirely negated.[109]

Before long the clash between Arminius and Gomarus was generating a theological tension which not only pervaded the Reformed Church throughout the United Provinces—and neighbouring areas of Germany—but also invaded Dutch domestic politics. For by 1605, Oldenbarnevelt, Uyttenbogaert, and their allies had decided the best way of dealing with the disputes threatening the unity of the public Church was to revise the

---

[107] Ibid. 271.
[108] Maronier, *Jacobus Arminius*, 186–7, 202.
[109] Van Deursen, *Bavianen en slijkgeuzen*, 228–9.

confession and catechism so that its theological base would become more flexible and accommodating. The idea was to calm tempers by convening a National Synod to resolve the issues and adjust the confession of the faith.

But most ministers of the Reformed Church, in Holland, as in the other provinces, opposed revising the confession and catechism; and the South Holland Synod demanded that ministers under its jurisdiction, and the theology professors, at Leiden, should subscribe to the existing confession before the convening of a National Synod.[110] In April 1606, the North and South Holland Synods refused to participate in a National Synod unless it was stipulated beforehand that the gathering would confirm the existing confession and catechism. This produced deadlock and an escalating conflict (see pp. 421–32 below) which eventually led on to the great political crisis of 1617–18.

The overthrow of Oldenbarnevelt in 1618 enabled the Gomarists to force a conclusion to the controversies within the public Church, driving out their opponents. The Church thereby became more stable and internally cohesive. But the new regime failed to forge a viable new ruling bloc, championing the Reformed Church, in the States of Holland (see pp. 480–2 below) so that although, for a few years, the anti-Catholicism of the regime intensified, and policies of intolerance were in the ascendant, before long more tolerant regent groupings again gained the upper hand in some Holland towns, causing the breakdown, at least in Holland, of the post-1618 politico-theological consensus. Consequently, some towns now became more tolerant than others and the confessionalization process entered a wholly new phase. In effect, the Reformed Church had become more cohesive within but without acquiring a tighter grip over the overall confessionalization process and at the cost of driving away large numbers who had formerly belonged to the public Church. Those estranged now moved confessionally in various directions. Some eventually joined the new Remonstrant Church when it was able to emerge into the open, in the late 1620s. But in the meantime, whilst Remonstrantism was vigorously suppressed, many of those affected had turned elsewhere and were permanently lost to both the Calvinist orthodox and the Remonstrants.

Many people living in towns which before 1618 had been dominated by Remonstrant preachers—such as Rotterdam, Gouda, The Hague, Alkmaar, and Hoorn—permanently defected from the public Church after 1618, the dramatic jump in Catholic allegiance at Rotterdam, around 1620, being expressly attributed by the Catholic leadership to the coming over of large numbers of former Remonstrants.[111] But some former Rotterdam

---

[110] Bangs, *Arminius*, 280–1.   [111] *Archief aartsbisdom Utrecht*, xii. 209.

Remonstrants went over to the Lutherans.[112] At The Hague and Gouda, too, large numbers, reportedly, went over to the Catholics after 1618 and, to a lesser extent, the Lutherans. Lutheran preachers, eager to reap the harvest, emphasized the closeness of Arminius' teaching on will and Grace to that of Luther.[113] The Lutheran minister at Haarlem was even found, in 1624, to be distributing Arminian tracts as part of his drive to win converts.

Nor was it only Catholics and Lutherans who gained a new flock from the expulsion and persecution of the Remonstrants. In the environs of Leiden, first in the village of Warmond and then, more permanently, at nearby Rijnsburg, formed a group of liberal Arminians who subsequently refused to enter the Remonstrant Church when it was able to organize openly from the late 1620s, preferring to remain outside any formal church body and dispense both with clergy and any fixed confession of faith.[114] This was the first congregation of 'Rijnsburgers' or, as they became more generally known, 'Collegiants'. In the 1630s, the movement spread to Rotterdam, where it drew its membership from Mennonite as well as Remonstrant ranks. In 1646, a third 'college' of Rijnsburgers was established at Amsterdam. Subsequently several members of the regent class, notably the Pesser family and Adriaen Paets at Rotterdam, and Coenraad van Beuningen at Amsterdam, showed a strong sympathy for the movement. The free character of their services and extreme flexibility on confessional matters remained their hallmark. John Locke noted, in 1684, that between their prayers 'anyone that finds himself moved, has the liberty to speak', adding that 'they admit to their communion all Christians and hold it our duty to join in love and charity with those who differ in opinion'.[115] Although there were only three 'colleges' in the middle decades of the century—at Amsterdam, Rotterdam, and Rijnsburg—and Collegiant numbers were few, they came to exert an appreciable impact on religious debate in the Republic, and attitudes to church matters, especially among the Remonstrants and Mennonites.

ANABAPTISM AND THE CONFESSIONALIZATION PROCESS

Most churches in the Republic, including the public Church, Catholics, Lutherans, and Jews, could look to securely established co-religionists in neighbouring lands such as France, Germany, the south Netherlands, and

---

[112] Pont, *Gesch. van het Lutheranisme*, 551.
[113] Limborch, 'Voor-reden', 5–6v.
[114] Van Slee, *Rijnsburger Collegianten*, 29–44.
[115] Van Strien, *British Travellers*, 307.

Switzerland for guidance, and help with confessional, organizational, and theological problems. For all except the public Church, this was a crucial factor, in the Dutch context, since they were dissenting Churches, lacking the support of the State, or any political means of restraining and disciplining dissidents within their ranks. The Anabaptists and, after 1618, also the Remonstrants also had sister communities, at any rate in north-west Germany, where both groups were established in a number of places. But these German offshoots of Dutch Remonstrantism and Anabaptism were neither sufficiently numerous and stable, nor sufficiently authoritative, to instruct, or buttress, their brethren within the Republic. This was particularly a problem for Dutch Anabaptism, which was widely scattered and derived from a number of different roots and traditions.

Theological and organizational cohesion, in the situation in which Dutch Anabaptists found themselves, was bound to be elusive and it is not surprising that they were more apt to fragment and, at the same time, even more preoccupied with congregational discipline than their rivals. In reaction to the chaotic diversity of the 1530s, Anabaptism, under the leadership of Dirk Philips and Leenart Bouwens, in the 1540s and 1550s, strove for both doctrinal and organizational unity. Bouwens, who baptized over 10,000 persons, between 1551 and 1582, throughout the north Netherlands and East Friesland, established many new congregations, displaying markedly authoritarian tendencies and making frequent use of the ban to expel members who failed to live up to his exacting standards. But his very severity generated a reaction. A more liberal wing emerged, during the 1550s, critical of Philips and Bouwens, which became known as the 'Waterlanders', after the rural district to the north of Amsterdam. The 'Waterlanders' stood for less total submission of the individual to the congregation and authority of the elders. A gathering of Mennonite leaders from all over the Low Countries and northern Germany, Menno himself among them, at Harlingen, in 1557, attempted to heal the split.[116] But Menno, now old and frail, failed and the rift between conservatives and Waterlanders widened.

The migration of Flemish and Antwerp Anabaptists to the north Netherlands, and East Friesland, after the coming of Alva, aggravated old, and created new, tensions concerning doctrine, organization, and life-style. The names 'Flemish' and 'Frisian' which increasingly came into use during the last third of the sixteenth century, to distinguish different streams of conservative Anabaptism, although originally a reference to geographical

---

[116] Kühler, *Gesch. der Nederlandsche doopsgezinden*, 317, 321.

origin, soon became mainly an indication, not of provenance, but of which confessional bloc one belonged to, precisely as with the Waterlanders. Thus, Philips, though not a south Netherlander, became the leader of the 'Flemish' Anabaptists, who split from the 'Frisians', under Bouwens, after another gathering at Harlingen, in 1566, each side placing the other under its ban.[117]

By the late 1580s, both 'Flemish' and the 'Frisians' had, in turn, each divided into warring hardline and moderate factions. There were, in fact, no fewer than six main confessional blocs within Dutch Anabaptism by the 1590s: the Waterlanders, Old Frisians, Old Flemish, Young Frisians, Young Flemish, and so-called High Germans,[118] and most of these survived, in some form, through the seventeenth century, though the situation remained fluid and, at local level, different groups were continually arguing, splitting, and merging. The Republic's greatest poet, Joost van den Vondel (1587–1679), born at Cologne, his parents Anabaptist refugees from Antwerp, belonged, during his early life, to the Waterlander community, at Amsterdam. Karel van Mander (1548–1606), painter, poet, and author of a celebrated book about painters and painting, published in 1604, was a Flemish refugee who belonged to the Old Flemish community at Haarlem, a city where all the different groups were represented, and where in the early seventeenth century the Anabaptist groups together constituted the second largest Church block, after the Reformed, amounting in 1620 to some 14 per cent of the population.[119] At Haarlem, the Anabaptists—like the Catholics—had an appreciably larger community than in most Holland towns. Salomon van Ruysdael (1602–70), the landscape painter, belonged to the Haarlem Young Flemish, as, probably, did his brother, father of the greatest of all landscape painters, Jacob van Ruisdael (1629–82). Numerous other artists derived from a similar background. Govaert Flinck (1615–60), the most successful of Rembrandt's pupils, in Amsterdam, was born into a Mennonite family, in Cleves. The Dordrecht painter Samuel van Hoogstraeten (1627–78), another pupil of Rembrandt, also a writer about art, was born, like Vondel, into a family of Anabaptist refugees from Antwerp. The ingenious townscape painter, and inventor, Jan van der Heyden (1637–1712), was the son of an Utrecht Old Fleming and brought up among the 'Flemish' in Amsterdam.

Striving for greater doctrinal stability, as well as discipline of life-style and submission to the community, all the groups sought, often in dialogue with

[117] Doornkat Koolman, *Dirk Philips*, 133–6.
[118] Van der Zijpp, *Gesch. der doopsgezinden*, 80–2.
[119] Spaans, *Haarlem*, 101.

each other, to define and elaborate their respective confessional positions. Among the Waterlanders, the two leading theologians were Hans de Ries (1553–1638) and Lubbert Gerritsz. De Ries, originally from Antwerp, from 1598 worked mostly in North Holland, especially at Amsterdam, Haarlem, and Alkmaar, until his death in 1638. Gerritsz, a linen weaver from Amersfoort, having left the Young Frisians for the Waterlanders, was the leading preacher of his community, at Amsterdam, from 1591 until his death in 1612. Together, De Ries and Gerritsz drew up the Waterlander Confession of 1610, one of the most important of the Dutch Anabaptist confessions of the Golden Age. On defining the Trinity, it stood closer to the Young Frisians and High Germans than to the Flemish communities. The main difference between the Waterlanders and the rest remained their conception of the community, putting less emphasis on binding the individual to the authority of the elders.[120] This became the main stumbling-block to a merger between what evolved into the two largest groupings among the Anabaptists. For during the first half of the seventeenth century, at Amsterdam and elsewhere, many of the Young Frisians joined the Waterlanders while, in 1632, most Old Flemish reunited with the Young Flemish; subsequently the remaining Young Frisians merged with the United Flemish. Although there were still stubborn remnants of the other groups, by the 1640s the great majority of the roughly 75,000 Anabaptists in the Dutch Republic—amounting to some 5 per cent of the population—belonged either to the new moderate-conservative block of United Flemish, Frisians, and High Germans, or to the Waterlanders. Ultra-orthodox splinter groups which refused dialogue and reconciliation remained locally strong in some places including Groningen, where the Old Flemish long remained entrenched.

---

[120] Meihuizen, *Galenus Abrahamsz*, 36–8.

17

The Separation of Identities:
The Twelve Years Truce

❖

THE PRESSURE TO NEGOTIATE

Despite spectacular economic success since 1590, the United Provinces, as Oldenbarnevelt explained in 1606 in a letter to the Dutch envoy in Paris, had, since 1598, experienced serious problems in meeting the escalating cost of the war against Spain: 'within the country matters are now proceeding with extreme difficulty, but we dare not raise taxation in the towns and villages any higher for fear of disturbances'.[1] Holland's Advocate added that 'more than half of the inhabitants in the towns and countryside are inclined towards peace and . . . should there be any further reverses, the rest will not remain firm, especially since the provinces have been stripped of all business, prosperity, and most of their navigation, by the [peace treaties] of France and England'. Here Oldenbarnevelt was referring to the increased impact of the Spanish embargoes on the Dutch economy, and diversion of traffic away from the Republic, since the revival of commerce between England and Spain following the treaty of 1604.

Oldenbarnevelt, thus far, had proved an outstanding statesman but within a fixed framework of conflict with Spain which, ever since 1588, had kept the Republic in a static posture in its external statecraft. The Dutch state had persevered with an arduous and slow-moving war, while simultaneously prospering from the great expansion of Dutch trade and industry. Hitherto, this inflexible stance had served the Republic well. Seeing no advantage in negotiation, or compromise, only danger and loss of momentum, the States of Holland had neither needed, nor wished, to reassess their priorities or consider any fundamental change of direction.

The rigidity, and fear of change, rooted in a prolonged situation of siege, should not be underestimated. It required a great pressure to shift

---

[1] Deventer, *Gedenkstukken*, ii. 69. Oldenbarnevelt to Van Aerssen, 18 Jan. 1606.

Oldenbarnevelt and the regents from their entrenched stance. But between 1598 and 1606 a new general strategic situation arose which exerted such strain on the Republic that Oldenbarnevelt and the Holland *Gecommitteerde Raden* were obliged to reconsider their premises. This sprang partly from the sharply escalating burden of military expenditure. Between 1597 and 1606, the Dutch army had doubled in size and spending on fortifications had quintupled. Yet, where the 1590s were a time of triumphant military success, by 1605 the Republic was pinned to the defensive and inexorably losing ground. The situation was probably not untenable militarily, but arguably was unsustainable financially and psychologically. At the same time, a slackening had now set in in the Republic's overseas commerce and shipping, the pillar on which the vitality, and strength, of the Republic rested. The initial consequences of the Spanish embargo of 1598, though serious, had been softened by the inclusion of the English, under an earlier ban. In 1604, however, Spain and England made peace and, under the terms of the peace treaty, it was agreed that while English ships were now free to sail to Spain and Portugal, they must not, under any circumstances, carry for Dutch merchants. English ships sailing to Spanish or Portuguese ports must show papers certifying that their cargo was neither Dutch, nor Dutch-owned, and English vessels which failed to comply could, without further ado, be confiscated by the Spanish authorities along with goods suspected of being Dutch.[2] Thus the English Crown accepted that the Dutch should not be allowed to share, indirectly, in the strong revival of English commerce with Spain and Portugal which now ensued and England's restored access to the fine goods of southern Europe, which threatened to undercut a large part of the Dutch 'rich trades' and, to some, seemed likely to bring Dutch world trade primacy to an early end.

In September 1606, Oldenbarnevelt, addressing a secret committee of the States of Holland, held that the Republic's financial position was no longer tenable. He apparently urged that the Republic must now either place itself under the sovereign protection of Henri IV or else seek some accommodation with Spain. Furthermore, at this very time Spain's position also shifted. Earlier, the Archdukes had insisted that their sovereignty, and the king of Spain's rights, over the north had to be acknowledged in some form before negotiations could be contemplated. But late in 1606, Philip III and his chief minister, the duke of Lerma, after much deliberation, resolved to concede sovereignty, recognizing the 'rebel' provinces as an independent state, if the Dutch met their price in the Indies, and this the Archdukes were now told

[2] Israel, *Dutch Primacy*, 82; Israel, *Empires and Entrepots*, 194–202.

to communicate to Oldenbarnevelt. Two main factors effected this change in the Spanish position.[3] Firstly, Spain too was labouring under severe financial strain. But the key development was the Dutch breakthrough in the East Indies, in 1605, when the VOC conquered Amboina, Ternate, and Tidore. For Spanish ministers realized that they utterly lacked the means to prevent the Dutch sway in the Indies spreading.

What Spain now proposed was to sell the Dutch their independence, in return for their agreeing to withdraw from the Indies. When first soundings met with a favourable response, Philip directed the Archdukes to concede what he called *el punto mas dificultoso* (the most difficult point) and offer the Dutch 'rebels' recognition of their independence.[4] These Dutch–Spanish contacts remained purely informal—though Maurits and Willem Lodewijk were brought into the discussions[5]—until December 1606. In that month they were put on a formal basis with Spínola negotiating with Oldenbarnevelt on behalf of Spain and the Archdukes. Oldenbarnevelt gave verbal assurances that, in return for recognition, and a full peace, the United Provinces would evacuate the Indies. Spínola communicated Albert and Isabella's secret declaration of 13 March 1607 that the 'Archdukes holding nothing dearer than to see the Netherlands and their worthy inhabitants released from the miseries of this war, hereby declare that they are willing to negotiate with the States General of the United Netherlands as, and considering them as, free lands, provinces and States, over which their Highnesses make no claim whether in the context of a permanent peace, truce or armistice for twelve, fifteen or twenty years'.[6] Finally, a cease-fire was signed in April 1607. On seeing the text Spínola had signed, however, Philip and Lerma (not to mention Lerma's hawkish critics) were horrified to find no substantive—let alone equivalent—Dutch concession with which to balance Spanish acceptance of the independence of the rebel provinces. Albert and Spínola explained that, in principle, Oldenbarnevelt had agreed to disband the VOC, and abort the projected WIC, but had refused to stipulate as much in writing in a mere preliminary armistice before peace talks proper. Hence the accord had been signed without any apparent concession to Spain.[7] Not surprisingly, it was greeted with amazement at the courts of Europe and widely deemed a humiliation for the Spanish crown.

Spanish indignation was then further aroused by the almost simultaneous news of the great sea battle won by a Dutch fleet, of twenty-six warships off

---

[3] Israel, *Dutch Republic and the Hispanic World*, 5–6.
[4] CODOIN xliii. 50, 52–4.
[5] Van der Kemp, *Maurits van Nassau*, iii. 4.
[6] ARH SG 12575–7. sec. declaration of Albert and Isabella, 13 Mar. 1607.
[7] Rodríguez Villa, *Ambrosio Spínola*, 156–7

the southern Spanish coast. Since their first long-distance naval offensive, in 1599, when a fleet carrying 8,000 men had been sent to the Azores and São Thomé, the States General had dispatched several fleets, mostly to the coasts of Spain and Portugal, but thus far without any notable success. But, in 1607, determined to offset in some measure the effect of Spínola's recent victories on land,[8] and perhaps also gain some prestige for the States of Holland, as distinct from the Stadholder, Oldenbarnevelt and his colleagues stepped up their naval offensive. Sailing right into the Bay of Gibraltar, the Dutch fleet, on 25 April 1607, virtually annihilated a Spanish force of almost as many ships carrying even more guns, destroying all ten of its large galleons. The death in action of the Dutch admiral, Jacob van Heemskerck, in the midst of his victory, provided the States of Holland, when the fleet returned, with the opportunity to put on an impressive state funeral which was, at the same time, a celebration of Holland's burgeoning might at sea.[9] Indeed, the Van Heemskerck obsequies marked the commencement of a republican cult of fallen admirals which was later to develop into a familiar method of countering the military prestige of the Stadholders.[10] Some 800 regents and officials participated in the funeral procession, including the entire Amsterdam city council, and directors of the VOC, the coffin being carried by fourteen naval captains. To perpetuate the glory of Holland's naval hero, the States commissioned a handsome marble tomb which was prominently installed in the Old Church in Delft.

The Spanish court's frustration increased when formal talks resumed at The Hague, in February 1608, and it emerged that Oldenbarnevelt's verbal undertakings counted for little. Having tested regent opinion, Oldenbarnevelt knew that it was out of the question to press for the dissolution of the VOC even for a full peace and *de jure* recognition of the United Provinces 'as a free state'.[11] To do so was simply not feasible politically because many regents and élite merchants had invested heavily in the enterprise. Oldenbarnevelt was ready, however, to abort the plans (then before the States of Holland and Zeeland), to set up a parallel West India Company, and also to halt the further expansion of the VOC in the East Indies. Not surprisingly, this going back on what he had provisionally conceded destroyed prospects of a full peace and almost wrecked those for a truce.

Spain and the Archdukes were hardly likely to yield full recognition for the limited quid pro quo now on offer. But even offering what he did

[8] De Tex, *Oldenbarnevelt*, ii. 554.567.
[9] Van Meteren, *Historie*, ix. 211–12.
[10] Lawrence, 'Hendrick de Keyser's Heemskerk Monument', 272.
[11] Veenendaal, *Johan van Oldenbarnevelt*, ii. 185.

involved considerable risks for Oldenbarnevelt at home. The Advocate's
relationship with Maurits, deteriorating since 1600, was now under severe
strain, and so was his relationship with both Zeeland and Amsterdam.
During 1607, the Stadholder's initial opposition to Oldenbarnevelt's policy
of accommodation with Spain had failed. He had tried to mobilize war
feeling in the militantly Reformed provinces of Friesland and Groningen,
with Willem Lodewijk's help.[12] But these provinces only briefly sided with
Zeeland in the States General, and by the autumn of 1607 had effectively
ceased their opposition to Oldenbarnevelt's policy.[13] Like Gelderland,
Overijssel, and Utrecht, these provinces exhibited many signs of war-weariness and shrank from further increases in taxation.[14] Maurits was compelled
to moderate his tone for fear of being left too isolated. Amsterdam, in the
vote on the cease-fire, in the States of Holland, in March 1607, found herself
totally isolated in resisting Oldenbarnevelt.[15] But Amsterdam was a formidable adversary and remained implacably opposed to the Advocate's
policy;[16] moreover, in other Holland towns there was considerable anxiety
in some quarters. In particular, Delft prevaricated, worried about the East
India trade, seeing, as an English observer put it, that the 'freedom of
commerce into Spayne [including Portugal] which is a consequent of this
truce will in a short time divert all their merchants and mariners from that
tedious and dangerous navigation'.[17] In Zeeland too, the colonial interest
was a potent factor, though there the principal motive for opposing the
truce was the fear that the hitherto flourishing wartime transit traffic to
Flanders and Brabant along the Scheldt and Zwin, the mainstay of the
province's prosperity, would evaporate the moment hostilities ceased and
the Dutch blockade of the Flemish seaports was lifted.

During 1608, Oldenbarnevelt's critics waged a vehement publicity campaign across the Republic, endeavouring to sway the people with arguments
commercial, military, and religious, trying every conceivable ploy to discredit the proposed Truce. The directors of the VOC and private Guinea
companies submitted petitions to the States of Holland and Zeeland
warning that the newly gained long-distance trade would be jeopardized.
The States of Zeeland, denouncing the Truce proposals as 'ruineulx ende
dangereulx', issued a commemorative medal displaying the arms of Zeeland
on one side, and the Trojan Horse being dragged into Troy on the other,

[12] Jeannin, *Négotiations*, i. 253–4.
[13] RAGr S.Gr. 3, res. S.Gr. 25 Nov. 1607 and 28 Feb. 1608.
[14] Van der Kemp, *Maurits van Nassau*, iii. 9.
[15] Res. Holl. 27 Mar. 1607.
[16] GA Amsterdam res. vroed. 29 Oct. and 22 Nov. 1607.
[17] BL MS Add. 40837, fo. 315v. Winwood and Spencer to Cecil, 17 Nov. 1608.

warning that catastrophe would ensue should the States General be duped into accepting the Spanish offer.[18] Maurits, in his open circulars to the Holland town councils, in the autumn of 1608, maintained that the proposed truce would undermine the Republic's security and perhaps even lead to the restoration of Spanish tyranny.[19] The main publicity vehicle, however, were the printed pamphlets which poured from the presses especially of Amsterdam and Middelburg. Several of the most effective were written by Willem Usselincx, the leading champion of the West India Company project (and himself a refugee from the south), who argued that the truce would severely damage the textile industries of Haarlem, Leiden, and Delft—by enabling those of Flanders to revive—as well as undermine Dutch interests in the Indies.

But it was Oldenbarnevelt's arguments which carried most weight amongst the Holland regents and it was they who decided. They needed little convincing that Generality finances were insufficient for the war to continue without major tax increases and this they deemed inadvisable. A twelve-year truce, Oldenbarnevelt admitted, might not be as attractive as a full peace, with recognition, but it would extricate the Republic from the financial impasse; release the Republic's forces enabling the States General to intervene more effectively, in defence of Dutch interests elsewhere, than was possible, whilst the war continued; and, of course, rescue Dutch commerce in Europe by lifting the Spanish embargoes thereby reviving Dutch navigation to the Iberian peninsula and Mediterranean. Oldenbarnevelt held that gains accruing in European trade from the lifting of the embargoes, would outweigh the losses from halting the VOC's expansion in the Indies.[20]

Having failed to secure disbandment of the VOC, Spain offered a Twelve Years Truce, in return for Catholics in the Dutch provinces being granted open and public toleration of their faith.[21] But, in the circumstances of 1608, this was just as impossible, politically, for Oldenbarnevelt to concede as dissolution of the VOC.[22] Again the negotiations verged on collapse. Finally, after much heart-searching, Philip and Lerma swallowed their pride and consented to truce terms which both foreign diplomats, and much Spanish opinion, deemed prestigious for the 'rebels' but not for Spain. The only tangible Dutch concessions were the aborting of the planned West India Company and the halting of the VOC's attacks on the Portuguese in Asia, though even this lasted only to 1613. The Truce was signed, amid

[18] Van Loon, *Beschryving*, ii. 40–1.
[19] Van Meteren, *Historie*, ix. 66–7.
[20] Deventer, *Gedenkstukken*, iii. 311.
[21] Rodríguez Villa, *Ambrosio Spinola*, 230–1.
[22] De Pater, *Maurits en Oldenbarnevelt*, 54–5.

much pomp and ceremony, at Antwerp, on 9 April 1609. But it left a bitter taste among broad sections of the political élite in both Spain and the United Provinces. As the Amsterdam city council complained, Spain's acknowledgement of the United Provinces 'as if' they were a sovereign state, in a truce agreement which, by its nature, was temporary, was virtually meaningless.[23]

THE POLITICAL AND ECONOMIC CONSEQUENCES OF THE TRUCE

Oldenbarnevelt's arguments were, in most respects, vindicated. Substantial gains accrued to the Republic, the most obvious of which, initially, was the enhancement of the Republic's international status. Since the 1590s the Republic had been one of Europe's major powers yet had lacked the trappings of great power status. Under the treaty of Nonsuch, the English Crown had not formally recognized the sovereign independence of the United Provinces and, officially, the Republic continued to be regarded as a temporary phenomenon, an interim rebel state, lacking legitimacy, whose envoys should not be treated as ambassadors.[24] Furthermore, opposing Spain's might in the Netherlands had so tied up the Republic's armed forces that (except for East Friesland) the rest of Europe had not yet directly encountered Dutch power. Also there were doubts whether the Republic could survive without English and French help and subsidies. All this changed in 1609. Spain grudgingly acknowledged the Republic, *de facto*, 'as if' it were a sovereign state; the rest of Europe, and the Muslim powers of the Near East and North Africa, saw the Truce as a full legitimization of the United Provinces.

In 1609 France and England acknowledged the Dutch envoys, in their respective capitals, as full ambassadors.[25] Soon after, the United Provinces established diplomatic relations with Venice and, in December 1610, with Morocco. Letters arrived from the Ottoman court inviting the States General to send out a resident ambassador to Constantinople, an offer acted on, the following year, when Cornelis Haga, the first Dutch ambassador to the Ottoman Porte, set out for his new posting.[26] The number of resident Dutch ambassadors remained very few (as was usual among the European powers at the time), but recognition also enabled the Republic to establish

---

[23] Res. Holl. 19 Mar. and 3 Apr. 1609.
[24] Wernham, 'English Policy and the Revolt', 29–35.
[25] Barendrecht, *François van Aerssen*, 228–9.
[26] De Groot, *Ottoman Empire and the Dutch Republic*, 104–6.

a network of consulates which were of great value to a maritime power such as the Dutch Republic. From this point on, resident Dutch consuls were able to send regular reports, assist Dutch merchants and skippers involved in legal or political difficulties, or business disputes, and act as diplomatic auxiliaries. Agents and consuls were posted in various cities in Germany and the Baltic and in Livorno (1612), Aleppo (1613), Cyprus (1613), Venice (1614), Genoa (1615), Algiers (1616), and Zante (1618).[27]

In other ways too there was now a wider deployment of Dutch power and influence. The Dutch had commercial interests across the world and were, or soon became, involved in major economic disputes with England, Denmark, and other powers which, until 1609, the Dutch could not afford to displease but now felt free to stand up to with full vigour. The Dutch reacted to the Danish king's interference with their shipping, and raising the Sound tolls, in 1611 by forging armed alliances with Sweden and the Hansa towns, threatening force unless Denmark gave way.[28] With the treaties signed in 1613–14, the States General established a powerful Dutch influence in the Baltic area, insisting that no state would be allowed to obstruct the trade or shipping of the others, setting themselves up as guarantors of freedom of the Sound and the estuaries. Similarly, when the English Crown, in 1614, adopted the Cockayne project, intending to prevent unfinished English cloth being exported for dyeing, and finishing, in the United Provinces, the Amsterdam city council, and States of Holland, reacted energetically, clapping a general ban on the importing of finished cloth, and kersies, from England.[29] This Dutch retaliation caused a severe slump in the English textile industry and eventually forced James I to abandon the Cockayne project.

Yet whilst vigorous in defending its economic interests, the Republic showed little inclination—whilst Oldenbarnevelt remained at the helm—to become the hub of a 'Calvinist International' or in any way pose as the protector of the Calvinists of Germany or France. The Republic might well have become the political leader of the German Protestant Union, centring on the Calvinist Palatinate, an organization which looked to the United Provinces, in the years after 1609, for support and guidance in combating the advance of the Counter-Reformation in the Empire.[30] But Oldenbarnevelt and the regents eschewed such a role. Nor did they try to build a non-confessional, anti-Habsburg axis. Oldenbarnevelt studiously ignored

[27] Heeringa, *Bronnen*, i. 51–4.
[28] Beutin and Entholt, *Bremen und die Niederlande*, 8, 31–2.
[29] GA Amsterdam res. vroed. 6 Oct. 1614; *Groot Placaet-Boeck*, i. 1170.
[30] Van Deursen, *Honni soit*, 18–21.

the efforts of the Moroccan sultan in 1609–10, and of the Ottoman court, in 1614, to draw the Republic into formal anti-Habsburg alliances.

However, there was one trouble spot from which Oldenbarnevelt could not afford to disengage—the neighbouring lower Rhine duchies of Jülich-Cleves, Berg, and Mark, where a succession crisis had begun in 1609 and there was bitter local strife between Catholics, Calvinists, and Lutherans. In 1610, Oldenbarnevelt yielded to French pressure for joint intervention in Jülich-Cleves because the Holland regents saw that leaving the duchies in the hands of the local Catholic and pro-Spanish party posed a direct threat to the security of the Republic. Cleves commanded the crossing-points on the lower Rhine at the point where the Republic, Spanish Netherlands, and Holy Roman Empire converged, and at which it was easiest for the Spaniards to cross the rivers and penetrate into the Dutch interior. In fact, Jülich-Cleves commanded the approach to the most vulnerable sector of the Dutch defensive ring, the invasion route by which Spínola had threatened the IJssel line, sowing panic in the Republic, in 1605–6.[31] The town of Jülich, jointly captured by the Dutch and French, in 1610, was garrisoned by the Dutch alone. A partition treaty was negotiated whereby the claimant supported by Spain and the Lutherans, the duke of Neuburg, received Jülich and Berg while his rival, the Elector of Brandenburg, supported by the Calvinists and Dutch, acquired Mark and the duchy most crucial to the Republic—Cleves. Meanwhile, Oldenbarnevelt's main concern was to avoid armed clashes with Spanish troops. Even in Jülich-Cleves, it was clearly his policy to minimize Dutch–Spanish friction rather than exploit Calvinist fervour, and antipathy to the Habsburgs.

When the fragile status quo in Jülich-Cleves collapsed, in 1614, and the rival claimants fell to blows, the 'Spanish party' expelling the Brandenburgers from Düsseldorf, Oldenbarnevelt, anxious to minimize Dutch involvement, was dangerously late in intervening. The Spaniards, determined not to be caught out this time, moved first. Spínola, on orders from Madrid (but in the name of the Emperor), toppled the Calvinists in Aachen, in August 1614, and occupied the towns of Orsoy and Wesel. The seizure of the latter caused a sensation in the Republic (see PLATE 9). The town, with its 6,000 inhabitants, was the centre of Calvinism on the Lower Rhine and the strongest crossing-point on the Rhine just below the Dutch frontier. Oldenbarnevelt's failure to defend Calvinism in Wesel (and Aachen) seemed inexplicable. There was widespread indignation. The setback was a serious blow to the prestige of the Republic and especially to Oldenbarnevelt and

---

[31] Vreede, *Inleiding*, ii. 260.

his supporters.[32] Maurits belatedly appeared, with an army, and occupied the towns of Emmerich, Hamm, and Lippstadt. A new partition treaty was drawn up, in November 1614, again assigning Jülich and Berg to Neuburg, and Cleves and Mark to the Elector, and providing for the Dutch and Spanish garrisons to remain indefinitely in the towns each side had occupied.

Not the least remarkable feature of the Jülich-Cleves crisis of 1614 was the movement of Spanish and Dutch forces in close proximity without any armed clashes.[33] Maurits and Spínola, evidently, were as anxious as Oldenbarnevelt and Lerma to avoid incidents which might escalate. It is a reflection also on the high level of discipline of the two armies.

Both Oldenbarnevelt and Lerma wanted to build on the Truce, hoping to create conditions for a permanent Dutch-Spanish peace.[34] Philip III was still willing to abandon his sovereign claims and recognize Dutch independence. What Spain wanted was Dutch withdrawal from the Indies: Madrid was coming, increasingly, to view Dutch transoceanic commerce as the principal menace to both the Portuguese and Spanish colonial empires.[35] Since 1609, the Dutch salt trade with the Caribbean had ceased, with the return of the Dutch salt fleets to Portugal; and the Spaniards, in the Caribbean, and the Portuguese, in Amazonia, had eliminated some of the Dutch outposts in the New World. But the Dutch remained entrenched, particularly in the western part of the Guyanas, and continued a flourishing trade with Santo Domingo, Cuba, and Puerto Rico. As for the East Indies, the truce there, effective initially, progressively broke down until, in 1614, the States General, blaming the renewed fighting in the Moluccas on the Spanish Crown, declared the truce in the East Indies to be at an end.

Lerma knew that without a comprehensive settlement friction in the Indies would be bound, sooner or later, to degenerate into renewed full-scale war. In 1611, he established secret contact with Oldenbarnevelt, again offering 'perpetual peace', and recognition of the United Provinces as a 'free state', in return for evacuation of the Indies.[36] The English soon learnt of these talks from which the Republic's French and English allies were purposely excluded.[37] The contacts managed by Spínola, and Lerma's favourite, Rodrigo Calderón, were carried on through a Portuguese New Christian friar, Martín del Espíritú Santo, who was escorted to, and from,

[32] Ten Raa and De Bas, *Het Staatsche leger*, iii. 32–4.
[33] Van Deursen, 'Val van Wezel', 14–15.
[34] Israel, *Dutch Republic and the Hispanic World*, 16–17.
[35] Ibid. 66–74.
[36] AGS Estado 2294. 'Relacion dell estado que tiene la negociacion' (Dec. 1611).
[37] Van Deursen, *Honni soit*, 79–90.

Oldenbarnevelt's lodgings, in The Hague, by an Amsterdam Jewish merchant, one of the leaders of the first Amsterdam synagogue, named Duarte Fernandes. At a later stage, another intermediary was the Dutch poet and playwright Dirk Rodenburg, a fluent Spanish speaker who in 1611–13 was in Spain as an unofficial Dutch representative.[38] He saw Lerma frequently and, in May 1611, was given an audience by Philip III. After returning to Amsterdam, in 1614, he became a central figure in the Amsterdam theatre world, a personality much detested by the Counter-Remonstrants. This secret dialogue between Madrid and The Hague continued for some time but was probably doomed from the start. There were two issues of substance: would the Dutch evacuate the Indies and would they permit the exercise of the Catholic faith at home?[39] On neither point was it possible for Oldenbarnevelt to make tangible concessions.

Dutch long-distance trade and the Zeeland transit traffic to the south Netherlands both suffered extensively from the Twelve Years Truce. By aborting the plans for a West India Company, in 1607, Oldenbarnevelt also undermined the chances of the Dutch carving out an extensive empire in the New World, for prospects for a breakthrough were much better at that time than later, in the 1620s. Between 1607 and 1621, both Spaniards and Portuguese successfully extended their network of forts in the areas which the Dutch had penetrated—the Caribbean, Venezuela, the Guyanas, and Amazonia—while the Dutch lost ground, especially in the 'Caracas' trade and the salt trade with Punta de Araya, and on the Amazon. In the East Indies, the VOC suffered some loss of momentum, as the Portuguese East India trade (temporarily) revived and Lisbon again, for the duration of the Truce, competed with Amsterdam as a distribution centre for pepper and spices.[40] On the Amsterdam Exchange the quoted price of VOC shares having climbed to 200 per cent of their original value, by 1608, fell back, in the wake of the Truce, to 132 per cent and subsequently remained depressed until the 1620s.[41]

These were significant setbacks. Yet, Oldenbarnevelt's forecast that the gains would outweigh the losses was, as we have seen (p. 313 above), proved correct, at least for Holland. The boost given to Dutch trade with southern Europe by the return of their ships and cargoes to Spain and Portugal, lower freight and insurance charges, and the rise of the Dutch Levant trade which followed, in turn reinforced Holland's dominance of the Baltic and Russia

---

[38] Worp, 'Dirk Rodenburg', 78–84.
[39] AGS Estado 2294. 'Advertencia de Don Rodrigo Calderon sobre sus despachos'.
[40] Disney, *Twilight*, 51, 162.
[41] Penso de la Vega, *Confusion de confusiones*, 21–2.

trades. The Truce years were one of the most flourishing of all the phases for Dutch seaborne commerce in European waters from Portugal to Archangel and from Scotland to the Ottoman Near East.

'SOUTH' CONFRONTS 'NORTH'

The Twelve Years Truce proved a crucially formative stage in the recovery and reconstruction of the south Netherlands. It provided the first real respite from struggle for nearly forty years and a precious opportunity to rebuild the south's blighted cities, economy, and culture. After 1609, the towns recovered rapidly. At the same time, this revival which brought with it far-reaching religious and intellectual changes created a new southern perception of the relationship between 'south' and 'north', based on the notion of a ruptured common 'Fatherland' of seventeen provinces.

The dislocation of war ended—for the time being—with the armistice of 1607. With the advent of the Truce, in 1609, the army of Flanders, the largest in northern Europe, was reduced from some 60,000 to under 20,000 men.[42] This permitted some relaxation of fiscal pressure on the war-weary land while, at the same time, allowing, without adding new burdens, a steep increase in spending on ecclesiastical and secular building, patronage of education and the arts, and the creation of new courtly and bureaucratic posts, in some cases diverting funds sent from Spain for the upkeep of fortifications and the army. Albert and Isabella aspired to win the approbation of the local nobility and civic élites, for both themselves and the Counter-Reformation, and assiduously courted local opinion.[43] While Albert took care not to convene the southern States General again, after 1600, he went to some lengths to foster good relations with the various provincial States. He consulted them, allowed them more leverage over the fiscal process, and permitted some airing of their constitutional pretensions. After Albert's death, one Spanish grandee commented sarcastically that he had been such a 'good prince' that he had treated the populace of the south Netherlands 'more like children than subjects'.[44]

Even before 1609, there were numerous signs of a robust reconstructed political, religious, and cultural framework emerging in the south and a new stability of structures in the Low Countries as a whole, as well as more opportunity to consider the future relationship of the two parts of the Netherlands. Already in his *Politicorum Libri Sex* (1589), written in the

---

[42] Parker, *Army of Flanders*, app. a.
[43] Brants, *La Belgique*, 52–7.
[44] AGS Estado 2037. Consulta of the Consejo de Estado, 14 Apr. 1623, fo. 3.

north, Lipsius had appealed to the rulers of his day (especially rulers of the Netherlands) to pursue civil peace and restoration of order as their supreme aims.[45] But the attributes he believed essential to attaining these goals—monarchical authority imperiously overriding conventional procedures, laws, and principles, and the enforcement of a purely outward religious uniformity—were totally at odds with the consultative, procedure-based rule by oligarchy then evolving in the north. Having placed his hopes first in Anjou, and then in Leicester, and twice been bitterly disillusioned, Lipsius came gradually to think in terms of the Spanish Habsburgs as the princely power best placed to rise above the fray of ideologies, propaganda, and confessions, and establish a new order of stability and peace.[46]

After his return to the south, in 1591, Lipsius concentrated, in his research and writing, on a historical phenomenon, the strength and durability of the Roman empire, which deeply fascinated thoughtful men amid the seemingly endless disruption of the Revolt. His researches, culminating in his *De Magnitudine Romana* (1598), on the roots of Rome's imperial greatness, identified that empire's great size and population, submerging of local differences, transcending of its republican past, and emphasis on military organization, and discipline, as the chief ingredients in its stupendous success. The experience and methods of Imperial Rome seemed, in his eyes, the key to ending the terrifying conflicts engulfing the Europe of his own day.[47] Ultimately, order must rest on imperial grandeur based on a military organization which no rebellion could challenge.

Lipsius was the most influential European philosopher of his age and, to an extraordinary degree, mirrored its fundamental dilemmas, forging an intellectual framework which exerted an immense appeal throughout Catholic, monarchical Europe, and not least in the Spain of Lerma and Olivares,[48] while at the same time having a special relevance to the emerging new cultural context in the south Netherlands. Lipsius came into contact with several leading Spanish figures, including Don Balthasar de Zúñiga, Olivares's uncle, who was posted in Brussels for several years early in the new century. He also called, discreetly at first but from 1605 publicly, by means of an open letter, for peace between the Spanish Crown and the 'rebels' in the Low Countries. But it was less his attempts to influence Spain's policy in the Netherlands, and end the strife between north and south, than his moral and political Neostoic thought itself which helped

---

[45] Tuck, *Philosophy and Government*, 56–60.
[46] Ibid. 60, 65.
[47] Oestreich, *Neostoicism*, 61–3.
[48] Elliott, *The Count-Duke of Olivares*, 22–3, 81.

shape an emerging new south Netherlands identity linked to Spain and
the cultural revival which gave the Spanish Netherlands its Silver Age
(1609–59). In 1604, Lipsius restated his moral philosophy with his two late
treatises on Stoicism which may be seen as a renewed appeal to all
Netherlanders to reject the fatal lure of patriotic sentiment (the basis of
pro-Revolt propaganda) and confessional zeal, cultivating instead a moral
outlook, based on avoidance of strife, and preservation of order, which
would lead of itself to acceptance of his princely, imperial concept in
political life.[49]

Lipsius was one of the first modern political writers to stress the
importance of population and economic well-being for political power and
stability and the emergence of a new political, religious, and cultural order
in the south during his last years was indeed intimately linked to the south's
demographic and economic revival. The rural population of Flanders and
Brabant began to recover from the disruption of the 1570s and 1580s after
1590. It has been estimated that the total population of Brabant, having
grown from about 370,000, in 1480, to 450,000 in 1565, was down to only
363,000 in 1615. But it was already rising rapidly by that date and
outstripped the level of 1565 at some point probably well before 1648. By
1665, it is estimated to have reached 475,000, after which population growth
in the south slackened until after 1750.[50] Meanwhile, the recovery of
agriculture proceeded rapidly. In Flanders land prices had fallen by well
over half between 1572 and 1590, and farm rents become severely depressed.
But both land prices and farm rents revived strongly in the 1590s and had
already recovered the level of 1565 by around 1605. Both the boom in land
values, and the expansion of agricultural activity generally, then continued,
albeit more slowly, until about 1640. Next came a quarter of a century of
static prices followed by a prolonged decline in land prices and farm rents
throughout Flanders and Brabant in line with the more general agricultural
depression which took hold in the 1660s throughout the Low Countries and
western Europe.

But the economic recovery of the south was by no means confined to
population and agriculture. Many of the industries for which Flanders and
Brabant, as well as the Walloon country, were famous revived, above all the
Flemish linen industry, which was to be the foremost industry of the south
throughout the seventeenth and eighteenth centuries.[51] Although the latter
was in part a rural activity, it helped stimulate trade and urban growth as

[49] Tuck, *Philosophy and Government*, 48, 54–6.
[50] Klep, 'Historisch moderniseringsproces', 19.
[51] Coornaert, *Centre industriel*, 493–4.

well as rural population increase. The fall of Antwerp, in 1585, and closure of the Scheldt estuary to maritime traffic, may have severely hampered the overseas commerce of the south and helped boost that of the north. It is true that after 1590, industrial activity in the north eclipsed that in the south for well over a century. But even so the south was reviving in both town and countryside and the eclipse of Spanish Netherlands by the north by no means appeared irreversible—at any rate in the period down to the 1620s. If the United Provinces had suddenly achieved an overwhelming commercial and industrial supremacy over the south, it was obvious that this was primarily due to the prevailing political and strategic circumstances. Change those circumstances and there seemed to be no reason why the economic superiority of the south should not be restored. By reducing the 'rebels', or at least weakening them, reopening the Scheldt and assisting Spain to drive them from the Indies 'east and west', the former glory and prosperity of the cities of the south could seemingly be regained. Not a few of the south's economic advantages had survived the closure of the Scheldt and exodus of Protestants with their skills and capital to the north. Compared with England, France, and Germany, the south Netherlands was still a land with a highly developed agriculture, exceptionally high crop yields,[52] and an industrious work-force inured to a wide range of industries and sophisticated techniques. The quality of Flemish manufactures remained impressive during the first half of the seventeenth century, signs of deterioration in the more specialized industries, such as tapestries, jewellery, book production, and silks, and of a narrowing of the range of the south's industrial capacity, becoming apparent only after 1648.[53]

At Antwerp, a partial, but sustained, recovery commenced in the 1590s, gathered momentum during the Truce, and then continued, albeit slackening, after 1625, down to 1648.[54] Antwerp's commerce displayed renewed vitality, though on a different basis, and smaller scale, than before 1585, Antwerp now serving as the principal conduit for the flow of goods passing between north and south. Admittedly, some of the city's industries suffered from heightened competition from the north with the lowering of tariffs, following the signing of the Truce in 1609, and a few, such as manufacture of tiles, never revived. Moreover, the business of finishing English undyed cloth, once diverted to the north, from 1585, was never won back. But Antwerp successfully held her own in a range of specialized industries, including silks, jewellery, tapestries, and fine furniture (at least until 1648)

---

[52] Vandenbroeke and Vanderpijpen, 'Agricultural Revolution', 167–8.
[53] De Nave, *Antwerpen en de scheiding*, 81–2.
[54] Baetens, *Nazomer*, i. 51–2.

and expanded dramatically as a centre for Catholic book production and religious art. Antwerp's population rose steadily, if not spectacularly, from 42,000 in 1585, to 47,000 in 1595, 54,000 by 1612, and 62,000 by 1648.[55] But Antwerp's revival was by no means an exception. On the contrary, Ghent and Bruges recovered at a comparable rate, similarly revitalized by the Truce. Ghent's linen industry flourished and her harbour filled with shipping from Holland and Zeeland. Ghent, like other cities in the south, experienced a vigorous boom in house construction, especially during the Truce, her population rising from 31,000, in 1600, to about 50,000 by 1670.[56] At Bruges, it was the 'new drapery' industry, fustians and especially 'says', which was the driving force. By about 1615 there were as many textile looms operative in Bruges as there had been on the eve of the Revolt.[57] The Bruges woollen cloth industry was to retain its renewed vitality down to the 1650s.

But no other aspect of the south's recovery was so imposing as the revitalization of the old faith and the Church. While some aspects of the Tridentine Decrees were not acted on until after 1609, the most crucial components of the Counter-Reformation in the south, the intensive re-education, and confessionalization, of the common people, was firmly under way well before that date. Schooling the children of the civic élites was taken vigorously in hand by the Jesuits and produced an entire new generation reared in a militant Catholic stance. Jesuit colleges sprang up in all the main towns. The number of Jesuits in Antwerp increased from three, shortly after the Spanish recapture of the city, in 1585, to thirty-one by 1603, the Antwerp Jesuit college moving into splendid new premises during 1608. The number of Jesuit pupils, in Antwerp, rose from zero, in 1585, to 300 by 1591, and 600 by 1613.[58] Torrents of devotional literature poured from Antwerp's presses. As early as 1587, the first steps were taken to ensure that all children in Antwerp, even the poorest and most neglected, received Catholic religious instruction. By 1606, a system of Sunday schooling, subsidized by the municipality, and attached to the parish churches, was in operation, catechizing the children, free of charge to the parents. To ensure that most were caught by the net, a system of listing, and fining, parents who failed to send their children to the weekly catechism classes was introduced.[59] By 1620, no fewer than 3,200 children attended these Sunday schools in Antwerp alone. At 's-Hertogenbosch, where the new Sunday

[55] Thijs, *Geuzenstad tot katholiek bolwerk*, 45.
[56] Dambruyne, 'Gentse immobilienmarkt', 163–5.
[57] Vermaut, 'Structural Transformation', 192–3.
[58] Thijs, *Geuzenstad tot katholiek bolwerk*, 65, 69.
[59] Ibid. 141–2.

school system was introduced in 1595, a new confraternity was established in the town, with the encouragement of the Jesuits, specifically to collect money from the affluent laity to provide free compulsory Sunday schooling for the children of the poor.[60]

In the towns, crypto-Calvinism remained a factor in the life of the south for another generation. During the Truce years, as many as 400 people at a time, from Antwerp, would attend Reformed services at the garrison church of the States' fort, at nearby Lillo; and these were only the most defiant souls. With some reason the regime in Brussels remained wary of the population of Antwerp for several decades after 1585. As late as 1622, an English observer noted that many people in the city hoped the Dutch would capture it, being sufficiently sympathetic to the Republic, and Protestantism, to want to see the Scheldt reopened by means of Dutch victories over Spain. It was not until the early 1630s that the bishop of Antwerp felt that Protestantism had been sufficiently marginalized no longer to pose a significant threat.

An essential aspect of the re-education process, and confessionalization of the population, was the use of visual means, art, architecture, and the devotional print. Just as the printing presses produced catechism books, and short texts, aimed at children and the man in the street, who was often only barely literate, they supplied masses of cheap prints suitable for display in the homes of humble folk.[61] By 1617, there were at least ten firms in Antwerp, some with many employees, producing great quantities of reproductions of saints and religious scenes. Since it was also an effective means of popularizing religious art—and the work of contemporary painters—the method attracted the attention of the south's leading artists, including Rubens. Antwerp's devotional prints were so successful they were exported in quantity not only to Spain and Portugal but also Spanish America and, by various routes, the Far East.

Also basic to the new culture in the south was the proliferation of new churches, chapels, and monasteries. The Revolt, and the iconoclastic outbreaks of 1566, 1576–8, and 1580–1, had devastated the monasteries and convents of Flanders and Brabant and stripped the images and altars from the parish churches and cathedrals. Almost the entire visual fabric of the Church awaited reconstruction. This could not begin immediately after the fall of Antwerp, in 1585, because of the slump, continuing fighting, and lack of resources. But, from around 1606, the process of rebuilding and renovation gained momentum and the south Netherlands began producing religious

[60] Nauwelaerts, *Latijnse school*, 65–6.   [61] Ibid. 98–100.

art and architecture on a scale, and of a quality, unparalleled anywhere else in Europe outside Italy. No fewer than thirty-five monastic establishments of one sort or another were erected in Ghent alone between 1590 and 1670;[62] and it was much the same in the other cities. Nor was there difficulty in finding sufficient artistic skills for the work of embellishment. In contrast to other groups, many artists tended to remain in Antwerp in 1585. There was no shortage of masters to train new talent and the stock of skills was further enhanced by the return of many south Netherlands artists from Italy. In 1616 no fewer than 216 painters belonged to the St Lucas guild, in Antwerp, twice as many as in 1584.[63]

Albert and Isabella backed the efforts to re-educate and confessionalize the populace, and heighten the impact of the Church, not least by pouring substantial resources into religious art and architecture. In both, especially architecture, they favoured the new baroque style, emanating from Rome, and were closely involved in shaping the programme of cultural renewal. In 1605, they summoned back the Antwerp artist-architect Wensel Cobergher (1560–1634) from Rome, appointing him their court architect and artistic adviser.[64] Cobergher and his younger relative Jacob Francart (1583–1651), also prominent in moulding the new religious architecture of the south, had trained in Italy and began by importing concepts current there; but, from around 1615, they were increasingly successful in blending Italian baroque style with local traditions, reflecting a wider tendency pervading the culture of the south of which Rubens, the pre-eminent artist of the south Netherlands but who was also closely linked artistically to Rome, Madrid, and Vienna, was the supreme manifestation.

Cobergher designed numerous buildings in Brussels, Antwerp, and other towns, one of his most striking being the new Augustinian church in Antwerp, begun in 1615. Francart too was associated with many large projects, foremost among them the Jesuit church in Brussels, the foundations of which were ceremonially laid by Albert and Isabella in 1606 and which they inaugurated, magnificently, just after the expiry of the Truce, in 1621; most sumptous of all was the Jesuit church of St Ignatius, in Antwerp, built largely according to Roman baroque taste, and approved by the Jesuit General in Rome, inaugurated shortly after Albert's death, amid great pomp, in September 1621.

The task of embellishing altars and images for so many new, and refurbished, churches and monasteries dominated the new art world of the

[62] Dambruyne, 'Versteningsproces', 44.
[63] Thijs, *Van Geuzenstad tot katholiek bolwerk*, 120.
[64] Plantenga, *L'Architecture religieuse*, 43–9.

south. On all sides artists were put to work serving the new crusade. Rubens's oil sketch of the conversion of St Bavo (1611), for the cathedral of Ghent, depicting Bavo exchanging armour for the vestments of a prelate, aptly symbolized the transition from arms to war waged with spiritual weapons, a war of religious and cultural confrontation with the north. Rubens, who returned from Italy in 1608, wrote to a friend in Rome just before the signing of the Truce, forecasting the end of hostilities and expressing his hopes that the 'obedient provinces' would 'flourish again'.[65] Art was at the forefront and Rubens's aptitude for unusually large canvases led to his being regularly employed, from 1609, painting the category of work which had the greatest impact on the public—vast pious tableaux for the principal churches. The altarpieces Rubens painted during the Truce surpassed both in number and grandeur those he painted in the rest of his career, revolutionizing religious art in Catholic northern Europe.[66] Many were commissioned for major churches in Antwerp; but he painted altarpieces also for Brussels, Mechelen, Lille, and Cambrai, as well as a St Francis for Cologne, the city where he had been born amongst the Netherlands refugee community. Dozens of assistants were needed to work on these vast pictures, some of whom were soon to achieve fame in their own right. His contract with the Antwerp Jesuits for the ceiling paintings of the Church of St Ignatius named as his chief assistant the gifted young Anthonie van Dyck (1599–1641).

The Counter-Reformation in the south was accompanied by the Counter-Reformation in the North Rhine area and Westphalia. There too a new culture was in the making since the 1580s, a rolling back of the tide of Protestantism and effective re-Catholicization of the populace with the aid of educational tools and cultural resources imported from Italy and south Germany. Here the process had tentatively begun slightly earlier with the promulgation of the Tridentine Decrees at Münster, in 1571. But the real start of the re-Catholicization programme came with the arrival of the Jesuits, in 1588, and their take-over of the principal schools.[67] Although most of the Jesuits active in Münster were local men, the 'Little Rome' they created there brought about major changes in the cultural profile of Westphalia. They inculcated a political and social outlook, in the sons of the Catholic nobility and merchant class who flocked to them from all over north Germany and the north-east Netherlands, hostile to toleration and the civic privileges and freedoms around them, an attitude militantly confessional

---

[65] Burckhardt, *Recollections of Rubens*, 200.
[66] Baudouin, *Pietro Paulo Rubens*, 65–111.
[67] Hsia, *Society and Religion in Münster*, 62–9.

and favourable to the new Catholic princely absolutism of the north-west German ecclesiastical states. The confrontational character of this culture led to a heightening of tension throughout Westphalia not only as between Catholic and Protestant states but within the bishoprics, where both Lutheran and Calvinist influence was strong, and there was a long tradition of civic autonomy. This confrontation and events such as the bishop of Paderborn's reduction of that city, in 1604, and the clashes between the Wittelsbach prelate-prince Ernst (of Cologne and Münster) and the city of Münster, in 1607, generated a conflict of political ideologies which inter-acted at many levels with the growing Catholic–Protestant polarization. On the cultural front, the Jesuits showed a marked preference for High German rather than the traditional Low German of the Westphalian region. In this way, the Counter-Reformation in north-western Germany tended to widen and accelerate the increasing divergence between the culture of this region and the north-eastern Dutch provinces, just as the Counter-Reformation of Albert and Isabella decisively separated the two cultures of the Netherlands.

The confrontational character of the new Counter-Reformation cultures of the south Netherlands and Westphalia arose from local circumstances as much as from the Spanish Crown, Papacy, and Habsburg connection. The south Netherlands saw itself as set against the north. In this sense, the Truce may be termed a continuation of the Eighty Years War by other means. Jesuit writers during the early seventeenth century interpreted the Dutch Revolt against their legitimate ruler as a catastrophe caused by the cancer of foreign heresy, seeping in from Germany, and the ambition of corrupt nobles.[68] Their programme of re-education was intended to lead ultimately to the downfall of Calvinism in the north Netherlands, Cleves-Mark, and the Protestant enclaves in and around Westphalia. As far as the Netherlands was concerned this implied the eventual reabsorption of the rebel north into the bosom of the Church and thus also into a political and ecclesiastical framework administered from Brussels. In this way, despite the deep rupture ensuing from the Revolt, the new high culture of the south fostered the notion of an overarching single Netherlands into which the north would eventually be reintegrated.[69]

This reconquest was envisaged as political and religious but also econ-omic. If one walked the streets of Antwerp, during the Truce, as Sir Dudley Carleton did, in September 1616, whilst on his way to The Hague to take up his post as English ambassador there, one could not fail to be aware of

[68] Andriessen, 'Jezuieten-auteurs', 44–6.
[69] Andriessen, *Jezuieten en het samenhorigheidsbesef*, 87.

the incompleteness of the south's recovery and the signs of the shift of vitality to the north.[70] The staunchly Catholic patricians who now ruled the southern towns were encouraged by the recovery but also convinced of the need for aggressive economic strategies—albeit preferably short of actual war—to regain what was lost and restore the primacy of the south. During the Truce, a confrontational anti-Dutch mercantilism became an integral part of the culture of the south, reinforcing feelings of separateness and sympathy for the Spanish Habsburgs' aspirations to weaken the United Provinces and eventually re-establish the common Fatherland. These were the men who proposed and supported Albert's programme of improving the canals linking the Flemish sea ports with Bruges, Ghent, and Antwerp to establish a viable maritime link bypassing the Dutch forts on the Scheldt estuary.[71] One of the most eloquent eulogists of such projects was Carlos Scribani (1561–1629), a native Netherlander though partly of Italian descent, head of the Jesuit province Flandro-Belgica in the years 1613–19 and fervent adherent of the notion that Antwerp would one day again be the supreme commercial metropolis of the Netherlands—and Europe.

The world of the south Netherlands in the era of Albert and Isabella was a highly ideological culture, locked in antagonism with what it rejected—the independence, Calvinism, and economic superiority of the north. Its consolidation during the Truce decisively widened the gulf between south and north while simultaneously nurturing the idea of a common Netherlands of seventeen provinces which had (allegedly) existed before 1572. Not surprisingly, the supreme advocates of the idea of seventeen provinces divided by rebellion and heresy, which should be reintegrated, were the foreign-trained Jesuits, with Scribani well to the fore.[72] But it had to be reunification on the basis of the south incorporating the north, that is under the auspices of the Spanish Crown and the Catholic Church, eliminating northern rebellion, Protestantism, constitutionalism, and toleration. For spokesmen of the new culture no form of coexistence of north and south on the basis of peace and the mingling of faiths was acceptable or even conceivable. The idea of a common Netherlands of seventeen provinces forming a single political entity, which had in the sixteenth century been the preserve of an unrepresentative fringe of courtiers and humanists, in this way became, in the seventeenth, integral to Counter-Reformation propaganda.

To an extent the idea of a common Fatherland of seventeen provinces was also an element in militant Protestant ideology in the north, but only

[70] Brown, *Van Dyck*, 16.
[71] Voeten, 'Antwerpen's handel', 70–1.
[72] Andriessen, *Jezuieten en het samenhorigheidsbesef*, 69–70, 79.

marginally. The wide spectrum of élite, and to a degree of popular, opinion expressed in the Dutch pamphlets of 1607–9 shows that, while the hope of restoring the unity of the Netherlands did exist in some quarters, usually among Protestant south Netherlanders who had taken refuge in the north, such notions were not a central feature of political thinking in the United Provinces.[73] Usselincx, one of the few writers in the north who did see the task of freeing the south from Spain as a continuing objective, and main priority, of the struggle, warned that if the United Provinces failed to drive the Spaniards from the Low Countries, and establish freedom of religion for the Reformed in the south, the independence and 'freedom' of the north could not be secure. But even Usselincx was more concerned with making the south safe for Protestants, and removing the south's new patricians, pawns of the Spaniards as he saw them, from control of the town councils, than with reabsorbing the south into the same body politic emerging in the north. In the Dutch Golden Age the idea of a common Fatherland of seventeen provinces played scarcely any part as an inspiration and motive force in culture and politics.

[73] Kaper, *Pamfletten*, 37–41.

18

Crisis within the Dutch Body Politic,
1607–1616

❖

The armistice of 1607 and Spain's entering into peace talks with the
Dutch, and then the concluding of the Truce in 1609, were regarded
throughout Europe as sensational successes for Oldenbarnevelt and the
Holland regents. The Truce confirmed the separation of north and south
indefinitely and the survival, at least north of the rivers, of the Revolt.
Furthermore, the Truce was an unquestioned triumph not only for Oldenbarnevelt and the Holland regents but for the Republic, government by a
consultative, decision-making process without an 'eminent head' or monarchical element. Yet, at this very moment there were already worrying signs
of rising tensions within the infant Republic which many believed could
soon undo all that had been achieved. The young Hugo Grotius (1583–
1645) was just one of many who predicted, in 1607, that the truce with Spain
would release a rising tide of faction, discord, and popular pressure.[1]

On one side, the Oldenbarnevelt regime faced the antagonism of the
Stadholder, Prince Maurits, a potentially quasi-monarchical figure, and, on
the other, the rising hostility of many preachers of the Reformed Church,
due to the regime's tolerant church policies, and both challenges commanded considerable popular support. Indeed, by 1607 it was already
conceivable that the two great dramas unfolding respectively in secular and
church politics might coalesce to engulf the regime in a major crisis of the
body politic. The United Provinces had, since 1588, been a fully-fledged
republic and by the first decade of the new century possessed, especially (but
not only) in the writings of Grotius, a republican political outlook to fit the
reality. In his *Parallela Rerumpublicarum* (1602), only a fragment of which
survives, the *De Antiquitate Reipublicae Batavicae* (1610), and other writings
of these years, Grotius developed the idea that liberty, stability, virtue, and

---

[1] Grotius, *Briefwisseling*, i. 85.

prosperity are best preserved when government is consultative and reserved to a closed oligarchy, such as the regents, with the resources, time, and education to devote themselves fully to public affairs, reverently abiding by the constitutional procedures of the republic. In this respect, Grotius considered the United Provinces to be like ancient Judaea, Athens, and Rome during the most flourishing and stable periods of their history.[2] In his eyes, the United Provinces were far from perfect as a republic and would benefit, in particular, from having a stronger directorate at the centre. In his unpublished essay, the 'De Republica Emendanda', written somewhere between 1600 and 1610, he advocated strengthening the *Raad van State* to this end.[3] But the existing United Provinces did embody what Grotius deemed most essential in a true republic and this, he argued in his tract of 1610 (which was widely read in Dutch translation), the Dutch had not only defended against the tyranny of Spain but inherited from the distant past, its origin lying in the liberty which the ancient Batavians—whom he claimed had been ruled not by kings but by *primores*—had defended in their revolt against the Romans.[4]

To preserve this patrician republic extolled by Grotius, Oldenbarnevelt had, on the one hand, to keep the Stadholder weak and, on the other, check the pretensions of Reformed preachers opposed to the policies of the regents. At the start of the negotiations with Spain, in 1607, Oldenbarnevelt was already simultaneously seeking to contain Maurits and trying to damp down the growing tension within the public Church. At that stage, he planned to solve the difficulties in the Church by convening a National Synod to revise the Netherlands Confession (*Confessio Belgica*) and make it theologically more flexible. As a first step, he convened a preparatory convention at The Hague in May 1607, intending to coax the rigidly confessional party into conceding a National Synod which would enable him to render the public Church both broader doctrinally and more subordinate to the provincial assemblies institutionally. But most of the convention insisted that Confession and catechism were unalterable and that the sole task of the projected National Synod should be their confirmation. Oldenbarnevelt promptly lost his eagerness for a National Synod.

But something had to be done to check the seething strife within the public Church. Already the quarrel between Gomarus and Arminius was arousing much disquiet among the public and the clamour against Arminius and his adherents was growing. In his address on laying down the rectorship of the university, at Leiden, in February 1606, Arminius condemned theological strife between Christians as the worst of ills, a scourge nurturing doubt, atheism, and despair.[5] But this served only to encourage talk that he was unsound in doctrine and tainted with 'Socinianism'. By 1607 he was being openly harassed by townsmen and students.[6] Arminius and his supporters turned to the States of Holland for help.

Oldenbarnevelt tried to quell the furore by submitting the controversy to the judgement of the States of Holland. This gave Arminius the opportunity to demonstrate his irenicist leanings and deference to civil authority, whose right to oversee the public Church, and sound doctrine, he endorsed. Predictably, the regents much preferred this attitude to Gomarus' insistence that the Church's doctrines were no business of the civil authority and that Arminius had lapsed into the heinous errors of the Pelagians and Jesuits on will, Grace, and Salvation, and should be silenced.[7]

The problems confronting Oldenbarnevelt in theological politics were aggravated during 1608, just as the Truce controversies reached their climax. The same stern Calvinists who insisted there should be no peace with Spain, and that the security of the state was being endangered, simultaneously strove to mobilize the provincial synods against Arminius and the plans to revise the doctrines and management of the public Church. The South Holland Synod demanded that any preacher with reservations about the Confession should declare them. The classis of Alkmaar, deeply split, even required its preachers to sign the Confession forthwith, or face suspension. This was an affront not only to the Arminian faction but to Oldenbarnevelt and the States who aspired to supervise ecclesiastical affairs.

Of the classis' twenty-five ministers, five refused to sign, including Adolphus Venator, a prominent figure at Alkmaar.[8] The classis, backed by the North Holland Synod, then suspended them, at which the States intervened, cancelling their suspension. The Synod retorted that the Church must not be ruled by the State or lack the authority to remove ministers unsound in doctrine. The States remained unmoved. Venator (who diverged further from orthodoxy than Arminius) retained his pulpit, supported by the *vroedschap*. But the latter remained divided and, in December 1609, the Stadholder, who until 1617 only rarely showed his preference for the Gomarists, exercised his authority to choose members of the *vroedschap*, after annual 'elections', from double lists, to install a predominantly

---

[5] Bangs, *Arminius*, 280–1.
[6] Ibid. 275–6.
[7] Itterszon, *Franciscus Gomarus*, 119–27.
[8] Rogge, *Johannes Wttenbogaert*, i. 323–4.

Gomarist town council.[9] This, and the consequent dismissal of Venator, was a clear setback for the States. But at this point the civic militia intervened, seizing the town hall and demanding the removal of the hardline Calvinists—who were generally unpopular in Alkmaar—from the *vroedschap*.[10] Oldenbarnevelt was happy to oblige, thereby reversing the Stadholder's intervention, despite the blatant infringement of the latter's prerogatives and dangerous precedent of allowing civic militias to impose their political and theological views and purge a regent government.

After Alkmaar, little doubt remained as to the capacity of the Arminian–Gomarist disputes to create political turmoil, or exacerbate tensions in society, and any that did linger was rapidly dissolved by the disturbances which erupted the following year at Utrecht. For centuries Utrecht had been a focus of social and political unrest and instability. 'Utrecht', remarked James I of England, 'hath always been given to sedition and mutiny.'[11] In Utrecht there was a long-standing tension between the guilds which since the 1580s had adhered to Calvinist orthodoxy and the wealthy patricians who mostly espoused the liberal, irenic theological tradition of Duifhuis. Besides social and theological stresses within the city, there were economic tensions between the city and the rest of the province. In contrast to Groningen, Utrecht possessed few staple privileges and it had been the policy of the noble-dominated States of Utrecht since 1572 to block every effort on the part of the city to claim a monopoly of brewing and other 'civic industries' in the province.

The dissatisfaction of the guilds boiled over into revolt in January 1610. Led by a group of strict Calvinists headed by a former burgomaster, Dirk Canter, who had links with the Stadholder, the dissidents, including much of the militia, seized the city and purged those regents known to be unsympathetic to the guilds and Calvinist orthodoxy.[12] Many regents and nobles fled the city, leaving the insurgents in control also of the provincial States.

The Advocate of the States, Ledenberg, appealed to Oldenbarnevelt for help. The States General nominated a commission to meet the rebels and 'reconcile' the parties. The guild representatives demanded numerous changes in the administration of the city, a ban on 'urban industries' in the countryside, and the strengthening of the city's voice in the States.[13] Seeing

⁹ Den Tex, *Oldenbarnevelt*, iii. 163–5.
¹⁰ Knevel, 'Onrust', 167–8.
¹¹ Kaajan, *Groote Synode van Dordrecht*, 12.
¹² Den Tex, 'De Staten', 72–3.
¹³ Vijlbrief, *Van anti-aristocratie*, 70–7.

little scope for compromise, Oldenbarnevelt, and the States of Holland, persuaded the States General to suppress the guilds by sending troops. Maurits, pleading illness, excused himself from leading the expedition, giving his younger half-brother, Frederik Hendrik, his first opportunity to enter the limelight. There was talk of a siege but the Utrechters' bravado rapidly evaporated on the approach of the soldiery. A garrison was introduced into the city. The regents and nobles who had fled returned. Finally, in May, the new Calvinist *vroedschap* was removed and the 'libertine' faction restored to power. Oldenbarnevelt had won the second round.

But having sensed their power to mobilize discontent within society against the 'libertines' and Arminians, the Gomarists increasingly sought to arouse the public against their opponents in both Church and government, denouncing them as heretics, Pelagians, and (in some cases) Socinians. A campaign developed to prevent theology graduates with Arminian sympathies obtaining preaching positions. The Arminian party within the Church, led by Uyttenbogaert—Arminius himself had died the previous year— backed by Oldenbarnevelt, decided at this point that their best course was to combat the precisians head-on, together with the States, defeat them, remodel the public Church, and eradicate confessional rigidity, thereby minimizing theological strife and its public consequences.

The result was the famous 'Remonstrance' of the Arminians to the States of Holland. The text, drawn up by Uyttenbogaert (probably at Oldenbarnevelt's prompting)[14] called for revision of the Netherlands Confession, asserted the authority of the State over the Church, and restated Arminius' position on predestination. The Remonstrance, signed by forty-four preachers of the public Church, was submitted to the States by Oldenbarnevelt, in July 1610. The Gomarists then accepted Oldenbarnevelt's proposal to hold a six-a-side theological disputation before the States to resolve the points at issue. The Arminian team was headed by Uyttenbogaert and the gifted young Simon Episcopius (1583–1643), the Gomarist side by the Amsterdam preacher Plancius and his Leiden colleague Festus Hommius.[15] It was at the opening of this disputation that the Gomarists presented their equally famous 'Counter-Remonstrance', setting out the anti-Arminian position, rejecting amendment of the Netherlands Confession, restating Gomarus' position on predestination, and condemning the Remonstrants' plea that nothing should be decided by provincial synods, or classes, until the controversy had been resolved by a National Synod. The

---

[14] Den Tex, *Oldenbarnevelt*, iii. 133–5.   [15] Wijminga, *Festus Hommius*, 104–7.

Counter-Remonstrants argued that the Church could not be required by the civil authority to retain ministers who rejected its teaching.[16]

Remonstrants and Counter-Remonstrants clashed over the theology of predestination and their rival conceptions of Church–State relations. In 1610, Uyttenbogaert published at The Hague an important tract, *On the Office and Authority of a Higher Christian Government in Church Affairs*, championing the authority of the State over the Church in the appointment of preachers, regulation of doctrine, calling of synods, and determining their agenda, and the right of the State to representation, and influence, in synods of the Church. Uyttenbogaert's Erastianism provided a theological basis for Oldenbarnevelt's efforts to thwart what he and his allies regarded as the would-be tyranny of the Church over its membership, to ensure individual liberty and encompass as much as possible of society within the public Church.[17] In Uyttenbogaert's eyes, the Church itself could possess no part of sovereignty: it might argue but not compel, convince but not command.

Initially, the Arminian–Gomarist quarrel was confined to Holland and Utrecht. But the close links between preachers in different provinces, and between universities, and the Counter-Remonstrants' endeavours to mobilize support for their position in the outlying provinces (where the civil authority was less likely to follow Oldenbarnevelt than in Holland and Utrecht), rapidly disseminated the controversy throughout the Republic, and at all levels of society. Episcopius, who had studied under Arminius at Leiden (and whose best student he was), personally brought the controversies to Franeker, where he went to further his studies, in 1609. No sooner had he arrived than he was dragged into encounters with the chief spokesman of Gomarist orthodoxy in Friesland, Sybrandus Lubbertus.[18] In rural Friesland, Remonstrantism had little impact. But in Leeuwarden, Franeker, and Dokkum the Arminians did gain a following. In 1610, after disturbances in Leeuwarden, a religiously liberal town council emerged which was opposed to the rigid orthodoxy favoured by Willem Lodewijk and eased the pressure on the Mennonites as well as favouring the Remonstrants.[19] This faction at Leeuwarden became known as the '*politique* Beggars'. When, in 1615, the States of Friesland, eager to impose Calvinist orthodoxy, intervened, attempting to restore the old magistracy—the strict Calvinist faction known as the 'Genevan Beggars'—the Leeuwarden 'libertines' turned to Oldenbarnevelt for support. Through the States General, the

---

[16] Keuning, *Petrus Plancius*, 40–1.
[17] Nobbs, *Theocracy and Toleration*, 47.
[18] Van Limborch, *Leven van Simon Episcopius*, 6, 9.
[19] Glasius, *Gesch. der Nationale Synode*, i. 238.

States of Holland sent a delegation to Friesland to warn the States not to violate the civic privileges of Leeuwarden. In September 1616, the States of Friesland forbade the appointment of any Reformed preacher in Friesland without his first signing, and swearing by, the Netherlands Confession.

In Groningen, Arminianism made little impact. But Overijssel and Gelderland were both deeply divided by the controversies. Kampen, where all the preachers, headed by the Leiden graduate Thomas Goswinius, took the Remonstrant side, was the chief centre of Arminianism in Overijssel, but the Remonstrants also had some support at Zwolle and in the countryside.[20] Nor was theological passion by any means confined to the preachers and regents. According to Baudartius, the boatmen and wagoners of Kampen were so fervently Remonstrant that, in 1617, they refused to transport goods belonging to tradesmen in the city who were known Counter-Remonstrants.[21] The Overijssel *ridderschap* was split; but, for the moment, pro-Oldenbarnevelt nobles dominated both the States and Delegated States, with the support of Kampen, and prevented measures being taken against the Remonstrants.

In Gelderland, by contrast, the balance of support favoured the Counter-Remonstrants. In Nijmegen most regents and preachers were pro-Remonstrant, as also were many nobles of the Nijmegen quarter, and also the towns of Tiel and Zaltbommel. Burgomaster Christoffel Biesman, who dominated the *raad* of Nijmegen at this time, was Oldenbarnevelt's most important ally in Gelderland together with the Remonstrant count of Culemborg. The town of Arnhem, where two of the preachers were Remonstrant, was divided. But the Arnhem quarter was predominantly, and the Zutphen quarter entirely, Counter-Remonstrant and Oldenbarnevelt's enemies dominated the Hof of Gelderland from the outset.[22] In 1612, the Counter-Remonstrants gained control of the provincial synod and ruled that all Reformed ministers in the province must sign a testimony of orthodoxy and adherence to the Netherlands Confession.[23]

Zeeland was staunchly Counter-Remonstrant. But the garrison towns of northern Brabant became the scene of furious quarrels among the Reformed communities. At Grave, both the preacher, Paludanus, and the Reformed schoolmaster, took the Remonstrant side. At Breda, a feud erupted between the Remonstrant preacher, Isaac Diamantius, and the hardline Gomarist, Henricus Boxhorn. In an attempt to quell the strife and spreading acrimony,

---

[20] Van den Sande, *Nederlandtsche Geschiedenissen*, 65.
[21] Baudartius, *Memoryen*, book ix, 88.
[22] Van den Sande, *Nederlandtsche Geschiedenissen*, 65, 81.
[23] Ibid. 65.

the magistracy, in December 1615, forbade any pronouncement from the pulpit touching on the national controversy. In the Brabant garrison towns at this time, the magistrates were, as a result of Holland's 'industry and practice' in the selection, often pro-Remonstrant.[24]

A new phase in the struggle began in 1611 with the battle over appointing a successor to Arminius' chair at Leiden. Oldenbarnevelt, guided by his son-in-law, Cornelis van der Mijle, a curator of the university, and Uyttenbogaert, chose the German theologian Conradus Vorstius (1569–1622), a man known since the 1590s both in Germany and the Netherlands, as an irenic liberal at odds with the orthodox Calvinist theology faculty at Heidelberg. His writings had influenced Arminius. His Erastianism was beyond doubt. Uyttenbogaert brought Vorstius on a visit to Leiden, and The Hague, to meet Oldenbarnevelt. Alarmed by the theological warfare raging in Holland, Vorstius himself hesitated to take up the appointment. But Oldenbarnevelt pushed it through, not realizing the danger to his own position posed by Vorstius' published work, which, since the 1590s, was marked by Socinian tendencies.[25]

Vorstius' appointment provoked a storm of protest from Counter-Remonstrant theologians, led by Lubbertus, Hommius, and the preacher of the English Presbyterian church in Amsterdam, Matthew Slade, a prominent supporter of the Counter-Remonstrant cause, as well as of the anti-Vorstius campaign. At this point, the Dutch controversies began to spill over into the international arena. James I of England, alarmed by the strife rending the Dutch Church, was horrified by the appointment of Vorstius, whom he regarded as an out-and-out heretic. Early in 1612, the king lodged a strong protest with the States General. This encouraged Lubbertus (who had links with the Calvinist party in England) to think that the Counter-Remonstrants might prevail in the United Provinces with the help of the English Crown. In 1613, Lubbertus published a Dutch version of his letter to the archbishop of Canterbury, denouncing the States of Holland for failing to protect the Dutch Church from the 'plague' of Vorstius' teachings and calling for English intervention.[26]

It was at this point that the now 30-year-old and already internationally renowned humanist scholar-regent Grotius was drawn into the strife. Since 1607, Grotius had been Advocate-fiscal, a senior law officer, of Holland and acquired a certain political importance. In 1613, he was appointed pensionary of Rotterdam, on Oldenbarnevelt's recommendation, and asked by the

[24] Carleton, *Letters*, 97.
[25] Kühler, *Het Socinianisme*, 57–9.
[26] Lubbertus, *Brief D. Sibrandi Lvbberti*, 6.

VOC to head its delegation to London to negotiate over the Anglo-Dutch differences in the East Indies. At the same time, Grotius was asked by Oldenbarnevelt to help persuade those close to James not to support the Counter-Remonstrants. Grotius (wrongly, as it turned out) believed that he had changed James's mind about the Counter-Remonstrants;[27] and when he returned to the Republic published a vigorous defence of the States of Holland, against Counter-Remonstrant criticism, attacking Lubbertus, in particular, for seeking to smear the Remonstrants as crypto-Socinians.[28] Under the title *Pietas Ordinum Hollandiae ac Westfrisiae Vindicata*, the tract appeared in October 1613, in both Latin and Dutch versions.

The Counter-Remonstrants reacted to Grotius' intervention with amazement. For Grotius had had his own doubts about Vorstius and, on his visit to Groningen and Friesland, in the autumn of 1611, established amicable relations with Ubbo Emmius and Lubbertus himself. It had been Grotius' policy to present himself neither as Counter-Remonstrant nor Remonstrant, but as the champion of peace within the public Church, the intermediary friendly with both sides. During 1612 and early 1613 he had scrupulously preserved his neutrality, and the respect of all, as the man above the strife.[29] Now, at a stroke, he abandoned his neutrality, siding categorically with Oldenbarnevelt and the Remonstrants. Althusius, Syndic of Emden, joined those who angrily rejected Grotius' admonitions and attempt to subordinate the Reformed Church to the secular authority.[30] He already disliked the Oldenbarnevelt regime for its Arminianism and having signed the Truce with Spain.[31]

Once committed, Grotius became an indefatigable participant in the fray. At Rotterdam, he led the fight against Counter-Remonstrantism, stiffening the attitude of the city council and consistory and reinforcing the city's reputation as a bastion of Remonstrantism.[32] He emerged as one of Oldenbarnevelt's principal supporters in the States of Holland. At the same time, it was especially Grotius who extended the struggle throughout the Dutch scholarly world, mobilizing like-minded humanists against the Counter-Remonstrants whom he regarded as a menace not just to the stability of the state and the public Church but also to individual liberty of conscience and humanist studies. Counter-Remonstrants frequently disapproved of the Erasmian legacy, Slade openly disparaging Erasmus as the

[27] Van der Woude, *Hugo Grotius en zijn Pietas*, 16–17.
[28] Grotius, *Pietas* (Dutch version), 6, 30.
[29] Van der Woude, *Hugo Grotius en zijn Pietas*, 8–9.
[30] Althusius, *Politics*, p. xvi.
[31] Antholz, *Politische Wirksamkeit des Johannes Althusius*, 124.
[32] Wijminga, *Festus Hommius*, 183, 186.

spiritual forefather of Arminianism, alleging that he would have rejoiced at his popularity amongst Vorstius' partisans.[33] Incensed by this assault on Erasmus, Grotius galvanized the Republic's men of learning.[34] Among those he drew out of their ivory towers was the eminent humanist Gerardus Vossius, rector of the Latin school at Dordrecht.

At Leiden university itself, meanwhile, curators and professors battled to keep the raging furore out of lectures and classes. They were assisted in this by Gomarus' departure for Middelburg, and the eventual cancelling, by Oldenbarnevelt, of Vorstius' appointment. The curators then chose the moderate Counter-Remonstrant Johannes Polyander, and the Remonstrant Simon Episcopius, to the two vacant chairs of theology. Officially, the theology faculty, and university, maintained a façade of unity, and neutrality; but behind the scenes this was increasingly splintered by fierce clashes that kept erupting at private gatherings, and over meals.[35]

Grotius did not advocate full religious toleration either at this stage, or later. He wanted to defend liberty of conscience but within a strong public (or state) Church which would overwhelmingly—to an extent coercively—dominate, in the sphere of religion, for purposes political and social, as much as spiritual.[36] To his mind the stability of state and society depended on this. His ideal in this respect was the Church of England. During his visit to London Grotius had heard much complaint about the allegedly pernicious effects of religious freedom as allowed by the Dutch. James and the English bishops were appalled by the seemingly anarchic religious situation prevailing in the United Provinces. Grotius himself accepted that the existing situation was intolerable and that it could not continue without highly damaging consequences. Grotius' solution was to regulate, and in some respects curtail, freedom of conscience, and expression, in such a way as to restore stability and order.[37] His idea, readily endorsed by Oldenbarnevelt, was for a States of Holland resolution which would tailor, and set limits to, toleration by balancing freedom and authority. His principle was to define, by decree, those doctrines which were, and those which were not, open to public debate. If the States of Holland were to separate doctrinal issues where differences of opinion could safely be ventilated publicly, from those where dissent would be contrary to the fundamentals of Christian faith, it would be possible to lay down rules as to what views could be

[33] Nijenhuis, *Matthew Slade*, 14.
[34] Van der Woude, *Sibrandus Lubbertus*, 260–2.
[35] Van Limborch, *Leven van Simon Episcopius*, 31.
[36] Nobbs, *Theocracy and Toleration*, 61.
[37] Grotius, *Oratie*, 26, 50, 52.

publicly discussed and which held only in private. The States of Holland could ensure toleration of tenets deemed publicly acceptable by forbidding polemics against such views whether from the pulpit or in print. Preachers who defied the States of Holland's directions as to what doctrines could be publicly held, and which not, whether Remonstrant or Counter-Remonstrant, could then be disciplined by the States and, if necessary, dismissed from their livings.

Grotius took this grand theologico-political concept with great seriousness and laboured long on the text of the placard 'For the Peace of the Church' which he laid before the *Gecommitteerde Raden*, and full States of Holland. His proposals were disparately received. The most ardently Remonstrant town councils, such as Leiden and Rotterdam, deemed his text insufficiently hostile to the Counter-Remonstrant position. But Grotius and Oldenbarnevelt, unlike the States of Utrecht, and some Holland towns, were not trying to crush Counter-Remonstrantism, but draw its teeth and confine theological conflict to the theological sphere, separating, as it were, theology from politics. It was an exercise in defusing tension which would be self-defeating if too blatantly one-sided. Indeed, the basis of Oldenbarnevelt's and Grotius' policy during the years 1614–17 whilst they were still, to an extent, in control of the situation was to try to restore, and maintain, unity within Holland by winning over the Holland Counter-Remonstrant towns to support their strategy for defusing the theologico-political conflict.[38] Nor was this a vain hope for while Amsterdam and Dordrecht backed the Counter-Remonstrants, this was partly, if not largely, for political, rather than theological, reasons and these towns too had cause to be disturbed by the growing disunity within the States of Holland and States General.

Oldenbarnevelt and Grotius not only succeeded in persuading Rotterdam and Leiden to drop their objections but almost succeeded in persuading the Counter-Remonstrant camp among the Holland regents to co-operate. With the promise that the placard would be applied in a balanced manner to Remonstrant as well as Counter-Remonstrant preachers, and that there would be a ban on doctrines declared heretical, Dordrecht agreed to support Grotius' concept. At the gathering of the States of Holland, in January 1614, Oldenbarnevelt and Grotius thus managed to split the Counter-Remonstrant party, securing the votes of Dordrecht, Schiedam, Purmerend, and Monnikendam.[39] Only Amsterdam, Enkhuizen, and Edam rejected the decree and at Amsterdam the decision to do so was taken, in the city

---

[38] Den Tex, *Oldenbarnevelt*, iii. 300–1.   [39] Ibid. 299–300.

council, by only a narrow majority. Yet this sufficed to deny Oldenbarnevelt and Grotius the façade of unity which was essential. Amsterdam, under Reinier Pauw and his faction, continued to insist that the conflict between the Remonstrants and Counter-Remonstrants could only be resolved by a National Synod.

The placard was formally adopted by the States of Holland over the objections of three towns. But, in practice, it took effect only in the Remonstrant towns and was used practically only against Counter-Remonstrant preachers. Nevertheless, it represented the best chance available to Oldenbarnevelt to restore unity in Holland and stabilize the Republic, meeting as it did with the approval of moderate Counter-Remonstrants, or some of them, and also with that of the king of England. But all subsequent attempts to persuade Amsterdam to come round were in vain. Opposition hardened, rather than weakened, with the passage of time. Oldenbarnevelt on occasion intervened to restrain the Remonstrant fervour of some town councils. But the conviction that the placard, even if non-partisan in appearance, was being used by the Remonstrants in a partisan manner, in practice, increasingly took hold, as more Counter-Remonstrant preachers in Remonstrant towns found themselves threatened with loss of their livings and expulsion.

19

The Fall of the Oldenbarnevelt Regime,
1616–1618

❖

In the years 1609–10 the Arminian–Gomarist dispute spread through the length and breadth of the United Provinces, throwing the public Church into turmoil and unsettling civic and provincial government. Following the intervention of Oldenbarnevelt, and the States of Holland, on the side of the Arminians, a series of political initiatives were taken between 1610 and 1614 which, for the moment, seemed to check the turmoil and stabilize state and society under the leadership of the Holland regents.

During these years, Oldenbarnevelt and other leaders of the States of Holland, from 1613 including Grotius, showed both determination and skill. The situation was complex, and fraught with pitfalls, but in encounter after encounter the Remonstrant regents, and party in the Church, worsted their opponents. The army was successfully used to quell unrest at Utrecht, in 1610. The Stadholder (though privately opposed to Oldenbarnevelt) had his hands tied. With the help of the Arminian factions in Overijssel and the Nijmegen quarter of Gelderland, Holland was able to prevent a majority of the Seven Provinces backing the call for a National Synod, at least whilst the Oldenbarnevelt party retained the initiative, down to 1617. Also, in Holland and Utrecht, Remonstrant control over preaching posts in the main towns led to a process of 'Remonstrantization' of the Church in places where the Remonstrants were strong. Finally, the English Crown, a potential ally of the Counter-Remonstrants, was, again until 1617, successfully kept at arm's length.

Though the Stadholder privately confessed he was unable to make head or tail of the theological controversy, his sympathies were already clear during the Alkmaar disturbances, in 1610, when Gomarists openly paraded their allegiance to the 'House of Nassau';[1] he also supported the anti-Vorstius

---

[1] Van Deursen, *Bavianen en slijkgeuzen*, 306.

campaign. But the Gomarists were defeated at Alkmaar and Utrecht, and during the years 1610–16 Maurits avoided committing himself too deeply.[2] There was no sense in destabilizing the state, and pushing things to extremes, if the other side appeared strong enough to win, or force a deadlock which could only lead to civil war, and a crippling of the state. Maurits, for the moment, had little choice but to be moderate; and since the Arminians controlled the public Church at The Hague, he continued attending the preaching of Uyttenbogaert, in the Binnenhof. Between 1610 and 1615 Oldenbarnevelt had some reason to be confident, though he was too apt to dismiss the Counter-Remonstrants as extraneous, a collection of 'puritans, mostly Flemish or Frisian'.[3] The overthrow of the Oldenbarnevelt regime was not a foregone conclusion and did not appear likely until 1616, or 1617. However, the roots of his defeat lay further back and it is apparent that his (and Grotius') political and ideological initiatives lost edge, and momentum, around 1615. From then on, the sway of the ruling group gradually weakened.

The defeat of Oldenbarnevelt and the majority faction of the States of Holland, the more liberal grouping in the Dutch political arena, may be attributed to three main factors. First, there was the failure to restore unity in the States of Holland. In the years 1614–16, following adoption of Grotius' placard 'For the Peace of the Church', the moderate Counter-Remonstrant grouping was overruled, albeit narrowly, by the hardliners, led by Burgomaster Pauw of Amsterdam, who preferred to align with the other provinces against Oldenbarnevelt rather than with Oldenbarnevelt to restore Holland's hegemony over the rest.[4] This factor had more to do with economic and political than religious or ideological considerations. Above all, the ruling group at Amsterdam, the sponsors of Petrus Plancius and his strident Counter-Remonstrantism, could not forgive Oldenbarnevelt for the Truce and his sacrificing the interests of colonial trade.[5]

Secondly, there was the continuing strength of Counter-Remonstrantism among the preachers, and consistories, of the public Church in Holland despite the progress of 'Remonstrantization' in many Holland towns. The regents exercised a great deal of leverage over preachers but only in the main towns. Outside these, they had no way of tackling the preponderance of Counter-Remonstrantism. Of the fifteen classes comprising the public Church in Holland, five were solidly Counter-Remonstrant—those of

[2] Van Deursen, 'Maurits', 106.
[3] Van Deursen, *Bavianen en slijkgeuzen*, 267.
[4] Den Tex, *Oldenbarnevelt*, iii. 298–302, 426.
[5] Israel, *Dutch Republic and the Hispanic World*, 60–4.

Amsterdam, Dordrecht, Enkhuizen, Edam, and Gorcum. In the rest the Arminian city councils purged the Counter-Remonstrant element from the towns or else, as at Leiden and Haarlem, devised a *modus vivendi* with predominantly Counter-Remonstrant consistories which, until 1617, avoided serious friction, but were unable to impose their will on the classes more generally.[6]

Wherever Arminianism was preponderant, the regents went on to the offensive against Counter-Remonstrant preachers who defied their authority, vigorously suppressing separatist tendencies among the Counter-Remonstrant citizenry. At Utrecht, the Arminian magistracy, after 1610, was as intolerant towards 'Gomarists', according to the Catholic leadership, as towards Catholics.[7]

At Hoorn, where the congregation, and consistory, split in August 1614, the *vroedschap* purged the consistory of Counter-Remonstrants, expelled the town's sole Counter-Remonstrant preacher, and broke up Counter-Remonstrant conventicles.[8] At Rotterdam, where the Counter-Remonstrant minority tried to secede, and set up a separate congregation, in 1614–15, Grotius enforced his philosophy of liberty of conscience without freedom of practice, countenancing no rift within the public Church.[9] At The Hague, the Counter-Remonstrant preacher Henricus Rosaeus and his supporters were effectively bridled by the Arminian consistory, until 1615; when it came to an open breach between Rosaeus and Uyttenbogaert, in that year, Rosaeus was stripped of his living and expelled. Not even a small Counter-Remonstrant congregation was established in The Hague until 1617.

But in rural and suburban Holland, including localities such as Delfts-haven and Rijswijk immediately adjoining Rotterdam and The Hague, Counter-Remonstrant theology reigned supreme. The English ambassador, Sir Dudley Carleton, exaggerated when he reported, in 1617, that the 'villages, as well of Holland as the other provinces [remain] universally for the Counter-Remonstrants'.[10] In fact there was a belt of villages, including Berkel, Hazerswoude, Warmond, and Zevenhuizen, stretching across South Holland and Utrecht to the countryside of the Nijmegen quarter of Gelderland, and also in Overijssel, where both preachers and villagers were Remonstrant in sympathy.[11] But it was true that most villages in South Holland, and nearly all villages in North Holland, were Counter-Remonstrant.

[6] Van Deursen, *Bavianen en slijkgeuzen*, 257–67, 298.
[7] *Archief aartsbisdom Utrecht*, xvii. 460.
[8] Trigland, *Kerckelycke Geschiedenissen*, 839.
[9] Den Tex, *Oldenbarnevelt*, iii. 401.
[10] Carleton, *Letters*, 89.
[11] Van Deursen, *Bavianen en slijkgeuzen*, 243–4.

As a result, there were no classes that were solidly Remonstrant. Of the ten classes that were not predominantly Counter-Remonstrant, four—those of Rotterdam, Alkmaar, Hoorn, and Brill—had divided into warring factions, by 1615, and two more—Gouda and Woerden—were to split over the next two years. In the remainder—Haarlem, Delft, and Leiden—the form of accommodation arrived at differed little, in practice, from an open rift.[12]

The third factor was the last to materialize and decisively tilted the balance. This was the increasing unrest amongst sections of Holland's urban population, a key element in the crisis of 1617–18 which destabilized the state, and gave Maurits his opportunity to topple Oldenbarnevelt without paralysing deadlock, or civil war. By 1616, social unrest in the Holland towns was causing the regents serious concern. One major element in this was the festering resentment of the now long-established south Netherlands immigrant population, which felt discriminated against in many areas of civic life including the militias, militia command, and civic welfare. The fact that Gomarus was Flemish and Arminius a Hollander typified a theologico-cultural split permeating the Holland towns. The consistories at Leiden and Haarlem were dominated by southerners and a militant Counter-Remonstrantism tinged with pique that those who had created the new textile wealth of these cities were excluded from civic government and regent circles. Oldenbarnevelt and Burgomaster Hooft were two of many Hollanders, on the Remonstrant side, who alluded with aversion to the Calvinist orthodoxy of the southern immigrants. When the Leiden *vroedschap* in 1615 asked the new Remonstrant professor of theology, Episcopius, to preach regularly in the town, he declined, remarking that he had no wish to be censured by the 'Flemish gentlemen' of the consistory.

But the Calvinist zeal of many immigrants was not a new element in the situation and, when Hooft or Episcopius complained of 'Flemish' influence, they were referring primarily to preachers and affluent manufacturers and merchants, in the consistories, rather than the immigrant working population.[13] Discontent in the manufacturing towns only became a major factor from around 1616 and has to be ascribed, at least in part, to economic causes. The Twelve Years Truce stimulated the growth of Dutch commerce within Europe—except the Zeeland transit trade. It was also a time of rapid expansion in manufacturing, especially the textile industries. But although the manufacturing towns grew rapidly, along with output, the Truce was also characterized by growing competition from the reviving industrial districts of the south Netherlands, due to the lowering of the Republic's

---

[12] Ibid. 267.　　　[13] Briels, *Zuid-Nederlanders*, 269.

import tariffs, in 1609, and resumed flow of Baltic wools, and other raw materials, to Flanders. After 1609, 'new drapery' products, and linen, poured on to the Dutch market, from Flanders and Brabant. This suited Dutch merchants, who now had two sources of supply for the cloth and linen they exported while cost prices sagged. But it meant that, for the working population, the Truce was a time of harsh downward pressure on wages, as well as rising rents, and increased exploitation by merchants.[14] There were also a few industries, notably brewing, which were not geared to exporting to overseas markets and which gained no benefit from the strengthening of the overseas trade system but yet faced the same problems of high costs, and increasing competition from the south, as other industries.

Thus, economic pressures led to worsening conditions among the artisan population in the manufacturing towns and this expressed itself, at least in part, in the form of a militant popular Counter-Remonstrantism. This phenomenon was by no means confined to the immigrant textile proletariat: it was widespread in the larger cities and some small towns. But it would be true to say that it assumed a particularly acute form among the immigrants. Thus, there were cases where the adverse impact of economic pressures was marked but the overflow into the theological and political arena limited. Serious rioting erupted in August 1616 at Delft, a town where there were relatively few immigrants but a particularly severe economic deterioration owing to the crisis of the brewing industry, the mainstay of the town's economy.[15] But, there, the theological component was not especially evident. The unrest which culminated in the pillaging of the town hall was essentially a protest about high bread prices, and worsening conditions among the working population, in which artisan wives played a prominent part. There were also cases where few, apart from immigrant textile workers, were strongly behind the Counter-Remonstrants, as we see in the case of Gouda, a predominantly Arminian town where the Counter-Remonstrants ventured to present a petition to the Stadholder, in January 1617, without informing the *vroedschap*, requesting permission to establish their own separate Reformed congregation. This challenge to the regents, backed by the claim that the *vroedschap* lacked jurisdiction in Church affairs, so infuriated the Gouda city council that it banished two leaders of the movement and stripped three others of their citizenship so that they could no longer be members of the town's guilds. Some eighty members of the Gouda Counter-Remonstrant grouping have been identified, about 60 per cent of whom were southern

---

[14] Israel, *Dutch Republic and the Hispanic World*, 56–60.
[15] Dekker, *Holland in beroering*, 28–30.

immigrants, mostly textile workers.[16] Yet, in all the larger manufacturing cities, and also Amsterdam, most of the working population were Counter-Remonstrant in sympathy even while anti-Arminian fervour was most marked amongst the southern immigrants.

By 1616–17 popular Counter-Remonstrantism posed an open challenge to the power of the regents in Holland. In the city of Utrecht, as yet, there was little sign of revival of popular Calvinist militancy, the only opposition being the trekking out each Sunday of a few dissidents to attend 'true Christian Reformed services' at nearby Counter-Remonstrant Vianen.[17] (By contrast, the neighbouring free lordships of Culemborg and Buren were staunchly Remonstrant.) But from many Holland towns large numbers of 'Mud Beggars' (*Slijkgeuzen*), as they were called, were now demonstrating their opposition by trudging out of town, in long columns each Sunday, to Counter-Remonstrant churches in the countryside. At The Hague by the summer of 1616, about 700 people walked each Sunday to hear Rosaeus preach at Rijswijk.

By early 1617 there was an unmistakable note of rebellion in the air. There were disturbances at The Hague and Brill, in January, in the latter case the local garrison commander refusing to help the magistracy without instructions from the Stadholder. At The Hague, the atmosphere was so fraught Uyttenbogaert was close to despair. On 9 July, a Counter-Remonstrant crowd forcibly seized the disused Cloister Church in the centre of The Hague and established a congregation there which the town government did not dare try to suppress. The services now organized in The Hague Cloister Church were, reportedly, better attended than Arminian services in the city's main church. This episode, together with Maurits's decision to attend the Cloister Church himself, made a deep impression, being clear signs of the growing weakness of the Oldenbarnevelt regime.

In Amsterdam Counter-Remonstrant mobs became active in February 1617. Crowds of youths began attacking Remonstrant conventicles.[18] Several Remonstrant houses were sacked. There was also a major disturbance at Arminius' birthplace—Oudewater—on 3 May 1617, when a mob of artisans compelled the Arminian *vroedschap* to cancel their dismissal of the Counter-Remonstrant preacher Johannes Lydius.[19] A military garrison was based nearby but, again, the regents received no assistance.

The growing involvement of the people was reflected in the steep rise in the number of Dutch-language pamphlets and tracts dealing with the

[16] Abels, 'Van Vlaamse broeders', 80, 85–6.
[17] GA Utrecht 2/121. res. vroed. 31 Mar. 1617.
[18] Nijenhuis, *Matthew Slade*, 41–8.
[19] Den Tex, *Oldenbarnevelt*, iii. 477.

Arminian–Gomarist controversies. From around fifty pamphlets published in 1613, and again in 1614, the quantity rose to eighty in 1615, over one hundred in 1616, to 175 in 1617, and more than 300 in 1618.[20] Both sides produced popular theologico-political tracts of unbridled vehemence, those of the Rotterdam preacher Nicolaes Grevinchoven, and his Utrecht colleague, Jacobus Taurinus, being especially intemperate on the Remonstrant side. But, strikingly, in a country teeming with artists—many of whom doubtless had strong political and theological views—and where the Revolt had provided ample practice in the arts of caricature and the political print, there was no parallel wave of visual material until after the crumbling of the regime, in 1618. The most accomplished exponent of the political print of this era, Adriaen van de Venne (1589–1662) began producing work such as the *Righteous Sieve* (1618)—showing a great sieve held up by members of the States General, assisted by Maurits, through which tumble Oldenbarnevelt and the Arminian leadership—only when the political contest was effectively over.[21] Van de Venne's earlier painting, *Fishing for Souls* (1614), places a batch of Remonstrant theologians, including Vorstius, on the same side as the Counter-Remonstrants, facing the Catholics, with no hint of strife, suggesting rather the unity despite differences which was Oldenbarnevelt's and Grotius' policy. Before 1618, no city council or provincial States, it would appear, whatever their theology, were prepared to allow the Advocate, or States of Holland, to be lambasted in published prints. This was paralleled by the fact that the printed polemics of the day were virulent about theology and theologians, but highly restrained in alluding to Oldenbarnevelt, and the States of Holland, as well as Maurits.

Grotius, an élitist to his fingertips, disdained the violent acrimony of this escalating propaganda war. Nevertheless, he entered the fray through the publication of what Slade called his 'long and elaborate Oration', an immense harangue, which he delivered, as head of a States of Holland delegation, before the Amsterdam city council, in April 1616, in a final effort to persuade Amsterdam not to oppose the church policies of the regime.[22] In this text Grotius expounded his republican ideology of the 'public Church', to the modern mind a bizarre mixture of toleration and intolerance, insisting on the indispensability, and indivisibility, of the public Church, and need for the State to uphold it over other Churches, being the foundation of social, moral (and ultimately also political) stability: 'even in kingdoms the division of the public religion is extremely damaging; but

[20] Ibid. 404.
[21] Royalton-Kisch, *Adriaen van de Venne's Album*, 58–60.
[22] Nijenhuis, *Matthew Slade*, 36–7.

in republics it is totally ruinous'.[23] But this outward uniformity must be combined with internal toleration and doctrinal elasticity. As long as the fundamentals of Christian dogma remain intact, what is secondary should be left open to debate. In a republic which grants liberty of conscience, he argued, there is a constant peril of fragmentation through seeking doctrinal uniformity: an uncompromisingly confessional approach can only lead to inward perforation so that, were the Gomarists to persist, they would break the public Church into warring pieces. He raised the spectre of the Dutch Anabaptists 'who already have so many sects among them that there is hardly anyone who knows their number, or all their names'.[24]

Grotius tried to separate the fundamentals of Christian belief, including the Trinity, from a secondary zone, including predestination, where confessional uniformity was inappropriate. At the heart of his Christian republican ideology was his harnassing humanist scholarship to a campaign to convince the public that the States of Holland, and public Church, as upheld by the States, adhered fully to Christian truth while, simultaneously, rejecting precisian intolerance, maintaining a broad, but also legitimate, toleration of disparate doctrines among its preachers. Assisted by Vossius, Grotius devoted much time, at this crucial juncture, to studying Pelagianism and Socinianism, with which, from the outset, Counter-Remonstrants had stigmatized Arminius, Vorstius, and all the Remonstrants. Grotius, who arranged Vossius' appointment as regent of the States College, at Leiden, in 1615, warmly encouraged his vast study of the Pelagian and semi-Pelagian heresies.[25] The aim of Vossius' 800-page *Historia Pelagianismi* (Leiden, 1618) was to prove that Remonstrants were not Pelagians. Similarly, Grotius' *Defensio . . . adversus Faustum Socinum*, published the previous year, was intended to show that Remonstrants were not Socinians and thereby cleanse Remonstrantism, and the regime, of his opponents' most damaging smear by unassailably establishing the truth of the Trinity.[26] However, he had such difficulty with his proofs that he ended up merely demonstrating the weakness of the arguments against anti-Trinitarianism.

Counter-Remonstrant theologians were assailed by Grotius, Vossius, and also Drusius, the leading light of Franeker, who, after prolonged silence, revealed his Remonstrant leanings with a blistering attack on Lubbertus, whom he (like Grotius) charged with unintentionally spreading, instead of checking, Socinian notions in the United Provinces. Lubbertus tried to

---

[23] Grotius, *Oratie*, 52.
[24] Ibid. 50.
[25] Rademaker, *Life and Work of Gerardus Joannes Vossius*, 123–5.
[26] Kühler, *Het Socinianisme*, 81–2.

orchestrate a theological counter-offensive in the universities,[27] but the Counter-Remonstrants lacked the scholarly muscle of their adversaries. Especially embarrassing were the efforts of the new professor, Hermann Ravensperger, at Groningen, who published a supposedly crushing reply to Grotius, on Socinianism, in 1617, which elicited such a withering riposte from Vossius as to damage the standing of the university.[28] The Groningen university senate had to order their mediocrity to keep silent.

The Arminians won the intellectual battle but lost the political. By the summer of 1617, after the disturbances at Amsterdam, The Hague, Brill, and Oudewater, and the Stadholder's open endorsement of Counter-Remonstrantism, the atmosphere was so menacing that Oldenbarnevelt, and his allies, felt under siege. The Holland leadership were losing their grip. To shore up their crumbling position they took the step, in August 1617, which precipitated the final act of the drama and led on to the collapse of the regime. This was the passing of the so-called Sharp Resolution over the strenuous objections of the six cities known to the Gomarists as the 'good towns'—Amsterdam, Dordrecht, Enkhuizen, Edam, Schiedam, and Purmerend. The 'Sharp Resolution,' of 4 August 1617, empowered the Holland towns to raise special troops known as *waardgelders* to maintain order in each town, the troops swearing their allegiance to the municipality which paid them.[29] The resolution also declared that units of the regular army under Holland's *répartition* owed their primary allegiance to the provincial States rather than to the States General. This assertion that sovereignty, in the United Provinces, lay entirely in the provinces infuriated the Counter-Remonstrant opposition. Always keen to appropriate the title of 'patriots', supporting the Union in politics, as they did Calvinist orthodoxy in the Church, supporters of the 'good cause' exploited the 'Sharp Resolution' to label their opponents traitors to the Generality and even covert collaborators of Spain. The Stadholder, Maurits, proclaimed the 'Sharp Resolution' an 'affront to the true Reformed religion and our person'.[30] By 1617, the Counter-Remonstrants spoke openly of the opposed 'Remonstrant' and 'true Christian Reformed religion' as if they were two separate religions caught in a conflict which had to be fought to the bitter end. There was talk of civil war. Maurits, seeing the danger, proceeded, as in (most of) his military campaigns, with immense caution.

The tension gripped all the larger Holland towns and also Utrecht which remained sullenly quiescent but where the city council, mindful that the

[27] Van der Woude, *Sibrandus Lubbertus*, 309–10, 322, 329.
[28] Rademaker, *Life and Work of Gerardus Joannes Vossius*, 122.
[29] Den Tex, *Oldenbarnevelt*, iii. 493–7.
[30] Smit, 'Prins Maurits en de goede zaak', 60–1.

situation 'in many places in Holland was leading more and more to strife and discord under pretext of religion',[31] and that unrest was likely in Utrecht too, proceeded, after the passing of the 'Sharp Resolution', to raise 600 *waardgelders* for service in Utrecht.[32] When the troops were in place, the *raad* proceeded to purge the city militia of Counter-Remonstrant militants, citing the alarming situation in Leiden as justification for its action.

The friction was indeed at its most acute in Leiden, a city accounted by Carleton the 'fountain of these dissensions'.[33] By September 1617, the *vroedschap* was so apprehensive of an imminent outbreak of mob violence, and an attack on the town hall,[34] it resolved to cordon off, and barricade, the heart of the city (see PLATE 11) using the *waardgelders* to man the barricades and keep hostile crowds at bay. On 3 October—the anniversary of the lifting of the great siege of Leiden—there were clashes between townsmen and *waardgelders* in which several soldiers were injured by flying stones and one person killed.[35] Unsure of the militia, the regents attempted to secure their position, in January 1618, by imposing a new oath. Discarding the vital phrase adopted during the Revolt, binding the militia to hold Philip II and his 'adherents' as enemies, the regents substituted the obligation to support the burgomasters in repressing all commotion, an obvious attempt to bind them to back the regents against Counter-Remonstrant protest among the citizenry.[36] Consequently, many refused to swear and some five to six hundred men were summarily purged from the militia. Soon after, the militia was purged also at Haarlem.

Society polarized during the summer of 1617 and so did the Holland regents. All pretence of unity was now gone and the States of Holland split into two warring blocks. Delft, where the preachers and most regents were Arminian, but the working populace, as in the other manufacturing towns, and Amsterdam, overwhelmingly Counter-Remonstrant, voted for the 'Sharp Resolution'. But, intimidated by the ugly mood among the populace, and a disturbance early in September, in the New Church in Delft (where the mausoleum of William the Silent was housed), most of the city council now abandoned the Arminians, overruling Burgomaster Ewout van der Dussen, a loyal ally of Oldenbarnevelt.[37] Delft retreated into a tense neutrality which soon veered towards support for the Stadholder, the Delft

---

[31] GA Utrecht 2/121. res. vroed. 28 Aug. 1617.
[32] Ibid. 30 Sept. 1617.
[33] Carleton, *Letters*, 82, 117, 307.
[34] GA Leiden Sec. Arch. 446, fo. 254. vroed. res. 6 Sept. 1617.
[35] Knevel, 'Onrust', 161.
[36] Ibid. 163–4.
[37] GA Delft 13/3, fo. 280. res. vroed. 11 Sept. 1617.

city council agreeing to support the call for a National Synod, in December 1617.[38] The hard-core Arminian towns—Rotterdam, Leiden, Haarlem, Gouda, Alkmaar, Hoorn, Brill, and Schoonhoven—began during the summer, holding separate gatherings of their representatives in The Hague.[39] The Counter-Remonstrant towns did likewise.

Maurits chiselled relentlessly at Oldenbarnevelt's shrinking power base, dispatching letters to Holland regents who opposed Oldenbarnevelt or might be persuaded to do so.[40] He was in constant touch with Burgomaster Pauw, at Amsterdam, and bombarded the town councils of Medemblik and Monnikendam, wavering towns, whose representatives had been absent from the Hague, on 4 August, when the 'Sharp Resolution' was passed, urging them to protest at the manner of the resolution's passing, as well as its content. He encouraged Counter-Remonstrant regents in Remonstrant towns—notably Jacob van Brouckhoven, at Leiden—to organize opposition to their colleagues and urged defecting towns, such as Delft, Medemblik, and Monnikendam, to back the call for a National Synod. In late November 1617, the Stadholder toured several South Holland towns accompanied by his personal guard, trying to accelerate the process of defection from the ruling Arminian block. His proceedings increasingly alarmed Oldenbarnevelt's supporters and there were persistent rumours about his intentions. In towns he visited, he harangued the regents on the dire catastrophe for Church and State which would result if there was not a prompt calling of a National Synod to settle the affairs of the Church. He also endeavoured, as Carleton put it, 'to discharge himself of the imputation cast upon him by his enemies of affecting the sovereignty of this country'.[41]

During the weeks following the 'Sharp Resolution' it was widely expected that Maurits would soon launch an armed coup to topple Oldenbarnevelt and the Arminians. Many expected this after the Leiden riot, in October 1617, when Maurits came in person to Brill, to change the garrison and assert his authority over it, precipitating a bitter clash with the *Gecommitteerde Raden* of Holland. But still the Stadholder held back, wary of the appreciable support the Oldenbarnevelt regime still enjoyed both in and outside of Holland. To avoid civil war and too blatant an overturning of all accepted procedures, Maurits felt the need to prepare the ground yet further.

Oldenbarnevelt suffered a series of defeats during the opening months of 1618. In January, Maurits travelled to Nijmegen and took a step which he

---

[38] Ibid., fo. 281v. res. vroed. 4 Dec. 1617.
[39] Groenveld, *Evidente factien*, 17.
[40] Smit, 'Prins Maurits en de goede zaak', 83, 89–90.
[41] Carleton, *Letters*, 203–4.

had not previously dared to—although he claimed the authority to do it under the terms of his 1591 appointment, as Stadholder of Gelderland. Accompanied by the Chancellor of Gelderland, Gerlach van der Capellen (1543–1625), leader of the Counter-Remonstrant *ridderschap* of the Zutphen quarter, Maurits purged the Nijmegen *raad*, replacing its Arminian membership with Counter-Remonstrants. The new *raad* reversed Nijmegen's stand on the question of the National Synod and, in April, sacked the city's three Arminian preachers.[42] Another humiliation for the Arminians took place at Heusden, then a distillation of the tensions infusing the Republic. The town had an Arminian *vroedschap* but predominantly Counter-Remonstrant population. It also had two of the ablest young Reformed preachers in the United Provinces, but on opposite sides, Johannes Grevius, from Cleves, one of the signatories of the Remonstrance of 1610, and the newly arrived Gisbertus Voetius, a zealous Counter-Remonstrant, destined in later decades to become the leading spokesman of Calvinist orthodoxy in the Republic. In order to avoid popular interference in the *vroedschap* elections for 1618, the Holland *Gecommitteerde Raden* sent a delegation, headed by Grotius, to supervise, and ensure the town's continued Arminian allegiance. A new Arminian town council was installed. But no sooner did the visitors depart than rioting erupted and a Counter-Remonstrant mob stormed the town hall, ejecting the Arminians and replacing them with Counter-Remonstrants. Lacking control over the army garrison in the town, the *Gecommitteerde Raden* had no choice but to accept the outcome of this daunting popular intervention in the political process.

It was clear the resolution of the great crisis could not be long delayed. The garrisons at Brill, Heusden, Oudewater, and elsewhere were refusing to obey the *Gecommitteerde Raden*. Town councils were being set aside, in Holland by popular intervention, and, in Gelderland, by the Stadholder. The eight resolutely Arminian towns of Holland, holding separate gatherings, in The Hague, asked their three leading pensionaries, Grotius, Hogerbeets, and Johan de Haen, of Haarlem, to compose a declaration denouncing the illegality of recent proceedings and threatening to withhold Holland's contribution to the Generality budget.[43] This was put to the full States of Holland, by the Haarlem delegation, on 23 January 1618. The Arminian towns also proposed the recruitment of more *waardgelders* and, for this, needed both justifying arguments and to divert funds from the coffers of the Generality. The strictly military value of the *waardgelders* might have been limited. But expanding their numbers was a means of

[42] Jenniskens, *Magistraat van Nijmegen*, 2, 7.   [43] Den Tex, *Oldenbarnevelt*, iii. 553.

exerting pressure on the Stadholder, and other provinces, by stepping up the threat of civil war. During March, accompanied by fierce encounters in the States of Holland, the Arminian towns resumed their recruiting, as did the city of Utrecht.[44]

For Maurits, the next step was to mobilize the five provinces against Holland and Utrecht. In March 1618 he attended the States of Gelderland in person, justifying his action in Nijmegen, and persuading the States to reject the protests of Holland, and the purged magistrates, and direct their delegates in the States General to support his call for disbandment of the *waardgelders* in Holland and Utrecht.[45] In May, Maurits attended the States of Overijssel, in person, and persuaded the still wavering *ridderschap* to support him. That left only the city of Kampen still resisting in the whole eastern part of the Republic. On 5 May 1618, the unwaveringly Arminian *raad* of Kampen, gathered with the town's Sworn Council, discussed a letter from Maurits, urging them finally to assent to the calling of a National Synod to resolve the religious differences unsettling the provinces and Union. Kampen replied that a National Synod would not resolve anything but simply create 'more disorder and disunity'.[46] The States of Overijssel then decided to go ahead without Kampen and join the provinces, calling for a National Synod and disbandment of the *waardgelders*.[47] Only in May, after bringing heavy pressure to bear by means of a delegation headed by three principal nobles of the province—Sweder van Haersolte (who was increasingly Maurits's right-hand-man in Overijssel), Hendrik Bentinck (*drost* of Salland), and Johan van Raesfelt—was Kampen's ostensible assent finally extracted.[48]

By the spring of 1618 morale within the pro-Arminian grouping of the States of Holland had been seriously eroded. In desperation Oldenbarnevelt and Grotius strove to steel their supporters' resolution. 'There is a discourse presented by Mons Barnevelt but penned by Grotius to the towns of Holland', reported Carleton in April, 'to puff up their spirits, telling them how the ancient Batavi were *socii Imperii Romani*, with such like pedantical stuff, concluding, because that Holland is more ancient, greater and richer than the rest of the United Provinces, ergo they must have no National Synod.'[49] The Arminians at the same time stepped up their campaign of

---

[44] GA Utrecht 2/21 fo. 196v. res. vroed. 9 Mar. 1618.
[45] ARH PR 8. res. S. Geld. 13 and 16 Mar. 1618.
[46] GA Kampen Oud-archief 24, fo. 92v. res. raad, 25 Apr. 1618.
[47] ARH PR 486, fos. 84–6. res. SO, 29 Apr., 5 and 7 May 1618.
[48] GA Kampen Oud-archief 24, fo. 94. res. raad, 6 May 1618.
[49] Carleton, *Letters*, 265.

innuendo about Maurits's personal political ambition. To this the Counter-Remonstrants retorted that the Stadholder was merely standing up for his rights and that the States of Holland, as Carleton put it, 'have for a long space undermined his authority and left him nothing in effect but the bare title of governor of the country'.[50]

As the wrangling over the National Synod and *waardgelders* intensified, other constitutional aspects of the struggle also received more attention than before. In June and September 1617, a bare majority of the provinces in the States General—Friesland, Groningen, Zeeland, and Gelderland (without the consent of the Nijmegen quarter)—had voted to convene the National Synod (in May 1618) and invite delegations to attend from the Church of England and Reformed churches of France, Geneva, the Palatinate, and Hesse.[51] By May 1618, this had become a more convincing majority, now including the Nijmegen quarter and Overijssel. But the Remonstrants (and Grotius in particular) argued that the vote in the States General was 'illegal'. Neither side held that decisions in the States General had to be unanimous; it would have been absurd for Grotius to do so, for many decisions had been taken in the States General, at Holland's prompting, since the 1590s, by majority vote, over the objections of other provinces, especially Friesland and Zeeland. Indeed, Grotius expressly asserted that neither the Dutch Republic, nor any republic, could function unless its highest deliberations were settled by majority vote, with the minority accepting the decision.[52] His argument was that sovereignty resided in the individual provinces and that it was solely in spheres where the provinces had agreed to delegate part of their sovereignty that majority voting in the States General was valid. Religion and church policy, however, did not pertain to the States General. In religion, each province was fully sovereign and there was no requirement for Holland to conform to the majority.[53] Equally, Holland, as a sovereign province, could do whatever her States deemed necessary to safeguard internal order and could do this without infringing the Generality's responsibility for the armed forces of the Union.

The Stadholder was interested in the practical aspects, rather than theory. Yet in his speech to the States of Overijssel, in May 1618, he refused to concede that sovereignty lay wholly in the individual provinces, though he granted that much of it did; Maurits asserted that the religious divisions within, and between, the provinces had to be settled by the States General 'as representing the highest government of the United Netherlands by whose authority all differences and difficulties of importance over the last thirty

---

[50] Ibid. 192.   [51] Grotius, *Verantwoordingh*, 6.   [52] Ibid. 86.   [53] Ibid. 26–7.

years have been settled'.[54] If it is to be left to each individual province to settle the religious differences then they cannot be settled and the unity of the provinces and state will be irreparably damaged. In effect, what Maurits claimed, as his party consistently maintained later, was that sovereignty in the United Provinces was divided between the provinces and the Generality.

On 9 July 1618 the States General began deliberating the disbandment of the *waardgelders* raised in Holland and Utrecht. These provinces protested the illegality of this proceeding, claiming that as sovereigns, they were entitled to raise, and maintain, troops, for internal reasons, as and when they saw fit. On this point, even Dordrecht agreed with Oldenbarnevelt. The other provinces, however, insisted that under the terms of the Union everything concerning defence, armed forces, and military command pertained to the Generality and Stadholders. The States General then voted through the disbandment of the *waardgelders* in Holland and Utrecht, by five provinces to two. Next the States General appointed a commission drawn from the five provinces to accompany the Stadholder on his intervention in Utrecht, where disbandment, on the orders of the Generality, was to begin.

Oldenbarnevelt, Grotius, and their adherents now revealed the fundamental inconsistency in their position. They claimed each province was sovereign. But the provinces did not have their own armies. There was only the one army of the Union, under the control of the Generality and the Stadholder. Not all the garrison commanders automatically supported Maurits. Some, including the commander of the English garrison at Utrecht, sympathized with Oldenbarnevelt and Ledenberg. In desperation, Oldenbarnevelt sent Grotius and Hogerbeets at the head of a supposedly States of Holland delegation (authorized in fact by only a minority of towns) with instructions for officers of army units in the province of Utrecht that their first obligation was to the province which paid them, that is (mostly) Holland, and that where there was a clash of authority they must ignore the orders of the States General and Stadholder. These instructions flatly contradicted what, since the mid-1580s, had been standard Dutch political and military practice. They were to provide the core of the subsequent treason charges which their enemies were to bring against Oldenbarnevelt, Grotius, and Hogerbeets, and were seen as clear evidence that they had overturned the fundamental principles of the Union. A meeting of Counter-Remonstrant Holland regents at the house of Gerrit

[54] ARH PR 486, fo. 84. res. SO, 29 Apr. 1618.

Witsen, Pauw's chief ally at Amsterdam, organized a counter-deputation to Utrecht to assure the troops there that Holland would not stop their pay.[55]

Maurits brought additional troops into Utrecht and then commenced enforcing his, and the States General's, authority. There was no resistance. Ledenberg and Taurinus fled to Holland. The city's 900 *waardgelders* were disarmed, watched by Maurits and a large military force on 31 July—a drama long to be remembered as a decisive event in the history of the city of Utrecht. All members of the Delegated States were purged. Maurits did not eject anyone from the Utrecht *ridderschap* but did put in seven new nobles of Counter-Remonstrant views.[56] Most pro-Arminian members of the city council were removed and replaced. Chastened, the States of Utrecht, now dominated by friends of Maurits, duly voted in favour of calling a National Synod. Ledenberg's successor as Advocate of the States of Utrecht, Anthonie van Hilten, a confidant of Maurits, had no previous connection with the province.[57]

Early in August, the *vroedschap* also accepted the petition of the Counter-Remonstrant citizenry, calling themselves the 'true Reformed Church of Christ in Utrecht', asking for one of the main churches to be assigned to them, the 'true Reformed'. The ecclesiastical position in the city was now indeed bizarre and was to remain so for many months. Officially, there was only one public Church. But, in practice, the *vroedschap* now ruled that there were two. The cathedral of Utrecht, the Dom, was, for the time being, left in the possession of the Remonstrants, who had not yet been condemned by a National Synod and saw themselves as the authentic public Church.[58] Apart from Taurinus, the other Remonstrant preachers in the city—and there were no Counter-Remonstrants—remained at their pulpits. Yet the city council accepted the charge that the religion provided in the city's public churches did not conform to the 'pure Reformed Christian Religion comprised in the Netherlands Confession and the Heidelberg Catechism', deemed Remonstrantism a religion apart from, and incompatible with, 'the true Reformed religion', and set up a separate Reformed community.[59]

Seeing that further resistance was hopeless, Oldenbarnevelt and his allies abandoned the struggle. Leiden and Rotterdam disbanded their *waardgelders* on 22 and 23 August and the other towns soon followed. Yet Oldenbarnevelt and Grotius still hoped to avoid complete capitulation.

---

[55] Den Tex, *Oldenbarnevelt*, iii. 606.
[56] Den Tex, 'Staten in Oldenbarnevelt's tijd', 86.
[57] Smit, 'Prins Maurits en de goede zaak', 52.
[58] GA Utrecht 2/121. res. vroed. 5 Aug. and 5 Sept. 1618.
[59] Ibid. 27 July 1618.

They finally acquiesced in a National Synod to settle the Arminian–Gomarist controversies, but still hoped to influence the proceedings and salvage something of Holland's leadership of the Union.[60] 'This business would prove Penelope's web', concluded Carleton, 'unless these men be layde hold on.'[61] The question was whether the States General could arrest the principal figures of the States of Holland, including their Advocate, without the consent of the States of that province. No such thing had ever occurred before. But the principle that sovereignty lay partly in the States General, and that Holland and Utrecht had infringed that sovereignty, was deployed to justify this step. The States General passed a secret resolution, on 28 August, authorizing Maurits and a Generality commission, appointed to secure the 'common good', to investigate recent actions of Holland and Utrecht subversive of the Union and take necessary action to ensure the security of the state. On the strength of this, Maurits proceeded, the next day, to arrest Oldenbarnevelt, Grotius, and Hogerbeets, at the Binnenhof, in The Hague, and Advocate Ledenberg, of the States of Utrecht, the following day.

[60] Vervou, *Enige Aentekeningen*, 132–3.   [61] Lee, *Dudley Carleton*, 256.

20

The Calvinist Revolution
of the Counter-Remonstrants, 1618–1621

❖

DOMESTIC POLITICS

Maurits kept his three principal prisoners at the Binnenhof, in The Hague, 'well-guarded', as Slade noted, and 'very pensive'. The Prince of Orange, as he now was (since the death in Brussels, in February, of his Catholic older half-brother, Philips Willem), wielded greater authority, from the summer of 1618 until his death in 1625, than any man in the United Provinces since his father's assassination thirty-four years before. Oldenbarnevelt was removed; Maurits was now the presiding figure in the state. This meant that he had to form his own ruling circle and methods of managing the complex political machinery of the Republic.

During 1617–18 Holland had been repeatedly overruled in the States General by a majority of provinces, and the prestige of the Generality had been much enhanced. But clearly, in the longer run, the United Provinces could not be managed by trying to subordinate Holland to the collective will of the lesser provinces, under the leadership of the Stadholder. Power and authority in the United provinces could only be based on Holland, with the rest playing a subsidiary role. Some historians have assumed from this that little changed in the political character of the Republic: whether Oldenbarnevelt or Maurits stood at the helm could make no difference to Holland's underlying dominance in terms of population and resources.[1] Outwardly, the constitutional forms and procedures of the United Provinces remained unchanged.[2] The Republic was still an intricate cross between confederacy and federal state in which one province, Holland, presided over the others.

Nevertheless, it is wrong to suppose that Maurits's coup changed little in the political character of the Dutch state. In fact, it marked one of the most

---

[1] Van Deursen, 'Maurits', 108. [2] Wansink, 'Holland and Six Allies', 151.

fundamental shifts of the Golden Age. Dutch institutions, since 1579, were so elastic that, without changing the outward façade, it was possible to transform the reality within, and this is what Maurits and the Counter-Remonstrants now did. Holland's previously unchallenged preponderance was ended and executive power, in effect, transferred to the stadholderate with many profound and in some cases enduring consequences. In the medium, as well as short, term the curtailment of Holland's hegemony in decision-making—especially in church affairs, foreign policy, and military matters—was far-reaching. The steps Maurits took to enhance his authority in Overijssel, Utrecht, and Gelderland, and subordinate the States of Holland to himself, as Stadholder, enabled him to forge an entirely new relationship between Holland and the rest, under his leadership. Having purged pro-Remonstrant nobles from positions of influence in Overijssel, Utrecht, and Gelderland, he brought to the fore Counter-Remonstrant nobles, already well-connected in their respective provinces, who, from this point on, assisted him to manage affairs in their quarters, provinces, and the Generality colleges. Especially prominent, in the new regime, were Sweder van Haersolte, pre-eminent in the States of Overijssel; Gerlach van der Capellen, Chancellor of the Hof of Gelderland; Arnold van Randwijk, who had played a chief part in pushing through Gelderland's vote in favour of a National Synod, and who represented Gelderland in the *Raad van State*; and Adriaen Ploos van Amstel (1585–1639), from 1618 Maurits's principal manager in the States of Utrecht. Ploos now headed the Utrecht delegation to the Generality and was nominated one of Oldenbarnevelt's judges; like Van Haersolte he was to continue as a leading figure of the new regime also after Maurits's death, in 1625.[3]

The Prince extended his new ruling group also to Holland, choosing comparable men with whom he could work, who would be subservient to his authority, but yet command sufficient influence in their province, to help him manage the *ridderschap* and States of Holland. Oldenbarnevelt's control of the Holland *ridderschap* had been an essential part of his power base. Until August 1618, Adriaen van Mathenesse (c.1560–1621), a friend of Oldenbarnevelt and, according to Carleton, a 'passionate Arminian', had headed the preponderant Remonstrant grouping in the Holland *ridderschap*, Mathenesse and his allies excluding from the college eligible noblemen from qualified families but of contrary theological leanings. These men Maurits now introduced, chief among them being Nicolaas van den Bouchorst, lord of Wimmenum, who in subsequent years acted as Maurits's regular manager

---

[3] Ploos, 'Adriaan Ploos van Amstel', 48, 59.

of the *ridderschap* and, together with Pauw, one of the two new chief figures of the States of Holland. Besides introducing four qualified Counter-Remonstrants, from old Holland noble families, the Prince also brought in two more dubious additions to the Holland *ridderschap*, François van Aerssen, the most experienced diplomat, and talented politician, in Maurits's entourage, a nobleman but a Brabanter (and a close friend of Van den Bouchorst), and Daniel de Hertaing, seigneur de Marquette, a Walloon army officer who was one of Maurits's most trusted aides.[4] At the same time, while Mathenesse himself was allowed to remain—he was old and sick—two younger Holland nobles who had opposed Maurits—Cornelis van der Mijle, a bitter foe of Van Aerssen, and Reinoud van Brederode (both sons-in-law of Oldenbarnevelt)—were expelled.

Maurits may not have remodelled the Holland *ridderschap*, as an institution, but he did alter its political and theological complexion, turning it into a pliant instrument of his authority. Moreover, while the Holland *ridderschap* had already been playing an important role in the States of Holland, under Oldenbarnevelt, under Maurits its influence increased. Maurits, who relied on noblemen to help him manage the States of Overijssel, Utrecht, and Gelderland, transformed the general tone and character of government at The Hague, enhancing the position of the *ridderschap* also in Holland. Under Maurits, from 1618, noblemen became more prominent (in the medium term), regents less so. Even the most important of Maurits's regent allies, the Amsterdam burgomaster, Reinier Pauw, was assigned only a relatively modest place in the new arrangements. This downgrading of the regents, inevitably, was both noticed and resented. A clandestine anti-Maurits tract published in 1620, according to Carleton a 'pernicious pamphlet', denounced Van Aerssen, Van den Bouchorst, Johan van Duivenvoorde, 'and all the noblesse of Holland as [Maurits's] instruments of tyranny, inciting the people to commotion for liberty'.[5]

But at the heart of the revolution was the purging of 'Arminians' from the town councils. The first purges in Holland, at Schoonhoven and Brill, commenced a few days after Oldenbarnevelt's arrest, Maurits, in consultation with Pauw, selecting 'well-affected' persons, especially men of strong Counter-Remonstrant leanings, to replace the ousted Arminians.[6] The role of the regents may now have been reduced, but until he had purged the *vroedschappen*, the Prince could not rely on the quiescence of the States of Holland which was essential to enforcing his authority and stable and

---

[4] Van Nierop, *Van ridders tot regenten*, 221–3.
[5] *Nootwendighe ende vrypostighe Vermaninghe*, 4–7, 9, 15; Carleton, *Letters*, 503.
[6] Nijenhuis, *Matthew Slade*, 91.

effective government. In a vote in the States of Holland less than a month after Oldenbarnevelt's fall, only nine of the eighteen voting towns of Holland approved of their Advocate's arrest.[7] Six towns, headed by Haarlem, Leiden, and Rotterdam, insisted that any charges against the arrested men should be heard by the States of Holland as the competent authority. Two more towns—Delft and Medemblik—had refrained from expressing a view. The situation, as of September 1618, scarcely provided a basis for stable government under Maurits leadership. He had no choice, having gone thus far, but to remove, or neutralize, the men who had opposed him.

During the autumn of 1618, Maurits systematically purged the Holland towns which had backed Oldenbarnevelt or where there were substantial 'Arminian' factions. The Prince's visitations marked the beginning of a new era in each town. Alkmaar was one of the first he visited. After securing the town with troops, Maurits staged his entry, on 18 October, accompanied by an imposing entourage and 180 musketeers. He summoned the *vroedschap* and removed sixteen regents 'for the service', as he explained, 'of the land and future tranquillity of the town's inhabitants'.[8] Only eight members of the old *vroedschap* remained, among them Pieter Jansz. Schagen, a zealous Counter-Remonstrant selected as one of Oldenbarnevelt's judges. The town militia was also purged and made to swear a new oath of allegiance.

The Prince sent troops into Leiden, on 20 October, and three days later arrived to purge the *vroedschap*, 'with much applause of the people', replacing no fewer than twenty-two of the city's regents. Next he descended with his entourage on Haarlem, assembling the *vroedschap* and justifying his action as necessary to curtail unrest; he expelled thirteen regents, introducing twenty new men.[9] At Rotterdam, where he appeared four days later, Maurits removed fifteen and brought in seventeen new men, including a well-to-do cloth merchant, Jan Jansz. Kalf, father of one of the greatest still-life painters of the Golden Age, Willem Kalf.[10] Most of the Gouda *vroedschap* was purged on 1 November. Amsterdam, though a Counter-Remonstrant city, also received an impressive visitation from the Prince.[11] For, there too, though a minority, there were supporters of Oldenbarnevelt, and toleration, in the *vroedschap*; seven noted 'libertines' were ousted, though the Prince spared the now old and ailing Hooft. As elsewhere, the Stadholder's visit was marked by banquets and elaborate festivities. The rhetoric

[7] Vervou, *Enige Aentekeningen*, 136, 149–50.
[8] GA Alkmaar inv. no. 42, fo. 236. res. vroed. 11 Oct. 1618.
[9] Spaans, *Haarlem*, 223.
[10] Lois, *Cronycke*, 121–2; Grisebach, *Willem Kalf*, 13.
[11] Wagenaar, *Amsterdam*, I, 471–2.

chamber *d'Eglantier*—in the past no friend of Counter-Remonstrantism—staged an allegory, proclaiming Maurits the 'champion of God's Church'.[12]

A direct result of these purges was the disappearance of regents with experience of government and administration, men educated and trained for the public sphere with the leisure to devote their energies to *vroedschap* affairs. They were replaced with inexperienced, and less educated, men frequently with businesses to attend to and apt to devote less time and attention to civic and provincial business than their predecessors, a not inconsiderable factor in the most striking political result of the coup of 1618—the reduced role of the Holland towns.

This shift was inherent in Maurits's overthrow of Oldenbarnevelt. After his coup, the Stadholder, eager to protect his power, took care to avoid being saddled with another strong leader of the States of Holland. For any competent figure leading the States would, sooner or later, be bound to emerge as a rival for the leadership of the Republic. It thus became a matter of high policy—and was to remain such until the late 1640s—to ensure the election of a Pensionary of Holland—for Oldenbarnevelt's title of 'Advocate' was now abolished—who would not just be less assertive but be an instrument in the Stadholder's hands. Also the Pensionary's functions were reduced.[13] It is indeed ironic that Andries de Witt, uncle of the greatest Pensionary of Holland of the second half of the seventeenth century—Johan de Witt—was co-opted, following Oldenbarnevelt's fall, to serve as acting Pensionary, precisely because he was a man of little experience and no weight whatsoever, a professed Counter-Remonstrant, only recently appointed Pensionary of Dordrecht.[14] De Witt continued in this function until January 1621, when an election was held to choose a new permanent Pensionary. It is striking that only one of the three candidates in this election—Reinier Pauw of Amsterdam—had much standing in the assembly, the others being Anthonis Duyck, a functionary without a power base in any Holland city, and, again, Andries de Witt. The last was the least able of the three but, as Carleton noted, the 'disabilitie he hath shewed doth no whit hinder him in regard there is the lesse suspicion of his attayning to his predecessour's greatness'.[15] The fact that Duyck was elected shows how far-reaching was the political revolution initiated by Maurits, and the Counter-Remonstrants, in 1618–19. For Duyck was a creature of the Stadholder, and the Generality, not a leader of the States of Holland, of which he had scant experience.

[12] Evenhuis, *Ook dat was Amsterdam*, i. 250.
[13] Den Tex, *Oldenbarnevelt*, iii. 773.
[14] Rowen, *John de Witt*, 6–7.
[15] PRO SP 84/98, fo. 148. Carleton to James I, 8 Jan. 1621.

The purges were by no means confined to the city councils and provincial States. The conflict of the Remonstrants and Counter-Remonstrants had pervaded the whole of politics and society as well as Church and education, and the process was bound to extend also to the civic militias, consistories,

TABLE 24. *The Advocates and Pensionaries of the States of Holland, 1513–1795*

Pensionary (before 1618 'Advocate')	Native town	Previous office	Term
Albrecht van Loo	—	jurist of the Hof	1513–24
Aert van der Goes	Delft?	jurist of the Hof	1524–43
Adriaen van der Goes	Delft	jurist of the Hof	1543–60
Jacob van den Eynde	Delft	pensionary of Delft	1560–8[a]
Paulus Buys	Amersfoort	pensionary of Leiden	1572–85
Johan van Oldenbarnevelt	Amersfoort	pensionary of Rotterdam	1586–1618
Andries de Witt	Dordrecht	pensionary of Dordrecht	1618–21
Anthonis Duyck	Hoorn	*griffier* of Hof of Holland	1621–9
Jacob Cats	Brouwershaven	pensionary of Dordrecht	1629–31
Adriaen Pauw	Amsterdam	pensionary of Amsterdam	1631–6
Jacob Cats	Brouwershaven	pensionary of Dordrecht	1636–52
Adriaen Pauw	Amsterdam	official of SH	1652–3
Johan de Witt	Dordrecht	pensionary of Dordrecht	1653–72
Gaspar Fagel	Haarlem	*griffier* of States General	1672–88
Michael ten Hove	—	pensionary of Haarlem	1688–9
Anthonie Heinsius	Delft	pensionary of Delft	1689–1720
Isaac van Hoornbeeck	Leiden	pensionary of Rotterdam	1720–7
Simon van Slingelandt	Dordrecht	treasurer-general of Generality	1727–36
Anthonie van der Heim	The Hague	treasurer-general of Generality	1737–46
Jacob Gilles	—	deputy *griffier* of States General	1746–9
Pieter Steyn	Haarlem	burgomaster of Haarlem	1749–72
Pieter van Bleyswijk	Delft	pensionary of Delft	1772–87
Laurens Pieter van de Spiegel	Middelburg	Pensionary of Zeeland	1787–95

[a] Died during his imprisonment by Alva in 1569.

schools, and universities, as well as the preachers of the public Church. Along with the *vroedschappen*, the militias were an urgent priority, being the guardians of law and order and civic awareness. The authority of the new regents would inevitably remain precarious until Arminians were removed especially from positions of command and replaced with

Counter-Remonstrants committed to the new regime.[16] This was done so methodically that the exercise affected even the militia group portraits. The Haarlem painter Frans de Grebber (*c.*1570–1640), having finished a large militia piece in 1615, from which he was subsequently asked to paint out four of the figures (who had been among the Counter-Remonstrants expelled from the Haarlem militia in 1617), was now required to paint the men in again.[17] The militia purges of 1618 were drastic yet in several cases initially insufficient. Faced by an outbreak of rioting in Hoorn and Alkmaar, in March 1619, Maurits sent Marquette, with troops, to restore order and purge the militias again.[18] Even then troops had to be kept in Hoorn, Alkmaar, and Schoonhoven for many months.

It was not only the personnel but also the colours and oaths of the civic militias which were changed. The St Joris militia company, of Haarlem, when painted by Frans Hals, in his first great militia piece (1616), wore sashes, and carried banners, sporting their own colours and those of the town. The tradition of the militias, under the Arminians, was essentially local and civic and, in the case of the Utrecht militia (who took an oath of allegiance to the States of their province as well as to the city), also provincial.[19] After 1618, Hals and the other painters of militia pieces show us the same companies now wearing the orange, white, and blue of the Generality or the orange of the Stadholder. The implication was that the militias were entrusted with more than simply upholding law and order locally: they were now also, as they had been during the war against Spain, defenders of the Union and the Generality.

Purging the militias was attended to urgently. Other elements of the Counter-Remonstrant revolution proceeded more slowly. Although the Counter-Remonstrants had been actively planning their National Synod, since March 1618, when Pauw convened a meeting in the Amsterdam town hall attended also by representatives from Leiden and Enkhuizen, this long-awaited assembly to end the dissension in the public Church gathered only in November and got round to formal condemnation of Arminian theology, only in the spring of 1619. Before this there was no authorized basis for sacking preachers, schoolmasters, and academics, so that the purges in the ecclesiastical and academic spheres tended to be long delayed. The commission to purify Leiden university began work only in August

[16] GA Utrecht 2/121. res. vroed. 2 and 12 Nov. 1618; GA Kampen Oud-archief 24, fo. 103. res. raad, 22 Sept. 1618.

[17] Knevel, 'Onrust', 166.

[18] Carleton, *Letters*, 345.

[19] GA Utrecht 2/121. res. vroed. 23 Nov. 1618.

1619. A recalcitrant schoolmaster at Kampen, who refused to teach the Netherlands Confession or, later, sign the acts of the Synod of Dordrecht, was not dismissed until August 1620.[20] Naturally, in the case of good teachers there was hesitation, and disagreement, as to how to proceed. But even those willing to sign the Acts of the National Synod were not necessarily safe from being purged. Dirk Schrevelius, rector of the Latin school at Haarlem and, since 1607, member of the Remonstrant *vroedschap*, was purged from the town hall in 1618 but not stripped of his rectorship until after prolonged deliberation, in 1620.[21]

Even so, the theological rift was too bitter and divisive simply to be shelved until the National Synod had done its work. On a *de facto* basis, 'cleansing' the Church began much earlier, even though it could nowhere be carried through, systematically, until well into 1619. At Leiden, a *de facto* division of the public Church began as early as 1614 when the two sides agreed to use the city's two large churches by turns.[22] In most Remonstrant towns, however, the regents had refused to permit any form of separation, to accommodate Counter-Remonstrant preaching. Accordingly, in these towns the Counter-Remonstrant public had neither preachers, nor school-masters, consistory, or even a church at their disposal at the time of Maurits's *coup d'état*.

Thus, the first priority of the new regime in church affairs was to establish Counter-Remonstrant congregations where these were lacking and assign to them the principal churches. At Utrecht, the (still predominantly Remonstrant) consistory was asked to surrender the cathedral to those of the 'true Reformed religion' voluntarily, to avoid disturbances, but refused. In September 1618, the new Counter-Remonstrant Pensionary harangued the consistory but the latter remained adamant that there was no basis on which they could be dispossessed of the city's main church before the National Synod had even commenced.[23] Eventually, the *vroedschap* expelled them but, for some months, still permitted Remonstrant services in the city's other public churches. Only in February 1619 did the *vroedschap* forbid Remonstrant preachers to conduct services, in the city, and only following the Synod were they stripped of their livings—and houses, where these belonged to the consistory.

At Utrecht, Haarlem, and Leiden, where there was strong Counter-Remonstrant support, the purging of Remonstrantism began early and

---

[20] GA Kampen Oud-archief 24, fo. 132. res. raad, 2 Aug. 1620.
[21] Spaans, *Haarlem*, 158.
[22] Wijminga, *Festus Hommius*, 180–1, 260.
[23] GA Utrecht 2/121. res. vroed. 3 Sept. 1618.

proceeded in stages. By contrast, in Rotterdam, Gouda, Alkmaar, and Kampen, where the citizenry were predominantly Remonstrant in sympathy, the town councils were much slower to act and had done little, or nothing, by the time the National Synod concluded its deliberations. At Alkmaar, no move was made until a special commission, including Petrus Plancius, arrived—amid the jeers of a Remonstrant crowd; Maurits had to send troops, to secure the city, before the commission could set to work.[24] Under armed guard, they examined the preachers of the classis, of whom they dismissed four. The first Counter-Remonstrant services in the main church at Alkmaar were highly charged events likewise conducted under armed guard. At Gouda, the new Counter-Remonstrant *vroedschap* proceeded with equal caution.[25] They dared not dispossess the Remonstrants of the great Sint Jans Church until after the formal condemnation of Remonstrantism and it was not until 28 July 1619 that the first Counter-Remonstrant sermon—delivered by a preacher borrowed from Delft—was read in the main church. Even then, the occasion was a disaster from the Counter-Remonstrant point of view.[26] Congregants jeered, and stamped their feet, the solemnities lapsing into uproar. Over the next weeks, the city seethed with unrest. Remonstrant conventicles were held and there were street disturbances. Worried, the *Gecommitteerde Raden* sent two of its members to the Gouda *vroedschap*, offering troops.

The trial of Oldenbarnevelt, Grotius, and Hogerbeets too proceeded slowly. It was a trial of great political significance and also one which posed some difficulty from a jurisdictional point of view, being unlike any previously conducted in the Republic. The first question to resolve was whether the men were being tried by the Generality or States of Holland. The latter pointed out that they were the judicial authority in Holland; but the other provinces argued that the treason, of which the defendants were being accused, had been perpetrated against the Generality.[27] Under the eventual compromise, it was a trial by the States General but with the States of Holland playing a special role. Twenty-four judges were chosen—twelve representing Holland and twelve the other six provinces, two from each—among them Pauw, Jacob van Broekhoven (leader of the Counter-Remonstrant party at Leiden). Adriaen Ploos (Utrecht), Goosen Schaffer (Groningen), and Maurits's proxy as First Noble of Zeeland, Adriaen Manmaker.

[24] Van der Ploeg, *Uit Alkmaars roemrijk verleden*, 45.
[25] GA Gouda OA 8 res. vroed. 23 and 28 Nov. 1618.
[26] Geselschap, *Gouda*, 306–7.
[27] Brandt, *Historie van de rechtspleging*, 53–5.

The trial dragged on for months. Oldenbarnevelt was dignified, even defiant. Grotius protested that the States General were not his sovereign and had no competence to try him, and his colleagues, but was otherwise submissive.[28] The judges held that sovereignty in the United Provinces was divided between the States General and the individual provinces, rejecting Grotius' view that each province possessed the sovereign right to settle the public Church as it saw fit, within its own borders. They also denied that individual provinces could legitimately raise troops or issue military orders. Oldenbarnevelt, Grotius, and Hogerbeets were found guilty of treason, on 12 May 1619. To Oldenbarnevelt's amazement (and that of many others), he was sentenced to death, the sentence to be carried out the next day, to avoid intercessions on his behalf. Even so, various personages at The Hague, including the French ambassador and Louise de Coligny, pleaded for his life. But Maurits remained adamant that reason of state required the old man's execution.[29] On 13 May 1619, Holland's 72-year-old Advocate was led out and beheaded, before a large crowd, at the Binnenhof.

Grotius and Hogerbeets were sentenced to life imprisonment. The great scholar was transferred to Loevestein castle but, being who he was, could not decently be denied great quantities of books and paper for his research and writing. Whilst in prison he wrote much of his *De Veritate Religionis Christianae* and his introduction to the law of Holland. Eventually, his guards tired of searching his chests of books and it was in an empty chest that his wife and servants effected his famous escape, in March 1621. He fled to Antwerp, where he lodged with the former Rotterdam preacher Grevinchoven. On the expiry of the Truce, however, not wishing to attract adverse publicity in the Republic by staying in the Spanish Netherlands, he removed to Paris, where he spent most of the rest of his life.

The purges, trial of Oldenbarnevelt, National Synod, and suppression of Remonstrantism imparted a new feel to the United Provinces, a changed atmosphere, reflected in many aspects of Dutch life. In the larger Holland towns, where the Stadholder's influence in *vroedschap* elections had lapsed to a formality, or altogether, before 1618, stricter regulation by the Stadholder was reimposed after 1618. At Alkmaar, where the States had been regulating *vroedschap* elections since 1610 but, in practice, leaving the *vroedschap* free to co-opt its own members, this freedom ended and the Stadholder took to choosing members from double lists presented to him each year.

---

[28] Ibid. 87.   [29] Ibid. 251.

Maurits was not particularly concerned to promote the glorification of his own person. Nevertheless, the change of regime, and his enhanced prestige, led to his portrait, and Orangist political allegories, engraved and painted, becoming more prevalent than before. Until August 1618, many people had displayed portrait prints of Oldenbarnevelt, Arminius, Uyttenbogaert, and Grotius in their homes. These were now removed.[30] Glorifying the House of Orange, through art chosen to embellish public buildings, and rich men's houses, became—together with honouring the National Synod and sundry Calvinist theologians—integral to Counter-Remonstrant civic culture. A notable example is a large political allegory, celebrating the House of Orange, commissioned by the Haarlem *vroedschap* from Hendrik Pot, in 1620; it extols the Christian virtues and political, as well as military, skills of leading members of the House since William the Silent, including his brothers, killed at Mook in 1574—a picture housed today (still in its magnificent original frame) in the Frans Hals Museum, in Haarlem. Several artists depicted Maurits overseeing the disbandment of the *waardgelders* at Utrecht, in July 1618, one of the graphic moments of the Counter-Remonstrant revolution, incorporating crowds of Counter-Remonstrant nobles, officers, and burghers, sporting orange cloaks, hatbands, plumes, garters, and sashes. Adriaen van der Venne produced a series of imposing engravings of Maurits and Frederik Hendrik in the years around 1620.

THE SYNOD OF DORDRECHT (DORDT), 1618–1619

The tensely awaited National Synod finally convened—at Dordrecht rather than Amsterdam, as Pauw had hoped—in November 1618. From the outset, the Counter-Remonstrants intended it to be an international Calvinist gathering, authoritative for the whole of Reformed Europe, as well as the United Provinces. Outside the Republic, the synod was to be of particular importance for the Reformed Churches' position in Germany. The Dutch participants were divided into ten 'colleges', one for each of the eight provincial synods, one for the Walloon Church (see p. 628 below), and the tenth for the theology faculties of the universities.[31] The foreign colleges comprised delegations from Britain, Switzerland, and Germany. It had been hoped that the French Reformed Churches would also participate but Louis XIII refused to allow the Huguenots to attend, so that their place had to be marked by a symbolic empty bench (see PLATE 13). The foreign colleges, especially the British, were by no means mere spectators and exerted a

[30] Harvard, *Michiel van Mierevelt*, 88.
[31] Kaajan, *Groote synode van Dordrecht*, 27, 33, 75.

certain moderating influence over the proceedings.[32] There were six official delegates from Britain, five from England and one, Walter Balcanqual, from Scotland. There were ten German delegates in three delegations, from the Palatinate, Hesse, and Bremen.

Each college drew up its views, on each point, and delivered a single vote. To preside, the gathering chose Johannes Bogerman, leader of the Frisian delegation, and a well-known Counter-Remonstrant controversialist. The synod was held under the auspices of the States General,[33] and in the presence of eighteen political commissioners, one of whom was Jacob de Witt, father of the future Pensionary of Holland. The agenda was by no means confined to the issue of Remonstrantism. Numerous other matters were dealt with including Church–State relations, procedures for appointing preachers, relations with the Lutheran Church, and, at a later stage (at the desire of James I of England), the question of bishops, and episcopal organization, in a Reformed context. Another theme was the need for an authorized 'States' Bible, that is a Dutch Bible approved by the public Church and States General.[34] There were already several Dutch versions of Scripture. But the synod took the view that an entirely fresh, and authoritative, translation, from the Hebrew, Aramaic, and Greek, was required, giving the appointed team of six chief translators, the exacting task of rendering Scripture into a standard Dutch. States Bible Dutch was to be a carefully crafted compromise, especially between Brabants and Hollands.[35]

Even so, the National Synod was dominated by the issue of Arminianism. The Remonstrant preachers still residing in the Republic—Uyttenbogaert had fled, the day after Oldenbarnevelt's arrest—chose their most formidable spokesman, Simon Episcopius, to lead their delegation. He was accompanied by other prominent Remonstrant preachers, including Bernardus Dwinglo and Johannes Corvinus, veteran publicists, from Leiden. Theological connoisseurs curious whether the Arminians would adopt a submissive, or defiant, stance learnt the answer, on 7 December, when Episcopius delivered a powerful address restating the Arminian case, demanding toleration within the public Church on all but the most fundamental points, and making some unflattering allusions to Prince Maurits. The Remonstrants had reacted to the official propaganda campaign against them by feeding the current of innuendo about the Prince's notorious sexual promiscuity. This lent bite to veiled remarks about him made in official contexts.

[32] Van den Berg, *Dordt in de Weegschaal*, 5.
[33] Van Gelder, *Getemperde vrijheid*, 8.
[34] Broek Roelofs, *Wilhelmus Baudartius*, 152–3.
[35] De Vooys, *Gesch. van de Ned. taal*, 108–9.

Uyttenbogaert, as former preacher at the Binnenhof, was amply informed about Maurits's compulsive pursuit of women of every description and the Remonstrants deliberately fed such talk—and the charge that the Prince aspired to sovereignty over the United Provinces—to impugn his reputation and integrity.[36]

That the National Synod would condemn Arminius and Remonstrantism was scarcely in doubt. Nevertheless, such a gathering could not proceed to do so until all aspects of the matter had been thoroughly considered. This was inevitable in a great international theological gathering, but, from the point of view of Maurits and the Counter-Remonstrants, hardly convenient. For the delay hampered suppression of Remonstrantism in Holland, Utrecht, and the parts of Gelderland and Overijssel where it was entrenched, allowing the Remonstrants a respite in which to organize and react. The news, in March 1619, of a rival Remonstrant synod, held in secret, at Rotterdam, only added to Counter-Remonstrant impatience. During March, the Republic was shaken by a wave of pro-Remonstrant disturbances at Rotterdam, Hoorn, Alkmaar, and Kampen.[37] Troops had to be deployed to restore order.

It was not until the 137th sitting of the synod, in May 1619, that the assembly finally condemned the Remonstrants as heretics, disseminators of false doctrine, and '*perturbateurs*' of state and Church. A list of Arminian preachers was drawn up together with a formula of submission to which those prepared to recant (and keep their livings), and remain within the public Church, would have to subscribe. The formula pledged adherence to the Netherlands Confession and Heidelberg catechism, and acceptance of the Acts of the National Synod. Of Remonstrants present at Dordrecht, only Henricus Leo, preacher at Zaltbommel, signed and kept his living. Those who refused were referred to the States General for banishment from the Republic. In June 1619, after 180 sessions, the thirty-one Dutch and twenty-eight foreign theologians gathered at Dordrecht concluded their deliberations and received the approbation of the States General, and provincial assemblies, for their resolutions or 'Acts'.

In all about 200 Remonstrant preachers were deprived of their livings and the right to preach by the Dutch provincial and civic authorities during 1619.[38] Of these, around forty were subsequently rehabilitated after complying with the formula of submission. Another seventy or so were permanently stripped of their pulpits but allowed to live quietly as private citizens

[36] Rogge, *Johannes Wttenbogaert*, ii. 278–9.
[37] Smit, 'Prins Maurits en de goede zaak', 143–6.
[38] Kaajan, *Groote synode van Dordrecht*, 183.

after signing a promise not to preach or engage further in theological dispute. The rest, those who refused to sign, or remain silent, totalling over eighty, were banished from the Republic, their expulsion being entrusted to the *Gecommitteerde Raden* and Delegated States of the respective provinces. Those who sought to evade expulsion, and continue preaching clandestinely, could expect to be hunted and, if caught, imprisoned.

Meanwhile, Uyttenbogaert, Episcopius, and their colleagues, in their places of refuge, had by no means given up the struggle. In October 1619, Uyttenbogaert convened a Remonstrant synod, at Antwerp, with permission of the Archduke Albert, who was eager to keep the Dutch theological strife on the boil. The Antwerp gathering was attended by some forty Remonstrant preachers. They drew up rules and procedures for their international Remonstrant Church in exile and initiated negotiations with the Danish Crown and several German towns, seeking permission for the public exercise of their faith. The Danish king permitted exiled Dutch Remonstrants to settle in his new port of Glückstadt, in Holstein, on the lower Elbe, below Hamburg. The Antwerp synod also agreed plans to arrange clandestine preaching in the main centres of Remonstrant support in the Republic, and secret fund-raising, with which to pay stipends to Remonstrant preachers whether within the Republic or in exile.[39] These efforts to organize met with some success. During 1621, the Dutch Remonstrant Church in exile collected over 20,000 guilders in Holland, the bulk from the five towns where Remonstrant support was strong—Rotterdam, The Hague, Gouda, Alkmaar, and Hoorn—but also from Amsterdam, where, since 1617, the Remonstrants had gained some support.[40] Very little was collected elsewhere and nothing at all from Dordrecht, where Remonstrantism was practically non-existent.

Joined by their families and a few businessmen, often relatives, the Remonstrant preachers in exile formed congregations at Antwerp, Waalwijk, a Brabant border village under the archduke's control (close to Heusden), Hamburg, Glückstadt, Friedrichstadt, and Wesel, in the duchy of Cleves, where the Spanish governor (who already allowed Reformed, as well as Catholic, worship)[41] was favourably disposed. But on the expiry of the Truce, in April 1621, most Remonstrants in the Spanish Netherlands departed in order to avoid the stigma of being on enemy territory.[42] Many migrated to north-western Germany; Uyttenbogaert and Episcopius, like Grotius, moved to France.

[39] Haentjens, *Simon Episcopius*, 55.
[40] Brandt, *Historie der Reformaties*, iv. 628.
[41] ARH Hof van Holland 5225, 'Examen Johannes Grevius', fo. iv.
[42] Van Limborch, *Leven van Simon Episcopius*, 120–1.

Until 1618 Remonstrant influence had been widespread in Holland and by no means only in the main towns. Remonstrantism had been strong also in Utrecht and, after 1619, the Remonstrant Church in exile was able to keep communities in being at Utrecht, Amersfoort, Wijk-bij-Duurstede, and also in the villages of Woudenburg and Bunschoten.[43] In addition, there were still pockets of Remonstrant support in Overijssel, the Nijmegen quarter, and at Dokkum, in Friesland. Also the Remonstrant Church in exile disposed of a number of preachers of exceptionally high intellectual and moral calibre. But while it proved possible to sustain links with the main centres of Remonstrant support within the Republic, it was difficult to do so—either from abroad or the main centres within the Republic—with the many small towns and villages where, prior to 1619, Remonstrant preachers had built up a following. Thus, it is by no means correct to say that the Counter-Remonstrant repression of the years 1618–21 was ineffective. On the contrary, it severely taxed the limited resources of the Remonstrant Church in exile and eroded its following, especially outside the main cities of Holland.

Counter-Remonstrant suppression of Remonstrantism, in the years after 1619, was far from brutal. But it was determined and real. Remonstrant preachers who defied the States, and continued working clandestinely in the Republic, needed courage and tenacity. Johannes Grevius, Voetius' rival at Heusden, returned, after the Antwerp synod, and secretly toured Overijssel and Gelderland. During his month in Kampen, he held eleven prayer-meetings in different private homes, each time preaching to around twenty 'brothers'. In order not to give themselves away, he and his secret flock dispensed with psalm-singing.[44] But eventually he was caught, tried, and imprisoned. Later he escaped, and settled in Hamburg; but, after years of sacrifice, he lost heart, abandoning the struggle. So did others. Thomas Goswinius, leading Remonstrant preacher at Kampen, gave up, under relentless persecution, in 1623. He signed his submission and retired to live as a private citizen. The difficulties, and defections, sapped Remonstrant morale. Not many could muster the resolve of the Leiden preacher (of Walloon extraction) Paschier de Fijne, who also attended the Antwerp synod and returned to preach clandestinely in the Republic. He was active in much of South Holland, a legendary figure who preached in the villages of Warmond, Oegstgeest, and Zoetermeer, as well as in the towns.[45] On a cold winter's day, at Gouda, he delivered a sermon in the open air, standing

[43] Tideman, *Remonstrantsche broederschap*, 305.
[44] ARH Hof van Holland 5225, 'Examen Johannes Grevius', fo. 2.
[45] De Fijne, *Eenige Tractaatjes*, i. 'Vaderlyk Onderwys', 21–3.

on a horse-drawn sledge, on an iced-over canal, escaping at speed over the ice before his pursuers could seize him. Remonstrantism survived as a significant force in Dutch life, but as a shrinking movement dying away in many places where it had formerly enjoyed support.

MAURITS, THE COUNTER-REMONSTRANTS, AND THE COMMENCEMENT OF THE THIRTY YEARS WAR

The Calvinist revolution of the Counter-Remonstrants altered the political balance within the Republic, made the Dutch Reformed Church a bastion of Calvinist orthodoxy, and changed the tone of Dutch life in the short and medium term. It also made the United Provinces the hub of international Calvinism, only temporarily, it is true, but at precisely the moment when the intensification of pressures within the Holy Roman Empire led to the onset of the Thirty Years War and when the international community—as well as the Dutch and Spaniards—began to focus their minds on the approaching end of the Twelve Years Truce. The Calvinist revolution in the Republic thus played a key role both in the making of the Thirty Years War and the outbreak of the second part of the Eighty Years War between the Dutch and Spain.

In Germany, the Lutheran states mostly adhered to a conservative policy of non-confrontation with the Habsburgs. Relations between Lutherans and Calvinists were difficult and tense. There were several areas of acute Protestant–Catholic rivalry, above all Bohemia and the middle Rhine, but the militant Protestant party, mostly Calvinists and semi-Calvinists, knew that they could expect little help or encouragement from most foreign Protestant powers. The Swedish Crown was absorbed in conflict with Poland. Denmark showed interest but lacked the resources to take the lead. James I of England made it clear that his policy was non-interventionist and conciliatory towards the Habsburgs. He tried to dissuade his son-in-law, Frederick, Elector of the Palatinate, and leader of the German Calvinist princes, from accepting the crown, offered to him by the Bohemian Protestant rebels. In the circumstances of 1618–20 the militant Protestant states in Germany could expect extensive backing from only one source: the United Provinces.[46] No one knew whether or not the Twelve Years Truce would be renewed on its expiry in 1621. But, in 1618–19, both Spain and the Dutch had their hands free to intervene in Germany and these two powers, deeply wary of each other, were the chief sources of troops, military

---

[46] Gindely, *Geschichte des Böhmischen Aufstandes*, i. 454 and ii. 235.

expertise, supplies, and money on the borders of the Empire. Since the fall of Oldenbarnevelt, the United Provinces were presided over by the Prince and Counter-Remonstrants, the men who had opposed the Truce, and avowed unswerving adherence to Calvinist orthodoxy, and hostility to Catholicism. Spain, still the pre-eminent European power, had little to fear, for the time being, from her traditional rival, France. Since the assassination of Henri IV, in 1610, France had withdrawn into an attitude conciliatory towards Spain and hostile to Protestantism.

In the circumstances, The Hague was the only place to which the Bohemian rebels and German Protestant Union could realistically look for support. By ousting Oldenbarnevelt, Maurits had not only placed himself at the helm of the Dutch state but at the centre of the European stage.[47] His every action was now being minutely scrutinized in Germany, England, France, Spain, and also Italy, where the Venetian Republic—at this time in confrontation with Spain and the Emperor—signed a defensive alliance with the Dutch in 1619, hoping, by drawing the Dutch in, to ease the pressure on themselves. The Remonstrants may have been right that Maurits had an unprepossessing character—vengeful, calculating, ambitious, and lustful— but it was, in many ways, ideal for the dangerous predicament in which the Republic now found itself. The unfathomable, and cautious, Maurits kept even the most astute observers guessing. A prince of great military experience and prestige, slow to act but capable of forceful measures, he preoccupied himself almost obsessively, and for long periods, with complex political problems. Sick with fever in January 1620, he 'ceaseth not', noted Carleton, 'most hours of the day to attend business'.[48]

Maurits liked to take decisions himself, consulting only with his circle of close confidants. In any case, he had little alternative, for his *coup d'état* had eliminated the regents with knowledge and experience of international affairs and running the Dutch military machine. The change in the Dutch body politic wrought by the events of 1618 was both drastic and fundamental, or so it seemed in the years immediately following. The French ambassador at The Hague, Du Maurier, reported to Paris late in 1619 that, since Oldenbarnevelt's downfall, the States of Holland 'estant à present si égaux en authorité et en ignorance', exerted practically no influence on Dutch statecraft.[49] Maurits and his inner circle—Van Aerssen, Van de Bouchorst, Ploos, Van Randwijk, and the Frisian Stadholder, Willem Lodewijk—all noblemen, decided everything, ensuring that nothing of

---

[47] Polisensky, *Tragic Triangle*, 185–208.
[48] Carleton, *Letters*, 441.
[49] Ouvré, *Aubéry du Maurier*, 308.

significance regarding the two great issues of the day—the Bohemian Revolt and expiry of the Truce—came before the provincial assemblies, or States General.[50] The only province which showed stirrings of independence during this period was Gelderland, which, in May 1620, concurred with the rest over the proposed West India Company but also expressed anxiety lest the project prejudice prospects for renewing the Truce;[51] in the autumn of 1620, the States of Gelderland instructed their deputies at The Hague to 'advance the renewing of the Truce all they possibly may'.[52] But the rest, including Holland, were inactive and quiescent.

Nevertheless, Maurits and the Republic, locked in strategic confrontation with Spain, without prospect of the pressure being relieved by France or England, and with a major conflagration commencing in Germany, faced a harsh dilemma. Whatever strategy was adopted regarding Germany, and Spain, carried great risks. The domestic arena too remained fraught with difficulties. The Remonstrants had been defeated; but tension between the rival politico-theological blocs persisted and in several Holland towns there were sporadic disturbances. Furthermore, not only Gelderland but Overijssel and Utrecht shrank from a resumption of war with Spain, and the attendant burdens and taxation. Opinion in these provinces favoured renewing the Truce,[53] while the newly dominant bloc in Holland, and the Zeelanders, out of maritime and colonial considerations, preferred to renew the war.[54] Maurits also had to contend with the perennial rift between Groningen and the Ommelands and a potentially dangerous split in Friesland, especially after Willem Lodewijk's death, in June 1620, left a worrying vacuum which local nobles, adhering to the traditions of the Roordists, exploited, concerting a campaign to appoint a new Stadholder, from outside the House of Orange-Nassau, in reaction to what many Frisians regarded as Willem Lodewijk's excessive subservience to Maurits, the Generality, and The Hague. Maurits contemplated intervening to arrange the stadholderate of Friesland to be conferred upon himself. 'But that will raise jealousy', noted Carleton, 'besides the inconvenience of having those parts governed by deputies.'[55] Two other candidates presented themselves from within the House of Orange-Nassau—Maurits's younger half-brother, Frederik Hendrik, and Willem Lodewijk's brother, Ernst Casimir (see Table 25). Friesland chose Ernst Casimir, a zealous Counter-Remonstrant who had assisted with

[50] Israel, *Dutch Republic and the Hispanic World*, 74–81.
[51] ARH PR 8. res. SGeld. 9 May 1620.
[52] PRO SP 84/98, fo. 145v. Carleton to Nethersole, 8 June 1621.
[53] Israel, *Dutch Republic and the Hispanic World*, 63–4, 74.
[54] Ibid. 77–81.
[55] Carleton, *Letters*, 473.

the purging of the Holland town councils. Groningen and Drenthe, however, chose Maurits, who promptly accepted, assuring Carleton that he had only desired the stadholderate of Groningen and Drenthe 'lest it should otherwise have gone out of the house of Nassau'.[56]

Internally, Maurits's great problem was the tenacity of Remonstrant opposition. Following riots in March 1619, there were further disturbances at Alkmaar and Schoonhoven in July, and at Rotterdam in October. Again troops were deployed, to suppress disorder, causing several deaths. In November 1619, the Prince turned to the last two town councils on his list to be purged—Zaltbommel and Tiel, Remonstrant towns in the west of the Nijmegen quarter. After that, all the town councils were controlled by Counter-Remonstrants. But Counter-Remonstrant regents in Holland, including his chief allies at Amsterdam, Pauw and Witsen, were beginning to be seen as spineless pawns of the Stadholder, so that opposing Counter-Remonstrantism, in Holland regent circles, was beginning to take on the air of a movement aimed at reviving Holland's power and influence. At Amsterdam, there was mounting criticism of Pauw and Witsen, on the part of *politique* and opportunist regents who were turning simultaneously anti-Pauw, anti-Orangist, and anti-Calvinist. Maurits warned that he would not permit the Amsterdam regents removed in 1618 to be brought back into the *vroedschap*.[57] In December 1619, the Prince closely regulated the *vroedschap* elections at Gouda, Hoorn, Alkmaar, and Kampen, all towns where Remonstrantism remained vigorous.

The external dilemmas confronting Maurits interacted with the internal pressures in a multiplicity of ways. Spanish ministers, seeing the continuing intensity of the theologico-political rift within the United Provinces, were inclined to count heavily on its disruptive effect, leading them to adopt more forward strategies than they might otherwise have done.[58] This, from Maurits's point of view, was an advantage, for it reduced the likelihood of Spain offering plausible truce proposals which would be bound to exacerbate the differences between the provinces. For, in that case, Gelderland, Overijssel, and Utrecht would wish to accept whilst the Counter-Remonstrant regents of Holland and Zeeland would not.[59] Other aspects of the interaction, however, were altogether unhelpful. One particularly worrying consequence of the riots was that the Prince had to keep a sizeable military force stationed in the interior of the Republic—at Utrecht, Hoorn, Schoon-

[56] PRO SP 84/98, fo. 148. Carleton to James I, 29 Dec. 1620.
[57] Smit, 'Prins Maurits en de goede zaak', 152.
[58] AGS Estado 2034. Bedmar to Philip III, Brussels, 1 Feb. 1620.
[59] KBH MS 75 k 83. 'Op Peckij propositie', fo. 2.

hoven, Alkmaar, and Oudewater—far from the main Dutch defensive ring, thus weakening the Republic's overall strategic position. In June 1620, Carleton reported that some forty companies of troops were tied down in Holland and Utrecht to control the 'Arminian towns'.[60]

Dutch policy diverged sharply from English policy in central Europe in 1618–19 and was also more important in shaping the opening phase of the Thirty Years War. The key to Maurits's statecraft was his need to minimize Spanish pressure on the Republic and, so far as he could, divert its impact into Germany. His overriding priority was to prevent an open split among the provinces, and Spain exploiting the Republic's continuing domestic difficulties.[61] Consequently, though James and English ministers had expected that, by helping the Counter-Remonstrants in 1617–18, they would achieve a harnessing of Dutch policy to English policy, in fact, as Carleton soon came to realize, Maurits's objectives in Germany and Bohemia had nothing in common with England's. On the contrary, Maurits sought to influence the Elector of the Palatinate, Frederick V (1596–1632), who was also his nephew (Frederick's father having married Louise Juliana Vom Nassau, eldest child of William the Silent's third marriage, and Maurits's half-sister; see Table 25), in a quite different direction. James, realizing the combustible implications, strove to restrain his son-in-law, warning that he could expect no help if he accepted the Bohemian crown. Maurits, designing to deflect pressure from the Republic by stoking up conflict in Germany, promised his nephew his full support.[62] Frederick hesitated many months before finally accepting the crown of Bohemia—a decision which hurled central Europe into a horrendous war and proved totally disastrous for himself and the Palatinate. During this period of hesitation, Maurits's intervention, and encouragement, was of decisive importance.[63] By offering the Bohemians a subsidy of 50,000 guilders monthly and, subsequently, a like sum to the German Protestant Union, and promising to send troops both to Bohemia and the Palatinate, Maurits and his entourage materially contributed to precipitating the great conflict. Money and troops were dispatched. The United Provinces also helped raise loans for Bohemia, in Amsterdam, and provided weapons and munitions. About one-eighth of the Protestant army which faced the might of the Emperor, and king of Spain, at the battle of the White Mountain, in November 1620, amounting to over 5,000 men, was Dutch or paid for by the Dutch.

[60] PRO SP 84/95, fo. 271v. Carleton to James I, 19 June 1620.
[61] De Boer, 'Hervatting der vijandelijkheden', 48–9.
[62] Van der Kemp, *Maurits van Nassau*, iv. 142.
[63] Aubéry du Maurier, *Mémoires*, 242–3; Ouvré, *Aubéry du Maurier*, 507.

TABLE 25. *Genealogical table of the House of Orange-Nassau in the Netherlands*

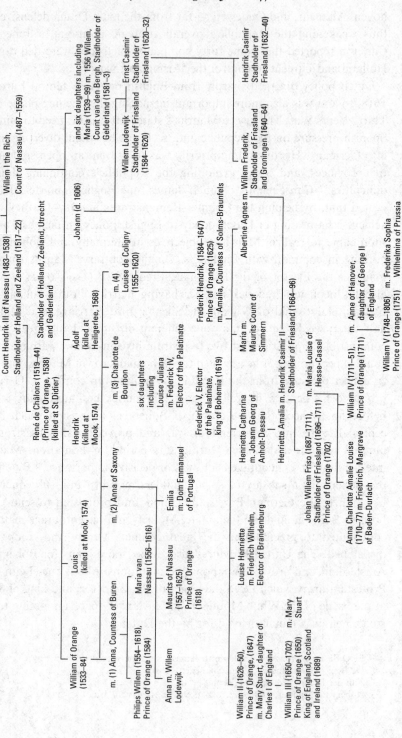

Even after the débâcle of the White Mountain, Maurits and his entourage hoped to gain from their investment in the German war. Maurits ordered the Dutch troops, garrisoning Pilsen to hold out in the hope of encouraging other Bohemian towns to resist. When Frederick and Elizabeth, the 'Winter King and Queen', fled to The Hague, with only half of the Palatinate occupied by Spanish and Bavarian troops, Maurits urged him to go back, and fight, instead of abandoning his lands 'too soon and lightly'.[64] Maurits laboured to mobilize international Protestant support for the Palatinate. Repeatedly he sent Arnold van Randwijk to confer with the princes of the German Protestant Union to harden their resolve. He exploited the mounting uncertainty over whether the United Provinces would agree to a new truce, promising the German princes that 'either they shall have the use, this next summer, of a good part of the [Dutch] army, in Germany, or the benefitt of a diversion in these parts, according as the ceasing, or renewing, of the Truce shall minister occasion'.[65] Maurits also pressed James to do more for his daughter and son-in-law and did much to facilitate the logistics of English intervention. The 4,000 English troops dispatched to the Palatinate, in September 1620, were armed, fed, and transported by the Dutch. Their march up the Rhine was covered by a column of Dutch cavalry commanded by Frederik Hendrik and Marquette. At the same time, Maurits sent Dutch troops to occupy the island of Papenmutze, in the Rhine between Cologne and Bonn, as a warning to the Elector of Cologne and other Rhenish ecclesiastical princes not to interfere.[66]

James was far from pleased by the trend of events. During the calamitous autumn of 1620, he partly blamed the Dutch for the reverses suffered in the Empire, by the Protestant cause, and admonished Maurits and his advisers to 'call to mind the encouragements they gave the Bohemians from time to time in the resolution they took of the election of a new king, of which the trouble of Germany is a consequence; and the promise they have given in writing to the princes [of the German Protestant Union] . . . if the enemy marched that way to assist them with troops'.[67] Maurits was reminded that the king of England had 'no part in the first motives of those troubles' and that the English king was not 'engaged, as they are, by promise' to send troops to the Palatinate.

Maurits deliberately veiled his intentions with regard to renewing the Truce, so as to cause maximum uncertainty and confusion. It was a form of statecraft in which he excelled. The Venetian ambassador at The Hague

[64] PRO SP 84/99, fos. 147 and 191. Carleton to Calvert, 11 and 21 Feb. 1621.
[65] PRO SP 84/99, fo. 191v. Carleton to Calvert, 21 Feb. 1621.
[66] Israel, *Empires and Entrepots*, 6, 217.
[67] Carleton, *Letters*, 475.

admitted he was completely baffled by Maurits's evasive and contradictory utterances.[68] The Archduke Albert, in Brussels, was at a loss to know what to make of Maurits's cryptic replies to his messages. There was continual contact between The Hague and Brussels during 1620–1, but Maurits confided what was happening only to his own inner circle—especially Van Aerssen, Van den Bouchorst, Marquette, and Duyck.[69] The States of Holland, and other provincial assemblies, were left completely in the dark. Maurits, devious, methodical, and circumspect, deliberately delayed the setting up of the West India Company during the years 1619–21 so as to avoid obstructing the new truce should he opt for renewal.[70]

Maurits's master-stroke was his invitation to Archduke Albert to send a representative to The Hague to negotiate an end to the war, in the Low Countries, on the basis of token recognition of the sovereignty of the king of Spain.[71] Albert, not realizing that Maurits was luring him into a trap, sent Chancellor Peckius of Brabant to address the States General along the lines Orange suggested. If Peckius had simply proposed renewal of the truce, stating Spain's demands for modifications to the existing terms, the divisions among the provinces would have been exposed for all to see. Maurits's aim was to prevent this and cause a rapid breakdown of formal talks, ending the role of the States General, and provincial, leading them to empower him to take sole charge of further contacts, deal secretly, and only disclose Spanish proposals to the provinces when he judged it appropriate to do so. The plan worked to perfection. The one issue capable of aborting formal negotiations immediately, and eliciting a totally unified response from the States General, was any form of Habsburg claim to sovereignty over the United Provinces. Peckius duly arrived and talked of sovereignty, instantly angering his hosts and destroying the negotiations. Holland's delegation prepared the States General's reply, employing a form of words which embodied the Counter-Remonstrant view of the Dutch state, the notion which was now the official view of the regime. 'Undoubtedly and indisputably the sovereignty and supremacy of the United Provinces', Peckius was told, 'resides in the States General and the respective provinces.'[72]

The States General then authorized Maurits to keep all further truce contacts with Albert and Spain secret, and in his own hands, only disclosing affairs to the States General, and the provinces, when he saw fit. Carleton

---

[68] Geyl, *Christoforo Suriano*, 306–7.
[69] Carleton, *Letters*, 488.
[70] PRO SP 84/94, fo. 16v. Carleton to Buckingham, 3 Jan. 1620.
[71] Israel, *Dutch Republic and the Hispanic World*, 76–81.
[72] Aitzema, *Historie*, i, 85.

had already noted, in August 1620, that 'though we have the body of the States, the soul may be said to be absent, because all power upon the present occurrences is in the hands of the Prince of Orange, and such of the States as are with him, who do not so much as give an account to these here, at The Hague, either of their deliberations or resolutions'.[73] This abrogation of power by the States of Holland was placed on a formal basis by a States General resolution of 25 March 1621. Enhancing the power of the Stadholder was, indeed, a Counter-Remonstrant strategy, rooted in fear that the 'very proposition of a new treaty', as Carleton put it, 'will distract them here very much in regard of their unsettledness and aptness upon any dispute to relapse into faction'.[74] A strong Stadholder had become essential to Counter-Remonstrantism.

Had Spain offered a straight renewal of the Truce, on the terms of 1609, Maurits told Peckius (and repeated in subsequent secret messages to Brussels), he, and the States General, would have responded favourably. This was probably true, since Maurits's complex manœuvring, delaying of the West India Company, and reluctance to open hostilities, in 1621, all pointed, as the most acute diplomatic observers (eventually) realized, to Maurits's preference for a new truce, on the same basis as the old, and a diverting of war to Germany. Should Spain propose 'renewing the truce in terms as it formerly stood', Carleton assured London, in March 1621, 'I find that [the Prince] will leane to the five provinces and oversway the other two'—that is, overrule Holland and Zeeland.[75] But in Madrid, the new Spanish ministers believed the Twelve Years Truce had been prejudicial to Spain and that the truce should not be renewed unless the 'rebels' made substantive concessions in the maritime and colonial sphere. The Spanish court made three demands in return for renewal of the truce, of which the first two were essential: Dutch evacuation of the Indies east and west; the lifting of the Scheldt restrictions; and toleration of public practice of the Catholic religion in the 'rebel' provinces.[76] Maurits was not prepared to discuss these terms, or see them debated in the provincial assemblies.

After the Truce expired, in April 1621, there was no immediate resumption of hostilities. Maurits continued sending messages to Brussels reiterating his concurrence in a new truce provided Spain ceased demanding concessions. Six months later, in September, Maurits intimated to (what was now, following the Archduke Albert's death, in July, again) the Spanish

[73] Carleton, *Letters*, 488.
[74] PRO SP 84/95, fo. 210. Carleton to Buckingham, 10 June 1620.
[75] Ibid. 84/100, fo. 34. Carleton to Calvert, 20 Mar. 1621.
[76] ARB SEG 185, fos. 24r–24v. Philip III to Albert, 4 Feb. 1621.

regime, in Brussels, that if Spain would agree to renew the truce he would consider lifting the Scheldt restrictions and, possibly, arrange some concession in the Indies.[77] Neither the States General nor the States of Holland had any precise knowledge of Maurits's dealings—partly through the great painter, Rubens, in Antwerp—with the Infanta Isabella, in Brussels, during the years 1620–3. But it did become widely known at The Hague, and the Dutch provincial capitals, as well as Antwerp and Brussels, that the Stadholder was conducting a secret dialogue with the Infanta and Spain, and that he was endeavouring to renew the truce.[78] The rumours worried hardline Counter-Remonstrants and pro-war regents eager to resume the struggle and set up the West India Company, and, behind the scenes, generated some caustic comment about the Stadholder's entourage and methods of running the Republic.

THE BEGINNINGS OF THE FURTHER REFORMATION

The Calvinist revolution of the Counter-Remonstrants altered the shape of the Republic's politics, imposed confessional discipline on the public Church, and influenced the outbreak of the Thirty Years War. In addition, it set up the West India Company and marked the commencement of the Further Reformation.

Maurits's *coup d'état* of 1618 enabled the Counter-Remonstrants to settle the doctrinal disputes within the public Church. But some Counter-Remonstrants felt that a broader programme of purification of religious life and society was needed than followed from merely settling the theological issues and expelling adherents of unsound doctrine. The foremost exponent of this view was the Zeelander Willem Teellinck (1579–1629), the 'Reformed Thomas à Kempis', as one of his chief admirers, Gisbertus Voetius—the future standard-bearer of the Dutch Further Reformation—was to call him. Teellinck shared all the usual Counter-Remonstrant intolerance of Arminians, Catholics, Lutherans, and Jews, and was as ardent as any for pure doctrine; but, at the same time, he yearned for a shift from purely doctrinal concerns to *theologia practica*, the reforming of life-style and morals. As a young man, he had studied for a time in Scotland, and England, and become strongly influenced by the attitudes of the English Puritans. Teellinck was convinced that much of the Dutch population had thus far adopted the Reformed faith more in name than spirit, not only failing to

---

[77] ARB SEG 186, fo. 99. Isabella to Philip IV, 22 Sept. 1621.

[78] Van der Capellen, *Gedenkschriften*, i. 11; *Nootwendighe ende vrypostighe Vermaninghe*, 4–7, 9; Israel, *Dutch Republic and the Hispanic World*, 75–85, 154–7.

strive for Reformed ideals in life-style but adhering to all kinds of 'superstitious' practices and undesirable survivals from the pre-Reformation era which, in his view, needed to be eradicated.[79] At the same time, desirable religious practice, above all proper observance of the Lord's Day, was being dismally neglected.

Teellinck argued that even the most blameless purity of belief and doctrine is worth little when unaccompanied by a pure and godly life-style. He was a prolific writer, and in works such as his *Eubulus* (1616) had already made an impact before 1618. After his death, no fewer than 127 publications were attributed to him. The most influential of these were written in the early and mid-1620s, a time of economic slump and hardship in the Republic, as well as of the resumption of the war with Spain. The gloomy circumstances admirably fitted Teellinck's message. In his *Zions Basuyne* (1621), for example, he assured the *Raad van State* that the Fatherland could be successfully defended only if the military effort were based on a thorough reformation of life-style and morals. The deepening gloom which followed merely intensified Teellinck's fervour and the appeal of his message. In his tract *Noodwendigh Vertoogh* (1627), he argued that the slump, and terrible disasters of the Thirty Years War, including the defeat of the Protestants in Bohemia, were signs of God's wrath at the deplorable state of society and morals.[80] His further Reformation aspired to curb not only adultery, prostitution, and drunkenness but all frivolity, ribaldry, and ostentation as well as suppress 'amorous books', violation of the sabbath, and 'superstitious festivals', including the widely popular St Nicholas Day feast celebrated in December.[81]

Teellinck's was the most strident voice calling for a Further Reformation but by no means the only one. Other influential preachers held similar views, notably Dionysius Spranckhuysen (1587–1650) at Delft and the Zeelander Godefridus Udemans (1580–1649), who besides demanding stricter sabbath observance, and a more puritanical society, at home, spoke out, in 1624, against toleration in Dutch Brazil.[82] Moreover, some Counter-Remonstrant regents shared their zeal, including the influential Van Lodenstein and Van Bleiswijk families, at Delft, and the incorrigible Amsterdam burgomaster, Frederik de Vrij (1579–1646). The latter, an ally of Reinier Pauw at Amsterdam, and elder of the consistory, in 1622 published a 442-page heroic poem, entitled *Anatomia*, exhorting his countrymen to strive to lead pure lives and help build a godly society.

[79] Bouwman, *Willem Teellinck*, 13–15.
[80] Ibid. 24.   [81] Exalto, 'Willem Teellinck', 24, 27.   [82] Boxer, *Dutch in Brazil*, 121.

Thus, the victory of the Counter-Remonstrants, in 1618, brought in its wake not only efforts to eradicate Arminianism and cut back the toleration allowed to the dissenting Churches but also a first blast of pressure to goad the secular authorities into combating a range of behaviour which had previously been unrestricted or looked on with greater leniency. On the confessional front, the new Counter-Remonstrant town councils took a harder line against Catholic conventicles than their predecessors. But it was by no means only the Remonstrants and Catholics who felt the change. Lutherans and Jews did too. The Lutheran church at Leiden was closed and that at Rotterdam demolished.[83] The States of Holland rejected the request of the Bodegraven Lutherans for toleration, in 1621 and 1624, ruling that Lutheran preaching and practice were forbidden everywhere in the country-side of Holland.[84] The synods persuaded the States to consider banning Jewish worship and, when it became clear that Amsterdam would block this, petitioned that the 'freedom of the Jews might be cut back and limited, as is done in other lands where they are permitted to reside'.[85] As regards behaviour and life-style, the consistories pressed for reforms across a broad front, hoping to achieve a shift in civic legislation towards more, and tighter, restrictions on feasting, dancing, music-making, and theatrical perform-ances, indeed the activities of the rhetoric chambers generally.[86]

In former Arminian towns, the Calvinist revolution of the Counter-Remonstrants also involved changing, or modifying, numerous features of church life and popular piety as these had developed in the decades since the Reformation. At Gouda, there was talk at this point of removing the celebrated stained-glass windows from the main church. At Utrecht, in November 1623, the new authorities brought in regulations on the celebra-ting of Christmas. Efforts to combat the highly popular St Nicholas Day feast seem to have little effect but were nevertheless taken seriously by some: in 1620, De Vrij tried to stop the sale of children's dolls on the eve of the St Nicholas Day feast in Amsterdam.[87]

After 1625, the repression of Remonstrantism weakened, the Counter-Remonstrant cause suffered political reverses, opposition to the attitudes of the Further Reformation stiffened. The great poet Vondel evinced a fierce antagonism towards Teellinck, his sons, and allies, influenced doubtless by their hostility to music, theatre, and the rhetoric chambers, though he may well have agreed with De Vrij that poets ought not be preoccupied with

[83] Loosjes, *Gesch. der Luthersche kerk*, 118–21.
[84] Knuttel, *Acta*, i. 6, 110.
[85] Ibid. 103–4.
[86] Bogaers, 'Kwestie van macht?', 114–15.
[87] Evenhuis, *Ook dat was Amsterdam*, ii, 119.

amorous themes nor fill people's heads with images of pagan gods and goddesses and their doings. Vondel's antipathy to the Teellincks, whom he deemed 'seditious seed' which will not 'leave freedom in peace', manifested itself in several of his anonymously published topical poems.[88] In one he accused the Teellinck clan of dragging in the 'Trojan Horse of the Scots', implying that by importing the bigoted zealotry of the Scots Presbyterians they were sowing division and therefore threatening the ruin of the Republic.

Yet whilst the political fortunes of the Counter-Remonstrants waned, after 1625, and both Arminianism and 'Barneveldist' principles revived, the voice of the Further Reformation did not fade away. On the contrary, during the 1630s and 1640s, in towns all over the Republic, especially in Holland, Zeeland and Utrecht, influential preachers and others took up Teellinck's message and gradually built up support in Reformed circles for a wide-ranging programme of social and moral reform to be achieved by Church and State working hand in hand and which would transform the conduct not only of the Reformed community but of society as a whole. The most prominent of these figures were Teellinck's sons, Maximilian and Johannes, both leading preachers in Zeeland, and, from the late 1630s onwards, the doyen of *theologia practica* at Utrecht, Gisbertus Voetius (1589–1676).

---

[88] Vondel, *Hekeldigten*, 80, 96–8, 124–9.

21

The Republic under Siege, 1621–1628

❖

MAURITS'S LAST YEARS, 1621–1625

The early and mid-1620s were one of the most sombre periods in the history of the United Provinces. It was a time when the Republic was effectively under siege and squeezed hard.

The reimposition of the Spanish embargoes, in April 1621, had a drastic effect on the Dutch overseas trading system, largely eliminating Dutch trade with the Iberian peninsula, destroying their Levant trade, and weakening their Baltic traffic, as well as the North Sea herring fishery, which was now short of suitable salt.[1] Spanish successes in the Caribbean, and Brazil, cutting off the supply of Caribbean salt, and (until 1630) thwarting the newly set up West India Company, together with Spanish attacks on the herring fishery, and the onset of the Dunkirk privateering offensive, in the mid-1620s, intensified the impact of the embargoes. The economic and maritime siege was further tightened by the river blockade mounted by the Spaniards in the years 1625–9, when the traffic along the Rhine, Maas, Waal, Scheldt, and Ems was halted by the ring of Spanish garrisons extending from the Scheldt to the Ems. The pressure remained severe until the Spanish defeats of 1629.

Practically all Dutch overseas trade—apart from the East India commerce—slumped in the 1620s, as did many industries, including sugar-refining, salt-processing, printing, shipbuilding, and herring-packaging. It was in the 1620s that the West Frisian ports of Hoorn, Enkhuizen, and Medemblik, hit by contraction of the salt trade and herring exports, commenced their long-term decline.[2] As from April 1621, when there was a sharp rise in Dutch freight rates, much trade controlled by the Dutch during the Truce was diverted to England and the Hanseatic ports of north

---

[1] Israel, *Dutch Republic and the Hispanic World*, 202–15; Israel, *Dutch Primacy*, 121–96; Israel, *Empires and Entrepots*, 101–48, 205–10.
[2] Lesger, *Hoorn als stedelijk knooppunt*, 61–2; De Vries, *Enkhuizen*, 72.

Germany. The onset of Phase Three in Dutch world trade primacy (1621–47) was one of contraction and drastic restructuring. 'If we cast our eyes over the whole land,' wrote Paschier de Fijne, in 1624, 'do we not see that trade, industry, and the crafts decline everywhere, become lifeless and decay?' 'Do we not hear', he continued, 'the seamen, citizenry, householders, and everybody complain?'[3]

But no less unremitting than the slump, and effects of the embargoes, was the financial exigency and burden of sustaining the Republic's defence. In 1621, the Spanish Crown expanded the army of Flanders, encircling the Republic from Flanders to Lingen, to 60,000 men.[4] Even though Maurits kept to the defensive, the States General were obliged to increase the Dutch standing army from 30,000 to 48,000 men just to hold the defensive ring.[5] At the same time, the fortifications right round, from Cadzand to Delfzijl, had to be refurbished, and strengthened. Despite the slump, and instability of the Republic internally, Maurits and the States General had no alternative but to increase taxation steeply.

To add to the sombre picture, there was the Republic's diplomatic isolation and the deteriorating strategic situation in Germany. Even after France and England had made peace with Spain, in 1598 and 1604, respectively, the Dutch had continued to receive French and English subsidies until 1609. But from 1621, they found themselves (for the first time since 1576) entirely on their own. Franco-Dutch relations had been frosty since the overthrow of Oldenbarnevelt. A States General delegation—consisting of Ploos, Pauw, and Manmaker—was sent to Paris to plead for aid but returned empty-handed.[6] At the same time, Anglo-Dutch relations, marred by economic disputes, were distinctly less cordial than in 1617–18. Yet the Republic had no alternative but to sustain both its own defences and the sagging Protestant cause in Germany. After the defeats in Bohemia and the Palatinate, Maurits and the States General could not simply abandon the German Protestants; for if the Habsburgs were to prevail in northern, as well as southern and central, Germany, the Republic would be in a far worse strategic and political plight than it was already. Thus, there was no choice but to persevere as general paymaster of the Protestant armies in Germany.[7] Even though Count Mansfeld's army in East Friesland remained largely inactive, it was better, for the Dutch, to pay to keep it in

---

[3] De Fijne, *Eenige Tractaatjes*: 'Broederlicke vermaninge', A5.
[4] Parker, *Army of Flanders*, 272.
[5] Ten Raa and De Bas, *Staatsche leger*, iii. 292–3.
[6] Maarseveen, 'Republiek en Frankrijk', 422–3.
[7] Polisensky, *Tragic Triangle*, 247.

being, than allow it to melt away and see the armies of the Emperor and German Catholic League advance to the eastern borders of the United Provinces.

The *malaise* gripping the Republic in the early and mid-1620s arose partly from external factors: it was a *malaise* of commerce, navigation, industry, finance, taxation, and other war-related burdens and a decidedly grim strategic situation. But it was more than this. For it was a crisis also of the body politic, society, and religion. For the time being, the States of Holland had indeed lost their 'soul' and ceased to lead. With every year that passed, it became clearer that the system forged by Maurits and the Counter-Remonstrants, in 1618, was fatally flawed and cracking under the strain. The Counter-Remonstrants had created a body politic excessively reliant on the person of the Stadholder, in whom power and authority were concentrated.[8] As Maurits's own health deteriorated, the system became increasingly inefficient. By 1623, the Prince's decrepit condition, and the expectation that he would soon die, had become a constant topic of conversation at The Hague. Carleton, in December 1623, accounted the Prince 'much broken'. In any case, once the Dutch–Spanish war resumed, it became obvious that command of the army could not efficiently be combined with presiding over government at The Hague. As commander, Maurits had to absent himself for long periods, to encamp with his troops and supervise the defensive ring, from where he could not fully control affairs at The Hague. Maurits had no alternative to delegating more responsibility, and power, to the *Gecommitteerde Raden*, and to Holland's Pensionary, Duyck, who was considered only slightly less inept than Andries de Witt.[9] Moreover, co-operation among the Prince's noble underlings and favourites was patently deteriorating. In particular, the former friendship between Van den Bouchorst and Van Aerssen had changed by 1621, into enmity, with the latter seeking to displace the former as head of the Holland *ridderschap*.[10] Van Aerssen tried to have Van den Bouchorst packed off to Paris, as Dutch ambassador, but Maurits, forced to choose, backed Van den Bouchorst and packed Van Aerssen off to Venice.

The root of the crisis was the inability of Maurits's regime to secure the close collaboration of the States of Holland and Holland town councils. Maurits and the Counter-Remonstrants had emasculated the States of Holland, and thus the Generality too, concentrating influence in the hands of the Stadholder and his entourage. But Maurits and his favourites still

[8] Groenveld, *Evidente factien*, 24.
[9] Reigersberch, *Brieven*, 2–4.
[10] PRO SP 84/102, fo. 171v. Carleton to Calvert, 5 Sept. 1621.

relied on the regents whom they had brought into the town councils, and *Gecommitteerde Raden*, to ensure stability in the towns, raise taxes, and provide the finance without which state and army could not function. The new men, brought in in 1618, however, were simply not up to the job. No doubt the scorn, tinged with snobbery, the 'Arminian' leaders heaped on those who had usurped their places was biased and exaggerated. Yet it had some basis in fact. There were few able men among them. The States of Holland remained weak and passive. By 1623, the *Gecommitteerde Raden* of Holland were experiencing acute difficulty in persuading the town councils to agree on new taxes to pay for the war.[11] The failure was due to political weakness, and drift, and the sharpening of faction fights in the city councils. Carleton reported 'disorders which are grown in these assemblies (particularly in this of Holland) through private interest and emulation which hindereth all publique proceedings'.[12] For the Stadholder the most worrying aspect of this deterioration was the fragmentation of the Counter-Remonstrant party in Amsterdam. Despite the arrival of more Counter-Remonstrants on the Amsterdam city council in 1618, it was clear, by 1621, that their regime in Amsterdam was in deep trouble. Pauw's problem was that the theological base of Counter-Remonstrantism in the Amsterdam city council had always been fairly limited. Pauw ruled with the support of *politique* regents, such as Hendrik Hudde and Hendrik Reynst, more interested in commerce, and the merchants' views, than theological polemics. The commercial slump at Amsterdam was severe and Pauw's group failed to weather it. The *vroedschap* fragmented and, with the New Year elections of 1622, Pauw's ascendancy was broken.[13] Three of the four new burgomasters at Amsterdam in 1622 were averse to Counter-Remonstrant attitudes and policies. Pauw retained some influence in 1622–3 but, by 1624, was a broken reed. Opponents of the Counter-Remonstrants now controlled Amsterdam. Weakened by slump, and the need to pile on heavy taxation, the regime was further undermined by the tenacity of Remonstrantism. Admittedly, the war heightened patriotic sentiment and fear of the consequences of internecine strife, both of which served to bolster Counter-Remonstrantism. Remonstrants were in danger of being cast as the unpatriotic party, in collusion with Spain, whose opposition was weakening the Republic. But, at the same time, Maurits had to transfer troops from garrison duty, in Holland and Utrecht, to the Republic's outer defensive ring, and this inevitably diminished repression of Remonstrant activity. Grotius,

[11] Res. Holl. 13 Oct. 1621 and 20 Mar. 1623.
[12] PRO SP 84/103, fo. 6. Carleton to Calvert, 4 Oct. 1621.
[13] Elias, *Vroedschap van Amsterdam*, i, p. lxxvii.

Uyttenbogaert, and Episcopius were acutely aware of the dilemma in which this placed them. They sensed the increasing weakness of the Counter-Remonstrant regime, and scope for their own party to stage a recovery,[14] but also saw the danger of disruption and risk this posed both to the Republic and themselves.

Given the intensity of the Counter-Remonstrant repression in the years 1618–21, and depth of grievance where Remonstrant support remained strong, it was impossible to relax the previous severity without disruptive effects. When the troops left Schoonhoven for the border fortresses, the Remonstrants 'assembled in the market-place', and began 'preaching before the statehouse until half a company [of troops] was sent thither out of Tergoes [Goes]'. 'It appears,' commented Carleton, 'the Arminian towns will be no longer quiet than they are bridled by garrisons, the charge whereof, added to the increase of their army, is insupportable; they doe now calculate, besides all other mischiefes caused by that faction, a debt growne unto the state of more than two millions [for extra troops].'[15]

In this chronic situation, Maurits could only stoke the fires of the German war, prodding England and Denmark to do more, and seek to distract Brussels with a stream of cryptic and prevaricating truce proposals. Constantly ill over the winter of 1622–3, Maurits sent messages indicating he was now ready to consider making substantial concessions to Spain.[16] Spínola and Peckius became increasingly optimistic, from late 1622, that the stream of secret notes emanating from Maurits augured a long truce with enough Dutch concessions to satisfy Spanish pride and end the fighting in the Low Countries.[17] At Madrid, Philip IV's ministers, facing grave financial difficulties of their own, were divided as to how to react to the reports from the Infanta and Spínola. Some of the king's ministers believed that a new truce could and should now be concluded. However, Philip IV's favourite, the influential count-duke of Olivares, took a hard line, insisting that there was still no satisfactory basis on which to negotiate.

From Spain's point of view he was right. For Maurits's offers of concessions, like Oldenbarnevelt's in 1606–7, were mere straws in the wind.[18] In reality, there was no possibility that Holland and Zeeland could be persuaded to make large concessions in the Indies, on the Scheldt, or with regard to Catholic practice, and Maurits knew this better than anyone.

---

[14] Evenhuis, *Ook dat was Amsterdam*, i. 258.
[15] PRO SP 84/102, fo. 201. Carleton to Calvert, 17 Sept. 1621.
[16] AGS Estado 2147. Isabella to Philip, 7 Apr. 1623.
[17] AGS Estado 2147. consultas of the special junta on Netherlands affairs, 4 and 14 July and 10 Aug. 1623.
[18] Israel, *Dutch Republic and the Hispanic World*, 157–60.

Probably, he never had any intention of proposing anything in the States General that was remotely likely to satisfy Spain. He was simply stalling, playing for time. Eventually, he admitted as much to Carleton, confessing that he had 'continually putt [Spínola's and Peckius'] papers into his pocket and so suppressed them (with the consent of some of the States of whome he was most confidant) lest such propositions being brought into their publick assemblies might have driven them into distraction and dispute . . . and thereby slacken their contributions wherewith they pay their army, and by consequence expose them to the mercie of thyr enemy'.[19]

Early in 1622, Spínola captured Jülich, cutting the Republic's line of communications with the Palatinate. Even though the army of Flanders suffered a serious reverse, later in 1622, when Spínola was forced to abandon the epic siege of Bergen-op-Zoom, after heavy losses in men and *matériel*, the strategic position of the Dutch continued to deteriorate, as the Habsburgs gained ground in Germany.[20] Mansfeld's army, in East Friesland, remained pinned to the Dutch border. For a time, Maurits and his entourage drew comfort from the progress of Christian of Brunswick, who had seized Lippstadt and forged a Protestant army in the Lower Saxon circle, attracting support from the still numerous Protestants of the Münsterland, during 1619–21. Christian seemed a useful shield for the Republic, and bridle on the Catholic ecclesiastical states of north-western Germany. By 1622, the States General were pouring money into this new Protestant army.[21] But Christian proved an even worse investment than Mansfeld. As the army of the Catholic League, under Tilly, advanced into Westphalia, Christian fell back towards the Dutch frontier, his army being overtaken and crushed by Tilly, on 6 August 1623, at Stadtlohn, practically on the Gelderland border, a disaster for Protestant arms in Germany, and Protestantism in Westphalia, which also spread panic through Gelderland and Overijssel. Thousands of fleeing soldiers, local Protestants, and Bohemian refugees poured into Gelderland and Overijssel, accompanied by droves of camp women and children. Twenty-four shiploads of refugees were shipped round from Amsterdam alone to the north German ports, during the ensuing weeks.[22]

The summer of 1623, when Grotius wrote his *De Jure Belli ac Pacis* at Senlis, near Paris, in the company of the young jurist Dirck Graswinckel, and Rembrandt neared completion of his training as an artist, was a time

[19] PRO SP 84/115, fo. 104. Carleton to Buckingham, 9 Dec. 1623.
[20] Israel, *Dutch Republic and the Hispanic World*, 104–5.
[21] ARH SG 3182. res. SG res. 26 June and 3 Aug. 1623.
[22] Wassenaer, *Historisch Verhael*, v. 171.

of pervasive gloom throughout the Republic. Maurits's statecraft, instead of deflecting Habsburg forces from Dutch borders, appeared to be drawing them directly down upon them. In the wake of Stadtlohn, additional troops had to be rushed to the IJssel where the dry weather, and low level of the river, posed an additional threat to the Dutch defensive ring. For Spain, it seemed a heaven-sent opportunity to squeeze the 'rebels' until the pips squeaked.[23] But (unaccountably in the view of his own subordinates, as well as his Dutch adversaries) Spínola made no move. Chastened by his losses at Bergen-op-Zoom, and believing Maurits to be on the point of agreeing to a new truce, on terms advantageous to Spain, Spínola remained inactive.[24] Only after another five months of exchanging secret messages with the Prince did the generalissimo, and Peckius, conclude that the Dutch Stadholder was leading them a dance. Spínola was not amused. He took revenge, in 1624, by ravaging the personal lands of the Prince of Orange, not only around Breda but also Grave and Moers, having previously (according to Carleton) protected these areas, during the years of secret dialogue 'as a souldier's curtisie'.[25]

Maurits, in his last months, languished in a strategic, and diplomatic, trap from which there appeared to be no escape. When Spínola besieged Breda, in August 1624, Dutch morale sank to its nadir. Plague raged at Amsterdam (where it is said to have caused 11,000 deaths) as well as in Leiden, Delft, and other main cities (see Table 32). While Spínola tightened his grip on Breda, a second Spanish army, operating further east, captured Cleves and Gennep, on the Republic's eastern flank. Meanwhile, the Republic's financial position steadily worsened. The slump in both Baltic and Mediterranean trade, already severe, grew worse. 'Leur ruyne ne fut jamais si proche d'eux', remarked the French ambassador, 'qu'à cette heure.'[26] Chronically short of cash to pay the troops, the provinces had to heap new taxes on the population, though the regents knew full well there was likely to be trouble. Holland's new butter tax, four guilders per vat, introduced in June 1624, provoked riots in Delft, Hoorn, Enkhuizen, The Hague, Amsterdam, and Haarlem. At Haarlem, the militia, in which the great portraitist Frans Hals was then serving, fired on the demonstrators, killing five and wounding many more,[27] causing jubilation in Brussels from where ministers reported to Madrid that the Dutch populace were on the verge of revolt. The year

[23] Alcalá-Zamora, *España, Flandes y el mar del Norte*, 187.
[24] AGS Estado 2037, consultas of 16 Sept. and 26 Oct. 1623.
[25] PRO SP 84/120, fo. 67v. Carleton to Prince of Wales, 4 Sept. 1624.
[26] Aubéry du Maurier, 'Rapport', 399.
[27] Schrevelius, *Harlemias*, 198–200; Dekker, *Holland in beroering*, 30–1.

1624, in which Hals painted his *Laughing Cavalier* (Wallace Collection), was the harshest of the first half of the Golden Age. 'Here is nothing but gloom for the present', commented Grotius' brother-in-law, 'and fear for the future.'[28]

More increases in the excises were introduced in Holland in the mid-1620s than at any other time between the 1590s and 1672. The States went as far as they dared. The sheer inadvisability of further burdening the common man, combined with the acute need for cash, helped inspire the invention of stamp duty, one of the key innovations in the history of European taxation.[29] This was devised in 1624 by a clerk of the States of Holland, adopted by the States, and imposed on all legal transactions and documents, being a means to tax the affluent without further burdening the poor.

But new taxes were not enough. There was a desperate need for additional alliances. Maurits dispatched an embassy extraordinary to Paris headed by Van den Bouchorst, early in 1624. This time the approach succeeded. The French court was becoming uneasy at the expansion of Habsburg greatness.[30] Under the treaty of Compiègne (June 1624), Louis XIII undertook to subsidize the ailing Republic to the extent of a million guilders yearly—equivalent to some 7 per cent of Dutch military expenditure—for three years.

THE COMMENCEMENT OF FREDERIK HENDRIK'S STADHOLDERATE

Maurits died, in April 1625, with the Republic's fortunes at a lower ebb than at any time since 1590. The country was tense, finance for the army, and fortifications, chronically short.[31] Breda, one of the most vital strongholds in the Republic's defensive ring, was not lost yet; but with Spínola encircling the city with 23,000 men in well-fortified siege positions, the outlook for its garrison of 3,500, one of the Republic's largest, looked bleak. In May, Frederik Hendrik, the new captain-general of the Union, made a last attempt to save the city but was forced back. Breda surrendered in June, bringing most of north-west Brabant under Spanish control.

Frederik Hendrik, the most attractive personality among the Princes of Orange second only to William the Silent, was to dominate Dutch politics

---

[28] Reigersberg, *Brieven*, 23.
[29] 't Hart, *Making of a Bourgeois State*, 128–30.
[30] Maarseveen, 'Republiek en Frankrijk', 443–7.
[31] Blok, *Frederik Hendrik*, 66.

for more than two decades. He possessed his older half-brother's cautious, methodical temperament but without its brooding, vengeful undercurrent. He was a statesman who invariably preferred compromise, and the middle path, to drastic measures and to whom Robert Fruin, the father of modern Dutch historiography, applied the dictum *fortiter in re, suaviter in modo*. A more stylish, grander figure than Maurits, he developed into a renowned soldier and one of Europe's leading courtly figures. A man of refined tastes—often with a pronounced French flavour, inherited from his mother, Louise de Coligny—and of intellectual interests, Frederik Hendrik incomparably surpassed Maurits as a patron of the arts. In later years, after the gloom of the 1620s had lifted, he spent lavishly, refurbishing his palaces and building new ones, notably Noordeinde, in the centre of The Hague, and, at the end of his life, the Huis ten Bosch, at its outskirts. Among the artists he patronized in the 1630s and 1640s were Rembrandt, Lievens, Honthorst, Van Campen, Van Poelenburgh, and Moreelse, though he also procured many paintings, of a more baroque character, from leading south Netherlands artists, including Rubens and Van Dyck. In artistic and intellectual matters he was guided by his cultivated secretary Constantijn Huygens (1596–1687), son of a refugee bureaucrat from Brabant, who had been a secretary of the *Raad van State*. Though Counter-Remonstrant,[32] as well as Orangist, Huygens was the Republic's leading connoisseur of art, architecture, and culture generally, as well as a major poet in his own right. Another key influence was the Prince's wife, Amalia von Solms, daughter of the Calvinist Count of Solms-Braunfels, whom he married three weeks before Maurits's death. Former lady-in-waiting, and a close friend of Queen Elizabeth of Bohemia, at her refugee court at The Hague, Amalia stimulated Frederik Hendrik's sense of grandeur and dynastic ambition and added to the air of splendour and refined elegance which came to characterize the Stadholder's court.

Initially, Frederik Hendrik was captain-general of the Union but not yet Stadholder, since each province had individually to confirm him in this capacity and draw up the terms of his 'commission'.[33] Thus, he succeeded immediately as Prince of Orange, and commander of the army, but not to Maurits's political authority. The stadholderate was, in effect, suspended for months, at a critical juncture in the Republic's history. By 1624, the Counter-Remonstrants had plainly failed to consolidate the power they had captured in 1618. Grotius learnt, a month before Maurits's death, from his brother-in-law, that the 'well-intentioned party' were now gaining ground

---

[32] Hofman, *Constantijn Huygens*, 21, 108–9.   [33] Poelhekke, *Frederik Hendrik*, 157–8.

not only in traditional centres of Arminian strength but also Dordrecht and several Zeeland towns where previously it lacked support.[34] Particularly encouraging to Remonstrants was the eclipse of Pauw, at Amsterdam, and fading of the Counter-Remonstrants, at Dordrecht, where there were scarcely any theological Arminians but where control was passing to a middle group of *politiques*.[35]

Dordrecht shows that the rise of political 'Arminianism' in Holland and Zeeland, in the mid-1620s, cannot be interpreted as the political manifestation of a resurgent Remonstrantism. For, as a confessional block, Remonstrantism retained its vitality, by 1625, only in a few towns and was everywhere in retreat in the face of repression, both geographically and in terms of popular support, even where the movement remained strongest in, and around, Rotterdam, Gouda, Alkmaar, Hoorn, and The Hague. Since 1618, there had everywhere been numerous defections of former Remonstrants to the Catholics and other confessions (see pp. 464–5 above).

Rather the rise of political 'Arminianism' in the mid-1620s must be treated as a separate, albeit connected, phenomenon. For the party-factions dominating the politics of the town councils were loose coalitions in which regent dynasties strongly linked to a particular confessional stance, like the Van Lodensteins, at Delft, or Steyn at Haarlem, rubbed shoulders with trimmers and *politiques* who deemed it opportune to join them.[36] Thus many regents (and others) had jumped on the Counter-Remonstrant bandwagon without necessarily being fervent adherents of Calvinist orthodoxy, or the political and social attitudes linked to Counter-Remonstrantism, such as zeal for the Union, Stadholder, colonial companies, and war against Spain, or enthusiastic for the suppression of Remonstrantism, Catholicism, and (outside a few prescribed places) Lutheranism, or Judaism, and other faiths.

Political 'Arminianism' stemmed from secular pressures and was in part a reaction against the eclipse of Holland following Maurits's coup of 1618, as well as the trade depression commencing in 1621. But, if the 'Arminianism' which captured Amsterdam, Rotterdam, and other town councils in the early and mid-1620s was basically a political and secular phenomenon, it nevertheless had far-reaching religious and ideological ramifications.[37] For political 'Arminians' still operated within a framework infused with theological tensions. Just as political 'Counter-Remonstrants' adopted attitudes which reached beyond religion, gaining support for this wider stance from

[34] Reigersberg, *Brieven*, 23–4, 38.
[35] Van Dalen, *Gesch. van Dordrecht*, ii. 818.
[36] Israel, *Empires and Entrepots*, 75–88.
[37] Evenhuis, *Ook dat was Amsterdam*, i. 283–8.

strict Calvinists, so political 'Arminians' attracted opponents of the remodelled Reformed Church and political attitudes linked to it. This was inherent
in the situation. Political 'Arminians', consequently, resisted the aspirations
of the public Church, promoted toleration, disliked the war, and aspired to
reassert Holland's predominance. Resenting the enhanced authority of
Generality and Stadholder, political 'Arminians' rejected the constitutional
principles of Maurits's coup, preferring those of Oldenbarnevelt and Grotius, asserting the absolute sovereignty of the States of Holland.

After 1618, the core of Maurits's power was his control of *vroedschap*
elections. But during the interval before Frederik Hendrik succeeded to his
political functions, this supervision lapsed, though it theoretically devolved,
for the interim, on the Hof of Holland. This suspension of the Stadholder's
authority enabled the political 'Arminians' to regain more of the ground, in
the *vroedschappen*, they had lost.[38] But to keep, and build on, their gains
they needed the friendship of Frederik Hendrik and, to secure this, had to
help check the disruptive effects of the Remonstrant religious resurgence.
Uyttenbogaert (who had been tutor to the young Frederik Hendrik, and
remained on friendly terms with him) wrote, from Rouen, promising that
he and his followers would not try to overturn the Synod of Dordrecht, or
alter the public Church as now constituted, desiring only freedom of
practice for their own Church.[39] Grotius also stressed the need to 'rein in'
the Remonstrant public at this crucial juncture so as to avoid clashes and
disturbances. 'But who', asked Grotius' brother-in-law, 'will have the
authority to restrain them?'[40]

During the summer of 1625, 'Arminians' gained control of the Rotterdam
vroedschap. At Amsterdam, the Counter-Remonstrant party was further
weakened by a quarrel between Pauw and one of those brought in in 1618,
Jacob Gerritsz. Hoyngh, a member of the consistory and zealous Counter-
Remonstrant. Arminians progressed also at Alkmaar, Hoorn, and Gouda.
There was, concurrently, a general easing of the pressure on Remonstrant
worship, in these towns, and writers and artists forced to keep silent since
1618 could now—to an extent—make their views known. Vondel caused a
general sensation by boldly publishing his poetic drama *Palamedes*, dealing
with the judicial murder of a thinly disguised Oldenbarnevelt by an
Agamemnon unmistakably resembling Maurits.[41] This was too much: the
Amsterdam magistrates punished Vondel with a heavy fine, though even this

[38] Reigersberg, *Brieven*, 50; Grotius, *Briefwisseling*, ii. 154–7, 441.
[39] Uyttenbogaert, *Brieven*, ii. 301–3.
[40] Reigersberg, *Brieven*, 51.
[41] Brandt, *Leven van Joost van der Vondel*, 14–16.

comparatively mild punishment was a sign of changed times. There are definite hints that Rembrandt's earliest known painting, his dramatic 'Stoning of St Stephen' (1625), is also a commentary on the harsh fate of Oldenbarnevelt.[42]

The Counter-Remonstrants were deeply apprehensive at the prospect of Frederik Hendrik succeeding to the stadholderate. His earlier links with Uyttenbogaert, and unwillingness to join Maurits in espousing Counter-Remonstrantism, were well known. At the very least, Frederik Hendrik was a *politique* with scant sympathy for Counter-Remonstrant theology and attitudes. The States of Holland decided to appoint Frederik Hendrik without changing their Stadholder's 'instructions' but wished to proceed, in this matter, jointly with Zeeland. In the States of Zeeland, however, a majority took the view that fresh 'instructions' should be adopted binding the Stadholder to uphold the Reformed religion as presently constituted by 'public authority' under the 'Acts' of the National Synod of Dordrecht, confirmed by the States General, and provincial assemblies.[43] Zeeland sent a delegation to The Hague (with Frederik Hendrik away on campaign trying to save Breda), to sway Holland. To avoid splitting their own assembly, though, the States of Holland preferred to stick to their original decision, compelling Zeeland to follow. The Prince took his oath as Stadholder of Holland and Zeeland (ironically at Waalwijk), on 2 June 1625.

In Overijssel and Gelderland, those nobles who had managed affairs for Maurits hastened to demonstrate their deference, and usefulness, to Frederik Hendrik. Sweder van Haersolte, who had clinched Overijssel's vote in favour of the National Synod, in 1618, and dominated the province's Delegated States, quickly secured Frederik Hendrik's appointment and personally brought his province's commission to the Prince, at Waalwijk, and administered the oath.[44] In Gelderland too, there was little difficulty, though the States did add to the 'instructions' a clause charging their new Stadholder to maintain the Reformed faith as 'presently in force in this duchy'.[45]

Matters progressed less smoothly, though, in the remaining provinces. Averse to the Prince's tolerant inclinations the States of Groningen, followed by those of Drenthe, discarded Frederik Hendrik, choosing instead the Frisian Stadholder, Ernst Casimir. In Utrecht, Maurits's commission had been revised after the coup, in 1618, to enhance his power to regulate

---

[42] Schwartz, *Rembrandt*, 36.
[43] Van der Capellen, *Gedenkschriften*, i. 352.
[44] ARH PR 486 res. SO. 5 and 9 May 1625.
[45] Blok, *Frederik Hendrik*, 72.

city council elections and manipulate the *ridderschap* and clerical chamber. Although all prominent 'Arminians' had been purged, there were still many nobles who disliked the changes and now backed moves to appoint Frederik Hendrik under the 'instructions' of 1590, thereby again cutting back the Stadholder's powers. The result would have been to transfer responsibility for adjudicating disputes about city council elections from Stadholder to *ridderschap*. But the city, under a firm Counter-Remonstrant regime, allied to Counter-Remonstrant elements in the *ridderschap*, held out for the commission of 1618. After protracted wrangling, a compromise was reached but inclining more to the terms of 1618 than 1590.[46] Frederik Hendrik was belatedly installed, as Stadholder of Utrecht, only in November.

When the Prince returned to The Hague, in July 1625, after the loss of Breda, he faced a domestic situation of daunting complexity. The 41-year-old Stadholder, born in the year of his father's assassination, was temperamentally averse to Counter-Remonstrantism and, in any case, could not now revert fully to the political system of his half-brother even had he wanted to. Political 'Arminianism' was now too strongly ensconced in the Holland *vroedschappen* for that. This meant that he had to find a political middle path between the party-factions. But how was he to accomplish this in the fraught situation of 1625? If he assisted, or failed to oppose, the resurgence of Remonstrantism he would be stirring up a hornets' nest of opposition in the town councils and provincial assemblies. For the revival of political 'Arminianism' did not mean that political 'Counter-Remonstrantism' was dead. Far from it. If political 'Arminianism' prevailed in the Holland ports (other than Enkhuizen), and where popular Remonstrantism had previously been strong, there were also key towns where the regents had been Arminian, before 1618, but the populace predominantly Counter-Remonstrant and where maritime commerce was less important than at Amsterdam and Rotterdam, where political 'Counter-Remonstrantism' remained deeply entrenched.[47] This was true, in particular, of Haarlem, Leiden, and, outside Holland, of Utrecht—all inland cities with large proletarian populations.

Somehow, Frederik Hendrik had to strike a balance which would accommodate both the 'Arminian' and 'Counter-Remonstrant' party-factions while providing the Republic with the internal stability which now, more than ever, was essential. He was willing to end the organized repression of Remonstrant conventicles, a repression continuing in most places outside

[46] Poelhekke, *Frederik Hendrik*, 87–8.
[47] Israel, *Empires and Entrepots*, 48–56, 79–81.

Amsterdam and Rotterdam, and cultivate links with the political 'Arminian' leadership. This had been evident from the outset, not least from his allowing his Remonstrant friend (Oldenbarnevelt's son-in-law) Cornelis van der Mijle to return to The Hague, showing him public favour—at, of all occasions, Maurits's funeral. But, at the same time, the Prince had no intention of leaning so far towards the Arminians as to drive the Counter-Remonstrants into outright opposition. From his perspective, such an outcome would have been disastrous. His objective was a *via media* which would leave the Counter-Remonstrants, and public Church, with enough of their previous gains for them to wish, and need, to co-operate with him. His goal was to make both party-factions dependent on himself, as the indispensable arbiter who held the balance.[48] Frederik Hendrik was, and remained, a *politique* through and through. If religious conviction influenced his politics, it was hard to discern where. The Venetian ambassador, Contarini, believed the new Prince of Orange had no religion other than 'ragion di stato'.[49]

It was typical of Frederik Hendrik to proceed adroitly, taking every precaution to avoid inflaming the situation. Through intermediaries, he intimated that, for the moment, he did not wish prominent Remonstrant exiles to return or create difficulties by agitating for this. When Uyttenbogaert did return from France, in September 1626, the Prince quietly protected him, while, at the same time, declining to meet him.[50] Predictably, Frederik Hendrik's deftness in distributing favours to both sides, what the younger Dudley Carleton called the 'indifferent and moderate course which his Excellency hath hitherto holden', was 'little satisfactorie to either' side.[51] But it was effective, giving both party-factions reason to refrain from criticizing his conduct of affairs and to defer to his authority.[52]

One major risk of the Stadholder's strategy was that the resurgence of Remonstrant gatherings would provoke the fury of the Counter-Remonstrant masses. For in the largest cities, including Amsterdam, most of the public remained Counter-Remonstrant in sympathy. The danger was made starkly evident in April 1626, when Amsterdam's most fervent orthodox preacher, Adriaen Smout, openly incited the populace to disrupt the Sunday prayer-gatherings of the Remonstrants.[53] There was rioting on 13 and 14 April in which the mob scattered a conventicle and demolished a house used

---

[48] Aitzema, *Historie*, ii. 67.
[49] Blok, *Frederik Hendrik*, 79.
[50] Ibid. 80.
[51] PRO SP 84/131, fo. 7v. Carleton to Conway, 18 Jan. 1626.
[52] Grotius, *Briefwisseling*, iii. 19.
[53] Brugmans, *Gesch. van Amsterdam*, iii. 40.

for Remonstrant services. The civic militia, the rank and file of which was also Counter-Remonstrant in sympathy, proved reluctant to obey the orders of an 'Arminian' *vroedschap* to suppress Counter-Remonstrant crowds.[54] When the city council asked the consistory to order preachers to admonish the people to eschew violence and be tranquil, the exasperated elders refused.

Frederik Hendrik made no attempt to persuade the States of Holland to cancel the placards forbidding Remonstrant prayer-gatherings, as Uytten-bogaert and Episcopius wished. On the other hand, he made no effort to enforce the placards, as his brother had done and Counter-Remonstrants demanded. Consequently, a glaring disparity of practice ensued. Where Counter-Remonstrant preponderance persisted, as at Haarlem, Leiden, Enkhuizen, Utrecht, Nijmegen, and Kampen, repression of Arminian con-venticles, in the name of the States General and provincial assemblies, continued as before. But where political Arminianism prevailed, Remon-strant gatherings occurred increasingly openly and, soon, practically un-disturbed. In the larger 'Arminian' towns of Holland neither the *Gecommitteerde Raden*, nor the States, could interfere. However, there were centres of Remonstrant agitation which formed a different category—be-cause of the presence of army garrisons. These included Nijmegen, Heusden, Utrecht, Schoonhoven, and Oudewater. The question arose whether, in such cases, Counter-Remonstrant town councils could call on army comman-ders—as they had under Maurits—to suppress Arminian gatherings. It thus marked a crucial shift when, in February 1626, Frederik Hendrik instructed officers in Utrecht that troops were no longer to be made available for quelling peaceful Remonstrant meetings.[55] The change was confirmed, in April 1627, when the Counter-Remonstrant *vroedschap* of Schoonhoven requested troops with which to suppress conventicles. The Prince ruled that troops were not to be used to break up orderly gatherings but only 'in case of publique tumults and violences'.[56]

By creating a balance, the new Stadholder was, in effect, siding with the Arminians, or at least the political 'Arminians'. He had to rein in manifes-tations of Remonstrantism, but, at the same time, deliberately encouraged the revival of political 'Arminian' power in the town councils. Wherever the Arminians were a force, Frederik Hendrik sought to advance their position and ease out the 'Church' party. In August 1626, Grotius noted that he was backing 'Arminian' regents in the power struggles between the party-

[54] Dekker, *Holland in beroering*, 104.
[55] Grotius, *Briefwisseling*, iii. 19.
[56] Israel, *Empires and Entrepots*, 79.

factions at Hoorn, Alkmaar, Gouda, and Brill.[57] In December 1626, the younger Carleton complained that 'at Utrecht and Delft . . . certain bitter Arminians are crept into the Magistracie by the nominacion of the burgers, but by the election of the Prince of Orange, whome the late Prince had in the time of reformacion displaced for Arminianisme'.[58] Similarly, at Nijmegen, early in 1627,[59] Frederik Hendrik reversed Maurits's intervention of 1618 and restored the Arminians, though in the longer run at Nijmegen, as at Gouda, the Counter-Remonstrants regained the upper hand.[60] The new regime, forged in the years 1625–7, rested on a deft balancing of party-factions; but it was yet weighted towards the Arminians.

Nevertheless, at the level of provincial managers, what is chiefly striking is the strong element of continuity with the regime of Maurits. Only two of Maurits's managers, François van Aerssen (for the moment) and Adriaen Manmaker, were discarded with the advent of Frederik Hendrik; and Maurits had already withdrawn his favour from the former. Two professed 'Arminians', Count Floris II of Culemborg, a foe of Maurits, and the poet-politician Simon van Beaumont (1574–1654),[61] Pensionary of Middelburg (where, recently, political Arminians had come to the fore), were brought into the inner circle of provincial managers and Stadholder's confidants. But, in most cases, the political bosses who managed the provincial and quarter assemblies for Frederik Hendrik were identical to those who served Maurits, confirming that the structures of influence and clientage in the provinces—whether regent or noble—remained largely independent of the Stadholder. Van den Bouchorst still dominated the Holland *ridderschap*, Ploos the States of Utrecht, and Van Haersolte the States of Overijssel. Goosen Schaffer, pre-eminent in Groningen under Maurits, and uniquely well connected with both the city and the Ommelander *jonkers*, remained pre-eminent under Frederik Hendrik. The States General committee which negotiated the alliance with England, in October 1625, included Duyck, Van den Bouchorst, Schaffer, Randwijk, and Culemborg.[62] The simultaneous alliance with Denmark was handled by a committee of seven including Van Haersolte, Randwijk, Schaffer, and Culemborg.[63]

Most towns became firmly tied to one party-faction or the other. Amsterdam, Rotterdam, Dordrecht, and Alkmaar were now 'Arminian'

---

[57] Grotius, *Briefwisseling*, iii. 64.
[58] Israel, *Empires and Entrepots*, 80.
[59] Van der Capellen, *Gedenckschriften*, i. 437–8.
[60] Jenniskens, *Magistraat van Nijmegen*, 17–18.
[61] Meertens, *Letterkundig leven in Zeeland*, 229–301.
[62] Aitzema, *Verhael*, i. 97–100.
[63] Aitzema, *Historie*, ii. 939.

towns, although Amsterdam remained unstable owing to the strength of Counter-Remonstrantism in the city. Haarlem, Leiden, and Utrecht, by contrast, and numerous smaller towns, remained solidly Counter-Remonstrant. But there were also towns where Frederik Hendrik's manipulations produced no clear outcome, other than conflict and instability which continued for years. Delft, Gouda, and Nijmegen were towns where the Stadholder's intervention temporarily weakened but, in the medium term, failed to break the Counter-Remonstrant ascendancy. The result was turmoil followed, notably at Gouda, by reversion to Counter-Remonstrant dominance. At Utrecht, the Prince's attempt to unseat the Counter-Remonstrants was supported by the provincial *ridderschap* in the years 1626–8 but ultimately failed to break the hold of Johan van Weede, the Counter-Remonstrant burgomaster who dominated the city. During this tussle, the Utrecht 'Arminians' were backed by two of the remaining four voting towns of the province—Amersfoort and Wijk-bij-Duurstede, the Counter-Remonstrants by Rhenen and Montfoort.[64] In Utrecht, Counter-Remonstrantism, partly a reaction to the strong Catholic presence in the city, also denoted zeal for the city's rights in the contest with the *ridderschap* for control of the deeply divided States and province.

But unquestionably the most chronic local instability in the late 1620s was that unsettling Amsterdam. By 1627, Rotterdam was openly defying other Holland towns, refusing to suppress Remonstrant gatherings.[65] But in Rotterdam Counter-Remonstrant support was sparse. Very different was the position in Amsterdam. As the Arminians tightened their grip on the city government, and battled to control the civic militia, tension and acrimony mounted. The burgomasters who emerged from the elections of February 1628, headed by Andries Bicker and Jacob de Graeff, led the city's 'Arminian' faction, which was to dominate Amsterdam's politics for decades to come. The city's preachers, led by Smout, incensed that the city's former stance was now being discarded in favour of a more liberal policy towards dissenting religious conventicles, none too subtly took to inciting the populace against the regents. On 8 March 1628, a Remonstrant prayer-meeting was again disrupted by rioting. The burgomasters, only too aware of the precariousness of their position, and the deep divisions within the civic militia, asked the Stadholder to come in person to restore calm. Frederik Hendrik arrived accompanied by two members of the *Gecommitteerde Raden*—one Arminian and one Counter-Remonstrant—and a retinue

---

[64] Uyttenbogaert, *Brieven*, iii, part 1, 138, 150–2, 174–5.
[65] GA Gouda OA 9, fo. 92. res. vroed. 5 Oct. 1627.

of nobles.[66] The Prince requested explanations from both sides: the burgo-masters blamed the trouble on rebellious preachers inciting the populace, the consistory on the *vroedschap*'s toleration of Arminian gatherings. A group of Counter-Remonstrant merchants, as well as the directors of the Amsterdam Chamber of the WIC, also petitioned the Stadholder to revert to his brother's policies and forbid Remonstrant meetings. The Prince urged both sides to moderation and calm.

But the effect of the visitation soon wore off. A new furore erupted when the burgomasters replaced a Counter-Remonstrant militia captain with a well-known 'Arminian', Jan Claesz. Vlooswijck, who had been purged from the Amsterdam militia in 1618. Part of Vlooswijck's company then refused to serve under a man whom they called a 'godless libertine' and were then also dismissed from the militia. The 800-man Amsterdam city militia was now dangerously agitated. Openly seditious pamphlets appeared, proclaim-ing the civic militia the true guardians of the people, public Church, and privileges of the city, recalling the decisive part they had played in the overthrow of the Catholic city council in 1578. Defying the burgomasters, a delegation of rebellious Counter-Remonstrant militiamen and citizenry, led by a physician, Carel Leenaertsz, proceeded to The Hague, in December 1628, formally protested to the States of Holland, and received a hearing from the Stadholder.[67] The petitioners, claiming to represent the burghers of Amsterdam, complained that the city council had broken their undertak-ing to the Stadholder, made in his presence, in April, to maintain the public Church, and be 'accommodating and pleasant' towards the populace.[68] They deplored not only the new leniency regarding Arminian conventicles, but also that towards Amsterdam's Catholics, who, they alleged, now enjoyed greater freedom than at any time since 1578, practising their 'superstitious idolatry as if they were in Spain', with services being held regularly in forty different houses in the city.

The petitioners also attacked the constitutional principles of the Arminian faction now controlling Amsterdam. The ideological battle revolved at this point around Grotius' *Apology for the Legitimate Government of Holland*, clandestinely published in 1622, which held that each of the Seven Provinces was fully sovereign within its borders, including in church affairs.[69] The book, banned by the States General, in November 1622, was resolutely suppressed by some towns of Holland but, the rebellious citizenry

---

[66] Wagenaar, *Amsterdam*, i. 496–7.
[67] Brugmans, *Gesch. van Amsterdam*, iii. 42.
[68] Leenaertsz, *Copie vande Remonstrantie*, A2–3.
[69] Grotius, *Verantwoordingh*, 14–15, 26–7.

complained, had been twice reprinted, in Amsterdam, and was being freely distributed as if it were the official version of the events of 1618–19 and the constitutional points involved. They denounced Grotius' book as trebly seditious, compromising the authority of the States General, Stadholder, and public Church.

Like Grotius, the 'Arminian' Amsterdam city council regarded the civic militia as purely civic in character. In their view, it represented neither the people nor the Union, and had no business seeking to defend the public Church, or appealing to the States of Holland or Stadholder. Faced by insubordination on such a scale, the burgomasters, seriously alarmed, sent a request to the Stadholder for troops to help them master the situation and restore calm. The Stadholder ordered in six regular companies of infantry. The dissidents' ringleaders were arrested. Leenaertsz was tried, heavily fined, and sentenced to perpetual banishment.[70] The civic militia was subjected to a further purge and a new oath of allegiance.

The suppression of the Amsterdam militia mutiny and the Stadholder's supporting the *vroedschap* with troops brought the debate about the Union, public Church, and role of the civic militias to fever pitch. Theologico-political pamphlets poured from the presses. Against the 'Arminian' town governments stood the increasingly exasperated Counter-Remonstrant city councils of Leiden, Haarlem, Gouda, and Utrecht.[71] In the States of Holland, the Counter-Remonstrants refused to condemn the actions of the Amsterdam militia, despite the defiance of a regent regime. Holland, more than any other province, was now deeply divided.[72] Yet in view of the perilous external situation of the Republic neither side wished to see the contest escalate to the point where it might seriously unsettle the regime or disrupt the mechanism of the State.

In the years 1625–8 the United Provinces remained under siege without and intense pressure within. There was little or no alleviation of either the trade depression or the dismal strategic situation both of which, in some respects, grew worse.[73] The Habsburgs extended their power over northern Germany. The commercial slump dragged on through the years 1625–9 when, besides the existing embargoes and dislocation caused by the Swedish–Polish conflict in the Baltic, the Spaniards mounted a sustained blockade on the rivers and stepped up their naval offensive. Privateers operating

---

[70] Wagenaar, *Amsterdam*, i. 500–4.

[71] GA Leiden Sec. Arch 917, res. vroed. 19 Jan. 1629; GA Gouda OA 9, fo. 112v, res. vroed. 26 Feb. 1629.

[72] De Fijne, *Eenige Tractaatjes*, ii. 200–1.

[73] Israel, *Dutch Republic and the Hispanic World*, 116–17, 190–4; Israel, *Empires and Entrepots*, 118.

from Dunkirk and Ostend captured numerous Dutch ships in the North Sea and Channel, forcing Dutch freight rates higher, and, in 1625 and 1627 particularly, inflicting great damage on the Dutch herring fleets. Even so, the worst of the crisis was now over. Frederik Hendrik showed patience and adroitness in coping with the difficulties, providing firmer, more resolute leadership than could Maurits in the last years of his life. Still more important, after capturing Breda, the Spaniards had been unable to continue their land offensive. At that stage the Republic had appeared to be in serious difficulty and Spanish ministers knew this. But the strain imposed by the resumption of war in the Low Countries on Spain's finances was immense and the insupportable cost in men and money of the Bergen-op-Zoom and Breda campaigns had persuaded even Olivares that the offensive had to be abandoned. In May 1625 the Council of State, in Madrid, agreed to cease offensive operations against the Dutch by land, place the army of Flanders on a defensive footing, and cut the funds provided from Spain by one-sixth. A third factor mitigating the crisis was that although the Spanish river blockade paralysed the Republic's river trade with the south Netherlands and the Rhineland, the damage was offset, as far as most of the population was concerned, by the resulting glut of victuals within the Republic. The Spanish action, in effect, engineered a sharp drop in food prices affording welcome relief to the hard-pressed urban population.

By the winter of 1628–9, there was unmistakable evidence that a basic shift in the balance of military power in the Low Countries was under way. While the Spanish army of Flanders, contracted after the fall of Breda, from 1626, the Dutch standing army grew. Where the financial predicament of the Spanish Crown steadily worsened, that of the States General eased, owing to the new excises introduced in 1623–4 and the French subsidy. Where the Dutch had fought alone hitherto, England entered the war against Spain, in 1625, in alliance with the Republic. The sensational success of the WIC fleet, under Piet Heyn, in capturing the Mexican treasure convoy off the Cuban coast, at Matanzas, in 1628, further depressed Spain's fortunes and encouraged the Dutch, the eleven million guilders in captured silver greatly enhancing the prospects of the WIC. But most decisive of all was the Franco-Spanish conflict which broke out over the Mantuan Succession (1628–31), resulting in a massive diversion of Spanish cash and troops to Italy which would otherwise have been committed to the Netherlands.[74] It was this—for Spain—disastrous Mantuan entanglement above all, which explains why the United Provinces achieved, rather suddenly

[74] Elliott, *Count-Duke of Olivares*, 366–7.

(albeit temporarily), a general superiority over Spanish arms in the Low
Countries at the end of the 1620s.

The Spanish army of Flanders, amounting to 70,000 to 80,000 men during
the years of the offensive, between 1621 and 1625, comprised only 50,000
men by 1628.[75] Spain still maintained a string of formidable garrisons in the
Low Countries, the largest being those of Breda, 's-Hertogenbosch, Wesel,
and in and around Antwerp (see Table 26). But there was now a less than
adequate field army to cover these somewhat widely separated bases and
they were also less well supplied than a few years earlier.

TABLE 26. *The Spanish ring around the Republic, 1626–1628*

Garrison	Dec. 1626	Feb. 1628	Future troop-levels planned in Apr. 1628
Lingen	2,000	1,353	2,200
Grol	1,500	(lost in 1627)	
Wesel	2,500	3,077	2,750
Rheinberg	800	1,695	1,800
Düsseldorf	600	581	200
Geldern	400	400	400
Roermond	400	506	?
's-Hertogenbosch	1,500	2,730	2,500
Breda	2,000	4,067	2,500
Antwerp with Zandvliet	600	3,518	2,360
Hulst	600	844	1,500
Sas van Gent	600	500	600
Bruges and the Bruges–Ghent canal	1,400	580	400
Damme	1,000	546	
Ostend	1,000	166	800

Note: The table shows actual reported troop-strength in the main Spanish fixed garrisons
around the Republic and the garrison strengths fixed in Madrid in April 1628 as
appropriate for a long-drawn-out war of attrition by Olivares, Spínola, and other
ministers.

Sources: AGS Estado 2041, *consulta* of the Cosnejo de Estado, 10 Mar. 1627; AGS Estado
2321, 'Relación de los oficiales y soldados', Mar. 1628; AGS Estado 2320, 'Relación de la
gente de guerra de guarnicion que se ha ajustado que es necesario que aya en los presidios
de los estados de Flandes', Apr. 1628.

Meanwhile Stadholder and *Raad van State* had persuaded the States
General, in March 1626, to increase Dutch troop-strength by 7,000 men,
from 48,000 to 55,000, making the army, for the first time, equivalent to or

[75] Israel, *Dutch Republic and the Hispanic World*, 162–5.

larger than the army of Flanders. Soon after, Dutch troops, under Ernst
Casimir, captured Oldenzaal, liquidating the Spanish presence in Overijssel.
The following year, the States General voted a further increase in troop-
strength to 58,000 men, so that the Dutch army was now appreciably larger
than the army of Flanders.[76] In 1627, after a short siege, Frederik Hendrik
captured Grol, clearing the Spaniards from the *Achterhoek* of Gelderland.
Yet, for the moment and during most of 1628, the wider situation still
favoured Spain.[77] For in 1627, the armies of the Emperor and Catholic
League, in Germany, advancing northwards, decisively defeated the king of
Denmark. The Habsburgs now dominated the whole of north Germany,
and the Dutch situation appeared as precarious as at any time since the
1580s.[78] Hence, during 1628, the States General were forced to concentrate
their forces in the north-east, ordering their commanders to keep strictly on
the defensive. The army of the Catholic League, with Imperialist contingents, entered East Friesland, occupying positions close to the Dutch
border. There was no fighting but the tension was acute. The States General
stopped the flow of provisions, beyond the Dutch garrisons, to the Ems
valley. From Madrid, Olivares laboured to arrange a joint Imperialist–
Spanish invasion across the Ems into Groningen, and beyond, a threat
which seemed very real to the Dutch during most of 1628.[79]

POLITICS, IDEOLOGY, AND THE GREAT DUTCH TOLERATION DEBATE OF THE LATE 1620S

Lacking the support of the Stadholder, the Counter-Remonstrants were
now heavily dependent on their ability to sway the public, and therefore on
publicity and propaganda. The effect was further to embitter and intensify
the war of ideologies fought through the printed word. Accused by
Uyttenbogaert of rejecting the Spanish king's faith but adopting his intolerant methods,[80] Counter-Remonstrants lambasted the Remonstrants as 'hypocrites' who, before 1618, had lorded over Utrecht, Rotterdam, Gouda,
Hoorn, Alkmaar, Tiel, and Zaltbommel, so intolerantly they had refused to
permit even one preacher 'of our persuasion'. The Arminians, they held,
were not really a Church at all but a political faction who had deliberately
divided the public Church in order to weaken the Union and control the

[76] Ten Raa and De Bas, *Staatsche leger*, iv. 355–6.
[77] Elliott, *Count-Duke of Olivares*, 331–5.
[78] ARB SEG 126. Olivares to Spínola, Madrid, 30 Apr. 1628.
[79] Van der Capellen, *Gedenkschriften*, i. 444, 451–2, 465; Grotius, *Briefwisseling*, iii. 236.
[80] Uyttenbogaert, *Ondersoek*, 23.

state. Bicker and De Graeff might claim to be members of the public Church but, Counter-Remonstrant propaganda assured the people, they were 'dissimulators', members of the same pernicious faction of 'Arminians' and 'Barneveldists' who had subverted the Union until 1618.[81] Meanwhile, in their own towns, Counter-Remonstrant city governments cracked down with all the means at their disposal. The men put in in 1618 at Leiden, according to Pachier de Fijne, were now the fiercest persecutors in Holland, relentlessly fining and banishing their own citizens in their unholy zeal to crush Arminian sentiment in the city.[82]

Among the leading Counter-Remonstrant controversialists of the late 1620s were Adriaen Smout and Jacobus Trigland at Amsterdam, Roseaus at The Hague, and, perhaps the most systematic as an anti-toleration publicist, Henricus Arnoldi of Delft.[83] Arnoldi, asked to write the South Holland Synod's remonstrance of July 1628, petitioning the States of Holland to enforce the ban on Remonstrant conventicles, denounced Remonstrantism as politically as well as theologically subversive, as it caused disturbances in the body politic—he cited recent riots in Rotterdam, Gouda, Delft, Warmond, Oestgeest, and Hazerswoude—and spread Pelagian and Socinian ideas.[84] He argued that toleration had now gone too far in the United Provinces and should, as a matter of urgency, be pruned back.

Arnoldi expounded his arguments most systematically in his tract *Vande Conscientie-dwangh*, published at Delft, in 1629. It is striking that he expressly bases his philosophy of intolerance on the principles of the Revolt and Union of Utrecht. Refusing freedom to gather, practise, publish, and teach, he insisted (contradicting Coornhert), in no way conflicted with the freedom of conscience enshrined in the Union of Utrecht.[85] Consequently, the toleration for which the Remonstrants were now calling—in contrast to their previous, pre-1618, stance—conflicted with the authentic legacy of the Revolt against Spain and was incompatible with the 'freedom' for which William the Silent, and the generation of the Revolt, had fought. He pointed out that neither the States General, nor provincial States, had ever authorized the 'free exercise of their pretended religions to the Lutherans or Mennonites, and still less to the godless Jews, in these lands; their conducting services in some places occurs only as a consequence of the secular authorities turning a blind eye'.[86] Nor was it only the Remonstrants who

---

[81] *Cort ende bondich verhael van de Arminiaansche Factie*, fo. A3v.
[82] De Fijne, *Eenige Tractaatjes*, ii. 200–1.
[83] Van Gelder, *Getemperde vrijheid*, 238–41.
[84] Knuttel, *Acta*, i. 239–45.
[85] Arnoldi, *Vande Conscientie-dwangh*, 20.
[86] Ibid. 93.

should be vigorously suppressed by the Generality and the provincial governments. He allowed that the Lutherans and Mennonites could safely be tolerated 'as long as they keep silent and do not concern themselves with political matters, or the public Church, and avoid all conspiracy against the state of these United Provinces'.[87] But tolerating Jews, he argued, damages all Christian society 'since they insult the name of Christ', so that Jews should not be tolerated anywhere.

Arnoldi rightly saw that the toleration the Remonstrants were now calling for differed from the pre-1618 toleration of Arminius, Grotius, and Uyttenbogaert fundamentally. He was correct also in discerning Episcopius rather than Uyttenbogaert as the true author of the new toleration. In Arnoldi's view, the Arminians, whatever they claimed, derived their new principles not from 'God's Word, or Scripture . . . but the books of Dierick Volckertsz. Coornhert'[88]—still a damning indictment in the eyes of many regents. Arnoldi made much of the inconsistency of Episcopius, Uyttenbogaert, De Fijne, and the other Remonstrant advocates of toleration, whom he accused of unremitting intolerance towards the Counter-Remonstrants before 1618. He also ridiculed the examples they offered the regents of the benefits stemming from toleration, insisting that it was absurd to cite Poland under King Stephen Bathory as a model of tranquil coexistence between Reformed, Lutherans, and Catholics since Poland was a land of chronic instability and turmoil.[89]

All the Remonstrant leaders participated in the new intellectual and publicity campaign in favour of toleration. They all argued for toleration in general and not merely a particular toleration for Remonstrants. Only Grotius, in Paris, persisted in adhering to the very limited concept of toleration which he had proclaimed before 1618, insisting that a public or state Church, supreme over the religious life of the bulk of society, was absolutely necessary to the stability of society and the body politic.[90] While he had conceded that the regime which he had served had 'connived' at Lutheran and Mennonite conventicles, for practical reasons, he had denied that these Churches were tolerated on any basis of principle or that they should be. For Grotius, the unchallengeable ascendancy of the public Church over society was more fundamental to its well-being than freedom for confessional minorities to organize or the individual openly to dissent. His ideal was an internally tolerant state Church, doctrinally soft-centred— he was resolutely opposed to the forcing of the individual conscience—but institutionally powerful, embracing the great majority of society. Thus, Grotius' toleration was no more than an acceptance of theological

[87] Ibid. 94.   [88] Ibid. 28.   [89] Ibid. 47–8.   [90] Grotius, *Oratie*, 52.

disparities, as far as practicable, within the public Church. This is the toleration he proclaimed in his early treatise *Meletius* (1611; a text only recently published), and to which he adhered throughout his life. Fundamentally, Grotius' toleration resembled that of Lipsius and Scaliger, advanced a generation earlier, subordinating theological dispute to the requirements of the public good and keeping dissenting Churches as peripheral and inconspicuous as possible. Grotius' treatise on the toleration of the Jews, of 1614, fits very much within this frame. On balance, he takes the view that it is right for a Christian society to tolerate Jews but he opposed the granting of full freedom of worship and stipulated harsh restrictions to ensure that Jews did not publicize their faith, convert Christians, or polemicize against Christianity.[91]

But even Grotius made some contribution to the great toleration debate which began with the onset of Frederik Hendrik's stadholderate and which (though it continued through the 1630s) was at its most intense and decisive phase in the late 1620s. Grotius advised his ideological allies inside the United Provinces to commence their campaign by extending the toleration accorded to Lutheran worship. Grotius, seeing that Luther's doctrine of will and Grace approximated to that of Arminius, believed that greater toleration of Lutheranism in the Republic would, of itself, eventually lead the States of Holland to accept the setting up of a separate Remonstrant Church.[92]

Meanwhile, Uyttenbogaert argued for a broader toleration and so did his colleagues, among them Paschier de Fijne, who in his tracts of these years vehemently denounced the intolerance and 'Calvinistic fury' of the Counter-Remonstrants, denouncing all religious persecution as destructive of human freedom and also of economic prosperity. Like Uyttenbogaert and Episcopius, he cited the commercial and industrial slump gripping Holland and Zeeland in the 1620s as unassailable evidence of the harmful effects of religious persecution, ascribing the economic malaise to the repression of Arminian merchants and artisans, some of whom had chosen to emigrate.[93] Both Uyttenbogaert and De Fijne pressed for toleration of other Churches besides that of the Remonstrants, Uyttenbogaert eventually coming round, in a tract which he addressed to Frederik Hendrik in 1639, to urge the full and unrestricted toleration of Catholic worship in the United Provinces.[94] Yet only Episcopius amongst the Remonstrant publicists of the late 1620s

[91] Grotius, *Remonstrantie*, 112–16.
[92] Grotius, *Briefwisseling*, ii. 154–7.
[93] De Fijne, *Eenige Tractaatjes*; 'Broederlicke vermaninge' (1624), A2–5; and 'Silvere Naalde' (1624), B3–8.
[94] *Archief aartsbisdom Utrecht*, ii. 1–25.

and 1630s can be said to have developed a fully fledged doctrine of toleration, breaking with the premises of the past, arguing for unrestricted freedom of practice, as well as of conscience, for all Churches and individuals, accepting the validity of variety of religions and human belief.[95] He was also the first since Coornhert, preceding Uyttenbogaert, to argue expressly in favour of tolerating Catholic practice as distinct from conventicles. Episcopius, reviving Coornhert, championed a wider concept of toleration, the tradition continued in the work of Philippus van Limborch, later in the century, which eventually influenced Locke.

The difference between Episcopius, in his key tract *Vrye Godes-dienst* (1627) and the *Apologia pro Confessione Remonstrantium* (1629), and Uyttenbogaert or De Fijne is that the Amsterdammer derives his toleration principles from his theology, working out the implications to make a consistent whole. According to Episcopius, Christians largely agree on the essentials of their faith, most contemporary theological dispute being about *non necessaria* over which consensus is neither needed nor possible. A wide variety of views may legitimately be derived from Scripture, which means that diversity of belief is not harmful, and indeed has a certain validity, in God's eyes, each strand comprising fragments of truth.[96] Consequently, the views of every individual about Scripture ought to have validity in the eyes of other individuals, Churches, and the State. Disparity in interpreting Scripture Episcopius thus elevates to a positive good, where for Arnoldi and the Counter-Remonstrants such diversity is a plague. From the outset, Episcopius' toleration had as much to do with the freedom of the individual, and the impermissibility of coercion, within any given Church, as with toleration of practice for each Church.

Episcopius' *Vrye Godes-dienst* (Free Religion) narrates a dialogue between a Remonstrant, and a Counter-Remonstrant, layman, evoking echoes of innumerable lay encounters pervading Dutch life—not least in town halls, taverns, and passenger-barges—for over two decades. The Counter-Remonstrant argues that society will be more stable, and the state stronger, if only one Church is permitted to hold divine service publicly, and preach, publicize, and teach its faith, backed by the state. By contrast, Episcopius' Arminian holds that allowing freedom of practice to all Churches, and free preaching and teaching, frees society from the pent-up stress, and frustration, inevitable when there are many views and beliefs but only one interpretation of Scripture finds public expression.[97] Where the state enforces one

[95] Nobbs, *Theocracy and Toleration*, 103–5.
[96] Van Limborch, 'Voor-reden', 2–4.
[97] Episcopius, *Vrye Godes-dienst*, 36–7.

particular confession, forbidding other views, resentment and disillusionment will inevitably grow within the public Church, as well as outside, in
those who reject it in their hearts. But also, within dissenting Churches, all
efforts to stifle internal criticism of articles of faith imposed by that Church's
authorities, in their desire to keep their Church's teachings uniform and
confessionally pure, are mistaken and violate the legitimate freedom of the
individual. For no human conscience, or intellect, is above another, or can
judge another.[98] Everybody has equal access to God's Word and God's
truth. Not only persecution, but ecclesiastical authority, imposed by any
form of coercion is wrong, and harms society, not just because it generates
resentment, and disrupts political and economic life, but, still more, because
coercion stifles true enquiry into Scripture, reducing the individual to an
unthinking cipher or worse, a hypocrite who, in his heart, rejects what
publicly he professes.[99]

Toleration, in Episcopius' view, strengthens the state because only that
state is secure whose citizens are content, and this can only be where
conscience, enquiry, and religious practice are free and untrammelled. In a
free society, nobody will resent the state and want to overthrow it. On the
contrary, its citizens, whatever their beliefs, will cherish and defend it. For
the hatred of the state which breeds conspiracy and subversion, and makes
citizens unwilling to support it, is the product of intolerance and lack of
freedom. It is only 'free minds and hearts', he insists, 'that are willing to
support the common interest'.[100] How does Episcopius square this with the
danger posed, in the midst of war with Spain and the south Netherlands, by
the hostility of Dutch Catholics? He takes the bull by the horns, arguing
that Catholics should enjoy the same freedom of exercise as others,
provided, in this case, that political precautions are taken. To safeguard the
state, Episcopius proposes that Catholics must 'declare that they will
conduct themselves as true and upright subjects according to the laws of the
country' and take an oath of loyalty before the magistracy 'with express
renunciation of all those maxims which would dispense them from such an
oath'.[101]

How can there be a public Church, under Episcopius' toleration, if there
can be no confessional discipline, or ecclesiastical authority? Episcopius
answered, in his *Apologia*, that Remonstrants did not deny the public
Church, or any Church, the right to impose discipline of belief and conduct,
based on spiritual authority. They denied only that the public Church, or
any Church, could legitimately coerce, or penalize, its members—with or

[98] Ibid. 43.   [99] Ibid. 36–7.   [100] Ibid. 37.   [101] Ibid. 44.

without the backing of the secular authority.[102] The sole ecclesiastical power which was valid was that to teach and persuade, the exercising of a purely spiritual sway.[103] Only this kind of authority, moreover, could elicit true and sincere compliance. Thus not merely did the secular authority have no right to impose any Church on the people, it had no business trying to influence, on theological grounds, the individual's life-style and private morality.

The great Dutch toleration debate of the late 1620s resounded through the length and breadth of the land, interacting continually with the wider political debate. On the constitutional side, the Counter-Remonstrants' most able publicist was the new Pensionary of Haarlem, Gillis de Glarges, one of the few south Netherlanders brought to the fore by Maurits's *coup d'état*. De Glarges demanded that the States General purge the Amsterdam *vroedschap*, as had been done in 1618. He lambasted Grotius, insisting the States General were, in part, a sovereign body.[104] Interestingly, he also rejected Grotius' principle that the regent city councils possessed an absolute right to 'represent', and speak for, the citizenry of the Holland towns, reminding readers that the Arminians had been happy enough to back popular insurrection, at Alkmaar and Leeuwarden, in 1609–10, when it suited them. For De Glarges, there were contexts in which the citizenry should express their views. Unmoved, Grotius wrote to Uyttenbogaert, in May 1629, reiterating that neither the Revolt against Spain, nor the Union of Utrecht, altered, or diluted, the powers and privileges of the city councils and provinces, and that the other provinces had no right to intervene in Holland, or change magistracies in the Holland towns, though it was legitimate for Holland to help other provinces to 'conserve their rights and authority'.[105] At times Grotius' juristic dexterity verged on double-talk, but at its heart was his burning conviction that toleration, in his limited sense, and the well-being and stability of society, could only be safe in the hands of the Republic's proper ruling élite, namely the regents, and that there was no basis on which the people could question the authority of the regents. As Grotius saw it, once tyranny was removed there was no longer any justification for the people to intervene in the political sphere.

[102] Nobbs, *Theocracy and Toleration*, 96–7.
[103] Van Limborch, 'Voorreden', 2.
[104] Grotius, *Briefwisseling*, iii. 45.
[105] Ibid. iv. 56–7.

22

The Republic in Triumph, 1629–1647

❖

FREDERIK HENDRIK VICTORIOUS
AND THE REGENTS DIVIDED, 1629–1632

Only over the winter of 1628–9, when the Catholic League forces withdrew, did it become clear how fundamentally the Mantuan war had altered the strategic balance in the Low Countries. The Dutch had remained continually on the defensive since 1604. Now, suddenly, there was the opportunity to break the Spanish ring encircling the Republic. At Brussels, the Infanta Isabella had, by February 1629, become extremely worried. She warned Philip that if the Dutch should besiege Breda or 's-Hertogenbosch, 'we see no way of saving either'.[1]

Frederik Hendrik hastened to profit from Spain's predicament. But at this point domestic difficulties threatened to interfere. Inevitably, a major offensive required additional troops, equipment, and supplies, and therefore funds. But following the recent furore at Amsterdam, the Counter- Remonstrant towns were in no mood to co-operate. In the circumstances they preferred a static war, at less cost, until what they regarded as the menace of resurgent Arminianism had been crushed. In the debates, over war-finance, of February 1629, the States of Holland split along ideological lines. Amsterdam and Rotterdam supported the Stadholder's request for resources, which they could scarcely refuse, given their dependence on his protection. By contrast, the Counter-Remonstrant towns—Leiden, Haarlem, Enkhuizen, Edam, and Schoonhoven—insisted there should be no offensive until 'religion and regime' had been placed on a sound basis.[2] Thus, they sought to impede the Stadholder's strategic plans as a weapon in their struggle with Remonstrantism and political Arminianism. Orange had to press hard, detaching Leiden, by working on Burgomaster van Brouckhoven, to win his majority.[3]

---

[1] ARB SEG 200, fo. 57. Isabella to Philip IV, 13 Feb. 1629.
[2] Res. Holl. 10 and 21 Mar. 1629.
[3] GA Leiden Sec. Arch. 447, fo. 99. res. vroed. 2 Feb. 1629.

With funds secured, additional troops were raised, bringing Dutch troop strength, by April 1629, to 77,000, half as much again as the army of Flanders. Commanding a field army of 28,000, and provided with a huge artillery train, the Stadholder swept down on 's-Hertogenbosch. In desperation, Isabella begged for Imperial assistance, which arrived in the shape of 16,000 men, under Count Montecuccoli. Together Imperialists and Spaniards launched a diversionary thrust across the IJssel, into the Dutch interior, the strategy the Dutch had most feared since Spínola's offensive of 1606, but which the Spaniards had not attempted to repeat until this point. Across the IJssel, the Spaniards hoped to sow sufficient panic in Holland to force Frederik Hendrik to pull back. But he stuck doggedly to his siege. The States of Holland hurriedly raised 5,000 civic militia men, sending them to garrisons in the south, drawing off regular troops which were then rushed to the IJssel line, Amsterdam dispatching 500 men to Heusden and Steenbergen.[4] Holland also borrowed thousands of seamen and WIC troops preparing for the invasion of Brazil launched the following year. At the height of the emergency, the States General, reportedly, had 128,000 men under arms. The Imperialists penetrated as far as Amersfoort, which promptly surrendered and where Catholic worship was briefly restored. But the Habsburg invasion collapsed when Dutch troops, far in the rear, surprised, and captured, Wesel, the principal Spanish base on the lower Rhine, in Cleves. This severed the Spanish supply lines, compelling the Imperialist and Spanish troops in Utrecht and Gelderland to withdraw to their IJssel crossing-points, though, from there, they still posed a threat. The 3,000-man garrison of 's-Hertogenbosch surrendered, after a five-month siege, in September.

This was a sensational event, a shattering blow to Spanish prestige, which caused deep dismay in Madrid.[5] The double loss of Wesel and 's-Hertogenbosch represented the first really large-scale Spanish defeat in Europe since the scattering of the Armada of 1588. Nieuwpoort was a battle lost but also one which proved the continuing strategic superiority of Spain in the Low Countries, and the qualitative edge of the Spanish infantry. The defeat of 1629 was 'epoch-making', showing that it was now the Dutch who enjoyed overall strategic superiority, at least while the Mantuan war continued. Spain had poured vast resources into 's-Hertogenbosch, building the most extensive and sophisticated fortifications—making no small use of Dutch designs—science could devise. The city was also the focus of the Counter-Reformation and seat of the only bishopric in north Brabant, besides being

---

[4] Aitzema, *Historie*, ii. 883–4.   [5] Elliott, *Count-Duke of Olivares*, 387–8.

the hinge of the line of Spanish strongholds running from the Flemish coast to Lingen, ringing the United Provinces until 1629 (see Table 26).[6] With its loss, there was a gaping hole in the middle. The Spanish strongholds no longer posed a credible strategic threat to the Republic. Deeply shaken, and abandoning all his Low Countries objectives pursued since 1621, Philip IV overruled Olivares, and resolved to extricate himself from the Netherlands quagmire by offering a long and (for the first time) unconditional truce—a truce being preferred to a full peace, at this stage, to circumvent the thorny matter of sovereignty.

The States General refused to negotiate, however, until all Spanish and Imperialist troops had evacuated the IJssel line.[7] On their withdrawal the States General passed on Philip IV's offer of a long and unconditional truce to the seven provincial assemblies. This signalled the start of one of the most divisive political debates of the Dutch Golden Age. The entire population participated, in one way or another, with dozens of pro- and anti-truce pamphlets circulating and much discussion in taverns and passenger barges. Frederik Hendrik's remarks in the States General and assemblies implied that he favoured the truce.[8] Some observers considered this merely a stratagem to mislead the Spaniards and panic the Counter-Remonstrant towns into loosening their purse-strings—as have modern historians. But if one scrutinizes those whom the Prince employed to bring his advice to the provinces, and quarter assemblies and their proceedings, it becomes clear that the Prince genuinely sought the truce, content to rest on the laurels he had already won and the strategic security which possession of 's-Hertogen-bosch conferred.[9] In Overijssel, Sweder van Haersolte secured a favourable vote in a few days. Frederik Hendrik's managers secured the approval of the Gelderland quarters in such haste as to leave no time for proper debate; Ploos organized matters, with the same result, in Utrecht. It is true that Friesland and Groningen rejected the proposal; but this was in spite, and not because of the Prince, as is clear from the speech delivered by Schaffer before the Groningen city council.[10] Zeeland, predictably, also rejected the truce but did so overruling the Prince's manager Simon van Beaumont, whose strenuous efforts to obtain a favourable vote greatly annoyed the regents and merchants of the province.[11] What conclusively proves that the Prince was in favour is that the head of the Holland *ridderschap*, Van den

[6] Israel, *Empires and Entrepots*, 174.
[7] GA Amsterdam Algemeen bestuur 11, fos. 182v–183.
[8] PRO SP 84/140, fo. 40; Poelhekke, *Frederik Hendrik*, 309–14.
[9] Israel, *Empires and Entrepots*, 45–56, 87–91.
[10] GA Groningen res. raad. 13 and 15 Oct. 1629.
[11] *Notulen SZ* 1629, pp. 363, 369–70.

Bouchorst, and the new Pensionary of Holland, Jacob Cats (1629–31; 1636–52), both totally subservient to Frederik Hendrik, laboured on behalf of the truce.[12]

But Frederik Hendrik, and his favourites, were hampered by the political split in Holland, which at this point was as acrimonious as at any time since 1618. The 1629–30 truce deliberations showed how profoundly the theologico-political split in the town councils affected the decision-making and general strategy of the state. The division of the States of Holland into warring Counter-Remonstrant and 'Arminian' factions made it impossible, in the end, to reach any decision about the truce. The *ridderschap* (reflecting the Prince's wishes) and 'Arminian' towns—Amsterdam, Rotterdam, Dordrecht, Alkmaar, and also Delft—came out in favour.[13] The Counter-Remonstrant towns, however, stubbornly rejected it. Frederik Hendrik tried to break the deadlock, in December, with a speech to the States of Holland, urging that the truce issue should be kept separate from the deliberations over 'regime and religion'.[14] The Counter-Remonstrants disagreed. Leiden insisted it was undesirable to enter into talks with Spain before a 'better order in the affairs of this state' was agreed, existing placards forbidding Remonstrant conventicles enforced, and the principle enacted that no non-member of the public Church could hold municipal, or provincial, office.[15] Haarlem, Schoonhoven, Schiedam, and several others likewise pressed for a 'good Church ordinance' before entering into negotiations with Spain.

As usual in Dutch Golden Age politics, the debate was also influenced by economic considerations. The pro-truce stance of Amsterdam and Rotterdam was rooted in the adverse effects of the war on trade and shipping. But equally Zeeland's attitude, that of the textile towns, and East and West India Companies, was linked to their economic interests. Zeeland had suffered during the Twelve Years Truce from the collapse of the transit traffic to the south. But from 1621, with the reimposing of the Dutch naval blockade of the Flemish seaports, this commerce, so vital to Zeeland's prosperity, had revived.[16] It was the fear of lapsing back into the slump of the Truce years which lay behind Zeeland's hostility to any new truce. Likewise Haarlem and Leiden benefited from the blockade of the Flemish coast and the war tariff reintroduced in 1621; for these together hampered

---

[12] PRO SP 84/140, fo 71–2. Carleton to Dorchester, 15 Oct. 1629.
[13] Israel, *Empires and Entrepots*, 90.
[14] RAZ SZ 2099. Zeeland deputies to SZ, The Hague, 10 Nov. 1629.
[15] GA Leiden Sec. Arch. 448, fos. 164, 167, 176 res. vroed. 6 Dec. 1629 and 7 Jan. 1630.
[16] Israel, *Dutch Republic and the Hispanic World*, 230.

the flow of wools and other raw materials from the Dutch entrepôt to the southern Netherlands, the north's main industrial competitor, while simultaneously impeding imports of finished textiles from the south, by (drastically) raising import duties, thus affording the Dutch textile towns double protection from Flemish and Brabantine competition.[17]

At the same time, the WIC, now preparing its invasion of Brazil, would have to cease its armed offensive in the New World and West Africa, in the event of a truce. This consideration may have cut little ice in Amsterdam, where the ruling clique had not forgiven the Company's siding with the Counter-Remonstrants against the *vroedschap*, in 1628; but in Zeeland, and various inland cities with sizeable holdings in the WIC, it was an appreciable factor. The truce controversy of 1629–30 sharpened the clash of interests between the merchants in European trade, which was in recession, and needed peace, and the colonial companies. This was fully admitted by Willem Usselincx, who argued, in several pamphlets published in 1629–30, that while it was undeniable that the war had seriously damaged their trade in Europe,[18] Dutch commerce as a whole could only flourish and be secure in the long term by expanding colonial commerce, since Dutch trade and shipping in European waters would always be vulnerable to the ambition and caprices of kings.

The most vociferous element outside civic and provincial government were, as usual, the preachers of the public Church. Urging the conquest of more of the Spanish Netherlands, and bitterly at odds with the 'Arminian' town councils, some preachers openly denounced the proposed truce from the pulpit, making plain their disapprobation of 'Barneveldist' regents. At Rotterdam, the burgomasters warned of severe measures if they did not desist.[19] At Amsterdam, the *vroedschap*, exasperated by the inflammatory sermons of Smout, banished him from the city in January 1630. This caused uproar in the public Church, two other leading Amsterdam preachers, Trigland and Cloppenburg, demonstrating their indignation by leaving the city also. The anti-truce towns deliberately chose this moment to introduce a new draft placard, banning Remonstrant conventicles, in the States of Holland, in a bid to rally the small towns, but were vigorously opposed by Amsterdam and Rotterdam together with the *ridderschap* acting in compliance with the Stadholder's wishes. The Haarlem *vroedschap* thereupon stepped up their campaign by taking the highly irregular step of publishing their resolution rejecting the Spanish truce offer, a text vehemently critical

---

[17] Israel, *Dutch Primacy*, 187–95.
[18] Usselincx, *Waerschouwinghe*, 1–5.
[19] GA Rotterdam res. vroed. 26 Nov. 1629.

of town governments which 'expel' Reformed preachers, and other 'honest persons', while permitting Arminians, and even Catholics, to 'creep' into the civic militia, and magistracy, sowing discord, instability, and ruin, in government and society.[20]

Haarlem's public denunciation of Amsterdam included a thinly veiled warning that popular unrest would increase until 'regime and religion' in the United Provinces were restored to the secure and 'godly' basis established by Maurits and the Synod of Dordrecht. The Haarlem city fathers saw the Republic's troubles as a direct consequence of the crumbling of the Counter-Remonstrant gains of 1618–19. By contrast, Grotius, observing from Paris, cited the deadlock as proof that Maurits's coup had divided and paralysed Holland, removing her experienced leaders, and reducing the province to the feebleness of the lesser provinces.[21] Maurits's coup, in Grotius' view, had 'enslaved Holland' to 'ignorant persons', by which he meant the Calvinist bigots of Haarlem and incompetent likes of Duyck.

The deadlock was total: on 7 December 1629, the States of Holland divided five against five, the rest assuming intermediate positions.[22] The Stadholder's efforts to break the impasse failed. Yet, as the months passed, contrary to Haarlem's prediction, popular unrest did not increase. Rather, during 1630, the tension between the opposing theologico-political blocs gradually subsided. It became clear that the attempts of Smout and Cloppenburg to incite the populace against the Amsterdam regents had been counter-productive. The conflict between the rival party-factions continued but lost intensity as the public slowly tired of interminable polemics after two decades of ceaseless tension and party strife, and the resulting impotence of the States of Holland. Remonstrantism and toleration remained divisive but no longer generated sufficient uproar to precipitate drastic solutions. Gradually, the grip of the 'Arminian' town councils on their cities strengthened, while popular Counter-Remonstrantism weakened. The Counter-Remonstrant towns could only dig in their heels and press their campaign of obstruction without hope of an imminent resolution of the tensions in State and Church.

The Stadholder backed the truce throughout. Philip IV's new chief minister at Brussels, the marqués de Aytona, assured Madrid, in June 1630, that Frederik Hendrik was endeavouring to push the truce through but being thwarted by the 'insolencia' of some Holland towns.[23] An English

[20] *Resolutie der Stadt Haerlem*, 10–13.
[21] Grotius, *Briefwisseling*, iv. 200–1.
[22] GA Leiden Sec. Arch 448, fo. 164v. res. vroed. 10 Dec. 1629.
[23] BRB MS 16149, fo. 32v. Aytona to Philip IV, 19 June 1630.

envoy to The Hague confirmed, in August 1630, that the Prince 'hath bin and is still affected to the Truce',[24] explaining the superficially baffling circumstance that it was the Arminian towns which supported Frederik Hendrik's call for additional funds, for the next campaign, while the Counter-Remonstrant towns, opposed to peace, refused every request for money, by observing that the Arminians were deliberately increasing taxation so that the 'common people will not be able to beare it, but . . . will conclude for a peace' while the Counter-Remonstrants, 'seeing this, will not by no means consent to the laying on of the hundreth penny, nor of making an offensive warre, or scarce thinking of putting their army into the field this year other than for defence'.[25] What the Counter-Remonstrants wanted was a long, static war which would also be cheaper than the offensive warfare Frederik Hendrik had waged in 1629.

The stalemate in Holland prevented the Stadholder taking the field in 1630. He had to be content with repairing the fortifications of Wesel and 's-Hertogenbosch. Meanwhile, the theologico-political conflict immobilizing Holland dragged on. Amsterdam and Rotterdam (supported, behind the scenes, by Frederik Hendrik) took up, during the summer of 1630, the Remonstrant leadership's plea that Holland's ban on Remonstrant prayer-gatherings now formally be lifted. The Counter-Remonstrants martialled their forces to resist. The political 'Arminians' won in the assembly of the *ridderschap*, overruling the Counter-Remonstrants led by Duivenvoorde;[26] but in the full States they lacked the support of sufficient towns. Dordrecht, ironically, and also Delft backed Amsterdam and Rotterdam. But hardly any other towns did so. Remonstrant gatherings now took place without hindrance, in Amsterdam, Rotterdam, and also at The Hague. But this was still not the case in most of Holland; the small towns, and Gouda, joined Haarlem and Leiden in insisting that Holland's prohibition of Remonstrant conventicles continue and be properly enforced, as at Haarlem and Leiden. But while this Arminian initiative was defeated, the majority were powerless to check the progress of Remonstrantism, and toleration generally, in Amsterdam and Rotterdam. Both Remonstrantism, and toleration, scored a notable victory, in September 1630, when the Amsterdam Remonstrants, backed by the *vroedschap*, completed their public church and the building was inaugurated by Episcopius. In the early 1630s, Remonstrantism again became an accepted part of civic life in some larger cities of Holland, and the portraits of the Remonstrant leaders, generally banished from sight,

---

[24] Israel, *Empires and Entrepots*, 91–2.
[25] PRO SP 84/141, fo. 89. Vane to Dorchester, 4 Mar. 1630.
[26] Grotius, *Briefwisseling*, iv. 230–1.

even in private homes, since 1618, reappeared. Van Mierevelt painted Uyttenbogaert in 1631 and had numerous copies made for sale. Rembrandt painted Uyttenbogaert's portrait in April 1633, adding an etched portrait soon after; of these, in contrast to most of Rembrandt's portraits, many copies were made and distributed.[27]

The cooling of tempers, during 1630, however, did nothing to remove the split among the Holland regents. The States of Holland, the Venetian ambassador reported to the Venetian Senate, continued to be totally paralysed by the rift between what he called 'Arminiani' and 'Gomaristi'.[28] To break the deadlock, the Stadholder planned another sensational military triumph for 1631. Initially, Haarlem and Leiden again blocked his request for additional funds.[29] But, backed by Amsterdam, Rotterdam, and Dordrecht, the Prince eventually obtained the cash needed for his offensive. His intention was to invade Flanders in force, as Maurits had done in 1600, besiege and capture Bruges or Dunkirk, and thoroughly humiliate Spain.[30] Amsterdam, Rotterdam, and also the States of Zeeland were keen to march on Dunkirk; for, since the mid-1620s, the town had become the principal base for naval and privateering attacks, from the South Netherlands, on Dutch shipping and the herring fishery. In scale, the invasion greatly eclipsed that led by Maurits in 1600. Frederik Hendrik descended the rivers into Flanders with 30,000 men, eighty field guns, and mountains of supplies of every type, on no fewer than 3,000 river ships. It was the most impressive display of the collective might of the United Provinces—and the incomparable efficiency of the Dutch state in organizing and transporting troops and equipment—yet seen. Disembarking at IJzendijk, the Stadholder penetrated to the Bruges–Ghent canal, spreading panic throughout Flanders. But the arrival of a sizeable Spanish force in his rear provoked an unseemly row between the Prince and Holland's deputies in the field, who insisted that the Stadholder must not risk the army, and therefore the state, by pressing on, and that the final say at such a critical moment must rest with the States General's deputies, not the Stadholder.[31] Furious, Frederik Hendrik ordered a retreat, having accomplished nothing after such vast expense and preparations. In his eyes it was humiliation less at the hands of the Spaniards than Holland's deputies. The summer of 1631—when Rembrandt moved his studio from Leiden to Amsterdam—afforded a foretaste of Holland's

---

[27] Tümpel, *Rembrandt*, 56–7; *A Corpus of Rembrandt Paintings*, ii. 91.
[28] *Capita Selecta Veneto-Belgica*, i. 152.
[29] Res. Holl. 13, 19, and 29 Mar. 1631.
[30] ARH SG 4562, fos. 199–200v. sec. res. SG 8 and 30 Apr. 1631.
[31] *Mémoires de Frédéric Henri*, 125–6; Van der Capellen, *Gedenkstukken*, i. 625–6.

pending revival as a counter-weight to the Stadholder, an inevitable development once the theologico-political strife in the province eased and a measure of unity was restored.

But the fray within Holland was not over yet. An event which did nothing to allay the worries of the Counter-Remonstrants, or help the Prince manage the States, was Grotius' attempt to return and resume life in the Republic. Uyttenbogaert and Episcopius had been allowed to return five years before, when Counter-Remonstrantism in Holland was stronger than it now was. But they were churchmen. Grotius was a statesman who, more than any other, embodied the principles of the Oldenbarnevelt regime. In Counter-Remonstrant eyes Grotius was both a heretical figure and a traitor to the state.

The statesman-scholar arrived in Rotterdam, ten and a half years after his legendary escape from Loevestein castle, in November. The sensational news reached The Hague at a moment when tempers were already frayed owing to the escape—also from Loevestein—of the remainder of the Remonstrant preachers held since Maurits's time, it was rumoured with the connivance of the Stadholder. Grotius' first outing in Rotterdam was to visit the town's celebrated statue to 'show my affection for the memory of Erasmus . . . who so well showed the way to the right kind of Reformation'.[32]

For six tense months, until April 1632, Grotius remained in Holland, hoping to be allowed to settle permanently. He knew that the Stadholder would (if possible) avoid arresting him and counted on friends, and the Arminian towns, to arrange matters. He lodged first in Rotterdam, then Delft (where his parents still lived and where political Arminianism was now in the ascendant), and finally, reckoning that he would be safest there from hostile pressures, at Amsterdam.[33] Whilst at Delft, his portrait was painted by Van Mierevelt, engraved, and widely distributed.

The 'Arminian' party proposed an amnesty for Grotius in the States of Holland. The Counter-Remonstrants moved to block it.[34] One of those most active in seeking the amnesty was the Rotterdam burgomaster, Gerard van Berkel, whom Frederik Hendrik had employed to conduct his secret contacts with the Archduchess Isabella during the years 1628–30. Behind the scenes, the campaign was supported by several members of the Prince's entourage, notably Van Beaumont, and also Uyttenbogaert and the playwright Hooft. In the end six Holland towns and also the *ridderschap*

[32] Becker, 'Rotterdamsche heyligh', 30.
[33] Hallema, *Hugo de Groot*, 116–22.
[34] Ibid. 123–4.

voted in favour of allowing Grotius to stay. But, once again, Haarlem, Leiden, and Gouda demonstrated not just their Counter-Remonstrant resolve but their ability to rally practically all the small towns, not least zealous Edam, Schoonhoven, and Enkhuizen. On the Grotius issue, the 'Arminians' were defeated in the States by twelve votes to seven, leaving Grotius with no option but hurriedly to depart.

In 1632, Frederik Hendrik succeeded in delivering that spectacular second blow for which he had striven since 1629. He prepared the ground well. To encourage the rising disaffection now evident in the Spanish Netherlands, and with the help of his Arminian allies, he persuaded a reluctant States General to publish a placard proclaiming that the public practice of the Catholic religion would continue, and be tolerated, in all places which fell to the States General that year.[35] He then used this placard to coax Count Hendrik van den Bergh into an anti-Spanish conspiracy designed to enable southern nobles to revolt against Spain, at the moment the Dutch invaded, without being accused of betraying their Catholic faith.

On 22 May, the States General published their 'manifesto', calling on the southern provinces to rise against the 'heavy and intolerable yoke of the Spaniards', promising that the Catholic clergy would remain and retain their churches and property in towns and districts which came over to the States. This manifesto greatly alarmed Spanish ministers in Brussels, for it was, above all, the Counter-Reformation, and strength of Catholic sentiment in the south, which ensured resilience in the face of Dutch pressure when Spain's military power in the Low Countries was at low ebb. Perceiving that Antwerp, his original objective, had been strongly reinforced, Frederik Hendrik switched instead to the Maas valley.[36] Commanding 30,000 men, he took Venlo early in June, and, soon after, Roermond, Sittard, and Straelen. Under the terms of capitulation, Catholicism remained intact and Church property, and revenues, in the hands of the Catholic clergy; each town was required only to hand over one church for Reformed worship.[37]

The Stadholder took up siege positions around the great fortress city of Maastricht, on 8 June. Count van den Bergh unfurled the banner of revolt against Spain, from Liège, issuing manifestoes, urging the nobility of the south to rise, and accusing the Spaniards of insufferable arrogance towards the nobles of the king's provinces. Other leading southern nobles were also plotting against Spain, but refused to follow Van den Bergh in colluding with the Dutch, preferring to conspire with Cardinal Richelieu than with

[35] ARH SG 4562. sec. res. SG 19 May 1632.
[36] ARH SG 4562, fos. 207, 209. sec. res. SG 5 Feb. and 21 Mar. 1632.
[37] Van Gelder, *Getemperde vrijheid*, 137.

heretics.[38] Thus, Frederik Hendrik's plan to unleash a general revolt in the south which would finally break Spanish power in the Low Countries, using religious toleration as his weapon, largely failed.

But the siege of Maastricht prospered. Once again the Spaniards faced a major humiliation. In a desperate effort to save Maastricht, the Spanish army of the Palatinate was summoned and the Emperor sent an additional force under his general Pappenheim. But the Dutch entrenchments were too strong to be stormed and all attempts to relieve the city failed. Meanwhile, the Dutch subjected the fortifications to unremitting bombardment, gradually advancing their trenches and underground shafts closer. Frederik Hendrik sprang his mines, on 20 August, blasting great gaps in the walls. The city capitulated three days later, like Venlo and Roermond, securing the public exercise of the Catholic faith and most of the Church's property.

Jubilation swept the United Provinces. Church bells rang throughout the land. Vondel, who had celebrated the capture of 's-Hertogenbosch with a stately poem, in 1629, and generally lauded Frederik Hendrik's tolerant and moderate proceedings in the late 1620s, now published a triumphal poem, the *Stedekroon van Frederick Henrick*, extolling the Stadholder, and contrasting his conduct with the cruelty and intolerance of the sack following Parma's capture of the city in 1579. Vondel eulogized Frederik Hendrik as the liberator of Maastricht but still more as the champion of toleration, and of peace, striving to bring the age-old war with Spain, and Catholicism, to an end—a theme the poet had already broached in his poem of 1629.[39] Desperately trying to shore up the king's Netherlands, the Infanta in Brussels, now in the last months of her life, sent her trusted intermediary, the artist Rubens, to Maastricht, to lay new secret truce proposals before Frederik Hendrik and the Dutch 'deputies in the field'.[40] But the Stadholder paid little attention to Rubens, detecting a more advantageous path to peace.

THE NEGOTIATIONS BETWEEN
NORTH AND SOUTH OF 1632–1633

After the defeats of the summer of 1632, Spanish power in the south was so debilitated that Isabella was unable to resist the pressure of the southern provinces for the convening of their States General. The southern States General duly met, in September, in Brussels, for what was to be their last

---

[38] Waddington, *République des Provinces Unies*, i. 146–50.
[39] Duits, *Van Bartholomeusnacht tot Bataafse opstand*, 172–5.
[40] Gachard, *Histoire politique*, 242–3, 248.

ever gathering under Spanish rule. Most of the provincial delegations urged immediate talks to end the war, to 'preserve' the southern provinces and the Catholic faith.[41] A delegation of the Brussels States General, headed by the duke of Aerschot and archbishop of Mechelen, then met the northern States General's 'deputies in the field', at Maastricht, offering to negotiate peace on the strength of Philip IV's authorization to Isabella of 1629. In fact, Philip IV and Olivares never authorized the negotiations which Isabella was now forced to permit, and secretly cancelled the authority given to her in 1629. Olivares always regarded the ensuing proceedings between the two States General as a usurpation of royal authority which posed a dire threat to the Spanish Crown and, from the outset, worked to undermine them.[42] But so weak was Spain's military position in the Low Countries at this point that he, and the king, had little alternative but to appear to approve, for the time being, until powerful reinforcements could be sent. Throughout the negotiations of 1632–3, Olivares was far more concerned with restoring Spanish authority in the south than seeking an accommodation with the Dutch.

Frederik Hendrik, by contrast, sought to seize the opportunity and draw the southern provinces into talks, at Maastricht, whilst his army remained at his side. Consequently, he desired the Dutch provinces to authorize immediate talks for a full peace. There was no problem with Gelderland, Overijssel, and Utrecht—the traditional 'peace' provinces—his usual 'managers' obtaining authorization within days.[43] But Zeeland, Friesland, and Groningen again refused and, as before, there was a deep split in the States of Holland. The *Gecommitteerde Raden* wrote to the town councils asking them to respond with maximum speed, within three days. All the Arminian towns did so—as did the *ridderschap*—reflecting Frederik Hendrik's wishes. But while only Leiden rejected talks outright,[44] the other Counter-Remonstrant towns (except Gorcum and Purmerend, which had voted with the latter on Remonstrant conventicles but now sided with Amsterdam, Rotterdam, and Dordrecht on peace talks) would permit the States General's delegates at Maastricht to do no more than hear the proposals of the Brussels States General.

The obstacles to prompt negotiations at Maastricht proved insuperable because Friesland, Groningen, and Zeeland, and the Holland Counter-Remonstrant towns, insisted that they would, in any case, negotiate only

[41] Gachard, *Actes*, i. 3–6.
[42] Israel, *Empires and Entrepots*, 179–80.
[43] RAZ SZ 2102. Zeeland deputies in The Hague to SZ, 19 Oct. 1632.
[44] GA Leiden Sec. Arch. 449, fos. 1–4, res. vroed. 9 Oct. 1632.

'States to States', excluding the king of Spain.[45] This was useless in the eyes of the Stadholder and Arminian towns, as it was obvious there could be no peace without the Spanish Crown being party to it, while for Amsterdam it was vital to include Spain, since one of the city's chief objectives was to restore commerce with the Peninsula and, through Spain, with Spanish America.

It took until November (the month Spinoza was born at Amsterdam) for the Dutch States General to agree to negotiate. The talks commenced at The Hague, in December. Adriaen Pauw (son of Renier) had succeeded Jacob Cats as Pensionary of Holland, in April 1631, and, considered a compromise candidate acceptable to both Arminians and Counter-Remonstrants, headed the Dutch delegation. Other key members were Van den Bouchorst, Beaumont, and Johan de Knuyt, Frederik Hendrik's representative, as First Noble in the States of Zeeland. At this stage the Stadholder got on well with Pauw.[46]

The Dutch side presented numerous preconditions for peace, including (at the insistence of the Counter-Remonstrant towns) the demand that the Reformed Church be tolerated in the southern provinces. There was initially an immense gap between the sides but gradually, over the winter months, both gave ground, discarding many of their original demands. Of course, the southern delegation, as the weaker party, began with fewer and yielded most. The only major point on which they were adamant—at Isabella's insistence and aware that otherwise the king of Spain would certainly repudiate any agreement which they signed—was that the Dutch must evacuate the part of Brazil which the WIC had conquered in 1630. In exchange, the Brussels assembly offered Breda and cash reparations to compensate the WIC.[47] The Dutch demands were more numerous, though the Arminian towns, impatient for peace, and the Stadholder ensured that many were soon dropped. But, as more and more of the initial list was jettisoned by Pauw, and his colleagues, the Counter-Remonstrant party-faction became increasingly agitated. The Zeelanders were indignant when the Holland peace towns proposed dropping the demand for mixed administration of the Flemish seaports, a device intended to ensure that tolls and imposts in those ports, in peacetime, matched those applying on the Scheldt, thereby preventing diversion of Zeeland's transit trade to the Flemish coast.[48] In April 1633, Pauw presented a much more moderate list of

[45] Ibid., fo. 13v, res. vroed. 7 Dec. 1632; GA Gouda OA 9, fo. 188v, res. vroed. 15 Nov. 1632.
[46] Fouw, *Onbekende raadpensionarissen*, 63–4.
[47] Gachard, *Actes*, i. 148–52.
[48] De Boer, *Friedensunterhandlungen*, 80–5.

desiderata than the southern side had been faced with at the outset. However, these had been agreed in the States General by only four provinces to three—over the objections of Zeeland, Friesland, and Groningen, while there was mounting criticism also from the Counter-Remonstrant towns within Holland and Utrecht. The States of Utrecht backed Frederik Hendrik and the Holland 'Arminians', with the *ridderschap* and small towns overruling the rigidly Counter-Remonstrant city.[49]

But while the Dutch had now considerably moderated their initial demands, they still insisted on annexing the whole of the sizeable territory of the Meierij (see Map 10), which Aerschot and the States of Brabant wished to keep in the south—claiming it as a jurisdictional appendage of 's-Hertogenbosch. In addition they demanded Breda and Geldern, tariff guarantees, and—given Spain's refusal to accept the WIC's gains in Brazil— limitation of the peace to Europe only, with the war continuing in the Indies. Throughout these months Frederik Hendrik professed (as he had in 1629) to be neutral on the main question, refusing to declare in the assemblies whether he preferred to conclude peace or not. Yet it was no less clear in the spring of 1633 than in 1629–30 that the Stadholder was endeavouring, with the Arminian towns, to negotiate an end to the war.[50] The Republic was no longer in danger. Since the Swedish intervention in Germany, in 1630, the Habsburg preponderance in central Europe had been drastically cut back. France, under Richelieu, was increasingly challenging Spain for hegemony in Europe. From the standpoint of Frederik Hendrik and the Arminian towns, the United Provinces could safely rest on their laurels, enjoy the fruits of past success, and profit from the escalating conflicts between France and Spain, and Sweden and the Emperor. In a tense meeting, in April, the Zeeland delegation to the States General reproached Orange for being too inclined to peace and neglecting Zeeland's interests. Frederick Hendrik admitted he was in favour of peace if a settlement could be reached which would be reputable and secure;[51] but he promised that he would sacrifice neither the essential interests of the 'state', nor Zeeland's interests in particular—a reference to tariffs in the Flemish seaports. By June 1633, the negotiations were on the verge of collapse. The Arminian towns urged further concessions for the sake of peace. This put pressure on the Prince to stipulate how far he was prepared to go, together with the Holland 'Arminians'. He advised that in his judgement the other

---

[49] ARH SG 12,548. Utrecht vroed. to SG, 27 May 1633.
[50] De Boer, *Friedensunterhandlungen*, 141–2.
[51] Israel, *Dutch Republic and the Hispanic World*, 247.

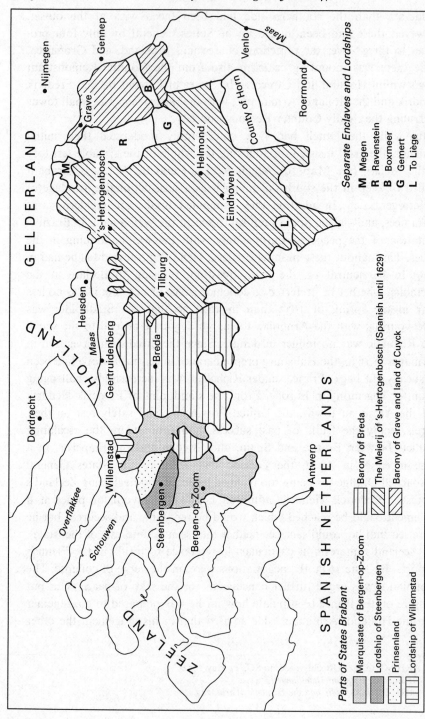

MAP 10. States Brabant after 1629

side must yield on three essential points if there was to be peace: the whole Meierij, tariff guarantees, and the WIC's conquests in Brazil.

At this point, for the first time in Frederik Hendrik's stadholderate, a significant gap opened between him and the 'Arminian' towns.[52] For Amsterdam, Rotterdam, and Dordrecht were so anxious, out of commercial considerations, to reach a settlement they were prepared to go substantially further than the Stadholder to achieve peace. Previously, from September 1632 to June 1633, the *ridderschap*, Amsterdam, and Rotterdam had commanded a solid majority in the States of Holland and nudged the hard-core Counter-Remonstrant towns—Haarlem, Leiden, Gouda, and Enkhuizen—into one concession after another.[53] At that stage, the 'Arminians' disposed of majorities in the States of Holland and Utrecht but partly because of the support of the Stadholder. Then, in the summer of 1633, over the Meierij, Flemish ports, and Brazil, the peace party's majority dissolved. Orange distanced himself from Amsterdam, and the 'Arminians', during August, declaring in the States General that if the Brussels assembly did not concede his three points within a month, the talks should be broken off.[54] Until August 1633, Richelieu had seen little prospect of coaxing Frederik Hendrik into allying with France against Spain. In March 1633, the French ambassador at The Hague confirmed that the Prince definitely favoured a settlement with Spain. Only from the late summer of 1633 did French diplomats detect signs of a fundamental shift in the framework of Dutch politics.[55] Suddenly, Frederik Hendrik was no longer deaf to the allurements of the French and Swedes.

The possibility of a break between the Stadholder and the Holland 'Arminians' had been on the cards since at least June, when the Amsterdam *vroedschap* made up its mind to press for evacuation of Brazil—with Spain paying compensation to the WIC—rather than let the peace process collapse.[56] Rotterdam and Dordrecht had also instructed their delegates to the States of Holland to agree to further substantial concessions to end 'this sorrowful and burdensome war', meaning that they too were ready to abandon Brazil.[57]

By August, the Holland towns had to decide what to do about their Stadholder's advice to break off the negotiations with the Brussels States General if his three conditions were not met. Haarlem, Leiden, and the small

---

[52] Israel, *Empires and Entrepots*, 92–4.
[53] Ibid. 62–3, 94–5.
[54] Ibid. 62, 94.
[55] *Archives*, 2nd ser. iii. 38–41; de Pange, *Charnacé*, 75–6.
[56] De Boer, *Friedensunterhandlungen*, 104.
[57] GA Rotterdam vroed. res. 9 June 1633; GA Dordrecht vroed. res. 6 June 1633.

towns accepted Frederik Hendrik's advice. But Amsterdam rejected it, as did Rotterdam, whose *vroedschap* insisted that the talks should not be abandoned and that 'with the aid of the Almighty a way to peace would be found'.[58] At this point, a fierce quarrel erupted between the Stadholder and Adriaen Pauw, who sided with Amsterdam and Rotterdam in wanting to persevere with the negotiations.[59] Much to the satisfaction of the French, the rift between Prince and peace towns could no longer be hidden and this changed the whole tenor of Dutch politics. By November, Orange was actively mobilizing his friends in the States of Holland and Utrecht against the 'Arminian' block.

In this way the peace negotiations between the two States General turned, during the autumn of 1633, into a struggle between the Stadholder and the 'Arminian' party-faction for control of the States of Holland and therefore of the Republic. It was thus only from this point on that the Holland 'Arminians' can be said to have again been, as they formerly were, in Oldenbarnevelt's time, the 'States' party in the sense that they stood for Holland's hegemony within the Union and ascendancy of the States over the Stadholder. The situation had not quite come full circle since 1618. For the moment, Orange was still at the helm. But, once again, the dominant element in the States of Holland was at odds with the Stadholder, and Calvinist orthodoxy. A further parallel was that there was, for the first time since Oldenbarnevelt's downfall, an energetic Pensionary leading the States of Holland in opposition to the Stadholder.

On 2 December 1633, the States of Holland voted on whether or not to break off talks with the southern States General. It was a victory for Pauw: only three Counter-Remonstrant (and now also Orangist) towns—Haarlem, Leiden, and Gouda—and the *ridderschap*, which switched with the Stadholder, voted according to the Prince's advice.[60] For the moment, the rest followed Amsterdam, Rotterdam, and Dordrecht. But Orange won in both Utrecht and Gelderland, where his influence over the *ridderschap* proved decisive. On 9 December, in the Prince's presence, the States General voted, by five provinces to two, to break off the talks. Just as in 1618, the Stadholder, backed by five provinces, confronted Holland supported by just one other—this time Overijssel.[61]

According to the French ambassador, Frederik Hendrik wavered for months, following his first clash with the Holland 'Arminians', in August,

[58] GA Rotterdam vroed. res. 10 Aug. 1633.
[59] Groenveld, *Evidente factien*, 34–5.
[60] Poelhekke, *Frederik Hendrik*, 404.
[61] De Pange, *Charnacé*, 83.

before going over, finally, to the war party and the Counter-Remonstrants.[62] He had good reason to hesitate. From 1625 to 1633, his overwhelming authority had rested principally on the split in Holland and his alignment with the 'Arminian' towns. He had played the Arminians off against the Counter-Remonstrants, exploiting the rift in Holland, to make himself the arbiter of all. The 'Arminians' had had no choice but to rely on his favour and protection. The new situation, by contrast, posed incalculable risks for the Stadholder. Pauw might mobilize enough support in the States of Holland to hamper seriously the Prince's conduct of affairs. It would be harder to secure funds for his military campaigns and he was apt to become excessively dependent on France. Hitherto, Orange had enjoyed the support of the Remonstrants, and other non-Calvinists, and faced the veiled disapproval of the Counter-Remonstrants. The danger now was that no segment would give him their unqualified support. Amongst those who cooled was Vondel.[63] Having penned numerous poems extolling the Prince as a hero of toleration and moderation, as well as war, down to 1632, Vondel pointedly left off doing so from 1633. Even at the time of the Stadholder's death, in 1647, Vondel published not a word about him, a silence rendered highly conspicuous by the fact that the Republic's most celebrated poet regularly wrote funerary poems extolling eminent personages when they passed on.

FREDERIK HENDRIK AND
THE REGENT PARTY-FACTIONS, 1633–1640

The year 1633—in which Rembrandt painted his first two large pictures for the Stadholder, the *Ascent* and *Descent from the Cross*—marks the great watershed in the stadholderate of Frederik Hendrik.[64] This was the year in which he abandoned the party-factional alliance which had sustained his authority hitherto and espoused the 'war party' and Counter-Remonstrants. It was the year in which the 'States party' tradition of Oldenbarnevelt was reborn and confrontation between Stadholder and States of Holland again became the central theme of Dutch politics. The Prince agonized long and hard before finally breaking with Pauw. There was nothing impulsive or haphazard about his shift over from one ideological bloc to the other. The process began with the quarrel over Brazil and the Meierij. But the real

---

[62] *Archives*, 2nd ser. iii. 38–41.
[63] Duits, *Van Bartholomeusnacht tot Bataafse opstand*, 177–9.
[64] Israel, *Dutch Republic and the Hispanic World*, 299–304; Israel, *Empires and Entrepots*, 94–7.

cause was the receding of Counter-Remonstrant support amongst the ordinary populace and growing confidence of the Arminian regents. Before the early 1630s, the Holland Arminians could not challenge Frederik Hendrik, needing his support and protection to survive. But, by 1633, what was now the leading group in the States of Holland was no longer dependent on the Stadholder and sufficiently confident to push for primacy in the Republic. The year 1633 was thus one of the key turning-points of the Dutch Golden Age.

The struggle between Frederik Hendrik and the Holland peace towns developed, during 1634, into a bitter tussle over relations with France. By the autumn of 1633, it was already clear that the alternative to peace with Spain was an alliance with France. Louis XIII was offering a close partnership and tempting subsidies. But the required quid pro quo involved locking the Republic into confrontation with Spain, and subordination to France, for years to come. The French alliance would presumably also bolster the Stadholder and 'war party', and therefore minimize the influence of Holland indefinitely. What the Arminian towns particularly objected to was the clause of the treaty stipulating that the United Provinces, in return for subsidies, must not negotiate with Spain, except 'conjoinctement et d'un commun consentement' with the French Crown.[65] Both faction-parties besieged the small towns of Holland for their support. Pauw boasted he had the backing of a majority of the States of Holland in opposing the alliance; Orange assured him he was supported by only four or five towns motivated by selfish commercial interests rather than the true interest of the state.[66]

The contest proved long and arduous. Orange's campaign managers in the States of Holland were Van den Bouchorst, who swung the Holland *ridderschap* behind Haarlem, Leiden, and Gouda, and François van Aerssen, who was highly regarded by Richelieu and now fully restored to the Prince's favour.[67] Gradually, the small towns were won over. Van Aerssen afterwards admitted that the outcome of the canvassing had long been in doubt and that, at times, he had despaired of success. The 'Arminians', he remarked afterwards, tried everything to block the alliance, and defeat the Stadholder, representing France as 'plus dangereuse à cet estat que l'Espagne mesme'.[68] Amsterdam's deputies in The Hague protested that if Holland approved the alliance, binding the Republic to negotiate with Spain only jointly with France, Amsterdam would repudiate the

[65] De Pange, *Charnacé*, 93–6.
[66] *Archives*, 2nd ser. iii. 47.
[67] Aitzema, *Verhael*, i. 287.
[68] *Archives*, 2nd ser. iii. 54.

decision and refuse to consider the commitment binding, insisting that her protest be entered in the resolutions of the States.[69]

The Prince won narrowly in Holland, more easily elsewhere. Ploos persuaded the Utrecht *ridderschap* to align with the Counter-Remonstrant city behind the Stadholder.[70] Van Haersolte swung Overijssel. Gelderland fell into line. The consent of Zeeland, Friesland, and Groningen was already assured.[71]

In the new situation, the Stadholder's effectiveness depended more than ever on the dexterity of his provincial bosses. Frederik Hendrik's managers needed no particular theology, or ideological consistency, but consummate adroitness with provincial factions, exploiting local tensions and distributing favours and offices. Consequently, his managers were long-standing adherents of the House of Orange and noblemen rather than regents whose influence was limited to a particular town. Influence and clientage were what mattered, so that the Prince's volte-face, ditching the 'Arminians' and espousing the Counter-Remonstrants—however half-heartedly on a theological and intellectual plane—produced few changes in his circle of confidants. There were one or two. Van Beaumont was too committed an Arminian to continue,[72] while Van Aerssen, too much of a Counter-Remonstrant to be used before 1633, was brought back. But otherwise the Prince's friends, including Floris, count of Culemborg, formerly an Arminian, changed course with him. Van Haersolte dominated the Delegated States of Overijssel until his death in 1643, several times serving as Overijssel's 'deputy in the field' with the army. As one of his rewards, the Prince nominated him *drost* of Lingen after Spain evacuated the county, in 1633, and it reverted to Dutch control. Van Haersolte's regime in Lingen, a predominantly Catholic enclave, became notorious for corruption. Also as before, Ploos van Amstel managed Utrecht, Schaffer Groningen, Culemborg the Nijmegen quarter, and the Counter-Remonstrant regent, Vosbergen, together with another famously corrupt noble, de Knuyt, Zeeland. The States General secret committee set up to finalize the French alliance, in 1634, included Van den Bouchorst, Ploos, Culemborg, de Knuyt, Pauw, and Willem Ripperda,[73] an Overijssel noble married to a daughter of Van den Bouchorst who deputized for Van Haersolte, in Overijssel, and later succeeded him as the province's leading figure. These provincial managers were the nuts and bolts of Frederik Hendrik's power.

[69] GA Dordrecht res. vroed. 7 Feb. 1634.
[70] Ploos, 'Adriaan Ploos van Amstel', 54–8, 66.
[71] Waddington, *République des Provinces Unies*, i. 221.
[72] Meertens, *Letterkundig leven*, 301.
[73] Aitzema, *Verhael*, i. 297.

The system of Generality 'secret committees' reached its apogee under Frederik Hendrik at this time and over the next few years. It was rooted in the divisions paralysing Holland and the ascendancy of the Stadholder.[74] Formerly, in the era of Oldenbarnevelt and Maurits, the States General had nominated secret committees but always on a short-term basis, to consider a specific issue, and usually to report back without taking decisions, as, for example, in the case of the committee of eight—two from Holland and one each from the other provinces—nominated to draft the Twelve Years Truce, in 1608. The difference between these and the 'secrete besognes' which flourished under Frederik Hendrik, from the early 1630s onwards, was that the new committees enjoyed *carte blanche* in a specified area of diplomacy, or military affairs, and continued as long as the committee itself deemed necessary.[75] There was never a single standing Generality secret committee, as historians once supposed, but there was much overlap between the committees, as well as with the 'deputies in the field', who accompanied the Stadholder on campaign, so that it was invariably the same men who were chosen—mostly the Prince's managers in each province and their deputies.

Frederik Hendrik himself oversaw these *secrete besognes* and had the chief say in choosing their membership. Usually, they comprised eight or nine members, with two or three representing Holland and one each for the rest. It would be wrong to suggest that these men automatically did the Prince's bidding on every occasion. There were differences of opinion—but not many. A characteristic (and significant) feature was that the Pensionary of Holland by no means figured prominently and was sometimes not a member at all. Thus, in terms of authority and distribution of power within the Republic, the revolution of 1618 remained largely intact, the *secrete besognes* confirming Holland's displacement and the consolidation of the Generality under the guidance of the Stadholder.

Power and influence were now concentrated in the hands of a handful of bosses favoured by the Stadholder who assisted him. Inevitably, this implied the continuing emasculation of the provincial assemblies. The Republic's political system, under Frederik Hendrik, was shaped by clientage, favours, courtly connections, and noble status, and characterized by a minimum of open debate. It was also a system open to foreign manipulation through corruption, more so than a broader-based, more consultative decision-making was apt to be. As the men who sat on the *secrete besognes*, or those

---

[74] Israel, *Empires and Entrepots*, 83–5; Groenveld, *Verlopend getij*, 75–84; De Bruin, *Geheimhouding*, 253–9.
[75] De Bruin, *Geheimhouding*, 253–4.

who mattered, were always the same, and the system was co-ordinated by the *griffier* of the States General, Cornelis Musch, it was easy for foreign diplomats to draw them into a web of bribery. The members of the *secrete besogne* set up in 1636 to renew the Franco-Dutch alliance—Van den Bouchorst, Haersolte, Ploos, Schaffer, De Knuyt, Cats, and Culemborg— were offered gifts of cash by Richelieu, after the treaty was signed, the amounts varying according to each member's usefulness to French inter- ests.[76] Van den Bouchorst and Ploos each accepted 10,000 livres, Cats 6,000, and de Knuyt 5,000; the largest sum, 20,000 livres, went to the notoriously corrupt *griffier* of the States General, Musch, a figure extremely useful to France, as well as to Frederik Hendrik, controlling as he did the corre- spondence, and records, of the federal assembly. The influence wielded by Frederik Hendrik's managers enabled them to amass enormous wealth. By the late 1630s Van Aerssen was, next to the Stadholder, the richest man in The Hague. Musch's greed was legendary. Ripperda was described by a Swedish diplomat, during the Münster peace congress, in the 1640s, as 'très avare', and continually alternating between France and Spain according to which offered the largest gifts.

France declared war on Spain in May 1635. Under the agreement reached in Paris, the previous February, the States General were committed to invade the south Netherlands jointly with France during 1635. Once again the south was offered freedom of religion and encouraged to revolt.[77] Should the southern provinces rise, they were also to be given their freedom as a league of independent cantons, on the model of Switzerland, but with the Flemish seaports, Namur, and Thionville annexed by France, and Breda, Upper Gelderland (Geldern), and the Waes district (Hulst) to the Republic. But should the southern provinces remain loyal to Spain, and be conquered, it was agreed they would be partitioned between France and the United Provinces, with the French-speaking provinces and western Flanders allo- cated to France, and Antwerp, the Scheldt estuary, and Ghent, Bruges, and Mechelen to the United Provinces.[78]

The latter scenario was particularly worrying to Pauw and the States party-faction which greatly disliked the notion of having France as an immediate neighbour, as well as the possibility of the Republic being enlarged with parts of Brabant and Flanders, which would be bound to enhance their Stadholder's power while further diminishing that of Holland. Doubtless Amsterdam also feared the prospect of Antwerp being freed from

---

[76] Waddington, *République des Provinces Unies*, i. 283.
[77] Blok, *Frederik Hendrik*, 164–6; Poelhekke, *Frederik Hendrik*, 429–31.
[78] Lonchay, *La Rivalité*, 68–9.

the Scheldt restrictions and regaining part of her former commercial greatness at Holland's expense. But in the form agreed in Paris the projected partition was also unpalatable to the Calvinist orthodox. For in areas transferred to the United Provinces, the States General undertook to preserve the 'Roman Catholic religion in its entirety', as it was at present, with all cathedrals, churches, monasteries, and other premises and resources of the Catholic Church remaining in Catholic hands. Richelieu had even refused to concede that the public exercise of the Reformed faith should be permitted, arguing that if he agreed to this he would seriously offend the Papacy and other anti-Habsburg Catholic powers. All that France had been willing to concede was that the private practice of the Reformed faith, in houses, would be allowed. Reformed opinion in the Republic was outraged. The Hague *predikant* (Dutch Reformed Church preacher) Rosaeus told Frederik Hendrik to his face that it was better not to acquire Anwerp at all than do so on such a basis.

But all this proved academic, the Spanish Netherlands turning out to be a harder nut to crack than expected. France hurled her forces across the southern border of the Spanish Netherlands. But the Spaniards neither caved in nor (as is often supposed) gave their main attention to fighting the French, downgrading the Dutch front in consequence. On the contrary, Olivares' strategy, after the victory of Nördlingen (1634) over the Swedes, in Germany, and the arrival of the Cardinal-Infante, Philip IV's younger brother, as the new governor of the Spanish Netherlands, with an additional 11,000 Spanish troops, and fresh funds, was to employ Spain's revived might in the Netherlands to squeeze the Dutch hard—while fighting purely defensively against France—forcing them into a separate, and early, peace with Spain.[79] Once the Dutch had settled, it was assumed France (not yet as strong as Spain militarily, or financially) would come to terms, as she would then be strategically at a disadvantage. Consequently, despite successive French invasions of the south Netherlands, from 1635, Spanish strategy over the next crucial few years was to concentrate against the Dutch and not against France.[80] Besides their calculation that this was the best way to defeat the combination of France and the Republic, Spanish ministers also preferred *guerra offensiva* against the Dutch, and *defensiva* against France, because of their need to shield Antwerp, Ghent, and Bruges—cities vulnerable to the Dutch but less so to France. They assigned lower priority to

---

[79] AGS Estado 2153, 'voto del Conde Duque', 16 Nov. 1635; AGS Estado 2052, 'voto del Conde Duque', 7 Oct. 1637; AGS Estado 2156, 'votos' of Olivares of 8 Jan. and 9 Mar. 1638; Israel, *Empires and Entrepots*, 182–5.

[80] Israel, *Empires and Entrepots*, 183–5; Israel, *Dutch Republic and the Hispanic World*, 251–8.

Artois, Hainault, and Luxemburg, provinces lacking cities of comparable importance. Also, attacking France, and defending against the Dutch, was apt to result in cities falling into heretic hands, whereas the opposite would not. Finally, territory taken from the Dutch could be absorbed into the Spanish Netherlands, and treated as the king's, whereas anything captured from France would simply have to be handed back under the eventual peace.[81]

During the late 1630s the army of Flanders totalled over 70,000 men and was more potent and numerous than at any point hitherto in the Eighty Years War.[82] The Cardinal-Infante, aided by the south Netherlands' formidable network of defences, convincingly thwarted the Franco-Dutch invasion of 1635. Once the invasion receded, the Spaniards emerged from their fixed garrisons, and mounted a pincer movement enveloping the Meierij and Cleves, encircling the Dutch garrisons in the Maas valley. The Dutch public was stunned by the rapid turn-around of the situation. Sensationally, on 26 July 1635, Spanish troops, from Geldern, captured the supposedly impregnable fortress of Schenckenschans, situated on an island in the Rhine, just below the Dutch–German frontier, one of the most vital links in the Dutch defensive ring, commanding access, along the north bank of the Rhine, into the Dutch interior. Over ensuing weeks, the Spaniards recovered most of the Meierij, Imperialist troops came up, and combined Spanish–Imperialist forces overran Cleves, extending their positions to link up with Schenckenschans.

Frederik Hendrik, dropping everything else, concentrated a huge force, blockading Schenckenschans on three sides, resigned to camping out in the cold all winter to recover the vital fortress. Over the next months, the Spaniards battled to hold on to their corridor through Cleves. Olivares assured the Cardinal-Infante (he was not joking) that it was more important to hold Schenckenschans than capture Paris.[83] For if the Spaniards consolidated their grip there, they would enjoy unobstructed access into Gelderland and Utrecht, the Dutch garrisons in the Maas valley would be encircled, and the Dutch 'will have to make peace or a truce as we would wish'.[84] The Hague artist Gerrit van Santen painted the dramatic scene of the bombardment of Schenckenschans, one of the largest winter operations of the century, which hangs today in the Rijksmuseum, in Amsterdam.

It was at this juncture, with Spain holding Schenckenschans, that Rubens, with his 'penchant irrésistible pour la politique', obtained the Cardinal-Infante's

---

[81] AGS Estado 2053, *consulta* of the *Junta de Estado*, 7 Mar. 1638, fo. 7.
[82] AGS Estado 2051, *consulta*, 12 Apr. 1636; Parker, *Army of Flanders*, 272.
[83] AGS Estado 2153, 'voto del Conde Duque', 16 Nov. 1635.
[84] BL MS Add. 14007, fo. 53. Philip IV to Cardinal-Infante, 25 Oct. 1635.

authorization for his last and grandest effort to mediate a Dutch–Spanish truce. By this time the great artist's reputation in The Hague was that of a go-between 'plein d'artifices' who needed careful watching. To circumvent the Franco-Dutch pact precluding informal Dutch contacts with Spanish representatives, Don Fernando approved Rubens's plan to travel to Amsterdam supposedly to inspect a recently arrived batch of Italian paintings, taking with him pictures ostensibly *en route* to London.[85] Once in Amsterdam, he designed to enter into secret talks with key figures of the States. Orange and the French ambassador soon saw what Rubens intended. His request for a passport to enter Holland, sent by the States General to the States of Holland, produced an inconclusive dispute between the Stadholder's friends and the 'Arminians'. The decision was then left to the Stadholder, who greatly admired Rubens's paintings but refused him entry to the United Provinces.

Olivares categorically ordered *guerra defensiva* against France, early in 1636, and a Spanish offensive beyond Schenckenschans, into the Veluwe and Overijssel, to widen the breach in the Dutch defences. It was never the intention in Madrid to invade France, in 1636, and the subsequent advance on Corbie, which sowed such panic in France, was a purely stop-gap measure, not part of Olivares' strategy at all. After a relentless bombardment, pounding it from river gunboats and both banks, Frederik Hendrik forced the surrender of Schenckenschans, in April 1636. Thus, what Olivares called the 'finest jewel which the king possessed in those lands with which to settle his affairs' was lost, 'a great blow', he lamented, 'for all Spain'.[86] He urged the Cardinal-Infante to try to retake Schenckenschans and fortify Helmond and Eindhoven to consolidate the Spanish hold on the Meierij.[87]

The fiasco of the joint Franco-Dutch invasion of the Spanish Netherlands, in 1635, was a severe check for the Prince, and adherents of the alliance with France, as were the revival of Spanish strength and setbacks in the Meierij and Cleves. No less frustrating, for the Stadholder, were the difficulties he now experienced in managing the States of Holland. From now on, clearly, the Holland regents were to be Frederik Hendrik's thorniest problem. To neutralize Holland, he needed above all to replace Pauw, as Pensionary of Holland, with a nonentity ready to do his bidding. The opportunity came with the expiry of Pauw's first term of office, in March 1636. To get Pauw out of the way, the States General set him on an embassy to Paris, refusing

[85] Gachard, *Histoire politique*, 259–60, 342–3.
[86] BL MS Add. 14007, fo. 57. Olivares to Cardinal-Infante, 25 May 1636.
[87] AGR SEG 214, fo. 565. Philip IV to Cardinal-Infante, 13 June 1636.

to let him return until it was too late to canvass support for his re-election.[88]
In his absence, Van Aerssen, Van den Bouchorst, and Cats, with the
pensionaries of Haarlem and Leiden, ensured that the States chose a
candidate more palatable to the Stadholder. Three candidates stood: the
'Arminian' Nanning van Foreest, of Alkmaar; a Counter-Remonstrant, De
Glarges of Haarlem; and Jacob Cats, who had been passed over, in 1631,
in favour of Pauw partly because he was a Zeelander. None secured enough
votes to win outright. Cats was then chosen—in effect by the Stadholder.[89]
In selecting Cats, the Prince knew what he was about. Renowned for his
verse, Cats was a fatherly, mild-mannered man, though viewed with
suspicion by other writers and intellectuals—and contempt by Grotius—for
having been a voice for moderation yet gone along with harsh Counter-
Remonstrant policies.[90] His poems extolled Calvinist values, and the Further
Reformation influenced by the theology of Willem Teellinck and Godfried
Udemans, though some found this hard to square with the romantic undercurrent of his writing.[91] But what mattered in Frederik Hendrik's eyes was
that he was an unassuming functionary, having served as Pensionary of
Middelburg and, since 1623, Dordrecht, without aptitude for leadership or
independent action, and largely devoid of knowledge of foreign affairs. His
obsequiousness and ties with the Stadholder's favourites—one of his
daughters married Cornelis Musch, another the personage Orange appointed *drost* of Breda—made him, from the Stadholder's point of view, the
ideal choice. Cats fulfilled his role to perfection. At times, rather than
Pensionary *of* Holland, it seemed almost as if he were Pensionary *against*
Holland. In December 1637, he went so far as to refuse to 'conclude' a
resolution unpalatable to Frederik Hendrik, reducing troop levels, despite
having no fewer than fifteen of the eighteen towns voting in favour.[92]

But a subservient Pensionary, and compliant *ridderschap*, were insufficient. Most of the time the Stadholder could rely on the group of towns
headed by Haarlem and Leiden to support his authority, but there were no
longer enough Counter-Remonstrant towns in Holland to keep the States
as divided as they had been in the early 1630s, nor were the old theological
disputes so divisive as formerly. In short, there was no way the Stadholder
could prevent a majority of the States of Holland pressing for troop cuts
and reductions in spending. The first major round of cuts since 1621 was

[88] *Archives*, 2nd ser. iii. 83–5; Poelhekke, *Frederik Hendrik*, 436–40.
[89] Grotius, *Briefwisseling*, viii. 70.
[90] Ten Berge, *Hooggeleerde en zoetvloeiende dichter*, 72–3, 104.
[91] Schama, *Embarrassment of Riches*, 436–7, 443.
[92] Van Deursen, 'De raadpensionaris Jacob Cats', 158–9.

forced through by the States of Holland over the winter of 1636–7.[93] The troops raised in 1629 were disbanded and the earlier augmentation, of 1628, cut by 20 per cent. Holland, manipulated by the Stadholder, may have submitted, for the moment, to the Prince's war policy and French alliance but could, nevertheless, dilute his statecraft by trimming the military budget.

A feature of the reduction in Dutch military spending, from December 1636, and the waning of Frederik Hendrik's military fortunes, after the recapture of Breda, in 1637, was that this occurred just as the economic boom which had commenced in the early 1630s gained momentum. If the keynote of Dutch life and politics in the 1620s was one of slump and gloom, that of the mid- and late 1630s was one of rising wealth and speculation. There was no change in the basic structure of Dutch commerce after 1630.[94] Throughout Phase Three (1621–47), the overseas trading system continued to be characterized by deep recession in Dutch trade with southern Europe and an emphasis on colonial trade, textile exports, and investment in agriculture, combined with a thriving Zeeland transit traffic to the south Netherlands (see pp. 314–15 above). But the mostly unfavourable circumstances of the 1620s gave way, in the 1630s, to a set of highly favourable conditions within the same general framework which gave new vigour to each of the existing main strands. These changed circumstances flowed from the lifting of the Spanish river blockade mounted from the Ems to the Scheldt (1629), the end of the Polish–Swedish war and its disruption of Baltic commerce (1629), and the outbreak of the Franco-Spanish war (1635) which had the important effect of closing the border between the south Netherlands and France, cutting off the route via Calais and Boulogne and compelling the cities of Flanders and Brabant to import, and export, more via the Dutch-controlled waterways and Scheldt estuary.[95] This adversely affected commerce and industry in the Spanish Netherlands, contributing to the slackening of the recovery of the south by forcing the south to pay the heavy wartime tolls and tariffs imposed on the transit traffic, by the States General, and gave Zeeland its most flourishing years of the entire Golden Age. Additional factors contributing to the Dutch economic boom of the mid- and late 1630s were the worsening situation in Germany, increasing demand for supplies and foodstuffs from the Dutch entrepôt, the resumed expansion of the VOC in Asia, and the WIC's success in the mid-1630s in generating a thriving sugar-export traffic from the conquered areas of north Brazil.

---

[93] Res. Holl. 15, 16 and 21 Dec. 1636.
[94] Israel, *Dutch Primacy*, 143–7, 194–6; Israel, *Empires and Entrepots*, 24, 123–6, 148–50.
[95] Israel, *Dutch Primacy*, 194; Israel, *Empires and Entrepots*, 130.

Yet it was a boom without basic restructuring and with limited outlets for new investment. For the main restrictions on the growth of Dutch European trade—the Spanish embargoes, high freight-rates, the Dunkirk privateering offensive, poor access to Italy and the Levant (where commerce continued to be dominated by the English)—remained in place. It was doubtless this which made it a boom with a marked speculative dimension.

Thus the return of confidence rapidly turned somewhat feverish. The late 1630s witnessed the most spectacular jump in VOC share values on the Amsterdam Exchange of the entire seventeenth century.[96] After a slow, halting rise between 1615 and 1630, shares in the Amsterdam Chamber doubled in value between 1630 and 1639, most of the increase coming after 1636, and rose by a further 20 per cent in 1640. At 229 per cent of face value in March 1636, the price stood at 412 per cent in August 1639, and reached 500 per cent a few months later. A similar phenomenon occurred in the case of large houses in Amsterdam. The prices of rich men's houses actually fell in the early 1630s, but then shot up, undergoing one of the two steepest rises of the seventeenth century (the other was in the late 1650s), in the late 1630s.[97] It is also against this background that one should view the celebrated tulip craze of 1636–7. The initial boom in tulip horticulture, and speculation in tulip bulbs, were signs of the growing sense of ease with the achievement of security and returning prosperity, combined with the rapid accumulation of large surpluses amid restricted investment opportunities. A rarity down to around 1630, in the mid-1630s cheaper varieties of tulip were widely marketed and tulip-fancying rapidly pervaded the middle strata of Dutch urban society. In an age in which investing in East and West India Company shares, drainage schemes, and large houses required impressive sums, and were reserved for the wealthy, tulip bulbs, powered by heavy demand and proliferation of varieties, lent themselves to widespread local speculation and became the mania of small-town dealers, tavern-keepers, and horticulturalists, what has aptly been described as a 'pastiche form of stockbroking'.[98]

Frederik Hendrik's own annual income, buoyed by the agricultural boom—most of his private money came from farm rents in north Brabant and south Holland—and the recovery of Lingen and Breda, reached a healthy 650,000 guilders yearly by 1637.[99] It was in the mid- and late 1630s that he embarked on some of his most grandiose projects with regard to his

[96] Aitzema, *Historie*, v. 198–9; Van Dillen, 'Effectenkoersen', 10–11.
[97] Lesger, *Huur en conjunctuur*, 77–87.
[98] Schama, *Embarrassment of Riches*, 359.
[99] Blok, *Frederik Hendrik*, 196.

palaces, art collections, and private gardens. His retreat at Honselaersdijk
was completed in 1638, the palace at Rijswijk (see PLATE 14) built between
1634 and 1638, the castle of Buren refurbished as from 1637, as was that of
Breda. The Noordeinde palace in The Hague, and the Stadholder's quarters
at the Binnenhof, were rebuilt and it was in the 1630s that his galleries filled
with Honthorsts, Poelenburghs, Rubens, Van Dycks, and Moreelses, spiced
with a touch of Rembrandt and Lievens. The Stadholder spent heavily on
his gardens and substantially on tapestries, one of his main disbursements
for art, in 1638, being 2,200 guilders paid to Van Honthorst for four
tapestry cartoons.[100] Amalia von Solms assembled a magnificent collection
of jewellery. Receptions and feasts at the Stadholder's palaces became
steadily grander, binding influential nobles closer to the stadholderate and
its patronage.

Yet, whilst the Republic's rising wealth financed the growing splendour of
the merchant élite, the Stadholder's court, and leading nobles, and powered
the VOC's invasion of Ceylon, in 1638, and the WIC's expeditions to West
Africa and against Bahia, in the late 1630s, Frederik Hendrik found himself
increasingly cramped in his statecraft, and as a military commander, in the
Low Countries. Part of his difficulty was that his alliance with the Holland
Counter-Remonstrant towns was so manifestly a marriage of convenience.
Given his past, he could scarcely pose as a champion of Calvinist orthodoxy, even had he been willing to abandon his previous tolerant approach
to religious and intellectual affairs; nor could the Counter-Remonstrants
ignore the fact that he had undermined the gains they had achieved under
Maurits, after 1618. The Prince's capture of Breda with a relatively small
army during the campaign of 1637—possible only because the Cardinal-
Infante (contrary to earlier instructions[101]) moved his main force away from
the Dutch front to face the French, in Artois—met with a muted response
in the Republic, which showed that his exploits were no longer being
applauded by any principal segment of Dutch opinion. The Counter-Remonstrants disliked his religious policy in the newly conquered areas.
Vondel remained silent. Huygens wrote from the Stadholder's camp, at
Breda, to Hooft, urging him to publish a triumphal poem celebrating the
taking of Breda, as he had that of 's-Hertogenbosch, remarking that the new
exploit was no less worthy than the other, but Hooft remained silent too.[102]

The Stadholder did make some adjustments to his religious policy in the
conquered areas. He did not again ask the States General, as he had in 1632

---

[100] Slothouwer, *Paleizen van Frederik Hendrik*, 338–40.
[101] AGR SEG 217, fos. 358–60, 'Discurso sobre . . . atacar Grave'.
[102] Groenveld, 'Breda', 106.

and 1635, to offer toleration of the Catholic faith, and retention by the Catholic Church of its clergy, buildings, and revenues in localities which threw off the yoke of Spain and submitted to the Republic. He did not concede Catholic toleration in his newly regained barony of Breda, refusing to allow any greater freedom for Catholic worship than had been permitted before 1625, so that Catholic services were again confined to the same two convents which Maurits had allowed.[103] Yet, the Stadholder remained a champion of tolerant attitudes as, indeed, his alliance with France required him to. If, formally, he imposed the same rules at Breda as applied before 1625, he was decidedly lenient in observing them, allowing several Catholic priests to remain and instructing his new *drost* to permit Catholic conventicles. The religious regime Frederik Hendrik maintained in his newly regained county of Lingen was acknowledged by the Dutch Catholic Mission, in Utrecht, to be exceptionally tolerant.[104]

For the orthodox Calvinist party, the post-1633 situation posed a dilemma. It was now, less than ever, in their interest to criticize the Stadholder. They felt bound to support him against the detested 'Arminians'. Yet their attitude remained lukewarm, characterized by an undercurrent of disapproval. The drift away from policies of intolerance, and coercion, in religious and intellectual matters clearly could not be reversed, or checked, without a fundamental change in policy on the part of the Stadholder and ruling group. For the moment there was no prospect of this. Yet orthodox Calvinists, including some Holland regents, adamantly refused to yield to the trend towards toleration, and religious freedom, at local level: in their towns and communities they continued to combat it. When the Leiden magistrates summoned the town's *schout*, in June 1633, asking him to explain his imperfect record in suppressing Catholic and Remonstrant conventicles in the city, he replied that with Catholics and Remonstrants allowed to gather without hindrance nearby, in The Hague, they had come to expect the same in Leiden.[105] The magistracy retorted that Leiden was not going to be like The Hague and that Leiden's Catholics and Remonstrants would not be allowed to gather.[106] Similarly, Haarlem, Gouda, and some smaller towns persevered with intolerant policies.

The States General no longer offered south Netherlanders Catholic toleration. But neither was there any hint that the Stadholder was waging war for the sake of the Reformed faith. This too orthodox Calvinists found

---

[103] *Geschiedenis van Breda*, ii. 181–3.
[104] *Archief aartsbisdom Utrecht*, xii. 429–30.
[105] GA Leiden Sec. Arch. 683, fo. 308, res. gerecht. 8 June 1633.
[106] Ibid; GA Leiden Sec. Arch. 684, fo. 158, res. gerecht. 13 Dec. 1637.

difficult to stomach. 'What kind of war are the United Provinces waging?' asked a Counter-Remonstrant pamphleteer, in 1637, answering, with rhetorical disgust: 'a Libertine war'.[107] The author considered this an evident symptom of sickness in the body politic. He lamented the open toleration of Catholicism, in Maastricht, and the Stadholder's permission for Catholic practice in the predominantly Calvinist town of Wesel, recovered from the Spaniards in 1629. He despaired of the town governments of Holland which, in his view, were full of 'libertines, Arminians, Atheists and concealed Jesuits'.[108] Both the 'Union' and Reformation were being subverted, he insisted, noting that in recent years Catholic prayer-gatherings had become more widespread, and open, not only in Amsterdam and Rotterdam, but also in The Hague, Dordrecht, and other towns, as well as the Holland countryside. Here he was certainly right. A Catholic report, of 1638, remarks that at Enkhuizen, a town where twenty years before there were practically no Catholics, there were now around 1,300.[109] In Dordrecht, the *vroedschap* had become far more lenient towards both Catholics and Mennonites since the death of Prince Maurits,[110] as was true also in Delft, Hoorn, Alkmaar, and even Utrecht.

Yet, Frederik Hendrik was heir to the political system created by the Calvinist revolution of the Counter-Remonstrants. He, and his entourage, remained firmly at the helm and persisted with their war in alliance with France. In 1638, Orange suffered a serious check when attempting to capture the forts on the Scheldt, below Antwerp; part of his army was surprised and routed in a battle at Kallo, in June, in which hundreds were killed and 2,500, troops, with eighty river craft, captured. Two months after this 'grand desastre', as Van Aerssen called, it, the Prince signally failed in his attempt to capture Geldern, the sudden appearance of an Imperialist army necessitating an undignified retreat. From his campaigns of 1639–40 he returned empty-handed, his repeated attempts on Geldern and Hulst ending in failure. During the unsuccessful siege of Hulst, in 1640, the Frisian Stadholder, Hendrik Casimir, was mortally wounded.

Thus, despite his recapture of Breda, in 1637, Frederik Hendrik's military achievements, in the late 1630s, were unimpressive compared with those of the years 1629–33. Indeed, his feats were overshadowed by the conquests of the VOC in Asia which secured a large part of coastal Ceylon from the Portuguese, in the years 1638–41, and Malacca in 1641. They were surpassed

---

[107] *Klare ende korte Aenmerckinge*, 6–7.
[108] Ibid. 8–9.
[109] *Archief aartsbisdom Utrecht*, xii. 420.
[110] Van Dalen, *Gesch. van Dordrecht*, ii. 803, 821–2.

also by the exploits of his cousin Count Johan Maurits van Nassau-Siegen, the WIC's governor-general of Brazil (1637–44), who considerably extended the area of northern Brazil under Dutch sway, bringing seven of the fourteen captaincies into which Brazil was divided under the WIC, though he failed—with dire consequences for the future of Netherlands Brazil—in his grandest undertaking, his attack on Bahia with 3,600 European and 1,000 Indian troops, in 1638. It was also Johan Maurits who sent across, from Brazil to Africa, the expeditions which captured Elmina (1637), on the Guinea Coast, and Angola (1641). Also eclipsing anything achieved by Frederik Hendrik after 1637 was Admiral Tromp's triumph, and that of the navy, in 1639 in destroying the great armada which Olivares had painstakingly built up over several years and which he sent to the Channel in the hope of wresting naval supremacy from the Dutch. The Spanish armada of 1639 numbered almost 100 ships, including some accompanying English transports, and carried over 20,000 Spanish and Italian troops, *en route* to Flanders. After the initial battle off Beachy Head, the armada took refuge on the English coast, at the Downs. Charles I, whose relations with Spain at this time were good, tried to protect the mauled Spanish fleet, warning the Dutch not to affront him 'in his own chamber'. But Tromp was sent secret instructions, by the Stadholder, to ignore English objections and, on 21 October, swept in and completed his victory.

THE CONTEST FOR
THE LEADERSHIP OF THE REPUBLIC, 1640–1647

But if the ageing Stadholder's military accomplishments waned, his zest for enhancing his court and dynasty, not least through imposing architectural projects and the arts, and his will to dominate the Dutch political scene showed no sign of slackening.

As the years passed, the Prince's courtly style, and establishment, became steadily grander. In 1636, Louis XIII upgraded the official French form of address for the Stadholder from 'Excellence' to 'Altesse', a mode normally reserved for minor sovereigns and their relatives. The States General followed suit in January 1637, changing the mode of addressing the Prince from 'Excellencie' to 'Hoogheid' (Highness).[111] More prestigious still, among Europe's courts, was the Prince's success, in 1641, in arranging the marriage of his son and heir to a daughter of Charles I of England. This was the first of the Orange–Stuart marriages, and the first time the House

---

[111] Waddington, *République des Provinces Unies*, i. 281.

of Orange-Nassau concluded a marriage alliance with a major royal line. The bride, Princess Mary, and her ladies, considered she was marrying beneath her rank. It is doubtful whether Charles would have agreed to the match had his own affairs not then been in such disarray and he in need of any help he could find. But the marriage none the less greatly enhanced the status of the House of Orange-Nassau. There was no objection to this, at the time, in the States General or States of Holland, the match being seen as a way of driving a wedge between England and Spain and therefore of political advantage to the Republic.[112]

The Prince acquired additional status by accumulating more stadhold-erates. He had been unsuccessful, in his first attempt, on Ernst Casimir's death in 1632, to acquire the stadholderates of Groningen and Drenthe. But after the death of Ernst Casimir's son, Hendrik Casimir, Stadholder of Friesland, Groningen, and Drenthe (1632–40), he had tried again, having paved the way by building up his clientele among local nobles and, in 1639, clinched the election of his protégé, Roelof van Echten, by the States of Drenthe, as *drost*. He was helped also by the fact that many Groningen *jonkers* had come to see Hendrik Casimir as an ally of the city. On the news of Hendrik Casimir's death at Hulst, the Prince's friends set to work canvassing support for him in the north. The States General, prompted by Van den Bouchorst, voted by five provinces (including Holland) to two to send a delegation to Friesland and Groningen, to urge both to appoint Frederik Hendrik their next Stadholder, in order to improve military co-ordination between the provinces, and enhance the unity of the Repub-lic.[113] Friesland and Groningen (the two which voted against sending the delegation) protested that they were sovereign provinces which ought to be left to decide their own Stadholders without interference from the Gener-ality.[114] The procedure failed utterly in Friesland. The States of Friesland hurriedly met to settle the question before the delegation arrived. The Frisian nobles who backed Hendrik Casimir's younger brother, Willem Frederik, exploited Frisian particularism, and the preachers' dislike of the Prince's tolerant attitude towards Catholics and Remonstrants, to such effect that the Generality commission arrived to find Willem Frederik already Stadholder of Friesland. They rushed on to Groningen, where a decision was yet to be made.

The States of Friesland also sent a delegation, appealing to Groningen to keep to the tradition, more than a century old (since 1536), of sharing the

---

[112] Groenveld, *Verlopend getij*, 99–100.
[113] Aitzema, *Historie*, v. 92.
[114] Blok, *Frederik Hendrik*, 205–7.

same Stadholder as Friesland. But, after vigorous canvassing, it was the Prince who was appointed. Soon after, the States of Drenthe also set aside the claims of the Frisian branch and chose Orange. In addition, in November 1640, the States General nominated him Stadholder of the Generality Lands of Wedde and Westerwolde.[115] The Prince visited the north-east, in November 1640, to receive his new dignities. At Groningen, his son, the future William II, who accompanied him on the trip, received the 'survivance', or right to succeed his father to the Stadholderate. This practice of conferring the succession beforehand, on a hereditary basis, was a recent innovation begun (at Van Haersolte's suggestion) in Overijssel, in 1631, and subsequently adopted (at Van den Bouchorst's suggestion) by Holland and then other provinces.[116]

In 1640, Frederik Hendrik acquired additional stadholderates and prestige. Yet, to an extent, it was status which was politically counter-productive.[117] Maurits had enjoyed the full support of Willem Lodewijk, and the Republic as a whole benefited from their close co-operation. Frederik Hendrik, by contrast, had sought to deprive Willem Frederik of the Frisian stadholderate and actually stripped him of those of Groningen, Drenthe, and Westerwolde, a circumstance his Frisian cousin was hardly likely to forgive.[118] From the outset, relations between the two stadholders were bad.

The façade seemed grander but the reality behind was growing weaker. After the failure of his military campaign of 1640, Orange found himself in renewed difficulties with the States of Holland.[119] Relations deteriorated as most towns pressed for further army cuts, clamouring for full disbandment of the fifty companies recruited in 1628. News of the Catalan Revolt and deepening predicament of the Spanish Crown only hardened the States of Holland's attitude. Amsterdam insisted that Spain no longer posed a credible threat and that the army could be safely reduced.[120] Only with difficulty did the Prince arrange temporary deferment of the disbandment.

Between 1629 and August 1633, the Stadholder had consistently been 'inclinable' to peace, or a new truce, with Spain and the south Netherlands. Subsequently, he became locked into a posture of war, fixed by the terms of the Franco-Dutch alliance, and responded negatively to all secret contacts from Brussels. As opposition to this policy in the States of Holland grew, the Prince became ever more anxious to maximize his leverage over the

---

[115] Van Winter, *Westerwolde*, 105.
[116] Aitzema, *Historie*, v. 93–4.
[117] Ibid.
[118] Lijndrajer, *Ontwikkeling*, 115–16.
[119] Blok, *Frederik Hendrik*, 215–16.
[120] Res. Holl. 13 and 30 Oct., and 22 Dec. 1640 and 2 Feb. 1641.

States General, and their secret committees, and ensure that every approach from Brussels was dealt with exclusively by his trusted confidants, with as few members of the States being involved as possible. When the Cardinal-Infante sent an envoy to negotiate at Kranenburg, in Cleves, during the winter of 1635–6 the latter had found himself confronting only a single Dutch representative, the venal Cornelis Musch.

Even if Frederik Hendrik had not tightly controlled the Kranenburg talks, it is unlikely that anything would have come of them since Olivares, with Schenckenschans in his grasp, was in confident mood, demanding the complete abandonment of Dutch Brazil, partial evacuation of the Dutch East Indies, and the return of Maastricht, Venlo, Roermond, and Rheinberg to Spain, in exchange for a long truce, Breda, and Schenckenschans, demands which stood no chance of being met.[121] Spain subsequently lost Schenckenschans and, in 1637, Breda, though the Cardinal-Infante in that same year retook Venlo and Roermond.

After 1637 the approaches from Brussels became more insistent while Frederik Hendrik became ever more anxious to prevent Spain working on the divisions in the States of Holland. In February 1639, the Cardinal-Infante assured Madrid that peace sentiment in Holland was strong, and becoming stronger, but admitted that he was baffled as to how to circumvent Frederik Hendrik's iron grip on the States General and its secret committees, so as to make contact with the Holland peace party.[122] After the Catalan and Portuguese revolts, Spanish ministers became frantic to detach the United Provinces, if at all possible, from the French alliance, and the Cardinal-Infante redoubled his efforts. But again the Stadholder, with the assiduous support of Musch who controlled all the States General's correspondence, and was lavishly compensated by Paris for his pains, deftly blocked every approach. In March 1641, the Cardinal-Infante reported pessimistically to Madrid that as long as the Prince of Orange remained tied to France and in control of the States General, he saw no way of reaching any settlement with the Dutch.[123] As seen from Brussels, the States of Holland were still paralysed.

Although Orange was 'inclinable' to a Spanish peace in the first phase of his stadholderate (1625–33), and opposed in the second (1633–46), there is nevertheless an important political continuity underlying the phases. The Dutch Republic was the creation of the States of Holland, which, until 1617–18, had effortlessly dominated the weak and divided lesser provinces.

[121] ARH SG 4563, fos. 359v, 367. sec. res. SG 19 Oct. 1635.
[122] AGS Estado 3980, Cardinal-Infante to Philip IV, 15 Feb. 1639.
[123] Israel, *Dutch Republic and the Hispanic World*, 348.

During the Twelve Years Truce, however, Holland had split, threatening the Dutch body politic with dissolution and chaos. Stability and cohesion had been restored by Maurits's *coup d'état* of 1618. This demonstrated there was an alternative basis on which the United Provinces could function. While still based on the wealth, and resources, of Holland, it was possible to forge a non-republican, non-consultative, quasi-princely system of government, in which the Stadholder and his confidants controlled decision-making and the processes of the state. Superficially, this alternative achieved greater unity among the provinces and an enhanced role for the Generality. Provincial sovereignty—a half-truth under Oldenbarnevelt—was an almost total fiction after 1618, under Maurits and Frederik Hendrik. But there was a fundamental flaw in the system created by Maurits: it depended on a divided Holland. If Holland was not split, it could not work. The moment Holland reverted to near unity, the 'princely' system ceased to be viable.[124] For its essence was denying Holland active leadership of the Union.

As Holland became less divided, the Prince's authority correspondingly waned. The Holland faction needing the Stadholder's help, and deferential to him, was bound to be the weaker group. Hence the volte-face of 1633. Until the early 1630s, the 'Arminians' were the weaker block in Holland; after 1633, the stronger.

During 1641 the Prince fended off pressure for further army cuts. Even so, his efforts to exploit Spain's now desperate predicament produced but meagre results: during 1641, he captured only Gennep, which belonged to Jülich but had been seized and fortified by the Cardinal-Infante in 1635. Over the winter of 1641–2, Amsterdam led new moves in the States of Holland, to reduce expenditure, and the army. Except for the *ridderschap*, which stood loyally by the Stadholder, almost all the States backed Amsterdam and, although the Prince received strong support from Zeeland and Utrecht,[125] he was eventually forced to accept the cutting back of the army from over 70,000 to 60,000 men. The news caused dismay in Paris. 'Son authorite se diminue beaucoup,' commented the French ambassador at The Hague.[126]

Nor was Holland's growing assertiveness confined to expenditure and the army.[127] Holland was now more unified than in the 1630s and there was no way the Prince could prevent her playing a more active role in affairs, even had his own deteriorating health not increasingly incommoded him. He retained the same confidants as before but, from this point on, sought to

[124] Israel, *Empires and Entrepots*, 98–9.
[125] Res. Holl. 14 Apr., 1 Aug., and 19 Dec. 1642.
[126] D'Estrades, *Correspondance*, 149.
[127] Ibid. 156.

avoid, or minimize, friction, trying to forge a *modus vivendi* which would accommodate Holland's increased role while preserving as much as possible of the quasi-monarchical façade built up in the 1630s. He was helped by the agreement of the main participants in The Thirty Years War, in December 1641, to commence peace negotiations at Münster and Osnabrück. There was now a formal negotiating framework—even if, for several years, little actual negotiation—involving France, Sweden, the Dutch, Spain, and the Emperor, which served to justify the Stadholder's continued blocking of direct peace soundings between Brussels and The Hague. Even though there was no substantive progress towards peace during the years 1641–4, Frederik Hendrik, and his allies, could now argue that they were negotiating peace with Spain, alongside France, in accordance with the Franco-Dutch alliance.

A key step in whittling down the Prince's authority was the erosion of the States General secret committees, which ensued as consultations began about the form, and commission, of the Dutch delegation to the Münster peace congress.[128] In August 1643, the States of Holland drew up new instructions for their deputies to the Generality forbidding them, any longer, to discuss matters of war, peace, truce, alliances, or sending diplomatic missions abroad, in the States General and its committees except as instructed by the States of Holland.[129] This pierced to the heart of Frederik Hendrik's system and paved the way for the growing ascendancy of the States of Holland during the mid-1640s. Other provinces soon followed Holland's lead regarding their deputies to the States General.

Formerly, the Stadholder had provided energetic leadership. But the changed political situation, and his declining health, imparted an air of drift and irresolution to the final years of his stadholderate. His own entourage was increasingly divided, especially over how far to accommodate Holland.[130] The chief item on the political agenda, in 1643, were the instructions for the Dutch delegation to the Münster peace congress. After lengthy deliberation the States General agreed to conclude peace with Spain, provided Philip IV ceded the whole Meierij—an area still largely in the hands of Spanish troops—recognized Dutch conquests in the Indies, accepted permanent closure of the Scheldt to maritime traffic, satisfied Zeeland regarding tariffs in the Flemish ports, and lifted the embargoes on Dutch shipping and trade,[131] Spain having already acknowledged the

---

[128] De Bruin, *Geheimhouding*, 258.
[129] Geyl, *Oranje en Stuart*, 31–2.
[130] Hofman, *Constantijn Huygens*, 192–4.
[131] Israel, *Dutch Republic and the Hispanic World*, 355.

sovereign independence of the United Provinces. The States General voted to continue hostilities until the king of Spain ratified any agreement negotiated at Münster.

But there was still disagreement as to whether these terms were fully binding on the Dutch plenipotentiaries or could be modified. By March 1644, six of the seven provinces accepted that not all the conditions had to be met in their entirety.[132] The Zeelanders, though, remained adamant that the plenipotentiaries must break off talks should Spain reject any of the conditions, fearing for their transit trade with the Spanish Netherlands, should other provinces be tempted to drop the condition about tariffs in the Flemish seaports. Zeeland reminded the States General that during the Twelve Years Truce her transit traffic had been diverted and 'Brabant, Flanders, and other provinces supplied with merchandise, even fish and herring, from the United Provinces through the Flemish ports'—that is, by Hollanders bypassing Zeeland and the Scheldt estuary.[133]

The Münster peace process enabled Frederik Hendrik to moderate friction with Holland over relations with Spain, the Spanish Netherlands, and France, during his last years. The civil war in England caused some disagreement between Holland and the Prince but no serious difficulty. A more substantial clash, however, erupted over the Danish Sound and the problems of Dutch Baltic trade. In 1638, the king of Denmark-Norway, Christian IV, had embarked on an aggressively anti-Dutch mercantilist policy, drastically increasing the tolls charged on foreign ships passing in, and out of, the Baltic, through the Sound—the largest proportion of which, of course, were Dutch.[134] Eventually, the States General sent a high-level embassy to Copenhagen, demanding cancellation of the increases, removal of a new Danish toll on Elbe traffic, at Glückstadt, and resolution of the long-standing Dutch–Danish dispute over the whaling grounds around Spitsbergen. The Danish king rebuffed the demands, signed an alliance with Spain, and began co-operating with the Spanish embargoes against the Dutch, imposing certificates, and checks, on ships bound for Spain, leaving Hamburg and the Elbe.[135] Yet, for years, the States General took no action. By 1644, there was widespread indignation amongst the merchants, skippers, and seamen of North Holland. Amsterdam insisted that a fleet should be sent to bring the Danes to heel. Frederik Hendrik demurred, claiming it was more important to concentrate on the Spanish war and maintain the

---

[132] ARH SG 4853. sec. res. SG 10 Mar. 1644.
[133] ARH SG 4853, 'Tot justificatie van . . . Zeelandt' (Mar. 1644).
[134] Kernkamp, *Sleutels van de Sont*, 19–20.
[135] Israel, *Empires and Entrepots*, 241–3.

Dutch naval blockade of the Flemish ports and privateering bases.[136] What is chiefly striking about this episode is the refusal of the States of Holland, as a whole, to assign such high priority to Baltic commerce as did Amsterdam and the West Frisian ports. The South Holland towns, including Rotterdam, did not consider the Baltic to be so very vital and, at this juncture, agreed with Zeeland that it was more essential to maintain maximum naval pressure on the Flemish privateers, and seaports, than send a fleet to deal with the Danes.[137] The eventual result was a compromise. Most of the navy remained in the Channel. But a makeshift second fleet, including six hired VOC ships, was eventually dispatched to Denmark, in the summer of 1645, forcing Copenhagen into a humiliating climb-down, and lowering of the tolls, albeit seven years after their introduction.

Frederik Hendrik was more sympathetic to the cause of Charles I in the English Civil War than the States of Holland but made no effort to become actively involved, contenting himself with a few minor gestures of support.[138] By far the most important issue in Dutch politics in the mid-1640s was the question of the terms on which to settle with Spain and the south Netherlands. Frederik Hendrik was eager to achieve some final prestigious conquests in the south, before peace was concluded, and therefore sought to delay further cuts in military spending and troop-strength as long as possible. Holland, however, was becoming increasingly restless at the delay in both reaching peace and cutting war expenditure. In his 1644 campaign, the Prince captured Sas van Gent, which was then incorporated into States Flanders, as was Hulst, captured at last the following year. But in the spring of 1646, Holland refused to approve the annual military budget until the remaining unresolved issues, holding up the peace with Spain, were settled.[139] In August, the Prince made a last, unsuccessful attempt on Antwerp. But, by this time, he had begun co-operating with Holland—going against French wishes, as well as some elements in the States General—in seeking to bring the Dutch–Spanish negotiations, at Münster, to a successful conclusion.[140] The Spanish plenipotentiaries first realized the Stadholder was now assisting the peace process when Johan de Knuyt (the Prince's personal plenipotentiary, as well as Zeeland's, at Münster) began working with Holland's chief plenipotentiary—Adriaen Pauw—rather than obstructing the process, as Zeeland intended.

[136] Aitzema, *Historie*, v. 637–41.
[137] Ibid.; Israel, *Dutch Primacy*, 148.
[138] Groenveld, *Verlopend getij*, 131–3.
[139] Res. Holl. 20 and 23 Mar. and 17 Apr. 1646.
[140] Poelhekke, *Geen blijder maer*, 10.

The acquiescence of the now old, and sick, Stadholder does not mean that there was no longer significant resistance in the United Provinces to peace with Spain, even though in Holland only Leiden remained obdurately against (after first Haarlem, and then Gouda, defected and concurred with the rest),[141] and from October 1646, Friesland and Groningen also ceased their obstruction.

Some of Frederik Hendrik's entourage were far from keen to break ranks with France and see the Republic's affairs run henceforth by Adriaen Pauw and the now pre-eminent figure at Amsterdam, Andries Bicker. The Prince's son and heir, William, remained fiercely opposed, assuring the French ambassador that he would remain 'fortement uni avec la France'.[142] Opposition to a Spanish peace remained strong in Zeeland, Utrecht, and the Zutphen quarter, as well as among the many Reformed preachers who yearned to liberate the south from Spain and the Papacy and introduce the Reformation there. In Gelderland, much of the wrangling over the peace terms sprang, according to Alexander van der Capellen, a leading noble in the Zutphen quarter, and later a prominent adherent of William II, from the rivalry between the quarters for leadership of the province.[143] The Zutphen and Nijmegen quarters traditionally leaned to opposite sides in Generality politics, as they had during the Twelve Years Truce, when Nijmegen sided with Oldenbarnevelt and Zutphen with the Counter-Remonstrants. At that time, Arnhem had adopted an intermediate position and did so again in 1646–8. The Zutphen quarter, during 1647, pressed not only for outright annexation of the Meierij and Overmaas but for Spain also to cede Upper Gelderland, or the Roermond quarter, the region (formerly the fourth quarter of Gelderland) which had remained part of the Spanish Netherlands and been re-Catholicized since the 1580s. By contrast, the Nijmegen quarter opposed the demand for annexation of Upper Gelderland and generally supported Holland.[144]

Obstruction was widespread enough, and disagreements between provinces, and quarters, sufficiently marked, to delay significantly finalization, and ratification, of the peace. The death of Frederik Hendrik, on 14 March 1647, scarcely affected the complex wrangling which continued throughout 1647 and into the early months of 1648. For the time being, Holland's ascendancy in the United Provinces was unchallengeable. But it was a hegemony amid acrimony, polemic, and the polarization of the Republic into warring

[141] GA Haarlem res. vroed. 15 Sept. 1646; GA Gouda OA 10, res. vroed. 15 Sept. 1646.
[142] Kernkamp, *Prins Willem II*, 71.
[143] Van der Capellen, *Gedenkschriften*, ii. 172–82.
[144] ARH SG 4856. sec. res. SG 12 and 28 Jan. 1647.

ideological blocs which were, at the same time, rival networks of influence and clientage at local level.

Frederik Hendrik received delegations from the States General and States of Holland for the last time three days before his death, closing with the words, 'I have been the servant of the States.'[145] Around his death-bed, during his last hours, gathered many of the protagonists of the Republic's subsequent politics, including Jacob Cats, representing Holland, Huygens, and the fervently Orangist Delft preacher Johannes Goethals, who subsequently published a detailed account of the Stadholder's last days. During the preparations for the funeral, which took place at Delft, on 10 May, there was disagreement between friends of the dead Stadholder and the States of Holland over the level of ceremony appropriate.[146] The Prince's side wanted plenty of pomp and triumphal display, paid for by the Generality, to glorify the dead Prince and make an impact on the public. But Holland insisted on more modest arrangements following the precedents of the public funerals of William the Silent (1584) and Maurits (1625). Eight illustrations of the procession were made by Pieter Post and subsequently published, in 1651. The cortège featured twenty parade horses bearing the coats of arms of the various lordships of the House of Orange-Nassau, including Breda, Grave, Geertruidenberg, Buren, IJsselstein, Leerdam, Lingen, Moeurs, Veere, and Flushing, as well as Orange, Nassau, and Dietz. The coffin was followed by William II, other family, including the Great Elector, then, walking solemnly behind, the States General, the *Raad van State*, and, finally, well to the rear, the States of Holland. The funeral procession included a strikingly large number of nobles and senior army officers, showing the public the extent of the influence of the Stadholder's court.[147]

[145] Poelhekke, *Frederik Hendrik*, 563.
[146] Van der Hoeven, *Hollands aeloude vryheid*, ii. 305.
[147] Mörke, 'Hofcultuur', 56–7.

23

Art and Architecture, 1590–1648

❖

THE PROLIFERATION OF ART

The Dutch Revolt, a revolution in politics and religion, was also a revolution in art and architecture. The fighting devastated hundreds of castles, residences, churches, cloisters, and civic buildings. It involved the suppression of the Catholic Church, which meant confiscation of its buildings, and art treasures, and their reallocation for civic use. The new public Church, the Reformed, adopted a totally different approach to church architecture, and adornment of churches, than its predecessor. The Revolt also led to the expansion, and enhanced status, of the civic militias which became the guardians and standard-bearers of the Revolt. It forged a new political rhetoric which demanded novel forms of civic art replacing what had gone before.

Yet, it cannot be said that 1572 marks the start of the Dutch Golden Age in art and architecture. On the contrary, the years 1572–90 were a period of turmoil and drastic change in which, as yet, there were neither the resources, nor demand, for a large artistic output. In the early years of the Revolt everything had to be done on a shoe-string budget. There were practically no wealthy merchants in the north Netherlands and officials with money to spare were unlikely to invest in art in such uncertain times. The urgency of the military situation meant that where gatehouses and sections of town walls had to be rebuilt, as at Haarlem, this was done quickly, cheaply, and, for the most part, merely following the pre-1572 designs.[1] At the same time, the large number of Catholic churches confiscated meant that the new public Church required no new buildings. The heroes and heroic feats of the Revolt could not, as yet, be glorified and commemorated in expensive works of art.

The waves of iconoclasm of 1566, 1572–4, 1577–80, and, in the inland provinces, 1590–4 resulted in massive destruction of paintings, images, and

[1] Ter Kuile, 'Werkzaamheid', 250.

sculptures. The taking into civic custody of the best of the ecclesiastical art which survived led to its being displayed—after sifting out what was too obviously Catholic—in civic buildings, especially town halls.[2] In this way a refurbished civic artistic identity emerged, using paintings of the pre-1572 period, with works of Lucas van Leyden, Jan van Scorel, Maarten van Heemskerck, and Anthonie van Blocklandt (1534–83) well to the fore. The paintings enhanced the interaction between civic officialdom and the public instead of between Church and faithful. At Delft, paintings by sixteenth-century masters filled the Town Hall throughout the Golden Age,[3] precluding any great need for new civic commissions which, in that town, were rarely forthcoming. The burgomasters' rooms in Leiden were hung with paintings by Lucas van Leyden, an artist in whom the city continued to take great pride.[4]

Nevertheless, the ground was prepared, during the 1570s and 1580s, for the tremendous flowering of the arts which began in 1590s—at the same time as the commencement of Dutch dominance in the 'rich trades'—a Golden Age in which artistic achievement and innovation in art proceeded on a scale, and with an intensity, which has no parallel in any other time, or place, in history. This is true not only in that a new ideological and religious framework was created but also in that an unprecedented profusion, and variety, of artists and artistic skills accumulated in the still comparatively poor northern Netherlands, during the 1580s. The refugee artists from the south, who arrived in large numbers in the years around 1585, were Protestants, or at least forced to adapt to a Protestant cultural milieu. But they brought with them much of the legacy of refined artistic skills and training of Antwerp, Bruges, and Ghent, cities which had for centuries been amongst the foremost artistic centres of Europe. At the same time, while the character and orientation of native north Netherlands art was transformed, there was a continuity of training and skills emanating from the studios especially of Van Heemskerck (who was still active in Amsterdam and Haarlem during the early 1570s) and Van Blocklandt, the artistic glory of Utrecht, who greatly influenced the flowering of art in that city, in the 1590s, through pupils such as Abraham Bloemaert.[5]

With resources so limited until the 1590s and the native studios surviving, things were far from easy for the mass of refugee artists in the north, which doubtless contributed to persuading a considerable proportion of the artists

[2] Freedberg, 'Art and Iconoclasm', 77–8.
[3] Boitet, *Beschryvinge*, 74–7.
[4] Orlers, *Beschryvinge*, 163.
[5] De Meyere, 'Utrechtse schilderkunst', 164.

of Antwerp, Ghent, and Bruges to remain in the south. Most of the émigrés had a hard time initially and were frequently reduced, as one of Rembrandt's pupils, Samuel van Hooghstraeten (himself the son of Flemish immigrants), recalled nearly a century later, to the lowest hack work and trifles.[6] One consequence of this was the proliferation, well before 1590, of the cheap print and mass-produced, low-cost etching, depicting heroes of the Revolt or Spanish atrocities. Another effect was that artistic talent was available in profusion, and at low cost, for temporary decoration and civic pageantry, enabling civic governments to use art as propaganda to impress the public, extolling the Revolt, freedom, and local patriotism, with all kinds of commemorative events and celebrations. Leicester, and his English entourage, were amazed at the elaborateness of the shows and displays which enlivened his progression from Middelburg to Utrecht, after his arrival in the northern Netherlands, in December 1585. On entering Haarlem, in March 1586, he encountered a bewildering array of triumphal arches, festive pyramids, and allegorical obelisks, representing Haarlem's heroism and suffering, during the siege of 1572–3.[7] Leicester's grand entries in Zeeland, Holland, and Utrecht were reproduced for the public by means of mass-produced prints.

Yet, there was also innovation, a series of isolated artistic breakthroughs which had only a limited effect, initially,[8] but which later, from the 1590s, lent momentum to the phenomenal growth and diversification of Dutch art. Particularly, at Haarlem, the leading trio—two north Netherlanders, Cornelis Cornelisz. van Haarlem (1562–1638) and Hendrik Goltzius (1558–1617), and the south Netherlander Carel van Mander (1548–1606)—developed new concepts, techniques, and approaches. One of the most notable pre-1590 achievements was Cornelis Cornelisz's astounding militia group portrait of 1583,[9] painted when he was only 21, the start of the tradition of lifelike militia pieces which was to culminate later in the militia group portraits of Frans Hals. Another was Goltzius's famous portrait of William the Silent, of 1581, rimmed with heroic symbols, simultaneously a masterpiece of art and political propaganda (see illustration no. 6).

Thus, when the general situation was transformed in the 1590s by the sudden tremendous flourishing of the 'rich trades', and massive resources became available, an abundance of artistic talent of stunning sophistication was already in place, making possible an outpouring of art, the like of which,

---

[6] Busken Huet, *Land van Rembrand*, 750.
[7] Van Dorsten and Strong, *Leicester's Triumph*, 65–7.
[8] Freedberg, 'Art and Iconoclasm', 78–80.
[9] Levy-Van Helm, 'Haarlemse schuttersstukken', 109.

in terms of quantity, quality, and variety, has never been equalled by any other society or age. Concentrations of talent were to be found in several towns. At Utrecht, there were Abraham Bloemaert (1564–1651), Joachim Wttewael (1566–1638), and Paulus Moreelse, the three pillars of Utrecht painting at the start of the Golden Age. Delft boasted Michiel van Mierevelt (1567–1641), son of a goldsmith, who had trained with Blocklandt, at Utrecht, in the early 1580s, was considered, by the nineteenth-century critic Busken Huet, the first great artist of the Golden Age,[10] and who, in turn, enriched Utrecht, by training Moreelse. Van Mierevelt established his reputation as Holland's leading portraitist, at Delft, in the 1590s. These were all northerners. But much of the flood of talent flowed from the south. At Amsterdam, initially, immigrant artists predominated.[11] Hans van de Velde, father of the more famous Esaias, emigrated from Antwerp, becoming a citizen of Amsterdam in 1586. David Vingboons (1576–1632), a key figure of the early Dutch Golden Age, and father of the architect Philips Vingboons, an emigrant from Mechelen, was trained by his artist-father, in Amsterdam, in the 1590s. Roelant Savery (1576–1639), from Kortrijk, trained at Amsterdam, in the 1590s, under his brother. One of the south Netherlands genres transferred to the north—the elegant garden party scene—was developed in the first two decades of the seventeenth century, at Haarlem, particularly by artists from the south, or sons of southern immigrants, notably David Vingboons, Esaias van de Velde, and Dirk Hals.[12]

Other south Netherlands artists migrated first to Germany, where prospects seemed brighter, in the 1580s, than in the north and transferred to the north Netherlands after 1590, when the situation there improved. Gillis van Coninxloo (1544–1607), one of the émigrés most esteemed by contemporaries, settled in Amsterdam, from Germany, only in 1595. Some southern artists stayed initially in Antwerp, after 1585, and moved north only later when the Dutch art scene gained its staggering impetus. In other cases, skilled, and relatively affluent, artisans from the south, seeing the new opportunities in painting created by the commercial boom of the 1590s, steered their sons to careers in art, as was probably the case with the brothers Frans and Dirk Hals. Haarlem's greatest painter, Frans Hals (1582–1666), arrived with his parents, from Antwerp, around 1586; he trained, reportedly, with Van Mander, presumably around 1600, though his earliest documented painting dates only from 1611.[13]

[10] Busken Huet, *Land van Rembrand*, 275.
[11] Brown, *Dutch Landscape*, 20–2; Haak, *The Golden Age*, 174.
[12] Keyes, *Esaias van den Velde*, 29–30, 34.
[13] Thiel-Stroman, 'The Frans Hals Documents', 375.

The Dutch art élite of the Golden Age, like the merchant élite, was thus a mixture of native-born and immigrants. Genres transferred, or adapted, from the artistic traditions of the south Netherlands certainly played a major role in the great flowering of art in the United Provinces. Nevertheless, at the time, the presiding figures at Utrecht, Haarlem, Delft, and Leiden tended to be north, rather than south, Netherlanders, not least the Leiden regent-painter Isaac van Swanenburg. Moreover, the training and orientation of the new generation of north Netherlanders was, broadly, more in the tradition of Blocklandt, Bloemaert, Mierevelt, Lastman, and the Van Swanenburgs than that of the Antwerp school.

This rapid escalation of artistic output in seven or eight centres, all at the same moment, in the 1590s, of course coincided with developments in society which made it both possible and sustainable. Dutch society became, within the space of a few years, far richer and more secure than previously; the towns began to grow rapidly and a wealthy merchant élite came into being. Together these social changes generated a spate of new buildings, refurbishment of confiscated monasteries for secular uses, a stream of public commissions for art works, of many types, and the rapid formation of connoisseur collections. These trends together fuelled the unprecedented proliferation of art. A related phenomenon was the rise of specialized luxury industries which were new to the north and which provided further scope for art and artists. Prominent among these were tapestry-weaving, transferred from Antwerp to Middelburg, and especially Delft, where François Spiering (son of an Antwerp burgomaster) led the way, and linen damask, the weaving of intricate patterns into fine linens, transferred from Kortrijk to Haarlem.[14] Damask became one of the emblems of civic pride at Haarlem, Frans Hals depicting a particularly fine example in his first big militia group portrait, in 1616 (Frans Hals Museum, Haarlem).

During the 1590s the regents of Holland, Zeeland, and Utrecht began assigning valuable commissions for public art. In the case of tapestries these were bound to go to south Netherlanders who dominated the craft. Among the largest projects in this sphere were the six great tapestries, illustrating sieges and battles of the Revolt in which Zeelanders had been prominent, ordered by the States of Zeeland for the assembly hall of the States, in the former abbey of Middelburg,[15] and twelve tapestries commissioned by the States General, in 1610, as a gift for the French envoy Pierre Jeannin, who figured prominently in the negotiations leading to the Twelve Years Truce. Some of the architectural commissions also went to south Netherlanders,

[14] Ysselstein, *Van linnen en linnenkasten*, 43, 57.
[15] Ysselstein, *Gesch. der tapijtweverijen*, i. 70, 79.

notably the Fleming Lieven de Key (c.1550–1627), who supervised numerous building projects at Haarlem and Leiden during the 1590s and first decade of the seventeenth century. But while expertise was essential, background and connections also mattered, and it is noticeable, especially in painting, that the best public commissions went not just to native Hollanders but men closely linked to the towns and their regent élites. At Leiden, Isaac van Swanenburg (1537–1614), member of the *vroedschap*, as well as the city's leading artist, influenced who received what, allocating the choicest patronage, including a series of paintings illustrating the revival of the Leiden cloth industry, to himself.[16] At Haarlem, there were numerous talented immigrants. But the valuable commissions nearly always went to Cornelis Cornelisz, a local man married to a daughter of one of the burgomasters. He painted a series of large pictures for the city council, including several of a distinctly anti-Spanish and anti-Catholic flavour hung in the former cloister converted by the *vroedschap* into Haarlem's Prinsenhof—lodgings for the Stadholder and other high-born guests, which the Haarlem town government simultaneously used as a repository of paintings by famous artists of the past, especially Maarten van Heemskerck—which had been confiscated from the Church and now served the new purpose of enhancing civic pride.[17] Paulus Moreelse, a local Counter-Remonstrant, who became a member of the *raad* of Utrecht, in the 1620s, gained handsomely, securing, among others, commissions to design a new city gatehouse and paint pictures for Amalia von Solms, on the occasion of her marriage to Frederik Hendrik. One of the principal surviving militia group portraits, of the Delft militia, painted in 1592, was commissioned from Jacob Willemsz. Delff (c.1550–1601), who became a Delft burgher (though in fact he came from Gouda, not Delft) long before the immigrant influx from the south.

ARCHITECTURE AND THE BUILDING BOOM

In the maritime zone, all the major towns grew, after 1585, at a furious rate and many civic institutions and establishments—town halls, militia quarters, Latin schools, and orphanages—were now too small or in need of being refurbished. At the same time the breakthrough in the 'rich trades', and rise of the new merchant élite, resulted, for the first time in the north, in opulent merchant residences being built and decorated, and in substantial numbers. The vast building boom was to continue until 1621.

[16] Schwartz, *Dutch World of Painting*, 29–30.
[17] Gonnet, 'Oude schilderijen', 140; Van Bueren, *Tot lof van Haarlem*, 200–5.

Church-building, as we have seen, was, in the main, an exception save at Amsterdam, where urban growth at this time was on an unparalleled scale. Three major new churches were built there, all designed by Hendrik de Keyser (1565–1621), who came from Utrecht, became Amsterdam's civic architect and sculptor, and, in his day, was the best-known architect and sculptor of the north Netherlands. Apart from these, and the New Church at Haarlem (1610–15), the architecture of the Republic at the end of the sixteenth century, and during the first third of the seventeenth, was over-whelmingly secular in character.

Not all prestige projects were commissioned in Holland and Zeeland. The stability of the post-1590 period generated a few notable buildings also in other provinces. Franeker built a fine new town hall in the years 1591–4; Zutphen commenced its civic showpiece, the tower known as the Wijnhuis-toren, during the Truce years. But the inland towns were in too depressed a condition for any large-scale public building before 1609 and it was only in Holland and Zeeland that economic growth, and urban expansion, sufficed to generate a massive wave of new construction.

Among the foremost developments were the new East India House (1606), Exchange (1608–11), and Haarlem Gate (1615–18), at Amsterdam, built to designs by Hendrik de Keyser. The new militia hall (1590), Prinsenhof, Meat Hall (1599), Weigh-House, New Church, and annexe to the Town Hall (1620–2), at Haarlem, were designed by Lieven de Key as was the Old Men's Home (1608), today the Frans Hals Museum.[18] Various new structures arose in Leiden commencing in the 1590s, including the new town hall.[19] Delft acquired the marble Mausoleum of William the Silent, in the New Church, executed by Hendrik de Keyser, and the new façade of the Town Hall. Scarcely less imposing were the new élite merchant residences. The grandest arose along Amsterdam's stately new canal the Herengracht, during the Truce years, among the most opulent being the Bartolotti House, completed in 1621 to designs by De Keyser.[20]

During the depression of the 1620s and 1630s, both public and private building slackened and Dutch architecture discarded the thrusting, extrovert confidence of the pre-1621 period for the austere, 'classicist' style which developed in the mid-1620s. The principal author of this architectural shift was the Haarlem architect-painter Jacob van Campen (1595–1657), who started the trend with his first major commission, the Coymans House, a double residence built for the élite merchants Balthasar and Jan Coymans

[18] Ter Kuile, 'Werkzaamheid', 246–51.
[19] Orlers, *Beschrijvinge*, 159–60, 168, 215.
[20] Fokkens, *Beschrijvingh*, 394–8.

in Amsterdam, in 1625.[21] Two other guiding figures were the Stadholder's secretary, Constantijn Huygens, who worked with Van Campen in designing his own house, at The Hague, in the mid-1630s, and the Haarlem architect-painter Salomon de Bray (1597–1664), also an enthusiastic promoter of the new classicizing tendency. Work on the Mauritshuis, the most famous example of Dutch classicist architecture, and today the main art museum in The Hague, began in 1633, to designs by Van Campen, with Huygens exerting an influence.

The slower tempo of urban development between 1621 and 1647 was a consequence of the resumption of the Eighty Years War, and the relatively depressed conditions of the 1620s and 1630s. It is no accident that the two towns which (at least after 1635) continued with major projects, Haarlem and Leiden, were textile towns which profited from the economic effects of the war (see p. 315 above), while the Holland maritime towns were mainly adversely affected. The great age of building in Leiden began with the upsurge of the fine cloth industry, which brought new prosperity to the town from the later 1630s onwards. The most outstanding edifices were the elegantly octagonal Marekerk, the first major Protestant church built in Leiden, begun in 1639, and the Cloth Hall (1639–40), a landmark in architectural history, marking the transfer of classicism from use for private and princely residences to civic and commercial use.[22]

An important aspect of Dutch art and architecture, during the 1630s and 1640s, was the work on the various palaces of the Stadholder, Frederik Hendrik. A new palace in the centre of The Hague, the Noordeinde, designed by Van Campen, was constructed, and decorated in the 1640s, and in the late 1640s work began also on the famous Huis ten Bosch, a *villa suburbana* set in the woods near The Hague. The Huis ten Bosch, one of the foremost examples of Dutch classicist architecture, was designed and built in 1645–7, by Pieter Post, a protégé of Huygens and Frederik Hendrik, taught by Van Campen, who worked on nearly all the Stadholder's palaces.[23] Originally a painter, and son of a glass-painter, he was an elder brother of the Frans Post who accompanied Count Johan Maurits of Nassau to Recife and became the best-known of the Dutch artists working in Brazil. Pieter Post was, together with Van Campen, Philips Vingboons, and Arent van 's Gravesande, one of the four chief exponents of Dutch Golden Age classicist architecture.

[21] Kuyper, *Dutch Classicist Architecture*, 58–60.

[22] Turck, 'Lakenhal in Leiden', 404–5.

[23] Slothouwer, *Paleizen van Frederik Hendrik*, 186; Terwen and Ottenheym, *Pieter Post*, 56–60.

Vingboons became the chief designer of opulent houses for Amsterdam merchants and patricians, in the late 1630s, an early influential design being the house of Michael Pauw, built in 1638, on the Herengracht, next to the Bartolotti House. In 1642, he built a splendid house for Joan Poppen the Younger, one of the richest men in Amsterdam. Vingboons also designed country villas for the wealthy of Amsterdam, but (presumably because he was a Catholic) never obtained significant patronage in towns outside Amsterdam and no major civic patronage within the city. Very different was the case of Arent van 's Gravesande, another talented architect who learnt his trade in the Stadholder's service amid the architectural milieu nurtured by Huygens. His first large commission, the Sebastiaensdoelen militia hall, in The Hague (1636), established his reputation. Another notable early achievement was his design for the small, but imposing, town hall of the little town of Middelharnis (1639). After Middelharnis, 's Gravesande worked principally as town architect in Leiden, designing both the Cloth Hall (1640) and the Marekerk, an imposing church, influenced by the famous Santa Maria della Salute in Venice, and yet unmistakably Dutch in flavour.

SPECIALIZATION IN PAINTING

The scale of artistic production in the United Provinces—principally Holland and Utrecht—in the early seventeenth century was astounding. Extrapolating from the numbers of paintings in family inventories in Delft, it has been estimated that, by 1650, there were approximately two and a half million paintings in Holland, most admittedly copies, or pictures of poor quality, but a sizeable proportion, some 10 per cent, pictures of quality.[24] Painting in the Dutch Republic, in the seventeenth century, was a major industry, as well as art, and great numbers of paintings (often of indifferent quality) were produced not only for the Dutch market but for export, to those parts of Europe, particularly Germany, where there was a Protestant civic culture which to an extent shared the tastes of Dutch civic society. In the early period, down to the 1620s, very few foreign rulers took much interest in Dutch artistic production, though a notable exception was Christian IV of Denmark.

There was, in the Dutch art world of the early seventeenth century, incentive both to produce huge quantities of mediocre art, and to strive for the most refined effects. It required more time, as well as skill, to paint

---

[24] Van der Woude, 'Schilderijproduktie', 20–5.

pictures of quality, and originality, appropriate for the connoisseur élite merchant or regent. But such pictures fetched far higher prices, and competition remained intense. By the Truce years, the best Dutch artists were vying not only with each other, for the attention of the connoisseurs, and the rich, but also with a swelling influx of art from Italy, Germany, and the south Netherlands. Amsterdam became the hub of the European art trade, just as the Dutch entrepôt was the hub of the 'rich trades' in general. Buyers on behalf of illustrious personages in England, France, Germany, and Scandinavia bought pictures of all kinds, at Amsterdam, not only the pick of Dutch art. In the past, secular painting in Europe meant painting for rulers, and the high nobility, whose taste gravitated to mythological, pastoral, and martial themes. The rapid diffusion of merchant and regent wealth in the Dutch Republic, however, from the 1590s onwards, created a new situation. The sheer extent of the new connoisseurship, and high prices remunerating those who succeeded in pleasing regents and élite merchants, generated totally new pressures and opportunities and it is these which gave the art of the Dutch Golden Age its special character.

Especially striking was the shift towards a previously unheard-of degree of specialization.[25] With numerous buyers and pressure to increase production to the maximum compatible with quality, most artists strove for novel and refined effects within a particular genre of painting. In a culture with comparatively few buyers of expensive pictures, and those buying possessing only a few paintings, there is little point in artists becoming more and more specialized. But here was a society in which, all at once, from the 1590s, unprecedented numbers of buyers were purchasing unprecedented numbers of pictures of quality. With so many new, and refurbished, buildings and houses, noble and civic as well as mercantile, in town and country, requiring fine décor, there was a constant spur to innovate and introduce more variety. There were collectors who liked to concentrate on a particular genre. But it was more usual for wealthy collectors and connoisseurs to seek variety. The collection of the Leiden humanist Petrus Scriverius was typical in including religious scenes, mythological subjects, still lifes, flower-pieces, genre, landscapes, seascapes, and portraits.[26]

The most prestigious (and expensive) paintings during the first surge of Golden Age art were grand, richly coloured mythological scenes, chiefly painted at Haarlem and Utrecht, the two leading, and most innovative, art centres of the north Netherlands in the early years, down to 1621. This imposing wave of 'late mannerist' mythological art welled up in the 1590s,

[25] De Vries, 'Art History', 265.   [26] Frederiks, 'Kabinet schilderijen', 62–3.

in the studios of Cornelis Cornelisz, Van Mander (who expressly sought to elevate and heroicize art), and Hendrik Goltzius, at Haarlem, and those of Abraham Bloemaert and, later, Joachim Wittewael (1566–1638) and Paulus Moreelse, at Utrecht.[27] The favourite themes were drawn from Greek mythology, the most frequently painted being *Diana and Actaeon*—a craze culminating in Rembrandt's masterpiece, painted in 1634 (at Schloss Anholt), *Venus and Adonis*, a subject which Cornelisz painted at least eight times between 1600 and 1630, and *The Judgement of Paris*. These pictures, produced for wealthy merchants and regents, featuring naked, frolicking goddesses and nymphs, in an erotically suggestive manner, were sharply criticized, after 1609, in Counter-Remonstrant circles.[28] It is doubtless no accident that they flourished chiefly at Haarlem and Utrecht, both Remonstrant cities. In Counter-Remonstrant Amsterdam Rembrandt's teacher, Pieter Lastman (1583–1633), also painted some mythological scenes in the Truce period but put more clothes on his goddesses, toning down the erotic element. The genre survived but declined steeply after 1618. The English ambassador, Sir Dudley Carleton, noted in 1616 that, at Haarlem, the 'painters were the chiefest curiosity, whereof there is one Cornelius, for figures, who doth excel in coloring but errs in proportions'.[29] Haarlem and Utrecht surpassed Amsterdam as art centres, during the first two decades of the century, Carleton going so far as to say that in Amsterdam there were many fine pictures 'but few good painters, that place being in this commodity, as in others, the warehouse rather than the workhouse'.[30]

Especially Haarlem stood at the forefront of artistic innovation, and the trend towards specialization. Among the most outstanding innovators was Hendrik Cornelisz. Vroom (1566–1640), creator of the realistic seascape, which he developed in the 1590s. Vroom went to appreciable lengths to refine his speciality, once sailing in a storm off Zierikzee, to improve his rendering of rough conditions.[31] The novel realism of his depictions of ships, and the sea, won him renown, and much profit, and he became something of a national and international celebrity. 'Vroom hath a great name for representing of ships', remarked Carleton, in 1616, amazed at the high prices his paintings fetched, 'and all things belonging to the sea, wherein indeed he is very rare.'[32] Uniquely skilled in his day at handling large masses of shipping, he frequently depicted the great maritime events of his age and

---

[27] Sluijter, *Heydensche fabulen*, 14, 24–5, 38; Miedema, 'Appreciation', 130–3.
[28] Sluijter, *Heydensche fabulen*, 279–90.
[29] Lee, *Dudley Carleton*, 218.
[30] Ibid.
[31] Russell, 'Hendrick Vroom', 119–20.
[32] Lee, *Dudley Carleton*, 218.

was commissioned to execute the cartoons for most of the Middelburg historical tapestries. His engraving of Maurits's invasion force being shipped in 1600 across the Scheldt estuary, to Flanders, sold widely, adding to his fortune. Vroom was also one of the inventors of the urban panorama, a genre popular with the regents.[33] One of the choicest of the early urban views, painted in 1615, was Vroom's panorama of Amsterdam highlighting the city's new 'Haarlem gatehouse'.

Haarlem's most celebrated painter, Frans Hals, can be said to have devised the spontaneous, lively portrait, capturing the fleeting mood. He was the first to portray personalities at a particular moment. Another Haarlem innovation was the 'Merry Company', depicting groups of extravagantly attired revellers making no secret of their enjoyment of earthly pleasures, cultivated in particular by Hals's younger brother, Dirk, and the gifted Rotterdam artist Willem Buytewech (1591–1624), who moved to Haarlem in 1612. Yet another, and more enduring, Haarlem genre was the realistic landscape, developed around 1614, by Esaias van de Velde (1587–1630), one of the foremost innovators of the Dutch Golden Age. Van de Velde proceeded from the older landscape tradition of Coninxloo, Vingboons, and Bloemaert, but effected a radical shift, from imagined landscapes, depicting a fantasy world, to observed landscape, reflecting the unspoilt remaining margins of the actual Dutch landscape.[34] He produced 'realistic' Dutch landscapes both as paintings and in a seminal series of landscape etchings. Other artists soon followed, producing great quantities of landscape prints.

Utrecht too, though no longer the unrivalled centre it had been in the sixteenth century, remained a major focus of innovation throughout the first main phase of Dutch Golden Age art (1590–1621). One of Utrecht's specialities was the so-called Italianate landscape, Mediterranean settings bathed in a warm, romantic glow and, in the early period, often adorned with mythological figures. Its primary originator was Cornelis van Poelenburgh (1586–1667), who developed it from the mythological picture. But Utrecht became especially renowned for the application of Caravaggesque chiaroscuro to genre scenes, imparting a dramatically lit theatrical quality.[35] The three principal Utrecht *Caravaggisti* were Hendrik Ter Brugghen (1588–1629), Gerrit van Honthorst (1590–1656), and Dirk van Baburen (c.1594–1624)—all of whom spent long periods, as young artists, in Italy, evolving an art pervaded with Italian influences without merely duplicating Italian styles. Ter Brugghen, a pupil of Bloemaert, the most original, was the

---

[33] Russell, 'Hendrick Vroom', 143.
[34] Keyes, *Esaias van den Velde*, 28–32; Freedberg, *Dutch Landscape Prints*, 28–34.
[35] Schneider, *Caravaggio und die Niederländer*, 32–4.

real inventor of the style. Honthorst, who returned to Utrecht, from Italy, six years after Ter Brugghen, in 1620, was renowned especially for his skill in rendering candle-lit night scenes. The numerous courtesan and brothel scenes painted by Honthorst and Van Baburen, in the 1620s, after the Counter-Remonstrant reaction, were not intended to titillate—the prostitutes are mostly clothed—but to dramatize the dangers of the seductive and venal, highlighting the message with hideous, grasping procuresses.[36]

THE SECOND PHASE IN GOLDEN AGE ART, 1621–*c*.1645

The first main phase of Dutch Golden Age art and architecture ended in the years around 1621. The transition from Phase Two (1609–21) to Phase Three (1621–47) of Dutch world trade primacy involved a fundamental restructuring of the whole of commerce, industry, and many aspects of retailing.[37] Inevitably, the pace and direction of Dutch art, being closely tied to the economic boom and rebuilding of the cities, were profoundly affected also.

The impact on art was partly the result of the slump, the contraction, and difficulties in commerce down to the early 1630s, which sharply curtailed spending and demand. Thus, one feature of the 'middle period' of Dutch Golden Age painting (1621–45) was a shift to smaller, cheaper pictures, and more modest subjects. The new period was also characterized by changes in subject-matter. The elegant 'garden parties' and 'Merry Companies' of the Truce era receded, to be replaced by battle views, skirmishes, and genre scenes featuring soldiers in taverns, brothels, and guardrooms. Another feature was the shift in colouring and tone. The most drastic change in Dutch overseas commerce in the early 1620s, was the collapse of the traffic with Spain, Portugal, the Caribbean, and Spanish America, and general decay of Dutch trade with southern Europe. In consequence, American and Mediterranean dyestuffs, including indigo, cochineal, Campeche and Brazil wood, became scarce and expensive in Holland,[38] as did diverse earth pigments, and rare substances for pigments, obtained from Italy and the Levant. It was in particular the most brilliant reds, blues, and yellows which were most affected by the sudden scarcity of exotic dyes and glazes.

The switch to monochrome, predominantly brown and grey pictures in the early 1620s was a broad phenomenon, cutting across many genres.[39] The vivid, rich colouring of the Truce years yielded, quite suddenly, to an

---

[36] Van de Pol, 'Beeld en werkelijkheid', 118–19.
[37] Israel, *Dutch Primacy*, 121–87.
[38] Israel, *Empires and Entrepots*, 28–9, 189.
[39] Bergström, *Dutch Still-Life Painting*, 112.

austerity of tone and colour which permeated the entire spectrum of Dutch art. The change is striking in the still life, with the splendour, rich hues, and brilliant flower-painting of the pre-1621 period being replaced by the modest still life of kitchen utensils, blocks of cheese, and books, objects which could be painted in yellowy-brown and grey. There was also the so-called monochrome banquet piece, painted in brownish hues, of which Willem Claesz. Heda (1594–1680) and Pieter Claesz (1597–1660) were the supreme exponents.[40]

Similarly in the landscape, Esaias van de Velde, now working at The Hague, switched to smaller, more modest scenes, painted in sombre colours. But it was especially his pupil Jan van Goyen (1596–1656) and Salomon van Ruysdael (c.1600–70) who, during the 1620s and 1630s, brought the modest, monochrome landscape to its zenith.[41] The same transition occurred in marine painting, with smaller themes as well as canvases—often depicting single vessels in rough weather, or fishing boats—painted in what has been called a 'tonalistisch-atmosphärisch' manner, with sombre expanses of grey replacing the grand, splendidly coloured panoramas of Vroom and Van Wieringen.[42] This new style of seascape was developed particularly by Jan Porcellis (1584–1632), followed by Simon de Vlieger (1601–53). Porcellis, an immigrant from the south, was one of the few talented artists working in the United Provinces, in the seventeenth century, known to have worked initially in extreme poverty. But in his case too art proved a ready route to affluence. His new style soon made him famous and, by 1629, he owned three houses.

At the same time, where expensive dyes and glazes continued to be used more time and care were lavished on their use, leading to the 'fine painting' concept—a highly polished and luxuriously coloured art for connoisseurs developed first by Rembrandt at Leiden, in the late 1620s,[43] and then, as Rembrandt discarded it, in the 1630s, by Gerrit Dou and his pupils. If Haarlem and Utrecht were the principal centres of artistic innovation, during the early period of Golden Age art, Leiden and Amsterdam came to the fore during the 1620s and 1630s. Besides the 'fine painting' manner, Rembrandt can be credited with introducing a new emphasis on gesture and posture, to heighten the dramatic effect of the 'history painting'. Rembrandt's first pupil, Gerrit Dou (1613–75), commenced studying with him in 1628, adopting the smooth, highly polished brushwork characteristic of Rembrandt at that time. Dou stayed in Leiden and became the leading

[40] Segal, *A Prosperous Past*, 121.
[41] Brown, *Dutch Landscape*, 22–3; Buijssen, *Between Fantasy*, 56–7.
[42] Bol, *Holländische Marinemalerei*, 91.
[43] Rosenberg, *Rembrandt*, 18.

painter there after Rembrandt moved to Amsterdam in 1631. By 1640, the fame of Dou's polished 'fine-painting' style had made him an emblem of civic pride.[44] Because of the meticulous effort lavished on each painting, and his renown, he painted only for collectors willing to pay very high prices.

Rembrandt's mastery was rapidly noticed at the highest levels in the Republic, as can hardly have been otherwise in a society so geared to artistic connoisseurship.[45] His genius came to the notice of Constantijn Huygens in 1629, when he was only 23. Huygens, in turn, brought Rembrandt to the attention of the Stadholder. During the 1630s, Rembrandt was, indeed, partly a court painter, especially during 1632 when he spent much of his time at The Hague, painting portraits amongst others of Amalia von Solms and Huygens's brother, Maurits. He painted several large pictures for the Stadholder, while remaining the leading, and most fashionable, painter at Amsterdam. During these years he made a great deal of money, married the daughter of a Leeuwarden burgomaster, and bought a fine house which he filled with his bizarre collection of art, armour, and exotica. Rembrandt never lost his reputation during the Golden Age as the most masterly and versatile Dutch artist of the time. But he was also considered a strange and difficult man prone to antagonize his patrons. *The Night Watch* (1642), the most famous and greatest of all Dutch militia pieces, was widely admired for its originality, virtuosity, and dramatic effect,[46] though it may have annoyed some of those who paid for it only to be hidden from view, immersed in dark shadow. Probably, his eccentric life-style and, possibly, his opinions contributed to his remaining out of favour with the Amsterdam regents, his being passed over in the assigning of most major commissions in the city, and his gradual withdrawal during the 1640s, into himself. There are hints that Rembrandt may have had Orangist views; and although its exact meaning remains in doubt, his political allegory, *The Concord of the State*, painted in the late 1630s, can be construed as criticism of Amsterdam for looming too large in the States of Holland and impairing the unity of the Union.[47]

Rembrandt, the towering genius, the greatest artist of the age, was highly versatile, a master of etching and drawing, as well as painting, and expert in biblical scenes, mythological scenes, landscape, genre, and the militia piece, as well as portraits and group portraits. His most gifted pupil, Carel Fabritius (1622–54), whose career was tragically cut short by the great

[44] Sluiter, *Leidse fijnschilders*, 15.
[45] Rosenberg, *Rembrandt*, 17–21.
[46] Tümpel, *Rembrandt*, 104.
[47] *A Corpus of Rembrandt Paintings*, iii. 341–56.

gunpowder explosion of Delft, was also versatile.[48] But specialization remained more usual and paid better. Emanuel de Witte (*c.*1617–92), son of an Alkmaar schoolmaster, was undistinguished as a general painter in the early phase of his career, in the 1640s, achieving success only after he concentrated on 'church interiors', after 1650.[49] Most specialized from the outset and rarely, if ever, ventured out of their sphere of specialization.

As the older genres evolved, new masters tended to aim for heightened realism and ever more sophisticated effects. The controversial artist Johan Torrentius (1589–1644), who was arrested in Haarlem, in 1627, and tried for blasphemous utterances, immoral conduct, and painting obscene pictures— one showed a naked woman with her foot on her knee—was widely, almost exclusively, known in Holland, before his arrest, as a 'miracle' of a painter, as Uyttenbogaert called him, in a letter to Grotius, in the still life.[50] He was credited with having introduced a stunning new realism which was greatly admired by Constantijn Huygens.[51] And as the still life evolved towards greater and greater realism so did the seascape, landscape, and household scene. At the same time, enterprising artists developed new specialities and angles. Among the novelties of the second quarter of the century was the church interior, and exterior, developed by Pieter Saenredam (1597–1665), a friend of Van Campen, the guardroom scene, and animal and poultry painting. The painting of animals was the speciality especially of Paulus Potter (1625–54). The leading Dordrecht artist Aelbert Cuyp (1620–91) specialized in painting sunlit views, frequently with cows. The Utrecht artist Herman Saftleven (1609–85) became the acknowledged master of sunlit forest scenes, meticulously rendering sunlight filtering through branches and leaves. Pieter de Hoogh (1629–83) specialized during the early part of his career in painting guardroom scenes.[52] Philips Wouwerman (1619–68), a Haarlem painter, amassed a fortune by painting hundreds of cavalry skirmishes for which, evidently, there was an inexhaustible demand. The Amsterdam painter Aert van der Neer (1604–77) tirelessly laboured at his two specialities—winter landscapes and landscapes by moonlight.

The art and artists of the Golden Age captured the whole of the physical, social, and cultural reality surrounding the Dutch burgher of the day, depicting his own household and civic world, the rural surroundings, and also what surrounded that—the soldiers, on the landward side, and ships and the sea on the other. In other parts of seventeenth-century Europe it

[48] Hoogstraeten, *Inleyding*, 291, 308.
[49] Manke, *Emanuel de Witte*, 7–13.
[50] Uyttenbogaert, *Brieven*, iii. 11.
[51] Bredius, *Johannes Torrentius*, 6–8.
[52] Sutton, *Pieter de Hooch*, 12.

1. Charles V combats heresy (1531).

2. *The Ship of the Church* (early 17th century).

3. The iconoclastic fury in Antwerp (August 1566).

4. *The Lamentation of the Devastated Netherlands*. Engraving by Hendrick Collaert (*c*.1570).

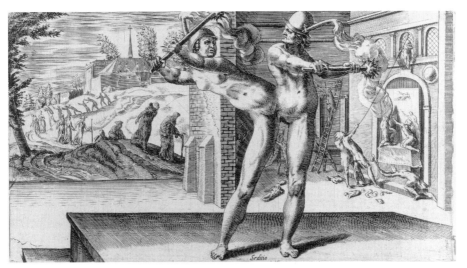

5. The Revolt as religious strife.

6. William the Silent. Engraving by Hendrik Goltzius (1581).

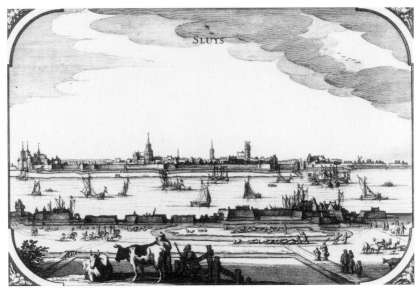

7. The Dutch defensive Ring: the town of Sluis in States Flanders.

8. The arms of the States and cities of Zeeland. Tapestry (1604).

9. *Vreemden handel* (Strange Business). Anti-Oldenbarnevelt print (1614).

10. *The Power of Peace* in both the Netherlands (1609).

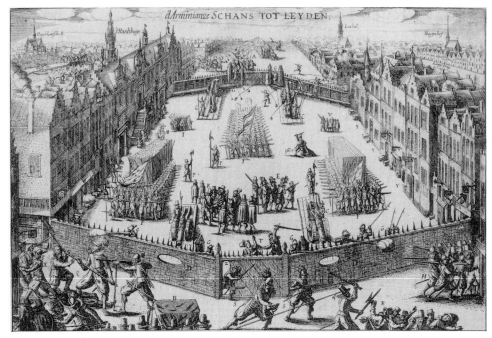

11. *The Arminian Redoubt at Leiden* (1617–18).

12. The occupation of the city of Utrecht by Prince Maurits and disbandment of the *waardgelders* (July 1618).

14. Frederik Hendrik's palace at Rijswijk (1634–44).

13. The Synod of Dordrecht (Dordt) of 1618–19.

15. The inauguration of the University of Leiden (1575).

16. Allegory of the birth of William III, by Govaert Flinck (1650).

18. *Only in a Republic are True Peace and Happiness to be Experienced* (1669).

17. Dutch shipbuilding in the later seventeenth century.

19. *The Great Assembly at The Hague* (1651).

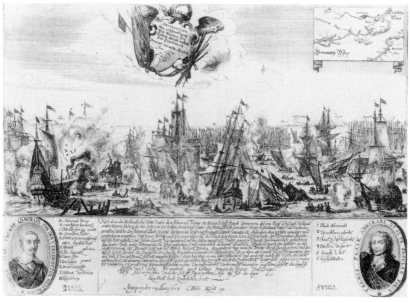

20. The Battle of Portland Bill (February 1653).

21. The Anglo-Dutch peace of 1667.

22. The Republican Triumph of Cornelis de Witt (1670).

23. An anti-De Witt political cartoon (1672).

24. William III becomes Stadholder (July 1672).

25. *Utrecht Restored*. Engraving by Romeyn de Hooghe (1674).

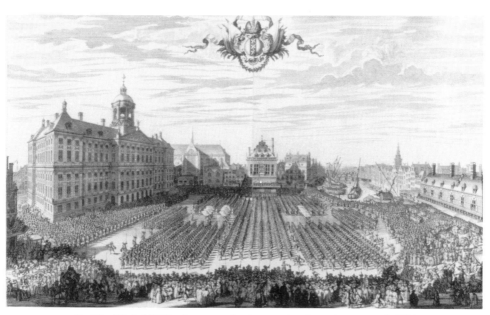

26. The Civic Militia drawn up in Amsterdam's main square (1686).

27. William III, the States General, and their allies thwart Louis XIV (1689).

28. *The Chief Occurrences of the Year 1692.* Engraving by Jan van Vianen.

29. The VOC storehouse and wharves in the early eighteenth century. Copy of an engraving by Petrus Schenck.

30. *William IV, Prince of Orange, Rescues the Dutch Maid* (1747).

31. Rioting in Amsterdam in June 1748.

32. Stadholder William V being welcomed by the States of Zeeland (June 1786).

was possible to live in a town or locality and not see, and sense, very much of what went on beyond. Life in Dutch society was very different, for the Republic was the entrepôt of world trade, with evidence of ships and the sea everywhere. Because the fisheries were so fundamental to the Dutch scene, reminders of the defensive ring, and fixed garrisons, ever present, and contact with other, neighbouring towns unavoidable, it was a society in which no one could live without continually sensing the interaction of land and sea, town and country, one town with the next, soldiers and seamen with burghers, the exotic with the mundane, and the foreign with the local. Art, by encompassing all of this, and reflecting it on everyone's walls, and in every tavern and public building, made explicit, and heightened awareness of, what everyone saw and felt.

But art by no means slavishly mirrored this teeming reality. Rather it strove to adapt and interpret the Dutch physical and social world of the time in terms of faith, nostalgia, and cultural values. Thus, art also sought to make real the worlds of the Bible, Greek and Roman mythology, and fantasy worlds nurtured by recollection of a lost past and vague notions of exotic places. Among the latter was the fantasy world of the Italianate landscape— sunlit and warm, with a hint of the erotic, a world pioneered by Poelenburgh and Nicholas Berchem (1622–74), and extended by Karel DuJardin (1622– 78), Johannes Lingelbach (1622–74), and Jan Baptista Weenix (1621–60). The realistic landscape of Van Goyen and Van Ruisdael was, in its way, a fantasy world too, for the Dutch rural setting of the seventeenth century, certainly in Holland, Zeeland, and Friesland, was mostly highly artificial, much of it intensively farmed polder.[53] The task of the landscape artist was to capture the unspoilt niches, in the dunes and river estuaries, or remote parts of the inland provinces, restoring to onlookers natural surroundings which had now largely disappeared, soothing their sense of loss.

Politics was one area which artists were generally not encouraged to depict, at least directly. Yet, here too, the man in the street was aware of developments, being ceaselessly bombarded with anonymous pamphlets, and hearing politics and theology discussed in taverns, and on passenger barges. Moreover, the rich and influential greatly enjoyed subtle political allusions. Thus this aspect of reality pervaded art too, albeit usually in surreptitious ways. We know the political and theological affiliations of only very few artists, among them the Counter-Remonstrant Adriaen van de Venne (1589–1662). Van de Venne produced paintings extolling the stadholderate, and glorifying Maurits and Frederik Hendrik, and several hard-hitting engravings, lambasting Oldenbarnevelt and the Arminians. But

---

[53] De Vries, 'Dutch Rural Economy and the Landscape', 86.

usually, in Dutch Golden Age art, the political message is harder to find, and the modern scholar reduced to conjecture. Even so it is hardly likely to be coincidence that a spate of *Samson and Delilah* paintings, including renderings by Rembrandt and his early rival, Lievens, were painted in 1629–32 during the Truce negotiations between the Republic and Spain when there was much argument about whether the Spanish offer was merely a trick to tempt the Dutch into dropping their guard.[54] The likelihood of a connection is strengthened now that it is known that Rembrandt's *Samson and Delilah* was painted after the Truce talks began, in 1629, and not (as according to the forged signature) in 1628.[55] Often these *Samson and Delilah* pictures were painted for the Stadholder or members of his entourage.

One major event which did bring art and politics into proximity was the conclusion of the Dutch–Spanish peace at Münster and the accompanying celebrations. One of the greatest artists of the Golden Age, Gerard ter Borch (1617–81), attended the Dutch delegation quartered in Münster during the years 1646–8, and served as a kind of informal artistic recorder of the event.[56] He painted portraits of many of the participants, including Adriaen Pauw, and the Spanish plenipotentiary, Peñaranda, as well as his famous picture of the ceremony of ratification in Münster town hall (National Gallery, London). Within the Republic itself, festivities, enhanced by art, were put on in all the main towns—except for Leiden, which refused to participate. At Haarlem, a Corinthian 'peace' temple, designed by Van Campen, was erected in the garden of the Prinsenhof where it stands today. At Amsterdam, celebrations on an unprecedented scale continued for two months. Three open-air stages were set up on the Dam for the performance of historical and political allegories and pageants, one of which, written by the Remonstrant poet and preacher Gerard Brandt, extolled the triumphs of the ancient Batavians in their fight for 'freedom' against the Romans. Vondel's 'peace' play, the *Leeuwendaalders*, was repeatedly performed. Two of the city's militia commanders, Cornelis Witsen and Joan Huydecoper, both major figures in Amsterdam politics, commissioned massively opulent militia pieces, depicting the banquets to celebrate the Münster peace. The picture showing Witsen and his men, painted by Bartholomeus van der Helst (1613–70), one of the most fashionable of the Amsterdam portrait painters of the middle years of the century, is accompanied by a poem, by Jan Vos, explaining that the participants are not only celebrating the Republic's triumph but also peace and reconciliation.

[54] Schwartz, *Rembrandt*, 82–3.
[55] *A Corpus of Rembrandt Paintings*, i. 253–7.
[56] Gudlaugsson, *Geraert ter Borch*, i. 52–63.

24

Intellectual Life, 1572–1650

❖

THE FORMING OF A NEW CULTURE

The Revolt opened a chasm separating north from south, creating two mutually alien and antagonistic cultures where, previously, there had been one. The result was a dichotomy rooted in the religious divide which permeated all aspects of education and cultural life, a separation in the intellectual sphere which paralleled the separateness in economic life and politics reaching back over centuries. After 1585, the civilization of the south Netherlands, both French and Dutch-speaking provinces, was exclusively Catholic, with a confessional grip on education, thought, and book censorship so strong as to render culture largely free of major internal stresses, aside only from the Jansenist controversies (see pp. 649–53 below). Also, this south Netherlands culture rapidly became integrated into the broader framework of Counter-Reformation education, art, thought, and censorship, encompassing much of continental Europe, with especially close cultural links with the German ecclesiastical states and Rome. By contrast, the cultural world of the north evolved into an uneasy blend of Protestant–Catholic confrontation, humanist–confessional antagonism, and Protestant anti-Calvinist dissent, which fragmented thought and education, creating a new kind of European culture fraught with powerful and insoluble internal stresses. The result was a highly dynamic, if initially unstable, culture, in many ways quite unlike that to be found in neighbouring Protestant as well as Catholic lands.

Naturally, the experience of the Revolt and Reformation, and the flood of warring ideological and theological tracts which accompanied these great processes, dramatically heightened the public's awareness of a wide range of intellectual issues, posing questions about the nature of political and ecclesiastical authority, status of Scripture, rights and wrongs of revolt, toleration, and freedom of conscience, and, not least, the problem of how to reverse the collapse of discipline and morality.

This dragging of the fundamentals into the public sphere was not at all to the taste of the most renowned scholar of the Low Countries, and Europe, of the late sixteenth century—Justus Lipsius (1547–1606). Lipsius, convinced that previous philosophy, at least since Roman times, provided little of use in coping with the disruption, and dilemmas, of the Low Countries wars, forged a recipe for moral survival amid religious and political upheaval,[1] a Neostoic system of ethics and politics, which exerted an extraordinary fascination on the generation of Dutch educators, writers, poets, and artists moulded by the Revolt. However, he saw it not as a recipe for the masses but for humanist scholars and the refined, publishing his books, including his key ethical work, the *De Constantia* (1584), solely in Latin. Moreover, he criticized Coornhert for advocating toleration and religious freedom—which Lipsius himself rejected—in Dutch-language publications designed to bring the debate about such fundamental issues into the minds and living-rooms of the common people.[2] When it was suggested to Lipsius that he might summarize his Neostoic philosophy in Dutch, rather than Latin, he haughtily replied that he had no wish for his learning to be discussed by innkeepers and sailors.

But Lipsius' horror of popularization and popular involvement stood in contradiction to the cultural and ideological realities of the 1580s. He believed that true scholarship required detachment from the concerns of society and the common man.[3] To cultivate learning, and his writings, he sought a 'safe tranquillity', refusing to commit himself publicly, and even in private conversation outwardly evading the central issues, religious and political, posed by the Revolt.[4]

Yet his very aversion to the strife, and ideological furore, around him led him to express, in *De Constantia*, an ethics devoid of Scriptural underpinning, neutral between the warring Churches, which answered one of the most basic needs of his time. It was ideal for concealed Catholics living among Calvinists and concealed Protestants under Catholics, and equally for the non-committed. Lipsius had links with the Family of Love and Saravia was quick to note that *De Constantia* could also be construed as a learned cover for Spiritualism, a camouflage for private religion hidden from society.[5] Lipsius rejected Coornhert's quest to enlighten his countrymen on ethical and spiritual questions. Yet his work fed precisely that impulse in the emerging new culture around him.

---

[1] Lipsius, *De Constantia*, 3–4.
[2] Güldner, *Toleranz-Problem*, 107.
[3] Van Dorsten, *Poets, Patrons and Professors*, 37.
[4] Mout, 'In het schip: Justus Lipsius', 55–62.
[5] Hamilton, *Family of Love*, 96–8.

Lipsius' Neostoicism could not be confined to his ivory tower of Latin. Hardly had *De Constantia* been published than two different Dutch versions appeared, one translated by a son-in-law of the famous publisher Christopher Plantin, prefaced by an ode on Stoic resolve by Jan van Hout, Pensionary of Leiden, an influential figure in civic politics and a leader of the new literary and intellectual culture in Dutch. Van Hout, poet, bibliophile, and champion of the Dutch language, idolized Lipsius but also William the Silent, and the Revolt, and aspired to mobilize the people behind the Revolt. He organized the festivities to mark Leicester's entry into Leiden, in 1586, an occasion culminating in a lecture on Tacitus by Lipsius.[6] The handsomely bound copy of *De Constantia* presented to Leicester on that occasion was a mark of the great significance of Lipsius not only for the infant university but for the Republic. Yet all the while Lipsius himself privately brooded, soon as disappointed in Leicester as he had been in Anjou, fearful lest his reputation be irredeemably damaged should he remain in the north and the war be won by Spain, as seemed quite likely at that juncture. Lipsius evidently pondered departure, and reversion to the Catholic Church, for years before he actually left in 1591.[7]

De Constantia heralded a wider quest for a way out of the moral maze created by the Revolt and collapse of the old faith. Coornhert propagated his ethical system for the individual, and the people, through his *Zedekunst* (1587), a treatise aimed at the general population, as well as more sporadically in his moralizing plays, which glorified what he called 'Christian philosophy' without either identifying with, or apparently criticizing, any specific branch of Christianity.[8] Stevin set out his moral recipe for the people, stressing the overriding need for order and discipline, in his *Het Burgherlick Leven* (1590). Another prophetic disciplinarian, galvanized by the threat of a general breakdown, was Hendrik Laurensz Spiegel (1549–1610), an Amsterdam patrician and merchant-poet who admired Lipsius, was a friend of Coornhert, and refused to acknowledge the legitimacy of the 1578 'alteration' in Amsterdam, remaining a Catholic all his life. Spiegel expressed his austere, non-biblical moral philosophy, with its stress on the rigorous schooling of the young as the foundation of a godly society,[9] in a vast moral heroic poem, the *Hertspiegel*, written in alexandrine verse around 1600, though not published until 1614. Like his friends Van Hout and Coornhert, Spiegel was much concerned with elevating, and refining, the

---

[6] Van Dorsten and Strong, *Leicester's Triumph*, 63.
[7] Kluyskens, 'Justus Lipsius' levenskeuze', 22; Mout, 'In het schip: Justus Lipsius', 61.
[8] Van der Meulen, *Comedies van Coornhert*, 70, 78, 110–11.
[9] Buisman, *Ethische denkbeelden*, 25–43.

Dutch language so that it should be a worthy instrument for serious literature. Through his many contacts with leading writers, artists, and scholars, he exerted a pervasive influence, among others on the young Hooft and Carel van Mander, the Flemish refugee artist of Haarlem who, in his book on art, published in 1604, urged his fellow artists to base their creative work on disciplined lives, eschewing the sensuality, disorderly life-style, and loose women traditionally associated with artists.[10]

The architects of the new north Netherlands civilization aspired to align literature and education in Dutch with the lofty standards of the neo-Latin writings of the humanists. Men like Van Hout, Coornhert, Stevin, and Spiegel, precisely because of the hopeless disparity of their religious convictions, resorted with deep seriousness to the people, to restore stability and discipline to society and make the best of the status quo in which there was, and for the moment could be, no firm confessional basis. They sought to mobilize the people and equip them morally, politically, and in every other way to succeed permanently in the great task of breaking free of Spanish tyranny. Stevin, who stood high in the regard of Prince Maurits, and was the Republic's leading scientist, mathematician, and engineer, also deemed it useful to propagate applied science among the people, publishing several of his scientific works in Dutch.[11] In his *De Thiende* (1585), for example, he stressed the usefulness of decimals, especially for achieving improved precision in land surveying, hydraulic management, and the laying out of fortifications.[12]

Yet, at the same time, these architects of culture, not least Stevin, desired the people to be not just disciplined but deferential to patrician authority, uninvolved in politics, and submissive in the face of the bewildering state of church affairs. This remarkable mix of values at the root of the new Dutch culture, blending Erasmian tolerance, freedom of conscience, outward submission, and an uncompromising stress on the high moral purpose of education and literature, culminated in the life and work of the patrician-author Pieter Cornelisz. Hooft (1581–1647), son of the Amsterdam burgomaster Cornelis Pietersz. Hooft. Hooft was another Neostoic, *politique*, and austere moralizer who aspired to elevate the people while simultaneously transcending the conflict of confessional theologies.[13] He was also the most gifted Dutch writer before Vondel and wrote some of the loftiest Dutch poetry and prose of the Golden Age. His aim was not just to refine literary

[10] Van Mander, *Het Schilder-Boeck*, 3–7.
[11] Dijksterhuis, *Simon Stevin*, 192–5, 211–14.
[12] Florin, 'Simon Stevin', 94–5.
[13] Cornelissen, *Eendracht van het land*, 77–9.

Dutch to a level comparable with the best literary French and Italian—at that time the only two modern languages which enjoyed international prestige as intellectual and literary vehicles—but to instil reverence for stability and order and ease theological passions and political tensions by advancing the austere ideals of Roman republican literature and philosophy.

Hooft was a moderate Orangist who believed that an 'eminent head', above the divisions in society, was indispensable to the orderliness he craved. He saw danger in the direction chosen by Oldenbarnevelt and his allies but, later, was also deeply disappointed by Maurits's failure to remain above the confessional conflict.

He first achieved mastery of the allegorical drama of ideas in his *Geeraerdt van Velsen* (1613), a play about tyranny but also the dangers of rebellion against tyrants, in the age of Count Floris V of Holland, which remained popular with Amsterdam theatre-goers throughout the seventeenth century. Even more topical was his play *Baeto* (1617) which proclaimed—as the struggle between the Remonstrants and Counter-Remonstrants neared its climax—that civil strife is the worst of evils, idealizing the individual with a sense of responsibility towards society, and the state, so strong he will even sacrifice his own interests for the greater good. A true Neostoic, Hooft always remained above the conflict but did decide, following Maurits's *coup d'état*, that he could no longer admonish directly and that the theatre no longer served his literary-philosophical purpose.[14] After 1618, he switched to writing his grand histories, that of the supreme *politique*, Henri IV of France, and that of the Dutch Revolt. Hooft, the patrician-writer, in a sense combined the legacies of Lipsius and Coornhert, reflecting a social and political ambivalence which lay at the heart of the Dutch Golden Age.

UNIVERSITIES AND CIVIC HIGH SCHOOLS

The conscious quest for a new and separate culture in the north Netherlands also led, in February 1575, to the founding of the first university north of the rivers, at Leiden. Holland's seat of learning, founded on the eve of the Breda negotiations, was expressly intended to bolster the political and religious separatism of Holland and Zeeland.[15] The new foundation was needed, on the one hand, to educate the regents and nobility, and train the office-holders and professionals who would staff the rebel state and, on the other, supply preachers for the public Church, which, as far as possible,

---

[14] Groenveld, *Hooft als historieschrijver*, 23–5, 45.
[15] Woltjer, *De Leidse universiteit*, 2.

preferred to recruit its preachers from amongst university graduates.[16] But whilst the needs of the new Church were a contributory factor, they were definitely not, as the States of Holland's resolutions show, the foremost motive. It was, from the outset, intended that the new academy should not only provide theology and law but also seek to attract the best scholars, and excel in humanist studies, mathematics, medicine, and history.[17] Inevitably, the Church wanted the new university placed under its supervision and specifically under the South Holland synod. But Orange and the States expressly rejected any such formal link, rendering the new university freer from ecclesiastical sway than any other in Europe.

The university's constitution vested control in seven curators, of whom three were nominees of the States and four of the Leiden burgomasters. This ensured (down to 1618) avoidance of a narrowly confessional approach and prevalence of what strict Calvinists called a 'libertine' attitude.[18] Indeed, Calvinist orthodoxy by no means dominated in the early years, especially not among the curators and professors. Neither Lipsius nor Bonaventura Vulcanius, another pillar of Leiden in the 1580s, were Calvinists at heart, while Thomas Sosius, appointed professor of Roman Law in 1584, was apparently a Catholic. Plantin noted, in 1585, that Catholic students were not subjected to any pressure at Leiden, while the leader of the Catholic revival in Holland, Sasbout Vosmeer, deplored the readiness of Catholics to study there.[19]

Yet, for some years, this liberal spirit debilitated the university, and especially its theology faculty. It is scarcely surprising that, initially, the new academy proved less flourishing than William the Silent and Dousa had hoped, given that the very survival of the rebel state remained doubtful before 1590. But Leiden's less than solid reputation amongst strict Calvinists—who mostly preferred Heidelberg or Geneva—exacerbated matters. Remarkably, student numbers at Leiden actually fell in the 1580s during the great influx of Protestant refugees from the south. Wilhelmus Baudartius, future Counter-Remonstrant theologian and translator, was one of the few immigrants who did study at Leiden.[20] But he stayed only briefly before moving on to the Republic's second university, inaugurated in 1585, at Franeker. A committee of curators, professors, and burgomasters was constituted at Leiden, in May 1586, to ponder the reasons for the univer-

[16] Groenhuis, *De predikanten*, 165–6.
[17] Res. Holl. 1575, 348–54.
[18] Lunsingh Scheurleer and Posthumus Meyjes, *Leiden University*, 2–4.
[19] Geurts, *Eerste grote conflict*, 26.
[20] Broek Roelofs, *Wilhelmus Baudartius*, 22–3.

sity's poor showing and how to reverse its decline.[21] Adrianus Saravia (*c.*1532–1613), the rigid Calvinist appointed professor of theology in 1584, and now *rector magnificus*, attributed the failure to recent Spanish military successes, rendering the country insecure, and to the new university of Franeker, diverting students from Leiden. The burgomasters, however, blamed the deficiencies of the professors, and especially the absenteeism of Saravia himself, who was often away conferring with Leicester, at Utrecht, instead of teaching.[22] Lipsius, asked to propose reforms—an indication in itself that scant attention was paid to orthodox views—recommended expanding the range of studies, introducing more classical learning and philosophy.[23]

The fragility of the universities in the north persisted until the early 1590s, culminating in Lipsius' departure from Leiden. Prospective theology students stayed away and there were few others. Saravia proved an unmitigated disaster, his career ending with his botched attempt, in 1587, to foment a pro-Leicester coup to seize the city. In the first twelve years (1575–87) only 131 students enrolled to study theology at Leiden. Franeker also languished. Founded by the Frisian States, and Stadholder, Franeker attracted only thirty-six students in its first year and still fewer through the late 1580s. It survived and, indeed, seemed likely to fulfil the States' main purpose, training young Frisians for careers in the province. But in its early years, Franeker drew practically only Frisians and Ommelanders.[24]

Matters improved dramatically, as with so much else, with the transformation of the military and economic situation, in the early 1590s. Suddenly, the Republic was secure and money available for new professors, books, and facilities. Student numbers rose sharply. In 1591, the States of Holland established a 'States College' at Leiden to accommodate thirty theology students studying with grants from the States of Holland and Zeeland.[25] Academic printing and bookselling at Leiden suddenly flourished and during the 1590s the Leiden University Library became one of the most considerable in Protestant Europe. Although the university had decided in 1587 to establish a *hortus academicus*, or botanical garden, in imitation of the university of Pisa (which had founded the first botanical garden in Europe, in 1543), and those of Padua, Bologna, Florence, and Leipzig which had done so since, it was not until 1594 that the gardens were laid out, rare

[21] Molhuysen, *Bronnen*, i. 45.
[22] Nijenhuis, *Adrianus Saravia*, 69.
[23] Dibon, *Enseignement philosophique*, 18.
[24] Fockema Andreae, *Album Studiosorum*, 13–18.
[25] Geurts, *Voorgeschiedenis*, 35.

varieties acquired, and planting began. Carolus Clusius (1526–1609), a native of Arras who had become the most famous expert on plants in Europe, working at Vienna and Frankfurt in the 1570s and 1580s, agreed to become director of the *hortus* and arrived in Leiden in 1593. Clusius' *Rariorum Plantarum Historia* (1601) was one of the first major scientific works to be published in the north Netherlands. Franeker too grew in reputation, increasing student numbers every year between 1590 and the middle of the seventeenth century.

The student population of Leiden expanded from about 100, in 1590, to over 500 by the 1640s. But while Leiden always boasted many more students than Franeker in absolute terms, the two universities expanded at the same rate, and phasing, down to the 1660s.[26] Franeker's student body remained at about one-quarter of that of Leiden. By 1609, Leiden was one of the biggest universities in Europe and, by the 1640s, the largest in the Protestant world. During the quarter-century 1626–50, 11,000 students enrolled at Leiden, compared with 8,400 at Cambridge, the largest university in Britain, and 6,700 at Leipzig, the largest in Germany.[27]

More striking, though, than the size of the student body was its international composition. Whereas Oxford and Cambridge were almost entirely British universities—and Leipzig and Heidelberg, German—Leiden, Franeker, and (later) Utrecht were international Protestant universities of a kind which only really existed in early modern times, for any length of time, in the north Netherlands. During the peak quarter-century at Leiden (1626–50), over half the total student body derived from outside the Republic, most from the German lands (3,016), Britain (672), and Scandinavia (621),[28] though, during the Thirty Years War, Leiden also drew appreciable numbers from France (434), Poland (354), and Hungary (231). By contrast, scarcely any arrived from Italy (19), Spain (3), or Portugal (3). Franeker too, from around 1620, became an international university. Descartes, who studied there briefly in 1629, was, in this respect, one of a crowd. Where in the years 1590–1624, over 75 per cent of Franeker's student population were Dutch (two-thirds from Friesland and Groningen), in the period 1625–50, nearly half Franeker's students were foreigners, mainly Germans.[29] Many of these German and other foreign students in the Dutch universities subsequently were prominent in their own, or other, lands. Andreas Gryphius, one of the principal German writers of the baroque era, spent six years at Leiden (1638–44) and wrote much of his poetry there.

[26] Bots and Frijhoff, 'Studentenpopulatie', 57.
[27] Wansink, *Politieke wetenschappen*, 9, 26.
[28] Ibid.
[29] Bots and Frijhoff, 'Studentenpopulatie', 61.

The third Dutch university, Groningen, was founded by the States of that province, in August 1614, partly to divert some of the flow away from Franeker, and partly to prevent Groningen youth being infected by the Arminianism rife at Leiden. Although Groningen never matched the international prestige of Franeker, it attracted nearly as many students, including many from adjoining parts of Germany. The founding father of the university was the theologian-historian Ubbo Emmius (1547–1625), son of an East Frisian Lutheran pastor converted to Calvinism at Geneva, by Beza. By the 1580s he was the leader of the Calvinists in East Friesland as well as a renowned anti-Mennonite controversialist and eminent scholar. After the capture of Groningen, in 1594, the new Reformed *raad* invited Emmius to reform the city's prestigious Latin school. He remained influential throughout the region, helping mould spiritual life and writing extensively about the history of Groningen, Friesland, and East Friesland. The Groningen *raad* promoted his reputation as a method of enhancing the city's stature, organizing an impressive public funeral, on his death, and placing portraits of him in civic buildings.

The fourth Dutch university in chronological order but, from the outset, second in status, was Utrecht. Proposals for a provincial university for Utrecht had been under discussion since 1602 but with a majority of the States preferring to locate it at Amersfoort rather than in the province's chief city. The project was long shelved, partly owing to the reluctance of the *ridderschap*, and lesser towns, to see that city's preponderance over the province enhanced further and partly owing to the inhibiting proximity of Leiden. When later, in 1632, the city announced plans for a so-called Illustre School, or high school, as a first step towards forming a university, asking the States to help financially, some of the latter still considered Amersfoort the preferable site.[30] Consequently, the city proceeded on its own, setting up the high school in 1634 and asking the States to endorse its conversion into a full university two years later. As a result, Utrecht was the one Dutch university which possessed an essentially civic rather than provincial character. The celebrated preacher Gisbertus Voetius, who was appointed to the chair of theology, remained over many years the presiding figure among its professors.

The rapid growth of the universities also created demand for civic colleges, the new 'Illustrious Schools', to prepare boys who had been through the Latin schools for university, especially by polishing their Latin. The setting up of these institutions was typically a phenomenon of the 1630s

---

[30] Kernkamp, *Utrechtsche Academie*, i. 47–8.

and 1640s. Among the most noted were the Deventer Illustre School (Overijssel, Zeeland, and Drenthe were the provinces which never acquired universities), which won renown especially during the rectorship (1642–58) of Johannes Fredericus Gronovius, a German humanist and follower of Vossius, who became a leading classical philologist in the Republic. Remarkably, of 450 boys who enrolled at Deventer, in Gronovius' time, over 20 per cent were foreign, including fifty-eight Germans, four Danes, and no fewer than twenty-seven Hungarians.[31] Another noted Illustrious School was that of Dordrecht, founded in 1635, with the scientist Isaac Beeckman (1588–1637) as its first rector. But the most renowned—as well as controversial—was the Illustrious School or Athenaeum, set up in Amsterdam in 1630–1. Again the purpose was to prepare the city's youth for university. But the Arminian *vroedschap*, aware that several celebrated scholars were available, having been fully, or partially, purged from Leiden for Remonstrantism, recruited them, in this way deflecting lustre from Leiden to Amsterdam, a strategy which Leiden, through the Hof of Holland, tried unsuccessfully to block. Vossius was appointed rector, in 1631, at the (previously unheard-of) salary of f2,500—the university of Utrecht in its first year paying its rector f1,300, and Voetius f1,200.[32] The Athenaeum also conferred a professorship on the scarcely less embattled humanist Caspar Barlaeus (1584–1648).

Universities—of which there were five with the founding of Harderwijk, in 1648—existed only in the provinces and not in Generality Lands. But Illustrious Schools arose also in the Generality Lands partly as civic institutions but jointly sponsored by the Generality, through the *Raad van State*.[33] Here they were a curious phenomenon. Intended to prepare future Reformed preachers, and administrators, for university, they were subsidized by the Generality, headed by noted Calvinist scholars, and assigned ample resources and prestigious premises; but they generally lacked students. Few young men from north of the rivers, or abroad, desired to study in the Generality Lands, whilst the local populace, predominantly Catholic, shunned them as bulwarks of Protestantism. The 's-Hertogenbosch Illustre School founded in 1636 by the town's new Reformed *vroedschap*, had as its first rector the noted Huguenot professor Samuel Maresius (1599–1673), formerly of Sédan, and later theological doyen of Groningen. The rival institution at Breda was inaugurated in 1646, largely on the initiative of the Stadholder, who aspired to turn his baronial town into the intellectual centre of north Brabant.[34]

---

[31] Van Slee, *Illustre School te Deventer*, 40.
[32] Kernkamp, *Utrechtsche Academie*, i. 57.
[33] Sassen, *Wijsgerig onderwijs aan de Illustre School te 's-Hertogenbosch*, 7–8.
[34] Sassen, *Wijsgerig onderwijs aan de Illustre School te Breda*, 1.

While most students attending the universities read theology, law, or the third great vocational discipline of early modern times—medicine—the greatest academic prestige stemmed from excellence in humanist studies— classical philology, biblical research, and philosophy. Renown in these spheres vastly enhanced the regional and international status of universities and civic colleges, attracting students from distant lands, especially where, as in Scandinavia and Lutheran Germany, little attraction was exerted by the Dutch theology faculties.

DUTCH LATE HUMANISM

In the 1580s Lipsius was the intellectual glory of Leiden and all Holland. Franeker's answer to Lipsius was Johannes Drusius (1550–1616), like Clusius, Barlaeus, Stevin, and other prominent intellectual figures of the Republic in the early seventeenth century, a refugee from the south. This celebrated philologist originally occupied a chair at Leiden, but was lured to Franeker, in 1584, despite William the Silent's effort to forestall this by urging the Leiden curators to increase his salary.[35] Drusius' expertise in Greek, Hebrew, and other Near Eastern languages, especially Syriac, eventually made Franeker famous throughout Europe, attracting students from as far afield as Scotland and Switzerland. Like Lipsius, Drusius avoided theological and confessional issues, sticking to classical studies and philological research.

Worried by Drusius' defection, and Franeker's progress, the Leiden curators appreciably increased their professors' salaries. This failed, however, to prevent Lipsius' departure in 1591. To replace Lipsius, the curators spared no effort to find a scholar of comparable worth, mobilizing the States of Holland to assist with the task. States and curators cast their eye on the renowned French humanist Joseph Justus Scaliger (1540–1609) and sought the aid of the French king in approaching him. Scaliger describes how he was 'besieged' for two years before agreeing to come at the unprecedented salary of 1,200 guilders—Lipsius was earning f1,000 yearly when he left— provided he would not be asked to lecture.[36] An irritable man who loathed most professors and liked marking venomous comments in the margins of his copies of colleagues' books, Scaliger found much to complain of in Holland, not least the cold, food, heavy drinking, and exorbitant rents.[37] But for the States, university, and city it was abundantly worth the high cost

[35] Molhuysen, *Bronnen*, i. 39.
[36] Scaliger, *Autobiography*, 37.
[37] Ibid.; Grafton, *Joseph Scaliger*, ii. 374–5.

of accommodating Scaliger and his library in one of the best houses on the stately canal, facing the university. For his reputation bestowed lustre on all three.

Scaliger did not lecture. But teaching small groups of specially selected students he established new standards of philological research in classical and Near Eastern texts, surpassing anything then found elsewhere in Europe.[38] His insistence on a wide knowledge of ancient languages, and scripts, as the basis of high scholarship, became as celebrated as his favourite method of disposing of a scorned colleague: 'il n'a pas bien entendu les langues.' Scaliger, reputedly the greatest expert on the New Testament of his age, produced masterly editions of classical authors, including Catullus, Tibullus, and Propertius, and, besides legendary expertise in Latin and Greek, imparted major impetus to the study of Hebrew, Syriac, Arabic, and other languages and literatures he deemed relevant to biblical study, including Coptic and Ethiopic. Of his works written at Leiden, his masterpiece was the *Thesaurus Temporum* (1614), establishing a general chronological framework for ancient history, a work which grew out of his efforts to establish a critical text of Eusebius.

Scaliger's principal legacy was his influence on his circle of gifted students. Through them, he exerted a lasting impact, in the Republic and beyond, in classical and biblical scholarship and study of Near Eastern languages. Pre-eminent among his students were Grotius, who arrived at Leiden in 1594, at the age of 11, an acknowledged child prodigy; Petrus Scriverius (1580–1655); and Daniel Heinsius (1580–1655), who arrived in 1598 and became Scaliger's foremost protégé. In 1605, at the age of 25, Heinsius was appointed Leiden's professor of Greek. Emulating Scaliger, he produced improved scholarly editions of numerous classical authors, including Horace and parts of Aristotle, but though he too became famous throughout Europe, he introduced no major innovation and lacked the depth of his mentor.[39]

In Near Eastern studies, Scaliger's leading student was Thomas Erpenius (1584–1624), who was appointed professor of oriental languages in 1613. His *Grammatica Arabica* (1613) remained central to Arabic studies in Europe for two centuries and was republished, in German, as late as 1771. He also prepared an Arabic New Testament published in 1616. Erpenius attracted many students and consolidated Leiden's position as the pre-eminent centre for Near Eastern studies in Europe. After his death in the plague epidemic of 1624, his star student, Jacobus Golius (1596–1667), continued

---

[38] Rademaker, 'Scriverius and Grotius', 47.   [39] Sellin, *Daniel Heinsius*, 14, 36.

the tradition.[40] On trips to North Africa, Syria, and Constantinople, in the years 1622–5, Golius amassed some 300 medieval Arabic, Persian, and Turkish manuscripts, forming the core of Leiden's celebrated collection of Near Eastern texts. Golius, who also did much to stimulate practical astronomy at Leiden, promoted interest in the history of science, exploring medieval Arabic texts which transmitted Greek scientific knowledge. In this way, he helped generate the close interaction between science and the humanities characteristic of seventeenth-century Dutch culture. But his crowning achievement was his *Lexicon Arabicum* (1654), which remained in use amongst western orientalists down to the nineteenth century. His chief follower was Levinus Warner, a Westphalian, from Lippe, who eventually became Dutch resident in Constantinople and collected numerous additional Near Eastern manuscripts for Leiden.

The close involvement of universities and Latin schools in civic and provincial life placed them at the centre of the Arminian–Gomarist storm. Virtually all the principal humanists and biblical scholars, in the tradition of Erasmus and Lipsius, disliked the rising dogmatism and Calvinist zealotry around them. Even Heinsius, who later assailed the Remonstrants, particularly Episcopius, and served as Latin secretary of the Synod of Dordrecht, was not a professed Gomarist before 1618 and was subsequently lambasted by Grotius, Vossius, and Barlaeus, not as a Calvinist zealot but betrayer of friends and shabby opportunist,[41] whom they denounced as a hypocrite, drunkard, and 'chaser after whores'. Their common teacher and guide in the world of scholarship, Scaliger, long an admirer of Erasmus, had, in his last years, made clear his own admiration also for Arminius and contempt for Gomarus.[42]

After Oldenbarnevelt's downfall, the new States of Holland changed the Leiden curators, in February 1619, and established a commission to eradicate Remonstrantism from the faculties, in July. A number of leading professors were marked men. Petrus Bertius, the Remonstrant regent of the States College, until 1615, was immediately dismissed from his chair, Barlaeus was sacked as deputy head of the States College, in July, and from his professorship, in August. Episcopius, having fled the Republic, was deemed to have dismissed himself. Vossius was sacked as regent of the States College but retained his chair, albeit with his writings under investigation by the South Holland Synod. The new curators, writing to the States of Utrecht, in August 1619, claimed to have purged their university of its

[40] Brugman, 'Arabic Scholarship', 213.
[41] Sellin, *Daniel Heinsius*, 79, 188.
[42] Grafton, *Joseph Scaliger*, ii. 376, 393.

'previous disorder', requesting that province to resume sending its students to study in Leiden.[43]

The Latin schools of Holland and Utrecht were similarly purged. At the renowned Hieronymus school at Utrecht, attended by some 300 pupils, rector and staff were dismissed, the new teachers including the young scientist and zealous Counter-Remonstrant, Isaac Beeckman, installed as deputy head in November 1619.[44] Similar purges took place at Haarlem, Leiden, Gouda, and Rotterdam. Following the dismissals at Rotterdam, Beeckman's brother, also a strict Calvinist, was appointed rector of the Latin school there.

Nor did the purges of 1618–20 end the feuding amongst the Republic's intellectual élites. Recrimination and acrimony continued to pervade Dutch cultural life down to the 1630s and beyond. With the advent of the stadholderate of Frederik Hendrik, in 1625, however, there was more scope for accommodation, and reconciliation. After all, Counter-Remonstrants could admire aspects of humanist enquiry, provided it avoided sensitive theological issues. Constantijn Huygens, a pillar of the Counter-Remonstrant faction at the Stadholder's court, and leading figure in literary circles, was among those most eager to bind the wounds and create an integrated, revitalized Dutch culture, known for learning and erudition. Shortly after Maurits's death, he helped Barlaeus, whose neo-Latin poetry he admired, and who was living in straitened circumstances giving private tuition in Leiden, by securing commissions to write Latin court poems, one of the first of which was the *Britannia Triumphans* (1625), celebrating the marriage of Charles I of England.

Huygens, Hooft, Barlaeus, Vossius, and others laboured to end the state of scholarly and cultural stasis and transcend the theological divide. A cultural phenomenon of considerable importance in this connection was the literary and intellectual group known as the 'Muiden Circle' which gathered around the *politique* poet, playwright, and historian Hooft. As *drost* of Muiden castle, near Amsterdam, he was well placed to host regular gatherings of writers and scholars, besides being the arch-*politique* who alone had remained neutral above the theological tirades and retained the friendship of both sides. For many years Hooft presided over a unique coterie, including Huygens, Barlaeus, and Vossius, and sought to guide Dutch literary and intellectual culture out of the aridity of past polemics into new worlds of intellectual, metaphysical, and poetic enquiry.[45] They

[43] Kernkamp, *Utrechtsche Academie*, i. 43.
[44] Van Berkel, *Isaac Beeckman*, 50.
[45] Cornelissen, *Eendracht*, 92–6.

avoided much and deliberately cultivated an air of refined frivolity but also replaced controversy with the ideal of secluded debate and pursuing truth through literature. Huygens, who admired the metaphysical verse of John Donne, aspired to bring similar depth to Dutch poetry. Hooft, by contrast, abandoned verse during the years of the Muiden Circle, concentrating in the 1630s and 1640s on inner wrestling with the political and ethical issues which had for so long preoccupied him and writing his history of the Dutch Revolt, which marks the zenith of Dutch Golden Age prose.[46]

Intellectually and culturally, the Arminian–Gomarist controversies resulted in a deadlock which, from the 1630s onwards, poetry, history-writing, theology, and humanist scholarship all strove to surmount in linked, similar ways. Vossius, with immense circumspection, quietly pushed on with his research. Generally within Dutch humanist enquiry, the emphasis shifted, from the late 1620s, towards searching for a more detailed grasp of the specific historical, linguistic, and religious context of Scripture and early Christianity, avoiding former battlegrounds.

This new sensitivity, a reversion to the discretion of Lipsius, Drusius, and Scaliger, showed on both sides of the theological divide. In 1627, the Huguenot professor Louis de Dieu, one of the orthodox replacements appointed at Leiden, in 1619, published his Syriac edition, and Latin translation, of Revelation, based on a manuscript discovered by Heinsius among Scaliger's papers, without making any polemical remark. Next, in three volumes (1631, 1634, and 1646), De Dieu published his *Animadversiones*, on the New Testament, again side-stepping all potentially divisive theological issues, elucidating obscurities exclusively by Scaliger's method of comparing ancient versions with related texts in Hebrew, Syriac, Arabic, Ethiopic, and Greek. Similarly, Heinsius' chief contribution after 1618 was his *Exercitationes* (1639) on the New Testament, which again eschewed doctrinal issues, arguing exclusively in philological and historical terms, while veiling his implied criticism of the official Dutch translation of the Gospel in the States Bible.[47]

Admittedly, Heinsius' circumspection did not prevent his work being fiercely attacked by Vossius, Grotius, and his new Leiden colleague, the Huguenot professor Claude Salmasius. But this fresh acrimony stemmed from personal rather than ideological animus, though there were also some philological issues at stake.[48] In what became a legendary academic feud Salmasius held that the New Testament was written in the standard common

---

[46] Groenveld, *Hooft als historieschrijver*, 32–8.
[47] De Jonge, 'Study', 94–7.
[48] Ibid.

Greek of the Hellenistic era, disparaging Heinsius' view that it was a Judaic Greek permeated with Hebrew and other Near Eastern constructions.[49] Vossius, who accused Heinsius of appropriating Scaliger's unpublished notes without acknowledging the fact, sided vigorously with Salmasius.

Meanwhile, Grotius refined his own biblical exegesis, his principal work in this field, his *Annotationes* on the Old and New Testaments, being (again) a product especially of the 1630s. Grotius' notes on the New Testament (1641) undoubtedly surpassed both De Dieu and Heinsius in depth, erudition, and originality. But here too one discerns the same determination to elucidate the difficulties and obscurities of Scripture, using philological methods and avoiding dogmatic issues, treating the text almost as one would a work of classical antiquity.

By creating a new biblical exegesis based on philological expertise, and confessionally neutral, the generation of Dutch humanists active after 1625 generated at least the possibility of building bridges, and genuine dialogue, between different confessional blocs. Yet, it has to be admitted that, despite this, no true inter-confessional dialogue proved possible in the Dutch Golden Age. The methodology was there but, by and large, it proved impossible for Calvinists, Remonstrants, Catholics, and Jews to break out of dogmatic confessional modes of thinking.

Such bridge-building as there was only proves how limited were the possibilities. A case in point is that of the Amsterdam rabbi Menasseh ben Israel (1604–57), a friend of Vossius after the latter's move to Amsterdam, in 1631, respected by Grotius and Barlaeus, on the Arminian side, and Salmasius and Constantijn L'Empereur (1591–1648), professor of Hebrew at Leiden from 1627, on the orthodox. Menasseh's book the *Conciliador* (1632), reconciling apparent contradictions in the Hebrew text of the Bible, was published in Spanish, with the approval of the Sephardic community, and was applauded by Vossius and Barlaeus, who urged him to publish a Latin version, a step normally not open to, or sought by, Jewish scholars. Menasseh had a Latin version prepared and asked the States of Holland for permission to dedicate the work to them. The States thereupon sent the Latin text to the Leiden theology faculty, which replied that the book was full of 'Jewish fables'. The States refused Menasseh's request, but without banning his book. Menasseh's decision to publish, albeit altering the place of publication from 'Amsterdam' to 'Frankfurt', annoyed both the Calvinists and the elders of the Sephardic community, whose policy it was that there be no Jewish publications of a sort liable to irritate the public Church.

[49] Ibid. 96–9.

Vossius noted that Menasseh was exceptional among Jews in being willing to debate with Christian scholars but also that, for that very reason, he was 'not much respected by those of his own faith'.[50] This was true. But it was equally true that Vossius, and still more orthodox Calvinists like L'Empereur, proved incapable of genuine dialogue with Judaism and rabbinic learning. Vossius' attitude was pervaded by a desire to convert the Jews to Christianity. L'Empereur may have been a professor of Hebrew but ignored contemporary intellectual developments among Dutch Jewry and was unable to step beyond a traditional, dogmatic anti-Judaism.[51]

Yet there was much in Dutch late humanism which was impressive. Not only did it greatly refine the tools of scholarly research, it created a new type of European intellectual environment. If it failed to generate authentic dialogue between confessions, and could not do so in the context of the time, it undeniably encouraged a milder spiritual climate in which everyday coexistence of rival theological and philosophical systems was not just conceivable but an established fact, a reality to which everyone had to adjust and within which a wide variety of religious traditions and cultural systems could separately flourish.

THE RISE OF THE MECHANISTIC WORLD VIEW

The late humanist outlook of Lipsius and Scaliger, with its retreat from dogma, emphasis on research, and resort to Neostoic and other non-Christian systems of ethics and politics, was fundamentally a symptom of the 'sceptical crisis' which pervaded western Europe from the end of the sixteenth century.[52] This, arguably the most decisive shift in European thought in early modern times, is best understood as stemming from the general deadlock of Protestantism and Catholicism which settled over France, Germany, the Low Countries, Britain, Switzerland, and east-central Europe by the third quarter of the century.[53] While Lipsius and Scaliger may be regarded as the classic representatives of this post-1570 crisis of the early modern mind, Coornhert, Stevin, Hooft, Vossius, and Grotius (with his vision of a non-dogmatic Erasmian Reformation) were all, in their different ways, also spokesmen of the 'sceptical crisis'. Almost everyone at the forefront of Dutch intellectual life, by the 1630s and 1640s, was trying to cope with the effects of the deadlock between Protestantism and Catholicism,

---

[50] Rademaker, *Life and Work of Gerardus Joannes Vossius*, 264.
[51] Van Rooden, *Constantijn L'Empereur*, 181–3.
[52] Popkin, *History of Scepticism*, 66–150; Tuck, *Philosophy and Government*, 30–65.
[53] Israel, *European Jewry*, 35–40, 53–6.

Calvinism and Lutheranism, and Arminianism and Gomarism. The general tendency, among the intellectual élite, was an intensified resort to the methods, and attitudes, of Lipsius and Scaliger. This meant that established authority was weak and that, by the 1630s and 1640s, the Dutch intellectual milieu was potentially receptive to a general overturning, and replacing, of existing theological, philosophical, and scientific systems of thought.

Science and mathematics had, of course, from the outset had their acknowledged place in the new Dutch high culture forged by the Revolt. These subjects had, since the founding of Leiden university, in 1575, figured prominently in Dutch academic life and, through Stevin, also more widely in Dutch high culture. The leading figure at the beginning of the century was the mathematician Rudolf Snellius (1546–1613), a native of Oudewater (like Arminius) trained in Germany, who had imbibed a strong Ramist influence. Snellius lectured uninterruptedly at Leiden, from 1580, teaching mathematics and his version of Ramism. Petrus Ramus (1515–72), a Huguenot logician slaughtered in the St Bartholomew's Day massacre in Paris, had devised a post-Aristotelian system of logic and knowledge which, despite its crudity, enjoyed vast popularity in late sixteenth-century Europe, and at the outset of the seventeenth, providing as it did a method of systematizing all branches of knowledge, emphasizing the relevance of theory to practical applications, a feature of particular interest to Snellius. The latter's son, Willibrord Snellius (1580–1626), also a leading mathematician and admirer of Ramus, continued the tradition established by his father, and Stevin, applying mathematics to a range of scientific problems. Having trained under the great Danish astronomer Tycho Brahe, some of his work was in the field of mathematical astronomy. He is chiefly remembered, however, for his path-breaking experiments on refraction of light, culminating in his formulation of the law of refraction which bears his name. Most of Snellius' work remained unpublished. According to Vossius and Huygens, Descartes subsequently made use of Snellius' discoveries in optics without fully acknowledging the fact.

Until the mid-1630s Dutch science and scientific ideas evolved quietly, without provoking any major furore, along the several fronts mapped out by Stevin and the two professors Snellius. Copernicus' view of the planetary system found an early and relatively favourable reception in the Dutch Republic but awareness of his ideas remained restricted to a tiny circle.[54] Ubbo Emmius attacked Stevin for adopting a Copernican standpoint but

---

[54] Vermij, 'Het copernicanisme', 357–62.

there was no public controversy. This was merely an early rumble of what was to follow. The situation began to change only after the papal condemnation of Galileo, in 1633, which sharpened debate, and increased awareness of the issues, especially following the introduction of lectures teaching the heliocentric conception at the Amsterdam Athenaeum. On several occasions in 1636, the Amsterdam Reformed consistory expressed alarm at the sudden upsurge of interest in the doctrines of Copernicus and Galileo and condemned the teaching of the heliocentric doctrine at Amsterdam.

This marked the commencement not only of the rapid and wide dissemination of the Copernican view of the universe in Dutch society but also of a strong reaction against it, in the Church and universities, which was soon to become linked to a more general conflict between Calvinist orthodoxy in alliance with traditional Aristotelian science and philosophy, on the one hand, and, on the other, a complex of new tendencies—scientific, philosophical, and theological—of which the heliocentric doctrine was an integral part.[55] The doyen of Utrecht university, Gisbertus Voetius, who was to emerge as the chief spokesman of both Calvinist orthodoxy and Aristotelian philosophy in the bitter controversies of the 1640s and 1650s, was at the same time the principal champion of the campaign against Copernicus and Galileo and their conception of the universe.

The most outstanding Dutch scientist between the younger Snellius and Christian Huygens (who established his reputation in the 1650s) was Isaac Beeckman. A pupil of Snellius and admirer of Stevin, Beeckman was skilled in a variety of practical applications, especially pumps, as well as pure mathematics. First as a businessman and later as a teacher in the Illustrious Schools of Utrecht, Rotterdam, and Dordrecht, he pursued his career and researches entirely outside the university context. He first met Descartes at Breda in 1618 and soon became closely involved in the great French philosopher's progress towards a fully integrated, mechanistic world-view based on mathematical laws.[56]

The mechanistic world-view, a mode of abstraction whereby all worldly reality is reducible to terms of extension, mass, and movement which can be expressed mathematically, first emerged in the years around 1630 in the minds of René Descartes (1596–1650) and Beeckman. Descartes, fearful of incurring the censure of the Catholic Church, in 1628 settled permanently in the Republic, as a land where he could freely develop his system. For most of the rest of his career, until 1649, he resided and worked on Dutch soil. Precisely how considerable Beeckman's role was will probably never be

[55] Benthem, *Holländischer Kirch- und Schulen-Staat*, ii. 57–8.
[56] Van Berkel, *Isaac Beeckman*, 44–7.

known for certain. But it is clear from Beeckman's journal (and Descartes's behaviour) that he did significantly influence Descartes and preceded him in some respects.[57] In 1630, Descartes angrily broke with Beeckman, refusing to accept that he had acquired part of his system from him. But what Beeckman certainly lacked, which Descartes possessed, was the ability to weld his mechanistic insights into an integrated philosophical system. By the time Descartes published his *Discours de la méthode*, in 1637, he was well on the path towards what was to prove the most revolutionary scientific-philosophical system of the seventeenth century. Orthodox Calvinists grew uneasy. Descartes's progress was followed with an increasingly hostile eye by the vigilant Voetius.

By the late 1630s, Descartes's philosophy was already generating controversy in the universities and amongst the intellectual leadership of the public Church. In 1639, Voetius organized a series of theological disputations at Utrecht on the subject of atheism, distinguishing between 'direct' atheism and atheism concealed behind belief in a remote deity, of which Vanini and Descartes were cited as the prime examples. Voetius condemned Descartes as doubly culpable for basing his philosophical system on doubt and discarding all traditional (Aristotelian) science and philosophy, including existing proofs of God's existence.[58]

Initially, Voetius' offensive had little effect. Descartes's scientific-philosophical-theological system was championed within the university by the professor of medicine, Henricus Regius (1598–1679). Descartes himself, who showed only contempt for Voetius, assured his friend Mersenne, in March 1642, that Regius' 'disciples, ayant gousté ma façon de raisonner, méprisent si fort la vulgaire, qu'ils s'en moquent ouvertement'.[59] Voetius persevered, however, aiming to provoke such uproar in Church and State as to force provincial and city governments into silencing his enemy. He developed several lines of attack, in particular inciting Maarten Schoock, professor of philosophy at Groningen, to publish a (supposedly) crushing refutation, and mobilizing the Utrecht *vroedschap* against Descartes, who was a familiar figure in the city. The Utrecht *vroedschap*, still Counter-Remonstrant through the 1640s, took up Voetius' cause. Schoock's *Philosophia Cartesiana* (1642) robustly denounced Descartes, assailing his mechanistic approach to the biological sciences, equating him with David Joris and the blasphemous still-life painter Torrentius, as a 'seducer' of ordinary folk, accusing him of seeking to tyrannize over all philosophy by publishing in French, and

[57] Ibid. 159–76.
[58] Verbeek, *René Descartes et Martin Schoock*, 30–1.
[59] Descartes, *Correspondance*, iii. 545–6.

appealing to non-academics, instead of sticking to Latin terminology.[60] Neither did he hesitate to call Descartes an 'atheist', styling him the new 'Vanini'.

Descartes assured friends in France that Schoock's book was contemptible and that he would not bother to reply were it only his own position which was at stake. However, he explained, since Voetius, whom he regarded as the true author, 'gouverne le menu peuple en une ville où il y a quantité d'honestes gens qui me veulent du bien, et qui seront bien aysés que son authorité diminue', he felt bound to enter the fray for their sake, to diminish Voetius' standing and increase 'freedom' to philosophize.[61] The war of Cartesianism and Aristotelianism now pervaded not only the whole of Dutch science, philosophy, and theology but was beginning to invade civic politics and the confrontation of party-factions, not only within the city council, and university, but also the States, consistory, and beyond. For Voetius' sway in Utrecht derived essentially from the Reformed man in the street, and his ability to mobilize the consistory. Cartesianism was thus now inseparable from the general ideological and political battle in progress in Utrecht and therefore the Republic. Despite having spent much of his life in Holland, Descartes had only a poor command of Dutch and was unable to follow the intricacies of the public debate in that language. Nevertheless, he desired that his reply should, with the help of friends, appear in Dutch, so as to damage Voetius' reputation as much as possible. His answer to Schoock took the form of an open letter to Voetius proclaiming the latter a benighted bigot, ignorant of science and philosophy, who abused his power as *rector magnificus* of the university to obstruct scholarship. But this served only to incense opinion and alarm the authorities.

The furore, now spreading well beyond Utrecht,[62] started to worry Descartes. In 1643, he appealed to his friend Constantijn Huygens, and through him the Stadholder, for protection for himself—and for Regius who, he feared, might lose his professorship and become the 'premier martyr de ma philosophie'.[63] He assured Huygens that where previously he believed 'que ces provinces fussent libres', now he saw that it was the spirit of the Inquisition which reigned, particularly at Utrecht. Regius was not sacked; but the university did order him to eschew philosophy and confine his lectures henceforth to medicine.[64] The Utrecht *vroedschap* also took steps

---

[60] Verbeek, *René Descartes et Martin Schoock*, 200, 316–17.
[61] Descartes, *Correspondance*, iii. 598–9.
[62] Van Berkel, *In het voetspoor van Stevin*, 46.
[63] *Correspondence of Descartes*, 210–11.
[64] Sassen, *Gesch. van de wijsbegeerte*, 144–5.

against Descartes which eventually led to Frederik Hendrik's intervention to protect him.

Whilst Frederik Hendrik lived, Descartes was safe and, indeed, able, with the help of the French ambassador, to counter-attack with some effect. He lodged complaints against Schoock with the Groningen university authorities which gained the support of the new *rector magnificus* there, Samuel Maresius, an orthodox Calvinist but also ardent foe of Voetius. Schoock was humiliated and compelled to admit that Voetius had put him up to write against Descartes.[65] By 1644, Descartes was also receiving favourable treatment in philosophical theses disputed at Leiden, his principal ally there being the brilliant young mathematician Frans van Schooten (1615–66), who had been close to Descartes since 1636, drawn the figures for several of his works, and translated the *Géométrie* (1638) into Latin. It was Van Schooten who, during the mid-1640s, taught the young Johan de Witt and Christian Huygens their mathematics and also doubtless something of his reverence for Descartes.

The Cartesian controversy in the United Provinces began earlier than elsewhere and attained an unparalleled intensity. In the Spanish Netherlands, a current of sympathetic interest in Cartesian science and philosophy was evident, at Leuven, by 1650, as well as a prevailing negative response, resulting in a general condemnation by leading figures of the university in 1652. Cartesianism was not eradicated from the south Netherlands universities. But neither did it escalate into a central issue in the culture of the south. It was not until 1662 that the papal internuncio in Brussels spurred the Leuven theology faculty to condemn a list of Cartesian theses and not until the following year that Descartes's works were placed on the Index.[66] But this served neither to eradicate Cartesian teaching from the Arts faculty at Leuven nor to generate a major intellectual furore. Reaction in the south remained muted.

In the north, the Cartesian controversy not only pervaded academic life but became a major issue in high culture and politics. The Cartesian question by no means drove theology from centre stage in the ideological warfare between the rival party-factions. But the feud between Descartes and Voetius did make philosophy and science key aspects of the rival thought-worlds based on competing theological systems, which infused, and helped shape, the party-factions. In the Dutch context, contrasting attitudes to the 'new philosophy', and Descartes, became part of the ideological

[65] Verbeek, *René Descartes et Martin Schoock*, 52, 55.
[66] Vanpaemel, 'Kerk en wetenschap', 184.

baggage of politics by the early 1640s and remained so until the beginning of the eighteenth century.

By the mid-1640s Descartes felt decidedly insecure. Conscious of Galileo's fate and the furore over the Copernican doctrine that the earth revolves around the sun, escalating in Holland since the mid-1630s, Descartes shrank from openly endorsing it in his *Principia* (1644).[67] After the death of Frederik Hendrik, in 1647, the great philosopher's anxiety increased. The new Stadholder thought differently from his father and allied himself with the Calvinist orthodox. In a letter penned shortly after Frederik Hendrik's demise, Descartes remarked that the United Provinces no longer provided the tranquillity necessary for philosophizing 'in freedom' which he had come there to find. Instead of enjoying calm he found himself entangled with a 'troupe de théologiens' intent on vilifying him in the eyes of the public. By late 1647, a full-scale offensive was under way against his ideas at both Utrecht and Leiden. He sombrely predicted that his Voetian adversaries would first secure condemnation of his system in the university senates, then, with academic backing, in the consistories, and, finally, with consistory support, oblige the regents to muzzle him and suppress his books.[68] In September 1649, with William II's star in the ascendant, a disillusioned Descartes boarded ship for Sweden.

BOREELISM AND THE 'THIRD FORCE'

One response to the sceptical crisis was the 'new philosophy' and mechanistic world-view, another that of Voetius, an anti-Cartesianism rooted in confessional orthodoxy and the authority of established Churches, in alliance with traditional Aristotelian science. But there was also a third response which has been aptly termed the 'Third Force'.[69]

This reaction also arose in the second quarter of the seventeenth century, initially especially in England. Based on radical spiritualist interpretations of Scripture, rooted in mystical methodologies, the Third Force, not least in its Dutch context, rejected the entire existing order of authority and learning, achieving certainty by fusing revealed truth, divine inspiration, and scientific knowledge in ways which often seem startling to the modern mind. The central figure in the United Provinces was Adam Boreel (1603–65), scion of a Middelburg regent family, deeply influenced by experiences in England during the 1630s. Boreel and the 'Boreelists'—the term was

---

[67] Vermij, 'Het copernicanisme', 364.
[68] Descartes, *Correspondance*, iv. 323–4.
[69] Popkin, *The Third Force*, 90–2.

commonly used in Holland from the late 1640s onwards—denied that any existing Church was the true Church of Christ but, at the same time, held that all existing Churches, including that of the Jews, possessed fragments of truth.[70] The true Church of Christ were the small informal groups, emancipated from the sway of clergy and constituted Churches, banded together in pursuit of a pure apostolic Christianity of which public preachers and Churches were the decayed and corrupted remnants. In Boreel's true Church of Christ there was general freedom of debate and speculation and all members were equal. Boreel set out his ideas in his book *Ad Legem et Testimonium*, published in Amsterdam, in 1645, shortly before he settled permanently in the city.[71] The book earned him the bitter hostility of the Reformed Church.

Boreel, who had studied in Leiden, found much in the existing Collegiant movement that fitted with his ideas and, on establishing his 'college' in Amsterdam, in the late 1640s, together with a group of liberal Mennonites, drew recruits from the same liberal Mennonite and Remonstrant circles as the Rijnsburgers. But he continually strove also to forge links with Lutherans, Jews, Quakers, and indeed Catholics. Endeavouring to penetrate to the absolute—but superficially hidden—certainties of Revelation, and prepare the Jews for their conversion to his true Church of Christ, Boreel placed particular emphasis on studying Hebrew and post-biblical Jewish literature. Among his intimates in Middelburg was the Sephardic rabbi Judah Leon Templo and in Amsterdam Menasseh ben Israel. Boreel laboured, over many years, preparing a series of Hebrew, Latin, and Spanish versions of, and commentaries on, the Jewish Mishnah, though only his vocalized Hebrew version was actually published, albeit without his name on the title-page, so as not to alarm orthodox Jews.[72]

A key Spiritualist ally of Boreel, in Amsterdam, was the mystical Chiliast Petrus Serrarius (1600–69), a former preacher of the Dutch Walloon Church expelled, in 1628, after being drawn into a Schwenckfeldian Spiritualism probably acquired during his years in Cologne (1626–8). After settling in Amsterdam, in 1630, Serrarius developed his own theology of the invalidity of constituted Churches, and of a hidden true Church of Christ which would ultimately transform the world and introduce a glorious new era.[73]

The ideas of Boreel and Serrarius lent themselves to the Millenarian speculative concerns which became increasingly characteristic of the north-

[70] Van Slee, *Rijnsburger Collegianten*, 138–41; Meihuizen, *Galenis Abrahamsz*, 43–8; Lindeboom, *Stiefkinderen*, 342–4.

[71] Lindeboom, *Stiefkinderen*, 342–3.

[72] Popkin, 'Some Aspects', 8–9.

[73] Van der Wall, *Mystieke Chiliast Petrus Serrarius*, 204, 208, 621.

ern European 'Third Force' in the 1640s and 1650s. While Serrarius evidently moved further in this direction than Boreel, the latter too frequented Millenarian circles and his writings were read in Millenarian terms by his allies.[74] A close associate of Boreel and Serrarius was the Dutch-Scottish Millenarian John Dury (1596–1680), who spent long periods in Cologne and other German cities, as well as in Holland and Britain. He too was a key figure in 'Third Force' circles in the Republic. In the winter of 1635 he had a long meeting with Descartes at which he strove to conquer the latter's scepticism, as he had his own, with his 'infallible way of interpreting' Scripture.[75] Dury failed to impress Descartes; but his method of construing biblical passages, and passion for fusing theology with science and philosophy to form an integrated, triumphant whole, along similar lines to Boreel, influenced many in the United Provinces and Germany as well as Britain. Dury and Serrarius shared with Boreel a mystical conception of science which included an abiding fascination with alchemistic experiment and strange medical remedies.[76] Science for these men meant revealing the hidden truths of nature, with the help of chemistry, a process akin to uncovering, by means of profound but elusive methodologies, the secrets of spiritual truth and divine Revelation.

The passion for alchemy which transcended faiths and political barriers infusing the souls of many prominent personalities in seventeenth-century Europe—not least Leopold Wilhelm, governor-general of the Spanish Netherlands in the years 1647–56, who turned Brussels for a time into a noted centre of alchemistic endeavour—was a central element in the religious and scientific outlook of the Boreelists and their allies. Alchemy lay at the heart, for instance, of the friendship between Serrarius and the dissident Brabanter Franciscus Mercurinus van Helmont (c.1614–98), a renowned mystic and alchemist whose reputation spread all over Europe. The latter's father, Johannes Baptista van Helmont (d. 1644), was also a leading alchemist whose collected works were published at Amsterdam in 1648. Attracted both to Jewish mysticism and the Quakers, the younger Van Helmont regularly visited Holland over many years, cultivating Boreel and Serrarius and becoming a stalwart of the world of radical religious dissent, mysticism, and pseudoscience.

Leading international figures of the Third Force such as Dury, Van Helmont, and the German Samuel Hartlib, who settled in England, acknowledged that the United Provinces, and especially Amsterdam, had a pivotal

---

[74] Ibid. 149–54, 338–42.
[75] Popkin, *The Third Force*, 95–6.
[76] Van der Wall, *Mystieke Chiliast Petrus Serrarius*, 291–7.

part to play in their plans to spread knowledge and spiritual truth, and prepare for the glorious day to come, being the world's general entrepôt not only of ships and commerce but also of books, printing, ideas, religions, and men who had seen the light. A towering champion of the quest for salvation by combining science and a new approach to education with new techniques for grasping revealed truth was the Czech refugee polymath and leader of the Moravian Brethren, Jan Amost Comenius (1592–1670). Exiled and traumatized by the Habsburg reconquest of Bohemia-Moravia, Comenius spent much of his subsequent life in Poland before permanently settling in Holland in 1656. But long before then, his personality, prophetic politics, and educational vision, fusing science with revealed truth, were well known to the Boreelists and Serrarius.[77] Comenius sought to forge a system of universal knowledge, a total reintegration of science and faith, again rejecting the entire existing order of authority, Churches, and academic learning.

One of Comenius' key early encounters in Holland, in 1642, was with Descartes. He himself describes how he walked together with Descartes for four hours in the countryside near Leiden. Descartes, who respected Comenius' personality if not his ideas, expounded his philosophy; Comenius countered with his 'pansophism', insisting that 'all human knowledge which is obtained by thought and reflection alone is imperfect' and that only through divine inspiration, and prayer, is a true universal synthesis attainable.[78] They parted on friendly terms, neither convinced by the other. Comenius composed his last, and most ambitious, work, his general *Consultatio*, addressed to humanity, mainly in Amsterdam during the 1660s. His final resting-place was in Naarden.

It is true that Boreelism and the Third Force were, by their nature, a fringe phenomenon of the Dutch cultural world of the mid-seventeenth century. The hostility of the established Churches, universities, and schools, and consequent lack of official backing, saw to that. Yet it is also true that the Third Force was a reflection of some of the most basic impulses within the European, including the Dutch, intellectual milieu of the time and, as such, an integral and vital factor. Serrarius participated centrally in an astounding range of theological and intellectual polemics. He was also, for many years, a close associate of Spinoza. Leading theologians of the Reformed Church, including two of the Republic's best-known university professors, Johannes Hoornbeek and Samuel Maresius, considered Boreel

---

[77] Ibid. 104; Evans, *Making of the Habsburg Monarchy*, 78, 395.
[78] Rood, *Comenius*, 134.

such a menace that they found it necessary to publish long refutations of his ideas. Finally, the Third Force's chief concern, reconciliation of theology, philosophy, and science, albeit in a mystical version, was ultimately a variant of the central preoccupation of seventeenth-century Dutch intellectual life as a whole.

PART III

The Later Golden Age
1647–1702

❖

MAP II. The United Provinces in the Golden Age

25

The Stadholderate of William II, 1647–1650

❖

The stadholderate of William II was brief but of great significance in the history of the Republic. For it produced the most severe crisis of the Dutch state between 1618 and the fall of the De Witt regime in 1672. It also renewed some of the former ideological intensity of Dutch politics after the calmer era of the 1630s and early 1640s.

Under the stadholderate of Frederik Hendrik, especially after his shift of course in 1633, the lines of political and ideological strife in Dutch society had, to an extent, become blurred. The Calvinist orthodox abhorred Frederik Hendrik's tolerant policies towards Catholics, Remonstrants, and, after 1642, Cartesians, and his willingness to shield these from the zeal of the Reformed preachers. But they scorned the 'libertine' regents of the Holland towns even more and felt bound to support the Stadholder in his quarrels with the States party-faction from 1633 onwards. But under William II the lines of political confrontation came to correspond, once more, as they had under Maurits, to the lines of ideological, and theological, strife permeating society and the rival factions in the municipalities and provincial assemblies.

William II first emerged on to the political stage, in 1645, when his father was sick and he attempted, backed by the French ambassador, to gain command of a field army with which to fight the Spaniards. His father had refused to permit this and during his last two field campaigns (1645–6) deliberately thwarted his son's desire for military command.[1] While relations between father and son deteriorated, the Stadholder, increasingly frail, began co-operating with Adriaen Pauw and the Bickers, who were now effectively directing the Republic. For his part, William leaned towards those amongst his father's entourage, such as Constantijn Huygens, who continued to oppose peace with Spain. After Frederik Hendrik's death, in March 1647, the Orangist court remained divided. The French envoy spoke

[1] Kernkamp, *Prins Willem II*, 48–9.

of a split between 'la mère [Amalia von Solms] et ceux de son parti', cultivating the interests and prestige of the House of Orange-Nassau, and legacy of Frederik Hendrik, in co-operation with the regents, on the one hand, and, on the other, 'le fils et ses dépendans'.[2] Among other things, the young Stadholder and his mother quarrelled bitterly over Frederik Hendrik's will, including the provision that, should William II die without legitimate heir, the whole legacy of the House of Orange-Nassau should pass to the line of his eldest sister Louise Henriette, wife of the Elector of Brandenburg.[3] At the same time, Amalia backed the moves towards peace with Spain whereas her son made no secret of his hostility to the pending treaty.

Though the Prince's haughty and irascible temperament showed clearly from the outset, initially he lacked the standing, never having commanded in the field, to exert much impact on the Republic's political course. Holland's dominance in 1647–8 looked unchallengeable. It was hard to guess, at that time, that within two years the Stadholder would be able to mobilize a powerful coalition against the Holland regents, bringing the Republic to the brink of civil war.

During the final stages of the Münster peace negotiations, the main opposition to Holland sprang not from the Orangist camp but provinces and quarters where local vested interests preferred to prolong the war.[4] In particular, Zeeland, fearful that peace would destroy her transit trade with the south Netherlands, as in 1609, and Utrecht, stubbornly resisted. The States of Utrecht, dominated by the Counter-Remonstrant city, held that the Generality's plenipotentiaries had failed to extract sufficient concessions from Philip IV, especially regarding the Meierij, Overmaas, and Roermond quarter, and the WIC, and that, besides, the Republic should stick to its treaty obligations and not proceed until France had settled her differences with Spain.[5] This line of thinking found favour also in parts of Gelderland, where the quarters were, as usual, deeply divided, with Zutphen opposing and Nijmegen supporting Holland, and the Arnhem quarter split.[6]

The final act of the Münster peace saga—ratification of the seventy-nine articles of the treaty—took place at The Hague, and Münster, during the spring of 1648. Five provinces voted to ratify, against the advice of the Stadholder, on 4 April, but it was felt that with two provinces still opposed this did not suffice, given the momentousness of the decision. The Holland

[2] Groenveld, 'Willem II en de Stuarts', 175.
[3] Ibid. 159; Blok, *Frederik Hendrik*, 246.
[4] Israel, *Dutch Republic and the Hispanic World*, 362–74.
[5] ARH SG 4856. sec. res. SG 22 Jan. 1647.
[6] Van der Capellen, *Gedenkschriften*, ii. 172–4.

regents brought pressure to bear on the States of Utrecht and its members, not least the town of Amersfoort. Finally Utrecht yielded, and the peace was signed by six provinces, over the continuing objections of Zeeland. Unable to influence the proceedings, William II deliberately absented himself from The Hague at critical moments in the tussle, so that his political impotence should be less obvious.[7] Zeeland had eventually to fall in line, publishing the peace with Spain a few weeks after the other provinces.

The ensuing peace festivities could be, and were, seen as in part signifying Holland's triumph over the House of Orange and the province's newly won leadership of the Republic. A celebratory medal, issued at Amsterdam, proclaimed the superiority of peace over martial glory, carrying the deliberately ambiguous inscription, *Pax una triumphis innumeris potior*, widely construed as a snub to the dead Frederik Hendrik. The regents now openly praised Oldenbarnevelt and there was talk of politics having come full circle, since 1618, with the principles of the States of Holland being again in the ascendant. An anonymous account of the life of Oldenbarnevelt, published in 1648, was dedicated to the Rotterdam magistracy because, the author explained, Rotterdam had, since 1618, been the city which had most resolutely defended 'freedom of conscience'.[8]

Only gradually did it emerge that Holland was not, after all, firmly in the saddle. This was partly due to the formidable influence of the stadholderate. But the causes of the Dutch political crisis of 1649–50 also lie in tensions within Holland, and between the provinces, which ultimately enabled William II to divide Holland and rally the rest against her. Some of these stresses were economic in character. If commerce and industry in Holland benefited from the economic effects of the peace (see pp. 610–12 below), this is by no means true of the other provinces. Zeeland, just as in 1609, suffered an immediate and severe slump because, as the States of Zeeland explained, 'all trade and commerce on the Schelde, Sas, and Zwijn [the waterways linking Zeeland with Bruges, Ghent, and Antwerp] diminish more and more, every day, being diverted to the Flemish seaports'.[9] For the lifting of the naval blockade of the Flemish coast again made possible the provisioning of the south with salt, wine, fish, grain, and Baltic naval stores from Holland and, by means of the Hollanders' ships, direct from the Baltic, bypassing Zeeland and the Scheldt estuary. Meanwhile, the swingeing cuts in garrisons and military spending spread recession throughout the great arc of the inland defensive ring, from Delfzijl to Sluis. Holland's failure to

[7] *Journalen . . . Willem II*, 447–8, 458–9.
[8] [C.P.T.], *Historie van Johan Olden-Barnevelt*, 3v.
[9] GA Dordrecht city council archives, 115/336. SZ to SG, 10 Oct. 1648.

rescue the WIC from its now disastrous plight in Brazil was an added grievance, especially in Zeeland and Groningen,[10] provinces where investment in the company was proportionately higher than in Holland.

Resentment generated by these contrary shifts was then aggravated by a run of wretched harvests due to cold, wet summers, followed by soaring bread prices, a phenomenon which affected the whole of Europe. For the poor artisan, feeding his family chiefly on bread, living standards slipped sharply in the years 1648–50 to one of the lowest points of the seventeenth century. The setback was no less marked, albeit much shorter, than that experienced by the working man during the recession of 1621–31.[11] Several contemporary pamphlets proclaimed the high food prices, and dismal weather, signs of God's displeasure at the ungodly peace of Münster. Antoine Brun, Spain's first ambassador to the United Provinces, reported, in February 1650, that the growing instability and potential for unrest in the Dutch body politic was mainly due neither to the Stadholder, nor the military element, but to the *gente mecánica*, ordinary artisans stirred up by the preachers.[12] Repeating this in a report to Madrid, a month later, he noted that most ordinary Dutch folk considered themselves worse off now than during the war because bread prices were now considerably higher.[13] Similarly, the historian Aitzema considered the common populace a key element in the Dutch constitutional crisis of 1650. He stressed that outside Holland the common folk were generally opposed to Holland and that inside Holland opinion was deeply divided.[14]

Another factor was the exasperation of the Calvinist orthodox.[15] The most vehemently anti-Holland pamphlets published in 1649–50 were often written by hardline preachers who openly attributed the high cost of bread, economic collapse in Zeeland, and débâcle in Brazil to God's wrath with the regents for failing to support the public Church sufficiently and for their ungodly tolerance of Catholicism and Protestant dissent.

At this point several issues mired relations between the regents and the Church. One source of acrimony was the limited progress of the Reformation in the Generality Lands—a major issue in the aftermath of the Dutch–Spanish peace. During the Münster negotiations, Spain had tried to surrender only 'temporal sovereignty' over the Meierij, the largest chunk of territory annexed to the Republic, seeking to protect the region's 300

---

[10] *Correspondência Sousa Coutinho*, iii. 56, 359.
[11] Nusteling, *Welvaart en werkgelegenheid*, 260–1, 263–4.
[12] Muller, 'Spanje en de partijen', 172.
[13] AGS Estado 2170. Brun to Philip IV, 25 Mar. 1650.
[14] Aitzema, *Herstelde Leeuw*, 90–1.
[15] Poelhekke, *Geen blijder maer*, 42–5.

churches, monasteries, and convents and their lands and revenues,[16] and it is likely that the Holland regents would have acquiesced in this were it not for the outcry in the other provinces and from the Church. 'Absolute sovereignty' was eventually conceded and, with the peace ratified, the attempted Protestantization of the Meierij began.[17]

The main effort to Protestantize not only the Meierij, but also the other annexed areas and Lingen, began only in 1648 because previously, with the war in progress, it had been impossible for Reformed preachers to operate outside fortified places held by Dutch troops. To promote the Reformation in the newly acquired territories the States General accepted the advice of the provincial synods not to create new synodal bodies but to place the Generality Lands under the existing synods.[18] Thus, States Flanders and Bergen-op-Zoom remained under the Synod of Zeeland, and the barony of Breda under South Holland, while the Meierij was split into two classes both assigned to the Synod of Gelderland. To ensure that Protestantization in the Generality Lands proceeded on a common basis as a collective undertaking of the Seven Provinces—which jointly exercised sovereignty in the region through the States General—a steering committee of representatives from all the provincial synods was set up.

Institutionally, the Reformation in the Generality Lands now proceeded briskly. In the Meierij the States General confiscated all 300 Catholic churches and cloisters, seizing their revenues and stripping them of altars and images.[19] The main churches were whitewashed and reinaugurated for Reformed worship. Consistories were established, Reformed bibles and catechisms replaced Catholic books in schools and civic libraries, and Catholic schoolmasters were removed. The first fourteen Reformed preachers installed by the Generality, in the Meierij, were in residence within weeks of the signing of the peace. Their number had risen to thirty-six by late 1648 and fifty-two by late 1649.[20] This was close to the maximum ever achieved; for at its height, in the eighteenth century, the Reformed Church in the Meierij never totalled more than sixty preachers. At the same time, the States General installed fifty-one Reformed schoolmasters to run the Meierij's schools.

Similar changes took place in the other recently secured Generality Lands, except Maastricht and the Overmaas, where Catholic worship was guaranteed by the States General's placard of 1632 and the Catholic Church

[16] ARH SG 4856, 'articulen', 27 Dec. 1646; *Correspondência Sousa Coutinho*, iii. 58.
[17] Aitzema, *Verhael*, ii. 188, 317–19.
[18] Knuttel, *Acta*, iii. 72–5.
[19] Beaufort, *Leven van Willem den II*, i. 369–71.
[20] Van Heurn, *Historie*, iii. 2–3.

remained intact. The transformation gained added impetus where the Stadholder wielded special influence. For Frederik Hendrik had been notably lenient towards the Catholics in his own domains. William II, who was notoriously dissolute, was anything but a Calvinist in life-style; but, unlike his father, made a point of aligning with the public Church, seeing the Calvinist orthodox as a valuable buttress to his authority. No sooner was peace concluded than the Prince instructed the *drost* of Breda to proceed 'immediately, without delay, to strip the churches of all images and papist adornment' and install Reformed preachers in the barony outside the town.[21] Before 1648, Reformed preachers in the Generality Lands were unable to operate outside the walls of the garrison towns. Consequently, despite the predominant Dutch presence from the 1590s until 1625, and again between 1637 and 1648, the Reformation in most of the barony of Breda and lordship of Steenbergen (see Map 10) effectively began only in 1648. The same was true around Hulst, Sas van Gent, and the other newly annexed districts of States Flanders. William II also promoted the Reformation in his county of Lingen, instructing his *drost*, Rutger van Haersolte, to remove the Catholic priests (whom his father had permitted to remain), strip the churches, and install Reformed preachers.[22] Since Lingen, a predominantly Catholic area, was wedged between the two main parts of the prince-bishopric of Münster, where the Counter-Reformation was now fully victorious, the changes in Lingen added to the tension between Reformed and Catholics throughout the eastern side of the Republic, and between the Republic and the prince-bishop.[23]

But it soon emerged that seizing churches, installing Reformed preachers, and introducing the States Bible and Reformed schools, would not suffice to change the religion of regions assiduously re-Catholicized since the late sixteenth century by the Counter-Reformation offensive in the Spanish Netherlands and territory of the prince-bishop. The end of the fighting signalled the arrival of the Reformation in the unfortified towns and villages of the Generality Lands, but was also a signal for Catholic priests to return from Catholic-held areas, and re-establish their authority over villagers and townsfolk; and for the local populace to bring out from hiding their holy objects and images and rebuild their religious culture.[24] Reductions of garrisons and military patrols only encouraged these tendencies.

This Protestant failure in the Generality Lands generated intense frustration within the public Church throughout the United Provinces. The

[21] Knuttel, *Acta*, iii. 76.
[22] *Archief aartsbisdom Utrecht*, iv. 148; Ter Kuile, 'Graafschap Lingen', 20–1.
[23] Kohl, *Christoph Bernhard von Galen*, 96.
[24] *Geschiedenis van Breda*, ii. 135–7.

Reformed synods took the view that the Reformation in the newly secured regions would only succeed if the States General adopted tougher measures, arguing that the Republic could not afford to see the Catholic Church triumph in the extensive, and strategically vital, areas concerned. In June 1648, the States General published a placard banning the entry of Catholic priests into the Generality Lands.[25] Spain protested that this violated the terms of the peace which guaranteed freedom of movement between the territory of the two sides. As the pressure of the synods for stronger methods increased, a reaction set in among the Holland regents who disliked the way the synods were determining policy in the Generality Lands, their pressure for coercion, and the negative effect on relations with Spain. A key issue was the proposal, backed by the synods, to exclude Catholics from all posts, municipal or administrative, in the Generality Lands. The measure was supported by several lesser provinces but opposed in the States of Holland. The majority in that assembly rejected the measure, against the advice of the Stadholder and also of Leiden and Haarlem.[26]

In their exasperation, orthodox Calvinists turned to the Prince of Orange, who was more than willing to respond.[27] When the Catholics of Breda petitioned the Prince to mitigate the anti-Catholic offensive in the barony, he pointedly refused, for which he was extolled by hardline preachers, such as Jacobus Stermond, at The Hague, as the 'protector' of the Reformed Church, a pious hero who wanted no part of his father's leniency towards Catholics.[28] But such gestures also whetted the appetite for more. At Middelburg, Maximilian Teellinck published an appeal to the Prince, in 1650, urging him not just to be the champion of the Reformation in Breda and the Meierij, but to initiate a new stage of Reformation throughout the Republic—a reforming of society, morality, and politics and elimination of the power of the 'Arminian' regents of Holland to 'control consistories, and choose preachers in their towns', the method by which they diluted the Church's influence and the 'exercise of discipline'.[29] Those preachers who fervently lauded William II invariably denounced the 'Arminians' dominating the States of Holland, not least Burgomaster Andries Bicker, of Amsterdam, whom they accused of 'impudently' obstructing the 'most necessary Reformation in the Meierij of Den Bosch'.[30]

---

[25] Knuttel, *Toestand*, 253.
[26] Res. Holl. 18 May 1649.
[27] Groenveld, *De Prins voor Amsterdam*, 93–5.
[28] [Stermond], *Lauweren-krans gevlochten*, 18.
[29] Teellinck, *Vrymoedige Aenspraeck*, 15.
[30] [Stermond], *Lauweren-krans gevlochten*, 15v.

In Holland, even strident opponents of toleration, such as Stermond, or passionate Orangists, such as Johannes Goethals, preacher at Delft for thirty-three years (1640–73), who had led the prayers at Frederik Hendrik's death-bed, were obliged, when preaching, to refrain from openly criticizing the regents. But preachers outside Holland, where the secular authority was on their side, could go further.[31] One of the most outspoken was Abraham van de Velde, who in a series of sermons delivered in Utrecht cathedral openly disparaged the Holland regents, denouncing the peace of Münster as a 'damned peace', and violation of the Republic's undertakings, so displeasing to the Almighty that it had rained incessantly ever since.[32]

TABLE 27. *The size of the Dutch standing army,*
1642–1661

Year	Infantry	Cavalry	Total
1642			(over 70,000)
1643	53,480	6,950	60,430
1647 (proposed)	34,550	4,250	38,800
1648	30,790	4,340	35,130
1650	26,250	3,000	29,250
1661	21,790	2,605	24,395

Source: Ten Raa and De Bas, *Het Staatsche leger*, iv. 158 and v. 407, 409, 441–4.

Against this background of economic restructuring, slump in the lesser provinces, falling living-standards for the ordinary man, and frustrated Reformation in the Generality Lands, the quarrel which developed between Holland and the Stadholder over further army cuts became one of crucial significance even though previously, in the years 1646–8, much larger reductions had already taken place (see Table 27) than were being argued over in 1649–50. The debate about the size of the army and levels of Generality military expenditure had continued uninterruptedly, since 1646. Shortly before his death, in 1647, Frederik Hendrik had urged the States General to agree to fix the future peacetime standing army at 39,000 men, over half the troop-strength on the Generality's payroll in 1642. But Pauw, Bicker, and the inner circle of the States of Holland wanted a considerably smaller force. By 1648, the army was down to 35,000 men; but the Holland regents considered this still too high and pressed for further reductions.

---

[31] Aitzema, *Historie*, vii. 53.
[32] ARH Hof van Holland 5266/8. 'Contra Abraham van de Velde'.

Disagreement became confrontation during 1649, with Holland demanding that the army be reduced to 26,000.[33] The Prince answered that the Republic's territory was now considerably larger than in 1609 and that, accordingly, more troops were required to garrison the now fifteen fortified towns and thirty-three forts constituting the Republic's outer defensive ring. Cuts of the order urged by Holland, he insisted, would jeopardize the security of the state.[34] During early 1649, both sides compromised, largely closing the gap. But, in the summer, deadlock resumed. The army was now down to 29,250 men, its lowest level since 1590. The remaining disparity between what the two sides proposed had shrunk to a mere few hundred men.[35] But neither side would concede anything more.

Clearly, the real issue now was not the size of the army, but who controlled the Republic. The constitutional question whether Holland, as a 'sovereign' province, had the right, under the Union of Utrecht, to dissolve those elements of the army for which she paid, without the agreement of the Generality, raised the most fundamental issues.[36] If a province could disband army units on its *répartition* unilaterally, disregarding the States General, *Raad van State*, and Stadholder, then the authority of each of these was no longer remotely what it had been in Frederik Hendrik's day. Furthermore, while regents normally referred to the United Provinces as a whole as 'this state', during the seventeenth and eighteenth centuries, and it had (undeniably) hitherto been a 'state', if henceforth each province could raise and disband troops, then it would not be a state any longer but a collection of 'states'.[37] This message was spelt out in several Orangist pamphlets.

The constitutional dimension mattered greatly not only to the provincial political élites, Generality bureaucracy, and Stadholder, but also to the army, navy, public Church, and common populace. As the fiery preacher Abraham van de Velde observed, if Grotius was right, and each province was fully 'sovereign', then each province would be free to go its own way not only in military matters, and expenditure, but also church policy. 'States' party ideas of provincial sovereignty implied the overturning of the National Synod of Dordrecht, and the whole concept of a public Church, maintained by the Union, with the Catholic Church suppressed on a common basis, throughout the provinces and Generality Lands.[38] For this reason, above all, Grotius' doctrine was reviled by the orthodox Calvinist bloc.

[33] Wijnne, *Geschillen*, pp. xii–xiv; Zwitzer, *Militie*, 175.
[34] Kernkamp, *Prins Willem II*, 100–6.
[35] Rowen, *Princes of Orange*, 85.
[36] Wijnne, *Geschillen*, p. xl; Groenveld, *De Prins voor Amsterdam*, 44–53.
[37] Aitzema, *Historie*, vii. 53–62; *Recht der souverainiteyt*, 5.
[38] [Van de Velde], *Oogen-salve*, 2v.

By the summer of 1649, it was clear that the balance within the Dutch body politic was beginning to tilt against the regents. William II had already decided, in the autumn of 1649, many months before he launched his *coup d'état*, to use the army to break Holland and secure control of the state. As early as October 1649, he confided to the Frisian Stadholder, Willem Frederik, his intention, should Holland proceed unilaterally, to dissolve army units, to stage a coup to save the Union and his authority.[39] Willem Frederik's journal shows that the Stadholder counted not only on the support of the six lesser provinces but on a widening rift within Holland. Dividing Holland was, indeed, the only basis on which there could be an enduring transformation of power relationships within the Republic. This was the lesson of Maurits's coup and the secret of Frederik Hendrik's authority until the mid-1640s. William II calculated that, in fact, only six Holland towns were sufficiently committed to the new principles to stand up to him in a real contest—Amsterdam, Dordrecht, Delft, Haarlem, Hoorn, and Medemblik. When it came to a trial of strength, he predicted, the Holland *ridderschap* and around seven Holland towns would rally to him.[40] He already planned, in the autumn of 1649, to paralyse the States party-faction, by arresting those regents he regarded as the backbone of the States party-faction. Already then he named nine prominent men he planned to seize, among them four Amsterdammers—Adriaen Pauw, Andries and Cornelis Bicker, and Anthonie Oetgens van Waveren.

Originally, the two Stadholders intended to act in the spring of 1650. But they recognized the need to stage their coup at the most favourable juncture, mobilizing maximum support and creating as much disarray as possible within Holland. William II saw the crucial importance of the common people in the unfolding drama, expecting to discredit the regents, and incite the populace against them, with a barrage of propaganda pamphlets.[41] Only when the population was thoroughly aroused, and the regents intimidated, would the Prince employ troops to surprise Amsterdam and seize his opponents. A bizarre feature of the plan was the intention to station a force at Texel to block any attempt by the English Parliamentary regime to send a fleet through to Amsterdam, to save the States party-faction. William II's declared aims were to restore his authority as Stadholder, subdue Holland, and purge the 'Arminian', pro-regent preachers at Amsterdam, replacing them with Orangist orthodox, who could be relied upon to persuade the people to support his authority.

[39] Groenveld, 'Enckel valsch', 113.
[40] Ibid.; Groenveld, 'Willem II en de Stuarts', 162.
[41] Groenveld, 'Enckel valsch', 113–15.

Few people knew of the conspiracy. But it was obvious, not least to the Spanish council of state, in Madrid, that the Republic was engulfed in a crisis capable, like that in England, of leading to civil war, and that, should William II triumph, he would repudiate the treaty of Münster, align with France (and the English royalists), and bridle Amsterdam, the chief backer and guarantor of the Dutch–Spanish peace. A decision was thus taken in Madrid that, should matters come to extremes, or civil war, in the Republic, the regime in Brussels would do what it could to assist Holland against the rest.[42]

The Prince seized every opportunity to step up the psychological pressure. Blame for the deteriorating situation in Netherlands Brazil, which was causing rising indignation in Zeeland, Groningen, and Utrecht, was pinned firmly on Holland.[43] The irascible admiral Witte de With, who besides his humble social origins held anti-Orangist views, was arrested, with several of his captains, for sailing back from the stricken colony, with part of the fleet with which he had been sent out, before receiving orders to do so from the States General and Stadholder. Several of his captains were locked up, on Orange's orders, by the admiralty college in Amsterdam, incensing the burgomasters, who insisted that no one could be arrested in Amsterdam except by the city magistracy and promptly released the prisoners. Witte de With himself, however, remained a prisoner of the Stadholder at The Hague.

More than a little unscrupulous was Orange's instigating in July 1650, a month before his coup, the publication of a forged document, purporting to be a secret pact between Amsterdam and the Parliament of England under which, in case of civil war in the United Provinces, England would send a fleet and 10,000 troops to help Holland fight the Stadholder and Generality.[44] This was one of several propaganda publications of 1650 directly sponsored by the Stadholder and his entourage.

During the weeks previous to Holland's vote to proceed with unilateral disbandment of army units intense pressure was bought to bear on waverers by both sides. Amsterdam was accused of going beyond accepted practice in influencing other Holland towns, both to stiffen resolve, at Dordrecht, and sway divided towns such as Haarlem, Gouda, and Schiedam.[45] Meanwhile, as predicted, the rift within Holland widened. In April, Orange assured Willem Frederik that Amsterdam and Dordrecht now barely commanded a majority of the States, having only ten votes against nine.

---

[42] AGS Estado 2072. consulta 16 Aug. 1650; Poelhekke, *Geen blijder maer*, 174.
[43] Boxer, *Dutch in Brazil*, 221–5.
[44] Groenveld, 'Enckel valsch', 115.
[45] [Stermond], *Lauweren-krans gevlochten*, 11v.

This was close to the mark and, without Amsterdam's leaning on Haarlem and Schiedam, the critical resolution would not have passed at all.[46] William's forecast of October 1649 proved remarkably accurate. The vote to disband, of May 1650, passed by only eleven votes to eight, with the *ridderschap* and seven towns—Leiden, Rotterdam, Enkhuizen, Gouda, Hoorn, Gorcum, and Schoonhoven—against.

Shortly afterwards, the *Gecommitteerde Raden* dispatched letters of disbandment to the captains of twelve cavalry, and thirty-one infantry, companies on Holland's list. The next day Prince and *Raad van State* informed the States General they had instructed all army captains to ignore orders from any particular province and obey only the commands of the States General and the Stadholder as captain-general of the Union. A critical decision was then taken in the States General by five provinces to two—over the protests of Holland and Gelderland—authorizing the Prince to enter, at the head of a Generality commission, every Holland town which had voted for unilateral disbandment, for the purpose of compelling these towns to accept that their resolution violated the terms of the Union, and was invalid, and to agree to adhere henceforth to the 'accepted' procedures of the state'.[47]

Orange sought to exploit this procedure of a grand Generality visitation to display his authority, power, and popularity and, by visibly mobilizing the public behind him, force the Holland regents to give in. It was a key instance, in the early modern context, of an attempt to use the common populace as the decisive instrument of politics. But, in Holland, the people were less solidly behind the Prince than elsewhere. He enjoyed some success at Dordrecht, the first town visited, where the guilds were traditionally Orangist. The Stadholder entered a city gripped by tension, with the regents thoroughly intimidated, accompanied by Generality representatives and an entourage of 400 nobles and troops. His right-hand-man Alexander van der Capellen, of the Zutphen *ridderschap*, a fervent champion of both Orangism and Calvinist orthodoxy, read out the Prince's address to the assembled *vroedschap* making abundantly clear the Prince's displeasure with Dordrecht in particular and Holland in general.

After Dordrecht, though, the inexorable build-up of pressure which the Stadholder intended failed to materialize. Delft agreed to admit the Prince, and hear his address, out of respect for his person, but refused to admit his military escort. Amsterdam sent word that Orange would be received in his capacity as Stadholder but not as the head of a Generality visitation, which

---

[46] Wijnne, *Geschillen*, p. xl.   [47] Kernkamp, *Prins Willem* II, 109.

Holland had voted against.[48] The Prince entered Amsterdam to find the entire civic militia out on parade and the burgomasters refusing to allow him to read his address. He was so incensed he stormed out of the city without stopping to partake of the banquet prepared in his honour.

The Prince staged his coup, ignoring Holland's last-minute attempt at compromise, on 30 July 1650. His officers arrested six principal regents, in the name of the States General, at the Binnenhof, including Burgomaster Jacob de Witt (father of Johan de Witt) of Dordrecht, and Albert Ruyl, Pensionary of Haarlem. Troops were deployed, to ensure calm, in The Hague. Meanwhile, 12,000 troops of the States General's army, drawn from garrisons in Gelderland and commanded by Willem Frederik, converged, during the night, on Amsterdam. They were already very close when the burgomasters were alerted by a routine postal courier who rode past the soldiery on his way in from Hamburg. Just in time the city gates were closed and the civic guard called out. Willem Frederik did not attempt to force his way in. The troops camped outside, awaiting the Stadholder. The episode certainly had its farcical side. Yet, despite the failure to surprise the city, the Prince could now negotiate from a position of strength. The outcome demonstrated that he was now master in the state.[49] His two arch-opponents—Andries and Cornelis Bicker—were purged from the *vroedschap*, and the city undertook to cancel Holland's disbandment orders and accept new troop and spending levels to be agreed by the Seven Provinces together, in the States General. Once Amsterdam had yielded, the Stadholder, and his troops, departed.

In justification of his coup, the Prince dispatched letters to the provincial assemblies, and major town councils, outside Holland.[50] In the lesser provinces, opinion was generally favourable. A good part of the population evidently nurtured feelings of envy and grievance if not outright antagonism towards Amsterdam. Van Lodenstein, a leader of the Further Reformation, at Utrecht, expressed joy at Amsterdam's humiliation.[51] The Prince was pleased by the sycophantic replies which he received, especially the congratulations of the States of Zeeland.[52] Nevertheless, some of the political élites outside Holland hinted their unease over what the Prince had done, even disapproval. At Zutphen, a stronghold of Orangism and orthodox Calvinism, support for the coup against Amsterdam was less than wholehearted and some even ventured to criticize Van der Capellen for participating in

[48] Rowen, *Rhyme and Reason*, 68.
[49] Ibid. 114; Van der Plaat, 'Lieuwe van Aitzema's kijk', 352.
[50] *Journalen . . . Willem II*, 530.
[51] Evenhuis, *Ook dat was Amsterdam*, i. 326.
[52] *Journalen . . . Willem II*, 530.

the Prince's visitation when his own province had voted against the procedure.

The pamphlet war continued unrelentingly.[53] The year 1650, together with 1618 and 1672, were the three peak years of the Golden Age for both quantity and vehemence of political and theologico-political tracts issuing from the Dutch presses. Much of the argument was about provincial sovereignty, the States party-faction maintaining, in the spirit of Grotius and Oldenbarnevelt, that sovereignty in the United Provinces resided in the individual provinces alone, Orangists and Voetians that the provinces, when joining together in the Union, had each surrendered part of their sovereignty, creating a 'supreme and general sovereignty'—what modern writers would call a federal government.[54] Orangists and Voetians took the view that this 'general sovereignty' lodged in the States General or, in some cases, in the Generality defined as the 'States General together with his Illustrious Highness'. Abraham van de Velde, like other Further Reformation ideologues, insisted that the United Provinces were a 'sovereign republic' under which lodged the 'particular sovereignty of each province'.[55] Not without justification, Orangists ridiculed States party ideologues' love of citing the Swiss Confederacy as a (defensive) league of sovereign cantons comparable to the United Provinces. The Swiss example at this time attracted the States party bloc—and later Pieter de la Court and Huber—because the Swiss had a States General too but one wielding little power, the sovereignty of the individual cantons remaining unchallengeable. Orangists dismissed Switzerland as irrevelant since the Swiss maintained no large, standing army, or navy, and each canton had a separate religious policy, whereas in the Dutch state all provinces were obliged to maintain the same public Church, on the basis of the Acts of the Synod of Dordrecht. Orangists agreed that the United Provinces formed a republic. They denied that the Stadholder was a monarchical figure, incompatible with the institutions of a true republic, arguing that there was an inherent need for an 'eminent head', and that the Dutch state shared this feature with Venice and Genoa, which likewise each had its 'doge'.[56] Endorsement, and condemnation, of Grotius abounded, serving (as also later) as a kind of ideological shorthand, enabling pamphleteers and commentators to indicate, in a word, their stance on a whole complex of political, ecclesiastical, and theological questions.

With his coup, William II demonstrably altered the balance of power in the Republic, much as Maurits had done in 1618. Over the next months the

---

[53] Groenveld, *Prins voor Amsterdam*, 42–5.
[54] *Recht der Souverainiteyt*, 7; Poelhekke, *Geen blijder maer*, 37–40.
[55] [Van de Velde], *Oogen-salve*, 4r–v.
[56] *Grondigh Bericht*, 4–7, 13.

States of Holland remained quiescent. The Prince held the six regents he had arrested at Loevestein, where Grotius had once been incarcerated. There was no further opposition to his fixing troop-levels, military expenditure, or making decisions in foreign policy. The Prince used his power to draw closer to France and create tension with Spain.[57] He also tightened the screw on his regent opponents, among other steps instigating a States General enquiry into the conduct of the Dutch plenipotentiaries at Münster, to determine whether they had accepted bribes from Spain. Recalling Olden-barnevelt's fate, Pauw was now a deeply worried man. He implored the Spanish ambassador that letters from, or concerning, himself in the keeping of Spanish ministers be closely guarded and that when referring to him, Spanish officials mention him not 'with praise but with much indifference'.[58]

But whatever his ultimate intentions, the young Stadholder died too soon to consolidate the change he had brought about. For several months, the 'good patriots', as the Orangists, and devout Calvinists, called themselves, were in euphoric mood. But the euphoria was cut short. In October 1650, William II came down with a fever which turned out to be smallpox. He died, at the Hague, on 6 November. To many Reformed, who believed in divine intervention on behalf of State and Church, the totally unexpected loss of their adored Prince was as devastating as it was inexplicable. A mood of shock and dismay persisted for months. For, with his death, the new political order, and prospects for the public Church, so lately established and seemingly firm, at once collapsed. Suddenly, the States party-faction were again at the helm. The First Stadholderless era had begun. As consolation, Orangists had only the birth, in December 1650, of William II's longed-for son, William III, a birth gratefully celebrated among large sections of the public (see PLATE 16).

[57] Poelhekke, *Geen blijder maer*, 167–9.
[58] AGS estado 2076. consulta, Madrid, 25 Nov. 1650.

26

Society

❖

THE ECONOMY

Dramatic changes in economic life set in in the late 1640s resulting from a general restructuring of overseas commerce and navigation. In the years around 1647, the Dutch–Spanish conflict ceased, and a new phase, Phase Four (1647–72) of Dutch world trade primacy, began, involving vast shifts in the pattern of maritime commerce which, in turn, had ramifications for all aspects of the Dutch economy, society, and culture.[1] Since 1621, during Phase Three, Dutch overseas trade had lapsed into recession (1621–32) and then recovered in the 1630s, albeit without regaining some strands of the 'rich trades' lost after 1621. Overall, the period 1621–47 was one of hesitant growth, the setbacks in European trade being compensated for, on the one hand, by the demand for Dutch-supplied provisions of all kinds in Germany and the south Netherlands and, on the other, by the gains in colonial commerce.

The new phase in Dutch commerce and navigation was chiefly shaped by the transformation of the international situation at the end of the Thirty and Eighty Years Wars, in 1646–8. The principal determinants of the general restructuring were the lifting of the Spanish embargoes (1647), the end of the Flemish privateering campaign against Dutch shipping (1646), the cessation of Dutch–Spanish hostilities in the New World (1647), a sustained and steep drop in Dutch freight charges and marine insurance rates, the lifting of the Dutch naval blockade of the Flemish coast (1647), and the conclusion of fighting, and disbandment of armies, in Germany and the north Netherlands.

While Dutch Baltic bulk freightage, and also Dutch agriculture, were adversely affected, the main consequence of the general restructuring of the late 1640s was a rapid revitalization and diversification of the Dutch 'rich

---

[1] Israel, *Dutch Primacy*, 197–207; Israel, *Dutch Republic and the Hispanic World*, 382–5; Israel, *Empires and Entrepots*, 148–60, 209–12, 383–409; Israel, 'New History', 473–6.

trades', and supporting industries, at the expense especially of the English, Hanseatics, and Venice. Amsterdam resumed her former direct commerce with Spain, using her many advantages in commodities, shipping, and freight rates, and her financial power, to dominate large sections of it, including the remitting of Spain's subsidies to the south Netherlands and the carrying of Spain's wool and dyestuff exports, all of which had (since 1630) previously been in the hands of the English. Simultaneously, there was a strong revival of Amsterdam's Italian and Levant trades, rooted in the fall in freight rates, and greater security of Dutch shipping entering the Mediterranean, helped by the Venetian–Turkish War of 1645–69, which paralysed Venetian navigation in the Levant, enabling the Dutch to capture much of Venice's former intermediary role. Furthermore, the Dutch could now participate on a large scale in the official Spanish transatlantic trade, via Cadiz, to Spanish America and, also in the late 1640s, captured a commanding position (for the time being) in Caribbean navigation, assisted by the English Civil War, which disrupted trade between London and the English Caribbean colonies. The great impetus imparted, from 1647, to the Spanish, Spanish–American, Levant, and Caribbean trades in turn gave Amsterdam commercial control over a range of key raw materials, including Spanish wool, Turkish mohair, Spanish-American dyestuffs, mercury from Venetian Dalmatia, and Caribbean sugar, strongly reinforcing those Dutch industries geared to exporting high-value goods. This then, in turn, translated into a deeper Dutch penetration of other major European markets such as France and Russia. The further strengthening of the Dutch trade with northern Russia after 1650, for example, was essentially a by-product of the general bolstering of the Dutch overseas trading system and of Holland's industries.[2]

The expansion of the 'rich trades' from the late 1640s, and their continuing prosperity down to the early eighteenth century, is indeed fundamental to any proper understanding of the Dutch Golden Age. For practically every single Dutch export industry of importance in the seventeenth and eighteenth centuries (except for salt-refining and Leiden 'new draperies') was at its height from the late 1640s down to the early—or in some cases the middle of the—eighteenth century, industrial performance being directly, and integrally, linked to the 'rich trade' framework. Thus, production of fine cloth, which was of much greater value, and employed many more people, than the cheap 'new drapery' branches, increased in the 1640s and 1650s, as did output of camlets, a very valuable product, silks, cottons, and Dutch

---

[2] Bushkovitch, *Merchants of Moscow*, 45–6.

fine linen.[3] Whale oil processed in Holland, Delftware, paper-making, tobacco-spinning, sail-canvas, Gouda pipes, and a host of others were only just beginning to attain real importance by the (late) 1640s, and sugar-refining, though already flourishing before, expanded further after the 1640s.[4] The story was the same with the tile industry, which expanded steadily in the first half of the seventeenth century, was at its height during the second half, and remained prosperous down to the early eighteenth.[5]

The changes of the late 1640s, structural changes resulting from shifts in international relations but reinforced by a range of economic factors, led to a fundamental restructuring of Dutch overseas commerce and export-orientated industry. But the same changes also had a profound effect on the inland economy, though here the results were of a very different sort. The strengthening and expansion of Dutch commerce and industry from the late 1640s chiefly affected Holland, plus the inland tobacco-growing areas and (somewhat later) the textile districts of Twenthe and the Meierij. By contrast, the reducing of the fixed garrisons, and decay of the Zeeland transit traffic to the south Netherlands, which were just as much consequences of the end of the Eighty and Thirty Years Wars as the expansion of the 'rich trades' and industry, depressed the economy of much of the Republic's periphery and Zeeland. The result was a drastic widening of the gap in vitality between most of Holland—and some other areas—on the one hand, and large segments of the periphery, on the other, a gap of economic structures and prosperity which was to have profound consequences for social life and also politics and culture.

The acceleration at the core, and general reversal of activity on the periphery, were both rooted in the peace process concluding the Eighty and Thirty Years Wars. Previously, since the 1590s, the outer ring of fortress towns and forts, stretching from Delfzijl, in the north-east, to Sluis, in the south-west, constituted a main source of economic vitality around the outer rim of the Republic. Until the mid-1640s army garrisons constituted a sizeable proportion, and often the majority, of the population of the strongholds—Sluis, Aardenburg, Sas van Ghent, Hulst, IJzendijk, Bergen-op-Zoom, Steenbergen, Willemstad, Heusden, Breda, 's-Hertogenbosch, Grave, Maastricht, Nijmegen, Arnhem, Doesburg, and Zutphen, and further north, Coevorden, Bellingwolderzijl, Bourtange, and Delfzijl, as well as

---

[3] Posthumus, *Geschiedenis*, ii. 930–1; Slicher van Bath, *Samenleving*, 59, 200–1; Israel, *Dutch Primacy*, 262–9.
[4] Wijsenbeek-Olthuis, *Achter de gevels*, 59, 419; De Jong, 'Walvisvaart', 313; Israel, *Dutch Primacy*, 259–69, 346–58.
[5] Hoynck van Papendrecht, *Rotterdamsche plateel*, 74, 126–32.

the towns garrisoned by the Dutch across the border, in the Empire. Inevitably, the local economies of these, and their hinterlands, depended heavily on military garrisons which were large, fixed, and regularly paid, and which continually had to be supplied and equipped. Outlay on the garrisons, fortifications, stores, and weapons, as well as the garrisons' food, horses, and forage, accounted for most of the Republic's military expenditure. Thus, spending on the defensive outer ring represented a massive transfer of resources from the Republic's dynamic core to the periphery. In these provinces, it was only in Overijssel that the garrison system was a less than vital element in the local economy.

Contraction of the garrisons began in 1642 when Holland pushed through the first general reduction in the level of forces maintained since 1629.[6] The cuts were already noticeably affecting the economies of the garrison towns by the mid-1640s. But the big reductions accompanied the Spanish peace in the years 1647–51. These were drastic. The garrison at Maastricht, after 1632 the Republic's largest, contracted from 5,300 men, in 1639, to less than half of this, around 2,500, by 1651.[7] Zutphen, the second largest garrison in Gelderland, after Nijmegen, fell from around 1,450, in the early 1640s, to a mere 560 men by 1651.[8] Given that many of the men also had female companions and children, the social and economic effects of the reductions were both many and far-reaching. Of course, some places were worse hit than others, Nijmegen, for example, suffering more than Arnhem,[9] but overall the impact was severe. The population of Nijmegen, including the garrison, contracted from over 14,000, in 1645, to little more than half of this, under 8,000, by 1660 (see Table 28). Population loss on this scale paralysed not only the city but its entire hinterland. The population of Maastricht fell back from 23,000, in 1645, to 18,000 by the mid-1650s.

Admittedly, not all the consequences of peace, around the outer rim, were negative. Traffic by road, and water, to and from neighbouring parts of Germany, and the Spanish Netherlands, was now less disrupted, border tolls were reduced, and the ravages of war itself had ceased. But the last mattered less in the Dutch context than in neighbouring Germany because it had had a quite different impact on the fabric of local life there. Where, in Germany, armies ravaged the countryside, and sacked villages, in the Low Countries the war was largely static and, by mutual arrangement, both sides spared the villages and crops of the other. The phenomenon of large, fixed, and

---

[6] 't Hart, *Making of a Bourgeois State*, 44.
[7] Ubachs, *Twee heren*, 20.
[8] Frijhoff, *Gesch. van Zutphen*, 92–3.
[9] Holthuizen-Seegers and Nusteling, 'Arnhem', 87–8.

regularly paid garrisons resulted in steady payment for food, clothes, horses, forage, and prostitutes, without pillage and rapine, stimulating local agriculture, trade, and crafts. Furthermore, some major garrison towns, such as Bergen-op-Zoom, Breda, and Coevorden, were poorly placed—with respect to rivers and main trade routes—to participate in the post-1647 growth in cross-border traffic. If there were now more river ships plying the Rhine, Maas, and Scheldt than before, this tended to benefit Dordrecht and Rotterdam rather than garrison towns closer to the borders.

TABLE 28. *Population and births at Nijmegen,*
1620–1699

Decade	Births per year (annual average)	Total population
1620/29	474	13,500
1630/39	456	13,000
1640/49	458	13,100
1650/59	292	8,357
1660/69	290	8,250
1670/79	371	10,600
1680/89	456	13,200
1690/99	362	10,350

Source: Engelen, *Nijmegen*, 12–13.

Consequently, peace brought few compensations to counterbalance the impact of the garrison cuts. Suddenly, there were far fewer soldiers to be maintained and less cash in circulation. Less food and forage was required and there were fewer customers for shops and taverns. The drop in beer consumption was staggering. At Breda, one of the towns hardest hit, the value of the tax-farm for the beer excise slumped from 21,000 guilders, in 1641, to only 9,800 guilders by 1655.[10] The value of the tax on use of Breda's Weigh-House, a good index of activity, fell by more than a third between 1640 and 1651 (see Table 29). In all the garrison towns, almost every activity—tailoring, saddle-, boot-, and belt-making, innkeeping, prostitution, and not least construction and repairs on the fortifications—was drastically curtailed. An uncle of Vermeer, a military supplier and engineer, who worked at various strongholds in the 1630s and 1640s, was bankrupt within two years of the peace of Münster.[11] 'The inhabitants of this town',

---

[10] GA Breda afd. 1/la H 2001 and H 2002.   [11] Montias, *Vermeer*, 94.

the magistracy of Breda assured the *Raad van State*, in 1649, 'find themselves in a very sober and desolate condition.'[12]

The municipalities of the garrison towns strove to alleviate the impact as much as possible, especially by the traditional method of towns in decay—strengthening the guilds and guild regulations to restrict competition from outsiders and between guild members. The guild of fishermen at Zutphen obtained a ruling from the *raad*, in 1648, forbidding non-guild members fishing within the town's jurisdiction.[13] The *raad* at Breda granted the appeal of the town's crane and wharf workers, in March 1651, to tighten rules on work practices, stipulating that a minimum of four men be used for unloading market barges from Dordrecht and Rotterdam and not fewer than six for wine barges. The *raad* explained that with the 'slackness of trade, guild members were daily becoming more impoverished and that it was now almost impossible to earn one's living' and that it was necessary to prevent some dockers grabbing all the work and others and their families being left with nothing.[14]

TABLE 29. *Annual value of the tax-farm for use of the Weigh-House at Breda, 1640–1660 (guilders)*

1640/1	1,200	1650/1	800
1641/2	1,110	1651/2	705
1642/3	1,200	1652/3	545
1643/4	1,145	1653/4	480
1644/5	1,100	1654/5	410
1645/6	930	1655/6	430
1646/7	890	1656/7	460
1647/8	930	1657/8	540
1648/9	940	1658/9	640
1649/50	760	1659/60	710

Source: GA Breda afd. 1 1a H 2001 and H 2002.

Another device was to establish higher education institutions to draw students from the surrounding area and, hopefully, further afield. The Breda Illustre School was opened in September 1646. The *raad* of Nijmegen, undaunted by the fact that the States of Gelderland decided in 1648 to upgrade the academy at Harderwijk into a provincial university, resolved,

[12] GA Breda Afd. 1/1a H 249. Breda *raad* to RvS, 29 July 1649.
[13] Frijhoff, *Gesch. van Zutphen*, 114.
[14] GA Breda Afd. 1/1a Acten Mag. 1634–59, fo. 237. res. raad. 23 Mar. 1651.

in 1655, to set up their own Illustrious School for the express purpose of drawing students from the rest of Gelderland.[15] The lesser towns and *ridderschap* of the Nijmegen quarter, regarding Harderwijk as an asset of the Arnhem quarter rather than of the province as a whole, agreed to help finance the new civic academy.

But the regents knew that the only real prospect of amelioration lay in securing increases in the garrisons. No sooner had Prince William II staged his military coup against Amsterdam, in the summer of 1650, than the Nijmegen *raad* congratulated him on taking 'Holland in hand' and requested him to 'send a good number of troops . . . into garrison here'.[16] Only with the resumption of protracted warfare, from 1672, did the garrison towns begin to revive, though even then, the signs are, it was not a full recovery.

The garrisons were again much larger between 1674 and 1713 than between 1647 and the French invasion of 1672. There was also a good deal of refurbishment.[17] The fortifications of Bergen-op-Zoom, Breda, Grave, Maastricht, and many other strongholds were extensively rebuilt between 1674 and 1702 to the most advanced designs in Europe planned by the 'Dutch Vauban', Menno van Coehoorn (1641–1704), one of William III's most trusted commanders and chief engineer, the inventor of the 'Coehoorn mortar'. Yet population and activity failed to regain pre-1647 levels, because the wars of the 1672–1713 were less static than those of the 1590–1647 period and because, from the mid-1670s onwards, especially between 1689 and 1713, much of the army was stationed in Spanish Netherlands fortresses rather than Dutch strongholds. At Nijmegen both population and birthrate, in the 1690s, were still appreciably below the levels for the period 1621–47 (see Table 27).

Not all inland areas of the Republic were adversely affected by the restructuring of the economy after 1647. The negative repercussions were balanced by the positive effects of a stronger overseas trading system on inland areas such as Twenthe, the Arnhem quarter, and the Meierij of 's-Hertogenbosch. The strengthening of Dutch commerce and shipping (except in the Baltic) from the late 1640s onwards imparted fresh impetus to industry, and the cultivation of industrial crops, and the stimulus was by no means confined to the maritime seaboard. In the Meierij, from the 1650s, Leiden and Haarlem textile entrepreneurs provided employment in spinning and weaving in and around Helmond, Tilburg, and Eindhoven, farming out

[15] GA Nijmegen 102. res. raad. 2 and 14 Feb. 1655.
[16] Ibid. res. raad. 18 Aug. 1650.
[17] Kappelhof, *Belastingheffing*, 289–92.

preliminary work, on a cottage basis, with a view to boosting output of finished woollen cloth and linen at Leiden and Haarlem. In the Twenthe quarter of Overijssel there developed, especially during the last quarter of the century, a thriving linen industry, provided with flax by the peasant farmers of the neighbouring Salland quarter.[18] In the Arnhem quarter and eastern Utrecht, there was a dramatic expansion, after 1647, in cultivation of tobacco, which was then spun and blended with better-quality American tobaccos in the workshops of Amsterdam. Between 1675 and 1710 tobacco output in these areas approximately trebled.[19]

For the inland areas of the Republic, the post-1647 restructuring of large sections of Dutch economic life thus had the double effect of depressing towns and districts which were the centres of activity before 1647 and stimulating districts which, before 1647, were of little account, sparsely populated, and economically stagnant. In the maritime west, the effect of the restructuring was also a double one. For the changes galvanizing the Dutch trading system, and industry, after 1647, expanded activity in the 'rich trades', and export-orientated industries, but depressed the traditional bulk-carrying traffic. Also in recession after 1647 was the Zeeland transit traffic to the Spanish Netherlands, which had been artificially boosted, during the war, by the Dutch naval blockade of the Flemish coast, which hampered ships supplying the Flemish ports directly by sea.

The decline of Dutch bulk-carrying, or at least the traditional grain, timber, and salt commerce, was partly due to the end of the German war and effects of this on agriculture, and subsistence, throughout northern Europe. With disbandment of the armies in Germany, and gradual recovery of German agriculture, there was a progressive fall in demand for the grain, meat, fish, and dairy produce which West Frisian, and Frisian, skippers freighted—especially from Hoorn, Enkhuizen, Medemblik, and Harlingen —to Hamburg, Bremen, Stade, and Emden, whence the supplies were shipped up the Rivers Elbe, Weser, and Ems, to the armies and garrisons in north and central Germany. This flow of foodstuffs rapidly dwindled after 1650. At the same time, freightage of Baltic grain contracted, partly because there was now no need for supplies for Germany, and partly because the grain-producing areas of Poland and the Ukraine were ravaged during the Chmielnicki troubles (1648–51) and subsequent Swedish invasion of 1655. An additional factor, depressing agricultural prices, in Holland, was the rise in agricultural output in the Spanish Netherlands and England. The contraction of bulk-carrying led, in turn, to a marked decline in shipbuilding

---

[18] Slicher van Bath, *Samenleving*, 59, 200–2.   [19] Roessingh, 'Tobacco Growing', 42.

in the West Frisian area.[20] This was a purely local phenomenon, however, more than compensated for by further growth of shipbuilding in Amsterdam and Rotterdam, and especially on the Zaan, the industrial belt to the north of Amsterdam which only really came into its own with the general strengthening of Dutch commerce after 1647. The further decline in the population of Hoorn and Enkhuizen after 1650, combined with falling demand for West Frisian dairy produce in Germany, had the additional effect of depressing agriculture north of the Zaan.[21]

As bulk freightage decayed, the branches based in the West Frisian area contracted faster than the commerce as a whole. Some of what was lost to the West Frisian ports migrated to Amsterdam. But most shifted to the Wadden Islands and Frisian ports, which means that the change was, in part, from large to small vessels.[22] The bulk fleets of Hoorn and Enkhuizen consisted of large and medium-sized *fluits*. But, as both volume and profit margins receded, small vessels proved more suitable. The Frisian fleet plying the Baltic consisted mainly of tiny vessels, often of less than 20 lasts. The total of Dutch voyages to the Baltic fell from a yearly average of 1,200, in the 1640s, to 895 in the 1650s, 681 in the 1660s, and a mere 595 in the 1670s.[23] At the same time, small vessels came to predominate, boosting the shares of Friesland and the Wadden Islands. West Friesland's share of Dutch traffic passing through the Danish Sound, dropping from 30 per cent in the 1620s to 20 per cent by the 1640s, had receded to only 15 per cent by the 1660s.

But the rapid waning of Dutch Baltic bulk freightage after 1650 was outweighed by the predominant trend in Dutch maritime trade and shipping after 1647. Overall commerce, shipping, and employment in shipping expanded with only brief interruptions—despite intense English and French hostility—until the French invasion of 1672 and subsequent fighting in the Republic (1672–7). During the years 1672–7 the overseas trading system, and the main towns, were seriously damaged and a long-term deterioration of the Dutch economy set in. Nevertheless, the Dutch 'rich trades' and industry rallied, temporarily regaining most of the lost ground during the 1680s. The permanent, irreversible decline of Holland as a maritime and industrial power commenced only in, or around, 1688 with the onset of the Nine Years War and its many harmful consequences for the Dutch economy. But, even then, activity and population in the main towns did not fall far below the peak attained in 1672, and again in the 1680s,

[20] Lesger, *Hoorn*, 159.
[21] Van der Woude, *Het Noorderkwartier*, i. 184.
[22] Lesger, *Hoorn*, 151, 171.
[23] Bang and Korst, *Tabeller*, i. 1–15.

until after 1720.[24] Broadly, the economic Golden Age lasted from 1590 to about 1740.

Although some 'rich trades'—notably the Levant traffic (from 1688) and Spanish trade (from 1700)—experienced drastic decline by the end of the century, and the overall influence of the Dutch trading system in world trade diminished, most of the 'rich trades', and connected industries, held up well after the 1670s, and in a few cases continued to expand. At the same time, while some industries closely associated with Dutch world trade primacy between 1647 and 1672 collapsed before 1700—notably the camlet industry—or else ceased to grow, as with the manufacture of fine cloth at Leiden, and the processing of whale products, overall there was a continued diversification of industry down to the early eighteenth century and some of the classic industries, such as paper and fine linen, continued to grow. The traditional manufacturing towns—Haarlem, Leiden, and Delft—were clearly past their peak after 1688. But industry at Amsterdam and Rotterdam held up and the Zaan industrial belt with its hundreds of industrial windmills, processing a proliferating range of items, did not reach its peak until around 1720. The number of paper-mills on the Zaan rose from five, in 1650, to seventeen by 1670, twenty-six by 1690, and thirty-six by 1700. The total number of windmills used for processing and manufacturing in the Zaan area rose steeply from the middle of the century, climbing from about 40, in 1620, and 160, in 1640, to 584 by 1731.[25]

POPULATION

The restructuring of the economy in the period from the late 1640s until the disastrous disruption of 1672 caused several basic shifts in activity, and hence vitality, both on the seaboard and inland. The overall result was a significant growth in population where the economy continued to expand, that is in the bulk of Holland (except the North Quarter and West Frisian ports), the Veluwe, Twenthe, and Helmond–Tilburg area, with urbanization proceeding in these areas, while, at the same time, population decreased and towns stagnated, or in the depressed districts where either bulk-freightage or garrisons had been the driving force behind the economy. Taking the Republic as a whole, the upshot was a marginal population increase, and impulse towards further urbanization, down to 1688 when the Republic became sucked into a vast new bout of European warfare. But more significant than this overall trend for our understanding the processes at

[24] Israel, *Dutch Primacy*, 292–358; Nusteling, 'Strijd', 10–12.
[25] Van der Woude, *Het Noorderkwartier*, ii. 490; Davids, 'Technological Change', 97.

work, and the course of future developments, was the widening gap between economically expanding and contracting zones.

The population of the principal cities rose during the period 1647–72 at an impressive pace. The catastrophic effects of the invasion of 1672 then abruptly reversed this trend so that these cities then fell back markedly, in every respect, between 1672 and around 1678. However, this did not mark the end of urbanization in the Dutch Golden Age. For a general economic recovery ensued which gained momentum in the mid-1680s and which brought the chief Dutch urban centres back to, or more likely slightly above, the levels of population attained by 1672. Final, long-term decline of the Dutch cities, de-urbanization in the Republic, commenced only with the resumption of general warfare in 1688.[26]

The total population of the Republic at the zenith of its economic development is estimated at about 1,950,000. In 1700 the total was about the same, or slightly lower. Meanwhile, the combined population of the Republic's thirty largest towns rose from about 36 per cent of the total population, in 1650, to about 38 per cent in 1688.[27] At the same time the eight largest cities increased their share of that total for the thirty largest towns from 61 per cent to over 64 per cent, with nearly all the growth in the five largest Holland cities (see Table 30).

The largest city, Amsterdam, increased fastest between 1647 and 1672, stimulated by the commercial boom, growing by a quarter from about 150,000, in the late 1640s, to some 200,000 by 1672.[28] After falling back somewhat in the 1670s, Amsterdam resumed her expansion, rising to around 205,000 by 1700. Leiden, the second largest city, grew from around 60,000, in 1647, to 72,000 by 1672, sagged in the 1670s, recovered to around 72,000 by 1688, and then fell back again, during the Nine Years War, to about 63,000 by 1700. Amsterdam's share of the total population of the Republic rose from 8 per cent, in 1647, to about 11 per cent by 1700.

In the countryside there was demographic growth in South Holland balanced by population loss in the North Quarter. Outside Holland, the predominant trend, from the 1640s down to the early eighteenth century, was one of increasing population, except in Friesland, which was in decline from around 1670.[29] Friesland's population fell, as near as we can tell, by some 12 per cent between the 1660s and 1714, from around 147,000 to 129,000. Harlingen, the chief port, declined from 8,823, in 1689, to 7,100 by 1714. Dokkum also shrank, though the provincial capital, Leeuwarden,

[26] Nusteling, 'Periods and Caesurae', 111.
[27] Ibid. 108.
[28] Nusteling, *Welvaart en werkgelegenheid*, 235, 237.
[29] Faber, *Drie eeuwen Friesland*, i. 57 and ii. 413–15.

grew from around 13,500, in 1689, to 15,700 by 1714. But the contraction of the rural population in Friesland (and Holland north of the Zaan) was untypical of the Republic's post-1650 demographic development more generally. In most inland areas, the pattern was one of steady growth, though (owing to the stagnation of the urban economy, outside Holland) not in the cities. Overijssel's population grew appreciably, from below 70,000, in 1650, to around 107,000 by 1720.[30] Significant growth was registered in all three Overijssel quarters but was most marked in Twenthe. Stimulated by the rise of the linen industry around Almelo, Enschede, and Oldenzaal, Twenthe's share of Overijssel's total population rose from under 25 per cent, in 1650, to over 30 per cent by 1720. Meanwhile, the combined population of the three chief towns fell as a proportion of the total for the province (having reached 38 per cent around 1500) to 30 per cent in 1600, 28 per cent by 1675, and 24.5 per cent by 1720.

TABLE 30. *The population of the main Holland cities, 1635–1700 (estimates)*

	1635	1647	1672	1688	1700
Amsterdam	120,000	140,000	200,000	200,000	205,000
Leiden	55,000	60,000	72,000	72,000	63,000
Haarlem	42,000	45,000	50,000	50,000	40,000
Rotterdam	20,000	30,000	45,000	50,000	45,000
Delft	21,000	21,000	24,000	24,000	19,000
The Hague	16,000	18,000	30,000	30,000	30,000

Sources: Hart, *Geschrift en getal*, 118; Posthumus, *Geschiedenis*, iii. 882; Wijsenbeek-Olthuis, *Achter de gevels*, 27; Nusteling, *Welvaart en werkgelegenheid*, 234–5; Nusteling, 'Periods and Caesurae', 92–112; Mentink and Van der Woude, *Demografische ontwikkeling te Rotterdam*, 38–9.

Drenthe's population also grew vigorously, as did that of much of Gelderland, eastern Utrecht, and the industrial belt of the Meierij. The number of households in Drenthe grew more rapidly in the last quarter of the century than any other period of early modern times, from 4,938, in 1672, to 5,629 in 1692 but, again, Drenthe's demographic expansion was exclusively rural.[31] Coevorden stagnated, like the main Overijssel towns, declining markedly as a proportion of the province's population. A similar pattern of de-urbanization, and strong rural growth, was seen in the Arnhem quarter of Gelderland. Overall, the population of this region rose from 40,000, in 1650, to around 54,000 in 1749, a much faster rate of

[30] Slicher van Bath, *Samenleving*, 53–60.
[31] Bieleman, *Boeren op het Drentse zand*, 65, 70.

increase than occurred in the period 1500–1650.[32] However, Arnhem itself, a city of around 6,000, in 1650, contracted sharply before recovering to around 5,600 by 1749, while Harderwijk declined from 3,000 to about 2,350. The combined total of the five towns of the Arnhem quarter fell, as a proportion of the quarter's population, from 32 per cent, in 1650, to only 26 per cent a century later.[33] The United Provinces, a land of continuing urbanization along the maritime seaboard down to 1688, the year of general reversal of the long-term trend towards growth and urbanization in the Dutch economy (see p. 618 above), was simultaneously, from the 1640s, a land of de-urbanization in its landward provinces.

WORK AND MIGRATION

The impressive growth of Holland's cities between 1647 and 1688—despite the setback of the 1670s—arose not from natural increase but economic growth, boosting activity and demand for labour. Economic expansion sucked in population from elsewhere. In Holland, the maritime and urban economy experienced a quarter of a century of sustained growth from the late 1640s, which resulted in Holland's urban economy needing a considerably larger labour force than ever before—despite the shrinkage of the Baltic bulk trade. This means that expansion of the 'rich trades', and urban industry, between 1647 and 1672 generated activity and employment at an appreciably faster rate than shrinkage of Baltic bulk-carrying reduced activity and employment. Surprising though it may seem, this applies even to the numbers of seamen needed. For new jobs were being created in Mediterranean and colonial trade, and the whale fishery and navy, at an impressively faster rate than jobs were being lost in Baltic bulk-freightage (see Table 31). There were, by 1672, hundreds fewer ships, and thousands fewer seamen employed on the Baltic run,[34] while the 'rich trades', admittedly, used only a fraction as many ships. But numbers of men per ship, in the latter case, were far greater. Some of the 'great ships' used in the Levant traffic, fetching mohair, cotton, and raw silk from Smyrna, were manned by as many as 200 men each. East India ships and the vessels which sailed to Cadiz, carrying textiles and spices for re-export to Spanish America, and returning with silver, dyestuffs, and wool, likewise carried large crews. Simultaneously, employment in the whale fishery and navy rose steeply. Consequently, despite the decay of the 'mother trade', employment in Dutch

[32] Roessingh, 'Het Veluwse inwonertal', 108–9.
[33] Ibid. 96, 102.
[34] Faber, 'Decline', 119.

shipping between 1635 and 1670 increased substantially, possibly by as much as 50 per cent (see Table 31).

TABLE 31. *Manpower employed in Dutch shipping (estimates)*

	1610	1635	1670	1725
European trade	20,000	21,500	25,000	20,000
Fisheries (except whaling)	6,500	7,000	5,500	4,000
Whale fishery	0	1,000	8,000	8,000
VOC	2,000	4,000	9,000	11,000
Navy	3,000	7,000	11,000	3,500
New World trade	1,000	2,500	3,000[a]	2,000
TOTALS	33,000	44,000	64,500	52,500

[a] Including the sailors on the fleet of Curaçao barques.

Sources: PRO SP 84/166, fo. 217. 'Navigation of the United Netherlands'; Lucassen, 'Zeevarenden', 132; Bruijn and Lucassen, *Op de schepen*, 14; Van Royen, *Zeevarenden*, 25.

This rise in employment in Dutch shipping took place at a time when more labour was needed for industry, and there was no compensating loss of labour elsewhere in the economy. Consequently, it was impossible to find enough men from amongst the Dutch population, and there was a sharp increase in the proportion of foreigners—especially Danes, Norwegians, and north Germans—finding employment in Dutch ports.[35] Foreign seamen signed on in all sectors but were especially numerous where wages were lowest, in the VOC, the WIC, and the navy. There was a sharp rise in the number of foreign seamen employed by the VOC in the 1650s, to over 40 per cent of the total.[36] This fell back in the 1660s but increased again from the 1680s. The navy became heavily reliant on foreigners. The English ambassador in Denmark-Norway claimed, in 1664, on the eve of the second Anglo-Dutch War, that 'all their Norway mariners are run in to the Hollanders' service, for want of employment at home, and if [the Danish king] should command them back, the States would not be able to put their fleet to sea'.[37] Nevertheless, in some parts of the Republic a very high proportion of the adult male population continued to be employed as seamen, nearly one-sixth of the menfolk of Friesland. In West Friesland, despite the decline in bulk-freightage, the proportion may have been as high

[35] Van Royen, *Zeevarenden*, 29.
[36] Bruijn and Lucassen, *Op de schepen*, 20-1.
[37] PRO SP 75/17, fo. 191. Talbot to Bennet, Copenhagen, 11 Oct. 1664.

as a quarter. Heading the list were Texel, Vlieland, and the other Wadden Islands, where over half the available manpower earned their bread at sea.[38]

But if the restructuring of the economy after 1647 boosted employment in shipping, expansion of the labour force in industry was much more marked. At Leiden, cloth output reached a peak of 138,000 pieces, in 1671.[39] But, besides the increase in quantity of output, there was the fundamental shift away from lighter, cheaper fabrics towards fine cloth, and camlets, and these products were more labour-intensive than the *says* and *bays* of the past. The number of looms operative at Leiden scarcely increased between 1614 and 1647; but after 1647 grew rapidly, rising from 2,675, in 1648, to 3,505 by 1661, and a still higher figure by 1671.[40] By 1654, some two-thirds of the textile work-force at Leiden were employed in the *laken* and camlet industries, and only one-third in the traditional cheap branches, with the total numbers employed climbing steeply.

The growth of the labour force at Amsterdam, Leiden, Haarlem, Delft, Gouda, The Hague, Rotterdam, and on the Zaan was simultaneous with the increase in demand for men for merchant shipping, the fisheries, and navy. The only way this could be coped with was by drawing in large numbers of people from outside the main towns—from the inland provinces and from abroad. 'It is certain', wrote the Leiden manufacturer and economic writer Pieter de la Court, in 1661, 'that our manufactures, fisheries, commerce and navigation, with those who live from them, cannot be preserved here without a continual immigration of foreign inhabitants—much less increased or improved.'[41] This was correct. The main Holland towns, like main towns elsewhere in Europe at the time, showed a regular excess of deaths over births. Were the influx from outside to cease, or drastically diminish, the populations of the main towns would immediately contract disastrously.[42]

The growth of all the main Holland towns between 1647 and 1672 is all the more remarkable when we consider that, until 1670, outbreaks of plague continued to be a major negative factor. The epidemics which struck were both virulent and prolonged. Pieter de la Court noted, during the 1663–6 epidemic, that the plague had the habit in Holland of lingering for unusually long periods, with deaths continuing at two or three times the normal rate for several years running. If the Leiden outbreak of 1655 was among the worst of the Golden Age, reportedly carrying off 11,000 people, nearly 20 per cent of the population in six months, the sickness which gripped the city

[38] Van Royen, *Zeevarenden*, 31.
[39] Posthumus, *Geschiedenis*, iii. 930–1.
[40] Ibid. 938.
[41] Rowen, *The Low Countries*, 209.
[42] Wijsenbeek-Olthuis, *Achter de gevels*, 83.

in 1663, though less devastating, proved unusually persistent, lingering until the end of the decade.

The last great plague, that of 1663–9, began at Amsterdam and had little effect initially. The impact grew, however, during 1664. With the prospect of plague, as well as war with England, looming, the English ambassador commented in May: 'there are dead this last weeke to the number of 338 at Amsterdam and if the plague thus increases within, and a warre with His Majestie without, there will be little need of that vast new towne which they are making there',[43] a reference to the ambitious extension of the city then under way. The double crisis intensified, making it all the more striking that there was no let-up in the great urban renewal programmes in progress.

TABLE 32. *Deaths and death-rates per thousand in Dutch cities during plague years, 1624–1667*

Year	Amsterdam	Leiden	Rotterdam	Enkhuizen	Utrecht
1624	11,795 (112)	9,897 (200)	—	—	—
1625	6,781 (60)	—	2,500 (115)	—	—
1635	8,177 (60)	18,000 (320)	3,500 (140)	—	4,000 (140)
1636	17,193 (140)		—	2,495 (131)	
1652	—	—	—	1,526 (85)	—
1653	—	—	—	1,280 (71)	—
1654	—	10,529 (165)		1,060 (64)	—
1655	16,727 (125)	11,591 (174)	2,200 (63)	—	1,000 (30)
1663	9,752 (60)	—	—	—	—
1664	24,148 (120)	—	2,450 (61)		1,300 (40)
1666	—	—	—	1,115 (67)	
1667	—	—	—	1,000 (61)	—

Sources: Noordegraaf and Valk, *De gave Gods*, 54–5; Willemsen, *Enkhuizen*, 111; Lois, *Cronycke*, 150; Rommes, 'Pest in perspectief', 265.

'There dyed this last weeke at Amsterdam 739', Downing reported, on 29 July, 'and the plague is scattered generally over the whole country even in the little dorps and villages, and it is gott to Antwerp and Brussels.'[44] At Amsterdam and Leiden the worst was over by 1665 but elsewhere it was yet to come. In places as widely dispersed as Enkhuizen, Flushing, and Zutphen, the epidemic peaked only in 1666, the year of the Great Plague in London. A final wave of epidemic swept Leiden in 1669, carrying off five university professors, including Cocceius.

---

[43] Lister, *Life and Administration*, iii. 319.   [44] Ibid. 331.

By the late seventeenth century, there were about 100,000 people employed in the main industries, over 5 per cent of the total population of the Republic, without counting employment in shipping, a proletariat which could be sustained only by means of continuous and large-scale immigration. At Amsterdam, while the number of foreign-born immigrants marrying in the city peaked in the 1640s, it remained high and the reduction was compensated for by the rising numbers originating in other parts of the United Provinces, particularly Overijssel and Gelderland. For demographic growth in the inland provinces was, in reality, greater than appears from the net increase of population there. Indeed, a major contribution of the eastern provinces to sustaining the Dutch entrepôt, and overseas trading system, was to supply part of the immigration on which Holland's economy depended. As a proportion of the total number of outsiders marrying in Amsterdam, immigrants from Gelderland and Overijssel increased from 20 per cent in the second quarter of the seventeenth century to 42 per cent by the first quarter of the eighteenth.

TABLE 33. *The Dutch urban industrial work-force, 1672–1700 (estimates)*

sector	Numbers employed	sector	Numbers employed
Woollen textiles	35,000	Delftware and tiles	4,000
Other textiles	20,000	Paper (Zaan and Veluwe)	2,000
Shipbuilding	8,000	Sugar refineries	1,500
Brewing	7,000	Other refineries	1,500
Gouda pipes	4,000	Sail-canvas	1,500
Tobacco workshops	4,000	Soap-boiling	1,000
Distilleries	3,000	Salt-boiling	1,000
		Printing	1,000
Total	94,000		

Sources: Van Zanden, 'Economic van Holland', 603; Israel, *Dutch Primacy*, 356.

Despite the rising level of immigration from the inland provinces, most immigrants in Amsterdam continued to be foreign-born. In the 1650s, 6,677 foreign-born men married in Amsterdam as against 4,252 newcomers born in the Republic outside Amsterdam.[45] For the 1690s, the comparable figures were 5,503 against 3,932. The majority of foreign immigrants in Amsterdam were German Protestants but there were also substantial numbers of Scandinavians and German (and Portuguese) Jews. By contrast, Leiden

[45] Hart, *Geschrift en getal*, 140–2.

attracted few Scandinavians, and debarred Jews, but attracted more immigrants from the south Netherlands than Amsterdam. A vital part in building up the camlet industry, in the late 1640s, and 1650s, was played by Walloon immigrants, chiefly from Liège, Lille, and Valenciennes.[46] Like Amsterdam and Haarlem, but unlike Middelburg, Leiden also attracted large numbers of German immigrants—Lutherans, Catholics, and Calvinists. The Leiden wine-dealer Jean de Parival, himself an immigrant from Lorraine, noted, in the 1650s, that whole sections of the *laken* industry, including the cloth shearers, were dominated by Westphalians and other Germans.[47] Similarly in the mid-, and late, 1680s, the main Holland towns attracted a disproportionately large share, indeed the great bulk, of the Huguenot influx into the United Provinces.

A high proportion of the VOC's soldiers and sailors came from the landward provinces and north-west Germany. Many non-Hollanders served under Van Tasman (himself an Ommelander) on the voyage which discovered New Zealand, in 1642.[48] Often such men, like Van Tasman himself, later settled, in retirement, at Batavia. Similarly, the VOC's colonists in South Africa reflected the predominance of the landward provinces and north-west Germany, as did the Dutch colonists in New Netherland and, to an extent, Surinam. The Cape Colony grew slowly under its first governor, Jan van Riebeeck (1652–62), but what colonization there was stemmed chiefly from the landward provinces and north-west Germany. A survey of settlers, compiled in 1664, lists 303 white people, of whom Hollanders and Zeelanders were a small minority. A majority of the native Dutch-speakers came from the landward provinces and over one-third were German or Scandinavian.[49] This pattern then persisted throughout the history of Dutch South Africa. As late as 1806 it was estimated that only about 50 per cent of the white population were descended from Dutch immigrants, most of the rest being German (27 per cent) or Huguenot (17 per cent).

THE HUGUENOT INFLUX

The Huguenot influx following the Revocation of the Edict of Nantes (1685) in France was a factor of some significance in Dutch history, but not as significant as has often been supposed. The total number of Huguenot refugees settling in the Republic in the decade following the Revocation has

---

[46] Posthumus, *Geschiedenis*, iii. 908, 913.
[47] Enschedé, 'Jean Nicholas de Parival', 82.
[48] Slot, *Abel Tasman*, 45, 58.
[49] Pauwels, *Verzamelde opstellen*, 52–3.

recently been estimated at between 35,000 and 50,000,[50] but may well have been less than 35,000. At most, Huguenot immigrants amounted to about 2 per cent of the total Dutch population and some 7 per cent of the population of the thirty largest towns. This was a substantial if not enormous accretion of urban population, all the more valuable to the urban economy because of the relative affluence of many of the immigrants and their high level of skills.

The Huguenot immigration occurred at a time when commerce and industry were recovering from the setback of the war of 1672–7. The population of the main towns had not yet fully regained the level of 1672, which, combined with the impact of the vast urban extension projects of the 1660s, meant that in all the main towns, including Amsterdam, house rents were markedly lower than in the past and accommodation and work premises easier to find.[51] The timing of the Huguenot immigration, in other words, was fortunate from the point of view of both the immigrants and the host society: a gap had opened up, before their arrival, which they were eminently suited to fill.

The Holland and Zeeland towns competed for Huguenots—and their money and skills—with each other and also with the inland towns. Occupied or besieged by the French and Munsterites in the years 1672–4, Utrecht, Amersfoort, Deventer, Zwolle, Nijmegen, Arnhem, Zutphen, and Groningen had suffered even greater damage than the cities of the maritime seaboard and now eagerly sought immigrants and new vitality. The States of Zeeland and Friesland, both provinces being now in the grip of deepening recession and population loss, were actively searching for ways to stimulate local economic life and showed keen interest in schemes to attract Huguenots. In February 1686, the Frisian States resolved to fund the salaries of ten Huguenot pastors willing to settle in the province and help establish Huguenot congregations.[52]

Creating French-speaking Reformed congregations, under the supervision of the Synod of the Walloon Church, affiliated to the Dutch Reformed Church and, in effect, an extension of the public Church, was a favourite method of drawing Huguenot immigrants. Most main Holland and Zeeland towns had originally acquired 'Walloon' communities and churches long before, during the great influx from the south Netherlands, in the 1580s. Some were even older. There had been a French-speaking Reformed congregation in Dordrecht since at least 1577. Subsequently, many garrison

[50] Buning, Overbeek and Vermeer, 'Huisgenoten', 357.
[51] Nusteling, *Welvaart en werkgelegenheid*, 262.
[52] ARH PR 383, fo. 317. res. SF 20 Feb. 1686.

towns also acquired 'Walloon' churches, Maastricht in 1633, Nijmegen in 1644, and Hulst in 1649. By 1640, there were twenty-five 'Walloon' congregations and thirty-five serving preachers under the Walloon Synod.[53] But, by 1685, many communities were in decay so that while, in the late 1680s, some towns were endeavouring to establish Walloon congregations, others, which had long possessed them, strove to provide better premises, facilities, and preachers' salaries. New 'Walloon' congregations arose in Gelderland at Arnhem (1684), Zutphen (1686), Tiel (1686), Harderwijk (1687), Zaltbommel (1687), and Doesburg (1688); in Friesland at Harlingen (1686), Sneek (1686), and Franeker (1686); in Zeeland at Veere (1686) and Tholen (1688); and in the Generality Lands at Cadzand (1686) and Bergen-op-Zoom (1686).[54] Even the States of Drenthe established a Huguenot congregation, complete with preacher and subsidized housing, at Dwingelo.[55]

But most of these new congregations remained extremely small. The bulk of the Huguenot immigrants in the United Provinces settled in just seven cities—Amsterdam, Leiden, Haarlem, Rotterdam, The Hague, Delft, and Utrecht.[56] Approximately one-sixth of the total, over 5,000, settled in Amsterdam. The Hague appears to have been the second largest community, numbering around 2,750, with Rotterdam third.

The influx of Huguenots had a substantial impact on Dutch economic life, their arrival coinciding with, and materially contributing to, the acceleration in the recovery of the 'rich trades' and industry in the years 1685–8. But the boom did not continue long after their arrival, the Dutch economy suddenly going into reverse, following the great Amsterdam crash of August 1688. The Huguenots undoubtedly did much to strengthen the Dutch silk industry. They opened many fashion boutiques in Amsterdam, The Hague, and elsewhere, and Huguenot dressmakers, hatmakers, wigmakers, and watchmakers introduced new standards of elegance and taste. Nevertheless, there was a tendency at the time (especially in France) to exaggerate the Huguenot contribution. Beyond the silk industry, and world of fashion, Huguenots, in fact, found relatively few openings for their capital and skills in the Republic. Although Huguenots had been prominent in the paper and glass industries in France, before 1685, and many Huguenots active in these industries emigrated, this had little impact on the Dutch scene. The major expansion of the Dutch paper industry, on the Zaan, in the last quarter of

[53] Enschedé, 'Jean Nicholas de Parival', 76.
[54] Buning, Overbeek, and Verveer, 'Huisgenoten des geloofs', 359.
[55] ARH PR 491 res. SO 5 Apr. 1688.
[56] Nusteling, 'The Netherlands and the Huguenot Émigrés', 21.

the seventeenth century, and early eighteenth, was not due to the Huguenots.[57] Huguenots did set up glass factories in the Republic but most soon
failed.[58] Moreover, the crash of 1688, and subsequent slump, caused heavy
losses on the Amsterdam Exchange, and through commercial bankruptcies,
to Huguenots no less than other Dutch businessmen. Many of the new
Huguenot silk enterprises failed at this point, including the chief Huguenot
business in Groningen. Following the Glorious Revolution in Britain, in
1688-9, not a few Huguenots who had previously settled on Dutch soil
moved on to England; also, where most Huguenots emigrating from France
previously chose the Republic as the most promising refuge, after 1688, new
emigrants preferred England, a sure sign that Britain was now replacing the
United Provinces as western Europe's foremost land of opportunity.[59] After
the setting up of the Bank of England, in 1690, Huguenots also preferred to
deposit their savings in London rather than Amsterdam, rates of interest in
England being appreciably higher.

WAGES AND LIVING STANDARDS

Wages remained extremely high, by comparison with neighbouring countries, especially in the main cities of Holland, and Dutch employers'
complaints that they had to pay their workers far more than did competitors
in England, Germany, or the south Netherlands, often twice as much, were
broadly correct. Proposals for glass manufacture in Haarlem, in 1679, noted
that where glass-workers in Liège received the equivalent of 8 to 10 stuivers
per day, their counterparts in Holland earned 18 to 24 stuivers per day.[60] A
comparably wide wage gap pertained throughout the industrial sector.

But the level of nominal wages in Holland was strongly influenced by the
high rents and heavy taxation, so that one must not conclude too readily
that real wages were especially high. Moreover, even if real wages did exceed
real wages elsewhere, it might still be argued that real earnings were being
progressively eroded not just by the generally harsher conditions, and
heavier taxation that applied from the 1670s onwards, but because Dutch
manufacturers, increasingly squeezed by English and French competition,
were forced to cut prices, and accept lower profits, and had little option but
to become more forceful in cutting costs, above all wage costs. Employers
had various ploys at their disposal and could count on the help of the town
councils. One of the few labour riots to break out at Leiden during the

[57] Enschedé, 'Papier en papierhandel', 186-8.
[58] Klein, 'Nederlandse glasmakerijen', 31-4.
[59] Nusteling, 'The Netherlands and the Huguenot Émigrés', 22, 25.
[60] GA Haarlem gildenarch. 35, Anthonie Maire, 'Propositien', fo. 2.

Golden Age occurred in October 1671, with cloth output at its peak. The rioters were children from the city's orphanages employed as temporary forced labour spinning yarn. They yelled that the 'Walloons' heartlessly exploited them, making them work too hard and providing insufficient food.[61]

During the 1650s and 1660s there was a definite tendency for some nominal wage rates to decline. According to a complaint submitted at Leiden, in 1663, 'wages of working folk here have been reduced by a full third over the last fifteen years'.[62] But it would be wrong to conclude from this that during the decades trade and industry flourished most the work-force conspicuously failed to share in the Republic's economic success, suffering declining living standards, while employers and merchants prospered.[63] For such complaints refer to piece-rates at a time when the general restructuring of the late 1640s, bolstering the 'rich trades' and connected industries, boosted demand for labour and entailed fundamental changes in the pattern of employment. At Leiden, most textile workers shifted over, during the 1640s and 1650s, from work in the declining 'new draperies' to the expanding *laken* and camlet industries, where piece-rates were far higher. Thus, even if nominal wages were receding, much or most of the work-force was still earning more by the 1660s than they had in the 1640s. Similarly, at Amsterdam, the rising industries—sugar-refining, diamonds, tobacco-processing, cotton and silk manufacture—required more training and expertise but were also better paid.

Besides the impact of the restructuring on patterns of employment, several additional factors affected living standards favourably. Thus, the purchasing power of wages was boosted by the general trend, after 1660, for agricultural prices, and food costs, to fall. This continued over a long period but was especially noticeable in the 1660s when grain prices on the Amsterdam Exchange fell precipitately, the price of Baltic rye by more than half.[64] Another significant factor, from the late 1660s (initially as a result of the urban extension programmes and the building boom), was the fall in the cost of housing and rents at Amsterdam, Leiden, Haarlem, and probably all the main Holland towns.[65] Cheaper housing was especially a feature of the 1680s (see Table 34).

Recent research relating to Amsterdam indicates that the purchasing power of workers' wages rose between 1650 and the 1680s by roughly 20

[61] *Briefwisseling . . . Van der Goes*, ii. 279.
[62] Posthumus, *Geschiedenis*, iii. 652.
[63] Ibid. 650–2; Nagtegaal, 'Stadsfinanciën', 101, 105.
[64] Posthumus, *Inquiry*, i. 574–5, 20.
[65] Nusteling, *Welvaart en werkgelegenheid*, 131, 137.

per cent.[66] Thus, after taking account of the restructuring of employment and making allowance for increased productivity, through technical innovation, which often made it possible to earn more even where piece-rates were reduced (as in some sectors of the Leiden textile industry), it appears likely that Phase Four (1647–72) generated a solid improvement in living standards for much of the working population. In the case of Leiden, this supposition is strengthened by the rapid increase in the number of affluent artisans in the city from the 1640s onwards (see Table 35). Whereas the proportion of rich men, with high tax assessments, in Leiden fell back sharply between 1623 and 1644 and then recovered by the 1670s, the increase in the numbers of modestly affluent, assessed at between one and three thousand guilders, continued throughout but accelerated rapidly from the 1640s. At Gouda, there was a similar general contraction of wealth during Phase Three with recovery commencing around 1648, and continuing to around 1688, albeit the proliferation of small fortunes was not so marked as at Leiden.[67]

TABLE 34. *Index of house-rents at Leiden,*
1640–1689

	Index		Index
1640/44	221	1665/69	222
1645/49	245	1670/74	219
1650/54	250	1675/79	210
1655/59	241	1680/84	194
1660/64	236	1685/89	193

Note: Rent levels of 1580 = 100.
Source: Posthumus, *Geschiedenis*, iii. 1019–21.

Real wages improved in Holland after 1650 in part because the cost of living decreased. But the latter did not fall as much as it might have done had the guilds been weaker than they were. There is clear evidence that the bakers' guilds in particular succeeded in increasing profit margins by preventing the full decline in grain prices from being passed on to the consumer in lower bread prices.[68] It has even been argued that workers in Holland and Utrecht were worse off than workers in the cities of the eastern provinces if differences in bread prices and other retail prices, as well as differentials in rents, are taken into account.[69] Though this may seem unlikely at first glance, given the continuous immigration to the western

---

[66] Posthumus, *Geschiedenis*, iii. 1010; Lesger, *Huur en conjunctuur*, 67.
[67] Klein, 'Heffing', 47–8.
[68] Van Zanden, *Rise and Decline*, 134–7.
[69] Ibid.

seaboard from the eastern provinces, it has to be considered as a real possibility. For it is indeed true that the higher margin of nominal wages in Holland needed to be very substantial indeed if it was to compensate for the higher food prices, rents, and excises on drink and tobacco. But the key issue here is not real wages but real earnings. For the towns in the east were stagnant and provided few employment opportunities either for newcomers or any increase in the native work force, the guilds, as in Holland, exercising a tight hold over wide sections of the urban economy. For the migrant skilled or unskilled worker, Dutch or foreign, the cities of Holland offered far greater opportunities than those in the east for finding work or, by changing one's employment, better-paid work.

TABLE 35. *Assessed wealth among Leiden householders,*
1623–1675

Tax Class	1623	1644	1675
1. Rich artisans/petit bourgeois (1,000–3,000 guilders)	576	617	824
2. Bourgeois (3,000–10,000 guilders)	697	669	687
3. The rich (10,000–50,000 guilders)	485	345	481
4. The very rich (over 50,000 guilders)	71	53	79

Source: Posthumus, *Geschiedenis*, iii. 1010.

RURAL SOCIETY

The combined effect of a growing rural population and shrinking urban economy in the east of the Republic was a mounting spiral of rural deprivation and poverty which became an increasingly striking feature of the Dutch scene after 1647. From the late 1660s, the agricultural slump also extended its grip over the maritime west and Friesland. But where, in the west, until 1688, the cities continued to expand as a proportion of total population, in the east the towns contracted and it was the rural population which inexorably grew as a proportion of the whole. In Overijssel and Drenthe population increased faster during the late seventeenth century than at any other period between 1500 and the early nineteenth century. There was little alternative but to bring more inferior, and previously barely used, land into cultivation. In Drenthe, over the century 1650–1750, approximately 8 per cent more land came under the plough, often of very poor quality.[70] Throughout Overijssel, during the late seventeenth century,

[70] Bieleman, *Boeren op het Drentse zand*, 65, 212.

and early eighteenth, there was a marked increase in the number of landless rural poor.[71] Even in the Meierij, where there was less population increase than in Overijssel, Drenthe, and Gelderland, the fall in dairy and grain prices, and consequent drop in the value of farms and demand for rural labour, led to a noticeable increase in rural poverty.

At the same time, as the relative political and economic weight of the towns in the east contracted, a phenomenon most marked in Overijssel and Gelderland, the grip of the *jonkers* on office-holding, taxation, and the administration of justice, above all in the countryside, inexorably increased. Doubtless the growing power of the nobles, noticeable particularly during the Orangist ascendancy between 1675 and 1702, was also in part a compensation for the decline in noble incomes from land. In 1683, the *ridderschap* of the Arnhem quarter pushed through new rules for rural taxation in their quarter, approved by William III as 'First Noble' of the quarter, which gave local *jonkers* an unprecedented degree of control over the setting of assessments and mechanics of collection.[72]

The great Dutch agricultural depression, still local, affecting only the inland areas, and north Brabant, in the 1650s and early 1660s, became general in the late 1660s. The end of the Thirty Years War, and falling off of agricultural exports, by sea, to north Germany undoubtedly exerted a negative influence already earlier. But the agricultural recovery in Germany and the south Netherlands took time to gather momentum and its effects were masked, during the 1650s, by disruption of grain imports from the Baltic caused by the troubles in Poland. After 1662, grain and dairy prices fell dramatically, as they did all over Europe but with a greater impact on Dutch agriculture, and rents, because the Republic had been the only west European country regularly exporting and re-exporting great quantities of agricultural produce. Also contributing to the glut and price slump, after 1660, was the emergence of England as a regular exporter of grain and dairy produce.

The Dutch seaboard was still cushioned, for a few years, by the second Anglo-Dutch War (1664–7), which paralysed seaborne commerce in northern Europe, curbing grain imports by sea. The temporary resurgence of grain and dairy prices, in Holland, even encouraged some new investment in agriculture and land reclamation.[73] But, with the end of the war, a precipitate decline in dairy, grain, and land prices set in, plunging the countryside into a slump which was to continue for a century. By January 1669, the hire value of prime agricultural land in Holland had sunk to some

---

[71] Slicher van Bath, *Samenleving*, 278.
[72] Verstegen, *Gegoede ingezetenen*, 64.
[73] *Briefwisseling . . . Van der Goes*, ii. 21.

30 per cent below the level of two years before, a ruinous drop for nobles, urban investors, and farmers alike. At a stroke, landed property lost its allure. The noble family of Van Mathenesse were obliged, in 1670, to hire out farms on South Holland polder land at scarcely more than half the 23 guilders per *morgen* accruing a few years before.[74] The board administering the property of the young Prince of Orange decided, in January 1671, not to rent out a batch of farms near The Hague, since the best offers amounted to little more than half the rent obtained five years previously.[75]

There was much talk among the nobility and rich farmers (and doubtless also among poorer farmers) as to the causes of the *malaise*. The prevailing view was that the crisis stemmed from the glut due to the simultaneous resumption of grain imports from the Baltic and of grain, and dairy, imports from Britain, as well as butter from Ireland. There were proposals in the provincial assemblies to help landowners and farmers by imposing higher duties on food imports.[76] It was easy to win support for such measures in the lesser provinces, where the nobility were politically dominant. The States of Friesland, for example, pressed, in November 1670, for a 25 per cent tariff increase on imports of butter, cheese, and meat, because of the 'general complaint of our good inhabitants concerning the wretched prices and sales of their dairy produce which is chiefly caused by excessive importing of English, Scots, and other foreign butter'.[77] But decisions about tariffs—and tariffs were a Generality matter decided in the States General—were made not by the nobility of lesser provinces but the regents of Holland, and they were more impressed by the advantages of cheap food for Holland's urban population, and the need to safeguard bulk-carrying and re-exports, than the consequences for nobles and farmers. By 1690, North Holland farm rents had dropped by 40 per cent since the 1650s.[78]

Owing to the fall of cheese and butter prices numerous rural wage labourers lost their jobs, and left the land, and, at least in the west, many farmers sold up and departed.[79] Depopulation of the countryside occurred particularly in the West Frisian region and coastal Friesland. Two features of the demographic decline in Friesland clearly point to the agricultural recession as the prime cause of depopulation: the decline was more marked in the countryside than the towns (down to around 1720)—when the main Dutch economic collapse began—and depopulation in the countryside was

[74] Baars, 'Gesch. van het grondbezit', 130.
[75] *Briefwisseling . . . Van der Goes*, ii. 221.
[76] Ibid. 76, 180.
[77] ARH PR 377. res. SF 19 Nov. 1670.
[78] Van der Woude, *Het Noorderkwartier*, ii. 530.
[79] Van Zanden, 'Prijs van de vooruitgang', 89.

confined to the richer, more productive area of clay soils, on the coastal side. On the poor soil of the area called the Wouden adjoining Overijssel and Drenthe, where production was for local use, there was, as in those provinces, demographic increase rather than loss.[80]

Another consequence of the agricultural slump was the sudden slackening in land reclamation, from the late 1660s, throughout Holland, Zeeland, Friesland, and Groningen. In the half century 1665–1714, land reclamation proceeded at only one-third of the rate of the previous half-century.[81] But the most crucial consequences of the slump for Dutch society were the contrasting responses in terms of land use, and tenure, as between maritime west and inland east. On the richer clay soils in the west, small farmers tended to sell up and leave the land, along with thousands of landless labourers, and move elsewhere, mostly to nearby cities. Larger landowners and nobles, having more staying power, were to some extent able to reinforce their holdings, buying adjoining small farms cheaply. Thus the trend was towards rural depopulation and larger farms. By contrast, in the inland provinces, and south-east Friesland, the tendency was for smallholders to proliferate, farms to become smaller, and the problem of rural poverty to grow more acute.

But in all provinces, and soil zones, landowners and farmers resorted to new agricultural strategies calculated to meet the crisis and yield improved returns. Labour-intensive solutions were useless in the maritime west. For here the pull of better wages in the still dynamic towns left no alternative but to shed labour. By contrast, further inland, where labour was cheap, and the option of non-agricultural work less immediately available, labour-intensive alternatives to producing food made good sense. In eastern Utrecht and the Arnhem quarter, as well as the neighbouring duchy of Cleves, the most favoured solution was to cultivate tobacco. The rate of increase in tobacco production in these areas after 1670 is, indeed, astounding. Between 1675 and 1710, tobacco output in Utrecht and Gelderland approximately trebled.[82] In Overijssel and northern Brabant the main shift was to flax for the linen industry. In Zeeland farmers grew more madder, a dyestuff used in the textile industry. The rapid spread of tobacco cultivation east of Utrecht further accentuated the rise of the small peasant farmer, and landless labourer, in the inland areas. For tobacco required an abundance of additional labour at certain times of the year. It was perfectly suited to regions where small holdings, a growing population, and low wages, allowed small peasant farmers to obtain cheap seasonal labour as and when needed.

[80]   Faber, *Drie eeuwen Friesland*, i. 61.
[81]   De Vries, *Dutch Rural Economy*, 194.
[82]   Roessingh, 'Tobacco Growing', 39–42.

27

Confessionalization, 1647–1702

❖

THE RISE OF TOLERATION

The Dutch Republic became a freer, more flexible society after 1630, at least as regards religion and thought, if not life-style. Remonstrants, Lutherans, Mennonites, Collegiants, Jews, and Catholics all benefited from this change. At Amsterdam, it first became usual for Catholics to have their children baptized not in the public Church but by Catholic priests in the late 1640s.[1] The same shift occurred in Rotterdam slightly earlier, in the 1630s,[2] and at Leiden, somewhat later, in the 1650s.[3] It was indeed during the 1650s that all the large former Counter-Remonstrant towns in Holland—Leiden, Haarlem, Gouda, and Enkhuizen—finally ceased breaking up Catholic conventicles and harassing Catholic priests. The Reformed consistory at Haarlem complained to the burgomasters, in June 1665, about the great change which had taken place in the city over the last ten years, with whole streets and quarters assuming a Catholic character and priests no longer concealing their activity.[4]

Yet, as the complaint of the consistory shows, there was still—even in Holland, and more so in the lesser provinces—widespread resistance to the growth of toleration. It would be wrong to suppose that toleration was now broadly accepted in Dutch society. Since the 1630s most regents in Holland were inclined to a tolerant policy but by no means all. A preacher at Utrecht observed in a pamphlet, in 1650, that while most Holland regents were 'Espanolized, libertine Arminians who have no religion in their hearts' and who, though nominally members of the public Church, deliberately excluded men zealous for the Reformed faith from positions of influence and power, there were also some who were 'well-intentioned'.[5] Nor did he

---

[1] Nusteling, *Welvaart en werkgelegenheid*, 237.
[2] Mentink and Van der Woude, *Demografische ontwikkeling*, 44.
[3] Posthumus, *Geschiedenis*, iii. 880.
[4] GA Haarlem kerkeraad 10/8. res. 9 June 1665.
[5] [Van de Velde], *Oogen-salve*, B, D.

despair of changing the balance. Rather his perception was of a continuing struggle for control of the public sphere, an unrelenting *Kulturkampf*, pervading politics, education, and life-style, as well as the public Church.

The Republic was a society in which theologically argued and politically concerted intolerance remained a potent force. Adherents of intolerance had had to retreat somewhat from the position of Saravia, Gomarus, or Arnoldi. But they had by no means given up the fight. Gisbertus Voetius, head of the anti-Cartesian campaign, doyen of the university of Utrecht, and chief spokesman of Calvinist orthodoxy, had by the 1640s retreated to a doctrine of limited toleration under pressure of trends which could not be reversed, but could perhaps be checked.[6] Catholic practice would remain under tight restriction, papist 'superstition' combated, above all those who denied the divinity of Christ, and the Trinity, should not be tolerated at all but rooted out. Moreover, in his view, not only must State, and public Church, eradicate professed Socinians and deists but also concealed 'Socinians' mingling amongst the Mennonites and Remonstrants.[7] The Reformed Church should assist the lesser Churches to reinforce, and purify, their faith in the divinity of Christ and doctrine of the Trinity.

The restrictions on Catholic worship, confining services to inconspicuous 'hidden chapels', as they were called, were not just a vestige of the past, a mere formality to veil the growing reality of toleration. Rather concealment, and the segregation which resulted, were fundamental to the fabric of Dutch life. There was still widespread opposition to Catholic worship, amongst large sections of the population, and 'Arminian' regents needed to be on their guard. During the 1650s, the Catholic Vicar Apostolic at Utrecht still distinguished between liberal towns in Holland, above all Amsterdam and Rotterdam, and cities such as Leiden and Haarlem where official and popular attitudes remained hostile.[8] It was still possible that the increased freedom Catholics had gained would be cut back, as happened at Utrecht, during the 1630s and 1640s, when the views of Voetius gained ground and anti-Catholic attitudes intensified.[9]

Furthermore, while orthodox Calvinists regarded most Holland regents as not 'well-intentioned', practically all claimed to be members of the public Church and its protectors. Without so professing one could not participate in civic government. Even Adriaen Paets, the most resolute champion of toleration among the 'Arminian' regents of Rotterdam during the third quarter of the century, a man of pronounced Remonstrant sympathies,

[6] De Jong, 'Voetius en de tolerantie', 115.
[7] Voetius, *Politica Ecclesiastica*, ii. 538–40, 542–4, 551.
[8] *Archief aartsbisdom Utrecht*, xi. 79, 87, 118, 151.
[9] Ibid. x. 179.

nevertheless attended services in the Reformed Church, a practice verging on hypocrisy but indispensable to his political career.[10] Even the most liberal of the States party ideologues, the Leiden manufacturer Pieter de la Court, a man outside active politics who argued the necessity of freedom of religion in republics, urging the need to tolerate Catholicism and attract more immigrants of diverse religions to the Holland towns, to nourish trade and industry, nevertheless accepted that the welfare of the Republic, of any republic, necessitated some not inconsiderable limitations on toleration.[11] De la Court affirmed that a republic required a state Church, favoured above other Churches, to which everyone in government and administration had to belong. He saw no alternative to excluding persons belonging to dissenting religions from public office. Furthermore, he accepted that tolerated Churches had to be closely supervised by the magistracy and, in the case of the Catholics, could be permitted to meet only in small gatherings, in the homes of reliable citizens, ministered to by priests supervised by civic government.[12]

Given the special status of the public Church, its resources and political backing, monopoly of preaching to large congregations, and possession of practically all buildings which looked like churches, it is not surprising that (except in the Generality Lands, Twenthe quarter of Overijssel, and eastern part of the county of Zutphen) the Reformed Church was the most successful in the race to confessionalize the populace. The Catholic Church was the only other which had some success, and then only to a modest extent. Other Churches and spiritual movements in the United Provinces either lost ground during the second half of the century, as in the case of the Remonstrants and Mennonites, or else gained in numbers only locally owing to immigration from abroad, as with the Lutherans, Jews, and Quakers.

Foreign observers often perceived the Republic as an open arena in which religions proliferated, and prospered, without hindrance. By the 1670s and 1680s, a few foreign writers, such as Sir William Temple or Gregorio Leti, viewed Dutch toleration with an approving eye; but most disapproved. The book which most emphatically claimed the United Provinces as Europe's haven of toleration *par excellence* was not a eulogy but a subtle exercise in defamation, the work of a Swiss Protestant officer, J. B. Stouppe, in the service of Louis XIV. Stouppe, in his *Religion des Hollandois* (1673), proclaimed the Republic the most tolerant of European societies not to extol

---

[10] Roldanus, 'Adriaen Paets', 153.
[11] De la Court, *Aanwysing*, 60, 65–6, 382, 398.
[12] Rees, *Verhandeling*, 36–7.

but to discredit it,[13] accounting Dutch toleration a product of the indifference, and insincerity, of the regents, the inevitable result of which was a fragmented society. He held that the Dutch were now split into three roughly equal groupings—Reformed, Catholics, and 'sectaires', by which he meant not only Mennonites, Remonstrants, Lutherans, and Jews but also Quakers, Socinians, Collegiants, Spiritualists, deists, and Spinozists.[14] Stouppe was actually the first writer to note the impact of Spinoza on Dutch society, characteristically adding that while Spinoza overturns 'absolument les fondements de toutes les religions', practically no one in the Dutch Republic took the trouble to refute him,[15] a charge subsequently rebutted by Bayle, in his attack on Spinoza, in his *Dictionnaire*.[16]

Stouppe's book elicited an angry response from Dutch Reformed critics. Jean Brun, preacher to the Walloon church at Nijmegen, published a rebuttal, accusing Stouppe of presenting a distorted picture. Brun observed that foreigners were always astonished by the religious diversity in the United Provinces, but had an exaggerated notion of it because the few places they visited—especially Amsterdam and Rotterdam—were precisely those where Remonstrants, 'sectaires', and Spinozists tended to congregate. Brun conceded that Catholics were numerous throughout the United Provinces, but insisted they amounted to nothing like one-third of the population.[17]

Leaving aside the Generality Lands and Twenthe, it is clear that (though increasing) Catholics indeed amounted to far less than one-third of the Dutch population. The Catholics increased most in Amsterdam where, after 1630, they enjoyed the greatest freedom. In 1656, the Catholic authorities themselves estimated Amsterdam's Catholics at 30,000, which, since the city was then over the 150,000 mark, was equivalent to around 20 per cent of the total.[18] By 1700 we can estimate the Catholic population of Amsterdam with greater accuracy from the baptism statistics—since by that date practically all Catholics were having their children baptized by Catholic priests. Making allowance for a Jewish population (which does not appear in the figures) amounting to around 3 per cent of the total, and a slight margin for other sects not included, we see that the city's Catholic population amounted to slightly under 25 per cent of the total, similar to the level attained in Haarlem (see Table 36).[19]

[13] Basnage, *Annales*, 135–7; Bots, 'Tolerantie', 660.
[14] Stouppe, *Religion des Hollandois*, 69.
[15] Ibid. 65–6.
[16] Bayle, *Dictionnaire*, iii. 2633.
[17] Brun, *Véritable religion des Hollandois*, 165–6.
[18] *Archief aartsbisdom Utrecht*, xi. 132.
[19] De Jongste, *Onrust aan het Spaarne*, 60.

Elsewhere in Holland—except Alkmaar and Hoorn—Catholics generally formed a smaller proportion of the population. In some cities, such as Leiden where they approached 20 per cent by 1700, or Rotterdam where the Catholic population has been estimated at 16 per cent,[20] proportions were not vastly less than at Amsterdam and Haarlem. But in Delft, in 1700,

TABLE 36. *Reformed, Lutheran, Remonstrant, and Catholic baptisms at Amsterdam, 1631–1700*

Decade	Reformed[a]	Lutherans	Remonstrants	Catholics	Total
1631/40	36,047	7,600	483	320	41,450
1641/50	44,543	11,878	646	1,512	58,573
1651/60	36,979	11,947	607	1,989	51,522
1661/70	41,060	13,025	463	6,153	60,701
1671/80	40,934	12,520	592	9,535	63,581
1681/90	41,043	11,700	565	12,027	65,335
1691/1700	43,618	11,778	506	15,031	70,933

[a] Including Walloons and Huguenots.

Source: Nusteling, *Welvaart en werkgelegenheid*, 237.

TABLE 37. *Protestant and Catholic baptisms at Leiden, 1640–1700*

Decade	Protestant	Catholic	Total
1640/49	20,777	217	20,994
1650/59	19,103	1,526	20,329
1660/69	20,553	3,063	23,613
1670/79	17,082	2,985	20,167
1680/89	18,307	3,714	22,021
1690/99	16,915	3,628	20,541

Source: Posthumus, *Geschiedenis*, iii. 880.

Catholics amounted to only about 9 per cent of the population;[21] and in Dordrecht and Enkhuizen (where, as late as 1656, Catholics still lived 'sub persecutione') less still. The report of 1656 tells us that there were only a few hundred Catholics in the towns, and districts, of Schoonhoven and Oudewater. Certainly there were parts of the Holland countryside, notably between Leiden and Gouda, and between Haarlem and Hoorn, where there were substantial numbers of Catholics. But there were also areas with very

[20] Mentink and Van der Woude, *Demografische ontwikkeling*, 47–8.
[21] Wijsenbeek-Olthuis, *Achter de gevels*, 413.

few. On the South Holland islands of Goeree and Overvlakee there were no more than a few hundred Catholics.[22] According to Brun, a more reliable source than Stouppe, The Hague in 1675 had a total population of 30,000, of whom only 4,000 were Catholics.[23] Thus, when De la Court, in his *Aanwysinge*, held that, even if Catholics were hostile to the Republic, they could not seriously threaten its security, amounting at most to 20 per cent of the population,[24] he would seem to have been reckoning by what he knew of his own city, Leiden, giving an estimate which was, in fact, too high, for the territory of the Seven Provinces as a whole.

Outside Holland and Utrecht, Catholicism was generally weaker. According to Brun, in Zeeland there were practically no Catholics. In fact, Catholicism did have some strength at and around Goes but, with the exception of South Beveland, there were, indeed, remarkably few Catholics in Zeeland.[25] In Friesland, the Catholic Church benefited from the substantial number of Catholic nobles. Nevertheless, the number of priests in the province, twenty-eight in 1640, still remained at twenty-eight in 1689, while Catholic numbers were static or declining, amounting in the late seventeenth century to about 10 per cent of the population.[26] Their distribution was uneven, however, and here accessibility may have been decisive. Catholic strength lay especially in the south-west corner of Friesland, the area most easily reached by missionaries coming from Holland, and in the towns, especially Leeuwarden, Harlingen, Sneek, and Bolsward. By contrast, north of the line Harlingen–Franeker–Leeuwarden, there were practically no Catholics.

In most of the east Catholicism was weaker still. In the 1650s Zwolle was alone among the Overijssel towns in having a comparatively large Catholic minority combined with a level of civic toleration comparable with Holland.[27] But, even in Zwolle, where in 1656 there were 'at least 1,200 Catholics', they constituted under 20 per cent of the population. At Deventer and Kampen, active repression continued and Catholic numbers remained meagre. At Kampen, reportedly, there were 'scarcely 500 Catholics', barely one-twelfth of the populace. Groningen still had a substantial Catholic community, estimated at around 2,000, but this represented at most 10 per cent of the city's population and, here again, civic policy was intolerant. Zutphen remained a stronghold of Calvinist intolerance, Catho-

---

[22] *Archief aartsbisdom Utrecht*, xi. 67, 70.
[23] Brun, *Véritable religion des Hollandois*, 168.
[24] De la Court, *Aanwysinge*, 401.
[25] *Archief aartsbisdom Utrecht*, xi. 171–6.
[26] Faber, *Drie eeuwen Friesland*, i. 80.
[27] *Archief aartsbisdom Utrecht*, xi. 205.

lics there, in 1656, numbering 'around 400' and 'enjoying minimal freedom of exercise'.[28] Arnhem, during the third quarter of the century, was more liberal, yet the Catholic population was estimated to have amounted, in the 1660s, to only about 15 per cent of the total.[29] Moreover, if Catholicism was generally weak in the towns of the eastern provinces, in much of the countryside, including the Ommelands, Drenthe, the Veluwe, and the Vollenhove and Salland quarters of Overijssel, the old Church had been largely eliminated.

Owing to their weakness in the eastern areas the Catholic hierarchy were forced, during the period of the French occupation (1672–4), to proceed cautiously. Louis XIV ordered the cathedral at Utrecht and main churches of Arnhem, Nijmegen, Zutphen, Deventer, and Zwolle to be taken from the Reformed and reconsecrated for Catholic worship.[30] But the other churches, in each town, were left in the hands of the Reformed. The policy introduced by the French (ironically) was one of general toleration, or 'religious peace' as it was called, with both Catholic and Reformed churches functioning as public churches, provisionally. In towns where no Catholic conventicles had been regularly held, and there was no resident priest, as at Rhenen, a priest was now sent and Catholicism formally established.

Under the French and Munsterite occupation Catholics enjoyed religious freedom for the first time since the early 1590s. Nevertheless they kept a low profile. Only where local Catholic support was relatively strong, as in the cities of Utrecht and Nijmegen, were there signs of popular Catholic militancy. At Utrecht there were several incidents in the autumn of 1673, with crowds of Catholic youths throwing stones at the Reformed or attacking Reformed churches where services were in progress.[31] But elsewhere there was little open friction.

Not only were Catholics conceded toleration together with the Reformed, under the French, so were Lutherans, Remonstrants, and Mennonites. The region was given a taste of full toleration but under provisional and abnormal circumstances. No sooner were the French and Munsterite armies evacuated, than the forces of intolerance surged back, strong enough to effect a general reaction. At Rhenen, Catholic practice was suppressed, the priest expelled, and the few Catholics in the town reduced to occasional contact with Catholic priests residing in the homes of the Catholic nobles of south-eastern Utrecht. At Arnhem, by 1677, Catholic priests had been expelled and Catholic worship again forbidden. Nor was this mere

---

[28] Ibid. 211; Frijhoff, *Gesch. van Zutphen*, 272.
[29] Holthuizen-Seegers and Nusteling, 'Arnhem', 92.
[30] Brun, *Conseil d'extorsion*, 32, 52; Frijhoff, 'Katholieke toekomstverwachting', 447.
[31] GA Utrecht kerkeraad 10, res. 1 and 7 Sept. 1673.

window-dressing. Arnhem was more intolerant in the last than in the third quarter of the century, and continued to suppress Catholic worship down to around 1720.[32] Similarly, the *raad* of Zutphen in 1676 expelled Catholic priests from the town and reimposed the pre-1672 ban on Catholic conventicles, persisting with this policy for several decades.[33] At Kampen, there were also moves, once again, to suppress Remonstrantism.[34]

Nevertheless, the clock could not be turned back altogether and occasionally, as at Nijmegen, occupation did prove conducive to greater toleration. There is also a wider sense in which the shock of the invasion served to advance confessional toleration. The near disintegration of the Dutch army, in June 1672, the loss of whole provinces, and peril facing the rest caused a surge of emotion among the public, a form of national feeling which expressed itself through special church services for the safety and well-being of the state. It was the intense response among the ordinary public, and militias, in the summer of 1672, as much as anything, which saved the Republic from collapse. Already before the invasion the populace of Utrecht crowded into the city's principal churches to attend special services and sermons.[35] In Delft, twice-weekly special services were laid on on weekdays to pray for the saving of the Republic, which drew crowds large enough for the consistory to consider using the city's two main churches simultaneously.[36]

This emotional tide, on the one hand, fed anti-Catholic sentiment. Reformed resentment of Catholic behaviour, in 1672, was intense. The Catholics of Nijmegen, according to Brun, welcomed the French as they had the Munsterites, in 1666, with open arms, displaying a 'rage furieuse contre ceux de la religion', revering Louis XIV as a Messiah come to save the Catholic faith.[37] But at the same time, it was noticed that other Churches were as stirred by the peril as the Reformed, and no less demonstrative of their commitment to the Republic. In one case, the Jews' patriotic conduct in 1672 was subsequently used as a justification for toleration. Stouppe laid special stress on Dutch toleration of Jews as part of his campaign of disparagement. Brun, in reply, cited the special services the Jews held in their synagogues in 1672, and their prayers 'pour le salut du pais', remarking that he wished that all native-born Christians had proved 'aussi bons patriotes' as the Jews.[38]

[32] Holthuizen-Seegers and Nusteling, 'Arnhem', 70, 92, 97.
[33] GA Zutphen 1st afd. 1/20. res. raad 28 Nov. 1676.
[34] GA Kampen kerkeraad 13, fo. 28. res. 1 May 1674.
[35] GA Utrecht kerkeraad 10. res. 4 May 1672.
[36] GA Delft kerkeraad 7, res. 13, 20, 27 June 1672.
[37] Brun, *Véritable religion des Hollandois*, 54–5.
[38] Ibid. 221–5.

The response of the Mennonites was also widely noted. They could pray for the saving of the state if not (owing to their beliefs) the success of its arms. They too sought to show their solidarity. For all the restrictions which the Republic heaped upon them, it still gave Anabaptists greater freedom than they enjoyed anywhere else. At Groningen, the Zaan, and Deventer, Mennonites raised large sums for the war effort.[39] In Friesland, the Mennonite community informed the States, at a time when the Amsterdam Exchange was paralysed, the normal money market had dried up, and it seemed the Republic itself might soon be overthrown, that they would willingly advance funds but also wanted some amelioration of their position.[40] The Frisian States took up the loan at the relatively low rate of 4 per cent interest. In return Mennonites were accorded formal toleration in Friesland and exemption on grounds of conscience from auxiliary duties connected with military operations. As Huber noted, this was a turning-point in the history of toleration in Friesland.[41] Anabaptist churches built after 1672 in Friesland were still 'hidden churches' in the sense of being discreetly tucked away, behind other buildings, and constructed so as not to look like churches. But now, in place of the harassment and uncertainty of the past, the Mennonites were a recognized Church in the province.

WILLIAM III AND THE CHURCHES

Confessionalization, toleration, the balance between Churches and theological streams, are fundamental social and intellectual processes which we do not normally associate with particular personalities. Yet while the play of social and intellectual forces sets the scene and largely determines what follows, the outcome can also be influenced by key personages, in the Dutch context particularly Stadholders and Pensionaries of Holland. De Witt personally was a factor in the liberalization of the 1650s and 1660s, building on foundations laid by William the Silent, Oldenbarnevelt, and Frederik Hendrik. De la Court considered William the Silent still relevant to the ideological debates of the 1660s because he had striven for toleration, and accommodation between the Churches, and this was widely known to the man in the street. States party writers, after 1650, found little good to say about Maurits, or William II, both of whom had demonstrated how great a change in politics and general culture, as well as religion, ensued when the Stadholder took sides with the Calvinist orthodox, but respected Frederik

<hr>

[39] Van der Zijpp, *Gesch. der doopsgezinden*, 147.
[40] Kalma and De Vries, *Friesland in het rampjaar*, 179–81.
[41] Huber, *Hedendaegse rechts-geleertheyt*, 21.

Hendrik for reverting to the tolerant principles of William the Silent.[42] Voetians, by contrast, hoped that Frederik Hendrik's policy was an aberration which would never recur. With the overthrow of De Witt, and accession to power of William III, in 1672, Voetians congratulated themselves that a new era of confessional and social discipline was at hand. But, as it turned out, they were to be disappointed. The new Stadholder did not develop into another Maurits, or William II, as regards confessional issues but another Frederik Hendrik.[43]

The forces of intolerance enjoyed their best opportunity to reverse the trend towards toleration, in the years following the Revocation of the Edict of Nantes (1685). This was a time of mounting Catholic–Protestant tension in Europe, more marked in Britain than in the United Provinces, but evident in the latter too.[44] The resurgence of anti-Catholic sentiment, in reaction to persecution of the Huguenots, in France, pervaded the entire religious and intellectual climate of the Republic.[45] It was further intensified by the influx of preachers and other Huguenots into the Republic, many of whom adopted a militantly anti-Catholic tone in their preaching and pamphlets,[46] intent on arousing the United Provinces to an 'English fury against Catholics'.

Many Dutch Reformed were alarmed by the coincidence of the new persecution in France, and Savoy, with the accession of the devoutly Catholic monarch, James II, in Britain, and a Catholic line to the formerly Calvinist electorate of the Palatinate. The consistories pressed the town councils to become alert to the rising Catholic threat in Europe, urging the need to cut back the freedom allowed to Catholics at home.[47] There was talk, as in England, of an international Catholic conspiracy aimed at the destruction of Protestantism. Pressure for action against Catholics, and especially the expulsion of Jesuits and foreign-born priests from the Republic, and suppression of Catholic schools, built up amongst the public and consistories, to the point where the regents conceded that Catholic freedom should now be curbed. The Leiden *vroedschap* voted to support anti-Catholic moves in the States, in August 1685,[48] Delft a few months later.[49] By September 1687 there was a majority in the States for a general placard

---

[42] De la Court, *Aanwijsinge*, 399–400.
[43] Israel, 'William III and Toleration', 134–5.
[44] *Archief aartsbisdom Utrecht*, v. 5.
[45] Barnouw, *Philippus van Limborch*, 42–3.
[46] Gibbs, 'Influences of the Huguenot Émigrés', 275.
[47] GA Haarlem kerkeraad 10/10. res. 15 June 1685.
[48] GA Leiden kerkeraad 7. res. 31 Aug. 1685.
[49] GA Delft kerkeraad 7. res. 30 Nov. and 5 Dec. 1685.

aimed at curtailing toleration of Catholicism, and expelling Jesuits and other 'regular clergy', leaving only the 'seculars', a step which, if enforced, would have halved the number of Catholic priests in the province.[50] Nor was the upsurge of anti-Catholic sentiment by any means confined to Holland. There was a fierce outbreak of anti-Catholic rioting, in Leeuwarden, in July 1687.

Holland's anti-Catholic placard was in an advanced stage of preparation, and would have been adopted by the States, had not William III intervened to stop it.[51] On this and, as the French ambassador admitted, also other occasions, William III played a decisive role in thwarting the forces of intolerance while simultaneously making use, for his own purposes, of Protestant fervour. By tilting the balance in the Republic—and from 1688 also in Britain—in favour of toleration, at a crucial moment, the Stadholder exerted an appreciable impact on the entire Dutch confessional and cultural scene. Partly he acted out of personal conviction. But defending and widening toleration in the United Provinces—and Britain—was also essential to the Prince's overall European strategy. For the success of his efforts to check the power of Louis XIV and make the United Provinces secure depended on his being able to form a Catholic–Protestant coalition against France and, in particular, retain the support of Spain and the Emperor.[52]

While the Stadholder, and Holland's Pensionary, Caspar Fagel, steadfastly opposed any general change, some local measures against Catholics were taken and the synods and consistories kept up the pressure to reduce toleration. At Leiden, the Jesuits were expelled, with several other priests, in November 1685.[53] When the anti-Catholic mood was at its height, in 1687, the North and South Holland Synods sent a delegation to Orange to urge him to assist the passage of the placard 'against all regular priests whether Franciscans, Jesuits, or of whatever order they may be'.[54] Characteristically, he suggested, instead, that Reformed preachers in Holland should stress, in their sermons, how grave was the peril confronting Protestant Europe. William sought to deflect the anti-Catholic pressure away from intolerance in a direction he considered useful for his international political strategy.

The recrudescence of anti-Catholic sentiment in the United Provinces in the years 1683–8 faced Dutch Catholics with an acute dilemma. If some prayed for Louis XIV and James II, it was not in the Catholic interest to

---

[50] *Archief aartsbisdom Utrecht*, v. 15.
[51] *Négociations . . . d'Avaux*, vi. 109–10.
[52] Israel, *Anglo-Dutch Moment*, 136–9.
[53] GA Leiden kerkeraad 7. res. 9 Nov. 1685.
[54] Knuttel, *Acta*, vi. 19–20.

appear disloyal. Some Catholics sought to show solidarity with the Republic and disapproval of the intolerance of Louis XIV. In the collection in Leiden, in December 1685, to raise money to assist Huguenot refugees arriving in the town, more than one-third of the 20,000 guilders raised was contributed by Churches other than the Reformed, nearly half by Leiden's Catholics. Where the Mennonites collected 13 per cent of the total and the Remonstrants 3 per cent, Catholics contributed 16 per cent, almost exactly reflecting their strength within Leiden's population.[55]

As in 1672, the momentousness of 1688 produced a heightened emotional state amongst the Reformed population, and show of support for the Republic. At Leiden, there were special services to implore God to bless the 'Fatherland, Reformed Church, and especially the great and important undertaking of the state, and His Highness, the Prince of Orange, in England';[56] these were held twice weekly during the evening, after work, through November and December 1688, and drew such crowds that the consistory had to use both of Leiden's principal churches simultaneously. At Delft too there was a massive response.[57] The regents were eager to encourage such fervour but, like the Stadholder, were at the same time anxious to avoid aggravating confessional tension. They did not want the populace to consider those outside the Reformed Church foes of the state. Catholic priests were assured, by the burgomasters, that they, and their congregations, would be protected. Following the eruption of anti-Catholic rioting in England, in December 1688 (which was widely reported in the Dutch press), the States of Holland instructed the burgomasters in the towns to warn the consistories there must be no stirring up of anti-Catholic feeling in sermons delivered in the Reformed churches, so that, as the Amsterdam burgomasters put it, no one listening to the preachers could claim 'this state had begun a war of religion against the Roman Church'.[58]

It was not just a question of preventing incitement to anti-Catholic agitation within the Republic. The lesser Churches were urged to demonstrate their solidarity with the Republic in its hour of need. At Haarlem, the burgomasters asked the preachers, and consistories, of the Remonstrant, Mennonite, and Lutheran communities to hold services for the state and explain the momentousness of the occasion to their congregations.[59] The Portuguese Jews at Amsterdam put on special services for the success of

[55] GA Leiden *Notulen* burgemeesterskamer (1682–98), fo. 89.
[56] GA Leiden kerkeraad 7. res. 19 Nov. 1688.
[57] GA Delft kerkeraad 7, fo. 175v. res. 20 Nov. 1688.
[58] GA Amsterdam inv. 376 no. 15, fos. 275–6. res. 19 Jan. 1689.
[59] GA Haarlem 10/27, fo. 88. res. burgomasters 13 Nov. 1688.

Stadholder and States General in their invasion of England, publishing a Dutch translation of their prayer for the state so that the public should know its content. Also noticed was the financial assistance given by Baron Lopes Suasso and other Sephardi Jewish financiers during the months the invasion armada was being prepared.[60] One States party writer later pointed out that, in 1688, Jewish financiers had done more to help the Dutch state than Christian businessmen.[61]

The Mennonites rallied likewise while, again, also seeking to bolster toleration. Their leaders had long been alarmed by the effect of the accusation, spread by the Reformed, that they were harbourers of 'Socinians'. They wanted the greater sense of security that would come with an easing of confessional tensions. The Anabaptist preachers, and deacons, of Amsterdam and Zaandam collectively wrote to Fagel, praising the famous open letter on toleration, *Letter to Mr Stewart*, which William III and Fagel had published for distribution in Britain, expressing pleasure at the Stadholder's support for 'freedom of conscience' and asking Fagel to advance toleration further by stopping Reformed preachers' attacks on Mennonites as 'Socinians'.[62] The Mennonite authorities professed no complaint against 'good and moderate' Reformed preachers who did not molest them but greatly feared the vehemence of hardliners, in the tradition of Petrus de Witte (1622–69), a preacher active at Delft and Leiden, who had attributed the great gunpowder explosion of Delft, in 1654, to God's anger at the town's immorality and who, in 1661, had published a blistering attack on 'Socinians' and crypto-Socinians. The Mennonite authorities stressed their support for the Republic and its intervention in England, urging Fagel to muzzle the Calvinist militants and, thus, enable Mennonites to enjoy the 'priceless freedom' which formed the 'foundation of this illustrious Republic from its beginning'.[63]

JANSENISM AND ANTI-JANSENISM

The formidable reaction against the Jesuits and other Catholic regular clergy in the Republic in the 1680s encouraged the shift, already noticeable earlier among sections of Dutch Catholicism, towards a more 'national' attitude, adjusting to the specific context and institutions of the United Provinces under the leadership of their own local hierarchy, based in

---

[60] Israel, 'Amsterdam Stock Exchange', 436–8.
[61] Van der Hoeven, *Hollands aeloude vryheid*, ii. 400.
[62] ARH SH 2939/18. Anabaptist preachers and deacons to Fagel, Amsterdam, 1 Nov. 1688.
[63] Ibid.

Utrecht, and therefore separated from the south Netherlands and also increasingly Jansenist in theology, moral attitudes, and views about the governance of the Church. During the second quarter of the century, Jansenism developed into a powerful current within the *Missio Hollandica*, tending towards accommodation with the secular authorities in the north, rejecting direction from Brussels and Münster, and antagonistic to ultramontanism in Church affairs—as well as to Louis XIV.

Jansenism is named after the Hollander Cornelis Jansen (1585–1638), a native of Leerdam who attended the Latin school at Utrecht before studying at Leuven. Later he rose to become seventh bishop of Ieper. His famous book, the *Augustinus*, from which the movement named after him stems, though only published after his death, in 1640, from then on had a far-reaching impact. It expounded an austere, pessimistic doctrine of Grace and will, based on Augustine, which directly clashed with the teaching of influential sections of the Church, especially that of the Jesuits, and provided a basis for a severe, inward-orientated approach to piety critical of what Jansenists deemed the excessive emphasis frequently placed on outward forms of devotion and veneration of images and saints. The theological furore surrounding Jansen's views rapidly spread beyond the borders of the Spanish Netherlands. Although Jansenism as a theological stream was to remain largely confined to the Low Countries and France (where Louis XIV emerged as its foremost adversary), the quarrel between Jansenists and Jesuits over whether Jansen's doctrines should be condemned by the Church soon spilled over to the papal court, Madrid, and later also Vienna.

By the mid-1640s, the Catholic Church in the Spanish Netherlands was deeply split over Jansenism and at all levels, including the episcopate.[64] The archbishop of Mechelen in the years 1621–55, Jacobus Boon, primate of the Church in the south, had long been an admirer of Jansenius—as he was called—as had the bishop of Ghent, Antonie Triest (1622–57), a stern disciplinarian and one of the leading figures of the Counter-Reformation in the south Netherlands since the time of Albert and Isabella. Jansenius' successor at Ieper was also a Jansenist. By contrast, other bishops were fiercely anti-Jansenist, not least the bishop of Antwerp, Gaspar Nemius (1634–51), and his successor, Marinus Ambrose Capello (1654–76). This doubtless contributed to the absence of Jansenist influence at Breda, which was within the see of Antwerp, though it should be noted that the Catholics of the Generality Lands, being outside the *Missio Hollandica*, and sullen towards the Republic, were generally much less responsive to Jansenism

---

[64] Ceyssens, *Première Bulle contre Jansénius*, pp. xxix–xxxvii; Spiertz, 'Jansenisme', 149–51.

than Catholics north of the rivers. Of the south's two universities, Leuven was predominantly pro-Jansenist, Douai firmly anti-Jansenist.

During the 1650s, there was a marked reaction against Jansenism, backed by some cardinals at Rome and the Spanish court as well as the most notable governor of the Spanish Netherlands after the Cardinal-Infante, the Austrian Habsburg Archduke Leopold Wilhelm (1647–56), a pupil of the Jesuits as well as soldier, dabbler in alchemy, and passionate collector of art.[65] In 1651, the see of Roermond, having long been left vacant, was filled with Andries Creusen, a leader of the anti-Jansenist campaign, who in 1655 was nominated to succeed Boon as archbishop of Mechelen. The Holy Office banned a long list of Jansenist literature including the *Lettres provinciales* of Blaise Pascal. In May 1656, the Spanish monarch instructed his new governor of the south Netherlands, his illegitimate son, Don Juan José, to 'proceed to extinguish this new doctrine of the *Jansenistas* and avoid promoting to high ecclesiastical office those who are reported to defend, or be inclined to, the teachings of Jansenism'.[66] In December 1656, the monument to Jansenius in the cathedral at Ieper was demolished by the authorities, to the distress of much of the citizenry.

Nevertheless, neither Papacy, nor Spanish Crown, wholeheartedly backed the anti-Jansenist campaign, and during the 1660s it slackened in the south Netherlands just as it gathered momentum in France. In the longer run, the hesitation of the Papacy, and mounting friction between the Papacy and Louis, as well as between Louis and Spain, meant that its enemies were unable to eradicate Jansenism from the bosom of the Church and a long and bruising conflict continued in France, the Spanish Netherlands, and the north Netherlands alike.

The Jesuits and most regulars in the north, like those in the south, were staunchly anti-Jansenist and formed a large part of the clergy in the area of the *Missio Hollandica*. But there had long been some tension north of the rivers between seculars and regulars as the latter, being subject to provincials in Brussels, and the Jesuit General in Rome, were less willing to defer to the Vicar Apostolic in Utrecht, and the leadership of the secular clergy of the *Missio*, than the local priesthood. From the outset jurisdictional disputes regarding the status and powers of the *Missio*, and its Vicar Apostolic, were a key factor in the battle between Dutch Jansenism and anti-Jansenism.

It was especially under the vicariate apostolic of Johannes van Neercassel (1661–86)—a Hollander from Gorcum and friend of such leading French

---

[65] Ceyssens, *Fin de la première période*, i, pp. v, xx–xxii.
[66] BL MS Add. 14007, fo. 189. 'Instrucción reservada . . . â Don Juan de Austria'.

Jansenists as Antoine Arnauld and Pasquier Quesnel—that Jansenist theology spread wide and deep throughout the *Missio*, and the shift towards an
accommodation between Dutch Catholicism and the secular authorities,
spurred by the friction between seculars and regulars, took place.[67] Neercassel frequently complained to Rome about the obstruction he encountered
in running the *Missio*, from the Jesuits and their Dominican and Franciscan
allies, and, in 1670, travelled to Rome in person to defend himself against
Jesuit accusations. During the 1680s, bitter local quarrels between Jansenists
and anti-Jansenists erupted in several main centres of Dutch Catholicism,
not least Delft, where Antoine Arnauld himself sought refuge in the years
1682–4 and where, even before that, Jansenism exerted a growing influence.[68] The regents of Holland and Utrecht, for their part, seeing that
Jansenists showed more deference for the authority of the States than their
adversaries and were less prone to inculcate hostility to the Republic, and
nurturing as they did a traditional dislike of Jesuits, tended to favour the
Jansenists—and all the more so for their having incurred the wrath of Louis
XIV.

It is true that during the French occupation Neercassel (successor of
Vicars Apostolic who had never formally accepted the legitimacy of the
United Provinces or had dealings with the Dutch state, or provinces)
showed an unseemly willingness to collaborate with Louis XIV.[69] He had
allegedly wanted Louis to restore the archbishopric of Utrecht, as it had
been under Philip II, with himself as archbishop—a change which, however,
was sure to be opposed by Spain and likely to be blocked by the Papacy.
When the French evacuated Utrecht, Neercassel departed also, albeit partly
through fear of an eruption of popular anti-Catholic violence. But after
1673 he rapidly discarded his former deference for Louis and finding the
authorities in the Spanish Netherlands unsympathetic, sought refuge in
Huissen, a locality enclaved within Gelderland, and part of the *Missio
Hollandica*, but conveniently part of Cleves-Mark and outside the Republic,
a place where the Elector of Brandenburg permitted the open practice of
Catholicism. By this means, he adroitly showed his neutrality as between
Louis XIV and the Republic (as well as Spain).[70] At Huissen, Neercassel
wrote his *Amor Poenitens*, an uncompromisingly Jansenist work subsequently much assailed by the Jesuits. After the French evacuated Gelderland and Overijssel, Neercassel radically changed the political orientation of

[67] Ceyssens, *Fin de la première période*, i. 1; Spiertz, 'Jansenisme', 153–9.
[68] Van Schaik, 'Johan Christian van Erkel', 138, 143–5.
[69] Spiertz, 'Katholieke geestelijke leiders', 8–9.
[70] Smit, 'Neercassel', 203–5.

the *Missio*, responding to William III's evident desire to detach Dutch Catholicism from its tutelage to France, for the first time, negotiating a formal *modus vivendi* with the Republic. From 1675 onwards, Neercassel exercised his office as Vicar Apostolic, supervising and touring the Dutch Catholic Church, with the formal consent of the Dutch state.[71]

This in itself helped exacerbate the now traditional friction between the mainly Dutch secular clergy, on the one hand, and the regular clergy and Jesuits, who were chiefly south Netherlanders and foreigners,[72] on the other. And this, in turn, encouraged the impulse within the Dutch Catholic Church towards a Jansenist stance. During the years Arnauld resided in Delft, Neercassel not only assisted him but enabled him to cultivate contacts with Dutch priests. The intellectual ties formed in the early 1680s between a generation of younger priests, with Arnauld and Quesnel, greatly enhanced Jansenist influence in north Netherlands Catholicism and helped lay the basis for the full-scale schism which split the Dutch Church in the eighteenth century (see pp. 1034–7 below).

In the 1690s, Quesnel emerged as the chief figure in international Jansenism and a hardening, even radicalization, of Jansenist attitudes, both in theology and with respect to papal and episcopal authority, set in, affecting both Dutch and south Netherlands Catholicism as well as the situation in France. This later Jansenism, or Quesnelism, came to be reviled by its opponents as virtually a form of crypto-Calvinism within the Church. At the same time, there began a new general offensive against Jansenism in the Spanish Netherlands, in France, and at Rome, which culminated in the pontificate of the uncompromisingly ultramontane Pope Clemens XI (1700–21).

THE WANING OF THE LESSER CHURCHES

The anti-Catholic and anti-Socinian campaign of the 1680s lost its momentum after 1689. From around 1690 the trend towards a more tolerant and flexible society resumed. Nevertheless, the lesser Churches were still subject to numerous restrictions. The Reformed Church, backed by the States General, and the provincial and civic governments, still exercised an overwhelming superiority over its rivals in public life, education, publishing, welfare, and preaching to large congregations. It was a situation in which the tendency to conform to the public Church proved stronger than any tendency, encouraged by growing toleration, to dissent. The Republic was

---

[71] Spiertz, 'Katholieke geestelijke leiders', 9–10.   [72] Ibid. 11.

not in reality an open arena in which rival religions were continually gaining more adherents, and a higher profile. On the contrary, the trend was chiefly the other way, with diversity diminishing and the Reformed Church steadily making progress in confessionalizing the Dutch populace.

In terms of confessionalizing the native-born Dutch population, only the Reformed Church and Catholics made headway. Support for the Collegiants, Quakers, and other new 'sects' grew, for a time, in Amsterdam and Rotterdam but failed to extend to any great degree elsewhere. 'Sortez hors d'Amsterdam, de Leyden et de Rotterdam, où il y a quelques sectaires,' observed Brun, 'vous en trouverez fort peu ailleurs. Dans les villages il n'y en a presque point, si ce n'est quelque peu d'Anabaptistes. Pour ce qui est des Luthériens, Borellistes et d'autres je ne crois pas que le nom y soit connu.'[73] Dutch Quakerism grew until around 1700 and then waned.[74]

Especially striking is the precipitate decline of the Remonstrants. This had begun with the repression of 1618–19 and had already progressed quite far by the 1630s. But even if we exclude developments before the Remonstrants were able to organize as a separate Church, in the 1630s, it is clear that this Church subsequently failed to retain, let alone increase, its following in Dutch society.[75] In many outlying towns and places where Remonstrantism had once been strong, opposition to the public Church waned rapidly during the 1630s and 1640s. Voetius remarked, in his farewell address to the Reformed congregation at Heusden, in August 1634, that whereas the town had formerly been deeply divided between 'Arminians' and 'Gomarists', in recent years the 'pure Word of God' had prevailed and many former Remonstrants become good Counter-Remonstrants.[76] Outside of Holland, Remonstrantism survived in the last third of the century, in isolated pockets at Kampen, Leeuwarden, Harlingen, Dokkum, and Nijmegen, and also at Friedrichstadt, in Schleswig, but scarcely anywhere else. Huber remarked, in the 1680s, that the Dokkum Remonstrants had declined noticeably in recent years.[77] Although Remonstrantism still evinced some strength in Gouda, Leiden, The Hague, and one or two other Holland towns, it cannot be said that Brun's claim that the 'Arminiens ne se trouvent qu'à Amsterdam et à Rotterdam; ailleurs le nombre en est presque imperceptible' was essentially untrue.[78] At Amsterdam, Remonstrant numbers held steady, initially, but, from the 1650s, showed a clear downwards trend in both

[73] Brun, *Véritable Religion*, 167.
[74] Kannegieter, *Gesch. van de vroegere Quakergemeenschap*, 321–5.
[75] Barnouw, *Philippus van Limborch*, 18, 139.
[76] Voetius, *Afscheydt Predicatie*, 14.
[77] Huber, *Hedendaegse Rechts-geleertheyt*, 21.
[78] Brun, *Véritable religion des Hollandois*, 166.

relative and absolute terms.[79] It can even be argued that Dutch toleration, as it developed in post-1630 Amsterdam, condemned Remonstrantism to decline, by confining Remonstrant worship to one inconspicuous 'hidden church', thereby syphoning off pressure from Remonstrants for freedom of worship, but denying them scope for confessionalizing large numbers. Amsterdam's toleration of the Remonstrants after 1630 was thus, in a way, a form of concealed intolerance which progressively marginalized the Remonstrant Church. Even more striking was the decay of the much larger Remonstrant congregation at Rotterdam. There the community seems to have held steady until 1672 but then suffered an accelerating decline during the last part of the century.[80] The Rotterdam Remonstrant community was still about 7,000 strong in 1670, slightly larger than the Catholic community, representing virtually one-sixth of the population. By 1700, they were down to around 6,000, less than one-eighth of the total, and already substantially smaller than Rotterdam's Catholic population.

The Mennonites too were declining.[81] They were an older Church than the Remonstrants and had long formed a substantial part of the population in Holland, Utrecht, Friesland, and Groningen. There were Anabaptists also in other provinces, with a substantial following in the north-west corner of Overijssel in and around Blokzijl and Giethoorn. Although, after 1673, the Mennonites were an officially tolerated Church in Friesland, and found greater acceptance in Holland, they still laboured under substantial disadvantages. A particular problem for the Anabaptists was their reliance on preachers, and guidance, from within the Republic. Unlike the Catholics, Lutherans, and Jews, they had no major centres of authority and learning outside the Republic, but nearby, from which they could draw sustenance. They had only limited access to educational facilities, and the press, and it was also difficult for them to establish new congregations where they had had none before, owing to resistance from the public Church and local authorities. Anabaptist efforts to spread their presence in Overijssel in the 1660s, especially in the districts of Enschede and Hengelo, met with vigorous opposition.

As a rule Dutch Anabaptism failed to establish a presence during the seventeenth century where it had not previously gained a foothold in the sixteenth. At the same time, there was a clear tendency for the Anabaptist communities to weaken, during the second half of the seventeenth century, even in their foremost centres. At Haarlem, one of the principal Mennonite

[79] Nusteling, *Welvaart en werkgelegenheid*, 237.
[80] Mentink and Van der Woude, *Demografische ontwikkeling*, 43, 45.
[81] Van der Zijpp, *Gesch. der doopsgezinden*, 96, 178–80.

centres in Holland, they accounted for some 15 per cent of the city's population around 1620. With the suppression of Remonstrantism, after 1619, the Mennonites, as well as Catholics and Lutherans, received former Remonstrants.[82] But later in the century they began to decline, amounting to less than 11 per cent of the city's population by 1707.[83]

In Friesland the Anabaptists lost ground in both town and countryside. In the late sixteenth century, the Anabaptists may have amounted to as much as 20 per cent of the total population. In 1666 there were approximately 20,000 Anabaptists in Friesland, living in seventy-two communities, representing about 13 per cent of the population. During the middle decades of the seventeenth century, Anabaptists were still a larger grouping in Friesland than the Catholics.[84] Yet, despite the failure of the Catholic Church to grow in Friesland, shrinkage of Mennonite numbers led eventually, around the middle of the eighteenth century, to the Catholics supplanting them as the second largest church grouping in the province.

A remarkable feature of the Dutch confessional scene in the late seventeenth century was the continued failure of the Lutheran Church to make any real impact on the Dutch populace, despite the proximity of Lutheran states in Germany and the large number of German and Scandinavian Lutheran immigrants. Official hostility was still a factor, especially outside the main towns of Holland. At Zutphen, Lutherans, mostly members of the garrison, held conventicles in the 1650s but were not permitted to invite Lutheran preachers from outside to hold formal services. What the *raad* was afraid of was precisely that Lutheranism might appeal to sections of the native populace. In July 1668, German officers at Zutphen were given permission to organize a service, with a Lutheran preacher from outside, provided they did so without publicity and without 'admitting any inhabitants'.[85] Only with the French occupation, in 1672, did the Lutherans of Zutphen gain the freedom to organize and only in 1681 did they acquire their first resident preacher. At Groningen the picture was similar. After 1672, there was no further repression of Lutheran conventicles in the city but it was not until 1687 that the *raad* finally legalized Lutheran worship.[86] The first Lutheran churches were built in Zutphen only in 1693, and in Groningen in 1696. In Overijssel only Zwolle was relatively tolerant towards Lutherans (as well as Catholics), allowing them to form a congregation

[82]　GA Haarlem kerkeraad 10/4 res. 6 Oct. 1623.
[83]　De Jongste, *Onrust aan het Spaarne*, 60.
[84]　Faber, *Drie eeuwen Friesland*, i. 82–3.
[85]　GA Zutphen 1/107. res. raad 11 July 1668.
[86]　Kramer, 'Luthersche gemeente te Groningen', 291.

in 1649.[87] At Deventer, Lutheran worship was forbidden until 1672 but, after the establishment of a Lutheran community during the Munsterite occupation, permitted after 1674.

Friesland was another province where toleration of Lutheranism arose grudgingly and late. A petition for freedom of worship submitted to the Franeker university senate, in 1650, by thirty-one German and Scandinavian students, was refused. Lutheran conventicles formed at Harlingen, which had close links with Norway and the Baltic, and Leeuwarden, around 1660. But the petition of the Leeuwarden Lutherans for permission to build a church, in 1668, was rejected.[88] The first Lutheran church to be built in Friesland was completed at Harlingen only in 1669. The city of Leeuwarden formally extended toleration to the Lutherans only in 1681.

In Holland the main limitation was the ban imposed by the States, in 1624, on Lutheranism in the countryside. By and large, except at Bodegraven and at Zaandam, the ban remained effective. Zaandam provides an interesting example of the limited character of Dutch toleration during the Golden Age, since it was not only a key industrial zone but, through its busy timber trade, had close links with Lutheran lands. Zaandam's Lutherans, however, met with persistent obstruction. When they began building a church and school in West Zaandam, in 1644, the classis of Haarlem complained to the Hof of Holland, which led to the States reissuing their general placard forbidding Lutheran worship in the countryside.[89] The Lutheran church was temporarily closed, in 1652. The general ban was reissued, again with specific reference to Zaandam, in 1655. Complaints continued down to the 1680s. By contrast, most of the Holland towns did tolerate Lutheran worship from the early seventeenth century onwards but even here there were exceptions. Dordrecht with its Rhine trade refused permission for a Lutheran church until as late as 1689.

Like the Lutherans, the Jews increased in numbers owing to immigration and, again like the Lutherans, mostly from Germany. The Sephardic or 'Portuguese' Jewish community in Amsterdam grew rapidly whilst the overseas trading system was at its height, in the period 1647–72, but scarcely increased thereafter. Moreover, though it remained more important in finance and overseas commerce than the German Jewish community, it was comparatively small, attaining a maximum of about 3,000, in the late seventeenth century. By contrast, the much poorer German Jewish

[87] Loosjes, *Gesche. der Luthersche kerk*, 108, 114.
[88] Ibid. 158–9.
[89] ARH Hof van Holland 5335/8, 'stukken rakende de Luthersche kerk te Zaandam'.

community began to grow rapidly from the last quarter of the seventeenth century onwards, both in Amsterdam and in the Republic more generally.

By 1672, German Jewish communities were firmly established in Rotterdam, Amersfoort, and Leeuwarden, as well as Amsterdam, and there were also small Sephardic congregations in Middelburg, Rotterdam, Amersfoort, Maarssen, Nijkerk, and The Hague, as well as Amsterdam. Yet many towns and rural areas in the Republic continued to exclude both German and Sephardic Jews. The city of Groningen did not finally lift its ban on Jewish settlement until 1711, that of Utrecht not until 1789, and Deventer not until the 1790s.[90] Among the Gelderland towns, only Nijmegen permitted Jews to settle in the late seventeenth century, Arnhem permitting this only after the town became confessionally more liberal in the 1720s. In Leiden, Haarlem, and Delft Jewish settlement was not permitted until the 1720s and 1730s. At Amsterdam the Portuguese and German Jewish communities were in rough balance by 1700, totalling around 6,000, representing about 3 per cent of the city's population. The Jewish population of the United Provinces grew steadily after 1648 but only in a handful of localities and, even then, often under stringent restrictions.

CHURCH POLITICS IN THE GENERALITY LANDS

An entirely different confessional situation prevailed in the Generality Lands, where the bulk of the populace remained staunchly loyal to the Catholic Church. Here it was not the provincial governments and town councils which determined church policy but the States General and *Raad van State*. Yet the Generality's attitude to confessional matters in the Generality Lands was decided collectively by the Seven Provinces, and especially Holland, so that it is not surprising to find similarities, in policy towards dissenting Churches, between the situation in the Generality Lands and that in the Seven Provinces.

The only districts where public practice of the Catholic faith was permitted—on the basis of the States General's decree of 1632 (see p. 515 above)—were Maastricht and the Overmaas. As a consequence, the confessional situation there differed radically from that in the rest of the Generality Lands. Maastricht was the one city in the Republic where many churches, and much property, remained in Catholic hands, where Catholic education and monastic life flourished. As a result, there were incomparably more Catholic priests there—in 1662, no fewer than 515 parish clergy and 'regulars'—than anywhere else in the Republic, indeed more than in all the

---

[90] Reijnders, *Van 'Joodsche Natiën'*, 135, 143.

rest put together.[91] For in the whole of the Dutch Catholic Mission—that is the Republic, minus the Generality Lands—there were only 379 priests, as late as 1701, and thirty-six of those were in the adjoining German territories of Lingen and Cleves.[92] Most of Maastricht's population adhered to the old faith, regarding Protestants as foreigners and occupiers. Even so, owing to the garrison—and the flight there, after 1633, of groups of German Calvinists—the Reformed community was substantial, amounting in the late seventeenth century to as much as 20 per cent of the total. The *Raad van State* undoubtedly wished to weaken the Catholic character of both city and hinterland but, remarkably, did not seek to achieve this by extending toleration to other dissenting Churches. An informal Lutheran community existed in Maastricht, from the 1640s, but the Synod of Gelderland (which was responsible for maintaining the Reformed Church in Maastricht) resisted all pressure for a Lutheran church and it was not until the French occupation, in 1672, that Lutherans were tolerated in the city.[93] Even after the French evacuation, though Lutherans were no longer obstructed in holding conventicles, it was not until 1684 that they were allowed their own church. Jews were not permitted to settle in Maastricht until the 1790s.[94]

Elsewhere in the Generality Lands Catholicism was officially forbidden. At the time of the definitive annexation of the Meierij to the Republic, in 1648, Catholicism was driven largely out of sight into private homes and makeshift premises, though concealment was often little more than perfunctory in the countryside, where the Reformed Church had no following beyond the soldiery and a few Generality officials.[95] In the main towns, there was a more substantial Reformed minority. But though the Generality went to some lengths to promote the Dutch Reformed Church and its adjunct, the Walloon Church, its policy was one of intolerance towards Protestant dissenting Churches and Jews. Jews were allowed to settle in States Brabant only from the end of the eighteenth century.

At 's-Hertogenbosch, Catholic conventicles usually took place undisturbed, except for occasional interference when the Reformed *raad* deemed them excessively large or blatant.[96] Officials seeking to prevent a gathering in a private home, in October 1673, were driven off by an angry crowd. Even so, the Catholic situation in 's-Hertogenbosch, or Breda, differed markedly from that in Maastricht; nor was this merely a question of fewer, and less

[91] Ubachs, *Twee heren*, 72.
[92] *Archief aartsbisdom Utrecht*, xix. 2–5.
[93] Loosjes, *Gesch. der Luthersche kerk*, 115.
[94] Reijnders, *Van 'Joodsche Natiën'*, 158.
[95] Van Heurn, *Historie der stad en Meyerye*, iii. 43.
[96] Ibid. 223.

conspicuous, priests: 's-Hertogenbosch's famous Catholic Latin school was suppressed and replaced by one with a militantly Reformed character;[97] secondary education for other confessions largely ceased. Intolerance became deeply embedded in the life of the city. Lutherans were finally conceded liberty of worship in 1686. But the community retained a strongly German flavour until late in the eighteenth century.

The question of Lutheranism in the Generality Lands is of special significance given the large numbers of German troops in the garrisons and proximity of Lutheran states. The *raad* of 's-Hertogenbosch strove (albeit without much success) to attract Huguenot immigrants, in the 1680s, but never tried to strengthen the Protestant presence by seeking Lutheran immigrants.[98] Only Breda, the city of the Nassaus, continued the tradition of toleration towards Lutheranism reaching back to the days of William the Silent. On recapturing the city from the Spaniards, in 1637, Frederik Hendrik reconstituted the Lutheran community, which subsequently showed some vitality. But, elsewhere, the Generality followed a policy of intolerance, reflecting fear of Lutheranism as a potential rival to the Reformed Church. In Bergen-op-Zoom Lutherans were unable to organize openly until 1698. Grave lacked a Lutheran congregation until well into the eighteenth century. In Westerwolde, Lutherans were barred until 1687, when William III allowed them a church, close to Winschoten—where the city of Groningen was trying to prevent Lutheranism establishing a foothold—provided they refrained from ringing bells and all other outward signs of 'public religion' and gave no offence to the Reformed Church.[99]

THE UNITY OF THE PUBLIC CHURCH

A constant preoccupation of provincial and civic government in the Dutch Republic was to safeguard the inner cohesion, and stability, of the public Church. For if the Reformed Church lapsed into turmoil, as it had during the Twelve Years Truce, then the entire body politic would be divided and society would be at war with itself.

In this respect, there was more similarity than dissimilarity between the two great party-factions, 'Orangists' and 'States' parties. The rival blocs in the Dutch Republic did not, of course, resemble modern political parties. They were informal groupings, inclined in the one case more, in the other less, towards the Stadholder, and his court, with differing views of the

---

[97] Sassen, *Wijsgerig onderwijs . . . 's-Hertogenbosch*, 6–7.
[98] Loosjes, *Gesch. der Luthersche kerk*, 108.
[99] Van Winter, *Westerwolde*, 13.

Union and the nature of the Generality. At the same time they were patronage and clientage networks concerned with control and distribution of public offices and local power. Both party-factions protected the public Church, disagreeing only over how much influence to accord the Church in public, social, and educational life and how much toleration to the dissenting Churches.

In the main Holland towns, civic government, by the 1640s, was mostly in the hands of the 'Arminians' or States party-faction. But this does not mean that those who stood for Calvinist orthodoxy had no prospect of regaining the upper hand. The attitudes of the regents were not necessarily the attitudes of the populace. Oldenbarnevelt's downfall, in 1618, had owed much to strong popular support for Counter-Remonstrantism in Amsterdam, Haarlem, Leiden, and Utrecht. After 1650 too, Calvinist hardliners could count on appreciable support from the mass of the Reformed community. Leiden's persistence, as the last large Holland town still combating Remonstrant conventicles in the 1660s, was less out of line with the underlying Dutch reality than it might seem. When Remonstrant conventicles began in Leiden, in defiance of the *vroedschap*, in 1662, there were demonstrations by children from the civic orphanages, a hotbed of militant Calvinism.[100] When the Remonstrants petitioned for toleration, in 1664, the *vroedschap* refused on the grounds that, in Leiden, Remonstrantism would cause rioting and disorder. In the disturbances at Rotterdam, in 1672, a key demand of the disaffected citizenry was that the rector and teachers of the city's Latin school should, henceforth, be loyal members of the Reformed Church.[101] The threat of popular pressure hung constantly over those who dissented.

There was already a tendency during the stadholderate of William II for Calvinist orthodox to align with the Orangists and more liberal preachers with the States party side. But, as yet, there was no theological polarization within the public Church apt to reinforce this dichotomy. The rift between Remonstrants and Counter-Remonstrants was vividly remembered, and there prevailed a general resolve to quell all signs of recurrence of such strife. Nevertheless, slowly but inexorably, tensions in the body politic began to interact, during the 1650s, with a fresh theological rift within the public Church.[102] On the one side stood Calvinist orthodoxy, anchored in the Netherlands Confession, with the redoubtable Gisbertus Voetius, doyen of the university of Utrecht, as its chief spokesman; on the other, the liberal

---

[100] *Leydsche Proceduuren*, 3–4, 13–14.
[101] *Request van de Borgerye*, point 18.
[102] Van Asselt, 'Voetius en Cocceius', 32–3.

stream in Dutch Reformed theology, the adherents of Johannes Cocceius (1603–69), since 1650 professor of theology at Leiden, and one of the most influential Calvinist theologians of the seventeenth century in Dutch and German lands. Cocceius, eschewing fundamentalism and dogmatism, and an expert in Near Eastern languages, and philology, held that the text of Holy Scripture was complex, and not always to be taken literally, and that its meaning could be properly grasped only by the skilled philologist. In particular, the nature of the covenant between God and godly, he argued in his influential *Summa Doctrinae de Foedere et Testamento Dei* (1648), has to be construed from the changing spiritual context through which it had evolved.[103]

The term 'Voetians' came into use first in the 1640s, and acquired a clear meaning before the emergence of the 'Cocceians' as a theological and intellectual bloc. The Voetians were the Calvinist orthodox who rejected liberal tendencies in theology, as well as Cartesianism in science and philosophy, and championed rigorous enforcement of anti-Catholic legislation. The full implications of Cocceian theology for society and politics emerged only in the 1650s. For many years the 'precisian', or 'Voetian', bloc within the Reformed Church, in Utrecht, Amsterdam, and other main cities, had also been pressing the secular authorities to impose godly ways on society.[104] They interpreted disasters, such as the great gunpowder explosion of Delft of 1654, as signs of God's anger, admonishing the States of Holland to curb swearing, prostitution, dancing, and dance-schools, and enforce stricter sabbath observance on the population.[105] The Voetians were thus also the champions of the 'Further Reformation', the movement to lead society to be more godly in life-style.[106] As pressure mounted for stricter enforcement of the Lord's Day, and government measures to discourage work and sport on the sabbath, however, dissenting voices began to be heard from Cocceius' side.

Eventually, disagreement within the Leiden theology faculty over sabbath observance, a dispute penetrating to the heart of the theological divide between Voetians and Cocceians, spilled over into the public sphere.[107] Voetius' ally at Leiden, Johannes Hoornbeeck (1617–66), in 1655 published a Dutch-language tract which was, in effect, an appeal to the public and the Church, against Cocceius, over the heads of the university. Cocceius had

---

[103] Cocceius, *Leer van het Verbond*, 231–2.
[104] Groenendijk, 'Petrus Wittewrongel', 66–7.
[105] Res. Holl. 3 May 1655 and 27 July 1656.
[106] Van Lieburg, *Nadere Reformatie*, 13–44.
[107] Visser, *Gesch. van den sabbatsstrijd*, 116–20.

already pronounced on sabbath observance in his *Summa* and other theological writings: for him, the Fourth Commandment was no longer in effect, as it had once been, and keeping the Lord's Day did not require the strict observance, and abstinence from work, demanded by the Voetians. This was inherent in Cocceius' theology; but he shrank from public polemics and, initially, avoided open dispute. But, once started, the controversy escalated, gaining a momentum which compelled the Cocceians to respond. Cocceius' ally, Abraham Heidanus, published his *De Sabbate* (1658) in Latin; but a Dutch version soon appeared and tempers flared. In defence of Hoornbeeck, a colleague of Voetius at Utrecht, Andreas Essenius, published a fierce attack on Heidanus, obliging Cocceius himself to intervene. Cocceius published a long Latin treatise on the nature of the Christian Sunday, detaching it and its obligations from the Jewish sabbath and the observance once binding on the Jews under a covenant now discarded.[108] He dismissed the stringency of the Voetians as lacking theological foundation, insisting that his account of the Lord's Day fully accorded with the Heidelberg catechism and Acts of the Synod of Dordrecht. Hoornbeeck reacted by publishing an expanded version of his treatise to which both Heidanus and Cocceius responded with further controversial publications.

By 1659 the Synods of North and South Holland, and Utrecht, were in uproar. The South Holland Synod, meeting at Gouda, in July, referred to the 'wretched disputes and growing dissension which have weighed so oppressively on the churches in these provinces, through the publications of professors and preachers regarding observance of the Lord's Day'.[109] Most of the Synod agreed with Hoornbeeck and Essenius that Cocceius' theology diluted the pure Word of God, legitimizing ungodly work, and pleasure, on the sabbath, in contravention of the Fourth Commandment. But the Synod, and still more the States of Holland's commissioners, attending its meetings, were less interested in pursuing the controversy than quelling it. The Synod tried to induce the professors to drop the matter, and refrain from publishing anything more on the subject.[110] But Hoornbeeck refused to desist. The States of Holland then instructed their commissioners to direct the North and South Holland Synods to cease debating sabbath observance, ruling that the matter was to rest on the (inconclusive) basis of the Acts of the National Synod of Dordrecht.[111] The Leiden university curators were required to ensure that professors made no further pronouncement on

---

[108] Cocceius, *Indagatio naturae Sabbati*, 123–7.
[109] Knuttel, *Acta*, iv. 130–1.
[110] Eekhof, *Theologische faculteit*, 323–6.
[111] Schrenk, *Gottesreich und Bund*, 117.

sabbath observance either in lectures or in print. While superficially neutral, the States of Holland's intervention was in effect—and was so regarded—a victory for the Cocceians.[112] For the result was that nothing further was done about tightening sabbath observance.

While, on the surface, the furore in Holland now subsided, it escalated in Utrecht and Groningen. After expelling Van de Velde and Johannes Teellinck, in 1660, the city, and States, of Utrecht took steps to curb Voetian influence in the consistory, classes, and university, which brought the theologico-political *Kulturkampf* in the city to fever pitch.[113] One of the States party-faction's measures was to appoint the German Reformed preacher, Frans Burman (1628–79), a militant Cocceian, to a chair in theology at Utrecht, in July 1662. Burman, a protégé of Heidanus (whose widowed daughter, Maria, he subsequently married), was brought to Voetius' university to combat Voetianism and did not fail to do so at every step.[114] His Cocceian *De Moralitate Sabbati* (1665) became one of the most embroiled of the mid-century books on sabbath observance, eliciting a hail of rebuttals from Lodenstein, Gentman, and other opponents. Eventually, *vroedschap* and States, weary of the controversy, forbade further publications on the subject, as well as discussion of it in the university and in preaching.

The States of Holland and of Utrecht checked the sabbath observance controversy. But they could not stop the spread of theological conflict, along a broad front, between the Voetian and Cocceian blocs within the public Church. The rift became fundamental not only in the church and academic spheres but in the body politic and the whole edifice of Dutch Golden Age culture. Everyone agreed that the theological conflict had to be contained. But, at the same time, there was an inherent tendency for States party-faction and Cocceians to combine; for both were endeavouring to soften confessional pressures and prevent Calvinist orthodoxy dominating society, politics, and the public Church. Equally, Orangists and Voetians were natural allies; for both were endeavouring to check the political dominance—with its confessional implications—of the States of Holland. The Arminian–Gomarist conflict of the early seventeenth century was noisier and more destructive than the Cocceian–Voetian rift of the second half of the century. But the latter, which infused Dutch Reformed theology, politics, and culture down to the middle of the eighteenth century, pervaded the Dutch scene for considerably longer.

[112] Goeters, *Vorbereitung*, 127.
[113] Visser, *Gesch. van den sabbatsstrijd*, 160–1, 167–70.
[114] Trimp, *Jodocus van Lodensteyn*, 111–13.

The continuing impact of the quarrel after the deaths of the two leading protagonists themselves (Cocceius in 1669, Voetius in 1676) not infrequently amazed foreign observers who hardly knew what to make of it. Outsiders, used to the intellectual worlds of France or Britain, found it both bizarre and baffling. One Huguenot writer in the Netherlands protested that in France and England learned men scarcely ever mentioned Voetius and Cocceius, let alone ceaselessly disputed their views.[115] Pierre Bayle mockingly warned a Swiss acquaintance, in 1693, that foreigners stood scant chance of obtaining professorships at Dutch universities since these were allocated exclusively on the basis of Cocceian–Voetian considerations. At Leiden, he explained, Voetianism had prevailed since 1672, so that 'toute place vacante est toujours un morceau réservé pour quelqu'un qui s'est distingué par son opposition, et par son antipatie, au cocceianisme'; at Franeker, on the other hand, 'c'est tout le contraire', with Cocceians excluding Voetians; and he added: 'et il est sûr qu'hors ce pais-ci, on ne sait guère ce que c'est que cocceianisme et voetianisme'.[116]

One Dutch Reformed writer countered that the French and English only esteemed their own books, so that Dutch publishers, knowing this, did not bother to send any Voetianism or Cocceianism to England or France; to compensate for this, he asserted, Dutch theologians were much debated in Germany.[117] Balthasar Bekker made the same point, remarking that foreign theology students carried back Voetian and Cocceian concepts from Dutch universities to the Reformed regions of Germany and also Hungary,[118] and, indeed, both Voetian and Cocceian methods and ideas were cultivated within the Hungarian Reformed Church until deep into the eighteenth century, with Voetianism generally in the ascendant.[119]

By contrast, in the German Reformed consistories on the lower Rhine it was Cocceianism which predominated. During the 1670s, the strength of Cocceianism in the Synod of Cleves, Mark, and Berg, and the intercession of the German Reformed Churches, helped moderate the Voetian reaction in the Republic following the downfall of De Witt.[120] There was also strong interest in Voetian–Cocceian matters in Emden, Bremen, and Hamburg. Cocceius' 'covenant' theology, his conception of salvation as emanating from a divine covenant with the faithful, evolving in stages through history, was to have a lasting impact on Protestant theology in Germany.

[115] [Joncourt], *Entretiens*, 6–7.
[116] Bayle, *Lettres*, ii. 511.
[117] *Chef des moqueurs démasqué*, 312.
[118] Bekker, *Kort Begryp* 36.
[119] Bánki, 'Utrechtse universiteit', 94, 99–101.
[120] Ypeij and Dermout, *Geschiedenis*, iii. 512.

For many years Cocceius had striven to avoid being drawn into a direct clash with Voetius himself. When an open quarrel finally ensued, in 1665, the two chief protagonists confined their dispute to the purely theological sphere, arguing about Grace, salvation, and the covenant.[121] But while the contest between Voetius and Cocceius was essentially theological, the pressure behind the Voetian reaction, after 1672, came not from the theology faculties of the universities but the consistories, classes, and synods, that is Reformed opinion in society at large.

To grasp the centrality of the Voetian–Cocceian controversies in Dutch culture, over so many decades, one must appreciate the depth of anxiety aroused among large sections of the Reformed public by the onset of the new philosophy and science. Cocceian theology appeared to be, and in some respects was, the ally of these new intellectual forces, which meant that in many people's eyes Cocceian theology was undermining faith and especially faith in the literal meaning of Scripture.[122] By diluting Scripture, Cocceian-ism was held to be helping to subordinate theology, and religion itself, to (Cartesian) philosophy and science. As Van der Waeyen showed, with his Dutch translation of Cocceius' first major work, the *Summa Doctrinae* (1648), which he published at Middelburg, in 1677, some of the Reformed public could be won over to a sympathetic understanding of Cocceius' theology. But this was mainly among the more sophisticated, often profes-sionals, lawyers, and regents. Only such people were likely to appreciate Cocceius' idea that parts of Scripture were intended only to be figurative and allegorical, tailored to the ignorance and superstition of the ancient Israelites, and that the real meaning and relevance can only be distilled by means of sophisticated exegetical methods. Much of the Reformed public was appalled that Cocceian preachers should intimate that God may not really have made the Red Sea part, or the sun stand still in the sky for Joshua.[123] Voetians saw this as tantamount to rejecting Scripture and encouraging disbelief and atheism.

The problem for the Voetians was that there were enough Cocceians amongst the preachers and elders to split key consistories and synods. Voetian pressure split the North Holland Synod, in 1673, the majority faction passing a resolution requiring classes to proceed with 'care and zeal' against 'offensive novelties'—coded language for Cocceian theology. (It was characteristic of the struggle throughout that both sides avoided using the

---

[121] Van Asselt, 'Voetius and Cocceius', 35–6.
[122] Gelazius Major, *Overtuychde ontrouw*, 10; Benthem, *Holländischer Kirch- und Schulen-Staat* ii, 57, 141.
[123] Cramer, *Abraham Heidanus*, 121–4.

terms 'Voetians' and 'Cocceians' in formal documents and discourse, since the doctrines of neither professor had been authorized, or condemned, by any official body.) Like a number of Holland classes, the classes of Zeeland began pressing for the suppression of 'offensive doctrines', demanding that candidates for preaching posts be required, by the synods, to sign undertakings to reject and avoid such teachings—by and large the twenty 'offensive' Cocceian-Cartesian doctrines drawn up by the Leiden university curators (without mention of Cocceius) in 1676.

In Holland and Zeeland, the consistories and classes were divided, as was also the case, it soon emerged, in Friesland and Groningen. Partly as a way of opposing the influence of William III, Hendrik Casimir and the Frisian Delegated States supported Cocceian theology. The consistories and synods, however, were dominated by Voetians who opposed their Stadholder's attitude.[124] A movement began at the meeting of the Synod of Friesland, in 1680, led by Henricus Brinck, for vigorous measures against the 'boldness' of the 'Cartesians and Cocceians'.[125] This led, at the 1681 meeting, to an acrimonious quarrel between Brinck and Hendrik Casimir's close adviser, Professor Van der Waeyen, and an anti-Cocceian offensive which resumed at the gathering of the Synod in 1682. Brinck's own classis, Zevenwolden, urged that Cartesian philosophy be banned 'following the example of the Swiss churches', at the university of Franeker, and measures be taken against theological 'novelties'. The Delegated States of Friesland had to intervene to rescue the Cocceian minority of the Synod. Meanwhile, in Groningen, Cocceians were similarly under pressure.[126]

With memories of the Remonstrant and Counter-Remonstrant battles still strong, a main concern of the provincial States, regents, and also William III, was to prevent a general escalation of theological strife. Here the Amsterdam *vroedschap* led the way, and its example was subsequently widely followed. Until 1677, Amsterdam's regents nurtured Cocceian sympathies and tended to block attempts by the predominantly Voetian consistory to appoint Voetian preachers. But when, in 1677, the consistory split, over the appointment of a new preacher, burgomasters and consistory forged a compromise designed to avoid such rifts in the future. Rules were drawn up, in six articles, to which all members of the consistory, including all twenty-five Reformed preachers in the city, were required to subscribe individually.[127] These laid down that the points in dispute were not of an

[124] Ypeij and Dermout, *Geschiedenis*, ii. 516–19.
[125] Van der Wall, 'Profetie en providentie', 34.
[126] Nauta, *Samuel Maresius*, 381–5.
[127] Knuttel, *Balthasar Bekker*, 140, 144.

'essential character', and did not affect salvation, and that it was therefore possible for adherents of both theological wings to live and work together within the same consistory, in harmony. The articles stipulated that only peace-loving candidates would be chosen and that when making appointments the consistory was not to favour one side or the other. To prevent manipulation and pressure, the *vroedschap* imposed a system of *alternativa*, that is that every preaching vacancy in the city had automatically to be filled alternately first by one side, then the other. Pieter de la Court had earlier described the clashes between Voetians and Cocceians over preaching appointments at Leiden as the battles of the '*Hoeks* and *Cabbeljauws*', apt to plunge the entire city in turmoil.[128] With their *alternativa*, the Amsterdam burgomasters hoped to prevent such unseemly altercations in their consistory, and thus also more widely in the city.

Over time, the Cocceians tended to divide into diverse strains. Voetian wrath was particularly aroused by the followers of Henricus Groenewegen (1640–92), a preacher at Enkhuizen from 1679 until his death. His grouping, known as the 'Green' or 'Leiden' Cocceians, emphasized Cocceius' allegorical and typological approach in their preaching, de-emphasized dogma, and were especially receptive to Cartesian ideas. They were also less austere in matters of dress and life-style than others. Then there were the 'severe Cocceians', a group which adopted Cocceius' theological apparatus but combined it with support for the Further Reformation and austerity in matters of life-style. Two of its leaders were David Flud van Giffen (1653–1701),[129] a favourite of Albertina Agnes and the Frisian court while a preacher at Sneek in the 1680s, later prominent at Dordrecht, and Johannes d'Outrein (1662–1722), a Zeelander who worked at Franeker, Arnhem, and Dordrecht, before becoming a preacher at Amsterdam. D'Outrein was one of the Cocceian leaders consulted by William III, and other leading political figures, in the 1690s over how to lessen Cocceian–Voetian strife in the Church. He was a supporter of the Further Reformation, yet in his preaching style a full Cocceian, making abundant use of allegory and typology.

A crucial factor in the Cocceian–Voetian conflict was the attitude of the Stadholder, William III,[130] whose sympathies throughout his stadholderate remained broadly pro-Voetian. Despite his tolerant leanings, he continued to reveal his Voetian preferences, particularly in the sphere of academic

---

[128] De la Court, 'Brieven', 126.

[129] Van der Wall, 'Profetie en providentie', 34.

[130] Ypeij and Dermout, *Geschiedenis*, ii. 506 and iii. 174–6; Van der Wall, 'Orthodoxy and Scepticism', 124.

patronage. But, during the 1680s, he substantially modified his position in church politics more generally, seeing the dangers inherent in escalation of the theological rift. His chief concern was to reduce the strife, as he made abundantly clear in the early 1690s when he refused to sponsor a clampdown on Cocceianism in the synods and consistories and collaborated instead with the States of Holland in drawing up a detailed *reglement*, in 1694, designed to regulate appointments to preaching vacancies, and other sensitive areas. This had the effect of taking the conflict off the boil in Holland and, to a large extent, throughout the Republic.

INTERNAL CONFESSIONALIZATION

The rift between 'precisians' and liberals dividing the Dutch Reformed Church from the 1650s was part of a more general intellectual phenomenon which affected the other Churches in not dissimilar ways. The Walloon Church was an adjunct of the public Church and here the town councils tended to support the authority of the Church's Synod and elders as they did that of the public Church itself. The Walloon Church in the Dutch Republic avoided becoming entangled in the Voetian–Cocceian controversies, at any rate down to the early eighteenth century.[131] For the Walloon Church, it was the Huguenot influx of the 1680s which posed a problem for internal unity, since the Huguenot pastors who arrived at that time were a heterogeneous group theologically and, though many were orthodox Calvinists, some were liberals, chiliasts, and even, it was suspected, in some cases Socinians. To ensure doctrinal purity, and unity, the Walloon Synod, meeting at Rotterdam in 1686, established a commission of surveillance, consisting of four pastors and four professors of theology, to censor preaching and publications.[132] The Synod also drew up an oath of conformity, known as the 'Declaration of Rotterdam', which by 1689 had been signed by no fewer than 202 refugee pastors.

The sole undisguised rift in the Walloon Church arose from the De Labadie affair, in the late 1660s. Jean de Labadie (1610–74), a former Jesuit, from southern France, who had converted to the Reformed faith in Geneva, and, in 1666, become a preacher at Middelburg, was a magnetic personality whose religious impact continued to trouble the United Provinces for decades. His thought displayed mystical, chiliastic tendencies combined with an intense asceticism and zeal to reform private and public life. Impatient with compromise, the slow progress of the Further Reformation, and the

---

[131] Goeters, *Vorbereitung*, 272.   [132] Cerny, *Theology, Politics, and Letters*, 62–3.

Walloon Synod's wariness of aligning with the Voetians in condemning Cartesian philosophy and science, De Labadie openly challenged the authority of the Walloon Synod.[133] His rebellion, stemming from inflexible fundamentalism, led in 1669 to his expulsion from the Church and the secession of his followers. The affair caused a sensation throughout the land and by no means only in Reformed circles. The Collegiant mystical Spiritualist Petrus Serrarius deemed his expulsion a glaring instance of the tyranny of organized Churches over the individual conscience.

The Walloon Church, alarmed by the threat posed by Labadism to its authority and unity, appealed to the provincial assemblies for support.[134] The secular authorities, sensitive to the theological interdependence of the Walloon and public Churches, intervened. De Labadie was expelled from Middelburg and then Veere. Labadist conventicles were banned in Utrecht as early as May 1669. Gelderland followed, enjoining the provincial Hof to keep a vigilant eye to prevent the distribution of De Labadie's publications in the province.[135] Before long, Labadist gatherings were officially prohibited throughout the Republic.

The Labadists were soon obliged to leave even Amsterdam, the main group migrating to Herford, in Westphalia, and then Altona, before returning to settle in the Frisian village of Wieuwerd, halfway between Sneek and Leeuwarden, in 1675. Locke visited the community, then of roughly one hundred, in 1684, finding them remarkable for their severity, sharing their goods in common, being 'much separated from the world', and finally for their discourse, which 'carries with it a supposition of more purity in them than ordinary and as if nobody were in a way to heaven but they'.[136]

De Labadie's following was small but fervent and select, attracting a few eminent personages. Among these was a sister of a governor of Surinam, Cornelis Aerssen van Sommelsdijk, who governed the territory in the years 1683–8. This redoubtable lady brought a Labadist colony out with her in the same year that Locke visited Wieuwerd. They established their community on a plantation which they called *La Providence*, forty miles up the Surinam river, beyond the zone secured by Dutch colonization. However, they failed to convert their hostile Indian neighbours, and eventually abandoned the plantation and left Surinam.

The intolerance shown towards De Labadie and his adherents was symptomatic of a profound nervousness arising at least partly from the fact that his rebellion expressed (albeit in an extreme form) a dissatisfaction

[133] Trimp, *Jodocus van Lodensteyn*, 121–3; Van der Wall, *Mystieke chiliast*, 453–4, 495.
[134] ARH SH 2606. Walloon Synod to SH, 3 Apr. and 8 Sept. 1669.
[135] ARH PR 15. res. S. Geld. 6 May 1669.
[136] Van Strien, *British Travellers*, 310–12.

prevalent in orthodox Calvinist circles. His break with the Walloon Synod stemmed from impatience with the compromises and moderation of the public Church which was, to an extent, shared by all the Voetian stream. Not the least disturbing aspect of the affair was that Anna Maria van Schurman (1607–78), celebrated paragon of Calvinist severity and one of the best known Dutch women of her time, as well as a long-standing friend of De Labadie, openly joined his group at Amsterdam, defying the authority of both the public Church and magistracies who had censured Labadism. Anna Maria (who as a young woman had amazed Descartes with her habit of reading Scripture in Hebrew) had for decades been Reformed society's 'docta sine exemplo femina', and a key role model as well as lay ally of Voetius Van Lodenstein, and other leaders of the Further Reformation. Voetius tried hard to dissuade her, fearing lest others should separate. In her answer to the summons of the Utrecht consistory, she sternly deplored the fact that worldly concerns for the Church as an organization should take precedence over fundamental spiritual values, scorning the Church's condemnation of the doctrinally pure 'house-church' to which she belonged, in Amsterdam, as 'schismatic', and attempts to suppress it, in a land where all manner of heretical sects were tolerated.[137] Anna Maria in 1673 published her autobiography, *Eucleria* (characteristically in Latin)—a Dutch version appeared in 1684—not failing to point out that Van Lodenstein and other leading figures of the public Church had long shared her frustration at the slow progress of a wider and purer reformation of Church and society.[138]

The provincial and civic authorities were determined to protect the cohesion of the public Church and its adjunct, the Walloon Church, and help shield them from the effects of inner controversy but, of course, showed less concern about the internal condition of the dissenting Churches. Even so, it would be wrong to suppose that they took no interest in the government of the lesser Churches. For they were anxious to maintain the stability of civic and rural society generally and felt a need to intervene in dissenters' internal disputes when these seemed likely to cause excessive disturbance.

The elders of the Mennonite churches themselves grew alarmed in the 1650s, with the growth of Collegiant and Socinian ideas among some of their followers and the resulting erosion of the authority of elders, congregation, and confessional discipline.[139] Reaction against these tendencies came to a head in Amsterdam, in the mid-1660s, where the Mennonite

[137] Leiburg, *Nadere Reformatie*, 126–7.
[138] Trimp, *Jodocus van Lodensteyn*, 98.
[139] Kühler, *Socinianisme*, 154–61; Van Slee, *Rijnsburger Collegianten*, 144–9.

conservatives organized a campaign against the popular teacher Galenus Abrahamsz de Haan (1622-1706), an enthusiastic, Anabaptist, participant in the Collegiant movement who believed in dialogue between Anabaptists and Collegiants and watering down confessional differences. The Mennonite precisians, or 'Old Mennonites' as they became known, were a confessional movement aimed at restoring the authority of congregation, elders, and dogma. They insisted on submission to the Confession of the Faith, drawn up by Hans de Ries and Lubbert Gerritsz.[140] An open rift occurred among the Amsterdam 'Waterlanders', in 1664, after which the Old Mennonites eschewed all further contact with the Collegiants, 'Socinians', and other rebels against what they regarded as the pure teaching of Menno. The split spread to Utrecht, Haarlem, and Leiden, and then further afield, also splitting the Mennonite communities in Zeeland.[141]

The Remonstrants too were caught in a swirl of theological controversy in the 1650s and 1660s, engendered by the Collegiant movement, anti-church attitudes, and Socinianism. The ensuing erosion of doctrinal cohesion and communal discipline plunged the Remonstrant Church into a phase of spiritual crisis which it was the life's work of Philippus van Limborch (1633-1712), the leading Remonstrant theologian of the second half of the century, to address. A not dissimilar rift opened up among the ranks of the Lutherans, where the orthodox traditionalist or 'Wittenberg' stream was challenged by a liberal movement which arose at Amsterdam, headed by Coenraad Hoppe (1621-70), which became known as the 'Dutch stream'. Hoppe was influenced by the liberal Helmstedt school of theology, in Germany, and like them pressed for dialogue with other Churches, flexibility in doctrine, a good library for the community, and a seminary for training a new type of Lutheran preacher. Until Hoppe, Lutheran preachers in the Republic had been trained and recruited in Germany; the very idea of training preachers in Amsterdam smacked of heresy to the traditionalists. For over three decades, a formal split was avoided but at the cost of continuing internal strife bitter enough, at Amsterdam, to cause the civic authorities to intervene several times. The struggle was complicated by the efforts of the Amsterdam Lutherans to lay down the law to the rest. Finally, in 1696, ten of the thirty-eight Lutheran congregations in the Republic—led by The Hague, Rotterdam, Gouda, Alkmaar, and Zaandam—seceded, setting up the so-called Hague Union of Lutheran churches.[142]

---

[140] Meihuizen, *Galenus Abrahamsz*, 103-8.
[141] Ibid.
[142] Loosjes, *Gesch. der Luthersche kerk*, 146-53.

Regents, and republican writers of the States party-faction, were not slow to see the parallels between the Voetian–Cocceian struggle within the public Church and the battles between precisians and liberals in the lesser Churches. On the one side were consistories and boards of elders seeking to impose confessional, organizational, and moral discipline; on the other, a plethora of dissidents, striving to create more flexible, less dogmatic structures. Ideologues of the States party-faction satirized the Voetian wing of the public Church as the 'Scots Devil', implying it derived from Scots Calvinism, which Dutch critics deemed the epitome of theological inflexibility and puritanical zeal.[143] One particularly vehement anti-Voetian pamphlet of the 1660s, the work, seemingly, of the Dordrecht regent Johan de Wit (1618–76; cousin of his more famous near-namesake, the Pensionary of Holland), bore the title *Den Schotschen Duyvel* (The Scots Devil). According to this tract, Voetius was the 'arch-mutineer', the prime mover of sedition against the regents, inflaming the people with his bigotry. 'Freedom is the true bond and aim of the Union', stated de Wit, accusing Voetius of preaching reverence for the Union of Utrecht while actually seeking to pervert it into a new tyranny, the yoke of confessional discipline and Calvinist orthodoxy. Advocating 'freedom', and toleration, the tract extolled the principles of Grotius, a figure abhorred by Voetians.

During the De Witt era, the orthodox often complained that the Holland regents deliberately selected Cocceians, rather than 'upright' candidates, for the 'best places', as preachers in the main towns. The regents were alleged to be oppressing the consistories, which had been 'stripped of their freedom' to appoint 'upright preachers'. Who were these 'upright preachers'? The *Schotschen Duyvel* replied that they were those like 'Voetius, Teellinck, Smout, Essenius, Lodenstein, Gentman, and Rysennius . . . all rebellious, frustrated, overweening, impudent, and shameless, vilifiers of persons high and low'.[144] 'That is what you call freedom,' charged De Wit, 'the freedom to enslave everybody.' Pieter de la Court even suggested that Voetians were not devout at all but 'godless men, much worse than atheists', who had perverted the Reformation, and meaning of Scripture, in their ruthless pursuit of power.'[145] The *Schotschen Duyvel* bracketed Voetians, strict Lutherans, and Old Mennonites together as all of a piece—all against 'freedom' and 'moderation'.[146]

---

[143] De la Court, 'Brieven', 131.
[144] [De Wit], *Schotschen Duyvel*, 62–3.
[145] De la Court, 'Brieven', 131.
[146] [De Wit] *Schotschen Duyvel*, 63, 68–9.

THE LATER STAGES OF THE TOLERATION DEBATE

At the close of the seventeenth century and beginning of the eighteenth, the battle for religious toleration in the United Provinces was, thus, by no means won. On the contrary, the toleration debate in the Republic only reached its climax in the 1680s, 1690s, and first decade of the new century, just as in England, France, and Germany. Advocating toleration, on principle, was becoming more frequent in the Dutch context, as in the English, and both Dutch and foreign writers resident in the Republic made numerous contributions to the European debate. On the one side, there was the secular republican toleration tradition of De la Court and Valckenier, continued by Ericus Walten, Gregorio Leti, and Gerard Noodt. Leti proclaimed the United Provinces the model European society, in his *Raguagli politici* (1700), the home of toleration, the *mater gentium*. Noodt, one of the Republic's leading professors of law, argued strongly for toleration in a famous address, in Latin, delivered at Leiden in February 1706 and subsequently published in abstract in Le Clerc's *Bibliothèque choisie*, in French, and, in Dutch, by Halma, in the *Boekzaal*, followed within two years by full French and English translations and, subsequently, by German versions. Noodt's was the culminating Dutch defence in secular, natural right terms, rather than theological principles.[147] He declared the Almighty 'le seul maître de nos consciences' and denied that any Church or ecclesiastical authority could have authority over the individual except 'celle des conseils, des exhortations'.[148] At the same time, there was a further strengthening of the theological toleration tradition stemming from Episcopius and the Arminians, in the writings of Philippus van Limborch, Locke's principal Dutch friend, and Le Clerc. In the eloquent oration Le Clerc delivered in Amsterdam, at Van Limborch's funeral in 1712, a text published in English the following year, he reminded the world how Van Limborch had continued Episcopius' work with his 1661 treatise on toleration, his publishing Episcopius' unpublished work, his *Theologica christiana* (1686), which remained one of the most discussed Dutch theological works in the early eighteenth century, his dialogue with the Sephardi Jewish anti-Christian controversialist Isaac Orobio de Castro, published at Gouda, in 1687, and his *History of the Inquisition*, dedicated to the Latitudinarian archbishop of Canterbury, Tillotson, in 1692.[149]

It was also Van Limborch, Le Clerc failed to add, who revived the memory of that long-forgotten Sephardi Jewish intellectual, Uriel da Costa

---

[147] Van den Bergh, *Life and Work of Gerard Noodt*, 224–38.
[148] Noodt, *Discours sur la liberté de conscience*, 332, 405.
[149] Le Clerc, *A Funeral Oration*, 8–13; Barnouw, *Philippus van Limborch*, 18, 24–7.

(*c*.1583–1640), whose *Examination of Pharisaic Traditions*, denying the immortality of the soul, published at Amsterdam (in Portuguese), in 1624, had been condemned by the Sephardic elders and publicly burned by the Amsterdam magistrates,[150] and who, in a fit of depression brought on by the degradation to which he had been subjected, committed suicide in 1640. The book had been effectively suppressed, indeed remained lost until the sole known surviving copy was discovered in Copenhagen, towards the end of the twentieth century. Van Limborch's purpose in publishing Da Costa's Latin autobiography, entitled *Exemplar humanae vitae* (a manuscript of which had survived amongst Episcopius' papers), in 1687, was primarily to demonstrate the evil of religious intolerance in whatever context by showing how the Amsterdam Portuguese Jewish elders and rabbis had crushed Da Costa's spirit, subjecting him to every humiliation. But the effect was to rescue from near oblivion a figure who, while arousing some sympathy, also now became widely notorious for having denied the immortality of the soul. Inevitably, his name was linked with Spinoza's and his text assigned to the growing list of books spreading unease among orthodox churchmen of all hues.

Finally, in addition to the native traditions advocating toleration, there was the towering genius of Pierre Bayle, who emerged in the 1680s and 1690s as the apologist *par excellence*, above all on philosophical grounds, of an unrestricted toleration of belief for every individual, including the right to be mistaken and hold ill-founded views.[151]

Yet much, or most, opinion in the Republic, including mainstream intellectual opinion among the Huguenots, did not accept either the republican toleration of De la Court, Walten, and Leti, or the theological toleration of Episcopius and Van Limborch, or the philosophical, sceptical toleration of Bayle. Regents, university curators, professors, and preachers were, in the main, more tolerant than their counterparts in the rest of Europe. But their principles were, at most, those of a semi-toleration of practical necessity, tempering somewhat intolerant inclinations and views. Up to a point one was allowed to discuss and propagate dissident religious opinions. It may be true that to foreign visitors used to more repressive societies, and greater religious uniformity, the degree of religious freedom allowed in the Republic often seemed, even at the end of the seventeenth century, horrifying and absurd. Stouppe had numerous successors who continued to elaborate on this theme. One English observer described Holland as a 'university of all religions, the fair of all the sectes where all

---

[150] Da Costa, *Examination*, 17, 311–18.   [151] Berkvens-Stevelinck, 'Tolerance', 257–8.

pedlars of religion have leave to vent their toys, their ribbons and phanatick rattles'.[152] But such reactions generally reflected the position in Amsterdam rather than in the rest of Dutch society and even in relation to Amsterdam and Rotterdam were greatly oversimplified. For there were stringent limits on what could be published, openly declared, or even uttered in conversation. One needed to take care not to overstep the mark. Even in Amsterdam, Bayle noted in 1701, anyone publicly contradicting the doctrine of the Holy Trinity stood an excellent chance of being sent to prison.[153] It was this ambivalent semi-tolerance which was the real hallmark of the Dutch Republic at the end of the Golden Age, a partial toleration seething with tension, theological and political, both within, and between, the principal church blocs and between these and their dissident offshoots.[154]

[152] *A Trip to Holland*, 12.
[153] Bayle, *Lettres*, iii. 828, 835.
[154] Bots, 'Tolerantie', 664; Berkvens-Stevelinck, 'Tolerance', 269.

28

Freedom and Order

❖

A DISCIPLINED SOCIETY

Descartes complained, in 1643, that the United Provinces were not as 'free' as he had originally supposed. Decades later, Spinoza and Bayle, not to mention Koerbagh and Walten (see pp. 919, 929 below) had still greater reason to lament the limited character of Dutch freedom. During the seventeenth century, and early eighteenth, foreign visitors routinely praised the comparative freedom, both for groups and the individual, prevailing in the Republic. But the more perceptive also noticed that this freedom was a complex phenomenon rooted in a deep preoccupation with order and discipline.

No aspect of Dutch freedom in the Golden Age struck contemporaries, especially foreigners, more than that enjoyed by women—of all classes and types. Dutch women, even young, unmarried women, were free to come and go, unaccompanied and unchaperoned, to work, conduct business, and engage in conversation almost like men.[1] Everyone agreed that, in Dutch society, wives were less subservient to their husbands than elsewhere. The German Heinrich Benthem, writing in the 1690s, sharply contrasted the way the Dutch and Germans went to church on Sundays, noting that in Germany husbands walked together, talking, whilst their wives followed, shepherding the children. Only in Holland, he noted, scornfully, did the women accompany each other to church gossiping whilst their husbands tended the children: 'for here the hen crows and the cock merely cackles'.[2]

Yet, as Leti, observed, it was precisely the personal freedom accorded to women, and girls, which most clearly revealed the connection between liberty and order. It was possible for women to enjoy a large measure of independence, coming and going as they pleased, for the same reason that

---

[1] Leti, *Raguagli historici*, i. 29–31.
[2] 'Denn hier krehet die Henne und der Hahn muss nur keckeln', quoted in Bientjes, *Holland und die Holländer*, 223.

the solitary male, or foreign traveller, could wander, day or night, in town or country with relatively little fear of being robbed, or assaulted: the individual was, and felt, secure.[3] 'On peut voyager librement par toute la Hollande', observed Jean de Parival, in 1669, 'seul et en compagnie sans crainte d'estre detroussé.'[4] The Swiss Albrecht von Haller, living in Holland, in the late 1720s, was amazed to find that in Leiden everyone went about unarmed and that one's possessions were so secure one could leave one's door unlocked and go away for days without anything being stolen.[5] Levels of crime were, and were perceived to be, low.

Not only was one safe outside the house; Leti remarked that it was also basic to Dutch freedom that one was less likely than elsewhere to be assaulted in the home. He claimed that wife-beating was uncommon in Holland, because neighbours would not tolerate it and would expose the husband to local Church and civil pressure. Thus, the fact that much of the population lived in closely regulated towns was a key factor in curbing misconduct. He also observed that servants were better treated and accorded more dignity than elsewhere, remarking that in Holland it was unacceptable to slap servants with or without other people present, as was usual, for example, in France. Significantly, an underground mock placard, printed in 1679, a piece of social protest, claimed that ill-treatment of servants in Holland was increasing owing to the new classicist-style villas and mansions, secluded from neighbours, and therefore encouraging abuse, for now masters could seduce, or beat, maidservants without anyone knowing and their wives stoop to 'cooling the fires of lust' with male servants.[6] Protection for servants lay in the strict attitudes of society.

Dutch freedom was thus rooted in the preponderance of cities and a high level of social discipline and control. Evidence of this discipline was to be seen everywhere, in the home, schools, churches, universities, merchant ships, and harbours, as well as in the navy and army. During the 1590s, there was a tussle of wills between the university senate and students, at Leiden, over the carrying of weapons. But, before long, backed by the States, the University succeeded in enforcing its ban on the wearing of swords, and other arms, by students.[7] There were also strict curbs on drinking. Parival remarked that German students at Leiden were obliged to be less rowdy than was customary at German universities.[8] Von Haller

[3] Leti, *Raguagli historici*, iii. 408–10.
[4] Parival, *Délices de la Hollande*, 174.
[5] Von Haller, *Dagboek*, 30–1.
[6] ARH SH 5318/ii, satirical placard, dated 30 Nov. 1679.
[7] Woltjer, *De Leidse universiteit*, 43–5.
[8] Enschedé, 'Jean Nicolas de Parival', 83.

commented on the orderliness, and lack of heavy drinking, characteristic of student life, at Leiden, a product, he thought, of the cold temperament and regimented life-style of the people. Discipline was particularly severe at the States College, where students were awakened at five in summer, and six in winter, for prayer and Bible reading, and expected to have tidied their rooms before breakfast.

Harder to discipline than students were the Republic's sailors, whether in the navy, VOC, WIC, merchant ships, whalers, or privateers, both on land and at sea. Yet no form of discipline was more essential both for the success of the Dutch overseas trading system and the well-being of Dutch society as a whole. Seamen constituted a large proportion of the population and appeared in droves in numerous Dutch towns as well as foreign ports. The results were far from perfect, particularly on privateers, which carried much larger crews than merchantmen, in more cramped conditions, but where the means to maintain discipline were less than was the case on warships and VOC vessels. Yet, by and large, the standard was high and Dutch ships became known all over the world not only for their spruceness but for the cleanliness and good order of their crews. There were separate, printed codes of discipline for not only the navy but the VOC, WIC, and privateers, and the men were made familiar with the articles before each voyage.[9] These were both detailed and rigorous. Even on the privateers, prayers and psalm-singing took place twice daily, morning and evening, with money fines for sailors absent without permission.

Among the eminent Dutch seamen of the age, there were, as one might expect, some notoriously unruly characters. But such men encountered no little pressure to improve. Michiel de Ruyter (1607–76), by his own admission, regularly behaved badly as a youth, was hot-headed and frequently involved in fights.[10] Though he came from a humble family background, at Flushing, he rose to the pinnacle of command in the navy, not least through his unrivalled ability to instil discipline in his men; he also became widely known, in later life, for the genuineness of his piety. By contrast, Abel Tasman tended to deteriorate. In 1642, he undertook his famous voyage, from Batavia, on which he discovered Tasmania and New Zealand. Six years later, in April 1648, he commanded the last major Dutch attack on the Spaniards of the Eighty Years War, an unsuccessful expedition to the Philippines on which he drank heavily, flew into a rage, and severely assaulted two of his own men. For this he was tried by the VOC's High Court of Justice, at Batavia, suspended from the service, and stripped

[9] Verhees-van Meer, *De zeeuwse kaapvaart*, 62–3; Bruijn, *Dutch Navy*, 140.
[10] Blok, *Michiel Adriaanszoon de Ruyter*, 11–12.

of his rank. The Reformed consistory at Batavia also refused to allow him to remain an elder of the Church. Later, he was taken back into the service but a further serious lapse, this time duelling, led to his being permanently disgraced by the VOC and stigmatized by the consistory.[11]

The greatest pressure to discipline sailors, students, soldiers, as well as orphans, apprentices, and many other groups, in order to ensure a well-ordered society, derived from the main towns and town councils. There were various levels of supervision, and agents of punishment, but arguably most crucial, in policing the towns, were the neighbourhood watches, local citizen organizations in the various quarters of the towns, headed by elected local burghers. The neighbourhood watches saw it as their task not only to guard their quarter, preventing robbery and crime, but also to enforce decency and apprise the town's *schout*, magistrates, or consistory of unacceptable behaviour. Policing had to devolve upon the neighbourhoods in this way.[12] For the civic militia, responsible for keeping order, and maintaining a guard at the town-hall and city gates, at night, would only be called out in the event of serious disturbances. The *schout*, or sheriff, and his handful of deputies, headed the policing effort, and made arrests in serious cases, but were too few to shoulder the main burden of policing. At Amsterdam, during the last quarter of the seventeenth century, the sheriff and his staff amounted, together with a few servants, to just eighteen persons.

As one of their main tasks, the elected citizens' committees in each quarter of a town organized a system of regular night-time patrolling of the streets. At Amsterdam, in the 1660s, there were approximately 300 lightly armed burghers on duty each night, around half of whom would be patrolling the streets at any one time. They were paid 5 stuivers per night for the work. Each of the neighbourhood watches had a primitive local gaol where miscreants could be locked up until the *schout* and his staff had had a chance to consider their offences. The citizenry participated in these neighbourhood watches, and co-operated with them, because they knew everyone involved, the watches were an inherent part of the local scene, and it was directly in their own interest to prevent rowdiness and crime.

It was taken for granted that little of what went on in a neighbourhood would escape the notice of the neighbourhood watches. This is the reason why wife- and servant-beating were relatively rare and blatant street prostitution (as opposed to concealed prostitution in taverns) was unusual. The system was effective at checking all forms of violent crime and abuse, including rape. A young woman alleging rape, when explaining pregnancy

[11] Slot, *Abel Tasman*, 78–83.　　[12] Spierenburg, *Judicial Violence*, 38.

outside of wedlock before a Reformed consistory, would not be found convincing unless she offered some reason why her cries for help went unanswered.[13] A seamstress who claimed to have been raped at night, in the streets of Amsterdam, in 1616, assured the consistory she had cried for help but that the strong wind blowing at the time had prevented her cries being heard. The crucial importance of neighbours, and neighbourhood watches, in curbing misconduct and maintaining the high level of social control typical of the Golden Age, and eighteenth-century Dutch society, is proven by the fact that statistics for assault, and other violent crime, tended to be considerably higher for the countryside than for large towns.[14] The civic ethic underpinned all.

The adoption of public street lighting, one of the outstanding examples of the successful application of technology to daily life in the Dutch Golden Age, was motivated by several considerations but especially a desire further to enhance orderliness and reduce crime—as well as the incidence of drunkards falling into canals and drowning at night. The world's first real system of public street lighting was devised by the Amsterdam artist-inventor Jan van der Heyden (1637–1712), who invented a street-lamp manufactured of glass and metal, with shielded air-holes, capable of letting out the smoke, without letting in the wind. The lamps burnt through the night on a mixture of vegetable oils with wicks of Cypriot cotton manufactured at Van der Heyden's lamp factory. The plans for lighting up Amsterdam were adopted by the *vroedschap*, in 1669, and took only a few months to implement.[15] By January 1670, the entire city was lit up by 1,800 public lanterns on posts, or affixed to walls of public buildings, Van der Heyden having calculated that maximum lighting efficiency, on a minimum expenditure of oil, was attained with lanterns placed 125 to 150 feet apart. A code of punishments was then published, that same year, for the new civic offences of vandalizing public lanterns, tying up boats, or horses, against the posts, or emptying garbage around them, thereby impeding the work of the public lamplighters and cleaners.[16] Each lamplighter lit twenty lanterns, so that 100 were required to service the entire city. By 1681 another 600 lanterns had been added. The system was a resounding success and the advantages for street security, at night, so manifest it was soon adopted by The Hague and other Dutch and German cities, though only partly in England, where the towns lacked the civic institutions, and finances, which

---

[13] Roodenburg, *Onder censuur*, 304.
[14] Noordam, 'Prostitutie in Leiden', 68.
[15] Multhauf, 'Light of Lamp-Lanterns', 238.
[16] Ibid. 240.

could undertake such large-scale schemes. Dordrecht installed the new street-lamps in 1674,[17] 's-Hertogenbosch did so, erecting 450 of Van der Heyden's public lanterns, in 1684. At 's-Hertogenbosch, the municipality employed eighteen municipal street-lamp 'lighters', who refilled and, every evening, lit twenty-five lanterns each at an annual cost of 3,000 guilders.[18] It took fifteen minutes to light up the entire city. Berlin and Cologne installed the Dutch street-lamps in 1682.

Dutch freedom was real but had stringent limits. Furthermore, Dutch society was often less permissive of errant, deviant, or flamboyant behaviour than of unorthodox ideas. In particular, Dutch society was not less, but more, prone than other European societies to repress bawdiness, eroticism, undisguised homosexuality, and street prostitution. Foreign observers— Trevisano, Saint-Évremond, Temple, and Leti—all remarked on the coldness, eschewing of all coquetry, and 'very general good fame' of the Dutch female. In fact what they discerned was a powerful repression of the erotic, and perhaps a necessary one if women were freely to go about their daily lives unchaperoned—to be matter-of-fact in routine, daily dealings with menfolk. Dutch women of the higher classes, after 1650, eagerly adopted French fabrics and fashion except, Leti noted, for one feature: Dutch society simply would not tolerate the plunging necklines and flaunting of the bosom prevalent, at the time, in France, England, and Italy.[19] In the Republic, high necklines were *de rigueur* for fine ladies and serving maids alike.

Prostitution was widespread in Dutch society but, in contrast to other European countries, characterized by a relative absence of soliciting in streets and a tendency to disguise brothels as something else.[20] At Amsterdam brothels offered music and were called 'music halls', drawing a discreet veil over what went on upstairs. Moreover, even at Amsterdam, there were no real 'red light' districts in which prostitutes flaunted their figures. In other towns, including Leiden, not only was street prostitution unusual but there were no brothels of any size. Rather prostitution was plied inconspicuously in inns and lodging houses, scattered about the poorer quarters and outskirts, usually with only one or two girls working in any one establishment.[21] More respectable districts, including, at Leiden, the university area, were generally free from prostitution, even though students were

[17] Van Dalen, *Gesch. van Dordrecht*, ii. 593.
[18] Van Heurn, *Historie*, iii. 287–8.
[19] Leti, *Teatro Belgico*, ii. 29.
[20] Van de Pol, 'Beeld en werkelijkheid', 136–7.
[21] Noordam, 'Prostitutie in Leiden', 71–4.

among the prostitutes' most frequent customers, in other parts of town. It is this reticence, doubtless, which explains the notoriety in the north Netherlands, in the early seventeenth century (before the authorities became stricter about prostitution also in the south), of Antwerp's city-centre brothel quarter.[22] This celebrated district, much visited by travellers, exhibited prostitution much more blatantly than was allowed north of the rivers. It was estimated, at the beginning of the century, that there were over 125 brothels in Antwerp.

The wide dispersal of houses of ill-repute, in the Dutch context, was essential if they were to remain discreet and inconspicuous, and thus for their survival. The girls who worked in them dressed like respectable women on their way to and from them, just as erotic pictures could be bought under the counter but not openly displayed. Dutch brothels of the Golden Age can be compared to the 'hidden churches' of the Catholics. Many people knew where they were. But they were tolerated only as long as they stayed seemingly innocuous and caused no disturbance.[23] Prosecutions of brothel-keepers (who were often women), and whores, frequently resulted from street brawls or other rowdy incidents scandalizing a locality.[24] It is significant that the Amsterdam Reformed consistory when considering complaints concerning alleged houses of ill-repute were often uncertain whether a particular address was, in fact, a brothel or not.[25] Leti, who asserts there were only around thirty brothels in Amsterdam in his day, far fewer than in Venice or 'so-called holy Rome', confirms that the chief difference between Italian and Dutch whoredom was that the Dutch pushed it out of sight, remarking that in Holland one simply did not see the brazen enticement of men from windows, and in streets, usual, he says, in Italy.[26]

Suppression of the erotic extended also to banning even mildly pornographic books and art.[27] It may be, as has been argued, that in the Republic, during the second half of the seventeenth century, suppression of erotic books, often of French origin, was less strict than in France itself.[28] But, even so, such works, including the most notorious, *L'École des filles* (1669), were prohibited, in both their Dutch and French versions, and remained forbidden throughout the following century. Erotic pictures, it would seem,

---

[22] Thijs, *Van Geuzenstad tot katholiek bolwerk*, 138.
[23] Van de Pol, 'Beeld en werkelijkheid', 131–40.
[24] Noordam, 'Prostitutie in Leiden', 66.
[25] Roodenburg, *Onder censuur*, 292–3.
[26] Leti, *Raguagli historici*, i, rag. 3, p. 269; Leti, *Il ceremoniale*, v. 734.
[27] Knuttel, *Verboden boeken*, 29, 39.
[28] Haks, 'Libertinisme', 86.

were more stringently suppressed than text alone. In a country with such a plethora of skilled artists, it was always likely that at least a few would pander to the taste for the titillating. But we know of remarkably few instances and, in both of the best-known cases, the artists concerned paid a heavy price for engaging in such work. One was the great still-life painter Jan Torrentius, who was sentenced to twenty years' imprisonment, at Haarlem, in 1628, essentially for blasphemy but, in part, also for having executed a series of pornographic paintings. The other instance involved the late seventeenth-century Orangist engraver Romeyn de Hooghe (*c.*1645–1708), whose prosecution by the Amsterdam magistrates was widely attributed to political animus; nevertheless, the substance of the charges was that he had produced, and sold, erotic engravings.

But also with the printed word ventures into the realm of the erotic had necessarily to be furtive. The eminent historian Aitzema, a known philanderer, hinted—but only in inconspicuous places buried deep in his voluminous published work—that sexual intercourse outside of wedlock is no sin. The one Dutch writer who flagrantly defied the rules in this sphere was the initially wealthy Zeelander Adriaan van Beverland (*c.*1652–1716), a remarkable personality of whom there survives a portrait by Ary de Vois, showing him as a young man sitting smoking an immensely long pipe, beside an elegant and provocatively *décolleté* prostitute.[29] Van Beverland, whilst a gentleman-student at Leiden, collected erotica (as well as medallions and sea shells), became an accomplished classical scholar, researched the history of prostitution in the Roman Empire, and published a book on original sin, his *De Peccato Originale* (1678)—which later also appeared in French and was banned in France—finding Adam and Eve guilty of no more than discovering sexual intercourse. His scepticism about the Church's doctrine of original sin, compounded in the second edition (1679) by his drawing on Hobbes and Spinoza for support, caused such offence that the States of Holland, under pressure from the South Holland Synod, asked the Leiden university authorities to arrest and interrogate him. The copies of his book were seized and burnt.[30] Banished from Holland, he moved to Utrecht but, before long, was expelled from there too. In 1680, he emigrated to England where he remained until he died, an impoverished freethinker, in London, in 1716. Van Beverland's brand of overt sexual libertinism, with what were seen as its insidious intellectual and religious implications, was simply not tolerated in the Dutch Republic. Nor was any obvious display of sexually

[29] Schwartz, *Dutch World of Painting*, 120.
[30] Benthem, *Holländischer Kirch- und Schulen-Staat* ii. 452–3.

provocative or dissolute behaviour, whatever went on out of sight. As the French nobleman Saint-Évremond remarked of Holland in the 1660s: 'la débauche s'y cache, la pensée libre s'y affirme, mais l'une et l'autre se pratiquent avec sérieux et à fond'.[31]

Another key agent of social discipline were the Reformed consistories. Backed by the neighbourhood watches, and supplied with additional information from the house-visits of the preachers and their assistants, the 'sick comforters', the consistories kept up a relentless pressure, at all levels, against immodesty, promiscuity, rowdiness, drunkenness, dishonest bankruptcies, and, not least, the low-cut dresses worn by a few fashionable ladies in courtly circles. The consistories were not unaware that many, or most, cases of adultery and fornication went undetected. They nevertheless believed that where instances came to light it was vital to investigate, and bring pressure to bear. For no open challenge to society's norms could be tolerated, especially—as in the case of Rembrandt and Hendrickje Stoffels— where there was an element of defiance.[32] The summoning of Rembrandt's housekeeper, in 1654, for living like a 'whore' with 'Rembrandt the painter' was a routine incident of its kind. The number of summonses before the Amsterdam consistory, for adultery, steadily increased in the period down to 1680, a major objective being to break up irregular liaisons, mobilizing social pressure to reduce offending individuals to penitence and willingness to reform.

For members of the public Church, anxious for their souls, banishment from the Lord's Supper, and public exposure as unchaste, was not only harmful to one's reputation and social standing, but damaged one's spiritual status. Many of those who suffered the Church's censure subsequently went to some lengths to show contrition and recover lost respectability. A young Haarlem widow who had a child out of wedlock and was barred from the Lord's Supper, in 1700, was obliged to live for three years without further blot on her reputation under scrutiny of her local preacher, to get the sanction removed.[33] In 1705, a Haarlem woman who gave birth out of wedlock, pleading rape, was similarly barred and placed under the scrutiny of her local preacher, with the admonition that she would be readmitted to the sacrament if she maintained a reputation for chastity over the next four years.[34]

---

[31] Quoted in Roldanus, *Coenraad van Beuningen*, 140.
[32] Roodenburg, *Onder censuur*, 281.
[33] GA Haarlem kerkeraad 10/11. res. 6 Apr. 1703.
[34] GA Haarlem 10/11. res. 7 July 1705.

SCHOOLS, LITERACY, AND THE RESHAPING OF
POPULAR CULTURE

Long before 1572 the Netherlands both north and south of the great rivers exhibited higher levels of literacy than neighbouring parts of Europe, owing essentially to the very high proportion of the population dwelling in towns. But unquestionably the Revolt and eventual triumph of the Reformed Church in the north, as well as the victory of the Catholic Church in the south, lent much additional impetus to schooling and pushed literacy levels higher still. Even so the parting of the ways in institutions and religion also led to a widening gap between north and south in respect of schooling and literacy. For if north and south were equally committed to the race to confessionalize the population, in the south catechizing was often oral whilst in the north the centrality of Bible and catechism-reading in the confession-alization process generated a more sustained and widespread effort to advance literacy in both towns and countryside. The resulting gap between north and south was still clearly evident in the middle of the nineteenth century. In 1843, 51 per cent of army recruits in Belgium were illiterate, to give one example, as against a comparable figure of 26 per cent in the Netherlands.[35] It is clear that in the Dutch Republic literacy among both men and women attained a level, and a literacy-based culture developed to an extent, which was wholly exceptional in Europe and which did not become normative elsewhere until centuries later. When the great scholar, Scaliger, arrived from France in 1593, he was astonished to find that in Holland even servant girls could read.

After the Revolt, the provincial States, town governments, and the public Church in the north all took a far greater interest in expanding and regulating the schools in both towns and countryside than had the secular and ecclesiastical authorities before 1572. The overwhelming motive for doing so was the pressure to confessionalize the population in a Reformed direction as rapidly and effectively as possible, both to counter the efforts of the dissenting Protestant Churches, and the Catholics, and to widen the base of support for the rebel state and the new public Church. It is for this reason that the chief emphasis in education at primary level was always on reading, instilling the catechism, and church-going. Learning to write was regarded as less essential, while arithmetic was not considered part of elementary education at all. But, if the motivation was confessional, it is also apparent that the great expansion of primary education in the United

---

[35] Van der Woude, 'Onderwijs en opvoeding', 258.

Provinces after 1590 coincided with the major expansion of the cities, and of the economy, and that the spread of literacy not only buttressed the confessionalization process but assisted the diffusion of many kinds of technical knowledge, including military and naval drill, and served to advance social mobility by increasing the opportunities available to able boys from humble backgrounds, not the least of whom was the great admiral Michiel de Ruyter. Majority literacy also had the effect of enabling humble men such as sailors, bargemen, and artisans to follow political and church developments by reading the numerous Dutch-language, and often popularly couched, pamphlets issuing from the presses from the 1570s onwards.

Educational strategy in the north, though shaped by the needs of the new public Church, was laid down and controlled by the provincial States and the town governments. Here we encounter a fundamental difference between north and south. For in the Spanish, and later the Austrian, Netherlands, the Church, at the insistence of central government in Brussels, exercised a direct control over the appointment and regulation of schoolmasters and mistresses, turning the existing schoolmasters' guilds in the towns into a strict regulatory mechanism without the provincial and civic authorities participating in the process.[36] In the north, by contrast, except at Middelburg, schoolmasters' guilds were everywhere absent from the picture.[37] The system in the south was designed to ensure that only strictly Catholic education was provided. The system in the north ensured that Reformed schooling everywhere predominated but nowhere exercised an absolute monopoly.

In the years following the Revolt, the northern provincial States drew up provincial 'school orders' and regulations intended to promote elementary education. They gave responsibility for administering the school system, appointing teachers in the 'public schools', and licensing private school teachers to the town governments and, in the countryside, to those who had inherited, or purchased, local lordly rights—which, in Holland and Zeeland, often again meant the town governments. But, at the same time, the provincial States assigned the public Church an important advisory role as regards appointments and measures to assist poor parents to send their children to school, and a dominant voice in determining the syllabus in the 'public schools'. Thus the States of Zeeland in their school order of 1583, renewed in 1590, declared that one of their prime responsibilities was to ensure that the youth of Zeeland should be 'educated and brought up in the

---

[36] Art, 'Volksonderwijs', 268. [37] Welten, *Hervormers*, 17.

fear and right knowledge of God' and that accordingly only 'approved' teachers would be permitted to teach in the province; that there should be a provincial system of village schools; and that the schoolmasters in the latter should be appointed by those who held local lordly rights—whether nobles or towns—but only with the approval of, and in consultation with, the local classis of the Reformed Church.[38] In the towns, it was laid down, no one was allowed to run a 'Dutch, Latin, or French' school without the permission of the magistracy. The States of Utrecht's school order of 1588 similarly aspired to create a province-wide elementary educational system controlled by the towns and, in the countryside, by local nobles but with extensive participation by the Reformed classes.[39]

The goal of the provincial States, town councils, and Reformed classes was to provide cheap, subsidized primary education, available to most children, which would instil reading, discipline, and confessional attitudes but not necessarily writing and rarely arithmetic. Parents who wished their children to be taught to write had to pay additional fees. In order to keep the 'school money', paid by parents for their children's education, as low as possible the policy was for the towns to pay 'public' schoolmasters a basic (albeit very low) salary. With the passage of time, and growth in additional subsidies from the consistories, it also became usual in some areas for schoolmasters of Reformed schools to be obliged to teach the children of the poor free of charge. Since together the salary and 'school money' paid to village schoolmasters were rarely sufficient to make ends meet, it was common for the latter to work also for the local consistory as church choir leader, bell ringer, and in other auxiliary roles.

The teaching method used in the primary schools consisted of putting boys and girls, separated by sex and age, into small groups all in one large room, with each group at a different stage. Learning chiefly by memorizing, the children followed a fixed system, beginning with the letters of the alphabet learnt from the so-called ABC books. The schoolmaster's job was chiefly to organize these groups, maintain order, 'hear' pupils reading, and to ensure, at a later stage, that prayers, psalms, and questions and answers from the catechism were being learnt by heart.[40] Teaching in the sense of explanation and elucidation rarely intruded. From the ages of 6 to 8 children concentrated on spelling, reading, and first elements of catechism. Elementary education was then completed with more advanced reading from the catechism and excerpts from Scripture. In many schools the

[38] *Notulen SZ* 1590, 90–1. res. SZ 20 June 1590.
[39] De Booy, 'Het "basisonderwijs" ', 209–12.
[40] Ibid. 212–14.

flavour of elementary education was uncompromisingly confessional in character, featuring question-and-answer sessions such as 'Who is the head of the Reformed Churches? Answer: Christ alone'. 'What then is the Pope? Answer: the Antichrist'.[41] However, by assigning control to the town governments, and those with lordly rights in the countryside, the provincial States had created a system which allowed wide variations in the manner and zeal with which confessional education was administered. Much depended on the ideological stance of the town in question and, at any rate in Holland and Utrecht, on the attitude of local nobles. Elsewhere, on the whole, the provincial Delegated States showed more determination in refusing to allow Catholic and crypto-Catholic nobles to appoint teachers with little zeal for the Reformed faith.

One of the most important factors in the progress of Catholic and Lutheran confessionalization in towns such as Haarlem, Leiden, Rotterdam, Gouda, and also Nijmegen (where the Catholic clergy were exceptionally successful), before 1618, was that the Arminian regents who then controlled these towns adopted a much more lenient attitude towards Catholic, Lutheran, and other non-Reformed private schools than did their Counter-Remonstrant counterparts. Moreover, in rural Holland and Utrecht Catholic nobles were sometimes successful in placing, and keeping, Catholic or crypto-Catholic schoolmasters in the village schools, as for example at Warmond and Wassenaar. Nevertheless, it is clear that large numbers of Catholic children did attend Reformed village schools. For if, in the course of time, there were numerous Catholic and other non-Reformed schools in the towns, in the villages there was normally only a single school. Thus, for example, in the predominantly Catholic Utrecht village of Odijk some sixty pupils attended the Reformed village school in 1660, a size fairly typical of village schools throughout the Republic. Yet some Catholic parents clearly preferred not to send their children to school, if only Reformed education was available, even though in localities with a large Catholic population Reformed schoolmasters often diluted the confessional content of their teaching so as not to alienate parents and thereby lose school fees. Thus while literacy levels amongst the Catholic population living in the United Provinces were higher than in the Spanish Netherlands, and than among Protestants living in Britain or Germany, they were nevertheless lower than among the Dutch Protestant population. In the late eighteenth century, roughly 57 per cent of Catholic bridegrooms marrying in rural Utrecht could sign their names, whereas the comparable figure for Protestant men was 75 per cent.[42] A similar but

---

[41] Ibid. 215.   [42] Ibid. 210.

somewhat narrower gap is evident also for the cities. At Amsterdam, it was already the case, by 1630, that 57 per cent of bridegrooms and 32 per cent of brides could sign their names; by 1680, the corresponding figures had risen to 70 and 40 per cent.[43] A century later, in 1780, 87 per cent of Reformed bridegrooms and 69 per cent of Reformed brides could append their signatures as against 79 per cent of Catholic grooms and 53 per cent of Catholic brides. Literacy figures in the Amsterdam Lutheran community in the late eighteenth century were only slightly lower than those for the Reformed. Among the Jewish community, 84 per cent of bridegrooms could sign but only 31 per cent of brides, a gap between men and women which was unique in Dutch life to the Ashkenazic Jews.

An essential feature of Dutch elementary education was the emphasis on discipline. One of the principal purposes of primary education was to bring the children into the Reformed churches, under the supervision of their teachers, in disciplined rows trained to sit through the (often extremely long) sermons and to sing together. But it was by no means only in church that a reverential attitude was insisted on. Children were required to show proper respect towards their elders and betters in and outside of school and outside of church. The Zeeland school order of 1583 required that children who failed to step aside and doff their hats, on encountering grown-ups on their way to and from school, should be reported and punished.

THE FURTHER REFORMATION AND SOCIETY

All the confessional blocks in seventeenth-and eighteenth-century Dutch society strove to instil social and moral discipline into their members. Church leaders may have been at odds over a range of theological and institutional issues but in the social sphere pursued broadly similar aims, albeit with differences of emphasis, all being adamant on the need for a highly disciplined, orderly society. Thus the Jewish congregations, however different in other respects, through their boards of elders likewise enforced a stern social and moral discipline. Among Protestants the most austere, and insistent on submission of the individual to elders and consistory, were the Mennonites. All the Anabaptist groups adhered to stringent moral codes and patterns of behaviour, eschewing taverns as well as wine and spirits, and discouraging laughter—endeavouring always to look stern.[44] They were the most austere in matters of dress, the most severe towards bankrupts. After

---

[43] Hart, *Geschrift en getal*, 131.
[44] *Lammerenkrijgh*, A3; Sprunger, 'Faillissementen', 108.

the split of 1664 both main streams of Dutch Anabaptism remained decidedly strict though the Old Mennonites were the most uncompromising, refusing any concession to fashion, display, or hint of luxury. It was claimed in the eighteenth century that a principal reason for the steady decline in Mennonite numbers was their uncompromising rejection of novelties such as coffee and tea, wearing wigs, and taking snuff.

But if the Mennonites were the severest, it was the Reformed who exerted the widest influence on society. Here, however, the situation was complicated by the deep rifts within the public Church down to 1619 and again from the 1650s. For these, if rooted in theological differences, nevertheless extended, to a degree, to the social sphere, especially on questions of life-style and sabbath observance.[45] Even so by the middle of the seventeenth century, the Further Reformation—the call for a reforming of manners and morals, and a more godly society—was gaining momentum and becoming more widespread throughout the Republic. Voetius and the other prominent preachers beside him at Utrecht—Jodocus van Lodenstein (1620–77), Andreas Essenius (1618–77), Cornelis Gentman (1617–96), Johannes Teellinck (d. 1674), and the incorrigible Abraham van de Velde (1614–77)—persevered with their crusade for stricter sabbath observance, reduced toleration, and above all a thorough purification of Church and society to make both more God-fearing and godly. Van de Velde, in publications such as his *Biddaghs-Meditatie* (1659), deemed Dutch society to be deeply mired by immodesty, extravagance, adultery, prostitution, and profanation of the sabbath, warning that God had already manifested his anger by taking from the Dutch their conquests in Brazil, and other punishments, and that worse would soon follow if there was no radical change of heart.[46] Van Lodenstein, a man of deeper spirituality, and a considerable poet, was milder but, by the 1650s, likewise feared that only some great disaster would exert enough pressure to compel the regents and the rest of society to accept a thorough reformation of morals and life-style.[47] Pre-eminent figures of the Further Reformation outside Utrecht, during the third quarter of the century, included Petrus Wittewrongel (1609–62), a Zeelander who had an appreciable impact as a preacher and writer on life-style, at Amsterdam,[48] Theodorus à Brakel (1608–69), from Enkhuizen, who laboured chiefly in Friesland, and the fervent controversialist Jacobus Koelman (1632–95), preacher from 1662 to 1674, at Sluis.

[45] Van Lieburg, *Nadere Reformatie*, 12–14, 57–8.
[46] Van de Velde, *Biddaghs-Meditatie*, A4, C3, D.
[47] Trimp, *Jodocus van Lodensteyn*, 79–81.
[48] Groenendijk, 'Petrus Wittewrongel', 66–9.

The Further Reformation was a puritanical movement within the Reformed Church for the reforming of life-style and morals. But it was inseparable from the rigid confessional stance with which its leading protagonists were imbued. Voetius, dominant in the Utrecht consistory, firmly coupled *theologia practica* with dogmatic fundamentalism.[49] He viewed purity of life as the fruit of true faith. The reformation of society, he and his adherents believed, required an unremitting onslaught on doubt, evasion, and heresy. In this way, Voetius' reformation of behaviour became tied to his attack on Descartes and the 'new philosophy', as well as Remonstrantism and other deficient theology, especially 'Socinianism', which he, like Essenius and Wittewrongel, identified on all sides. But in Holland and Utrecht, the foes of faith were protected by the 'Arminian' regents, as were ungodly living and 'whoredom'. Thus, Voetius, like Van de Velde and Lodenstein, felt bound to enter the political sphere. To combat the 'Epicureans, atheists, libertines, heretics, and Spiritualists' with any hope of success, and carry through their reformation of life-style, they had to capture the town halls and overthrow the regent policies which encouraged libertinism, practical and theoretical, to flourish.

The Further Reformation worked through the consistories and laity, mobilizing support, to exert pressure on the regents, to act both against unseemly conduct and reprehensible beliefs. The basic strategy pursued by Voetian consistories was to present petitions to town councils requesting tough civic edicts designed to curb immorality and misbehaviour by imposing penalties and fines. Typical was the remonstrance submitted, at Voetius' prompting, to the Utrecht regents in 1665, demanding the appointment of more preachers, stringent regulations against smoking, drinking, swearing, blasphemy, and violation of the sabbath, and also the closure of taverns on Sundays, effective suppression of Catholic conventicles, and, finally, that 'adultery be vigorously combated . . . and that just as placards exist against brothels and such whoredom . . . there should be strict penalties for ordinary whoredom'.[50] 'Ordinary whoredom' was the name which the consistories gave to adultery as distinct from prostitution. One of their chief goals was to have adultery made a civic offence punishable by fines.

But to mobilize the consistories against the 'Arminian' regents of Holland and Utrecht, they had first to overcome their opponents in the consistories. Thus, Voetians regarded Cocceius' theology as a brake on the reformation of society and the presence of Cocceians in the consistories as an obstacle to their labours. To succeed they felt they needed to sweep Cocceian

---

[49] Van 't Spijker, 'Voetius practicus', 250.
[50] Duker, *Gisbertus Voetius*, iii, pp. xxxvi–xl.

theology aside, capture the consistories, and, mobilizing the people, exert irresistible pressure on the regents. Cocceian theology, in their estimation, not only undermined sabbath observance, and encouraged the spread of Cartesian philosophy and science, but directly obstructed the drive against extravagance and immodesty. By the late seventeenth century, it was claimed, one could distinguish Cocceian and Voetian preachers from across the street, since the one wore wigs, and made other concessions to fashion, which the other did not. Concerning seemly and unseemly conduct disagreement was, of course, usually a matter of degree. With regard to dancing, for example, Voetians rejected dance and dance-halls outright, as ungodly, and would not tolerate dancing at weddings, while Cocceians considered dancing acceptable in moderation 'with care as to time, place, and persons'.[51] At Amsterdam, the consistory no longer summonsed congregants for the sin of dancing, after 1650; but several preachers kept up an unrelenting campaign from the pulpit. In 1681, the Amsterdam consistory laid down that when, at wedding receptions, guests began to dance, any preacher of the public Church present must immediately depart to show his disapproval.[52]

Another ingredient of Dutch life decried by the Further Reformation was the theatre. Prior to the 1640s, there had been a sporadic campaign especially against Vondel and other known adversaries of Counter-Remonstrantism connected with the stage. But a more general polemic against the theatre arose only during the middle decades of the century inspired by Voetius and led, at Amsterdam, by Petrus Wittewrongel who, especially in his *Oeconomia Christiana* (1655), a handbook of Christian purity, strongly disapproved of the violence, paganism, and marital infidelity so often depicted in plays. During the First Anglo-Dutch War, Wittewrongel admonished his countrymen that the Almighty would inflict on them terrible retribution unless they renounced their sinful ways, eschewed whoredom and heavy drinking, and suppressed the stage. After the war, the warnings lost none of their stridency, as trade recovered, anxieties waned, and from 1655, for the first time in the history of the Dutch theatre, and several years before they did so in England, women began appearing on stage. Aroused by the mounting controversy, Vondel, in 1661, published an uncompromising defence of the theatre which provoked several angry rejoinders. During the plague of 1664, the *vroedschap* had to shut the theatre, allowing performances to resume only in 1666. But adversity soon again came to the aid of the Further Reformation. Closed during the emergency of 1672, the

---

[51] Van Leenhof, *Zedig en Christelik verandwoordschrift*, 122.
[52] Roodenburg, *Onder censuur*, 323.

theatre remained shut, under Voetian pressure, for five years.[53] It was only allowed to reopen, after a determined campaign led by Van Beuningen and Hudde, on condition nothing was staged which could be deemed harmful either to morals or the public Church.

The Further Reformation failed to close the Amsterdam theatre permanently. Nevertheless, it had a pervasive impact on the Dutch stage. If the consistory succeeded only once in persuading the burgomasters to suppress a particular play—Vondel's *Lucifer*, banned after two performances, in February 1654, for representing heaven and angels on stage[54]—the sustained pressure, and intermittent closures, of the 1660s and 1670s compelled the theatre board to become exceedingly cautious. They exercised a self-censorship which prevented anything in the least objectionable or bawdy reaching the playhouse at all. Nothing remotely like the bawdiness of English Restoration comedy was possible in the Dutch theatre of the period. Moreover, the Further Reformation ensured that outside Amsterdam, The Hague, and Rotterdam, stage performances occurred increasingly infrequently and that in some cities, such as Utrecht, from 1662, the stage was banned outright.[55]

Another issue which led to much wrangling, even in small towns, was that of organs and organ-playing in the churches of the public Church. Under the Acts of the National Synod of Dordrecht of 1578 it was forbidden to use organs for divine service. But in most main churches the organs had not actually been removed and were regularly played, to enliven church-going, before and after services. The greatest Dutch composer, the organist Jan Pietersz. Sweelinck (d. 1621), earned his living at the Old Church, in Amsterdam, in precisely this way. But this left an unresolved argument which intensified in the 1640s, following publication of a treatise championing the use of organs to accompany services which Constantijn Huygens published, with the approval of Hooft and other members of the Muiden circle, in 1641. Frederik Hendrik also seems to have looked favourably on the use of organs in the churches. But most preachers opposed using organs to accompany services and many actively urged their removal. Where Voetius and Huygens were agreed was in holding that it was illogical to enhance church-going with organ-playing before, and after, services if the organ was a papist embellishment unfit to accompany divine service.[56] Voetius and the Further Reformation launched a counter-campaign for the

[53] Schenkeveld-van der Dussen, 'Inleiding', 13–15.
[54] Evenhuis, *Ook dat was Amsterdam*, ii. 292.
[55] Worp, *Drama en toneel*, ii. 96.
[56] Huygens, *Gebruyck of ongebruyck*, 14–34.

removal of the organs from the churches, provoking endless debates in consistories and town councils. A main aim of Koelman, a pupil of Voetius and uncompromising anti-Cocceian, during his twelve years as a preacher at Sluis, was to secure the removal of the organ from the main church.[57]

The Further Reformation was at its height in the second half of the seventeenth century. It pressed most strongly at times of national emergency—during the Anglo-Dutch Wars, the French invasion of 1672, and, again, in 1688. It reached all parts of the Republic and levels of society. No province was unaffected by its rise. For despite the United Provinces' highly decentralized political structure, in some respects the country was more, rather than less, integrated than the great monarchies of Europe and by no means only in the spheres of passenger travel, communications, transport, finance, and commerce. It was also culturally highly integrated. The system of appointing preachers according to their reputations as communicators to the people made the consistories throughout the Republic (who never knew when they might next have to fill a preaching vacancy) connoisseurs of preachers' skills, and careers, in all the provinces, and rendered the influential preacher's activity a matter of 'national' rather than purely local or provincial interest. Perhaps more than any other occupational group, preachers moved from province to province, often embracing three or four provinces during the course of a career. Joannes Teellinck, for example, served as preacher at Flushing (1649–55), Utrecht (1655–60), Arnemuiden (1660–1), Kampen (1661–74), and Leeuwarden (1674).

Locally, the extent of the impact of the Further Reformation had much to do with the political balance between the rival politico-theological blocs in the towns and town halls. When regents sympathetic to the Voetian outlook controlled the town government, the scope was obviously greater than when their opponents were in the ascendant. But it should not be supposed that wherever the States party-faction prevailed in the town hall, the Further Reformation was then without influence. If it held sway in the consistory, this was bound to mean that it was supported by a large segment of the town's populace. Thus, Voetius and his adherents secured more co-operation from the Utrecht regents in the 1640s, and again after 1673, when the city was dominated by the 'Church' party, than in the intervening period when the 'Arminians' were in charge. Yet despite this, and the frustration felt by Lodenstein and others, at their defeats, the Further Reformation gained some notable successes at Utrecht during this time, including an intensified drive against prostitution, placards banning theatre

[57] Krull, *Jacobus Koelman*, 32–4.

and restricting dancing, and, in 1659, a ban on cock-fighting.[58] At Amsterdam, the consistory exerted greater pressure during the decades 1650–90 than either before, or after, through its enquiries and summonses, on adulterers, unmarried mothers, and girls pregnant on marriage. It was during the same period, moreover, that it spurred the city into trying to curb at least the more blatant forms of prostitution.[59] During the second half of the seventeenth century, between eighty and two hundred brothel-keepers and prostitutes were prosecuted by the magistracy annually, amounting to about 20 per cent of all arrests in the city.

Nevertheless, a shift in political control could make a great difference to the culture and flavour of a town. Arnhem, relatively liberal during the third quarter of the century, experienced, like the other towns occupied by the French and Munsterites in the years 1672–4, a certain loosening of discipline, and the full religious toleration, which prevailed in those years. Even so (whatever some Reformed divines said afterwards), the city was hardly a sink of iniquity. The French soldiery were reasonably disciplined, despite finding the local womenfolk mostly unresponsive, even in the taverns. One disgruntled French officer wrote to a friend, of the women of Arnhem, that one 'can see nothing of their bosoms since they cover them up so carefully that they all look like saints'.[60] Nevertheless, after the French evacuation, the consistory, backed by the new Orangist town government, exploited the reaction against the French, Catholicism, and alleged deterioration of morals to engineer a lasting change in attitudes in the town, not least by warning their congregants that only by means of a thorough reform of morals and life-style could they deflect future visitations of God's anger.

In the subsequent period, the Arnhem *raad* became more active than they had been prior to 1672 in breaking up Catholic conventicles and combating adultery, prostitution, merry-making, and dance. That this was not mere window-dressing is indicated by the evidence of the town's baptismal registers. After 1675, there was a noticeable falling off of births out of wedlock, and conceptions before the date of marriage, indicating a decrease in extramarital sex in Arnhem which was not reversed until after the end of the period of confessional intolerance around 1720.[61] At the height of the campaign, in 1678, the Voetian consistory petitioned the town council to emulate 'other towns' and impose civic fines for the offence of 'fornication' among couples intending to marry.

[58] Bogaers, 'Kwestie van macht', apps.
[59] Van de Pol, 'Beeld en werkelijkheid', 131–3.
[60] Kotte, 'Gelderse bloem', 93.
[61] Holthuizen-Seegers and Nusteling, 'Arnhem', 76–8.

A typical feature of the Further Reformation was the demand for consistory and pulpit to be free of control by the town councils. For, in Voetian eyes, it was the power of unsympathetic, or insufficiently supportive, regents which chiefly obstructed the Church's progress. 'Arminian' regents, backing the De Witt regime, were viewed with often vehement hostility by the Voetians. One preacher remarked, in 1672, that though the regents who dominated the States of Holland, and sought to muzzle the consistories, were nominally members of the public Church, in fact they were not 'true believers' but hypocrites who subverted society, state, and Church. He claimed that, since the peace with Spain, in 1648, 'Arminians, together with their supporters, the Socinians and Atheists, have crawled into the consistories and town halls and, so as more easily to coax our youth into accepting novel opinions, encouraged the study in our universities of the seducer Descartes'.[62] The only cure for the 'sickness' afflicting Dutch society, he assured his readers, was to restore the pulpit to its 'former liberty and freedom'. The 'hypocrites' within the consistories were, of course, the Cocceians, whom Voetians regarded as accomplices of the States party-faction. Some Voetians were inclined to view Cocceian collaboration with the 'Louvesteiners' as part of a sinister theologico-political conspiracy designed to abolish the stadholderate, subvert the Union, undermine the consistories, overturn the National Synod of Dordrecht, replace Aristotelian philosophy and science with the 'new philosophy' of Descartes, and pervert the moral fibre of society.

The last major surge of the Further Reformation in Holland—elsewhere it retained its grip longer—coincided with the rising fear of Louis XIV, and the supposed international Catholic offensive, in the 1680s. The plight of the Huguenots alarmed Dutch opinion, creating a sense of insecurity, and at the same time intensified pressure for the 'necessary reformation' of society. At Delft, the consistory submitted a petition to the *vroedschap*, in November 1685, demanding stronger curbs on Catholic freedom, closure of brothels, tighter sabbath observance, stricter enforcement of fines for adultery, and placards banning celebration of the December St Nicholas feast, and other 'superstitious festivals'. The *vroedschap* was also asked to act 'in conformity with many other towns' to ban comedy-players, jugglers, and tightrope walkers during the annual fair.[63] Suppressing prostitution was a particularly high priority. But whoredom in Delft was so inconspicuous that the town's *schout* could assure the *vroedschap* that, as far as he knew, there were no addresses where prostitution was practised there.[64]

[62] *Genees-Middelen voor Holland*, 6.
[63] GA Delft kerkeraad 7, fos. 147v–148v. res. 30 Nov. 1685.
[64] GA Delft kerkeraad 7, fo. 151v. res. 5 Dec. 1685.

Similar pressures arose at Amsterdam, especially during the tense month of November 1688, as William III's armada for the invasion of England nervously awaited a favourable wind. The consistory agreed, 'since Fatherland and Church are threatened by very dark clouds', to petition the burgomasters for more vigorous moral reform, especially suppression of prostitution, 'closure of taverns and other places of debauchery on the Lord's Day', and suppression of dance-halls.[65] Part of the consistory also wanted to renew the attack on the city's theatre, but others preferred to leave that for the moment. In March 1686, even Leiden's predominantly Cocceian consistory felt some need to respond to the prevailing mood and pressed for closure of the town's (Huguenot) dance-halls—but only on Sundays, a characteristically Cocceian twist.[66]

The advance of the Further Reformation, and resulting pressure on morals and life-style, led critics to ask by what right the public Church, and its allies within civic government, sought to direct the life of the community and individual. The most influential opponent of consistory power was the Utrecht regent, and physician, Lambert van Velthuizen (1622–85). Though nominally a member of the Reformed Church, he was a strong supporter of toleration, a friend of Collegiants, and fervent Cartesian. Velthuizen argued, in several tracts of the 1650s and 1660s, that no church body had authority to coerce the individual and that compulsion in civil society could legitimately derive only from the secular authority.[67] He considered it essential that the consistories be firmly subordinated to the city councils.

The conflict between the rival ideological blocs within the Dutch body politic during the mid-seventeenth century was not a gentlemanly affair. Much was at stake and both sides were apt to use intemperate language. Voetians called the States party 'hypocrites, libertines and heretics', while their opponents styled the Voetians advocates of the Genevan yoke, subverters of freedom, and allies of immoral Stadholders. The 'Louvesteiners' cast no slur on William the Silent and Frederik Hendrik, who had defended 'freedom' and resisted many demands of the public Church. But precisely those Stadholders, Maurits and William II, who had championed the Church, and whom the orthodox glorified, were more than a little vulnerable to critical innuendo. The lawyer Johannes Uytenhage de Mist, a friend of Pieter de la Court, alluded, in several of his republican tracts, to the promiscuity of Maurits and William II, princes whose unbridled lust had

[65] GA Amsterdam 376/15, fos. 269–70. res. kerkeraad 11 and 18 Nov. 1688.
[66] GA Leiden kerkeraad 7. res. 15 March 1686
[67] Velthuysen, *Apologie*, 9–11.

been the constant talk of The Hague. The public were asked to wonder what trust they could have in the Calvinist zeal of preachers who professed to revere such men.

29

The Republic at its Zenith, I: The 1650s

❖

THE MAKING OF THE `TRUE FREEDOM´

No sovereign prince (to Lipsius' distress) attained sovereign power in the north Netherlands after 1572. The States of Holland assumed charge of the government, in that year, with Orange directing the war, and heading the executive, but with the promise to act only in consultation with the States 'who best know the situation of the land and inclinations of the people'.[1] Holland, with Zeeland and Utrecht, unlike Brabant and Flanders, firmly refused to transfer sovereignty to Anjou. Nevertheless, government in the north between 1572 and 1587 was not yet fully republican in character. This was less because Philip II was still acknowledged as sovereign in theory, until 1581, than because Orange—and briefly also Anjou and Leicester— loomed large in the processes of decision-making, military command, and appointments. Only with Leicester's departure, in 1587, did a fully republican system evolve in which the States of Holland, led by Oldenbarnevelt, emerged in practice, if not in theory, as the principal decision-making body. Moreover, this first bout of real republican rule acquired a political philosophy to match in the pre-1618 writings of Grotius and also the remarkable tract *De Republica Ebraeorum* (1617) by the Leiden professor Petrus Cunaeus, which has been called the 'most powerful public statement of republican theory in the early years of the Dutch Republic'.[2] But this opening phase of republican government foundered despite its many successes. It ended, after thirty years, with Maurits's *coup d'état* of 1618, which fundamentally changed the structure of power at all levels in the United Provinces, replacing a fully republican with a quasi-republican 'Caesarean' system. It also halted the flow of republican writing in the tradition of Grotius and Cunaeus. Now the Stadholder controlled decisions and ap-

---

[1] Bremmer, *Reformatie en rebellie*, 226.
[2] Tuck, *Philosophy and Government*, 169.

pointments through his tiny circle of confidants and favourites, mostly nobles and military men, and political discourse changed accordingly.

Maurits's system of decision-making, clientage, and influence continued under Frederik Hendrik, albeit in a modified form, without Maurits's theological base and yielding some ground to Holland. But Holland remained in an essentially subordinate position, with major appointments and decisions being made by the Stadholder and his favourites. The distribution of influence in the United Provinces under the Orangist system, in other words, was fundamentally different from under the republican system restored in 1650. Foreign courts and diplomats in mid-seventeenth-century Europe were acutely aware of the gulf between these contrasting versions of the Dutch Republic because under the system of the Stadholder the latter effectively controlled Dutch diplomacy (even though officially ambassadors dealt with the States General) and the Stadholders took major military decisions (apart from provision of funds), whereas under the rival system, restored in 1650, it was the committees of the States of Holland which controlled diplomacy and the use of the army.[3]

The system of the Stadholders undoubtedly allowed speedier decisions than the more consultative and formalized republican alternative, and made it much easier for the Dutch state to cloak its high-level decision-making in secrecy.[4] But, as against this, it also exhibited appreciable weaknesses. Under Stadholders, most power and influence in the Republic was wielded by a small clique, often nobles linked to the Stadholder's court, representative of no broad groups or entities in the population and answerable, in practice, only to the Stadholder. Consequently, government was, and remained, remote from Holland's civic society where wealth was created and most of the Republic's vitality, in all spheres, lay. An inevitable consequence was that military matters vital to the Stadholder and his favourites received higher, and the maritime interests of Holland lower, priority than they would have under the republican system in which Holland not only provided the resources but controlled their use.

Another effect of the concentration of influence in few hands under the Stadholders was that policy-making became more susceptible, than under the republican system, to corruption from without. It is true that under the republican system corruption was also rife, that, after 1650, the corridors of power at The Hague became notorious for trafficking in state documents and secrets, and that in the cities corrupt dealings in the disposing of offices

---

[3] BL MS Add. 14006, fos. 258v–259. 'Relazión del govierno de los Estados Generales' (Nov. 1663).
[4] Ibid., fo. 254.

and favours were rampant. Yet here the susceptibility was much more to the power of corruption from within, so that the Republic remained distinctly less vulnerable to venal manipulation by foreign courts than under Stadholders. A prodigiously corrupt figure such as Cornelis Musch, secretary of the States General under Frederik Hendrik, who made his fortune chiefly out of his influence over the conduct of diplomacy, was a typical symptom of the Orangist system. The French envoy, Chanut, noted this distinction in 1653, pointing out that under Maurits and Frederik Hendrik, the foreign diplomat at The Hague always knew 'qui distribuoient les charges et les graces', so that bribery in high places was an apt means of conducting diplomacy; under the States party-faction, by contrast, power—and thus also corrupt power—was more diffuse, with the result that such bribery became a less effective instrument: 'aujourd'hui', concluded Chanut, 'cette dépense serait infinie et infructueuse'.[5]

Dismantling the system based on the stadholderate commenced during Frederik Hendrik's last year as Holland took charge of the Münster peace talks and reduced the army. The Stadholder's court, during the years 1646–8, lost much of its previous leverage. But then a struggle for control ensued in which William II triumphed and briefly succeeded in restoring the system prevailing between 1618 and 1646, with the Stadholder making key decisions and appointments and Holland eclipsed. The Stadholder's death in November 1650, however, undid his work, the structure of government then reverting immediately to its more republican mode, nullifying the changes brought in by the Counter-Remonstrant revolution of 1618. Thus William II's death precipitated a much more fundamental change than his sensational coup, a fact quickly grasped by leading regents and subsequently stressed by Aitzema in his great chronicle.[6] The new era of republican rule was to last twenty-two years.

The States of Holland, so recently humiliated, seized the opportunity which presented itself with alacrity.[7] The Holland *Gecommitteerde Raden* moved to assert their authority over the army and summoned the full States to an emergency session. The regents incarcerated by William II at Loevestein were released and restored to their previous offices except in the case of the Brothers Bicker—who had enemies as well as friends in the Amsterdam *vroedschap*—and resumed only their *vroedschap* seats; henceforth, it was the equally republican-minded brothers De Graeff, and their following, who dominated Amsterdam. Within days of the Prince's death Holland

⁵ Quoted in De Bruin, *Geheimhouding en verraad*, 377.
⁶ Van der Plaat, 'Lieuwe van Aitzema's kijk', 354–7.
⁷ Poelhekke, *Geen blijder maer*, 182–3.

proposed in the States General that the provinces should gather in a special 'Great Assembly' to determine how best to maintain the Union in the unprecedented situation in which the United Provinces now found themselves. Preparations were made for a special convention at The Hague to take place early in 1651.

But the basic restructuring of government, and power relationships, took place during the crucial months between William II's death and the convening of the Great Assembly, leaving the latter with little more to do than acquiesce and formalize the restoration of Holland's ascendancy over the confederate state. Thus, the majority of the States of Holland showed no desire to appoint anyone as Stadholder to succeed the dead Prince and the decision to leave the stadholderate in Holland indefinitely vacant was already taken in November. Immediately after doing so, Holland sent a delegation to Zeeland to forestall moves there to appoint a Stadholder,[8] following the birth of William III.

Having laid both stadholderate and captaincy-general in abeyance, the States of Holland proceeded to assume the political and military functions of the stadholderate within their province.[9] Previously, the Stadholder had supervised *vroedschap* elections and, in most towns, enjoyed the prerogative of selecting the civic magistrates (*schepenen*) from double lists, as well as the right to appoint the key rural magistrates—the *drosten* and *baljuws*. None of the States of Holland wholly opposed the appropriation of these functions by the States, though the *ridderschap* objected to the relegation to the towns of unrestricted control over their elections urging active supervision by the States (which would have given the *ridderschap* some influence in the proceedings), while Leiden held that the transfer of powers should be provisional only 'in the hope that eventually the newly born Prince will serve the Republic in the same functions as had been conferred respectively on his father, grandfather, great-uncle and great-grandfather, in their lives'.[10] No other Holland town remained so incorrigibly Orangist.

The States took over the Stadholder's powers within the province, on 8 December 1650, issuing charters to voting towns which applied, allowing them to elect their own *vroedschap* members, magistrates, and burgomasters, without outside intervention, under ultimate supervision of the States.[11] In this way, the regents arrogated to themselves full control over distribution of offices, and influence, within their towns. Holland towns unrepresented

---

[8] Groenveld, *Evidente factiën*, 43.
[9] Fruin, *Gesch. der staatsinstellingen*, 269–70.
[10] GA Leiden Sec. Arch. 451, fo. 57. res. vroed. 28 Nov. 1650.
[11] Res. Holl. 8 Dec. 1650.

in the States—Geertruidenberg, Oudewater, Woerden, Naarden, Heusden, and Middelharnis—were to continue submitting double lists of nominations from which the choice of regents would be made as before, but now by the States, instead of the Stadholder.[12] The States likewise took responsibility for appointing *baljuws* and *drosten*.

All this signified a considerable change in the structure of power, in both towns and rural areas. The grip of the regents was reinforced; other influences of which the Stadholder was apt to take account—including in some contexts guild and militia bodies—were eliminated. In Dordrecht, where the guilds still had a residual voice, there was strong resistance and, in April 1651, rioting in support of the guilds and the college, called the *Goede Lieden van Achten*, of guild representatives (chosen, until 1650, by the Stadholder, from nominations submitted by the guilds), which had retained a say in the selection of burgomasters. The Dordrecht regents quelled the disturbances with the support of the States.[13]

The *baljuws* and *drosten* were powerful figures in rural Holland and elimination of the Stadholder entailed a transfer of power which simultaneously affected many smaller towns. At Gorcum the *drost*—in 1650 still the same nobleman that Maurits had put in, in 1617—had hitherto lorded over the town, as well as the countryside around.[14] This ended in 1650; the new *drost*, appointed by the States, was without authority in the town, which followed the rest in obtaining a States charter enabling its regents to hold their own elections, and choose burgomasters, without the *drost* intervening.

Holland also endeavoured, in advance of the Great Assembly, to encourage similar changes in Zeeland. Orangist sentiment was traditionally strong in Zeeland; but many regents wished to emulate Holland, and profit from the Stadholder's death, to enhance their local power and influence. Consequently, only two, of the six, voting towns—Flushing and Veere—were eager to appoint the infant William III Stadholder.[15] A majority of the States of Zeeland voted to leave the stadholderate vacant, abolish the vote of the First Noble (that of the Prince of Orange), reducing the States from seven votes to six, and follow Holland in authorizing the towns to co-opt their own regents and burgomasters, powers which were refused by Flushing and Veere.[16] The Zeeland nobles, at this point, submitted a petition claiming that the First Noble had been the representative of the Zeeland *ridderschap*

---

[12] ARH SH 2709/3. Oudewater to SH, 28 Apr. 1653.
[13] Melles, *Ministers aan de Maas*, 105.
[14] De Wit, *Gorcums heren*, 6.
[15] *Notulen* SZ res. SZ 23 and 24 Mar. 1651.
[16] Kluiver, 'Zeeuwse reacties', 410.

and that his vote should now be transferred to them, an argument which failed to impress the States. From 1650 to 1672, the States of Zeeland were the Republic's only provincial assembly in which towns alone were represented. Zeeland society as a whole, however, was deeply divided by the changes of 1650 and, from April 1651, Middelburg experienced several months of instability and riots.

But it was not only the Holland and Zeeland regents who sprang into action. There was, in fact, intense politicking, in all the provinces. If Amsterdam struck a medal, representing William II as the Greek god Phaeton, who, through pride, and exceeding his powers, fell from glory to disaster, adding the tag 'Magnis excudit ausis' as an expression of relief at William II's disappearance from the scene, many prominent men in the inland provinces wanted to preserve the system of Maurits, Frederik Hendrik, and William II, and likewise manœuvred to gain advantage in advance of the Great Assembly. Backed by the States of Friesland, Willem Frederik urged the States of Groningen and Drenthe to choose a new Stadholder without delay, preferably by appointing himself. A Frisian delegation, of three *grietmannen*, a Sneek burgomaster, and the secretary of the Delegated States, hastened to Groningen, to extol the virtues of the House of Nassau.[17] Shortly after, Groningen conferred its stadholderate on Willem Frederik, followed by the States of Drenthe. At the same time, the count appealed to the élites in other provinces not to leave their stadholderates vacant. Three days after the birth of William III, he wrote to the States of Utrecht, appealing to them to appoint the infant prince 'Stadholder of Utrecht', and himself 'lieutenant Stadholder' to exercise the Stadholder's powers, until the Prince came of age.[18] He pursued the same aim in Gelderland and Overijssel, where efforts were made, on his behalf, by local Orangist nobles.[19] But no other province followed Groningen and Drenthe in choosing a Stadholder in advance of the Great Assembly.

Of course, Holland by no means left this to chance. Delegations were sent to the inland provinces as well as Zeeland. The new leading figure in the Holland *ridderschap*, Jacob van Wassenaer, lord of Obdam (1610–66), worked skilfully on nobles with seats in the States of Gelderland and Overijssel. A military man, since 1643 *drost* of Heusden, and soon also governor of the garrison, he was particularly successful in winning over younger nobles with promises of commissions, and promotions, in the army. Obdam, and Cornelis de Graeff, who accompanied him to Gelderland, also

---

[17] RAGr. Arch. Sgr 11. res. SGr. 15 and 19 Nov. 1650.
[18] RAF stadhold. arch. 37/1/2d. Willem Frederik to SU, The Hague, 17 Nov. 1650.
[19] RAF stadhold. arch. 37/1/4k. Linteloo to Willem Frederik, 21 Nov. 1650.

exploited the resentment of the Nijmegen *raad* over William II's backing for the college of *Gemeensluyden*, the representatives of the guilds, which had traditionally had a voice in the election of *raad* members.[20] The regents of Nijmegen aspired to control their city like regents elsewhere, unencumbered by the influence of guild representatives, and discarding the stadholderate was the obvious way to achieve this. Caught between contradictory pressures but swayed most by Holland, the States of Overijssel voted to postpone their decision on the stadholderate.[21]

The Great Assembly was the first occasion, since 1579, when the provinces gathered to debate the form and structure of the Union. Inevitably, there was much disagreement. Even the status of the delegations provoked acrimonious dispute. The full States of Holland participated. But while Holland had urged the others also to attend as 'full States', empowered to make decisions without referring back to their provincial capitals, none were willing to do so. Four provinces—Friesland, Groningen, Utrecht, and Zeeland—designated their representation 'extraordinary delegations' of their provincial States.[22] Overijssel initially sent only her ordinary States General delegation but subsequently upgraded this to an 'extraordinary' status. The most bizarre was Gelderland's representation. The three quarters, bitterly divided—with Nijmegen supporting Holland, Arnhem undecided, and Zutphen Orangist[23]—failed to agree, so that delegations arrived from the Nijmegen and Arnhem quarters designated (in defiance of the Hof of Gelderland) members of the full States of Gelderland gathered in The Hague, while Zutphen's representation attended as members of Gelderland's normal delegation to the States General.

The Great Assembly opened at the Binnenhof, at The Hague, in January 1651 with an address in which Holland's Pensionary, Jacob Cats, used his literary skills to extol republics as inherently superior to monarchies, citing the glories of the ancient and medieval republics of Athens, Sparta, Rome, Florence, Venice, Switzerland, and Genoa.[24] Whether or not Cats himself perceived the sublime irony of his claiming this, hardly anyone present can have been unaware of his own abject subservience, over so many years, to Frederik Hendrik, and, as a consequence, Holland's eclipse.

The first item on the agenda was the stadholderate. Since November 1650, Friesland, most cohesive of the lesser provinces in the mid-seventeenth

---

[20] GA Nijmegen 102, fos. 513, 524. res. raad 11 and 14 Dec. 1650.
[21] ARH SG PR 488 fo. 159. res. SO 18 Nov. 1650.
[22] Aitzema, *Herstelde Leeuw*, 127.
[23] Van der Capellen, *Gedenkschriften*, ii. 334.
[24] Aitzema, *Herstelde Leeuw*, 133.

century, had led the opposition to Holland, concerting moves in support of the House of Orange-Nassau. To enable the Frisian delegation to respond promptly to the Hollanders' moves, they were authorized, by the Delegated States, to confer secretly with Willem Frederik, and act without referring back to Leeuwarden for approval.[25] Friesland and Groningen insisted the issue of whether or not to appoint a Stadholder was not a purely provincial matter, since the stadholderate was also a Generality institution.[26] The stipulation, in articles 9 and 21 of the Union of Utrecht, that disputes between provinces should be settled by mediation of the Stadholders, was interpreted by these provinces to mean that, under the Union, every province was obliged to have a Stadholder.[27] Given the incomparable services of the House of Orange-Nassau to the state, since 1572, the Frisians added, these obligatory Stadholders should be chosen from that house. They also argued that military discipline required that the army have an 'eminent head', a commander of appropriate standing and prestige, if it was to be effectively led. They urged that William III be appointed captain-general and admiral, with the Frisian Stadholder as acting captain-general until he came of age.

But Friesland was no match for Holland in exerting pressure on other provinces. The Gelderland *ridderschap* declined to back Willem Frederik, partly owing to the 'advancement to army companies which [Obdam and de Graeff] had promised some nobles'.[28] The States of Overijssel resolved, in March 1651, that appointing a Stadholder was not obligatory, under the Union, and that Overijssel's stadholderate would remain vacant indefinitely.[29]

The second main theme was religion. Advocates of Calvinist orthodoxy had lost their Prince but by no means abandoned their schemes for a confessionally and morally more disciplined society. Here, the Hollanders could expect stronger criticism than in any other sphere; for the view in the lesser provinces was that, in Holland, support for the public Church was inadequate and toleration excessive. The States of Overijssel, divided over everything else, united in backing Friesland's call for stronger measures to combat Catholicism and Protestant dissent.[30] The Orangist Pensionary of Zeeland, Johan de Brune (1649–58), accomplished poet and orthodox Calvinist, saw there was no chance of unifying the States of Zeeland around

[25] ARH SG PR 374, fo. 889. res. SF, 25 Apr. 1651.
[26] Van Slingelandt, *Staatkundige geschriften*, ii. 225.
[27] ARH SG PR 374. res. SF 6 Dec. 1650.
[28] Van der Capellen, *Gedenkschriften*, ii. 349–50.
[29] ARH SG PR 488, fo. 165. res. SO 11 Mar. 1651.
[30] Aitzema, *Herstelde Leeuw*, 155–6.

an Orangist platform at that juncture, but that he could rally Zeeland behind a drive for more stringent church policies.[31] On a key issue worrying the Reformed synods at this time—the spread of Socinian literature and ideas—Zeeland led the way whilst the Great Assembly was in progress, proclaiming severe punishment for propagating Socinian doctrines and books.[32]

The consistories and synods of the Reformed Church strove to influence the Great Assembly. Consistories submitted their advice to the synods, which then prepared a joint petition to lay before the Great Assembly. Voetius himself was asked to write the advice of the Utrecht consistory. He wanted the Great Assembly to confirm the Acts of the National Synod of Dordrecht as the basis of the public Church and the Generality to be given a greater role in protecting, and advancing, the Church. In particular, Union and provinces, in his view, needed to combat Catholicism more effectively, promote the Reformation in the Generality Lands more vigorously, and meet the growing Socinian threat.[33]

The joint petition of the synods to the Great Assembly insisted that Catholicism was reviving and that its suppression should be taken more energetically in hand throughout the provinces and Generality Lands.[34] In the latter, exclusion of Catholics from all offices, blocked since 1649, should now take effect. At the same time, the synods wanted the Great Assembly to rule that no tolerated congregations of Lutherans, Mennonites, and Remonstrants could be established, where these did not already exist, to prevent their spreading further and that the Jews, as 'blasphemers against Christ', be forbidden the public practice of their faith throughout the United Provinces,[35] as well as to take vigorous steps to suppress Socinianism. Finally, regarding life-style, the synods demanded placards to tighten observance of the Lord's Day, curb extravagant dress and prostitution, and close the dance-schools.

Friesland and Groningen championed the demands and urged greater co-ordination between the provinces in church affairs generally, arguing that it made little sense that the provinces should have the same public Church, and rules for combating Catholicism, but possess no Generality machinery for supervising practice throughout the United Provinces to ensure enforcement of placards, on a common footing.[36] Overijssel too approved. But

---

[31] Op 't Hof, 'Godsdienstige ligging', 44–9.
[32] *Notulen SZ* res. SZ 25 Mar. 1651.
[33] Duker, *Gisbertus Voetius*, iii. 148–9.
[34] Basnage, *Annales*, 204–5.
[35] Aitzema, *Herstelde Leeuw*, 151.
[36] Ibid. 160; RAGr. arch. SGr. 11 res S.Gr. 22 Mar. 1651.

Holland, unwilling to expand the role of the Generality, firmly rebuffed Friesland's plea for a 'harmony and unity to be established jointly by the United Provinces'. The public Church was denied much of what it wanted. Holland did agree, though, to confirm the Acts of the National Synod of 1618–19 as the sole basis of the public Church throughout the United Provinces, allaying fears that there might be attempts to dilute the Counter-Remonstrants' gains of 1618–19, and to a ruling that tolerated Churches—Lutheranism, Anabaptism, and Remonstrantism—'in future will not be permitted in any other places than where they are already practised', implying exclusion of these faiths from many towns and most of the countryside,[37] as a general policy of the Union.

A third main concern of the Great Assembly was the organization and command structure of the army. No province wished to weaken the principle of a common army and system of defence. But the provinces disagreed as to how, without a Stadholder, the Generality would run the army and appoint, and promote, its army officers.[38] Several provinces, especially Gelderland, which provided a high proportion of the army's Dutch officers, sought to minimize Holland's leverage by transferring responsibility for commissions and promotions to the States General, where Holland possessed one vote out of seven. But Holland, backed by Zeeland, advising a less cumbersome method, pressed for promotions to be assigned to the *Raad van State*, where Holland possessed two votes out of eight. Eventually, a compromise emerged, with army appointments to be made jointly by the States General and *Raad van State*.

Holland's approach to army issues provoked fierce criticism from some nobles and military men, in the inland provinces, who deemed it transparently political. Van der Capellen complained that the Holland regents not only lacked the experience, and expertise, necessary to evaluate candidates for promotion but cared less about military efficiency than advancing relatives and friends and would turn the army into a web of political patronage 'paying little regard to merit'.[39] The change in the structure of power in 1650–1 did indeed carry far-reaching implications for the relationship between the army and society. Holland, having drastically reduced the army in size, now also sought to emasculate it politically, and lower its status. Besides gaining control of the machinery of commissions and promotions, the Holland regents were anxious to neutralize the army's Orangist inclinations and especially to prevent Willem Frederik being

[37] Aitzema, *Herstelde Leeuw*, 157–8; Van Gelder, *Getemperde vrijheid*, 95.
[38] Fruin, *Gesch. der staatsinstellingen*, 272; Poelhekke, *Geen blijder maer*, 237–8.
[39] Van der Capellen, *Gedenkschriften*, ii. 371–2.

appointed 'acting captain-general' or obtaining any influence over the army. No one had forgotten that, in 1650, it was he who had led the troops against Amsterdam. By arranging for Jan Wolfert van Brederode to command under the title of 'Field Marshal', Holland ensured that no politically formidable figure led the army or could deploy soldiers against the civilian authorities. The Great Assembly further reduced the status of the military by ruling that, in garrison towns, city keys, and responsibility for opening city gates at dawn and dusk, be transferred from the military governors to the burgomasters.[40] Similarly, the army's jurisdiction over soldiers charged with offences was reduced to the barest minimum—desertion and insubordination—cases of assault, theft, rape, and murder involving soldiers being transferred to the civil magistrates.[41]

The Great Assembly also debated the question of representation in the States General and Generality colleges. Since the early days of the Union, the number of voting provinces had remained fixed at seven. But should other regions, notably States Brabant and Drenthe, be permanently excluded and, if so, with what justification? Since 1648, the towns of States Brabant, headed by 's-Hertogenbosch and Breda, had canvassed support, among the provincial assemblies, for admittance as a voting member of the Generality. Much was at stake for the province, for representation in the States General would bring not only enhanced status but political influence and the same right to self-administration, and taxation, as the existing Seven Provinces possessed. At their gathering, at Tilburg, in January 1651, the towns of States Brabant agreed that, even if they failed to secure acknowledgement as a full voting province it would still be advantageous to gain 'at least the freedom to administer themselves, and collect their own taxes', like Drenthe.[42] Drenthe also sent delegations to the various provincial assemblies seeking admittance as a full voting member.

At the Great Assembly, there was extensive backing for both regions. Drenthe's delegation to Leeuwarden, in April 1651, had been favourably received and the Frisian delegation, at The Hague, was instructed to lend Drenthe full support.[43] States Brabant also met with a positive response from Friesland, Groningen, Zeeland, and Gelderland. Indeed, it was only Holland which firmly rejected both provinces' applications. The Brabanters spared no effort to win the Hollanders round, compiling whole treatises, employing every conceivable juridical, political, fiscal, and historical argu-

[40] GA Nijmegen stadsarch. 103, fo. 44. res. raad 26 Mar. 1651.
[41] Ibid.; Schulten and Schulten, *Het leger*, 59.
[42] Wagenaar, *Vad. Hist.* xii. 190.
[43] ARH SG PR 374, fo. 889. res. SF 25 Apr. 1651.

ment. Among other things, they pointed out that taxation by the Generality infringed the ancient privileges of Brabant, was directly contrary to the principles of the Union of Utrecht, and could eventually embitter the local population 'against the state'.[44]

That only Holland opposed States Brabant's application shows that, whatever was alleged, the region's exclusion owed nothing to religious considerations. The city councils of 's-Hertogenbosch, Breda, Bergen-op-Zoom, and Grave consisted exclusively of adherents of the Reformed Church, as eager as anyone to combat Catholicism. In the United Provinces, every province subscribed to the Dutch Reformed Church on the basis of the National Synod of Dordrecht, and officially banned Catholicism, and there was no possibility of any province going its own way. One might question the claim that admittance as a full province would strengthen the Reformed faith in the region. But there was no way the region's political élite could have ceased to be other than exclusively Reformed. Holland did allege Brabant's Catholicism as grounds for opposing admittance, but the real reason for Holland's unwavering refusal to admit States Brabant (and Drenthe) was her unwillingness to add votes to the total in the Generality, which would be bound, in some degree, to dilute Holland's preponderance.[45] An additional motive regarding States Brabant was the industrial potential of Tilburg and Helmond. Whilst States Brabant remained under the Generality, Holland could manipulate the affairs of these textile towns in the interests of Leiden and Haarlem. If, however, north Brabant became a full province, she would soon rival Holland as a textile producer, with the advantage of far lower wages.

During the course of the Great Assembly several provinces lapsed into chronic internal instability. The dissension among the Gelderland quarters intensified. Deep rifts appeared in Groningen, on the one hand between city and Ommelands, over the provincial Hof, or *Hooftmannenkamer*,[46] and, on the other, among the Ommelander *jonkers*, with one faction opposed to Willem Frederik and another headed by Osebrand Jan Rengers, lord of Slochteren, richest noble of the Fivelingo quarter, and right-hand man of the Stadholder.[47] Zeeland too fell prey to internal splits. Unrest spread to much of the province, including Zierikzee and especially Tholen, which was now in constant ferment, the States intervening several times to calm the populace and guilds. At Middelburg, during these months, the populace,

[44] Christ, *Brabantsche Saecke*, 220–8.
[45] Ibid. 253–60.
[46] RAGr Ommelander arch. 319 res. Ommelands, 21 Nov. 1651.
[47] De Boer, *Woelingen in Stad en Lande*, 7–11.

dismayed by the effects of Zeeland's economic slump and encouraged by
several élite groups—including the city's preachers, who were then in the
midst of a row with the burgomasters—turned against the ruling faction. In
June 1651, in riots involving several thousand people, Burgomaster Hendrik
Thibault, who had been William II's principal ally in Zeeland, was overthrown, control of the Middelburg *vroedschap* passing for the moment to
the brothers Veth, leaders of the pro-Holland grouping. Delighted, Johan
de Witt pronounced the Middelburg coup a 'manifest miracle and work of
God's hand'.[48] The voting towns of Zeeland were now split three against
three: Flushing, Veere, and Goes remained broadly Orangist, while Middelburg, Zierikzee, and (waveringly) Tholen leaned the other way.[49]

The utter precariousness of the lesser provinces underlined the significance
of the Great Assembly as a symbol of the unity of the United Provinces, the
gathering having at any rate secured agreement as to how, in the new
circumstances, Generality and army were to be run. It was obvious that the
lesser provinces were, in themselves, inherently weak and unstable. Hence,
the cohesion, and stability, of Holland were, now more than ever, the rock
on which everything rested—the pillar of the Republic and its trade,
shipping, colonies, international standing, and military and naval power.
For regents sitting in a fractured States of Zeeland, or noblemen in a
deadlocked Groningen or Gelderland, the Great Assembly represented
more than a remote, federal concept, rather the Union under Holland's
leadership offered the only realistic hope of internal stability as well as
military security. Thus, the Great Assembly ended amid a sincere enough
show of harmony and loud calls for unity. Amsterdam, until the end, was
determined to exact retribution for the use of the army against herself in the
summer of 1650, with Friesland stubbornly justifying Willem Frederik, the
chief remaining culprit in Amsterdam's eyes. In the States of Holland,
Leiden was initially alone in calling for an amnesty.[50] But the acutest minds
amongst the Holland leadership saw that their province had more to gain
from conceding an amnesty than pursuing Willem Frederik, Van der
Capellen, and other leaders of the coup of 1650. The able young regent
Johan de Witt, whose political career had just begun, on his becoming
pensionary of Dordrecht, in December 1650, was one of the most active in
persuading the States of Holland (including his own father, who remained
doubtful) of the advantages of the proposed amnesty.[51] The measure
enabled the Great Assembly to end on a note almost of euphoria.

[48] Van der Bijl, *Idee en Interest*, 18; 't Hart, 'Autonoom', 56–8.
[49] *Notulen SZ* res. SZ 21 Sept. and 2 Oct. 1651.
[50] GA Leiden Sec. Arch. 451, fo. 118. res. vroed. 25 July 1651.
[51] Rowen, *John de Witt*, 53.

To mark its conclusion, the States of Zeeland issued a remarkable commemorative medal, both the design, and inscription, of which were devised by the province's poet-Pensionary De Brune, depicting a sturdy rock, with the coats of arms of the Seven Provinces affixed, on which stood a graceful female figure, holding aloft the Liberty Hat, under the sun of prosperity.[52]

THE FIRST ANGLO-DUTCH WAR (1652–1654) AND THE EXCLUSION CRISIS (1654)

A major consequence of the restructuring of the Dutch overseas trade system in the late 1640s, at the close of the Eighty Years War (see pp. 610–11 above), was a basic change in relations between the Republic and England.[53] During the previous period, Phase Three of Dutch world trade primacy (1621–47), the relative weakness of Dutch commerce with the Iberian peninsula, Mediterranean, and Near East had made possible a fundamental division of labour between the two maritime nations which had removed most sources of friction between them. After 1621, England had suffered more and more in her traditional markets in the Baltic, Germany, Russia, and Scandinavia, the Dutch going from strength to strength. But this had caused no great difficulty, since England's losses were compensated by her new dominance, especially after 1630, of the maritime commerce of southern Europe and the Levant. The withering of English trade with the north was matched, so to speak, by the withering of Dutch trade with south. The same division of labour was also neatly reflected in the re-exporting of East India commodities. The Dutch prevailed in the market for pepper and spices in northern Europe; while the English sold theirs, virtually free of competition, in the south.

But this comfortable accommodation was inherently precarious. The United Provinces were, at that time, basically a much stronger trading power than England, with more shipping, lower freight rates, a better financial system, lower interest rates, and, on the whole, a wider range, and higher quality, in manufactures. As some observers in the 1640s realized, English hegemony in southern European trade, particularly in Spain, Portugal, and Italy, was based to a large extent on the Spanish embargoes and effects of the Flemish and Spanish privateering campaign against Dutch shipping. Remove the political underpinning and the whole structure was bound to collapse.

[52] Van Loon, *Beschryving*, ii. 362.   [53] Israel, *Dutch Primacy*, 197–207.

This supplanting by the Dutch of English maritime primacy in the south took place in the late 1640s, and with breath-taking speed.[54] The impact was evident everywhere from Portugal to Aleppo but was most marked in the case of Spain and the trade in Spanish American products. A graphic example was the carrying of Spain's wool exports. 'Whereas we formerly brought home foure or five thousand baggs of cloth wooll and the Hollanders scarce a thousand,' complained one Englishman, in 1650, 'which they had then by re-shipping, theirs being prohibited, they now carry away five or six thousand and wee bring not past 12 or 1500 in the yeare at most.'[55] At the same time, sales of English textiles in Spain, which had generated the purchasing power to buy up Spain's wool and American dyestuffs, slumped as English manufactures were replaced by Dutch. A reversal on such a scale, and so rapidly, severely affected London, English shipping, and England's cloth industry, and there was no chance that it would be accepted without a bitter and powerful reaction. Since the goods of Spain, Italy, and the Levant, and even the wine of the Canary Islands (then much drunk in England), could now be shipped more cheaply to Holland than England, there began all at once, at the end of the 1640s, a massive influx of such merchandise from Holland into England, where, before 1647, there had been no trace of such traffic.

By 1651 the slump in England, and disgruntlement of the merchants, shippers, and clothiers, had brought Anglo-Dutch relations under severe strain. Initially, the Parliamentary regime in London sought to redress the situation by political means. If the Dutch would accept political subordination to England, there would be no need for confrontation. A political union between England and the United Provinces was proposed of the sort which Parliament had recently imposed, by force, on Scotland. A Parliamentary mission arrived in The Hague, in March 1651, whilst the Great Assembly was in progress, demanding a 'more strict and intimate alliance and union' between the two countries. The Dutch negotiators made no response to the political demands but sought to discuss ways of easing the now acute tension souring the Anglo-Dutch relationship. The English, for their part, made it clear that if the Dutch would not accept political subordination, then pressure of another sort would be brought to bear.

This was not long in coming. In August 1651, the month that the Great Assembly concluded, Parliament passed the Navigation Act. This had a specific purpose and was geared to a particular situation, being designed to stop the importing of colonial products and fish into England on Dutch

---

[54] Israel, 'England's Mercantilist Response', 50–6.
[55] *A Brief Narration of the Present Estate*, fo. 2.

ships and prevent the shipping of Italian raw silks, Turkish mohair, Spanish commodities, Zante raisins, Naples olive oil, and Canaries wine from the Dutch entrepôt to England. It prohibited all Dutch carrying of southern European products to English ports and outlawed the newly flourishing Dutch commerce with the English colonies in the Caribbean.

The Navigation Act aroused indignation amongst merchants and the shipping interest in the United Provinces. But this alone would not have brought about the First Anglo-Dutch War.[56] For while it was a serious blow to the Dutch it did not fundamentally threaten their trading system, England being much less important to the Dutch as a market than France, Spain, or the Baltic. What made war certain was the mounting interference (encouraged by the Navigation Act) with Dutch shipping, on the high seas, by the English navy and privateers. This harassment was England's answer to her losses at Dutch hands since the late 1640s, and steadily escalated, during 1651 no fewer than 140 Dutch merchantmen being seized by the English on the high seas, in the Channel, Atlantic, Irish Sea, and the Caribbean.[57] These were brought into English ports on charges of infringing the Navigation Act, trading with Royalists in the Caribbean, shipping munitions to Ireland and Scotland, and like pretexts. Despite repeated protests from the States General, Parliament showed no inclination to stop the harassment, quite the contrary. In January 1652 alone, another thirty Dutch vessels were brought in. It was this which made the First Anglo-Dutch War inevitable. Either the Republic was able to curb such disruption of her shipping or it was not. If not then Dutch world trade primacy was at an end.

Despite the initial confidence in this conflict of a public accustomed to triumphs at sea in the war against Spain, nearly all the strategic advantages lay with England. During the years 1649–51 Parliament had considerably expanded, and improved, the English navy in order to deal with the royalist threat at sea. By contrast, at this very time, the Dutch navy had been run down rapidly, the admiralty colleges selling off many of their vessels, including Tromp's flagship, the *Aemilia* (600 tons; 57 guns), after the peace with Spain.[58] At the outset of the new war, they had only seventy-nine ships at their disposal and most of these were old and in a poor state of repair. The situation was so bad that the English navy then had no fewer than fourteen 'first-rates' which equalled, or surpassed, in fire-power the most heavily armed vessel in the Dutch fleet. Moreover, the English 'first-rates'

[56] Wilson, *Profit and Power*, 58.
[57] Groenveld, 'English Civil Wars', 561.
[58] Bruijn, *Dutch Navy*, 62–3, 69–71.

not only had more but also heavier guns. Added to this, lying as they did to the windward of the United Provinces, astride the Dutch maritime lanes, and with the wind blowing most of the year from the west, the English were better placed to disrupt the commerce and shipping of their foe than vice versa. Finally, the Dutch with their extensive bulk-carrying fleets, and fisheries, and need to secure the Danish Sound—more vital to them than to the English—were driven to disperse their strength much more than their adversary.

The Dutch admirals, notably Tromp and De Ruyter, showed flair, and resolve, but could find no answer to the greater English fire-power and concentration of strength. Each time the mighty fleets clashed in the North Sea and Channel, the Dutch were shattered, holed, and dismasted at a faster rate than their foes. The large numbers of dead and maimed steadily sapped morale in the home ports of Holland and Zeeland. The heaviest defeats occurred during 1653. Having returned 'much torn and shattered' from the battle off Portland Bill, with the loss of twelve ships, in February, the Dutch were beaten off Harwich, in June, and Scheveningen, in August. In this last, crushing reverse, they lost their commanding admiral, Tromp, eleven warships, and four thousand men.

The war, and loss of hundreds of merchant vessels, caused a catastrophic slump in the Republic. The Amsterdam burgomasters afterwards calculated the total loss of Dutch merchant and fishing vessels during the war at around 1,200—a devastating setback to commerce. The herring fishery, and traffic, were paralysed. A large part of Dutch long-distance trade had to be suspended for the interim. Moreover, unable to reinforce what remained of Netherlands Brazil, the States General, and WIC, suffered the humiliation of seeing their once prosperous colony finally reconquered by the Portuguese.

Both the losses, and the cost, of the war were immense. Yet Holland could not accept defeat. For to do so would mean giving up her commanding position in the 'rich trades', the foundation of the Republic's prosperity and greatness. Somehow, the war had to be fought to an acceptable, if not successful, conclusion, one which would fully safeguard Dutch shipping, colonies, and trade. At massive cost, plans were laid for a fundamental reorganization of the navy and the construction of an entire new war fleet.[59] The States General ordered the building of thirty new men-of-war in February 1653 and another thirty the following December. Yet still the pleas of the admirals for bigger, and still more powerful, ships were ignored, none

[59] Bruijn, *Dutch Navy*, 72–4.

of the new vessels being larger than Tromp's last flagship, the *Brederode* (600 tons; 54 guns). The regents preferred to stick to their policy of dispersal of fire-power so as to maximize the protection of sea-routes and trade. In January 1654, the States General declared the sixty new ships the property of the Generality, forbidding the admiralty colleges to sell them off after the war as they had many of their vessels after 1609 and 1648.

But whilst the war was at its height most of the new ships were not yet ready. Also, owing to the heavy casualties, it became progressively harder to find men willing to face the English guns, despite the redundancy of thousands of seamen caused by the war. The Dutch admiralty colleges, unlike the English naval administration, were not permitted to use the press-gang to man their fleets, this being deemed incompatible with the 'freedom' which was the proclaimed basis of the Republic. The States accordingly had no alternative but to raise naval wages to unheard-of levels and increase the compensation for wounds received in action, a procedure established since 1645. Under the improved list published in September 1653, men maimed with the loss of a left arm fighting at sea received 266 guilders (or roughly a year's wages for an artisan) and 333 guilders for a right, 1,066 guilders (three to four years' wages) for the loss of both, or both eyes, and half this amount for the loss of both legs, on the principle that a man without legs is better able to earn his bread than a man without arms or eyes.[60] These compensation payments were later raised again, in 1664, on the eve of the Second Anglo-Dutch War, those who lost both arms, or eyes, receiving 1,500 guilders.

The defeats and mounting gloom rebounded against the government of the regents, generating a powerful surge of popular indignation and anti-regent, Orangist sentiment. This popular disgruntlement was energetically fomented by some Reformed preachers. Jacobus Stermond delivered a sermon at The Hague in March 1652, openly criticizing the regents, which resulted in his immediate dismissal from his living, though this was subsequently cancelled after he promised to refrain from ever again broaching politics in his sermons. Orangist support increased with every month which passed. In July 1652, the Frisian Stadholder was assured by a supporter in Zeeland that not only there but also 'en beaucoup de villes d'Hollande on commence à changer de langage: ils voyent qu'ils ne peuvent estre sans chef'.[61] The Delft preacher Johannes Goethals, an ardent Orangist, reported

---

[60] Ibid. 138; see the SG's placard of 26 Sept. 1653 in BL Printed Proclamations, D n 2/1 no. 32.

[61] RAF Stadhoud. arch. 37/1/4k. Manmaker to Willem Frederik, Bergen-op-Zoom, 8 July 1652.

to Willem Frederik, also in July, that to his joy he had found, at the recent gathering of the South Holland Synod, that 'nearly all the brothers professed great affection for the House of Orange-Nassau and Your Excellency's person in particular'.[62] He added that Johannes Teellinck (a political activist, as well as leader of the Further Reformation) was mobilizing popular feeling in Zeeland against the regents, commenting that 'when the matter is ripe there, more good friends and reliable people will be spurred to advance the cause in other provinces, and the States General'.[63] Goethals admitted that he had not expected such a marked shift in popular sentiment in Holland and Zeeland 'in such a short time'.

Since Teellinck, Goethals, Stermond, and their ilk could not openly denounce the regents from the pulpit, their preferred method of attacking the government was through anonymous published pamphlets, 'serving to open the eyes of the common folk, more and more, to the saving of the land', and encourage 'pious regents'—that is, regents favourable to Calvinist orthodoxy, the Further Reformation and House of Orange.[64] But, in Holland, there was still the problem that most printers were afraid to publish such material, prompting Goethals to ask Willem Frederik if he could arrange for political tracts written by himself, and other Orangist activists, to be printed in, and distributed from, Friesland.[65]

Willem Frederik sought to foment popular anger against the regents but without arousing suspicions that he designed to usurp the rightful place, and inheritance, of the infant William III. He wrote to the States of Zeeland and Groningen, assuring them that he aspired only to become lieutenant-general of the army, and acting admiral of the navy, and would not in any way prejudice the young Prince's position.[66] He assured Zeelanders that the House of Orange-Nassau had brought the United Provinces from the 'deepest and most abject slavery' to the sublimity of the 'most glorious, law-based, freedom'.

By late summer, the agitation in favour of the House of Orange, orchestrated by Teellinck, had thoroughly intimidated the States party bloc in Middelburg, where the *vroedschap*, led by Adriaen Veth, yielded to the pressure to propose the elevation of William III to the stadholderate, and Willem Frederik to the lieutenant-stadholderate, of Zeeland. Deeply worried, the States of Holland sent a delegation to Zeeland, which included Johan de Witt and Joan Huydecoper, a leader of the republican faction at

[62] RAF Stadhoud. arch. 37/1/4k. Goethals to Willem Frederik, Delft, 7 Aug. 1652.
[63] Ibid.
[64] Ibid.
[65] Ibid.
[66] RAF Stadhoud. arch. 37/1/4k. Willem Frederik to SZ, 14 July and to S.Gr. 5 Aug. 1652.

Amsterdam. Their arrival provoked angry demonstrations, at Flushing and Veere, as well as Middelburg, with numerous redundant sailors and fishermen, and wives of maimed seamen, taking part.[67] An ugly situation developed in which De Witt, only 27 years of age, displayed a coolness and presence of mind well beyond that of his older colleagues. The pro-Holland leadership, at Middelburg, insisted they had not abandoned the cause of 'freedom' but that, for the moment, the populace were so enraged that they had no alternative but to bend before the wind. Zeeland, accordingly, voted for the appointments of William III, and Willem Frederik, in the States General, provided—a useful escape clause—other provinces (meaning Holland) were of a like opinion. Holland urged the States of Zeeland to think again and, this time, take precautions to prevent persons 'outside the government' interfering with their deliberations.

In fighting the Orangist upsurge, De Witt and his colleagues restated their 'States' party ideology with renewed vigour. By late 1652, De Witt was standing in, as acting Pensionary of Holland, for Adriaen Pauw; Pauw had taken over from Cats the previous year, and was still a symbol of Holland's defiance of the Stadholders but was now old and sick. Like Grotius, and Graswinckel, De Witt categorically upheld the principle of provincial sovereignty, in May 1652 reproving the Dutch envoys in England for allowing Parliament to refer to the United Provinces as a *respublica*, instead of in the plural, as the *Respublicae Foederatae*.[68] He also stressed the right of the States to supervise the public Church, and insisted that where control is concentrated in the hands of one man, an 'eminent head', there can be no responsible exercise of power through representatives, and assemblies, and no means of correcting misrule, except by dangerous popular unrest. For De Witt, the essence of what he later called the 'True Freedom', that is, republican government, was the sharing of power amongst those fitted by background, education, and training to exercise it, this dispersal of influence and the consultation, and compromise, that goes with it being the most effective mechanism for checking abuse and misgovernment.[69]

The Orangist upsurge of 1652–3, in the United Provinces, was generated by the pressures of the war with England but also restrained by them. The States of Gelderland, at their gathering in September 1652, split, with Nijmegen supporting Holland, Arnhem divided, and Zutphen Orangist.[70] But even the staunchly Orangist *raad* of Zutphen, eager though it was to see

---

[67] Rowen, *John de Witt*, 83.
[68] Ibid. 58.
[69] Ibid. 86–7.
[70] Wagenaar, *Vad. Hist.* xii. 229.

William III appointed Stadholder, and Willem Frederik Lieutenant-Stad-holder, was concerned, in the midst of the war, not to plunge the Union into dangerous turmoil, urging caution and the use of all possible arguments to persuade provinces which did not agree (that is Holland) to change their view.[71] The States of Groningen, predictably, joined Friesland and Zeeland, in urging, in the States General, that William III and Willem Frederik should be appointed captain-general, and lieutenant captain-general, of the Union.[72] But three entire provinces, Utrecht and Overijssel, as well as Gelderland, were too divided to adopt a clear stance.

A further twist to the political conundrum was added in the spring of 1653. On hearing of the Dutch defeat off Portland Bill, Charles II, pretender to the thrones of England, Scotland, and Ireland, living in exile, in Paris, wrote to the Dutch ambassador there, declaring himself 'heartily sorry' and promising, 'if the States will assigne me some ships . . . I will engage my own person with them, in the company of their fleets, and either by God's blessing prevaile with them, or perish in the attempt'.[73] Parliament in England was deeply worried precisely lest such an alliance should be formed, for in such a case, the expectation was, much of the English navy would desert to the king. Orangists, of course, were eager to ally with Charles II. But De Witt, and the leadership of the States of Holland, rejected this recourse, seeing that it would inevitably embitter, and prolong, a war from which they were anxious to extricate themselves at the earliest opportunity.[74] Neither did they wish to see collaboration between English royalists and Dutch Orangists strengthened.

The most dangerous period for the Holland States party was the summer of 1653, when the heaviest defeats were suffered at sea. Riots erupted at Dordrecht, The Hague, Rotterdam, Alkmaar, Hoorn, Medemblik, and—most spectacularly—at Enkhuizen, where the mob, in an anti-Catholic, as well as anti-regent, frenzy, took over the town for several days. There were riots also in Zeeland, at Middelburg, and Zierikzee, and at Bergen-op-Zoom. No less worrying for the Holland *Gecommitteerde Raden* and De Witt—who was installed, as full Pensionary, in July—was the spread of Orangist agitation to the navy itself. This not only increased the risk of mutiny and insubordination but hampered co-operation among the admir-als, Tromp and Jan Evertsen being Orangist in sympathy, and De Ruyter, and Witte de With, firmly aligned with the States party. After Tromp's

[71] GA Zutphen 1/13. res. raad 21 Sept. 1652.
[72] RAF Stadhoud. arch 37/1/22 a/b res. S.Gr. 23 Dec. 1652.
[73] PRO SP 84/159, fo. 149. Charles II to Boreel, Paris, 6 Mar. 1653.
[74] Geyl, *Oranje en Stuart*, 87–9.

death, the States of Holland painstakingly searched for someone to replace him as commander, who would be politically safe but, at the same time, possess status above other admirals and the capacity to pull the navy together.[75] This may have been the most tremendous naval conflict the Republic had yet fought but so fraught was the domestic political arena that it seemed more vital to appoint a head of the navy with the right political and social credentials than one with practical naval expertise. There was, indeed, a long delay until, finally, De Witt persuaded Obdam, the pre-eminent noble of the Holland States party-faction, and a capable man but one totally lacking in experience of the sea, to lead the fleet of one of the world's two great naval powers.

Caught between the English, without, and the Orangists, within, the 'True Freedom' of the republicans was saved by the cohesion of Holland, the lack of cohesion of the lesser provinces, and the vulnerability of England to maritime counter-pressure. Their backs to the wall, the Holland regents closed ranks. Even Leiden, though Orangist, had no wish to open the door to the mob pressure which had swayed Zeeland, or impair Holland's unity at such a dangerous juncture.[76] Holland stood firm while other provinces, including Groningen, which had a Stadholder, sank ever deeper into turmoil. Where then, De Witt asked his opponents, was the unity that went, according to them, with installing an 'eminent head'?

England won the battles in the North Sea but failed to win the war, owing to the impact of the Dutch strategic and maritime counter-offensive further afield. While the Dutch kept on fitting out their home fleet, the English could not disperse their strength to break the Dutch hold on the main sea-lanes, away from home waters. As a result, England's shipping and commerce were paralysed to an even greater extent than those of the Dutch. Eventually, it became impossible to go on with the war. Allied to Denmark, and keeping a strong force at the Danish Sound, the Dutch closed down English trade with the Baltic completely. During 1653 not a single English ship passed through the Sound. In the Mediterranean, the Dutch were equally successful. Having trapped a returning English Levant fleet at Livorno, Admiral van Galen crushed the relief fleet sent out to rescue it, off Livorno, in March 1653. After this, the English gave up the Mediterranean for the remainder of the war.[77] In the East Indies, the VOC quickly won maritime supremacy from the Persian Gulf to the China Sea. Furthermore, even in the North Sea by the summer of 1653, Dutch privateers were

---

[75] Oudendijk, *Johan de Witt en de zeemacht*, 52–3.
[76] GA Leiden Sec. Arch. 451, fo. 230. res. vroed. 5 Aug. 1653.
[77] Thurloe, *State Papers*, i. 437, 458.

beginning to capture English merchant ships as fast as the English privateers were capturing Dutch ships.

By November 1653, Cromwell and Parliament had had enough and began to think in terms of making peace without making great gains from the war.[78] As peace negotiations dragged on, month after month, the English leadership had to abandon all thought of material gains. By the spring of 1654, the sole remaining demand was that the Republic should never again appoint a Prince of Orange to the 'high charges' of the state—the stadhold-erate or captaincy-general—or any member of the House of Orange-Nassau. When this desideratum became known in the Republic, uproar ensued. Orangists assumed (probably rightly) that the demand originated with De Witt, rather than Cromwell, or at least in collusion between the two. There was a flood of bitter recrimination.

Seeing the lesser provinces would never accept such a proviso, De Witt had it dropped from the formal negotiations. Thus, the published text of the peace treaty carried no hint of an Exclusion of the House of Orange. But the States General did not know that De Witt had conceded a secret annexe, obliging the States of Holland alone to pass an Act of Exclusion, with respect to their province, stipulating that Parliament would not ratify the peace until Holland had done so.[79] Of the Generality's four plenipotentiaries in England, one, the Zeelander, had died before this was agreed, and had not been replaced, while, of the others, two were Hollanders. Of these, Hieronymus van Beverningk, of Gouda, one of the ablest men in the States of Holland, had proceeded in secret contact with De Witt, leaving his colleagues, especially the fourth—the Frisian, Jongestal—in the dark. In this way it came about that the States General ratified what they thought was the peace treaty, on 22 April 1654, unaware of the secret condition governing its ratification in England.

The leadership in Holland rallied the States behind the Exclusion. The 'chiefe among the Excluders' were reported to be De Witt, De Graeff, Obdam, and the army commander, Brederode.[80] Amsterdam, Dordrecht, and Gouda lent solid support. But most of the other towns were initially dubious, or hesitant. When it came to the first vote, only half the Holland towns supported De Witt, no fewer than nine towns—Leiden, Haarlem, Delft, Rotterdam, Gorcum, Alkmaar, Hoorn, Enkhuizen, and Edam—voting against.[81] In the college of the *ridderschap*, six of the ten nobles

[78] Farnell, 'Navigation Act', 451.
[79] Geyl, *Oranje en Stuart*, 103–4.
[80] Thurloe, *State Papers*, ii. 272.
[81] BOX MS Rawl. A.13, p. 332. 'Intelligence', 5 May 1654.

supported Exclusion—Obdam, Brederode, Duivenvoorde, Wimenum, Van der Mijle, and Merode—the other four—Beverweert, Noordwijk, Schagen, and Warmond—being opposed. Observers were surprised at Warmond's stance, since he was a Catholic, and his family had never been on friendly terms with the House of Orange-Nassau. De Witt set to work to win the majority he needed, swaying Delft, Rotterdam, and Gorcum. But the rest continued to oppose his advice, Leiden protesting that the Act of Exclusion was a violation of the sovereign independence of the United Provinces, in general, and Holland, in particular. Haarlem too resisted. Albert Ruyl, pensionary of Haarlem, although one of the six 'Louvesteiners' locked up, by William II, in 1650, had afterwards 'always showne himselfe very much devoted to the House of Orange and was one of the great opposers of this Act of Seclusion'.[82] Yet the six towns which fought the Exclusion made no appeal to the Generality against the majority in the States of Holland. If the minority bloc in Holland agreed with the view of the States of Friesland, Groningen, and Zeeland that the Exclusion violated the terms of the Union of Utrecht, and the accepted procedures of the State, they preferred not to split their province, or align with others against their own.[83] The States of Holland passed its Act of Exclusion on 4 May 1654.

The outcry in the country, and public Church, against the Exclusion and especially De Witt, Beverningk, and Obdam was predictably fierce, but De Witt was never one to be deterred by a furore. He went quietly about the task of persuading the other provinces to accept the situation. A week after the Exclusion, he conferred for two hours with Willem Frederik, at The Hague, but failed to allay the latter's indignation or his suspicion that it was really De Witt who was behind the whole business.[84] The most vehement response came from the Delegated States of Friesland, which felt thoroughly duped by Holland. On 18 May, Friesland submitted in the States General a vitriolic protest which De Witt termed 'a certain impertinent and exorbitant paper'. At the end of May, in an emergency session, the full States of Friesland endorsed the stance of their Delegated States and called on the States General to repudiate the Exclusion and hold an enquiry into the conduct of their plenipotentiaries in England.[85]

The reaction against the Act of Exclusion amongst large sections of the public was strong, but in the provincial assemblies relatively muted. Only Friesland vigorously opposed Holland's conduct.[86] The strength of De

[82] Ibid.
[83] GA Leiden Sec. Arch. 451, fos. 342–3. res. vroed. 30 Apr. and 9 May 1654.
[84] Sypestein, *Geschiedkundige bijdragen*, i. 64–7.
[85] ARH SG PR 375, pp. 271–2. res. SF. 27 May 1654.
[86] BOX MS Rawl. A.16, p. 74. 'Intelligence', 14 July 1654.

Witt's position—and this was always Holland's strength—was that the lesser provinces were unable to react in a coherent manner because of their own internal divisions. Owing to disagreement between the quarters, the States of Gelderland failed to produce a declaration supporting Friesland until late July.[87] Groningen, paralysed by the province's double split, produced a declaration condemning Holland only in August. The States of Utrecht were unable to respond with a single voice at all. The Utrecht *ridderschap*, traditionally Orangist, deplored the Exclusion as a usurpation of the powers of the 'Generality, and collectivity of the provinces, which alone have responsibility for making peace'.[88] But the new pro-Holland Utrecht city council firmly dissociated itself from this.

All these splits, however, were child's play compared to the turmoil which now engulfed Overijssel. In Overijssel, there were five *drosten*—of Salland, Twenthe, Vollenhove, IJsselmuiden, and Haaksbergen—and, in September 1653, the death of the then *drost* of Twenthe precipitated a bitter quarrel in the States, over the choice of a successor, which had deep roots in the past. The principal candidate to succeed to the powerful and lucrative office was the Orangist noble Rutger van Haersolte, who was already treasurer of Salland and *drost* of Lingen. He had the backing of Zwolle and Kampen but was opposed by Deventer, which, at the time, was aligned with the Holland States party. At the gathering of the States of Overijssel, in April 1654, two of the three voting towns, and the *ridderschap* of two of the three quarters, supported Haersolte. But Deventer persisted and a rift ensued which led to the departure of the representatives of Zwolle and Kampen, and the Haersoltist nobility, who convened instead at Zwolle, even though that year it was Deventer's turn to host the States.[89] The minority remaining at Deventer, including the *ridderschap* of Twenthe, then declared the Zwolle gathering 'illegal' and issued a placard forbidding the inhabitants of Twenthe to obey their 'illegally' appointed new *drost*.

Thus, it transpired that, aside from Friesland and Holland, only Zeeland participated coherently in the constitutional debate, between the provinces, over the Exclusion. Like the Frisians, the Zeelanders condemned the Exclusion, and Holland's dealings with London, as violations of the Union of Utrecht and accepted procedures of the Republic. Even so, Zeeland's critique was couched in muted terms very different from the vehemence of Friesland. Observers perceived that Zeeland was not in earnest, denouncing

---

[87] RAF Stadhoud. arch. 37/ii/48 a/c. res. S.Geld. 28 July 1654.
[88] RAF Stadhoud. arch. 37/ii/48 a/c res. Utrecht ridderschap, 18 July 1654.
[89] De Vries, *Gesch. van Zwolle*, ii. 49–50.

Holland only *pro forma*, to placate popular feeling in the province.[90] Many Zeeland regents, not to mention the populace and preachers, strongly disapproved of what Holland had done. But Zeeland's shipping had suffered severely from the war and, in the context of 1654, few Zeeland regents—or merchants—were willing to press their support for the House of Orange to the point of endangering the newly concluded peace. Just to make sure, a letter from Cromwell, to the States of Zeeland, arrived, at this point, absolving De Witt from responsibility for the Exclusion and threatening to renew the war should it be rescinded. The letter was construed by Orangists as yet another example of De Witt's deviousness but proved none the less effective for that.

Zeeland's 'Well-Reasoned Deduction' was compiled by Adriaen Veth, who was by no means an Orangist. The text accused Holland of breaking articles 9 and 10 of the Union of Utrecht, clauses forbidding any individual province to negotiate separately, or form 'confederacies or alliances' with foreign powers.[91] It also accused the Hollanders of violating the Particular Union of Holland and Zeeland, of 1575, and showing great ingratitude to the House of Orange-Nassau.

To justify Holland's conduct, De Witt compiled a lengthy text which he presented first to the States of Holland and then distributed widely, in the name of the States. De Witt's *Deduction*, which contains several important claims and principles, was debated by the States of Holland in a five-hour session and approved by nearly the whole assembly, with only Leiden and Edam opposing publication. Enkhuizen, earlier one of the most vehement in criticizing De Witt, lapsed into an unexpected silence not unconnected, observers concluded, with the town's just having received a provincial subsidy for its herring fishery. According to De Witt's *Deduction* of July 1654, the Union of Utrecht was no more than an alliance of seven 'sovereign states', each of which remained free to make its own arrangements regarding Stadholders, and approve, or disapprove, of any candidate for captain-general, without reference to other provinces. De Witt held that when tested against the 'touchstone of true and unfalsified freedom', the 'true aims' of Holland's critics were manifestly damaging to 'our dearly bought freedom'. Discoursing on past republics, especially Florence under the Medici, De Witt insisted that 'everyone should realize that, according to the judgement of all political writers of sound mind, high positions cannot be assigned, in a republic, to those whose ancestors held these posts, without considerable

---

[90] BOX MS Rawl. A.20, p. 113. 'Intelligence', 20 Nov. 1654.

[91] Kluiver, 'Zeeuwse reacties', 411–20.

peril to freedom'.[92] The hereditary principle, and that of the 'eminent head', he argued, had destroyed the Florentine republic and was inherently dangerous to republics.

De Witt had survived the Orangist surge of 1652–3, carried the Exclusion, and made peace with England, without making any concession to England's maritime and colonial interests. The episode was a triumph for De Witt and Holland's sense of purpose, and solidarity. Nevertheless, it left a bad taste in the mouth of the public. The official festivities held at the end of May, to mark the peace with England, were a frigid affair by comparison with the celebrations for the peace with Spain, in 1648, with which they were widely compared. As on the earlier occasion, Leiden refused to participate in the celebrations at all.[93] The inhabitants of Rotterdam, an Englishman reported, 'burnt pitch barrels . . . but it was slightly done, most of the understanding people being dissatisfied with the conditions of peace'.[94] 'Not one citizen or particular person did make any bonfire or demonstration of joy,' it was alleged, 'but only those . . . who either depended upon the magistrate or the admiraltie.' At Dordrecht, the 'young men were so bold as to sett up the Prince of Orange his colours upon the street and De Witt durst not pull them downe'. Only at Amsterdam was there more zest in the festivities with 'thousands of people abroad in the streetes to heare and see the showes upon the Dam'.[95] The text of the peace was read out to the multitude 'with the sound of trompets and the discharging of the great guns', after which came 'bonfires and fireworks . . . throughout the cittie'. The trumpeters also played the 'Wilhelmus' to the bewilderment of the crowds, who were unable to make out whether this was being done on the orders, or in defiance, of the *vroedschap*. But in Amsterdam too, it was remarked that 'there was more joy showne amongst the citizens, at the publishing of the peace between Spayne, and this state, then there was now'.

DE WITT'S SYSTEM DURING THE LATER 1650s

At Dordrecht, Rotterdam, and other Holland towns, much of the common populace strongly disapproved of the Exclusion and conduct of their regents. At Enkhuizen, a Reformed preacher who omitted the traditional prayer for the Prince of Orange, after the Exclusion, was told by local sailors that, if he did so again, they would throw him in the sea; the next week he

---

[92] Rowen, *The Low Countries*, 196.
[93] GA Leiden Sec. Arch. 451, fo. 359. res. vroed. 27 May 1654.
[94] BOX MS Rawl. A.14, pp. 266–7. 'Intelligence', 28 May 1654.
[95] Ibid.

recited a longer prayer than usual for the Prince, even though this went against his inclination. The Enkhuizen regents, it was reported, in May 1654, had opposed the Exclusion despite being privately in favour of it, 'pour complaire à leur peuple'.[96] This was reminiscent of the behaviour of the Zeeland regents, who were said to have denounced the Exclusion purely out of deference to the people. De Witt and his colleagues had much of the populace of Holland, as well as the nobles and regents of the lesser provinces, against them. Yet, the Holland States party was in a far stronger position than Oldenbarnevelt and his adherents during the crisis of 1616–18. For Holland was now able to bend the other provinces almost as she chose, instead of their being able to intervene in Holland, as in 1618; and, then, 'Barnevelt and the States of Holland were not masters of the militia [that is, the army] as the States of Holland are at present'.[97]

The later 1650s were one of the most flourishing periods of the Dutch Golden Age, at any rate for Holland. Once the pressure of the English war was removed, Dutch dominance of the world's 'rich trades' resumed and was, indeed, reinforced by the Anglo-Spanish War of 1655–60, which disrupted what remained of English commerce with Spain and southern Italy, and through Spain, with Spanish America. The ultimate irony of the First Anglo-Dutch War is that it was precisely in its aftermath—the later 1650s—that Dutch gains at English expense, especially in Spain, Spanish America, Italy, and the Levant, were greatest. Whether or not there was a winner of the war, it was unquestionably the Dutch who won the peace. It was also in the late 1650s that the Dutch completed their conquest of Ceylon, gaining a monopoly of the world cinnamon supply, and strengthened their position in India. Only in Portugal, which was in conflict with the Republic (and with Spain), did Dutch commerce fail to gain ground. All the Holland towns continued to grow and increase in wealth. At Amsterdam, rents for cheap housing during the 1650s remained stable. By contrast, the value of expensive houses, along Amsterdam's prestigious canals, began to soar, particularly at the end of the 1650s, despite the rapid construction of more and more mansions, or *herenhuisen*.[98]

The result of the Exclusion Crisis, in Dutch politics, was the strengthening of De Witt's position, in Holland, and of Holland's position, within the Republic. By late 1654, De Witt had swayed Enkhuizen, and mollified Haarlem, leaving Leiden in isolated, and impotent, opposition to the States party bloc within Holland.[99] De Witt, writing to the Dutch ambassador in

[96] Ibid. 270.
[97] BOX MS Rawl. A.16, pp. 439–40. 'Intelligence', 7 Aug. 1654.
[98] Lesger, *Huur en conjunctuur*, 67, 83.
[99] Thurloe, *State Papers*, ii. 650.

London, in April 1655, surveyed the scene with undisguised satisfaction. Opposition to Holland's policies had everywhere abated and the States General subsided into a 'peaceable mood'.[100] Of the lesser provinces, all except Friesland were in the grip of internal strife. From De Witt's point of view, this was advantageous rather than detrimental to the viability and vigour of the United Provinces as a whole. For the other provinces had no alternative but to defer to Holland and seek her guidance and help. In Zeeland, the towns were split three against three, with Middelburg, Zierikzee, and Tholen allied to Holland, and the rest Orangist.

But there was a limit to how unstable and turbulent the lesser provinces could safely be allowed to become; and, here, Groningen, and especially Overijssel, gave cause for concern. In October 1654, the 'States of Overijssel' gathered at Zwolle endorsed Van Haersolte's proposal that the way to overcome the 'disorders which daily increase in this province' was to appoint William III Stadholder of Overijssel and Willem Frederik Lieutenant-Stadholder.[101] This alarmed De Witt, and the *Gecommitteerde Raden* of Holland, who dispatched a circular to the Holland town councils, warning that the latest developments in Overijssel could have perilous consequences for Holland and summoning an emergency session of the States.[102] These gathered in a sombre mood, the city of Delft having been shattered a few weeks before by the great gunpowder explosion which killed hundreds of people and demolished a large part of the city.

As the Holland regents pondered what to do about Overijssel, Willem Frederik hastened to Zwolle where he was fêted and took his oath as 'Lieutenant-Stadholder', swearing to uphold the province's 'instructions', for the now 4-year-old 'Stadholder of Overijssel', until the infant William III should reach his 'capable years'. Having secured Zwolle and Kampen, the Frisian Stadholder proceeded to Deventer, early in November, seeking to win the city over with 'expedients and promises'. But, lacking cash for bribes, and hampered by the strife among the towns and *ridderschap*, he made little progress, especially as the opposition was strongly encouraged by Holland.

Willem Frederik, Stadholder of Friesland, Groningen, and Drenthe, and acting Stadholder (at least according to two-thirds of the States) of Overijssel, by no means had an easy task in challenging De Witt and the ascendancy of the States party-faction. In Groningen, his authority had all but collapsed, by 1655, pulverized by the splits in the Ommelands and

---

[100] *Brieven geschreven ende gewisselt*, iii. 41.
[101] Bussemaker, *Gesch. van Overijssel*, i. 68–9.
[102] GA Gouda OA 11. res. vroed. 26 Oct. 1654.

between the Ommelands and city.[103] His hopes of progress in Utrecht, where the *ridderschap* and chapters voted to confer the stadholderate on William III with himself as 'Lieutenant-Stadholder', in July 1654, were dashed by the (since 1651) pro-'States' city of Utrecht, which blocked every Orangist initiative.[104] In Gelderland, there was the usual bickering among the quarters compounded by divisions within them, for, in both the Arnhem and Zutphen quarters, the main towns—Arnhem and Zutphen—argued that their votes were equivalent to those of the small towns combined while Harderwijk, Wageningen, and other small towns insisted on one town one vote. As in the past, Zutphen remained Orangist, Nijmegen anti-Orangist, and Arnhem divided. Equally unavailing were Willem Frederik's efforts to exploit the Orangism of Leiden, Haarlem, and Enkhuizen. In vain, he bemoaned the 'timid attitude' of the 'good towns' of Holland, meaning their refusal to combine with Friesland against the majority of the States of Holland.[105]

Orangist debility increased with the mounting strife within their own camp. Princess Mary detested Willem Frederik, whom she suspected of seeking advantages for himself, at the expense of her son. Amalia von Solms, still a force in Orangist circles, was also at odds with the Frisian Stadholder, as was Friedrich Wilhelm, the Great Elector, in Berlin, who, as husband of Louise Henriette (1627–67), eldest daughter of Frederik Hendrik, and aunt of William III, rejected the Exclusion and took a keen interest in Dutch internal politics. Several meetings were arranged between the Frisian Stadholder, two princesses, and representatives of the Great Elector and William III's maternal uncle, Charles II of England. But intrigue and suspicion continued to poison their relations. Among other steps to reassure the Orangist public, Willem Frederik, through the Delegated States, arranged for the Reformed preachers of Friesland to introduce into their services, alongside existing prayers for the provincial States and Stadholder, prayers for the Prince of Orange, although this had never previously been the practice in that province.[106]

The affairs of Overijssel continued to deteriorate. The 'States of Overijssel' gathered at Deventer denounced the appointments of William III and Willem Frederik by the 'States' gathered at Zwolle as a violation of the laws of the province.[107] The Twenthe *ridderschap*, led by Adolph Hendrik van

[103] Aitzema, *Histoire*, viii. 217, 357.
[104] Wagenaar, *Vad. Hist.* xii. 342.
[105] Sypestein, *Geschiedkundige bijdragen*, i. 86.
[106] BOX MS Rawl. A.17, p. 232. 'Intelligence', 21 Dec. 1654.
[107] Bussemaker, *Gesch. van Overijssel*, i. 69–70.

Raesfelt (*c*.1625–82), heer van Twickelo, accusing Van Haersolte of all manner of misconduct, resolutely opposed his authority in Twenthe, where local administration had now largely broken down. As tension mounted, the Deventer 'States' worried that their adversaries would resort to force. A delegation from Deventer appeared before the States of Holland, in March 1655, asking for deployment of more Generality troops in the province to forestall a possible coup against the city. The States of Holland agreed (over the objections of Leiden), and persuaded the States General to send a force, though its dispatch was held up for a time by the *Raad van State*.[108] Holland also demanded that Willem Frederik abandon the Zwolle 'States' and renounce his 'illegal' appointment and title, as 'Lieutenant-Stadholder of Overijssel'.

Holland's key lever was control of the Generality's army, as became more than ever obvious in September 1655, when Field Marshal baron van Brederode died. The Frisian Stadholder wished to become commander of the army, in succession to Brederode, and had been contemplating improving his position, by means of a *rapprochement* with De Witt, since the spring of 1655, when Holland had helped him restore order in Groningen. A Generality commission, headed by De Witt, had travelled to Groningen to hear all parties to the disputes and organize a compromise package, thereby (temporarily) restoring the Stadholder's authority in the province. But De Witt perceived, in the aftermath of Brederode's death, a chance to strengthen his own party and to aggravate further the dissension amongst the Orangist leadership. As bait, he suggested to the Frisian Stadholder that he might become commander of the army were he to acknowledge the illegality of William III's, and his own, respective appointments as 'Stadholder' and 'Lieutenant-Stadholder' of Overijssel.[109]

The course which De Witt now pursued seemed highly dubious to many on his own side. Amsterdam was appalled at the suggestion that the man who had led the military, during the coup of 1650, should be named Field Marshal of the army by his former victims.[110] The *vroedschap* set up a special committee of senior regents, headed by Cornelis de Graeff, to study the question of the command of the army. They acknowledged that it was necessary to find an experienced and prestigious commander for the States General's forces quickly to maintain the army's discipline and organization at a time when the lesser provinces of the Union were in turmoil. But the man appointed Field Marshal had, in their opinion, to be politically safe.

[108] GA Leiden Sec. Arch. 451, fos. 54, 57. res. vroed. 22 Mar. and 20 Apr. 1655.
[109] Sypestein, *Geschiedkundige bijdragen*, i. 101–2.
[110] GA Amsterdam res. vroed. 11 and 14 Sept. 1655.

Consequently, Amsterdam proposed Willem Frederik's only plausible Dutch rival—Count Johan Maurits of Nassau-Siegen, former governor of Netherlands Brazil, and now Stadholder of Cleves for the Elector of Brandenburg. The count was no friend of Willem Frederik, and had long been amenable to the States of Holland.

But De Witt persuaded Amsterdam's deputies to the States, at The Hague, that if Holland did not use the opportunity to appoint Willem Frederik, while simultaneously neutralizing him by imposing tough new constitutional limitations on the authority of the commander-in-chief, there was a real risk that Friesland and Groningen would rally enough other provinces for their Stadholder's candidacy to force his appointment through, without new constitutional safeguards, leaving Holland isolated and vulnerable. De Witt's objective was to reinforce the 'True Freedom' by fully subordinating the army to civilian control. After confidential talks with Willem Frederik, he assured Amsterdam that the Frisian Stadholder would accept command, under the limitations Holland would propose, and 'in such a case would renounce the government of Overijssel'.[111]

The negotiations between De Witt and Willem Frederik resulted in a package presented to the States General, in December 1655.[112] The agreement stipulated that the States General would draw up new 'instructions' for the Field Marshal of the army; that the Field Marshalship could not, in future, be combined with the office of Stadholder, or Lieutenant-Stadholder (except in this first instance, with respect to Willem Frederik being Stadholder of Friesland and Groningen); that Willem Frederik would renounce his title as 'Lieutenant Stadholder of Overijssel'; and that there would be no further dispute about Holland's Act of Exclusion—implying its tacit acceptance by Willem Frederik and the States General. Finally, the blocking of the appointment of the dextrous (and soon very rich) Van Beverningk, as treasurer-general of the Generality, was to cease.

This package, known as the 'Harmony' of 1655, excited some lively discussion throughout the Republic, particularly as to who was duping whom. De Witt encountered many sceptics on his own side, including his father, who doubted that making Willem Frederik commander of the army was a way of strengthening the 'True Freedom'. De Witt's confidence in his 'precautions and clauses for the preservation of freedom', and conviction that his 'Harmony' implied acceptance of the Exclusion by the Generality, was not shared by other observers. The historian Aitzema, who was also a diplomatic agent, bon vivant, libertine, and spy, regarded abroad as one of

---

[111] GA Amsterdam res. vroed. 19 Nov. 1655.   [112] Japikse, *Johan de Witt*, 111–12.

the remarkable personalities of the Republic, told De Witt to his face that steel was stronger than paper, and that once Willem Frederik commanded the army he would use it, to master the Republic, by degrees.[113] Yet, even before the 'Harmony' was adopted by the States General, it bore fruit in the shape of heightened strife among the Orangist leadership. To Princess Mary, and her entourage, Willem Frederik's dealings with the Pensionary were a betrayal of her son. While Amalia—who was not on good terms with her daughter-in-law—was rumoured to back the 'Harmony', the Orangist grouping of the Holland *ridderschap*, led by Mary's personal adviser, Lodewijk van Beverweert, and the heer van Noordwijk, opposed the arrangement.[114]

Steering the 'Harmony' through the States General proved no easy task. De Witt and the Frisian Stadholder devised a compromise package for ending the troubles in Overijssel, in February 1656, cancelling the appointments of a 'Stadholder' and 'Lieutenant-Stadholder', and the appointment of Van Haersolte as *drost* of Twenthe. But this merely provoked a break between the Frisian Stadholder and the Haersholtists, who refused to accept that William III was not Stadholder of Overijssel, Van Haersolte not *drost* of Twenthe, and the Zwolle 'States' not the States of Overijssel.[115] As the deadlock continued, Willem Frederik became disillusioned with his deal with Holland's Pensionary. By late 1656, he had switched back to opposing Holland and trying to mend his bridges with the Orangists. Rejecting De Witt's 'Harmony', the States of Friesland pressed, in January 1657, for the appointment of their Stadholder as commander of the army, on the same basis as Brederode. At a moment when the president-of-the-week of the States General was an Orangist, and willing to countenance a vote with only five, of the seven, provincial delegations present, Willem Frederik's supporters carried his appointment as Field Marshal, without new constitutional safeguards and outside the 'Harmony', overruling Holland by four provinces to one.[116] The Holland *Gecommitteerde Raden*, and De Witt, reacted vigorously, warning the States General that regiments in Holland's pay would not obey the orders of an 'illegally' appointed Field Marshal. A circular was sent to the other provincial assemblies, condemning the appointment as invalid, and a violation of accepted procedure. Friesland denied this, taking the opportunity to reaffirm the validity of majority voting in the States General, even when some provincial delegations were absent.[117]

[113] Rowen, *John de Witt*, 368.
[114] BOX MS Rawl. A.17, pp. 278–9. 'Intelligence', 20 Dec. 1655.
[115] Sypestein, *Geschiedkundige bijdragen*, i. 109.
[116] GA Amsterdam res. vroed. 15 Jan. 1657.
[117] ARH SG PR 375, p. 595. res. SF, 17 Feb. 1657.

The ideology of the 'States' party was rooted in the claim, buttressed by Grotius and Graswinckel, that each province of the United Provinces was sovereign. This was a manifest fiction and everyone knew it to be a manifest fiction. There had always been majority voting in the States General and this was unavoidable if the Republic was to function. Holland regularly participated in majority votes in the Generality. But this was when Holland was with the majority. The reason the doctrine of provincial sovereignty was so vital to the Holland States party, and De Witt, was that they could not accept that Holland could be overruled in the Generality, by a majority of lesser provinces, or even all the other provinces together. If the majority could overrule Holland, then Maurits's *coup d'état*, of 1618, was legitimate and so were William II's actions against Holland, in 1650. The reality was that the provinces were not sovereign—or at least the lesser provinces were not—and that decisions went by majority vote in the Generality, provided Holland was among the majority, but not when she was not. There was no way this could be justified, in theoretical terms; and the only way it could be buttressed, in constitutional theory, was to insist on the fiction of provincial sovereignty. Speaking in the States General, De Witt warned the other provinces that an attempt, by the majority, to overrule Holland would lead, as in 1618 and 1650, to 'serious confusion in the state'.[118]

Holland's Pensionary resolved the tangle in the States General by working on the lesser provinces and, on 1 February, the earlier decision, to appoint Willem Frederik, was cancelled by four votes to three, with now only Friesland, Groningen, and Zeeland supporting the appointment. But the strife in Overijssel and Groningen was not so easily resolved. Moreover, the adverse effect of the ferment in those provinces, for the Republic as a whole, was greater now than previously, owing to developments across the border, in the prince-bishopric of Münster. The efforts of the new prince-bishop, Christoph Bernhard von Galen, to forge an absolutist state in the large, and agriculturally rich, territory of the Münsterland, by suppressing the autonomy of the city of Münster, and vigorous advancement of the Counter-Reformation, was causing concern throughout Overijssel, Drenthe, Groningen, and Gelderland, and beginning to pose a potential threat to the United Provinces as a whole; not least since Von Galen was actively reviving Münster's claims to Borculo.[119]

As the turmoil in Overijssel continued, the Deventer 'States' began encouraging the small towns to the north of Zwolle—Hasselt and Steenwijk—to rebel against Zwolle and seek voting status in the States of

---

[118] Rowen, *John de Witt*, 372.   [119] Bannier, *Landgrenzen*, 260.

Overijssel.[120] These towns began sending their fiscal contributions to Deventer, instead of Zwolle. In the spring of 1657, fearing a strong reaction, Hasselt also obtained a garrison from Deventer. Van Haersolte replied by gathering a force and bombarding Hasselt for three days, with four artillery pieces, firing off 700 cannon-balls, and causing substantial damage to the town. Deventer sent a second force to relieve the siege, which led to a small battle nearby, in which there were several killed and numerous wounded. Hasselt sent letters to Holland imploring relief from the 'gruesome tyranny' of Zwolle and Kampen.

Hasselt capitulated to the Zwolle 'States', on 7 June 1657. But Van Haersolte and his colleagues had overplayed their hand. De Witt and the *Gecommitteerde Raden* of Holland had had enough. At Holland's insistence, the States General formed a commission to end the turmoil in Overijssel, headed by De Witt and De Graeff.[121] The two leaders of the Holland States party heard submissions from all factions and duly presented their 'compromise'. This nullified the appointments of William III and Willem Frederik as 'Stadholder' and 'Lieutenant-Stadholder' of Overijssel, reunited the States of Overijssel on the basis of the status quo ante, with exclusion of Hasselt and Steenwijk, cancelled Van Haersolte's appointment as *drost* of Twenthe, ruled on the fiscal dispute, and declared a general amnesty for the events of 1653–7.[122] It was also agreed that the texts each side had published, denouncing the other, be recalled and suppressed. It was less a 'compromise' than slapping down of the Overijssel Orangists. But Zwolle and Kampen acquiesced, participating in an elaborate ceremony of reconciliation of the warring parts of the States of Overijssel—appropriately enough in the hall of the States of Holland. In Overijssel quiet was restored, though the province remained deeply divided.[123]

Holland also intervened, yet again, to check the turmoil in Groningen. The compromise *reglement* which the Generality commission, headed by De Witt, had imposed in May 1655 had soon broken down. By 1656, Groningen was more turbulent than ever. In August 1656, the Ommelander faction headed by Rengers, had a sufficient stranglehold over the Hunsingo and Fivelingo quarters to purge their opponents from the rural magistracies.[124] The city responded by stepping up its support for the anti-Rengers faction in the Ommelands, to which Rengers replied by stirring up the guilds against the ruling faction in the city *raad*. Though Rengers and his

---

[120] De Vries, *Gesch. van Zwolle*, ii. 52.
[121] *Brieven geschreven ende gewisselt*, iii. 400.
[122] Bussemaker, *Gesch. van Overijssel*, i. 177–84.
[123] Ibid.
[124] De Boer, *Woelingen in Stad en Lande*, 23–32.

adherents, as Ommelander *jonkers*, rejected the staple privileges the city claimed over the Ommelands, they by no means opposed the pretensions of the guilds within the city, seeing this as a useful means of weakening the *raad*. Serious rioting erupted at Groningen, in March 1657, in which a burgomaster was almost killed and his house ransacked. Willem Frederik, as Stadholder, sent troops into the city, but when these were attacked by a stone-throwing mob, decided to withdraw, lest they should have to open fire and cause a massacre.[125]

To settle Groningen, the Generality sent a commission, drawn from four provinces, including Holland. After lengthy investigation, the Generality commissioners, who included the dextrous Van Beverningk, drew up a radically new *reglement* which was published in March 1659. The essence of the new arrangements was the splitting of the Ommelander quarters into sub-quarters, with jurisdictional boundaries, designed to prevent any over-mighty *jonker*, in the future, accumulating offices, and influence, across the quarter. To distribute power more effectively, the new *reglement* laid down detailed rules for electing judicial and fiscal officers at under-quarter, as well as quarter, and provincial, level, prohibiting interference by one under-quarter in the affairs of another, as well as of one quarter in another.[126] The effect was indeed to disperse power in the Ommelands but, at the same time, to reinforce the grip of *jonker* families over particular administrative posts and localities.

At the same time, Holland intervened in the Münsterland. Normally, neither the Generality, nor states of Holland, made it their business to oppose princely absolutism, and support 'freedom', outside their own territory. But the German lands immediately to the east of the Republic, historically closely intertwined with the eastern Dutch provinces, were a special case. The strategic and economic importance of the Ems estuary, and valley, of the lower Rhine duchies, and the Münsterland, together with the Calvinist county of Bentheim, as well as the ceaseless, triangular contest of Catholicism, Calvinism, and Lutheranism throughout these regions, from East Friesland to Aachen, entwined the politics of these German states inextricably with those of the inland areas of the Republic (see Map 12). In the case of the prince-bishopric matters were made worse by the intractable problem of the enclaves along the border. Especially contentious were Borculo, Bredevoort, Anholt, Lichtenvoorde, and the castle of Bevergern, which Frederik Hendrik had annexed to Lingen, but was claimed by Münster and in 1652 had been seized by Munsterite troops.

---

[125] Aitzema, *Historie*, viii. 985.
[126] Ibid. ix. 622–3; Feenstra, *Adel in de Ommelanden*, 81–2.

The struggle which developed in the 1650s between the prince-bishop and city of Münster troubled the Dutch for three reasons. Should a strong absolutist state emerge in the Münsterland, Munsterite pressure on the border enclaves would grow;[127] activity of Catholic missionaries in Twenthe and eastern Gelderland, already a source of friction, would escalate; and third and most serious, consolidation of a hostile power, controlling a large area on the eastern side, raised the spectre of an alliance between this power and a potential adversary, such as England, to the west, trapping the Republic, in pincers, between the two. It was not long before it was seen just how serious a strategic threat this posed.

The struggle in the Münsterland culminated in 1661, when the prince-bishop successfully besieged the city whose privileges De Witt had sought to defend.[128] Christoph Bernhard triumphed over not only the city but Holland's efforts to protect its autonomy, De Witt having gone so far, in October 1657, as to threaten to send troops to the city's assistance. One lesson of the Münster saga of the 1650s and early 1660s was that Gelderland and Overijssel, on their own, were totally incapable of standing up to the prince-bishopric. As they were outside the Holy Roman Empire, their interests could only be safeguarded by Holland. Yet Holland's concerns were primarily maritime and not all her towns supported De Witt's interventionist policy in the Münsterland. Amsterdam, in particular, opposed Holland's vote to threaten force against the prince-bishop, in 1657,[129] disagreement which the latter adroitly exploited.

During the late 1650s, De Witt found himself continually juggling troublesome situations within the Republic with challenges to Dutch interests without, which taxed his political dexterity to the limit. Amsterdam refused to give as much weight to the problem of Münster as De Witt, but was deeply worried by the struggle unfolding in the Baltic and around the Danish Sound. The Republic intervened in the Baltic, sending a fleet, under Obdam, to Danzig, in the summer of 1656, to prevent Danzig, and the Vistula estuary, falling to the Swedes. When Charles X of Sweden, in a lightning campaign, overran much of Denmark, in 1658, and closed in on the Danish Sound, setting siege to Copenhagen, Obdam was sent with a fleet to relieve Copenhagen, and keep the Sound out of Swedish hands. When an English fleet was sent to Danish waters, in 1659, to stiffen the Swedes, a second Dutch fleet was sent out, under De Ruyter, to bolster the Danes,

---

[127] Schilfgaarde, *Graven van Limburg Stirum*, i. 127.
[128] Schröer, *Korrespondenz*, 60–2.
[129] De Bruin, *Geheimhouding en verraad*, 439–40.

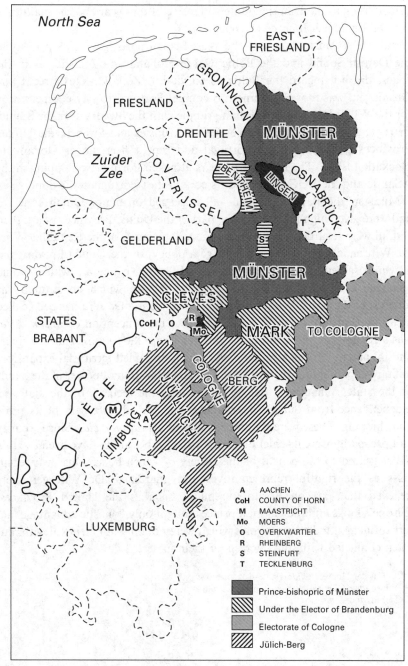

MAP 12. The German states bordering the Republic in the mid-seventeenth century

contributing to the Danish counter-offensive of that year and the making of the Danish–Swedish peace of 1660.

But whilst Amsterdam, and the West Frisian ports, gave high priority to the Danish Sound and the Baltic, South Holland and Zeeland, as in the 1640s, did not regard the Baltic as so vital.[130] Zeeland, like Utrecht and Groningen, was more concerned to compel Portugal to pay compensation for the WIC's losses in Brazil than grapple with the Swedes over the Sound. In 1657, about to threaten force against Münster and Sweden, the United Provinces declared war on Portugal and sent a fleet, under Obdam, to blockade Lisbon. The Dutch privateers attacked Portuguese shipping in the Atlantic and the VOC completed its conquest of Portuguese Ceylon.

Münster, the Baltic, Portugal—all impinged on major Dutch concerns and were given high priority by one part of the United Provinces or another. But all were regarded as less vital by much, or most, of the Republic. What De Witt endeavoured to do was forge a policy for the United Provinces as a whole, albeit giving preference to Holland's concerns, which would reconcile divergent interests, creating a balance which constituted the 'interest of the state'. With considerable justification De Witt has been called a *raison d'état* politician.[131] So he was. But his conception of *raison d'état* was a republican one, profoundly different from the *raison d'état* of princes and monarchs. It was a *raison d'état* which disdained territorial expansion, military capability for its own sake, and concentration of power in the hands of the state. What he strove to ensure was the security of the state, its independence from outside interference, and the advancement of its trade and shipping. These were the three pillars of his *raison d'état*. Since security and prosperity were its chief objects, it can also be said to have been a *raison d'état* geared to the benefit of the society of which he saw his own regent class as the rightful representatives and guardians. De Witt genuinely believed that, in contrast to a republic such as the United Provinces, Europe's kings and the German princes sought only dynastic advantage and territorial aggrandizement, goals which were not only not identical with, but often conflicted with, the interests of their subjects.[132]

---

[130] Van der Hoeven, *Bijdrage*, 98–102, 106.
[131] Boogman, 'De *raison d'état* politicus', 389–93.
[132] Ibid. 399–407.

30

The Republic at its Zenith, II: 1659–1672

❖

A new era commenced in both parts of the Netherlands with the end of the great Franco-Spanish war of 1635–59. The peace of the Pyrenees (1659) which concluded the Franco-Spanish conflict, a struggle which dominated the affairs of western Europe for a quarter of a century, also signalled a fundamental change in Spain's role in the Netherlands and in that of the Republic in the southern provinces. Before 1659, the Republic had had no role in the south and, since 1648, it had been free of any entanglement by land liable to threaten its security or commerce. The Dutch had come under heavy pressure from England. But the English threat, severe though it was, was confined to the maritime sphere and the Indies. Until 1659, Spain had shouldered the burden of containing French power in western Europe and of fortifying the south Netherlands.

Spain had, until the peace of the Pyrenees, adhered unwaveringly to her old policy of employing the southern Low Countries as the hammer and anvil of the Spanish monarchy and the bridle of France. She had done so by maintaining her principal army in the Spanish Netherlands and committing the bulk of her military expenditure to this arena. Even the shock of the revolts of Catalonia and Portugal against Spanish Habsburg rule, in 1640, had failed to shake Spanish ministers' belief in this strategy as the best means to maintain Spain's position in Europe. The struggle in Portugal, continuing desultorily, had been given relatively low priority.

There was even a late revival of Spanish power in the south Netherlands during the governorship of the Archduke Leopold Wilhelm (1647–56), who was provided with the troops and money to take advantage of France's temporary weakness during the Frondes (1648–52). Spanish troops regained some of the ground lost in the 1640s and, in 1652, the year in which Philip IV retook Barcelona, Leopold Wilhelm recovered the strategically vital and heavily fortified port of Dunkirk. It was the inability of the French to gain the upper hand in the 1650s which gave Cromwell the opportunity to bring England into the war to tilt the balance against Spain. Only with the battle of the Dunes, outside Dunkirk, in June 1658, were Spanish arms in the Low Countries decisively defeated.

But, after 1659, the picture changed both rapidly and radically. The flow of silver remittances from Madrid to Antwerp, which had lubricated Spain's military machine since the days of Alva, dried up. Don Juan José of Austria, governor-general at Brussels in the years 1656–60, was the last governor of

TABLE 38. *The governors-general of the Spanish Netherlands from Alva to Max Emmanuel*

Governor-general	Status	Dates
Alva, Don Fernando Alvarez de Toledo, duke of	Castilian grandee	1567–73
Requesens, Don Luis de	Catalan noble	1573–6
Austria, Don Juan de, Catholic commander at Lepanto	bastard son of Charles V	1576–8
Parma, Alessandro Farnese, Prince and duke of	nephew of Philip II	1578–92
Mansfelt, Peter-Ernst, count of (acting)	Stadholder of Luxemburg, army general	1592–4
Ernst of Austria, Archduke	nephew of Philip II	1594–5
Albert of Austria, Archduke	nephew of Philip II	1595–8
Albert and the Infanta Isabella (Philip II's daughter)	as joint sovereigns	1598–1621
Infanta Isabella	as regent for Philip IV	1621–33
Aytona, Don Francisco de Moncada, marqués de	Castilian soldier-diplomat	1633–4
Cardinal-Infante, Don Fernando de Austria, the	brother of Philip IV	1634–41
Melo, Don Francisco de	Portuguese adviser to the Cardinal-Infante	1641–4
Castel Rodrigo, Don Manuel de Moura y Cortereal, marqués de	Portuguese diplomat	1644–7
Leopold Wilhelm of Austria, Archduke	cousin of Philip IV	1647–56
Austria, Don Juan José de	bastard son of Philip IV	1656–60
Caracena, Don Luis de Benavides, marqués de,	Castilian noble	1660–4

Governor-general	Status	Dates
Castel Rodrigo, Don Francisco de Moura y Cortereal, marqués de	diplomat	1664–8
Velasco, Don Iñigo de, Constable of Castile	Castilian grandee	1668–70
Monterrey, Don Juan Domingo de Zúñiga, conde de	son of Luis de Haro	1670–5
Villahermosa, Don Carlos de Gurrea y Aragón y Borja, duke of	grandee	1675–8
Parma, Alexandre Farnese II, Prince of	allied prince	1678–82
Grana, Otto Heinrich, marquese di	Imperial diplomat	1682–5
Gastañaga, Don Francisco Antonio de Agurto, marqués de	cavalry general	1685–92
Max Emmanuel, Elector of Bavaria	allied prince	1692–1706

the Spanish Netherlands to command a powerful army. Almost as soon as the peace was concluded, Spanish ministers switched their priorities, having decided to use the men and resources previously committed to the Netherlands in a sustained effort to reconquer Portugal and her colonial empire. In the event, the great Spanish offensive against Portugal proved a humiliating failure and, in 1668, Philip IV resolved to cut his losses and recognize Portuguese independence. But Spain was now exhausted and the army of Flanders, having been cut back to the point that it no longer represented a significant force in international affairs, was never subsequently restored to anything like its previous dimensions or strength.

The army of Flanders shrank from over 70,000 men in 1658 to 33,000, by 1661,[1] and, before long, to scarcely 20,000. The last Spaniard to hold the post of governor of the Spanish Netherlands, the marqués de Gastañaga (1685–92), admitted early on in the Nine Years War (1688–97), in which Spain was allied with the Dutch, Britain, Austria, and Brandenburg, against France, that Spain could play only a minor role in defending the south Netherlands, which was regarded as the bulwark of Germany, Italy, and Spain, as well as of the Dutch Republic, against Louis XIV.[2] In December 1690, he estimated Spain's effective troop strength in the Low Countries at

[1] Parker, *Army of Flanders*, 272.
[2] ARH SG 7086/1. Dijkvelt to SG, Brussels, 24 Dec. 1690.

no more than 15,000. During 1692–3, the French committed 100,000 men to campaigning in the Low Countries and the allies around 75,000, a figure which rose to 90,000, in 1694, and 120,000 in 1695. Yet the Spanish contribution to this, by far the largest and most important army of the anti-French coalition, failed to grow—through lack of remittances from Spain—so that the proportion of the allied army shouldered by Spain continued to dwindle. By late 1695 the once mighty army of Flanders had sunk to only about 6,500 effectives.[3]

Yet even at this dismal level, it proved impossible to finance Spain's war effort with funds raised by the Spanish Crown. The States of Flanders and Brabant voted substantial sums towards the war but so diminished were the credit and prestige of the Spanish Crown that the Antwerp money market— since 1659 only a shadow of its former self—proved largely unwilling to provide the required advances. It was literally impossible to bank on promised remittances from Spain. Consequently, it proved necessary to borrow over eight million guilders on the Amsterdam Exchange, with the help of the Dutch authorities, though even in Amsterdam there was remarkably little enthusiasm for lending to the king of Spain. In the event much of the finance was raised by Baron Francisco Lopes Suasso, the leading financier of the Sephardi Jewish community of Amsterdam, who had played a notable part in organizing the finance for the Dutch expedition to England in 1688. Lopes Suasso's father had been the first Jew to be made a baron by the king of Spain. In July 1696, the Council of State in Madrid acknowledged that Lopes Suasso had almost single-handedly saved the Spanish military machine in the Low Countries from collapse.[4]

Yet despite the weakness of Spain in the south Netherlands after 1659, and repeated French invasions from 1667 down to 1712, the south continued to show remarkable resilience both as a political and cultural entity and as an economy. Much damage was caused by the fighting, and movement of armies, but mainly in the Walloon areas. In Flanders and Brabant agriculture entered the same long depression, after 1660, as gripped the north Netherlands and the rest of western Europe, but over the next half-century rural rents and land prices in Flanders and Brabant fell considerably less sharply than they did in the north Netherlands (see pp. 634–5 above) and the high productivity of Flemish agriculture remained unaffected. It is true that there set in, after 1648, a marked qualitative deterioration in the more specialized urban industries such as tapestries,

[3] De Schryver, *Jan van Brouchoven*, 104.
[4] AGS Estado 3890. *consulta* of the Consejo de Estado, Madrid, 2 July 1696.

silks, jewellery, and book production;[5] but this was compensated for by the further growth of labour-intensive industries where much of the work could be done by the still growing rural population, above all the linen industry.[6] As exports of French linen to Spain and Spanish America declined, after 1688, Flemish linen, like Dutch linen, benefited from the increased opportunities for sales in the Spanish empire.

As Spain's grip weakened, there were also increasing signs of restlessness among the States of Flanders and Brabant and the civic élites of Antwerp, Brussels, and Ghent at the deterioration of public administration and especially the lack of support given by the regime to commerce, industry, and shipping. Few officials of the regime, whether local or Spanish, showed great ability. But there was a conspicuous exception in the shape of the remarkable Jan van Brouchoven, count of Bergeyck (1644–1725), who was described, in 1701, by the French officials sent by Louis XIV to take over the administration of the south Netherlands, in the name of the new Bourbon king of Spain, Philip V, as 'le seul homme capable' to be found at Brussels.[7] As the minister most relied on by a declining Spanish regime and by the provincial States alike, Bergeyck became the chief focus, and co-ordinator, of the pressure for change. With his help, States and civic élites sought to forge a more active role for the south Netherlands in both the commerce of the Spanish empire and international commerce more generally. There were several initiatives relating to Spanish America. In September 1686, for example, the States of Flanders petitioned the king to allow direct navigation between Ostend and Buenos Aires as well as other Spanish ports which were not visited by the official transatlantic convoys sailing from Spain. They asked also to be allowed to colonize Santo Domingo as part of Spain's effort to prevent the island being overrun by the French. Both aspects were extensively discussed in Madrid albeit without result. By the end of the 1690s Spanish authority was so reduced that the last governor-general of the Spanish Netherlands, Max Emmanuel of Bavaria—who had been brought in as an emergency measure, at the request of the Stadholder-king, William III, and who had few links with Spain—guided by Bergeyck, actually issued a charter, in 1699, setting up a Flemish East India Company, a forerunner of the later Ostend Company, in the name of the king of Spain but without his permission.[8] Inevitably, this move caused both consternation and anger at The Hague, where the States General promptly issued an edict forbidding Dutch subjects to participate in the Flemish initiative in any way.

[5] De Nave, *Antwerpen en de scheiding*, 17, 81–2.
[6] Vermaut, 'Structural Transformation', 193–7.
[7] De Schryver, *Jan van Brouchoven*, 478.
[8] Ibid. 476.

The civic élites of the south desired more opportunities in long-distance trade, resented the continued closure of the Scheldt to maritime traffic, and also disliked the passive tariff policy of the Spanish regime in the 'obedient' provinces. The merchants and manufacturers of Flanders and Brabant wanted far more extensive protection on the part of the king, especially from Dutch products and competition, and, as the Spanish sway weakened, pressure for such protectionism increased, despite Madrid's reluctance to offend the Dutch and (after 1688) also Britain. In 1699 Bergeyck convened a gathering of civic delegates to debate trade, industry, and tariffs which resulted in the promulgation of new tariffs to replace the tariff list of 1680 (which was favourable to the Dutch) designed to curb imports of Dutch textiles, refined salt and sugar, and other products.[9] As regards salt at least, these measures violated the terms of the treaty of Münster, which included a clause by which Spain made concessions to the Zeeland salt industry. The States General at The Hague retaliated by banning imports of glass, paper, linen, and woollen cloth until Brussels' measures were lifted. This growing friction between north and south over tariffs then became subsumed, from 1700, into the wider conflict over the Spanish Succession and the future of the south Netherlands.

The United Provinces had a vital interest in upholding the terms of the treaty of Münster, especially the closure of the Scheldt to maritime traffic, and in keeping the south in a position of economic subordination. This means that the Republic was strongly committed to preserving the Spanish regime in the south; for the Spanish Crown was the only party bound by the treaty to enforce its clauses in the south. At the same time, the Republic had a vital strategic interest in preserving the south as a buffer against France. Yet this by no means meant that the Dutch regents, or the merchant élite, were eager for military collaboration with the Spanish regime in the south Netherlands. In the first place it was fundamental to De Witt's view of the Republic's essential interests that it should avoid becoming locked into the system of long-term military commitments and rivalries, and the territorial ambitions, which were the perennial sport of kings.[10] Moreover, Spain was now severely weakened and there was inevitably scepticism as to her continued usefulness as an ally. From both a strategic and economic point of view it seemed to De Witt—and many others—that the Republic's overriding concern was to avoid becoming entangled in conflict with France. It was thus, above all, the Stadholder William III (1672–1702) who emerged as the great champion of close strategic links between north and south.

---

[9] Despretz-Van de Casteele, 'Het protectionisme', 311.
[10] Japikse, *Johan de Witt*, 172–7.

The resilience of the south Netherlands in the later seventeenth century was economic and political but, above all, religious and cultural. The early fervour of the Counter-Reformation in the south Netherlands inevitably ebbed somewhat, after around 1650. But by that time it had accomplished its task and rendered the south an impregnable bastion of Catholic orthodoxy, the sole major problem on the religious and cultural front being the vexed divisions within the Church and universities between Jansenists and anti-Jansenists (see pp. 650–1 above). If the great wave of church-building and commissions which began with the onset of the Twelve Years Truce ended in the middle of the century, and there was now far less call for artists and craftsmen to work on churches, chapels, images, and other appurtenances of the faith, a culture had been formed which had, and retained, an unbreakable hold on every section of the population. At least in the towns both elementary and secondary education, galvanized by the re-Catholicization programme, had attained impressive dimensions. In the decade 1656–65, the school population of Antwerp stood at over 4,000, representing about half of all Antwerp children between 7 and 15.[11] Virtually all children received religious instruction on Sundays.

The ascendancy of the Catholic faith was now such that the presence of large Dutch Protestant garrisons in many towns from 1689 onwards aroused no fears and had little if any effect on urban society. Needless to say, no form of disrespect towards the Church was tolerated on the part of non-Catholics. Nor was the Portuguese New Christian community of Antwerp, at least part of which was crypto-Jewish, permitted to cast off its public veil of allegiance to the Church, as was allowed, from the 1640s onwards, in the case of the Portuguese New Christian communities in France. The pressure against such backsliding made the ecclesiastical and civic authorities in Antwerp extremely sensitive to evidence of contacts between Portuguese New Christians in Antwerp and Dutch Sephardic Jews who were, in some cases, close relatives. By the 1670s there was a tiny group of professed Jews in Antwerp who refused to have their children baptized or kneel, or take off their hats, before images. The bishop was unable to persuade the Secret Council in Brussels to expel them from the Spanish Netherlands. But both ecclesiastical and civic authorities applied sufficient pressure to ensure that Jewish worship took place only in secret.[12]

The Spanish Netherlands was not Spain. Some scope for dissent existed, provided it was sufficiently veiled. If the Papacy complained to Madrid, in April 1671, that the regime in Brussels was turning a blind eye to clandestine

[11] Put, 'Het fundament', 15.   [12] Dequeker, 'Heropleving', 159–60.

Jewish worship in Antwerp,[13] French Cartesians noted, in 1670, that despite the Church's condemnation of Cartesian philosophy and science there were crypto-Cartesian professors at Leuven who concerned themselves with forbidden ideas discreetly but also unhindered.[14] But the fact remained that neither the authority, nor the teachings, of the Church could be openly challenged. Thus while the anti-Cartesian offensive which began in the academies of the south, at the prompting of the papal internuncio, in 1662, failed to eradicate Cartesian influence, it was nevertheless the case that only attacks on Descartes could be published. No southern academic could openly espouse Descartes's doctrines and there was absolutely no parallel in the south to the raging philosophical and scientific controversies gripping the universities in the north.

Open dissent was simply not tolerated and there were few instances of it. One of the most remarkable was that of the French Calvinist heretic, of alleged Jewish extraction, Isaac de la Peyrère (1596–1676). La Peyrère came to the Spanish Netherlands as secretary to Prince Louis de Condé, one of the principal nobles of France, who fled to Brussels following the collapse of the Frondes. La Peyrère had written a sensational book, the *Prae-Adamitae*, arguing that there were men on earth before Adam and that the Bible we possess is but a corrupted version of God's original revelation, transmitted by fallible scribes. The work was published at Amsterdam, in 1655, and instantly banned as blasphemy by the Hof of Holland. At that point La Peyrère himself was staying at Namur, where the bishop had his book publicly condemned in all the churches of the city, a month after the Dutch condemnation. La Peyrère returned to Condé's side, in Brussels, but was seized and imprisoned there in February 1656. After months of interrogation he broke, renounced his heresies, and converted to Catholicism.[15]

Perhaps the most bizarre cultural encounter of the seventeenth century, at Brussels and Antwerp, was that involving that extraordinary personality Queen Christina of Sweden. She was present in the Spanish Netherlands in 1654–5 shortly after abdicating from the Swedish throne. Both Leopold Wilhelm and the Church authorities applauded her official mission, which was to undergo Catholic indoctrination and renounce the Lutheran faith in which she had been brought up. But Christina nurtured mystical, messianic theologico-political ideas and spent much of her time at Brussels seeking to promote her grandiose schemes for reconciling Catholicism and Protestantism, Christianity and Judaism, and—for good measure—also Spain and

[13] AGS Estado 2115. *consulta* of the Consejo de Estado, Madrid, 13 May 1671.
[14] Vanpaemel, 'Kerk en wetenschap', 184.
[15] Popkin, *Isaac La Peyrère*, 48–9.

France, deliberating over her goals with such men as the Amsterdam rabbi Menasseh ben Israel and Condé's secretary, La Peyrère, who also acted as political intermediary between her and Condé, to whom she assigned an important role in her plans.[16] And as if all this was not disturbing enough for the Spanish authorities, she made known, after her secret conversion to Catholicism at Brussels, on Christmas Eve, 1654, her desire to be appointed viceroy of the Spanish Netherlands in succession to Leopold Wilhelm, who was about to depart.

The slackening of Church and court commissions after 1648, and the general deterioration of the specialized industries of Antwerp, Brussels, and Ghent in the late seventeenth century, in turn ensured the decline of both the decorative and fine arts south of the rivers. But given the imposing scale, and superb quality, of artistic achievement in the Spanish Netherlands in the early seventeenth century there was room for extensive shrinkage without the arts of the south becoming in any way insignificant. Rubens died in 1640, Van Dyck in 1641, and there were no more major baroque architectural projects after the completion of the magnificent church of the Béguines in Brussels in the late 1650s.[17] An era had come to an end. But the fine arts continued to flourish, albeit at a lesser level, in both Antwerp and Brussels, throughout the third quarter of the century. It was not until the 1680s that the great artistic flowering which accompanied the Counter-Reformation in the south Netherlands was finally at an end.

The most notable of the artists working in the south during the third quarter of the century was David Teniers the Younger (1610–90), a prolific painter of genre and landscape scenes whose early career was spent at Antwerp but who moved to Brussels, in 1651, on becoming court painter to Leopold Wilhelm, a noted collector and connoisseur. He was afterwards also court painter to Don Juan José, for whom he painted a number of grand military scenes. The Antwerp art world was presided over, after Van Dyck's death, by Jacob Jordaens (1593–1678), a lesser but still substantial artist who had worked under Rubens and painted some of the largest religious pictures to be found in Antwerp's churches. A perhaps finer Antwerp artist was Gonzales Coques (1618–84), a favourite of Leopold Wilhelm who was later also patronized by the count of Monterrey. Like Jordaens, Gonzales Coques also worked at the Huis ten Bosch, at The Hague, in the early 1650s, on the grand paintings glorifying the heroic achievements of Frederik Hendrik. As a court portraitist, Gonzales Coques was a refined and worthy successor to Van Dyck.

[16] Akerman, *Queen Christina*, 204–6.   [17] Plantenga, *L'Architecture religieuse*, 261.

After the treaty of the Pyrenees, and departure of Don Juan José, the previous glitter of the Spanish court at Brussels ebbed away and the brilliance of Antwerp faded. The Silver Age of the south Netherlands, which had begun with Albert and Isabella, and the return of Rubens from Italy, ended definitively in the 1670s. Yet, the underlying resilience, cultural and economic, of the south remained and formed the basis for glimmerings of remarkable new developments towards the turn of the new century.

PARTY AND FACTION IN THE EARLY 1660s

The peace of the Pyrenees, and Stuart restoration in Britain, offered the Republic cause for both optimism and anxiety. Orangists, of course, could hope for a revival of their fortunes since England's new king was an uncle of the young Prince of Orange, now aged 10. Charles II could be expected to favour the boy's interests and political prospects. But, at the same time, the merchant and regent élites could hope for peace in Europe, undisturbed commerce and sea-routes, and better relations with England.[18] The Cromwellian regime had been feared, and detested, by both Dutch and the south Netherlanders, for its aggressive maritime policies, which had inflicted great damage on the commerce and shipping of both parts of the Netherlands. Nor was anyone disposed to underestimate England's capacity to attack Dutch commerce, and the colonial empire, also in the future. Accordingly, many regents and merchants considered it of the greatest importance to win the friendship of the new king and establish harmonious Anglo-Dutch relations. Some optimists in the Amsterdam city council even believed that manifest good-will might persuade the 30-year-old monarch to rescind the detested Navigation Act of 1651.[19]

Charles spent two months on Dutch soil, in the spring of 1660, at Breda and The Hague, before embarking, from Scheveningen, for England, in June. During these weeks, provincial assemblies and town councils vied with each other in their efforts to please the new king, laying on receptions, banquets, and all manner of ceremonies in his honour. Now in retirement at his villa at Zorgvliet, Jacob Cats (who, in contrast to Vondel, practically never touched on matters of state in his poetry)[20] composed a poem celebrating the 'king of Great Britain', and urging a pact of friendship between Britain and the Republic. Charles responded pleasantly to the attention; but, at the same time, emphasized his affection for his young

---

[18] Japikse, *Johan de Witt*, 162–9.
[19] GA Amsterdam res. vroed. 21, 28, and 31 May 1660.
[20] Van Deursen, 'De raadpensionaris Jacob Cats', 157–8.

nephew, Orange, and intention to favour him and his mother, the 'Princess Royal', Mary, his sister. The States of Zeeland, disappointed Charles had not accepted their invitation to return to London via Zeeland, hastened to show more regard for William than they had hitherto. In June, the States of Zeeland instructed their *Gecommitteerde Raden* to peruse all their resolutions about the stadholderate since 1650 and prepare recommendations.[21]

Most worrying for De Witt was the willingness of the many opportunists among the regents to show deference to the House of Orange now that its fortunes were reviving in the wake of the English Restoration. Such men justified their compliant attitude as pragmatic and in the interests of the Republic's commerce, shipping, and colonies. De Witt still had some staunch allies in the Amsterdam *vroedschap*, notably Cornelis and Andries de Graeff, Jan Huydecoper, and the new Pensionary, Pieter de Groot, son of Grotius, all firm republicans out of principle—and deep suspicion of the political and dynastic ambitions of the House of Orange.[22] But these men were a minority of the city council. Traditionally, most of their colleagues took a more flexible view of the city's needs and interests and were more impressed with the advantages, political and economic, of better relations with England than any threat an Orangist revival might pose to the internal stability of the Republic and ascendancy of Holland. As De Witt saw it, there was now a real danger that, in her eagerness for friendship with England, Amsterdam might sponsor imprudent courses which could ultimately undermine the States party regime.

De Witt's unease mounted in June, when Amsterdam joined Haarlem and Leiden in inviting Princess Mary, and the Prince, to make an official visit.[23] Amsterdam put on a lavish show, extolling the splendour of the House of Orange and its glorious past,[24] a clear sign that Holland's greatest city, having assiduously boycotted the House of Orange since 1650, now wished to mend its bridges with William III. Cultivating Orange was, indeed, an integral part of Amsterdam's 'English' strategy in 1660–1, culminating in the plan, readily accepted by the rest of the States, to dispatch an embassy extraordinary to London, bringing a gift for the king, from the Generality, so magnificent as to eclipse all previous gifts, erase recollection of Dutch reluctance to help Charles in his difficult times, and lay foundations for a new beginning. The *vroedschap* nominated a committee, headed by Cornelis

---

[21] *Notulen* SZ res. SZ 18 June 1660.
[22] Epkema, 'Pieter de Groot', 178–9.
[23] Aitzema, *Historie*, ix. 933–5.
[24] Mörke, 'Hofcultuur', 51–2.

de Graeff, to draw up a 'concept' of the kind of treaty of friendship which Amsterdam hoped Charles would accept. The main points were a defensive alliance against third-party aggression, 'unrestricted trade', meaning abrogation of the Navigation Act, and the principle of Free Ship, Free Goods (*Vrij schip, vrij goedt*) to apply whenever one of the two powers was engaged in hostilities with a third.[25] This last grew out of the experience of the Anglo-Spanish War of 1655–60 when the English had frequently boarded Dutch ships, searching for, and sequestrating, cargoes found to be from Spain, or the Spanish Netherlands, or belonging to Spanish subjects. From 1660 onwards, it was one of Amsterdam's chief priorities in foreign affairs to persuade England to accept the principle that the ships of the Republic, when neutral, and cargo carried, whatever its provenance, should be exempt from boarding and inspection.

The 'Dutch Gift' of 1660–1 was a prodigious gift, the most splendid ever presented by the States General to a foreign ruler. Amsterdam's regents spared no effort or expense to ensure the success of their scheme. Cornelis and Andries de Graeff were friends of Govaert Flinck and, like many Amsterdam regents, enthusiastic connoisseurs of art. They planned the gift in consultation with Gerrit Uylenburgh, the best-known art dealer in the city, and former sponsor of Rembrandt and other leading artists. The choicest Italian paintings in the Republic, including a Titian and a Tintoretto, were purchased for the gift, together with Graeco-Roman antiquities from the famous collection, housed on the Herengracht, belonging to former burgomaster Gerard Reynst, a renowned connoisseur who had specialized in trade with Venice. The States paid 80,000 guilders for this part of the present alone. To this abundance of Italian and ancient art were added four 'modern' paintings—an Elsheimer and three Dutch pictures, one by Saenredam and two by Gerrit Dou, Leiden's, and now the Republic's, most highly reputed artist.[26] Dou, who like many contemporary artists was also a dealer, was engaged to assess the price of the Saenredam which the States bought from Andries de Graeff. To complete the 'Dutch Gift', Amsterdam supplied a handsome yacht, the *Mary*. At the ceremony of presentation, at Banqueting House, Whitehall, in November 1660, Charles talked with the States General's ambassadors, 'heartily thank'd them for so worthy a present, and express'd his willingness to enter into a nearer Alliance with them'.[27] The Dous—one was *The Young Mother* (Mauritshuis)—reportedly made as great an impression as the Italian paintings, on king and court.

[25] GA Amsterdam res. vroed. 2 July 1660.
[26] Sluijter, *Leidse fijnschilders*, 37–8.
[27] Logan, '*Cabinet*' *of the Brothers*, 81.

For her part, Princess Mary sent a circular to each provincial assembly asking that her son be designated to the high offices, and dignities, which the Princes of Orange had held in the past, pointedly omitting any request for Willem Frederik to deputize. Zeeland voted, on 7 August, to press in the States General for designation of William as future Stadholder and captain-general of the Union, the 'high charges' to be conferred on his reaching his eighteenth year.[28] Friesland followed, urging also that the Prince be assigned a seat on the *Raad van State*, from the age of 16 (or earlier, if the other provinces would agree), adding that Frisians were proud to show their 'old and enduring' affection for the 'houses of Orange and Nassau', as they consistently had since 1650—an allusion to Zeeland's inconsistency.[29] Overijssel and Gelderland voted likewise. All this was followed with an intent eye by Charles II, who wrote to the States of Zeeland thanking them for their efforts on behalf of his nephew.[30]

De Witt found himself under mounting pressure. Other than Holland, no province had adopted an Act of Exclusion while, even in Holland, the rising enthusiasm for designating Orange to the 'high charges' signified that Exclusion was now a dead letter. Leiden and Haarlem chose this moment to propose that the Prince be designated for the stadholderate, knowing that several smaller towns would support them.[31] De Witt, together with Cornelis de Graeff and allies in the *ridderschap*, manœuvred to prevent Leiden's proposal gaining wide support in the States of Holland. Deflecting the pressure, by offering as bait a handsome pension for the Prince, from the States of Holland, De Witt drew Princess Mary into an arrangement whereby the Prince would, for the time being, only be designated a 'Child of state', to be educated, and trained, for high station by the States of Holland, with the implication that he would eventually fill high office.[32] With this expedient, De Witt and De Graeff hoped to mollify Mary sufficiently for her to urge her brother to be accommodating in the negotiations under way in London. Consequently, at the end of September, Holland revoked the Act of Exclusion and undertook the maintenance and education of the Prince.

Mary's deal with De Witt obtained some solid advantages both for her son and the stability of the Republic. There was much grumbling about her acquiescence, however, not only on the part of those (including many

[28] *Notulen* SZ res. SZ, 7 Aug. 1660.
[29] ARH PR 375, p. 856. res. SF 8 Sept. 1660
[30] PRO SP 84/163, fo. 35. Charles to SZ 1 Oct. 1660
[31] GA Leiden Sec. Arch. 452. res. vroed. 16 and 17 Sept. 1660.
[32] Rowen, *John de Witt*, 514–19.

Voetian preachers) for whom supporting Orange was chiefly a means of opposing the Holland regents, but also from Orangist regents who felt that Mary had betrayed their long efforts on her son's behalf, by doing nothing to enhance their influence.[33] Their indignation mounted when it emerged that the States of Holland committee nominated to supervise the Prince's education included De Witt, De Graeff, and other States party regents, but none of Holland's Orangists. The Princess Dowager, Amalia von Solms, berated her daughter-in-law for allowing herself to be tricked by De Witt into abandoning the House of Orange-Nassau's tried and trusted friends in Holland—Leiden, Haarlem, and Enkhuizen.[34] The Elector of Brandenburg was also annoyed; for De Witt's scheme denied him influence, too. In vain, the Elector and Princess Dowager proposed a different committee to control the Prince's tutors and entourage, comprising Amalia, Willem Frederik, Burgomaster van der Aa of Leiden, and deputies from the *ridderschap*, Haarlem, and Enkhuizen.

But just as De Witt had seemingly surmounted one hurdle, all was again thrown into confusion by the sudden death of the Princess Royal, from smallpox, in January 1661. Mary had named her brother, the king, her son's guardian, and this confronted De Witt with a host of new dilemmas. Since Leicester's time, no foreign power had possessed such leverage, within Dutch domestic politics, as did now the English monarch. Plainly, Charles would not be easy to deal with. The Anglo-Dutch negotiations in London, on which Amsterdam had placed such high hopes, were not going well. Far from repealing the Navigation Act, the king was about to reissue it, under his own name. The old wrangling between the two East India Companies showed no sign of abating, indeed was increasing. Added to this, major new tensions had arisen in the Caribbean, West Africa, and over New Netherland. The West Frisian ports, Maas fishing towns, Zeeland herring ports— Zierikzee and Brouwershaven—and again Amsterdam were also deeply dismayed about the bill which had come before Parliament, prohibiting fishing by any but subjects of the English Crown, within ten miles of the English coast.[35] Moreover, within the States of Holland, the Orangist party-faction had gained considerable ground since the late 1650s. De Witt's proposals for the maintenance of the Prince of Orange were opposed as insufficient by seven towns—Leiden, Haarlem, Enkhuizen, Rotterdam, Gorcum, Schoonhoven, and Purmerend.[36]

[33] PRO SP 34/163, fo. 54. Amalia to Mary, 29 Sept. 1660.
[34] GA Amsterdam res. vroed. 6 Jan. 1661.
[35] PRO SP 84/163, fos. 147v, 189.
[36] Aitzema, *Historie*, ix. 966–7.

To add to all this, there was the unpalatable news that Charles had chosen as his ordinary ambassador at The Hague, Sir George Downing—a former supporter of the Cromwellian regime, turned royalist, known for his abrasive style and animosity towards the Dutch. On his arrival, in June, armed with instructions to mobilize the Orangist camp to pressure Holland into submitting to supervision of the Prince's upbringing by the now three guardians—Charles, Amalia, and the Great Elector—he at once entered into all kinds of surreptitious dealings with Orangist deputies and military men. In one of his first reports from The Hague, he remarked, 'this is certain that as much dirt as can be must be thrown on De Witt.'[37]

By the autumn of 1661, it seemed that Charles had the Holland States party trapped between the rising tide of English pressure at sea, and the upsurge of Orangist sentiment within. Already many in Amsterdam regretted the outlay on the 'Dutch Gift'. A leading member of the Frisian delegation to the States General predicted, in November 1661, that if war should break out between the Republic and England, the 'provinces of Zeeland, Friesland, Overijssel, and Groningen will not take up arms against England and will contribute nothing to the war'.[38] Moreover, Gelderland, and also Utrecht, where the *ridderschap* was strongly Orangist but the city 'un peu hollandisée', were hopelessly divided.

The thorniest issue dividing the Seven Provinces, during 1661, aside from the future status of the Prince of Orange, was the draft peace for ending the war with Portugal. Until May, four provinces—Zeeland, Groningen, Utrecht, and Gelderland—had adamantly refused to settle without restitution of former Netherlands Brazil. It was Downing's other main task, in 1661, to play on this rift, and turn it to England's advantage, by doing everything possible (whilst his master also applied pressure on Portugal) to block the peace.[39] In this way, England could simultaneously prevent the Dutch recovering their trade with Portugal, and gaining commercial privileges there equivalent to those of the English, and widen the divisions between the provinces, weakening the Republic internally.

De Witt, closely assisted by Pieter de Groot, eventually managed to detach Utrecht and half of Groningen from the opposition, but this still left Zeeland and Gelderland. In an epic five-hour debate in the States General, on 23 June 1661, involving besides the regular provincial delegations twenty-six extraordinary deputies from Zeeland, three from Utrecht, and the entire States of Holland,[40] Zeeland and Gelderland refused to settle

[37] Rowen, *John de Witt*, 539.
[38] PRO SP 84/163, fo. 148v. [Willem van Haren?] to Williamson, Leeuwarden, 4 Nov. 1661.
[39] Japikse, *Verwikkelingen*, 120–6.
[40] Grever, 'Structure of Decision-Making', 143.

'without restitution of the lands of Brazile', insisting 'that it was against the articles of the Union that peace, or warre, should be made but by the consent of all the provinces'. The Hollanders reminded the gathering that in 1648 'the peace with Spaine was made by the plurality of voices without the consent of Zeeland and Utrecht'.[41] Finally, the president-for-the-week, the head of the Groningen delegation, Schuylenborgh (who, for reasons of self-interest, sided with Holland, opposing the city of Groningen's backing for the WIC), concluded, ruling that the States General had made peace with Portugal, by a majority of five provinces to two.

As the months passed, it emerged that De Witt's position was less precarious than it had previously seemed. The quarrel between Holland and Zeeland, over Portugal, subsided, and it became clear that the twin strands of Charles II's Dutch policy—squeezing the Dutch in the maritime sphere, whilst simultaneously dividing them internally—were, to an extent, mutually contradictory, at least in the maritime provinces.[42] At Amsterdam, regents, merchants, and directors of the WIC and VOC, seeing that their 'Gift' brought no advantage, and facing escalating confrontation, rather than reconciliation, in trade, lost interest in the Prince of Orange and rallied behind De Witt, a strong, united Holland now being their only recourse. Much the same happened also elsewhere in Holland, and Zeeland.

In Zeeland, Orangist fervour was traditionally strong. But Zeeland stood to lose more from English maritime expansion, and gains in the Caribbean and West Africa, than from doing without a Stadholder, despite the Zeelanders' distaste for Holland's tolerant religious policies. In August 1661, the States of Zeeland expressed serious alarm over the encroachments of the newly formed English Royal Africa Company, on the Guinea Coast where the the WIC had, since the 1630s, dominated the lucrative gold and slave traffic. They voted to co-operate closely with Holland to resist the growing English pressure.[43] The more Charles encouraged the ambitions of London's merchants and companies, the more Zeeland was alienated from both England and Orangism.

Zeeland's shifting mood resulted in fresh changes in the balance of the party-factions in the town councils. At Middelburg, the anti-English, States party bloc, which gained ground from late 1661, urging co-operation with Holland, was led by none other than Hendrik Thibault, who had been William II's right-hand man in Zeeland, in 1649–50, and was overthrown by the States party-faction, in 1651, as a staunch Orangist. This astounding

[41] BL Ms Egerton 2537, fo. 349. Downing to Nicholas, 24 June 1661.
[42] Geyl, Oranje en Stuart, 149.
[43] Notulen SZ res. SZ 3 and 4 Aug. 1661.

volte-face reflected the complexity of party-factional politics and the strong influence of popular opinion in Zeeland. The rival groupings in the town halls were a mélange of ideological, theological, financial, family, and place-seeking sentiment, coloured also by the immigrant factor. An English observer, writing in August 1663, went so far as to interpret Middelburg politics as a tussle between regents who were 'natives', that is descended from old-established Zeeland regent families, and a newer bloc, comprising 'Walloons and French', the 'natives' led by Veth, the Walloons by Thibault.[44] He explained Thibault's vigorous Orangism in 1649–50 as due to popular pressure and his new attitude, in 1662, to the fact that the 'Prince of Orange's . . . interest is so low that Mons. Thibault fears it not'. By January 1662, only Flushing and Veere of the six Zeeland towns still adhered to an Orangist stance, the rest all inclining to the States party side. Downing became uneasy over the growing co-operation between Holland and Zeeland, and what he called 'a notable plot for the making of a kind of a new act of seclusion of the Prince of Orange'.[45]

As the Anglo-Dutch negotiations in London dragged on, and Anglo-Dutch relations increasingly soured, De Witt resolutely resisted Charles's demands for compensation for affronts and damages in the East Indies, while Friesland and the Orangist camp pressed for Dutch concessions, hoping to secure an Anglo-Dutch treaty of friendship which would resolve the maritime disputes, and open the way for the Orangists to make gains in the domestic political arena as friends of the English connection and the treaty. Thus, through most of 1662, the confrontation between the rival politico-theological blocs in Dutch politics turned on whether or not to respond to English demands for compensation for damages suffered in the Indies.[46] In April 1662, the States party-faction gained fresh ground through De Witt's success in concluding a treaty of alliance with France, including a clause guaranteeing the Dutch fisheries in the North Sea. De Witt and what Downing called his 'junto' of leading regents—Pieter de Groot, Van Beverningk, of Gouda, and the Pensionary of Dordrecht (a cousin of De Witt's, Govaert van Slingelandt)—began insisting that if the Dutch plenipotentiaries in England could not conclude under their existing instructions, they should be recalled. De Witt, and his supporters, preferred heightened friction, even war with England, to yielding to Charles's pressure. They were supported by Zeeland and Utrecht and opposed by Friesland, Gelderland, Overijssel, and Groningen.[47]

[44] PRO SP 84/167, fo. 240. Bampfield to Williamson, Middelburg, 16 Aug. 1663.
[45] BL MS Egerton 2538, fo. 16. Downing to Nicholas, 3 Feb. 1662.
[46] Japikse, *Verwikkelingen*, 178, 191, 219.
[47] BL MS Egerton 2538, fo. 45. Downing to Nicholas, 21 Mar. 1662.

Fundamentally, it was a split between maritime and landward provinces. But the latter were too fragile internally, and externally, long to resist De Witt and the Holland leadership. While Overijssel wavered, Groningen lapsed yet again into chaos, major riots erupting in the city in July, in which the guilds, demanding 'abatement of their taxes . . . and that the government shall not be monopolized into some families', overthrew the magistracy and paralysed the States.[48] The city remained in uproar, until November, when Willem Frederik succeeded in entering with a strong force of troops and restoring quiet. De Witt exploited the turmoil to win the province's vote so that, by August, it was just Friesland and Gelderland still adamant they would not break with England over maritime disputes affecting only Holland and Zeeland.

During the summer of 1662, Downing remained confident De Witt and his supporters would crack under continued pressure and that they were caught in pincers from which there was no escape. In August, he reported the words of a Frisian deputy that De Witt and his 'junto' should 'looke what they do for that if a breeche should happen, they must not onely not expect any assistance from them, but . . . the contrary'.[49] 'In Holland itself,' Downing assured ministers in London, '(however Mr Dewitt carries it) there is nothing of inclination to breake with England, to say no more, they love themselves and their trade too well and know they have more reason to thinke of ways, and good husbandry, of paying that infinite debt which yet lies upon them than to contract more . . .' The taxes, imposts, 'and excises', he explained, 'are to this day as high in Holland as ever they were and yet their frontiers are very slightly garrison'd and yet not assur'd but in actual dispute with every one of their neighbours, all which they know very well'. This last alluded to the unresolved issue of the Overmaas, still in dispute with Spain, and enclaves contested by the bishop of Münster, who in 1661 had finally mastered the city of Münster and was stepping up his quarrel with the Republic.

This was all true; and yet Downing's assessment that Holland would fold under English pressure was wrong. It was not easy to judge the extent of disunity in Holland since it was in the interest of the Orangists to play up their alleged weight. Downing noted, in August 1662, that 'Haarlem and others said they would be no more blindely led into a difference with England' but failed to explain why they had been thus far and why they had assisted him so little.[50] If we scrutinize Downing's confidants among the

[48] De Boer, *Woelingen in Stad en Lande*, 41–9.
[49] BL Egerton MS 2538, fo. 117. Downing to Nicholas, 22 Aug. 1662.
[50] Ibid., fo. 120. Downing to Nicholas, 29 Aug. 1662.

Dutch regents, we see that he had good contacts among the Frisian delegation, in The Hague, and at Leeuwarden, being in regular touch with two leading Frisian deputies, Epo van Bootsma and Willem van Haren, but that (despite the alleged venality of the Holland and Zeeland regent class) he was largely unsuccessful in penetrating, and finding collaborators, among the States of Holland and Zeeland.[51] The reality was that, by the summer of 1662, Holland and Zeeland were unified behind De Witt to a degree which enabled him to pursue a resolute policy, step up naval armaments, and defy the English king. English tactics had, in fact, undermined the Orangist party. As one of Downing's Frisian confidants expressed it, in June, De Witt 'afferme de jour à autre son party en les Provinces Unies et celuy de Sa Majesté, et Monsieur le Prince d'Orange, commence à decliner'.[52]

This was confirmed by the events of the autumn of 1662. The Anglo-Dutch treaty of alliance was finally signed, in September, but in so fraught an atmosphere, and after so long a delay, with so many new disputes arising on all sides, that it failed to provide that stable basis of friendship which the Orangist camp needed. Meanwhile, the States of Holland and Zeeland reached agreement over the stadholderate as well as ratification of the peace with Portugal. Earlier, Downing had reported that the 'agreement between the two pensionaries [De Witt and Veth] hath been againe this assembly hott sett on foote and pressed in the Estates of Zeeland but without effect, the townes of Flissing and Ter Vere remaining stifly against it, whereupon the Princesse Dowager hath written a letter of very hearty thanks to them'.[53] In September, he reported, sombrely, that despite his, and Amalia's, efforts to prevent it, the two pensionaries had now succeeded, and De Witt 'made report in the Assembley of the Estates of Holland that . . . neither Province will speake of bestowing any charge upon the Prince of Orange until he come to eighteen years of age [that is not before 1668]'.[54] Thibault and the Middelburg *vroedschap* backed the agreement, which was approved in Zeeland by four towns to two, overruling Flushing and Veere. Throughout the mid-1660s De Witt worked harmoniously with Thibault and the dominant faction at Middelburg and in the States of Zeeland.

Meanwhile, the peace with Portugal again seemed on the verge of collapse, with England obstructing finalization and three provinces—Zeeland, Groningen, and Gelderland—refusing to ratify.[55] The impasse was

[51] De Bruin, *Geheimhouding en Verraad*, 363, 376.
[52] PRO SP 84/165, fo. 324. [Van Haren?] to Williamson, 24 June 1662.
[53] BL MS Egerton 2538, fo. 45. Downing to Nicholas, 21 Mar. 1662.
[54] Ibid., fo. 131v. Downing to Nicholas, 12 Sept. 1662.
[55] Groenveld, *Evidente factiën*, 53.

broken, again by the collaboration of the Pensionaries of Holland and Zeeland. Over the objections of Flushing, and bitter recriminations of Groningen and Gelderland, Holland and Zeeland agreed that (in return for Zeeland ceasing to oppose ratification, and co-operating over the stadhold-erate) a new method be adopted for sharing out the salt conceded by Portugal, under the peace, to compensate the WIC for its losses in Brazil, which especially favoured Zeeland.

By the time the new French ambassador, Godefroy d'Estrades, arrived in January 1663, De Witt had pulled off a remarkable string of political and diplomatic successes. Besides his treaties with Portugal, France, and England, he had finally also settled the Overmaas dispute with Spain, unresolved since 1648. As late as 1658, Spain had still endeavoured to retain most of this territory, spurred by the religious orders in the south Netherlands which were concerned for the numerous monasteries and ecclesiastical lands in the area. But, after the peace of the Pyrenees, Spain changed tack on this too, putting improved relations with the Republic above other considerations.[56] Under the Dutch–Spanish partition agreement of December 1661, the territory was divided half and half, assigning the towns of Valkenburg, Heerlen, and Dalhem to the Dutch.

D'Estrades was much struck by De Witt's dexterity and the apparent eclipse of the House of Orange. 'Je vois bien à présent', he reported, in February, 'que c'est une Maison entièrement détruite, et qu'il ne faut pas songer à prendre d'autres mesures qu'avec Messieurs les États, c'est à dire avec Monsieur de Witt.'[57]

IDEOLOGICAL CONFLICT IN THE EARLY 1660S

Another consequence of the Orangist revival of 1660–1 was a recrudescence of ideological warfare which permeated politics, society, and culture, generating the most extensive and important debate of the Golden Age about the nature of the Dutch state, hereditary power, and republics. By the early 1660s over a decade had elapsed since the demise of William II; the 'True Freedom' had had a chance to establish itself, and its legitimacy, in the public mind. Yet, as the Orangist upsurge of 1660–1 showed, the people's yearning for an 'eminent head', descended from the Father of the Father-land, who would preside over State and Church, was as deeply rooted as ever. At the same time, republican ideas were gaining ground among segments of the professional and intellectual élites in the United Provinces,

---

[56] Haas, *Verdeling*, 224–9.   [57] D'Estrades, *Lettres*, ii. 152.

as in England. One sign of this was a heightened interest in the works of the great Florentine political thinker Machiavelli, a new Dutch edition of whose writtings appeared in 1652.[58]

The feverish ideological battle of the early 1660s drew its impetus partly from the political context, the improved prospects for the House of Orange, after the English Restoration, followed by the renewed slump in Orangist fortunes, with the resurgence of Anglo-Dutch tension; but it was shaped also by a wider, cultural stasis resulting from the bitter philosophical and theological debates of the 1650s. The Orangist revival demonstrated the continued ascendancy of older traditions over the popular mind; the obvious response was to combat Orangism by seeking to undermine the people's reverence for figure-heads, hereditary power, and the authority of the Reformed Church. But this, in turn, provoked a furious theologico-political reaction on the part of Orangists and Calvinists, of a sort to make the sceptical onlooker wonder whether this was an argument the States party-faction could realistically hope to win. Aitzema, ever sceptical about De Witt's 'True Freedom', and impressed by the Restoration in England, declared in the sixth volume of his great history—a volume published in 1661—that the Dutch were not suited to dwell in a republic, having no previous experience of such a thing: in Rome, Venice, Genoa, and Switzerland, he argued, republics had flourished because republican forms and ideas had deep roots. The English Commonwealth, by contrast, had soon collapsed, lacking roots in the English past, while the Dutch were simply unwilling to be governed by those whom they did not regard as their social superiors. They needed, and wished, to be ruled by an 'eminent head' whom they revered.[59]

The two most noticed publicists on the republican side were the Leiden textile manufacturer Pieter de la Court (1618–85) and his friend, The Hague lawyer Johan Uytenhage de Mist. The latter, second to none in assailing the House of Orange, not least in his *Stadhouderlijke regeeringe in Hollandt* (1662), which held that William the Silent was neither the founder, nor protector, of 'Dutch freedom',[60] was otherwise a routine publicist. But De la Court was a writer of international significance whose ideas touched every aspect of contemporary political, economic, and cultural life. He provoked an unprecedented furore throughout the United Provinces with his 272-page *Interest van Hollandt*, published at Amsterdam in 1662, arguing that Holland was, and would always be, better off without a Stadholder. The text

---

[58] Haitsma Mulier, *Nederlands gezicht van Machiavelli*, 12.
[59] Van der Plaat, 'Lieuwe van Aitzema's kijk', 353.
[60] [Uytenhage de Mist], *Stadhouderlijcke regeeringe*, 30–2.

had been shown to De Witt before publication and the Pensionary had personally helped revise it,[61] toning it down in places, but broadly agreeing with its political philosophy that republics are intrinsically superior to, as well as more trustworthy than, monarchies; that kings and captains-general, wielding greater influence when their countries are at war, keep the whole world in perpetual conflict; and that the courtiers, favourites, nobles, and soldiers who surround rulers necessarily subsist off the productive activity of ordinary folk. De la Court's remarks about the stadholderate incensed much of the public and provoked a flurry of publications, most notably Jean de Parival's *Le Vray Intérêt de la Hollande*, published in Dutch and French editions, both in 1662.

More significant, from a theoretical standpoint, however, were the *Political Discourses* (1662), a reworking by De la Court of a text by his brother Johan, written in a direct, straightforward Dutch, addressed to a broad public, expounding a republicanism deeply influenced by the writings of Machiavelli and Boccalini.[62] In De la Court's eyes all monarchy and quasi-monarchy harms the true interests of the citizen, for any element of hereditary power subordinates freedom and the public good to dynastic concerns. Thus, republics have citizens, monarchies subjects—for De la Court an absolute distinction. Finally, he asserted that if 'freedom' and the public good were to prosper, it was necessary to curb the influence of the established Church in the public domain outside its proper sphere.

Not surprisingly, the public Church hastened to show its disapproval. Censured by the Leiden consistory, for attacking Reformed preachers as power-seekers, and enemies of freedom both individual and public, De la Court found himself debarred from the Lord's supper and under pressure. Through his regent friend De Groot, Grotius' son, he appealed to De Witt.[63] But Holland's Pensionary, eager though he was to promote republican ideas in Dutch life and, by degrees, to widen the scope of intellectual (if not political) freedom, took care not to associate his person, or the States, with De la Court's full-frontal attack on the House of Orange and authority of the Church. De Witt's strategy, rather, was to stand by the Church, outwardly, while seeking to promote its liberal Cocceian-Cartesian wing within.

The battle over De la Court's books proved but a prelude to a wider controversy over the form of the State, and place of the Church, which erupted the following year. Since the subsiding of the sabbath observance

[61] Rowen, *John de Witt*, 391–5.
[62] Haitsma Mulier, *Myth of Venice*, 127–35.
[63] Van der Bijl, 'Pieter de la Court', 73.

controversy, the struggle between the opposing wings of the Church had lapsed into a quieter smouldering phase which left much unresolved. But one type of disparity the States of Holland decided not to tolerate—disarray in public prayers for the secular authority. In early modern societies prayers for the government were an important aspect of political, and popular, culture and the United Provinces, in this respect, were no exception. The problem was that, despite the lack of a Stadholder, Voetian preachers still included prayers for the Prince of Orange and doctored those for the States of Holland, in ways which did not please the States party-faction.[64] To achieve uniformity in this weighty matter, a States of Holland committee drew up an approved formulary for use by the Church throughout the province. This formulary was then sent to the town councils, in March 1663, with instructions to require the consistories to ensure obedience and uniform practice.[65] Claiming that many preachers recited public prayers 'as if the States General were the lawful, supreme government over this province . . . such as might give the impression to simple, uneducated, and unsophisticated people that the *ridderschap* and towns of Holland are not the unquestioned sovereign and (next to God) only supreme authority in this our province',[66] the States laid down that henceforth the prayer for the States of Holland, 'our lawful, supreme government', must always be recited first among prayers for the public authorities. Next was to come that for the well-being of the States of the other provinces, Holland's partners in the Union, and only third that for the States General.[67] Public prayers were to conclude with a prayer for the magistracy of the town where one dwelt (or, if in a village, the *drost* or *baljuw*) with no prayer for the Prince, or House, of Orange.

In Holland, scarcely any preachers protested openly, from the pulpit, knowing they faced immediate dismissal if they defied the States before their congregations. De la Court noted the sullenness with which those at Leiden complied.[68] But there was much complaint in the consistories, the preachers at Amsterdam and Haarlem maintaining the new formulary conflicted with the Acts of the National Synod of 1619. At Leiden, the preachers appealed to the *vroedschap*, distinguishing, deferentially, between the 'political' aspects of the matter, which they conceded were not their business, and the manner in which the States had proceeded, insisting this should have been

---

[64] Ypeij and Dermout, *Geschiedenis*, ii. 503.
[65] Knuttel, *Acta*, iv, p. xvii.
[66] GA Leiden Acta Kerkeraad v. res. 6 Apr. 1663.
[67] Aitzema, *Historie*, x. 582.
[68] De la Court, 'Brieven', 109.

through the synods and in consultation with them. They also rejected the implication in the circular that preachers of the public Church had deliberately fomented 'serious discrepancies in prayers for the supreme and secondary authorities', in order to spread 'among the people' the misconception that the States General were the supreme government in Holland which, they commented, was an allegation frequently heard from dissenters outside the Church.[69] It appeared, they complained, the States wished to render them 'suspect' in the eyes of the people.

It was chiefly in the lesser provinces that the furore erupted in the public domain. The Frisian States denounced Holland's formulary as incompatible with authority of the States General, claiming it contradicted over eighty years of usage in the churches of the United Provinces, the Acts of the National Synod of 1619, confirmed by the Great Assembly as the foundation of the public Church, and also the States Bible. Friesland denied sovereignty resided in the provinces alone, recalling that the States of Holland themselves had drafted the resolution, of 25 March 1621, answering Chancellor Peckius with the formula that 'supremacy and sovereignty in the United Netherlands reside incontestably in the States General and the States of the separate provinces'.[70] The States General were the 'highest and sovereign authority over all the United Provinces', insisted the States of Friesland, demanding that Holland rescind her formulary and restore precedence to the Generality in the prayers for the regime. They instructed their deputies, at The Hague, to concert with other provincial delegations to put pressure on Holland.

The Frisians stirred the other provinces, prompting De Witt and the Holland *Gecommitteerde Raden* to intervene to prevent resolutions condemning Holland's formulary. De Witt wrote to Zeeland's Pensionary, presuming that Zeeland would not dispute that the States of Holland were sovereign in their province as the other provincial States were in theirs, flatly rejecting Friesland's argument that sovereignty lay partly in the States General, and denying any formulary was to be found in the Acts of the Synod of Dordrecht.[71] Flushing and Veere sought to align Zeeland with Friesland; but the other Zeeland towns hesitated. They too had always resisted the argument that sovereignty lay solely in the provincial States and did so now, but shrank from antagonizing Holland at this juncture. In Middelburg, most preachers sided with the Veth faction, which reportedly had nine votes in the *vroedschap*, while the Thibault faction, with fifteen

[69] GA Leiden Acta kerkeraad 5, res. 13 Apr. 1663.
[70] Aitzema, *Historie*, x. 616–22.
[71] Rowen, *John de Witt*, 431–2.

votes, stood closer to De Witt.[72] But in the end, neither grouping supported Flushing and Veere. Rather, the States of Zeeland prevaricated, opposing Friesland's view that there was an established formulary which Holland had violated, but simultaneously holding that the 'several sovereign provinces, through their close confederacy, are so closely bound together that they have, thereby, composed themselves as if they were one body, one state, one government, and one republic, without, however, abdicating from their right of sovereignty', the partial sovereignty of the States General being evident from the fact that the 'noblest and most essential parts of sovereignty' had been assigned to the Generality.[73] Thus, Zeeland agreed with Friesland that sovereignty lay partly in the States General and partly in the individual provinces. Middelburg, Zierikzee, Tholen, and Goes were content to leave it there 'and not bother the gentlemen of Holland with it any further', much to the disgruntlement of most of the Zeeland public, preachers, and regents of Flushing and Veere.

The controversy, avidly followed by the public, dragged on in the States General, provincial assemblies, town councils, consistories, and in the case of Gelderland, which in September joined Friesland in condemning Holland's formulary, in the quarter assemblies. De Witt tirelessly asserted that the provinces were sovereign—except in the Generality Lands, where the States General were sovereign. His stance was reinforced by the timely publication of a hefty three-volume work, the *Public Gebedt* (Amsterdam 1663–4) by his namesake and fervently anti-Orangist cousin, Johan de Wit (1618–76). This work too was personally vetted by the Pensionary and used every conceivable argument to demonstrate that sovereignty, in Holland, resided in the States of Holland, 'that is, in the *ridderschap* and towns, with the regents of the towns collectively represented by the States of Holland'. De Wit held that the 'aristocratic republic', such as 'Holland', was the most excellent form of state and had been chosen by God himself 'for his people, the children of Israel',[74] and cited Tacitus' maxim that prayers for any but the sovereign power, in public ceremonies, weaken the state itself. De la Court was especially pleased with the second volume, published in November, believing that the public, through reading it, would 'more and more esteem the conduct of their lawful government and detest the harsh dominance, and tyranny, sought by the other provinces, over Holland'.[75]

---

[72] PRO SP 84/167, fo. 240. Bampfield to Williamson, Middelburg, 16 Aug. 1663.
[73] *Notulen* SZ res. SZ 26 June, 5 Sept., and 8 Nov. 1663.
[74] De Wit, *Public Gebedt*, ii. 2.
[75] De la Court, 'Brieven', 143.

At the height of the controversy, during 1663, Uytenhage de Mist published several more uncompromisingly republican books. He too cited Roman political wisdom and Tacitus, urging the need, if 'freedom' is to be maintained, for subordination of the public Church to the secular authorities. The essential 'interest' of the Republic, argued Uytenhage de Mist, was to remain at peace, administer justice well, tend the public finances responsibly, allow its citizens to become wealthy, and, above all, ensure 'freedom of life and conscience, and, especially, of religion'.[76] One of his main reasons for urging that Holland's interests were better served by not having a Stadholder was that it was chiefly through the stadholderate that the influence of the public Church over society would expand: 'where now', he taunted, 'are those zealous preachers who, in 1650, did not scruple to denounce the States of Holland from the pulpit?'[77]—a reminder that, under William II, the preachers had been both bolder and more influential.

The most erudite work claiming a wider role for the public Church, published in 1663, was the first volume of Voetius' *magnum opus*, his *Politica Ecclesiastica* (4 vols., 1663–76). This resoundingly rejected the Erastianism of the States party, defending the autonomy, and broad responsibilities, of the public Church,[78] however in Latin. But there was no lack of Dutch-language, popular Voetian literature, streaming from the presses in reply to De Witt, De Wit, De la Court, and Uytenhage de Mist. One of the most hard-hitting was the 'Resurrected Barneveld', a tract written by someone close to Voetius, or possibly Voetius himself, which vitriolically attacked the principles of Grotius, 'maxims pernicious for the land and contrary to the Union', accounting the doctrine of provincial sovereignty a device to reduce the six lesser provinces to being dependent 'planets' revolving around the 'sun of Holland'. This tract denounced the new prayer formulary as a violation of the States General resolutions of 1618, and 1651, holding that the public Church, in so far as it was the concern of the secular authorities, *was* a matter for the Generality,[79] and, once again, reminded readers that it was the States of Holland themselves who had drafted the States General's answer to Peckius, asserting that sovereignty in the United Provinces 'unquestionably lay in the States General and those of the particular provinces'. Such vigorous propaganda led to Voetius, and what opponents called his 'Reformed Jesuits', being accused of aspiring to subject regents and populace to the sway of the Church, and subvert the authority of the

[76] [Uytenhage de Mist], *Apologie*, 58.
[77] Ibid. 156.
[78] Bouwman, *Voetius over het gezag der synoden*, 23.
[79] *De Ver-resenen Barnevelt*, 31.

States. As part of their campaign they were alleged to be insidiously inculcating in the minds of the young, and ignorant, the notion that Oldenbarnevelt was a 'traitor, rascal, and enemy of the land, and of religion, who was justly sentenced and executed'.[80]

At this point Voetians had little choice but to defend the execution of Oldenbarnevelt for the episode was now, more than ever, a favourite theme of States party publicity. Vondel's *Palamedes* (see p. 488 above), suppressed between 1625, and 1650, having been reprinted in 1652, was reissued in 1660, 1662, and 1663. Its first stage performances took place, amid intense controversy, at Rotterdam in 1663 and at Amsterdam in February 1665. Inevitably, with Rotterdam and Amsterdam resounding to *Palamedes*, an Orangist theatrical counter-thrust followed. This took the form of the tragedy *Wilhem, of gequetste vryheyt* (1662) by Lambert van den Bosch, the vehemently anti-Catholic co-rector of the Dordrecht Latin school. His play glorified William the Silent, reminding the public how much Dutch 'freedom' owed to him, and the House of Orange, and endeavouring to boost reverence for the stadholderate.[81] It was amid this feverish atmosphere that Vondel wrote his last political play, *The Batavian Brothers, or Suppressed Freedom* (1663). Here Vondel celebrated the Batavian revolt against Roman oppression in a way which enabled him, by power of association and allusion, to defend the 'True Freedom' against Orangism. He styles the Roman governor whose cruelty, corruption, and extortion precipitated the revolt a 'Stadholder', whose power was based on control of the army, and whose illegal actions were encouraged by self-seeking favourites.[82] As Vondel's anti-Orangism was directed chiefly against Maurits and William II, the stress on illegal conduct was also a way of steering popular disapproval especially towards these two Stadholders.

The ideological strife between the party-factions culminated in 1663. But whilst the Orangists remained weak politically, they could not effectively attack the 'True Freedom'. As De la Court tersely remarked, 'vana sine viribus ira'.[83] Moreover, as the months passed, the States of Friesland met with less and less success in their efforts to mobilize opposition to Holland's ascendancy among the other provinces. For besides the recrudescent English menace, there was the rising tension in the Dutch–German borderlands stemming from the growing power and aspirations of Christoph Bernhard, prince-bishop of Münster. Both overseas, and down its eastern side, the

---

[80] [De Wit?], *Schotschen Duyvel*, 52.
[81] Duits, *Van Bartholomeusnacht tot Bataafse opstand*, 121, 134–6.
[82] Ibid. 254–68.
[83] De la Court, 'Brieven', 143.

Republic faced an insecure, and uncertain, future and, with every month that passed, it became more obvious that the only way these challenges could be met was by accepting Holland's leadership. At their gathering in July 1663, the States of Gelderland had already shown alarm at the aggressive, militantly Catholic policies of Münster. Having mastered the city of Münster, and amassed one of the strongest armies in Germany, the prince-bishop was now being courted by the kings of England and France. Gelderland and Overijssel may have claimed to be sovereign provinces but they also knew they were helpless in the face of Munsterite power and pretensions without the protective umbrella provided by Holland. Christoph Bernhard formally demanded the return of Borculo in February 1664. 'Those of Gelderland', reported Downing, 'say they will hazard all rather than they will part with it, it being upon their frontiers and an exceeding strong place.' 'But yet,' he noted, 'Holland seems to be somewhat indifferent in the matter, hopeing thereby to force Gelder to comply with them in the businesse of the new prayer, and to revoke their resolution against it.'[84] It soon became clear that Holland's protection mattered more to Gelderland than pursuing the controversy about public prayers, a subject on which the States of Gelderland suddenly fell remarkably quiet.

THE SECOND ANGLO-DUTCH WAR, 1664–1667

The Second Anglo-Dutch War commenced, officially, in March 1665 but, in reality, early in 1664. Ever since England had made peace with Spain, in 1660, and resumed peacetime maritime expansion, tension between the rival English and Dutch empires of trade had been acute. The friction was world-wide, but especially intense in West Africa, the Caribbean, and the East Indies, a global confrontation, snarling and acrimonious, that had seemed likely to lead to a new war ever since 1661, and the coolness following the 'Dutch Gift'. It was one of those wars everyone had expected, and prepared for, over many years. By 1664, English harassment of Dutch shipping, and colonies, had reached such a pitch that there was an all but inevitable slide into conflict. By the time Charles II declared war officially, some 200 Dutch ships had already been brought in and several Dutch colonies overrun, including New Netherland, the previous autumn, the name of its chief town, New Amsterdam, being changed to New York. The mood in England, and the English colonies, was vehemently anti-Dutch. Samuel Pepys did not exaggerate when he wrote, in 1664, that both the royal court and city of London, expecting big gains, were 'mad for a Dutch war'.

---

[84] Lister, *Life and Administration*, iii. 278.

As in 1652–4, other European powers (except Portugal and Münster), needed little convincing that the Republic was in the right, but observed that England had the might and nearly all the strategic advantages.[85] The Republic, spurred by Holland, had continuously striven, since 1653, to strengthen and expand its navy and naval administration, placing the admiralty colleges, and their shipyards, arsenals, and stores, in a readier state.[86] The Dutch now had a much larger standing navy than before, with more professional naval officers, more and better purpose-built warships, and heavier guns. Yet the English too had poured in resources, to prevent the Dutch closing the gap, and, on the whole, retained their advantage, especially in weight of guns. In April 1665, the Royal Navy possessed eight 'first rates', mounting over seventy guns, as against only four on the Dutch side.[87]

The Holland regents had considerably improved their navy. But what they could not do was purge it of ideological tensions, any more than they could the Republic as a whole. These threatened to be as chronic as during the first war. When the captain of the *Gouda* (56 guns) ran up the States flag at the commencement of the first battle in the North Sea, his men refused to fight until he replaced it with the Prince's colours. After the initial defeats, bickering intensified as republican admirals sought to pin the blame on Cornelis Tromp and Jan Evertsen, their Orangist colleagues.[88] Relations between De Ruyter and Tromp became exceedingly strained. Reports that the latter had 'underhand, stirred up divers to talke . . . that they should have some illustrious person for their chief, and so bring in the Prince of Orange' almost led to Tromp's arrest in June 1665.[89] Eventually, in the midst of the war, in August 1666, he had to be dismissed from the navy, for insubordination, though a capable commander and popular with the men.[90] He remained in disgrace as long as the republican regime lasted, only re-entering naval service after William III reconciled him to De Ruyter, in 1673. The younger Tromp relished being painted as much as any of his colleagues and sat for numerous artists including Caspar Netscher and Samuel van Hoogstraeten. But here too ideology intruded. In one painting, Abraham Willaerts (Rijksmuseum, Amsterdam) depicts him in Roman costume, sporting a blazing orange cape.

[85] Barbour, *Capitalism in Amsterdam*, 103; Israel, *Dutch Primacy*, 276–7.
[86] Bruijn, 'The Dutch Navy', 50, 54; Bruijn, *Dutch Navy*, 75–9.
[87] Boxer, *Anglo-Dutch Wars*, 25.
[88] Oudendijk, *Johan de Witt en de zeemacht*, 111–12.
[89] Lister, *Life and Administration*, iii. 387.
[90] Rowen, *John de Witt*, 590.

Most foreign observers took it for granted the Republic was the weaker party and, being representatives of monarchs, and disdainful of republics, assumed that its decentralized, consultative structure would fatally hamper its effectiveness. If republican regents deemed republics superior to monarchies, the typical European diplomat of the time believed otherwise, particularly as regards power and military capacity. And compared to Venice, or Genoa, the Dutch Republic appeared doubly hindered by its three-tiered structure. Downing predicted, before war broke out, that if the king remained unyielding, the Dutch would capitulate without a fight; and that, if they fought, they would be hopelessly divided and rapidly defeated.

Downing adduced numerous arguments to support his assessment.[91] He noted that De Witt's collaboration with Amsterdam had slackened since the death of Cornelis de Graeff, in 1664, and that, even in Holland, 'every towne [is] jealous of the other, and nothing more easy then, by complying with one, to draw them from the other'. Since 1660, the number of Orangist towns in Holland—now comprising Leiden, Haarlem, Rotterdam, Enkhuizen, Gorcum, Schoonhoven, and Purmerend—had appreciably increased. But most crucial of all, he urged, was the system of provincial government, the weakness of the inland provinces, and their lack of interest in fighting England. Downing assured his masters that each province was sovereign and that the inland provinces would contribute neither financially, nor in other ways, to the war. Finally, he stressed that the populace were already saddled with heavy taxation and the Generality, and States of Holland, with huge debts.

The opening great battle, off Lowestoft, in June 1665, seemed amply to confirm the predictions of English superiority and justify the confidence of English merchants and colonial governors. The Dutch sent out the most powerful fleet they had ever assembled: 103 ships, mounting 21,613 men—a number equivalent to about one-third of the total manpower on the Dutch merchant and fishing fleets—and 4,869 guns.[92] But the Dutch capital ships could not match the fire-power of the English three-deckers. Seventeen Dutch warships were sunk or captured. Obdam's flagship, the *Eendracht* (84 guns; 500 men), blew up with the loss of the admiral and all but five of the crew, the blast reportedly being heard as far away as The Hague.

Morale slumped in the navy, on the Amsterdam Exchange (see Table 39), and throughout the Republic. By the 1660s merchants and regents, as well as foreign diplomats, had become accustomed to view movements in share prices, on the Amsterdam stock exchange, especially shares in the Amsterdam Chamber of the VOC, as a pointer to confidence in the prospects of

---

[91] Lister, *Life and Administration*, iii. 305–6.   [92] *Kort en Bondigh Verhael*, 59, 62–3.

the Republic as a whole, as well as of the great colonial companies. At the beginning of 1664, VOC shares remained high, at 498 per cent, reflecting the prosperity, and political stability, of the early 1660s. The WIC share price had recovered somewhat from its disastrous slump in the late 1640s and 1650s. During the spring of 1664, however, as the two maritime powers moved towards war, there were sharp falls in share prices, leading to bankruptcies and huge losses.[93] There was a temporary rally in the WIC share price in the autumn, following De Ruyter's success in West Africa, when he recaptured the forts the English seized from the Dutch the previous year. 'Knowing men' bought WIC shares after De Ruyter's triumph but did not tarry long before selling them again.

During the spring of 1665, VOC and WIC share prices resumed their fall. After Lowestoft, business confidence slumped, the VOC share price falling from 336 to 322, one of the lowest points recorded for the second half of the seventeenth century. Yet, before long, both general morale, and business confidence, rallied. This had mainly to do with the Republic's naval build-up, much of which had not yet been brought to bear in the opening battle. Seeing that most of the fleet that fought survived intact 'and that the great ships now building at Rotterdam, and the three great ones lately launched at Amsterdam, will be very suddainly ready to joine with them, and the hopes that their fleet will be suddainly againe at sea, hath already raised the East India actions againe from 336 to 348'.[94] To find enough seamen, the admiralty college at Amsterdam raised naval wages to the unheard-of level of 30 guilders monthly. Late in the summer morale rose further on the news that the returning East India fleet, sailing north, around the top of Ireland and Scotland, had eluded the English fleet and reached the relative safety of the Norwegian harbour of Bergen. VOC shares rose to 395.[95]

The war began in defeat and amid much gloom. Yet the internal disarray and lack of cohesion predicted by Downing failed to materialize. It was perfectly true, as he insisted, that the inland provinces had no direct interest in fighting England. But the United Provinces were, after all, not a league of 'seven sovereign allies', and the Generality, prodded incessantly by Holland, furnished men, and resources, in proportion to population, at much higher, not lower, levels than was at that time possible in monarchies such as England, France, or Spain.[96]

[93] Lister, *Life and Administration*, iii. 300, 319.
[94] Ibid. 382, 387.
[95] Ibid.
[96] Grever, 'Committees and Deputations', 33.

Admittedly, the co-operation of Gelderland, Overijssel, and Groningen—though not of Utrecht and Friesland—can be partly explained by the threat posed by the prince-bishop of Münster. But Münster was not a new, or unexpected, element in the situation but a long-term factor, shaping the reality of the Dutch Republic. The eastern provinces knew now—but had long known—that no one else was going to protect them from the quarrelsome and militantly Counter-Reformationary prince-bishopric or any other powerful eastern neighbour, if Holland did not, and that Holland would shield them only if they gave co-operation in return.

De Witt and the States General had sought to dissuade the prince-bishop from joining England by means of a show of strength in the east. Early in 1664, Christoph Bernhard had expelled the Dutch from a fort in the Ems valley, the Dijlerschans, garrisoned on behalf of the count of East Friesland. In May 1664, Dutch troops, under the Frisian Stadholder, penetrated the Münsterland and recaptured the fort. But the prince-bishop was unimpressed, and with reason. For the Holland regents had run the Generality's army down not only quantitatively, but qualitatively, to such an extent it no longer represented a credible deterrent. In September, Von Galen officially demanded restitution of Borculo-Lichtenvoorde; receiving no satisfactory answer, he declared war. Next, backed by English subsidies, he invaded Gelderland and Overijssel with 20,000 men.

The Dutch army in the east, commanded by the now elderly Johan Maurits of Nassau-Siegen, retreated in disarray behind the IJssel line. Munsterite troops occupied Oldenzaal, Almelo, and much of the Twenthe quarter and, further south, also Bredevoort, Doetinchem, and much of the *Achterhoek* of Gelderland. The failure of the army to protect the eastern provinces damaged the Holland States party's standing, provoking a fresh controversy over who should command the army and how it should be organized. Much of the criticism adhered to De Witt's brother who, as one of the States General's 'deputies in the field', had authorized the pull-back to the IJssel.

After this the prince-bishop overran Drenthe, or as the indignant Spinoza put it 'foolishly entered Frisia, as Aesop's goat entered the well'.[97] Panic gripped large parts of the Republic, not least Groningen which now came under threat. It took the arrival of a French auxiliary force, in November, to stabilize the front, and evaporation of English subsidies, to force the Munsterites into the undignified withdrawal which Spinoza had assured his correspondent in London would follow.

[97] Spinoza, *Correspondence*, 213.

But while the Munsterite threat explains the increased propensity of Overijssel, Gelderland, and Groningen to co-operate with Holland, it does not account for the wider, popular support for the De Witt regime during the war, the weakness of the surge in Orangist support in 1665–6, compared to that during the First Anglo-Dutch War, or the solidarity of Friesland. The States of Friesland had long known that war with England would harm the Orangist cause in the Republic. In October 1664, Friesland had pressed for more concessions to England to restore 'peace and friendship'.[98] But before long Friesland too was caught up in the wave of patriotic sentiment stirring the Republic. Some of the States of Friesland opposed payment of Friesland's share of the cost of the De Ruyter expedition to West Africa, on the grounds that the forts there had nothing to do with Friesland. But the majority took the view that the English attacks in Guinea were aggression against 'our common dear Fatherland' and the 'entire state of the United Netherlands', and that Friesland should pay her share.[99]

Generality military, and naval, expenditure rose, in 1665, to some two and half times the level of 1664. Friesland's 11.6 per cent quota—the second largest after Holland's—totalled over 3 million guilders that year, compelling the States to raise special loans. The bulk of what Friesland raised was then spent on the navy. The admiralty college at Harlingen, two-thirds of its money coming from Friesland, and one-third from Groningen, fitted out fourteen warships, mounting 3,115 men and 700 guns, in June 1665, representing about one-seventh of the manpower, and guns, which fought on the Dutch side at Lowestoft. By the summer of 1666, the Frisian-Groningen contingent of the Dutch navy had increased to twenty-eight ships, mounting 5,000 men and 1,100 guns.[100] The conduct of the Frisian States reflected the mood of the Frisian public.

The crucial factor in the Republic's surviving the setbacks of 1664–6, without caving in, and finally emerging triumphant, was indeed the attitude of the populace. The French ambassador saw the importance of this early on, writing, in January 1665, that 'les peuples sont fort animez, et accordent pour cette guerre tout ce qu'on leur demande'.[101] The result was that leading Orangist and pro-English figures, such as the Frisian deputy Willem van Haren, a member of the *Raad van State*, and one of Downing's closest allies in the Republic, found themselves out of step with sentiment in their provinces and the Generality. The war reduced the influence of the Orangist

---

[98] ARH SG PR 377, p. 192. res. SF 7 Oct. 1666.
[99] Grever, 'States of Friesland', 16.
[100] Ibid.
[101] D'Estrades, *Lettres*, iii. 17.

nobility in Friesland, strengthening the so-called Aylva faction of *grietman-nen* and nobles, dominated by the Aylva and Grovestins families, who were also broadly the pro-Holland party in Friesland. Willem Frederik died in 1664 and although his supporters were still influential and his widow, the Countess Albertina Agnes, as regent for their young son, Hendrik Casimir II (1664–96), anxious to defend the interest of the Frisian stadholderate, for the moment, the anti-Holland party had no alternative but to adopt a low profile.

A particularly thorny matter, not only for De Witt and the Orangists, but also the English court, was the role of the young Prince of Orange. De Witt was anxious to minimize any upsurge of sentiment in favour of the House of Orange. Orangists had no wish to support De Witt; but neither could they afford to dissociate themselves from the war. The very strength of popular support for the war made it imperative, from their point of view, to detach the Prince from Charles II rather than the war effort. The awkwardness of the situation was clear to all when it was proposed, in April 1665, that the 15-year-old Prince should visit the fleet at Texel. Republican regents, we learn, 'doe not shew any satisfaction or good liking of his goeing; on the other hand, no doubt, if he should goe, he would be put upon drinking the prosperity of the fleet, and such kind of things as his Majesty would have no great excuse to be oversatisfied with'.[102] But expedients were devised which satisfied De Witt and the Orangists while simultaneously providing scope for de-emphasizing the Prince's English links in favour of the Brandenburg connection. In May 1666, there were great festivities aboard the fleet, at Texel, when the Prince visited De Ruyter's flagship accompanied by the Elector of Brandenburg, in person, as well as the duke of Holstein and other German princes.[103] For once, full-strength beer was dispensed to men, which doubtless enhanced the cheering.

Gradually, during 1666, the strategic situation of the Republic improved. French intervention, and the drying up of English subsidies, forced the prince-bishop into a humiliating withdrawal. States General negotiators, headed by Van Beverningk, in April 1666, concluded the peace of Cleves with Christoph Bernhard, whereby he abandoned the places he had occupied and his claims on Borculo. All neutral commercial centres—Hamburg, Lübeck, Venice, Livorno, Genoa, and Cadiz—apart only from Lisbon, remained strongly pro-Dutch. Denmark-Norway, instead of siding with England, as Charles II had hoped, again allied with the United Provinces, helping to repulse the English from Bergen, and closing the Sound to

[102] Lister, *Life and Administration*, iii. 375.
[103] Blok, *Michiel Adriaansz. de Ruyter*, 259.

English shipping. The Dutch auxiliary force sent to Danish waters ensured that England could not force the Sound. During 1666, not a single English vessel passed in, or out of, the Baltic.[104] In the East Indies, the VOC again swept the English from the seas and captured several English forts. In the Mediterranean, both sides paralysed the trade and shipping of the other—to the temporary advantage of Genoa and the French. In northern waters, the Dutch privateers, more numerous and better organized than in 1652–4, began capturing English vessels at an appreciable rate.[105] Altogether, around 500 English merchant vessels were captured, including the twenty-seven taken by De Ruyter off West Africa, and in the Caribbean. A significant number of captured English ships were auctioned off in Spain, twenty-eight at Corunna alone.

For a time, shutting down England's trade had no great effect on the English naval effort. The vast sea battles, portrayed in a series of masterly paintings by Willem van de Velde, continued to be bitterly fought. The Dutch, under De Ruyter, had the edge in flair and deployment, but the English still in weight of guns. The Dutch marginally triumphed in the 'Four Days' Battle, of June 1666, but again were defeated, with heavy losses, in the St James's Day Fight (4 August 1666). Soon after, the Dutch suffered a major disaster when the English admiral, Holmes, penetrated between the North Holland islands and burnt 150 merchantmen sheltering behind Terschelling. But whilst the Dutch had the money, munitions, and stores to keep on fitting out their fleets, Charles II and Parliament were unable to keep it up. The cost was tremendous and English maritime commerce almost completely paralysed. Loss of trade and ships, shortages of stores, and the impact of the Great Plague and Fire of London all contributed to undermining the war effort. The mood was not improved by the lack of coal to heat London over the winter of 1666–7, the colliers being kept away by the Dutch navy and privateers. Psychologically, the Dutch had already won by the end of 1666.[106] It remained only to use the initiative now in their hands.

During 1667, the Dutch blockaded the south-east of England, as far north as Harwich. In June, De Ruyter carried out his famous raid up the Medway, breaking the defences, penetrating to Upnor Castle, burning installations and five Royal Navy vessels, and towing away the *Royal Charles*, the English flagship. The Republic erupted in jubilation, ringing of church bells, victory bonfires, and the burning of King Charles in effigy. The tide turned

[104] Bang and Korst, *Tabeller*, i. 1–12.
[105] De Bruijn, 'Dutch Privateering', 79–86; Israel, *Dutch Primacy*, 278.
[106] Ibid. 275–9.

also in the Caribbean. In 1665, it had seemed that the English governors in the New World were about to 'root the Dutch out of all places in the West Indies'. Before long, New Netherland, St Eustatius, Saba, Essequebo, and Pomeroon had fallen and the king was 'full of hope shortly to hear of the like success against Curaçao'.[107] In contrast to his success in West Africa, De Ruyter's expedition to the Caribbean achieved nothing. But Curaçao held and eventually the Dutch recovered Essequebo and Pomeroon. In 1667, a Zeeland expedition of seven ships, and 1,000 men, seized the English fort at Paramaribo and, with it, the whole of the potentially sugar-rich colony of Surinam. The WIC also reoccupied Tobago.

Peace was signed at Breda in July 1667. Under the terms, England kept New York, but returned St Eustatius and Saba, ceded Surinam and the former English West African base of Cormantine, now 'Fort Amsterdam', surrendered her long-standing claim to Pola Run in the Banda Islands, conceded the principle of 'Free Ship, Free Goods', and agreed to modify the Navigation Act to allow Germany to be defined as part of the Republic's natural hinterland.[108]

The peace of Breda was a triumph for the Republic, the Holland States party-faction, De Ruyter and the navy, and the brothers De Witt personally. Cornelis de Witt, humiliated in 1665, at the IJssel, was now honoured by having an allegorical victory painting, depicting him as the States General's deputy to the fleet, presiding over the raid (see PLATE 22) on the Medway, and being crowned with a laurel wreath, hung in Dordrecht town hall. The navy, and not least De Ruyter, were fêted. One of the victory allegories painted at the time, today in the Rijksmuseum, shows De Ruyter and the other admirals symbolically bringing the fisheries back to life, hauling in a net full of herring.

By contrast, for Orangists the war ended in embarrassment and humiliation. In the early stages the young Prince, and the Princess Dowager, had steered immaculately between the Scylla of appearing to be tools of De Witt, on the one side, and the Charybdis of appearing half-hearted about the war, on the other. During the Munsterite invasion, when attention had focused on the deplorable state of the army, and the weakness of the Republic's defences in the east, there had even been some scope for advancing the Prince's cause. The general clamour for an illustrious personage to take command of the army was hard to resist. But the Prince was still only 16 and the States party argued that military experience was more vital than

---

[107] Cal. St. Papers. *America and the West Indies* (1661–8), 328.
[108] Van Winter, 'Acte van Navigatie', 44, 53.

glorious forebears. To deflect attention from the Prince, the names of two famous foreign generals who might be approached—Marshal Turenne and the Swedish general Wrangel—were proposed.[109] The republican notion had arisen among the States party-faction, in the 1650s, that the way to solve the question of the command of the Republic's army was to find a foreign general with great military prestige but who could pose no political threat to themselves. It was a tradition that would one day saddle them with Marlborough.

Considering the position, in March 1666, the Leiden *vroedschap* concluded there was little prospect of the Prince being appointed to a high charge in the near future but that the outlook might well brighten before long. In this connection, they believed it vital to persuade the Princess Dowager to send everyone with close English links away from the Prince, and especially his governor, Willem van Nassau, heer van Zuylenstein, and that the Prince should be solely under the guidance of principal personages 'of this state'.[110]

Undoubtedly, Orangists were more inclined than the States party-faction to press for an early peace with England, even if this meant accepting defeat. In August 1666, a low-point in the Republic's fortunes, the Haarlem *vroedschap* recommended 'all possible efforts' to procure peace, the 'continuation of the war with that crown being the total ruin of our beloved Fatherland'.[111] But few Orangists thought in terms of active collusion with England. The main significance of the 'Buat conspiracy', uncovered in August 1666, is that it shows that there was, despite party-factional feuding, a fairly highly developed sense of loyalty to 'this state'.[112] Henri Buat was a French officer in the States General's service, attached to the young Prince's household, and a passionate Orangist, who was at the centre of a plot orchestrated by the English minister, Lord Arlington, designed to bring about an Orangist *coup d'état* which would overthrow De Witt, end the war, renew Anglo-Dutch friendship, and restore the stadholderate. Buat gave himself away in the most farcical circumstances, having mixed up his letters in a moment of haste and himself handed to De Witt, in error for another, a secret communication from Lord Arlington which revealed all. He was arrested and the names of his accomplices discovered. But it was found that apart from two regent extremists at Rotterdam—one of whom was Johan Kievit, who managed to escape to England—those prepared to conspire

[109] GA Haarlem vroed. res. 21, fo. 93. res. vroed. 2 Feb. 1666.
[110] GA Leiden Sec. Arch. 453. res. vroed. 1 and 29 Mar. 1666.
[111] GA Haarlem vroed. res. 21, fos. 141–2. res. vroed. 23 Aug. 1666.
[112] De Bruin, *Geheimhouding en verraad*, 537–8.

against the regime were neither numerous nor important. The episode nevertheless caused a sensation and was to remain cause for acrimony among the party-factions for years to come.

The revelation of the Buat affair, at least in the short term, greatly strengthened De Witt's hand. In a letter to the Princess Dowager, written on 30 August—the day before the funeral of Frans Hals, in Haarlem—he described its discovery as a 'manifest miracle of God's working'. Before Buat's arrest, there had been persistent pressure for the Prince to be placed at the head of the army, some of it from within Holland. Thus, in April 1666, De Witt and the *Gecommitteerde Raden* had had to expound 'several important principles of statecraft', that is, republican concepts, to convince the States of Holland to reject out of hand the proposal, urged especially by Zeeland at that point, that Orange should be made captain-general but not Stadholder.[113] In the months after Buat's arrest, all such pressure collapsed. De Witt and his allies were able to tighten their grip over the Prince's entourage and education, finally getting rid of Zuylestein and other undesirable Orangists. De Witt continued to assure the Princess Dowager that he took the Prince's education with the utmost seriousness and that Holland was excluding him from military command not out of animosity towards the House of Orange but only 'principles of statecraft'. Reviewing the situation a few months later, the Leiden *vroedschap* judged it pointless for the time being even to press for Orange to be seated on the *Raad van State*, concluding that they would have to wait 'until a better opportunity'.[114]

THE REPUBLIC IN CONFLICT WITH LOUIS XIV

During the opening years of Louis XIV's personal rule (1661–1715), it had appeared that the former coolness prevailing between France and the United Provinces since 1647–8 (when the latter had concluded their separate peace with Spain) had ended. France and Republic were once again, following the Franco-Dutch treaty of 1662, officially allies and this benefited the Dutch in many ways. In confrontation with England, the States party-faction found in the French alliance a counter-weight to the Stuart connections of the Orangists both at home and abroad. During the Second Anglo-Dutch War, the French alliance assisted the Republic more indirectly than directly, but was nevertheless of considerable value. French forces did not fight the English (except in the Caribbean) but Louis lent support, at

[113] GA Gouda OA 11. res. vroed. 5 Apr. 1666.
[114] GA Leiden Sec. Arch. 453, fo. 247. res. vroed. 29 Nov. 1666.

least in the early stages, behind the scenes, not wishing to see the Republic overwhelmed and England emerge as mistress of the seas; above all, he helped check the forces of the prince-bishop of Münster. The situation was thus reminiscent, for a few years, of the alignment during the Twelve Years Truce when England sided with Maurits and France with Oldenbarnevelt and the 'Arminians'.

Initially, Louis sought the friendship of the Holland States party-faction. In the 1660s, the Spanish monarchy was still regarded as France's principal adversary, at least until 1668, and the Spanish Netherlands as the chief focus of great power rivalry. Moreover, as was obvious to all Europe, French supremacy would be greatly facilitated should the United Provinces become, in some degree, a client state of France. Louis unsuccessfully offered De Witt—who prided himself on being above corruption—a generous annual pension. As part of this strategy of rendering De Witt an instrument of French policy, the French envoy, d'Estrades, carried instructions, on his arrival in the Republic, in 1663, to help reconcile the warring Veth and Thibault factions, at Middelburg, so as to improve co-operation between Zeeland and Holland, to the advantage of the States party-faction and detriment of the Orangists.[115] At this time, Louis enjoyed a generally favourable press in the Republic.[116]

Yet, from the outset, tensions arose to disturb this incipient amity between France and the Republic. Two principal sources of friction, one strategic and territorial, the other economic, eroded Franco-Dutch concord and proved decisive in shaping the subsequent course of great power politics. The first was the future of the Spanish Netherlands. With Spain's withdrawal of most of her forces from the Low Countries, a power vacuum arose in one of the most strategically crucial zones of Europe which became a source of dangerous instability, Spanish strength ebbing away just as Louis was forming the largest and most potent army of the then world. The result was a fundamental shift in the balance of power. Since the 1540s, the south Netherlands had served as Spain's, and also Europe's, bridle on French expansion, thwarting French ambition throughout the continent. Now, suddenly, the bridle had fallen away and there was seemingly no check to French ambition and territorial expansion.

Spain's weakness in the south Netherlands had troubled De Witt since as early as 1663.[117] Louis showed every sign of nurturing designs on the region, though, at this stage, not averse to discussing his expansionist schemes with

---

[115] D'Estrades, *Lettres*, iii. 17.
[116] Van Malssen, *Louis XIV d'après les pamphlets*, 6–12.
[117] Rowen, *John de Witt*, 479–80.

his Dutch ally. De Witt judged it prudent to enter into talks about reviving the Franco-Dutch partition treaty of 1635 (see p. 527 above) whereby the larger part of the Spanish Netherlands would be annexed by France and the area north of the line from Ostend to Maastricht, including Bruges, Ghent, Mechelen, and Antwerp, to the Republic.[118] He also discussed with Louis the possibility of allowing the southern provinces to become 'free' cantons, on the Swiss model, under Franco-Dutch protection. But the regents harboured strong doubts and reservations about such notions, arising not least from Amsterdam's fear that Antwerp might recover her former greatness were the city to be incorporated into the United Provinces and thus released from the Scheldt restrictions obstructing her trade since 1572. For the closure of the Scheldt to maritime traffic would continue, seemingly, only so long as Antwerp remained under Spain and the terms of the treaty of Münster in force. Even more daunting, were the south to be partitioned, would be the prospect of having an expanded France immediately adjoining the Republic.

Dutch anxiety mounted, in the spring of 1663, when Louis cancelled his renunciation, solemnly entered into when marrying his Spanish Habsburg bride, of her inheritance rights in the Spanish Netherlands, on the grounds that her dowry had not been paid.[119] The Spanish Crown, its forces committed in Portugal, tried to counter French pressure by drawing the United Provinces into guaranteeing the borders of the Spanish Netherlands, playing on Holland's fear of having France as an immediate neighbour. But De Witt, believing it would be fatal to tie the Republic's future to the decaying Spanish monarchy, rejected Madrid's proposals for a Dutch–Spanish defensive pact to protect the south from France.[120] The Pensionary told the Spanish ambassador, Don Esteban de Gamarra, that if Spain could not defend the southern provinces, they should either become an autonomous confederacy, on the Dutch or Swiss model, the solution known as 'canton-ment', or else be transferred to the Emperor, who would be better able to protect them. When, in December 1663, Gamarra again urged a Dutch–Spanish alliance, De Witt replied that he did not judge it 'a good plan to lean against a wall which was about to collapse'; to which Gamarra retorted that precisely because it was precarious the Dutch should prop it up, for, if it fell, they 'would be caught under it'.[121]

The other source of tension was commerce and colonies. Before 1662, the French Crown had been so anxious to secure Dutch collaboration against

[118] Lonchay, *La Rivalité*, 206–7.
[119] Haley, *An English Diplomat*, 44–8.
[120] Israel, *Dutch Republic and the Hispanic World*, 404–9.
[121] AGS La Haya xlvii, fo. 421. Gamarra to Philip IV, 25 Dec. 1663.

Spain, it had avoided taking any vigorous steps to check the growing Dutch penetration of the French market, or Dutch predominance in the carrying of France's bulk exports—wine, brandy, and salt. Nor, as yet, had the French Crown put much energy into building a rival empire of trade, navigation, and colonies overseas. But this changed with the onset of Louis's personal rule. Dutch friendship was now less essential to France than in the age of Henri IV and Richelieu, while, especially since the 1640s, sales in France of Dutch textiles, East India wares, fish, whale products, tobacco, earthenware, and refined sugar, as well as Baltic stores, had greatly expanded. By the 1660s, this increasing success of Dutch commerce in France was causing widespread resentment among French merchants, and manufacturers, while at the same time Louis, eager to match the maritime power, and colonial expansion, of the Dutch and English, embarked on an ambitious programme of mercantilist initiatives which clashed at many points with Dutch interests in both Europe and the Indies.

The beginnings of Franco-Dutch economic conflict reached back to before the Second Anglo-Dutch War. But, at that stage, Louis avoided the undisguised rivalry which so poisoned relations between England and the Republic. In 1664, Colbert's new general tariff was introduced, under which increases were kept at levels just tolerable, albeit with some grumbling, to the Dutch:[122] only in the case of imports of refined sugar into France was a prohibitively high tariff adopted. This dealt a severe blow to the Amsterdam sugar-refining industry, which since the 1640s had been selling much of its output in France. But Amsterdam had been receiving much of her raw sugar, in French eyes illegally, from the French West Indies, the output of which Louis wished to reserve for the French refineries, not in itself an unreasonable aim. Also in 1664, Louis set up the new state-backed French East, and West, India Companies, marking the commencement of a regular French East India traffic and a new and more dynamic phase of French trade and colonization in the New World. French expansion overseas greatly accelerated. Again, this alarmed Dutch merchants, but could not, in itself, be grounds for official complaint. For the moment, French colonial policy was peaceful enough—with one exception. In 1664, Louis sent an expedition to Cayenne (claimed by France but which had, for some years, been colonized by the WIC), seizing the colony from the Dutch. But, with war with England and Münster looming, and French help indispensable, this was an affront to which De Witt chose to turn a blind eye. Amsterdam already suspected the French monarch designed to 'damage the commerce

---

[122] Elzinga, 'Tarif de Colbert', 221–3.

of this state and . . . divert it there',[123] but De Witt saw no alternative to putting up with the situation with the best grace he could muster.

By the spring of 1667, however, Louis saw there was no longer a risk the English might overwhelm the Dutch, seize their colonies, and dominate the world's maritime commerce (a prospect widely feared in Europe) and decided to profit while he could from the absorption of the English and Dutch in the last stages of their war. The king began advancing French interests more aggressively than before, both on land and by sea, within Europe and without. In particular, two initiatives transformed the situation: the publication of Colbert's second tariff list, in April 1667, and the entry of French troops into the Spanish Netherlands. Colbert's new list imposed draconian increases on imports of foreign goods into France, especially on Dutch fine cloth, camlets, herring, whale products, Delftware, tobacco, Gouda pipes, and East India wares. Since France was the Republic's largest market for many of these,[124] the new tariff list produced shock and indignation in the Dutch ports, substantially reduced the volume of Dutch trade with France, and adversely affected numerous Dutch industries.

It was also in April 1667 that French troops crossed into the Spanish Netherlands. They did not advance far, initially, but in the summer the invasion began to look more menacing, especially after Lille capitulated to Louis on 28 August. The States of Holland's committee for French affairs frantically searched for a means to halt the invasion, without irrevocably offending the French monarch, ignoring all pleas from Spain for assistance. When Gamarra threatened, on instructions from Brussels, that if the Dutch did not assist, Spain might abandon the south Netherlands to France, in exchange for Roussillon, and French Navarre, De Witt retorted he considered this a bluff, not a serious possibility.[125] He judged correctly: when ministers at Madrid heard about it they administered a sharp rebuke to the governor-general at Brussels, the marqués de Castel Rodrigo, for suggesting something potentially so hazardous for morale in the southern provinces. The Spanish court instructed Castel-Rodrigo to try again to negotiate a defensive pact with the Republic, authorizing him to hand over Ostend, Bruges, and Damme to the Dutch, to be garrisoned by their troops, as collateral for a loan of a million guilders and military assistance.[126]

De Witt and the Holland leadership at this point entered negotiations with Spanish ministers not because they seriously contemplated intervention

[123] Brugmans, 'Notulen', 191, 268.
[124] Elzinga, 'Tarif de Colbert', 246–8.
[125] AGS Estado 2203. consulta 16 Sept. 1667.
[126] AGS Estado 2203. consultas 1 and 27 Oct. 1667.

against the French but to exert psychological pressure on France, and stake out a zone of Dutch influence, should Spanish authority in the south Netherlands collapse, and there be no alternative to partition. Should this indeed happen, the Dutch intended to annex the parts of Flanders close to the Republic, including Ostend, and also Upper Gelderland (the Roermond quarter). De Witt pointedly obtained the approval of the States of Holland to send in Dutch troops to garrison Ostend, Bruges, Blankenburg, and Geldern, as a pledge of repayment of a Dutch loan to Spain.

Neither De Witt, nor Amsterdam, wanted intervention, or partition.[127] Finally, forced to act, however uninviting the courses open to him, De Witt opted for what became known as the Triple Alliance of 1668. This was an armed coalition of the Republic, England, and Sweden, formed to mediate between France and Spain. The Triple Alliance demanded an immediate cessation of hostilities, calling on Spain to cede either Luxemburg or the Franche-Comté, together with the extensive territory the French had already conquered—Douai, St Omer, Lille, and Cambrai (see Map 13). Louis was required only to halt and be content with what the allies would compel Spain to yield. The ultimatum was thus a device to placate France, at the expense of Spain, but with a sting in the secret annexe, engaging the coalition to intervene militarily against France, should Louis refuse to agree.[128] De Witt tried by this means to stop Louis without sacrificing the Republic's officially still friendly relationship with France. Indeed, De Witt continued to see it as a vital Dutch interest to avoid conflict with France and preserve some semblance of Franco-Dutch friendship for the sake of the Republic's security, in order to dispense with the need for a large and powerful army, and, not least, to retain France as a counter-weight to what he called the 'usual arrogance of the English nation'. The signing of the Triple Alliance by no means implied that De Witt supposed there was no further need to check 'English bad principles'.

Differences of view as to how to deal with France and Spain, between De Witt and Amsterdam, developed into serious tension within the States party bloc during 1668. The influential regent Coenraad van Beuningen (1622–93), who had been Dutch ambassador in Paris, and was the Republic's most experienced diplomat, argued, in his secret report to the States General of September 1668, that even if Louis accepted the ultimatum put to him by the Triple Alliance, his underlying attitude to the United Provinces was now so hostile that there was no longer any point in half-measures or pretending

---

[127] Rowen, *John de Witt*, 686–94.
[128] Haley, *An English Diplomat*, 172–3.

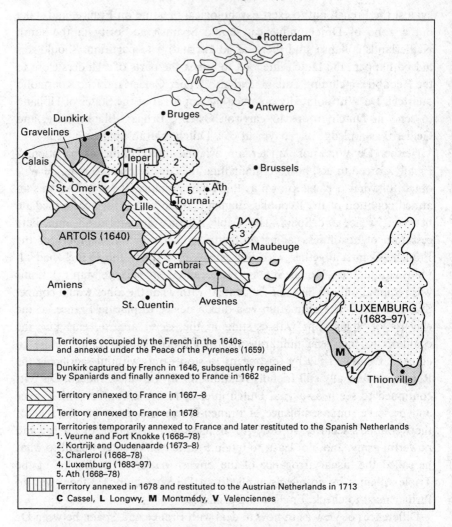

MAP 13. French conquests in the Spanish Netherlands in the seventeenth century

that the Franco-Dutch friendship of 1662 was still alive.[129] Van Beuningen advocated a resolutely anti-French stance in alliance with Spain, and the Emperor, and a vigorous programme of maritime and tariff retaliation to force Louis to moderate his mercantilist measures. At Amsterdam, Van Beuningen's approach was preferred to De Witt's, because the new French tariff list had aroused particular anger there and, also, because Spain and

---

[129] Franken, *Coenraad van Beuningen's . . . aktiviteiten*, 91–2.

Spanish America had, since 1647, become two of Amsterdam's most important markets. Also, Dutch merchants would enjoy greater advantages in the Spanish America trade—in fact they had lost quite a lot of ground to the French since 1659—if the United Provinces formed a close relationship with Spain.

Louis bowed to the Triple Alliance and halted the advance of his armies in the south Netherlands, but barely concealed his fury at the Dutch role in his being thwarted.[130] From this point on both his diplomacy and mercantilism assumed an aggressively anti-Dutch character. The French West India Company, assisted by the Crown, mounted regular patrols in the Caribbean to keep Dutch ships away from Martinique and other French colonies.[131] A powerful expedition was prepared for the East Indies which set sail, in March 1670, with instructions to seize permanent bases, and establish commerce in Ceylon and southern India (a preserve of the VOC)—using force if necessary. In 1669, Colbert set up the Compagnie du Nord, a maritime organization, backed by the Crown, designed to cut Dutch shipping out of the carrying traffic between France and the Baltic.

At the same time Louis sought allies amongst the Republic's eastern neighbours. The German states of the lower Rhine were indeed fertile ground for Louis's new policy of fomenting hostility to the Republic. The Elector of Brandenburg resented the continued Dutch occupation of Wesel, Rees, Emmerich, and Orsoy, and the fortress of Schenckenschans, in his duchy of Cleves. But it was especially the electorate of Cologne and bishopric of Münster which became focuses of French diplomacy. The regents knew what to expect from Christoph Bernhard, a prince 'toujours mal intentionné pour les Estats', as the French ambassador at The Hague expressed it.[132] In 1668, the prince-bishop, exploiting dissension in the Calvinist county of Bentheim, persuaded the count—previously a client of the Dutch—to convert to Catholicism, occupied the county, and reintroduced the Catholic faith.[133] Meanwhile, he steadily expanded his army, and not least his famous artillery train, including the sixty siege howitzers which subsequently earned him his nickname of 'Bombing Berend'. Louis also egged on the Elector of Cologne to demand Dutch evacuation of Rheinberg and the transfer of part of the Overmaas to the bishopric of Liège, and encouraged the Elector's efforts to master the Imperial Free City of Cologne, which was surrounded by his territory. To counter French

[130] Haley, *An English Diplomat*, 149, 176.
[131] Mims, *Colbert's West India Policy*, 195–6.
[132] Pomponne, *Relation de mon ambassade*, 159–60.
[133] Kohl, *Christoph Bernhard von Galen*, 297–9; Schröer, *Korrespondenz*, 138.

influence, the Republic backed the city of Cologne. Just as in the 1650s, the Holland States party tried to save the city of Münster from the encroaching absolutism of the prince-bishop, so now De Witt sought to defend Cologne's autonomy against the Elector. Arrangements were made for Cologne to accept a Dutch garrison should the Elector threaten force.[134]

De Witt's chief priority, however, was to mend his fences with Louis by agreeing to resume talks about the future partition, or cantonment, of the Spanish Netherlands. The French ambassador at The Hague, Arnauld de Pomponne, was instructed to negotiate so as to lull De Witt into a false sense of security and embroil the United Provinces further with their neighbours. And, indeed, De Witt was slow to grasp the full extent of the peril the Republic now faced. A crucial failing of the Dutch state apparatus, at this time, was the poor quality of the intelligence the ruling group at The Hague received from England.[135] By the autumn of 1669, Louis and Charles had agreed, in principle, to launch a combined land and sea attack on the United Provinces to break their power, punish the Dutch for their 'ingratitude', and take some of their territory and colonies. Yet the elderly, and ineffectual, Dutch ambassador in London, hopelessly misled, was still assuring De Witt, on the eve of the signing of the secret Anglo-French treaty of Dover (June 1670), that England would faithfully adhere to the Triple Alliance.

Another problem for De Witt was the growing *rapprochement* in the States of Holland between Amsterdam and the Orangist towns, Leiden and Haarlem, a development linked to the menacing economic situation. Van Beuningen and Gillis Valckenier, increasingly prominent at Amsterdam, rejected De Witt's conciliatory approach towards France, advocating instead a mercantilist counter-offensive, which both Leiden and Haarlem were keen to support, their textile exports being severely hit by Louis's tariffs. Against De Witt's advice, a States of Holland committee was set up to consider methods of economic retaliation against France, which, in November 1669, recommended banning imports of French silks and imposing punitively high tariffs on French wine, brandy, salt, vinegar, and paper, as well as an edict directing Holland's hospitals, orphanages, and old people's homes to boycott French products and consume only items of Dutch manufacture.[136] Amsterdam's own committee on commerce, headed by Van Beuningen and Valckenier, agreed to the ban on French silk, and action against French brandy and salt, but, before additional measures were taken, urged enquiries to see whether sufficient supplies of paper could be obtained

---

[134] O'Connor, *Negotiator out of Season*, 45–7.
[135] Rowen, *John de Witt*, 725, 731.
[136] GA Amsterdam res. vroed. 2 Nov. 1669.

elsewhere and to assess the effects of a ban on French wine. Owing to Amsterdam's worries (and opposition from Rotterdam, the city which now handled the lion's share of the French wine traffic), the States General published their initial package of economic retaliation against France, in January 1671, without banning French wine, the principal product imported from France.[137] But Amsterdam soon veered behind a wider ban, to include French wine, paper, vinegar, and sail-canvas, in addition to the action already taken, and, after reaching agreement on how to compensate Rotterdam, a second and more sweeping package of retaliation against France was voted through in November 1671.

Late in 1671, De Witt's brother, Cornelis, led an embassy extraordinary to Cologne, in a bid to end the quarrels with Cologne, and Münster, and dislodge these states from their alignment with France, but failed.[138] Louis completed his plans for the encirclement, and breaking, of the Republic, with his alliance with Cologne of January 1672.[139] France and England, together with Cologne and Münster, were now poised to overwhelm the Republic, destroy its power and independence, and despoil it of substantial territory and most of its colonies. The prince-bishop was promised the entire Borculo-Lichtenvoorde enclave, including Grol and Bredevoort; the Archbishop-Elector, ready to invade with 18,000 men, was to recover Rheinberg, and annex Maastricht and the Dutch Overmaas. Charles II, under the treaty of Dover, was due to receive parts of Zeeland and States Flanders.[140] Louis's intended annexations went unspecified in the treaties but were bound to be more extensive than those of his allies, whose investment in terms of money and troops was small compared with his own.

THE TWILIGHT OF THE 'TRUE FREEDOM'

The last years of the 'True Freedom' saw a recrudescence of ideological warfare and now, also, a deepening theologico-political and philosophical debate closely linked to the ideological context. In eclipse during the Second Anglo-Dutch War, Orangism revived strongly after 1667, helped by both the Republic's seemingly improved relationship with England and her fearful predicament, confronted by the growing hostility of France and the ecclesiastical princes of the lower Rhine. William III was now nearing his majority and, however adroit De Witt's expedients, a decision about

[137] Elzinga, *Voorspel*, 281–2, 284.
[138] Van der Hoeven, *Leeven en Dood*, 310–11.
[139] O'Connor, *Negotiator out of Season*, 50.
[140] Haley, *An English Diplomat*, 265.

how, precisely, he was to be incorporated into the Republic's power structure could not be postponed much longer. This renewed sparring around the House of Orange, combined with the intensifying wrangling over religious toleration, Church authority, and personal liberty, produced a feverish intellectual atmosphere and flurry of key publications.

Besides the Calvinist Orangism of the Voetians, there now also throve a secular, republican Orangism, rebutting the out-and-out republicanism of De la Court, which appeared in its most developed form in Valckenier's *'t Verwerd Europa* (1668). Petrus Valckenier (1638–1712), Dutch resident in Switzerland, agreed that republics were superior to monarchies and that 'freedom' and 'prosperity' were the attributes of republics;[141] but he insisted also on the need for the stadholderate, to lend cohesion. He accepted that toleration was essential but held also that the Holland regents had not been as supportive of the public Church as they should, allowing 'atheism and libertinism' to advance too far.[142] In later editions, he added that De Witt personally bore much of the responsibility for the excessive toleration now prevailing, observing that when the pressure began in the States of Holland, for banning De la Court's uncompromising defence of toleration, the *Aanwysinge*, De Witt had tried to prevent its suppression.

De la Court's *Aanwysinge der heilsame politike Gronden* (1669), a reworked version of the *Interest van Holland*, was banned by the States of Holland, in May 1669, at the request of the South Holland Synod, for its criticism of the public Church and uncompromising plea for the 'free practice of all religions and sects'.[143] But the work infuriated Orangists, as well as Voetians, containing an intensified attack on the stadholderate and many remarks linking Orangism with the intolerance of the militant Calvinists. As part of his campaign to discredit the Voetian wing of the Church, De la Court highlighted the antagonism between William the Silent and the Calvinists, during the Revolt, and reminded readers that the Calvinist orthodox had aligned with Leicester.[144] In any case, toleration was essential, he held, to stimulate the immigration so urgently needed to sustain the economy and population of Holland's cities.[145]

That intolerance and Calvinist orthodoxy were a danger to the true interests of 'Holland', and had always been the political ally of the House of Orange, De la Court's message, spread also through various anonymous

[141] Valckenier, *'t Verwerd Europa*, 16–19, 116–17.
[142] Ibid. 228–9, 236, 249.
[143] Rees, *Verhandeling*, 41–2; Japikse, *Johan de Witt*, 278–9.
[144] De la Court, *Aanwysinge*, 399–400.
[145] Ibid. 60, 65–6, 382, 398.

tracts published in the late 1660s by committed republicans. One such derided the Zeelanders' complaint that Holland had become too tolerant, holding that 'no Hollander need feel ashamed that his province is alleged' to be a 'free province where not only all Christians enjoy freedom but also the Jews, Persians, and Turks, who come here—that is our glory'; it was entitled (recollection of the Buat affair still being vivid) *Den Zeeuwsen Buatist* (1668), thereby postulating a link, in the mind of the public, between intolerance, Orangism, and Calvinist orthodoxy, on the one side, and treachery on the other.[146]

But by far the most devastating critique of intolerance and ecclesiastical power was, of course, Spinoza's *Tractatus Theologico-Politicus* (1670), a work of crucial importance in Dutch and European history, not only for the radical character of its biblical criticism, uncompromising republicanism, and the force of its attack on Church authority but also because of the marked democratic tinge which Dutch republicanism here assumes. Spinoza's contention that 'democracy is of all forms of government the most natural and most consonant with individual liberty', and generally the most apt to generate the 'benefits of freedom in a state',[147] was integrally linked to his defence of toleration and attack on Church authority. For Spinoza grasped that concepts of the State not based on promoting the welfare of the citizenry, and preservation of individual liberty, must rest on an ecclesiastical sanction.

Spinoza's philosophy and biblical criticism were deeply enmeshed in the wider campaign mounted by Dutch radical Cartesians and republicans gathering momentum during the 1660s, and which also now began to clash increasingly with what we may term the élitist, regent republicanism of Grotius, De Witt, and De Groot. The most famous anti-Orangist ideologue of the time, De la Court, was in this context something of an in-between figure, a writer more democratic and opposed to Church authority than the regents but not so democratic, or philosophically systematic, as the radical republicans, an intellectual coterie which crystallized around 1660, first at Amsterdam and soon also at The Hague, Rotterdam, and Leiden around Franciscus van den Enden, Spinoza, and such allies as Lodewijk Meijer, Jan Hendrik Glazemaker (another reputed 'atheist' and the translator of Descartes's works into Dutch), Abraham van Berkel, who translated Hobbes's *Leviathan* into Dutch (a work published in 1667, causing a considerable stir in Holland), and Adriaen Koerbagh, who was arrested for blasphemy after

---

[146] *Den Zeeuwsen Buatist*, 27–8.
[147] Spinoza, *Political Works*, 137.

publishing his *Bloemhof van Allerley Lieflijkheid* (1668) and who died in gaol, in Amsterdam, in 1669.[148]

The oldest member of the group, and after Spinoza the most important, was Franciscus van den Enden (1602–74), an ex-Jesuit from Antwerp who had taken refuge in Amsterdam in the 1640s and who, for many years, earned his bread as a teacher of Latin, one of his pupils being the young Spinoza. According to a report of 1662, Van den Enden was, at that time, regarded as the leader of the philosophical 'atheists' in Amsterdam.[149] His republican tract the *Vrije Politijke Stellingen*, published in 1665, is of great importance because of its intellectual sophistication, its foreshadowing of Spinoza in several respects, and perhaps most of all for its strongly democratic character, this being one of the very earliest systematic statements of democratic republicanism in the western world.[150] For Van den Enden, government should not only be for the good of the citizenry, and based on republican virtues, but should create equality of opportunity and be controlled by the people.[151] Like De la Court and the English classical republicans, Van den Enden was much taken with the formulations of Machiavelli. This remarkable man clashed several times with the regents in Amsterdam and, in 1670, moved to Paris, where he subsequently, in 1673, became involved in a mismanaged conspiracy to rid France of Louis XIV. He was hanged in the Bastille, in 1674, at the age of 72.

In the late 1660s, Spinoza and his circle were undoubtedly ideological and political allies of De Witt and the States party-faction—there was no other strategy open to them—but, at the same time, they clearly desired to go much further towards undermining Church authority, and broadening toleration and individual liberty, than was prudent for the regents to contemplate. Consequently, few if any regents approved of their views and a tension developed which focused on practical points, such as book censorship, as well as profound philosophical issues. De Witt and his regent allies were trying to broaden freedom of the press and liberalize book censorship up to a point. But, equally, they were determined to draw a line beyond which intellectual enquiry—as well as criticism of the regents and sexual libertinism—must not penetrate. De Witt tried to prevent De la Court's *Aanwysinge* being banned but failed. Koerbagh was severely dealt with; but then he had blatantly overstepped the mark regarding blasphemy. But Meijer's critique (see pp. 918–19 below), more discreetly worded (albeit

---

[148] Meinsma, *Spinoza en zijn kring*, 317–19.
[149] Klever, 'Inleiding', 27.
[150] Ibid. 86–109.
[151] Van den Enden, *Vrije Politijke Stellingen*, 207–15.

published in both Latin and Dutch), was not banned and nor, as yet, was the Dutch edition of Hobbes. For Spinoza, the great tactical question of the 1660s was how to deliver his intended supreme blow against the scriptural basis of Church authority, and constraining of individual liberty, without his work being banned by the secular authorities and attracting a general hue and cry. He had laboured on his *Tractatus* since the early 1660s, or earlier, and shown the manuscript on occasion to various liberal, republican-minded regents (including Adriaen Paets) who, however, were far from eager to see it published.[152] For years, Spinoza held back, encountering only discouragement from his regent friends, acutely aware that the public reaction could severely harm, rather than further, his cause. His finally taking the plunge, in 1670, may well have been prompted by his anger at the treatment meted out to Koerbagh;[153] certainly, the famous words of his preface, proclaiming the 'rare happiness of living in [the United Provinces] where everyone's judgment is free and unshackled, where each may worship God as his conscience dictates and where freedom is esteemed above all things dear and precious', were meant in some degree ironically or even sarcastically.[154] Spinoza's chief objective in the *Tractatus* is to demonstrate that the combination of theological zeal and ecclesiastical power which destroyed the Oldenbarnevelt regime (an episode to which he alludes in the closing sections)[155]—and which now threatens the De Witt regime and the advance of philosophical enquiry—is spuriously based and that its scriptural foundations ought not to be respected. Thus, the same freedom which protects toleration and individual liberty ensures legitimate government. 'Not only can such freedom be granted without prejudice to the public peace,' he assures his audience, 'but also without such freedom piety cannot thrive nor the public peace be secure.'[156]

Spinoza published his sensational book in 1670, following a careful strategy. The book was published anonymously and he took steps to ensure that the work should be confined to Latin only, for it was clear from the experiences of Meijer, Koerbagh, and others that the authorities would stomach bolder contentions in Latin than in Dutch. When he discovered, in February 1671, that an unknown translator was preparing a Dutch edition for publication, without his permission, he implored one of his allies to help trace and stop the translator, explaining that 'this is not my request

[152] Roldanus, 'Adriaen Paets', 159.
[153] Meinsma, *Spinoza en zijn kring*, 317–26.
[154] Spinoza, *Tractatus Theologico-Politicus*, 51; Francès, *Spinoza*, 61.
[155] Spinoza, *Tractatus Theologico-Politicus*, 297.
[156] Ibid. 6–7.

only but also that of many of my good friends who would not like to see the book prohibited, as will, without doubt, happen, if it is published in Dutch'.[157] Spinoza asked help to block the Dutch edition not only for his own sake but that of 'our cause'. Prohibition of books in the Dutch Republic may not have eradicated sales but it certainly blighted the status and reputation of both book and author in respectable society.[158] That the text remained confined to Latin was essential to Spinoza's political-philosophical strategy.

Among leading republican regents who edged further than De Witt in forming links with republican writers, and opponents of the public Church, were Pieter de Groot, Adriaen Paets, Coenraad van Beuningen, and the Utrecht philosopher-regent Lambert van Velthuysen. De Groot was close to De la Court both before and after 1672, when both men took refuge in Antwerp. Van Beuningen came from a strongly pro-Remonstrant background, was an admirer of Erasmus, Coornhert, and Grotius, a well-known defender of free enquiry in theology, friend of the Collegiants (like Paets and Spinoza), and a devotee of Cartesian philosophy.[159] Van Velthuysen was also a keen Cartesian, defender of toleration, and foe of ecclesiastical power.

Yet all these men were intensely aware of the dangers of the path along which De la Court, the radical Cartesians and Spinozists were advancing. De Groot did more than De Witt to assist De la Court in his battles with the Leiden consistory but also restrained him and expurgated his work. Van Beuningen shrank from too open a display of radical ideas. Paets and Van Velthuysen were veteran ideologues of the States party-faction and champions of toleration and the new philosophy. But they were also deeply uneasy at the new, more radical intellectual tendencies emerging in Holland in the late 1660s. When the Rotterdam Collegiant preacher Jacob Ostens (1630–78), an Anabaptist surgeon and suspected Socinian, close to the republican regents of Rotterdam,[160] and a fierce anti-Orangist, wrote to Van Velthuysen in 1671, asking his opinion of the *Tractatus*, the Utrecht regent (who had, for decades, battled against Voetian influence) penned a vigorous critique, denouncing the book as a work which 'abolishes and absolutely subverts all worship and religion and clandestinely introduces atheism'.[161] Ostens then sent Van Velthuysen's reply to Spinoza, with whom he was friendly and who indignantly compared Van Velthuysen's rebuff with Voetius' assault on Descartes.

[157] Spinoza, *Correspondence*, 260–1.
[158] Groenveld, 'The Mecca of Authors?', 72–3.
[159] Roldanus, *Coenraad van Beuningen*, 156–7.
[160] Van Bunge, 'Rotterdamsche collegiant', 74.
[161] Spinoza, *Correspondence*, 253–4.

All along De Witt had sought to curb radical manifestations of Socinianism, Cartesianism, and republicanism, so as to protect, and nurture, the
essential core of the 'True Freedom'. Open expression of extreme ideas
could only undermine stability, and the regime, and, in the end, destroy
'freedom' itself. At the same time, defending stability and the regime, as well
as freedom, depended, no less, on neutralizing the upsurge of Orangism in
alliance with Voetian orthodoxy. To achieve this he had somehow to
accommodate Orange within a power structure controlled by the Holland
regents which would placate the Orangists while simultaneously precluding
all prospect of restoration of the stadholderate. In the long run the 'True
Freedom' could survive only if the political and ideological tension which
had so long permeated the body politic, church affairs, universities, and
intellectual life was neutralized.

In the final years of his regime, De Witt's quest for political stability under
the leadership of the Holland regents centred around his 'great concept of
harmony'.[162] This was a formula whereby the young prince would be
assigned a seat in the *Raad van State*, a special position in the state, and the
eventual likelihood of being appointed captain-general but only on the basis
of exclusion from the stadholderate of every province.

In the version of the 'Harmony' laid before the States of Holland, in July
1667, the Prince was deemed insufficiently prepared for the captaincy-
general until he had reached 23, rather than 18 (or one year on), as the
Orangists were insisting. But the key feature of the 'Harmony', as it evolved
in Holland, was the celebrated additional clause which abolished the
stadholderate in the province for ever. This addendum, introduced—in
one of the supreme ironies of the Republic's history—not by De Witt but
by Caspar Fagel, Pensionary of Haarlem, and Gillis Valckenier, later key
figures in William III's regime, nevertheless came to be regarded as the
constitutional centrepiece of De Witt's 'True Freedom'.[163] In the summer of
1667, the Orangists were still in eclipse and there was scant opposition
to the measure in the States of Holland. In their deliberations, on 2 August,
the Leiden city council noted gloomily that while a few other towns—
Enkhuizen, Alkmaar, Schoonhoven, and Edam—were unenthusiastic, only
Leiden categorically opposed abolition of the stadholderate on principle.[164]

The 'Perpetual Edict . . . for the Preserving of Freedom', as the law was
entitled, was duly passed and promulgated. Its three chief points were
abolition of the stadholderate, permanent separation of the captaincy-

---

[162] Japikse, *Johan de Witt*, 287–8; Rowen, *John de Witt*, 788–92.
[163] Geyl, *Studies en strijdschriften*, 141.
[164] GA Leiden Sec. Arch. 453. res. vroed. 2 Aug. 1667.

general from the stadholderate of all provinces, and the transfer of the political functions of the Stadholder of Holland to the provincial States.[165] A few Orangist towns, notably Leiden, fought a lengthy rearguard action against the new oath for civic office-holders, in Holland, introduced together with the abolition of the stadholderate, by which civic office-holders swore to uphold the 'Perpetual Edict'. Here there was, indeed, a vital principle at stake. The doctrine of Grotius, Graswinckel, and De Witt held that the States were absolutely sovereign within the province and could therefore bind magistrates and other office-holders to uphold the basic principles of the state. But Orangists rejected this notion of the full sovereignty of the States not only with respect to the Generality but also the lower authorities within the province. Leiden argued that the States were not fully sovereign but representatives of the *ridderschap* and towns wherein provincial sovereignty ultimately lay. This meant, according to the Leiden *vroedschap*, that the deputies to the States were only spokesmen for their 'principals' in the town councils and could not therefore exercise sovereign authority over them.[166]

The Perpetual Edict of 1667 came to be seen by writers, poets, and artists, as well as regents, as the supreme embodiment, and crown, of the 'True Freedom'. One enthusiast was the Rotterdam Collegiant poet Joachim Oudaan (1628–92), an admirer of De Witt, Paets, and Ostens, who wrote a jubilant eulogy entitled 'Freedom established on its throne'.[167] Extolling the Perpetual Edict went hand in hand with celebrating the recently concluded peace of Breda, another of Oudaan's themes, for the peace seemingly ended England's former role in Dutch domestic politics, making possible a more definite curtailment of the stadholderate than had been possible, previously, at any point since the Stuart Restoration of 1660. Oudaan also eulogized Pieter de Groot, publishing a poem to mark the latter's arrival in his new post, as pensionary of Rotterdam, in 1670, as embodying the triumph of the States party in the city and return of Grotius' 'principles of freedom'.

By January 1668, Utrecht, Gelderland, and Overijssel, as well as Holland, accepted the 'Harmony' and it passed, by four provinces to three, in the States General. But, during the course of 1668, De Witt's position weakened again, leaving various matters connected with the 'Harmony' unresolved, including that of whether the Prince was to have a merely advisory, or 'conclusive', vote in the *Raad van State*. In Overijssel the split between Orangists and States party-faction produced an outburst of renewed turmoil

---

[165] *Perpetual Edict*, clauses 1–3.
[166] GA Leiden Sec. Arch. 454, fos. 33–4. res. vroed. 30 Dec. 1667.
[167] Melles, *Joachim Oudaan*, 76–9.

reminiscent of that of 1653–7. The Prince was now approaching his eighteenth birthday, and legal majority, and this, in itself, heightened tension as his advisers and supporters encouraged him to build his influence and manœuvre for position. Friction developed also between out-and-out republicans and States party pragmatists inclined to veer as the Prince gained ground. A small incident redolent of what was to come enlivened a dinner party held in the castle of a Utrecht nobleman, in 1668, at which all four Amsterdam burgomasters were present.[168] In the midst of the repast, William III unexpectedly arrived in person. Three of the burgomasters, including Gillis Valckenier, hastened to their feet, raising their glasses and declaring themselves the Prince's 'servants', while the fourth, Cornelis van Vlooswijck (1601–87), a more principled republican, adroitly extricated himself from his predicament by courteously explaining that, had he also declared himself the Prince's 'obedient servant', he would have meant it sincerely.

Even before December 1668, the Prince and his entourage began acting as if he had already reached his majority. In September, he travelled to Zeeland where he was fêted by the States and received the title of 'First Noble of Zeeland'. He named the son of Beverweert, Willem Adriaen, heer van Odijk, to act as his proxy in the States of Zeeland and cast the now restored seventh vote. In October 1668, the Princess Dowager formally laid down her guardianship. Holland, however, denied that the Prince had yet reached his majority, keeping him out of his designated seat, in the *Raad van State*, through 1669, despite the protests especially of the Frisians and Zeelanders.

Gradually, as both the external peril and internal rift, over relations with France, intensified, De Witt's position weakened. The Amsterdam *vroedschap*, split between pragmatists and republicans, was led by Valckenier and Van Beuningen into a tactical alliance with the Orangists to change the direction of policy towards France, strengthen the Republic's military alliances, and compromise with the Prince. In May 1670, it was settled that the latter would take his seat in the *Raad van State* with a 'conclusive' vote. As Orange gained, and he lost, ground, De Witt strove to win Valckenier and Van Beuningen back into his own camp. When this failed, and the break between him and Valckenier became open, he worked to unseat them and, initially, seemed to be successful in doing so. In the Amsterdam municipal elections of February 1671, Valckenier and Van Beuningen lost and the hard-core republican faction of Andries de Graeff and van

---

[168] *Briefwisseling van Reede van Amerongen*, 114.

Vlooswijck gained control.[169] But with the *vroedschap* deeply divided, this, in itself, did little to bolster De Witt's deteriorating position.

The growing threat of war with France, by late 1671, stirred a powerful new movement in the provinces for the appointment of the Prince of Orange as captain and admiral-general. Enkhuizen proposed this in the States of Holland on 4 December. Most of the provinces voted in favour over the next few days. De Witt tried at first to block the proposal outright, arguing that such an appointment would violate the Perpetual Edict, since the Prince already held high political office as a member of the *Raad van State*. Then, seeing he could not prevent it, De Witt supported a proposal for a temporary appointment, for the coming campaign season only, rejecting the captaincy-general for life urged by the Orangists. The issue of whether to nominate the Prince captain-general 'ad tempus' or 'ad vitam' was furiously debated in the provincial assemblies; the States of Utrecht,[170] like most of the other lesser provinces, voted for the latter during December. Following this the States General, in January 1672, asked Holland to conform with the majority of provinces and proclaim the Prince permanent captain-general. Holland, still dominated by the States party, with Dordrecht and Delft the most obdurately anti-Orangist, refused, offering the Prince a temporary appointment only.[171] But this the Prince declined. The deadlock continued for a few more weeks; but finally, with the external situation continually worsening, Holland yielded. On 24 February 1672, the States General formally appointed the Prince of Orange captain and admiral-general, albeit under strict supervision by the Generality's 'deputies in the field'.[172]

This settled, minds turned to the Republic's ominous situation and to strategy. The Republic's position was now so perilous that virtually no potential allies were willing to lend support. The army was seriously under strength and most fortifications in a lamentable state of disrepair. In the key garrisons on the IJssel and Rhine, troop-strength, stores, and morale were all disastrously low. The VOC share price at Amsterdam plunged even before the French and English declarations of war, in April, though they staged a tiny rally in May when letters from London revealed that Charles II's alliance with France was unpopular in England. The regents became locked in discussion during these spring months of 1672, as to whether it was better to divert men and resources to construct an additional, inner, line of defence, running via Utrecht and the Vecht, to Naarden, or else stake

[169] Porta, *Joan en Gerrit Corver*, 6.
[170] *Briefwisseling van Reede van Amerongen*, 78.
[171] Japikse, *Johan de Witt*, 311.
[172] Van der Hoeven, *Leeven en Dood*, 324–7.

everything on the IJssel line. No one yet suspected the situation was so grave that both the IJssel line and the Vecht were about to fall, with scarcely a struggle, into the hands of Louis XIV.

31

1672: Year of Disaster

❖

The year 1672 was the most traumatic of the Dutch Golden Age. It was a year of military collapse, of almost complete demoralization, the moment when the overthrow of the Republic, if not in its entirety, then certainly as a major power, seemed at hand. It was the year of the greatest crash on the Amsterdam Exchange of early modern times, paralysing Dutch commerce and finance, the year when public building ceased and the art market withered, with consequences for art, artists, and architecture noticeable for decades to come. It was also a year of sensational domestic political events and feverish ideological conflict. Finally, it was the year when the common populace and militias intervened in the political process, and ideological warfare, more extensively than at any time since the 1580s, with lasting consequences for political and social life.

The full gravity of the threat to the prosperity, independence, and very existence of the Republic became clear only in March 1672, a month after William III's elevation to the captaincy-general. It emerged that Louis had formed a coalition which ringed the Republic and was about to attack with overwhelming superiority of force. The Republic was on the point of being invaded and blockaded, its trade and fisheries ravaged, its territory dismembered. On 23 March, without warning, the English navy descended on the returning Dutch Levant convoy, off the Isle of Wight. For two days guns thundered ominously in the Channel, signifying that England was joining France in the onslaught, in resumption of her quest to capture control of the seas and commercial hegemony. Louis declared war, publishing remarkably vague grievances,[1] on 6 April; England followed. In May, Louis led his army, the largest and best in Europe, across the Spanish Netherlands towards Maastricht. At this point, it was still unclear whether the main invasion would come from the south or from the east, along the Rhine valley. Louis crossed the Maas north of Maastricht on 22 May. As he

---

[1] Sonnino, *Louis XIV and the Origins*, 192.

advanced, the prince-bishop of Münster declared war on the Republic, on 18 May, the Elector of Cologne shortly after.

Louis XIV's invasion army, without counting the troops of Münster and Cologne, deployed further north, amounted to 118,000 infantry and 12,500 cavalry, outnumbering the then Dutch regular army by four to one. Besides this, the Dutch soldiery was qualitatively inferior, and dangerously dispersed around the defensive ring. Emergency steps were taken, during May, to raise several thousand civic militiamen in Holland, and Utrecht, and rush them to stiffen the garrisons to the south and east. The States of Gelderland tried to raise 3,000 armed burghers, within their province, to bolster the frontier strongholds. But it was all too little too late.

It was decided also to bring out the war fleet and try to strike at the English before the French could join them. De Ruyter was too late to prevent the French, under the comte d'Estrées, with thirty-six ships, mounting 11,000 men and 1,926 guns, joining the English fleet, under the king's younger brother, James, duke of York. The Dutch were now heavily outmatched in weight of ships and fire-power. Nevertheless, De Ruyter and the States General plenipotentiary, Cornelis de Witt, concluded they had no alternative but to attack. It was a brave decision which led to one of the most critical battles of the Anglo-Dutch Wars, off the English east coast, in Solebay, on 6 June. De Ruyter's victory was not decisive. But the Dutch reduced Charles's flagship, the *Royal James* (100 guns), to a burning wreck and damaged enough of the other English 'first rates' to prevent a full-scale descent on the Republic, from the sea, during the ensuing months.[2] On De Ruyter's return to port, most of the fleet's seamen and troops were rushed to various strongholds to reinforce the land defences.

The main land offensive developed on the lower Rhine early in June. The Dutch garrisons in Cleves—Rheinberg, Orsoy, Emmerich, Rees, and Wesel—having defied Spain for decades, fell to Louis in under a week. These towns were never to return to Dutch control, reverting subsequently to Brandenburg.[3] The Munsterites simultaneously overran Lingen, invaded Overijssel, and joined the French in besieging Grol, which fell on 9 June. The French stormed across the Rhine at Lobith, south of Arnhem, on 12 June, under the eyes of Louis, the Dutch losing 1,500 men killed and wounded in the battle. With the French across, in the Betuwe, the IJssel line was effectively outflanked. The States of Holland and States General decided to abandon the IJssel, pull the depleted army back, and stake all on the defence of Holland, Zeeland, and Utrecht. Substantial garrisons still

---

[2] Boxer, *The Anglo-Dutch Wars*, 47–8. [3] Bannier, *Landgrenzen*, 306.

manned the great strongholds along the eastern frontier. But morale had disintegrated. As the French approached Arnhem, the citizenry rioted, refusing to try to hold the town.[4] The city capitulated, without a fight, on 15 June.

The army entrenched on the IJssel, having been ordered to retreat, some 9,000 men marched overland to Utrecht; the rest were shipped, from Overijssel, across the Zuider Zee. The French advanced rapidly behind them entering Amersfoort on 19 June. The collapse in civilian morale seriously hampered defensive operations also in Utrecht. The citizenry rioted, on 15 June, and took over the city, refusing to permit preparations for a siege. Having unsuccessfully tried to rally the city, Orange had no choice but to order a further retreat, towards the so-called five posts, selected as the pivots for the defence of Holland. The French army entered Utrecht, in triumph, on 23 June; the same day Munsterite and French troops captured Zwolle and Kampen.

The Utrecht city council resolved on a policy of submission and non-provocation. They instructed the consistory, a bulwark of Voetian orthodoxy, still dominated by Voetius in person, to discontinue the special services being recited in the churches, for the preservation of the state and success of its arms.[5] The Utrecht regents also ordered the consistory, and preachers, to be extremely prudent, in preaching, and on no account incite the people against the French, but rather instil 'steadfastness of faith, godliness, and obedience to the authorities'.[6] Cardinal de Bouillon, the most senior ecclesiastic accompanying Louis, fresh from inaugurating the main church of Arnhem, for Catholic worship, on 9 July celebrated the first Catholic mass held in Utrecht cathedral since the 1570s. As in Arnhem, and indeed all the occupied towns, Louis granted freedom of worship to the Reformed, and their retaining most churches, but assigned the principal church to the Catholics, who likewise now enjoyed full freedom of worship. The Munsterites had already reinaugurated the churches of Grol and Bredevoort for Catholic worship, before the end of June.[7]

Holland was saved, initially, by sheer luck, and subsequently, by effectively inundating the stretch of terrain, the so-called water-line, running from Muiden, in front of Amsterdam, on the Zuider Zee, via Bodegraven (where the Prince established his headquarters), and Schoonhoven, to Gorcum, on the Waal. At first, the Republic's last line of defence was in a state of

---

[4] Kotte, 'Gelderse bloem', 52–3.
[5] GA Utrecht kerkeraad res. 17 June 1672.
[6] Ibid., res. 20 June 1672.
[7] Kohl, *Christoph Bernhard von Galen*, 362.

hopeless disarray which presented no real obstacle to the French. The castle of Muiden, at the northern end, the last position before Amsterdam, was almost lost without a shot being fired, being completely empty just before the French vanguard arrived—and without Muiden the entire 'water-line' was useless. The ageing Count Johan Maurits rushed troops in with two hours to spare. Over the next fortnight the French could still easily have crossed the 'water-line'; for although the dikes and sluices were opened— after some resistance, particularly around Gorcum, from armed peasants reluctant to see their land ruined—the water level rose only slowly owing to the dry summer weather.

The towns of Holland and Zeeland were gripped by a mixture of fear, pandemonium, and popular fury. The people were incensed with both the army and the regents. There were accusations of scandalous neglect of duty and even blatant treason.[8] The surrender of the stronghold of Schencken-schans, one of the strongest on the lower Rhine, on 21 June, without a shot being fired, was ascribed to its having been placed in the charge of an inexperienced, and drunken, youth, the son of a Nijmegen burgomaster allied with De Witt and the States party. The regents were allegedly going through the motions of preparing the towns for defence, but were not doing so in earnest. At the same time, to provide men for the 'water-line', while simultaneously strengthening the watches on the town gates and walls, and carrying out last-minute repairs, large numbers of additional men were recruited into the civic militias, and hastily armed and drilled.

Defeatism was most pronounced in the towns closest to the enemy, such as Gouda, Leiden, Schoonhoven, and Gorcum, irrespective of whether these were of States party or Orangist allegiance. The Orangist Leiden *vroedschap* were prepared to capitulate to Louis, on whatever terms the Republic could obtain, counting on the mercy of the Prince's uncle, the king of England.[9] The States of Holland, against De Witt's advice, already opened negotiations with Louis before the fall of Utrecht, Pieter de Groot being assigned the role of chief negotiator with the French ministers, Louvois and Pomponne. On returning to The Hague, after the fall of Utrecht, De Groot claimed there was no alternative to surrender and submission to Louis's demands. The Holland *ridderschap* agreed, proposing that the Republic try to keep the Seven Provinces—and the public Church within the provinces— intact, 'letting the rest go', that is, signing away the Generality Lands.[10] Most of the town governments concurred.

[8] Roorda, *Partij en factie*, 100–1.
[9] Vivien and Hop, *Notulen*, 110–11.
[10] Wicquefort, *Histoire*, iv. 424–30.

It was at this point that the role of the common people proved decisive. Protests at the perfunctoriness of the defence, and shortage of arms, began at Dordrecht and developed into riots against the States party regents and in favour of making the Prince Stadholder. The people were stirred up by artisan guild leaders, preachers, and militiamen. Numerous women and girls participated. The unrest soon spread to Rotterdam and Amsterdam. At Rotterdam, the civic militia and populace, aroused against De Groot, Burgomaster van de Aa, and other leaders of the States party-faction, demanded a more resolute defence of the Republic and forced the *vroed-schap*, at gunpoint, to swear that they would not give up the city to the French without the agreement of the whole citizenry.[11] (The Rotterdam city council nevertheless voted, that same day, to send De Groot back to Louis's camp authorized to sign away the Generality Lands.) Even more crucial was the impact of popular intervention, and that of the civic militia, in Amsterdam. Evidently morale among large sections of the Protestant population was firmer than among a considerable portion of the *vroedschap* itself. Whether or not it is precisely true that the *vroedschap* split, in the crucial vote of 26 June, by twenty votes to sixteen, in favour of sending De Groot back to capitulate to Louis, but that the minority, led by Valckenier, reversed this decision by threatening to call in the militia, it is certain that the *vroedschap* was deeply divided and that the vote to break off talks with the French, and fight, was carried owing to pressure from the militia and populace.[12] The agitation in Amsterdam, as in the other towns, continued day after day.[13] Valckenier became the hero of the city not because he was regarded as an Orangist but because he stood for going on with the war. His rival, Burgomaster de Graeff, was threatened with mob violence, being regarded as a key States party figure and suspected of defeatism, the two being linked in the mind of the populace.

The vote of 26 June in the States General, when four provinces—Holland, Utrecht, Gelderland, and Overijssel, only one of which was still resisting the enemy—ignoring the protests of Zeeland and Friesland, and in the absence of Groningen, resolved to send back De Groot to sign away the Generality Lands and offer a large war indemnity, made an abject impression, further inflaming popular indignation. As it happened, Louis was unimpressed also, and, on Louvois's advice, sent De Groot back empty-handed, pronouncing the regents' offer insufficient, demanding besides much of the Nijmegen quarter and public toleration of the Catholic faith throughout the Republic.

[11] Roorda, *Partij en factie*, 114.
[12] Salomons, 'Rol van de Amsterdamse burgerbeweging', 206–8.
[13] 'Een dagboek', 51–4.

The populace were now thoroughly aroused. In Amsterdam, there was further popular pressure, through June and July, but mostly without the unruly scenes, and sporadic violence, which marked the disturbances elsewhere.[14] By contrast at Dordrecht, where, as at Rotterdam, popular fury with the regents was especially intense, there were massive demonstrations which soon compelled the *vroedschap* to agree to vote to set aside the Perpetual Edict and elevate the Prince to the stadholderate.[15] On 29 June, serious rioting erupted in Schiedam, Rotterdam, Gouda, and Delft. At Schiedam, Orangist banners were unfurled, the streets filled with demonstrators, and Burgomaster Willem Nieuwpoort (who, together with Van Beverningk, had negotiated the undertaking to enact the Exclusion of 1654) was attacked and beaten. At Rotterdam, crowds denounced the six 'traitors' who wanted to hand the country over to the French—Pieter de Groot, Willem van de Aa, Johan Pesser, Arent Sonmans, Willem Bisscop, and Adriaen Vroesen. Again women played a notable part in the disturbances,[16] as did the militia who closed the city gates against a force of cavalry, sent by the States of Holland, to restore order. The homes of Burgomasters van der Aa and Sonmans were plundered. Here too, the main cry was for setting aside the Perpetual Edict and elevation of the Prince.

At Gouda, furious peasants, whose land had been flooded, joined with artisans, and working women, to take control of the streets; the Prince came in person to persuade the peasants to leave. Delft was also seized by a combination of women, workmen, and peasants, stiffened with out-of-work fishermen pouring in from Schiedam and Delftshaven.[17] The crowds swamped the town hall, forcing the regents to set aside the Perpetual Edict and vote for restoration of the stadholderate. There was unrest also at Haarlem (where the opulent house of a cousin of De Witt, Van Sypestein, was pillaged), Leiden, and Monnikendam. In several small towns, such as Hoorn, Gorcum, Purmerend, and Brill, the *vroedschap* was compelled to renounce the Perpetual Edict by the militia alone, without popular intervention. There were also riots in Zeeland, at Middelburg, Flushing, and Veere.

Populace and militia had often played a part in the past, notably in 1566, 1572, 1576–7, the 1580s, and 1617–18. But 1672 was different. This was the first time widespread unrest, encouraged by political agitators, shaped events in a sustained fashion, over a period of months. Of course, both main party-factions in Dutch life were undemocratic in that they saw no regular place for the people, or militias, in provincial or civic politics. Nevertheless,

[14] Ibid. 206–9.
[15] Van Dalen, *Gesch. van Dordrecht*, ii. 1137–8.
[16] Roorda, *Partij en factie*, 107, 162.

the pamphlet literature of 1672, and subsequent party-faction propaganda, show that there was a difference of attitude, between the blocs, towards the people. The States party-faction stressed the absolute authority of the States, deploring any constraint on the sway of the regents, whether from the Generality, or from below. States party writers subsequently condemned the popular movement of 1672 as something illegitimate, and dangerous, often with some allusion to Middelburg being taken over by peasants and Delft by 'fishermen'.[18] By contrast, Orangist publicists styled the populace 'true patriots', an invaluable check (on occasion) to regent presumption, hinting that, at least in emergency situations, popular intervention did not lack legitimacy. For it was the people who made the Prince Stadholder in July 1672, transforming the structure of power.

Zeeland made William III Stadholder on 2 July. The next day, thoroughly intimidated, the States of Holland set aside the Perpetual Edict and proclaimed Orange Stadholder of Holland. Six days later William took the required oath. The disturbances continued, however, especially at Dordrecht and at Rotterdam, where De Groot and Adriaen Vroesen were threatened by the mob. De Groot moved about under militia guard, and a guard was placed at his house; even so, his position became impossible and, later in the month, he fled to Antwerp.[19] On 11 July riots erupted at Zierikzee and Tholen in which, again, fishermen and peasants, streaming in from outside, played a large part.[20] The Zierikzee regents were compelled to follow Tholen and Goes and allow representatives of the guilds and consistory to sit in and observe what was said in meetings of the *vroedschap*.

For a few days after becoming Stadholder, the Prince supported the sitting town governments, trying to calm the unrest. But it soon emerged that restoration of the stadholderate, and the decision to go on with the war, and wage it more vigorously, were only part of what the adherents of 'Prince and Fatherland' were pressing for. Popular Orangist ideology ruled the streets, an ideology which condemned the 'Louvestein faction' as 'traitors' and enemies of the public Church, champions of toleration for Catholics and dissenters, who had abandoned Brazil and committed innumerable other crimes against the 'Fatherland'. The flood of printed pamphlets circulating during July and August 1672 condemning the persons and principles of the 'Loevestein faction' shows that the political impulse behind the popular movement went far deeper than a mere desire for the elevation

[17] Wagenaar, *Vad. Hist.* xiv. 79.
[18] Van der Hoeven, *Hollands aeloude vryheid*, ii. 376.
[19] Melles, *Ministers aan de Maas*, 129.
[20] Vos, *Vroedschap van Zierikzee*, p. xlv; Roorda, *Partij en factie*, 129–30.

of Orange. Militias and guilds wanted changes in the character of civic government.[21]

The return of Jan Kievit to Rotterdam was greeted with rowdy enthusiasm, in the city, and followed by further attacks on the houses of unpopular regents. The Rotterdam militia began pressing for the purging of nine States party regents from the *vroedschap*. There were more disturbances at Dordrecht, with the homes of two leading States party regents being sacked. During the third week of July, the Prince ceased supporting the sitting magistracies, motivated possibly more by anxiety to restore order quickly, without diverting troops, than desire for revenge. At Amsterdam there were further disturbances early in August, with the civic militia showing itself more and more antagonistic to the 'Loevestein faction', who were still the majority in the *vroedschap* if one counted both the De Graeff and Hooft factions as 'Loevesteiners'.

The resurgence of unrest reached its peak in late August and early September. De Witt had ceased playing an active role in events since he was wounded in a knife attack, at The Hague, on 21 June. He laid down his office as Pensionary of Holland on 4 August, 'all his vast plans in ruin, the principles of his conduct of affairs destroyed, and amid a change of scene so bewildering that he could only play the part of a mute or fool where once he had led the company'.[22]

In rioting at The Hague, on 20 August, De Witt and his brother, Cornelis, were caught by an angry crowd which included a number of militiamen, outside the prison, opposite the Binnenhof. They were beaten, stabbed, and shot to death. The corpses were dragged to a nearby scaffold and pulled up by the feet to be displayed to the people, and then mutilated, parts being roasted and eaten in a frenzy of cannibalistic hatred. The brothers De Witt were dead. But, as one observer noted, amid it all, order was 'maintained amidst disorder'. No one else appears to have been killed at The Hague and it is an astonishing fact that, throughout the months of disorder affecting most of the Holland and Zeeland towns, only a handful of people were killed and that the violence, on the whole, was both carefully directed and restrained.

The slaughter of the brothers De Witt lent new impetus to the popular movement throughout Holland. Backed by large demonstrations, the Rotterdam militia captains forced the convening of the *vroedschap*, on 22 August, and removal of the remaining 'traitors'.[23] The men purged by the militia—Van der Aa, Bisschop, Pesser, Paets, and Vroesen—were

[21] Kurtz, *Haarlem in het rampjaar*, 7.   [22] Wicquefort, 'Mémoire', 285–6.

undoubtedly supporters of De Witt and his regime, but were also regarded as the defenders of toleration and chief protectors of the Collegiants, Remonstrants, and other dissenters. Fearful of being attacked, the Collegiants suspended their gatherings for several weeks. After consulting the Prince, the *vroedschap* vacancies were filled with avowed Orangists and orthodox Calvinists.

On 27 August the States of Holland empowered the Stadholder to 'persuade, dispose, and, if necessary, oblige' such changes in the town councils as he should deem necessary to restore order. The Prince delegated this task to two close confidants, his treasurer, Johan Wierts, and a member of the Hof of Holland, Albrecht Nierop. It was during the days just before the main series of purges—between 5 and 8 September—that the popular movement reached its climax with a series of massive demonstrations at Delft, Leiden, Haarlem, and Amsterdam. These largely non-violent insurrections demanded the purging of the 'Loevestein faction' from public life but also presented the town councils with mass petitions, or 'requests of the burghers', ranging over a variety of issues.[24] These 'requests' were, in part, political. Those who convened the burgher and militia meetings which drew up the petitions, mostly professional men—lawyers, printers, or, like the Amsterdam writer Abraham Poot, doctors—aspired to tie regent government more closely to certain attitudes among the middling strata of the citizenry. They demanded restoration of the ancient privileges, and independence, of the civic militias,[25] regarding these as the principal check on regent power, and mouthpiece for the citizenry as a whole, which, in the past, had rightly wielded influence in city government, not least in Amsterdam, in 1578, when the militias had taken the lead in changing the *vroedschap* and giving Amsterdam its Reformed character. Here was that hint of democratic tendencies which, by 1672, was an integral feature of Dutch Orangism.

Some of the 'requests' also confirm the importance of confessional attitudes, and church politics, in shaping the popular movement. At Amsterdam, as at Rotterdam, many leading States party figures had been cool towards the Reformed Church and, during the 1660s, Collegiants and other dissenters had gained ground and more freedom. The petitioners wanted more firm Calvinists in the town councils and more Reformed content in town government. The printer of several of the Rotterdam

---

[23] *Den Oprechten Patriot*, app.

[24] Kurtz, *Haarlem in het rampjaar*, 24–34.

[25] Ibid.; GA Delft vroed. res. 5, fos. 88v, 89v. res. vroed. 30 Aug. 1672; GA Leiden Sec. Arch. 445, fos. 73, 75. res. 6 and 11 Sept. 1672.

Orangist-Voetian pamphlets, and requests, was Johannes Borstius, son of the preacher who was one of the chief instigators of agitation in the city.

The purges carried out under the Prince's direction attracted much attention during September 1672. The process began at Dordrecht, on 9 September, fourteen out of the forty members of the *vroedschap* being replaced. These included those who had been particular targets of popular denunciation but by no means all those who had supported the previous regime. At Delft, the next day, half of the *vroedschap* of forty were changed. At Amsterdam, also on 10 September, ten members of the thirty-six were replaced. These did not include Valckenier and others who had jumped on the Orangist bandwagon in the summer of 1672, nor some moderate republicans, but only the out-and-out republicans of the De Graeff faction.[26] At Leiden and Haarlem there was relatively little to do, only five regents in the first case, and one in the second, being removed. At Gouda, too, the purge was relatively light, only six *vroedschap* members being changed.

The removal of republican regents took place also in the smaller Holland towns, though not in all cases. At Brill, eight out of eighteen *vroedschap* members were changed, at Schoonhoven, nine. At Hoorn, too, the purge was extensive, but, at Purmerend, even though the militia drew up a petition, demanding that personages 'who followed the maxims of Mr Jan de Witt' should not continue in the *vroedschap*, the Stadholder made no change.[27] At Monnikendam, among the most embattled of the small towns, the Prince removed twelve regents. But at Schiedam, also a town where there was much disturbance, only Burgomaster Nieuwpoort was replaced.

In several Zeeland towns there were extensive purges in response to a widespread movement of popular protest. At Zierikzee, long a centre of States party-faction sentiment, eight regents were changed by the Stadholder, at the prompting of the militia. By contrast, at Middelburg, the purge resulted not from the Stadholder's intervention but directly by pressure of the guilds, which were traditionally stronger there than in the Holland towns; seven regents were removed, by guild pressure, despite the Prince's disapproval of the way that this was effected.[28]

No less significant than the question of who was removed was that of whom the Prince put in. Here a distinction has to be made between Amsterdam and other towns. For at Amsterdam, there was no Orangist bloc, and there it was less Orange than Valckenier who selected the new men; six of the newcomers at Amsterdam, including Valckenier's protégé,

---

Louis Trip, were élite merchants.[29] But elsewhere, the purges led to ideological change and the strengthening of the Prince's authority. In Rotterdam, a city where, as in Utrecht and Leiden, ideological pressures were acute,[30] the new men were, reportedly, less wealthy than those they had supplanted, but tended to be zealous Orangists and Voetians, among them the former conspirator Johan Kievit, who now became town pensionary in place of De Groot. From 1672 onwards, for many years, Rotterdam remained under the sway of the Orangist-Voetian bloc. Dordrecht, too, now remained subservient to the Prince for a considerable period. Everywhere the republicans, the 'Louvestein faction', subsided into defeat and humiliation.

[29] Edwards, 'Amsterdam City Government', 6.   [30] Price, *Holland*, 79–80.

32

The Stadholderate of William III, 1672–1702

❖

FROM THE 'YEAR OF DISASTER' TO THE PEACE OF NIJMEGEN, 1672–1678

The catastrophe of June 1672 was followed by further defeats. In July, the French captured Nijmegen, and part of north Brabant, whilst the Munsterites overran Coevorden, Drenthe, and much of Groningen. By late summer, the greater part of the Republic was in French, or Munsterite, hands and the rest gripped by riots and political turmoil. The only province both unoccupied and untouched by rioting was Friesland. But even there there was profound unease, voiced especially by the Reformed preachers. The purging of *Arminianen*, as they were still commonly called, from the town councils of Holland and Zeeland, under pressure from a popular movement convinced that the 'Loevesteiners' had betrayed the Fatherland, through corruption, blatant negligence of the country's defences bordering on treachery, and designing to 'change the Reformed religion, as established by the Synod of Dordrecht, and restore to the Papists free exercise of their religion', caused strong reverberations also in Friesland.[1] Preachers, and 'reformateurs', demanded thoroughgoing reform of the administration of the province and a drive against corruption. The criticism worried both the Delegated States and, more generally, the Frisian nobility who, since the middle of the seventeenth century, were more and more gaining a stranglehold over the province's rural magistracies. At this juncture, Friesland's great jurist Ulricus Huber published, anonymously, at Franeker, where he was professor of law, a much noticed pamphlet calling for calm and proclaiming that the politics, and constitution, of Friesland were entirely different from those of Holland and that disaster would ensue, if the disorder, and disrespect for authority, gripping Holland, should spread to Friesland.[2]

[1] Kalma and De Vries, *Friesland in het rampjaar*, 137–9.
[2] Huber, *Spiegel van Doleancie*, 120–4.

Conditions in the occupied areas rapidly deteriorated. Groningen became a war zone with the city under siege. The countryside of Gelderland, Overijssel, and Utrecht, and also Drenthe and States Brabant, was ravaged by enemy soldiery, even though their commanders were at some pains to restrain the pillage and rape which ensued. The fine mansions and country villas along the River Vecht, the 'Arcadia' of the Amsterdam patriciate, between Utrecht and Muiden, were plundered and ruined.[3] Economic activity, almost everywhere in the inland areas, was severely disrupted.[4] Additional dislocation was caused by the flight of numerous magistrates and office-holders, from both town and countryside. French military governors, in the occupied zone, issued proclamations ordering absent burgomasters and magistrates to return to their posts, threatening dismissal if they failed to comply. This posed a thorny dilemma. If office-holders resumed their normal duties, they risked being branded as collaborators and incurring the Stadholder's displeasure. If they disobeyed, and stayed away, as many did, they risked losing not only their offices, but property and influence as well. Numerous nobles, and magistrates from inland areas, did seek refuge in Holland, only returning after the French evacuation. Others stayed without permanently compromising their reputations, among them Everard van Weede van Dijkvelt (1626–1702), in Utrecht, later one of William III's closest confidants. But those who remained, under the French, and had previous links with the States party-faction, did tend to be discredited, among them Lambert van Velthuysen, in the city of Utrecht, and the nobleman Godard Willem, heer van Welland, who eventually became leader of the anti-Orangist wing of the Utrecht *ridderschap*.[5]

After the purges, the young Stadholder held the States of Holland and Zeeland firmly in his grip. Of 460 regents in Holland, in 1672, he had replaced 130 as politically undesirable. Some never subsequently regained their previous influence, including the once powerful De Graeff family, at Amsterdam, and those so closely identified with the De Witt regime that they had felt obliged to flee abroad. Besides Pieter de Groot, the former Rotterdam burgomasters Pesser, Vroesen, and Gael, together with their families, all found refuge in Antwerp.[6] Large sums of regent, as well as merchant, capital left the Republic in 1672.

But if many were removed Orange could not abolish the division of the regent body into rival ideological and clientage blocs. In the first place, by

[3] Brun, *Le Conseil d'extorsion*, 19.
[4] GA Nijmegen vroed. res. fo. 448, res. vroed. 27 Aug. 1672.
[5] Van der Bijl, 'Utrechts weerstand', 140–2.
[6] De Groot, *Lettres*, 92, 101.

no means all adherents of the 'maxims of De Witt' were purged. In the second, many new men put into *vroedschappen* were fresh to municipal government and lacked the experience, influence, and often also the time to manage public affairs. Furthermore, as Pieter de Groot observed, depriving locally influential family networks of offices and perquisites, to which they were accustomed, and deemed themselves entitled, was bound, in the broader context of civic society, to intensify rather than suppress party-factional acrimony.[7] Finally, the ideological roots of rivalry between the factional blocs—the tension between opposing wings of the public Church, and controversies over toleration and discipline, in society—were too pervasive for any purge to obviate the tendency to polarize, whether at local, provincial, or Generality level.

The Stadholder's purges ended the rioting and political turmoil; but the disturbances of the summer of 1672 left a lasting impression on Dutch society and not least on the political élites themselves.[8] The spectacle of mass insurrection against unpopular office-holders and policies excited ambition in some, and anxiety in others, which did not simply vanish in September 1672. Veteran observers such as De Groot or Huber, men deeply attached to the institutional forms of the Republic, and convinced of the rightness, and advantages, of rule by a narrow, wealthy, entrenched oligarchy, detested popular pressure in politics as a menace to the Republic they extolled,[9] but at the same time perceived the Republic to be a benefit for all. Restating his republican credo in his letters, early in 1673, De Groot remained as convinced as ever that republics are superior to monarchies and that the universally envied prosperity of the Dutch derived largely from their republican system of government.[10] Only republics, in his eyes, could guarantee liberty of conscience, and security of private possessions, func-tions he deemed the twin pillars of prosperity, the inestimable advantages the Dutch state bestowed on its subjects. For De Groot 'liberté de conscience et la sûreté des biens' were the essence of the Republic, and the essence of his republicanism was his belief that 'il est impossible que cette liberté, et cette sûreté, demeure sous le gouvernement d'un souverain'.[11] But could stability return under a Stadholder who had stripped many Holland regents of their posts? De Groot argued that such purges undermined the Republic, whatever their short-term effects. For by driving rivalry, and

[7] Ibid. 93, 100, 107.
[8] Ibid. 100, 107.
[9] Huber, *Spiegel van Doleancie*, 123.
[10] De Groot, *Lettres*, 93–5, 99–100.
[11] Ibid.

contention, deeper into civic society, and rendering civic government more factional, the rival political blocs were compelled more and more to respond to pressures from, and enlist support among, the people, generating instability.

De Groot held that William III's coup could not lead to stable government, for several reasons. In the first place, it was improbable the initially great popularity of the Stadholder, erupting with such tumultuous force in 1672, could last. During the De Witt years, he argued, Holland's trade and shipping had flourished more than before.[12] This was true and remained a staple contention of States party writers subsequently. But now, instead of the prosperity and expansion of the De Witt years, the population suffered war, dislocation, and hardship. The purged States of Holland had no choice but to pile on heavier and heavier taxation. Furthermore, not only Mennonites, Remonstrants, and Catholics, but also the Cocceian wing of the public Church, was afraid that the new regime might heed the call of the Voetian bloc to curb toleration and dissent. By February 1673, according to De Groot, there were already signs of a popular reaction against Stadholder, Orangists, and Voetian preachers.[13] He warned that if purged regents remained barred from civic government there was a real danger their anger would coalesce with popular discontent and the grievances of the Catholics, Remonstrants, and Mennonites who, he claimed, all supported the States party-faction. The result would be a new age of disorder and strife such as had poisoned the life of the Italian republics in the era of the Guelfs and Ghibellines, and the north Netherlands during the later Middle Ages: 'toute la province se séparera', he predicted, 'en deux parties tel qu'ont été autrefois les Houx et Cabelliaux.'[14]

The underlying tension in the Dutch Republic—political, social, and ideological—remained. What William III did achieve with his coup of 1672 was a greater leverage over Holland, and a more dominant position in politics, than any Stadholder had had, with the possible exception only of Maurits, in the years 1618–25, in the history of the Republic. But even where the Prince's authority was unassailably entrenched there was a tendency, from the outset, for his favourites, and their often corrupt methods, to provoke disgruntlement which, in some degree, filtered through to the town councils. At Hoorn, thirteen regents were purged by the Stadholder, in 1672. The Prince's subsequent strategy was to rely heavily on his local favourite—François van Bredehoff—who combined the offices of *schout* and burgomaster with various lesser posts and a directorship in the VOC. Van Bredehoff packed the *vroedschap* with staunch Orangists, even

¹² Ibid. 389–90.   ¹³ Ibid. 99–100.   ¹⁴ Ibid. 107.

bringing in, in 1681, one of the assailants who had knifed De Witt, in June 1672.[15] But his corrupt stranglehold on the town also caused resentment, rekindling regent antipathy to the Stadholder's regime. At Gorcum, ten regents were purged, and a new *drost* appointed, in the shape of Lodewijk Huygens (a son of Constantijn), an underling of the Prince who at the same time restored the *drost*'s former powers curtailed in 1650.[16] But Huygens's blatantly corrupt regime provoked indignation, some of which, before long, rubbed off on to the Stadholder. The Holland regents of the De Witt era may have been corrupt too. But it was not long before many observers concluded that the Stadholder's underlings were decidedly worse and by concentrating local power in few hands, were forging petty despotisms and creating more disorder and resentment than their predecessors.

Placing favourites at the helm and excluding the men of the past proved easier in small and medium-sized towns than in the chief Holland towns where the Stadholder's influence was inherently less. In large towns, pressure to erode the Prince's grip and secure greater independence arose as early as 1673. At Delft, the *vroedschap* tried, in November 1673, to reinstate several regents removed the previous year, which led to the question of the purged regents being discussed in the States of Holland.[17] The Prince, professing to want to keep them out only so as to avoid a resurgence of popular unrest, warned the States, and Delft specifically, that he did not wish any of those he had removed to be brought back in, declaring that only 'honourable patriots', with no links with the previous regime, should be appointed. Delft complied but grudgingly and, before long, it was obvious that the Stadholder's leverage in the town was slipping. The next year he reprimanded the *vroedschap* for electing three men of whom he disapproved.[18] Besides Delft and Amsterdam (over which no Stadholder exerted much influence), other large towns where Orange's influence rapidly waned included Leiden, which had since 1618 been solidly Orangist, but now became increasingly fertile ground for republican views, and Middelburg, where the 1672 changes had been directed by local opponents of Veth, not by the Stadholder. The effect of the purge at Middelburg had been to weaken the Veth, and bolster the Thibault, grouping; this led, in the mid-1670s, to Middelburg developing into a haven for republican ideas and Cocceian theology.[19]

---

[15] Kooimans, *Onder regenten*, 43.
[16] De Wit, *Gorcums heren*, 18-21.
[17] GA Delft 1st afd. 13/5, fo. 107. William III to SH, 13 Dec. 1673.
[18] GA Delft 1st afd. 13/5, fo. 111. res. vroed. 30 Dec. 1674.
[19] Van der Bijl, *Idee en interest*, 25-6.

Whilst much of the Republic remained under French, and Munsterite, occupation, opposition to the Stadholder remained muted. Attention focused on the war. Almost miraculously, the Republic was saved. Despite the initial shambles, the 'water-line' held. From the autumn of 1672, the French found all routes into Holland blocked. Alliances signed by the States General, with the Emperor and Brandenburg, in 1672, bore fruit late in the year, when the advance of Imperialist and Brandenburg forces, on Cologne, forced Louis to divert part of his army to the south. Over the winter of 1672–3, the Dutch defences hardened. Marshal Luxembourg, commanding the French army in the Republic, after Louis's departure, had a brief opportunity when the inundated land thwarting his advance froze solid, but was unable to concentrate his troops with sufficient speed. He belatedly thrust forward with 10,000 men, penetrating as far as Zwammerdam, near Leiden, before a sudden thaw forced him back.

During 1673, England and France mounted a combined effort to crush the Republic at sea. His defensive campaign of that year was, arguably, De Ruyter's greatest achievement.[20] Under his leadership, the Dutch navy reached the peak of its effectiveness as a fighting force. Assailed in the Zeeland shallows, early in June, by an overwhelmingly superior Anglo-French fleet, of seventy-six sail, mounting 4,812 guns, De Ruyter exploited his greater speed and manœuvrability to thwart and batter the allies. In a second battle, off Zeeland, a week later, the result was the same. In the third and final trial of strength, the English and French threw everything into clearing a path for a seaborne invasion of Holland. An English expeditionary force gathered at Yarmouth, ready to embark should De Ruyter be beaten. The English and French came on together eighty-six sail, mounting 5,386 guns. De Ruyter engaged, off Texel, with a far smaller fleet, mounting 3,667 guns. For eleven hours a continuous thunder of guns could be heard in much of North Holland, a sombre backdrop to the special prayers in the churches. Again De Ruyter pulled it off, shattering enough of the English three-deckers to force abandonment of the offensive. The effect of the three victories of 1673 was far-reaching. In England, the setbacks, combined with the impact of the Dutch privateering campaign, on English seaborne commerce, not only in home waters, but off North America, Spain, and in the Caribbean, an impact considerably greater than in the previous two Anglo-Dutch Wars,[21] made it impossible for Charles II to continue. English trade and shipping were severely disrupted and, in some sectors, paralysed, rendering the war so unpopular in England that Charles had no alternative

[20] Boxer, *The Anglo-Dutch Wars*, 52–8.   [21] De Bruijn, 'Dutch Privateering', 85–93.

but to withdraw. The Anglo-Dutch peace of February 1674 reflected the Dutch successes at sea.[22] The treaty, despite the Dutch collapse in 1672, brought England no gains at all.

Meanwhile, in August 1673, Spain entered the war, alongside the Emperor and the Republic, compelling the French further to reduce their army in the United Provinces and enabling William III to take the offensive. His first success was the capitulation of the 3,000-man French garrison, holding Naarden. Later in the autumn, Imperialist and Dutch forces invaded the electorate of Cologne, which finally forced the French to evacuate their positions on the 'water-line' and withdraw to the IJssel. Catholic mass was celebrated in the Dom, at Utrecht, for the last time on the morning the French pulled out; hours later, a citizen mob poured into the cathedral, stripped the images, paintings, and vestments and heaped them all on a bonfire outside.

Two months after England, Münster was forced into a comparably humiliating withdrawal from the war.[23] Until the autumn of 1673, the prince-bishop had confidently expected to annex not only Grol, Bredevoort, Lichtenvoorde, and Borculo, but also Westerwolde and Lingen. But under the peace of April 1674 he was forced to abandon everything and all his claims. In May 1674, the French evacuated the IJssel line and the whole of Gelderland and Overijssel. As they marched out of Arnhem, the Reformed citizenry poured into the main church, stripped the altar and images, hung a large orange banner 'as a sign of joy' from the spire, and held a thanksgiving service.[24] Dutch troops reoccupied the strongholds the French vacated and helped prevent reprisals against the Catholic population. Dutch troops also reoccupied the county of Lingen.[25]

Thus far William III had consolidated his popularity and prestige through his resolute conduct of the country's defence. With the recovery of the IJssel line, Gelderland, and Overijssel, the Stadholder's authority and power in the Republic were at their peak. By June 1674, of all his Dutch conquests, Louis retained only the two fortress towns of Grave and Maastricht. The Dutch army had improved dramatically in two years and was now again a large and efficient force. The Republic had alliances which shielded it from any possible resumption of the French invasion. There was general praise of the young Prince. Prompted by Fagel, the Stadholder's right-hand man in the States, Haarlem proposed, in January 1674, that the stadholderate of

[22] Israel, *Dutch Primacy*, 297–9.
[23] Kohl, *Christoph Bernhard von Galen*, 389, 416.
[24] Kotte, 'Gelderse bloem', 103.
[25] Ter Kuile, 'Graafschap Lingen', 24.

Holland now be made both perpetual and hereditary in the male line of the house of Orange-Nassau. The States of Holland unhesitatingly voted in favour.

Yet William's very success in defending the country, and consolidating the stadholderate, prepared the ground for a renewal of opposition to his authority. With its back against the wall, the Republic had shown unsuspected reserves of resilience. But ending the peril which had forced the regents to submit to the Prince and unstintingly support the war created a securer atmosphere in which it was conceivable again to fear an overmighty Stadholder and the threat to 'freedom'. From the summer of 1674, the man in the street lost interest in what now seemed a remote and irrelevant war and began to wonder why he should go on paying the high taxes required for its continuance.

With the end of the French occupation, and prospect of reintegrating Utrecht, Gelderland, and Overijssel, party-factional and ideological tensions revived. On the entry of Dutch troops into Utrecht, in November 1673, part of the Reformed citizenry drew up a petition resembling those submitted in the Holland towns in the summer of 1672, complaining that the 'old regents' had mismanaged the affairs of the city, neglected the public Church, and permitted an 'excessive' degree of toleration.[26] The States General suspended all the colleges of the provincial government—States, Delegated States, Hof, *ridderschap*, and city council—pending an investigation of their conduct under the French, to be conducted by the Stadholder. The consequence was a power vacuum, which lasted until early 1674, in which virulent party-factional ideological strife flourished. Dubbed 'those of the Voetian community' by their opponents, the Utrecht petitioners labelled their adversaries 'Arminians', 'libertines', and foes of Stadholder and public Church, who had backed De Witt and the Perpetual Edict, surrendered too promptly to the French, tolerated Catholics and dissenters, and oppressed the 'Voetian' consistory and preachers.[27]

The States General agreed to readmit the three recently liberated provinces to the Union, in April 1674; but, at the same time, required them to submit to changes to their provincial systems of government which the Generality, on the recommendation of the Stadholder, deemed advisable.[28] The States General thus not only authorized the Stadholder to purge those of whose conduct he disapproved, from the provincial assemblies, and lesser colleges, of the three provinces, but entrusted him with revising their

[26] Van Klaveren, 'Utrecht zonder regeering', 98.
[27] Ibid. 100–3.
[28] Hartog, 'Prins Willem III', 126.

procedures, enabling him to secure greater leverage than any previous Stadholder had had. Altogether 120 office-holders were removed, under the Prince's supervision, in Utrecht alone, a much higher number, in proportion, than had been purged in Holland and Zeeland, in 1672.[29] Twenty-one regents, among them Lambert van Velthuysen, were removed from the city council alone. The new general *reglement* for the province of Utrecht was drawn up by William and his advisers and then instantly approved by the (then four voting provinces of the) States General. Numerous office-holders and regents were summarily dismissed from their posts also in Gelderland and Overijssel. But in these provinces, instituting the new *reglementen* was delayed for many months by the onset of the campaigning season.

During these months, before finalization of the new regime in the east, the Prince's friends were extremely active building his, and their, influence, and advancing the Orangist-Voetian bloc. With the ground well prepared, Orange attended the Gelderland quarter assemblies, and then the full gathering of the States, in January 1675. Amid a swirl of effusive deference, the States of Gelderland proffered the Prince the title of 'duke of Gelderland' and formal sovereignty over their province. The move was bound to create a sensation throughout the Republic. But the response was not what the Prince had expected. Despite earlier indications that the Louvestein faction was reviving somewhat, Orange and his supporters were astounded by the force of the negative response, in Holland and Zeeland especially. Some of this was voiced by regents, and the Stadholder noted with displeasure that many of those whom he had refrained from purging, in 1672, thinking that henceforth their deference to his wishes was assured, were among the most vocal.[30] But the real opposition flowed from deeper down, from the higher and middle strata of civic society. The merchants of Amsterdam were reportedly appalled that the Stadholder should aspire to sovereign power over Gelderland, taking the view that the vesting of sovereign power in a hereditary ruler, rather than the States, was detrimental to business and financial confidence. Rumours circulated that conferring the title of 'duke of Gelderland' was merely a first step towards princely sovereignty over all the United Provinces which, among other effects, precipitated a slide in States of Holland bonds on the Amsterdam Exchange.[31] Despite all this, the Stadholder, given his grip over the smaller towns of Holland, could have forced compliance with his wishes had it been worth the expenditure of political capital. But as it was, the affair served

---

[29] Van der Bijl, 'Utrechts weerstand', 139.
[30] Van der Hoeven, *Hollands aeloude vryheid*, ii. 379.
[31] Barbour, *Capitalism in Amsterdam*, 58.

only to reveal the limitations of the Stadholder's influence in the larger towns. Not only Amsterdam, but also Delft, Leiden, and Haarlem, opposed acceptance of the ducal title. At Amsterdam, Valckenier and Hooft—usually at odds—joined forces to present a united front. The Amsterdam *vroedschap* were reported to be 'very positive and resolute in their opinion of dissuading the Prince from it, showing that it was a direct breach of the Union'. A majority was mustered, in the States of Holland, in favour of the Prince's acceptance; only six towns voted against, and 'it was not allowed that each town's opinion should be represented to the Prince'. But Amsterdam ignored this, sending the Prince a missive with the reasons 'there deduced against His Highness accepting the Dukedom'.[32]

If the Prince was displeased by Holland's reaction, he was incensed by that of Zeeland. There, too, the public played an important part, revealing unexpectedly strong republican tendencies. As in the days of De Witt, the towns split three against three, Flushing, Veere, and Tholen siding with the Prince's friends and Middelburg, Zierikzee, and Goes against.[33] Replying to the objections expressed by the States of Zeeland, the Prince did not trouble to hide his pique. This proved a further blunder. For his reply was published and, reportedly, 'lost him in a great measure the affection of that province and of the people, who cry up their magistrates for their advice to the Prince and assure them they will stick by them'.[34]

The business of the 'sovereignty of Gelderland' proved a costly mistake on Orange's part. The Prince's having travelled to Gelderland, 'in person', one observer commented, 'is held a great imbecillity, whereas, if he had sent for them to come to The Hague, and refused this offer, without the advice of any, he would have gained all mens esteeme'.[35] The Louvesteiners gained a psychological and propaganda victory, having swayed many to 'look now upon the Prince as a man of great dissimulation, and of great ambition, but, since the businesse of Guelderland, not of that prudent conduct he was esteemed for'.[36] The Prince's *faux pas* elicited a spate of satirical comment, and pasquinades, which incensed the regime.[37] One tract, sarcastically referring to the Stadholder as 'His Majesty King William III', caused such offence that the States of Holland offered a thousand guilders for the name, and whereabouts, of the printer. Orangists, incensed that 'we daily find more and more that evil persons are busy spreading rumours among the good

---

[32] PRO SP 84/200, fos. 79–80. Temple to Williamson, 19/29 Feb. 1675.
[33] Hartog, 'Prins Willem III', 142–4.
[34] PRO SP 84/198, fo. 288, 'A relation of the present State of Affairs'.
[35] Ibid.
[36] Ibid.
[37] Wagenaar, *Vad. Hist.* xiv. 366.

inhabitants', alleging the Stadholder aspired to 'souvereiniteyt' over the Fatherland, accused the Prince's critics of attempting to sow dissension and render the populace unwilling to pay taxes. The States General issued a stern placard, forbidding any person to say, or repeat, that the Prince aspired to sovereignty over the provinces, under threat of severe punishment.[38] The United Provinces had never allowed free speech in the modern sense: dissenters were not permitted to speak ill of the public Church, anti-Trinitarians to deny the Trinity, Jews to dispute Christianity, blasphemers to blaspheme, and, in many towns, swearing was subject to municipal fines; nor was it allowed to speak disrespectfully of the political authorities. But this was the first placard which sought to muzzle political discussion as such.

The Prince appeared before the States of Gelderland, on 20 February 1675, at Arnhem, declining the ducal title, on the grounds that acceptance would create misunderstanding as to his intentions. But he was none the less thorough, for that, in completing his purge and devising a new *reglement* for Gelderland, appropriating, as Stadholder, an unprecedented degree of control at every level. In all, 126 members of town councils were replaced with known Orangists as the Stadholder's managers, the new men being selected in consultation with the militias, and colleges of representatives of the guilds. The *reglement* assured the Prince the main say in appointing most provincial and rural officers, and allowed him to nominate members of the colleges of *gemeenslieden* which chose the members of the town councils.[39] Master of Gelderland, the Prince proceeded to assume comparable powers in Overijssel, where a new general *reglement* was imposed, at the meeting of the States, at Zwolle, in March. As a finishing touch to the imposing new edifice of the Stadholder's power and influence, the States General, on 20 April, declared the offices of captain- and admiral-general of the Union henceforth hereditary in the male line of the Prince of Orange.

The Prince had never sought to flatter the people. Certainly, during 1672, he took advantage of popular support and worked, in some cases, with civic militias, against the sitting regents. But he had ignored most of the content of the popular petitions, and, by 1675, it was clear that Prince and people were drifting apart. This was, partly, inherent in the situation. But it was accelerated by the Prince's sullen, misanthropic temperament which, as time went on, became less and less inclined to cultivate the populace. His brusque departure from the festivities to mark the centenary of the university of

---

[38] *Groot Placaet-Boeck*, iii. 524; Wagenaar, *Historische verhandeling*, 53.
[39] Van den Bergh, *Life and Work*, 14–15; Rowen, *Princes of Orange*, 138–9.

Leiden, in February 1675, reportedly further estranged many ordinary folk in the city.[40] 'Tis not to be believed', noted one observer, 'how strangely the people's affections are alienated since that attempt of making the Prince Duke of Guelderland.'[41] Where, initially, his popular appeal had been his foremost weapon, after 1675, William III relied chiefly on behind-the-scenes influence, power of patronage, and twisting arms. His waning popularity was not helped by the fact that despite sizeable cuts in military spending, in the years 1675–6, the unprecedented scale of the state debt precluded reductions in taxation, a predicament which the man in the street was hardly likely to view understandingly. The Dutch, it was reported in London, 'look back with compassion on De Witt's fate, they begin to lament his losse, and consider his principles beyond what could be expected'.[42]

With the danger passed, high levels of taxation and military expenditure became a decisive factor shaping the political mood in the Republic. For the burden appeared insupportable. If De Witt and his colleagues had run the army, and land fortifications, down to minimal levels, William III and the States General had, in three years, restored the Republic's status as a major land power, as well as sea power. Fortifications and equipment had vastly improved. Huge numbers of men were recruited, Dutch troop-strength rising to around 100,000 men. Generality expenditure, in 1673, exceeded 100 million guilders or more than five times Holland's annual revenue—despite the fact that half of the Republic was under enemy occupation. The army was trimmed to 68,000 men, by 1675, and Generality expenditure to 50 million guilders.[43] But this did nothing to alleviate the existing intense fiscal pressure. With Holland's annual revenue running at 18 million, and that of the Seven Provinces, at under 30 million guilders, the public debt was still rapidly escalating. 'The expenses of this state in the warre,' predicted Sir William Temple, in February 1676, 'joyned to the diminution of their trade, seems to disable them from prosecuting it any longer than the next campaign.'[44] The French calculated likewise. But both were wrong. Not only did William III keep the Republic in the war during 1676 but, for 1677, the army was expanded, rising to 90,000 men.

The plight of the overseas trading system, and the rest of the economy, was serious. The catastrophe of 1672 had resulted in a slump of great severity. With the improvement in the Republic's fortunes, during 1674, the

[40] Japikse, *Prins Willem III*, 362.
[41] PRO SP 84/199, fo. 6. Intelligence, 7 May 1675.
[42] PRO SP 84/198, fo. 288. 'A Relation of the present state of affairs' (Apr. 1675).
[43] Ibid.
[44] PRO SP 84/200, fo. 147v. Temple to Williamson, 11 Feb. 1676.

economy too revived. Yet, the recovery in commerce, industry, and shipping, after England and Münster made peace, was only partial.[45] The
Republic was now safe but its shipping remained in grave danger, indeed,
in a sense, more so than before; for, during 1672–4, it was so perilous to
venture out that the States General kept the merchant and fishing fleets in
harbour, leaving practically nothing for the English and French to capture.
After the peace with England, Dutch shipping reappeared. But, for precisely
that reason, French privateers, based at Dunkirk and St Malo, inflicted
mounting losses on merchant shipping and the fishing fleets. There was also
a sustained French onslaught in the Caribbean. Consequently, the revival of
business confidence, the Amsterdam Exchange, and the value of shares in
the VOC and WIC, remained sluggish. In May 1675, shares in the Amsterdam Chamber of the VOC were stagnant at 428 per cent of face value (see
Table 39) while, as late as March 1676, States of Holland bonds languished
at only 80 per cent of face value.[46]

Orange needed to shore up his domestic support, and the public's
willingness to stick by Spain and the Emperor, until France was defeated.
In his eyes, it was the wider political and strategic contest in Europe which
chiefly mattered, a view of the Republic's essential interests which diverged
fundamentally from that of De Witt and the States party-faction. Anxious
to sustain Dutch commitment to the war, the Prince cultivated the English
court, hoping to embroil England, in some measure, if only as a mediator,
with France. In this connection, he began pressing, early in 1676, for the
hand of Princess Mary, daughter of the heir to the throne, James, duke of
York.

It was also in the hope of boosting support for the war, and his
position more generally, that the Prince cultivated the Voetian bloc within
the public Church. Preachers zealous for Orange, the Union, and a hardline
Calvinist stance, could, through their sermons, do much to promote
patriotic ardour and acceptance of heavy taxation. Thus, Orange, as an
English observer put it, in April 1675, 'doth very much court . . . the
predikants'.[47] This, in turn, led the Prince to intervene in the endemic strife
between Voetians and Cocceians which had now divided the public Church
for virtually a quarter of a century. This he did most notably at Middelburg,
where the wrangling was, at this time, especially virulent. Until the 1670s
Zeeland had been the province of the Further Reformation *par excellence*.[48]

[45] Israel, *Dutch Primacy*, 299–302, 306; Israel, 'Amsterdam Stock Exchange', 421.
[46] PRO SP 84/204, fo. 167v. 'An account' (Mar. 1676).
[47] PRO SP 84/198, fo. 289v. 'State of the United provinces' (Apr. 1675).
[48] Op 't Hof, 'Nadere Reformatie in Zeeland', 40–68.

But there had been a marked change since 1672, due partly to the gains of the Thibault faction and partly to the efforts of the charismatic Johannes van der Waeyen, a former Voetian preacher, from Friesland, turned Cocceian, who, since 1672, had set about changing the views of the consistory, preachers, and populace of Middelburg with such effect, helped by the anti-Orangist mood, the Middelburg consistory had become predominantly Cocceian. The result was a confrontation with the mainly Voetian classis of Walcheren Island, to which Middelburg was subject, which developed into a bitter clash, in 1676, when the Middelburg *vroedschap*, and consistory, appointed a well-known Cocceian, Wilhelmus Momma, to fill a preaching vacancy in the city against the wishes of the classis. The ensuing furore provided Orange with a pretext, in November, to intervene in person. The Prince not only expelled both Van der Waeyen and Momma from Zeeland—Momma retreated to Delft where he died the following year—but purged six States party, pro-Cocceian members of the *vroedschap* and also the consistory. Then, the following year, 'judging the consistory of Middelburg not sufficiently purged of those who were engaged for the said minister', he wrote to Middelburg from his camp at Charleroy, ordering a further purge of Cocceian elders and deacons.[49] Voetian views subsequently predominated in the Middelburg consistory, and throughout Zeeland, down to William III's death in 1702.[50]

Another strategy adopted by the Prince was to extend his influence into Friesland, and especially Groningen and Drenthe, so as to preclude opposition to his policies coalescing around the figure of the young Frisian Stadholder, Hendrik Casimir II (Stadholder 1664–96). In the past, Princes of Orange had mostly collaborated closely with their cousins and counterparts, the Stadholders of Friesland. But this pattern was broken, after 1672, by a growing tension between William III and the Frisian court. Following the death of Willem Frederik in 1664 (he accidentally killed himself in his bedroom, inspecting new pistols) his widow and cousin, Albertine Agnes, one of the three daughters of Frederik Hendrik, presided over the little court of Leeuwarden, as guardian of her 7-year-old son. He was educated to be a soldier and statesman but showed far less aptitude, in both capacities, than his older cousin who was constantly held up to him as a model and whom he grew increasingly to detest.[51]

What began as personal antipathy developed into political tension, as Orange exploited Hendrik Casimir's youth, and inexperience to interpose

---

[49] PRO SP 84/205, fo. 105. Meredith to Williamson, 14 Sept. 1677.
[50] Van der Bijl, 'Kerk en politiek', 181, 192.
[51] Guibal, *Johan Willem Friso*, 19–20.

his own influence in what traditionally was the sphere of the Frisian Stadholder. This began during the French invasion, in July 1672, when the States General appointed Orange Stadholder of Westerwolde, even though, previously, Westerwolde had invariably had the same Stadholder as Groningen, to which Hendrik Casimir had been designated.[52] Hendrik Casimir reached his majority in 1675, and, in the same year, the States of Friesland declared the stadholderate hereditary in his male line. Groningen and Drenthe, however, did not confer the 'survivance' on the count; and, in 1676, the States of Drenthe conferred theirs on William. Meanwhile, the influence of the Frisian court in the States of Groningen had greatly diminished. Indeed, by the mid-1670s, conditions in the province, as so often before, were so chaotic that the States General intervened repeatedly, to defend the Generality's interests, providing Orange with further pretexts to extend his influence. When the Prince indicated a wish to head the States General commission sent to Groningen, in February 1677, to compose the latest rift between the city and Ommelands, it was immediately assumed that 'his aim is to be made hereditary Stadholder of that province upon this occasion'.[53] For the moment there was little that Hendrik Casimir could do to check his cousin's influence. Even in Friesland, his authority was in tatters, owing to popular agitation in the towns, encouraged by Voetian preachers, directed against his mother and himself, as well as the civic patriciates. Since Orange favoured the Voetian tendency, Hendrik Casimir preferred Cocceian theology. In 1677, Johannes van der Waeyen, whom the Prince had expelled from Middelburg, was appointed to a chair at Franeker. Before long, Friesland's new Cocceian professor of theology had become one of Hendrik Casimir's closest advisers.

Despite the growing unpopularity of the war, there was no effective opposition to Orange until 1677. During 1675–6, the Prince's ascendancy remained unimpaired owing to the sparseness of the 'commonwealth party', as the English called it, in the town halls, as well as the weakness of Hendrik Casimir. But the ineffectiveness of the States party-faction during those years turned out to be due not just to Orange's hold over the small Holland towns, but also to the split in the Amsterdam city council, where the rivalry between Valckenier and Hooft deprived the city of much of its capacity to make its weight felt. This changed in January 1677, however, when a grand gathering of the regent patriciate achieved a 'friendly reconciling of all differences among them', and 'an order for electing burgomasters'.[54] In the

[52] Van Winter, *Westerwolde*, 106.
[53] PRO SP 84/204, fo. 121. Meredith to Williamson, 19 Feb. 1677.
[54] PRO SP 84/204, fo. 92. Meredith to Williamson, 2 Feb. 1677.

ensuing elections, of February 1677, Hooft, the real leader of the republican tendency at Amsterdam, emerged as presiding burgomaster with the backing of a majority of the *vroedschap*.[55] As in 1622–3, the economic slump helped to distance the city from the Stadholder, strengthening the States party bloc.

Hooft could now orchestrate real opposition to William III's leadership. There was, indeed, much to contest; for it was, by now, abundantly clear how great was the contrast between the Republic, and its statecraft, under a dominant Stadholder, and a republican, stadholderless regime. Besides disquiet over the prolonging of the war for reasons which meant little to the man in the street, insupportably heavy taxation, and the plight of commerce, the regents disliked the authoritarian style of the Prince's leadership. This applied not only to his manipulation of provincial assemblies and *vroedschap* elections but also his foreign policy and running of the army.[56] Before 1672, a committee of States General 'deputies in the field' had always accompanied the captain-general on campaign and participated in taking major military decisions. By contrast, since the fall of De Witt, 'deputies in the field' had been dispensed with and the Generality's participation in military decisions effectively ended.[57] Similarly, the Prince's diplomacy diverged strikingly from that of the stadholderless period. Much now transpired informally, through unofficial envoys, reporting to, and working for, the Prince, rather than the Generality.[58]

A frequent complaint was Orange's 'preferring of strangers and soldiers of fortune in the army who may solely depend upon his favour, and rejecting the Netherlanders'.[59] William assiduously recruited German noblemen into the army, often favouring them above others, even in making major military decisions, especially trusting Georg Friedrich, count von Waldeck. William's Dutch favourites, above all Hans Willem Bentinck and Dijkvelt, did wield influence in military, as other, matters, but again, it was a question of informal links, through the Stadholder, rather than formal military patronage in the assemblies and *Raad van State*. Finally, Orange took it upon himself to assign commissions in regiments paid by Friesland and Groningen, a blatant infringement, as Hendrik Casimir saw it, of his own authority.

Many aspects of the new regime were open to criticism, and, early in 1677, as opposition stiffened, the Prince suffered a serious military setback. The

---

[55] Edwards, 'Amsterdam City Government', 12.
[56] De Bruin, *Geheimhouding en verraad*, 269–70.
[57] Van Slingelandt, *Staatkundige geschriften*, iv. 83–4.
[58] Roorda, 'Willem III', 166–9.
[59] PRO SP 84/205, fo. 295. 'The Commonwealth Party'.

French had invaded the Spanish Netherlands, captured Valenciennes, and set siege to St Omer. William, with 30,000 Dutch, Spanish, and Austrian troops, attempted to relieve the city, but was repulsed with heavy loss, in April, at the battle of Mont Cassel. The defeat 'worked much to the Prince's prejudice' and encouraged disparagement of his method of running the army.

By 1677, Orange's authority was more than a little frayed, as was shown by a further bout of turbulence in Groningen. The instability in that province was now more chronic than ever. While the Ommelands paid more than the city in taxes, the city wielded 'halfe the authority of the province' and the presence of the provincial treasury, and its officers, within its walls ensured an undue influence over the province's financial administration. Also unresolved was the Ommelanders' claim to the 'right of precedence, of giving their voices first, of signing and sealing first'. The Generality commission sent to Groningen, in February 1677, recommended that the province be divided, for administrative purposes, with the Ommelands being permitted to set up a separate revenue chest, and receivers, and keep separate tax records from the city. This new Generality intervention, guided by Orange, pleased the Ommelands but incensed the city, which closed ranks with Friesland and Hendrik Casimir to oppose the Prince.

The vote in the States General, permitting the Ommelands a separate financial administration, passed by majority vote, with Holland's acquiescence, at a time when the States of Holland were not in session. The city of Groningen and Hendrik Casimir vehemently protested. On the convening of the States of Holland, in July, the Prince hurried back from the army, anxious to 'prevent any resolution of these States which might prove favourable to the city'.[60] The Ommelander assembly ordered that no more payments from the Ommelands be made to the provincial chest, in the city, in accordance with the Generality resolution. Hendrik Casimir thereupon 'ordered them the contrary'. When the Ommelanders defied their Stadholder, he sent 'officers from Groningen to seize all their chests and papers which they accordingly did and carried them to the Stadhouse of that city'.

In the States of Holland, meanwhile, Orange and Fagel swayed the *ridderschap* and small towns but not the large towns, 'those of Amsterdam having delivered theirs against the separation . . . some other towns, and among them Leiden, have taken further time to consult their principals upon that subject'.[61] With Amsterdam and Leiden joining Friesland in

---

[60] PRO SP 84/205, fo. 18. Meredith to Williamson, 29 June 1677.
[61] PRO SP 84/205, fo. 56. Meredith to Williamson, 27 July 1677.

blocking the Generality decision, and others wavering, it began to look doubtful whether Orange would get his way. Hendrik Casimir reminded the States General that dividing the financial administration of a province into two violated the doctrine that each province was 'sovereign as in the year 1651 was established as a fundamental principle of the state'.[62]

Orange hoped to strengthen his hand—in, and outside, the Republic—by clinching his long-projected marriage to Princess Mary. He left for England, with the permission of the States General, in October. Charles II would have preferred to wait until France and the Republic had made peace, not wishing to be dragged into the denouement of the struggle in whatever capacity. But Orange persisted and the wedding took place in London, in November. He also persuaded Charles to participate in the peace-making process and help try to sway Louis to restitute, to Spain, most of the border fortresses he had captured. The Prince insisted on restitution of Valenciennes, Charleroi, Tournai, Kortrijk, and Oudennaarde.[63] An Anglo-Dutch treaty formalizing the new closer relationship was signed at The Hague, on 10 January 1678.

Louis countered by exploiting the rift between the Prince and Amsterdam. He hoped to coax the States party-faction into breaking ranks with the Republic's allies, Spain, the Emperor, and Brandenburg, and signing a separate peace with France. As bait, he offered Holland's deputies at the Nijmegen peace congress cancellation of the tariff list of 1667, to be replaced by that of 1664, a concession with great appeal for Holland, and especially Amsterdam and Leiden, where there was now mounting anxiety at the slackness of trade and England's success, as a neutral power, since 1674, in diverting traffic from the Republic. Peace on the basis of Colbert's 1664 tariff list was thus, for the Holland towns, an offer too tempting to resist. In addition, Louis offered to evacuate Maastricht and return Valenciennes and Tournai to the Spaniards.

During the spring of 1678, the rift between Orange and Amsterdam became open and bitter.[64] Burgomaster Hooft, leading the peace drive, swayed most Holland towns to press for acceptance of Louis's offer. The Prince warned the provincial assemblies of the harm that would be done to the Republic's reputation and interests, should it leave its allies in the lurch. For some months, he succeeded in holding up the peace talks as well as the large army cuts proposed by Holland.[65] But, during June, the States

---

[62] PRO SP 84/205, fo. 46, undated copy of Hendrik Casimir to SG (July 1677).
[63] Japikse, *Prins Willem III*, ii. 61–2.
[64] Van der Bijl, 'Willem III, Stadhouder-koning', 171.
[65] Roorda, 'Peace of Nijmegen', 24–5.

party-faction in the States of Holland, led by Hooft and Paets, secured a vote in the States General for the immediate cessation of hostilities.

Just when it seemed that Holland had won, Louis threw everything into confusion by announcing that he would neither lift the siege of Mons, nor evacuate towns he had agreed to relinquish, until his ally, Sweden, received back most of what she had lost to Brandenburg. Incensed, the States of Holland promptly cancelled the cease-fire, voting that there could be no peace without prior evacuation of the agreed 'barrier' towns. On 2 August, the Prince, with the full backing of the States of Holland, including that of Hooft, advanced on Mons commanding 35,000 Dutch, Spanish, and Brandenburg troops. Perceiving his error, Louis hurriedly agreed to withdraw from the stipulated towns and cancel the 1667 tariff list. The peace treaty, ending the war, was finalized at Nijmegen, soon after. Four days later, but lacking official confirmation of the rumours of peace, the Prince attacked the French lines at Mons. The battle, bloody and inconclusive, led to a bitter exchange of accusations of bad faith.

The Hollanders had their political victory and prized tariff reductions. The latter were undoubtedly of great value to the Republic, and contributed substantially to the economic recovery of the 1680s. But the price was high. Orange's mortification was shared by the Emperor and Spain as well as the Elector of Brandenburg who, owing to the separate Franco-Dutch peace, failed to gain western Pomerania—France being free to support Sweden's refusal to give it up.[66] For years afterwards the Republic was burdened with the reputation of being an untrustworthy ally, concerned only with its commercial interests.

FROM NIJMEGEN TO THE REVOCATION OF THE EDICT OF NANTES, 1678–1685

William III returned to The Hague, in August 1678, determined to repair his diminished authority. Europe was still tense and so was the Dutch domestic arena. The continuing friction between the party-factions arose partly from the unresolved dilemma posed by French expansionism in the south Netherlands and Germany. The States party-faction, in the tradition of De Witt, desired to consolidate and strengthen the peace, minimizing Franco-Dutch antagonism, believing this the surest means of safeguarding the Republic's well-being and trade. They saw also that peace with France would dispense with the need for a large and expensive army and the web

---

[66] Troost, 'William III, Brandenburg', 308–11.

of informal diplomacy woven by the Prince. Orange and his entourage, by contrast, regarded the peace more as an armed interim, pending a fresh conflagration, with France remaining the principal menace to the security of both parts of the Netherlands.

This disparity of views provoked renewed wrangling even before the treaty of Nijmegen was ratified, due to fresh disputes between France and Spain over border localities of the Spanish Netherlands. Orange pressed the States General to delay ratification, to support Spain, and put pressure on France, while opponents preferred to sweep aside whatever might obstruct implementation of the peace.[67] When the stipulated six weeks allowed for ratification had almost expired, Amsterdam threatened, out of exasperation, to boycott all other business until the peace was finalized, reminding regents apt to support the Stadholder that failure to ratify would not only jeopardize the peace but reverse the recent rise in VOC shares, and States of Holland bonds, so that they, as well as the merchants, stood to lose should the treaty falter.

Domestic issues also contributed to the continuing friction between the party-factions, including a dispute about Maastricht and the Overmaas. The French having only recently evacuated these localities, Orangists urged that their office-holders be purged, just as had those of Utrecht, Overijssel, Gelderland, and Drenthe. Amsterdam, by contrast, anxious to block any further extension of Orange's authority, insisted this be dispensed with. On this issue, Orange's sway over the small towns of Holland led to Amsterdam being easily defeated. Among the provinces, Friesland and Groningen backed Amsterdam but the rest supported the Stadholder. The States General—by a majority of four provinces to two—then authorized the Prince to carry out the purges.

Maastricht demonstrated, yet again, the gulf between the style and methods of the De Witt era and those of the revived stadholderate, where the form of the Republic was preserved but much of the substance changed and the Stadholder was able, through his political bosses, to concentrate power and patronage, reaching across provinces, into his own hands. William III's favourites, both at provincial and local level, were often unpopular. But this did not, apparently, disturb the Prince, provided they carried out his wishes and secured him the votes he needed. He tolerated the blatant corruption, for which his favourites became notorious, as inherent in the web of influence, and clientage, on which his authority depended. Odijk, his proxy as First Noble, and manager, in Zeeland, son of one of Maurits's illegitimate offspring, was widely detested in Zeeland.[68] Yet,

[67] Res. Holl. 9, 14, 19 and 23 Sept. 1678.   [68] Busken Huet, *Land van Rembrand*, 662.

seemingly, his ability to manipulate the provincial States remained unaffected. Not infrequently Middelburg, Zierikzee, and Goes, the towns which backed Amsterdam, in 1675, and again over the Nijmegen peace talks, in 1677, were overruled in the provincial assembly by four votes to three, with Odijk's as the clinching vote. In Utrecht, Gelderland, and Overijssel there was deep resentment against the new political arrangements and the Prince's bosses.[69]

While it is hard to know whether the Prince's favourites were especially corrupt by European standards of the time—for it was normal for officials to supplement their emoluments by means of corrupt practices at the expense of those under their sway—it is clear that peculation amongst William III's underlings was a public issue even before the peace of Nijmegen, and remained so throughout his stadholderate. Since the advent of the stadholderless regime in 1650, a tendency towards combating official corruption, an incipient shift towards a more modern notion of public morality, seems to have heightened sensitivities among the public, enabling De Witt to gain politically from his reputation for rectitude. The reversion to more traditional methods and practices, after 1672, then resulted, it would appear, in a clash between expectations and reality.[70]

While Odijk remained unscathed, others of Orange's favourites scandalized opinion to the point that the Stadholder was forced to withdraw his favour—if only temporarily. The extortionate practices of Lodewijk Huygens led to his being arraigned before the Hof of Holland, in 1675, and found guilty, though this did not prevent his being restored as *drost* of Gorcum, in 1678. A *baljuw* Orange had appointed in 1672, a great enemy of De Witt, was 'much talked of for having placed loose women in several houses of which he paid the rent, upon condition that when any married persons, that might be good prey, come to them, they should give him notice'. This method neatly combined extortion with the Further Reformation; for the social stigma involved in being prosecuted, and fined, for infringing municipal edicts against both 'ordinary' and double whoredom induced many men of standing to 'redeeme themselves with great summes rather than undergo the infamy which the laws here impose upon adultery'.[71] It was remarked that this *baljuw*'s 'affection to His Highnesse, having advanced him to his place, gave him confidence that he would not lose His Highness' support in which he now findes himself mistaken'. Even so, the Prince was extremely slow to discard even his most reprobate underlings.

[69] Roorda, 'Willem III', 127.
[70] Dekker, 'Private Vices, Public Virtues', 492–3.
[71] PRO SP 84/204, fo. 248. Meredith to Williamson, 18 May 1677.

Orange's reverse at Amsterdam's hands, in 1678, showed that if he was fully to restore his grip, he needed to win over some of the opposition and broaden his base of support. Politically, he made several adjustments, after Nijmegen, aimed at narrowing the rift between the party-faction blocs, leading him to modify his previously inflexible attitude to regents whom he had purged in 1672 and his former readiness to back the Voetian stream within the public Church and local politics. Until 1678, the Prince resisted all pressure for the reinstatement of the men whom he had removed, and expected his underlings and allies to do likewise. Even at Amsterdam, Valckenier had, until 1677, vigorously opposed Hooft's desire to bring back regents purged in 1672.

By 1679, however, the Prince, aware he could not control the larger Holland towns, or Middelburg, with the methods he was accustomed to use in smaller towns, sought a *modus vivendi*, a way of sharing influence and power in key cities, while preserving the core of his authority. In a letter to the Delft *vroedschap*, of December 1679, he remarked that Delft had been the most adamant of the towns in seeking reinstatement of regents removed in 1672, admitting that these were often better qualified than others for public service, and that pressure for their reinstatement emanated from the respectable citizenry as a whole, and not just the regent body.[72] With this, Orange virtually concurred in the widespread opinion that those whom he had 'put in were generally of less abilityes than those he turned out'.[73] He announced he would no longer block the return of four leading Delft regents purged in 1672—Gijsbert van Berestein, Adriaen Bogaert, Gerrit van der Aal, and Johan van der Dussen.

The Prince thereby nullified Holland's resolution of December 1673, on which he himself had insisted, rejecting Delft's plea that reinstatement of the purged men be allowed. This was confirmed soon after in a meeting of the *Gecommitteerde Raden* with the Prince, and formalized in a new resolution of the States.[74] The Prince then sent letters to all the towns, expressly permitting rehabilitation of those whom he had purged.[75] The quest for a *modus vivendi* was helped by the death of Hooft, in 1678, and of Valckenier, in 1680; though Valckenier was something of an ally, both were strong personalities, jealous of Amsterdam's independence, who had not wanted the Stadholder to wield any influence in the city. The situation changed after their deaths, the new leading men, Johannes Hudde (1628–1704) and

[72] GA Delft 1st afd. 13/5, fos. 147v–148. William III to Delft *vroedschap*, 14 Dec. 1679.
[73] PRO SP 84/205, fo. 294v, 'The Commonwealth Party in the United provinces'.
[74] Res. Holl. 22 Dec. 1679.
[75] GA Leiden Sec. Arch. 917/x/6. William III to Leiden, 11 Feb. 1680.

Nicolaes Witsen (1641–1717) being of a milder type, known for preferring *rapprochement* to confrontation and aspiring to reduce both political, and Cocceian–Voetian, tension in their city.

The lull in the international arena lasted only briefly. Late in 1679, with the Emperor distracted in Hungary, and Brandenburg coaxed for the moment into a pro-French stance, Louis commenced a general encroachment along the borders of the Spanish Netherlands, Lorraine, and Alsace. These local annexations, called 'réunions', were justified on the grounds that the peace of Nijmegen had allocated conquered border towns to France, without demarcating the border, so that districts legally 'dependent' on these conquests could legitimately be absorbed into France. At the same time, Louis offered the Dutch a treaty of friendship. Amsterdam, and the States of Friesland and Groningen, wished to sign but the Prince persuaded the rest not to do so. The new French ambassador at The Hague, the comte d'Avaux, warned Fagel, in January 1680, that Louis would not tolerate procrastination. If the Republic failed to respond within fourteen days, His Majesty 'would use all his power to bring advantage to his subjects' commerce'.[76] Once again, the French monarch threatened to use French tariffs as a lever with which to manipulate the Republic. If the Dutch desired trade with France on favourable terms, then they must not oppose the king's territorial claims in the Spanish Netherlands, Lorraine, and the Empire. There was no response from the States General.

The French envoy ascribed Amsterdam's now more conciliatory stance towards Orange to the new principal burgomasters. Finding in him little inclination to oppose the Stadholder, d'Avaux dismissed Hudde as a regent of 'extraordinary timidity'. But the calm which descended over Dutch domestic politics in the years 1680–2 is attributable, rather than to personalities, to recognition, by all parties (except perhaps Hendrik Casimir), that accommodation offered more than confrontation. It was also a time of growing international tension and pessimism about the economy. Amsterdam's merchants remained nervous. VOC shares drifted back below levels reached in 1678–9, to 408 per cent of face value by April 1681.[77] Amid the general unease, William and Fagel could expect Holland to co-operate in bolstering the Republic's system of alliances—even if Hendrik Casimir would not. Ratification of the alliance with Sweden passed in October 1681, with Amsterdam's support, by five provinces to two, over the objections of Friesland and Groningen. With the French annexation of Strasburg, in

[76] *Négociations . . . d'Avaux*, i. 294 and iv. 358.
[77] BL MS Add. 37981, fos. 12v–14. Carr to Blathwayt, Amsterdam, 21 Mar. 1681.

November, pessimism deepened, the VOC share price sank further to 395 per cent (see Table 39). The value of wealthy homes at Amsterdam slumped.[78]

Never was Louis's position in Europe stronger than in the early 1680s. The Stadholder's contention that Nijmegen made France stronger, and the coalition opposing her primacy weaker, proved substantially correct.[79] In February 1682, the French stepped up their pressure on the Spanish Netherlands, blockading Luxemburg. Spanish ministers turned to The Hague, demanding military assistance—the 8,000 troops stipulated in the Dutch–Spanish pact of 1673. This precipitated further wrangling in the north, with Amsterdam, and other towns, opposing the dispatch of the expeditionary force.[80] In a speech in the States of Holland, on 7 March, the Prince declared that it was a vital Dutch interest to bolster Spain, and check France, for otherwise all Europe would soon be reduced to slavery. If the Republic stood idly by whilst Louis absorbed the Spanish Netherlands and adjoining lands, the Republic would gain only the contemptible reward of being swallowed last. Orange's advice was accepted, in the States of Holland, over the objections of Amsterdam, Rotterdam, and Dordrecht, and, in the States General, by five provinces to two, opposed by Friesland and Groningen. Nothing happened, however, as Louis, at this point, lifted his siege of the city of Luxemburg.

Early in 1683, Louis again massed troops on the borders of the Spanish Netherlands, knowing that the Emperor, embroiled with the Turks, would not interfere. The Turks (secretly encouraged by Louis), to the dismay of the Dutch, at this point launched a big offensive, culminating in the second siege of Vienna. The Amsterdam Stock Exchange oscillated wildly, in response to these shifts, VOC shares having recovered, to 462, late in 1682, following Louis' apparent withdrawal (and the Dutch capture of Bantam, in the East Indies), dropped to 402 per cent, after Louis resumed his pressure on the south Netherlands, in May 1683, and to 395 per cent on the besieging of Vienna, in July.[81]

On the resumption of the French encroachments, the Spanish governor-general, in Brussels, Grana, again requested the dispatch of the stipulated 8,000 troops. Orange responded precisely as before, the States of Holland approving the Prince's advice—over the objections of Amsterdam, Delft, and Leiden. The States of Friesland split; but the majority, and the

[78] Lesger, *Huur en conjunctuur*, 83–4.
[79] Roorda, 'Peace of Nijmegen', 25.
[80] Drossaers, *Diplomatieke betrekkingen*, 73.
[81] GA Amsterdam PJG 334, accounts of Manuel Levy Duarte, fo. 688.

Delegated States, backed Hendrik Casimir in opposing Dutch intervention in the Spanish Netherlands, setting up a secret committee of six *grietmannen* and two burgomasters to co-ordinate opposition to William III.[82] The troops were sent, but kept in reserve.

The Prince now decided that it was essential to raise extra troops and improve the army's readiness, if the United Provinces were to persuade either Louis, or potential allies, that they were serious about checking French might in the Low Countries. Prince and *raad* urged the provinces to expand the army by 16,000 men and vote the necessary funds. The request swayed the *ridderschap*, and a large majority in the States of Holland, but not the three towns now forming the core of opposition to the Stadholder— Amsterdam, Delft, and Leiden—and, since it was a financial measure (so that agreement had to be unanimous), it failed to pass. In Friesland, two quarters—Oostergo and Zevenwouden—backed Hendrik Casimir enough to block the States' agreement.[83] In Groningen, there was the usual split between city and Ommelands, the latter backing William and the city Hendrik Casimir.[84]

Attention now focused on Amsterdam. At this point the leading figure in the *vroedschap* was Coenraad van Beuningen, who was as little inclined to accept William III's assessment of the European situation, in 1683, as he had been to accept De Witt's in 1668. As a major investor in VOC shares, he also needed no reminding that the Prince's policy was depressing the stock market. Amsterdam's deputies argued against raising the 16,000 men, in the States, on 4 November: such a move, they insisted, would make war more, not less, likely and this, with Brandenburg and Denmark siding with France and the Emperor distracted, would be not just perilous but ruinous for both Dutch security and commerce. In his reply, Orange indignantly accused Van Beuningen of being a scarcely less eloquent spokesman, for France, than d'Avaux himself. He conceded that 'commerce is the pillar of the state' and that the Republic's foreign policy had to take account of trade and shipping, but insisted that if the security of the state were undermined then its commerce would be lost also.[85]

Eager to encourage resistance to the Prince, d'Avaux sent reassuring messages to Amsterdam, and assured the States General, on 5 November, that his master would take only what was due to him, Luxemburg and Namur, leaving untouched the fortified towns in Flanders, specified in the treaty of Nijmegen as a 'barrier' for the Dutch. But scarcely had he

[82] ARH PR 383, p. 59. res. SF 9 Aug. 1683.
[83] RAF M 2/32. res. Mindergetal, Leeuwarden, 9 Oct. 1683.
[84] RAGr. arch. SGR 378. res. S.Gr. 18 Dec. 1683.
[85] Kurtz, *Willem III en Amsterdam*, 67–8.

pronounced, than French troops occupied two of the 'barrier' towns—Kortrijk and Dixmuiden. A majority of the States of Holland, shepherded by Fagel, voted to send an extraordinary delegation, headed by the Stadholder, to exert pressure on Amsterdam. Prince and Pensionary duly arrived in the city, accompanied by two deputies from each of the nine towns which supported the Stadholder's policy, and three delegates of the *ridderschap*. The *vroedschap* closed ranks around Van Beuningen, who was now seen as embodying the dignity and independence of Amsterdam. In several tense meetings, in the city hall, the *vroedschap* insisted Louis would not be deterred by an extra 16,635 men and that the Republic should not risk war with France, and disaster for its trade, for the sake of a few enclaves of the Spanish Netherlands.[86] The Prince's ill humour was aggravated by the obvious signs that the ordinary people of Amsterdam backed the *vroedschap*. It was rumoured in the streets that Orange 'affects the sovereignty' and was 'unfortunate in the last war'. The surge of 'insolent and desperately seditious discourses upon the Dam, the Exchange, and other publiq places against the Prince while he was there' apparently 'terrified some in the [city] government' who were otherwise inclined to comply with the Prince.[87] Some citizens reportedly took the view that 'Amsterdam was a great republique and powerful and would rather separate from the rest of the provinces, and joyne with Freezland and Groningen and have another Stadholder [that is Hendrik Casimir] than continue under the Prince'. Mindful of 1650, the burgomasters watched for any sign of unusual troop movements anywhere in the Republic. Having staged a grand, quasi-monarchical entry into the city, the Prince stormed out in a fury, having been, as one observer put it, 'bitterly and scandalously reproached by the common people'.

William now switched to persuading majorities of the assemblies of Holland and Zeeland that the 16,000 men were an issue resolvable by 'plurality', or majority vote. Under intense pressure, Leiden yielded, Orangist regents urging, as a precedent for overruling Amsterdam, Leiden's treatment 'at the time of the peace with Spain', in 1648, when she was overruled.[88] Though six towns resisted initially—Amsterdam, Leiden, Delft, Alkmaar, Enkhuizen, and Schiedam—the Stadholder whittled this down to three—Amsterdam, Delft, and Schiedam—enabling Fagel to 'conclude' on 31 January 1684.[89]

Amsterdam protested vehemently, dispatching a circular to other towns condemning the vote by 'plurality' as a violation of the procedures of the

[86] Roldanus, *Coenraad van Beuningen*, 43.
[87] PRO SP 84/218, fos. 145, 148v. Bampfield to Hughes, Leeuwarden, 9 and 12 Dec. 1683.
[88] GA Leiden Sec. Arch. 458, p. 8. res. vroed. 27 Jan. 1684.
[89] Kurtz, *Willem III en Amsterdam*, 84.

provincial States laid down in 1581 and 1651. At the same time, delegates were sent to stiffen the resolve of Friesland and Groningen. While Orange's grip on the provinces 'reformed' in 1673–4 remained unassailable, his heavy-handed methods elsewhere proved counter-productive. Backed by the *Mindergetal*, Hendrik Casimir finally rallied all the Frisian quarters against raising the 16,000 men, to prevent a 'ruinous war' for which Friesland, depleted by agricultural slump, was unable to pay (see p. 635 above) and which could not be won, owing to lack of allies.[90] Hendrik Casimir, helped by Amsterdam, also swayed the Ommelanders, so that, in March, a united States of Groningen voted against the measure.[91]

In Zeeland, too, the Stadholder encountered stubborn resistance. Initially, four Zeeland towns approved the raising of the 16,000 men, with only Middelburg and Goes against. Goes was soon swayed. But Middelburg proved obdurate. In March 1684 the Prince travelled to Zeeland, in person, to overawe Middelburg.[92] He interviewed each member of the *vroedschap* individually, trying to persuade them to change their minds. When this failed he demanded that the Pensionary, De Huybert, conclude by 'plurality', in the States of Zeeland, as Fagel had done in Holland. On his refusal, William personally took the chair, passing the resolution by six votes to one, over the protests of Middelburg.

Since late 1683, Amsterdam's deputies in The Hague had held several secret meetings with d'Avaux. The Prince now sought to turn this to advantage, using the text of an intercepted letter, from d'Avaux to Louis, alluding to his contacts with Amsterdam, to discredit Amsterdam's proceedings in the States and her opposition to his policy.[93] Reading the text aloud to the States, on 16 February, the Stadholder accused Amsterdam of collusion with a hostile monarch and divulging the secrets of the state. In the ensuing uproar, the *ridderschap* proposed the city's conduct be investigated by the States, which should at once seize the papers of the burgomasters to prevent disappearance of incriminating evidence. By a majority of five, the States voted to circulate copies of the intercepted letter and impound the papers of the city's deputies at The Hague. The latter walked out; Amsterdam formally withdrew her delegation to the States.

Yet, for all the arm-twisting, it was clear, by April, that the Prince had lost. Despite Orange's majorities, Amsterdam succeeded in blocking his path essentially because public opinion in the chief cities of Holland and

[90] ARH PR 383, p. 85. res. SF 16 Feb. 1684.
[91] RAGr. arch SGR 378. res. S.Gr. 21 Mar. 1684.
[92] *Notulen* SZ, res. SZ 20 Jan. and 23 Mar. 1684.
[93] De Bruin, *Geheimhouding*, 360–1.

Zeeland was against the Stadholder and behind the States party-faction. By April, Rotterdam, the scene of a bitter tussle between Orangists and Louvesteiners, had shifted and come under the republican sway of Adriaen Paets. At Leiden, there was a strong reaction against the Prince's manipulation of the city.[94] There was much talk, at this time, in the inns and taverns of Holland, of curbing what many people now regarded as the excessive authority the Prince had acquired in 1672. Not a few spoke of him as a 'tyrant, murderer of the De Witts', and 'betrayer of his trust and country . . . with no friends but the miserable Spaniards', and of 'taking from the Prince (if they can) the power of choice out of the nominated persons [in the towns of Holland] which, if effected, half his power is taken away'.[95] On 13 May, the States of Holland passed a secret resolution forbidding the Dutch troops sent to the Spanish Netherlands to engage in hostilities with the French, so as to prevent their being used in an attempt to break Louis's resumed siege of the city of Luxemburg.

Friesland and Groningen, meanwhile, were locked in dispute with the States General. Ironically, it was now Orangist Holland which insisted that Friesland must abide by Generality decisions, taken by majority vote, and Friesland which quoted past resolutions of the States of Holland proclaiming the sovereign rights of each province. Friesland and Groningen demanded the recall of troops, on their *répartitions*, which had been sent to the Spanish Netherlands—not just to the territory of the Republic but their respective provinces.[96] They threatened to strike off the payroll soldiers who refused to obey the orders of the province which paid them, insisting that the articles of the Union of Utrecht, establishing a common defence, and army, did not cancel their 'sovereign right' to dispose of the troops for which they paid. The States of Friesland also passed a secret resolution forbidding troops in Friesland to leave the province, whatever the Generality or captain-general might order, unless authorized to do so by the province.[97]

All prospect of mobilizing an effective coalition to block Louis XIV's acquisition of Luxemburg had, by May 1684, evaporated. The argument between the two sides of the Dutch political spectrum now chiefly concerned what accommodation with France could be made regarding disputed districts of the Spanish Netherlands. The city of Groningen pressed, in the States of Groningen, for a treaty of friendship with France, along the lines

[94] Woltjer, 'Willem III en Leiden', 419–21.
[95] PRO SP 84/218, fo. 219. Bampfield to Hughes, Leiden, 29 Apr. 1684.
[96] RAF SF s4/i 'Secreet resolutie-boeck'. res. SF 15 and 25 Mar. 1684.
[97] Ibid. res. SF 19 Apr. 1684.

offered by Louis in 1679.[98] But what Louis offered now was a twenty-year truce in the Spanish Netherlands, with France keeping Luxemburg, and other recently annexed localities. On 5 June, d'Avaux announced that his master was granting the States General twelve days to decide on his offer. Amsterdam urged acceptance; the Stadholder recommended that the States General offer Louis a different truce, which would apply also to France's border with the Empire, and provide compensation for damage to the Prince's estates in Luxemburg and the principality of Orange.

The States of Holland voted, on 16 June, to accept the French offer, a resolution carried by Amsterdam, Dordrecht, Enkhuizen, Alkmaar, Schiedam, Brill, Delft, and Edam, in disregard of the Prince's advice.[99] William, for the moment, had lost his grip on the province. He also, temporarily, lost his hold on Utrecht, where, during April, vigorous endeavours were in hand to 'take off the province . . . from the Prince and joyne it with Freez, Groningen and Amsterdam'. At first, the States split, the towns siding with Holland, and the *ridderschap* with the Prince. But a delegation from Holland clinched Utrecht's vote. Even Overijssel wavered. On 24 June, the States General adopted Holland's proposal to accept the French offer, by five provinces to two, over the protests only of Zeeland and Gelderland; and the truce was duly signed.

The Stadholder fought to regain the upper hand, rendering the contest over ratification a classic cliff-hanger. He succeeded in winning back the States of Utrecht. Odijk clinched the States of Zeeland, which rejected ratification, by four votes to three, overruling Middelburg, Zierikzee, and Goes, which (as usual) backed the Holland States party.[100] But, on 19 August, the last remaining day for ratification, Overijssel—where the States had passed a secret resolution, instructing their deputies to hold out, for the Prince's interests, as long as possible, but not to let the truce collapse—came out in favour.[101] With Overijssel, the States General ratified by four provinces to three.

Orange had suffered another serious blow to his prestige, The European crisis was settled, in August 1684, in a manner favourable to France—at the insistence of Amsterdam. His foes could look forward to further reductions in the Stadholder's power. In the wake of ratification, Amsterdam sent an envoy to Leeuwarden, to confer with Hendrik Casimir, and his Cocceian adviser, Professor van der Waeyen, on other States party objectives,[102] such

---

[98] RAGr. arch. SGR 18, res. S.Gr. 25 Apr. 1684.
[99] GA Haarlem vroed. res. 25, fo. 91v, res. vroed. 19 June 1684.
[100] *Notulen* SZ res. SZ 14 July 1684.
[101] ARH PR 491, fo. 45, sec. res. SO 7 July 1684.
[102] Kurtz, *Willem III en Amsterdam*, 222.

as further army cuts, improved relations with France, restoration of Utrecht, Overijssel, and Gelderland to their pre-1674 constitutional status, and the dismissal of Waldeck, who was unpopular and reputedly a principal advocate of anti-French policies.[103]

But the Prince, intent on restoring his authority, learnt from his mistakes and adjusted his domestic strategy accordingly, switching from confrontation to dialogue and compromise. The events of 1683–4 taught him that he could not effectively lead the Republic, and confront the ambition of Louis XIV, at odds with Amsterdam and his alienated cousin. Clearly, he needed to build a broader-based consensus which offered enough to Amsterdam, and Hendrik Casimir, to win their co-operation and, until he achieved this, the United Provinces would remain distracted and divided. Mastering his irritable disposition, he began patiently extending the middle ground, entering, in particular, into contacts with the two leading figures (apart from Van Beuningen) at Amsterdam, Witsen, and Hudde. His new tack was helped by the fact that many Amsterdam regents felt uneasy over what had transpired and judged that, in the longer run, Van Beuningen's confrontation with the Prince served the interests of neither the Republic nor Amsterdam.[104]

Over the winter of 1684–5, there was intense debate among the provinces about military and naval expenditure. In 1682, at the Stadholder's insistence, naval spending had been trimmed, and army expenditure raised to 960,000 guilders monthly. Amsterdam, backed by Friesland and Groningen, now pressed for hefty cuts in military spending. In the States of Holland, Amsterdam was supported by Delft, Leiden, and Dordrecht. The Prince pointedly steered a middle course. The *Raad van State*'s petition to the Generality for 1685 requested only 775,000 guilders monthly, reducing the army to under 40,000 men.[105] When Amsterdam, Friesland, and Groningen then pressed for still further cuts, the Prince resisted, supported by Utrecht, Gelderland, and Overijssel. But he accepted Amsterdam's argument that, through inadequate naval expenditure, the Republic was allowing its navy to fall behind and the English to become 'masters of the seas'. He showed his willingness to meet Amsterdam half-way, bringing pressure to bear on the inland provinces to agree to substantial increases in naval spending.

William III was never again to undertake a major initiative without first securing the collaboration of Amsterdam. At this point he also offered to come to terms with Hendrik Casimir. The Frisian Stadholder being so taken

---

[103] PRO SP 84/218, fo. 255. Chudleigh to Sunderland, 20 Oct. 1684.
[104] Wagenaar, *Vad. Hist.* xv. 283–4.
[105] Ten Raa and De Bas Het *Staatsche leger*, vi. 154, 157–8.

with Professor Van der Waeyen as to be practically ruled by him, Orange sent Waldeck to Van der Waeyen to negotiate a set of compromises to serve as a basis for future co-operation between the two Stadholders. No doubt the Prince also intimated that his pro-Voetian stance in church and intellectual matters would now be further diluted. The result was a formal contract under which William yielded power of patronage in the Frisian and Groningen regiments of the army to his cousin and generally agreed to respect his position.[106] William wrote to him of his pleasure 'que vous estes satisfait de ce que Mr van der Waeyen a convenu avec moi sur les differens qu'il y avoient entre nous'.[107]

With his chief adversaries placated, Orange was free to rebuild his influence, and that of his supporters in the Holland town councils, by balancing the factions, sharing offices, and patronizing both wings of the public Church. It was no simple matter to damp down the bitter party-factional strife. One thorny problem was the tense situation persisting in Dordrecht.[108] This city's defection to the States party-faction camp had greatly annoyed him. He mobilized the Hof of Holland, in November 1684, to investigate what he claimed were irregularities in the nominations of the burgomasters of whom he disapproved. His opponents at Dordrecht then sent a circular to the other Holland town councils, accusing the Stadholder of subverting Dordrecht's 'privileges and rights and the peace and tranquility of the city'.[109] Orange responded with his own circular to the town councils, deploring the 'immoderate zeal' of Dordrecht's *vroedschap*, and efforts to stir up resentment against him among the Holland towns, questioning the city's motives, and assuring the States that he had respected, and would continue to respect scrupulously, the proper limits of his authority in the province.

This stress on constitutional propriety, and the need for moderation, determined the Prince's method of dealing with regent groups who had opposed him. His approach now was to balance the contending cliques, encouraging them to negotiate and draw up 'contracts of correspondence' for the sharing of civic offices between party-factional blocs. A prime instance was his confrontation with Leiden. During 1683–4, the Stadholder's relations with Leiden were continuously strained and whereas, during 1685, his relations with Amsterdam improved, those with Leiden

---

[106] ARH arch SH Collectie Fagel 496, 'Stukken betreffende . . . de Prins van Orange en Hendrik Casimir'.
[107] *Archives*, 2nd ser. v. 589.
[108] Van Dalen, *Gesch. van Dordrecht*, ii. 1139–40.
[109] GA Leiden Sec. Arch. 917/x/b. William III to Leiden vroed., 12 Nov. 1684.

worsened, becoming, for some months, the focus of Dutch domestic politics, an affair, which, d'Avaux reported, 'fait bien de bruit'. Ideologically, Leiden, at this time, was one of the most deeply divided cities in the Republic. The States party republican bloc in the *vroedschap*, in 1685, were reported to outnumber their rivals by twenty-six to thirteen.[110] As in other towns, the ideological, clientage, and theological splits in the *vroedschap* also pervaded the militia and consistory. In 1685, Leiden's eight militia captains were said to be divided four on either side and the city's twelve Reformed Church preachers, seven 'for the town' (Cocceian) and five 'for the Prince' (Voetian).

This confrontation reached its climax when the *vroedschap* presented Orange with a double list of nominations for the magistracy, as procedure required, but, in the Prince's view, denying him proper choice, by including two men disqualified by birth and background. He gave the *vroedschap* three weeks to amend their list and when they refused proceeded to select his own nominees. Leiden reacted in 'heat and fury', accusing the Stadholder of violating Leiden's privileges and subverting the autonomy of the Holland towns.[111] The burgomasters doubled the militia watch, deliberately stirred up a mood of crisis, and avowed themselves ready to sacrifice life and property for their civic freedom. The Prince, who absented himself from the States of Holland for over a year after his defeat, in 1684, suddenly appeared, in October 1685, adamant that he had acted correctly over the Leiden magistracy, promising that when towns submitted nominations to him in proper form, he would punctiliously adhere to names on their lists. Not only did the Prince succeed in isolating Leiden in the States, he forced the *vroedschap* to accept his mediation between the warring parties in the city.

For this task, Prince and States chose Van Beverningk, a former Louvesteiner who had made his peace with the Stadholder, a Cocceian, adroit diplomat, and expert in 'contracts of correspondence'. Van Beverningk declared the election of November 1685 void and imposed a compromise, involving the nomination of two burgomasters from either faction. One of these, Jacob van der Meer, subsequently emerged as the Prince's right-hand man in Leiden and the most influential figure in the city until his death, in 1696.[112] But it is the way Prince and Van Beverningk broke the ascendancy of the States party-faction which is chiefly significant. The guiding principle was avoidance of one-sidedness, with election of burgomasters 'according to

[110] *Négociations . . . d'Avaux*, v. 176.
[111] PRO SP 84/220, fo. 12v. Skelton to Sunderland, 16 Oct. 1685.
[112] Prak, *Gezeten burgers*, 61.

order and rank as is proper', with the Stadholder to ensure that balance was maintained.[113] No doubt most of the *vroedschap* adjusted to the new situation without great difficulty. In most cases self-interest prevailed. D'Avaux remarked, in December 1685, that only four or five members of the Amsterdam *vroedschap* could be described as 'bons républicains' in the sense of being immune to the blandishments of the Stadholder and consistent in their principles. The rest trimmed according to the wind: 'leur interest particulier, ou leur foiblesse, les oblige souvent à avoir de la complaisance pour le Prince'.[114] In Leiden the balance between principle and self-interest—when the two collided—was doubtless much the same.

Balancing the party-factions in the town councils implied balancing the theological factions also. For the one went with the other. The practice of alternating between Voetians and Cocceians, when appointing new preachers, as a way of balancing the parties and minimizing friction, was first adopted in Amsterdam in 1677. By the mid-1680s, alternating was favoured by many town councils, and the Stadholder, as a means of rendering Cocceian–Voetian conflict less combustible. In Leiden, though, consistory and *vroedschap* had for some years exclusively chosen Cocceians. The new burgomasters changed this in the spring of 1686. The procedure when a preaching vacancy arose was for the consistory to draw up a list of candidates which was then submitted to the burgomasters for approval. When the consistory did so in March 1686, though, the burgomasters rejected the list, remarking that they preferred that not all the candidates should be 'of that sort'. When presented with a revised list the response was the same, the burgomasters adding that they did not question the erudition of the candidates 'but that they were not of the sort which they wished to see and that they thought they had spoken clearly already as to what sort they preferred': with the Church divided between those called 'Voetians' and those called 'Cocceians', they judged the second list 'again weighted everything on to one side', which was not what they intended.[115] They then required the consistory to 'put on the nomination three preachers of the sort called Voetians'.

The consistory expressed 'surprise and sorrow' that the burgomasters should consider the public Church to be divided between 'Voetians' and 'Cocceians', averring 'they had never used these names ... but, rather, believed it dangerous to the peace of the Church to do so'.[116] They

[113] Woltjer, 'Willem III en Leiden', 420–1.
[114] *Négociations ... d'Avaux*, v. 196.
[115] GA Leiden kerkeraad 7. res. 13 and 17 Mar. 1686.
[116] GA Leiden kerkeraad 7. res. 15 Apr. 1686.

undertook to comply with the burgomasters' wishes. But on perusing their third list the burgomasters, to their amazement, could still find no 'Voetians'. They then named several and insisted the consistory include them, and it was one of these, Isacus Zevenhoven, at Flushing, who was duly appointed.[117]

From 1685 onwards, leading up to the Glorious Revolution (1688–91), the Prince could rely on a good working relationship, and effective co-oper-ation, with Amsterdam, Leiden, Dordrecht, Delft, all the Holland towns with which he had been so sharply at odds during the early 1680s. Local factors contributed. But the change was also partly due to a shift in the public mood arising from the Revocation of the Edict of Nantes, in France, and the increasingly sombre outlook in international politics. Louis XIV's intolerance and the plight of the Huguenots made a deep impression on the Dutch public.[118] D'Avaux and other diplomats frequently remarked on this. 'They beginne to exclaime very loudly here', noted the English envoy, Skelton, in October 1685, 'against the usage which the French Protestants have in France and a day of humiliation and fasting is to be appointed throughout these provinces by reason of that persecution.'[119] As a result, Fagel was relieved to see, d'Avaux 'lost much of his credit with those of Amsterdam'. The Huguenots who settled in the United Provinces included numerous preachers, professionals, and army officers, who did much to reinforce the growing hostility of Dutch opinion to Louis XIV.

The mass immigration of Huguenot refugees, with their graphic tales of persecution and harassment, contributed to the change of atmosphere and helped lend cohesion to the Dutch body politic during the years preceding the Glorious Revolution. But its importance should not be exaggerated. The Amsterdam burgomasters themselves told d'Avaux that Louis XIV's treat-ment of the Huguenots 'avoit changé la face des affaires de ce pays'.[120] D'Avaux knew his relationship with Amsterdam was not what it had been. Nevertheless, he remained confident, not only in 1685–6, but down to the autumn of 1687, that William III was powerless to mobilize Holland against his master's policies. In assessing the situation, d'Avaux placed most weight on the fact that Amsterdam, Rotterdam, Middelburg, and Leiden, and also Delft and Gouda, all had a large stake, given the importance of their trade with France, in preserving the existing peace. The Amsterdam burgomasters on several occasions renewed their assurance that provided Louis adhered

[117] GA Leiden burgomasters' *notulen*, 1682–98, fos. 95–6 (21 Mar. and 1 Apr. 1686).
[118] Van Malssen, *Louis XIV d'après les pamphlets*, 43–53.
[119] PRO SP 84/220, fo. 12v. Skelton to Sunderland, 16 Oct. 1685.
[120] *Négociations . . . d'Avaux*, v. 203, 215.

to what had been agreed at Nijmegen, and the Dutch continued trading with France on favourable terms, they would see to it that the Prince could, and would, not drag the Republic into an armed coalition against France.[121] The Huguenot refugees, and Voetian *predikanten* and their followers, may have fulminated against Louis; but the regents who had opposed Orange in 1683–4 were not zealous Calvinists and not interested in generating hostility towards Catholics and Catholicism. Religion was a potent factor in the situation. But in their religious attitudes the Dutch ruling groups, and common citizenry, were divided. 'Tous les bons républicains', as d'Avaux expressed it, 'sont Arminiens',[122] by which he meant nominal rather than committed members of the public Church, men opposed to the Calvinist militancy of the Voetians.

THE REPUBLIC AND THE GLORIOUS REVOLUTION, 1685–1691

In the years 1688–91 the course of both Dutch and British history was dramatically changed by one of the great events of world history—the Glorious Revolution. The dethroning of the last male Stuart monarch in Britain, and the enthroning, by Parliament, of William and Mary, were to have far-reaching consequences and not only for Britain and the United Provinces but for many other lands as well. What occurred in 1688–9 changed Britain fundamentally, creating, for the first time, a stable, and powerful, constitutional monarchy, with Parliament increasingly in the ascendant. This contrasted sharply with what had gone before; for, under Charles II and James II (1685–9), England tended towards absolutism, the weakening of Parliament, since the 1660s, together with religious tensions, rendering England, as well as Scotland and Ireland, divided and unstable. These stresses were then further aggravated by the religious policies of James, a staunch Catholic ruling over a largely Protestant population with often violently anti-Catholic instincts.

As with any great turning-point in history, some of its preconditions and causes reached far back into the past. Many of the political and religious tensions in Britain had been acute for decades. Also William III, the prime mover of the Glorious Revolution, being himself a nephew of both Charles and James, as well as the husband of the latter's eldest daughter, had long taken a keen interest in the future of the British thrones.[123] It was natural that he should privately harbour ambitions as to his future role in Britain

---

[121] Ibid. v. 250, 302 and vi. 12, 18, 100–2.
[122] Ibid. i. 3, 153 and iv. 321.
[123] Haley, *The British and the Dutch*, 133–5.

since (until the birth of James II's only son, in June 1688) the Prince's wife, Princess Mary, was the next in line to the three thrones of England, Scotland, and Ireland.

Yet, despite this, there was little sign that anything like the Glorious Revolution was even remotely possible, either in Charles II's reign or during the opening two years of that of James. Charles's position was unchallengeable, and while the Whigs tried to bar James's succession, on the grounds of his Catholicism, they were defeated. The failure of the Monmouth Rebellion in England, in 1685, not only further weakened the opposition but provided James with the pretext to raise, and retain, a standing army of 40,000 men, the first large standing army in England under monarchical rule, and a major enhancement of his power. Nor was there any prospect of active collaboration between the English Whig opposition and the Dutch Stadholder at that stage. The Prince of Orange could not intervene anywhere, even on a modest scale, using the troops and warships of the United Provinces, without the agreement, and co-operation, of Holland, including Amsterdam, and the events of 1683–4 had rendered it unlikely that this would be forthcoming for any major foreign intervention, let alone intervention across the sea in a land where the Stadholder had dynastic ties but the regents, and States of Holland, had no obvious interests at stake. That Holland should incur vast risks, and go to great expense, to advance the dynastic concerns of the House of Orange, in Britain, was inconceivable. Consequently, during 1685–7 there was no prospect of Orange undertaking a large-scale military expedition to Britain. It became a possibility during 1688 only because of startling new developments in France.[124]

For the Dutch public and regents it was not Britain, but France which was the focus of attention. But from 1685 until late 1687 Louis XIV (and James II) could safely rely on Orange's inability to bring the Republic into a European coalition against France. For Amsterdam and the *bons républicains* would block it. During 1686 Amsterdam refused to permit any increase in military expenditure while, as late as the summer of 1687, only half of the thirty-six new warships agreed in 1682 were being built. The States of Holland neither expected, nor wished, to be dragged into a major foreign entanglement. Rather the Dutch political climate was one of drift. 'In the yeare and a halfe that I have lived amonst them', an English diplomat reported, in October 1686, 'the States have not taken any one resolution, but only proposed, and debated, matters without concluding anything . . . they are in a grave arreare to their army', he added, 'their navy is rotting, their

---

[124] Israel, *Anglo-Dutch Moment*, 105–15.

shipping being in soe ill a condition that, to build new ones, the charge would not be much greater than to repayre the old, and all their magazines are empty.'[125] All efforts 'for the raising of money' proved fruitless. Some Holland towns proposed taxes which others rejected. Others wanted no new taxes, proposing instead that interest payable on States of Holland bonds be reduced (in line with other interest rates), from 4 to 3 per cent.

Moreover, international developments during 1685–7 tended to reinforce the likelihood of Dutch neutrality in case of a new war between Louis XIV and the Habsburgs. The death of the Elector Karl II of the Palatinate, in May 1685, led to that formerly Calvinist electorate passing into the hands of a Catholic prince, Philip-Wilhelm, duke of Jülich-Berg, who was closely allied to the Emperor, while the League of Augsburg, formed in July 1686 by the Emperor, various German princes, Spain, and Sweden, mounted an open challenge to the French grip on Alsace, Strasburg, and the upper Rhine. The Emperor's victories over the Turks in Hungary, in 1687, and rising prestige, only heightened the prospect of a full-scale conflict between France and the Emperor on the Rhine.[126]

While Holland, and the States General, made no move to strengthen their armed forces in the mid-1680s, commerce went from strength to strength. Initially, Dutch recovery from the war of 1672–7 had been slow and hesitant, and never really extended to the agricultural sector, public building, or the art market. Prices for rich men's houses, in Amsterdam, reached a nadir in 1683 and recovered only marginally in the years 1684–8.[127] But recovery in overseas commerce, shipping, and industry accelerated in the mid-1680s, the best results being achieved by the two great colonial companies and exports to western Europe, the Mediterranean, and Spanish America. VOC and WIC shares on the Amsterdam Exchange rose dramatically in the years 1685–7.

But it was a recovery in which Baltic bulk traffic, now much diminished, and the fisheries contributed little, a boom based chiefly on the 'rich trades' and manufacturing.[128] France, moreover, was one of the principal markets, fuelling the revival, absorbing great quantities of Dutch fine cloth, camlets, whale products, East India commodities, Gouda pipes, processed tobacco, dyestuffs, naval supplies, and much of the herring catch. Both for this reason, and also because Dutch gains in Spain and Spanish America accrued chiefly at the expense of French products, the Dutch boom of the

[125] BL MS 41814, fo. 40v. Skelton to Middleton, 15 Oct. 1686.
[126] Symcox, 'Louis XIV and the Outbreak', 186–7.
[127] Lesger, *Huur en conjunctuur*, 84.
[128] Israel, *Dutch Primacy*, 301, 340–1, 350–8.

1680s was inextricably entwined with the economic crisis gripping France. This French slump had several causes but was certainly aggravated by the massive haemorrhage of Huguenot capital and skills during the mid- and late 1680s. No less certainly the lowering of the French tariffs, in 1677, contributed to both the Dutch boom and the French crisis, even if the actual influence of tariffs was less than contemporaries supposed. France gained appreciably from the treaty of Nijmegen politically, but seemingly at great cost economically.

It was only a matter of time before a new Franco-Dutch *guerre de commerce* erupted, with incalculable consequences. Louis XIV's reversion to an aggressive anti-Dutch mercantilism began in August 1687, fifteen months before the commencement of the Glorious Revolution and Nine Years War, in November 1688.[129] They were to prove fifteen momentous months. The process began with a ban on importing of Dutch herring into France, except when certified as having been salted with French salt. Then, in September, Louis reimposed Colbert's general tariff list of 1667, at a stroke doubling the duties on Dutch fine cloth and drastically increasing duties on all Dutch manufactures entering France.[130] The reaction in the United Provinces was immediate and furious. For Louis had broken his undertakings under the treaty of Nijmegen and, in effect, torn up the treaty. Nevertheless, it was possible for Holland's regents, merchants, manufacturers, and skippers to hope initially that this was but a passing setback to Franco-Dutch relations, that Louis would relent, and Dutch commerce with France recover. Many of the Amsterdam *vroedschap* hoped for this not only on economic, but also on political, grounds; for if Louis persisted with fiercely protectionist measures and Franco-Dutch relations deteriorated, this could only justify, and strengthen, the Prince of Orange. Hudde was doubtless sincere in promising d'Avaux, in October 1687, to do his utmost to preserve the post-1677 relationship between the Republic and France. In d'Avaux's presence the four Amsterdam burgomasters toasted 'la bonne union entre sa Majesté et la République à la confusion de tous ceux qui la veulent traverser'.[131]

But Louis redoubled rather than relaxed his new mercantilist offensive. Additional protectionist regulations, and increases in tariffs on particular items, further depressed imports of Dutch manufactures, fish, and other commodities into France. In December 1687, Dutch factors at Paris, Metz, Lyons, and Lille reported that it was no longer possible to sell Dutch textiles

[129] Israel, *Anglo-Dutch Moment*, 114–16.
[130] Ibid. 114.
[131] *Négociations . . . d'Avaux*, vi. 102.

of any sort in France. In the States of Holland, Leiden's deputies complained, in March 1688, that the new French tariff 'in effect means an absolute ban on the sale of our *lakens* in France'.[132] Exports of herring to France collapsed, causing heavy loss to the South Holland herring fishery and Rotterdam. As the months passed, it also became harder to believe that this was anything but a planned, enduring, systematic onslaught on Dutch commerce. Fagel urged the States of Holland, in May, that all diplomatic means were now exhausted and that it was time to contemplate stronger measures.[133] D'Avaux was now less confident, but still hopeful, despite the indignation Louis's policy had aroused, that Amsterdam, backed by Rotterdam, Delft, and others would block retaliation and prevent an escalating confrontation between the Republic and France.

By early summer, the Dutch mood was hardening, convinced that Louis designed, as d'Avaux put it, to 'detruire leur religion et surtout leur commerce'. Dutch worries increased further with the international furore which erupted over the electorate of Cologne, following the death of the Elector Max Heinrich, in June 1688. Cologne was a strategically vital crossroads for France, Germany, and the Low Countries, as well as the leading ecclesiastical state of the Rhineland, and it was essential to Louis that it remain a protectorate of France. When his candidate to succeed Max Heinrich was thwarted by the Emperor and Pope, Louis threatened to use force. Although French troops did not occupy the electorate until September, when they did so as part of a more general invasion of the Rhineland, the menace of a French descent on Cologne alarmed the States General, as well as Brandenburg and the Emperor, who all mobilized large forces on the middle and lower Rhine.

At the same time, increasing tension with France of itself made the States of Holland, and States General, more nervous about England. James II may have faced growing domestic opposition but, for precisely that reason, he appeared increasingly dependent on the support of Louis XIV; he also possessed a formidable navy, and sizeable army. Memories of 1672, and previous Anglo-Dutch antagonism, rendered the regents all too ready to exaggerate the least sign of Anglo-French collusion, and to regard it as being directed against themselves.[134] Whether or not William III seriously believed there was a risk of a new joint Anglo-French attack on the Republic—James II later publicly denied any such conspiracy—he undoubtedly exploited apprehension on this score among the regents. Such

[132] Res. Holl. 18 Mar. 1688.
[133] GA Leiden Sec. Arch. 488, p. 359, res. 11 May 1688.
[134] Groenveld, 'J'equippe une flotte', 238–40.

fears were heightened by James's request to the States General, in February 1688, for the repatriation of the English and Scots regiments serving in the Dutch army. When the States General refused to release them, the king replied by issuing a general proclamation commanding his subjects serving in the Dutch army and navy to return home, a measure which materially heightened Anglo-Dutch friction.

Yet, all along, the decisive factor determining Dutch policy with regard to Britain was the escalating conflict over commerce between the United Provinces and France.[135] It was Louis's new *guerre de commerce* against the Dutch which made real the possibility of war between France and the Dutch and, in turn, rendered the possibility of Anglo-French collusion against the Republic dangerous. Both politically, and strategically, the economic war between France and the Dutch was the pivot on which everything turned, enabling the Stadholder to combine with Amsterdam, join a general coalition with the Habsburgs against Louis, and prepare his invasion of England. D'Avaux sensed a profound change, at Amsterdam, long before he had concrete evidence. In June 1688, Orange took three of the four Amsterdam burgomasters into his confidence, initiating a secret strategic collaboration of momentous importance in European history, in which the Prince's two closest confidants, Bentinck and, above all, Dijkvelt, consulted closely with the burgomasters, especially Hudde and Witsen.[136]

For the moment, the Amsterdam city council, divided among themselves, followed a middle course: holding up the proposed measures of retaliation against France but, behind the scenes, co-operating with the Stadholder's strategy of rearming the Republic, making alliances with German states, and amassing an armada for a possible invasion of England.[137] It was not until late August that d'Avaux grasped the full extent of the collusion between Amsterdam and the Prince, but before that he saw that Rotterdam had switched to supporting the proposed ban on French imports; that now only Amsterdam and Delft were holding it up; and that Amsterdam was no longer to be depended on to block William III's military and strategic plans. D'Avaux warned his master that the regents and merchants were 'trop aigries sur les affaires du commerce pour attendre une opposition vigoureuse de la part de la province de Hollande'. The ambassador tried stirring up Friesland and Groningen but found that Hendrik Casimir preferred to stick to his accommodation with the Prince.

[135] Israel, *The Anglo-Dutch Moment*, 110–19.
[136] Gebhard, *Het leven*, i. 320–7.
[137] Israel, *The Anglo-Dutch Moment*, 115–19.

But William III was also worried. If the Amsterdam burgomasters no longer opposed his policy, and were co-operating in the military and naval build-up, Hudde and Witsen were also appalled by the risks involved in attempting an autumn invasion of Britain, and Orange was in agonies of doubt as to whether he could count on them. Over the summer, with Amsterdam's support, he had been able to negotiate a series of troop-hire agreements with Brandenburg, Hesse-Cassel, Celle, and Württemberg, providing 14,000 seasoned German troops to serve under the flag of the States General, at Dutch rates of pay.[138] With these he hoped to assuage Amsterdam's fears that the eastern strongholds would not be sufficiently strongly held, after the Republic's best regiments were drawn off, to embark on the invasion fleet destined for England. Early in September, the Prince wrote from 'Minden to the magistrates of Amsterdam assuring them to have perfected the alliances with the Princes of Germany, that therefore they should come to the assembly of Holland . . . with an unanimous resolution for the prohibition of the French commodities'.[139] This helped stop the disastrous crash on the Amsterdam Stock Exchange which had begun on 25 August (see Table 39), but still Amsterdam hesitated.[140]

On 19 September the Prince and Fagel revealed part of their strategic plan to the full States of Holland in secret session. Orange held that France had inflicted great damage on Dutch commerce, shipping, and fisheries, and that the Republic had no alternative but to arm for war, leading him to negotiate the hire of 14,000 crack troops from four German principalities.[141] As previously arranged, Amsterdam approved of what the Prince had done and emergency meetings of the provincial assemblies followed over the next few days. The Prince had sent Hendrik Casimir Fagel's speech, to the States of Holland, asking him to use the same arguments to win over the States of Friesland. The Frisian Stadholder, in the ensuing secret session of the States of Friesland, stressed especially the 'conspiracy which the two kings of France and England have formed against this state'.[142] Friesland likewise approved the Prince's proceedings.

The Amsterdam *vroedschap* was split. At their meeting, on 24 September, a hard core of States party regents still refused to allow the ban on French imports to proceed, arguing that it was not yet too late and demanding fresh talks with d'Avaux, to search for a way 'so that the tariffs introduced in

---

[138] Ibid. 107–8.
[139] BL MS Add. 41816, fo. 179. D'Albeville to Middleton, 14 Sept. 1688.
[140] GA Amsterdam res. vroed. 21 and 24 Sept. 1688.
[141] *Secreete Resolution*, iv. 226–7.
[142] RAF arch. SF S4/1 'Secreet resolutie-boeck, 1671–99' res. 25 Sept. and 5 Oct. 1688.

France might be cancelled'.[143] But at the critical moment Louis played right into Orange's hands. Incensed at the Holland regents' 'insolence' in daring to consider measures of economic retaliation against France, Louis clapped a general arrest on Dutch ships in French ports, seizing over a hundred vessels, mostly loading wine, at Bordeaux, La Rochelle, and Nantes. With that the die was cast. The outrage amongst the Dutch public, and merchant

TABLE 39. *Movements in the VOC share price at Amsterdam, 1639–1690*[a]

Date	Political context explaining movements	Price fluctuations (% of face value)
Aug. 1639	Gains in Ceylon	412
Mar. 1641	Impact of Portuguese secession from Spain	481
Apr. 1648	Dutch–Spanish peace	539
Dec. 1649	William II confronts Holland	410
Mar.–May 1654	End of First Anglo-Dutch War	400–450
July 1660	Baltic peace; English Restoration; gains in E. Indies	370–480
Mar. 1664	Rumours of war with England	498–81
June 1665	English North Sea victories	348–322
Sept. 1666	Breda peace talks begin	400
Sept. 1667	End of Second Anglo-Dutch War	462
Aug. 1671	High returns from the East Indies	570
June 1672	Louis XIV's invasion of the Republic	250
May 1675	Intensifying maritime war with France	428–443
Nov. 1681	Threat of general European war	395
May 1683	Quarrel between William III and Amsterdam	427–402
Oct. 1684	End of Dutch domestic political crisis	470
Apr. 1688	No political fears trouble the Amsterdam Exchange	560–568
13 Aug. 1688	Optimism about VOC return cargoes	582
25 Aug. 1688	Rumours of pending Dutch invasion of England	580–500
26 Aug./5 Sept. 1688	Stock Exchange crash caused by fears of war with France and England combined, as in 1672	500–365
Oct. 1688	French army diverted to the Palatinate	420
July 1690	Battle of Fleurus	496–487

[a] Quotations are for shares in the Amsterdam Chamber of the VOC.

Sources: Israel, *Dutch Primacy*, 255; Israel, 'Amsterdam Stock Exchange', 440.

[143] GA Amsterdam res. vroed. 24 Sept. 1688.

community, was such that there was no further possibility of delaying economic retaliation against France, which in turn probably meant war with France. It also meant—since Orange, Fagel, and the States were agreed that Britain was the weak link in Louis XIV's European system—that there was no further prospect of opposing the invasion of Britain. On the news of the arrests of the ships in France, the Amsterdam *vroedschap* immediately approved the ban on French imports, and a general arrest of French ships, in Dutch ports, and sent additional senior deputies to The Hague, so that a secret committee could work with the Prince and Fagel, on the plans to invade England, without referring back further to the *vroedschap*.[144]

The full strategic plan was revealed to the States of Holland, in secret session, on 29 September. Orange's argument was that France had inflicted vast damage on Dutch commerce, shipping, and fisheries; as a result, war with France was now unavoidable; but, if the Republic adopted a defensive posture the likelihood was the two kings of France and England would overwhelm it, as they almost had in 1672; it was better, in the Prince's judgement, to invade England whilst England was divided, and weak, and before James could pack Parliament and overcome his domestic opposition; by invading, breaking the 'absolute power' of James II, and establishing an anti-French, and anti-Catholic, parliamentary monarchy, in Britain, the Republic could turn England round against France.[145] This, then, was the Dutch logic in throwing everything, the pick of their forces, into their invasion of England, launching the Glorious Revolution. As the States of Holland secret resolution expressed it, the aim was to make the English 'useful to their friends and allies, and especially to this state'.

The English ambassador at The Hague, the marquess d'Albeville, had, by early October, grasped what the regents expected to achieve: 'an absolute conquest is intended under the specious and ordinary pretences of religion, liberty, property and a free Parliament, and a religious, exact, observation of the laws; this, and [drawing England into] war against France, they make account, will be but a work of a month's time'.[146] The invasion army consisted of 14,352 regular Dutch troops, a massive artillery train, and 5,000 Huguenot, English, and Scots volunteers, making a total of over 21,000 men.[147] It was an army designed to be as large as, or larger, and better equipped and trained than, any army James II could put into the field. To

[144] GA Amsterdam res. vroed. 3 and 15 1688; GA Haarlem res. vroed. xxvi, fos. 217–18, res. 28 Sept. and 11 Oct. 1688.
[145] *Secreete Resolutien*, iv. 230–4.
[146] BL MS Add. 41816, fo. 232. D'Albeville to Middleton, 15 Oct. 1688.
[147] Israel, *Anglo-Dutch Moment*, 337–8.

carry the invasion force across to Britain, the admiralty colleges, chiefly of Amsterdam and Rotterdam, amassed some 400 transport vessels (ninety alone for the horses) and a war fleet, of fifty-three vessels, to escort them.

Diplomatic observers at The Hague were stunned by the speed and efficiency with which the Dutch armada of 1688 was fitted out. In terms of ships the Dutch invasion fleet was some four times as large as the Spanish armada of 1588. The secrecy with which much of the operation was prepared, and intricate planning which went into devising such a vast undertaking, were much commented on even before the invasion fleet set sail. 'Il faut convenir', commented one diplomat at The Hague, 'que ce projet ne peut être ny plus grand ny mieux concerté.'[148] Measured as an organizational accomplishment, the Dutch invasion of Britain, in November 1688, marks the high-point of the Republic's effectiveness as a European great power. Stadholder, regents, admiralty colleges, army, navy, and in several crucial instances—not least the commandeering of merchant shipping to transport the troops, artillery, and horses—the town governments, all worked impressively closely. When all dimensions are considered—military, naval, financial, logistical, diplomatic, domestic—together with the clever propaganda offensive master-minded by Bentinck, which had an important effect in England,[149] it was arguably one of the most impressive feats of organization any early modern regime ever achieved. D'Albeville perceived early on that a major difficulty for James and his ministers was simply to grasp what they were up against. 'There is not in Christendom a better army of the number,' he warned James's secretary of state; 'you may thinke what you please, they dont believe they will meet with great opposition.'[150]

The States General, States of Holland, and Stadholder took an immense risk in sending across all the best regiments of the Dutch army, together with the pick of the Republic's field artillery—fifty heavy guns, some 5,000 horses, and much of the war fleet to British shores amid the stormy weather to be expected in late autumn. The Whig opponents of James in England promised extensive support for the invasion; but William and the regents knew that they could not necessarily rely on this support materializing; and the Dutch leadership tended (after decades of Anglo-Dutch hostility) to regard all the English as highly unreliable. Thus, they had to ensure that the invasion force was sufficiently strong to defeat James even if they received only minor British support. At the same time, the army had to have

---

[148] BL MS Add. 38495, fo. 30. Moreau to Polish king, The Hague, 12 Oct. 1688.
[149] Israel, 'Propaganda', 169–73.
[150] BL MS Add. 41816, fo. 224. D'Albeville to Middleton, 9 Oct. 1688.

sufficient staying power to hold the balance should there be civil war in Britain. Meanwhile, the Dutch forces (and German and Swedish auxiliary regiments) in the Low Countries had to be mobilized for war. For it was virtually certain that France would declare war on the Republic once the invasion was launched, Louis having already warned the States General, in September, that he would do so should they move against England.[151] The Republic thus knowingly precipitated a simultaneous war with the kings of both England and France, believing that this strategy, however risky, gave it the best chance of transforming the balance of power in Europe and turning the tables on Louis XIV. Louis duly declared war on the United Provinces a fortnight after the invasion fleet set out.

The great armada of nearly 500 vessels assembled at Hellevoetsluis, south of Rotterdam, in late September. This process took weeks and, once complete, the armada was held up by adverse winds for an entire month, the soldiers and horses suffering considerable hardship. On 11 October, d'Albeville reported from The Hague that Dutch 'Catholics pray ardently for His Majesty's preservation and for the success of [James's] army against his enemies; the wind continuing contrary all this while they call it a "popish wind" '.[152] After further damage resulting from an unsuccessful attempt to get out, thwarted by a storm, the fleet finally departed, early in November, backed by a strong easterly, which was soon dubbed the 'Protestant wind'. No final decision had been taken as to whether to land in Yorkshire or Devon, William and Bentinck having planned only to land in one or the other so as to disembark out of reach of the English army (which was concentrated in the south-east), leaving the rest to the winds. The invasion fleet first proceeded up the east coast of England, as far as Harwich, and then doubled back. The English war fleet, caught in the Thames estuary by the strong easterly, watched it go by twice but was unable to get out to intercept it.

Orange swept through the Strait of Dover in style, stretching out his vast fleet in a line from Dover to Calais, twenty-five deep, the warships on either flank thundering their guns in an ironic salute to Dover Castle and Calais simultaneously, the Dutch regiments standing in parade formation on deck with 'trumpets and drums playing'. The army landed uneventfully in Devon and, before long, had seized Exeter. During the first three weeks, until it became clear that William's army was stronger than James's, English support for the invasion indeed proved sparse. But, as Orange himself told

---

[151] Israel, 'Amsterdam Stock Exchange', 431–2.
[152] BL MS Add. 41816, fo. 231. D'Albeville to Middleton, 10 Oct. 1688.

the gentry of Devon, Somerset, and Dorset, in a speech at Exeter, ten days after the landing, he did not need their 'military assistance', only their 'countenance and presence' to justify his expedition and actions.[153] During the first month after the landing the outcome seemed highly uncertain. There is little doubt that had James acted more resolutely both his army and fleet would have fought the Dutch. But his fatal irresolution led, during December, to his power crumbling away as William advanced inexorably towards London.

The Glorious Revolution reached its climax on 18 December, the day Orange and his army entered London in triumph. All the English regiments in the capital, including the palace guard, had been ordered, by Orange, to withdraw, to more than twenty miles outside London. Only Dutch troops were in the city; Whitehall, St James's Palace, and the rest of London were to remain guarded by Dutch troops for many months to come.[154] Orange was master of England, in control of the country's army, navy, and finances long before Parliament met and hesitantly agreed to make him king in place of James, to rule as joint sovereign together with Mary. During January 1689, before Parliament met, William and Bentinck were already planning to dispatch a large part of the English army to Flanders to boost the Republic's 'Barrier', and the Spanish Netherlands, against the expected French invasion.[155]

Officially, William became joint sovereign of England in February. In May, he brought England and (separately) Scotland into the war against France. But the Stadholder-king, as he now was, was nevertheless compelled to keep the Dutch troops he had brought over in Britain (and, from 1689, also Ireland) throughout the years 1689–91. For strong Jacobite opposition to the new regime developed not only in Scotland and Ireland but also in England itself. Many of the English nobility, and also the Church of England, were distinctly lukewarm in their attitude to the dethroning of James and his replacement with William and Mary. In the first year and half after James's flight from London not only many English, Scots, and Irish but also Louis XIV, d'Avaux, and, indeed, the Stadholder-king himself believed that without the Dutch army in Britain—and an additional force hired from Denmark—the revolution in Britain would falter and quite possibly collapse, since such English support as it enjoyed initially tended to diminish during 1689.[156] In Dutch eyes, and those of all Europe, William

[153] Israel, *Anglo-Dutch Moment*, 124.
[154] Ibid. 2, 125–8, 145–6.
[155] Ibid. 134.
[156] Ibid. 142–58.

III's position in Britain—and with it the fate of the Dutch Republic and the European balance of power—remained highly precarious, at least until the battle of the Boyne (July 1690), which decisively tilted the balance in Ireland.

The presence of a large, and the best, part of the Dutch army in Britain and Ireland for three years whilst the Republic was at war with France posed a host of new strategic and logistical problems for the States General and States of Holland. Amsterdam, and the rest of the States of Holland, had backed the invasion of Britain because they saw they had to fight France and that the best way of winning was to break the 'absolute macht' of James II, transform England into an anti-Catholic parliamentary monarchy, and turn Britain round against France. Thus there were good prospects the close collaboration prevailing between Orange and the States of Holland, since June 1688, would continue along with the struggle in Britain and Ireland. Indeed, in the new strategic context, Holland had no choice but to commit her forces to the defence of the Glorious Revolution. Nor was cost a problem, since January 1689, when William arranged for the 17,000 Dutch troops remaining in Britain to be paid for by the English taxpayer rather than the Dutch.[157] Yet many features of the new situation aroused anxiety in the regents; and, in the longer run, once the new regime in Britain was secure, and the main focus of the European struggle shifted back to the Low Countries, there was bound to be a growing divergence of approach and outlook as between the Stadholder-king and the Holland regents, or at least elements among them.[158] The dividing of the Dutch army between Britain and the Low Countries until the end of the war in Ireland, in 1691, created a complicated situation in which the Dutch remained pinned to the defensive on the Continent, leaving their allies, the Emperor and Brandenburg, to take the initiative throughout the north-west German theatre of conflict. Also, it meant that William and his Dutch noble favourites, especially Bentinck, Dijkvelt, and Ginkel—commander of the Anglo-Dutch army in Ireland during 1691—were freer than before to make key strategic decisions without consulting closely with the States. Furthermore, whilst it suited William III that the Dutch should provide the larger land force to defend the 'Barrier' in the south Netherlands while England played the chief role at sea, providing naval power in a ratio of five to three *vis-à-vis* the Dutch, this locked the Republic into a position of maritime inferiority to England which caused considerable unease in the Republic.[159]

[157] Res. Holl. 7 Dec. 1688.
[158] Pr :, 'William III', 72, 75.
[159] Rietbergen, 'A Fateful Alliance', 465–7.

Thus, the underlying contradiction in attitude between Stadholder-king and Holland regents regarding the fundamental interests of the United Provinces remained unresolved. While the former remained chiefly concerned with the European balance of power, and defeating Louis XIV, Amsterdam and the Holland towns were preoccupied with the security of their state and protecting its shipping and trade.

A further worry among many regents was that William III, as king of England and effective commander simultaneously of the armies of both England and the Republic, might now be more strongly placed than before 1688 (rather than weaker, as other regents hoped) to expand his power and influence, as Stadholder, in the Republic. This was an anxiety French propagandists sought to exploit, one writer commenting, in 1689, that the regents had enabled Orange to become king not only of the three kingdoms of England, Scotland, and Ireland but also of 'a fourth', meaning the United Provinces.[160] And, indeed, in many respects the structure of Orangist power and influence in the Republic did continue to grow after 1688. It is true that William III had already wielded an unprecedented sway over the army, military strategy, and promotions, when compared to previous Stadholders. But during the 1690s William III and his Dutch favourites possessed, in addition, an unprecedented leverage over war finance and the secret diplomacy of the state.[161]

THE LAST YEARS OF WILLIAM III'S STADHOLDERATE

The Stadholder-king's trump card in Dutch domestic politics between 1688 and 1697 was that scarcely any regents believed it possible to strike a deal with Louis XIV, or trust him at all, until France was weakened and his ambition curbed. Since it was impossible to accomplish this except through their English alliance, and hand-in-hand with Orange, there was no way the Stadholder's authority, or the web of favouritism, patronage, and influence forming the basis of his power, could be attacked. In these circumstances, there was little prospect of replacing the Stadholder's system with a more consultative, Holland-orientated framework in the tradition of the 'True Freedom' of De Witt.

Nevertheless, signs of a reviving Holland regent opposition to the Stadholder reappeared briefly, in 1689–90, at Amsterdam, Rotterdam, and Leiden. Indeed, over the winter of 1689–90, Orange became distinctly worried lest his entire European and British strategy be endangered by a

---

[160] Sainte Marthe, *Entretiens*, 18.   [161] De Bruin, *Geheimhouding*, 346.

fresh power tussle in the Amsterdam *vroedschap*, in which his friends, Witsen and Hudde, briefly lost ground to a more republican-minded grouping led by Jan Huydecoper (1625–1704) and Gerard Bors van Waveren (1630–93).[162] The first real clash between William and Amsterdam since 1684 occurred in December 1689 when the *vroedschap* ventured to deny that the Stadholder could still select the city's seven magistrates, from double lists of nominations (as reimposed in 1672), whilst residing, as he was now, abroad. In the States of Holland, Amsterdam's deputies argued that, with the Stadholder absent, Holland's civic magistrates should be selected, from double lists, either by the States, or the Hof, of Holland. Circulars were sent to the other Holland towns. 'I am so alarmed by Amsterdam's conduct,' wrote William to Anthony Heinsius, Holland's new Pensionary, in January 1690, 'seeing what the consequences could be, not only for myself but for all Europe, that I have decided to send [Bentinck] to The Hague.'[163] Bentinck's mission was to concert measures with Heinsius and head off any threat from the States party-faction to the Stadholder's authority in general and the imminent second Anglo-Dutch invasion of Ireland, in particular. The Stadholder-king could not afford difficulties with the States of Holland at any stage between 1688 and 1691 but least of all at this moment. For not only did he need the States General's approval to use the bulk of the Dutch troops in Britain as the spearhead of his offensive in Ireland—at the Boyne it was the Dutch Guards who led the attack—but he also required more of the very big guns not then produced in Britain, and ships suitable for transporting artillery and horses, all of which had first to be shipped from the Republic to England.[164]

Huydecoper and Bors van Waveren responded to Bentinck's arrival by attempting to prevent his assuming his seat in the Holland *ridderschap*, claiming he was no longer entitled to do so, being a naturalized subject of the English Crown. This imbroglio caused consternation throughout the Republic not least on the Amsterdam Exchange, where share prices tumbled in anticipation of a new rift within the Dutch body politic.[165] But the Amsterdam regents proceeded with immense caution, not wanting to undermine either the Anglo-Dutch alliance or the general strategic position of the Republic. The Leiden *vroedschap*, where republican sentiment at this point was also resurgent, was caught in the same dilemma, and Bentinck could soon reassure his master that while some regents opposed his

[162] Gebhard, *Het leven*, i. 389–90, 411–13.
[163] *Archives*, 3rd ser. i. 45–6.
[164] Israel, *Anglo-Dutch Moment*, 150–3.
[165] PRO SP 84/221, fo. 21. Aglionby to Warre, The Hague, 27 Jan. 1690.

authority in Dutch domestic politics 'dans la grande affaire ils sont bien'.[166] Nor was this surprising, for neither Amsterdam's trade with France, nor the sale of Leiden *lakens*, could be resumed until the French Crown was compelled to cease its mercantilist drive against Dutch commerce. With the Amsterdam *vroedschap* elections of February 1690, the tide ebbed back in favour of Witsen and Hudde. In a subsequent vote over whether Amsterdam should persist with defying the Stadholder in the matter of the magistrates, Huydecoper and Bors van Waveren were defeated by nineteen votes to twelve.[167] The Prince's friends in the States of Holland were jubilant and so was the Amsterdam financial community: 'we hope very well of the Amsterdam businesse,' reported one observer to London; 'Monsieur Witsen labours in it steadfastly; the actions at Amsterdam are risen prodigiously upon the hopes of an agreement.'[168] To save face, the Amsterdam *vroedschap* sent their double list of fourteen nominations to the States of Holland 'to do with it, as their soverains, what they should thinke fit'. French propaganda could only lament that 'les bons républicains qui ont encore quelques bluettes de l'esprit de De Witt sembloient vouloir respirer, mais ce n'a été qu'un petit soupir d'agonizant'.[169]

The inhibitions of the States-party faction at this time were further reflected in the striking paucity of anti-Orangist pamphlets and caricatures, especially by comparison with the outpourings of 1675 and 1683–4. By contrast, Orangist discourse and art became ever more effusive. The foremost Dutch political writer of the 1690s, Ericus Walten, extolled English-style constitutional monarchy, eulogized the Glorious Revolution, and hinted that there was no great gap between the political systems of England and the United Provinces, the essence of stable, responsible government being an 'eminent head' who scrupulously observes the constitutional limits on his authority. For Walten, illegitimate government was the arbitrary rule of the likes of Louis XIV. Romeyn de Hooghe (1645–1708), the foremost engraver of the later Golden Age, was also a leading Orangist propagandist who published numerous engravings exalting the exploits of the Stadholder in the field. When the Stadholder-king visited the Republic, in February 1691 (for the first time since 1688), unprecedentedly elaborate celebrations were laid on at The Hague,[170] featuring processions, poetic eulogies (including several penned in Spanish, by literati of the Amsterdam Sephardic Jewish com-

[166] Woltjer, 'Willem III en Leiden', 423.
[167] Porta, *Joan en Gerrit Corver*, 10–11.
[168] PRO SP 84/221, fo. 51. Aglionby to Warre, The Hague, 10 Mar. 1690.
[169] Le Noble, *Pierre de touche*, ix. 35.
[170] Japikse, *Prins Willem III*, ii. 327–8.

munity), and triumphal arches, obelisks, and other heroic décor, which De Hooghe helped design and were redolent of a growing personality cult of William III reminiscent of that of Frederik Hendrik. Amongst the grander literary offerings celebrating 1688 was the long heroic poem *Il Prodigio* (Amsterdam, 1695), composed in Italian, at Amsterdam, by the tireless Gregorio Leti, and the 9,000-verse effusion *Willem III*—the first full-length epic in Dutch—by the Amsterdam poet Lucas Rotgans (1654–1710), son of a merchant (whose villa on the Vecht had been sacked by the French, in 1672), the opening four books of which appeared in 1698, the rest in 1700.

Meanwhile, in 1692, the elderly Collegiant poet, Oudaan, contemplated, on his death-bed, the fate of his unpublished manuscripts, including his tragedy, the *Haagsche Broeder-Moord*, written in 1672–3, dramatizing the murders of the brothers De Witt. Besides the sheer impossibility of publishing in the 1690s a work glorifying the De Witts and peppered with hostile allusions to Orange, and his favourites,[171] it was untimely also in that Oudaan had, latterly, learnt to appreciate some of William III's qualities, particularly his robust defence of toleration. Oudaan could see no other course but to instruct his daughter to destroy the text. In fact, she did not do so; but it remained unpublished until 1712.

Thus, Orange's position in Dutch domestic politics in the 1690s, bolstered by international economic and strategic factors, was further strengthened by the policy of toleration which he pursued with consistency and vigour from the mid-1680s in both the Republic and Britain. The Stadholder demonstrated that (despite his preference for Voetian theology and professors) he was the chief protector of the Republic's Catholics, Mennonites, and Jews and, on several occasions, went out of his way to reinforce this message. It was also he who protected the Cocceians within the Church from the full brunt of the Voetian reaction. By following this course, the Stadholder-king deprived the anti-Orangist opposition of much of its traditional following. Dissenters not only came to look upon him favourably but, in many cases, including that of Oudaan, openly eulogized him as the glorious defender of toleration and liberty against the intolerance and despotism of Louis XIV.[172]

The 'True Freedom', plainly, was in retreat. Checked at Amsterdam and Leiden, it was further rebuffed at Rotterdam following an outbreak of serious rioting, in the autumn of 1690, against one of the Prince's most detested favourites, the *baljuw* Jacob van Zuylen van Nyevelt. This officer who specialized in combining a sanctimonious facade of Calvinist orthodoxy with extortion and manipulating prostitutes had his house wrecked by

---

[171] Gemert, 'Haagsche Broeder-Moord', 272–6.   [172] Ibid. 154–5.

an indignant mob incited by local political opponents. Among these, was the young Bernard Mandeville (1670–1733), who later became a famous writer in England. Mandeville caused a sensation by posting up on walls his vehement satire lambasting the *baljuw* as a 'money-grubbing tyrant'.[173] After the riots the *baljuw* was tried by the Hof of Holland for peculation but released, on the intervention of the Stadholder, who also compelled the Rotterdam *vroedschap* to pay an exorbitant sum in compensation. In the aftermath of the affair, in 1692, the Prince purged the *vroedschap*, removing seven republican regents, and the Pensionary, and replacing them with staunch Orangists.[174] This was followed by a general political, ideological, and theological reaction, presided over by the new Pensionary Isaac van Hoornbeeck, son of the Voetian professor Johannes van Hoornbeeck. Voetian values were now in the ascendant and the legacy of Paets and other champions of the 'True Freedom' under attack. Mandeville had probably already departed. Pierre Bayle, the 'philosopher of Rotterdam', long at odds with the Calvinist hardliners among the Huguenots, found himself a marked man in the eyes of the newly purged Dutch consistory. His professorship had been arranged by Paets. He was one of the principal champions of toleration in the Europe of the day. The following year, the *vroedschap*, at the request of the consistory, dismissed him from his professorship at the Illustrious School.[175]

The public accepted the necessity of the war against Louis XIV. Nevertheless the deterioration of the Dutch economy in the decade after 1687 was such that there were bound to be difficulties. Louis's renewed *guerre de commerce*, and the onset of the Nine Years War (1688–97), in fact mark the turning-point in the history of the Dutch overseas trading system.[176] Between 1590 and 1687–8, despite severe interruptions, and the restructuring between phases, the underlying trend in the economy and civic life had been consistently towards expansion. The conclusive proof of this is that the process of urbanization in Holland continued without let-up until the late 1680s—albeit with the sharp temporary reverse of 1672–4. By contrast, after 1687–8, even though faster or slower during different phases, the basic trend, until the end of the Batavian Republic in 1805–6, was one of contraction and absolute decline, and the conclusive proof of this is that the Republic, from the late 1680s, experienced a continuous process of de-urbanization (see pp. 1006–7 below).

[173] Dekker, 'Private Vices, Public Virtues', 485–8.
[174] Melles, *Ministers aan de Maas*, 139–41.
[175] Thijssen-Schoute, *Uit de Republiek*, 115.
[176] Israel, *Dutch Primacy*, 341, 359; Israel, 'Amsterdam Stock Exchange', 422–5.

The deterioration of the 1690s brought many adverse social consequences in its wake. The statistics of the drop in real wages and living standards at Amsterdam, in the 1690s show that this process began in the year 1688 precisely.[177] Despite the abrupt fall in real wages, poor men's rents at Amsterdam rose after 1688 while prices for large houses dropped substantially—a sure sign of diminishing prosperity.[178] At Haarlem and Leiden there was a marked contraction in employment in several textile branches, especially camlets, the supply of mohair, as with other raw materials from the Levant, being disrupted by the maritime conflict in the Mediterranean.[179] A riot at Haarlem in 1690 which began as a protest against a civic Further Reformation measure, banning smoking in the city's streets and in boats on its canals, on pain of a 6 guilder fine, ended with working men shouting down the burgomasters' efforts to calm them with cries that they had no work.[180] There were not many urban riots in Holland during these years but there were enough to show that the populace felt the impact of the changed circumstances acutely. The worst disturbances erupted at Amsterdam, in February 1696, in response to the laying on of additional taxation for the war.[181] The city was in uproar for a week with repeated mob attacks on the residences of excise collectors, one or two Jewish financiers, and the English 'agent' in the city.

The war dragged on, causing mounting hardship in the Republic as in France. In Britain and Ireland, the Jacobites, backed by the French, were crushed in the campaigns of 1690–1. But in continental Europe, the result was a stalemate, the combined might of the Republic, Britain, the Emperor, Spain, and Brandenburg proving insufficient to defeat France. Consequently, William III, working closely with Heinsius, who was adept at collaborating with the Stadholder while outwardly maintaining the dignity of the States of Holland, and of his office, entered into a series of complex secret negotiations with the French court in the latter part of 1693. The remarkable feature of these dealings, which, over the next three years, created the framework for peace, is that neither Parliament in England nor the Dutch provincial assemblies, or States General, played any part in, or had any idea about, the proceedings. The Stadholder-king employed Dijkvelt as his chief negotiator and otherwise involved only Heinsius, Bentinck and—just sufficiently to retain their confidence—the Amsterdam burgomasters.[182] Only when broad

[177] Nusteling, *Welvaart en werkgelegenheid*, 264.
[178] Lesger, *Huur en conjunctuur*, 67, 84.
[179] Israel, *Empires and Entrepots*, 158–61.
[180] Dekker, *Oproeren*, 12–13.
[181] Dekker, *Holland in beroering*, 32–4.
[182] De Bruin, *Geheimhouding en verraad*, 348–9.

agreement with Louis XIV had been reached were Parliament and the Dutch assemblies brought into the picture and did the formal negotiations at Rijswijk, Frederik Hendrik's palace near The Hague (see PLATE 14), begin.

When first made public, the ensuing peace terms appeared to satisfy all the essential war aims of the States General. The French agreed to evacuate the duchy of Luxemburg and strategic border fortress towns of Charleroi, Mons, Kortrijk, Ath, and Chiny, together with numerous dependent border castles and villages. Louis renounced his claims over the Spanish Netherlands. The Anglo-Dutch alliance was confirmed and Louis obliged to recognize William III as king of England, Scotland, and Ireland. Finally, and of particular importance to the Dutch, Louis consented to cancel the French tariff list of 1667 so detested by Dutch merchants and manufacturers, guaranteeing the 1664 tariff list and normal trading relations between the Republic and France, in a separate forty-five-clause treaty of commerce.

The Dutch had their 'barrier' and thought they had their trade concessions. The Franco-Dutch treaty of commerce stipulated that the 1667 tariff was to be abolished and a new tariff, acceptable to the Dutch, negotiated within three months; should agreement prove impossible, 'le tarif de l'an 1664 aura lieu pour l'avenir'.[183] This seemed clear and was approved and ratified by the States General. But after the three months had elapsed, Louis's ministers stunned Dutch diplomats by interpreting the crucial clause to mean that the 1664 tariff list would apply wherever the 1667 list had not previously been superseded with respect to particular commodities. Since many Dutch exports to France had been burdened during the years since, with even higher imposts than under the 1667 list, construing the treaty in this way completely nullified the gains the States General thought they had extracted. The return of a Dutch vessel from France, with a cargo of Gouda pipes still on board, because the French port authorities had insisted on payment of the prohibitive wartime duty decreed in 1692, utterly appalled the Dutch merchant and manufacturing community.[184]

Louis offered to negotiate; a States General commission was sent to Paris and Dutch and French negotiators argued about tariffs in Paris thrice weekly for many months without the least progress. In a private interview with the Dutch ambassador, in October 1698, Louis in person discoursed at length about whale blubber and Spanish wool imports into France, declining to yield the low tariffs the Dutch were demanding. The States General, meanwhile, refused to relinquish the base of Pondicherry, in India, which the VOC had captured from the French at great cost, in 1693, but which the Republic was due to return to France under the terms of the peace treaty. Not until June 1699 did the United Provinces and France finally settle on a new list, fixing France's tariffs on Dutch fine cloth and most other commodities at roughly half-way between the levels of 1664 and 1667. It was the best the Dutch could get; but the episode left a sour taste, reinforcing the impression in the Republic that it was impossible to trust Louis XIV and that the security of the Republic and its shipping and commerce had not yet been assured.

The international situation did indeed remain tense. In 1697, William III's status in the international arena, and prestige, appeared to stand higher than ever. But neither the personal duel between Louis XIV and the Stadholder-king nor the contest for hegemony in Europe and the Indies had been settled and, with the childless king of Spain, Carlos II, increasingly sickly, the approaching Spanish Succession crisis cast its shadow not only over Europe but the entire globe. The uncertainty prevailing during the short interval (1697–1700) between Rijswijk and the death of Carlos II, precipitating global conflict over the future of Spain, the Spanish Indies, and the Spanish Netherlands, doubtless contributed to the striking absence of any real revival of republican sentiment in the United Provinces in those years.

After 1697, during the last years of his life, both the authority and the reputation of William III tended to diminish, especially outside the United Provinces. In the first place, his position in Britain was now substantially weaker than in the early 1690s. Parliament, feeble in 1688–91, had by the late 1690s emerged as the dominant force in English politics and more and more limited the Stadholder-king's power, at least in domestic affairs. In the second place, his reputation suffered, beginning in 1697, through persistent rumours that he was conducting a scandalous homosexual relationship with his new favourite, the Gelderland noble Arnold Joost van Keppel, Lord Albemarle, and the public estrangement between the monarch and Hans Willem Bentinck, his right-hand man for over thirty years, who detested, and was jealous of, Albemarle.[185] But while this rampant innuendo was actively fomented in England and by the French court, and abounded at The Hague, it was not reflected in any surge of hostile propaganda or publicity in the Republic, where there was no shift in domestic politics comparable with that evident in England or Ireland. On the whole, the end of the war brought remarkably little slippage in the Stadholder's position in Dutch domestic politics. At Amsterdam, there were signs, by 1700, that the

[185] Japikse, *Prins Willem III*, ii. 390–5.

group around Joan Corver, successor to those who had challenged Witsen and Hudde in 1690, were reviving marginally, but, in general, the Stadholder's grip remained intact. At Leiden, the *vroedschap* remained remarkably submissive to his authority down to his death in 1702.[186]

The most ambitious international initiative undertaken by the Stadholder-king after the peace of Rijswijk was the attempt to forestall a fresh global war, over the future of the Spanish monarchy, by negotiating a partition agreement (which was never put into effect) with Louis XIV. Two treaties were negotiated in Paris in 1698 and 1699, and, again, only a tiny circle of confidants were involved while, during the course of the talks, both Parliament and the Dutch assemblies were left in the dark.[187] This time even Dijkvelt was excluded and Bentinck (who as William III's ambassador in Paris was supposedly spokesman for England's interests), though involved, carried less weight than before. The Amsterdam burgomasters also were largely left to one side, the Stadholder-king relying chiefly on Heinsius. When they were eventually told what was going on, of course neither the Emperor nor the king of Spain was at all pleased to see what William III and Louis were intending to commit them to: a division of the empire between the Dauphin and the Emperor's heir.

---

[186] Woltjer, 'Willem III en Leiden', 424–7; De Jong, *Met goed fatsoen*, 49–54.
[187] De Bruin, *Geheimhouding*, 349–50.

33

Art and Architecture, 1645–1702

❖

URBAN EXPANSION, TOWN PLANNING, AND THE ARTS

A new phase in Dutch art and architecture, as in economic activity, commenced in the late 1640s, the austerity of the previous quarter century ending in the mid 1640s. The new stage in the unfolding of the Dutch Golden Age was to be one of larger-scale, grander effects, richer and more varied colouring, and a striving towards yet greater sophistication in terms of both detail and perspective. As we have seen, between 1647 and 1672, Dutch commerce (except Baltic bulk-carrying) was in a more expansive and dynamic phase than during the previous quarter-century—as Aitzema, Pieter de la Court, Pieter de Groot, and other contemporaries noted—and it was as a direct result of this, as Emmanuel van der Hoeven observed, at the beginning of the eighteenth century, that most of the finest, largest, and most splendid buildings and sculptured monuments not only of his own city, Amsterdam, but also of The Hague, Leiden, Haarlem, and Dordrecht, materialized in the 1650s and 1660s.[1] This was also the most expansive period of the Dutch Golden Age for urban development and planning. Moreover, what applies to town-planning, architecture, and sculpture applies also to painting and the decorative arts. This new phase in art and architecture, which marks the zenith of Dutch artistic achievement in terms of scope, sophistication, and international impact, was to continue without faltering until the great crash (artistic as well as financial and political) of 1672.

Not surprisingly, there had been a marked tendency during the economic slow-down of the 1620s and 1630s, with the Spanish conflict and Thirty Years War in progress, for projects of urban development and construction of large buildings to be postponed. Agriculture flourished as never before and work on schemes for land reclamation and drainage accelerated. But the towns were under pressure and disinclined, throughout the quarter of a

[1] Van der Hoeven, *Holland's aeloude vryheid*, ii. 356.

century from 1621, to envisage major alterations, or demolish old and dilapidated structures, to create space for new development. Thus, even though the period was one of exceptionally rapid increase in the urban population of the maritime provinces, city councils, on the whole, shelved projects for new housing, walls, town gates, churches, harbour facilities, and educational institutions. In Amsterdam, and no doubt also other towns, the post-1621 slow-down in housing construction meant increased overcrowding in the poorer parts of the city.

The best-known instance of such postponement were the plans for Amsterdam's new town hall. The existing town hall was inadequate for its expanded functions long before the *vroedschap* decided, in 1648, the year of the peace of Münster, to allocate the resources for construction of a new town hall of appropriate size and splendour.[2] But there are numerous other examples. In the case of Leiden, it was obvious long before 1647 that the decaying gatehouses needed to be replaced but only after 1648 did construction of the new gatehouses begin. There had also been a pressing need for a major new church to accommodate the increasing numbers of Reformed worshippers. Designs for the Leiden Marekerk, first of the series of great monumental churches built in Holland and Zeeland, during the middle years of the century, were ready by 1639; but most of the work was left to the late 1640s, and the imposing façade, which cost most, to the 1650s, when an array of other large-scale projects were simultaneously in progress in the city.[3]

In some cases, shelving construction of new churches created appreciable problems of overcrowding. In Flushing, Reformed services were held only in the main church, until 1616, and then also in a second church which was enlarged in the 1620s. But, though it was not until after 1648 that construction of Flushing's third church began, it had long been impossible, by that date, to fit all the congregants in, obliging the *vroedschap* to ask the Stadholder to permit his residence in the town, the Prinsenhof, to be used to hold services for the overflow.[4] Flushing's third Reformed church was built in the years 1650–4.

The impetus behind the rapid urbanization, and development, characteristic of the new phase, beginning in the late 1640s, was thus economic and social, in the first instance. In cities such as Leiden, Haarlem, and Delft, where manufacturing formed the basis of urban prosperity and growth, regents and manufacturers viewed development schemes as a means of

---

[2] Fremantle, *Baroque Town Hall*, 23.
[3] Terwen, 'Ontwerpgeschiedenis', 247.
[4] Vrolikhert, *Vlissingsche kerkhemel*, 118–19.

stimulating further growth of manufacturing, as well as accommodating the existing population.[5] To thrive, these cities had to draw in labour, skills, and investment from elsewhere, and in the race to attract immigrants, competed against each other. The much discussed plans for laying out new quarters of Leiden, during the 1640s and 1650s, were warmly sponsored by textile bosses, such as Pieter de la Court, who warned the burgomasters that rents paid by textile workers for their houses were rising too fast, and that if the city failed to initiate large-scale urban expansion, and provide more cheap housing, then Leiden's prospects for growth, and vitality, would be fatally impaired. Still more protracted debates about urban renewal ensued at Haarlem, with Van Campen, Pieter Post, and Salomon de Bray providing architectural expertise and plans.[6] After completing several large projects in the city centre, the *vroedschap* decided, in 1671, to embark on a massive extension of the city, prompted by the vitality of the city's textile industry and the need for more cheap housing for textile workers, and inspired by the hope of attracting more industrial activity to Haarlem. It was a risky decision, unfortunately timed, which proved far too ambitious. But no one could know that in 1671. The urban extension programme embarked on in Amsterdam, in 1663, the biggest extension of Amsterdam in the seventeenth century, and the talking-point of the city for many years, was predicted by the English envoy, Downing, to be over-ambitious; but he was proved wrong. The new canals, and extensions of old canals, laid out at this time in Amsterdam came rapidly to be lined with handsome houses, including many of the finest town residences in the Republic.[7] In the mid- and late 1640s, before large-scale expansion had got under way, prices of large houses in Amsterdam had risen sharply; in the 1650s, they rose steadily; in the late 1660s, rich men's houses in Amsterdam eased back in value slightly, but basically held steady down to 1672.[8]

Major projects were undertaken also at Rotterdam and The Hague. Dordrecht was less ambitious but Van der Hoeven rightly included the city in his list, since there too civic extension projects commenced in 1647, the harbours were extended to accommodate the post-1647 increase in river trade, and the city built a number of new gatehouses. Besides the main Holland towns, Middelburg, and Groningen—which embarked on a major new church, Utrecht also hosted much debate about urban extension and renewal, in the 1650s and 1660s. The deliberations of the Utrecht city fathers

---

[5] Taverne, *In 't land van belofte*, 216, 377.
[6] Gonnet, *Wallen en poorten van Haarlem*, 8, 59.
[7] Fokkens, *Beschrijvingh*, 398–9.
[8] Lesger, *Huur en conjuctuur*, 83.

typified the mixture of economic, social, political, and cultural motivations which governed the Dutch urban development projects of this period. Utrecht regents were anxious to provide more cheap housing for artisans to facilitate the expansion of activity, and to attract wealthy men by building fine houses. But also they worried lest Utrecht be eclipsed by the Holland towns in grandeur, aspiring to beautify their city to add to its prestige and enhance civic pride.[9]

Thus, rivalry between the towns was economic but also political and artistic. Practical considerations weighed heavily but aesthetic judgements counted for a great deal also. Many regents, such as Gerard Reynst, Joan Huydecoper, and Cornelis and Andries de Graeff, at Amsterdam, or Govaert van Slingelandt, Pensionary of Dordrecht, were noted art connoisseurs.[10] But art, for these men, was not just a private matter. It was also directed towards the enhancement of their cities. This desire to enhance, on a large scale, so typical of the Dutch context at the zenith of the Golden Age, explains the high degree of interaction between architecture, sculpture, painting, and the decorative arts which is a further feature of the post-1647 period.

A typical feature of the culminating phase between the mid-1640s and 1672 was the series of great churches. Most of the major churches built in the Dutch Republic between 1572 and its downfall, in 1795, were constructed, and embellished, in the years 1645–75. They were the result of population growth and progress of confessionalization, but, in the case of the major non-Reformed churches (including the two great synagogues in Amsterdam), were also a product of the increasing toleration typical of the First Stadholderless period. The series began with the Marekerk at Leiden, a striking octagonal building, on a large scale, designed by Arent van 's Gravesande, working together, in part, with Jacob van Campen, the greatest of the five principal architects of mid-seventeenth-century Dutch classicism;[11] then followed the New Church at Haarlem, designed by Van Campen, and built in the years 1645–51. Next, and one of the most beautiful, was the Oostkerk erected at Middelburg in the years 1647–67, just when the number of Reformed preachers in the city reached its peak, rising from ten to eleven. This, the Republic's second large octagonal church, was designed by 's Gravesande and Pieter Post, largely on the model of the Leiden Marekerk.[12] The beautiful New Church, of The Hague, the third of

[9] Taverne, *In 't land van belofte*, 252–4.
[10] Houbraken, *Groote Schouburgh*, ii. 22–3, 162 and iii. 56; Von Moltke, *Govaert Flinck*, 11.
[11] Terwen, 'Ontwerpgeschiedenis', 231, 242–9.
[12] Ozinga, *Protestantsche kerkenbouw*, 85–8.

the city's major churches, and the first to be built for centuries, was constructed in the years 1649–56, on the joint initiative of the *vroedschap* and the Hof van Holland, to designs by Pieter Noorwits, a brother of 's Gravesande. Amsterdam, unlike the other towns, had built several new churches during the early seventeenth century; but there too, with the continued expansion, there was a need for another, the Reformed Ooster-kerk arising in the years 1669–71.

But, at Amsterdam, what was chiefly remarkable during this period were the huge, monumental churches built for the non-Reformed communities of the city. Especially striking were the magnificent round church built by the Lutheran community in the years 1667–71, a building with an impressive cupola which made a considerable impact on architectural connoisseurs, a church built to accommodate 5,450 people;[13] the main Ashkenazic syna-gogue, designed by Elias Bouman (1635–86), constructed in the years 1669–71; and the great 'Portuguese Synagogue', one of the largest buildings in Holland, begun in 1671, also to designs by Bouman, but completed only in 1675, owing to suspension of work during the French invasion of 1672–4. These two synagogues were not only the first imposing synagogues built in the Republic, but the first in western Europe—for those permitted in the Italian cities, including Venice and Rome, were handsome only within.[14] It had not been permitted that they should make an outward impact.

Accompanying the great churches, a variety of other monumental build-ings and structures were built during the quarter of a century after Münster. At Amsterdam vast sums and resources were lavished on the new town hall, which was undoubtedly the single most imposing architectural venture ever undertaken in the Republic. By the time work began, in October 1648, the burgomasters had been deliberating the designs for their vast new headquar-ters, together with Van Campen, Vingboons, and other architects, for a decade. The States party bloc which dominated the Amsterdam city council, and especially Cornelis de Graeff, who chiefly influenced the final outcome, intended the edifice to be the grandest in the Republic and express not only the greatness of Amsterdam but the secular values, and civic pride, of the citizenry and its élites and regents.[15] But during the late 1640s some concession had to be made to the strict Calvinist element in the *vroedschap*, for the city's New Church, next to the site where the town hall was to be built, had been damaged by fire in 1645, and required substantial restora-tion, and enhancement, lest it be completely overshadowed by what many

[13] Commelin, *Beschryvinge*, i. 495.
[14] Israel, *European Jewry*, 220.
[15] Fremantle, *Baroque Town Hall*, 23–35.

preachers and Calvinist orthodox saw as the excessive pomp of the planned town hall. Van Campen, and the sculptor Quellinus, who supervised the work on the town hall, were also commissioned to refurbish the neighbouring church. The main addition to the latter, however, intended to counterbalance the grandeur of the town hall, was abandoned after the death of William II, with the new ascendancy of the States party bloc.

The Amsterdam Town Hall, the largest architectural and artistic undertaking of the era, was also, in its stately grandeur and classicizing style, deeply representative of the culminating phase of the Golden Age. Working on an unprecedented scale (for there was no real model for what was intended), Van Campen successfully harmonized diverse Palladian, and other Italian, classicizing influences into a coherent whole with an unmistakably Dutch flavour.[16] The new building was inaugurated, amid much ceremony—official, artistic, and literary—including the reciting of commissioned verses by Vondel, in 1655. But that was just the architectural shell. Most of the work on the sculptures, and large public paintings, within was executed during the late 1650s and 1660s.

But Amsterdam was alone, in the core of the Republic, in needing a new town hall in the mid-seventeenth century. More typical of urban projects outside Amsterdam between the 1640s and 1672 were gatehouses, weighhouses, charitable premises, and ornamental entrances, such as that designed by 's Gravesande to adorn the medieval fort in the centre of Leiden. After Amsterdam, Leiden and Haarlem went furthest in renovating, and enhancing, their civic profiles. Urban development in Leiden may have been chiefly intended to enlarge the city, and its stock of cheap housing, but enhancement also had high priority. Remarkably, Leiden, then one of the largest manufacturing towns in Europe, could be described by the winedealer Jean de Parival (with pardonable enthusiasm) as 'cette ville la plus nette et la plus plaisante qui soit en l'Europe', especially in consequence of 'la beauté des édifices'.[17] The prosperity of the *laken* and camlet industries, since the 1640s, paid for this splendour; the vision, and architectural inspiration, derived from civic pride—the desire to surpass Haarlem, The Hague, and Delft, and vie with Amsterdam.

Laying out new canals, and streets, at Leiden, culminated in the 1650s, and early 1660s, before the plague outbreaks of the mid-1660s.[18] The *vroedschap* assigned the principal architectural commissions to 's Gravesande, who was civic architect in the years 1638–55, and later Pieter Post. 's Gravesande, who had learnt his trade working on Frederik Hendrik's

[16] Swillens, *Jacob van Campen*, 171–81.
[17] Parival, *Délices*, 39.
[18] Taverne, *In 't land van belofte*, 231.

palaces, during the 1630s, had won wide recognition with his designs for the Marekerk. He was also the architect of the Leiden Lakenhal (Cloth Hall), built to accommodate the headquarters of the burgeoning new *laken* industry, in the early 1640s. Sucked into a frenzy of architectural work in Leiden, during the early 1650s, he designed the first of the new city gatehouses, the Doelenpoort (1648); a civic hostel for official visitors, the Heerenlogement (1652); a civic gaol (1654); an elegant library, the Bibliotheca Thissiana (1655); and several stately houses, along the city's most prestigious canal—the Rapenburg. After 's Gravesande left, Post came to the fore, designing the Weigh-House (1657) and the nearby Butter House.

's Gravesande's Doelenpoort was the first of eight prestige gatehouses, encircling Leiden, built between 1648 and 1672.[19] They were constructed of expensive materials and designed to impress.[20] The Zijlpoort (1667) was adorned with a magnificent marble relief, festooned with baroque trophies, lions, and cannon, executed by Rombout Verhulst, the foremost sculptor active in the Republic during this period and the most influential, not least through his sculptures for the Amsterdam Town Hall. In embellishing Leiden, the *vroedschap* developed a veritable mania for public clocks and clock-towers. One was installed at the top of the White Gate (1650), near where passenger barge traffic loaded and unloaded, to encourage punctuality of barge departures. One of the largest of the Leiden public clocks, manufactured at The Hague, was affixed to the octagonal tower of the Marekerk, in 1648.

At Amsterdam, the new Town Hall overshadowed everything else (see PLATE 26). Nevertheless, there were many other large projects in progress, from the late 1640s down to 1672, besides this, the churches, and synagogues. Both of the city's main orphanages were replaced with larger buildings, the Reformed orphanage built to designs by Elias Bouman, in 1657, being designed to accommodate 800 children, the population of an entire village.[21] A vast new admiralty building, with an imposing façade reminiscent of the Town Hall, was constructed, to cope with the expanded functions of the Amsterdam admiralty after the First Anglo-Dutch War, in the years 1656–61. On this occasion too the *vroedschap* commissioned Vondel to write verses to be recited at the inauguration of the building. To adorn the interior, Ferdinand Bol was commissioned to paint four huge allegorical paintings, for which he was paid 2,000 guilders.[22]

[19] Van Mieris, *Beschryving*, i. 15–23; Parival, *Délices*, 78.
[20] Van Oerle, *Leiden*, i. 377–8.
[21] Commelin, *Beschryvinge*, i. 588, 594.
[22] Blankert, *Kunst als regeringszaak*, 36–7.

Much of the new urban area which arose as a result of the city extension embarked on in 1663 was auctioned off, in large lots, for the building of wide-fronted mansions for élite merchants, financiers, and regents. For the most successful men in the city, there was now a strong incentive to build on, and move to, the prestigious new stretches of the Herengracht and Keizersgracht, or at least build elsewhere, on a comparable scale, if they wished to keep up status. Among the most imposing new houses were that built for the brothers Trip (the Trippenhuis), begun in 1660, to designs by Justus Vingboons, and the residences of Joseph Deutz and Jeronimus Haase, built in 1670–2, on the Herengracht, by Philips Vingboons.[23] The Trippenhuis was embellished with paintings by Nicolaes Maes and Caesar van Everdingen, and the famous portraits of Jacob Trip and his wife, which Rembrandt painted, for this house, in 1661.

Amsterdam and Leiden surpassed the rest in grandeur. But much rebuilding, including many large-scale projects, was embarked on also in other towns. Much of the centre of Delft had to be extensively rebuilt, following the great gunpowder explosion of 1654 which demolished hundreds of houses and killed many citizens, including Rembrandt's most talented pupil, Carel Fabritius. Several projects were carried through in Gouda, notably the large new Weigh-House, designed by Post, built in 1668, the spot where possibly more cheese was piled, over the next half-century, than anywhere else on earth. Rotterdam too acquired new canals, streets, and fine buildings in this period, among them the Schielandshuis, designed by Post, and built in the years 1662–5, one of the masterpieces of Dutch classicist architecture.

Of particular importance were the architectural and artistic projects in progress at The Hague. If the Amsterdam Town Hall was the supreme embodiment of civic pride and republican virtue, the glory of the House of Orange attained its fullest expression in the elegant Huis ten Bosch, half-finished at the time of Frederik Hendrik's death in 1647, and completed by Amalia von Solms during the 1650s. The parallels between the two great undertakings were heightened by the fact that Van Campen was architect, and in overall charge of artistic activity, also at the Huis ten Bosch. The artistic centrepiece of the palace was the so-called Hall of Orange (*Oranjezaal*), which was covered with murals extolling the exploits of Frederik Hendrik.[24] Several of these were painted by the Antwerp artists Jacob Jordaens and Gonzales Coques, others by Dutch artists—Van Campen, Gerrit Honthorst, Caesar van Everdingen, Salomon de Bray, Jan Lievens, and Pieter Soutman.

[23] Ottenheym, *Philips Vingboons*, 53.   [24] Swillens, *Jacob van Campen*, 127–8.

The Huis ten Bosch and the New Church were two major projects in hand, at The Hague, in the 1650s—but there was also a third, the Hall of the States or *Statenzaal*. This was the hall, in the Binnenhof complex, where the States of Holland held their meetings. Johan de Witt was one of the most active of the States committee which supervised this extensive refurbishment, liaising in particular with the architect Pieter Post.

The prosperous Holland towns were in such close proximity to each other, and passenger barge transportation—which reached the peak of its development in the 1660s[25]—made confortable sightseeing so easy, that it was possible for an ordinary member of the public to savour the new architecture, public and private, comparing changes in one town with another. Pipe-smoking, chatting passengers, sitting in barges, also were able to view many of the country villas going up in Holland and Utrecht. In this way, these two provinces were turned into a kind of showcase in which formal gardens also became an integral feature.

These country villas, and their gardens, were dotted around the countryside especially to the north of Haarlem, around The Hague, and along the River Vecht, between Utrecht and the Zuider Zee, especially around Maarssen and Breukelen. Most of these mansions, often crammed with paintings, hangings, porcelain, and other décor, belonged to Amsterdam merchants, and regents, of Reformed background, including one of the finest, Goudestein, in Maarssen, which belonged to the Amsterdam burgomaster Johan Huydecoper and was repeatedly painted by his artist protégé, Jan van der Heyden. But there were also residences, and gardens, along the Vecht belonging to Catholics, Mennonites, and Portuguese Jews.

The fashion for building arcadian retreats had begun in the late 1620s and 1630s—once the danger of a Spanish invasion of the interior receded—but the classic age of the Dutch country mansion extended from the mid-1640s to 1672. During those years many of the finest were built and some of the earlier ones, including Huydecoper's Goudestein, redesigned and refurbished. The villas were an expression of mercantile wealth, and patrician status, but also of the wealth of the The Hague bureaucracy and high office. Among those near The Hague were Sorghvliet, built for Jacob Cats in the early 1650s, and Constantijn Huygens's residence, Hofwijck. Huygens lent impetus to the fashion for country villas by writing a country house poem, in 2824 alexandrines, in 1651, idealizing rural and disparaging city life.[26] Among the more notable villas north of Haarlem, was Vredenburgh, in the

[25] De Vries, *Barges and Capitalism*, 347–8.
[26] Kuyper, *Dutch Classicist Architecture*, 153.

Purmer polder, built for Frederik Alewijn, whose family had been amongst the most important investors in the project to drain the polder; both Philips Vingboons and Pieter Post produced designs for this house, which was completed around 1652. Another renowned villa was Elswout, near Haarlem, built in the late 1650s for the great Amsterdam merchant Gabriel de Marcelis, 'Agent' of the Crown of Denmark.

The scale and intensity of architectural activity, particularly in Holland, but not exclusively so, from the 1640s onwards, together with the plans for urban extensions, generated an upsurge of connoisseurship, and study, of architecture. In contrast to most European lands, where major building commissions would be decided by princes, noblemen, and powerful ecclesiastics, conferring privately with artists and architects, the practice in the Dutch towns was for regent committees to supervise commissions. As a result, there was more discussion, formal competitions between architects, and comparison of models. Jacob van Campen, most widely reputed of the architects, exerted a presiding influence over architecture at Amsterdam, The Hague, and on the Vecht, in the province of Utrecht, besides his home ground, at Haarlem. But his design for the New Church, built in Haarlem in the 1640s, was nevertheless chosen in competition with designs, and models, by Post and De Bray.[27]

A key feature of the urban reconstruction, and expansion, was that all the architects, planners, and artists consulted in connection with major projects were trained in the northern Netherlands. Palladian and other Italian classicizing influences were a crucial ingredient. But there was no close emulation of Italian, French, or English models.[28] Constantijn Huygens, an influential figure in the formation of Dutch architectural taste in the second quarter of the century, deliberately nurtured an authentic, and distinctive, north Netherlands classicist style. Foreign architectural textbooks played a part; but the chief influences on regents' decisions were the latest developments in neighbouring Dutch towns. Similarly, regents and merchants about to build rural residences contemplated neighbouring villas rather than foreign designs. It is this which explains the distinctiveness, and coherence, of Golden Age Dutch architectural development and the intense interest in new architectural projects throughout the United Provinces even before the buildings themselves materialized.

The example of Hendrik de Keyser, who through his book *Architectura Moderna* (1631) had made his designs known throughout the Republic, was emulated by Van Campen, Post, De Bray, and Philips Vingboons, a

---

[27] Swillens, *Jacob van Campen*, 128.   [28] Turck, 'Lakenhal in Leiden', 402, 406.

comprehensive edition of whose designs was published by the Amsterdam art dealer Clement de Jonghe, in 1665. The lesser provinces, Generality Lands, and also neighbouring German Calvinist towns such as Emden and Cleves drew their inspiration likewise, where major new building projects were undertaken, from Holland, albeit with a notable time lag. Thus, in 1643–7, Emden built its New Church on the model of the Amsterdam Zuiderkerk, construction of which had begun over forty years before; while Groningen's Noorderkerk, built in 1660–5, was modelled on the Amsterdam Noorderkerk, work on which had begun in 1620.

Altogether more up to date and expressive of the stately classicism characteristic of Dutch Golden Age architecture at its zenith was the beautiful Oostkerk at Middelburg, built chiefly under the supervision of Van 's Gravesande in the years around 1660. Though strongly influenced by the Leiden Marekerk, the Middelburg structure also displays a number of novel features and is even more impressive, indeed one of the foremost buildings of the Dutch Republic erected outside the province of Holland. Predictably, a print showing the architectural designs for the Middelburg church was circulating in Holland by 1657, long before the structure itself neared completion. Another indication of the tight architectural cohesion of the United Provinces was the choice of Pieter Post to design the new Maastricht Town Hall, built in the years 1659–64. Maastricht was remote from Holland. Even so, Post's designs were soon as familiar to Holland's regents and architectural connoisseurs as his other work, through the impressive engraving of the building he published in 1664.

PHASE THREE: THE ZENITH IN PAINTING, c.1645–1672

Urban development and the surge of new architecture, as well as the general restructuring of Dutch commerce during Phase Three of the overseas trading system (see pp. 610–19 above), was bound to affect painting fundamentally and on many levels. An obvious expression of the transformation of the Dutch urban scene, in painting, was the rise of the new genres of townscape and urban panorama, and growing interest in architectural painting. Pieter Saenredam (1597–1665) had pioneered the latter genre, first developing the 'realistic architectural' picture in the 1620s. He continued painting minutely measured, and spaced-out, church interiors and exteriors, uninterruptedly, throughout his career. But a wider vogue for such painting began only in the late 1640s with a group of artists of whom Gerard

[29] Osinga, *Protestantsche kerkenbouw*, 45–6, 50.

Houckgeest (*c.*1600–61), Emmanuel de Witte (*c.*1617–92), and Hendrik van Vliet (*c.*1611–75) were the most accomplished and formative in introducing the new and more complex perspectives used in Dutch architectural painting from around 1650 onwards.[30] Townscape painting as a distinct genre first arose in the 1650s and achieved its zenith, in terms of sophistication and grandeur, in the same decade in which urban development itself reached its zenith—the 1660s. In part, the new genre can be regarded as a response to the transformation and enhancement of the main town centres and the impact of the new views and perspectives. Thus, the grandest of the architectural projects, the new Amsterdam Town Hall, was one of the most popular subjects for architectural pictures. The leading masters of this new genre were Job Berckheyde (1630–93), who painted numerous views of Amsterdam, including the newly renovated Exchange, in 1668, his brother Gerrit (1638–98), who painted a panorama of the vast Haarlem redevelopment in 1671, and the ingenious artist-inventor Jan van der Heyden (1637–1712), who executed magnificent views of Amsterdam. Saenredam, too, exhibited a keen interest in the new buildings arising on all sides. On the completion of Van Campen's New Church, at Haarlem, in 1649, Saenredam executed no fewer than three paintings and eight drawings of the exterior and interior.[31] One of the chief concerns of both architectural painters, and painters of urban views, was to depict buildings which were symbols of civic pride, well lit, and from enhancing perspectives. A vogue developed among the Delft church painters for views of the interior of the city New Church, often providing a glimpse of the mausoleum of William the Silent, a sentimental attraction, doubtless, for Orangist buyers.[32]

One of the most original of all the genres of the Dutch Golden Age was the urban panorama of the 1660s and 1670s, the most sophisticated examples of which were painted by Jacob van Ruisdael, Holland's greatest master of the landscape.[33] These pictures, subtly conveying a sense of the interaction of town and country, and the fleeting effects of cloud and light, brought the conquest of physical reality by the artist to new heights, in some cases literally so. One of the finest of Ruisdael's panoramas was painted in the mid-1660s, on top of the scaffolding round the tower surmounting the new Town Hall, or at least based on drawings made there. Another, painted around 1675, reveals the transformed profile of the city from the south,

---

[30] Wheelock, *Perspective, Optics and Delft Artists*, 222–3, 226.
[31] Swillens, *Jacob van Campen*, 154.
[32] Giltaij *et al.*, *Perspectiven*, 43, 201, 221.
[33] Slive, *Jacob van Ruisdael*, 22.

showing the new gatehouses and fortifications, and the Portuguese Synagogue.

Few paintings were needed for the new churches or gatehouses. But, for
the Amsterdam Town Hall, the magnificent new houses on the Herengracht,
and country villas, large quantities of a rather grander kind of art than had
been painted in the past were required. If the second main phase of Dutch
Golden Age Art (1621–47) is that of monochrome austerity, the small-scale,
and intimate, the third (1647–72) was the age of the lavish and sophisticated.
This does not mean that there was no further demand for small pictures,
still lifes of kitchen utensils, and rowdy scenes; room could always be found
for such pictures. But the tone, and direction, of painting shifted, as the
market came to be dominated by wealthy merchants, regents, and sophisticated connoisseurs whose requirements were for large, opulent, and refined
paintings. At the same time, for official buildings, such as the Amsterdam
Town Hall, or the new Amsterdam Admiralty Building, there was a need
for a new kind of grand public picture with a republican message.

The change was manifested in many genres. In the still life, the sober
colouring, and modest utensils, of the 1620s and 1630s gave way, in the
1640s, to the the so-called *pronk stilleven* (Sumptuous Still Life), of which
the three great masters were the Utrecht painter Jan Davidsz. de Heem
(1606–83), Abraham van Beyeren (1620–90), and Willem Kalf (1619–93).[34]
De Heem's paintings in particular sold for high prices. Nearly all of Kalf's
sumptuous still lifes, which were also highly prized, were painted in the
1650s and early 1660s.[35] In landscape, the change was from the monchrome
sobriety of Van Goyen to the grander, more poetic effects of Van Ruisdael
and Hobbema. In seascape, there was a shift from small pictures, with few
and modest vessels, to the grand marine style of Willem van de Velde the
Younger (1633–1707) and Ludolf Bakhuysen (1631–1708).[36] Van de Velde
worked, for a long period, with his father, Willem van de Velde the Elder,
who, encouraged by the admiralty authorities, viewed the great battles of
the Anglo-Dutch wars from yachts close by, and made numerous sketches.
This enabled his son to achieve a high degree of realism and make his great
naval scenes, to an extent, a historical record. They were frequently
purchased to be hung in public places such as town halls and admiralty
college premises.

Another aspect of the artistic restructuring of the 1640s was the proliferation of the Italianate landscape and rise of the Mediterranean harbour

[34] Bergström, *Dutch Stll-Life Painting*, 260; Segal, *A Prosperous Past*, 142, 197.
[35] Grisebach, *Willem Kalf*, 143–4.
[36] Bol, *Holländische Marinemalerei*, 230.

scene. A crucial change in commerce and shipping in the late 1640s was the strong revival of Dutch Mediterranean trade, and it can hardly be an accident that the vogue for Mediterranean harbour views arose at precisely that time.[37] These southern port scenes, and the new generation of more grandiose Italianate landscapes—a genre previously restricted to Utrecht, but now, from the 1640s, intensively produced also in Haarlem and Amsterdam—were polished, costly paintings destined for the houses of élite merchants and regents, such as Jan Reynst, one of Amsterdam's principal traders with Venice, a close friend of Karel DuJardin (*c.*1622–78),[38] the wealthy artist who, along with Jan Baptista Weenix (1621–60), Adam Pynacker (1625–73), Jan Both (1615–52), Johannes Lingelbach (1624–74), and Nicholas Berchem (1620–83) was a principal exponent of the new style. These glowing paintings, with their antique ruins and fettered galley slaves, can hardly be called 'realistic'. Rather the intention was to evoke an exotic, but serene, world, bathed in glittering light, gently distracting their owners from their normally more business-like preoccupation with the south. To this was added a discreet strain of eroticism, especially in the work of Weenix and his son Jan Weenix (1642–1719), taking advantage of the exotic setting, remote from contemporary Dutch society, to feature dark-skinned women in low-cut, flimsy dresses, their breasts partly exposed and not infrequently being caressed by shepherds.[39]

Numerous Dutch artists won renown and wealth in the quarter-century after Münster. Their success enhanced not only their lives but the towns where they worked. Even though two of the Dutch art centres—Haarlem and Utrecht—produced prolifically for the Amsterdam market and for export, there was, nevertheless, a marked tendency, even in the case of Haarlem, for a high proportion of artistic output to be purchased, and to remain, in the town where it was produced.[40] Collectors and connoisseurs nurtured a different attitude to, and greater fondness for, artists living and working in their own towns than artists elsewhere. The vitality of local schools of artists at Dordrecht, The Hague, Rotterdam, and Middelburg, as well as the five chief centres—Amsterdam, Haarlem, Utrecht, Leiden, and Delft—was partly due to the strong sense of civic identity and pride of each town. This was particularly true with respect to prominent artists. The more, accordingly, a painter was esteemed by princes and nobles abroad, the more he was in demand among the connoisseurs of his own city, in some cases pushing prices for his pictures staggeringly high. A striking example of such connoisseurship were the Dou collections. Dou won a European reputation and sold his paintings for astronomical prices. Yet the most avid collectors of his work were in Leiden itself and wished all of Leiden to know it. The two most determined were the Remonstrant leader Johan de Bye and the famous professor of medicine Franciscus de le Boë Sylvius. This professor owned a large house on the Rapenburg and, by the time of his death, 162 paintings including many by Dou and Van Mieris, the other Leiden painter of his time, with a European reputation.[41] De Bye was a remarkable man who greatly annoyed the Leiden *vroedschap*, in the early 1660s, with his efforts to win toleration for Remonstrant worship in the city. In a subtle contest with the city government, he put his entire collection of twenty-nine paintings by Dou on public display, in 1665, in rooms opposite the town hall, advertising his exhibition to art-lovers in other towns.[42] It was a way of saying that no one cultivated Leiden's reputation and glory more than he.

The fame of local painters was a source of prestige but also of embarrassment to city governments. In 1669, the art-loving Cosimo III, future grand duke of Tuscany, on a tour of the Republic, visited Leiden, and one of the things he desired to see was the atelier of Van Mieris. That was an honour for Leiden as well as Van Mieris. The Leiden *vroedschap* subsequently resolved, specifically because both Van Mieris and Dou enjoyed such renown abroad and throughout the Republic, to commission a picture from each of them so that the city should possess examples of their work. The *vroedschap* continued discussing the matter for several months but then dropped the whole idea, presumably because of the very high prices asked.[43]

Other painters came to be recognized widely in Holland but were purchased chiefly in their home town. Most of Vermeer's paintings remained in Delft during his lifetime and the last quarter of the century, a high proportion—including the *Milk Maid*—in the collection of his local patron, the wealthy Delft *rentenier* Pieter Claesz. van Ruijven, who also owned several pictures by Emanuel de Witte and Simon de Vlieger. Others were in the possession of a Delft baker, who also owned at least two pictures by another famous Delft artist, Anthonie Palamedes.[44] Dordrecht exerted a remarkable hold over the batch of gifted artists which it produced. Aelbert Cuyp (1620–91), who painted many attractive views of the city and its environs, spent nearly his whole life there, married a lady from Dordrecht

[41] Sluijter, *Leidse fijnschilders*, 37.
[42] De la Court, 'Brieven', 148; Martin, *Leven en werken van Gerrit Dou*, 65.
[43] Sluijter, *Leidse fijnschilders*, 40.
[44] Montias, *Vermeer and his Milieu*, 251–6, 364–5.

regent circles, became a member of the Reformed consistory, and sold most of his pictures to local prominent men.[45] Samuel van Hoogstraeten (1627–78) trained with Rembrandt, in Amsterdam, in the 1640s, and travelled abroad extensively, but whilst in the Republic lived mainly in Dordrecht, where he held a post in the provincial mint; he painted at least two large group portraits, of Dordrecht mintmasters, to adorn the walls of the mint. Nicolaes Maes (1632–93) also trained with Rembrandt but returned to Dordrecht to work as an independent master, remaining there from 1653 until after the collapse of the art market following the French invasion of 1672, when he moved to Amsterdam.[46] Godfried Schalcken (1643–1706), a highly successful artist, son of a Dordrecht Reformed preacher and rector of the Latin school, trained under Van Hoogstraeten and then Dou, whose highly polished technique he adopted. He too settled in Dordrecht and became a prominent man, serving as an officer in the militia; only towards the end of his career did he move to The Hague. This artistic rootedness in particular towns, mirroring the distribution of urban vitality more generally, was encouraged by the system of St Lucas guilds which had the effect (at any rate outside Amsterdam) of restricting sales of pictures in each town, in the main, to those who belonged to the local guild and who were, therefore, citizens of the town.[47]

Most painters of quality derived from middle-class backgrounds and affluent homes. But it is striking that, in many cases, their skill as artists increased their wealth and, often, their status. During the third quarter of the century, more Dutch painters gained recognition abroad than previously, and this recognition both heightened their standing in civic society and increased the zeal of local regent and merchant connoisseurs, and possessors of famous art 'cabinets', as well as the prices they were willing to pay. A point made by Van Hoogstraeten in his book on art, published in 1678, was that, in the Dutch context, art was a path to fame, gaining access to the homes and tables of prominent and powerful men, and being noticed by foreign courts.[48] This phenomenon of foreign acknowledgement reinforcing civic pride, and the local standing of artists, is especially striking in the cases of Honthorst, Dou, Van Mieris, Van de Velde, Bakhuysen, De Heem, Van der Heyden, Flinck, Bol, Van der Helst, Ter Borch, Maes, Netscher, and Schalcken.

The fame and wider standing of artists reinforced civic identity and pride. But besides stocking the 'cabinets' of regents, élite merchants, and bureau-

[45] De Groot, 'Schilderijen van Aelbert Cuyp', 56, 70, 78, 80, 86.
[46] Haak, *The Golden Age*, 420.
[47] Montias, 'Art Dealers', 247.
[48] Van Hoogstraeten, *Inleyding*, 353–4.

crats, leading artists were also required to provide large public paintings for town halls, admiralty buildings, and other institutions. Such commissions tended to be well paid and conferred great prestige on the artists employed. Since, during the period 1650–72, there was no Stadholder in Holland and Utrecht, the two provinces where the bulk of the artistic activity was in progress, and the States party-faction needed to enhance the public's awareness of their political and social ideals and values, this also meant the rise, in the 1650s, of a specifically republican Dutch public art, a phenomenon especially pronounced at Amsterdam.

The most grandiose exercise of this sort were the pictures needed for the *Burgerzaal*, the public gallery of the new Amsterdam Town Hall. This part of the building, as we see from a view of it painted by Pieter de Hoogh, around 1670, was open to the general public and casual visitors, even dogs. The brothers De Graeff and their colleagues of the *vroedschap* earnestly pondered this commission, which was above all intended to extol 'freedom' and republican virtue. They wanted the pictures to form a coherent series and chose as their theme the story of the Batavian fight for freedom against the ancient Romans, a favourite topic of the Holland States party, since it emphasized Holland rather than civic particularism but without bringing in the other provinces, idealized the fight for freedom as the centrepiece of Holland's history, and provided no scope for Orangist propaganda. Flinck, a friend of the brothers De Graeff, and the most prestigious artist of the city—Rembrandt being under something of a cloud—was commissioned to paint the entire series but died, in 1660, shortly after commencing.[49] The *vroedschap* then decided to split the commission up and assign particular episodes of the Batavian Revolt to different artists. Rembrandt was allocated the first in the series—the conspiracy of the Batavian leader, Claudius Civilis, against the Romans. The painting was briefly hung in the *Burgerzaal*, in 1662, but provoked criticism, was removed, and returned to the artist, who remained unpaid.[50] The objection may well have been the incongruous crown which Rembrandt had set upon Claudius Civilis' head and his dominating the scene, hardly features of a consultative, republican attitude.

A central function of Dutch republican art for public buildings was to extol public spirit, probity, and civic virtue. For this, early Roman history was regarded as most appropriate and it remained a fertile source of inspiration. Various famous Romans were renowned as paragons of uncorruptibility and public virtue. A notable example was the large picture

[49] Haak, *The Golden Age*, 50.   [50] Schwartz, *Rembrandt*, 318–20.

painted by Ferdinand Bol, in 1656, for the burgomasters' chamber in Amsterdam, for which he was paid 1,500 guilders; the painting recounts the story of the Roman envoy who steadfastly resisted every attempt of King Pyrrhus of Macedonia, first to bribe, and then to frighten him.[51] Bol's pictures for the admiralty building, in Amsterdam, were of similar character.

Of course, stirring events of the Revolt against Spain, and historical episodes important to local civic identity, also claimed attention. The main rooms in the Leiden, Haarlem, and Delft town halls were all extensively refurbished in the 1660s and, at that time, a number of new paintings and tapestries were commissioned and installed. Dutch republican art was also intended to exalt some of the heroes of the contemporary Dutch Republic though not, as a rule, regent leaders themselves. Few official portraits of burgomasters, or other regents, were commissioned for public buildings, an exception being the fine group portrait of the Deventer *raad*, almost unique of its kind, which Gerard ter Borch painted, in 1667, and which still hangs in the Deventer town hall.[52] Usually portraits of regent politicians, including the marble bust of De Witt, sculptured by Quellinus, in 1665, and today in the Dordrecht Museum,[53] were intended for private use, as were pictures of well-known regents acting on behalf of the state such as Ter Borch's painting of the arrival of Adriaen Pauw at Münster in 1646, or Caspar Netscher's painting of Van Beverningk being received by the Spanish queen in 1671. Distinctly out of step with accepted practice was the painting of Cornelis de Witt 'triumphant at the Medway' (about which Charles II complained) hung in the Dordrecht town hall in 1670. It failed to survive long, being destroyed by the mob in the riots of 1672.[54]

Nor were the regents inclined to glorify military exploits, since the whole tenor of the republican regime, after 1650, was to play down military values, and the role of the army, in the life of the state. In any case, extolling military feats would have meant enhancing the image of the Princes of Orange, who until 1650 had commanded the army, and other commanders, who, when not foreigners, were usually noblemen from provinces other than Holland. Thus the group favoured for glorification in the public art of the Republic, during the First Stadholderless period, were the admirals who were Hollanders and Zeelanders and played no part in the political process. They were extolled both in paintings and in sculpture. After the Four Days Fight, in 1666, Ferdinand Bol was commissioned to paint an official portrait

[51] Blankert, *Kunst als regeringszaak*, 27–9.
[52] Haak, *The Golden Age*, 51.
[53] Rowen, *John de Witt*, 511–12.
[54] Van Rijn, *Atlas van Stolk*, iii. 47.

of Admiral de Ruyter, copies of which were then hung in all five admiralty colleges of the Republic. Of special importance were the monumental public tombs, installed by the States General and States of Holland and Zeeland, to commemorate leading admirals who had died in battle, or in the service of the Republic. After Tromp's death, fighting the English, in August 1653, the States General decided to perpetuate his fame by installing a large public monument in the Old Church at Delft. Rival designs by Van Campen, Post, and Verhulst were exhibited to the States General, in March 1654, the concept of Verhulst being chosen.[55] Verhulst brought to fruition a magnificent baroque tomb, featuring a bas-relief in marble of Tromp's last sea-battle. This was the beginning of a series of such splendid admirals' tombs, installed amid great ceremony, at Delft, Amsterdam, Utrecht, and in Zeeland. The most magnificent of all was the De Ruyter tomb, again executed by Verhulst, which was installed—where it remains to this day—in the New Church at Amsterdam.

ART AFTER THE CRASH OF 1672

The French invasion of 1672 disrupted the Dutch art market and art world generally, just as it paralysed commerce and public building, and undermined financial confidence. The panic led to a run on the banks. Society was in turmoil. Great quantities of finery, jewellery, and art, as well as cash, were transferred abroad, temporarily, to Antwerp and Hamburg. At Haarlem, work on the great urban extension project, begun in 1671, was halted.[56] At Amsterdam, the elders of the Portuguese Jewish community, seeing that all other public building in the city had ceased, deemed it hardly fitting for work on the great synagogue to continue and that too was interrupted for two years.

The intricate mechanism of the art market was dislocated. No one wanted to buy; everyone wanted to sell. Most of the opulent villas along the Vecht were pillaged by the French soldiery and much of the décor and art with which they were crammed pilfered and presumably sold for low prices, not least in Utrecht. At Amsterdam, prices for art slumped disastrously. Gerard Uylenburgh, the leading art dealer in Amsterdam, went bankrupt in 1672, with fifty statues and paintings by Titian, Tintoretto, and Rubens, as well as Rembrandt, Dou, Van Mieris, and Metsu, in stock. Uylenburgh attested, in a notarial deed, in January 1673, that prices of everything 'especially paintings and such rarities have greatly declined and slumped in value, as a

---

[55] Van Notten, *Rombout Verhulst*, 12.   [56] Taverne, *In 't land van belofte*, 375.

result of these disastrous times and the miserable state of our beloved Fatherland'.[57]

All the Dutch art centres were severely hit, and numerous artists ruined or uprooted. Jan Davidsz. de Heem retired to Antwerp. Willem van de Velde the Younger migrated to England. Karel DuJardin returned to Italy, in 1674, spending the last four years of his life in Venice. Others stayed put, and struggled to survive. Soon after Vermeer's death, in December 1675, his widow testified that 'her husband during the war with the king of France, and the next years, had been able to earn very little, or almost nothing, so that the works of art which he had previously bought, and in which he dealt, had had to be sold off, at very great loss, to feed their children'.[58] Vermeer's own works were auctioned off, in Delft, in several sales in 1676–7 (the auctioneer being none other than the famous scientist Van Leeuwenhoek), at greatly reduced prices.[59]

Nor was the crisis merely temporary. During the 1680s and 1690s far fewer new paintings were being sold in Dutch towns than previously. There was a remarkable decline in the proportion of paintings listed in Amsterdam inventories painted by contemporary artists, from a still dominant proportion in the 1660s, to 42 per cent in the 1670s, to a mere 14 per cent in the 1680s.[60] Moreover, once down to this level, the incidence of contemporary artists did not subsequently recover. The number of artists being trained, and entering the profession, probably began falling in the 1660s. But, during the 1670s, the contraction accelerated. There was less demand for paintings of all types. The most esteemed masters of the past, including Rembrandt, continued to sell at relatively high prices but, nevertheless, much lower prices than before 1672 and, in this respect, the market remained flat through to the early eighteenth century.

If some emigrated, other artists enjoyed status and wealth enough to retire from art, and live comfortably by other means or, at least, paint less than before. Willem Kalf's output declined from the mid-1660s but fell off further in the 1670s, and now qualitatively as well as quantitatively.[61] By 1672, the age of the 'sumptuous still life' was over.[62] Particularly frequent, after 1672, was an unmistakable tendency, evident in many artists, to degenerate by becoming repetitive, bestowing less care on effects of light and shade, and their figures, and also in use of colours and brushwork. The faltering of

[57] Bredius, 'Italiaansche schilderijen in 1672', 92.
[58] Montias, *Artists and Artisans*, 215.
[59] Van Peer, 'Drie collecties schilderijen', 94–7.
[60] Montias, 'Works of Art', 343; De Vries, 'Art History', 264.
[61] Grisebach, *Willem Kalf*, 162–3.
[62] Segal, *A Prosperous Past*, 196–7.

inspiration has often been noted, both as a general phenomenon, and with regard to particular masters. Pieter de Hoogh, who painted some of the finest examples of Dutch genre painting in the 1650s and 1660s, painted 45 per cent of his surviving *œuvre*, seventy-five pictures, in the years 1670–84; but this part of his work shows a clear deterioration in terms of care, polish, and overall quality.[63] Nicholas Berchem also painted a good deal after 1672 but, in contrast to his Italianate views of the pre-1672 period, now churned out uninspired routine work. Jacob Ochtervelt (1634–82), in his post-1672 art, shows a similar deterioration in both composition and rendering figures and shadow.[64] We can be sure that much of this erosion of quality stemmed from reduced readiness to lavish time, and the best materials, striving for refined effects. The occasional great masterpiece of the late seventeenth century, such as Meindert Hobbema's *The Avenue Middelharnis*, painted in 1689, were painted almost incidentally, in Hobbema's case, by an artist now earning his living by other means who had almost entirely retired from painting. The changed circumstances of the art market were the main factor behind this degeneration. But emigration could also lead to loss of quality. The art of Willem van de Velde deteriorated, after his move to London, in 1672, it has been suggested because of the inferior paints and glazes then used in England.[65]

A number of genres flourishing before 1672 sharply declined thereafter, among them the landscape, still life, and low-life scenes. But other genres, better suited to the taste of the Dutch élites, in the more restricted circumstances of the late seventeenth century—mythological painting, flower painting, townscapes, and, in some respects, genre painting—survived better. If the Dutch art world was disrupted by the events of 1672, it was by no means decimated. The expertise in preparing materials, and the training provided in the best ateliers, assets garnered over a century, did not suddenly vanish and were not easily matched abroad. The reputation of Dutch art and artists remained, in fact, very high down to the early decades of the eighteenth century. It is a point worth emphasizing; for European taste in the nineteenth and twentieth centuries, and principles of selection followed by the modern world's public collections, have had the effect of screening out of our awareness a substantial artistic production which in terms of quality, and also the high standing it enjoyed throughout eighteenth-century Europe, represents a genuine and not unimpressive prolongation of the Golden Age. Modern taste and museums, in other words, have

---

[63] Sutton, *Pieter de Hooch*, 35–6.
[64] Kuretsky, *Paintings of Jacob Ochtervelt*, 23–7.
[65] Percival-Prescott, 'Art of the Van de Veldes', 31.

created an impression of truncation of activity, and quality, around 1672, more total than was, in reality, the case.[66]

So great had been the number of artists working in the United Provinces during the middle decades of the seventeenth century that even with a drastic contraction in the 1670s, a reduction, it has been estimated, to roughly only one-quarter of the level of the 1650s,[67] far more art was still being produced in the Republic than anywhere else in northern Europe, and the Republic also still possessed many of Europe's most highly reputed painters. The most glittering success story was that of the Rotterdam artist Adriaen van der Werff (1659–1722), a miller's son whose renown began, in 1696, when Johann Wilhelm, Elector of the Palatinate, on a tour of Holland, was so taken with one of his pictures, which he bought in Amsterdam, that he went to Rotterdam, to visit the artist in his atelier. The Elector assigned him a court pension which rose to 6,000 guilders yearly, bought many of his pictures, brought him frequently to his court, at Düsseldorf, and eventually ennobled him. But whilst he became a favourite of the Elector, he nevertheless chose to remain in Rotterdam, where his reputation abroad—his atelier was visited also by August, Elector of Saxony and king of Poland, and Duke Anton Ulrich of Wolfenbüttel—secured him high status. He became a militia officer, and governor of the Old Men's Home, and received commissions from the *vroedschap*, the most important being his designing of Rotterdam's new Exchange. Shortly after the battle of Blenheim (1704), Marlborough had his portrait painted by Van der Werff—in Rotterdam.

But Van der Werff was merely part of a wider phenomenon. Romeyn de Hooghe remained active in the closing years of the seventeenth and opening years of the eighteenth century and was universally known as one of Europe's most accomplished engravers. Schalcken was still active, and held in the highest esteem in the years around 1700, when the Rotterdam admiralty college commissioned from him a series of portraits of the Princes of Orange. Ludolf Backhuysen was also active into the opening years of the new century; he enjoyed great renown and was visited in his atelier by the Grand Duke of Tuscany, and several German princes, as well as Peter the Great.[68] Rachel Ruysch (1664–1750), daughter of the scientist Frederik Ruysch, and of Maria Post (daughter of the architect), began painting in the 1680s and, despite having ten children, achieved great success

[66] De Vries, 'Art History', 261.
[67] Ibid.
[68] Bol, *Holländische Marinemalerei*, 301.

with her meticulous flower-pieces both in the Republic and abroad. One of the best-known figures at Amsterdam and The Hague during the 1670s and 1680s, and most successful, was Gerard de Lairesse (1641–1711), an immigrant from Liège. De Lairesse was famous for his emphasis on the need to integrate painting with architecture and for his innovations in large ceiling paintings.[69] He specialized in rendering allegories in a refined, classicizing style—though expressly rejecting the manner of the Italians—which fitted well with the general shift to a more aristocratic art and architecture after 1672. In his book, compiled from his lectures on art, given after he became blind, in 1690, he sought to reduce Rembrandt's status as the artist best known to the public, eulogized Van Dyck for his elevated, refined style, and rejected the realism of the past.[70] He was in fact one of the most representative figures of the post-1672 fourth, and last, phase of Dutch Golden Age painting.

Like painting and engraving, architecture survived the trauma of the 1670s, and showed more vitality than is commonly realized down to the beginning of the next century. But there was a change of emphasis. During the third quarter of the century, with the Dutch overseas trading system at its height, new architecture arose chiefly in the cities of the maritime provinces and Utrecht or, as an extension of this, as country villas, belonging to élite merchants and regents. After the peace of Nijmegen, by contrast, attention shifted to the building and rebuilding of the Stadholder's palaces and the rural residences of his favourites, and senior Generality officials. New developments in architecture and the decorative arts, as well as gardens, now emanated from a rural and noble rather than civic context and mirrored, to a greater extent than before, French and other foreign courtly influences. Yet, despite this, and William III's partiality for the Huguenot artist Daniel Marot (1663–1752), who from the time of his arrival in the United Provinces, shortly after the Revocation of the Edict of Nantes, stood high in the Prince's favour, much Dutch architecture of the last quarter of the century may nevertheless be regarded—like painting—as an authentic extension of the civic classicism of the third quarter. Marot did become a sort of general artistic adviser to the Stadholder but his influence predominated much more in the sphere of interior décor, garden design, and taste in statuary than architecture proper.

The two key architects shaping the post-1677 Dutch classicist architectural revival were Steven Vennecool (1657–1719) and Jacob Roman (1640–1715). Both learnt their trade, and designed a few buildings, in Dutch towns

---

[69] De Lairesse, *Groot Schilderboek*, i. 47, 71.   [70] Ibid. i. 17–18, 41 and ii. 168–74.

as well as working for William III and his favourites. Vennecool's chief civic building was the new Enkhuizen town hall, built in the late 1680s, a jewel of late Dutch classicism.[71] Roman, whose father had been a sculptor, working on the palaces of Frederik Hendrik, was appointed Leiden town architect in 1681. Leiden's era of expansion, with major projects, was over. He received only small commissions in the city but built elegant structures, very much in the classicist tradition, which led to his being appointed chief architect to the Stadholder-king in 1689.

Roman worked extensively on all of William III's Dutch palaces. Het Loo, designed and built in the late 1680s, was the result of several architects' efforts and it remains a matter of dispute whether Roman or Marot played the larger role. Roman also designed the elegant palace at Zeist which belonged to Odijk, and various imposing rural residences, most notably De Voorst, near Zutphen, built in the late 1690s for Arnold Joost van Keppel, Lord Albemarle. Both Vennecool and Roman were commissioned to work, together with Romeyn de Hooghe and other artists and writers, on the triumphal arches, and other structures, erected in front of the Binnenhof, in The Hague, in 1691, as part of the celebrations to mark the first stay of William III in the Republic since 1688.

Foreign visitors, who as a rule saw more of Holland than the other provinces, noticed little that was new, or of note, architecturally, in the years around 1700, other than fine gardens, which did impress. Most of the internationally influential gardens were in the vicinity of The Hague and in easy reach for foreign diplomats and nobles. The gardens of Duinrel, the elegant house of Cornelis de Jonge van Ellemeet, receiver-general of the States General, north of The Hague, designed by Roman in the early 1680s, were regarded as both innovative and very fine. Still more praised were the gardens at Sorgvliet, the former house of Jacob Cats, purchased by Bentinck in 1674, and extensively remodelled. Bentinck, who was made superintendent of the royal gardens in England, in 1689, was regarded as one of the principal connoisseurs of gardens in the United Provinces and strongly influenced the lay-out at Het Loo.[72] Another famous garden near The Hague was that of House Clingendael, one of the first to show a marked French influence, laid out in the 1670s, and belonging to Philips Doublet, receiver-general of the Generality and connoisseur of French gardens. The Dutch garden, which reached its zenith in the last quarter of the seventeenth century and first quarter of the eighteenth, undoubtedly owed much to

[71] Kuyper, *Dutch Classicist Architecture*, 173, 541.
[72] De Jong, 'Nederlandish Hesperides', 29.

French example, yet, in several respects, differed fundamentally from the French. Instead of being highly unified and centrally planned, Dutch gardens were compartmentalized, with little overall unity, and high hedges which turned gardens into what has been called a series of 'green rooms'.[73] Dutch fine gardens were small, formal, and crammed with oddities and rarities, not only plants, rocks, and fountains, but shells, figures, and grottoes. A noted feature of Bentinck's gardens were the displays of shells and coral housed in special pavilions.

While the best-known gardens were those grouped around The Hague, as regards architecture and décor it was the new activity in progress in Utrecht, Gelderland, and Overijssel which was most important, the building and refurbishment of inland country houses being indeed one of the most formative, and typical, cultural phenomena of the Republic during the last quarter of the century. The French occupation of these provinces in the years 1672–4, and Munsterite incursions into Groningen and Drenthe, had led to the pillaging and devastation of numerous noble residences. Admittedly, the severe agricultural recession, since the late 1660s, profoundly affected the nobility. But, during the stadholderate of William III, Orangist nobles were able to recoup their losses, and build new wealth, as commanders of his armies, military governors, and diplomats and, like Odijk, Bentinck, Dijkvelt, and Keppel, handsomely profited from the opportunities accruing from political power and patronage. Not a few nobles, accordingly, were in a position to design and build more imposingly than before and did not hesitate to do so, frequently adding gardens imitating the refined elegance of Het Loo and Zeist, including numerous potted orange trees, an emblem closely associated with the Stadholder, who was known to stroll often in his gardens at Het Loo.[74]

Among the notable examples of such refurbishment was the castle at Middachten, near Arnhem, sacked in 1672. It was entirely rebuilt, at great expense, to designs by Vennecool, by Godard van Reede van Ginkel, one of William's most trusted generals, whom he made earl of Athlone in 1691. Also badly damaged, in 1672, was the old castle at Amerongen, in Utrecht, which was handsomely rebuilt in the late 1670s to designs by Maurits Post, the architect son of Pieter Post. In some cases, as with the castle at Batenburg, the exterior survived but the interior had to be entirely renovated. At Batenburg this was undertaken by another of William III's military favourites, Willem Adriaen, count of Horn, who succeeded in

[73] Dixon Hunt, 'Reckoning with Dutch Gardens', 45–51.
[74] De Jong, 'Nederlandish Hesperides', 23–4.

turning the castle again into a main focus of elegant noble living in Gelderland.

Architecture and gardens in the 1680s and 1690s reflected the reality of the power shift which had taken place in the Republic in 1672. Even though Holland remained the treasury and the driving force of the state, for the time being it was the new élite of noble favourites, generals, and bureaucrats who set the tone in Dutch culture.

34

Intellectual Life, 1650–1700

❖

INTELLECTUAL CRISIS

The seventeenth century, the age of the 'New Philosophy', 'Scientific Revolution', and 'Crisis of the European Mind', marks one of the most decisive shifts in the intellectual, cultural, and religious history of the western world. But the transition did not occur simultaneously in all western Europe. Rather the process was highly uneven. Three countries, in particular, stood at the forefront—England, France, and the Dutch Republic—and, in some respects, the last was in advance of the other two. Consequently, the intellectual and scientific history of the United Provinces in the seventeenth century is crucial to any proper grasp of Europe's intellectual crisis as a whole.

It was in Holland and Utrecht that Descartes researched, wrote, and published his major works and there that Europe's Cartesian battles—about the mechanistic world-view—began in earnest, several decades before this happened in France itself. After the initial struggle between Descartes and the Voetians in the early 1640s, it was clear the effort to crush Cartesian mechanistic philosophy in the Dutch academic arena had, for the moment, failed. Far from being suppressed, awareness of Descartes's ideas, and controversy about them, invaded all the universities and Illustrious Schools and spread to more and more spheres of thought and research. By the late 1640s, a sea-change had taken place in Dutch intellectual life.

Voetians insisted that Cartesianism was based on doubt and meant abandoning the principles of Aristotelian science and philosophy, amounting, at bottom, to a form of concealed atheism. But while they convinced the university authorities that Cartesianism undermined the very basis of what traditionally had been taught in the universities, and threatened faith itself as well as harmony within the Church, leading the university senates to ban Cartesianism, this could not prevent, or conceal, the escalating conflict of ideas electrifying the Dutch academic world or, behind the scenes, the swift progress of Cartesian philosophy and science. Thus, a glaring disparity arose between official academic policy and what was actually being taught and discussed behind the scenes. The regent of the States College at Leiden complained to the curators, in June 1648, that a colleague, Johannes de Raey, was openly expounding Cartesianism in lectures 'whereby the good intention of your excellencies to eradicate these sects from the university is being frustrated'.[1] The university reaffirmed its ban but could not enforce it. 'In the university of Leiden', noted Van Velthuysen, in 1656, 'almost all students reading philosophy are Cartesians.'[2] The problem was highlighted in June and July 1651, when the count of Nassau-Dillenburg, faced with the spillage of Cartesianism from the Dutch universities into the Calvinist academies of Germany, had to decide whether to allow the teaching of Cartesianism in his university of Herborn. He proposed to follow the lead of the Dutch, as was usual at Herborn, and, to ascertain their position, sent a circular to all five Dutch universities enquiring what their policy on Cartesianism was.[3] All five replied that Cartesianism was prejudicial and had been banned, Utrecht citing its judgement of 1642, condemning Cartesian thought as incompatible with *philosophia recepta*, and orthodox theology, and Leiden its negative ruling of 1648, while Harderwijk denounced Cartesianism as 'pestilential'. The Groningen authorities somewhat spoilt the effect, however, by adding that their academy, unlike Leiden and Utrecht, also adhered to its ban in practice.

The anti-Cartesian campaign was thwarted by key professors who, increasingly openly, propagated Descartes's ideas, bringing over a large part of the student body, and thus the Republic's (and Calvinist Germany's) intellectual and political élite, to Cartesianism. The atmosphere improved for Cartesians at Utrecht, following the victory of the States party-faction in the *vroedschap*, in 1651, enabling men such as Henricus Regius, professor of medicine and hitherto surreptitious champion of Cartesian science, to emerge more into the open.[4] At Leiden, one of the three professors of theology, Abraham Heidanus (1597–1678), a close ally of Cocceius, soon came out openly on behalf of Cartesianism. As early as 1653, Christopher Wittichius (1625–87), who was to be one of the leading lights of Dutch Cartesio-Cocceianism, published a controversial work, in Latin, arguing that the scriptural passages Voetians cited as incompatible with Cartesianism should not be construed literally.[5] Even at Groningen, a leading professor,

[1] Thijssen-Schoute, *Nederlands Cartesianisme*, 125.
[2] Van Velthuysen, *Bewys*, preface, p. v.
[3] Tepelius, *Historia Philosophiae Cartesianae*, 70–9.
[4] De Vrijer, *Henricus Regius*, 42–4.
[5] Wittichius, *Dissertationes duae*, 246–54; Du Boys, *Schadelickheyt*, 11–12.

Tobias Andreae (1604–76)—a German Calvinist like Heidanus and Witti-chius—took the plunge in 1653, emerging, in response to Revius' attacks, as a defender of Cartesianism. Regius, Heidanus, Wittichius, and Andreae all remained virulently embroiled with Voetian theologians, and advocates of Aristotelian philosophy and science, for the rest of their careers.

During the early 1650s the university authorities at Leiden and Utrecht favoured, or at least did not oppose, the spread of Cartesianism but did so without reversing earlier official condemnations of Descartes's ideas.[6] Not surprisingly this provoked furious disagreement as to whether the teaching of Cartesianism was permitted or not. At Utrecht, Lambert van Velthuysen, prominent in the new *vroedschap*, held that Cartesianism was now allowed.[7] Voetius insisted it was not.[8] In a sense, both were right. One leading professor of theology, Maresius, at Groningen, an enemy of both Voetius and Cocceius whose judgements about Descartes were ambivalent, was claimed by both sides. In the Illustrious Schools of Nijmegen, Breda, 's-Hertogenbosch, and Deventer there was a similar tendency to have it both ways, with official connivance at the propagation of Cartesianism by some of the professors.[9]

This uneasy ambivalence led to Leiden's bizarre response to the publica-tion, in 1654, of De Raey's *Clavis Philosophiae*, a book dedicated to the university curators, in which the author argued that Descartes was the renovator of philosophy, and a hero of freedom, but also that the gulf between the new philosophy and Aristotelianism was not as great as opponents of Descartes supposed. The curators first accepted De Raey's dedication, and awarded him a grant, but then had second thoughts, requiring him to delete Descartes's name from the title-pages of copies as yet unsold. It was in 1653, in the midst of this struggle, with Aristotle half toppled, that Rembrandt painted his famous picture of Aristotle contem-plating the bust of Homer, an allusion perhaps to the elusiveness of philosophical truth.

The centrality of this intellectual conflict in Dutch life and culture stemmed from Voetius' insistence that Cartesianism subverted all estab-lished religion, philosophy, and science. It was precisely this that the Dutch academic Cartesians—Heidanus, Regius, Wittichius, and Tobiae—denied. They were sincere adherents of the public Church and believed that Descartes had detached philosophy from theology, leaving the structure of

[6] Bekker, *De Philosophia Cartesiana*, 116, 145.
[7] Velthuysen, *Bewys*, preface, pp. v–vi.
[8] Du Boys, *Schadelickheyt*, pp. ix–xiii.
[9] Sassen, *Wijsgerig onderwijs aan de Illustre School te 's-Hertogenbosch*, 28–30.

faith and theological doctrine intact. Andreae, in his defence of Descartes of 1653, enraged the Voetians by describing them as 'children of darkness'. The Voetians denounced the Cartesian professors for spreading pestilential doctrines in Latin, and Velthuysen for spreading the sickness in Dutch. 'It has not been enough for these new philosophers to propagate these novel ideas in the universities, and among the students,' fulminated an anti-Cartesian *predikant*, at Leiden, 'but they also aspire to convert the ordinary man into a Cartesian.'[10] This was indeed a particular worry of the Voetians at this point; for it was in 1656 that there appeared the first version of Descartes in Dutch, translated by the Amsterdam Anabaptist Jan Hendrik Glazemaker (*c*.1619–82) who later also translated Spinoza.[11] Descartes's *Discours, Meditationes*, and *Passions de l'âme* all appeared in Dutch that year, followed the next by the *Principia Philosophica*. Also published in 1656, at Utrecht, was Van Velthuysen's reply in Dutch to the anti-Cartesian onslaught, assuring the public that neither Descartes's principles, nor the (increasingly contentious) doctrine that the earth revolves around the sun,[12] conflict with 'God's Word' and that various illustrious professors of the universities of Utrecht, Harderwijk, and Groningen, as well as Professor Wittichius, at the Nijmegen academy, sanctioned Cartesianism.[13]

The Cartesian claim which most enraged Voetians was precisely that which formed the link connecting Cartesianism with Cocceian theology: the contention that parts of Scripture should not be construed literally but interpreted figuratively and in terms of historical context. Since miracles transcended the mathematical laws of nature as determined by Descartes, Cartesians adopted a sceptical attitude towards the miracles recounted in Scripture, which generated great friction. Ordinary, unsophisticated folk, Voetian preachers complained, were now sitting in their homes and taverns excitedly discussing whether perhaps the earth revolves around the sun, whether God really turned Moses' staff into a serpent, and whether, at Joshua's request, he really made the sun stand still, for an hour, in the sky.[14]

A strong reaction gathered, among the classes and synods of the Reformed Church, during the mid-1650s. The classis of The Hague led the way, calling on the synods, in April 1656, to urge the States of Holland to halt the undermining of the authority of Scripture and dissension among professors and students at 'various universities'.[15] The movement in the

[10] Du Boys, *Schadelickheyt*, 3.
[11] Thijssen-Schoute, *Uit de Republiek der letteren*, 202, 236.
[12] Wittichius, *Dissertationes duae*, 251–4.
[13] Van Velthuysen, *Bewys*, 1, 4, 25–6.
[14] Du Boys, *Schadelickheyt*, 11–12.
[15] Cramer, *Abraham Heidanus*, 66–8.

South Holland Synod greatly alarmed Heidanus who appealed to De Witt and the States party leadership. De Witt took the threat with great seriousness, devoting much attention to this matter over ensuing months. He fully grasped that the new philosophy and science caused major dissension in the public Church, and society, that this had political implications also, and that, from the States of Holland's vantage point, it was necessary to find some means to moderate the strife among the professors, and the exasperation accumulating in the synods.[16]

Nor was this a purely Dutch issue. At the meeting of the synod of Cleves, Mark, Jülich, and Berg, in July 1656, the German Calvinist churches on the lower Rhine condemned Cartesianism as dangerous to the faith of the ordinary man, agreeing to follow whatever action the Dutch Reformed synods decided on.[17] Heidanus hoped De Witt would persuade the States of Holland to intervene to forbid the South Holland Synod to pass a resolution condemning Cartesian philosophy and science, claiming that philosophy was not a proper topic for a provincial synod, being national, and international, in scope. To win De Witt, a devotee of Cartesian mathematics, to the wider Cartesian cause, Heidanus sent him a copy of his *Bedenckingen* (1656), or reflections on Cartesian philosophy; De Witt recounts that he immediately read the book to brief himself for the contest ahead.[18]

De Witt's chief concern, his letters reveal, was to ease intellectual tension and find 'peaceful' solutions. But within this context, he pursued a basically 'Cartesian' strategy, aligning closely with Heidanus throughout. The Cartesians, for the moment, were in a relatively strong position. The South Holland Synod found itself split, some members being 'moderate', to use De Witt's favourite theological term, or at least amenable to 'moderate' arguments. Moreover, the Leiden curators backed Heidanus, denying the contention of The Hague classis that the professors were hopelessly divided or that, at Leiden, theology was now the handmaiden of philosophy—instead of the other way around, as in the past.[19] Heidanus also had the support of his colleague Cocceius, who perceived that the Voetian attack on Cartesian philosophy was linked to the offensive against Cocceian theology.[20] De Witt wished to preserve freedom to philosophize, and philosophers, from the censorship of preachers and synods; but took the view that to achieve this the States needed to enforce the separation of philosophy and theology implied in Cartesian teaching.

[16] ARH SH 2647, fo. 248. De Witt to Heidanus, 21 July 1656.
[17] Du Boys, *Schadelickheyt*, 3.
[18] ARH SH 2647, fo. 248. De Witt to Heidanus, 21 July 1656.
[19] Molhuysen, *Bronnen*, iii. 112.
[20] Res. Holl. 30 Sept. 1656.

While Heidanus and Cocceius, together with De Witt, wanted a States of Holland edict separating theology from philosophy, Leiden's third professor of theology, Johannes Hoornbeeck (1617–66), vehemently dissented, insisting that only Aristotelian philosophy and science should be taught at Leiden. But to the relief of De Witt and Heidanus, Hoornbeeck was persuaded not to dissent formally from the advice of the Leiden theology faculty so that the States of Holland were able to legislate in accordance with the entire faculty's 'guidance'.[21] All the Holland town councils approved the draft edict except for Orangist Leiden, which strongly demurred, despite De Witt's tactfully describing the text, in a letter to the Leiden burgomasters, as designed to 'prevent abuse of freedom to philosophize to the detriment of true theology and Holy Scripture'.[22] The edict, adopted in October, proclaimed that philosophy and theology each had their proper sphere, and should be kept separate, but that where unavoidable overlap occurred, and apparent disparity between theological and philosophical truth arose, philosophy professors must defer to the theologians and refrain from interpreting Scripture contentiously 'according to their principles'. The South Holland Synod accepted De Witt's formulation as a way of preserving unity in university and Church, and preventing damaging rifts,[23] even though Hoornbeeck, and many others, saw that the placard's apparent subordination of philosophy to theology was only superficial and that the essential point was the separation, and therefore freeing, of philosophy from its tutelage to theology.

The Leiden curators circulated copies of the placard to the six theology and philosophy professors, summoning them on 8 January 1657, to sign, and swear an oath, that they would comply with its provisions. This the three theologians—Heidanus, Cocceius, and Hoornbeeck—and the three philosophers—De Raey, Heereboordt, and Bornius—duly did.[24] What it all amounted to was the removal of obstacles to teaching and discussion of Cartesian philosophy and science, provided explicit references to Descartes, and his books, and problematic references to Scripture were avoided. By compelling theologians and philosophers to disengage, and moderate their polemics, De Witt had, in effect, defeated the attempts to ban Cartesian philosophy and restrict freedom to philosophize in the universities.

Between 1657 and 1672 the Cartesian controversy entered a quieter phase at Leiden and Utrecht, while becoming more virulent in Gelderland,

---

[21] ARH SH 2647, fo. 276. De Witt to Heidanus, 29 July 1656.
[22] ARH SH 2647, fo. 324. De Witt to Leiden burgomasters, undated [Aug. 1656].
[23] Knuttel, *Acta*, iv. 35–6.
[24] Molhuysen, *Bronnen*, iii. 118.

Groningen, and especially Friesland. In 1656, Velthuysen claimed that Cartesian philosophy was now dominant at Groningen, as well as Leiden and Utrecht, was openly taught at the Calvinist university of Duisburg, and that the Illustrious School at Nijmegen had sanctioned Cartesianism by appointing Wittichius professor of theology there, the year before.[25] A rumbling campaign developed against Wittichius in Gelderland during the late 1650s, but the Synod of Gelderland ruled in his favour in 1660.[26] In Friesland, by contrast, it was not until the appointment of the controversial Johannes Wubbena as professor of philosophy at Franeker, in 1666, that Cartesianism seriously affected the university. Wubbena's lectures provoked a strong anti-Cartesian reaction among the preachers and, in April 1668, the classis of Leeuwarden declared Cartesian philosophy a threat to faith and learning, pressing for a provincial *reglement* banning Cartesianism in the province and obliging candidates for preaching positions formally to deny a list of proscribed Cartesian theses.[27]

The Synod of Friesland, however, in response to pressure from the Delegated States, decided not to take such action for the moment. An eloquent defender of Cartesian philosophy appeared, at this point, in the shape of a young preacher at Franeker, who was to play a role of great importance in Dutch intellectual life during the last third of the seventeenth century—Balthasar Bekker (1634–98). In his book *De Philosophia Cartesiana* (1668), Bekker argued that theology and philosophy each had their separate terrain and that Nature can no more be explained from Scripture than can theological truth be deduced from Nature. He conceded that certain authors in recent years, calling themselves 'Cartesians', had published novel doctrines damaging to faith and the public Church but he held that Cartesian philosophy itself could not damage faith.[28] He wrote approvingly of Heidanus, Wittichius, and his former teacher, Andreae, as upright men, loyal to the public Church, and 'Cartesians'. Those who go beyond what is in Descartes's philosophy and cause damage, he argued, were not entitled to be called 'Cartesians'.[29] Bekker was now a marked man in Friesland.

Meanwhile, a furious polemic raged, at Groningen, between the professors of theology, Samuel Maresius, and Bekker's friend and mentor, Jacobus Alting, an unseemly furore within the leading faculty which troubled the States of Groningen, not least because of the damage to the reputation of

[25] Velthuysen, *Bewys*, p. vi.
[26] Bekker, *De Philosophia Cartesiana*, 145.
[27] Knuttel, *Balthasar Bekker*, 43–9.
[28] Bekker, *De Philosophia Cartesiana*, 28, 116, 145.
[29] Bekker, *Friesche Godgeleerdheid*, 698.

the university.[30] Alting was a Cartesio-Cocceian who had studied under Andreae. In the past Maresius had been guardedly favourable to Cartesianism, and at least as hostile to Voetius (whom he had detested for decades) as Cocceius. He now produced a book entitled *De Abusu Philosophiae Cartesianae* (1670) in which he both praised, and deplored, Descartes but defining the damaging element in Cartesianism in broader terms than Bekker, two years before, in particular virulently attacking Wittichius.[31] At the same time, he redoubled his onslaught on Cocceius, whose theology he accounted 'pestem teterrimam Ecclesiae et Religionis'.

The curators at Groningen submitted Maresius' charges against Alting to the theology faculty at Leiden. Cocceius and Heidanus, not surprisingly, backed Alting. This so antagonized Maresius that he allowed himself to be reconciled to his old enemy Voetius. The two agreed that Cocceius and 'abuse of Cartesian philosophy' were now the two great perils threatening the public Church and that all Calvinist orthodox must rally to defeat these evils.[32] Three accounts of the Maresius–Alting quarrel were published at Amsterdam in 1669, much to the consternation of the States of Groningen, which feared a damaging split within the provincial synod. The States asked the States of Holland to suppress the books, promising that should Holland desire Groningen to help ban any books the province would be only too willing to comply.

The intellectual atmosphere changed palpably with the overthrow of the De Witt regime and elevation to the stadholderate of William III.[33] From 1672 a Voetian reaction gathered at Leiden and Utrecht though decidedly not at Franeker. University authorities in Holland and Utrecht avoided Cocceians and Cartesians when appointing their professors. At Leiden, the influence of the theologian (and university librarian) Frederik Spanheim (1632–1701) now predominated. Spanheim was a disciple of his father (and namesake), a hardline Calvinist, originally from the Palatinate, and also of Johannes Hoornbeeck, firmly opposed to both Cartesianism and Cocceianism. The 'moderate' Reformed Cartesians were out of favour and under pressure. At the same time, they themselves grew more adamant in attacking radical Cartesians and Spinozists, in order to distance themselves from them—and in their own defence. Spinoza complained of this in a letter of September 1675, where he mentions that the Reformed preachers were denouncing him to the Prince of Orange, as well as town magistrates, adding

[30] ARH SH 2711. S.Gr. to SH, 4 May 1669.
[31] Thijssen-Schoute, *Nederlands Cartesianisme*, 481.
[32] Nauta, *Samuel Maresius*, 381–5.
[33] De Vrijer, *Henricus Regius*, 80–1.

that the 'Cartesians, because they are believed to be in my favour, and in order to free themselves from this suspicion', now fiercely assailed his doctrines.[34] The Cartesio-Cocceian condemnation of radical Cartesianism and Spinozism was to become more and more vehement through the last quarter of the century.

By 1675, signs of the reaction against both Cocceio-Cartesianism and radical Cartesianism, and Spinozism, were abundantly evident. At Utrecht, the new professor of philosophy, Gerardus de Vries, a Voetian and fierce anti-Cartesian, eradicated Cartesian influence from the philosophy courses there. In January 1676, spurred by Spanheim, the Leiden curators drew up a list of twenty Cocceio-Cartesian doctrines they proposed to ban from the teaching of theology, philosophy, and science, as especially pernicious, including the propositions that 'Scripture speaks according to the erroneous prejudices of the common folk' and that philosophy should be the interpreter of Scripture.[35] The Prince of Orange approved the list of proscribed views and the curators' new policy to appoint only professors who agreed to eschew Cocceian and Cartesian tenets.[36]

The Voetian reaction was an academic development but one with a wide impact on the educated public, and classes and synods, where there was mounting agitation, at this time, against Cocceian theology and Cartesianism. The twenty propositions banned at Leiden were drawn as much from debates in the classes deploring new notions circulating among the public, and doctrines disputed by Voetian preachers in pamphlets, as lectures of university professors. The bookshop windows of Amsterdam, during the 1670s, were reportedly filled with Dutch-language books and pamphlets discussing the Cartesian and Cocceian controversies. The Leiden curators' resolution of January 1676 itself became a bestseller, 2,000 copies being sold at Amsterdam within days, some of its avid readership unkindly speculating that Spanheim and Anthonie Hulsius (the sole two professors consulted by the curators) were moved more by jealousy (students preferring Cocceio-Cartesian lectures to theirs) than zeal for God's truth.

In Zeeland, too, there was intense interest in the controversies and a fierce reaction against the Cocceio-Cartesian stream. In September 1673, the classis of South Beveland complained that the doctrine that the earth circles the sun was being used to convince humble folk that Scripture should not be read literally and that where one finds incompatibility between Scripture and the laws of Nature Scripture is figurative or false.[37] Such irreverence for

[34] Spinoza, *Correspondence*, 334.
[35] Cramer, *Abraham Heidanus*, 102–3.
[36] Ibid. 103–5, 152.
[37] Ibid. 124–8.

the Word of God the classis deemed to flow partly from Descartes, and partly from Cocceianism and especially from the lectures of Professor Wittichius—the most detested Cocceian since the death of Cocceius himself. The Zeeland classes advised Zeelanders studying at Leiden to boycott Wittichius' lectures.

In defence of the Cocceio-Cartesian world-view, Heidanus, Wittichius, and Burchardus de Volder (1643–1709)—the professor who introduced practical experiments in physics at Leiden, and established the university *theatrum physicum* (1675)—together wrote a long reply to the curators, also published in 1676, maintaining that the twenty banned doctrines were distilled from Descartes, Meijer, and others who were not university professors, and did not reflect the content of teaching at Leiden.[38] Heidanus (who accepted sole responsibility for the anonymous publication) was summoned before the curators and stripped of his professorship. This only encouraged interest in the book, however, which was twice reprinted during 1676. Nor did Heidanus' dismissal prevent Cocceianism and Cartesianism continuing to pervade lectures at Leiden and most of the more creative minds. But the reaction did place Voetianism incontestably in the ascendant and drive Cartesio-Cocceians to resort increasingly to allusions and circumlocutions.

At Leiden and Utrecht, Cartesianism and Cocceianism were now under a cloud. But William III's preference for Voetianism inevitably worked a contrary effect in Friesland, where the Frisian Stadholder and court exhibited a growing partiality for Cocceianism. In 1677, at the wish of Hendrik Casimir, Van der Waeyen was appointed professor of theology at Franeker, introducing a period of Cocceian ascendancy at the university, which accorded ill with the fundamentalism of the Frisian Synod. Van der Waeyen was more important politically and as an ideological standard-bearer than as a creative mind. But the German Cocceian Herman Alexander Röell (1635–1718), a student of Wilhelmus Momma, the Cocceian William III ejected from Middelburg in 1676, became a major force in Dutch intellectual life, following his appointment as professor of philosophy at Franeker, in 1685. Röell went further than any previous Cocceian theologian in forging a theology linked to reason and in trying to reconcile the new philosophy with Reformed theology. He defended the divinity of Christ and argued against the Socinians but in a manner which shocked Voetian sentiment. He also became locked in fierce disputes with Huber and

---

[38] Thijssen-Schoute, 'Cartésianisme aux Pays-Bas', 208.

Campegius Vitringa (1659–1722), who emerged as the academic champion of conservative Cocceianism in Friesland. Huber, the great legal scholar and Franeker's leading conservative light, reproached Van der Waeyen and Röell with applying the Cartesian method to theology, which Descartes himself had never ventured to do.[39] Huber was not an anti-Cartesian as such but was profoundly uneasy at the direction which Dutch Cartesianism was taking. The Delegated States of Friesland had repeatedly to intervene to calm the Franeker disputes. On the publication of his *Aphorismi* (1688), a work designed to appeal to a general audience and which appeared in five Latin and four Dutch editions, Vitringa became one of the best-known Cocceian theologians in the Republic.

THE UNIVERSITIES

During the seventeenth century, the Dutch Republic was renowned in Europe, amongst much else, for its universities and academic culture. As in England and France, many major developments in thought took place outside the formal academic sphere. But, in the Dutch case, the contribution of the universities was relatively more important than in England or France. If we consider all aspects of intellectual achievement, the United Provinces rank, together with France and England, as one of the three chief centres of European thought from the end of the sixteenth down to the early eighteenth century. But if we focus only on universities, the Republic arguably outstripped all other European countries, including England and France, in the scope and general significance of academic achievement. The religious division of Europe, in the wake of the Reformation, meant that there was no longer a shared, pan-European academic world, in the sense that there had been in the Middle Ages. The universities, and Illustrious Schools, of the United Provinces were Protestant institutions. Yet, the three leading Dutch universities—Leiden, Utrecht, and Franeker—collectively formed an academic forum which was international, and pan-European, at least within the Protestant sphere, to a greater extent than was found anywhere else.

During the half century in which the Dutch universities were at their height, from around 1620 to 1672, the number of students at the five institutions slightly exceeded the total studying at the two English universities—Oxford and Cambridge—which, in the quarter-century 1626–50, received approximately 16,000 students. Of the five Dutch universities,

[39] Ibid. 251–2.

Harderwijk never acquired the standing of the others and remained very small, hosting, in 1650, only eighty-four students; though established by the States of Gelderland, Harderwijk was really just a local university for the Arnhem quarter. Leiden, at the opposite extreme, was much the largest, though Utrecht, Franeker, and Groningen also attracted substantial numbers, approximately 40 per cent of the total. As we have seen (see pp. 572–3 above) it was also Leiden which received the highest proportion of students from abroad, though the others too were remarkable for their large numbers of foreign students. Almost exactly one-third of the 6,400 students who studied at Groningen between its founding and 1689 were German. By the last quarter of the seventeenth century, however, the pull of the Dutch universities on the rest of Protestant Europe had perceptibly waned,[40] though, owing to the simultaneous decline in the number of Dutch students enrolling (see Table 40), the proportions of foreigners were still very high, over 40 per cent at Leiden and some 36 per cent at Franeker, reflecting the fact that the Dutch universities continued to enjoy great international prestige. This applies especially but by no means only to Leiden. When John Locke visited Franeker, in 1684, he was unimpressed with the university's buildings and libraries but remarked that this shows that 'knowledge depends not' on such things 'since this university has produced many learned men, and has now some very learned amongst its professors'.[41]

The non-Dutch student population of the universities, and Illustrious Schools, came from all over Protestant Europe. However, the attraction was by no means spread evenly. The Dutch academies drew an uninterrupted stream of students from France, England, and Scotland. But these countries had their own renowned Protestant universities, at any rate (in the case of France) down to 1685, so that the role of the Dutch universities in shaping academic life was secondary, and supplementary. The position was otherwise in parts of Germany and in Denmark-Norway, Sweden-Finland, and Hungary-Transylvania, where Dutch academic influence was pervasive and, in some disciplines, exercised a general preponderance.

The largest component of the foreign student population at the Dutch academies consisted of Protestant Germans. During the quarter-century 1626–50, 5,713 foreign students enrolled at Leiden alone, of whom a majority, around 3,000, came from Protestant Germany.[42] The position was similar at Franeker, where, in the half century 1620–70, Protestant Germans

---

[40] Bots and Frijhoff, 'Studentenpopulatie', 57.
[41] Van Strien, *British Travellers*, 309.
[42] Wansink, *Politieke wetenschappen*, 9.

amounted to 56 per cent of the total foreign student population.[43] These students came from all over Protestant Germany but especially the German Baltic lands (East Prussia, Courland, and Danzig) and the Calvinist regions adjoining the Republic—East Friesland, Cleves-Mark, Jülich-Berg, and Bentheim. Besides Germans, the main groups among the foreign student population—leaving aside the French, English, and Scots (who at Leiden comprised nearly 20 per cent of the total but were a lower proportion elsewhere)—were the Swedes, Danes, Poles, and Hungarians. At Leiden, the Hungarians were the fourth largest group until 1650 and then third, after Polish students disappeared from the scene during the third quarter of the century. But where, for other nationalities, Leiden was the principal attraction, the Hungarians, who were numerous at all the Dutch academies, developed especially close links with Utrecht—and not least Voetius, a figure held in high esteem by the Reformed Church in Hungary-Transylvania. Hungarians were also disproportionately strongly represented at Franeker, where no less than 26 per cent of all foreign students during the half-century 1620–70 came from Hungary-Transylvania. Between 1643 and 1795 over 700 Hungarians studied at Utrecht.[44] Hungarians remained numerous at both Utrecht and Franeker down to the 1770s.

TABLE 40. *Student enrolments at Leiden per quarter-century,*
1575–1794

Quarter-century	Total	Dutch	Foreign	Average per year
1575–1600	2,725	1,705	1,020	105
1601–25	6,236	3,546	2,690	249
1626–50	11,076	5,363	5,713	443
1651–75	9,940	6,381	3,559	398
1676–1700	8,108	4,533	3,575	324
1700–25	6,722	3,558	3,164	269
1726–50	5,915	3,236	2,715	238
1751–75	3,845	2,713	1,132	154
1776–94	2,686	2,152	534	141

Sources: Colenbrander, 'Herkomst der Leidsche studenten', 276–8; Wansink, *Politieke wetenschappen*, 7.

In proportion to population of the home country, Hungarians formed the largest category among the foreign student population. But Hungarian

[43] Bots and Frijhoff, 'Studentenpopulatie', 59.
[44] Banki, 'Utrechtse universiteit', 94, 99–100.

students in the Republic tended to concentrate in the theology faculties.[45] Most were training to become Reformed preachers in Hungary-Transylvania. The theology faculties were also the prime attraction for students from the Reformed regions of Germany, where universities, such as Herborn in Nassau-Dillenburg, or Duisburg, in Cleves, tended to follow the Dutch universities in their teaching, theological approach, and book acquisitions. But where Dutch academic preponderance in Hungary-Transylvania and Calvinist Germany was primarily theological, the position was very different regarding students from Lutheran countries and regions. A few Danes and Swedes read theology in Dutch universities but most Scandinavians, as well as Lutheran Germans, congregated in other faculties. The latter chiefly gravitated to the law and medical faculties,[46] Danes and Swedes especially to the Arts faculties, though they too were numerous among the medical students. The universally acknowledged supremacy of Leiden in medical studies was especially due to the high standard of practical instruction and clinical research, evident particularly after the setting up of the university hospital, in 1637, and under the impact of Professor Franciscus de le Boë Sylvius (1614–72; the collector of Dou paintings), who heightened the emphasis on practical instruction and stressed the uses of chemistry.[47]

Danes and Swedes were spread across the faculties but were especially attracted to classical and philological studies. Something of the ascendancy of Dutch academe in the Scandinavian context can be gauged from the fact that between 1640 and 1660 practically half the professors at Uppsala had studied at Leiden, as had half of those approached to take up chairs at the new university of Åbo, established in Finland, in 1640.[48] Practically all Danish mathematicians, medical men, and scientists of any standing in the mid-seventeenth century had trained in the United Provinces.

A proportion of both Dutch and foreign students officially enrolled to study law and medicine, the key disciplines for the secular professions, also studied scientific subjects, or philosophy, out of intellectual interest. From the middle years of the seventeenth century, as the new Cartesian philosophy spread, a sense of intellectual excitement became a distinguishing feature of Dutch university life and remained so for several decades. Many leading Dutch regents of the second half of the seventeenth century were noted for their strong interest in the new subjects and this they mostly acquired as students at Leiden.

[45] Ridder-Symoens, 'Buitenlandse studenten', 74.
[46] Schneppen, *Niederländische Universitäten*, 15, 27.
[47] Woltjer, *Leidse universiteit*, 23.
[48] Wansink, *Politieke wetenschappen*, 10.

SCIENCE

Cartesian philosophy and science exerted an immense impact on Dutch culture in the 1640s and 1650s and for many decades subsequently. But, besides Cartesianism, there were two other major factors shaping the great age of Dutch science, which extended from the early Cartesian controversies of the 1640s down to the first quarter of the eighteenth century. One was the effect of technological advance linked to the mid- and late-seventeenth-century expansion and refinement of Dutch industry. The constant search for new techniques and methods in many areas of production, especially in capital-intensive and precision industries, and the public interest in new inventions such as Van der Heyden's street-lamps and fire-fighting pumps, acted as a stimulus to science, providing new instruments and devices which, in turn, suggested new kinds of research. It is often remarked that the university of Leiden was amongst the first where professors used instruments, and gave practical demonstrations, in teaching medicine and physics. And so it was; but this is scarcely surprising in a society in which exceptional emphasis is put on technological innovation. The third fundamental factor was the cultural impact of the 'rich trades' during Phase Four (1647–72) and Phase Five (1672–1702) of the Dutch overseas trading system. Success in long-distance trade generated a craze among élite merchants and regents for collecting and classifying 'rarities'—flora, fauna, fossils, shells, and minerals—from the world beyond Europe which lasted until deep into the eighteenth century and was to be one of the most important Dutch contributions to the European Enlightenment.

The greatest Dutch scientist was Christiaan Huygens (1629–95), son of Frederik Hendrik's secretary Constantijn Huygens. Huygens pursued a comprehensive approach to science, mathematics, and technology, based on the Cartesian tradition, seeking the mechanistic principles which lay behind the visible world.[49] He was a great mathematician, trained by Van Schooten, and made advances in several areas, especially in the mathematics of curves. He was also an accomplished astronomer and renowned in making, and improving, telescopes and microscopes. In 1655, using a giant 12-foot telescope, he discovered the rings, and one of the moons, around Saturn, and first became widely known, through his book on Saturn and the planetary system, his *Systema Saternium* (1659).

Huygens combined proficiency in mathematical theory with skill in practical experiment. In 1656, he invented the pendulum clock, showing its capacity to keep time with greater precision than all earlier types of clock.

---

[49] De Vries, 'Christiaan Huygens', 10–11.

Together with an expert clock-maker, Salomon Coster, at The Hague, and armed with a patent from the States of Holland—which in these years frequently issued patents for inventions—he began manufacturing pendulum wall-clocks in the late 1650s. Until 1672, The Hague and Leiden were the chief centres in Europe for making precision clocks. The oldest surviving Dutch standing (long-case) clock—which is also the earliest equipped with a second hand—was constructed in 1670 on the Rapenburg, in Leiden, opposite the main university building (The Clock Museum, Zaanse Schans).

De Witt, the regents, and soon also the English admiralty authorities began taking a lively interest in Huygens's pendulum clocks as he produced more refined models, during the 1660s, and demonstrated their use in determining longitude, at sea. Spinoza was asked, in a letter from Henry Oldenburg, secretary of the Royal Society in London, in September 1665 (shortly after the outbreak of the Second Anglo-Dutch War), what he thought of the 'pendulums of Huygens, especially the kind which are said to measure time so precisely that they can be used for finding longitude at sea'.[50] Spinoza worked closely with Huygens on optical instruments, at The Hague, during the mid-1660s, but can hardly have wished to discuss Huygens's work in letters to England at that juncture.

Later in his career, Huygens worked for many years in Paris, on a pension from Louis XIV, before retiring, in his last years, to The Hague. His most enduring contribution was in the field of optics, a lifelong preoccupation. Here, too, he built on Descartes, who had attempted to incorporate the phenomenon of light into his mechanistic philosophy, explaining light in terms of matter and motion, using mechanistic analogies. Huygens developed, and refined, the Cartesian conception, formulating his celebrated wave theory of light, and eventually the laws of reflection, refraction, and double refraction, in mathematical form. He summed up the results of his work in his *Traité de la lumière* (Leiden, 1690).

Huygens respected Descartes as an 'auteur qui voulait tout réduire à des raisons mécaniques',[51] but, in his later years, was positively disdainful of Cartesian metaphysics, insisting on a philosophy more purely mathematical and empiricist. Though outwardly a member of the Dutch Church while in Paris, he seems not to have regarded Scripture as divine revelation and to have been a deist rather than a Christian in any real sense.[52] With his revisionist attitude to Descartes, and view of the human condition, which precluded any direct relation between God and Man, Huygens may be

[50] Spinoza, *Correspondence*, 204.
[51] De Vries, 'Christiaan Huygens', 6–9.
[52] Ibid.

compared to his philosophical contemporary Spinoza, not least in his tendency to give primacy to mathematical concepts rather than experiment.

Huygens was one of numerous prominent men in contact with Spinoza at The Hague during the 1660s. It is tempting to assume that the great scientist took an interest in the ideas of the great philosopher. But there is no proof that this was so. Possibly, the sole reason Huygens cultivated Spinoza was his interest in the latter's lenses and microscopes. Spinoza showed an abiding interest in the practical side of scientific research. In a letter written just prior to the death of Rembrandt, in 1669, he describes an elaborate experiment he had just conducted on water pressure, using specially constructed tubes and requiring the help of two assistants. But if, in physics, he was an amateur, when it came to microscopes and telescopes, the philosopher was regarded as one of the chief experts in the Republic. Huygens acknowledged that, in some respects, Spinoza's microscopes were more advanced than his own.[53]

The microscope had been invented early in the century by the most ingenious of the early seventeenth-century Dutch inventors, Cornelis Drebbel (*c.*1572–1633)—who had also invented the thermometer—but it was only in the 1660s, after improvements introduced by the Amsterdam regent mathematician and scientist Johannes Hudde (1628–1704), that its potential as an instrument of scientific research began to be realized.[54] Both Huygens and Spinoza contributed to the early development of the microscope but the key figure in exploiting the new device was the scientist Jan Swammerdam (1637–80), son of an Amsterdam apothecary renowned for his outstanding natural history collection. Swammerdam studied anatomy, clinical practice, and dissection under the famous Leiden professor Le Boë Sylvius and, like Huygens, was fascinated both by the Cartesian vision and the research possibilities offered by the new devices and lenses. Exploring the mechanics of bodies, he opened up whole new fields of anatomy and physiology and was the discoverer of red corpuscles in blood and the structure of human brains, lungs, and spinal marrow. Many of his findings in anatomy did not become widely known, however, until much later when his unpublished work appeared under the title *Biblia Naturae* (1737–8). Tiring of the acrimonious polemics for, and against, Descartes plaguing anatomy, Swammerdam switched to studying insects, dissecting and investigating the structure of their bodies, establishing a tradition which became one of the glories of Dutch science. His major work, the *Algemeene Verhandeling van*

[53] Klever, 'Insignis opticus', 50–2.
[54] Cook, 'New Philosophy', 132–3.

de bloedeloose dierkens (1669), laid the foundations of the science of entomo-logy, eventually, in the 1680s, appearing also in Latin and French editions.[55]

Exploring insects, Swammerdam revealed a new world. He also exhibited it more effectively than anyone had before, preserving specimens by means of the ingenious preparations for which he became renowned. In the 1670s, however, he abandoned science to devote himself entirely to religion. His place was taken by Anthonie van Leeuwenhoek (1632–1723) of Delft, a self-taught researcher, who knew little Latin and was treated conde-scendingly by other men of science; but this did not prevent his winning international fame as a researcher. During his visit to Holland in 1697, Tsar Peter the Great travelled to Delft specially to see his microscopes, much as, in 1668, Grand Duke Cosimo of Tuscany, on his visit to Holland, had visited Swammerdam to peruse his.[56] Researching indefatigably in anatomy, entomology, and botany, Van Leeuwenhoek adopted a scientific outlook likewise pervaded by the Cartesian mechanistic world-view.[57] His methods he took largely from Swammerdam and other predecessors. Like Huygens and Spinoza, he was highly skilled in working with lenses and casings but surpassed them, gradually increasing his level of magnification from a starting-point of 40 times. He constructed approximately 520 microscopes, with copper and occasionally silver casings; of those that survive, the most powerful magnifies up to 270 times; but it appears that he achieved up to 500 times.[58]

Van Leeuwenhoek began making major advances in the 1670s; his most important publications appeared in the 1680s. Continuing where Swammer-dam had left off, he investigated further the structure of blood. In 1676, a year in which he auctioned off, in his capacity as a minor civic official, a number of Vermeer's paintings, he discovered bacteria. The following year, that of Spinoza's death, he revealed the structure of human sperm. After-wards, he worked on the structure of the blood and sperm of dogs, rabbits, frogs, and fish.[59] He also went beyond Swammerdam in investigating the mechanics of insects' bodies and wings. Recognizing his achievement early on, the Royal Society, in London, made him a corresponding fellow in 1680; he later left the society twenty-six of his microscopes. The Republic itself possessed no academy or corresponding body for science.

With Van Leeuwenhoek at Delft, Huygens (from 1666) in Paris (but also spending periods, and from 1681 residing permanently, in The Hague), the

[55] Schierbeek, *Jan Swammerdam*, 185–6, 226.
[56] Ibid. 27–8.
[57] Snelders, 'Antoni van Leeuwenhoek's Mechanistic View', 59–61.
[58] Schierbeek, *Antoni van Leeuwenhoek*, 31.
[59] Ibid. 87.

principal figure at Amsterdam, after Swammerdam, was Frederik Ruysch (1638–1731). Ruysch was *praelector* of anatomy in the city, and among other tasks, supervised the city's midwives. Also following Swammerdam, Ruysch researched many areas of human anatomy, and physiology,[60] and, using spirits to preserve organs, assembled was one of Europe's most famous anatomical collections (see p. 1044 below). He published a good deal, his crowning achievement being his *Thesaurus Anatomicus* (10 vols., 1701–15). Ruysch was also a botanist and, in 1685, was appointed head of the new Amsterdam *hortus botanicus* which was one of Europe's most important centres for botanical study. His famous daughter, Rachel Ruysch, recreated, as it were, his passion for plants, setting new standards of exactness in the painting of flowers.

Another expert classifier who improved methods of preserving specimens, though not a professional scientist, was the Anabaptist Levinus Vincent (1658–1727). Vincent created what was perhaps the most celebrated of all the Natural History 'cabinets of rarities' in late seventeenth-century Holland.[61] He turned Swammerdam's passion for insects into one of the most fashionable activities of late seventeenth-century Amsterdam, preserving and displaying great quantities of insects in new ways. His collection also included shells, birds, herbs, and lots of flower-pictures. Peter the Great and several lesser European princes visited Vincent's museum in the 1690s. He published his catalogue of the collection, the *Wondertoneel der Nature* (1706), adorned with a handsome title-page designed by Romeyn de Hooghe.

Amsterdam regent circles, especially Burgomaster Hudde, favoured the Cartesian approach and assisted new research, investing public money to provide facilities. Van Beuningen was one of Swammerdam's chief backers. Regents were also amongst the foremost collectors of rare plants and insects, the insect museum of the Witsen family being especially noted.[62] They followed the new developments in botany, and helped promote them. Here the key figure was the affluent apothecary Johannes Commelin (1629–92), one of the new regents put into the city council in 1672. He was prominently involved in the setting up of the new Amsterdam *hortus*, in 1682, and the subsequent rapid development of the garden, on scientific lines. An outstanding botanist, he contributed extensively to the *Horti Medici Amstelodamensis Rariorum Descriptio* (1697), the general catalogue of rarities in the Amsterdam *hortus* on which Ruysch and his nephew, Caspar Commelin, also worked.

[60] Schama, *Embarrassment of Riches*, 526–7.
[61] Freedberg, 'Science, Commerce and Art', 386.
[62] Ibid. 379.

Classifying rare and exotic plants, and illustrating them, emerged as one of the chief specialities of Dutch science. The tradition reached back to the early seventeenth century, but first matured with the botanical sections of the famous publication *Historia Naturalis Brasiliae* (1648), the general compendium of the research carried out in Dutch Brazil sponsored by Johann Maurits van Nassau-Siegen whilst he was governor there. The treatises on the plants, birds, and animals of Brazil were of exceptionally high quality, and mainly the work of a German scholar trained at Leiden, Georg Markgraf, whose work marks the beginning of the great age of Dutch botanical research and publications.

The most monumental project, before 1700, was the *Hortus Indicus Malabaricus* (Amsterdam, 1678–93), a comprehensive survey, magnificently illustrated, in twelve volumes, with no fewer than 1,794 plates. The project was funded, and inspired, by Hendrik Adriaen Reede tot Drakenstein (*c.* 1636–91), a VOC officer on the Malabar coast who rose in the 1660s to become commander of the Dutch fort at Cochin. He returned in 1678 to the Netherlands, where he was briefly active in the *ridderschap* of Utrecht, but subsequently returned, as a high official, to south India. His great project to survey the flora of Malabar was assisted by the Amsterdam regent Commelin, who contributed some of the plates and text. The work was so vast it remained largely confined to Latin, plans for Dutch and English versions being abandoned at an early stage.

But perhaps the most creative of all the researchers in botany was Georg Everard Rumphius (*c.*1627–1702), the so-called Pliny of the Indies.[63] Rumphius was a German employee of the VOC who spent most of his adult life in the Moluccas. He became a passionate botanist and general natural scientist and, even after becoming blind, in 1670, continued his research with the help of the authorities at Batavia, who provided financial and other assistance. His *magnum opus*, a vast study of the plants of Amboina, the *Amboinsch Kruidboek*, was almost lost several times. When it was partly destroyed in a fire which burnt down much of Amboina, in 1687, Rumphius had to redo all his drawings. It was then lost again, in 1692, *en route* from Batavia to Holland on a ship sunk by the French. Happily, the sole copy survived at Batavia and years later safely reached the *Heren XVII* in Amsterdam. Daunted by its size, however, they merely buried it, unpublished, in their archives. It finally appeared, produced by a consortium of publishers, in six monumental volumes, in the 1740s. Rumphius also predeceased publication of his other book, his *Amboinsche Rariteitenkamer*,

---

[63] Ibid. 381; Boxer, *Dutch Seaborne Empire*, 181–2.

a study of the fish, coral, and minerals of Amboina based on meticulous research carried out over forty years. It was published in Amsterdam in 1705. A scientist of the Golden Age, his legacy became known to Europe only during the Enlightenment.

By the first decade of the eighteenth century, Dutch science, like art and philosophy, was still in full flood. There was no sign yet of any lessening of vitality or creativity. It was also still the leading science in Europe in many sectors, particularly microscopes, anatomy, botany, insects, optics, some areas of chemistry, and—the aspect most widely noticed—in clinical methods and application of science to medicine.

THE ANTI-SOCINIAN CAMPAIGN

By the 1640s, hardline Calvinists, under the impact of Frederik Hendrik's tolerant policies, the Remonstrant revival, and lapsing of active persecution of Catholic conventicles, had had to retreat some way from the uncompromising intolerance of the Counter-Remonstrants of 1619. Voetius himself, during the 1640s, had evolved a somewhat grudging, limited doctrine of toleration which he later set out in his *Politica Ecclesiastica*.[64] After the, for them, shattering event of the early death of William II, orthodox Calvinists of the Voetian mould had to accept that they lived in a state which granted freedom of practice to dissenting Churches and that Catholic services held in private homes (as long as attendances were not too large) were beyond their reach. But Voetius and his followers drew the line at doctrines which, in their view, undermined the fundamentals of Christianity, especially those denying the divinity of Christ, the Trinity, and original sin, thus Socinianism and deism, as well as concealed and unconcealed atheism. The anti-Socinian campaign which gathered momentum in the United Provinces, in the years around 1650, remained a major element in Dutch thought and culture for over half a century, becoming a main engine, and justification, of policies aimed at restricting, and cutting back, intellectual and religious freedom.

One of the central principles of Voetius' *Politica Ecclesiastica* is that Socinianism, and anti-Trinitarianism generally, cannot be allowed, or tolerated, in a Christian society.[65] This meant, for Voetius, that tolerated dissenting Churches, such as the Remonstrants and Mennonites, who lacked the theological discipline, and authoritarian structure, of the Reformed and Lutherans (as well as the Catholics), had to be kept under constant

---

[64] Voetius, *Politica Ecclesiastica*, ii. 536–55 and iv. 596–9.   [65] Ibid. ii. 544–51.

surveillance, and pressure, to prevent the propagation of anti-Trinitarian thought in their midst, and induce them to purge themselves of their anti-Trinitarian members. Additionally, intellectual influences, including Erasmus,[66] in any way conducive to Arian and Socinian ways of thinking should be discouraged by the public authorities. Voetius argued that the eradication of Socinianism and other anti-Trinitarianism from society—and in the first place from their natural haven, the dissenting Churches and their offshoots, the Collegiants—was the duty of the state and had to be pursued, with or without the collaboration of the Mennonite and Remonstrant leadership. In a letter of 1664, he was glad to be able to praise the Dutch Mennonite leadership for co-operating with the public authorities in combating Socinianism within their own ranks.[67]

Cocceians were less rigidly intolerant on a practical level, but from a theological standpoint were as opposed to anti-Trinitarianism as the Voetians. Much of Cocceius' *Summa Doctrinae de Foedere* (1648) reads like a dialogue with Socinus and other Socinian writers.[68] In his exegetical passages, Cocceius refers continually to what he deemed the Socinians' errors in interpreting Scripture and failure to see references to the Trinity. Voetius and Cocceius were equally adamant that the divinity and coming of Christ are inherent in the Old Testament, as well as the New, and that the Socinian view of Christ as lacking divine attributes, and of the Old Testament as a mere preface, of little significance compared to the New, subverted the fundamentals of Christian faith. Heidanus, doyen of Cocceio-Cartesianism, considered anti-Trinitarianism the chief threat to Christianity and devoted much intellectual energy to combating it. Röell too, later in the century, justified his radical innovations as being the best defence against Socinianism and anti-Trinitarianism.

Evidently, by the 1640s, Socinian and anti-Trinitarian views were widely held in Dutch society, at any rate in the maritime provinces and Friesland. Johannes Sartorius, a Polish Socinian preacher who took refuge in Amsterdam, reported in 1638 that many men there privately rejected the Trinity, and were thus concealed anti-Trinitarians, or 'Nicodemites', as he calls them.[69] The States party-faction, in the ascendant in the late 1640s, and again after the death of William II, in 1650, were advocates of toleration. But they were also worried by the damage to their reputation, amongst the populace, which the Reformed preachers were capable of inflicting. In the

[66] Ibid. iv. 598–9.
[67] De Jong, 'Voetius en de tolerantie', 114–15.
[68] Cocceius, *Leer van het Verbond*, 40–50 *et passim*.
[69] Van Slee, *Rijnsburger Collegianten*, 384.

years around 1650, there are many indications of the States of Holland's nervousness on this score. In a placard of July 1653, the States denounced the campaign of insinuation mounted by certain preachers to 'discredit the sincere intentions and salutary decisions of the States of Holland' and 'spread sinister notions regarding the piety and uprightness of the regents of this province'.[70] Voetian preachers considered the Holland regents woefully inadequate when it came to championing religion, and the public Church, and the States felt vulnerable to such criticism. Several times the preachers of Holland were warned to show the 'proper respect and obedience that subjects owe their legitimate sovereigns'[71] both in their sermons and private discourse.

The centrality of the Socinian issue in the late 1640s and 1650s was partly due to the influx of Polish and German Socinians to Amsterdam, as a result of intensifying persecution in Poland and Brandenburg, and the publication in the Republic of several Socinian works, in Dutch. The books were printed and sold clandestinely and destroyed when intercepted by the authorities. In 1645, the Rotterdam burgomasters discovered a stock of 100 copies of a work by Crellius, in Dutch translation, and had them destroyed. But it was also due to the spread of the Collegiant movement, especially, in the 1640s, to Amsterdam, and mounting evidence that some Dutchmen were being influenced by Socinian doctrines.[72] Zeeland had already acted by the time the North and South Holland Synods petitioned the States of Holland, in 1653, to combat this 'sickness', which they called the most dangerous, and most 'Jewish', of all Christian heresies, alleging that it was spreading rapidly, especially in Holland, Friesland, and Groningen, an indication that Mennonites were regarded as particularly susceptible to Socinian arguments.[73]

In September 1653, the States of Holland duly prohibited Socinian and other anti-Trinitarian 'conventicles', warning participants they would be charged with blasphemy and as 'disturbers of the peace'.[74] Booksellers found stocking anti-Trinitarian books were to be fined 1,000 guilders, printers of anti-Trinitarian literature 3,000 guilders. The edict was aimed at Collegiants, and others who were susceptible to anti-Trinitarian influences, as well as avowed Socinians, meeting in groups. There was a crack-down on anti-Trinitarianism throughout Holland, as well as in neighbouring Utrecht,

[70] Res. Holl. 3 July 1653.
[71] Ibid.
[72] Kühler, *Socinianisme*, 148–9.
[73] Eekhof, *Theologische faculteit*, 65, 249.
[74] Van Gelder, *Getemperde vrijheid*, 176–7.

which continued through the 1650s and undoubtedly had a considerable effect. At Rotterdam, the consistory of the 'Flemish' Anabaptists felt obliged to conform to the edict and closed the free Anabaptist discussion college, which had been meeting weekly.[75] The Rotterdam Remonstrant consistory split, with some liberals wanting to defy the edict (with the support of the young Adriaen Paets), but the majority decided to defer to the authorities and close the 'Friday College'. At Amsterdam, too, the Collegiants were for some years forced to meet in smaller groups than before, in private homes, and be more circumspect.[76] The Reformed classes reported, at the meeting of the South Holland Synod at Dordrecht, in 1656, that enforcement of the anti-Socinian placard by the authorities was satisfactory, at least in the larger towns, which confirms that there was an evident change in the intellectual atmosphere at Rotterdam, The Hague, and elsewhere.[77] The crack-down on anti-Trinitarianism extended also to the countryside. The *baljuw* of Alkmaar wrote to De Witt, in March 1655, reporting his enquiries in the villages around the city, with the help of the 'regents of the principal villages', as to whether there were any Socinians, or anti-Trinitarian books, in the vicinity, concluding there were not.[78]

The States of Holland, like those of Zeeland and Utrecht, considered it prudent to act against anti-Trinitarianism, as also did the States of Friesland and Groningen. This they did, in part, as a political measure, to defend their reputations and, in part, out of real intolerance of anti-Trinitarianism in all but the most liberal regent circles. However, this by no means implies that the States party-faction was deferential to the public Church in such matters. The synods wanted stronger measures, especially with regard to book censorship, but the States refused to accord greater influence to the synods than they had already, through the States and city councils. In December 1654, the States of Holland rejected the joint request of the Holland synods for a provincial board of censorship, or *visitadores librorum*, to act as a permanent watch-dog, asserting that 'such practice in these lands would have very dangerous consequences'.[79]

In Holland, in contrast to other provinces, the drive against Socinianism, and all but the most outspoken anti-Trinitarianism, slackened after a few years. At Amsterdam, it proved impossible to halt the flow of Socinian publications for long. At the end of the 1650s, Frans Kuiper, a former

[75] Van Bunge, 'Rotterdamse collegiant', 68–9.
[76] Meinsma, *Spinoza en zijn kring*, 101.
[77] Knuttel, *Acta*, iii. 491 and iv. 21.
[78] ARH SH 2710/1. Baljuw to De Witt, Alkmaar, 19 Mar. 1655.
[79] Res. Holl. 14 Dec. 1654.

Remonstrant preacher turned Socinian, began publishing a series under the general title 'Bibliotheca Fratrum Polonorum', printing and distributing the books clandestinely. The series included the works of Socinus himself, as well as of Crellius, Jonas Schlichting, and other leading Socinian theologians. In 1659, the Collegiant Jan Cornelisz. Knol published a Dutch version of the Rakow catechism, the credo of the Polish Socinians. Also in 1659, a former official of the Hof of Holland, and a nobleman, Lancelot van Brederode, anonymously published a 563-page book assailing the public Church and rejecting the doctrine of the Trinity.[80] The book, printed in 900 copies, was consigned for distribution to Collegiant booksellers in Amsterdam. Both the States and Hof of Holland reacted vigorously. The book was immediately banned, its author discovered, tried, and heavily fined, and efforts were made to seize the copies in circulation, though the authorities failed fully to suppress it.

Collegiant meetings in large groups, or 'colleges', revived in the early 1660s. In 1661, the Amsterdam Reformed consistory complained to the *vroedschap* of the 'exorbitance of the Socinian gatherings, in which Quakers and Boreelists mingle, such that one hundred, one hundred and fifty, and sometimes even greater numbers attend them'.[81] What was at issue here was not the existence of Collegiant groups, as such, but that there was no longer sufficient pressure to compel them to meet only in small groups, in private homes. The consistory warned of dangerous consequences 'which can already be perceived among the Mennonites'—a reference to the growing tension over the Trinity among the Amsterdam Anabaptist communities. It is true that by no means all the Collegiants were anti-Trinitarians. The founders of the Collegiant movement in Amsterdam, in the 1640s—Daniel de Breen, Adam Boreel, and the Mennonite leader Galenus Abrahamsz. de Haan—had not been professed anti-Trinitarians. During the 1660s, the Boreelists and leading figures such as the mystical Millenarian Petrus Serrarius continued loosely to subscribe to the doctrine of the Trinity.[82] Yet the Reformed consistory regarded the Collegiant revival as a major change in the religious life of the city. The essence of the Collegiant movement lay in the ideal of a Christianity of Bible study and modelling one's life on Christ, divorced from all church authority and confessional differences.[83] The movement of the Rijnsburgers was the antithesis of church authority, creating an atmosphere in which anti-Trinitarianism flourished. At Amsterdam,

[80] Zilverberg, 'Lancelot van Brederode', 232, 237.
[81] Kühler, *Socinianisme*, 189.
[82] Van der Wall, *De mystieke chiliast*, 202, 234–5.
[83] Ibid. 202.

a large part of the Collegiant movement, including Kuiper, Knol, and Spinoza's ally Lodewijk Meijer, were professed anti-Trinitarians.

The anti-Socinian campaign relaxed somewhat, between 1660 and 1672, at least in Amsterdam, Rotterdam, and some other places in Holland. But in most of the Republic, repression of anti-Trinitarianism remained a fundamental aspect of religious, cultural, and political life throughout the late seventeenth century and early eighteenth. In the 1680s, the Synod of Overijssel was alarmed about the growth of Socinian influence among the Mennonites in the north-western part of the province, around Blokzijl.[84] The Rijnsburg-style 'college' established at Groningen in the 1680s was vigorously combated by the Groningen 'Old Flemish' Mennonites and repeatedly accused of anti-Trinitarianism, though the Groningen Collegiants insisted that they had no confession, or dogmas, but simply believed that Christ was the son of God, 'our prophet, high priest, and king'. In 1702, the Groningen *raad* suppressed the college and continued to break up the Collegiants' meetings until around 1712.[85] But it was especially in Friesland that Socinianism became a major issue in provincial life. In Friesland, Socinian, Quaker, and Collegiant influences gradually gained ground, especially among the liberal Anabaptists. A fierce placard was issued in 1662 by the Frisian States against Socinians and Quakers, which not only threatened heavy fines and imprisonment, but authorized the province's Reformed preachers to 'examine . . . persons upon whom suspicion falls' before the magistrates, a kind of informal method of inquisition never introduced in Holland.[86] The placard of 1662 was reissued in 1687 at a time of rising controversy about the new liberal Mennonite 'colleges' which arose in the 1680s at Leeuwarden, Harlingen, and several smaller places.

A key episode in the anti-Socinian campaign, particularly significant in that it shows that one did not need to be a professed Socinian or anti-Trinitarian to suffer repression, was the case of the Frisian Foecke Floris (*c.*1650–*c.*1700). Floris was a liberal Anabaptist preacher, a smith by calling, who established a following, or 'college', at Grouw. The Reformed preacher of Grouw accused him of being a 'Socinian', at first with little effect. However, in 1687, at Leeuwarden, Floris published a book, his *Bescherming der Waerheyt Godts*, in reply to his adversary's printed attacks on the 'cancer of the Socinian heretics' in general and himself in particular.[87] On the evidence of his book, the Synod of Friesland condemned Floris as

[84] ARH PR 491, fos. 28v, 73. Res. SO, 3 Apr. 1684 and 19 Mar. 1686.
[85] Van Slee, *Rijnsburger Collegianten*, 227.
[86] Van der Zijpp, *Gesch. der doopsgezinden*, 159.
[87] Kühler, *Socinianisme*, 177–9.

a 'Socinian'. The Delegated States banned the book, ordering all copies to be burnt, and forbade Floris to preach. He was also briefly imprisoned, at Leeuwarden, before being expelled from the province. He then migrated to Holland and resumed preaching in the Zaan area. The North Holland Synod at once complained to the *baljuw* of Kennemerland, who began to investigate. Floris, with the help of Galenus Abrahamsz, appealed to William III, who was then at Hellevoetsluis, preparing the great fleet for the invasion of England. William, who especially at that time wished to emphasize his tolerationist principles, ordered the proceedings suspended. In the early 1690s, however, the synod resumed its pressure and, in August 1692, the *baljuw* forbade Floris to preach. Later Floris resumed preaching and the affair ended inconclusively. His group at Grouw were repeatedly investigated for 'Socinianism'.[88]

There were two main grounds for banning books which were non-political and non-erotic in the United Provinces, during the second half of the seventeenth century—anti-Trinitarianism and 'atheistic' philosophical tendencies. The formal proscription of Socinianism and anti-Trinitarianism became in the 1650s, and then remained for many decades, the pivot of intellectual and theological censorship, even in Amsterdam. In 1669, the Hof of Holland complained to the *schout*, at Amsterdam, that volumes of the *Bibliotheca Fratrum Polonorum* were being almost freely distributed in the city, in defiance of the placard of 1653, ordering him to make surprise raids on bookshops to seize copies, and punish offending booksellers.[89] The Amsterdam burgomasters felt obliged to go along with this, at least formally. The practical effect was mitigated, however, by 'Arminian' regents warning the booksellers that the searches were to take place.

The Dutch Republic was undoubtedly freer than other European societies of the time and tolerated more churches and religions than any other, allowing numerous faiths to publish their books and rival interpretations of Scripture. Nevertheless, the Republic adhered to a comprehensive censorship which created a real and formidable barrier to the expression of certain kinds of religious and philosophical ideas. When, in 1678, the city of Utrecht reissued the anti-Socinian placard published by the city and States of Utrecht, in 1655, the *vroedschap* described their censorship policy as intended to suppress all 'Socinian, Arian, blasphemous, and entirely pernicious books and, in particular, the *Bibliotheca Fratrum Polonorum*, the *Leviathan* [of Hobbes], the *Philosophia Scripturae Interpres* [of Meijer], the

---

[88] Van Slee, *Rijnsburger Collegianten*, 215–17.
[89] Kühler, *Socinianisme*, 187–8.

Tractatus Theologico-Politicus, of Spinoza, together with B.d.S[pinoza], *Opera Posthuma*'.[90]

RADICAL CARTESIANS AND SPINOZISTS

Cartesian principles and Cocceianism together generated a broad stream of liberal thought in philosophy, theology, and science in the Dutch Republic, during the second half of the seventeenth century, which was theologically flexible, tolerant of philosophical innovation, and eager to elaborate Descartes's mechanistic world-view. Nevertheless, this broad liberal stream in thought and science, vigorous if not unchallenged in, and outside, the universities, civic government, and the public Church, also subscribed to rigidly defined frontiers beyond which the philosopher, theologian, scientist, and poet was not permitted to step. Chief among these were the divinity of Christ, the Trinity, original sin, immortality of the soul and divine authorship of Scripture. The limits were upheld by the provincial governments, public Church, and universities alike, and sanctioned by Cocceius, Heidanus, and Röell, as well as Voetius and the Voetians.

From this there arose, given that Cartesian principles could also be applied in ways which involved crossing these frontiers, a fundamental separation in the Dutch (and German Reformed) context between moderate and radical Cartesianism. Moderate Cartesians and Cocceio-Cartesians not only insisted on this distinction but claimed that those who overstepped the mark had no right to call themselves 'Cartesians' at all. But these radical Cartesians, though they had both Voetians and Cocceio-Cartesians against them, became, during the 1660s, a central feature of the Dutch cultural and intellectual scene.

Thinkers who ventured over the limits entered dangerous territory. The earliest and ablest of those who followed Lancelot van Brederode into this forbidden realm were Franciscus van den Enden, Lodewijk Meijer, Adriaen Koerbagh, and, above all, Spinoza. Spinoza, born into the Portuguese Jewish community in Amsterdam, had been expelled from the synagogue, for treating God 'philosophically' and questioning Scripture and rabbinical authority, in July 1656—a few weeks before the States of Holland issued their placard segregating philosophy from theology. After his expulsion from the synagogue, Spinoza mixed in Collegiant circles, first in Amsterdam and then Rijnsburg, near Leiden. Whilst at Rijnsburg, during the Brederode affair, he wrote his *Short Treatise on God, Man and his Well-Being* which he

---

[90] Van de Water, *Groot Placaat-Boeck . . . Utrecht*, iii. 432.

was still amending in 1662.[91] Already here, Spinoza defined God, and the world, in terms which departed totally from traditional Jewish and Christian views, ruling out divine intervention in human affairs as well as the existence of Satan and devils.

Spinoza, seeing the measures being taken against fellow Collegiants in Amsterdam and Rotterdam, was under no illusion as to what would happen should he publish his treatise. 'I do not separate God from Nature', he informed his correspondent in London, Henry Oldenburg, 'as everyone else known to me has done';[92] however, 'I do not have any definite plan regarding publication . . . I fear, of course, that the theologians of our time may be offended and with their usual hatred attack me, who loathes quarrels.' Oldenburg urged Spinoza not to worry about 'arousing the pygmies of our age' and to rely on that freedom for which the Dutch Republic was celebrated. But Spinoza knew his Republic better than Oldenburg and left his treatise unpublished. It did not finally appear in print until the mid-nineteenth century.

Spinoza was an immensely powerful thinker who made a deep impact on those around him. By 1662–3, he had succeeded in forming a circle, at both Amsterdam and Rijnsburg, of followers devoted to reading, and discussing, his manuscripts and ready, as one of them, Simon de Vries, expressed it, to 'defend truth against those who are superstitiously religious . . . and stand against the attacks of the whole world'.[93] Spinoza was by no means a philosophical hermit, withdrawn from the cares of the world, content to keep his ideas to himself. On the contrary, he was a determined, as well as great, philosopher, ambitious to make his mark and a realist constantly sizing up the Dutch political, theological, and philosophical scene around him. His whole strategy, in his writing and publications, was geared to the contemporary Dutch scene.

He disliked quarrels and knew he had to tread carefully to avoid not only risking the tranquillity he needed for his philosophizing but being attacked, vilified, and crushed. But his goal was to make an impact comparable to that of Descartes, revolutionizing every aspect of thought and science in the society around him. Obviously the best, and safest, way to secure a position of strength, at the centre of the Dutch intellectual arena, was to veil his own philosophy, for the moment, and appear before the public as a mainstream Cartesian. In this way, Spinoza hoped to gain acceptance and win highly placed friends among the many regents and academics who were committed to defending *philosophia cartesiana* against the Voetians. 'Perhaps it will

[91] Spinoza, *Collected Works*, i. 142–55.   [92] Ibid. 188.   [93] Ibid. 190–1.

convince some who hold high positions in my country', he explained to Oldenburg, 'to want to read other works I have written, which I acknowledge as my own, so that they would see to it that I can publish without danger of harassment.'[94] If he succeeded in this, it was Spinoza's intention to publish his philosophy as soon as possible but, if not, he intended to be 'silent rather than force my opinions on men against the will of my country and make them hostile to me'. Meanwhile, he worked steadily on his principal philosophical work, the *Ethics*.

Hence it was no accident that Spinoza's first published work was his exposition of the philosophy of Descartes (1663). The book aroused interest; but the results, from Spinoza's point of view, were inconclusive. He became a known figure. The Latin version was followed, the next year, by a Dutch translation, prepared by Pieter Balling, one of his followers, a Mennonite businessman with connections in Spain. Yet still the outlook seemed forbidding. He showed drafts of his manuscripts to influential friends but held back from publishing his own philosophy because of the opinion 'ordinary folk have of me; they never stop accusing me of atheism, and I am forced to refute this accusation as much as I can'.[95] He was still also wary of the 'prejudices of the theologians, for I know of no greater obstacle to men's applying their minds to philosophy'.[96] Deciding that he could not publish his *Ethics* even in the relatively liberal intellectual climate prevailing in the 1660s, Spinoza, like Meijer, embarked on the kind of biblical criticism which questions divine authorship, undermining the claims of the theologians, in order to weaken the people's veneration for the public Church, and, by this means, open the way to the publication, and acceptance, of 'philosophical truth'. The Reformed preachers of the United Provinces held sway armed with Scripture as divine revelation. Show that Scripture was not divine revelation and the preachers would be disarmed.

Meijer entered the fray first—and very possibly without Spinoza's approval—with his *Philosophia S. Scripturae Interpres*, which was published anonymously, at Amsterdam, in 1666. The book caused a general outcry. In his preface, Meijer claimed to be applying Descartes's method to the one area to which it had not, as yet, been applied—theology. Theology, the 'princess of learned disciplines', urged Meijer, was now in a state of such disarray, with so many rival interpretations of Scripture, that ordinary folk were becoming deeply confused and filled with doubt. The remedy, he held, was to follow Descartes and strip away everything it was possible to doubt

---

[94] Ibid. 207.   [95] Ibid. 350.   [96] Ibid.

until one arrived at truth so evident that it cannot be doubted.[97] Since Scripture was the basis of theology, he proposed to examine Scripture as a philosopher, suspending knowledge that it was divine revelation. The conclusion of this exercise was that Scripture is full of contradictions, discrepancies, and imperfections and that God, if the original author, cannot be regarded as the author of the text as we have it.[98] With this, Meijer provided the Voetians with the best proof they had yet that if philosophy was not rigorously subjected to theology, then philosophy would soon subjugate theology.

Voetians and Cocceio-Cartesians alike deplored Meijer's book. The condemnation issued by Leiden university theology faculty was signed by Cocceius and Heidanus. Bekker was among dozens of preachers, of both main streams, who denounced the work. Trinitarian Collegiants were also appalled. The mystical Millenarian Petrus Serrarius, at Amsterdam, who knew Meijer and Spinoza well (and probably knew who the author was) accused the author of bowing down before the idol of philosophy.[99] Serrarius agreed that the Churches were in a state of sickness but argued that the prevailing spiritual confusion had nothing to do with discrepancies in Scripture but arose from reading Scripture without being infused with the Holy Spirit.

The book was immediately banned in Friesland and more sporadically suppressed in Holland. Meijer was followed by another of Spinoza's circle, Adriaen Koerbagh (c. 1632–69), whose work shows a marked partiality for Collegiants and Quakers, and hostility to the public Church. Koerbagh's *Bloemhof van Allerley Lieflijkheid* (1668), recklessly published under his own name, was full of anti-Church, anti-Trinitarian, and Spinozist concepts. A second, even more radical work was on the press when the outcry against the first persuaded the printer to inform the authorities. Koerbagh went into hiding, was discovered, arrested by magistrates in Culemborg, and handed over to their colleagues in Amsterdam. Sentenced to ten years' imprisonment, and a 4,000 guilder fine, he died, in prison, to the distress of his allies, in October 1669. His brother Johannes was also imprisoned for anti-Trinitarianism but released by the Amsterdam magistrates on the principle that in the United Provinces persons who have not written books, or convened gatherings, cannot be punished for godless opinions.

Koerbagh attacked the doctrine of the Trinity, subordinated theology to philosophy, accounted Scripture a source of confusion, and was more

---

[97] Thijssen-Schoute, *Uit de Republiek der letteren*, 181–2.
[98] Meijer, *Philosophia S. Scripturae*, 56–7.
[99] Van der Wall, *De mystieke chiliast*, 478–83.

categorical than Meijer that Scripture was not divine revelation,[100] urging that this be explained to the people, to prevent their being further misled by churchmen.[101] He had asserted all this in Dutch and paid the price. It was in the aftermath of Koerbagh's harsh fate and perhaps partly as a consequence that Spinoza entered the field with his *Tractatus Theologico-Politicus* (1670), published anonymously at Amsterdam with the place of publication falsely given as 'Hamburg'. Spinoza himself tells us, in his preface, that his purpose was to liberate the individual, and society, from 'superstition' fostered by fear and, by freeing society from superstition, liberate the individual from intellectual servitude.[102] Alluding to the Cocceian–Voetian battles, he remarks that the theologians of his time 'harangue, not caring to instruct the people, but striving to attract admiration, bring opponents into scorn, and spread novelties and paradoxes', all of which he deems pointless. He accuses the Churches of perverting religion so that 'faith has become a mere compound of credulity and prejudice'.[103] By bringing the light of reason to the study of Scripture and discarding the 'principle that it is in every passage divine and true', Spinoza aspired to put an end to theological controversy and the hatred, intolerance, and divisiveness which accompanied it.

The publication of Spinoza's *Tractatus* provoked an immediate uproar throughout the length and breadth of Holland even though Spinoza had purposely published only in Latin and took energetic steps to prevent its publication in Dutch (see pp. 789–90 above). The Dutch version (by Glazemaker) did not finally appear until 1693. In Leiden, as in Haarlem, the Latin text was discussed by the outraged consistory in May 1670.[104] A delegation was sent to the burgomasters, who agreed that the passages brought to their attention were intolerable and arranged for the book to be seized from the bookshops. When the South Holland Synod convened some weeks later, at Schiedam, the *Tractatus Theologico-Politicus* was held up as the single most offensive of all the recent wave of 'foul and blasphemous books' which the consistories were determined to check.[105] It was resolved that Leiden's example should be generally followed. The delegates were asked to ensure that all the town magistracies actively suppressed the book under the existing anti-Socinian legislation as, assuredly, most of them did.

[100] Vandenbossche, *Adriaan Koerbagh*, 2.
[101] Ibid. 7–8.
[102] Spinoza, *Tractatus Theologico-Politicus*, 49–51.
[103] Ibid. 53–4.
[104] GA Leiden Acta Kerkeraad v, res. 9 and 16 May 1670; GA Haarlem Acta Kerkeraad ix, Res. 27 May 1670.
[105] Knuttel, *Acta*, iv. 531.

Meanwhile Spinoza refused publicly to acknowledge that he was the author. Nevertheless, he increasingly became an object of opprobrium and suspicion. He moved at this time from Voorburg to the centre of The Hague, doubtless at least in part so as to be under the very noses of the States and De Witt, thereby minimizing the risk of harassment by any purely local body. There he spent his last years, lodging in the house of an elder of the Lutheran consistory.

But the book caused a sensation in more than just a negative sense. Clearly it had a wide impact and swayed many of those who read it. Bekker later noted that Spinoza's influence penetrated deeply, 'seducing' many of the best minds.[106] As early as 1673, Stouppe reported that Spinoza 'a un grand nombre de sectateurs qui sont entièrement attachez à ses sentimens'.[107] As part of his campaign to damage the reputation of the United Provinces, Stouppe added that although the *Tractatus* 'a pour but principal de détruire toutes les religions, et particulièrement la Judaique et la Chrétienne, et introduire l'Athéisme, le libertinage, et la liberté de toutes les religions', Dutch theologians had made remarkably little effort to refute his arguments, an assertion hotly contested by Brun.

After the overthrow of the De Witt regime in 1672, an event which Spinoza found deeply distressing, his *Tractatus* was definitively banned, in 1674, by the States and Hof of Holland together with Meijer's *Philosophia* and Hobbes's *Leviathan*. A year later, though, during the months of the resurgence of republican sentiment and reaction against William III, in 1675, he made a final effort to have his *magnum opus*, his *Ethics*, published at Amsterdam. But the mere rumour that he was about to do so caused such a reaction, especially among preachers, that he decided the climate was just too forbidding.

After the great philosopher's death, in February 1677, Meijer and other allies lost no time in preparing his philosophical legacy for the press. Ten months after his burial at the New Church, in The Hague, they published the *Ethics* and unfinished *Tractatus Politicus*, together with his letters and Hebrew Grammar, in both Latin and Dutch editions but giving no place of publication or name of translator or publisher. All editions were definitively banned by the States of Holland in June 1678, as containing 'very many profane, blasphemous, and atheistic propositions, whereby not only the unlettered reader might be misled from the one and true path to salvation'.[108] The States' placard also prohibited all future translations and extracts from Spinoza.

[106] Bekker, *Kort Begryp*, 39.
[107] Stouppe, *Religion des Hollandois*, 65.
[108] *Groot Placaet-Boeck*, iii. 525.

There is every sign that this decree, however imperfectly implemented—
and clearly Spinoza's works continued to be sold and read—had an
appreciable impact. It was not advisable to propagate, or defend, Spinoza
publicly and no one with worldly ambitions thought it prudent to be
associated with Spinoza's ideas. The barrage of refutations pouring from
Voetian, Cocceian, Anabaptist, and Jewish quarters continued unabated. In
1680, Van Velthuysen, encouraged by Paets,[109] published his *Tractatus*
against Spinoza; the Sephardic publicist Isaac Orobio de Castro emerged as
one of the leaders of the anti-Spinoza campaign with his *Certamen philo-
sophicum* (1684); in 1690, Wittichius published his *Anti-Spinoza*. But still
Spinoza continued to penetrate deeply and, in the 1690s, to a much greater
extent than before among the ordinary public as is shown by the fact that
the furore now shifted from Latin to Dutch.[110] In 1693–4, two different
Dutch versions of the *Tractatus Theologico-Politicus* appeared, followed in
1694 by a translation of Wittichius' *Anti-Spinoza*.[111] But what caused the
greatest commotion was the publication in 1697 of the sequel to the
philosophical-theological novel *Het leven van Philopater* (The Life of Philopater) by Johannes Duijkerius (*c*.1661–1702).

The first part of this remarkable work, describing the stages in the
spiritual development of a young man who begins as a Voetian zealot, had
caused offence by presenting the Voetian–Cocceian battles as futile polemics
reminiscent of the medieval feuding of the *Hoeks* and *Cabeljauws*. But the
book had sold well and its success encouraged both author and publisher
to think in terms of a sequel which was assured of a ready market and might
be a powerful vehicle for propagating forbidden ideas amongst the general
public. Duijkerius, a trainee preacher of the public Church (unable to obtain
a post owing to his stammer) and unemployed schoolmaster, lived in
poverty in Amsterdam, eking out a living by grinding lenses—just as had
his hero, Spinoza.[112] The publisher, the Amsterdam bookseller Aart
Wolsgryn, a well-known supplier of Cocceian, Cartesian, and radical
Cartesian literature to the Amsterdam public (and likewise a fervent
Spinozist), had already slipped Spinozist notions into the epilogue of the
Dutch translation of the famous Italian pastoral poem, *Il Pastor Fido*, which
he published in 1695.[113] But the sequel to *Philopater* was a much bolder
move. The book openly expounds at length what has been termed an

[109] Bayle, *Dictionnaire*, iii. 2641.
[110] Halma, *Aanmerkingen*, 1–3.
[111] Thijssen-Schoute, *Uit de Republiek der letteren*, 198.
[112] Maréchal, 'Inleiding', 11–16.
[113] Ibid. 16–18.

'extreme materialist' interpretation of Spinoza, adopting his approach to Scripture, rejection of miracles, and many of his formulations, but also, like Uriel da Costa, denying the immortality of the soul, more bluntly than Spinoza had in his *Ethics*.[114]

It was a foregone conclusion that such a blatant attempt to popularize Spinoza would be suppressed by the authorities with the utmost rigour. Ever since Van den Enden, radical philosophical 'atheists' had pondered how they could most effectively popularize challenging new concepts. Van den Enden had formerly entertained high hopes of the theatre in this regard.[115] But the Dutch theatre remained tightly restricted. With his philosophical novel, Duijkerius had hit on a new avenue which promised brilliant possibilities.

The book appeared at Amsterdam, in 1,500 copies, in December 1697. That very month, the Rotterdam consistory reacted in alarm, urging the magistracy to take action. The Hague consistory shortly after obtained the backing of that *vroedschap* for an appeal to the Hof of Holland. The Hof ordered the book's suppression, asking all the municipalities of Holland and Zeeland to seize the stock. The copies confiscated at Rotterdam were burnt by the authorities at the town hall in May 1698. The Delegated States of Friesland also banned the book. Meanwhile, though the title-page withheld the publisher's name, and falsely declared the place of publication as 'Groningen', the Amsterdam magistracy had discovered the identity of the publisher. Wolsgryn was arrested, interrogated, and, in April 1698, sentenced to eight years' imprisonment to be followed by banishment from Holland for twenty-five years, besides a 4,000 guilder fine, all under the terms of the 1653 placard against Socinianism—*Philopater*, quite apart from anything else, being undeniably anti-Trinitarian.[116] Thus, Holland's anti-Socinian legislation remained the linchpin of the Republic's intellectual censorship. Duijkerius himself was also summonsed but adamantly denied being the author. He went unpunished by the secular authorities, though disgraced by the consistory. He died in impoverished circumstances in 1702.

The spread of a simplified Spinozism in Dutch, and even more the fierce reaction it provoked from the secular and ecclesiastical authorities, was a phenomenon which had profound consequences for the subsequent intellectual and cultural history of the United Provinces. Something of the atmosphere generated by the Spinoza ferment of the 1690s is captured in an anecdote recounted years later by the great Herman Boerhaave, the

---

[114] Ibid. 29–30.
[115] Klever, 'Inleiding', 70–2.
[116] Thijssen-Schoute, *Uit de Republiek der letteren*, 197; Maréchal, 'Inleiding', 33–4.

Republic's most celebrated medical scholar. Whilst aboard a passenger barge, as a student, in 1693, he overheard a lively discussion among the passengers about Spinoza. The views expressed were so vehemently negative he asked one of the critics whether he had actually read any Spinoza. At this, another passenger asked Boerhaave's name, noting it down, with the result that he became suspected at Leiden of being a Spinozist, and lost his chance of a career in the public Church.[117]

The mounting campaign in the 1690s to demolish Spinoza and his following was not principally the work of Voetians but Cartesians, Cocceians, and other main representatives of the Early Enlightenment in the Republic. By combating Spinoza and Spinozism, the Republic's intellectual leadership could blunt the attack of the Voetians, show that the new philosophy and science did not lead to atheism, and pose as the defenders of the religious and moral order. The single most widely influential critique of Spinoza written in the Republic at this time was that by Pierre Bayle, the 'philosopher of Rotterdam'. Bayle's article on Spinoza was the longest and one of the most important in his *Dictionnaire historique et critique*, the first edition of which appeared in 1696. A leading Dutch translator, from French, of the time, François Halma, bookseller and compiler of Dutch–French dictionaries, then translated and published Bayle's essay in Dutch as a separate booklet. In his preface, Halma wrote of his deep consternation at the spread of Spinoza's ideas among the public, since the publication of *Philopater*, and belief that a Dutch version of Bayle's essay was the best antidote available.[118] It was suspected at the time that Bayle put such zeal into tarring Spinoza with the brush of 'atheism' in order to deflect accusations of atheism being directed by Pierre Jurieu and other Huguenot critics against himself.

Bayle's denunciation of the *Tractatus Theologico-Politicus* as a 'livre pernicieux et détestable ou [Spinoza] fit glisser toutes les sémences de l'Atheisme qui se voit à decouvert dans ses *Opera Posthuma*',[119] marked the culmination of the attack on Spinoza in print. Bayle himself explained that his purpose was more to combat the 'Spinozists' of his own time than Spinoza himself,[120] and this was certainly also the intention of Halma and of Pieter Rabus, editor of the main Dutch-language review of books in the 1690s, the *Boekzaal van Europe*, and a key figure of the early Dutch Enlightenment.[121] Halma and Rabus orchestrated a secular anti-Spinoza

[117] Lindeboom, *Herman Boerhaave*, 46.
[118] Halma, *Aanmerkingen*, 20, 26, 78.
[119] Bayle, *Dictionnaire*, iii. 2633.
[120] Bayle, *Lettres*, iii. 906–10.
[121] De Vet, *Pieter Rabus*, 176–81.

crusade, which lent added impetus to the efforts of the theologians and academics, and the effect of which on Dutch culture as a whole was to be clearly visible down to the late eighteenth century and even beyond.

THE DEATH OF THE DEVIL

One of Spinoza's prime contributions to European thought was his denial of Satan and of devils in general. As it transpired, the foremost intellectual controversy of the early Dutch Enlightenment was fought precisely on the issue of the Devil, and erupted in the early 1690s when the Spinoza controversy was at its height.

The Cartesian movement had created a broad intellectual milieu in the United Provinces capable of looking on Satan, demons, witchcraft, and also angels, with growing detachment and scepticism. One of the bones of contention between Voetians and their Cocceio-Cartesian opponents within the public Church had been that the latter tended to regard angels as a figurative adornment, mentioned in Scripture for poetic effect, which did not, in reality, exist.[122] A further step towards undermining popular notions about the supernatural was taken by the Haarlem Anabaptist physician Anthonie van Dale (1638–1708), described by Jean Le Clerc as an 'ennemi juré de toute sorte de superstition' in his *De Oraculis* (1683), a work which argued that the oracles mentioned in Roman and Greek books had been based on the superstitious credulity of the people and that the priesthood had exploited the people's belief in demons and magical powers for their own selfish ends. Dutch and French editions of Van Dale's book appeared in 1687. In the 1690s, Rabus was to celebrate Van Dale in the *Boekzaal* as one of the chief champions of the fight against popular superstition.

The fight against superstition had begun, but in the 1690s most of society, including the preachers, was still saturated with belief in Satan, devils, angels, and often also witchcraft. Consequently, the most sustained and systematic attack on the Devil to be written and published in the United Provinces, Balthasar Bekker's *De Betoverde Weereld* (1691), had a sensational effect. It was one of the key books of the Early Enlightenment in Europe, and almost certainly the most controversial.

Bekker held back from asserting categorically that Satan, demons, and angels do not exist. But no one previously had examined the whole question of the Devil so methodically or argued so cogently, mostly from Scripture itself, that the Devil, demons, and angels which invade men's notions, fears,

---

[122] Cramer, *Abraham Heidanus*, 124.

and dreams are not real spirits but figments of the superstitious imagination. His central proposition, expounded at immense length, was that all allusions to Satan, demons, and angels in Scripture turn out, on meticulous examination, to be purely figurative, poetic allegories of sin and sinfulness, and the power of God.[123] Neither Job, Paul, Christ, nor anyone else described in the Bible had really ever encountered the Devil. In arriving at these conclusions, Bekker stretched the capabilities of Cocceio-Cartesian allegorical exegesis to the limit, portraying Scripture as full of poetic licence and figurative speech tailored to the credulous notions of the ancient Hebrews.

Bekker was steeped in Cartesian thought and Cocceian theology, and a declared foe of Cartesian radicals and Spinozists. Consequently, he was deeply shocked to find his book causing the greatest intellectual furore in the Republic for decades and under attack from mainstream Cocceians, as well as Voetians. He was accused of opening the floodgates to the atheistic views of Hobbes, Spinoza, and Koerbagh, ideas he himself viewed with abhorrence.[124] Several critics also linked Bekker's denial of the Devil with the biblical libertinism of David Joris, whose *Wonder-Boeck* lived on in the thought-world of the Dutch Early Enlightenment as the epitome of pre-philosophical free-thinking and perversion of Scripture.[125]

Both Voetians and Cocceians rounded on Bekker. Yet there was a considerable difference in tone, and line of attack, between the two. Bekker had been a principal *bête noire* of the Voetians since his spirited defence of Cartesianism in Friesland, in the 1660s. They saw him also as a convenient stick with which to assail Cocceio-Cartesianism in Dutch culture, as a whole. Voetians stressed both the Cocceian and Cartesian roots of Bekker's denial of the Devil. Cocceians, by contrast, had regarded Bekker as one of their own, until the publication of his tract on the prophecy of Daniel, in 1688.[126] In this work, Bekker agreed that the prophecies of the Old Testament prefigure the coming of Christ, but rejected Coccedius' view that Daniel prophesied the rise of the Christian Church. More generally, he concurred that much of the Old Testament was couched in terms adapted to the superstitious notions of the ancient Israelites, but, at the same time, charged Coccedius and his followers with overdoing their allegories and not sticking sufficiently to the plain meaning of Scripture, maintaining that Daniel relates only to the history of Israel.[127] Hence, the Cocceians, notably Groenewegen and Johannes van der Waeyen—who published a 651-page

[123] Bekker, *De Betoverde Weereld*, 559, 578, 625.
[124] Koelman, *Wederlegging*, 120–37; Bekker, *Nodige Bedenkingen*, 30.
[125] Bekker, *Kort Beright*, 46.
[126] [Walten], *Aardige Duyvelary*, 9.
[127] Knuttel, *Balthasar Bekker*, 178–9.

refutation of Bekker, at Franeker, in 1693—assailed him as a false Cocceian who had perverted Cocceius' methods and exegesis.[128] Both Voetians and Cocceians blamed Bekker for publishing in Dutch, thereby spreading the poison of Spinoza and Koerbagh—Koerbagh was continually mentioned alongside Spinoza in the attacks on Bekker—among the poor, uneducated, and semi-literate.[129] The fundamentalist Koelman accused Bekker of encouraging every mediocre theology student to maintain that this, or that, passage of the States Bible had been incorrectly translated from the Hebrew or Greek.[130]

There was a double offensive against Bekker. But the two prongs of attack had both different motives and distinct aims. Voetians, through Bekker, strove to bracket Cocceio-Cartesianism with Spinoza and Koerbagh; Cocceians, by affixing Bekker to Spinoza and Koerbagh, hoped to excise him from their midst, leaving Cocceio-Cartesianism intact. Bekker, driven from Friesland years before, had, since 1679, been a Reformed preacher at Amsterdam. His new book turned virtually the whole Amsterdam consistory against him. But while the Voetians demanded strong measures, others, especially the lay members of the then forty-nine-member body, urged the North Holland Synod to settle the affair without formal condemnation of the book or expelling Bekker from the ministry. The moderates wanted Bekker to retract certain passages, and amend others, in subsequent editions and sign 'clarifications' which would enable him to remain as a Reformed preacher. Bekker, for his part, expressed readiness to provide clarifications 'in order to remove all suspicion of Spinozism'.[131]

But moderation lost the day. The Voetian consistories of Rotterdam and Utrecht initiated a wider campaign to suppress Bekker and his book, amplify the allegations of Spinozism, and damage Cartesianism and Cocceianism as much as possible. Rotterdam sent circulars to other consistories throughout the Republic deploring Amsterdam's circumspection and maintaining that if Bekker was not condemned, and stripped of his ministry, respect for Scripture would decline and Spinozism spread further among the people. The militancy of the Rotterdam and Utrecht consistories was strongly backed by Middelburg, Kampen, Leeuwarden, and Groningen.[132]

The reaction within the public Church was overwhelmingly hostile. But, outside the Church and theology faculties, Bekker had many supporters and thus it happened that, in the eyes of a growing number of the 'enlightened'

[128] Van der Waeyen, *De Betooverde Wereld ondersoght*, 14.
[129] Leydecker, *Beckers Philosophise Duyvel*, 117–19.
[130] Koelman, *Wederlegging*, 197–8, 218.
[131] Knuttel, *Balthasar Bekker*, 296–9.
[132] Koelman, *Wederlegging*, 330, 339; Bekker, *Kort en Waarachtig Verhaal*, 21.

public, Bekker became a heroic figure who assailed Satan and defied an army of obscurantists. Duijkerius, in *Philopater*, admiringly calls him the 'Frisian Hercules'. Bayle had previously noted the tendency of Leiden students and 'ceux qui se piquent d'esprit' to rebel against the Voetianism of the regime and university authorities by favouring the lectures of Wittichius, which were full of 'cartésianisme' and 'cocceianisme';[133] at Leiden, many students and educated laymen reacted in the same way to the hue and cry against Bekker, rallying to his defence.[134] Bekker himself observed that, at Amsterdam, it was the sophisticated lay population who supported him whilst the Calvinist lower middle class, the traditional stronghold of Calvinist fundamentalism, backed the Voetian preachers.[135]

That large sections of the public were interested in the Bekker controversy is abundantly evident. There were two editions of *De Betoverde Weereld* in 1691, and all 5,000 copies of the Amsterdam edition, and 750 copies of the Frisian edition, quickly sold out.[136] An assortment of prominent laymen and publicists sprang to Bekker's defence. On the initiative of such men, among them Ericus Walten, Anthonie van Dale, and Pieter Rabus, several commemorative medals were struck celebrating Bekker's demolition of the Devil. Van Dale, denounced by Koelman as a libertine who speaks 'atheistically and blasphemously', had supplied Bekker with material. He now stood by him, linked his name with Bekker's, and later brought out a follow-up book to his own attack on superstition, his *De Origine et Progressu Idolatriae et Superstitionis* (1696), a study of the origin and varieties of religious 'superstition' in which he accused the Churches, including the Reformed Church, of deliberately encouraging popular credulity.

Bayle and the Huguenot publicists were unable to intervene in the Bekker controversy because it was mainly carried on in the Dutch language, of which they had remarkably little command. However, Rabus as editor of the only Dutch-language periodical gave Bekker valuable support. Rabus, under attack himself from the Voetian consistory in Rotterdam, had to tread carefully. His review of the Bekker controversy was a model of quiet circumspection. This did not, however, prevent the Rotterdam consistory reacting angrily to his pro-Bekker stance and petitioning the burgomasters for the suppression of the *Boekzaal*. For several years, Rabus and his allies had to battle for the survival of his journal.[137] Finally, in March 1694, the

---

[133] [Bayle], *Nouvelles de la République des Lettres*, iv. 2879–80.
[134] *De gebannen Duyvel*, 1.
[135] Bekker, *Nodige Bedenkingen*, 7–8.
[136] Knuttel, *Balthasar Bekker*, 267.
[137] De Vet, *Pieter Rabus*, 270–3.

Rotterdam *vroedschap* decided not to shut the *Boekzaal* down but ordered Rabus not to publish anything, in future, which had not previously been checked by the consistory's *visitadores*. In effect, the Voetians muzzled the Republic's only Dutch-language journal.

Bekker's most outspoken ally was the republican writer and eulogist of the Glorious Revolution, Ericus Walten. Though an Orangist, Walten was anything but an ally of ecclesiastical authority or Voetianism. Rather he was a passionate supporter of toleration and fierce critic of the influence of preachers in Dutch society. In 1691, he anonymously published a hard-hitting pamphlet, the *Aardige Duyvelary*, supporting Bekker and deriding his opponents.[138] Bekker admitted that Walten 'opened many eyes' to the truth about the Devil and the reality of what was happening but also saw that Walten gave the entire controversy a dangerous new twist with his harsh comments about Reformed preachers and consistories. Walten subsequently gave the affair an even more dangerous twist by drawing attention to the political undertones of the controversy.

During the early 1690s, the Voetians mounted a concerted campaign, in all the provinces of the Republic, to enlist William III, and the Orangists, for decisive action to end the disputes within the public Church. For the last time in the history of the Republic, the Calvinist orthodox endeavoured to draw the regime into proscribing their theological enemies, silencing them, and expelling them from the public Church.[139] Bentinck, the Stadholder-king's favourite, was widely held to favour a more energetically pro-Voetian stance than his master was inclined to. In 1692, as the Voetians exploited the Bekker affair, to step up the pressure on Cocceianism and Cartesianism, Walten impetuously published an open letter to Bentinck in which he held that, just as the Jacobites in Britain plotted to dethrone the Stadholder-king and bring back James II, Bekker's foes designed to suppress toleration and restore the dethroned Devil. Were the Prince to support the Devil-defenders, Walten admonished, not only would Bekker be vanquished but his foes would overthrow all professors and preachers in the United Provinces of whom they disapproved. In the past the Stadholder had defended toleration; let him be its champion, urged Walten, also in the future. With this outburst, he made himself a marked man and lost the favour of those who could protect him. The Voetians stepped up their campaign against him. He was arrested by the Hof of Holland in March 1694, the same month in which the *Boekzaal* was placed under Voetian censorship. His papers were

---

[138] [Walten], *Aardige Duyvelary*, 1–5.
[139] Ypeij and Dermout, *Geschiedenis*, iii. 174–5; Van der Wall, 'Orthodoxy and Scepticism', 124.

seized; he was tried for blasphemy, maligning the public Church, and spreading atheistic ideas about Scripture, one of the charges being that he had described the New Testament story of Christ being tempted by the Devil as 'bagatelles'.[140] Ericus Walten, the most uncompromising champion of toleration, constitutional rule, and curbing ecclesiastical power, of the early Dutch Enlightenment, died in prison at The Hague, three years after his arrest, in 1697, a few steps from where Johan and Cornelis de Witt had been murdered by the mob a quarter of a century before.

In Holland, the battle over Bekker and the Devil moved towards its climax. Rotterdam pushed hard for outright condemnation. But many consistories in Holland were split, or predominantly Cocceian. Delft and Dordrecht refused to support the moves to mobilize the South Holland Synod to put pressure on the North Holland Synod. The Delft consistory took the view that the matter should be left to the Amsterdam consistory to settle.[141] Bekker accused his Voetian opponents, in Holland, of inciting hostile interventions from the classes of Leeuwarden, Groningen, and Middelburg, in order to 'vanquish those who follow the teaching of Descartes and Cocceius' by coupling them with Hobbes and Spinoza, and also seeking to stir up an outcry in Reformed circles in Germany.[142]

Little by little, feeling in the North Holland Synod hardened against the moderation of the Amsterdam consistory. The classis Hoorn (at this time Voetian and fundamentalist, in contrast to Cocceian Enkhuizen) led the campaign for the humiliation of Bekker. At the gathering of the North Holland Synod, at Alkmaar in July 1692, the majority rejected Amsterdam's stance and Bekker himself was driven to deny the Synod's right to censor what he had published. He was duly condemned and declared unfit to be a preacher of the Reformed Church. The Synod requested the Amsterdam *vroedschap* to strip him of his pulpit. The Amsterdam burgomasters felt they had to comply; for if they were to insist on allowing Bekker to continue preaching, in defiance of the Synod, they would be at odds with the public Church and there were likely to be disturbances in the city. On the other hand, they had no wish to seem entirely subservient to the Synod either, and had to allow for the fact that much of the city, and *vroedschap*, sympathized with Bekker. Consequently, they suspended him, continuing his salary, without formally stripping him of his post, and refused to ban the book as the Synod asked. Utrecht and some other towns did locally ban the

---

[140] Knuttel, 'Ericus Walten', 437.
[141] GA Delft Kerkeraad 7, fos. 207v–210v, res. 9 and 12 Mar. 1692.
[142] Bekker, *Nodige Bedenkingen*, 53–5.

De Betoverde Weereld.[143] But Amsterdam and the States of Holland never did so.

THE TWO DUTCH ENLIGHTENMENTS

The furore over Bekker's *De Betoverde Weereld* was one of the most sustained and far-reaching of Early Enlightenment Europe. The book created an unprecedented uproar. Approximately 170 books for and against Bekker, and for and against belief in the Devil, appeared within three years of its publication. Some of the replies, including those of Koelman and Van der Waeyen, were even longer than *De Betoverde Weereld*. Yet this enormous upheaval in ideas and attitudes caused scarcely a ripple in France or England. An English translation of the first part of Bekker's book, entitled *The World Bewitched*, appeared in 1695, but interest in Britain was slender and soon the book 'seemed forgotten'.[144] The French version (1694) also seems to have made little impact. Even today, it is usual in Britain and France, when discussing the Early Enlightenment, to ignore the Dutch controversies completely.

This is symptomatic of a curious parting of ways which bifurcated much of the Early Enlightenment especially in the United Provinces. Bayle and the other Huguenot writers and intellectuals in Holland who did so much to promote new modes of thinking in Europe found it difficult to come to grips with the late Cartesian and Cocceian movements in the Republic. Part of the problem was the avalanche of material appearing in Dutch which placed it largely beyond the reach of the Huguenot intelligentsia with their poor grasp of that language. Bayle found this somewhat frustrating,[145] but also contributed more than anyone else to advancing the process whereby the Dutch controversies were screened out from what Huguenot, other French and English intellectuals regarded as contemporary issues. A striking feature of Bayle's great work, his *Dictionnaire historique et critique* (which did more than any other to set the agenda as to what to read and discuss in Early Enlightenment Europe) is that the Dutch controversies and participants to them are neither given entries nor mentioned. Apart from Spinoza and Wittichius, the rest—Cocceius, Heidanus, Röell, Vam Limborch, Meijer, Koerbagh, Van Dale, Walten, and Bekker—were simply erased from the picture. It was a tendency reinforced by the rule imposed by the Walloon Synod in the United Provinces that the French-speaking preachers

---

[143] Van de Water, *Groot Placaat-Boeck . . . Utrecht*, iii. 433.
[144] Trevor-Roper, *European Witch-Craze*, 102–3.
[145] Labrousse, *Pierre Bayle*, i. 169–70.

must refrain from entering into the Cocceian–Voetian disputes and related matters.

Yet a major intellectual transformation took place in the Republic at the end of the seventeenth century, virtually unconnected with the Huguenots, the effects of which were not confined to the United Provinces. It was a change in the ideas of Dutch-speaking élites but also, to an extent, a change in popular ideas. As the Voetian preacher Jacobus Leidecker pointed out, in 1692, the fact that many ordinary church-going folk, and some Reformed preachers, no longer believed in angels or Satan could not simply be blamed on Spinoza and Hobbes. It was Cartesianism and Cocceianism, the movements permeating every nook of the Dutch cultural world, and, above all, the work of Cocceius, Röell, and Bekker, which had done this.[146] Furthermore, the sea-change in the Republic, while exerting little direct impact on Britain and France, did have an appreciable effect in central Europe where Dutch cultural influence had long been more marked than in England or France and was still pervasive in the early eighteenth century. Bekker's *Betoverde Weereld*, almost contemptuously dismissed by Bayle,[147] was regarded in Germany as a major event. The first German translation appeared at Amsterdam in 1693 and a second at Hamburg, in 1695. In the years 1694–5, a lively debate about Bekker and the Dutch controversies ensued in the influential Leipzig journal, the *Acta Eruditorum*, in part reporting the discussion published in Rabus' *Boekzaal*, a review unknown in Britain and France but, again, much discussed in Germany.[148] Most German participants in the Bekker controversy reacted in the same way as the Dutch Voetians, insisting that Bekker was the heir of Hobbes and Spinoza and the champion of a new atheism.

But in Germany, too, the Enlightenment was stirring and, although French and English influences were considerable, Dutch intellectual influence during the initial stages was probably greater than either. This is especially true of the impact of radical ideas during the 1690s and opening years of the new century. A leading German Lutheran divine observed in the preface of a new theological journal, in 1701, that twenty years before, the German public and clergy had been in blissful ignorance of the dangers to come. Then they had learnt with astonishment of the uproar in that 'excessively free' country 'Holland' caused by a flood of pernicious new books, next heard with horror of the ideas of a 'certain Spinoza', and those of Beverland, Da Costa, and Hobbes and finally, 'in the last ten years', seen

---

[146] Leydecker, *Bekkers Philosophise Duyvel*, 29–30, 134–5.
[147] Bayle, *Lettres*, i. 417, 431–2.
[148] Zobeln, *Declaratio Apologetica*, 4–9, 38–9.

godless, 'heartless' texts pour into 'all the bookshops of our Protestant Germany'.[149] Spilling over into Germany, the Bekker controversy not only lent added momentum to this Dutch invasion of German bookshops but noticeably increased the impact of the new notions on ordinary, unsophisticated folk. Several of Bekker's German critics justified the added publicity they gave to his works on the grounds that his attempt to seduce pious folk into concluding that Satan and angels did not exist was already having a widespread and disturbing effect on German society. Friedrich Ernst Kettner's *De Duobus Impostoribus, Benedicto Spinosa et Balthasare Bekkero, Dissertatio* (Leipzig, 1694) ranked Bekker with Spinoza as one of the two principal intellectual threats to German piety and peace of mind.[150] Enoch Zobeln, in his *Declaratio Apologetica* (Leipzig, 1695), similarly held that Protestant Germany was being undermined by wicked outpourings from 'Holland', coupling Bekker's name with those of Spinoza, Hobbes, and (remarkably) David Joris.[151]

But by no means the whole German scholarly world took such a negative view, at any rate of Bekker. Christian Thomasius, leader of the intellectual campaign to discredit belief in witchcraft in Germany, cites Bekker cautiously but positively in his *De Crimine Magiae* (1701). Nor was Bekker entirely forgotten in Germany during the later Enlightenment. Just as Lessing and other leading spirits of the *Aufklärung* arrived at a more positive assessment of Spinoza so, in the late eighteenth century, there was some tentative recognition of the contribution of Bekker. Johann Moritz Schwager, a Reformed preacher in the county of Ravensberg, published a sympathetic account of Bekker's life in 1780, holding him up as a key figure of the Early Enlightenment in Germany and one of those who had done most to combat superstitious belief in the Devil and witchcraft. Schwager explained the fact that Bekker was no longer widely remembered as a consequence of the ungainly and inaccurate renderings of his work into German.[152] Schwager prepared a new translation which he published at Leipzig in 1781.

[149] Bell, *Spinoza in Germany*, 1.
[150] Kettner, *Duobus Impostoribus*, pp. A2, B, B2–4.
[151] Zobeln, *Declaratio Apologetica*, 1–2, 6–8, 38–9.
[152] Schwager, *Beytrag*, 3–4, 131–3.

35

The Colonial Empire

❖

In the years around 1640 it appeared that the Dutch were well on the way to consolidating a vast and profitable colonial empire in the western as well as another in the eastern hemisphere. Netherlands Brazil, or 'New Holland' as it was named, stretching from the Amazon estuary to Fort Maurits, at the mouth of the São Francisco river (about half-way between Recife and Bahia), seemed both secure and flourishing under WIC rule, especially during the largely successful term (1637–44) of the Company's first (and last) governor-general of New Holland, Count Johan Maurits van Nassau-Siegen, the same who was subsequently a senior commander of the Dutch army and the Elector of Brandenburg's Stadholder of Cleves-Mark. With possession of northern Brazil, the Dutch totally dominated the European sugar market. The WIC also seemed set to dominate the trans-atlantic slave trade and was by far the strongest European power in Africa. After conquering Elmina from the Portuguese in 1637, Chama and Boutry in 1640, and Axim in 1642, the Dutch were in full control along the Guinea coast and, in May 1641, an expedition of 3,000 men, sent from Brazil under the WIC's one-legged commander Pieter Cornelisz. Jol (d. 1641), also conquered Angola from the Portuguese. Meanwhile, to the north of Brazil, the Dutch retained their small settlements of Essequebo, Demerary, and Berbice in the Guyanas and, following their capture of Curaçao (1634), had acquired several other small Caribbean islands, so that by 1648 all six of the modern Dutch Antilles—the three 'Curaçao' islands—Curaçao, Aruba, and Bonaire—and the more northerly 'Leeward' group—St Eustatius, Saba, and half of St Martin—were under the Dutch flag. Finally, there was 'New Netherland' (Nova Belgica), from where the WIC controlled the North American fur trade from its two bases at Manhattan (New Amsterdam) and Fort Orange, which is today Albany.

But this imposing empire on both sides of the South Atlantic collapsed even more suddenly than it had arisen. In 1645, the Catholic Portuguese planters of northern Brazil rebelled against Company rule, as well as against Dutch Protestants generally and Portuguese Jews, both of which groups they resented for economic and religious as well as political reasons, commencing a war which rapidly swept across the cultivated regions of New Holland, devastating the sugar plantations. By the end of 1645, the WIC had effectively lost control of most of northern Brazil, the Dutch and Jews being blockaded in Recife and a few other fortified strongholds. Though it was widely hoped in the United Provinces that the end of the war with Spain, in 1648, would enable the States General to send sufficient forces to Brazil to rescue the WIC and suppress the revolt, the forces sent, though substantial, were unable to accomplish the task. After the arrival of the Generality expedition under Witte de With, in March 1648, the Dutch army in Brazil totalled over 6,000 men. But in their attempt to drive the Portuguese back from the environs of Recife, the army, under its German commander Sigismund von Schoppe, was defeated by a smaller Portuguese force at the first battle of Guararapes (April 1648) while, shortly after, a Portuguese expedition sent from southern Brazil forced the surrender of the Dutch garrison in Angola. The second attempt to end the blockade of Recife, the second battle of Guararapes (February 1649), resulted in an even more demoralizing defeat than the first and one which effectively sealed the fate of Netherlands Brazil. For it was now hard to see how Company rule and stability could be restored in the region. These three great colonial defeats of 1648–9 of course had a sensational effect in the Republic, materially affecting the developing political crisis there, enabling William II and the States of Zeeland, Utrecht, and Groningen, the three provinces chiefly supporting still more vigorous Generality intervention in Brazil, to pin much of the blame for the Republic's humiliation on the leaders of the States of Holland. Between 1645 and the final demise of Dutch Brazil, with the capitulation of Recife in 1654, the Company's shares lost almost all their value and the public's confidence in its enterprises all but vanished.

Yet, however bleak the outlook in those years, and despite the loss of all prospect of a large Dutch empire in the western hemisphere, the WIC nevertheless succeeded in the 1650s and 1660s in building a flourishing transatlantic empire of trade in collaboration with private merchants in the Republic (see p. 944 below). The WIC abandoned for good its grandiose aspirations and former methods and style. In contrast to the VOC, it ceased to be a significant military or naval power. But its small Caribbean islands and Guyana colonies, and its West African fortresses, developed into a network of trading posts and depots which enabled the Dutch to remain as one of the principal European Atlantic trading powers.[1] Especially important, from the late 1640s, was the Dutch carrying traffic in the Caribbean, and soon also between the Caribbean and the Spanish American mainland, both of which were based especially on Curaçao, and the Dutch transatlantic slave trade, via Curaçao, to the Spanish American colonies. The latter developed in conjunction with the *asiento*, a fixed-term supervised slaving monopoly, maintained by the Spanish Crown.[2] The WIC continued to reserve to itself the Dutch slave traffic, and also the Guinea gold trade and all navigation to its West African forts.

Meanwhile, in the East Indies, the VOC achieved impressive gains in the 1630s and early 1640s, capturing three of the six chief Portuguese strongholds in Ceylon in the years 1638–41, in alliance with the king of Kandy, ruler of the Sinhalese interior, and, in 1641, after a long and costly siege, the great Portuguese base of Malacca, commanding the straits between the Indian Ocean and the China Sea. Thus, by the 1640s, the Dutch were solidly entrenched in the Indian subcontinent and Malay peninsula as well as in Indonesia (and until 1662 Taiwan). In the 1650s, the Company continued to concentrate its main military effort in fighting the Portuguese in Ceylon. After the epic siege of Colombo (1655–6), the VOC controlled the whole of the cinnamon-producing zone of the island. During the war of 1657–61 between the United Provinces and Portugal (chiefly over Brazil) and its epilogue of fighting in south India, the Dutch not only completed their conquest of coastal Ceylon but conquered and annexed the whole of the string of Portuguese fortified bases—Negapatnam, Tuticorin, Cannanore, Cranganore, and Cochin—around the tip of India (see Map 14). From around 1660 until the 1720s, the Dutch were to remain the leading European power in India.

Consequently, despite the loss of Netherlands Brazil in 1654, Taiwan in 1662, and New Netherland in 1664, the Dutch colonial empire was at its height during the second half of the seventeenth century and first quarter of the eighteenth. During this period Dutch commerce and shipping expanded in both the eastern and western hemispheres and the contribution of colonial enterprise to the functioning of the Dutch trading system, as a whole, steadily increased. In the Indonesian archipelago, the VOC considerably extended its sway, in particular with the conquest of Macassar in 1667 by a force under Cornelis Speelman (1628–84), rival of Rijcklof van Goens (1619–82), who had led the Dutch victories in south India, and the annexation of Bantam in 1682. Meanwhile, in the west, the Dutch expanded

---

[1] Israel, *Dutch Primacy*, 236–44.
[2] Emmer, 'West India Company', 83–6; Postma, *Dutch Atlantic Slave Trade*, 27–45.

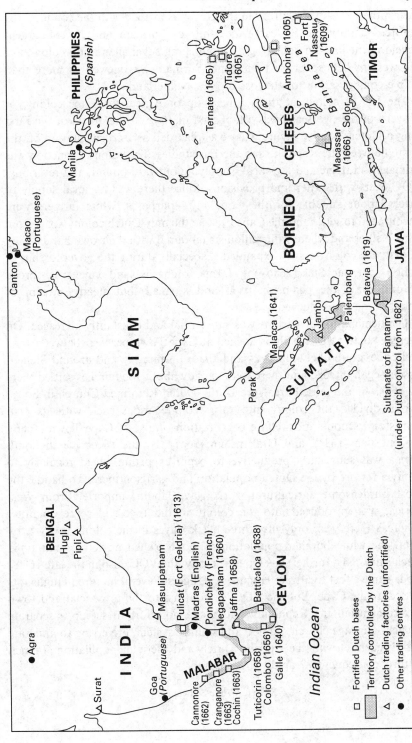

MAP 14. The Dutch empire in Asia at its height around 1688

their hitherto slender territory in the Guyanas in 1667 with the conquest (by a force sent by the States of Zeeland) of Surinam and its subsequent development into one of the most flourishing sugar plantation colonies of the western hemisphere. At the time, Surinam was viewed as more than ample compensation for the loss of New Netherland.

The VOC's colony at the southern tip of Africa, the Cape colony, or 'Tavern of the two seas', was established in 1652, at the outset of the First Anglo-Dutch War, to secure what was regarded as a crucial station on the route between the Republic and the East Indies. The colony's function was primarily strategic and logistical, supplying outward-bound, and returning, VOC fleets with water and provisions. Since there was no local supply of black labour suitable for the Company's purposes, white farmers were encouraged to settle and the Cape became the only Dutch colony apart from New Netherland where white colonists laboured with their own hands. Tiny at first, the colony slowly expanded. Especially during the governorship of Simon van der Stel (1679–99), farms, orchards, and vineyards spread beyond the Cape peninsula itself and a small, but steady, stream of immigration was achieved.

The demand for provisions was substantial and constantly increased. On average some 33 Dutch ships docked at Cape Town per year between 1652 and 1700 and 69 between 1715 and 1740. Farming in and around Stellenbosch began in 1680 and there were already about 100 families settled there by 1685. As the settled area spread, the Dutch Reformed Church in South Africa divided the colony into three congregations each with its own consistory, school, and welfare organization—those of Cape Town (1666), Stellenbosch (1685), and Drakenstein (1691). By the 1690s Dutch South Africa was sufficiently productive to begin exporting wheat regularly to Batavia for use by the Dutch population and garrison there. To handle the most burdensome agricultural work, slave labour, imported from West Africa, was introduced into the colony in the 1690s, in some quantity. Whereas there were only fifty-three black slaves in the colony in 1672, by 1711, the white burgher population of 1,756 owned no fewer than 1,781 black slaves.[3] To further develop the colony, the VOC, also in the late 1680s, made some effort to attract Huguenot refugees. Several hundred Huguenots settled at the Cape. But the VOC, in contrast to the provincial and town governments in the Republic itself, made no effort to set up a separate French-language church, school, and welfare system, preferring to integrate the Huguenots with the existing Dutch and German population. French culture, consequently, rapidly disappeared.

[3] Katzen, 'White Settlers', 201.

In Asia, Dutch power attained its zenith in the 1680s with the occupation of the sultanate of Bantam and assertion of Dutch power in Sumatra. In 1688, the VOC possessed over twenty fortresses in Asia of over 100 men, its principal bases being at Batavia and north-west Java, Amboina, Macassar, the Banda Islands, Malacca, Ceylon, and the southern tip of India (see Table 41). In South Africa, the VOC maintained a garrison of about 200.

TABLE 41. *The VOC's employees in the ten principal Dutch possessions in Asia,*
　　　　1688

Territory	Troops	Seamen and artisans	Administration and trade	Approx. totals
Java				
Batavia	1,900	600	200	2,700
Bantam	340	75	10	425
Japara	660	170	15	845
The rest of Indonesia				
Amboina	600	150	50	800
Banda Islands	500	150	30	680
Macassar	350	100	20	470
Sumatra	235	200	35	470
Ternate-Tidore	290	100	25	415
South India				
Negapatnam and the Coromandel coast	500	70	100	670
Cochin and the Malabar coast	420	150	50	620
Ceylon				
Colombo Negombo Jaffna Galle Batticaloa	1,700	600	150	2,450

Sources: Van Dam, *Beschryvinge*, ii, part 1, 320–1; Gaastra, *Gesch. van de VOC*, 85.

In addition, the Company had a string of trade factories without forts in north India and Siam as well as the only European factory in Japan. Altogether, the VOC had some 11,500 employees in Asia, of whom one-third were based on the island of Java and a slightly higher proportion, just over one-third, in India and Ceylon.

The turning-point, marking the beginning of Dutch decline in Asian trade, can be dated, as in West Africa (and with the Dutch overseas trading system as a whole), from the Nine Years' War (1688–97). The erosion of the VOC's sway began with the late seventeenth-century shift in the pattern of demand for Asian products in Europe, stimulating imports of commodities such as cottons, muslin, raw silk, tea, and coffee from regions where the Dutch possessed no garrisons. In the changed situation, particularly in the case of the China tea trade, the Dutch showed noticeably less dynamism than the English and French in opening up new strands of commerce. The receding of Dutch primacy was already clearly noticeable in the 1690s, and in southern India from around 1700.[4] Although the Dutch captured the French base of Pondicherry in 1693, holding it until 1699, they had little prospect, in the longer run, of checking either French or English expansion while the withdrawal of the main Dutch force on the Coromandel coast, from Pulicat to the base of Negapatnam, further south, virtually meant abandoning Dutch influence on the central and northern stretches of the Coromandel coast.[5]

By contrast, for Surinam, Dutch western Guyana (Essequebo, Demerara, Berbice, and Pomeroon), and the six Caribbean islands, especially Curaçao and St Eustatius, the first two-thirds of the eighteenth century were a golden age, at any rate for the white colonists and planters. For Surinam and western Guyana, prosperity was built on sugar, coffee, and black slaves, in Curaçao and St Eustatius on seaborne trade with the rest of the Caribbean area and with New York, Philadelphia, and Boston, in North America. The number of plantations in Surinam grew from around fifty in 1680 to over 600 by 1800, though sugar exports reached their peak in the 1750s. Coffee output rose dramatically during the first half of the eighteenth century but tended to stagnate thereafter. Colonization also proceeded in western Guyana, though it remained a less important and prosperous territory than Surinam down to its definitive acquisition by Britain in 1815. A report of 1782 gives the number of plantations in Dutch western Guyana as 387 with a total of 34,000 slaves.

COMMERCE, SHIPPING, AND SEAMEN IN THE INDIES

In 1657, the VOC had no fewer than 160 ships in Asian waters.[6] Trade and ships were the heart of the Dutch colonial empire, the principal motive and

---

[4] Israel, *Anglo-Dutch Moment*, 420–7.

[5] Arasaratnam, 'Dutch East India Company and its Coromandel Trade', 326, 337, 346.

[6] Aalbers, *Rijcklof van Goens*, 19.

impulse behind its rise and development. But the flourishing mercantile systems which the Dutch created in Asia, Africa, and the New World were always based on possession of colonies and on fleets and routes rigidly regulated by the Republic, and its two great colonial companies, within an unrelenting imperial framework. The Dutch mercantile system in non-European waters was literally an empire of trade.

During Phase Three (1621–47) of Dutch world trade primacy, the Dutch emerged as by far the strongest European power in Asia but, owing to the Spanish embargoes, with a sharply reduced supply of silver bullion reaching the Republic from Spain and the Spanish Indies, a situation which created serious difficulty for the VOC's financing of its purchases of pepper, spices, and raw silk for the European market. For Asians wanted few goods from Europe, in the seventeenth and eighteenth centuries, and all Europeans in Asia were in the position of having to purchase with cash. To sustain its expansion, on a reduced flow of Spanish silver, the main source of bullion in Europe, the Company moved in a direction which no other European nation did on a comparable scale in early modern times, forging a vigorous inter-Asian trade, in order to amass the additional buying power required.[7] Thus, in contrast to the English East India Company which always concentrated on its direct traffic between England and Asia, the VOC developed a network of inter-Asian trade routes, becoming an Asian trader on a large scale.

During the second quarter of the seventeenth century, the most important elements in this Dutch inter-Asian trade were the shipping of south Indian cotton textiles to Indonesia, Chinese raw silk from Taiwan to Japan, in exchange for Japanese silver and copper, at the VOC factory at Nagasaki, and Indonesian spices to India and Persia to help pay for Indian textiles and Persian raw silk, the latter mainly for the European market. After 1660, Dutch trade with China, via Taiwan, and with Japan declined, as did the inter-Asian trade based at Malacca. Despite this, the VOC's expansion in Asia continued, fuelled, from 1647, by the revived flow of Spanish silver to the United Provinces. Thus, the relative importance of the Dutch inter-Asian seaborne traffic also diminished. From 56 ships, in 1641, the number of VOC vessels engaged in inter-Asian trade increased to a peak of 107, around 1670, after which it gradually decreased.[8] But the loss of traffic in the China Sea was partially compensated for, after the VOC's conquest of Ceylon and the southern tip of India, by the new inter-Asian trade between

[7] Prakash, *Dutch East India Company and the Economy of Bengal*, 15–23.
[8] Gaastra, *Gesch. van de VOC*, 118.

these areas and northern India, especially Bengal, which, from the 1650s onwards, became the main source of the raw silk which the VOC exported, in ever increasing quantity, to the Republic. Consequently, though the number of Dutch ships involved in inter-Asian trade fell off, it remained impressive until well into the eighteenth century, falling to 66 in 1700, 52 in 1725, 43 in 1750, and 30 in 1775.[9]

While the Dutch inter-Asian traffic flourished, most of the VOC's ships were employed in sailing between one part of Asia and another. This was still the case in the 1680s but, by 1700, the balance had shifted, as the inter-Asian traffic shrank and the direct commerce between the Republic and Batavia expanded. By 1725, less than a third of the VOC's shipping was primarily used for the inter-Asian traffic. Most of the VOC's ships were large, well-armed, heavily manned ships, though some smaller vessels were used within the Indonesian archipelago. Consequently, the number of seamen the VOC required to man both its direct and inter-Asian traffic was, by early modern standards, vast, far larger than could be supplied from the overstretched stock of native-born Dutch seamen. Small numbers of Asian seamen were employed by the VOC in the eighteenth century but for the most part, for seamen almost as much as for soldiers, the Company relied on recruiting Protestant Germans, Scandinavians, and other non-Dutch Europeans.

In 1688, the VOC had some 12,000 employees in its fortresses and trading posts in Asia but besides these, another 6,000 on its outward- and homeward-bound fleets, together with another 4,000 manning the 80-odd ships engaged in inter-Asian trade, making a grand total of almost 22,000.[10] Of these, more than one-third, almost 8,500, were seamen (see Table 42). By 1750, while the numbers of seamen employed on Dutch merchant shipping, and the fisheries, in European waters had fallen appreciably since the 1680s, the number of seamen employed by the VOC had increased, since 1688, by a third. As a proportion of all seamen employed on Dutch merchant shipping, the number working for the VOC rose from a modest 6 per cent of the total, in 1610, to 17 per cent by 1680, and no less than a quarter of the total by 1770.[11]

The volume of VOC shipping sailing to Asia doubled from 117 per decade in the 1620s to 235 per decade in the 1690s; subsequently the volume increased further until the 1720s, after which it gradually declined, though with a sharp fall in the 1740s. Similarly, the volume of shipping returning

[9] Ibid.; Arasaratnam, *Dutch Power in Ceylon*, 161–3.
[10] Gaastra, 'VOC in Azië tot 1680', 200–1.
[11] Bruijn and Lucassen, *Op de schepen*, 14.

from Asia to the United Provinces—they were not allowed to call in anywhere else in Europe—doubled from 70 per decade in the 1620s to 140 per decade in the 1680s, increased further down to the 1720s, and then fell off, especially in the 1740s.[12] But while the VOC's fleets declined after 1730 in terms of size (and still more so in terms of profitability, though this trend had begun earlier), it is striking that the proportion of foreigners amongst the Company's seamen continued to grow, comprising around half by 1770.[13] The great majority of these were Lutheran Germans and Scandinavians.

TABLE 42. *Seamen employed by the VOC, 1688–1780*

Year	In Asian bases	Inter-Asian trade	Outward-bound fleet	Homeward-bound fleet	Total
1688	1,400	3,500	2,490	1,050	8,440
1700	1,400	3,500	2,790	1,230	8,920
1753	3,500	2,500	4,860	1,860	12,720
1780	2,900	1,000	4,320	1,530	9,750

Sources: Gaastra, 'VOC in Azië tot 1680', 200–1; Bruijn and Lucassen, *Op de schepen*, 135–7; Gaastra, *Gesch. van de VOC*, 82.

In Asian waters the VOC restricted all Dutch navigation to its own shipping. In a report on the Company's position, in 1662, Pieter van Dam, secretary of the Amsterdam Chamber of the VOC, and later author of the most comprehensive account of the VOC written in early modern times, proposed allowing private Dutch entrepreneurs and colonists to use their own vessels in the coast-to-coast trade within Asia.[14] But the directors chose not to move in this direction. By contrast, the WIC, after the loss of Dutch Brazil, in 1654, confined navigation to its own ships only with respect to West Africa, where it strove to maintain an absolute monopoly, and in the closely connected Dutch transatlantic slave trade. Private ships were allowed, were indeed vital, not only within the Caribbean to carry Curaçao's extensive inter-island traffic and commerce with the Spanish American mainland but also in the long-distance traffic between the Republic and the Caribbean.

In the seventeenth century, and at the beginning of the eighteenth, the Dutch slave trade was largely a WIC monopoly, although there was always some interloping, especially by Zeelanders, who (unable to put in at any of

[12] Gaastra, *Gesch. van de VOC*, 115.
[13] Bruijn and Lucassen, *Op de schepen*, 21.
[14] Van Dam, 'Concept', 270–1.

the Dutch Caribbean colonies, with their slaves), often used the Danish island of St Thomas as a depot. The Dutch slave trade during the period of the WIC monopoly, in contrast to that of the English and French, was chiefly orientated towards the Spanish American market, especially Cartagena, Venezuela, and Panama. During the last quarter of the seventeenth century, the WIC dispatched three to four slave ships per year to the Caribbean, from West Africa, without counting its shipments to the Dutch colonies in the Guyanas.[15] Since all the WIC's activities were shared among the five chambers, according to a rota system on a basis of ninths, with the Amsterdam chamber responsible for four-ninths of activity, Zeeland two-ninths, and the other three chambers—the Maas, North Quarter, and Groningen—one-ninth each (a pattern reflecting the apportioning of seats on the WIC's federal governing board), the WIC's slaving voyages, from the Republic to West Africa, and on to the Caribbean, were planned in series of nine, according to a fixed order, with Amsterdam organizing four, Zeeland two, and the rest one each, Amsterdam's ships taking the first, third, fifth, and ninth slots and Groningen the eighth.

Besides the WIC's slaving ships, and other vessels voyaging to the Guinea coast, the Company, as well as private firms, regularly sent large vessels to the Guyanas and Caribbean, especially Curaçao, laden with textiles, brandy, and other European goods. Most of this merchandise was intended not for the Dutch colonies but for stockpiling in the warehouses of Willemstad—which had one of the best-protected large harbours close to the Spanish American mainland—for distribution all over the Caribbean area and especially to Venezuela, New Granada (Colombia), Puerto Rico, Santo Domingo, St Thomas, and the English colonies, including those in North America. Although, under English laws, such traffic was illegal, numerous ships sailed to Curaçao from New York, Boston, and Philadelphia laden with flour, pickled pork, and other provisions (which were in short supply in the Curaçao islands), carrying back Dutch spices and manufactures to English North America.[16] Thus, one of the main cogs in the wheel of the commercial empire of the west was the fleet of barques and sloops, many of them Jewish-owned, based at Curaçao, which distributed cargoes all over the Caribbean area, returning to Willemstad with their cargoes of Venezuelan cacao, dyewood, sugar, indigo, and silver. At its height, in the 1680s and 1690s, the Curaçao-based fleet consisted of some 80 barques, manned by 15 to 80 men each.[17]

---

[15] Postma, *Dutch in the Atlantic Slave Trade*, 45.
[16] ARH WIC 206, fos. 8–16.
[17] ARH WIC 203, fo. 291v. Beck to Amsterdam directors, 4 Jan. 1710.

The *kleine vaart* (local trade) in the Caribbean was carried on using privately owned craft manned by seamen based in Curaçao. The *grote vaart*, the transatlantic traffic, consisted of a mixture of WIC ships and large private vessels paying fees and taxes to the Company. Also in contrast to the VOC, WIC ships mainly carried goods not for the Company but on behalf of private merchants who booked space for their goods, through brokers. From 1707 onwards, the traffic between Amsterdam and Curaçao was partly organized in convoys provided with naval escorts. At Curaçao, at the end of the seventeenth century and beginning of the eighteenth, the chief factors were Protestants, often Germans, but the majority of the middling and lesser merchants at Willemstad were Sephardic Jews, usually closely related to families in both Amsterdam and Surinam.

During the eighteenth century St Eustatius also attained great importance as a general entrepôt, both for the Caribbean area and North America. From around 1720 onwards, large numbers of ships came there to unload colonial produce for the European market and load with merchandise shipped out from the United Provinces. But, in contrast to Curaçao, which chiefly used its own fleet, St Eustatius was basically a convenient rendezvous, most of the shipping which docked there being French, English, Spanish, American, or Dutch, rather than local to the Dutch Leeward Islands. In the year 1773, for example, 146 ships docked at St Eustatius, one-third of them from the French colonies of Martinique and Guadeloupe and a substantial proportion American ships from New England and the Middle Colonies.[18] During the great eighteenth-century wars between France and Britain, St Eustatius was one of the principal loopholes through which French colonial produce continued to reach the European market.

Another main strand of Dutch transatlantic commerce was the traffic between the Republic and Surinam (and western Guyana), lands of sugar and—after 1700—coffee plantations. These exported their sugar and coffee exclusively to Holland and Zeeland, importing European goods solely from the Republic and, until the WIC's legal monopoly of the Dutch slave trade ended, in 1730, officially obtained slaves only through the WIC. With the steady expansion in sugar and coffee production, the number of vessels sailing from these colonies to Amsterdam rose to over 20 per year, after 1720, and over 40 per year, whilst these colonies were at their height, between 1740 and the 1780s, making the Amsterdam–Surinam route one of the most important in eighteenth-century Dutch long-distance navigation.[19]

Under pressure from private merchants, the States of Holland and Zeeland, and States General, were won round, by 1730, to the opening up

[18] Goslinga, *Dutch in the Caribbean*, 199.　　[19] Oldewelt, 'Scheepvaartsstatistiek', 131.

of the slave trade, expecting by this means to increase the flow of slaves to the Dutch colonies, reduce prices for slaves, and render the Dutch plantations more competitive in relation to French and English plantations.[20] Henceforth, Dutch merchants—it was especially the Zeelanders who specialized in this traffic—were obliged only to pay for a WIC pass to buy slaves in West Africa. This resulted in a marked increase in the flow of slaves to Surinam and western Guyana, Curaçao, though, never regained its former prominence as a slaving depot, after the transfer of the slave *asiento* for Spanish America to Britain under the terms of the treaty of Utrecht (1713). During the peak decades, from 1750 to 1780, slaving ships reached Surinam at rate of a dozen per year, bringing yearly some three to four thousand slaves.[21]

POWER, POLITICS, AND PATRONAGE

Throughout the Dutch empire in Asia and South Africa, the VOC was the only, and supreme, authority, under the sovereign supervision of the States General. The VOC was governed by a federal board of directors, the so-called *Heren XVII*, in the Republic, constituted of representatives of the Company's four constituent chambers (see pp. 321–2 above). Furthermore, while all the chambers were located in Holland or Zeeland, it was always the policy of the *Heren XVII*, and States General, that the Company constituted, and federated, the commerce and diplomacy of the whole of the United Provinces in Asia; and that, as a military power, maintaining armies, fleets, and garrisons, it was an extension of the Generality. Thus all the governors, military commanders, naval commanders, and diplomats of the VOC in Asia and South Africa acted always in a double capacity, and under a double oath of allegiance, to the Generality of the United Provinces as well as to the VOC. When in 1619 Jan Pietersz. Coen, governor-general of the Dutch East Indies (1619–23 and 1627–9), established the Company's permanent headquarters at his new fortified harbour, at Jakarta, his own choice of name for the new city, 'New Hoorn', after his own native town, was overruled by the *Heren XVII*, who chose 'Batavia' precisely because of its general north Netherlands connotations. The Company's principal base in India, in the early decades, at Pulicat, on the Coromandel coast, was called 'Fort Geldria'. In order to represent investors from provinces other than Holland and Zeeland, the rule was followed from 1613 onwards that

---

[20] Postma, *Dutch in the Atlantic Slave Trade*, 51–2, 54.
[21] Goslinga, *Dutch in the Caribbean*, 422–3.

Utrecht, Friesland, and Gelderland each held one of the twenty seats on the directorate of the Amsterdam Chamber, while from 1647, Groningen had a permanent director in the Zeeland chamber, and Overijssel was represented in the Delft sub-chamber. There were also rules whereby specific towns in Holland and Zeeland, where there was no chamber, had permanent representatives in the chambers. Thus, from 1648 Haarlem and Leiden each had a permanent seat in the Amsterdam chamber while the twelve directors of the Zeeland chamber from within the province were assigned nine to Middelburg, two to Flushing, and one to Veere.[22]

After the early years, it became usual at Amsterdam, and still more so in the smaller chambers, for the directors to be regents.[23] This meant there was always a close link between regent politics and interests, in Holland and Zeeland, and the running of the empire in Asia, and that civic patricians, mainly concerned with local government and administration, rather than active merchants, were in charge. It also meant, after the early decades, that directors obtained their posts through influence in civic government rather than experience in commerce or administration. Among the most powerful figures in the running of the VOC in the late seventeenth century were such leading Amsterdam regents as Coenraad van Beuningen, Joan Huydecoper, and Joanes Hudde. From the outset, the VOC thus reflected the dispersal of power typical of the Dutch confederate state as a whole. Down to 1795, the Dutch colonial empire was never run either by bureaucrats, at The Hague, or by the city of Amsterdam, crucial though Amsterdam's influence invariably was.

Since the Republic itself, and the chambers of the VOC in Holland and Zeeland, eschewed the principle of monarchy, in matters of government, administration, and patronage, in favour of dispersal of power, and decision-making by consultation, it was natural that neither the VOC, nor the WIC, should wish their governors-general and local governors, in the Indies, to resemble the powerful viceroys and governors of the Spanish and Portuguese empires. Both Companies insisted on the exercise of power, and making of decisions, in the Indies, by consultative procedure, the governors-general at Batavia and lesser governors being required to act only jointly with their 'political councils'.

At the apex of government in the East Indies stood, jointly, the governor-general and *raad* (council) of the Indies, at Batavia. In contrast to a Spanish or Portuguese viceroy, or governor, the VOC's governor-general was regarded as merely the 'first person' of the *raad* and was not allowed to

---

[22] Gaastra, *Bewind en beleid*, 32.   [23] Ibid. 32–4; Gaastra, *Gesch. van de VOC*, 31.

make decisions, or reports to the *Heren XVII*, on his own. Official communications and edicts had to be in the name of the governor-general and *raad*.[24] The next most senior member of the *raad*, the director-general, supervised the Company's commerce throughout Asia. The rest of the *raad* comprised a visitor-general, in charge of accounts, the president of Batavia's *raad van justitie*, or council administering justice, and the heads of the Company's military and naval forces.

This system of consultative government was then duplicated at regional level throughout the empire. When in 1651, the *raad* at Batavia learned that the then governor of Dutch Ceylon was taking decisions without the approval of the *raad* of Ceylon, he was told that 'in future you will not undertake or decide any matters of importance, except with previous consent and common decision of the council—as happens here and everywhere where good order is maintained'.[25] All communications of any importance from the main Dutch bases in Asia had to be sent to the governor-general and *raad* of the Indies, at Batavia, and signed both by the local governor and his 'political council'. In South Africa, too, the colonial government consisted of a *raad* sitting together with the governor. The same council, minus the governor, also functioned as the 'council of justice'. From 1685 onwards, first two, and later three, burgher representatives sat on the latter regularly, but were only occasionally permitted to represent the settlers on the presiding 'political council'.[26]

Who were the governors-general and governors? In the Spanish, Portuguese, British, and French colonial empires of the seventeenth and eighteenth centuries, viceroys and governors were invariably noblemen and represented their monarch. But this was not the case with the Dutch empire, where the governors, as a rule, were not nobles. Control over the Companies in the Republic lay in the hands of regents together with a few non-regent élite merchants. Inevitably, the directors at home exercised their influence on behalf of friends and relatives, procuring posts, especially in the Companies' commercial organization in the Indies (where corruption was widespread), to an extent on the basis of favour rather than ability. A few officials were appointed to senior posts at Batavia without having had previous experience in the Indies.[27] Nevertheless, especially before the Orangist revolution of 1747, because the *Heren XVII*, and regional chambers, had their eye in the first place on profit, and profits required

---

[24] Gaastra, *Gesch. van de VOC*, 66.
[25] Goonewardena, *Foundation of Dutch Power in Ceylon*, 141–2.
[26] Boxer, *Dutch Seaborne Empire*, 253; Schutte, *Nederlandse Patriotten en de koloniën*, 64.
[27] Gaastra, *Bewind en beleid*, 273, 276.

competence, they preferred men of experience and proven ability in the senior administration and military affairs of the empire. Consequently, the governors-general, and governors, tended to come from relatively modest, and in a few cases quite humble, backgrounds, provided they were sufficiently formidable men. The longest-serving governor-general the lawyer Joan Maetsuyker (1653–78), came from an undistinguished Catholic family and when first proposed for a senior legal post at Batavia, in 1636, was objected to by one of the *Heren XVII* as only nominally a member of the Reformed Church.[28] Owing to exceptional ability he rose rapidly through the Company's legal and diplomatic administration to become governor of Ceylon (1646–50) and then director-general of commerce at Batavia (1650–3). Rijklof van Goens, commander of the Dutch forces in Ceylon and India in 1657–63, and again in 1672–5, conqueror of the Malabar coast, governor of Ceylon (1653–72), and, finally, governor-general at Batavia (1678–81), was the son of a junior Frisian army officer, born at Rees, in the duchy of Cleves; orphaned, at Batavia, when 10 years old, he worked his way up from clerk to senior buyer, in the 1640s, becoming VOC commissioner in Siam, in 1650.[29] A third famous governor-general, Cornelis Speelman (1681–4), came from a Rotterdam burgher family and sailed to the East Indies, at the age of 18, to spend the rest of his life there. He started as a junior official, obtaining the post through the Rotterdam chamber; but he rose through his ability, becoming governor of the Coromandel forts (1663–5) and commander of the expedition that conquered Macassar in the years 1667–9. Governor-general Joannes Camphuys (1684–91), a devout Calvinist, had arrived in Asia in 1659 and held posts in various places, including Japan, before becoming a member of the *raad* at Batavia, in 1678. One of the very few noblemen who held high functions in the Dutch empire in the second half of the seventeenth century was a member of the Utrecht *ridderschap*, the remarkable Hendrik Adriaen van Reede tot Drakenstein, who entered the VOC's service in 1657, becoming commander of the VOC's forces on the Malabar coast, and after whom the Drakenstein mountains in South Africa are named (see p. 908 above).

In the empire of the west, it was originally intended, in 1622, that one trading Company, the WIC, should exercise supreme authority, again under the ultimate sovereignty of the States General. But in this case, in contrast to the East Indies, there were from the outset a number of fringe colonies and zones of influence which were not administered directly by the WIC. In order to profit from the efforts of private enterprise in less crucial regions,

[28] Boxer, *Jan Compagnie*, 30–2.   [29] Aalbers, *Rijcklof van Goens*, 34.

the WIC granted patents to certain merchant patrons prepared to undertake the colonization of stipulated localities, under the general auspices of the WIC but taking care of the administration themselves. None of these became flourishing colonies. But a few did develop at the fringes of the Dutch empire. One of these grants was that conceded to the Zeeland regent Abraham van Pere, in 1627, assigning him the estuary of the Berbice River in western Guyana. The small colony at Berbice continued to be governed by the Van Pere dynasty for many decades. In 1650, another Zeeland regent family, the Lampsins, were given a grant to colonize Tobago, which they renamed 'New Walcheren'. For most of the period (1654–78) that Tobago was held by the Dutch it was directly administered by the Lampsins, the main fort on the island being called Lampsinsberg.

Furthermore, whilst Netherlands Brazil and the forts on the Guinea coast were administered by the WIC as a whole, in the case of other WIC territories, or zones of influence, there was a tendency to assign responsibility to one or another of the five chambers—Amsterdam, Zeeland, the Maas, North Quarter, and Groningen. In this way, the Amsterdam Chamber had special responsibility for the Curaçao islands and New Netherland, while the Zeeland chamber took charge of western Guyana and, in the early period, the Dutch Leeward Islands. Among the zones of trading influence, the Gambia region of West Africa was assigned to the Groningen chamber.

In 1657, the Zeeland chamber transferred its responsibility for western Guyana to the three cities of Middelburg, Flushing, and Veere, which set up a joint directorate, dominated by their burgomasters, to manage the region under its new name 'Nova Zeelandia', which, besides Essequebo and Berbice, included a settlement which the Zeelanders established further west, at Pomeroon. When the original WIC was liquidated and the New WIC set up, in 1674, western Guyana came for the first time under the direct administration of the WIC, except for Berbice, which remained under the Van Pere proprietorship.

Matters became even more complicated after Surinam was conquered by the Zeelanders in 1667. The new colony was managed first by a directorate of the three Walcheren cities—Middelburg, Flushing, and Veere—until the New WIC was set up in 1674, when it came under the direct administration of the States of Zeeland. Finally, in 1682, a new body was established, called the 'Society of Surinam', in which the WIC and city of Amsterdam jointly were the main partners but in which the Aerssen van Sommelsdijk family also had a large stake.[30] Meanwhile, the Dutch Leeward Islands—St

---

[30] Goslinga, *The Dutch in the Caribbean*, 271–2.

Eustatius, Saba, and St Martin—remained under proprietorships, until they
were captured by the English in the Third Anglo-Dutch War. When they
were recovered, under the 1674 peace treaty, ownership of St Eustatius and
Saba was divided half-and-half between the WIC and the Van Pere family.
The Van Pere proprietorship was then sold to the Company in 1683,
bringing all three islands, for the first time, under the direct rule of the
WIC.[31]

But despite this more fragmented picture, some principles of colonial
administration in the west, at least in the main colonies, resembled the
position in the East Indies and South Africa. Again the Company's
governors and chief functionaries were not nobles and government was
consultative. The Dutch bases on the Guinea coast were administered from
the castle at Elmina by the WIC's director-general on the Guinea coast. But
he was supposed to take major decisions only conjointly with the *raad*, also
at Elmina. Similarly, the governor of Curaçao, who was also responsible for
Aruba and Bonaire, was appointed by the federal board of the WIC, to
whom he gave his oath of allegiance jointly with the States General. But he
was bound by instructions to govern the islands jointly with the *raad* in
Willemstad, which included, besides the commander of the garrison and the
WIC's commissioner for the slave trade, three representatives of the
citizenry. The position was similar in Surinam, defence, justice, and policing,
including the suppression of slave insurgency, being jointly under the
governor and *raad* in Paramaribo.

RELIGION AND DISCIPLINE

The VOC and WIC may have been devoted chiefly to trade, but profits on
the scale they sought were not to be had, in Europe or the Indies, without
military and territorial power; and, in early modern times, religion was one
of the most potent implements in the control of territories and peoples.

The charters granted to the VOC (1602) and WIC (1622) delegated the
States General's sovereign authority over the military and naval forces, as
well as the diplomats, in their employ in the Indies. All military and naval
undertakings by the VOC and WIC in Asia, Africa, and America, and
diplomatic activity, were carried out in the name of the States General as
well as the relevant Company. But in other respects, too, the great colonial
companies were extensions of the Dutch confederate state. Thus, both
Companies were bound by their charters, and the instructions of their

---

[31] Ibid. 31.

directorates, to promote, and protect, the Dutch Reformed Church as the sole public Church in their colonies, as well as to grant liberty of private conscience in accordance with the Union of Utrecht. Nor did the Companies and their colonial governments fail to commit some of their resources to maintaining and extending the supremacy of the public Church. Indeed toleration in the Dutch colonial empire was scarcely less limited and grudging (and in New Netherland, and South Africa, more so) than in the Republic itself.

The VOC's ships and garrisons, as well as its senior officials, were, in spiritual matters, all subordinate to the Dutch Reformed Church. Even though large numbers of foreigners were recruited, as seamen and soldiers, into the Company's service, neither Lutheran nor Catholic religious services were permitted in the VOC's ships and garrisons. In the period down to 1660, some 65 per cent of all the soldiers, and 35 per cent of the seamen, recruited for service in the East Indies by the VOC were foreign Europeans, and though the Dutch element increased somewhat between 1660 and 1700, the proportion of Germans and Scandinavians was always high. Yet not a single Lutheran church was permitted anywhere in the Dutch empire in Asia,[32] or in South Africa, during the seventeenth century, or the first part of the eighteenth.

Codes of discipline imposed in the garrisons, and on the ships of the VOC, and punishments for offences, were laid down by the States General.[33] On the VOC's ships, there were to be no words of blasphemy, or contempt for the Reformed faith or its preachers, under pain of fines and other forms of punishment. Permission could be obtained for absence from Reformed services, on certain grounds, but absence without permission meant being fined. There were punishments also for causing arguments about religion. Besides fines, offenders were apt to find themselves spending entire days working on the ship's pumps or sitting high in the masts. There were stiff penalties also for drunkenness and gambling.

Among non-Europeans under the VOC's rule in Asia the bulk were non-Christians and many of the rest Catholics. Up to a point, the Company had no choice but to accept liberty of worship among the non-European population. Yet, even as regards non-Europeans, the attitude of both the directors in the Republic and the ruling *raad* and governor-general, at Batavia, was far from being one of benign tolerance. In the first place, the Company, particularly in the early decades, saw itself as the declared foe of

---

[32] Troostenburg de Bruyn, *Hervormde kerk in Nederlandsch Oost-Indië*, 562–3.
[33] Bruijn and Lucassen, *Op de schepen*, 98–101, 158.

the Catholic Church. Catholic priests, mainly Portuguese, were expelled from Amboina, and other islands occupied in 1605, from Malacca in 1641, from the Dutch zone of Ceylon in 1647, and from the rest of coastal Ceylon after the Dutch completed their conquest in 1658.[34] Edicts were issued proclaiming severe punishment for harbouring Catholic priests. The Dutch authorities, even those who were not particularly devout, could not fail to be struck by the great impact which Portuguese missionaries had had in many of the territories which came under the rule of the VOC and the large number of Catholics among the native population on a number of Indonesian islands, in Ceylon, and at the southern tip of India. Inevitably, Catholicism was seen as a political and strategic, as well as spiritual, challenge to the interests of the Company. From the moment the Reformation began in Ceylon, in the 1640s, sizeable numbers of both Tamils and Sinhalese were converted, at least superficially, to the Dutch Reformed faith. But it was clear that it was practically only former Catholics who were susceptible to conversion, Buddhists, Hindus, and Muslims remaining largely impervious. At the same time, many former Catholics remained clandestine Catholics or waverers who could be pulled either way without difficulty. The Dutch Reformed Church in the East Indies, and their Catholic rivals, were thus competing for the same constituency, representing a large proportion of the native population especially on Amboina and in Ceylon. Only in the case of Taiwan did the Dutch succeed in winning a substantial flock for the Reformed Church among non-Christians where Catholicism had not previously prepared the way.[35]

The VOC's intolerance of Catholicism, and measures against Catholic priests, were thus a major plank of its imperial policy and remained so until late in the eighteenth century. There was, moreover, some similarity between the mechanics of the contest between Reformed Church and Catholicism in the Dutch East Indies and the Republic itself. Where a former Catholic population could not be cut off from regular contact with Catholic clergy nearby, as at the southern tip of India, overt Catholicism flourished. Where, as in Ceylon, access to Catholic clergy could be curtailed, the Reformed Church registered more success, at any rate until contact with Catholic clergy from outside became easier. The Reformed Church did best where, as in Amboina, there was a Catholic population that could be effectively insulated from the Catholic world outside. Eventually, Calvinism in Amboina, preached in Malay, put down enduring roots.[36]

[34] Aalbers, *Rijcklof van Goens*, 165, 219.
[35] Boxer, *Dutch Seaborne Empire*, 144–5.
[36] Troostenburg de Bruyn, *Hervormde kerk in Nederlandsch Oost-Indië*, 23, 381.

Besides Ceylon, Taiwan (until 1662), and Amboina, the Dutch Reformed Church in the East Indies achieved substantial success at Batavia, if not amongst the Chinese (who provided few converts to Calvinism), then certainly amongst the mixed and Malay-speaking population as well as the whites. In 1652, the number of Reformed preachers at Batavia was raised to five, in 1675 to seven, and in 1683 to ten; by 1730, the number had reached seventeen, more than in any Dutch city except Amsterdam.[37] The total number of Dutch Reformed preachers in the East always remained small but rose steadily, from seventeen, in 1647, to forty-one, in 1683, and forty-eight, by 1727. The preachers were supplemented, as in the homeland, by assistants called *ziecken-troosters* ('sick comforters') as well as school-masters who, in the east, were usually Tamils, Amboinese, or other natives.

Catholicism was combated with some effect at Batavia, Amboina, and in Ceylon, less so at Malacca, Timor, and in south India. But it was not only Catholicism and Protestant dissent that the Company sought to repress. If Buddhism and Hinduism had to be tolerated as necessary evils, the VOC adopted a markedly more hostile stance towards Islam. To an extent this was inherent in the religious dialectics of the East. Islam had begun to spread rapidly in the Indonesian archipelago, and to a lesser extent elsewhere in south Asia, during the sixteenth century, in reaction to the missionizing of the Catholic Portuguese. Under the Dutch, Islam continued to be seen by all concerned as a form of political (and economic), as well as theological, opposition to the Europeans. Although the Company's anti-Islamic placards had little effect in most of Indonesia in the long run, it was sporadically successful in checking the advance of Islam in places, notably Ceylon, where the Company was much severer towards Muslims than Buddhists and Hindus.[38]

Nor was the policy of the WIC in the Dutch empire of the Atlantic one of toleration. In Netherlands Brazil (1630–54), the WIC had granted Catholics liberty of conscience, as they were obliged to do under their States General charter, but not formal liberty of worship. When Dutch Brazil's one and only governor-general, Count Johann Maurits van Nassau-Siegen, nevertheless preferred to emulate Frederik Hendrik and show leniency regarding Catholic practice, he met with stiff opposition from the Calvinist consistory of Recife. Various restrictions on Catholic worship and proselyt-izing remained in force, though local Catholics did enjoy greater freedom than in the Republic. The exceptionally large (Sephardic) Jewish community which established itself, with the encouragement of the WIC, at Recife was

---

[37] Ibid. 13–14.   [38] Arasaratnam, *Dutch Power in Ceylon*, 220.

also granted more extensive freedom than they enjoyed in the United Provinces; but this too was opposed by the Reformed Church and was not regarded as a general concession applying in other WIC territories. In the Dutch possessions in America, the Jews made more rapid progress than other groups, owing to the special working relationship they developed with the WIC in commerce, and because Jews, unlike Catholics, Lutherans, and radical dissenters, could be religiously segregated from the rest of the population. Nevertheless, it was not until 1659 that the WIC granted liberty of worship for Jews at Curaçao, even though Jewish refugees had been leaving stricken Netherlands Brazil since 1645, many migrating to Barbados and other territories under the English.[39]

However, only Jews enjoyed formal liberty of worship, besides the Reformed Church, in Curaçao; moreover, with Brazil lost, Curaçao was, for some time, the only WIC territory where this freedom existed. During the third quarter of the seventeenth century, Jews enjoyed as much, or greater, freedom in certain of the English colonies as in the Dutch. When the Zeelanders captured Surinam, in 1667, some of the Jews living there migrated to other English colonies and those that stayed laboured under severe restrictions whilst the colony remained under the States of Zeeland, down to 1682.[40] It was only in that year, when the colony came under the control of the 'Society of Surinam', an organization controlled jointly by the WIC and city of Amsterdam, that the Jews acquired full liberty of worship in Surinam.

In New Netherland until the 1650s the position was the same as in South Africa subsequently: no other Church was allowed than the Dutch Reformed Church. Under the 1640 charter for New Netherland, the WIC had ruled that no other religion 'shall be publicly admitted in New Netherland except the Reformed as it is at present preached and practised by public authority in the United Netherlands'.[41] When in 1653, 'adherents of the Augsburg Confession' in Manhattan petitioned the governor, Pieter Stuyvesant, for permission to organize their own congregation, and appoint a preacher, Stuyvesant enquired of the *Heren XIX* who, pressed by the classis of Amsterdam (which had spiritual responsibility for the colony), answered negatively.[42] When this then led to repressive steps to break up Lutheran conventicles in the colony, the WIC ordered Stuyvesant to desist, ruling that Lutherans, and by implication other dissenters, were to possess 'free

---

[39] Emmanuel and Emmanuel, *History*, i. 45–8.
[40] Van der Linde, *Surinaamse suikerheren*, 102–31.
[41] Smith, *Religion and Trade*, 190–1.
[42] Ibid. 193–4.

religious exercise in their houses'. When the Lutheran community in Amsterdam then appealed to the WIC, requesting freedom of exercise for the Lutheran faith not only in New Netherland but all the Company's territories, the Reformed Church authorities at Amsterdam did all they could to prevent 'public worship' by Lutherans and not without success: the first Lutheran minister to reach New Netherland, sent by the Lutheran congregation in Amsterdam, was expelled by Stuyvesant, on the orders of the WIC, in 1659.

The first group of Jews to arrive in New Amsterdam were refugees from Brazil, who arrived in 1654. They were allowed to stay and trade, and practise their religion in their houses, but, the WIC ruled in 1656, could not own shops or build a synagogue.[43] But this was generous compared with the treatment meted out to radical dissenters. During the years 1658–62, Stuyvesant mounted a vigorous persecution of the group of Quakers who had settled on Long Island.

There was no Lutheran church in Curaçao, Surinam, or anywhere in the WIC's territories during the seventeenth century or at the beginning of the eighteenth, just as there were not in the territories of the VOC. Catholicism, too, was officially under a general ban even on Curaçao, where the Catholic religion had already been established, by the Spaniards, amongst the black and mixed population on the island, before the Dutch occupation in 1634. An effective ban against Catholic priests visiting Curaçao, from Venezuela, was maintained for several decades, the Church in Venezuela gaining access only from the 1670s.[44] In 1690, the WIC gave formal permission for priests to work on Curaçao provided they did not wear their vestments in public. There were few Catholics amongst Curaçao's white population, which included German Lutherans, as well as Dutch Reformed and numerous Sephardic Jews. But Catholicism rapidly became the main religion of the black population and poor half-castes. Thus a situation arose where the majority of the island's population was Catholic but yet, until 1730, no Catholic church could be built on the island.

---

[43] Ibid. 215–16.
[44] Cardot, *Curazao hispánico*, 393–4; Goslinga, *Dutch in the Caribbean*, 258.

PART IV

The Age of Decline, 1702–1806

❖

36

The Republic of the Regents, 1702–1747

❖

THE NEW REGIME

William III died at Hampton Court, in England, on 19 March 1702. The news was communicated to the people of the United Provinces by a prolonged tolling of church bells. Six days after his death, Heinsius, Pensionary of Holland, appeared before the States General, announcing that the States of Holland had decided to leave the stadholderate vacant. This was against the expressed wish of the dead monarch, who had already tried, in 1701, to persuade Holland to designate the young Frisian Stadholder, Johan Willem Friso (1687–1711), son of Hendrik Casimir, his successor as Stadholder of Holland.[1] But the Holland regents preferred to do without a Stadholder, and suspend the political functions of the stadholderate, precisely as in 1650. Ever since the death of Hendrik Casimir, in 1696, the childless William III had, in all provinces, been grooming Johan Willem Friso as his successor.[2] The Stadholder-king's last testament, opened in a special ceremony at The Hague, in May 1702, in the presence of the British and Prussian ambassadors, declared Johan Willem Friso William III's sole 'general heir'.

In this, as in other respects, the demise of William III heralded a profound change in the character of the United Provinces. Under William III's tutelage, the difference between the Republic under Stadholders, and without the stadholderate, had come to seem even more marked than formerly. After Leicester's departure, Oldenbarnevelt and the Holland regents had forged a fully republican regime, in which Holland had led the Union and controlled its foreign policy and resources. With his coup of 1618, Maurits had fundamentally altered the character of the state, reducing Holland to a passive role in decision-making, patronage, foreign policy, and matters of war and defence. The Stadholder and his entourage had replaced the States of Holland at the heart of government. This had continued under

[1] Rogier, 'Ware Vrijheid als oligarchie', 300.   [2] Guibal, *Johan Willem Friso*, 64–5.

Frederik Hendrik until, in the years 1646–8, under the leadership of Adriaen Pauw, a republican States party regime, with Holland making the decisions, had again emerged. This had then been briefly reversed by William II. But his early death led to the First Stadholderless period (1650–72), the classic era of the 'True Freedom', with Johan de Witt as the pre-eminent figure. Next, the upheavals of 1672 again transformed the Dutch state, concentrating power and influence in the hands of the Stadholder and his favourites, weakening the formal procedures of the Republic, and reducing the influence of regents linked with the republican tradition and the 'True Freedom'. This, in turn, had bred its own reaction and, in 1702, the 'True Freedom', the fully republican regime, was restored, this Second Stadholderless era lasting until 1747.

Thus, the year 1702 was a key divide in the history of the Republic not just because of the demise of William III and the onset of the War of the Spanish Succession (1702–13), the last great European conflict in which the Republic participated as a major power, but also for the release of pent-up tensions which had accumulated since 1672. In Holland, the change in the system of government occurred rather smoothly, with only a minimum of popular involvement, instantly producing a partial redistribution, and greater dispersal, of power and influence. In several towns, the *vroedschap* was re-elected so as to readmit former regents, or their younger relatives, excluded by the Stadholder since 1672. There was a minor disturbance or two at Haarlem.[3] At Leiden, the 'contract of correspondence' imposed by William III in 1685, was immediately discarded and replaced with a new 'contract' designed to minimize friction between the *vroedschap*'s rival States party and Orangist blocs, balancing contending family and clientage networks, by imposing an order of rotation of offices with greater formality and precision than had been attempted in the past.[4] Whereas, before, the Stadholder had regularly intervened in civic politics in Holland, to concentrate power in the hands of small, informal regent cliques, subservient to the stadholderate, now the objective was to disperse power, regularize rotation of offices, and stabilize relations between the regent blocs.

Holland's Pensionary, Anthonie Heinsius, was by 1702 an internationally renowned statesman of wide experience. Though he had worked closely with William III, he had never been a mere tool of the Stadholder and was deemed to have defended the interests of Holland—up to a point.[5] Never-

---

[3] Schutte, 'Republiek', 269.
[4] Prak, *Gezeten burgers*, 263–6.
[5] Lademacher, 'Wilhelm III von Oranien', 265–6.

theless, he was identified with the policies of the Stadholder-king and, after 1702, his influence diminished, though less than that of others of William III's close confidants. In the States of Holland, the balance of power tilted sharply away from the Stadholder's friends to the States party bloc. In the *ridderschap*, Baron Jacob van Wassenaar (1646–1707), leader of the anti-Orangist nobles, now became the presiding figure, arranging admittance of several other anti-Orangist nobles whom William III had kept out. The new 'contract of correspondence' at Leiden may have formalized rotation of offices, and balanced the blocs, but there was no doubt about which predominated in the years after 1702. Of all the Holland towns, Leiden now became the most vociferous in opposing the stadholderate and ambitions of Johan Willem Friso. At Amsterdam, William III's friends, Witsen and Hudde, had been re-elected burgomasters only a month before the Stadholder-king's death. But from that moment they were overshadowed by the leaders of the republican bloc in the *vroedschap*—Joan Huydecoper, Jacob Hinlopen, and the adroit Joan Corver.

William III's favourites did not abandon their power and influence, or opportunities for money-making, without a fight. They endeavoured to shore up their position with the argument that the United Provinces, on the brink of war with Bourbon France and Spain, needed an illustrious figure as captain-general and admiral, urging that the States General appoint Prince George of Denmark, consort of Queen Anne, the new monarch in England, to this high office.[6] The proposal, backed by Heinsius as well as Dijkvelt, Odijk, Bentinck, and Keppel, was designed to salvage some of their leverage by introducing a kind of surrogate Stadholder. Dijkvelt was sent to Amsterdam to win the *vroedschap* to the idea: the Amsterdam regents split; but Corver and Huydecoper carried the majority and the Orangists were defeated.

In contrast to 1651, the States of Friesland and Groningen made no effort to persuade the other provinces that they were obliged, under the terms of the Union of Utrecht, to appoint Stadholders. But the two northern provinces did advance the interests of their young Stadholder, wanting him acknowledged as 'Prince of Orange' and in May 1703 pressed for his appointment as a general of infantry in the army, with rank above that of the Republic's other generals, as preparation for eventual advancement to the captaincy-general and more stadholderates.[7] This was vigorously opposed by republican regents in Holland, Zeeland, and the eastern provinces. The

---

[6] Porta, *Joan en Gerrit Corver*, 38–9.
[7] ARH SG PR 387, p. 579. res. SF, 17 Mar. 1703.

Leiden *vroedschap* took the view that no special appointment or recognition should be conferred on Johan Willem Friso, since this would offend 'our great and powerful neighbour and ally', the king of Prussia.[8] The anti-Orangists deftly exploited the rift which had arisen as a result of William III's naming the Frisian Stadholder his general heir. For Johan Willem Friso's right to the legacy, lands, and title of 'Prince of Orange' was disputed by the new king of Prussia who (as son of Frederik Hendrik's eldest daughter, Louise Henriette) claimed the inheritance and title for himself, and, in March 1702, occupied Lingen.

Holland, through the States General, was in a position to arbitrate over the disputed inheritance and it suited Holland to drag the proceedings out. Indeed, the ensuing suit lasted thirty years. In the meantime, Holland and the other four provinces with no Stadholder, refused to address Johan Willem Friso as 'Prince of Orange' or 'Highness', or accord him the dignity that would be his due as Prince. The young Stadholder was made a general in the army but not placed above the other generals. A most delicate point was to avoid offending the king of Prussia. The States General could hardly refuse to accept the letters of this powerful ruler despite his emphatically adding 'Prince of Orange' to his titles. This was handled by accepting his letters but scrupulously omitting the title 'Prince of Orange' from the replies.[9]

The change in the structure of politics in 1702, however quietly accomplished, was fundamental. As one would expect, the redistribution of influence and patronage, dispersal of power, and formalization of decision-making also revived interest in the republican idea, ideological traditions of the States party bloc, and consultative institutions of the Republic. This was reflected in a wave of publications. There were the works of Emanuel van der Hoeven (*c*.1660–*c*.1728), who in 1705 published the first serious study of Johan de Witt, including official documents, and in 1706 his two-volume *Hollands Aeloude Vryheid*, arguing for a republic without Stadholders, glorifying Oldenbarnevelt and Grotius, and, when discussing medieval history, showing a strong bias in favour of the Hoeks (who had opposed the Burgundians and early Habsburgs). There was a new edition of the political works of Machiavelli (1703–5)[10] and Romeyn de Hooghe's two-volume *Spiegel van Staet* (1706) extolling the institutions of the Republic. There was also the *Diocletianus et Maximianus* (1704) by the great legal scholar Gerard

---

[8] GA Leiden Sec. Arch. 462, fos. 43–4. 87. res. 20 and 23 Mar. 1704.
[9] PRO SP 84/231, fo. 274. Dayrolle to Tilson, 29 June 1708.
[10] Haitsma Mulier, *Nederlandse gezicht van Machiavelli*, 13.

Noodt (1647–1725), a critique of corruption in criminal justice which was, in part, an attack on the corrupt methods of William III's *baljuws*.[11]

In Holland, the redistribution of power occurred peacefully without disrupting government and administration. This was not the case, though, in the four other provinces, which in 1702 resolved to discard their stadholderates in reaction to William III. Here the concentration of power in the Stadholder's hands, and those of his favourites, was too extensive and formalized for a smooth transition to a new framework to be possible. The Stadholder and his favourites had imposed systems of control on provincial, quarter, and town governments which had generated a considerable pool of discontent which soon led, especially in Gelderland and Zeeland, to widespread unrest.

Most of Zeeland now lapsed into turmoil. While Flushing and Veere adhered to their traditional Orangist stance, the other towns witnessed a fierce struggle between Orangist and anti-Orangist factions. A number of formerly Orangist regent families, such as the Van Citters and De Huybert, switched (albeit often only temporarily) to an anti-Orangist stance. The disturbances were often instigated by former regents, or members of families of regents, purged from the town councils in 1672, and (in Middelburg) in 1676, against rivals put in by William III who now refused to make way. As was traditional in Zeeland, both sides appealed to the citizenry and militias, Orangists rallying their following among the shopkeepers, seamen, and fishermen, anti-Orangists often among the more middle elements of the urban population. Skilled agitators appeared, distributing lampoons, in coffee-houses and taverns, stoking up political passion with their speeches, and organizing petitions.

The unrest began at Tholen, in April 1702, and spread to Goes and Middelburg. The principal agitator at Middelburg, Daniel Fannius, was a son of Johan de Witt's closest confidant in Zeeland and an uncompromising republican. The ferment incited by Fannius and his adherents in Middelburg's coffee-houses split the civic militia and led, in July 1702, first to riots and then to the purging of the Orangists from the *vroedschap*. By late 1703, however, Middelburg's Orangists, assisted by Flushing and Veere, had instigated a strong reaction, intent on recapturing the town hall and restoring orthodox Calvinist values.[12] Further rioting erupted, in January 1704, when Orangists briefly seized the town hall, but the 'new stream', as their opponents were called, rallied enough militia men and burghers to

[11] Van den Bergh, *Life and Work of Gerard Noodt*, 217–23.
[12] Van der Bijl, *Idee en interest*, 102–7.

drive them off. By the spring of 1704, the republicans, for the moment, enjoyed an unsteady ascendancy in the province.

Still more unruly were events in Gelderland. Like those of Utrecht and Overijssel, the States of Gelderland lost no time in cancelling the regulations William III had imposed when these provinces were reincorporated into the Union in 1674–5.[13] The structure of power, and political procedures, in Gelderland were supposed to revert to the situation as it had been before 1672, during the First Stadholderless period. But no moves were made by the States to remove the men whom William III had put in or restore the many regents and office-holders he had purged. A complicating factor was that, in the eastern provinces, the patrician oligarchy did not form an exclusive regent élite in the same way as in Holland and Zeeland. On important matters the *raad* in the eastern towns had for centuries been supposed to consult colleges of citizens' representatives, or *gemeenslieden*, who also, in varying degrees, exercised a role in annual elections of burgomasters and members of the *raad*. Since the sixteenth century, colleges of *gemeenslieden* exercised less influence than formerly. But they remained a significant element in civic life in Gelderland and Overijssel towns, as in the city of Groningen, a political forum for the citizenry and guilds.

William III had not only gained a firm grip on the States, quarter assemblies, and town councils but also the colleges of *gemeenslieden*. The subsequent re-emergence of the latter as representative bodies, capable of mounting pressure on civic government, was to be a key factor in eight-eenth-century Dutch political life. For it was in the eastern towns that there began the early stirrings of democratic tendencies which were to become a central feature of the Dutch scene in the 1780s and 1790s.[14] There was, in the eastern provinces in 1702, a stratum of civic society, affluent, literate— often highly articulate lawyers—who felt that William III and his favourites had stripped them of an influence in civic government to which they were entitled by tradition, privileges, and law.[15] At the outset of the First Stadholderless period, the Nijmegen *gemeenslieden* had opposed the efforts of the city *raad* to suppress their role, insisting that it was their duty to ensure that suitably qualified men, who were loyal members of the Re-formed Church, were elected to the *raad*.[16] One of the members of that college, in 1650, was the father of the republican jurist Gerard Noodt. In 1702, the *gemeenslieden* again saw themselves as upholders of an urban

---

[13] ARH SG PR 23. res. S.Geld. 8 Apr. 1702.
[14] Wertheim-Gijse Weenink, 'Een kwarteeuw burgerverzet', 410, 415.
[15] Van den Bergh, *Life and Work of Gerard Noodt*, 15.
[16] GA Nijmegen raad 102, fos. 513, 516, 524. res. 10, 11, 12, and 14 Dec. 1650.

representative tradition whose task was to ensure legitimate, and good, civic government.

The States of Gelderland abolished the *reglement* of 1675 soon after the Stadholder-king's death, but the province's town governments simultaneously tried, as they had after William II's death, in 1650, to end the role of the *gemeenslieden* as well. Beginning at Nijmegen, this provoked protest and agitation which was partly support for the *gemeenslieden* against the sitting regents but also an attempt by the men purged by William III, in and after 1674, to oust those whom he had put in control of the civic governments.[17] From Nijmegen, the rioting spread also to Tiel and Zaltbommel and before long the 'New Crew', as they were termed, dominated the Nijmegen quarter. The turmoil then spread to Zutphen and Arnhem. An added factor in the Arnhem quarter, where the *jonkers* exercised a high degree of leverage over the fiscal machinery, was a stirring up of the rural populace by the 'New Crew' in the city against the *jonkers*. The Arnhem *ridderschap* retorted by boycotting the quarter assembly.

By the spring of 1703, all three Gelderland quarters were in uproar and the unrest spread also to Utrecht, especially Amersfoort, where burgher and militia groups demanded that their representatives should again have the right to choose the magistracy, as they formerly had, before Charles V had incorporated Utrecht into the Habsburg Netherlands.[18] Armed burghers seized the city in July 1703. The States of Utrecht suppressed the movement with the aid of troops sent by the States General. There was unrest also in Overijssel, especially Deventer, where former patricians and *gemeenslieden*, backed by the guilds, wrested control from the men put in by William III.

A feature of the turmoil in the lesser provinces, in 1702–7, was the growing tendency towards political collaboration between disaffected groups in different provinces. A key orchestrator of anti-Orangist agitation was the Utrecht noble Godard Willem, heer van Welland, whom William III had purged from the Utrecht provincial government, in 1674. He emerged not only as leader of the anti-Orangist bloc in the States of Utrecht but a leading ally of radical republicans in both Zeeland and Gelderland. Opponents in Holland accused him of conspiring to subject Holland to rule by Utrecht, Gelderland, and Zeeland, together with Groningen and Overijssel. It is indeed striking that his outlook, and that of his allies, was infused with a marked strain of anti-Holland sentiment. The interplay between the various movements, moreover, was a matter of not only personalities but also ideas. Several radical pamphlets published at

---

[17] Brants, *Bijdrage*, 56–61.   [18] Wertheim-Gijse Weenink, *Burgers in verzet*, 29.

Middelburg, in 1703–4, deplored the effects of William III's regime on the Republic as a whole. In part, such publications were simply reviving the Louvestein ideology of 1650, De Witt, and the 'True Freedom'. But it is also true that they introduced a new element. Fannius, his allies in Zeeland, and the more radical 'New Crew' elements in Gelderland supplemented De Witt's 'True Freedom' with the notion *'majestas penes populum'*, that 'sovereignty had devolved upon the people', whose right it now was to make and unmake civic government in the public interest.[19]

For Holland, the unrest in the lesser provinces, especially in Gelderland, was inconvenient. With a great European war in progress, and a crucial struggle in the south Netherlands, the Generality needed stable domestic conditions and a smooth collection of revenues whereas, by 1704, Gelderland was paralysed and the regiments on Gelderland's *répartition* were no longer being paid. Yet, many Holland regents showed sympathy for the 'New Crew', and, even more, antipathy for their opponents, a factor which inhibited Generality intervention in the Gelderland troubles throughout the period 1703–6.

Meanwhile, the democratic tendency evident in Gelderland was spreading. In January 1703, the guilds of Harderwijk pressed the *raad* for restoration of all rights and powers which the *gemeenslieden* had exercised before 1672. In a petition drawn up in April, they demanded that henceforth, in Harderwijk, burgomasters and *raad* should be appointed by the *gemeenslieden* and guilds as was happening at Arnhem, Nijmegen, Wageningen, and other towns, and even that henceforth every citizen resident in the town should be eligible for election to the city government.[20] The *raad* at Harderwijk was purged by the guilds, in April 1703, six 'Old Crew' regents being expelled and seven new men brought in.

The struggle between the 'Old Crew' and 'New Crew' in Gelderland escalated further during 1704. In many towns there were gatherings and demonstrations of guild and militia members against the 'Old Crew'. In February 1704, armed guild members seized the Harderwijk town hall. In June 1704, with the *jonkers* boycotting the quarter assembly, the towns of the quarter agreed to begin collecting taxes in the countryside in defiance of the *ridderschap*. In August, the 'New Crew' *raad* at Arnhem raised a force of armed citizen volunteers to defend their gains in the city and the quarter.[21] The *ridderschap* also assembled a force, which approached Har-

[19] Van der Bijl, *Idee en interest*, 185–7.
[20] Vrielink, 'Harderwijk', 9–11.
[21] Ibid. 15–17.

derwijk. There was an armed clash at Putten. But still the States General held back from intervening.

A major weakness of the 'New Crew' movement in Gelderland was the ancient tension between the three head towns' of Gelderland—Arnhem, Nijmegen, and Zutphen—and the small towns of their respective quarters. This was a factor of considerable importance in the climax of the struggle in Gelderland which began in October 1707, when the 'New Crew' *raad* at Arnhem decided to send a citizen volunteer force, armed with cannon, to Wageningen to topple the 'Old Crew', who had just regained control there. The Arnhem militia seized Wageningen and arrested the 'Old Crew' magistrates. But most of the States of Gelderland condemned Arnhem, desired to suppress the burgher volunteer companies, and appealed to the States General. The States of Holland, finally losing patience, agreed to the sending in of Generality troops to end the disorder, the leading 'New Crew' cities, Arnhem and Nijmegen, failing to mobilize enough support in Holland, Zeeland, and Utrecht to block the decision. States General troops occupied Arnhem, in December 1707, and Nijmegen, in January 1708, suppressing the turmoil, arresting agitators, and expelling some 'New Crew' members from the two city councils. The final result in Gelderland was an unresolved and uneasy stalemate imposed by Holland.

In the last stages of the conflict in Gelderland, the 'Old Crew' drew strength from a noticeable revival of Orangist sentiment in the Republic, crystallizing around the figure of Johan Willem Friso, who reached his legal majority in August 1707. For some time Friesland had argued that the youth should be assigned a seat in the *Raad van State*, by virtue of being Stadholder of Friesland.[22] On reaching his majority, Johan Willem Friso claimed the seat 'his predecessors always possessed as Stadholders of Friesland and Groningen', but Holland, backed by Zeeland, Utrecht, Gelderland, and Overijssel, refused, arguing that Friesland and Groningen, each of which already had a seat on the *Raad*, should not have any advantage over the other provinces by virtue of having a Stadholder.[23] The latter, styled by his adherents the 'Prince of Orange', was now a major factor in the Republic's politics. In February 1708, he was formally proclaimed Stadholder, at Groningen, though the occasion was marred by a row between the city and Ommelands over his 'instructions'.

He was an able young man who, in more than one respect, aspired to follow in the footsteps of William III. In April 1709, he married Maria Louisa of Hesse-Cassel and—after having the princely quarters in Leeuwarden

[22] ARH SG PR 387, p. 736. SF to SF deputies at The Hague, 22 Aug. 1705.
[23] PRO SP 84/229, fo. 367. Dayrolle to Harley, 29 July 1707.

refurbished under the direction of Daniel Marot—installed his bride and court in that city in 1710.[24] He divided his time between Friesland, cultivating his interests at The Hague, and his career as a general in the States General's army, spending long periods in the allied camps in the south Netherlands, often with Marlborough. All the while he pursued his legal battle with the king of Prussia over the legacy of William III. If the king of Prussia was in a position to seize William III's possessions on the German side of the border, the Frisian Stadholder had the advantage on the Dutch side. In December 1710, the States of Gelderland found in his favour with regard to the palace at Het Loo.

But the hopes the Orangists pinned on Johan Willem Friso were dashed in July 1711. Summoned to The Hague, from the army, to assist the States General's efforts to negotiate a compromise with the Prussian king over William III's legacy, he capsized while sailing across the estuary, near Moerdijk, in a sudden storm and drowned. His remains, which took a week to find, were solemnly buried at Leeuwarden. A posthumous son—one day to become Stadholder of all the provinces—was born six weeks after his father's death, consoling dejected Orangists with the memory of the birth of William III, sixty-one years before, after his father's death. In accordance with the States of Friesland's decision of 1675 to make the Frisian stadholderate hereditary in the male line of Hendrik Casimir,[25] the infant automatically became Stadholder designate of Friesland and his mother, Maria Louisa, regent of the Frisian stadholderate. She christened the boy Willem Carel Hendrik Friso, deftly commemorating William III, Charles II of England, Frederik Hendrik, and the boy's father, all in one.

THE WAR OF THE SPANISH SUCCESSION, 1702–1713

For the United Provinces a great deal was at stake in the world struggle over the Spanish Succession which broke out in May 1702. In that month, the Republic declared war on France and her ally, Bourbon Spain, in alliance with Britain, Austria, and Prussia.

The Dutch entry into the war against the Bourbon monarchies has often been described as a continuation of the European policy of William III. This is not entirely untrue since William III's policy, since 1688, was based on achieving consensus with Amsterdam, and the States of Holland, and Holland was the driving force behind Dutch participation in the war of 1702–13. But Holland's interests were not the same as William III's and it

---

[24] Guibal, *Johan Willem Friso*, 136.　　[25] Ibid. 64–5.

was not the traditions of William III but the interests of Holland which determined the Dutch role in the new conflict.

At the moment of William III's death, two months before the outbreak of the war, the strategic position of the United Provinces, and the future of their overseas trading system, seemed more insecure, and in doubt, than at any point since 1672. The last Habsburg king of Spain, Carlos II, had died in 1700, leaving the throne of Spain and the Spanish empire in Europe, and the Americas, to the grandson of Louis XIV, who now became Philip V of Spain. Philip received backing from France in his bid to consolidate his grip over Spain and her empire. In 1701, French troops entered the south Netherlands and the Dutch were forced to evacuate their 'barrier' garrisons. There was now no longer a buffer between France and the Republic and no means by which the United Provinces could keep the Scheldt trade restrictions in force. Equally menacing to Dutch interests was the situation in Spain and the Spanish Indies. The merchants of Amsterdam, who dominated Dutch commerce with Spanish America, via Cadiz, and Curaçao, took the view that a Bourbon king in Spain meant that the Spanish market, and Spain's trade and colonies, would, sooner rather than later, come under French control. To an extent, this had already happened. In 1701, Philip V transferred the *asiento*—the monopoly of the slave traffic to Spanish America—from a Portuguese consortium which had co-operated with the WIC, and bought a large percentage of its slaves in Curaçao, to the French Guinea Company.[26] During the years 1700–2, the confidence of Dutch (and English) merchants trading with Spain and Spanish America had slumped to such a point that they had closed down their warehouses in Cadiz, Seville, Alicante, and Malaga and transferred responsibility for their merchandise in the Spanish Indies to neutral Genoese and Hamburg firms.[27] By means of a war to remove the Bourbon claimant to the Spanish throne, Holland's regents and merchant élite aimed to restore the favourable pre-1700 position of the Dutch in commerce of the Spanish Indies and confirm the Scheldt restrictions, as well as achieve strategic security, curb French power, and force Louis to moderate France's trade tariffs.

It seemed vital to check France and reverse the Bourbon Succession in Spain. But it was scarcely less vital to prevent the Republic's nominal ally, Britain, making all the gains outside Europe, should the Bourbon powers be defeated. Britain was now rapidly emerging as a faster-growing and more dynamic maritime, colonial, and commercial power than the Republic, and

[26] Palacios Preciado, *Trata de negros*, 136–8.
[27] ARH SH 2548 fos. 138v, 155, Dutch consul at Cadiz to SG, 14 and 29 Mar. 1701.

rivalry between the English and Dutch, especially in India, West Africa, and the trade of Spanish America, was as acute as ever.

At the same time, it was necessary to forge a *modus vivendi*, an acceptable balance of power in the north-west German borderlands along the Republic's eastern frontier. For the old power vacuum in these regions which had so well served Dutch interests, and for so long, was now definitely gone. Between 1591 and the mid 1630s, the Dutch and Spain had balanced each other, both garrisoning numerous towns, in different parts of the border zone. During the 1630s, the Spaniards had evacuated Lingen, Lippstadt, and Hamm, and been ejected from Cleves, so that from the late 1630s, until 1702, the Republic alone had dominated the belt of territory from Cleves-Mark and Moers, in the south, to East Friesland, in the north, albeit the prince-bishop of Münster had seriously challenged this Dutch hegemony during the 1660s and early 1670s. Since the prince-bishop's defeat in 1674, Dutch influence had been generally dominant not only politically and economically but, in the Calvinist areas, also in religion, and in culture through the entire zone. But in 1702 Prussia emerged as the principal power in the border regions.

On the death of William III, King Friedrich I of Prussia annexed the counties of Lingen and Moers, on the grounds that Frederik Hendrik's last testament had stipulated, should his direct male descendants become extinct, that the legacy of the House of Orange-Nassau, in his line, should fall to the descendants of his eldest daughter, Louise Henriette, wife of the Great Elector.[28] The States General and States of Overijssel protested but the king deterred Dutch counter-pressure by threatening to withdraw from the alliance against the Bourbons. The differences between the Republic and Prussia, and Prussian primacy in the region, grew with the campaigns of 1702–3, in which Prussian troops conquered most of the former Roermond quarter of Gelderland from the Bourbons, including the city of Geldern, which was now permanently annexed to Prussia.[29] Dutch troops secured Roermond and a few other enclaves but the entire relationship between the Republic and Prussia in the border zone remained highly uncertain.

In terms of men and resources, the Republic mounted the largest and most sustained military and logistical effort in its history, during the war of 1702–13. The Generality's army was expanded from its peacetime strength of 40,000 to over 100,000 men. To finance this effort, Generality expenditure and the contributions of the provinces rose to unprecedented levels. Yet, despite the raising of expenditure and troop-levels, it was clear the Republic

---

[28] Ter Kuile, 'Graafschap Lingen', 27.
[29] Jappe Alberts, *Gesch. van de beide Limburgen*, ii. 52.

was failing to keep pace with the growth of the armies, and power, of France, Britain, Prussia, and Austria. Early on in the new contest, the regents had to adjust to the Republic's occupying a less senior position in the allied coalition than during the previous war. On land, Britain, Austria, and Prussia all provided more troops, in proportion, than they had previously, while at sea Britain's preponderance, inherent in the circumstance that the Dutch had to commit a larger proportion of their war expenditure to their land forces, became ever more marked. The Anglo-Dutch naval agreement of April of 1689, whereby the two maritime powers were to provide capital ships for joint operations in a ratio of five to three,[30] ensured and formalized a steadily widening gap in naval might and resources.

The Republic's army had never been so large, being more than double that of the British on the Continent: over 100,000 men as against 40,000. In 1708, the Dutch army reached its all-time peak for the early modern period of 119,000 as against some 70,000 British.[31] To achieve this the provincial assemblies borrowed heavily from the public through provincial bonds, expanded the standing army of 45,000 to 75,000 men, supplementing this with some 42,000 men hired in contingents from the German Protestant principalities. About 15,000 temporarily hired men were paid from contributions exacted in the occupied areas of the southern Netherlands. Marlborough was appointed overall commander of the allied armies in the Low Countries. But, under the secret Anglo-Dutch agreement of June 1702, he was not allowed to move, or commit, the Dutch forces without the assent of both the Dutch generals and the States General's 'deputies in the field'.[32] The latter were instructed by the Generality to co-operate with Marlborough but refuse to participate in anything contrary to the interests or dignity of the United Provinces.

The Dutch were still a great power and major partner in the alliance against France. Yet the Republic's relative decline was already apparent during the opening years of the War of the Spanish Succession. Britain now provided a considerably larger share of the subsidies paid to the Emperor, and allied German principalities and sent more troops, and money, to the war in the Iberian peninsula, though Dutch troops also participated in the capture of Gibraltar. (Until 1713, Gibraltar was considered part of the Spain of 'Charles III', jointly occupied by the British and Dutch—there was even a 'music hall' at Gibraltar for the entertainment of the Dutch

---

[30] Warnsinck, *Vloot van den koning-stadhouder*, 21, 77.
[31] Zwitzer, 'Militie van den staat', 176.
[32] Jones, *Marlborough*, 63.

troops—rather than British.) There were also Dutch contingents in the allied army in Catalonia.

Ever since the 1650s the States party-faction had been drawn to the idea of appointing a foreign general to command the Dutch army, a figure militarily competent but incapable of challenging the Holland regents in domestic politics. Hence, to an extent, the appointment of Marlborough as joint commander in the Low Countries can be seen as part of the political reaction following the death of William III in 1702, foreshadowed by the schemes to appoint Turenne, or a Swedish general, in the 1650s. William III had gained a tighter hold over the Dutch army than any previous Stadholder and been able to dispense with the system of 'deputies in the field'. Also part of the reaction of 1702, these were now restored, though in place of the committee of seven or eight usual in the decades before 1672 there were now only four: one representing Holland and three for the other six provinces chosen in rotation.[33] Yet there was no hiding the fact that the appointment of Marlborough also marked a form of subordination of Dutch power to that of Britain.

It rapidly became clear that this new conflict, with its immense cost, the collapse of trade with the vital French, Spanish, and Spanish American markets, and the severe disruption of navigation to the Mediterranean, was causing unprecedented damage to the Dutch trading system, cities, and industries.[34] The States of Holland refused to continue with the Anglo-Dutch trade embargo on France and in 1704 the States General reached agreement with Louis XIV for a partial resumption of Franco-Dutch trade during the war.[35] But this provided alleviation mainly for agricultural exports and the wine trade. France, like Spain, continued to exclude Dutch manufactures and colonial goods. Awareness of the gravity of the slump was widespread throughout the Republic. Yet, despite this, merchants, manufacturers, and the public remained solidly behind the States of Holland in going on with the war.[36] Amsterdam merchants were convinced that the Dutch trading system of past decades could not survive without the defeat of France and removal of the Bourbon king from the Spanish throne, closure of the Scheldt, and restoration of Dutch commerce with Spanish America. Dislodging Philip V, and securing the Austrian candidate 'Charles III', in Spain, the south Netherlands, and American viceroyalties seemed a prize on which it was worth staking immense effort, sacrifice, and funds.

---

[33] Van Slingelandt, *Staatkundige geschriften*, iv. 83–4.
[34] Israel, *Dutch Primacy*, 359–76.
[35] Ibid. 364–5.
[36] PRO SP 84/229. fo. 456v; Helvetius, 'Mémoire', 185.

For, if the Bourbon Succession was not reversed, it seemed the old system would be done for anyway. Consequently, the anti-Orangist faction in the Holland *ridderschap*, and anti-Orangist regents, like the merchants, concurred wholeheartedly with Heinsius and Keppel: France and Bourbon Spain had to be defeated, in conjunction with Britain, Prussia, and Austria, and new guarantees and terms of trade arranged in the south Netherlands, Spain, and Spanish America.[37]

Despite the grievous slump, the War of the Spanish Succession appeared to succeed, in the early years, beyond the Amsterdam merchants' wildest expectations. Commencing with Marlborough's sensational victory over the French at Blenheim (1704), the allies went from victory to victory. The year 1706 saw the culmination of an almost miraculous string of military and naval successes. Anglo-Dutch forces, supported by Prussians, crushed the French army at Ramillies, freeing nearly all of the south Netherlands from Bourbon control. During the summer, the allied armies based in, and supported by, Catalonia and Portugal overran much of central Castile and captured Madrid. At the same time, the allied fleet gained control of the Mediterranean, while an Anglo-Dutch mixed occupation was established in Flanders and Brabant with its administration in Brussels, in which the Dutch interest predominated, especially in the economic sphere. Dutch economic control of the south in the years 1706–13 was regarded in The Hague as a partial compensation for the rapidly growing British ascendancy, political and economic, over Portugal, Catalonia, Savoy, and in Gibraltar, Minorca, and other conquered places in Spain. Brussels was forced, under Dutch pressure, to restore the Spanish Netherlands tariff list of 1680, a list favourable to Dutch commerce.[38]

But the States of Holland sought, as their reward for their investment in the war, and attendant sacrifices, not only to turn the south into a captive market of the Dutch trading system, a sort of equivalent to Britain's dominance of Ireland and Portugal, but to limit future Habsburg political control by means of new and more extensive 'Barrier' provisions designed to create a mixed Dutch–Habsburg political condominium. As originally envisaged in 1706, Holland wanted, in exchange for guaranteeing the Protestant Succession in Britain, British support for a Dutch right to garrison whichever, and as many, towns and fortresses in the south Netherlands as the States General chose.[39] In its final form (October 1709), the 'Barrier treaty' between the Republic and Britain exchanged a Dutch

[37] Aalbers, 'Factieuze tegenstellingen', 419–20.
[38] Huisman, *Belgique commerciale*, 69–72.
[39] Geikie and Montgomery, *The Dutch Barrier*, 49–51.

guarantee of the Protestant Succession in Britain, for a British guarantee of a future Dutch 'Barrier' in the south, to consist of a substantial number of towns and forts. These formed three groups: first, a group of strongholds—including Ghent, Lier, and Damme—flanking the southern side of the Scheldt estuary and Bruges–Damme canal, designed to bolster Dutch control of the estuary and a line of communications with the outer line of garrisons facing France; secondly, Ieper, Nieuwpoort, Lille, Tournai, and Valenciennes, securing Dutch control of the western end of Flanders and Walloon Flanders; and finally, further south, Charleroi and Namur, intended to secure Dutch control of the Meuse and Sambre valleys.[40] To finance the upkeep of these garrisons, the Dutch were to possess the revenues of any recovered former parts of the Habsburg Netherlands under French control at the time of the death of Carlos II plus an additional lump sum to be paid each year by the provinces of the Spanish Netherlands as they were in 1700. Finally, all restrictions applying to the Scheldt stipulated in the peace of Münster of 1648 were confirmed.

But if the war prospered in the south Netherlands, Germany, and Italy, it went badly in Spain and the New World. The Castilian population backed Philip, as his Habsburg rival, 'Charles III', increasingly came to be seen as an invader and ally of Catalans, Valencians, and Portuguese, as well as of Protestants and Jews. Philip V recaptured Madrid. The allied armies in Spain were driven back by the Franco-Castilian armies, into Catalonia and Portugal. Eventually, French fortunes recovered somewhat also on the northern front. By 1710, this first truly global war had turned into a vast deadlock which exhausted all the participants, especially the French and Dutch.

For several years, until 1710, Louis endeavoured to break the coalition ranged against him by offering the Dutch a separate peace advantageous to them, a strategy reminiscent of that he had successfully pursued in 1677. During several rounds of secret Franco-Dutch talks, culminating in the Geertruidenberg negotiations, of the spring of 1710, Louis declared himself ready to accept Philip's removal from the Spanish throne and recognize 'Charles III', if Philip were compensated with the Habsburg territories in Italy, and that the Dutch should have their 'Barrier', the French tariff of 1664, and other advantages. The Dutch leadership showed keen interest. But the talks of 1709–10 never seemed likely to succeed.[41] Quite apart from the prospect of incurring the bitter enmity of Britain and Austria, there was simply too much distrust of Louis amongst the regents. What if the Dutch

---

[40] Ibid. 156–8.　　[41] Stork-Penning, *Het grote werk*, 275, 301–2, 376.

laid down their arms, breaking with their allies, and Louis broke his promises to the Republic? The Sun King's record in such matters was far from reassuring. A further stumbling block was that of how Philip would actually be removed from Spain. Louis refused to join in any military operation to force his grandson to give up his Spanish possessions. In the final analysis, the most influential Holland regents—Heinsius, Corver, and the Pensionary of Gouda, Bruno van der Dussen—saw no alternative but to reject the French offer and fight on with Britain and Austria.[42]

After 1710 Louis, tired of the Dutch, focused his attention on London. When it emerged, during the formal negotiations between the powers at the peace congress at Utrecht in 1712, that France and Britain had struck a deal between themselves, bitter disillusionment swept the Republic as well as Austria. It transpired that the Tories, now in power in Britain, were willing to allow Philip V to remain king of Spain and the Spanish Indies in return for extensive advantages for Britain in particular, including Gibraltar, Minorca, and the slaving *asiento* for the Spanish Indies. There were anti-British riots at The Hague and talk of a Fourth Anglo-Dutch War. Together with Austria, the Republic briefly tried to continue the war against France, without Britain, but the remaining allies found both their forces and funds insufficient. The regents were left with no choice but to accept the Peace of Utrecht (1713) as tailored by Britain and France.

THE AUSTRIAN NETHERLANDS AND THE NORTH AFTER 1713

During the period from 1659 until 1701 the south remained locked into a position of strategic and economic subordination to the United Provinces. The Spanish Crown openly admitted its inability to defend the south, against France, without Dutch help. The treaty of Münster guaranteed the permanent closure of the Scheldt to maritime traffic and a variety of other economic restrictions on the south. Anxious to court the Dutch, the tariff lists adopted by the Spanish Crown in the south Netherlands, in 1669 and 1680, continued to favour the entry into the south of Dutch manufactures, fish products, Baltic materials, and East India goods.[43]

It was a politico-economic relationship expedient for both Spain and the Dutch but, in many ways, prejudicial to the commerce, shipping, and manufactures of the south. Psychologically, it had the effect of widening the gulf between north and south, generating both popular resentment,

---

[42] Porta, *Joan en Gerrit Corver*, 67–9.
[43] Despretz-Van de Casteele, 'Het protectionisme', 307.

reinforced by the religious difference, and deep frustration amongst the merchants and manufacturers of Antwerp, Brussels, Bruges, and Ghent. The advent of Max Emmanuel—who nurtured the ambition of eventually succeeding Carlos II, as sovereign in the south Netherlands, and wished to bolster the region's resources and strategic potential, for his own eventual benefit—was the signal for what may be deemed the first political revolt of the south against the economic and strategic tutelage of the north. On Bergeyck's initiative, the civic élites were consulted, and plans laid, and, in 1699, the regime in Brussels published a package of mercantilist measures designed to free the south from economic subjection to the north.[44] These included high tariffs against Dutch, and other foreign, manufactures, and steps to compel the Flemish linen producers to cease sending their un-finished linens to Holland for bleaching and distribution. The pressure to break away from tutelage to the north gained momentum with the death of Carlos II, in 1700. The Bourbon Succession enjoyed strong support, at all levels of society, in the south Netherlands; for the new regime could be expected to make sweeping changes in administration and institutions and, not least, put an end to commercial and maritime subordination to the Dutch. Philip entrusted care over his interests in the country to Louis, and when French troops then invaded the south, in February 1701, they were welcomed by the authorities and local populace, who helped them to enter the Dutch-garrisoned 'Barrier' towns and take them over, forcing the Dutch to evacuate their forces without a fight.[45]

The installing of Philip V's French-backed regime in Brussels, in 1701, did indeed precipitate a flurry of far-reaching changes. Bergeyck, who had lost no time in declaring his support for the Bourbon Succession, was made superintendent of finances and minister of war, becoming the mastermind of the Franco-Spanish-Bavarian alliance in the Low Countries. Whilst Max Emmanuel was absent in Bavaria in the crucial years of reform (1701–4), Bergeyck was, in effect, acting governor-general on behalf of Philip V.[46] In two years he built up, from scratch, a new South Netherlands army organized according to a general code of military practice in 134 articles which he drew up and published in December 1701. After obtaining approval from Versailles, he abolished the three Habsburg 'Collateral Councils', in the summer of 1702, replacing them with a single royal council of only six members, directly presided over by the governor-general, or his proxy, which meant, in practice, by himself. A new tariff regime was in place by April 1703.

⁴⁴ Ibid. 311.   ⁴⁵ De Schryver, *Jan van Brouchoven*, 228.   ⁴⁶ Ibid. 478.

Inevitably, the raising of troops, and laying on of new taxes, somewhat diminished the initial enthusiasm for the new order, as did the adoption of a strongly anti-Jansenist policy in church and intellectual matters in accordance with Louis's inclinations.[47] Nevertheless, the regime retained the support of the provincial States and civic élites. That the reforms proved short-lived, as well as far-reaching, was purely the result of military defeat. For everything changed with the crushing reverse suffered by the French and south Netherlands forces at the hands of the Anglo-Dutch army at Ramillies, near Tienen, on 23 May 1706. So weakened were the French, by this defeat, that contemporaries called it a 'revolution', an event which transformed the situation in the Low Countries fundamentally and at a stroke. In a matter of days, Leuven, Brussels, Mechelen, Antwerp, Ghent, Bruges, and Oudenaarde opened their gates to the allies and recognized 'Charles III' as king of Spain and ruler of the south Netherlands. By July 1706, when Ostend surrendered, only the three remaining Walloon provinces—Hainault, Namur, and Luxemburg—plus Nieuwpoort remained in Max Emmanuel's hands.

Bergeyck and Max Emmanuel transferred what remained of the administration of the Bourbon south Netherlands to Mons. At Brussels an Anglo-Dutch condominium was established to administer Flanders, Brabant, and Limburg provisionally in the name of 'Charles III'. The new royal council established in 1702 was promptly abolished and the three Habsburg 'Collateral Councils' restored. British and Dutch garrisons were posted in all the main towns. Almost immediately the States of Holland also took steps to ensure the cancellation of Bergeyck's tariffs and mercantilist measures.[48] The old tariff list was reintroduced by the new Brussels regime as early as July 1706. But not satisfied with this, Holland subsequently arranged for the 1680 list to be replaced with that of 1669 which was still more favourable to Dutch interests. If in the case of Portugal, in 1703, under the Methuen treaty, the British won most of the commercial advantages at the expense of the Dutch, under the arrangements imposed on Flanders and Brabant, in 1706, it was the Dutch who gained most in point of trade, as indeed was widely complained of in Britain.[49]

Neither the allied garrisons, nor the new administrative, fiscal, and tariff arrangements, were to the liking of the Flemish and Brabantine towns. From Mons, Bergeyck skilfully played on the disaffection, building a

[47] Houtman-de Smedt, 'Zuidelijke Nederlanden', 333.
[48] Veenendaal, *Het Engels-Nederlands condominium*, 71–3.
[49] Ibid.

formidable web of pro-Bourbon conspiracy.[50] Through collusion with
elements of the citizenry, the French succeeded in surprising, and seizing,
both Ghent and Bruges in July 1708. It cost Marlborough two lengthy sieges
before he regained the towns early in 1709. The Anglo-Dutch condominium
restored its grip. But there are many indications that hostility to the allies
in the Flemish and Brabant towns remained widespread down to, and after,
the end of the war and that this became a factor in weakening the Dutch,
and strengthening the Austrian position, in the post-1713 negotiations to
determine the future of the south Netherlands.

At the end of the war Philip V remained on the throne of Spain. But the
south Netherlands, after virtually two centuries, were detached from Spain
and assigned to the Emperor albeit under various limitations to satisfy the
Dutch and also Britain. The south thus now became the 'Austrian Netherlands'. Under the Austro-Dutch treaty of Antwerp, of November 1715, the
Emperor solemnly accepted Spain's obligation to abide by the treaty of
Münster of 1648, including the closure of the Scheldt to maritime traffic,
and the 1680 tariff list, an agreement which provided the basis for a renewed
Dutch trade supremacy which was to continue for several decades.[51]

Another major issue, of vital concern to the Dutch, settled through
arduous negotiation at the end of the war, was that of the restoration of the
cordon of Dutch-garrisoned 'Barrier' towns. Under the treaty of Antwerp,
the Emperor agreed that he and the Republic would be jointly responsible
for the defence of the Austrian Netherlands, that the land would be
defended by a standing force of 35,000 Austrian and Dutch troops in
peacetime, of which 14,000, or two-fifths, would be Dutch, a considerable
increase on the numbers (around 8,000) of Dutch troops stationed in the
Barrier towns under the 1697 peace treaty. The States General, which took
the view that the Grand Alliance of 1702 had together conquered the
Spanish Netherlands so that they should be a 'rampart and Barrier to
separate France from the provinces of the States General', had expected to
obtain rights not only in the Barrier towns proper but also at Ghent and
elsewhere in Flanders to secure their lines of communication, and extend
their influence.[52] This, though, the Emperor resolutely opposed, backed by
the British, who were anxious to deny the Dutch control over the canal
network linking Ostend, Bruges, and Ghent, the chief artery for British
manufactures entering the south Netherlands. Nor did the Dutch obtain as
many Barrier towns as they had hoped. The 'Barrier' of 1715 extended from

[50] De Schryver, *Jan van Brouchoven*, 355–8.
[51] Huisman, *La Belgique commerciale*, 69–73.
[52] Geikie and Montgomery, *The Dutch Barrier*, 326.

MAP 15. The Dutch 'Barrier' in the Austrian Netherlands as agreed in 1715

Veurne, near the coast, via Fort Knokke, Ieper, Waasten, Menin, and Tournai, to Namur (see Map 15).[53] In these towns the States General were entitled to post military governors, and control the administration, but not to establish the public practice of the Reformed faith. Protestant services were countenanced under the treaty only in private homes, on the same basis as in the reign of Carlos II. Finally, the Dutch were assigned an annual subsidy of one and a quarter million guilders from the Austrian Netherlands revenues towards the upkeep of their Barrier garrisons.

A further matter resolved through negotiation after the war was the future of the former Roermond quarter, or Overkwartier (Upper Gelderland), an area retained by Spain in 1648 which was claimed by the Dutch but which

[53] Ibid. 356–7.

had been under Prussian occupation since 1702. Prussia, having annexed Moers and Lingen in 1702, seemed well on the way towards amassing an extensive territory in, and adjoining, the Low Countries, a prospect which caused the States General deep unease. But, here again, the Dutch were thwarted, the British, for their own reasons, supporting Prussia's claims. Under the final partition, the Dutch acquired only Venlo and Stevensweert, with partial sovereignty over Roermond, the proviso in that city being that Catholic churches and property were to remain intact. Part of what remained went to Austria but most, including Geldern, was annexed to Prussia.

The first governor-general of the Austrian Netherlands was Prince Eugene of Savoy, one of the outstanding men of the age, who held the post for a decade (1716–25). A famous soldier and administrator, he was also known as a connoisseur of art and books with a taste for the ideas of the Early Enlightenment. However, his influence in Brussels was limited since he was absent much of the time in Hungary, fighting the Turks. In contrast to the flurry of changes following the introduction of the Bourbon regime, in 1701, the transition to Austrian rule, in the years after 1713, brought little immediate alteration to the status quo reimposed by the Anglo-Dutch condominium in 1706, apart from somewhat more vigorous direction, from the court at Brussels, than had been the case under the Spanish regime after 1659.

Nevertheless, enthusiasm for the new regime rapidly cooled under the autocratic rule of Eugene's lieutenant and minister plenipotentiary, the Italian Ercole di Turinetti, marquis de Prié. In the first place, the Barrier treaty itself was unpopular, being widely seen as the sacrificing, by the Emperor, of the interests of the southern provinces, for the sake of his wider statecraft and dynastic concerns.[54] The provisions regarding the Scheldt, and tariffs, were much disliked, as was the subsidy to the Dutch Republic. Secondly, the country rapidly tired of the Dutch and Austrian garrisons on its soil. Thirdly, under instructions from Vienna, Prié pushed hard on the fiscal front and was soon being accused of violating the privileges of the towns. Disillusionment and fiscal pressure combined led to a series of disturbances in 1717–18 in Ghent, Antwerp, and especially Brussels, in which resentment at high bread prices fuelled opposition to the Austrian authorities. There were several riots in which the residences of a number of officials and grain merchants were pillaged. But the unrest frightened the civic élites and, with their support, the government quickly mastered the

---

[54] Hasquin, 'Temps des assainissements', 79.

situation, in the spring of 1719. The crack-down was relatively moderate, however, only a handful of rioters being executed, together with one of the prime instigators of the unrest, François Anneessens. Some weeks later, Prié wrote triumphantly to Eugene that the 'populace se tient fort en repos et n'a fait le moindre mouvement après qu'elle a été intimidée par cette exécution'.[55]

In the economic sphere, the new regime steered a middle course, neither openly opposing, nor actively abetting, Dutch commercial dominance. The Emperor was bound by treaty regarding the Scheldt estuary, and tariffs, and knew that any repudiation of these undertakings would destroy the whole basis of Austro-Dutch co-operation in the Low Countries. Nevertheless, Eugene and his successors did find ways to support the merchants and manufacturers of the south Netherlands. The most celebrated venture was the setting up, in December 1722, of the Imperial East India Company in the Austrian Netherlands, commonly known as the 'Ostend Company'. The south's merchants had been investing in East India voyages ever since 1714 on a small scale; now, with official backing, they attempted to build something more substantial. In the mid- and late 1720s about a dozen ships sailed to Canton, for tea, and Bengal for silks and calicoes. Prince Eugene himself invested heavily in the enterprise. But the high hopes were soon soured. A mixture of commercial error and Anglo-Dutch counter-measures undermined the Company's position and, in 1731, the Emperor, who then needed Anglo-Dutch support in the European arena, consented to suppress the Company.

Eugene was succeeded by the Emperor's elder sister, Maria Elisabeth (1725–41). This corpulent lady, sporting the famous Habsburg protruding chin, convened a meeting of the States General, in Brussels, at the outset of her term, which was to be the last in the Austrian Netherlands until the turmoil of 1789–90. She renewed the privileges of the southern provinces, confirming that it was not her, or her brother's, purpose to alter the existing institutional framework in the land. But she came with decided ideas on religious and cultural matters and rapidly established a grander (and more expensive) court in Brussels than the south had seen since the mid-seventeenth century. Maria Elisabeth aspired to be a new Isabella, an illustrious head, presiding over the life of the country, and a grand patroness of the arts. Certainly, a new era had begun but there were now neither the resources, nor the need, for an extensive programme of building, and the arts at Antwerp, Ghent, and Bruges were at low ebb. The age of Rubens

[55] Ibid. 81.

and Van Dyck had long since passed and so had their successors; in most respects, the south had become distinctly lack-lustre in painting and all the decorative arts. Nevertheless, Maria Elizabeth had a considerable impact. She introduced the stiff formalism of the Viennese court and an array of Italian and central European artists and musicians who imparted a quite new tone to cultural life in the south. A particular favourite of the archduchess was the Brussels opera, founded in the time of Max Emmanuel, her taste being for Italian opera. Yet, few large projects of any sort were embarked on under Maria Elisabeth. Until the 1750s, there was something distinctly provisional about the courtly culture of the south. Even after the disastrous fire, in 1731, which destroyed the Burgundian-Habsburg palace in Brussels (and along with it several works of Rubens), the archduchess merely contemplated building a new palace without actually commissioning any building.

TABLE 43. *The governors-general of the Austrian Netherlands, 1716–1794*

Governor or regent	Relation to Austrian ruler	Dates
Prince Eugene of Savoy		1716–25
Archduchess Maria Elisabeth	sister of Emperor Charles VI	1725–41
Charles Alexandre of Lorraine	brother-in-law of Maria Theresa	1741–80
Archduchess Maria Christina	sister of Joseph II	1780–93
Archduke Karl	third son of Leopold II	1793–4

It was, above all, in the sphere of religion and intellectual life that Maria Elisabeth made her presence felt. If, in the arts, she followed Eugene in promoting Italian and central European influence, in church and academic affairs she sharply reversed the pro-Jansenist intellectually liberal stance of her predecessor. Eugene had openly favoured the Jansenists and regalist opposition to the papal claims set out in the Bull *Unigenitus* of 1713.[56] He had also protected the Leuven jurist Zeger Bernard van Espen (1646–1728), chief spokesman of the anti-ultramontane wing of the Catholic Church in the south Netherlands, whose tracts stressed the duty of Catholic princes to minimize the jurisdiction of external ecclesiastical authorities over their subjects. The archduchess, by contrast, guided by her Hungarian Jesuit confessor, Stephan Amiodt, who was continually at her side (even at the opera), pursued a rigidly anti-Jansenist, anti-regalist, pro-papal line.[57] She purged the university of Leuven with such vigour that Van Espen and a dozen other Jansenist academics were forced into exile in the United

[56] Roegiers, 'Jansenistische achtergronden', 431–2.   [57] Ibid. 433–4.

Provinces, the traditional refuge of Jansenists. Several prelates and abbeys were investigated and disciplined. Censorship of books was tightened to try to shut out of the country the works of the early French Enlightenment as well as anything smacking of Jansenism or regalism. But her anti-Jansenist drive ended with her governorship. Under her successor, Charles Alexandre, Jansenism once again returned to favour at Brussels.

Especially under Charles-Alexandre the central administration of the Austrian Netherlands became more streamlined and the first moves were made towards institutional rationalization in some aspects of provincial and fiscal administration. While the three Collateral Councils restored in 1706 and again, after a brief attempt to do away with them, in 1725, remained in form, after 1740, the Council of State seldom met and control passed definitively to a now reduced Secret Council consisting of six officials under the chairmanship of a *chef-président*.[58] This shift was part of a wider tendency, on the part of the Austrian regime, to dispense with the services of the local nobility and rely on professional officials. The third body, the Council of Finance, remained unchanged, consisting of four officials under the treasurer-general. Ever more prominent at Brussels was the secretary of state and war, the governor-general's powerful deputy and assistant.[59]

But if the central administration at Brussels became more compact, and professional, in the decades after 1715, it also became essentially functional in character, losing most of the former diplomatic and strategic importance it had retained from the days of Alva down to Max Emmanuel. This was one of the effects of another notable change—Charles VI's decision, in 1717, to set up a council in Vienna charged with overseeing the administration of the Austrian Netherlands. This council remained until 1757, when its functions were transferred to the Imperial Court Chancellery, which conti-nued closely corresponding with, and supervising, officials in Brussels.

At provincial level, the changes were less obvious. The provincial States continued to meet and they retained their former functions, notably the right to grant the ruler subsidies and oversee their collection. Nevertheless there was an unmistakable decline in their influence during the middle decades of the century, not least owing to the transfer of some of the former powers of the Brussels administration to Vienna, and the declining role of the Brabant and Walloon nobility. In the case of the States of Flanders, the grip of the principal towns—Ghent and Bruges—was further weakened (a long-standing aim of the Brussels administration) by assigning increased representation in the States to the smaller towns of the province such as

[58] Houtman-de Smedt, 'Zuidelijke Nederlanden', 351.   [59] Ibid. 352.

Aalst, Kortrijk, and Dendermonde. The political leverage of Ghent and Bruges was indeed a mere vestige of what it had been in the sixteenth century.

Under the Austrian regime, there were noteworthy changes in both administration and culture long before the more radical reforms, influenced by Enlightenment ideas, which the Emperor Joseph II introduced in the 1780s. But the most striking signs of renewal and growth were to be seen in economic life and the expanding population. Where the north had been markedly more dynamic than the south, both economically and demo-graphically, during the first century after the Revolt, and both parts of the Netherlands slackened between 1672 and 1720, after around 1720 the south was more vigorous economically and demographically than the north (albeit lacking the north's colonies and long-distance commerce), the contrast becoming dramatic after 1740 when 'rich trades' and industry in the north entered their phase of almost complete collapse.

Both parts of the Netherlands had sunk into a prolonged agricultural depression in the 1660s which then continued until deep into the eighteenth century. But whereas in Flanders and Austrian Brabant rural rents and land prices recovered strongly from around 1720,[60] in the north agricultural recovery began much later, from only around 1750, and was also distinctly more hesitant. In Friesland and North Holland, for example, farm rents were still falling in the 1730s and 1740s. After 1720, the rural population of the south, in marked contrast to the north, began to grow steadily and relatively rapidly. In Flanders this growth was most marked where the linen industry was widespread, and was clearly stimulated by it. In several parts of the French-speaking area, notably around Charleroi, Liège, and Verviers, a slowly accelerating growth in woollen textiles, coal, and iron-working was taking place which was to culminate in the early nineteenth century in full-scale industrialization. In these regions too industry, here both rural and urban, stimulated population growth. Yet, in Austrian Brabant, where industrial activity was not a major factor, and where the already high level of crop yield ratios left little scope for any further increase in agricultural productivity, there was also a rapid, and sustained, increase in the population.

But neither the spread of rural industry, nor the growth of population, were signs of an improvement of living standards, or rising prosperity, for the mass of the rural and urban work-force. On the contrary, there are numerous indications of a general rise in poverty, and criminality linked to

---

[60] Daelemans, 'Pachten en welvaart', 168; Aerts and Delbeke, 'Problemen', 585–8.

rural poverty, in the south as in the north. That the growing population could be fed was in no small measure due to the potato, which began to be adopted in Flanders and Brabant in the early eighteenth century and became widespread in the middle decades.[61] But the increasing use of the potato as the basis of poor families' subsistence, notably in the 1740s, when there was a sudden deterioration in conditions due to the onset of the War of the Austrian Succession (1740–8), was seen as an unavoidable necessity, it would seem, a resort to a cheap staple consumed *faute de mieux*, rather than as an enhancement of diet. As in Ireland later, the potato in the eighteenth-century Austrian Netherlands was above all a means of ensuring a maximum rate of survival amidst depressed, even wretched living standards.

NEUTRALITY AND DOMESTIC STABILITY, 1713–1746

Once the War of the Spanish Succession was over, the States General lost no time in disbanding most of the Dutch army. Troop-strength fell from 130,000, in 1712, to 90,000 in 1713, and 40,000 by 1715, the bulk of those retained being Dutch, Swiss, and Scots.[62] What remained of the Dutch army once again settled down to an uneventful, sedentary life of garrison duty in the fortress towns of the south, the Generality Lands, and Gelderland.

In itself, the reduction of the army to such levels represented no great change in the Republic's history. After the peace of Münster, in 1648, the army had been cut, eventually, to little more than 30,000 men. Now, as then, the shrinkage had a seriously adverse effect on economic life in border areas, especially the Generality Lands and Gelderland. Yet, in another sense, the change was fundamental. For relative to other European armies, and the military capacity of other states, the army's contraction marked a conclusive break with the past. Throughout the period from 1590 to 1713, in both peace and war, the United Provinces had, at all times, possessed one of the largest and most proficient armies in Europe. But after the treaty of Utrecht, the Dutch reversion to pre-1688 levels of peacetime spending and size of establishment, while Prussia, Austria, Britain, Russia, and other powers maintained considerably larger armies than in the past, meant that the Republic assumed the status of a lesser power and ceased to carry the weight it had, only a few years before, in European affairs, though it is also true, as regards the period down to the 1750s, that historians have often tended to exaggerate the extent of this decline. The United Provinces were far from being the power that they had been before 1713 but, until the 1750s,

[61] Ibid. 588–9.   [62] Goslinga, *Slingelandt's Efforts*, 9.

remained a middle-ranking power of considerable importance in European and world affairs.

Military expenditure was cut drastically. Yet, the provinces' public debt remained at an unprecedentedly high level while the provincial governments showed no inclination to increase taxation so as to be able to reduce the funded debt. While the war of 1672–8 had left Holland with a public debt of 38 million guilders, by 1713 this had risen to a staggering 128 millions, a burden which had a paralysing effect on the Republic's diplomacy and military establishment.[63] This was part of the price for having fought the War of the Spanish Succession principally on credit, avoiding large increases in taxation. Furthermore, the army cuts, and continuing high level of debt, provoked new inter-provincial tensions. For while Holland, Overijssel, and Gelderland (the province which benefited most from the presence of the garrisons) maintained their allocated quotas of troops, the rest unilaterally trimmed their respective portions of the army beyond what had been agreed, throwing more of the burden on to the provinces willing to pay. Friesland was especially obstreperous, complaining that her provincial quota in the Republic's finances was too high, as indeed it was.[64] The quota system had not been altered since 1616. But since then Holland's population and resources had increased in relation to Friesland, Zeeland, and Utrecht. Overijssel and Gelderland, by contrast, with their more vigorous demographic growth since the late seventeenth century, were better placed to meet their quotas. Friesland's payments fell far behind the province's official contribution.

It was against this background of unilateral, as well as collectively agreed, troop and financial cuts, massive public debt, complaints about quotas, and deteriorating co-operation between the provinces that (on the suggestion of Overijssel) a series of special gatherings of the States General were convened in the years 1716–17, to consider the state of the Union and proposals for reform. At the time (and since), these gatherings were called the second Great Assembly, though strictly speaking the gatherings of 1716–17 were never anything other than extraordinary meetings of the States General while, in concept, the Great Assembly of 1651 had been supposed to be a congress of the provincial assemblies. But, certainly, the gatherings of 1716–17 were the second Great Assembly in the sense of being only the second general review of the functioning of the Union and the state of co-operation between the provinces.

A leading part in the proceedings was played by Simon van Slingelandt (1664–1736), since 1690 secretary of the *Raad van State*, a vigorous

---

[63] Aalbers, *Republiek en de vrede*, 5.   [64] Ibid. 3.

administrator from a prominent Dordrecht regent family, his father being a cousin of Johan de Witt. Although his family had in the past been States party, Van Slingelandt largely detached himself from the ideological blocs, making a point of adopting a neutral position. During the war, he had worked closely with Heinsius and subsequently emerged as the chief figure in Generality politics after the Pensionary himself.

Van Slingelandt, with his wide experience of Generality affairs, was well placed to evaluate the structure and institutions of the Union from a collective, rather than purely provincial point of view. He and the *Raad* showered the States General with memoranda and proposals for institutional reform.[65] Van Slingelandt also sharply criticized the general trend of policy since 1713, arguing that the reductions in the Republic's military and naval strength had been so far-reaching as seriously to weaken its influence in international affairs.[66] He insisted that the Generality was now too weak and co-operation between the provinces wholly inadequate. One of his arguments was that in the early years of the Republic majority voting among the provinces, in the States General, had been more common than it now was, the tendency towards greater provincial particularism exerting a debilitating effect on the Generality.[67] The *Political Discourses* which Van Slingelandt composed at this time—though not published until 1784—reveal not only a remarkably detailed knowledge of the history and institutions of the Republic since 1572 but genuine reverence for the constitutional traditions and principles of the United Provinces. He saw the Revolt against Spain as the vital step by which the Dutch had become a 'free people and free government' and as being the key to restoring the crumbling republic of his own day. The United Provinces were declining, in his view, because they were betraying those first principles, moving towards a sterile emphasis on provincial particularism which was the one part of the legacy of Grotius and De Witt of which he disapproved. What Van Slingelandt wanted was to revert to the stronger *Raad van State* and Generality concept, which he believed had prevailed until perverted by the unfortunate English interference of 1585, which had introduced two English ministers on to the *Raad*.[68] He urged the provinces to vest more authority in the Generality, reform the Generality's finances, and restore the Republic as a leading military and naval power, while at the same time reducing the public debt.[69]

---

[65] Ibid. 62–3.
[66] Lademacher, *Geschichte der Niederlande*, 168–71.
[67] Schutte, 'Republiek', 277.
[68] Leeb, *Ideological Origins*, 50–2.
[69] Van Slingelandt, *Staatkundige geschriften*, ii. 127 ff.

But, though there was much debate, in the end the efforts of Van Slingelandt, the *Raad van State*, and the second Great Assembly came to nothing. In effect, the assembly was a decisive defeat for those who wished to reshape the United Provinces into a more integrated federal entity. Several lesser provinces took the view that they were already unfairly treated in decision-making and the matter of quotas, and were more interested in expedients to check Holland's preponderance than in enhancing it by strengthening the Generality. At the same time, the humiliation of 1712–13 rankled and helped to generate neutralist sentiment. The one major decision to emerge from the debates of the second Great Assembly was to reduce the army by another 6,000 men (mostly Swiss), bringing Dutch troop-strength down from 40,000 to 34,000 men.[70]

Those who aspired to rebuild the Republic's military and naval might— Heinsius, Van Slingelandt, and Van Duivenvoorde, a leading figure in the Holland *ridderschap*—saw its military role as essentially still a check to French expansionism combining this with a pro-British, but not necessarily Orangist, stance.[71] Britain encouraged the States General to continue playing an active role in European diplomacy and power politics, seeing this as a means of extending British leverage in Europe. Thus, it was partly under British pressure that the United Provinces almost entered the so-called Quadruple Alliance of 1718 aimed at checking Spanish Bourbon ambitions. The resolution to join the Quadruple Alliance gained a majority in the States of Holland and passed in the States General by five provinces to two, over the objections of Zeeland and Utrecht.[72] But Amsterdam, deeply concerned about the sluggish revival of Dutch trade with Spain and Spanish America, since 1713, and the deterioration of Dutch commerce generally, opposed joining a European coalition against Spain. The dominant faction in the Amsterdam *vroedschap*, led by Burgomaster Nicolaas van Bambeeck (1665–1722), was at odds with Heinsius and Van Slingelandt and wished to distance the Republic from Britain. Amsterdam had her way.

Keen interest was taken in the election of a successor to Heinsius, as Pensionary of Holland, after his death in 1720, not only among the rival blocs in the States but also in foreign capitals. The man favoured by Heinsius' friends, Van Slingelandt, was regarded as the 'British' candidate, the man who stood for greater Dutch participation in the international arena. His rival, backed by Amsterdam and the faction in the Holland *ridderschap* led by the heer van Noordwijk (which opposed Van Duiven-

[70] Wagenaar, *Vad. Hist.* xviii. 136.
[71] Van Arkel, *Houding van den Raadpensionaris*, 21.
[72] Ibid., pp. xviii, 173.

voorde), was Isaac van Hoornbeeck, Pensionary of Rotterdam, who was also the choice of the French.[73] Hoornbeeck was an competent regent administrator, a Voetian and former Orangist with little experience, or knowledge, of foreign affairs. He was chosen in preference to Van Slingelandt because he could be relied on to depart from the tradition of Heinsius and stick to non-intervention abroad.

Between the death of Johan Willem Friso, in 1711, and the early 1720s, Orangism was a latent, rather than active, force in Dutch politics. For the moment, the old rivalry between the party-factions had become less acute. Even so, in the years after 1713, there was a noticeable reaction against the republican tendencies of the post-1702 period. This was particularly evident in Gelderland, where the position of 'Old Crew' regents, and *ridderschap*, became stronger after 1713, and in 1717 the States of Gelderland abolished the rule that members of the town councils had to be re-elected every three years by the *gemeenslieden*, which marked the final defeat of the anti-Orangist, democratic forces which had plunged the province in turmoil in the years 1702–8. In 1718, the now 7-year-old Prince of Orange was designated future Stadholder of Friesland and, the following year, of Groningen. In 1722, he was also designated by the States of Drenthe, and Orangists in Gelderland urged that the States of Gelderland should follow. This was an important development because for the first time it was proposed that the Frisian stadholderate ought now to be merged with the lapsed stadholderate in the other provinces. The States of Holland, Zeeland, and Overijssel intervened to stiffen the opposition of the anti-Orangists in Gelderland, warning that designation of a new Stadholder of Gelderland would sow division in the United Provinces generally. The States of Gelderland ignored this, however, and proclaimed the Prince future 'Stadholder of Gelderland' but, at the same time, drew up new 'instructions' assigning their future Stadholder only a fraction of the authority which William III had possessed under the *reglement* of 1675.[74]

The Stadholder of Gelderland, under the 'instructions' of 1722, wielded little influence over the *gemeenslieden* in town council elections, appointments at provincial or quarter level, or selection of Gelderland's representatives on Generality committees. Even so, Gelderland's decision caused widespread unease amongst the regents. The States of Utrecht reaffirmed their resolutions of 1651 and 1702 to dispense with their stadholderate. Holland adopted a resolution, in March 1723, subsequently backed by Zeeland, Utrecht, and Overijssel, undertaking to co-operate with other provinces, and quarter-assemblies, to maintain the Stadholderless regime.

[73] Aalbers, 'Factieuze tegenstellingen', 442–3.   [74] Gabrieëls, *Heren als dienaren*, 67.

Until the mid-1720s, the regime of the Holland regents was relatively secure internally, and internationally, and could still count on Holland's great commercial, industrial, and financial strength. In the mid-1720s, however, Holland's regent leadership came under the treble pressure of reviving Orangism, rising international tension, and the progressive crumbling of the Dutch overseas trading system. Between 1713 and 1725, the Republic's slack and passive defensive posture, its small army and neglected fortifications, had rested on the premiss of French exhaustion and Austrian friendship. But in the later 1720s, the United Provinces entered a highly uncertain situation. There was increasing frustration at Austria's trimming what the Dutch claimed were their rights in the south Netherlands and concerning the Ostend Company. This set the Republic against the new alliance of Spain and Austria (1725). But at the same time, there were worries that the rival European coalition of Britain, France, and Prussia would not only confront the Emperor but favour the claims of the king of Prussia, against those of his rival, the Elector of the Palatinate, in the new Jülich-Berg Succession crisis. From 1725, the States General were deeply uneasy lest Prussia should acquire Jülich-Berg.

Although British and French diplomats habitually viewed the proceedings in the States of Holland, and States General, in terms of whether they were favourable to Britain or France, Dutch attitudes, and the Dutch predicament, had basically very little to do with partiality for either. The real Dutch dilemma in Europe was how best to protect Dutch interests in the south Netherlands, and prevent the region becoming an economic competitor to the Republic, and, at the same time, prevent Prussia annexing not only Jülich and Berg but the accompanying lordship of Ravenstein, enclaved within northern Brabant. Three Dutch territories—Maastricht, Venlo, and Roermond—were already separated, and enclaved, within Prussian territory (see Map 15) through Prussia's acquisition of most of Upper Gelderland. Prussia was also tightening her links with Emden and East Friesland from where the subjects of the king of Prussia plied their long-distance trade with West Africa and the Caribbean in rivalry with the Dutch. If Prussia, in addition, seized Jülich, Berg, and Ravenstein, not only would Friedrich Wilhelm, with his superior army, dispose of an expanded mass of territory down the eastern side of the Low Countries but yet another slice of the Generality Lands would be enclaved within Prussia. Dutch anxieties were heightened, in October 1726, when the Prussian king switched alliances, and signed a pact with the Emperor, hoping by this means to strengthen his hand in Jülich-Berg.[75]

---

[75] Aalbers, *Republiek*, 103.

The Republic had no alternative but to re-enter the European arena as a substantial power. In 1726, the States General decided to join the Alliance of Hanover, endeavouring, by this means, to check both Austria and Prussia. Holland and the lesser provinces agreed to enlarge the Dutch army by 20,000 men, and by 1727 had brought effective troop strength up to 54,000.[76] When Hoornbeeck died, in 1727, the prevailing view was that a stronger and more prestigious Pensionary was now required. Van Slingelandt was elected Hoornbeeck's successor as Pensionary of Holland in preference to a more committed anti-Orangist republican candidate, the Dordrecht regent François Teresteyn van Halewijn (who, it was feared, would prove divisive), but only after giving verbal assurances to the States party-faction that he would work to block the Prince of Orange and his supporters. Having thrown in his lot with the republicans, he gained the support of Jan Hendrik van Wassenaar van Obdam (1683–1745), leader of the *ridderschap* and a key anti-Orangist. Thus, a politician with little ideological commitment to the 'True Freedom' of De Witt, formerly inclined to believe that the Republic needed an 'illustrious head', became, in terms of practical politics, the leader of the States party-faction.[77]

As tension rose around the borders, and internationally, and the trading system faltered, party-faction strife intensified internally. The Prince of Orange, William IV (1711–51), came of age, at 18, in 1729, and was duly proclaimed Stadholder of Friesland, Groningen, Drenthe, and Gelderland. Latterly, he had been studying at the universities of Franeker and Utrecht, as his father had before him; but now he took up residence in the Prinsenhof, at Leeuwarden, and commenced playing an active political part. Anxious to check his rise, the Holland regents barred him from the *Raad van State* and other sources of influence. But little by little the Orangist cause gained ground. A development which distinctly raised the temperature was the agreement reached in Berlin, in 1732, ending the thirty-year-old dispute between the Frisian branch of the House of Orange-Nassau and the king of Prussia, who was now increasingly at odds with the Holland regents.[78] Under the compromise, William IV accepted Prussia's acquisition of Lingen and Moers, and abandoned all rights and claims to William III's legacy in Germany. The Prussian king reciprocated by abandoning his claims to the Orange-Nassau legacy in both the United Provinces and Austrian Netherlands. The problem of titles was solved by agreeing that both the king and

[76] Ibid. 109; Zwitzer, '*Militie van den staat*', 176.
[77] De Jongste, 'Bewind op zijn smalst', 45–6.
[78] Van Arkel, *Houding van den Raadpensionaris*, 36–40.

Frisian Stadholder, and subsequently their respective heirs, should have the right to call themselves 'Prince of Orange'.

The settlement signed in Berlin raised the spectre of future political collaboration between the Frisian Stadholder and king of Prussia against the Holland regents. An added worry in Zeeland was that the removal of Prussian objections opened the way for the Prince to claim the political functions in Zeeland attached to his possession of the marquisate of Flushing and Veere.[79] After William III's death, the States of Zeeland had discussed proposals to appropriate the marquisate, and political rights of the Prince of Orange separate from the stadholderate, in Zeeland, by purchase. This had been resisted by the States of Friesland as well as the Zeeland Orangists.[80] But now the matter became urgent. Zeeland offered the Prince 250,000 guilders for the rights; but he refused to sell. The States then insisted, purchasing compulsorily and depositing the money, in the Prince's name, in the Middelburg Bank.

No less worrying, from a political, and ideological, point of view, than the Prince's bargain with Berlin was his interest in marrying the daughter of the king of England. When the British court first raised this possibility, in 1728, Van Slingelandt reacted so negatively that the project was shelved for several years.[81] But the Hanoverian dynasty in Britain was none too secure in the affections of its English and Scots subjects, nor secure internationally. The Jacobite rising of 1715 had been suppressed, but a further Jacobite revolt seemed a real possibility; moreover, Spain and Austria were courting the Jacobites. In this situation, the idea of building on the traditions of William III, and the Glorious Revolution, was attractive to the British court and Parliament, especially as a marriage between George II's daughter, Anne, and the Prince of Orange could be expected to strengthen British influence in the United Provinces and, through the Dutch, in Europe.

For precisely these reasons the prospect of the Prince concluding such a marriage alliance was extremely disagreeable to Van Slingelandt, Amsterdam, and the Holland regents generally. But by 1733 there was nothing more they could do to prevent it. The wedding of the Prince and Anne of Hanover (1709–59) was celebrated at St James's Palace, in London, in March 1734. Holland, and the majority in the States General, resolved that the marriage should be marked in the Republic with as little ceremony as possible, contenting themselves with merely congratulating George II on choosing as a home for his royal daughter a 'free republic such

[79] Schutte, 'Republiek', 294.
[80] ARH SG PR 387, p. 731. SF to SH, 20 June 1705.
[81] De Jongste, 'Bewind op zijn smalst', 52.

as ours'.[82] On their arrival in the United Provinces, the newly wedded pair were coolly received at The Hague and Amsterdam, finding a warmer welcome only on reaching Friesland. To her dismay, the British Princess Royal, daughter of the monarch of what was now the proudest and richest empire in the world, found herself marooned in a minuscule court, at Leeuwarden, surrounded by décor and an establishment which she deemed infinitely beneath her station. Her isolation in Friesland was to last thirteen years.

Van Slingelandt remained what the French called 'le premier homme de la République'. The United Provinces had enlarged their forces and adopted a more purposeful stance. But despite his energy and resolution, Van Slingelandt found himself powerless either to rebuild the Republic's army and navy on a sound basis or to carry through the basic reforms for which he had so long pressed. The crisis of the Dutch trading system, and crumbling of Holland's urban economy, in progress since the 1720s, was a permanent structural change which destroyed Holland's economic vitality and capacity to cope with the financial commitments with which her previous great-power status, and European concerns, had saddled her.[83] From the 1720s the main Holland towns, and their trade and industry, rapidly declined in absolute as well as relative terms. Amsterdam was, in some respects, less severely affected than other towns. But this served only to create friction within Holland as the more rapidly declining towns, especially Dordrecht and Haarlem, tried to induce Amsterdam to shoulder more of the fiscal burden.[84]

The stronger political leadership provided by Van Slingelandt did ameliorate the situation in one respect, lessening the rift between Amsterdam and the other main Holland towns. But the Republic's economic and financial difficulties proved insuperable, blocking all prospect of revival. The only major reform carried through during Van Slingelandt's term as Pensionary (1727–36) was the revising of Holland's *Verponding*, the province's main direct tax on houses and land. The registers had not been revised for a century, since 1632; given that Amsterdam had grown more than other cities since then, the existing assessments assigned a disproportionately small share of the burden to Amsterdam. Van Slingelandt induced Amsterdam to consent to revision of the urban *Verponding*—the registers for the countryside were left unchanged—by underlining the dire financial situation in which the Republic now found itself and promising that the States would

---

[82] Schutte, 'Willem IV en Willem V', 192.
[83] Israel, *Dutch Primacy*, 376–98; Nusteling, 'Strijd', 9–14, 19.
[84] Aalbers, *Republiek*, 100–26.

give more vigorous support to efforts to suppress the Ostend Company.[85] So fragile were the Republic's finances that despite the continuing tension with Prussia and Austria, Holland decided, in January 1733, to prune the army back by 10,000 men, over the objections of Gelderland and Overijssel. Though this decision had to be cancelled, owing to the outbreak of the War of the Polish Succession (1733–5), and the generally precarious situation in Europe, the financial, political, military, and naval paralysis of the Republic was becoming more evident with every year that passed.

Following Van Slingelandt's death, in 1736, it took months of canvassing and intrigue in the States of Holland before a new Pensionary emerged in the shape of Anthonie van der Heim (1737–46), a nephew of Heinsius. Van der Heim sprang from the same élite of senior Generality functionaries as his predecessor, and had been his successor as treasurer-general of the Generality. Remarkably, before his appointment as Pensionary he had never once attended a meeting of the States of Holland. A notable feature of his instructions as Pensionary, of February 1737, was the stipulation by the States, for the first time in writing, that their Pensionary must strive to uphold the Stadholderless form of the regime, Van Slingelandt having had to do so only verbally.[86]

Van der Heim was very much a compromise candidate, intended to mitigate friction between the ideological blocs and provinces. He was a competent administrator and possessed a good knowledge of the Republic's institutions and procedures. He boasted ties with all groupings, though Amsterdam considered him too pro-British and his wife came from a Frisian noble family with close links with the Stadholder's court. Yet compromise candidates often serve merely to perpetuate deadlock and so it proved in this case, at least until 1742.

By 1737, there was a widespread expectation of further economic decay and an Orangist revival. Such serious problems of urban deterioration flowed from the structural difficulties of commerce and industry (see pp. 1006–8 below) that a deep social, and political, frustration was becoming prevalent amongst the common people of Holland. Memories of William III's regime were fading and it was natural to pin the blame for the growing economic difficulties on the regents who had now controlled the Republic for a third of a century. Whether, as some historians have argued,[87] there had also been a marked deterioration in the quality of regent government, with a noticeable increase in corruption and nepotism in public

---

[85] De Jongste, 'Bewind op zijn smalst', 47.
[86] Suijkerbuijk, *Archief van Anthonie van der Heim*, pp. v–vi.
[87] Rogier, 'Ware Vrijheid', 310.

life (which may be doubted), it is certainly the case that the cities of Holland and Zeeland were in the grip of a profound *malaise* stemming from the fact that the 'rich trades' and industry, and therefore the whole basis of Dutch primacy in world trade, and the prosperity of the Golden Age, had been irretrievably undermined. It was also undeniable that the provincial States, and States General, had lapsed into a sterile state of deadlock and that the standing of the United Provinces internationally had greatly diminished. If republicans had previously argued, with justification, that the Republic's greatest prosperity had occurred under the First Stadholderless regime, Orangists could now just as convincingly maintain that it was under the Second Stadholderless regime that the Republic's commerce and industry had crumbled to the point that the cities of Holland were in steep decline.

What remained in the ideological arsenal of the republicans was their claim to be the protectors of 'freedom'. Under De Witt, the 'True Freedom' had comprised, essentially, two elements: the upholding of a measure of religious and intellectual toleration and the principle that power is more responsibly wielded, and more likely to be exercised in accordance with the true interest of the state, if dispersed, with the dynastic element, inherent in the stadholderate, removed. Now a third element was added in a posthumous book, on freedom in civil society, by the fervently anti-Orangist regent Levinus Ferdinand de Beaufort (1675–1730), a former member of the Zeeland *Gecommitteerde Raden*, published at Leiden in 1737. De Beaufort claimed that the States party were also the upholders of civil freedom and the dignity of the individual.[88] De Beaufort's book was fiercely attacked by Orangist writers, which in turn provoked several further republican works maintaining that 'freedom' was indeed the central principle of the Republic and that the Stadholders had always threatened this freedom, reminding readers that William III had usurped an unacceptable measure of power.[89]

Thus, the regime of the regents became gradually more vulnerable in the years preceding the outbreak of the general European War of the Austrian Succession (1740–8). The United Provinces may have done nothing to provoke this great European conflict, and harboured a strong desire to stay neutral, yet they were bound in some degree to become embroiled, since in the 1740s the Republic was still an integral part of Europe's system of alliances and a key arena in Europe's diplomacy. With the entry of Britain into the war in 1744, all four of the Republic's powerful neighbours were fighting each other, with Austria aligned with Britain, and Prussia with France. With the United Provinces saddled with incontrovertible treaty

---

[88] De Beaufort, *Verhandeling*, 4–5, 228.
[89] Crispeel, *Politiecque Reflectien*, 217–19; Leeb, *Ideological Origins*, 56.

obligations to defend the Austrian Netherlands against France in conjunction with Britain, the diplomatic pressures became intense. France promised to renew the Franco-Dutch commercial agreement of 1739 (which was highly favourable to the Dutch) if the Republic ignored its obligations to Austria and Britain. But a majority of the States of Holland, and States General, did not believe it prudent to break the Republic's undertakings, or woo France at the cost of incurring the wrath of both the king of England and Austria. The States General, in September 1741, rejected the French offer.

Being pressured by four warring great powers, which were all neighbours, was disquieting in the extreme, but at least the Republic's predicament temporarily cured the political paralysis into which it had lapsed. In March 1742, the States General agreed to expand the army by 20,000 men and, soon after, to cope with the cost without further exacerbating the Republic's swollen public debt, by introducing a new form of tax, the *Personeel Quotisatie* of 1742, a notable early instance of income tax (albeit not intended to be permanent) imposed on all annual incomes in Holland higher than 600 guilders, the rough dividing-line between the artisan and the modestly affluent. By 1743, the army had been brought up to 84,000 men.[90]

Throughout the war the Republic continued paying military subsidies to Austria, for the defence of the south Netherlands, under the terms of the treaties. With its measures of 1742–3, the Republic showed that it was still a power of some consequence in European affairs. But by meeting its treaty obligations to Austria and Britain, the Republic also placed itself in an untenable, even absurd, position in the southern Netherlands. In fact, for much of the war, the Dutch had more troops garrisoning the country than did either the Austrians or British. It was inevitable that the United Provinces, while not formally at war with France, should be dragged into the thick of the conflict. France, naturally enough, regarded the Dutch Barrier garrisons as a vital part of both Austria's defences and Britain's continental posture.

The fact that the States General, and Dutch army, had no desire to fight the French only rendered them a soft target for the latter while simultaneously poisoning relations between the Dutch and their allies.[91] When the French advanced in 1744, the Dutch garrison at Menen (Menin) put up only a feeble defence, surrendering after a week, while that at Ieper capitulated after nine days. In April 1745, the French again invaded, this time via Mauberge, setting siege to the 7,000 poorly prepared Dutch troops holding

---

[90] Zwitzer, '*Militie van den staat*', 176.
[91] Browning, *War of the Austrian Succession*, 173, 206–8.

Tournai. A joint Anglo-Dutch-Austrian army then advanced to relieve Tournai, precipitating a full-scale battle at Fontenoy (11 May 1745) in which the French were victorious, the British attributing the allies' defeat (not entirely unreasonably) to the 'degeneracy of the Dutch troops'.[92] The French then captured Tournai, Ghent, and Ostend in rapid succession.

The subsequent outbreak of the Third Jacobite Rebellion in Scotland and the Highlanders' invasion of England (backed by a small French force) caused panic in London and the withdrawal, before the end of the year, not only of most of the British troops in the Austrian Netherlands but also some of the Dutch, so as to make up the 6,000-man expeditionary force the Republic was obliged, under the terms of the Anglo-Dutch alliance, to send in support of the regime, to Britain.[93]

During 1746, the French occupied Brussels and Antwerp and, after their further victory at Recour, practically all of the Austrian Netherlands except Luxemburg. Then, in April 1747, the French government, as a warning to the United Provinces to desist from their armed support for Britain and Austria, sent a comparatively small army of 20,000 men into States Flanders, seizing Hulst, Axel, and Sas van Gent. The French intended no more than a minor operation in pursuit of specific diplomatic and political goals. There can have been little inkling in Paris, London, or The Hague of its imminent vast and spectacular consequences. For whilst the States General tried to organize an effective defence, expanding the Dutch army to 95,000 men,[94] the people became greatly agitated. The prevailing mood turned strongly against the regents. The Dutch Republic was about to become the only European country to undergo a full-scale revolution in the middle of the eighteenth century.

[92] Haley, *British and the Dutch*, 211.
[93] Carter, *Neutrality or Commitment*, 731.
[94] Zwitzer, *'Militie'*, 176.

37

Society

❖

ECONOMIC DECLINE—RELATIVE AND ABSOLUTE

Most fundamental changes in Dutch society during the eighteenth century were consequences of the faltering of the Dutch overseas trading system—and the industries and fisheries tied to it. Throughout the Golden Age, since 1590, the phases of the overseas trading system had been the chief factor shaping population distribution, urbanization, employment, prosperity, poverty, and urban vitality generally, and this was equally true during the latter phases of the Republic's economic and social development, beginning with the collapse of Dutch world trade primacy, in the decades 1720–40.

After reaching its zenith in the period 1647–72, the Dutch world trade system had evolved through several phases, weakening slowly but largely continuing to function.[1] It is true that some key 'rich trades' of the Golden Age, such as the Levant and Guinea traffic, dwindled disastrously after 1688, the year which marked the definitive end of Dutch economic expansion. The Spanish American trade, flourishing in the 1690s, suffered severe contraction after 1700. But such setbacks, serious though they were, were partially compensated for by the continuing vitality of Dutch commerce within northern Europe, bolstered by further technical and industrial improvements, maintaining the technological lead over most of the rest of Europe. The number of industrial mills on the Zaan continued to increase until around 1720. Many Dutch export industries—Delftware, tobacco-processing, sugar-refining, paper, sail-canvas, Gouda pipes, silk, cotton, and linen—continued to expand during the first quarter of the new century. The United Provinces, rather than Britain, was still the world's technological showcase down to around 1740, and the technical gap between the Dutch economy and those of neighbouring countries remained considerable.[2] At

---

[1] Israel, *Dutch Primacy*, 292–376; Nusteling, 'Strijd', 9–14.
[2] Davids, 'Technische ontwikkeling', 32–3.

the same time, the VOC maintained its lead as the foremost European commercial organization trading in Asia, again down to the 1720s.

A description of Holland written by a Languedoc priest, Pierre Sartre, in 1719, gives a vivid impression of the country, as it seemed to an outsider, at the last point at which the economic system of the Golden Age was still functioning. What struck him above all was that 'dans ce pays tout est nouveau'.[3] Novelty, innovation, cleanliness, prosperity, the magnificence of the towns, and relative absence of poverty compared to neighbouring countries: these were the hallmarks of Dutch society around 1720. Zaandam, Europe's first real industrial zone, in the sense of being an area where industry was overwhelmingly the main activity, struck him as truly 'merveilleux'.[4] He reports that there were then reckoned to be 1,200 industrial windmills in operation on the Zaan—the real number was nearer half that—expressing his admiration for the speed with which the new timber saws cut planks.

But the situation changed radically during the second quarter of the century.[5] During the 1720s set in an accelerating collapse of most of the 'rich trades' and consequently of most export-orientated industry, as well as a disastrous contraction in the fisheries, which marks the end of the economic system of the Golden Age. Amsterdam merchants rapidly lost their previously extensive leverage over large areas of international commerce. Amsterdam's processing industries were devastated. The number of tobacco-processing plants in the city shrank from around thirty in 1720—half of them Jewish-owned—to only eight by 1751. The number of cotton presses slumped from eighty, in 1700, to twenty-one by 1770, and only twelve by 1796. The recently flourishing silk industry fell into decay.

The shrinkage of activity at Amsterdam, however, was slight compared with the harsh contraction, verging on disintegration, of the urban economy elsewhere. Leiden's vitality was destroyed in the 1720s and 1730s. Output of Leiden fine cloth plunged from 25,000 rolls yearly, in 1700, to only 8,000 by the late 1730s, owing essentially to failure to sell in what previously had been the three principal markets—France, Spain, and Ottoman Turkey.[6] Leiden's second main export product of the Golden Age, camlets, plunged from 36,900 pieces annually, in 1700, to just 12,600 by 1750, and a pitiful 3,600 by 1770—scarcely 10 per cent of the level of production of seventy years before.[7] Nor was the position better at Haarlem, where the fine linen and

[3] Sartre, *Voyage en Hollande*, 20, 25.
[4] Ibid. 34.
[5] Nusteling, *Welvaart en werkgelegenheid*, 90–7.
[6] Posthumus, *Geschiedenis*, iii. 1098–9.
[7] Ibid.

bleaching industries disintegrated in the 1730s and 1740s, the number of major linen firms falling in twelve years from seven to three.[8] Salt-refining at Enkhuizen, Dordrecht, and Zierikzee collapsed: by the 1740s, Dutch exports of refined salt were down to only one-fifth of the level of the late seventeenth century. At Zierikzee, where forty salt-boiling kettles were in operation in the mid-seventeenth century, only nine still functioned by 1750. On the Zaan, whale oil, sail-canvas, rope-making, and shipbuilding were all in steep decline by the 1750s. Total Dutch exports of tobacco in processed form, including snuff, plummeted.

Nor was the collapse confined to Holland and Zeeland. During the second half of the seventeenth century, much of the Dutch inland economy had also become harnessed to the overseas trading system and, despite the much lower wages prevailing in these areas, it was inevitable that they should be dragged down too. The Twenthe linen-weaving industry, flourishing in the last quarter of the seventeenth century and first quarter of the eighteenth, fell back in the 1720s, recovered somewhat temporarily (when the War of the Austrian Succession paralysed the linen output of Silesia), and then disintegrated in the 1750s and 1760s.[9] In north Brabant, the linen-weaving industry first reacted to the challenge of rapidly rising output in neighbouring Flanders and Westphalia by switching to technically more complex fabrics, a mixed linen and cotton weave, but, after 1740, textile activity at Helmond, and nearby, rapidly decayed.[10] The disintegration of the inland linen-weaving industry had a paralysing effect on economic and social life in large areas of Overijssel and north Brabant. Harlingen, the main industrial town in Friesland, survived slightly longer but also entered into steep decline after 1750.

It is often assumed that even if the 'rich trades' and industry collapsed, the bulk-carrying trade at any rate survived intact, so that an important part of the seventeenth-century economy continued as before. But this is a misconception. The apparent buoyancy of the Dutch Baltic grain and timber traffic in the middle decades of the eighteenth century stemmed from the rise in the number of small vessels employed in this traffic, sailing from Friesland and the Wadden Islands.[11] The main Dutch bulk-carrying traffic, based on Holland, and using larger ships, contracted sharply as Dutch herring, salt, and wine exports all dwindled. The impact of this contraction on Holland's secondary ports was devastating. The Hoorn bulk-carrying

[8] De Jongste, *Onrust*, 18–20.
[9] Slicher van Bath, *Samenleving*, 201–10.
[10] Harkx, *Helmondse textielnijverheid*, 42–5.
[11] Faber, *Drie eeuwen Friesland*, ii. 602.

fleet shrank from around 10,700 lasts, in the 1680s, to a mere 1,856 lasts in the 1730s, and only 1,201 lasts by the 1750s.[12] Enkhuizen, ruined by the collapse of the herring fishery and bulk-carrying, was a mere shadow of its former self. Even Rotterdam, the Dutch city which coped best with the situation, suffered a 30-per-cent decline in its main business, the carrying of French wine, between 1720 and 1760.[13]

The only expanding sector of Dutch overseas trade in the eighteenth century was in imports, and re-exports, of sugar, coffee, tobacco, tea, and cacao from the Americas and the Far East. The Republic, like every European country, including Austria and Finland, experienced a massive increase in consumption of these products, sugar consumption increasing by several times, owing to changes of habit and fashion. Moreover, because the Republic served as the gateway to the Rhineland and the interior of much of Germany, its levels of imports and exports benefited from this even more than did those of other countries. Yet despite this huge injection of fresh volume, levels of imports and exports at Amsterdam, where most of the new trade was drawn, failed to rise. The nominal value of imports and exports at Amsterdam remained static in the eighteenth century,[14] an age when the commerce of Britain, France, Russia, Prussia, Sweden, and indeed all the others bloated by the new consumables, rose by between two-and-a-half and five times. This means that Amsterdam's share of international trade slumped to a tiny fraction of what it had been before 1720, the vast influx of sugar, tea, and coffee being counter-balanced by the collapse of the strands of commerce the Dutch had formerly dominated. Moreover, a large proportion of the new commerce in tropical products was carried in British, French, Swedish, and other foreign vessels, to and from the Dutch entrepôt, rather than in Dutch. On top of which a price had to be paid for the new habits of consumption, not least in the shape of diminished demand for home-produced beer and imported wine (see Table 45).

The decline of the old Baltic carrying traffic was less abrupt—and less specific to the period 1720–50—than the collapse of the 'rich trades' and disintegration of Dutch industry, but it was no less absolute than decline in these other areas and no less destructive of the urban vitality of Dutch civilization. The waning of bulk-carrying, of course, inevitably brought with it the decline of shipbuilding. The Zaan shipbuilding industry, after growing rapidly in the first half of the seventeenth century, and attaining its most flourishing period—like the Dutch overseas trading system as a whole—in

[12] Unger, 'Publikatie', 170–95; Lesger, *Hoorn*, 150–1.
[13] Hazewinckel, *Geschiedenis*, ii. 210.
[14] Heeres, 'Annual Values', 270–1.

the period 1647–88, began to decline in the 1690s. The number of seagoing ships being built remained impressive down to the 1720s, ebbed markedly during the middle decades of the century—albeit with a temporary revival during the War of the Austrian Succession when the Dutch carried much of the colonial produce of France—and then plunged to minimal levels in the 1790s.[15] The number of shipyards on the Zaan fell from over forty, in 1690, to twenty-seven by the 1730s, and twenty-three by 1750. Still more spectacular, and even more conclusive, was the disastrous fall in the volume of the timber trade on the Zaan, the number of timber auctions falling from over thirty per year, around 1720, to under ten by the 1760s.[16]

   The root cause of the collapse of the Dutch overseas trading system after 1720 was the expansion of industrial activity in the south Netherlands, Germany, and Britain and the wave of industrial mercantilism which swept northern Europe, and especially Prussia, Russia, Saxony, Sweden-Finland, Denmark-Norway, Britain, and (in the 1750s) the Austrian Netherlands during the 1720–60 period.[17] Although Britain had previously been a closed market for the Dutch, in many products, long before 1720, she had continued to be one of the most important importers of two key Dutch export products—linen and sail-canvas; but, gradually, culminating in the 1750s, this outlet too was now closed off. Admittedly, as far as her exports were concerned, Britain also had to cope with the unfavourable effects of new strongly protectionist policies in states such as Prussia, Russia, and Sweden. Confident in its newly won great-power status, Prussia, from the 1720s, shut out practically all foreign textile products. But Britain was able to compensate for declining exports of manufactures to northern Europe, through selling more in her fast-growing American colonies and tightening her grip over Ireland, Portugal, and the Portuguese Atlantic trade with Brazil, as well as India and large parts of the Caribbean. The United Provinces simply lacked the vast imperial power, large navy, and populous colonies necessary, in the new circumstances, to sustain economic growth along the lines achieved in Britain. By 1760, as the Amsterdam Sephardic Jewish economic writer Isaac de Pinto (1717–87) noted, every one of the main props of the Dutch Golden Age economy—long-distance trade, Baltic commerce, the herring and whale fisheries, and industry—had been largely ruined, the only exception being the still flourishing East India traffic.[18] Even the Surinam trade was in terminal decline by the 1760s.[19]

---

[15] Van Braam, 'Over de omvang', 38–9, 43.
[16] Van der Woude, *Het Noorderkwartier*, ii. 477.
[17] Israel, *Dutch Primacy*, 383–8.
[18] De Pinto, *Traité*, 242.
[19] Cohen, *Jews*, 70–8.

A further symptom of economic collapse was the astounding increase in the transfer and depositing of Dutch capital abroad. Amsterdam banking houses with foreign connections plied a roaring business throughout the eighteenth century in exporting the capital the United Provinces had accumulated during the seventeenth. During the Golden Age, Dutch interest rates were the lowest in Europe, comparable rates in other European lands, including Britain, always being several per cent higher. But such was the insecurity of investing abroad due to the absence of large financial institutions of a sort in which Dutch investors could have confidence, and the vitality of domestic trade and industry, that capital surpluses had tended to remain within the United Provinces. From the early eighteenth century onwards, however, the lack of attractive investment opportunities at home combined with improved confidence in investing abroad—in the case of Britain chiefly as a result of the establishment of the Bank of England in the 1690s—generated a vast and continuous outflow of funds seeking the higher returns which could now only be obtained abroad. Thus, Dutch finance remained a major force in the world for many decades after 1720 but it served to fuel growth and create employment elsewhere, especially but by no means only, in England, rather than in the Republic.

If commerce—high-value and bulk, shipbuilding, the timber trade, and practically all export-orientated industry slumped disastrously between 1720 and 1760, the fate of the Dutch fisheries was certainly no less dismal. One of the chief props of the Dutch economy from the early fifteenth century down to the early eighteenth, after 1713 the Holland and Zeeland herring fishery rapidly ceased to dominate the herring grounds of northern Europe, suffering especially from Swedish, Danish, and Norwegian competition. Already greatly reduced by the early eighteenth century, Holland's herring fleet underwent a decisive further contraction in the 1750s, dwindling in a few years from around 225 to a mere 140 busses.[20] By the 1760s, Holland's annual herring catch amounted to less than a third of the catch normal in the middle of the seventeenth century. Enkhuizen was especially hard hit, her herring fleet having shrunk, by the 1750s, to less than one-quarter of its size of a century before.[21]

Agriculture, however, presents a somewhat different picture, though one which likewise indicates, in many ways, the crumbling of much of the rest of the economy. During the first half of the eighteenth century, the rural depression which had gripped the Dutch countryside since the late 1660s not only continued but tended to intensify during the second quarter, amounting

[20] Faber, 'De achttiende eeuw', 128.   [21] Willemsen, *Enkhuizen*, 56.

in some areas, such as North Holland, to a veritable agrarian crisis.[22] Furthermore, besides the continuing depression, persisting longer than in almost any other part of eighteenth-century Europe, Dutch agriculture was stricken by two different sets of natural disasters. By and large the flood defences of the Golden Age had succeeded in preventing the large-scale floods and inundations which had intermittently struck in the fifteenth and sixteenth centuries. But by the early eighteenth century there were signs of some deterioration of the sea-dikes and a rising incidence of serious breaks and floods, albeit not on the scale experienced before 1590. In 1715, the dikes of the Zeeland island of Schouwen broke and much of the island was flooded. In 1717, storms caused extensive damage in Friesland. But the costliest calamity afflicting the low-lying areas was the sudden infestation which began in 1731 of the timber supports of the sea-dikes by the 'pile-worm', a sea worm which rapidly rotted the wooden piles, seriously weakening the dikes. From the 1730s onwards, the dike and drainage boards were forced to raise the 'dike tax' levied on their villages substantially in order to lay out the huge sums required to import suitable rocks and stone, from Scandinavia, with which to buttress the dikes. The solution was effective, though, and there was a noticeable decrease in dike breaks and floods during the second half of the century.

Much the harshest natural disasters to afflict the Dutch countryside in the eighteenth century, however, were a series of great outbreaks of a cattle virus which decimated herds throughout the Republic, first in the years 1713–19, then, the severest epidemics, in the years 1744–65, and finally, and less virulently, in the years 1768–86.[23] The outbreak of 1744–5 reportedly wiped out 135,000 cattle in Friesland alone and that of 1769 another 98,000, causing the province's farmers millions of guilders of losses. Though the data are less specific, the indications are that in neighbouring provinces the dimensions of the disaster were no less. The outbreaks had a devastating impact on Drenthe. The virus spread extremely rapidly and very little was known about how to isolate and combat the sickness. The technique of vaccination, developed in the last third of the century, proved effective up to a point, but it was at that time not yet possible to apply the technique on a large scale.

Yet, unlike the rest of the economy, agriculture began to pull out of the depression in the 1750s and to expand, albeit distinctly more sluggishly than in the Austrian Netherlands and other neighbouring lands. At first glance even such a relatively weak recovery may seem a surprising phenomenon

[22] Van der Woude, *Het Noorderkwartier*, ii. 593–601.
[23] Faber, *Drie eeuwen Friesland*, i. 155–76; Bieleman, *Boeren*, 315–21.

given the shrinkage of the cities. But eighteenth-century Europe as a whole experienced rapid population growth and urbanization as well as (from around 1740) a steep, general rise in food prices which was inevitably reflected in the Republic too. Consequently, the Dutch agricultural recovery of the second half of the eighteenth century was an essentially passive phenomenon which went hand in hand with the decline of imports of Baltic grain into the Republic and the contraction of several of the most specialized sectors of the Golden Age rural economy geared to industry and commerce. The classic instance here is the case of tobacco-growing which, by the early eighteenth century, was one of the most important crops grown in Utrecht and Gelderland, as well as Jülich-Cleves and Mark. Dutch tobacco-growing suffered a sharp contraction in the 1720s, which roughly halved the level of output attained in the opening two decades of the century. Production then stabilized until around 1750. But whereas, around 1700, over 80 per cent of Dutch home-grown tobacco had been processed at Amsterdam, and a large proportion then exported, by 1750, despite reduced output, no more than a quarter of the crop was processed in the Republic.[24] In other words, until 1750, Dutch tobacco-growing survived the collapse of the Dutch tobacco industry by exporting most of the tobacco leaves unprocessed to countries such as Sweden, where tobacco-processing was now flourishing but cultivation of domestic tobacco still at a rudimentary stage. Consequently, after 1760 there was a noticeable further decline in Dutch tobacco output as Prussia and Sweden expanded their domestic production and needed fewer Dutch unprocessed leaves. Finally, after 1776, Dutch inland tobacco recovered to levels attained early in the century owing to the War of American Independence, which disrupted the supply of Virginia tobacco to Europe and revived demand for the Dutch product, especially in France.

Other industrial crops, like flax, ran a similarly meandering course or, like hops, sharply contracted. Consistent expansion of activity and output in Dutch agriculture after 1750 was confined to basic foodstuffs such as rye and potatoes. Potato cultivation certainly expanded vigorously in many parts of the Republic, including Zeeland, Drenthe, and Friesland, and indeed began to do so earlier than in the Austrian Netherlands, being already quite widespread by 1740.[25] But here again, as in Flanders and Brabant, it is arguable that the spread of the potato, which tended to accelerate when grain prices were particularly high, was to some extent a symptom of the general impoverishment, a sign of a society increasingly reliant on the cheapest foodstuffs.

[24] Roessingh, 'Tobacco Growing', 39, 44–9. [25] Bieleman, *Boeren*, 536–7.

URBAN DECAY

The crumbling of the overseas trading system of the Golden Age, and the processing and manufacturing which sustained it, reduced activity in the towns and also several previously vigorous sectors of agriculture. Thus, one of the main effects of the structural transformation of the middle decades of the eighteenth century was to end the urbanization process which had gone on continuously in the northern Netherlands for centuries, causing a general decline in urban population, noticeable even in Amsterdam. Worst hit were inland manufacturing towns such as Leiden, Haarlem, and Delft, which all sustained massive losses of population between 1720 and 1750. But maritime centres such as Middelburg, Zierikzee, Enkhuizen, and Hoorn, and fringe textile towns, such as Almelo and Helmond, also suffered heavy loss of population. At the same time, the three largest cities, Amsterdam, Rotterdam, and The Hague, continued to draw vitality away from more severely affected towns; so that while the proportion of the Dutch population living in the thirty largest cities was now declining, the proportion of the urban population living in these three cities increased, rising from 36 per cent in 1672, to 42% by 1732.[26] Collectively, the thirty largest Dutch towns showed a sudden fall in population and vitality which can be dated fairly precisely, to the three decades 1730–60.[27] The proportion of the Dutch population living in the Republic's thirty largest cities, having remained almost unchanged between 1690 and 1730, contracted from around 36.3 per cent of the total population of the United Provinces, in 1730, to 32.8 per cent in 1755.[28]

From the 1720s, de-urbanization led, in turn, to the rapid depletion of entrepreneurial wealth outside Amsterdam, Rotterdam, and The Hague. The contraction of textile industry at Leiden and Haarlem greatly reduced the number of wealthy manufacturers, dyers, and bleachers in those cities, largely removing what had formally been the backbone of civic wealth.[29] At Haarlem, in 1715, there were ninety manufacturers assessed as earning over 1,000 guilders yearly; by 1742, this figure had dropped to fifty-two. Similarly, at Leiden, in 1715, there were fifty-three manufacturers in this category, a figure which had dropped, by 1742, to only twenty-nine.

The decay of the maritime economy and manufacturing had the effect of rendering non-productive regents, and property-owning *rentiers*, the main grouping among the urban wealthy. By 1742, there were still sixteen pottery

[26] Nusteling, 'Periods and Caesurae', 96.
[27] Ibid. 97, 101, 109.
[28] Ibid. 109.
[29] Oldewelt, 'Beroepsstructuur', ii. 218

owners classed as earning over 1,000 guilders yearly at Delft; but these were increasingly overshadowed by the regent rich. In both Haarlem and Leiden, by 1742, regents far outstripped the handful of remaining wealthy manufacturers in the top tax class, earning over 4,000 guilders yearly. The growing preponderance of *rentier* wealth was reflected in the much increased proportion of civic wealth deposited in securities, bonds, and shares. At Hoorn, by 1742, there were only twelve merchants remaining among householders earning more than 1,000 guilders yearly; not a single active merchant was to be found amongst those earning over 4,000 guilders. The members of the town *vroedschap*, a large proportion of those who formed the top tax category, held some 57 per cent of their assets in States of Holland bonds and VOC shares.[30] The typical mid-eighteenth-century Leiden regent family had half its wealth in States of Holland bonds, over 25 per cent in shares, obligations, and foreign funds, and a mere 12 per cent in land and houses.[31]

TABLE 44. *The population of ten Dutch maritime and industrial cities, 1688–1815 (estimates)*

	1688	1720	1732	1749	1795	1815
Amsterdam	200,000	220,000	220,000	200,000	200,000	180,000
Leiden	70,000	65,000	60,000	36,000	31,000	28,500
Rotterdam	50,000	45,000	45,000	44,000	57,500	59,000
Haarlem	50,000	45,000	40,000	26,000	21,000	17,500
The Hague	30,000	—	38,000	—	—	38,000
Middelburg	30,000	—	—	25,000	20,146	13,000
Delft	24,000	20,000	20,000	13,910	14,500	12,850
Gouda	—	—	20,000	—	11,700	—
Enkhuizen	14,000	—	10,400	—	6,800	5,200
Zaandam	20,000	—	—	12,500	10,000	8,974

Sources: Hart, *Geschrift en getal*, 185–6; Diederiks, *Stad in verval*, 7–10; Posthumus, *Geschiedenis*, iii. 1038; Wijsenbeek-Olthuis, *Achter de gevels*, 27; De Jongste, *Onrust*, 59; Mentink and Van der Woude, 'Demografische ontwikkeling', 39; Nusteling, *Welvaart en werkgelegenheid*, 235, 248; Willemsen, *Enkhuizen*, 100, 178.

The Dutch civic élite of the mid-eighteenth century, including that of The Hague (where there was practically no entrepreneurial wealth in the top tax brackets, the backbone being formed by the eighty-one Generality and States officials and office-holders), thus held an astonishingly high proportion of their assets in paper securities. This meant that, at least in Holland and Zeeland, the country's wealthy were to a high degree dependent on the

[30] Kooijmans, *Onder regenten*, 19.   [31] Prak, *Gezeten burgers*, 132.

state, and the VOC, for sustaining their wealth. As De Pinto stressed, bonds, obligations, dividends, shares, and foreign funds were the linchpin of civic wealth and status, the principal pillar of the social system, a situation quite unlike that existing in other European countries.[32] De Pinto was already predicting, in the 1760s, the disaster that would ensue for Dutch society, and its élite, should the state and the VOC encounter major difficulties. For the collapse of Dutch Generality and provincial bonds would effectively mean the destruction of regent, and much other élite, civic wealth.

The contraction of the urban economy in the decades 1720–70 threatened the middle sector of urban society, shopkeepers, millers, bakers, and the like, as well as artisans and labourers, with the prospect of insecurity, ruin, and poverty. Many middling occupations were closely linked to levels of consumption, so that shrinkage of population inevitably reduced demand for their services. At Haarlem, 130 bakers belonged to the city's bakers' guild in 1707, a number which had dwindled to 70 by 1759.[33] In October 1731, the millers' guild in Leiden resolved the city's ten windmills then grinding flour for the bakers should be reduced to eight, agreeing to purchase two simply to demolish them.[34] Brewers were doubly hit, by the fall in consumption and the shift away from beer to more fashionable beverages—tea, coffee, and gin. Between the 1650s and 1770, there was a staggering fall in beer and wine consumption in Leiden, many times more than could be explained just from the population decline (see Table 45). It is true that there was also a rise in gin consumption; but, from the standpoint of the civic economy, this was small compensation. For the local brewers who went out of business were not being replaced with local distillers. Most of the gin being drunk in the United Provinces was produced in one locality—Schiedam. A leading Dutch writer of the late eighteenth century, Elie Luzac, claimed that coffee, tea, and gin between them destroyed 'more than three-quarters of the breweries of Holland',[35] an estimate which may not be far off the mark. At Delft, the number of breweries in operation fell from fifteen, in 1719, to only two by 1798.[36] Having fallen substantially during the first part of the eighteenth century, the total number of breweries operative in Holland declined from more than one hundred, in 1748, to only fifty-six by 1786.[37] In Leeuwarden, a city

[32] De Pinto, *Traité*, 242–4, 246.
[33] De Jongste, *Onrust*, 39.
[34] GA Leiden Sec. Arch. 113. Geregsdagboek 1730/3, pp. 94–5.
[35] Luzac, *Hollands Rijkdom*, iv. 119.
[36] Wijsenbeek-Olthuis, *Achter de gevels*, 417.
[37] Faber, Diederiks, and Hart, 'Urbanisering', 264.

which produced much of the beer consumed in Friesland, breweries dwindled from fifty, in 1700, to only eighteen by 1760.[38]

TABLE 45. *Returns on Leiden beer, wine, and gin excises, 1650–1790 (guilders)*

Year	Beer	Wine	Gin
1650	64,826	12,400	4,700
1670	47,600	22,600	17,800
1690	30,000	6,796	18,000
1710	14,979	10,700	15,600
1730	10,555	10,000	16,200
1747	8,532	5,700	16,500
1770	8,602	8,615	21,793
1790	5,521	7,656	21,571

Source: Posthumus, *Geschiedenis*, iii. 1156.

The reduction in activity meant that more and more of the work-force were discarded and workplaces abandoned. According to one estimate, some 9,000 textile workers became redundant at Haarlem between 1710 and 1753, for the most part falling into extreme poverty and often leaving for elsewhere.[39] The total work-force employed in the Leiden cloth industry fell by more than half, from around 36,000, in the 1680s, to 17,000 by 1752. The decline in shipbuilding on the Zaan, during the middle decades of the eighteenth century, meant that fewer men were needed not only in the shipyards but also in the timber mills. During the middle decades of the century, a considerable number of the windmills on the Zaan fell into disuse and were demolished.[40] One by one the Delft potteries were abandoned. 'La ville de Delft', noted one author in the 1770s, 'est pour ainsi dire une ville morte.'[41]

In Friesland too the towns were declining. Overall, while the total population of Friesland rose slightly from around 128,000, in 1689, to 135,000 by 1744, and then faster, during the second half of the century, to 157,000 by 1796, the combined population of the eleven Frisian towns fell from 43,000, in 1689, to 41,000 by 1744, recovering to only 45,000 by 1796.[42] Harlingen and the provincial capital, Leeuwarden, were proportionately

[38] Faber, *Drie eeuwen Friesland*, i. 245.
[39] De Jongste, *Onrust*, 50.
[40] Faber, 'De achttiende eeuw', 144.
[41] Accarias de Serionne, *Richesse de la Hollande*, i. 265.
[42] Faber, *Drie eeuwen Friesland*, ii. 414–15.

among the hardest hit. The north Brabant textile towns suffered severely from the commercial and industrial slump, Helmond losing one-third of its population between 1730 and 1780.[43]

Urban decay in the inland provinces mostly followed a different pattern, however. Here there had been less export-orientated industry to begin with, so there was less that could be directly undermined by the collapse of the overseas trading system. The decline of Maastricht from around 14,000 population, in 1713, to 11,000 in 1760 can be mainly attributed to the impact of the garrison cuts.[44] At Zutphen, the decline was the result of the general economic deterioration. The excise returns at Zutphen reveal a city static between 1688 and the 1720s which then entered a period of marked contraction of activity and population. While Zutphen's population stagnated, between 1688 and the 1720s, there were various efforts to establish

TABLE 46. *The proportion of Overijssel's population in the province's main cities, 1475–1748 (%)*

Date	Three main cities	Salland	Twenthe	Vollenhove	Total
1475	38	31.3	21.2	9.5	100
1675	28	32.5	25.5	14	100
1723	24.5	31.5	30	14	100
1748	20.5	28.5	40	11	100

Source: Slicher van Bath, *Samenleving*, 60.

new urban activities in the city—glass and soap works and silk enterprises—with the aim of profiting from the low wage rates applying on the Ijssel, compared to Holland.[45] After 1720, the dynamism (such as it was) evaporated, and the town lapsed into a more passive state. The city's population shrank to about 6,400 by 1780. In Overijssel, Deventer declined in absolute terms,[46] whilst Zwolle grew slightly. Overall, the population of the three cities of Overijssel remained static during the eighteenth century, despite the fact the province's total population grew vigorously. The result was a marked fall in the proportion of Overijssel's population living in the province's cities, from around 30 per cent in the 1680s to some 20 per cent by the middle of the eighteenth century (see Table 46).

[43] Harkx, *Helmondse textielnijverheid*, 56.
[44] Philips, 'Eenige aanduidingen', 32–3.
[45] Frijhoff, *Gesch. van Zutphen*, 96, 117–18.
[46] Te Brake, *Regents and Rebels*, 12–13.

By the third quarter of the eighteenth century, the decay of the Dutch cities was abundantly obvious and much noticed by foreign visitors. During a century when the population of western and central Europe was rapidly expanding, and most cities steadily gaining in dynamism and population, it was altogether remarkable, indeed amazing, to find, in the most developed part of Europe, the phenomenon of cities fast shrinking, and losing activity. 'Most of their principal towns are sadly decayed,' reported the young Boswell, in 1764, 'and instead of finding every mortal employed, you meet with multitudes . . . of poor creatures who are starving in idleness. Utrecht is remarkably ruined.'[47]

The shrinkage, and deterioration, of the cities of the United Provinces is all the more dramatic when looked at against the background of the general trend in eighteenth-century Europe towards urbanization. In a century in which many European cities doubled and trebled in size, and some grew much more spectacularly, the process of de-urbanization evident in both parts of the Netherlands was indeed a striking development. While London is estimated to have reached almost 900,000 by 1790, and Paris over 600,000, while St Petersburg grew from nothing to around 220,000, a level attained also by Vienna, Berlin expanded to about 150,000, and Hamburg to over 100,000, the main cities of the Low Countries, once the envy and wonder of all Europe, began to seem small and provincial—even, incipiently, in the case of Amsterdam.

The only part of Europe where there was a remotely comparable process of de-urbanization was the south Netherlands. But in contrast to the Republic both the economy and total population of the Austrian Netherlands grew significantly during the eighteenth century, hesitantly at first, more steadily after 1748. By 1784, the total population of the south, excluding the prince-bishopric of Liège, had reached 2,273,000 (62.5 per cent Dutch-speaking, 31 per cent French-speaking, and 6.5 per cent German-speaking),[48] as against a total of approximately 2,080,000 for the north.[49] Thus, despite the loss of territory to France, after 1659, the south slightly increased its former demographic edge over the north. But while agriculture, rural industry, industry in the Walloon towns, and the rural population expanded, the old high-value, sophisticated urban industries, including tapestries, luxury textiles, jewellery, and book-production, decayed and, on the whole, were not replaced. As a result Antwerp, Ghent, and Bruges all declined in the eighteenth century, while Brussels grew remarkably slowly

---

[47] Pottle, *Boswell in Holland*, 281.
[48] Bruneel, 'L'Essor démographique', 166.
[49] Van der Woude, 'Demografische ontwikkeling', 125.

compared with other European capitals. It may be true that the Low Countries still had a higher proportion of their total population living in towns than the rest of Europe. But, despite this, the cities of the Netherlands, where outside the Walloon area there was little to be seen, after 1740, which was new, were rapidly being marginalized in the general context of European urban life and development, and declining in relation to the local rural population. The proportion of the population of Austrian Brabant dwelling in cities fell from around 45 per cent, in 1700, to 34 per cent by 1755, and only 31 per cent by 1818.[50] Yet, striking though the decadence of the towns was also in Flanders and Brabant, neither there nor anywhere else in eighteenth-century Europe was the process of de-urbanization of remotely such severity, and its social consequences so unsettling, as in the Dutch Republic.

TABLE 47. *Population of the main cities of Flanders and Brabant, 1615–1784*

	1615	1690	1755	1784
Brussels	50,000	65,000	58,000	74,000
Antwerp	54,000	66,000	43,000	50,000
Ghent	31,000	52,000	39,000	50,000
Bruges	30,000	36,000	30,000	31,000
Leuven	10,000	15,000	15,000	15,000

Sources: Hélin, 'Demografische ontwikkeling', 175–80; Bruneel, 'Essor démographique', 164–6; Van Houtte, *Economische en sociale geschiedenis*, 211; Klep, 'Urban Decline', 274.

WEALTH AND POVERTY

The crippling of commerce and industry between 1720 and 1740, and of the fisheries, had the inevitable effect of reducing employment and prosperity, creating harsher conditions in town and country. But, as yet, there was no massive increase in urban poverty. That came only later, especially from the 1770s. Before that, contraction of the economy was reflected chiefly in the shrinkage of the towns. As employment opportunities dwindled, men moved elsewhere, in search of work, taking their families with them.

Many of those who left decaying towns migrated to Amsterdam, The Hague, and Rotterdam. Others, including many highly skilled artisans, emigrated to Britain, Scandinavia, Prussia, or Russia. Dutch shipbuilding

---

[50] Klep, 'Het historisch moderniseringsproces', 20.

workers and carpenters were in heavy demand throughout northern Europe. Soon the highly skilled were also leaving Amsterdam. When Sweden banned imports of processed tobacco, in the 1740s, entire workshops, with their men and machinery, removed to Stockholm.[51] The less skilled emigrated also to the New World. The Amsterdam Sephardic community in the 1740s stepped up its policy of assisting emigration of members who lacked employment opportunities in the Republic to Surinam and Curaçao.[52]

An initial effect of the shrinkage of urban activity and population, paradoxically, was to an extent to push up living standards for those that remained. The town governments had invested heavily in increasing housing, and expanding the general fabric of civic life, during Phase Four (1647–72) of Dutch world trade primacy, when it had appeared that the rapid growth of the cities was set to continue. This development had been designed to accommodate populations larger, in some cases twice as large, as those which now inhabited the towns. One consequence was to depress urban rents to the advantage especially of the poor man in a cheap house. Even in Amsterdam, where the downward pressure was least, the general deterioration of the economy caused real rents for cheap housing, from about 1730, to become substantially cheaper; real rents for artisans in Amsterdam did not regain the level of 1734 until as late as 1794.[53]

Because demand slackened faster than supply, prices for foodstuffs and fuel also fell sharply from the 1720s and remained low, in real terms, for about half a century.[54] This was inherent in the shrinkage of the urban population whilst that of the countryside increased. De-urbanization is indeed inherently prone to boost real wages—as distinct from real earnings—and it is not surprising that these rose substantially in the 1720s and 1730s as a result of the commercial-industrial collapse. At Amsterdam, real wages rose sharply in the 1720s and remained appreciably higher than they had been in the half-century 1670–1720 throughout the half-century to 1770.[55] This was part of a general Dutch phenomenon both in the maritime zone and the inland provinces.

But real wages are very different from real earnings, the one being the value of a given wage, the other what is actually earned; thus, one could only benefit from rising real wages if one worked as much, and under the same conditions, as before, a highly questionable premiss in the second quarter of the eighteenth century. For workers who remained in work, the

[51] Westermann, 'Memorie', 74.
[52] Cohen, *Jews*, 18–31.
[53] Lesger, *Huur en conjunctuur*, 68–9, 74–5.
[54] Posthumus, *Geschiedenis*, ii. 1005, 1082.
[55] Nusteling, *Welvaart en werkgelegenheid*, 264–5.

great challenge of the decades after 1720 was to defend wage rates and conditions the bosses had conceded in the past. From the 1720s, there was intense pressure not just to lay off workers wherever possible but to lower labour costs by compelling those that remained to accept worse pay and conditions and also by employing more children, youths, and cheap immigrant labour. In 1739, the Haarlem silk workers complained bitterly that their livelihood was being threatened by 'strangers' from northern Germany who were being given work in the industry.[56] Employing immigrants was also a means of circumventing guild regulations and, in some cases, of opposing the setting up of guilds. In 1742, for example, the claim that the workers were 'mostly strangers and of the worst sort' was used by the Haarlem ribbon-manufacturers as an argument against the setting up of a guild for that industry.[57]

The bosses' efforts to prune back wages and conditions previously conceded generated a new type of social conflict leading to worker actions and strikes which often had a distinctly modern ring, though it was a phenomenon unique to the peculiar situation of Dutch society in the eighteenth century and a temporary phenomenon which largely ceased by 1770. Moreover, it was as much a conflict between native workers, used to high wages and favourable conditions, and immigrants accepting low wages, as a conflict between workers and bosses. The numerous textile workers arriving in Haarlem and Leiden from Helmond, Almelo, and other decaying inland textile centres were just as resented as the Germans and, being willing to work for low wages, just as readily received by the bosses. The Leiden textile workers organized strike actions in 1700, 1716–18, 1724, 1730, 1741, 1744, 1747–8, 1761, 1764, and 1770.[58] After 1770, the Leiden textile industry was so decayed there was nothing left to contest. The Amsterdam cotton workers struck in 1729 and again in 1744, on the last occasion holding out well over a month because the bosses refused to stick to the agreement on wages and conditions reached in 1729, in particular by employing too many cheap-rate youths and children.[59] As in other Dutch strikes of this period, the Amsterdam cotton textile workers chose strike leaders, set up a strike fund, and consciously fought for improved wage conditions. Eventually, the strike leaders were arrested by the city authorities.

To protect their livelihoods and living standards, workers not only organized actions against the bosses but also, and this time with the encouragement of the city governments, sought to tighten guild restrictions and, where there were gaps, set up additional guilds. A complementary trend was the tendency of some city governments to lay down more

---

[56] De Jongste, *Onrust*, 35.   [57] Ibid.   [58] Dekker, 'Staking', 33.   [59] Ibid. 28–30.

stringent rules for the granting of citizenship, a precondition of entry into the guilds. This defensive reaction is well illustrated by the proliferation of guilds and guild-membership at Amsterdam. In 1688, the city boasted thirty-seven guilds with 11,000 members; by 1750, this had risen to fifty guilds with well over 14,000 members, though the total population remained unchanged.[60]

As the pressure of demand on civic and Church welfare institutions escalated, there was also a growing tendency among workers, encouraged by civic government, to set up more chests and funds to provide sickness and accident insurance. The first half of the eighteenth century in the United Provinces witnessed a remarkable proliferation of workers' societies designed to protect the established Protestant worker. The Leiden say-workers set up a 'bourse', in 1700, renewed in 1736, which was restricted to members of the Reformed Church 'of good moral reputation', over the age of 40, able-bodied and willing to submit to medical examination as a condition of entry.[61] Whilst in work, members paid two stuivers weekly, from their wages, into the chest, from which they received two and a half guilders weekly for up to six months, should they become unable to work through sickness or accident, provided the cause of the disability was not drinking or brawling. Another Leiden textile workers' society, set up in 1711, accepted Remonstrants and Mennonites, as well as Reformed, among its membership, but once again excluded Catholics. This society also paid out 50 stuivers weekly, in case of sickness or accident preventing work, interestingly forbidding 'brothers' in receipt of assistance to visit inns or gin-parlours 'except for one glass of beer to quench thirst, consumed standing, without lingering'.[62]

In the past, Dutch workers had enjoyed an appreciably higher standard of living than their counterparts in Germany, the south Netherlands, or Britain, and they showed determination to defend what they had. Even out of work, and on welfare, they evinced a tendency to be choosy and expect assistance, which was noted by numerous foreign observers, including Boswell, who remarked in 1764 that in Utrecht one saw great numbers of 'wretches who have no other subsistence than potatoes, gin, and stuff which they call tea and coffee; and what is worst of all, I believe they are so habituated to this life that they would not take work if it should be offered to them'.[63]

---

[60] Nusteling, *Welvaart en werkgelegenheid*, 155.
[61] GA Leiden Sec. Arch. 115, p. 37.
[62] Ibid. 43.
[63] Pottle, *Boswell in Holland*, 281.

This further encouraged Dutch employers to seek immigrant and seasonal labour from northern Brabant, Overijssel, and Gelderland, and especially from adjoining regions of Germany, which was used to more menial work and worse conditions and pay. It is indeed one of the most typical features of Dutch society in the eighteenth century that, whilst there was a large-scale outflow of skilled Dutch labour, emigrating abroad, there was no decline in the previous high level of immigration from north-west Germany. What changed was the composition of this German immigration. During the seventeenth century German settlement in Amsterdam had been, to a considerable extent, maritime and mercantile in character, including many seamen and persons working in commerce, often migrating from Hamburg, Bremen, Emden, Schleswig-Holstein, or the lower Rhine Calvinist duchies. After 1720, by contrast, there was a sharp fall in immigration from the German maritime zone, compensated by an increase in the number of often extremely poor Catholics, Jews, and Lutherans, arriving from the Münster-land, rural areas of Lower Saxony, and Hesse.[64] In the eighteenth century, seasonal labour from the Münster area became a major factor in the Dutch economy, especially in the most lowly jobs such as peat-digging and weaving, and not only in Holland. At Harlingen, in Friesland, for example, there was a notable strengthening of the Catholic presence during the first half of the eighteenth century which was almost entirely due to settlement in the city of Catholics from the Münsterland.[65]

Dutch society in the eighteenth century was a society dominated by the *rentier*. Whether regents, nobles, descendants of mercantile families who had abandoned commerce, or heirs to money made in manufacturing but no longer involved in active business, most of the wealthy in the eighteenth-century Dutch Republic were men who had no active economic role. They lived, often in great affluence, in elegant rural villas, as well as fine town houses, employing cooks, servants, coachmen, and gardeners, on the interest and dividends paid on their States of Holland bonds, obligations, colonial company shares, and deposits in foreign funds, often the Bank of England.

By and large, those businesses and industries which survived in part, or intact, down to the middle of the eighteenth century supplied few new-comers to the Republic's élites of wealth. A good deal of bulk-carrying remained, of course, but bulk freightage had never provided more than modest affluence for individual families, while those industries which sur-vived longest tended to be concentrated in just one or two localities, as with the Schiedam gin distilleries, or Gouda pipes, and were divided between a

---

[64] Hart, *Geschrift en getal*, 167–9.
[65] Faber, *Drie eeuwen Friesland*, i. 78.

large number of mostly small firms. The clay-pipe industry had been the principal economic activity of Gouda since the mid-seventeenth century and remained flourishing to around 1750, after which it rapidly declined. But it was an industry consisting of hundreds of small workshops whose bosses remained firmly among the middle strata of society.[66] In a city such as Gouda in the eighteenth century, regents and their relatives were almost alone amongst the ranks of the wealthy.[67]

Living off the legacy of the past, the Republic was still an affluent society compared with neighbouring countries. But it was a society in which the middle strata were being squeezed and wealth becoming more polarized than had been the case in the Golden Age. The deterioration of the urban economy, contraction of the towns, and reduced demand for rural produce inevitably meant rising poverty in both the towns and countryside. Initially, whilst the Republic still had a technical edge over the rest of Europe, those becoming redundant were more likely to migrate elsewhere than to go on poor relief. At Haarlem, between 1710 and 1750, approximately 9,000 weavers became redundant but only a small proportion stayed in Haarlem on charity.[68] But, after 1750, there was nothing with which to replenish the reservoir of skill and technological expertise, few skills left with which to emigrate, and, thus, more incentive to stay, on poor relief, than migrate. Thus, urban poverty built up relatively slowly in the decades in which commerce and industry were disintegrating (1720–70), but accelerated rapidly thereafter. At Amsterdam, the proportion of the city's population on poor relief increased only marginally between 1700 and 1770 but then dramatically from the 1770s, those receiving winter poor relief, of bread and fuel, rising from 9.5 per cent of the city's population, in the 1760s, to 13 per cent by the 1780s, and no less than 16 per cent by 1795.[69]

By contrast, the rise in rural poverty, in the inland provinces, was steady but relentless. In Overijssel, while the three main cities—Deventer, Zwolle, and Kampen—accounted for a dwindling proportion of the province's population, their share of the province's taxable wealth remained static. Thus, where in the 1680s they collectively comprised 30 per cent of Overijssel's population, but possessed 40 per cent of taxable wealth, by 1748 they still possessed 40 per cent of wealth but amounted to only 20 per cent of the population, implying the rural population as a whole was becoming poorer in relation to the cities. Simultaneously, the wealth of Overijssel's

---

[66] De Jong, *Met goed fatsoen*, 99.
[67] Ibid. 103–5.
[68] De Jongste, *Onrust*, 50.
[69] Nusteling, *Welvaart en werkgelegenheid*, 169, 265.

substantial independent farmers noticeably increased while the number of small independent farmers diminished (see Table 48). The consequence of these trends, combined with the overall increase in the province's population, was a steady escalation in rural destitution. Those registered by the States of Overijssel as too poor to pay the province's direct taxes rose from 25 per cent of the population, in 1675, to no less than 38 per cent by 1758. A similar trend is discernible in Gelderland where, as in the Veluwe, the towns stagnated but the rural population vigorously increased. In Drenthe, there was no rise in the numbers classified by the fiscal authorities as 'poor'. Nevertheless, there was, as in Overijssel, a fall in the number of independent farmers and a large increase in the number of landless labourers and crofters. In States Brabant, one of the classic areas of growing impoverishment during the eighteenth century, the registers again reveal hefty increases in the numbers of registered poor exempt from direct taxes.

TABLE 48. *Changes in distribution of wealth in Overijssel, 1675–1758*

Social group	1675		1758	
	% of population	% of taxable wealth	% of population	% of taxable wealth
Nobility	1.1	41.2	0.6	19.2
Rich burghers	1.8	31.6	1.0	31
General bourgeoisie and farmers	25.5	27	20	49
Artisans and small farmers	46.5	—	42.7	—
Poor	25.1	—	35.7	—

Source: Slicher van Bath, *Samenleving*, 273–9.

38

The Churches

❖

DUTCH REFORMED, PROTESTANT DISSENTERS, CATHOLICS, AND JEWS

During the eighteenth century, the Dutch Reformed Church, the public Church, retained the allegiance of the majority of the population throughout the Republic except the Generality Lands, Twenthe, and the southern fringe of Gelderland beneath the Waal. Nevertheless, with the growth of toleration, a marked feature of Dutch life in the eighteenth century, there was a noticeable tendency, virtually throughout the Republic (except Friesland), for the preponderance of the Reformed majority to be reduced.

In effect, the typical pattern of the period 1572–1700, with the Reformed Church being generally the most successful confessionalizing bloc, ceased to apply after 1700. It was now no longer the support of the provincial and civic authorities for the public Church which told most in determining the confessional balance in society but the growth of toleration and impact of immigration from Germany. As a result, the second largest Church, the Catholic, gained ground on the Reformed in all the provinces (except Friesland), and two smaller confessional blocs—the Lutherans and Jews—grew vigorously. However, the Anabaptists and Remonstrants, two major Churches of the Golden Age which did not benefit from immigration, not only failed to grow in the new circumstances but rapidly dwindled.

Though pruned back, the predominance of the Reformed remained considerable in most of the Republic. Outside Holland and Utrecht, there were many towns and localities where over 80 per cent of the population belonged to the public Church. In all the larger towns of the Republic, including most of the cities of Holland, it was still usual, at the end of the century, for the Reformed to comprise 60 to 80 per cent of the population (see Table 49). Haarlem, with its strong Catholic tradition, was something of an exception, but even in Haarlem, the most Catholic city in Holland, the Catholics amounted to only 25 per cent at the beginning of the century, rising above 30 per cent only in the 1790s (see Table 50). Amsterdam was also exceptional, the percentage of its population belonging to the public Church (with the exception of Nijmegen) being lower than in any other major city within the Seven Provinces. But this was not because the proportion of Catholics was high. As in all the main cities of Holland during the eighteenth century, Amsterdam's Catholics gained ground but increased from only 18 per cent of the total, in 1726, to 21 per cent by the end of the century.[1] The proportion belonging to the Reformed Church in Amsterdam was exceptionally low only because of the large Lutheran and Jewish communities in the city.

TABLE 49. *Confessional allegiance in eight Dutch Cities at the end of the eighteenth century (%)*

	Amsterdam	Rotterdam	Utrecht	Deventer	Zutphen	Leeuwarden	Harlingen
Reformed	54	61	65	75	82	75	73
Catholic	21	27.5	31	20	14	16	16
Lutheran	11	5.5	3	1	4	3	1
Jewish	10	3.5	0.5	0.5	0.75	4	1
Anabaptist	1	0.5	0.5	0.5	0.5	3	8
Remonstrant	0.25	1.5	0	0	0	0	0

Note: Based on the censuses of 1798 and 1809.

Sources: Mentink and van der Woude, *Demografische ontwikkeling*, 34; Faber, *Drie eeuwen Friesland*, i. 428; De Kok, *Nederland op de breuklijn*, 392, 429, 347.

The proportionate rise of the Catholic population at Amsterdam and Haarlem during the eighteenth century reflected a trend common to all the large cities. It applied both in towns where Catholicism was strong and where it was weak. Thus, in Enkhuizen, the Holland town where Catholics were least numerous, they increased, between 1726 and 1775, from roughly 4 to 10 per cent, and, in Dordrecht, from 5 to about 10 per cent by the 1790s.

As in the seventeenth century, Catholics continued to be fairly numerous in the countryside of Holland and Utrecht, but markedly less so in the rest of the Seven Provinces, always excepting Twenthe and the Catholic fringes of Gelderland. There were 97,000 Catholic communicants in the province of Holland in 1726, when the population of the province stood at around 800,000, which means, allowing for the Catholic children, that the Catholic

[1] De Kok, *Nederland op de breuklijn*, 203.

population amounted to approximately 18 per cent of that of the province. There were sharp variations, however, in the smaller towns and villages and also from area to area. Thus, about 30 per cent of the North Quarter minus West Friesland was Catholic,[2] while very few Catholics were to be found on the South Holland islands. In a number of small Holland towns, such as

TABLE 50. *Confessional allegiance at Haarlem, 1707–1809*

	1707		1791		1809	
Reformed	23,500	(61%)	12,100	(58%)	11,000	(54%)
Catholics	9,400	(25%)	6,200	(30%)	6,700	(33%)
Anabaptists	4,026	(10.5%)	965	(4.5%)	937	(5%)
Lutherans	1,089	(3%)	1,032	(5%)	1,093	(5.5%)
Remonstrants	184	(0.5%)	67	(0.3%)	55	(0.3%)
Jews	0		114	(0.6%)	152	(0.8%)

Sources: De Jongste, *Onrust*, 60; De Kok, *Nederland op de breuklijn*, 328.

Naarden, Oudewater, Geertruidenberg, and Heusden, a high proportion, up to half the population, was Catholic by the late eighteenth century.[3] But, equally, in other small towns, such as Schoonhoven, Brill, Maassluis, Middelharnis, and also the Zaan industrial belt, Catholics represented less than 15 per cent of the population. The contrast was even more extreme in the case of villages. There were villages, such as Wassenaar or Warmond, near Leiden, or Heemstede, Castricum, and Bloemendaal, near Haarlem, which were overwhelmingly Catholic.[4] But there were also places where there were no Catholics, including the islands of Vlieland and that of Marken, near Amsterdam.

The Catholic population of Holland rose from about 18 per cent to about 23 per cent during the course of the eighteenth century. Among the provinces, only Utrecht surpassed Holland in the size of its Catholic presence (see Table 51). The city of Utrecht was almost one-third Catholic (see Table 49), while Amersfoort had a still higher Catholic percentage, and the little towns of Montfoort and Wijk-bij-Duurstede were predominantly Catholic, as were many Utrecht villages, including Houten and Odijk. On the other hand, there were also some strongly Protestant localities, including Rhenen where, as late as 1809, there were only fourteen Catholics listed in a population of 1,850. In the mid-eighteenth century there were about

[2] Schutte, *Hollandse dorpssamenleving*, 92.
[3] De Kok, *Nederland op de breuklijn*, 311, 319, 437.
[4] Ibid. 322, 326–7.

27,000 Catholics in Utrecht out of a total population of 83,000, comprising about 35 per cent of the total.

Compared to Holland, Utrecht had a proportionately very large Catholic population; the rest of the provinces, though, had a smaller Catholic presence. The Catholic community in Zeeland remained meagre throughout the eighteenth century but grew at an appreciable rate, more than doubling in size, and reaching over 10 per cent of the province's population, by 1809 (see Table 52). This increase was particularly marked in Middelburg and other main towns, especially Flushing and Zierikzee. Some Zeeland villages, such as Domburg, Ellemeet, Kruiningen, Yerseke, Burgh, and Colijnsplaat, were listed, as late as 1809, as containing no Catholics at all.

TABLE 51. *Catholic communicants in the provinces of the 'Holland Mission', 1726–1800*

	1726	1758	1775	1800
Holland	97,000	105,000	113,000	120,000
Utrecht	18,500	19,000	21,000	25,000
Overijssel				
(minus Twenthe)	9,000	9,000	10,000 ⎫	30,000
Twenthe	15,000	19,000	20,000 ⎭	
Gelderland				
(north of the Waal)	9,000	12,000	13,000	—
Friesland	12,000	11,000	12,000	11,000
Groningen-Drenthe	4,750	5,000	5,000	6,000
Zeeland	2,000	3,500	4,000	5,000
Cleves-Mark	—	14,500	—	—
Lingen	15,650	17,000	19,680	—

Sources: *Archief aartsbisdom Utrecht*, x. 11–40; Polman, *Katholiek Nederland*, ii. 115, 161; Faber, *Drie eeuwen Friesland*, i. 81; De Kok, *Nederland op de breuklijn*, 466.

In the eastern provinces, Catholic populations were relatively small and grew less rapidly than in Zeeland, Holland, or Utrecht. Nevertheless, they did noticeably increase. In Overijssel, all three main cities had a substantial Catholic presence by the late eighteenth century, of 15 per cent or so in Kampen, 20 per cent in Deventer, and 22 per cent in Zwolle.[5] Twenthe, by the late eighteenth century, was roughly half Catholic but with sharp variations, Enschede and Almelo being mainly Reformed, Oldenzaal predominantly Catholic. Two-thirds of all the Catholics in Overijssel lived in

[5] Ibid. 392, 398, 407.

the Twenthe quarter. By contrast, the Vollenhove quarter was overwhelmingly Reformed, the small towns of north Overijssel, Blokzijl, Giethoorn, Hasselt, and Steenwijk, containing only tiny Catholic communities. As in Drenthe and the Ommelands, many villages in this area had no Catholics at all. In Gelderland, where the States formally tolerated Catholic practice under a placard of 1731,[6] the Catholics also increased in numbers, especially in the main towns and most dramatically in Nijmegen, where the Catholics became the majority during the second half of the century, the Reformed dwindling from some 60 per cent at the beginning of the century to only 40 per cent of Nijmegen's total population by 1800.[7] Nijmegen henceforth was the only major city of the Seven Provinces with a Catholic majority. Apart from Zeeland, Groningen was the province where there were least Catholics, though the Catholic proportion of the population of the city rose to about 15 per cent by the late eighteenth century. In Friesland the Catholics remained static at about 10 per cent of the total population.[8]

The Generality Lands were heavily Catholic in character in the seventeenth century, and remained so in the eighteenth, except for the two predominantly Protestant areas—Westerwolde and States Flanders. Though western States Flanders retained its Reformed character after 1700, the region showed the same tendency for the Catholic proportion of the population to increase as the Seven Provinces overall. The Catholic population of States Flanders rose from about 30 per cent of the total, around 1700, to 45 per cent by 1800.[9] Sluis, Aardenburg, IJzendijke, and Terneuzen, though, remained essentially Protestant towns.

Besides the Catholics, two other confessional groups, the Lutherans and Jews, significantly expanded their presence in Dutch society during the eighteenth century. Whereas, in the past, Lutheran growth had been chiefly confined to Holland, after 1700, as Holland-style toleration took hold in the outer provinces, the progress of the Lutherans became a general phenomenon throughout the Republic. In some places, the growth of the Dutch Lutheran Church was spectacular. In Rotterdam, for example, the Lutherans trebled in number from one to three thousand during the course of the eighteenth century.[10] In Leeuwarden, Lutherans approximately doubled between 1680 and 1770. Many of the main Lutheran churches in the United Provinces, including those of Rotterdam, The Hague, Delft, Utrecht, and

[6] Thielen, *Gesch. van de enclave Groenlo*, 158.
[7] De Kok, *Nederland op de breuklijn*, 422.
[8] Faber, *Drie eeuwen Friesland*, i. 80–1.
[9] De Kok, *Nederland op de breuklijn*, 143.
[10] Mentink and Van der Woude, *Demografische ontwikkeling*, 47–8.

Leeuwarden, were rebuilt or enlarged during the middle decades of the eighteenth century to accommodate the rapidly increasing numbers.[11] Among the middle-sized Dutch Lutheran communities, Middelburg obtained a second preacher in 1710, Gouda in 1750, and Breda in 1764. Among the larger congregations, The Hague obtained its third preacher in 1739, and Amsterdam, where the Lutherans were now the third largest Church in the city, its sixth, in 1740.[12] Owing to the proliferation of congregations employing more than one preacher in the eighteenth century it became much easier than in the seventeenth for the Dutch Lutheran Church, on the one hand to preach in Dutch and assume a more Dutch character and, on the other, to continue to cater for new immigrants from Germany, with preaching in German. For while the new immigrants were mostly unable to follow sermons in Dutch, children and grandchildren of German immigrants into the Republic could usually follow sermons better in Dutch than German.

As in the seventeenth century, Lutheranism in the eighteenth was largely confined to the main towns, but not exclusively so. In parts of North Holland, especially the Zaan industrial belt and Groningen, Gelderland, and also States Flanders, Lutheranism evolved also as a rural phenomenon. In Groningen, by the late eighteenth century, there were Lutheran congregations in several villages, the twin villages of Old and New Pekela becoming a centre for rural Lutheranism in the province, and acquiring a permanent preacher by 1760. One of the most notable of the rural Lutheran congregations was at Groede, in States Flanders. This was founded following the expulsion of the Lutherans from the archbishopric of Salzburg, in 1731. The following year, some 800 exiles from Salzburg settled in States Flanders, at the invitation of the States General, though many soon moved on or ceased to be Lutherans. The Lutheran church at Groede was inaugurated in 1743. During the late eighteenth century, and early nineteenth, Groede counted as one of the five main Lutheran congregations in Zeeland and States Flanders, together with Middelburg, Flushing, Veere, and Ziereikzee.[13] In neighbouring States Brabant there were four sizeable Lutheran congregations, at Breda, Bergen-op-Zoom, 's-Hertogenbosch, and Grave, all main towns.

A clear indication the United Provinces were becoming a more flexible and tolerant society, after 1700, was the growing willingness, in all the provinces, and in both town and countryside, to accept Jewish settlement and ease the restrictions (though by no means dismantle them entirely) on

---

[11] Loosjes, *Gesch. der Luthersche kerk*, 163.
[12] Ibid. 182.
[13] De Kok, *Nederland op de breuklijn*, 353, 356, 360.

Jewish activity. At the end of the seventeenth century, it was still usual in most Dutch towns, in Holland as well as in the outer provinces, to forbid Jews to settle, visit temporarily, or trade, and it was by no means uncommon for this policy to be reconfirmed in the early eighteenth. Thus, Gouda and Utrecht both passed civic laws in 1712, forbidding Jews to settle, lodge in inns, or enter for purposes of trade.

The steady increase in the Jewish population was almost entirely due to immigration from Germany. There were still some New Christians arriving from Portugal and Spain who reverted to normative Judaism in the Republic, during the first third of the eighteenth century. But this Sephardic immigration, joined by a handful of Jews from other parts of the Mediterranean world, was balanced by a constant stream of Sephardic emigration to Curaçao and Surinam and also to the British colonies in the New World, as well as to London. The continuous growth of the Jewish presence in the United Provinces, after 1700, was thus entirely due to Ashkenazic immigration, principally from Germany. While the Sephardic population remained static, at around 3,000, and the number of Sephardic congregations constant, at seven—Amsterdam, The Hague, Rotterdam, Middelburg, Maarssen, Nijkerk, and Naarden—German Jewish congregations proliferated all over the Republic, and the size of the Ashkenazic population steadily increased.

Most of the Jewish immigrants from German lands were desperately poor. Escaping from harsh restrictions, and often wretched conditions, in Germany, the United Provinces—decline or no decline—was for them a land of opportunity.[14] Most Jewish men in the Republic, during the eighteenth century, earned their living by peddling, carrying packs on their backs and selling—often imperfect and second-hand—goods, at low prices, to the less well off. This assured them a steady niche in Dutch life, albeit at a humble level, but also earned them the bitter enmity of Christian shopkeepers belonging to guilds, whose overheads were higher, and who found themselves being undersold by itinerant Jews whose shops were their back-packs. In 1733, the Leiden *vroedschap*, bowing to pressure from the city's linen and cotton goods retailers, forbade the city's Jews to sell these goods. But four years later, the same shopkeepers' guild again bitterly complained that they were being ruined by Jews selling in the streets 'carrying their wares under their arm'.[15] Most of the anti-Jewish legislation passed by Dutch provinces and towns in the eighteenth century was thus essentially economic in character, designed, in particular, to protect the guilds and Christian shopkeepers.

---

[14] De Vries, *From Pedlars to Textile Barons*, 28–9.
[15] GA Leiden Sec. Arch 114, fos. 75–6. res. gerecht, 24 June 1733.

Overijssel, Gelderland, Groningen, and Drenthe all strove to limit Jewish activity in the countryside at provincial level. In 1724, the States of Overijssel expelled vagrants, and itinerant Jews, from outside the province. In 1739, the States of Overijssel ruled that no Jews could establish themselves, or trade, in the countryside of the province, limiting their activity to those towns which would accept them.[16] In 1726, the States of Gelderland forbade Jews from outside the province to settle in rural areas, making an exception only for the village of Nijkerk, where there was already a substantial, mixed Sephardic–Ashkenazic community, active in the tobacco-buying business.[17] The States of Groningen issued placards against vagrants and Jews from outside the province in 1710 and 1713.

Most Dutch towns began allowing Jewish settlement at the end of the seventeenth century, or beginning of the eighteenth, but continued to restrict their numbers and activity in various ways, in particular by excluding them from guilds and shopkeeping. In Holland, Haarlem, Dordrecht, and Leiden permitted Jews to settle from the early eighteenth century onwards. A 'public synagogue' was allowed, and detailed *reglement*, restricting Jewish life in the city, adopted, in Leiden, in 1723 and, at Dordrecht, in 1728. At The Hague, the German Jews obtained their first 'public synagogue' also in 1723. However, at Haarlem a 'public synagogue' was not conceded until considerably later, in 1765, and Gouda and some other Holland towns continued to prevent Jewish settlement throughout the century.

In the province of Utrecht, the two important Jewish communities were those of Amersfoort, where they were mainly involved in the tobacco business, and Maarssen, the village with probably the highest proportion of Jews of any Dutch village, by the late eighteenth century, rising to about 10 per cent by the Napoleonic period. By contrast, the city of Utrecht continued its traditionally illiberal policy, officially excluding Jews until as late as 1788.[18] In Zeeland, Middelburg encouraged Jewish settlement from the beginning of the eighteenth century, but Flushing, Veere, Tholen, Zierikzee, and Goes excluded Jews. There was also a good deal of resistance to Jewish settlement in States Brabant and other Generality Lands. 's-Hertogenbosch, Tilburg, and Eindhoven all excluded Jews until late in the eighteenth century.[19] In 1767, the States General ruled that while there were a few Jews in some places in the Meierij outside the towns, there was no general permission for Jews to settle and trade in the area. Maastricht,

---

[16] Reijnders, *Van 'Joodsche Natien'*, 63–4.
[17] Ibid. 64–5.
[18] Gans, *Memorboek*, 253.
[19] De Vries, *From Pedlars to Textile Barons*, 32.

Venlo, and Roermond continued to forbid Jewish settlement throughout the eighteenth century.

The provinces where the Jewish presence was most pronounced were Holland, Friesland, Groningen, Overijssel, Gelderland, and also Drenthe. Although a grudging, restrictive attitude persisted, all the main cities in the east of the Republic switched over to accepting and regulating Jewish settlement during the course of the eighteenth century. In 1754, the city of Groningen ruled that all German Jews who had lived less than five years in the city, or one of its dependent jurisdictions, must depart within six weeks. It was not until 1756 that Groningen permitted a 'public synagogue'. Zwolle adopted a more tolerant policy towards Jews (as towards Catholics) than Kampen or Deventer, allowing Jewish settlement from the end of the seventeenth century and a 'public synagogue' in 1747. Kampen and Deventer became more tolerant towards Jews only in the later eighteenth century. Nijmegen, more tolerant than Arnhem or Zutphen, allowed Jewish settlement, on a restricted basis, from the end of the seventeenth century; Arnhem followed after the general liberalization in the city council's attitude towards dissenting religions, in the 1720s.

Village Jews were hardly to be found in Friesland but became fairly common in Holland, Groningen, Drenthe, and parts of Overijssel and Gelderland. Old Pekela, in Groningen, noted for its substantial Lutheran congregation, had an even larger German Jewish congregation (of 190) by 1809. In Drenthe, this phenomenon became so widespread that practically every village in the province had a Jewish community by the end of the eighteenth century. A curious feature, in Drenthe, was that the Jews, in much of the province, became the second largest Church after the Reformed.[20] In Hoogeveen, for example, in 1809, the great majority was Reformed; the rest consisted of 11 Catholics, 10 Lutherans, and 116 Jews. In Meppel, there was one listed Catholic, 41 Lutherans, and 178 Jews. In the village of Rhoden there were 1,100 Reformed, 3 Catholics, 4 Mennonites, 10 Lutherans, and 14 Jews. A still smaller Drenthe village, Eelde, had 873 Reformed, 1 Catholic, 2 Mennonites, 3 Lutherans, and 20 Jews. In Gelderland and Overijssel, the situation in this respect was very different. Even in Nijkerk, the largest Gelderland village Jewish community, where in 1809 there were more Jews than in Arnhem or Zutphen, the 214 Jews were heavily outnumbered by Catholics, as well as the Reformed.

While Catholics, Lutherans, and Jews benefited from the growth of toleration and assumed a greater role in Dutch life in the eighteenth century than previously, two other major Churches of the previous century, the

---

[20] De Kok, *Nederland op de breuklijn*, 385–8.

Anabaptists and Remonstrants, not only failed to benefit from the general easing of confessional tensions in the new century, but precipitately declined. In the case of the Anabaptists this can perhaps be explained by the fact that the Church's unrelenting emphasis on austerity and discipline, and opposition to new fashions and novelties, was increasingly at odds with the secular flavour of eighteenth-century life. Dozens of Anabaptist congregations, in many parts of the Republic, became extinct during the course of the century. Of twenty-seven Anabaptist communities in South Holland, in 1700, only three remained by 1800.[21] In Amsterdam, the Anabaptist community dwindled from about 3,000 in the mid-1660s to 2,218 by 1742, and only 1,868 by 1809, or under 1 per cent of the city's population. The Mennonites of Flushing, a vigorous community of 260, in 1660, had diminished to 125, by 1730, and only 49 by 1809, a drop from around 4 to 0.6 per cent of the town's population.

Overall, the most serious setback was the shrinkage of Anabaptist allegiance in Friesland. The Mennonite population of Friesland is estimated to have declined from about 20,000, or 13 per cent of the province's population, in 1666, to 12,800, or 8 per cent, by 1796.[22] At the same time, the number of Anabaptist congregations in Friesland dwindled from seventy-two in 1666 to fifty-five by 1789 while their stock of preachers shrank from 162, in 1739, to only 90 by 1789, and 59 by 1815.[23] The ultra-orthodox 'Old Flemish' community had 1,400 members in the province of Groningen in 1710, a number which had fallen to 642 by 1767.

Though they became thinner on the ground, the Anabaptists still remained an integral part of the confessional scene in Groningen, and north Overijssel, as well as Friesland, Holland, Utrecht, and Zeeland. In Overijssel, in 1809, there were still sizeable Mennonite communities at Blokzijl, Giethoorn—one of the very few towns in the Republic where the Anabaptists formed the majority of the population—Almelo, and Hengelo, where they were 10 per cent of the population. By contrast, the Anabaptist congregations in Deventer, Kampen, and Zwolle were minute.

No less spectacular was the collapse of Remonstrantism. The waning of the Remonstrants was already noticeable during the latter half of the seventeenth century but accelerated after 1700. At Rotterdam, the largest Remonstrant congregation, they were still the second most numerous Church, outstripping the Catholics, during the third quarter of the seventeenth century, when they numbered around 7,000, some 15 per cent of the

[21] Van der Zijpp, *Gesch. der doopsgezinden*, 178–9.
[22] Faber, *Drie eeuwen United Friesland*, i. 82.
[23] Blaupot ten Cate, *Gesch. der doopsgezinden*, 244.

total population.[24] By 1809, there were a mere 900 Remonstrants left, the
tiny remnant of a once great community, representing no more than 1.5 per
cent of the city's population. At Amsterdam only around 500 Remonstrants
remained by 1809. The only other Remonstrant congregations with over one
hundred members by 1809 were Gouda (461), Leiden (129), Hoorn (137),
and the village of Nieuwkoop, all in Holland. The Remonstrants in
Amersfoort had dwindled to thirty-three and in the city of Utrecht to a mere
twenty-seven. Well before 1800, Remonstrantism was extinct in Overijssel,
including Kampen, and almost so in Gelderland (see Table 52). The last
Remonstrant congregation in Friesland, at Dokkum, survived until 1796,
when the remaining ten members dissolved their congregation and merged
with the Anabaptists.

TABLE 52. *Breakdown of the population of the Kingdom of the Netherlands in
1809 by religious confession*

Province	Population						
	Total	Reformed	Catholic	Lutheran	Mennonite	Remonst.	Jews
North Holland	387,660	208,825	100,370	40,030	10,610	900	23,680
South Holland	401,240	289,560	90,780	10,240	470	3,056	5,890
Utrecht	107,940	60,880	42,160	2,110	180	80	1,210
Zeeland	80,180	69,360	8,830	1,380	270	0	270
(former) States							
Flanders	30,000	16,050	13,500	300	100	0	50
Friesland	172,980	141,520	16,310	880	13,050	0	1,020
Groningen	130,890	113,220	10,130	1,970	3,860	0	1,720
Drenthe	44,640	43,390	330	130	40	0	750
Overijssel	143,830	89,630	49,620	1,010	2,110	0	1,650
Gelderland	248,620	153,490	90,310	2,020	190	15	2,230
North Brabant	294,960	34,600	258,350	970	6	10	1,010
Limburg	162,570	1,870	159,740	360	0	0	600
East Friesland	126,380	25,530	1,970	96,070	480	0	1,740
TOTAL	2,205,500	1,222,210	840,210	61,790	30,890	4,080	39,600
(excluding East Friesland)		(55.4%)	(38.1%)	(2.8%)	(1.4%)	(0.18%)	(1.80%)
TOTAL	1,717,977	1,169,682	408,624	60,264	30,780	4,060	37,940
(excluding East Friesland and former Generality Lands)		(68%)	(23%)	(3.5%)	(1.8%)	(0.24%)	(2.2%)

Source: De Kok, *Nederland op de breuklijn*, 288.

[24] Mentink and Van der Woude, *Demografische ontwikkeling*, 43-5.

THE LOOSENING OF INTERNAL CONFESSIONAL BARRIERS

The tension between Voetians and Cocceians which had been such a major element in Dutch church and university politics in the late seventeenth century had been eased by the States of Holland's *reglement* of 1694 (see p. 669 above). Even so Voetian-Cocceian polemics remained a significant factor far beyond the sphere of pure theological debate, permeating church, academic, and local politics until the mid-eighteenth century,[25] and lingering in the background even in the closing decades. The death of William III, in 1702, precipitated a general reaction against his methods and principal supporters throughout the United Provinces, and led, consequently, to a shift in favour of the Cocceians throughout the Church, society, and universities.

This was especially the case in Zeeland and Utrecht. In June 1695, the States of Utrecht had adopted Holland's *reglement*, for the preserving of 'peace' in the 'Church and academy of this province', admonishing the professors to eschew the use of 'Voetian' and 'Cocceian' labels in their teaching. Nevertheless, the university of Utrecht remained, for the moment, a Voetian stronghold, dominated by men such as Melchior Leydecker, a leading Voetian opponent of Bekker. When, in 1698, the *vroedschap* tried to appoint the Franeker Cocceian, Campegius Vitringa, to a newly vacant professorship in theology, William III personally intervened, summoning one of the burgomasters to see him, at Het Loo, to block the appointment.[26] After William's death, the *vroedschap* promptly sought a leading Cocceian and, failing to procure Vitringa, secured the doyen of Reformed liberal theologians (though strictly speaking, not a genuine Cocceian), Herman Alexander Röell (1653–1718), at a salary of 2,200 guilders, which was much more than any other Utrecht professor then earned. This appointment, in 1704, reinforced Cartesianism in Utrecht, but provoked uproar in the theology and philosophy faculties and furious strife in the consistory, prompting the regents to warn Leydecker and other Voetian hardliners of firm 'measures' if they refused to live 'in peace and friendship' with Röell.[27] The academic atmosphere at Utrecht became milder only after Leydecker ceased lecturing, in 1716, and Röell died, two years later. By the 1720s, the university was calm. Yet Voetian and Cocceian credentials remained a prime factor in determining academic appointments for several decades more.

In Zeeland, the anti-Orangist reaction, after 1702, led to a brief Cocceian ascendancy at Middelburg which then faded temporarily with the Orangist

---

[25] Van der Wall, 'Orthodoxy and Scepticism', 124–6.
[26] Kernkamp, *Utrechtsche Academie*, i. 289.
[27] Ibid. i. 301; Sluis, *Herman Alexander Röell*, 42–3.

revival after 1713. After this came a further bout of bitter Cocceian–Voetian strife in the years 1715–20, followed, in the 1720s, by a renewed Cocceian ascendancy over the consistories and classes of Zeeland which continued down to the revolution of 1747.[28] During the later eighteenth century, Cocceian–Voetian antagonism was no longer so fundamental in Dutch culture as formerly. Even so, it is noteworthy that William IV, and later also William V, endeavoured in Zeeland, as in Holland, to revive and strengthen the Voetian stream within the public Church.

The same swing towards a Cocceian ascendancy occurred, albeit less dramatically, also in Holland. After 1702, Cocceians gained the upper hand at Leiden, backed by the *vroedschap*, which in the early eighteenth century was one of the most republican-minded in the province. In 1712, Leiden's Cocceian consistory, with the approval of the regents, voted to put up a stone memorial plaque, embellished with a carved portrait of Cocceius, in the city's principal church. Voetians were outraged, considering this a blatantly provocative, even 'Catholicizing', move, manifesting a desire to 'canonize' Cocceius.[29] The overriding consideration in regent minds after 1702, however, was to damp down Voetian–Cocceian conflict as much as possible, using the placard of 1694. Intermittent attempts to rekindle the flames were rigorously quelled. One highly inflammatory onslaught on Cocceianism published after 1702 was the *Entretiens* (1707) of Pierre de Joncourt, a Huguenot minister at The Hague. De Joncourt poured scorn on Cocceian methods of biblical exegesis, remarking that nobody in France or England took any interest in Cocceianism.[30] De Joncourt was instantly assailed by various Cocceian theologians. Alarm at the possible ramifications of this affray permeated the Walloon Church of the United Provinces at its annual gathering at Goes, in May 1707. Hitherto, Huguenots in the Republic had remained scrupulously neutral in the Voetian–Cocceian controversies and De Joncourt's outburst was viewed as a threat to both the neutrality and the internal unity of the Walloon Church. The synod took care not to censure De Joncourt's anti-Cocceianism as such, condemning, and disciplining, him purely for defying the Church's rule against meddling in the Voetian–Cocceian disputes.

With De Joncourt silenced, the figure who took up the cudgels against D'Outrein and emerged as the foremost Voetian controversialist of the early eighteenth century was Jacobus Fruytier (1659–1731), a pupil of Leydecker, and (like him) a Zeelander, whose father had played a prominent part in

---

[28] Van der Bijl, 'Kerk en politiek', 191–3.
[29] *Journal Littéraire*, i. 476–7.
[30] [De Joncourt], *Entretiens*, 6–7.

stirring up opposition to Momma in 1676. Fruytier, appointed by the then
rigidly Voetian consistory to a living in Rotterdam, in 1700, published his
principal attack on the Cocceians, his *Sions Worstelingen*, there, in 1713. He
charged Cocceians with undermining faith and the Church's authority by
dragging in the 'Trojan Horse of reason', denouncing, in particular, Bekker
and Röell. He also assailed Oldenbarnevelt, and his party, for policies which
had weakened the Church, planting the seeds of decay which had developed
into Cocceianism, a tampering with Scripture and dogma which had
culminated, as he saw it, in the poison of Bekker and the denial of Satan.
He predicted that, as doubt spread, and the Church became more divided
inwardly, honest Cocceians would eventually admit their error in allowing
the rationalists into their midst and renounce Cocceius.[31] Fruytier continued
polemicizing against the Cocceians, and Röell's rationalism, until his death,
but after 1715 was compelled by the South Holland Synod to considerably
moderate his tone.[32]

After 1716, when Henricus Ravesteyn, a Reformed preacher at Zwolle,
published his *Philadelphia*, a plea for an end to the theological Eighty Years
War which had divided the Dutch Reformed Church since the 1640s, calls
for reconciliation and harmony became increasingly frequent. The labels
'Voetians' and 'Cocceian' continued to be widely used down to the 1750s,
but with less vehemence than in the past. A notable contribution towards
this result was the book *Eubulus* (1737) by the Gelderland preacher
Johannes Mauritius Mommers.[33] Mommers listed seventy-six propositions
drawn from Cocceius' writings which had proven particularly divisive. He
then examined each in turn, arguing that, when studied in a spirit of
detachment and good-will, the differences turned out, in each case, to be less
fundamental than was commonly supposed.

The alleviation of the feuding within the public Church, from the 1720s,
went hand in hand with the ending of policies of intolerance on the part of
the provincial and civic authorities in the lesser provinces and easing of
antagonism (at any rate after 1750) between the main confessional blocs
within society. During the first half of the eighteenth century, there were still
moments of acute tension between Protestants and Catholics, especially the
1730s, when the Republic was swept by a wave of anti-Catholic sentiment.
In June 1734, the Reformed population was gripped by a collective state of
panic fed by rumours that the Catholics were planning a general mutiny to

[31] Fruytier, *Sions Worstelingen*, 763–5.
[32] Sluis, *Herman Alexander Röell*, 118.
[33] Van den Berg, 'Godsdienstig leven', 331, 335.

take over the state and the public Church.[34] There were various disturbances. States party regents accused the Orangists of being behind it all, and
deliberately inflating fears as a political and psychological ploy to heighten
the appeal of the House of Orange and stadholderate in the eyes of the
Protestant populace.[35] The Leiden city council mounted special patrols to
protect Catholic prayer-houses in the city from attack. Later, there were
again anti-Catholic disturbances during the Orangist revolution of 1747.
But, as in England in the eighteenth century, such anti-Catholic agitation,
based on a mixture of fear and popular hostility, was essentially a social and
political phenomenon. It no longer played a central role in high culture and
intellectual life.

The easing of internal confessional friction, and advance of toleration,
encouraged the growth of dialogue between the main confessional blocs,
first among the most literate part of the population, and then within society
as a whole. All these phenomena were aspects of a single process. As the
Enlightenment gathered momentum, and awareness of the new philosophy
and science spread, the sway of both theological dogma and ecclesiastical
authority, in society, slowly weakened.

The change was especially evident among the Anabaptist and Lutheran
communities, which were both less deeply divided than during the seventeenth century. Among the Anabaptists, the eighteenth century, the age of
toleration and Enlightenment, was an age of decline in numbers but also of
reconciling the old internal splits. The divisions of the seventeenth century
did not disappear. From the time of the Amsterdam rift of 1664, the
so-called *Lammerenkrijg*, down to the end of the eighteenth century, Dutch
Anabaptism was divided into three main blocs—the 'Lambs', or the more
liberal grouping; the 'Sunists', or conservatives who were, in turn, divided
internally into moderate and conservative wings; and, finally, the ultra-
orthodox remnants of the Old Flemish and Old Frisians.[36] But only the last
grouping (who were especially strong in Groningen) stuck to the absolutes
of the past, still seeing themselves as the only true followers of Menno
Simons, a holy community in a sinful world which must remain isolated
from it and eschew dialogue with the rest. Most Anabaptists, both 'Lamists'
and 'Sunists', no longer saw themselves as the only true church of Christ
that should live in intellectual and religious isolation from others. The last
major eruption of inter-Anabaptist wrangling in the Republic, a fierce
polemical exchange in Groningen, in the years 1735–42, was mainly

[34] Frijhoff, 'Paniek van Juni 1734', 170–3.
[35] Polman, *Romeinse bescheiden*, i. 305.
[36] Van der Zijpp., *Gesch. der doopsgezinden*, 163–6.

provoked by hardline 'true Mennonites' protesting over the changes to which other Anabaptists were adapting.

A number of Anabaptist ministers were among the most enthusiastic advocates of friendly relations, and discussion, among the confessions in the Republic during the eighteenth century. A notable instance was Johannes Deknatel, preacher at 'The Lam', on the Singel, in Amsterdam from 1726 until his death, in 1759. Deknatel put much effort into cultivating better relations between the different Anabaptist groupings, promoting links with the Collegiants, to whom he was close, and establishing dialogue with pietists and Cocceians within the public Church. Like Isaac le Long, who wrote extensively on economic as well as religious matters, Deknatel saw himself as the champion of all victims of religious intolerance and was active in the moves to bring a group of persecuted Moravian Brethren—'Hernhutters'—to settle, in the late 1730s, in Amsterdam.[37] He became a close friend of Count Nicholas Ludwig von Zinzendorf, the 'founder' of the 'Hernhutter' sect in Holland.

But no confessional bloc was more divided, internally, in the early eighteenth century, than the Catholics; and among no other was the easing of tension, in the middle years of the century, more sudden. Like the feud between Voetians and Cocceians within the Reformed Church, the great rift in Dutch Catholicism which arose in late seventeenth and early eighteenth centuries had its origins in theological controversy reaching back to the middle of the previous century. But, where strife among the Reformed had waned since the 1690s, that dividing Jansenists and anti-Jansenists within the Dutch Catholic Church escalated further after Pope Clement XI (1700–21) took a more resolutely anti-Jansenist line than his predecessors, forcing the rift in the Republic into the open.[38] In 1702, at the outset of the War of the Spanish Succession, with the Bourbon monarchs, and the new regime in Brussels, adopting a harshly anti-Jansenist stance in theology and church affairs, the Papacy suspended the then Vicar-Apostolic of the Dutch Catholic Church, Pieter Codde, despite his strong support among local secular clergy, on account of his Jansenist leanings. Codde, who had studied in France and been deeply influenced by Arnauld and Quesnel, had indeed done much, since becoming Dutch Vicar-Apostolic, in 1688, to promote Jansenist attitudes and theology, appointing Jansenists to senior posts, and harbouring French Jansenist refugees.[39] At this point, there were 466 priests

[37] Van der Berg, 'Zinzendorf en de Hernhutters', 77–8.
[38] Spiertz, 'Achtergronden', 183.
[39] Polman, *Katholiek Nederland*, i. 18–20.

in the *Missio*, 340 seculars, fifty-nine Jesuits, and sixty-seven other regulars.[40]

Codde's removal had been pressed for for years by the Jesuits and other anti-Jansenists. One of his chief opponents, Theodorus de Cock, was appointed Vicar-General in his place. But the latter encountered opposition not only from local Catholics but also the Holland regents, who had always been hostile to Jesuits and disapproved of forceful papal intervention in a matter which so deeply divided Dutch Catholics. In August 1702, the States issued a placard forbidding their Catholic subjects to recognize anyone as Vicar-General unless approved by the *Gecommitteerde Raden*. De Cock assured Brussels that the rift between Dutch Jansenists and anti-Jansenists was becoming also a split between 'Roman Catholics' and 'States Catholics'.[41] In the view of the ecclesiastical authorities in the Bourbon Netherlands, only a minority of the Catholic priests on Dutch territory could be classed as 'Jansenists' in theology. Nevertheless, in the years after 1702, those who found it expedient to be considered 'Jansenists', by the Dutch authorities, formed a majority of secular clergy and were especially strong in the traditional centres of post-1572 Dutch Catholicism, Utrecht and Haarlem.

Leading Dutch secular priests committed to the idea of the freedom and separateness (from Brussels) of the 'Batavian Church', men such as Johan Christiaan van Erkel (1654–1734), turned to Heinsius. Ordinary Catholics now had to decide whether to obey the Pope, and recognize the authority of De Cock, or obey the States and refuse to acknowledge him.[42] In 1704, the *Gecommitteerde Raden* examined a batch of priests, including three Jesuits, who had been appointed by De Cock, in disregard of the placard of 1702, suspending eleven from preaching and expelling two from the province. In 1707, and again in 1709, the States of Holland refused to allow the papacy's choice as Vicar-Apostolic to be acknowledged. The Pensionary of Amsterdam informed the Catholic authorities in Brussels that only a 'Jansenist' would be acceptable. Jesuits were also locally expelled, in 1708, from Amsterdam—where the city council was following a strongly pro-Jansenist policy—and Gouda. In 1717, the papacy appointed another Vicar-Apostolic, Joan van Bijlevelt, against the wishes of many Dutch secular clergy, and in violation of the 1702 placard, and Holland again forbade his being acknowledged. In February 1720, he was expelled from Utrecht at the States of Holland's request. In 1720, the States General and

---

[40] Spiertz, 'Katholieke geestelijke leiders', 20.
[41] Polman, *Katholiek Nederland*, i. 20.
[42] Van Schaik, 'Johan Christiaan van Erkel', 147; Spiertz, 'Anti-jansenisme', 240–1.

States of Holland proclaimed a general expulsion of the Jesuits, though it was not very strictly enforced and some were able to remain. This action was justified on the grounds that the Papacy and Jesuits were seeking to compel the consciences of Dutch Catholics, and make them submit to an authority which lay outside the Republic, and that this conflicted with the basic principles of the Republic by which the conscience of the individual must not be compelled.

The tension within the Dutch Catholic Church culminated in the formal schism which took place in April 1723, when the leaders of the 'refractory' clergy appointed one of their number, the Amsterdammer Cornelis Steenhoven (1651–1725), 'Archbishop of Utrecht' and head of what subsequently came to be known as the 'Old Catholic Church'.[43] All attempts to end the schism proved abortive. When Steenhoven died, the Old Catholic clergy appointed as their second 'Archbishop of Utrecht' the still more aggressively Jansenist Cornelis Barchman Wuytiers (1693–1733), a protégé of Pasquier Quesnel. There were now two rival hierarchies in the Holland Mission, one obeying the Vicar-Apostolic appointed by the Pope, and retaining the allegiance of the majority of the Catholic population, and a Jansenist 'Old Catholic Church', refusing to obey the Pope and obedient to its own 'Archbishop of Utrecht'. The Papacy deployed every means to weaken the 'Old Catholic Church', calling on loyal Catholics in the Republic to reject the refractory clergy and mobilizing the kings of France, Spain, Portugal, and Poland, besides numerous other lesser potentates, to protest to the States General at the official encouragement being given to the splinter Church. But, as Louis XV's chief minister, Cardinal Fleury, observed, in 1726, the Holland regents had no intention of facilitating a restoration of unity, preferring to see the Dutch Catholic population divided, sympathizing with the quasi-Calvinist characteristics of the Jansenist clergy, and citing freedom of conscience as justification for blocking efforts to end the schism.[44]

The schism became permanent. The Dutch 'Old Catholic Church' survived as a separate Church, outside the Catholic Church, down to the present day. Nevertheless, it rapidly lost much of its original support and influence. In 1725, seventy-eight of the priests in the Holland Mission were classified as 'refractarii', nearly a quarter of the total in the Mission. But Bijlevelt succeeded in obtaining more priests from 's-Hertogenbosch, Roermond, Münster, Mechelen, and elsewhere with which to replace the defectors and by 1726 the number of priests obedient to Rome had risen to nearly

---

[43] Polman, *Katholiek Nederland*, i. 284–6.   [44] Ibid. 291.

300.[45] The campaign in progress, since 1703, to persuade Catholic parishioners not to receive the sacraments from the hands of the 'Jansenists' was stepped up and led to an effective boycott throughout the Republic. At Amsterdam, in 1723, less than 10 per cent of the Catholic population were reported to be adhering to the schismatic Church. At Rotterdam, around a quarter of the Catholic population were classified in 1726 as 'Old Catholic', that is, took communion with 'refractory' priests. But by the 1750s this had dropped sharply, to less than 10 per cent of the total, and, by 1800, only 3 per cent of Rotterdam Catholics belonged to the schismatic Church.[46] Although there had been substantial Jansenist support among the Catholic population at Zwolle and other places in the east of the Republic in the late seventeenth century, it is striking that in 1726 there were no 'Old Catholic' priests in Overijssel, Gelderland, Groningen, Zeeland, or in Cleves-Mark, and only two in Friesland. Overwhelmingly, the schismatic Church was confined to Utrecht and Holland.[47] In 1809, there were still 867 'Old Catholics' in the city of Utrecht, and 141 in Amersfoort, but these were the only two remaining 'Old Catholic' congregations in the province. In Holland, the only 'Old Catholic' congregations with over one hundred members were at Dordrecht (112), Gouda (123), The Hague (126), Rotterdam (444), Amsterdam (125), Den Helder (where they were the majority of the Catholic community), Hilversum (517), and, largest of all, curiously, the village of Egmond-aan-Zee, the only place where they constituted a majority of the population, outnumbering the Reformed and Roman Catholics combined.[48] Outside Holland and Utrecht, the only 'Old Catholic' congregations existing at the beginning of the nineteenth century were at Culemborg, where over 10 per cent of the Catholic community (who made up over half the population of the town) belonged to the 'Old Catholics'.

[45] Ibid. 322–3.
[46] Mentink and Van der Woude, *Demografische ontwikkeling*, 44.
[47] *Archief aartsbisdom Utrecht*, x. 29, 31, 33–4, 37.
[48] De Kok, *Nederland op de breuklijn*, 303–29.

39

The Enlightenment

❖

THE DUTCH IMPACT

The Enlightenment was one of the most crucial intellectual and general cultural shifts in the history of Europe. It was a vast and many-sided phenomenon which can perhaps usefully be summed up under four heads—a shift to toleration, secularization, classification of knowledge, and popularization, the last particularly as regards science.

All European countries were deeply affected by the Enlightenment. But some played a larger role in generating, and propagating, the new ideas than others. In contrast to most of the rest, the influence and vitality of the Dutch Enlightenment in the eighteenth century was of decreasing, rather than increasing, importance. In this respect, the Dutch somewhat resembled the English (as distinct from the Scottish) Enlightenment, being rooted in major intellectual breakthroughs of the late seventeenth century, and exerting a powerful influence on the European Enlightenment early in the eighteenth, but having much less impact later. For Europe, the Dutch Enlightenment may be said to have been fundamental in the first third of the eighteenth century, of some, but diminishing, importance in the second, and marginal by the third.

A striking feature of Dutch cultural and intellectual life at the close of the Golden Age, and a continuing peculiarity of the Dutch Enlightenment during the early eighteenth century, was the split between the intellectual flowering in the French language, on the one hand, and Dutch and Latin, on the other. The principal Huguenot minds in the Republic—Bayle, Basnage, and Marchand—were by no means working in isolation from their Dutch context. They had Dutch patrons and associates and, in many ways, adapted to their new environment. They were also avidly read and discussed by the Dutch theologians, philosophers, scientists, and regent intellectuals around them. Yet they took no part in the Dutch Cartesian, Cocceian, and Bekkerite debates, they rarely taught in the Dutch universities, and their work scarcely ever appeared in the Dutch language. Only in the controversy about Spinoza did the Huguenots, particularly Bayle, figure prominently. Most failed to master Dutch. Bayle managed to live twenty-five years in Rotterdam without speaking any Dutch.[1] Prosper Marchand (1678–1756), the last great Huguenot mind to arrive, appeared in 1709, and spent half a century in the Republic, where he was a major figure. Yet he never learnt to speak Dutch and remained heavily orientated, in his work, towards Bayle, and other Huguenots, rather than Dutch writers, though he collaborated with several of those, notably Justus van Effen and the physicist Willem Jacob van 's Gravesande, who worked in both languages.[2]

A major aspect of the European Enlightenment was the change which took place, from about 1700, in debate about religion. Positive appreciation of toleration increased, confessional zeal receded, discussion emerged from the arena controlled by Churches and churchmen, and, above all, there was a new awareness and interest in the variety of religion and relationships between different religious traditions and theological systems. The impulse to classify and compare theological standpoints received new impetus from Bayle's *Dictionnaire* and remained much in evidence down to the middle of the eighteenth century.

A key figure in this process was Bayle's friend Jacques Basnage (1653–1723), son of a Rouen Huguenot jurist, and preacher to the French Reformed community in Rotterdam, from 1685 to 1709, who was then brought by Heinsius (who held him in high regard) to be minister at the Walloon Church in The Hague. This noted champion of toleration compiled *L'Histoire et la religion des Juifs depuis Jésus-Christ jusqu'à présent* (5 vols.; 1706–11), the first general account of post-biblical Jewry written in Europe and remarkable for its objective tone, notably the detached attitude to the seventeenth-century Sephardic anti-Christian polemicists Elie Montalto, Saul Levie Morteira, and Isaac Orobio de Castro. Basnage himself was aware of the novelty of his enterprise and deliberately stressed the injustice and persecution to which Christians had subjected the Jews, in order to make Christians think about the relationship in a new way.[3] For the same reason, he gave considerable space to the arguments against Christianity put forward by Isaac Orobio de Castro in his famous debate with Van Limborch in (or around) 1684. The knowledge of Jewish writers' rebuttal of Christianity which became a feature of the French radical Enlightenment after

---

[1] Labrousse, *Pierre Bayle*, i. 169–70.
[2] Berkvens-Stevelinck, *Prosper Marchand*, 167–8.
[3] Basnage, *Histoire des Juifs*, preface to 2nd edn.

1750, especially of the work of the Baron d'Holbach, can be said to have entered the world of the Enlightenment through Basnage and his circle.[4]

Another central figure in classifying and reappraising religions was the Swiss Jean Le Clerc (1657–1736). Le Clerc was a Genevan Calvinist pastor who, through reading Grotius, Stephen Curcellaeus, and Episcopius, became persuaded of the truth of Remonstrantism. Unable to declare himself a Remonstrant in Switzerland, he settled in Amsterdam, at the prompting of Van Limborch, in 1684, and became the great spokesman of Remonstrantism in French. He married Maria, daughter of Gregorio Leti, and followed his friend Van Limborch, and Episcopius, as a leading champion of toleration. One of his projects was the first general edition of the works of Erasmus (10 vols.; 1703–6), long the hero of the Remonstrants. His chief importance, however, was as a reviewer of religious and philosophical literature. His journal, which appeared in its mature period under the title *Bibliothèque choisie* (28 vols.; 1703–13), and later as the *Bibliothèque ancienne et moderne* (29 vols.; 1714–27), went beyond Bayle's *Nouvelles* in providing systematic and objective reviews.

A striking example of the new approach to religion was the monumental *Cérémonies et Coutumes religieuses de tous les peuples du monde*, published at Amsterdam, in thirteen volumes, in 1723. This work, largely written by Jean-Frédéric Bernard (1683?–1744) and magnificently illustrated by the engraver Freemason Bernard Picart (1673–1733), was remarkable for reviewing religious practices and rites systematically, treating Christianity as just another religion alongside Judiasm, Islam, and Freemasonry.[5] Picart went to some lengths to ensure the authenticity of his illustrations, participating personally, for example, in a Passover *seder* night service in the home of a leading Amsterdam Sephardic elder, in order to be able to depict the scene. A further contribution to the Enlightenment's reappraisal of religion was Marchand's principal work, his *Dictionnaire historique* (2 vols.; The Hague, 1758–9), a supplement to Bayle, embodying a secular critique of Catholicism—for its intolerance and tradition of persecution—and a dispassionate treatment of Socinianism.

Dutch, as distinct from Dutch Huguenot, Enlightenment writers were, on the whole, less preoccupied with religion and more concerned with science. The point at which the two wings of the Dutch Enlightenment met was in the campaign against Spinoza. This intellectual offensive, spearheaded by Bayle, continued without let-up throughout the first quarter of the eighteenth century. Many works of the period attest to the pervasive presence of

---

[4] Kaplan, *From Christianity to Judaism*, 451–6.
[5] Jacob, *The Radical Enlightenment*, 196.

'Spinozists' in Dutch society, equating 'Spinozists' with free-thinkers. It was usual also to deplore the openness with which 'Spinozists' dared express their opinions.[6] Although the Republic resembled England, during the first two decades of the eighteenth century, in being a country where deism, and rejection of revealed religion, were commonly perceived to be widespread phenomena, Dutch society was unique in mounting such a sustained anti-deist and anti-atheistic offensive. It was pressed home despite—or perhaps because of—the fact that many figures of the intellectual mainstream, including Bayle and Marchand, were suspected of being more inclined to free-thinking themselves than they cared to admit.

As a consequence of the campaign against the 'Spinozists', deism and rejection of revelation in the United Provinces, which were equated with Spinozism, became an underground movement, a clandestine stream which has aptly been called the 'Radical Enlightenment'.[7] Reacting against Spinoza, the Dutch mainstream Enlightenment never frontally questioned divine revelation, but sought, rather, to combine a conventionally pious—albeit tolerant and non-confessional—belief that God is omnipresent in nature and society with zeal for empirical science and the *esprit systématique*.[8] The principal early exponent of this 'physico-theology' in the United Provinces, the regent philosopher Bernard Nieuwentyt (1654–1718) of Purmerend, wrote two long, and influential, books to refute Spinoza and the other 'many atheistic books' pervading the Dutch scene, promoting empirical science in conjunction with veneration for a revealed God who is also evident in every detail of nature, *Het Regt Gebruik der Werelt Beschouwingen* (1715) and the *Gronden van Zekerheid* (1720). These enjoyed great popularity in the Republic and, unlike later Dutch books, appeared in English and German, as well as French and Dutch, and had a certain impact in France.[9] Originally a Cartesian, Nieuwentyt in these books categorically rejected Cartesian science, as based on a priori reasoning, advocating instead the *philosophia experimentalis* of the 'famous Mr Boyle in England',[10] that is, empiricism. Nieuwentyt's importance lies not in his originality—a similar physico-theology had already been propagated in France, by Fénelon, in his *Démonstration de l'existence de Dieu par les merveilles de la Nature* (1712), and in England by writers such as John Ray and William Derham—but rather in his lasting impact on Dutch culture.[11] For, in

[6] Aalstius, *Inleiding*, 4–7; Nieuwentyt, *Regt gebruik*, 6.
[7] Jacob, *The Radical Enlightenment*, 51–3.
[8] Mijnhardt, 'Nederlandse Verlichting', 252–3, 260.
[9] Vercruysse, 'Fortune de Bernard Nieuwentyt', 224–7.
[10] Nieuwentyt, *Gronden van Zekerheid*, 1–2.
[11] Bots, *Tussen Descartes en Darwin*, 5–17.

contrast to France, Nieuwentyt's comfortable conjunction of questing empiricism with an unquestioning faith which avoided the challenging issues raised by Spinoza, Huygens, Bayle, and Bekker continued to dominate the whole of the Dutch mainstream Enlightenment. Nieuwentyt explained in the preface of *Het regt gebruik* that he wrote in Dutch specifically in order to influence his compatriots and check the spread of 'atheism' in Dutch society.

The growing reliance of the Dutch trading system on industry, and technological sophistication, during the last phases of Dutch world trade primacy, down to 1740, imparted an impetus to applied and theoretical science and technology which went beyond anything found elsewhere in continental Europe during the first half of the eighteenth century. In physics, the role of the Dutch was to package, and propagate, Newtonian science. Here the two key figures were Willem Jacob van 's Gravesande (1688–1742) and Pieter van Musschenbroek (1692–1761). 's Gravesande, the son of a Generality official at 's-Hertogenbosch, did more than anyone before Voltaire to spread awareness of Newton's principles in Europe, partly through the *Journal de la République des Lettres*, which he established together with Marchand and Van Effen in 1713. 's Gravesande had visited England, conferred with Newton, and, after becoming professor of physics, in 1717, drew hundreds of foreign students to Leiden to imbibe the new science through his lectures. In 1719, he published a famous handbook of physics which made him the chief exponent of Newtonian science on the Continent, a role he retained through the 1720s and 1730s. Musschenbroek had also met Newton and, whilst professor at Duisburg (1719–23), and especially as professor of mathematics at Utrecht (1723–40), became the second internationally famous Dutch exponent of the new science.

Besides teaching and popularizing, 's Gravesande was a theorist of some stature, who introduced several refinements to Newton's laws, and an inventor who devised an array of pumps, steam-machines, and cranes.[12] He also attempted to integrate Newtonian science with philosophy, taking care to warn his students against Spinoza, whose ideas he denounced as 'très dangereuses', and whom he accused of abusing the mathematical method.[13] Musschenbroek also published a handbook of Newtonian science, his *Elementa physico-mathematica* (1726), and was a famous inventor. His two most notable contrivances were the pyrometer, a device for measuring high temperatures, in furnaces, and the atmometer, an instrument for measuring evaporation from moist surfaces.

---

[12] Davids, 'Universiteiten', 12–13.
[13] 's Gravesande, *Œuvres philosophiques*, ii. 22, 355.

Voltaire's main object in visiting the United Provinces (for the third time) over the winter of 1736–7, was to attend 's Gravesande's lectures, and visit the great Boerhaave, in preparation for his own Newtonian handbook, the *Éléments de la philosophie de Newton* (1738).[14] Voltaire owed a large debt to 's Gravesande and had no doubt that he and Boerhaave were the two leading men of Dutch science, reporting to the young Frederick the Great, in Berlin, in January 1737, that between them the two professors had attracted four or five hundred of the foreign students then to be found in Leiden.

In physics, the Dutch Enlightenment was the intermediary between Britain and the Continent.[15] But in microscopical science, botany, anatomy, and medicine, the Dutch Enlightenment may fairly be described as the instructor of Europe, including Britain. The tradition of Huygens and Van Leeuwenhoek in lenses and microscopical science was continued especially by Nicolaas Hartsoeker (1656–1725), son of a Remonstrant preacher at Gouda. After spending many years at Paris, making telescopes for the observatory, he had his own observatory assigned to him, by the *vroedschap* in Amsterdam, in the years 1696–1704, before becoming court mathematician to the Elector of the Palatinate, at Heidelberg. He spent the last part of his life (1716–25) back in the Republic. Hartsoeker was both a leading anti-Newtonian and critic of Van Leeuwenhoek who in his *Conjectures Physiques* (1707) and subsequent works strove to build an alternative scientific system.[16] Among other disputes with Van Leeuwenhoek, he claimed to have preceded him in discovering sperm.

In botany, the traditions of Commelin, Rumphius, and others were continued in the early eighteenth century by Ruysch, Commelin's nephew Caspar Commelin (1668–1731), also a leading botanist, and Boerhaave who, among his other roles, became head of the Leiden *hortus botanicus* in 1709, subsequently publishing his celebrated catalogue of the 3,700 species then to be found in the university gardens. It was above all owing to the large number of exotic and rare plants, preserved as dried specimens in Dutch collections, and grown in regent, patrician, and academic gardens, that the famous Swedish botanist Carl Linnaeus (1707–78), who was chiefly known as a classifier of botanical species, spent several years in the United Provinces (1735–8) researching and completing two books the manuscripts of which he had brought with him from Sweden. His *Systema Naturae* was published at Leiden, in 1735, and his *Fundamenta Botanica*, the following year.

[14] Vercruysse, *Voltaire et la Hollande*, 36–7, 127.
[15] Mijnhardt, 'Dutch Enlightenment', 203.
[16] Van Berkel, 'Intellectuals against Leeuwenhoek', 195–7.

Herman Boerhaave (1668–1738), another preacher's son, and an enthusiast for religious toleration as well as science, was one of the principal figures of the Dutch Enlightenment and, in his day, the most famous medical man in Europe. The importance of 'le célèbre Boerhaave', as Voltaire called him, lies not in any particular discoveries but rather in his unrivalled grasp of the scientific knowledge of his time and conception of medicine as a clinical science based on knowledge of all the sciences, understood in an empirical rather than deductive sense.[17] He placed great stress on demonstrations in chemistry, as well as anatomy, botany, and microscopical science. Among the most influential of his many books were his medical *Aphorismi* (1709), notes on diagnosis and treatment, and his *Elementa Chemiae* (1732) which was admired by Voltaire,[18] translated into various languages, and remained, for much of the eighteenth century, one of Europe's principal handbooks on chemistry. Like 's Gravesande and Musschenbroek an enthusiast for Newton, Boerhaave taught Voltaire and the rest of Europe how Newtonian principles applied in chemistry.[19] He was visited in Leiden by Peter the Great, in 1717, and accompanied the Tsar on his tour of the Leiden *hortus*, and its museum. The rise of Boerhaave, who by the 1720s was the foremost figure of Dutch academe, marked the final overthrow of Cartesian deductive science in the United Provinces and its replacement with the empirical *esprit systématique* of the eighteenth century.[20]

Several of Boerhaave's pupils led famous careers in Germany and at St Petersburg. Among the most able was Gerard van Swieten (1700–72), a native of Leiden who spent many years there first as a student and later a practising physician whilst Boerhaave was at his height. As a Catholic, he was excluded from a professorship in the Republic, but, after Boerhaave's death, was appointed personal physician to the Empress Maria Theresa and director of the Imperial Library, in Vienna. During the 1740s, Van Swieten remodelled the medical faculty of the university of Vienna on the Leiden pattern, applying the principles of Boerhaave. Van Swieten's chief published work was his commentary on Boerhaave's *Aphorismi*, which he published at Leiden (6 vols.; 1766–72), towards the end of his life.

The Dutch medical and anatomical collections, with their attendant drawings and prints, were no less celebrated than the collections of rare plants and insects with their accompanying paintings. Building on Swammerdam's methods,[21] Ruysch won particular renown for his skill in preserv-

[17] Lindeboom, *Herman Boerhaave*, 70, 95–101.
[18] Vercruysse, *Voltaire et la Hollande*, 119–20.
[19] Lindeboom, *Herman Boerhaave*, 270.
[20] Ibid. 366–7.
[21] Schierbeek, *Jan Swammerdam*, 85.

ing and displaying anatomical organs as well as other physiological, entomological, and botanical specimens. His celebrated natural history collection was sold to Tsar Peter the Great, in 1717, for 30,000 guilders. He then built up a new museum which was sold, after his death, in 1731, to the Polish king, for 20,000 guilders. The natural history collections, and 'cabinets of rarities', were celebrated features of early eighteenth-century Amsterdam and Leiden and the most impressive in Europe. But such collections were not confined only to those cities. The craze for collecting 'rarities' spread throughout the maritime provinces and beyond. One of the chief attractions of Utrecht for diplomats attending the peace conference in 1712–13 was the museum of the Huguenot Nicholas Chevalier, renowned for its stuffed rare birds and animals, as well as coins, Chinese sculpture, and oriental weapons.[22] François Valentijn (1666–1721), the Reformed preacher who spent many years in the East Indies, translated the Bible into Malay, and wrote the famous compendium about the Dutch empire in the east, the *Oud en Nieuw Oost-Indien* (1724–6), won fame, after retiring to his native Dordrecht, in 1714, as a collector of marine shells and plants.[23] He founded a society of conchologists at Dordrecht called Neptune's Cabinet.

The essence of the Dutch mainstream Enlightenment was the overthrow of Cartesian deductive science and its replacement with *philosophia experimentalis*, a mania for scientific classification which spilled over beyond the realm of the natural sciences. A typical exponent of eighteenth-century *esprit systématique* was Lambert ten Kate (1674–1731), one of the founding fathers of modern linguistics. A friend of the painters Van der Werff and Jan van Huysum—the latter as renowned as Ruysch's daughter, as a flower painter—Ten Kate carried out pioneering research in ancient Gothic, early German, old Dutch, and Anglo-Saxon, and was the first to classify the Germanic languages in terms of sound shifts, attempting to establish their relationships and evolution. In his introduction to his main work, Ten Kate spoke of his pride in the Dutch language and impulse to uncover its linguistic evolution by means of research into old Germanic languages.[24] Boswell was struck by the originality of Ten Kate's work on arriving in Utrecht, more than half a century later.[25]

Another respect in which the Republic served as the hub of the European Enlightenment, until around 1740, was as the headquarters of Europe's learned periodicals and book reviewers. During the Early Enlightenment, a

[22] Van Klaveren, 'Nicolaas Chevalier', 156.
[23] Boxer, *Dutch Seaborne Empire*, 182.
[24] Ten Kate, *Gemeenschap*, 18; Ten Kate, *Aenleiding*, i. 11–12, 14.
[25] Pottle, *Boswell in Holland*, 135.

general exchange of bibliographical news and reviews was, in a way that it ceased to be later, an essential element in the spread of ideas and diffusion of knowledge about books. For while Latin was slowly being replaced by modern vernacular languages, Europeans were still remarkably parochial in distributing and acquiring books, a situation aggravated by the prevailing ignorance of languages other than Latin and French. England had suddenly (since the last quarter of the seventeenth century), become of vital importance in European culture as a whole. But, as a lingering residue from the past, few people on the Continent knew English, and English books were rarely to be seen.[26] The situation regarding German was no better and, in the case of lesser languages, usually worse. It was, in fact, extremely difficult to learn about new books published in other countries and no easy matter to obtain them.

It is this which explains the astonishing profusion of journals and reviews of books in the United Provinces, beginning with the *Nouvelles de la République des Lettres*, which Bayle established in 1684, down to the 1740s. Europe's principal journals came to be concentrated in this way in the United Provinces partly because the Dutch entrepôt, the general reservoir of goods for Europe, was the hub of the international book trade and a leading centre of book production in several languages, and partly because Early Enlightenment attitudes had progressed further in the United Provinces than almost anywhere else, generating an exceptionally large local market for book news. The Dutch reviews were international in scope but still heavily reliant on the local market for their sales. Additional factors were the relative freedom of the press and presence of numerous Huguenot *érudits* with close links with France, Switzerland, and England.

As a rough rule of thumb about half the books reviewed in the Dutch journals were published in the Republic.[27] Of the rest, most were published in France with smaller quantities in England and Germany. Of the books reviewed by the *Journal Littéraire* (1713–37) of The Hague, for example, 55 per cent were published in the United Provinces (albeit often in French), and almost one quarter in France.[28] A mere 8 per cent of the books were published in Britain and around 7 per cent in Germany. Apart from the odd Italian volume, books produced outside the United Provinces, France, England, and Germany played practically no part in the Early Enlightenment at all.

A crucial function of the Dutch Enlightenment was the introduction of English ideas and culture to the Continent. All progressive minds in Europe

[26] Bots, 'Rôle des périodiques néerlandais', 54–5.   [27] Ibid. 53.   [28] Ibid.

wanted to learn about Newton, Boyle, and Locke but were usually unable to do so directly. To assist the process, a journal specializing in English publications, the *Bibliothèque angloise*, was established at Amsterdam, in 1717. Michel de la Roche, the editor, explained that the venture was needed 'parce que les éditions anglaises n'étaient jusque-là guère connues en dehors de l'Angleterre'.[29] A similar need was felt in the case of German books, a specialized *Bibliothèque germanique* being launched in 1720.

THE ʿRADICALʾ ENLIGHTENMENT

The mainstream Dutch Enlightenment was fundamental to the Early Enlightenment as a whole and one of its chief sources. But there was another stream of Dutch intellectual impact on Europe, of significance in the early eighteenth century, that of the 'Radical' Enlightenment. Where the Dutch mainstream Enlightenment was chiefly scientific, a manifestation of *esprit systématique*, and reverential towards revealed religion, the Dutch 'Radical' Enlightenment—essentially a popularization of Spinoza's critique of revealed religion—was the most vehement attack on Christianity of the first third of the eighteenth century. This aspect of the Dutch Enlightenment was of great importance also especially, so far as the rest of Europe is concerned, in relation to France.

Spinoza, who met Saint-Évremond in 1670, Stouppe in 1673, and others in the circle around the Prince de Condé, at Utrecht, during the French occupation, may himself have had a hand in preparing the influential French version of the *Tractatus Theologico-Politicus*, published in 1678, a version banned in France as well as in the Republic.[30] Several personalities who helped spread Spinoza's influence, after his death in 1677, were French exiles or had close links with France. Among them was Jean Maximilien Lucas (c.1646–97),[31] who knew Spinoza and to whom the earliest biography of the philosopher is attributed, a work which amongst much else is the chief source of the tradition—the veracity of which has been doubted—that among the regents who protected, and consulted, Spinoza was the Pensionary of Holland, Johan de Witt himself. Lucas's biography was not published until 1719, when it was brought out, in Holland, together with what was arguably the most sensational text of the Radical Enlightenment, the *Traité des trois imposteurs* [alluding to Moses, Jesus, and Mohammed], *ou L'Esprit de M. Spinosa*. This book, a concoction of Spinoza's most provocative

---

[29] Ibid. 54–5.   [30] Popkin, *The Third Force*, 146–7.   [31] Ibid. 136, 145, 270.

ideas, including sections translated from the *Tractatus* and *Ethics*,[32] spiced
with a little Vanini, was suppressed with more than usual zeal by the States
of Holland, most of the copies being seized and destroyed. It was rigorously
banned also in France. As a result, it circulated chiefly in hundreds of
manuscript copies, many of which are to be found today, in numerous
variants, in libraries all over the Netherlands, France, Britain, and Germany.[33]

The principal compiler of the *Traité* appears to have been Jan Vroesen
(1672–1725), son of the Rotterdam States party burgomaster Adriaen
Vroesen, purged by William III in 1672, a regent's son with a complete
mastery of French.[34] Other participants in the venture, several of whom
added sections of text, were the Huguenot radical Jean Rousset de Missy
(1686–1762),[35] a former soldier who had fought in the Dutch army against
the French at Malplaquet, and later become a leading journalist, at The
Hague and Amsterdam, and Jean-Frédéric Bernard, at Amsterdam, who,
besides collaborating with Picart in the great illustrative work on the
religions of the world, published in 1723, also translated Adriaan Beverland's book, denying original sin (see p. 684 above), into French.

In this way a debased, as well as drastically abbreviated, 'Spinoza' was
turned by a group of Dutch and Huguenot free-thinkers into a potent
subterranean force, the main engine of the Radical Enlightenment in the
United Provinces and an engine, if not *the* engine, behind the first broad
wave of anti-Christian writing in France. Dutch mainstream religious and
philosophical writers of the early and mid-eighteenth century invariably
assert that it was Spinoza, in popularized versions, and not any other
thinker, who was the chief source of the insidious poison which seemed to
them to be undermining Dutch religion and society and which they strove
to combat.[36] In France, the impact of Spinozism as a clandestine intellectual
current runs parallel with that in the Republic. Spinozism became established in France in the 1690s when figures such as the comte de Boulainvil-
liers (1658–1722), in Normandy, immersed themselves in Spinoza, coming
up with the same truncated, virulently anti-Christian Spinoza—leaving aside
his complex metaphysics and focusing on his critique of revealed religion—
as evolved in the Republic. But the phenomenon was largely confined to the
first third of the eighteenth century. After 1730, there were many new

[32] Ibid. 145.
[33] Wade, *Clandestine Organization*, 114, 124–6.
[34] Berti, 'Jan Vroesen', 537–8; Berti, 'Scepticism', 216–21.
[35] Jacob, *Radical Enlightenment*, 52, 187, 196.
[36] Aalstius, *Inleiding*, 4–7; Nieuwentyt, *Het regt gebruik*, 6; Nieuwentyt, *Gronden van
Zekerheid*, 2, 244, 303.

developments in France and the simplified 'Spinoza' of the early eighteenth-century Dutch and French Spinozists became increasingly marginal to the progress of atheism, deism, and anti-Christian ideas. At the same time, in the Dutch Republic, the Radical Enlightenment gradually faded, dying away under the combined stranglehold of Voetian orthodoxy and physico-theological moderation.

Nevertheless, it remained a significant undercurrent of Dutch cultural life at any rate down to the 1750s. One of its notable personalities was the rakish littérateur and wit Jacob Campo Weyerman (1677–1747). Born in William III's encampment near Charleroi, the son of a Dutch army officer, Weyerman acquired an unrivalled knowledge of the Dutch literary and cultural scene as well as a reputation as a free-thinker. A gifted writer, with a flair for pungent satire, he edited a series of Dutch-language periodicals, making himself a somewhat feared as well as notorious personality. Arrested by the Hof of Holland, for libel, in 1738, he spent his remaining years in prison. But the most outstanding figure continued to be Rousset de Missy, who developed, after 1719, into a fierce critic of regents and regent corruption, as well as of traditional thought.[37] He played a prominent part in the disturbances at Amsterdam in 1747–8, and became the foremost popularizer of John Locke's radical political ideas in the Republic (see p. 1074 below). His 1755 French version of Locke's *Two Treatises* became one of the most widely used editions of the eighteenth century. Yet, through it all, Spinozism—or pantheism, as he called his creed—was still the central unifying strand in his life and work. He remained the standard-bearer of the tradition of the *Traité des trois imposteurs*.

THE DECLINE OF THE UNIVERSITIES

In 1737, Voltaire was struck by the unparalleled capacity of the Dutch professors and universities to attract foreign students by offering new ideas and methods, especially in science and medicine. At that time neither Britain nor France could compete with the United Provinces in providing academic instruction in recent advances and thought, for both home and foreign students.

But the golden age of the Dutch universities was already over and what Voltaire glimpsed was the final glitter of a phenomenon which, since the 1720s, was already in decline, though the most dramatic phase of contraction began only after his 1737 visit, in the 1740s. During the first quarter of

---

[37] Jacob, 'Radicalism', 229–30.

the eighteenth century, 3,164 foreign students studied at Leiden, only slightly less than the number of home students, and down only marginally on the numbers of foreign students studying at Leiden during the second half of the seventeenth century.[38] During the second quarter of the eighteenth century, foreign student numbers at Leiden were still substantial, at 2,715, but with a disastrous slump setting in in the 1740s. By the third quarter of the century, only 1,132 foreigners studied at Leiden, amounting to less than one-third of the level of a century before. By the last quarter of the century, the decadence of Leiden was complete and irreversible, foreign student numbers being down to less than 10 per cent of the figures achieved a century before.

The story was much the same at the other universities. Utrecht, flourishing at the end of the seventeenth century, was in steep decline by the middle of the eighteenth. Franeker never fully recovered its former ability to attract German and other foreign students after 1672, among other setbacks losing virtually all its Hungarians to Utrecht. But Franeker did stage a partial recovery in the period 1690–1760 and, in the middle of the eighteenth century, strove to modernize its scientific and medical teaching, in particular by appointing Petrus Camper (1722–89) as professor of philosophy and medicine in 1749. Camper, a declared enemy of Cartesianism, 'Newtonian' and follower of 's Gravesande, Boerhaave, and Musschenbroek, who used 's Gravesande's *Philosophia Newtoniana* as the basis of his teaching, had some impact. But he disliked Franeker's isolation and stayed only until 1755. By 1760, the university was in full decline.[39] Boswell's observation, in 1764, that the 'universities here are much fallen' was, in every respect, justified.[40]

This catastrophic deterioration was a reflection of the decay of the Republic, and its society and economy, more generally. Several reports suggest that financial pressures, hampering investment in new buildings, equipment, and foreign professors, were a major factor in the process. The disintegration of the overseas trading system, and industry, and the end of the Dutch role in technological innovation, imparted an increasingly redundant, antiquated, and ruined feel to the university towns. Especially ruinous was the winding down of the medical faculties in the period after Boerhaave's death. Camper was not the only capable follower of Boerhaave and

---

[38] Colenbrander, 'Herkomst der Leidsche studenten', 278–87; Wansink, *Politieke wetenschappen*, 7.

[39] Ridder-Symoens, 'Buitenlandse studenten', 77.

[40] Pottle, *Boswell in Holland*, 282; I am indebted also to conversation with Karel Davids on this point.

Musschenbroek available to fill university chairs in the mid-eighteenth century. But the provincial and civic authorities would, or could, not provide the funds necessary to invest in the increased number of professors in medicine and science, and the new laboratories and equipment, characteristic of the best German and other foreign universities during the latter part of the eighteenth century.

THE DECLINE OF THE VISUAL ARTS

That the Dutch visual arts experienced steep decline in the eighteenth century has never been disputed. But this needs to be viewed not as an isolated phenomenon independent of society and the economy but rather as a process moving together with the decline of the trading system, industries, and civic vitality. For it was a staged, fading process, proceeding hand in hand with the lapsing of intellectual achievement, science, and the universities. Dutch art, in other words, remained one of the three foremost schools of Europe—with the Italians and French—until the 1740s, declined precipitately during the middle decades of the century, and, like almost everything else, was prostrate, in full decadence, after 1770.

At the beginning of the eighteenth century, the United Provinces were still regarded by contemporaries as the chief centre of artistic activity in northern Europe, certainly in painting, etching, engraving, and *grisailles*. The three cities which best weathered the economic storms of the 1670s and 1690s, and retained most general vitality—Amsterdam, The Hague, and Rotterdam— also tended to enhance their relative position, in the Dutch art world. Yet, other centres also retained some vitality. At Leiden, a group of artists continued the tradition of Dou, Van Mieris, and Metsu, in highly polished genre painting. Among the most notable were Willem van Mieris (1662– 1747), second son of Frans. He lived his entire life in Leiden, though his work was known, and sought after, also at Amsterdam and The Hague.[41] Jacob Toorenvliet (1640–1719), an older member of the group, spent the 1670s abroad, working in Rome, Venice, and Vienna, but afterwards returned permanently to Leiden, and was still a key figure in Leiden's guild of artists in the second decade of the eighteenth century. Arnold Houbraken (1660–1719), who trained in his native city, Dordrecht, under Van Hoogstraeten, when the crisis in the art market was at its worst, in the mid-1670s, remained for most of his career in Dordrecht, though his principal patron, the regent Johan Witsen, an avid collector of art and 'rarities', eventually

[41] Sluijter, *Leidse fijnschilders*, 152.

persuaded him to move to Amsterdam. Houbraken spent many years collecting information, albeit often rather unreliable, about the lives of the Dutch painters, and sought out Rachel Ruysch, and others who were still alive, to research their life-stories. His account of their lives, the *Groote Schouburgh der Nederlandsche konstschilders*, was published in three volumes in 1718–20.

Rachel Ruysch enjoyed her greatest success in the early eighteenth century, selling her pictures for over 1,000 guilders each, such was her renown both at home and abroad. She was named one of the court painters of Elector Johann Wilhelm of the Palatinate, in 1708, and was several times his guest at his court in Düsseldorf. He was accustomed to give her pictures as presents to other princes. The Amsterdam painter Jan van Huysum (1682–1749) also notably contributed to the further development and refinement of Dutch flower-painting in the early eighteenth century.

Dutch collectors in the mid-eighteenth century were still under the spell of the seventeenth-century masters.[42] As in intellectual life and political ideology, eighteenth-century Dutch art shows a remarkable sense of cohesion and continuity with the past without, at its best, being purely derivative. Jan van Gool, the leading Dutch art critic of the age, who published a sequel to Houbraken's *Schouburgh* in 1750–1, claimed that Dutch art was still flourishing but had nevertheless considerably declined, chiefly, he argued, because collectors prized seventeenth-century masters so much— avidly collecting Dou, Van Mieris, Metsu, and Ter Borch, the masters of the genre piece, in particular—that they lent insufficient support to contemporary artists.[43] Not surprisingly, nearly all eighteenth-century Dutch artists preferred to adhere to, and further develop, the traditions of the Golden Age rather than branch out in new directions. Thus, the main achievement of eighteenth-century Dutch art, as with Ruysch and Van Huysum in flower-painting, or Willem van Mieris in genre, was the continuing of the main lines of development of the seventeenth century. Only some of the old specialities lived on, however. The still life, apart from flower-painting, died away, as did marine painting after the deaths of Van Bakhuysen, in 1708, and Abraham van Storck soon after. The one figure who does stand out conspicuously for his originality was Cornelis Troost (1697–1750), who painted household and street scenes in a strongly satirical and theatrical style. Another noteworthy painter of this period was Jacob de Wit (d. 1754),

---

[42] Grijzenhout, 'A Myth of Decline', 327–8.   [43] Ibid. 328–9.

who, besides 'history' paintings, executed some eye-catching, innovative ceiling decorations.

A key feature of the Dutch art scene from the 1690s onwards, resulting from the declining demand for contemporary paintings, was a shift to new kinds of decorative work for the homes of the wealthy and especially engravings and coloured illustrations for publication in books.[44] Until the mid-eighteenth century, the United Provinces remained the leading centre of book production in Europe and, during the Early Enlightenment, the fashion amongst the courts and nobilities of Europe for acquiring collections of 'rarities', supplemented with handsomely bound books presenting surveys of topography, geology, insects, medals, coins, and much else, provided increasing scope for sophisticated, and often luxurious, book illustrations. This development necessitated a new type of intensive specialization combining art with the systematic observation of the scientist. One of the most impressive achievements in this sphere was that of Maria Sibylla Merian.[45] This intrepid lady, originally from Frankfurt, came to Amsterdam, to peruse the famous collections of exotic insects, especially that of Jonas and Nicholas Witsen. Constantly refining her skill in depicting tropical insects, in 1699 she boarded ship for Surinam, where she spent several months hard at work. The fruit of her labour, her celebrated book on the insects of Surinam, was published at Amsterdam, in 1705. It stands out as one of the triumphs of Early Enlightenment art and entomology combined.

After the deaths of Van Huysum, Ruysch, Willem van Mieris, Troost, and De Wit, who all died in or around 1750, the decline of Dutch art was precipitate and total. All the old specialities died away. The gifted flower-painter Gerard van Spaendonck (1746–1822), scion of one of the principal families of Tilburg, trained in Antwerp and worked briefly in Breda, but never ventured north of the rivers. Though his Catholic background may have played a role, there is little doubt that, to his generation, the Dutch towns had ceased to be an attractive, or viable, milieu in which to train or work.[46] He eventually decided that Paris offered the best prospects and it was there that he achieved lasting success, being named 'peintre en mignature' to the French court in 1774. During the late eighteenth century, leading members of the Dutch patriciate had their portraits painted by foreign, usually French-speaking, artists visiting the Republic.[47]

[44] Freedberg, 'Science, Commerce and Art', 377–9.
[45] Ibid. 379.
[46] Van Boven and Segal, *Gerard en Cornelis van Spaendonck*, 13–15.
[47] Grijzenhout, 'A Myth of Decline', 329–30.

THE ENLIGHTENMENT IN THE AUSTRIAN NETHERLANDS

In contrast to the Dutch Enlightenment, that in the south Netherlands began late and had little wider European impact. Yet it nevertheless had considerable importance in our context. For not only did it exert great influence on the historical development of the Austrian Netherlands, but also in defining the changing relationship between, and growing separation of, the two parts of the Netherlands. When the Dutch Enlightenment began to lose its wider significance for Europe, around 1740, the Enlightenment in the Austrian Netherlands had indeed not yet begun.

With his habitual acerbity Voltaire characterized the south, in 1740, as a land 'privé d'esprit, rempli de foi', and, certainly, in the early eighteenth century the country was proverbial in Europe for its lack of an intellectually active élite, absence of bookshops and periodicals devoted to scientific and literary concerns, and the Church's unchallengeable grip over higher education. The vigorous anti-Jansenist campaign during the governorship of Maria Elisabeth only strengthened the reactionary tendencies in the Church and universities and generally deterred all forms of intellectual controversy.

But after the end of the War of the Austrian Succession, in 1748, the picture changed rapidly. From the outset, the Enlightenment in the south drew its main impetus from above, from the court of the new governor-general, Charles Alexandre de Lorraine, and a number of key high officials both in Brussels and at the court of Maria Theresa, in Vienna. Apart from Charles Alexandre himself, the two guiding spirits of the Enlightenment in the Austrian Netherlands were Maria Theresa's principal minister at Brussels in the years 1753–70, Karl Johann Philipp Cobenzl (1712–70), and Patrice-François de Nény (1713–84), a high functionary of Irish extraction who became president of the Secret Council, in Brussels, in 1758.

The Enlightenment of Cobenzl and Nény was a moderate, intellectually conservative movement inspired by a neo-Jansenist, Catholic reforming outlook which was strongly regalist, intent on curbing the influence of the Church and Papacy outside the sphere these ministers deemed proper to its role, and eager to promote science and secular education in order to improve administration and stimulate commerce and industry. Nény, and the entire regime in Brussels, remained resolutely hostile to the ideas and attitudes of the French *philosophes*, especially Voltaire, whose works began to circulate fairly widely, if semi-clandestinely, in the cities of the south Netherlands from the 1750s onwards.[48]

---

[48] Hasquin, 'Joséphisme et ses racines', 218–19.

The ending of Maria Elisabeth's anti-Jansenist campaign, and the espousing of pro-Jansenist attitudes by the court in Brussels in the 1750s, was thus the intellectual mainspring of the official Enlightenment in the south. The great library, which Charles Alexandre amassed in Brussels, in several respects epitomized the intellectual character and spirit of the south Netherlands Enlightenment. The governor-general being a renowned enthusiast for scientific experiment, it evinced a marked interest in applied science, and the popularization of science, and a powerful encyclopaedic tendency in spheres such as natural history, geography, travel, navigation, and history. But it tended to avoid philosophical and theological dissident literature, though it contained a few volumes of Montesquieu, Voltaire, and others.[49] The personal libraries of Nény and Cobenzl were of similar stamp on a smaller scale, except that they showed less interest in science than the governor-general.

Despite widespread opposition and numerous setbacks, the main Enlightened initiatives of the Brussels regime in the 1750s and 1760s had a profound effect on Church–State relations, administration, education, medicine, and the prevailing intellectual atmosphere in the country, notwithstanding the partial frustration of much of what was attempted. One of Nény's prime aims was to reform the university of Leuven. Having been summoned to Vienna in 1750, to serve on the council for the Netherlands there, he was present in the years 1751–3 when the reforming of Vienna university, entrusted by Maria Theresa to her Dutch Catholic adviser, Van Swieten, reached its decisive point, extending to the theology faculty. Back in Brussels, he launched a sustained drive to transform Leuven from the 'citadelle de l'ultramontanisme', into which Maria Elisabeth's measures had turned it, into an outward-looking, Catholic reforming university in which the Church's influence would be less and that of the new science, medicine, and other secular studies much stronger.[50] Typical measures were the banning of various ultramontanist works and the rehabilitation of the publications of the Jansenist regalist Van Espen. In 1759 were established at Leuven a university press, a chair in experimental science, and a physics theatre. Such measures failed to turn Leuven once again into a leading European university but nevertheless did introduce a livelier atmosphere and considerably broaden the scope of secular studies.

Cobenzl's efforts to establish in Brussels a literary and scientific periodical press were unsuccessful at first, owing to lack of readers, but gradually the habit of reading such matter took hold in some circles, particularly among

[49] *Charles-Alexandre de Lorraine*, 96–105.
[50] Roegiers, 'Jansenistische achtergronden', 450–4.

the nobility, and close to the court, and became a significant feature of the cultural scene. He also helped set up a Brussels literary society in 1769 which, in 1771, was upgraded into a full academy, backed by the State and devoted to the promotion of science, literature, and historiography, though here again its impact was limited and achievements modest. One of the most crucial changes, though again one which failed to have quite the effect for which its progenitors had hoped, was the secularization of secondary education following the dissolution of the Jesuit Order by the Papacy, in 1773. Even so the setting up of some fifteen new 'Theresian colleges', staffed by lay teachers, did reduce the old emphasis on Latin and the disciplines chiefly stressed, since the end of the sixteenth century, by the Counter-Reformation, and led to more teaching of modern languages, science, mathematics, and history, invariably using French-language textbooks.

Gradually, both the official Enlightenment of the regime and clandestine Enlightenment, emanating from the writings of the French *philosophes*, gained ground not only among high functionaries, the nobility, and civic élites but also, albeit very patchily, among the middle strata of society. There are many indications that the works of the *philosophes* were circulating if not widely, then fairly freely in all the main cities by the 1760s, if not earlier. A number of Voltaire's works were also reprinted in the south Netherlands both in French and Dutch. The new periodical press became more firmly established and, again, by no means solely in French. One of the chief manifestations of the spread of Enlightenment attitudes in the south Netherlands was a Dutch-language journal, the *Vlaemsche Indicateur*, published at Ghent from 1779 onwards, a periodical which enjoyed a wide success, selling at a low price aimed at the ordinary burgher and even the artisan. It provided summaries of what was to be found in foreign books and journals about the arts and sciences, especially agricultural, industrial, and commercial improvements, and debates, and also discussed such political issues as the American War of Independence and the Scheldt question. During the 1780s the *Indicateur* became closely identified with the radical reforms of the Emperor Joseph II.

A sure sign that the Enlightenment was filtering down through at least urban society was the rise of a Catholic anti-Enlightenment semi-popular press in the 1770s. At that time several priests entered the fray as journalists dedicated to combating the *philosophisme* which they alleged was undermining religion and morals and therefore society itself. The most able of this new breed of polemicist was the Luxemburg Jesuit François-Xavier de Feller (1735–1802) who, from 1773 onwards, edited the anti-Enlightenment *Journal Historique et Littéraire*.

The grip of the Church, and attitudes inculcated by the Counter-Reformation, were palpably weakening. Up to a point, the endeavours of Cobenzl and Nény prepared the ground for the more far-reaching enlightened measures introduced in the 1780s by Joseph II. Yet, it was only very slowly, and perhaps marginally, that the attitudes and intolerance of the past were receding. Consequently when, in October 1781, Joseph II published his Toleration Edict for his empire, and this was followed by another, specific to the Austrian Netherlands, in November, there was a broadly hostile reaction.[51] Led by the cardinal-archbishop of Mechelen, the bishops and anti-toleration press were able to sway the city councils and also the States of Brabant, Namur, Hainault, and Luxemburg into officially opposing the edict, which in effect reduced Catholicism from being the Church of the state to being merely the dominant Church in society.

The Enlightenment in the Austrian Netherlands produced some important changes. But one respect in which it had virtually no effect was in breaking down the cultural, religious, intellectual, and psychological barriers separating the two parts of the Netherlands. The Enlightenment in the south led to an easing of confessional pressures, and of censorship, and greater openness to external influences. Yet the cultural barriers between north and south remained virtually intact. It is no accident that the only Dutchman to have any influence on the south Netherlands Enlightenment, Van Swieten, did so via Vienna. It is true that there was a mild interest in the Dutch-speaking provinces in one or two seventeenth-century Dutch literary figures, notably Vondel, but there was none in more recent Dutch writers. The evidence of the book trade confirms that whilst the Republic exported great quantities of books to much of the rest of Europe, there was practically no demand for Dutch books, even Jansenist and other Catholic literature, in the south Netherlands. Intellectual and literary contact between Enlightenment figures in the two parts of the Netherlands, all the evidence indicates, was minimal.

THE ENLIGHTENMENT IN THE COLONIAL EMPIRE

A crucial change came about in the religious, cultural, and eventually also the political, life of the Dutch colonial empire during the middle decades of the eighteenth century as a result of the spread of Enlightenment attitudes, and activities, from the Republic to the colonies. The religious and cultural rigidity of the past gradually dissolved and a more varied, tolerant, and intellectually active culture took its place.

---

[51] Hasquin, 'Joséphisme et ses racines', 229–34.

In the East Indies, the new era began with the arrival, as governor-general, of Gustaaf Willem, baron von Imhoff (1744–50), a Lutheran with broad cultural interests who started the habit of reading, as a fashionable activity, at Batavia and established a news-bulletin. One immediate change that followed his arrival was the permission given to the large German community in Batavia to organize a Lutheran congregation, under the proviso that their ministers be procured only from the United Provinces.[52] The first Lutheran preacher to work in the Dutch East Indies, sent out from Middelburg, delivered his inaugural sermon, in Batavia, in August 1746. Also in the mid-1740s, Lutherans on the Coromandel coast, and in Ceylon, obtained permission to organize congregations, and invite ministers from the Danish factory at Tranquebar to take services, provided they uttered nothing derogatory about the Dutch Reformed Church. Although there was still no public Catholic church at Batavia for many years (not until 1809), it was also in the middle years of the century that Catholic services in private homes became an accepted part of life at Batavia.

The easing of the old rigidity in church matters was almost simultaneous in the western colonies. In Surinam, a group of Moravian Brethren were admitted in 1735 to work at converting both Indians and blacks. The first Lutheran minister in Surinam arrived in 1742 and Paramaribo's Lutheran church was inaugurated in 1747.[53] It was also the middle of the eighteenth century which was decisive in Curaçao. When the first Lutheran minister to attempt Curaçao arrived in 1685, he was expelled on the orders of the WIC; a second was ejected in 1704. The WIC finally relented, agreeing that the Lutheran Germans of Willemstad should be permitted to organize a congregation, with its own institutions, in the 1740s, though the first professional Lutheran minister licensed to preach in Curaçao arrived (from Leeuwarden) only in 1757.[54]

The position of the Catholics also generally improved, though the Catholic community of Paramaribo were not allowed to convert a large building for use as a Catholic church until as late as 1787. In Curaçao, where the first Catholic church, under Dutch rule, was inaugurated in 1730, access for Catholic priests from outside remained difficult, and priests on the island scarce, often only one or two, until 1776, when a group of (Dutch) Franciscan friars were allowed to settle and work on the island, to minister to the (mainly Catholic) black population.[55]

---

[52] Troostenburg de Bruyn, *Hervormde kerk in Nederlandsch Oost-Indië*, 53–4.
[53] Goslinga, *Dutch in the Caribbean*, ii. 518.
[54] Ibid. 256–7.
[55] Cardot, *Curazao hispánico*, 410.

The last colony to abandon the uncompromising religious and cultural rigidity of the past was South Africa. The white population of the colony grew steadily during the eighteenth century, from 1,756, in 1701, to 9,721 by 1778, making it the equivalent of a medium-sized Dutch town of the time.[56] But despite the fact that a large proportion of this population was of German Lutheran extraction, no Lutheran church or school was permitted until 1780. For most of the century the only churches and schools in the colony were those of the (by 1745) five Dutch Reformed congregations. Moreover, it was practically only elementary Reformed education which was available. The Latin school established in Cape Town in 1714 was closed in 1742 for lack of students. While the Lutherans eventually obtained their own congregation, Catholic influence in the colony remained negligible and Jews continued to be excluded until the proclamation of general religious toleration throughout the Dutch empire in 1803.

As in all European colonial societies, participation in the intellectual and spiritual world of the Enlightenment was highly derivative and selective, always a pale reflection of developments in Europe. Nevertheless, it was real and exerted a profound influence, especially on the upper strata of colonial society but, through these, more broadly changing burgher attitudes and awareness. A Freemasons' lodge was established in Cape Town in 1772, a Society for Arts and Sciences founded amid much official pomp at Batavia in 1778. The latter may have been narrowly utilitarian in outlook but it none the less promoted the fashion for reading, obtaining recently published books from Amsterdam, learning French, and setting prize competitions. Furthermore, it remained in close contact with societies of arts and sciences in the Republic. One of the more remarkable men of the Enlightenment at Batavia was the innovative and widely read J. C. M. Radermacher (1741–83), a member of the *raad* of the Indies, a founding member of the Batavian Society for Arts and Sciences, and the founder also of Freemasonry at Batavia in 1764.[57]

The beginning of the vogue for obtaining, and discussing, new Dutch and French books coincided with the shift to a broader toleration, in the 1740s and 1750s. One of the leading figures of the Dutch colonial Enlightenment, the Sephardic Jewish writer David Nassy, author of the *Essai historique sur la colonie de Surinam* (2 vols.; Paramaribo, 1788), pinpointed the start of the Enlightenment in Surinam to the governorship of Jan Jacob Mauricius (1742–51), a contemporary of Von Imhoff, at Batavia, when the fashion

---

[56] Katzen, 'White Settlers', 206.
[57] Mijnhardt, *Tot Heil van 't Menschdom*, 135, 181, 189.

caught on for obtaining new books from Holland. Because copies of such books, in the colony, were few, as interest spread it became usual to read, and discuss, texts in groups which led, in turn, to the founding of reading and lecture societies on the model of those in the Republic. Several such societies were established in Surinam, including one for research in natural history in 1780. A number of interesting publications by Nassy and others appeared at Paramaribo, enabling the president of the local literary society to claim, in 1786, that over 'a hundred years there have not appeared from, and in, our colony, as many printed works as in these last four years'.[58] Enlightened reading became equally fashionable among Protestants and Jews, the latter constituting (in 1791) a slight majority of the 2,000 white population of Paramaribo.

David Nassy's library, one of the best in the colonies, was inventoried in 1782.[59] It included works by Boerhaave, Van Swieten's commentary on Boerhaave, and a French edition of Hume, as well as numerous volumes of Montesquieu, Voltaire, d'Holbach, and Rousseau, and those of Isaac de Pinto. Very few libraries in the colonies could stand comparison with Nassy's and no doubt there was some justification for the often disdainful attitude of WIC and VOC officials regarding the cultural level of colonial society. Yet everywhere the influence of Enlightened ideas and toleration in religion slowly gained ground through books, periodicals, clubs, and by word of mouth, during the middle decades of the century. Two notable figures reflecting this trend in South Africa were Joachim van Dessin, a native of Rostock who was secretary of the Cape Town orphanage in the years 1737–57 and amassed a collection of nearly 4,000 books and fifty paintings, and J. H. Redelinghuys, a Cape schoolmaster and, later, baker who developed into an able political propagandist and, finally, in the late 1790s, in Amsterdam, into a leading hardline Jacobin.[60]

The first stirrings of political opposition to the colonial regime of the VOC and WIC began in South Africa in direct response to the American Revolution as well as local stresses, with the distribution in Cape Town, in 1778, of copies of a pamphlet written by Elie Luzac many years before, justifying popular action against corrupt and deficient government in the context of the Amsterdam Orangist risings of 1747–8. But the causes of the unrest which grew in subsequent years were deeply rooted in South African colonial society.[61] Dutch South Africa was ruled, much as it had been in the

[58] Cohen, *Jews*, 95–7.
[59] Ibid. 181–250.
[60] Schutte, *Nederlandse Patriotten en de koloniën*, 71, 75.
[61] Ibid. 61–4.

second half of the previous century, by the VOC without any participation by the white settlers. These can be grouped into three broadly separate milieux. There was the world of Cape Town; that of the affluent farmers, producing grain and wine, owning the land close to Cape Town and supplying provisions to the VOC; and finally there were the mostly poor and homespun frontier *Boers*, who were the least touched by reading and the new ideas. Enlightened influences, and down to the 1790s also political activism, were almost entirely confined to Cape Town itself and its environs.

Opposition to the VOC regime in South Africa under its Orangist governor, Baron J. A. van Plettenberg (1771–85), arose principally from economic resentment over the VOC's monopoly of importing and exporting and sway over the market for agricultural produce. Since the VOC's need for provisions was limited to the fairly static requirements of its fleets, the Company's economic stranglehold over the colony not only kept prices of imports high, and for local produce low, but, in effect, discouraged expansion of production and further colonization. This led, in turn, to political frustration over the exclusion of local men from the governing Political Council, thereby rendering the Cape a fertile breeding-ground for the slogans and ideas of the American Revolution. In addition, the fact that, after 1747, colonial governors were chosen by the Stadholder, and were firm Orangists, only encouraged the tendency which developed, after 1780, to align ideologically with the Patriot movement in the United Provinces.

Secret meetings to concert opposition to the governor and the VOC took place regularly in Cape Town from 1778 onwards and the following year four delegates were sent, under pretence of private business, to present a petition of protest to the VOC directors in the Republic. But it was not long before the opposition in Cape Town lost all faith in the directors too. Ways were sought to circumvent the VOC in the quest for greater political and economic 'freedom'. In 1783, a sensational pamphlet, with which Redeling-huys was closely connected, was published in Holland under the title *L'Afrique hollandaise*, the Dutch version following immediately, warning the Dutch regents and public that 'les Anglo-Américains peuvent être imités par les colons des deux Indes; leur exemple peut devenir contagieux', and that this was especially likely in South Africa.[62] In 1784, the Patriot leadership in Cape Town submitted petitions directly to 'our high and lawful sovereign', the States General.

During the 1780s political unrest arose also in Curaçao and other Caribbean colonies, the white population dividing into Patriots and Orangists.

[62] Ibid. 78–81.

The defeat of the Patriot movement in the United Provinces, and Orangist restoration, brought about by Prussian intervention in 1787, cut off all prospect of pressing for reforms in the colonies through the regime in the Republic for the time being. But this did nothing to arrest the further growth of both Enlightenment views and Patriot sympathies in the colonies.[63] Patriot groups formed in Surinam, where there was serious tension by the early 1790s, and in western Guyana. Criticism of the Republic's colonial system became increasingly strident virtually throughout the Dutch colonial world.

THE LATER DUTCH ENLIGHTENMENT

After about 1740, Dutch intellectual and scientific developments were no longer an important influence on the progress of the Enlightenment elsewhere in Europe. Moreover, in the reception of books and ideas emanating from France, Britain, and Germany, especially the more radical aspects of the French Enlightenment, Dutch intellectuals showed great reserve. For in the United Provinces, the physico-theology of the early eighteenth century remained dominant and was buttressed by the still formidable power of the public Church. A number of physico-theological variants emerged. Particularly influential, in the 1750s,[64] was the optimistic teaching of the German philosopher Christian Wolff (1679–1754), who enjoyed the favour of Frederick the Great and became chancellor of the university of Halle in 1743. Wolff, influenced by his mentor, Leibniz, strove to combine empiricism with an integrated, systematic approach to accumulated knowledge, guided by reason, and pervaded by a conventional Protestant piety. Like the Dutch physico-theologians, he saw science and philosophy as a bulwark of conventional religion and he was enthusiastically acclaimed in the Dutch, as well as German, universities. There were still numerous Hungarian students at Utrecht, in the 1750s, but typically what they chiefly learned, besides Reformed theology, was the philosophy of Wolff.[65]

Among later Dutch writers affirming the physico-theological approach were the Leiden professor Johan Lulofs (1711–68), who published his *Primae Linae Theologiae Naturalis Theoreticae* in 1756, claiming that empirical research, guided by reason, can never clash with the dictates of Christian revelation, and the Zutphen Reformed preacher Johannes Florentinus Martinet, who modernized Nieuwentyt in his *Katechismus der Natuur*

---

[63] Goslinga, *Dutch in the Caribbean*, 309–10, 459.
[64] Mijnhardt, 'Nederlandse Verlichting', 253.
[65] Bánki, 'Utrechtse universiteit', 111.

(1777), a book which was continually reprinted and was to remain popular throughout the nineteenth century.[66]

Of course, there were deists, free-thinkers, and materialists in the Republic, as in France and Britain; but Spinozism was now weaker than at an earlier stage, and Dutch free-thinkers had learnt to be circumspect. The Sephardic Jewish writer Isaac de Pinto (1717–87) was a discreet deist who emphatically attacked materialism and atheism. In his *Précis des arguments contre les matérialistes* (The Hague, 1774), De Pinto feared lest posterity judge the eighteenth century 'le plus pervers et le plus corrompu qui se soit écoulé dans le vaste océan de la durée', deploring Spinoza but averring that some more recent *philosophes* were worse. 'Ils ont beau faire l'éloge de la morale,' he insisted, 'la vertu n'a point de base, si Dieu n'existe pas.'[67]

Several incidents warned off bolder spirits from dabbling with the ideas of the radical *philosophes*. The publisher and journalist Elie Luzac (1723–96), one of the leading figures of the later Dutch Enlightenment, in 1748 published La Mettrie's *L'Homme machine*. Luzac opposed La Mettrie's materialist views but believed that it was right to publish and refute them.[68] The Walloon Church consistory at Leiden disagreed and instigated vigorous moves against him. Luzac published his *L'Homme plus que machine* (1748), to defend himself against charges that he was propagating materialism, and also quarrelled with La Mettrie over a money matter. But this did nothing to check the outcry, which reached such proportions that he found it prudent to move to Germany for two years until the affair blew over.

Another of the best minds of the later Dutch Enlightenment, and its most cosmopolitan figure, was Rijklof Michael van Goens (1748–1810), great-grandson of the governor-general of the Dutch East Indies and son of a president of the Hof of Utrecht. Van Goens showed such brilliance, at an early age, that he was appointed professor of history at Utrecht at only 18. He was a prodigious reader, who assembled an immense library, corresponded with various *philosophes*, and became the foremost sympathizer, if not champion, of Voltaire, d'Alembert, and Hume, in the Republic. But he paid a heavy price for his sympathies, of which he revealed glimpses in several publications. The Voetian camp instigated such an agitation against this admirer of godless French philosophers that he was forced in 1776 to resign his professorship and, during the last ten years he remained in the Republic, found himself in some difficulty. In 1786 he emigrated, subsequently living in Switzerland and Germany. Diderot (who knew Van

---

[66] Wiechmann, 'Van Academia naar Akademie', 54.
[67] De Pinto, *Précis*, 14.
[68] Marx, 'Elie Luzac', 76, 86.

Goens well), after spending six months in Holland, in 1774, wrote in his *Voyage d'Italie et de Hollande* (Paris, 1775) that the Dutch nation 'est ennemi de la philosophie et de la liberté de penser en matière de religion; cependant on ne persécute personne', adding that disbelievers in Christianity are 'plus rares et plus haïs' than in France.[69]

The pressure to conform to certain attitudes in theology and philosophy had the effect of turning Dutch scholars and publicists away from many of the broader issues debated intensively in France, and elsewhere, rendering the Dutch intelligentsia increasingly inward-looking. There was still interest in scientific experiment and, especially, in consolidating the natural history collections assembled in the past. But the chief thrust of the later Dutch Enlightenment—abundantly evident in the work of Luzac, De Pinto, Van Goens, and others—was concerned with the specific moral, economic, and political problems of Dutch society itself. There was also extensive research into the institutions of the Republic. Ultimately, the principal preoccupation of the later Dutch Enlightenment was the decline of the Republic and how to achieve national regeneration.[70]

No feature of the later Dutch Enlightenment was more typical than the profound awareness of economic decay and its effects on Dutch society. Luzac and De Pinto dedicated their largest books to this subject and it permeated every facet of Dutch writing in the period. Especially characteristic was the special emphasis given to what were deemed the moral roots of Dutch decline. This tendency first matured in the Dutch-language journalism of Justus van Effen who, after years of successful publishing of French-language journals, switched to Dutch, establishing what was to prove one of the key journals of the mid-eighteenth century, the *Hollandsche Spectator*, modelled on earlier English periodicals, such as the *Spectator*, and which, in turn, became the model for numerous subsequent Dutch journals. Van Effen set out to combat prejudice and intolerance amongst broad sections of the Dutch populace, and above all improve morality.[71] He envisaged mankind as morally perfectible, provided reason, backed by a tolerant, non-dogmatic religiosity, is systematically applied to conduct. An integral part of his message was that the Dutch should take pride in their forebears, and the glories of the seventeenth century, as well as in their language and nationality, and reject imitation of French manners and morals.[72]

[69] Brugmans, 'Autour de Diderot en Hollande', 65.
[70] Mijnhardt, 'The Dutch Enlightenment', 205–11.
[71] Bisschop, *Justus van Effen*, 173–5.
[72] Van Sas, 'Vaderlandsliefde', 473.

The Dutch spectatorial press which took up Van Effen's call, and also popular literary figures such as the enterprising woman writer Betje Wolff (1738–1804), the first important Dutch novelist, vigorously rejected both the materialism and deism of the French Enlightenment, as well as French cultural influence more generally. But they also condemned the orthodox Calvinism of the past, wanting religion to promote virtue, and moral improvement, here and now, without diverting attention to dogmatic issues, or the hereafter. That there was work for this moderate Enlightenment to do is shown by the persistence of the strongly disapproving Voetian opposition and, during the 1760s, renewed pressure for tighter censorship of theological, philosophical, and scientific books. Wolff combined her moralizing with zeal for popularizing science.

One last feature of the Dutch Enlightenment needs to be noted: the proliferation, during the second half of the eighteenth century, of philosophical, literary, and scientific societies.[73] These bodies, which appeared in many towns, were typical expressions of the sociability of the Enlightenment and equally of the Dutch obsession with their national decline. Initially, these bodies, such as the Holland Society of Sciences (Haarlem, 1752), or the Zeeland Society of Sciences (Flushing, 1765), were essentially organizations for the patrician élite, patronized by regents and linked to the public Church. Like similar societies all over Europe, the societies built up libraries and collections, organized lectures, published the treatises of members, and arranged competitions for prizes. On the whole, they tended to be non-controversial, even timid both politically and philosophically.

An important further development, however, was the establishment of the Maatschappij tot Nut van 't Algemeen (Society for the Public Good), in 1784, in the midst of the Patriot agitation. This was the first society set up without regent participation with the intention of promoting reforms in the public sphere independently of the regime. This organization advocated the spread of enlightened education among the populace, in order to combat ignorance and prejudice, foment moral improvement, and encourage initiatives which would contribute to economic recovery. It criticized the older societies for failing to spread useful and morally improving ideas amongst the common populace and being concerned with the refinement of the individual rather than what was useful to society.[74] The new body was strongly utilitarian, more popular, and, to an extent, non-denominational, taking in large numbers of Mennonites and other Protestant dissenters,

---

[73] Mijnhardt, 'Dutch Enlightenment', 216–20.
[74] Mijnhardt, *Tot heil van 't menschdom*, 260–74.

though hardly any Catholics, even in Amsterdam and Utrecht, its two largest centres and cities where Catholics were especially numerous. After ten years of existence, the Nut had over twenty-five sections in different towns with a total of over 2,500 members.

40

The Second Orangist Revolution, 1747–1751

❖

In any highly urbanized, formerly prosperous society, unsettled by rapid economic decline and decay of its cities, as well as lack of work, the revolutionary process can be triggered by relatively unimportant occurrences. So it was in 1747. In April 1747, a small French army, sent as a warning to the States General rather than a serious invasion, entered States Flanders. In terms of French intentions, and the modest scale of the operation, the situation hardly compared to 1672. But in terms of impact on Dutch domestic politics the effect was shattering. The humiliating weakness of the Dutch defences revived painful memories of the Year of Disaster. Fear and anger swept the Zeeland towns. At Veere, the militia confronted the *vroedschap*, warning there would be rioting unless the regents complied with the wish of the citizenry, and militia, that Veere should press for the restoration of the stadholderate. The town councils of Veere and Flushing promptly yielded. At Middelburg and Zierikzee, it required more pressure, a wave of rioting, in which seamen figured prominently, before the regents gave way. The States of Zeeland proclaimed the restoration of the stadholderate on 28 April.[1]

The unrest in Zeeland touched off an immediate reaction in Holland. Two days after the events at Veere, on 26 April, the populace of Rotterdam took to sporting Orange cockades and ribbons. The unrest mounted so rapidly that within three days the *vroedschap* was goaded into proposing restoration of the stadholderate in the States of Holland. Rotterdam was bedecked with Orange banners and streamers, the ships in the harbour thundering their guns, church bells rang continuously, to stop people proceeding with their normal activities. By 27 April, The Hague too was covered in Orange banners and cockades. The States party-faction were not defeated yet. But when the States of Holland assembled, on 29 April, the atmosphere was so menacing, the crowds yelling 'Hoezee', 'Hoezee', 'Vivat Oranje!' so insistent,

---

[1] Rousset de Missy, *Relation historique*, 20–3.

that the regents were thoroughly intimidated. The *Gecommitteerde Raden*, staring out gloomily from the windows of the Binnenhof, considered summoning troops to clear the surrounding area but rejected this as liable to result in serious violence and bloodshed.[2] The Prince of Orange's two principal representatives in The Hague, Willem Bentinck van Rhoon and the Frisian delegate, Willem van Haren, were asked to address the crowds and try to calm them.[3]

The huge demonstrations at The Hague, and the next day at Dordrecht, left the Holland regents shaken and demoralized. The Dordrecht magistracy announced to the crowds, from the town hall, that they would support restoration of the Stadholder, an announcement met with thunderous applause. Dordrecht too was covered in Orange banners. Vigilante groups began touring the streets collecting 'fines' from persons unwilling to display Orange emblems on their attire. Popular pressure on such a scale was not easy to resist. When the *Gecommitteerde Raden* of the North Quarter gathered, at Hoorn, to discuss the situation, on 28 April, and a burgomaster of Enkhuizen seized a goblet and proposed the health of the Prince, most of those present coldly declined to respond. Yet only two days later, the same body publicly announced their support for the restoration of the stadholderate. On 1 May, Haarlem, Leiden, Alkmaar, Hoorn, Enkhuizen, and Gorcum all followed the example of Rotterdam and Dordrecht. Even the proud burgomasters of Amsterdam were thoroughly cowed.[4] On 2 May an Orange banner was unfurled from the Amsterdam town hall. A large crowd filled the Dam square. Amsterdam too, it was announced, would support restoration of the stadholderate. Again guns thundered in the harbour. Celebrations went on through the night. A number of republicans and Catholics, who refused to wear Orange emblems, were thrown in the canals.

By this time the entire *Gecommitteerde Raden* at The Hague were wearing Orange cockades and ribbons. Van Haren wrote to the Prince—who was still at Leeuwarden—recounting his amusement on seeing hardened States party regents who, a few days before, would not even deign to speak to him, or Bentinck, now walking the streets bedecked in Orange emblems.[5] Following the official proclamation of William IV as Stadholder of Holland, by the States, on 3 May, virtually the whole of The Hague erupted in fervent celebrations. Prominent men put on banquets and firework displays. Special

[2] Bleyswijk, *Memoiren*, 187–90.
[3] Wagenaar, *Vad. Hist.* xx. 85–6.
[4] *Archives*, 4th ser. i. 10.
[5] Ibid.; Bentinck, *Briefwisseling*, 256–8.

services were put on at The Hague's Portuguese synagogue. The entire Sephardic community, wearing Orange badges, the doors of the ark open, recited special prayers for the well-being of the Prince and States General followed by Psalms 117, 75, 144, and 67. That evening the façade of the synagogue complex, like most buildings in The Hague, was festively illuminated.[6]

Rousset de Missy called the events of the spring of 1747 'une grande révolution' and so it was. The States of Utrecht and Overijssel lost no time in following the example of Zeeland and Holland. By mid-May, William IV had become the first Stadholder of all the provinces of the Union. The populace supported the Stadholder. But they also expressed their fury with the regents and resentment towards Catholics. The people wanted the House of Orange, certainly, but this, in the Dutch popular mind of the time, implied more than simply restoring a princely house to power. It meant changes to strengthen popular participation in civic government, reforms to curb regent corruption and financial abuse, reassertion of the Republic's strength and dignity, repression of Catholicism, a programme to revive commerce and industry, and a call, especially in Leiden, Groningen, and Drenthe, for more Voetian preachers and stricter curbs on swearing and desecrating the sabbath.[7]

Thus far, there had been intimidation but little actual violence. Rousset de Missy proudly compared the non-violent character of the events of April and May 1747 with the violence of 1672. Not unreasonably, everyone, from the outset, compared 1747 with 1672.[8] Yet, as early as May, perceptive onlookers, including the Prince's most able adviser, Bentinck van Rhoon, saw that the people's expectations had been raised to such a pitch, and their resentment against the regents was so vehement, that they would not be satisfied merely with the restoration of the stadholderate.[9] Initially, the popular agitation vented itself in a mass of small incidents, directed especially against Catholics. This occurred in Utrecht, Overijssel, and Groningen, as well as Holland. A riot in Haarlem, on 6 May, was provoked by a Catholic innkeeper uttering disrespectful words about the Prince and encouraging his clientele to drink the health of the king of France. The crowd smashed his windows and would have wrecked the inn had not militia guards arrived.

Yet the Prince took no steps against regents or Catholics. If he believed the agitation would die down of its own accord, his inaction, and the

---

[6] Rousset de Missy, *Relation historique*, 32.
[7] De Jongste, 'Restoration', 55.
[8] Ibid. 56–7.
[9] *Archives*, 4th ser. i. 5.

progress of the French in the siege of Bergen-op-Zoom, were soon seen to be having a contrary effect.[10] Local agitators fanned the flames of popular resentment against the most hated members of the States party regime. Bentinck van Rhoon was particularly anxious that the Prince should purge Holland's anti-Orangist Pensionary, Jacob Gilles (1695–1765), Adriaen van der Hoop, secretary of the *Raad van State*, Burgomaster Hieronymus Karseboom, and two other regents of Dordrecht, Abraham van Hoey, pensionary of Gorcum, the baron van Duin of the Holland *ridderschap*, and Unico Willem, heer van Twickel, of Overijssel. But, of these, only Van der Hoop was actually removed.

The fall of Bergen-op-Zoom, in September 1747, set off a new wave of unrest and still more insistent calls to 'deliver the Fatherland from these rascals'. Again much of the violence was directed against Catholics at Utrecht, Deventer, and Groningen, as well as several Holland and Zeeland towns.[11] Shops and homes were attacked. Individuals were beaten and thrown in the canals. A States of Holland placard of 22 September condemned both Catholic provocation and Protestant retaliation, threatening all who disturbed the peace with punishment. But already the focus of popular agitation, steered by skilful coffee-house demagogues such as Laurens van der Meer, in Rotterdam, and Rousset de Missy and Daniel Raap, at Amsterdam, was beginning to shift. A delegation of Rotterdam burghers, led by Van der Meer, went to see the Prince, complaining that the most detested regents were still in their posts and that 'everything was still on the old footing'.[12] They demanded a general reform of civic government.

Bentinck van Rhoon, in close contact with the agitators, became increasingly worried. He saw that the people had made the revolution and given the Stadholder his power in order to punish the regents, purge the town councils, and find ways to curb regent corruption and abuse of power.[13] He continually reminded the Prince that, in the spring, he had helped calm the populace by urging them not to take matters into their own hands but await the Stadholder 'qui leur feroit justice'. The Prince's reluctance to purge the regents, in Bentinck van Rhoon's view, was positively dangerous as it threatened to undermine the new regime in the affections of the populace even before it had become securely established.[14] But still the Prince hesitated even to dismiss Gilles.

[10] Geyl, 'Agent Wolters', 57–8.
[11] Wagenaar, *Vad. Hist.* xx. 118.
[12] De Voogd, *Doelistenbeweging*, 80.
[13] Rowen, *Princes of Orange*, 173.
[14] *Archives*, 4th ser. i. 222–7. Considerations de W. Bentinck (July 1748).

Nevertheless, both the Prince, and Princess Anne, willingly established contact with the agitators, taking the view that the common populace was tied to the House of Orange and would prove an infallible means of intimidating the regents whenever they ventured to obstruct the wishes of the Stadholder and his court. William was more than satisfied with the obsequious deference to which his regent opponents had, for the moment, been reduced, assuming that he would have no difficulty in keeping them meek and pliant.[15] In England at the time, William was mockingly labelled 'Prince of the Mob' and—for all his aversion to violence and illegality— there was some truth in this. In November 1747, when it was proposed to make the stadholderate hereditary in both the male and female lines, among the Prince's issue, and Amsterdam alone dared express reservations, a new wave of unrest erupted, orchestrated by Rousset de Missy and Raap. Raap, a porcelain merchant and deist, headed a group of burghers who submitted a petition to the *vroedschap*, similar to that being agitated for at Rotterdam. They demanded a fully hereditary stadholderate, the choosing of the militia captains and officers from among the citizenry rather than members of regent families, rotation of seats in the town council, which should be allocated by public auction so as to raise money for the civic chest, and restoration of the guilds to their former privileges. Raap's adherents posted up notices all over the city summoning the populace to gather in Dam Square, in front of the town hall, at an appointed hour, on 9 November, to demonstrate in favour of the demands. The event fizzled out, though, degenerating into a minor disturbance which was easily dispersed by the militia.

At this stage the only concession to popular demands was a States of Holland placard condemning corrupt practice in the assigning of civic offices and requiring the town halls to submit lists of their civic offices and the perquisites attached. Meanwhile, the Stadholder concentrated, with considerable success, on building up his authority throughout the Republic. In May 1747, the States of Utrecht were compelled to readopt the old *reglement* of 1675 in unchanged form, giving William IV the same tight grip over the States and States deputies in The Hague as William III had possessed.[16] In Gelderland, a struggle developed between the Orangist *ridderschap*, who urged restoring the *reglement* of 1675, and the towns, which resisted this. But little by little the Prince and his friends wore down the resistance of the Nijmegen and Arnhem regents by both regular and

---

[15] Schutte, 'Willem IV en Willem V', 199.
[16] Gabriëls, *Heren als dienaren*, 65.

irregular means.[17] Riots broke out at Arnhem in January 1748. Before long the States of Gelderland too voted to restore the *reglement* of 1675, making the Prince master of the province, and its colleges, and arbiter of membership of the town councils.

A struggle also developed, from late 1747, in Groningen, between the *raad* of Groningen and the ruling *jonkers*, on the one side, and a combination of opposition *jonkers*, city guilds, and rebellious peasants, on the other. For the moment the States of Groningen, like those of Friesland, refused to follow Holland in making the stadholderate in their provinces fully hereditary. Rioting erupted in March 1748, in both city and Ommelands, where the houses of several *jonkers* were plundered. The city asked the Prince to send troops to help restore order: he refused; soon after, the States of Groningen declared the stadholderate fully hereditary. In May 1748, the *raad* of Groningen made some far-reaching concessions to the populace. It was promised that the college of *Taalmannen*, Groningen's equivalent to the *gemeenslieden* of Gelderland and Overijssel, would be restored to its former role and influence, that civic office-holding would be reformed, that disagreements between city and Ommelands would, in future, be referred to the Stadholder, and that the guilds would be restored to their ancient privileges.

Compared to Groningen and Gelderland, and also Drenthe, where there were disturbances and a strong protest movement against rule by a narrow clique of nobles (leading to a number of changes, including a hereditary stadholderate in both lines), Overijssel was largely quiescent.[18] Facing little opposition, the regents and nobles held out for a time but, eventually, they too were forced to cave in and restore the *reglement* of 1675, handing over effective power to the Stadholder.[19]

A new phase of the revolution began in May 1748 in Friesland, when rioters in the countryside began attacking the residences not only of *grietmannen* but also of tax-farmers (*pachters*).[20] In June, there was serious rioting in Harlingen. The States of Friesland asked the Stadholder to send troops: he refused. The burghers of Harlingen sent a deputation to the States, demanding full hereditary status for the stadholderate, abolition of the tax-farms for the excises, and restoration of various allegedly lapsed ancient privileges. Other towns also selected delegates and a general assembly of burgher representatives was convened in the main church of Leeu-

---

[17] *Journal van Mr Justinus de Beyen*, 37–41; Porta, *Joan en Gerrit Corver*, 249.
[18] Gabriëls, *Heren als dienaren*, 70.
[19] Te Brake, *Regents and Rebels*, 30.
[20] Guibal, *Democratie en oligarchie*, 138–89.

warden. The burgher representatives presented States and Stadholder with a list of seventy-two demands, concerning a wide range of judicial, fiscal, and financial matters, but calling with particular stridency for abolition of the tax-farms for the excises. The Stadholder was unenthusiastic about the fiscal and many of the other demands. But the alliance of Prince and people held for the moment. The States were forced to empower the Stadholder to draw up a *reglement* to curb abuse in the provincial and civic government of the province. This was submitted by the Prince, and approved, in December 1748. It stipulated that henceforth the qualified voters in each *grietenij* would elect three qualified candidates from whom the Stadholder would choose one.

It was the attacks on the tax-farmers in Friesland which triggered the real burgher movement of the summer and autumn of 1748, in Holland. An angry mob in Haarlem attacked the *pachters'* offices and houses on 13 June. The drums calling out the militia sounded but the response was patchy and many even of those who turned out refused to help defend the *pachters'* houses. A number were plundered, large quantities of elegant furniture, paintings, porcelain, and books being carried off, smashed, or thrown into the canals. Instead of suppressing the rioters, the burgher-guards began organizing meetings and formulating demands to put to the burgomasters.[21] When rumours circulated that troops were approaching, the militia closed the town gates. The *vroedschap* was forced to suspend the excises, and also municipal taxes, enabling the bakers and grocers to sell food at reduced prices. Soon the meetings of militia and burghers spread to other Holland towns. In Leiden, the people, as the local artist Frans van Mieris the Younger put it, began exacting 'revenge' on the *pachters*, on 17 June, by plundering their houses. Not only did the civic militia refuse to act against the mob, they played a principal role in formulating the people's political demands. These consisted of ten points, the most important of which were that the regents should no longer appoint themselves to command the militia, that the body of militia themselves should have the main say in the appointing of officers, that there should be delegates of the citizenry appointed to check the tax registers to prevent the regents under-assessing their own liabilities and thereby shifting too much of the burden on the rest of the citizenry, that the civic privileges be published so that all the citizenry would know their rights, that the powers of the guilds be restored, placards against swearing and violating the sabbath be enforced, and finally that more preachers of the 'old study'—that is Voetian preachers—be appointed

---

[21] De Jongste, *Onrust*, 181–5.

in the city.[22] The whole tenor of the demands was that regent government should be made answerable to the citizenry and supervised, as it were, by the body of the militia and other representatives of the people.

The riots in Haarlem, Leiden, and also The Hague, where three *pachters'* houses were sacked, in turn precipitated a new round of disturbances in Amsterdam.[23] Again the civic militia refused to fix bayonets or fire on the mob. During the first two days of renewed rioting in Amsterdam, 24 and 25 June, some twenty *pachters'* houses were sacked in the city.[24] Contemporary illustrations depicting the plundering show women well to the fore, wrecking costly furniture, tossing grandfather clocks into the canals, and raining choice porcelain from upper windows, as well as pilfering the odd item for themselves (see PLATE 31). On the second day, when the mob began to attack the houses of other rich men, the militia did finally open fire, killing and wounding several rioters. On the same day, the Prince of Orange appeared before the States of Holland to advise immediate abolition of the tax-farms. The text of his speech was printed and distributed amongst the populace. The States suspended the tax-farms.

It was now clear there were two distinct streams, or levels, of protest and agitation in progress.[25] On the one hand, Orangist agents and publicists, orchestrated by Bentinck and the Stadholder's court, were continuing to intimidate the regents with a view, especially, to weakening the Amsterdam *vroedschap* as a political force and consolidating all political power into the Stadholder's hands. A spate of pamphlets at Amsterdam vehemently denounced the regents as selfish and corrupt, interested only in monopolizing lucrative offices and lining their own pockets. It was at this point, the day after the worst violence in Amsterdam, that Rousset de Missy, eager to spread the influence of John Locke, reminded Bentinck that he had summoned him to The Hague, some time before, to discuss the immediate reprinting of a French edition of Locke's *Two Treatises on Government*, a work asserting the ultimate sovereignty of the people, as an ideological justification for enlisting the people on the Orangist side.[26] Rousset had now arranged with an Amsterdam publisher for a popular edition and was only awaiting Bentinck's signal. But Bentinck, it seems, held back. Nevertheless, Locke remained the intellectual prop of Orangism in 1747–51 and was warmly espoused by Luzac in the 1750s.[27] Only later did Luzac and the

---

[22] Prak, 'Burgers in beweging', 177–85.

[23] Porta, *Joan en Gerrit Corver*, 255–7.

[24] Wagenaar, *Vad. Hist.* xx. 222–4.

[25] De Voogd, *Doelistenbeweging*, 107–11.

[26] BL MS Egerton 1745, fo. 486. Rousset de Missy to Bentinck, Amsterdam, 26 June 1748.

[27] Velema, 'Elie Luzac and Two Dutch Revolutions', 125–8.

Orangist intelligentsia drop Locke. In the 1780s, through writers such as Price and Priestley, who gained considerable popularity in the Republic, Locke was to be appropriated, in turn, by the anti-Orangist Patriots.

In 1748, Locke was one of the ideological implements with which Orangists hoped both to justify, and control, their alliance with the people. But, at the same time, a more genuinely democratic impulse was surfacing, often with the respectable 'bourgeoisie' egging on 'le petit peuple',[28] a pressure arising from the professional and shopkeeping strata who, if less active, were no less eager than the mob to sweep away the tax-farms, reform the militias, and make civic government answerable to the citizenry.[29] The more radical political demands were propagated amongst the populace by means of pamphlets, handbills, and innumerable meetings in inns and coffee-houses, as well as in the assembly halls of the militia companies. There was much rousing talk of the spirit of 1572 and 1672 when the people had risen, led by the militias, and fought for their freedom. At Amsterdam eleven demands were submitted to the *vroedschap*, the most far-reaching of which were that the citizenry themselves should choose the burgomasters from amongst the *vroedschap*, that the regents should not appoint the militia officers, who should be chosen by the burgher-guard companies themselves, and that the citizenry should choose the directors of the Amsterdam Chamber of the VOC and WIC from amongst experienced merchants, a way of saying that merchants, not regents, should control the great colonial companies.

Bentinck van Rhoon was deeply worried by July 1748, feeling that the common populace had now lost patience with the Stadholder and were becoming alienated from him and the Orangist party as a whole,[30] and not without reason. The citizen committees organizing the agitation in Amsterdam, who were known as the *Doelisten* after the militia target halls where they chiefly met, were now split into two opposing wings. The moderates continued to follow the wishes of the Stadholder's court and the directions of Bentinck van Rhoon. The more democratic wing was increasingly drawn into conflict with the Stadholder and the Orangists. The moderates, led by Raap, Laurens van der Meer, who came to Amsterdam to assist, and a brother of the historian Jan Wagenaar, strove to target the continuing unrest towards securing reforms in civic office-holding and the ending of regent control over the militia companies, as well as transfer of the city's postal service into the hands of the Stadholder.[31] The radical *Doelisten*, led

---

[28] BL MS Egerton 1745, fo. 462. Report on the situation in Leiden, 20 June 1748.
[29] De Voogd, *Doelistenbeweging*, 106–7, 115.
[30] *Archives*, 4th ser. i. 221–2.
[31] De Voogd, *Doelistenbeweging*, 110–11.

by Hendrik van Gimnig, a Haarlem textile worker with a flare for demagoguery, pressed for the conceding of all eleven demands and the effective subordination of civic government to the militias and citizenry.[32]

The States of Holland, on 31 August, requested the Prince to go in person to Amsterdam 'to restore order' by whatever means he deemed necessary. On arriving in Amsterdam, the Prince held talks with spokesmen for both wings of the *Doelisten*. He reacted unenthusiastically, however, to Van Gimnig's vehement denunciation of the regents for oppressing the citizenry in every conceivable way. The huge popular demonstrations which took place in Amsterdam whilst the Prince was present, in the first weeks of September, though, clearly favoured the radical *Doelisten*, a tendency which became more pronounced as it became apparent that the Prince preferred spending his time being wined and dined by the burgomasters to talking to the citizenry. Eventually, the Stadholder was brought round to see that he had to dismiss the burgomasters, and purge the *vroedschap*; but the way in which he did this only heightened popular disillusionment.[33] The Prince retained nineteen of the former *vroedschap* of thirty-six, bringing in seventeen new men, some of whom were from mercantile backgrounds and had not previously been part of the regent class, but others of whom, including all four new burgomasters, emanated from long-entrenched regent families.[34]

The Prince's obvious reluctance even to concede a militia council independent of the *vroedschap* caused bitter disappointment. On 9 and 10 September, there were further huge demonstrations, this time in favour of a 'free' militia council, but the Prince refused to budge. The Stadholder returned to The Hague, leaving the populace of Amsterdam dissatisfied and confused. A reaction set in against the constant turmoil and in favour of the new *vroedschap* and a return to order. The focus of unrest now shifted to Leiden and Haarlem. These were the towns where the economic decay in progress since 1720 had gone furthest and where the frustration of the citizenry, accordingly, was greatest. Driven by slump, pressure of taxation, and fear of pauperization, the citizenry and *schutters* in the manufacturing towns strove to achieve a restructuring of civic and guild administration which would afford them fiscal relief and if not economic revival then at least more institutional protection from the harsh effects of the economic collapse.[35] The Prince undertook to investigate civic government in these

[32] *Billyk verzoek der Amsterdamsche Burgery* (Oct. 1748), demands 1, 4, and 7.
[33] Porta, *Joan en Gerrit Corver*, 265–6.
[34] De Voogt, *Doelistenbeweging*, 180–3.
[35] De Jongste, *Onrust*, 216–36.

two towns, in response to the continuing disturbances, and, during October, seven men were purged from the Haarlem *vroedschap* and five in Leiden.[36] But this seemed an inadequate purge to the populace and most of their other demands were rejected. In Leiden there was a major disturbance on 10 November, and intimidating presentation of demands to the burgomasters, which was much noticed throughout the Republic.[37] In response to the pleas of the new burgomasters, the Stadholder sent a thousand troops, who entered the city on 16 November and restored quiet.[38] The magistracy banned all further meetings and demonstrations.

On the surface, nearly all the major changes resulting from the Orangist revolution of 1747–51 were gains for the Stadholder and the Orangists. In Zeeland the Stadholder again became First Noble and resumed control of the seventh vote in the States suppressed in 1702. The Prince also demanded a strong say in the choosing of Zeeland's delegates, as also those of other provinces other than Holland attending the States General. Negotiations about this dragged on until June 1751, when the States of Zeeland finally accepted the obligation to obtain the Stadholder's approval beforehand for all persons nominated for the *Gecommitteerde Raden* of the province and colleges of the Generality. In Utrecht, Overijssel, and Gelderland, the Stadholder had not only secured the reimposition of the *reglement* of 1675 but even acquired additional powers beyond what William III had possessed, in Gelderland becoming First Noble of the *ridderschap* in each quarter.[39] In Drenthe, too, the Stadholder acquired far more power than in the past, across the entire administration of the province.[40] Finally, sweeping changes took place in Groningen, the province where previously the Stadholder's authority had been weakest. Under the *reglement reformatoir* to which Groningen was obliged to submit in November 1749, the Stadholder, for the first time, acquired extensive leverage over the appointing of office-holders.[41] In the city of Groningen, the Sworn Council was to continue each year to choose half of the *raad* while the *raad* still chose the burgomasters; but under the new *reglement*, all members of the *raad* and Sworn councils had, as in Overijssel and Gelderland, first to be approved by the Stadholder, who retained the right—should he disapprove—to appoint someone else of his own choosing. Far from being 'seven sovereign allies', the Orangist revolution of 1747–51 turned the Republic into what

[36] Prak, *Gezeten burgers*, 97–8.
[37] Hardenbroek, *Gedenkschriften*, 27.
[38] Prak, 'Burgers in beweging', 390.
[39] De Jongste, 'Restoration', 41–2; Te Brake, *Regents and Rebels*, 31.
[40] Smit, *Bestuursinstellingen*, 73.
[41] Feenstra, *Adel in de Ommelanden*, 91.

was really more of a constitutional monarchy without a crowned monarch. At the university of Groningen, as with the other universities, the Stadholder was now assigned the main influence in the appointing of professors.

For those who believed the solution to the Republic's social and economic problems lay in concentrating power at the centre, in the hands of a Prince of Orange whom serious Orangist projectors of reform, such as Bentinck van Rhoon, fondly imagined was eager to listen to, and follow, their advice, the situation by 1750–1 was one glowing with promise, the sole constitutional arrangement, as Isaac de Pinto, a prominent enthusiast, expressed it, 'par laquelle la république peut conserver son lustre et sa splendeur'.[42] De Pinto hoped especially for a rapid revival of Dutch finances, manufactures, and navigation, seeing this as the way to ease social tensions and distress and promote the arts and sciences. But the revolution which such men supported and longed to see bear fruit could not be fully consolidated. To the utter dismay of his supporters, the Stadholder died unexpectedly, at The Hague, at the age of only 40, on 22 October 1751.

[42] Nijenhuis, *Joodse* philosophe, 102–3.

41

The Faltering Republic and the New Dynamism in the 'South'

❖

POLITICS DURING THE MINORITY OF WILLIAM V, 1751–1766

The character of the Republic and its institutions had been fundamentally altered by the Orangist revolution of 1747–51.[1] Yet the fears and grievances which had brought it about had not been removed. The decay of Dutch industry continued as before. As early as 1750, the merchants of Amsterdam appeared to be reverting to their former pessimistic view of prospects for the Republic's trade and shipping. The slide in the value of VOC shares at Amsterdam, from 584 to 492 per cent, between January and July 1750, was interpreted as a sign of lack of confidence in the Republic and its commerce[2] and equally in the newly reformed structure of the VOC which followed from the naming of the hereditary Stadholder as 'Chief Director' (*Opperbewindhebber*) of the United East India Company, in 1749, with power to influence the choice of the other directors and, in Zeeland, to choose them outright.[3]

But while the causes of discontent and anxiety remained, what had grown impressively was the ability of the regime at The Hague to suppress protest and disturbance. The United Provinces, in their decayed state, were now a volatile land, potentially highly unstable (as de Pinto stressed), prey to a host of economic and political tensions which, in the eyes of the new regime, necessitated prompter and tougher methods of dealing with unrest than had been employed by the provincial assemblies in the past. When, for example, a fresh militia and burgher movement began to stir at Haarlem, in January 1750, the burgomasters soon lost control: but not so the regime at The Hague, which reacted vigorously, sending troops to occupy the city.[4] The

[1] Te Brake, 'Provincial Histories', 81–4.
[2] Van Hardenbroek, *Gedenkschriften*, 60.
[3] Gaastra, *Gesch. van de VOC*, 164.
[4] De Jongste, *Onrust*, 321–4.

delegates sent by the Haarlem militia companies to The Hague to present their demands to the Stadholder were simply arrested.

To an extent, the death of a Stadholder in his prime, leaving an infant son aged only 3 in the care of his mother, who now bore the title 'Princess-gouvernante', but was a foreigner, was bound to weaken regime and stadholderate.[5] Anne of Hanover assumed much of the responsibility of the stadholderate, on behalf of her son, but it was impossible she should exercise as much real power as had her husband since 1747. To guide her, an informal steering committee, or 'conference', took shape, the principal members of which were Bentinck van Rhoon; Pieter Steyn, the new Pensionary of Holland (1749–72); the presiding member of the Holland *ridderschap*; and the famous general Duke Ludwig Ernst von Braunschweig-Wolfenbüttel, known to the English as Brunswick, formerly in Austrian service, who had commanded the allied troops in States Brabant and Flanders during the French invasion of 1747–8.[6] William IV and Bentinck van Rhoon had been much taken with him and persuaded the Empress Maria Theresa to release him, in 1750, so that he could assume permanent command of the States General's army. Although Anne of Hanover initially regarded him with suspicion, she later came to consider him as the pillar of the regime and the most reliable upholder of the interests of her son and the House of Orange-Nassau.

Despite his contrasting ideological stance, Bentinck van Rhoon was a true successor of Van Slingelandt in that he too was deeply committed to reforming the institutions of the United Provinces so as to create a more integrated federal structure and provide stronger, more streamlined direction at the centre.[7] Bentinck van Rhoon had tried continually, since 1747, to persuade William IV to set up a Stadholder's cabinet, a formal committee of ministers to act as central executive for the state. William IV had had the power, and opportunity, to do this but lacked the will and vision, being content that decision-making should largely continue along the old consultative lines, as long as the regents and nobles showed him due deference and looked to his court as the fount of patronage. The 'conference' of the early 1750s represented a last chance to create a central ministry for the state but it was never formally recognized by the States General and was further weakened by the Princess-gouvernante's habit of frequently following the advice of court favourites outside the 'conference', often men with strong English links. The 'conference' continued to meet twice weekly down to

[5] Schutte, 'Willem IV en Willem V', 218–19.
[6] Gabriels, *Heren als dienaren*, 101–2.
[7] Rowen, *Princes of Orange*, 167, 172, 192.

Anne of Hanover's death in 1759. But Bentinck van Rhoon, the moving spirit behind it, was already bitterly disillusioned with it by 1753.[8]

In the aftermath of William IV's death, and still more after Anne's death, in 1759, the regents and nobles in the provinces saw their opportunity to claw back some of the influence they had lost since 1747.[9] The former Orangist fervour of the populace had cooled to such an extent by the early 1750s that there was little to obstruct their progress. In March 1752, the States party-faction regained control of the Amsterdam *vroedschap*, with a measure of popular support, and drew up a new 'contract of correspondence' to determine the selection of burgomasters, excluding the Princess and her advisers from the process. In August 1755, twenty members of the Haarlem *vroedschap*, including several professed Orangists who had come in only in 1748, combined to break the influence of the court by drawing up a new 'contract of correspondence', shutting ten Orange loyalists out of power.[10]

All this had its implications for foreign policy as well as for Dutch domestic politics. The court was strongly pro-British and all along, especially in the mid-1750s, with the European Seven Years War about to erupt, Bentinck van Rhoon and the duke of Brunswick had been eager to augment the army and strengthen the Republic's fortifications. By contrast, the States party-faction, especially at Amsterdam, gave priority to the interests of commerce, shipping, and colonies and was pervaded, like the merchants and shipping interests, by widespread anti-British sentiment. Most Holland regents had no desire to go to war with France, preferring a policy of neutrality which, however, found scant favour with Anne of Hanover and her advisers. The position of the States party-faction in this respect was much enhanced, though, by the collapse of the 'Barrier' negotiations between the Republic, Britain, and Austria, in 1753–4. Britain was anxious that the Empress Maria Theresa renew the old alliance, and allow the Dutch to revive and strengthen their 'Barrier' garrisons in the South Netherlands. But Austria, drawing closer at that time to France, showed little interest and refused the financial and administrative concessions requested.

The atrophy of the old system of alliances, and effective loss of the 'Barrier', inevitably served to intensify the sense of uncertainty, decline, and drift prevailing in the United Provinces. The court of The Hague showed an undiminished zeal for exercising its extensive patronage, and grip over all important appointments, without being able to give a lead, or undertake any

[8] De Voogd, *Doelistenbeweging*, 242.
[9] Kooijmans, *Onder regenten*, 74; De Jong, *Met goed fatsoen*, 77–9.
[10] De Jongste, *Onrust*, 344–5.

meaningful initiatives, in matters of policy. The favourites of the Princess, and her son, were often military men and their growing ascendancy tended to blur the dividing line between political and military promotion and favours. One group of courtiers with whom Bentinck van Rhoon repeatedly clashed were almost exclusively interested in the business of patronage. This was the so-called Frisian cabal, a coterie which had emerged at Leeuwarden before the revolution of 1747 and which subsequently followed William IV to The Hague.[11] Their leader, the *jonker* Douwe Sirtema van Grovestins (1710–78), busied himself tirelessly with exchanging favours for money, on one occasion, in 1756, reportedly receiving 70,000 guilders for securing the governorship of Ceylon for a friend.

It was inherent in the Orangist revolution of 1747–51, and the concentration of patronage in the Indies and lesser provinces, at The Hague, that followed, that for the first time in the Republic's history there should emerge a court nobility increasingly resembling the court nobilities of neighbouring monarchies.[12] The court at The Hague was now so important for the *ridderschap* of Gelderland that the States of that province allocated special emoluments to enable each quarter to appoint a noble to reside at The Hague and form part of the Stadholder's normal entourage. The Nijmegen quarter chose the son of the leading nobleman of the quarter, Frans Godard, baron van Lynden van Hemmen. The other quarters did likewise, as did Groningen, which was similarly anxious that a leading *jonker* of the province should be in constant attendance at The Hague. At the same time, Dutch noblemen holding senior commands in the army could, for the first time, expect automatic prominence at court. Sirtema van Grovestins himself was such a senior officer, as was Hans William van Aylva Rengers, who became William V's chamberlain.

To organize patronage and influence in each province, the court also needed provincial managers of the more traditional type cultivated by Maurits, Frederik Hendrik, and William III. In Utrecht, the court's favourite was Johan Daniel d'Ablaing van Giessenburg (1703–75), who was not a member of the old Utrecht nobility but son of an officer in the service of the VOC who had become governor of the Cape colony. The most influential of the court's favourites in Gelderland was Baron Andries Schimmelpenninck van der Oye van de Pell (1705–76), a member of the Veluwe *ridderschap*, who was continuously a member of the Delegated States of the Arnhem quarter from 1748 to 1774 and, in 1758, became *drost* of the Arnhem quarter. He was described by the French ambassador, in

---

[11] Gabriels, *Heren als dienaren*, 126–8. [12] Van Hardenbroek, *Gedenkschriften*, 48.

1762, as 'l'homme qui gouverne la Gueldre'. In Overijssel, the pre-eminent personage initially was a brother of Bentinck van Rhoon, Count Carel Bentinck van Nijenhuis (1708–79), who in 1748 became *drost* of Twenthe. He was eclipsed, however, in the mid-1750s (after Anne of Hanover took a dislike to him) by Count Frederik van Heiden van Ootmarsum (1696–1769), son of an army officer from Cleves who had procured entry to the *ridderschap* of Overijssel as recently as 1720 by purchasing the noble estate of Ootmarsum. He succeeded Bentinck's brother as *drost* of Twenthe in 1754.

As regards Holland, Bentinck van Rhoon had advised William IV to govern by selecting in each town council 'une personne par qui tout doit se faire' who could dispense the Prince's patronage. In fact, as at Amsterdam, Haarlem, Gouda, and Leiden, the court failed to secure a lasting grip.[13] But, in some cases, the strategy met with more success. At Dordrecht, Hieronymus Karsseboom, who in 1747 was reviled as a 'Louvesteiner', subsequently became a fervent Orangist who won William IV's favour, accumulated offices, and dominated the town for years. Similarly, at Hoorn, nearly all those brought in by the Orangist purge of 1749 were protégés of Burgomaster Joan Abbekerk Crap, who became the court's trusted confidant in the town.[14] However, Brunswick did not care for Crap and his reign at Hoorn ended with the death of Anne of Hanover, in 1759.

North of the rivers, the inexorable rise of Brunswick dominated politics in the 1750s. In 1755, the Princess-gouvernante named the duke guardian of the then 9-year-old William V and her other children. After her death, Ludwig Ernst presided over the Republic until the young Prince came of age, in 1766, in his double capacity as guardian of the Prince and captain-general of the army. But he was not able to prevent further erosion of the House of Orange's gains from the revolution of 1747–51. During the years of his guardianship, the Holland towns sent their double lists of candidates for municipal office to the States of Holland, not the court, as happened also in Zeeland. The *raad* members of the three chief towns of Overijssel, since there was no Stadholder to review nominations, and make changes each year, were allowed to remain in office as if they were a permanent oligarchy, filling vacancies themselves without reference either to the court or colleges of *gezworen gemeente*.

Brunswick, for many years, continued to collaborate with Bentinck van Rhoon. Relations between the two were less than cordial but each needed

---

[13] De Jong, *Met goed fatsoen*, 77–9; Prak, *Gezeten burgers*, 101–3.
[14] Kooijmans, *Onder regenten*, 75–6.

the other. Bentinck could see that Brunswick was the only figure capable of preserving at least the core of the political gains of 1747–51 and that he had no alternative but to try to work with him. Brunswick also needed Bentinck, who as the principal personage of the Holland *Gecommitteerde Raden* was still an influential and persuasive voice. Only in 1766 did the relationship degenerate into open antagonism, when Bentinck van Rhoon discovered that the young Prince of Orange (over whom he had hoped to exert a guiding influence) had signed a secret contract with the duke making him his principal adviser and special confidant.[15]

After the turbulence of the late 1740s there were three decades in which Dutch society seemed stable and the people withdrew from direct involvement in politics. For the moment, the economic and social tensions in society ceased to translate into popular protest. The people had their Prince and therefore the solution, as they had supposed, to all that was wrong. On the surface all was calm for the moment. But beneath the surface much of the people's dissatisfaction remained much as before so that when, eventually, the Orangist regime had alienated a large part of the common populace and the turmoil resumed, it proved impossible to absorb the renewed revolutionary impact within the existing institutional framework. In this sense, it is possible to say that by the 1750s, the Dutch Republic had, in its existing form, become fundamentally outmoded. This does not mean that successful solutions could not have been found and that it was impossible, in the second half of the eighteenth century, for the Republic to have evolved into a form of democratic, or more democratic, federal republic. But it does mean that the Orangist republic of the 1750s was inherently hollow and precarious. Bentinck van Rhoon fully realized that the revolution he had helped lead had failed to retain the support of the people, or meet their grievances, and that that failure, if not rectified with radical reforms, could only have fatal consequences for the new regime.[16]

For the moment the rival party-factions were locked into a delicate balance. One effect was to sublimate their conflict into an ideological war fought between the two sides' intellectuals and publicists. The fiercest outburst in this strife was the 'war of De Witt' which broke out in 1757. This clash involved several writers, but above all the Leiden publicist Elie Luzac, on the Orangist side, and the Amsterdam historian Jan Wagenaar (1709–73), on that of the States party. Both men were leading intellectual figures with national reputations. Both believed in progress, civilized values, and toleration. Both lamented the decline of their Republic and were key

---

[15] Rowen, *Princes of Orange*, 196–7; Leeb, *Ideological Origins*, 111–12.
[16] *Archives*, 4th ser. i. 218–27.

representatives of the Dutch Enlightenment. But they adhered to opposing sides in the ideological war, their bitter clash, in print, about the true nature and historical significance of Johan de Witt, and what Luzac called the 'Louvestein faction', seizing the public's attention.

According to Luzac, the principles espoused by Johan de Witt, and his eighteenth-century followers, including Wagenaar, undermined the very foundations of 'our state', weakening not only the Generality but, worse, the sovereignty which springs from the people and which, he argued, they had entrusted, at the time of the Revolt, to the Generality, as much as the provincial States, and to the care of Prince William I.[17] For Luzac, sovereignty, and legitimacy, derived from the 'people'. It was the ordinary folk, he insisted, who had changed the regime in 1572, 1618, and 1672; what they had done was legitimate, and all legitimacy in the Republic derived from the people.[18] He scorned the idea that the provincial States, and the regents and nobles who sat in them, were entitled to any kind of absolute sovereignty above the wishes of the people. Wagenaar, replied by ridiculing this legitimacy which Orangists claimed to derive from the people, though he willingly agreed that ultimately sovereignty came from the people. The people could not be permitted to intervene continually to modify the shape of sovereignty, for its views and loyalties are inherently shifting and inconsistent.[19] For Wagenaar, sovereignty lay absolutely in the hands of the provincial States as the representatives of the people, precisely as Grotius had held.[20]

Remarkably, during the period from the late 1750s to the 1770s, there occurred an almost complete reversal of these competing views, as to the role of the common people. Orangist ideologues continued to look back on the revolution of 1747–8, and popular intervention to restore the House of Orange, approvingly, even in the midst of the controversies over popular participation during the Patriot revolution of the 1780s.[21] But Luzac shifted his ground, from the 1760s onwards, abandoning Locke, and theories of popular sovereignty, in favour of Montesquieu and a more conservative view of institutions, leading him to endorse the revolution of 1747–8 in more guarded terms than before.[22] Simultaneously, especially during the 1770s, Locke, as radicalized in the works of Richard Price and Joseph Priestley, was appropriated by future Patriot leaders such as Joan Derk van der

---

[17] Luzac, *Zugt*, 2–12.
[18] Ibid.; Luzac, *Het oordeel*, 106–12; Leeb, *Ideological Origins*, 70–1.
[19] Wagenaar, *Vrymoedige aanmerkingen*, 102, 113; Leeb, *Ideological Origins*, 79–80, 90–7.
[20] Velema, 'Elie Luzac and Two Dutch Revolutions', 129–30, 146.
[21] *Ouderwetse Nederlandsche Patriot*, iii. 297.
[22] Velema, 'Elie Luzac and Two Dutch Revolutions', 129–30, 146.

Capellen and Pieter Paulus. Even the very term 'Patriots', an Orangist label in 1747–9, changed its meaning and came to be adopted by the anti-Orangists.[23] When the Orangists established a regular paper to combat the Patriot press, in 1781, they called it, significantly, the 'Old-Fashioned Dutch Patriot' (*Ouderwetse Nederlandsche Patriot*).

But, shifting responses to Locke and popular sovereignty notwithstanding, the ideological conflict raged uninterruptedly, around the heroes and institutions of the Republic's past. The growing preoccupation of leading intellectuals with the Republic's history, and research into its documents, served both to refine, and spread, knowledge of the Republic's origins, and leading figures, and intensify the ideological strife. The Batavian myth was shown to be largely a distortion which had the effect of making the Revolt appear a more authentically revolutionary event. A number of major historical works were produced, foremost among them Jan Wagenaar's *Vaderlandsche historie* (1749–59), a twenty-volume history of the Republic, designed to show how 'freedom' in the Netherlands had been oppressed and upheld, over the centuries.[24] It was a history neither of rulers, nor of a state, but of the 'freedom' of a people, even though, for Wagenaar, the people that mattered were the magistrates, merchants, and professionals, and definitely not the 'ignorant masses'. Pieter Paulus, in his study of the Union of Utrecht (4 vols.; Utrecht, 1775–7), set out not just to explain the Union as an institution but to elucidate what he saw as the principles of the Revolt, the enshrining of the principle of popular sovereignty. Paulus proclaimed Grotius a true champion of popular sovereignty and the right of resistance to despotic authority despite his contradictions.[25] Paulus also expressed amazement that the great jurist Huber should have endorsed the provincial *reglementen* imposed by William III in 1674–5.

On the other side, Luzac's 'enlightened conservatism' was reinforced by Van Goens and the researches of Adriaen Kluit. Kluit's central contention was that the medieval counts of Holland had held absolute power which, with the Revolt, had been transferred to the provincial States, which in turn delegated certain powers to the Stadholder. This left no room, in his view, for popular participation, or pressure from below, for curbing the Stadholder's powers, or widening toleration or freedom of the press.[26]

Johan de Witt and other heroes bitterly quarrelled over in the past— Oldenbarnevelt, Maurits, and William III—remained controversial, indeed

---

[23] Kossmann, *The Low Countries*, 41–2.
[24] Haitsma Mulier, 'Between Humanism and Enlightenment', 176.
[25] Paulus, *Verklaring der Unie*, i. 97, 185–7.
[26] Haitsma Mulier, 'Between Humanism and Enlightenment', 181.

fundamental to Dutch political and ideological discourse, throughout the late eighteenth century. During the Patriot revolution of the 1780s, the Orangist press continued its attack on De Witt, and the 'True Freedom',[27] while, on the Patriot side, veneration of Oldenbarnevelt and De Witt showed no sign of abating. During the 1780s, the English pottery manufacturer, Josiah Wedgwood, developed a lively business supplying ideological artefacts to both sides, Wedgwood busts of Oldenbarnevelt and De Witt, to the Patriots, and lockets with portraits of the Stadholder, and his family, to their adversaries.[28]

NEW DIRECTIONS IN THE AUSTRIAN NETHERLANDS

Meanwhile, the 1750s and 1760s witnessed a decisive shift in the relationship of north and south in the Low Countries which was economic, as well as political and strategic, and which was to have major repercussions in the future. For it was especially during the middle decades of the eighteenth century that the steady population growth under way in Flanders, Brabant, and the Walloon region alike, and the (from the 1750s) rapid expansion of industry, trade, and agriculture began to reduce appreciably the previously overwhelming superiority of the north in virtually every sphere. It is true that the United Provinces still greatly surpassed the south in maritime trade, as a naval and colonial power, and as a financial centre. But its industries were ruined, its 'rich trades' in collapse, its cities decaying, and agriculture relatively stagnant, whereas in the south the scene was one of growth and increasing dynamism, especially in agriculture and rural industry (see p. 984 above). These contrasting trends, and the changed diplomatic situation, encouraged the regime in Brussels, and ministers in Vienna, to seek increasingly to circumvent, or weaken, the various commercial and tariff constraints imposed on the Austrian Netherlands under the Austro-Dutch treaty of 1715, albeit for the moment without calling into question the continued closure of the Scheldt estuary to maritime traffic, the point on which the Dutch States General showed greatest sensitivity.[29]

One crucial effect of the changes of the 1750s was to remove the Austrian Netherlands from the epicentre of great-power conflict. During the century since the peace of the Pyrenees (1659), the south had been Europe's chief strategic barrier against France, defensible only with the aid of Britain and the Republic—and then not always successfully. At the commencement of

---

[27] *Ouderwetse Nederlandsche Patriot*, iii. 288–94.
[28] Van Sas, 'The Patriot Revolution', 117.
[29] Carter, *Neutrality or Commitment*, 81.

his long term as Austrian governor-general, Charles Alexandre of Lorraine (1741–80) suffered defeat and humiliation. The French invaded the south Netherlands in 1745, defeated the Austrians and their allies, and occupied most of the country, before going on to invade States Flanders, precipitating the Orangist revolution in the north. Between 1756 and the 1780s, by contrast, the south was stable, secure, and prosperous, an oasis between a friendly France, on one side, and neutral Republic, on the other. For the Franco-Austrian treaty of Versailles, of May 1756, not only effectively neutralized the frontier between France and the South Netherlands but, by shifting Austria's strategic weight eastwards, against Prussia, ended the South Netherlands' two-centuries-old role as the strategic pivot of Europe, introducing a period of peaceful development undisturbed by the threat of French expansion.

With the coming of peace, and quickening of economic growth, Charles Alexandre had the opportunity to preside over, and encourage, a process of reconstruction and revival, at times deliberately recalling the era of Albert and Isabella. Again there were signs in the air that the south might become a separate sovereignty under a cadet branch of the imperial dynasty. Charles Alexandre was the first governor in Brussels since Albert and Isabella to give energetic backing to numerous projects to stimulate trade and industry and, likewise, give a strong lead in the cultural sphere, promoting a general reorientation. These latter aspects of his activity were, indeed, closely linked. The court helped promote the economic revival through its aggressive tariff policy, shutting out foreign iron, in 1750, Delftware and Dutch tiles in 1758,[30] and British coal in 1761; and also improved the harbour at Ostend, and initiated a series of new canals as part of a wider plan to stimulate the flow of trade between the coast, Brussels, and the lower Rhine. The new Leuven–Mechelen and Ostend–Ghent canals were both laid out in the early 1750s. To emphasize the link between the court and these new engineering undertakings, Charles Alexandre issued several handsome medals, including one marking the inauguration of the Leuven–Mechelen canal, in 1753, with his bust on one side and the canal on the reverse and another, in 1772, celebrating completion of the Ostend lighthouse.[31] Besides the usual crystal, porcelain, and other luxury industries patronized by eighteenth-century European courts, Charles Alexandre set up a salt works at Ostend, a chemical works in Brussels in which he took a close interest, and invested heavily in coal-mining at Mariemont. And last, but not least, he gave the

---

[30] Hoynck van Papendrecht, *Rotterdamsche plateel*, 125.
[31] *Charles-Alexandre de Lorraine*, 78–9, 220–1.

Austrian Netherlands what, by 1780, was the densest, most modern road network anywhere in western Europe.[32]

In Flanders, the linen industry remained by far the most important industrial activity. Developing along traditional lines (except that the linen was now increasingly bleached in the south, instead of sent to Haarlem for finishing), output expanded steadily, if not spectacularly, by some 50 per cent between 1700 and 1775.[33] But the key developments in the industrial sphere, opening the way to the subsequent industrialization of Belgium, took place mainly in the Walloon areas; and here the changes of the 1750s and 1760s were of decisive importance. Particularly striking was the upsurge of coal-mining and iron-working in the districts of Charleroi, Namur, and also Liège. It was precisely in the 1750s that coal production began to rise rapidly in the Austrian Netherlands, doubling, and then trebling, in just a few years.[34] Also highly significant was the rapid expansion of fine cloth manufacture in the Verviers–Eupen–Aachen triangle, beginning immediately after the steepest falls in fine cloth manufacture in the United Provinces, in the middle years of the century. After 1750, the triangle was the leading, and most dynamic, fine cloth manufacturing area in Europe, output rising by over a third between 1750 and the late 1780s, at the expense of France as well as of the Republic.[35] Though Verviers, situated in the prince-bishopric of Liège, was the chief centre, nearby Eupen, in Austrian Limburg, also registered impressive rises in output, specializing in middling fine cloths for the Levant.

While coal, iron, and textiles were the driving force behind these crucial trends which brought the south Netherlands to the threshold of the Industrial Revolution, there were dramatic changes also with respect to processing industries, such as salt, tobacco, and sugar-refining, and also potteries. Previously, the south, like much of the rest of Europe, had simply imported processed goods from the Republic or England. But now, all commencing at the same time, in the 1740s and 1750s, and mostly successfully—the tobacco workshops being established chiefly at Brussels, Bruges, and Charleroi—the processing industries in the south took over the supplying of the Austrian Netherlands market, nurtured, on the one hand, by the vigorous new mercantilist stance of the regime and, on the other, by the collapse of industry in the United Provinces.

Having been raised at Nancy, and being heir to the dynastic world of the House of Lorraine, Charles Alexandre was noticeably less addicted to

---

[32] Houtman-de Smedt, 'Zuidelijke Nederlanden', 368–9.
[33] Dorban, 'Les Débuts', 126; Vermaut, 'Structural Transformation', 195–6.
[34] Dorban, 'Les Débuts', 130–40.
[35] Chorley, 'The Shift', 97.

Viennese tastes than Maria Elisabeth and more willing to cultivate local talent and traditions. In his major architectural initiatives, the overriding external influence was that of the courtly world of Nancy and Lunéville.[36] These were sufficiently compatible with the tentative neoclassicist tendencies embodied in the extensions undertaken by the south Netherlands nobility, since the 1720s, to generate a successful fusion of Lorraine and local styles, leading to the rise of a full-blown Belgian neoclassicism. At the forefront of this cultural regeneration was the work on the three royal palaces. This was directed by local architects, principally Jean Faulte (1726–66), from Bruges, and the prolific Laurent Benoit Dewez (1731–1812), who besides being court architect, designed dozens of neoclassicist additions to noble residences and abbeys throughout the south Netherlands—and the lighthouse at Ostend. Having purchased the Nassau palace in Brussels to serve as his chief residence, in 1756, Charles Alexandre rebuilt it in an opulent neoclassicist style in the years 1757–61, allowing plenty of space for his renowned library and numismatic and natural history collections. At Tervuren he rebuilt the old ducal palace, one of the favourite residences of Albert and Isabella, installing, nearby, a porcelain factory and silk works. Most striking of all, he built an entirely new neoclassical palace at Mariemont, which came to be widely considered one of the handsomest buildings of the Habsburg empire. Though there were no major painters to patronize, Charles Alexandre imparted new impetus to the applied arts, especially in Brussels, which he aimed to turn into one of the leading cultural centres in Europe; he assembled a large collection of old masters, including numerous seventeenth-century Flemish paintings; and commissioned sculptures from Laurent Delvaux (1696–1778), perhaps the most notable artist at his court, a prolific sculptor who successfully blended Flemish baroque traditions with the new neoclassicist tendency. Among Delvaux's chief commissions was a colossal Hercules, incarnating Charles Alexandre, installed in the new palace in Brussels in 1770.

THE EARLY YEARS OF WILLIAM V'S STADHOLDERATE, 1766–1780

An altogether less confident personality was the young Stadholder William V, who came of age in 1766, an event accompanied by constitutional modifications which, once again, strengthened the position of the Stadholder and his court—and of Brunswick, as the dominant influence over

---

[36] *Charles-Alexandre de Lorraine*, 25–43.

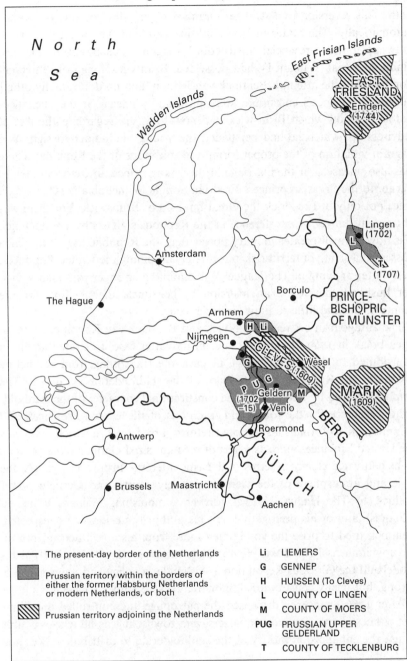

MAP 16. Prussian territory in and adjoining the Low Countries in the eighteenth century (showing dates of acquisition)

both. This reversion to a stronger Orangist regime did not always proceed automatically. The States of Friesland, in 1766, had the temerity to try to draw up a new provincial 'instruction' assigning less power to the new Stadholder than William IV had possessed. Brunswick's vigorous intervention quashed the attempt. Bentinck van Rhoon, and no doubt many others outside the Prince's entourage, were profoundly uneasy at the unchallengeable position which Brunswick had now built up, regarding the Act of Advisership, which he had persuaded the young Stadholder to sign, as a flagrant violation of the proper forms and traditions of the Republic. There was also unease over the marriage of the young Prince, in October 1767, in Berlin, to the Prussian princess Fredrika Sophia Wilhelmina (1751–1820), a niece not only of Frederick the Great but also of Brunswick. For there was an evident danger of interference in the Republic's affairs by a state which was now a much greater military power than the Republic itself and which possessed a string of territories immediately adjoining the United Provinces. Soon after arriving at The Hague, Wilhelmina, a stronger personality than her husband, developed an aversion to her uncle there.[37] But, for the moment, this did little to limit his ascendancy.

The antagonism between Brunswick and Bentinck van Rhoon came to an open break in 1769. Personality and, in the latter case, frustrated ambition contributed to this. Nevertheless, in part, the rift sprang from conflicting visions of the Republic and the place of the stadholderate within it.[38] The emphasis placed by Bentinck on the constitutional character of the stadholderate, reverence for the forms and traditions of the United Provinces, and commitment to formal, institutional reform jarred on Brunswick, who saw the United Provinces more as a sort of medium-sized German dynastic state to be cultivated chiefly in terms of dynastic interests. Brunswick brought the style and atmosphere of the German princely courts, and German power politics, to The Hague. He was forever admonishing William V not to relinquish any of his prerogatives lest his authority no longer be respected. Bentinck tried to prise the young man loose from his abject dependence on the now immensely fat duke. He urged the Prince to adopt William III as his model and the Glorious Revolution as his guide to policy and statesmanship. Strong, but firmly constitutional, monarchy was Bentinck's ideal.[39]

After 1766 Brunswick dispensed the patronage and controlled the Orangist cliques in the provinces, quarters, and towns. It was he who was able to use the enhanced authority of the stadholderate to distribute offices and

[37] Schutte, 'Willem IV en Willem V', 214.
[38] Rowen, *Princes of Orange*, 197–8.
[39] *Archives*, 5th ser. i. 109–11.

cultivate loyalties so as to tighten links between the court and supporters in the country. For this he needed provincial political bosses who would be loyal tools in his hands, putting the interests of court and faction above provincial considerations. The States of Zeeland—whom Anne of Hanover had permitted to appoint a successor as First Noble, should the sitting incumbent die during William V's minority—had, in 1764, combined the offices of Pensionary of Zeeland and First Noble in the hands of Willem van Citters (1723–1802), head of what was now the most powerful regent dynasty in the province. But Brunswick preferred to deal with noblemen whose outlook was not shaped by the civic preoccupations and traditions of a Van Citters. He organized a campaign against him and broke his influence. In Gelderland and Overijssel he worked chiefly with noblemen who were court favourites but, at the same time, relatively new to the provincial scene. As a Zwolle regent put it, in 1782, three men 'disposed and directed everything in Overijssel'; these were Count van Heiden Hompesch, son of Count van Heiden van Ootmarsum, whom he succeeded as *drost* of Twenthe, the former's cousin Count van Heiden Reinestein (1741–1813), and, after becoming *drost* of Salland in 1779, Dirk, Baron Bentinck van Diepenheim (1741–1813).[40]

In Holland, too, Brunswick's ascendancy was overwhelming. Pieter Steyn (1706–72), member of a wealthy Haarlem regent dynasty, and Holland's Pensionary, from 1749 until his death in 1772, owed his position above all to Bentinck. Neither Anne of Hanover, nor Brunswick (nor, after 1755, Bentinck) were on particularly good terms with him. He was adept at serving the interests of the House of Orange (and his own) while at the same time placating Amsterdam and the regents. However, Brunswick and William V regarded him as insufficiently subservient to the court. For, on occasion, when he considered that constitutional propriety was at stake, he was prepared to stand up to them. On Steyn's death, Brunswick picked Pieter van Bleyswijk (1724–90), a member of an old Delft regent family, who owed his position as Pensionary of Delft to Bentinck but had deserted him for the duke, to succeed as Pensionary, confident he had found a function-ary who was completely spineless. Only in merest form was Van Bleyswijk the choice of the States. Initially, he was indeed unabashedly subservient to the duke, but, in the late 1770s, as opposition to Brunswick and the stadholderate in the States began to harden, the Pensionary showed signs of going against the court.[41] By the beginning of the 1780s this born weather-cock had become the tool of the Patriot bloc in the States.

[40] Gabriels, *Heren als dienaren*, 236. [41] Miller, *Sir Joseph Yorke*, 34.

But while, in terms of patronage, the court continued to have everything its own way, politically there were increasing signs that the stadholderate was very much on the defensive by the late 1770s. Since Europe's 'Diplomatic Revolution' of 1756, Austria, and therefore also the Austrian Netherlands, had been in alliance with France. Prussia, formerly France's ally, entered into alliance with Britain. The change, sensational at the time, made nonsense of all the strategic assumptions and plans, current since 1713, based on the premisses that the south Netherlands would serve as a barrier between the Republic and France and that the Republic's security depended on close ties with Austria and Britain. It was a shift which undoubtedly increased the attractions for the Dutch of remaining neutral between both Britain and France, and Austria and Prussia.[42] But it was by no means seen as an invitation to retire from the arena of international power politics and neglect the Republic's armed forces. On the contrary, not only were both Britain and France regarded as overweening competitors, and possible adversaries, but there was now also apprehension as to Austria's intentions, as well as the long-standing unease regarding Prussian power around the Republic's borders. Anxieties regarding Austria increased from 1775 when the first serious disputes arose over the Austro-Dutch border in the Overmaas and Flanders. These were a prelude to the friction which developed, in 1781, when the Emperor Joseph II demanded the final dismantling of the Barrier system, and 1784, when he demanded the return of territory in the Overmaas and States Flanders, as well as Dutch evacuation of Maastricht and the reopening of the Scheldt. Far from creating an easier situation, the Diplomatic Revolution, it was clear by the early 1770s, had trapped the Republic in a four-way 'stretch' between the principal powers of western and central Europe.

Thus, neither the Stadholder's entourage, nor the leadership of the States party-faction, believed it sensible to neglect the Republic's defences. On the contrary, with a large colonial empire extended temptingly across the oceans and borders, some disputed, with lands under both Austria and Prussia, there were pressing reasons to expand and modernize both the navy and the army. Yet it was precisely this which posed the thorniest dilemma in Dutch deliberations in the 1770s. For there was no consensus as to whether the maritime or land forces should be given higher priority. A principal objective of the Orangist regime which had come to power in 1747, and of its British backers, was to build up the army. Yet, in fact, little was done to improve or enlarge it in the years after 1751, while, at the same time, scant

[42] Carter, *Neutrality or Commitment*, 84.

progress was made with plans to re-equip the navy with twenty-five ships of the line agreed as far back as 1741. By 1756, only a handful of the new warships had been built, while by 1759 the army, which had been substantially increased during the 1740s—the last occasion in European history when the Dutch counted as an important military power—had shrunk back to only 40,000 men.[43] In 1772, the army stood at 41,000.

During the 1770s, William V and Brunswick strove to secure agreement, and funds, to expand both the land and sea forces. But the States of Holland and Zeeland, and especially Amsterdam, were distinctly less eager to spend on the army than the navy, while the inland provinces preferred to spend on the army, albeit real determination to expand the army substantially was confined to Gelderland. But the crux of the problem was that William V was unwilling, or unable, to pressurize the inland provinces into consenting to increases in naval, as well as military, spending and, without it, Amsterdam simply refused to assent to army augmentation.[44] The consequence of this was a paralysis of the state, with neither the army nor navy receiving attention. When, in 1778, the Stadholder pressed for a hefty augmentation of the army, without increased naval spending, he was resolutely blocked by Amsterdam.

By the late 1770s, the United Provinces were caught in a *malaise* which extended into every dimension of national life. The sense of the Republic being in a steep decline became pervasive. In the States General, the provinces and Stadholder languished in a sterile deadlock. The Republic still possessed valuable assets, not least in the shape of its colonial empire and remaining shipping, which were vulnerable to Britain's growing imperial dominance outside Europe. At the same time, the United Provinces were boxed in between the rising continental powers of Austria and Prussia. This combination of economic, political, and imperial crisis facing the Republic in turn generated a degree of ideological tension which rendered the United Provinces more immediately vulnerable to revolutionary turmoil than probably any other European country at the time, even France. For this was a society in steep decline but decline from a very high level, experiencing massively adverse economic pressures amid the remnants of prosperity and much sophistication. Moreover, unlike other western European countries, this was a land in which the existing regime was looked on without respect, or affection, by large sections of the urban populace. Not surprisingly, in this context, the spectacle of the revolutionary movement in the American colonies caused particularly strong shock waves, which affected Dutch life at many levels.

[43] Zwitzer, *Militie*, 176.   [44] Bartstra, *Vlootherstel*, 265, 280.

In the form it took, the American Revolution was bound to sharpen tensions both between Britain and the Republic and, within the Republic, between Orangists and opponents of the Stadholder. From the outset, the insurgents in America obtained much of their weaponry and munitions from the Republic, mainly indirectly, via the West Indies, especially the island of St Eustatius. This led to a growing British pressure on the States General to halt these shipments, backed by threatening bluster and intermittent boarding and seizure of Dutch vessels on the high seas, in violation of the 1674 treaty, establishing the principle of 'Free Ship, Free Goods'.

At the same time, the American Revolution aroused sympathy amongst many sections of the Dutch public, an attitude stiffened by the Anglophobia prevalent amongst the mercantile element in Amsterdam. The Dutch trading system and colonial empire, like that of France, had been undermined, and stunted, by Britain's now overwhelming maritime superiority. The American Revolution seemed to afford both relief and the chance to alter the balance. It also served to sharpen the Dutch domestic ideological conflict. If Simon Stijl (1731–1804) in his complacent *Opkomst en bloei der Vereenigde Nederlanden* (Rise and Flourishing of the United Netherlands; Amsterdam, 1774; enlarged edition 1778) eulogized the Dutch Republic as a timeless haven of 'freedom', content with the States party-faction's traditional veneration for Grotius and the 'True Freedom' of De Witt spiced with a dose of Montesquieu,[45] a new note was struck by the Overijssel noble Joan Dirk van der Capellen tot den Poll (1741–84), a leading opponent of British policy in America, who was deeply influenced by Richard Price's *Observations on Civil Liberty* (1776), a work rooted in Locke and evincing strong democratic and pro-American tendencies.[46] Van der Capellen translated and published Price's work under the title *Aenmerkingen over den Aart der Burgerlicke Vrijheid* (Leiden, 1776), in support of the American cause.

Orangist publicists, including the Sephardic Jewish writer Isaac de Pinto, defended British policy in America. De Pinto warned the Dutch public (and his fellow Jews) that the collapse of the British empire in America would entail the eventual collapse of all the European empires in the Americas, destroying what remained of the Dutch trading system and devastating the Amsterdam stock market. But the Orangists were in a difficult position. Besides the unpopularity of the regime, and dire condition of the Republic's commerce, industries, and colonies, British policy was so bludgeoning that it became practically impossible for the Stadholder's court to oppose the wave of anti-British feeling. In February 1777, the British ambassador at

---

[45] Leeb, *Ideological Origins*, 122–36.
[46] Schulte Nordholt, *Dutch Republic and American Independence*, 25.

The Hague, Sir Joseph Yorke, presented a memorial from the British Government to the States General, demanding immediate action to stop the flow of munitions via St Eustatius, and the recall of its governor, accusing the States General of tacit collaboration in the seepage of supplies to the Americans and threatening that if the Republic could, or would, not stop the flow, Britain would do so by means of unrestricted boarding and seizure. Van Bleyswijk noted that the tone of the British ultimatum was so imperious that 'it creates here a very great sensation'.[47] Brunswick despairingly told William V that the text was the most overweening he had ever seen from one sovereign power to another. A flurry of pamphlets appeared furiously denouncing British arrogance and tyranny.

From this point on Anglo-Dutch relations edged inexorably towards war. Despite his strongly pro-British inclinations, the Stadholder had no alternative but to authorize the preparation of the navy to defend Dutch shipping from attack. At the end of 1779 a large Dutch convoy bound for the West Indies was fired on by the British in the Channel and forcibly escorted into Plymouth. Finally, unrestricted boarding, together with revelations, in the autumn of 1780, showing the full extent of the complicity of Amsterdam merchants, and financiers, in assisting the American Revolution, made war all but certain.[48] The appeal of a war against the Dutch, for the British in 1780, was the expectation that Dutch shipping and colonies could be captured quickly, and with ease, and then used to offset the losses, and dented prestige, resulting from the setbacks at American and French hands. Thus the steady deterioration of Britain's prospects in America only made the outbreak of war between Britain and the United Provinces more likely.

When it came, the Fourth Anglo-Dutch War (1780–4) proved an unmitigated disaster for the Dutch. In the first full month of the war (January 1781) the British navy and privateers captured no fewer than 200 Dutch vessels, completely paralysing what remained of Dutch shipping.[49] In February 1781, Admiral Rodney captured St Eustatius, seizing numerous ships and a vast store of merchandise and supplies. Further disasters followed. The British captured all the West African forts of the WIC, except Elmina, and the west Guyana colonies, though these were subsequently reconquered, for the Dutch, by the French. In the East Indies, the damage was less than it would have been without French assistance, but several bases were lost in southern India and Ceylon, including Negapatnam, and richly laden VOC ships taken with a combined value of 10 million guilders.

[47] Miller, *Sir Joseph Yorke*, 51.
[48] Schulte Nordholt, *Dutch Republic and American Independence*, 150–6.
[49] Ibid. 155.

42

The Patriot Revolution, 1780–1787

❖

On the morning of 26 September 1781, copies of a revolutionary booklet entitled *Aan het Volk van Nederland* (To the People of the Netherlands), published anonymously but written by Baron van der Capellen, were found posted up, and strewn, all over the Republic. Its political message was uncompromising. There had been a time, before the coming of the Habsburgs, when the Dutch people had enjoyed a high level of civil liberty and political freedom, being able to hold the rulers of the different provinces in check by means of the colleges of sworn representatives of the citizenry, the militias, and the influence of the guilds. The basis of this inestimable 'freedom' had been the unrestricted right of the citizenry to gather, organize, form committees, choose representatives, and express their views. The people had been stripped of their freedom by Charles V and, especially, Philip II. But the Revolt of 1572 had failed to restore their 'freedom'.[1] Although the quest to regain it had provided the essential impulse behind the Revolt against Philip II and the power of Spain, and there was much that was inspiring in it, from the people's point of view it had ended in failure. Popular participation in civic and provincial government, momentarily revived by the citizens' guilds and militias, had been suppressed once more by William the Silent and the regents.[2] The moment of disaster, according to Van der Capellen, had occurred exactly two hundred years before, in 1581, when the States of Holland issued its edict forbidding town councils any longer to consult on important issues with the militia companies and guilds (see p. 216 above). That was the moment when the Dutch Revolt betrayed itself, and its own basic principles.

Van der Capellen proclaimed the suppression of Dutch freedom, since 1572, to be chiefly the work of the Princes of Orange using the standing army: 'he who has the army may do as he pleases'.[3] In order to regain their

[1] Kossmann, *Politieke theorie*, 253.
[2] [Van der Capellen], *Aan het Volk van Nederland*, 6–7, 10.
[3] Ibid. 19.

'freedom', and participate once more in civic and provincial government, the people had to create a people's militia devoted to the principles of 'freedom' and effective enough to act as a counter-weight to the regular army. It was a message obviously inspired by the spectacle of the American militias resisting the might of the British army in the American colonies, and Van der Capellen expressly urged the Dutch to model themselves on the Americans. He called on the people to take their fate in their hands and begin a democratic agitation in every town and locality, a revolutionary process which would work from the bottom up. A country and its government, the baron assured his readers, belong to all who dwell in it—rich and poor—but the people will only control the state, and be free in their own country, if they create and maintain a citizens' militia highly motivated enough to use their bayonets for the defence of the people's freedom. That can only happen if the citizenry emulate the Americans (and Swiss) by drilling seriously and learning to use their weapons, especially on Sundays after church, and choose their own militia officers.

The baron's inflammatory pamphlet may have contained nothing new from the standpoint of political theory, but in Dutch society at the time it was startling for the force with which it drew a revolutionary message from familiar facts, addressing a situation which had caused deep frustration, throughout the Republic, ever since the Orangist revolution of 1747–51. The baron's pamphlet can almost be said to have been the manifesto of the Patriot Revolution of the 1780s, especially in its stress on the need to make government answerable to the people, by creating people's organizations at local level and forming citizens' militas, and its identification of the Stadholder and House of Orange as the principal enemy of freedom. The baron rebuked the regents too, but saw them as a subsidiary entity which could be pulled either way, towards the Prince or the people. In his view, Oldenbarnevelt and De Witt had in some degree served the interests of the people and, even though, during the First and Second Stadholderless periods, the regents had excluded the citizenry from participation in public affairs, the States party-faction were willing to help recover 'freedom' by allying with the people against the Stadholder.[4] Van der Capellen's insistence that without reforming the militias, and placing them under citizen control, no progress towards regaining freedom was possible, was to be the central tenet of the Dutch Patriot revolutionary press. As one leading Patriot periodical, *De Post van den Neder-Rhijn*, advised the Gelderland Patriots, in August 1784: 'they must investigate what violations of popular

---

[4] Ibid. 11, 25; Leeb, *Ideological Origins*, 159–60.

rights had occurred in each locality', through research in historical sources, but, above all, they must 'train in the use of arms whereby our good regents will be supported and the good-for-nothings silenced'.[5]

Meanwhile, the Fourth Anglo-Dutch War (1780–4) continued, and popular indignation and outrage over the crushing and disastrous setbacks at British hands escalated. The run-down and neglected state of the Dutch navy, and failure of the WIC and VOC to maintain their garrisons and fortifications adequately, were the principal cause and for this the regents and colonial companies were partly to blame.[6] But the public had been conditioned, and the Patriot press now conditioned them further, to blame the Stadholder and his court for the débâcle, including the severe economic recession in Holland and Zeeland which ensued from the disruption of shipping and the fisheries.[7]

Patriot agitation gained momentum during 1782 especially in Holland, Utrecht, Gelderland, and Overijssel. From the first it was the Patriot press, whose newspapers and periodicals deluged the public with criticism of the Stadholder and his regime, which spearheaded the Patriot movement.[8] This was a revolution led by journalists, lawyers, and other professionals, appealing to the literate, urban, middle strata of society, not least the shopkeepers. It was a revolutionary process, welling up from below, throughout a large part of Dutch urban and, more patchily, rural society, highly articulate, and aimed at radically remodelling the country's institutions and system of government, albeit within the framework of what were taken to be the founding principles of the Republic. The Patriots saw their movement as essentially a revival, continuation, and completion of the Dutch Revolt against Spain. The basic purpose of the Revolution was to wrest control of civic and provincial life from the hands of the Stadholder's favourites, and the regent oligarchies, and transfer power to those who regarded themselves as the spokesmen and representatives of the people.[9]

But while Patriot ideology was rooted in the Dutch past, and based on what were taken to be the essential principles of the Revolt and the Republic, it displayed several striking new features.[10] Especially important were its idealization of the 'people', an ideological tendency which was marked in the Dutch context since the middle of the eighteenth century, and, closely linked to this, its democratic tendency and a form of national

[5] *Post van den Neder-Rhijn*, 6/270 (1784), 992.
[6] De Wit, *Nederlandse revolutie*, 22.
[7] Van Sas, 'The Patriot Revolution', 97–8.
[8] Ibid. 99–104; Popkin, 'Print Culture', 287–91.
[9] Ter Brake, 'Provincial Histories', 85–7.
[10] Van Sas, 'The Patriot Revolution', 111–15.

feeling more akin to the liberal nationalism of early nineteenth-century Europe than any sense of identity which prevailed in the United Provinces during the Golden Age.[11] The Patriots viewed the 'Dutch people' as the whole body of the nation in which Lutherans (who were very active in support of the Patriots), Mennonites, and Catholics belonged as much as did the Reformed populace. They rejected formal discrimination against religious minorities and rejected also institutional discrimination against those parts of the Republic, the Generality Lands, which had a lower status than the seven voting provinces. Supporters of the Stadholder's regime, including Orangist Reformed preachers, the Patriot press termed *Antipatriotten*. Nor was this reaching out the hand to the non-Reformed population mere lip-service. It was, rather, part of the Patriots' political strategy to bring the religious minorities, and Generality Lands, into the revolutionary process and draw on their support in pressing for their goals. One way of doing so was to stress that not all the great heroes of the Republic belonged to the Reformed Church. The *Post van den Neder-Rhijn*, one of the most influential Patriot papers, published at Utrecht by Pieter 't Hoen, asked rhetorically, in November 1785, was not Admiral Zoutman, the sole naval hero of the late disastrous war, a Lutheran, was not William III's famous military engineer, Coehoorn, a Mennonite, were not the old States party's heroes, Oldenbarnevelt and Grotius, Remonstrants?[12]

The Patriot Revolution's method was to spread democratic awareness among the people through the press, turn the civic militias into an instrument of the people's will, and finally compel the Stadholder's representatives and the regents to restore the control of the citizenry in local, and therefore also provincial and national, politics.[13] The new militias, or Free Corps, as they were called, differed from the old civic militias in four ways: they were not to be under the control of the regents, but under burgher defence councils which were to select the officers; they were to shed their previously strongly Reformed character, becoming open to Dutchmen of all religious confessions, including Catholics; they were to participate directly in civic politics in support of the 'good regents' and against the *Antipatriotten*; finally, they were to drill more intensively and acquire more up-to-date weapons, so that they could be used not only to maintain order within towns but to oppose regular troops—Dutch or foreign—should this be necessary. The new-style Free Corps were also to be larger than the old civic

---

[11] Velema, 'Revolutie, contrarevolutie', 524–7; Van Sas, 'Vaderlandsliefde', 476–82.
[12] *Post van den Neder-Rhijn*, 8/391 (Nov. 1785), 700.
[13] [Van der Capellen], *Aan het Volk van Nederland*, 19–21; Te Brake, *Regents and Rebels*, 51, 81–3; Van Sas, 'The Patriot Revolution', 116.

militias. Dordrecht, a leading centre of Patriot agitation, became the first town, in January 1783, to set up a new-style Free Corps in place of the old *schutterij*; it soon comprised over 1,000 men.

One of the chief Patriot centres was the city of Utrecht. Utrecht had one of the main Patriot papers, one of the foremost Patriot clubs—the *Pro Patria et Libertate*—and built up one of the largest of the Free Corps. It was also at Utrecht that the series of national conventions of delegates of the Free Corps, from all over the Republic, met, from December 1784 onwards. With some justification Utrecht has been called the 'cockpit of democratic politics' during the Dutch Patriot era.[14] It was at Utrecht that the Patriots, in alliance with the 'good regents', posed their first major challenge to the authority of the Stadholder by rejecting the Orangist *reglement* which William III had imposed on the province in 1674 and which had been reimposed in 1748.[15] The Patriot press invited the citizenry to submit proposals for a new constitutional system for the province. Typically, the Patriots condemned the *reglement* as unconstitutional, and illegal, because it had been imposed against the wishes of the people and without citizens' bodies being consulted, as they always had on important matters, it was alleged, before the age of Charles V.[16]

As in 1748, the Patriots flooded the towns where they were strong with leaflets and posters announcing the times and places where petitions were to be submitted to the town councils, none too subtly summoning the people to turn up in great numbers and apply psychological pressure. This in itself was reminiscent of 1748. But this time there was much more emphasis on power being transferred to the people, a more confident legitimization of crowd pressure, and a more explicit threat to use force if necessary. Many Free Corps members attended these mass demonstrations carrying their weapons. When the Utrecht Patriot leader, Pieter Philip Ondaatje, warned the *vroedschap* that 'we are not '48-ers',[17] he meant that this time the citizenry would not be so easily fobbed off and thwarted as they had then.

If Van der Capellen's tract was the clarion-call of the Dutch Patriot Revolution, its weightiest publication was the famous two-volume *Grondwettige Herstelling* (Constitutional Restoration; 1784), a work compiled by various leading Patriots, including Van der Capellen, but published anonymously and, arguably, one of the most important political texts of pre-1789 Enlightenment Europe. It was a work which rested on the premiss that the

[14] Schama, *Patriots and Liberators*, 75, 427.
[15] Te Brake, *Regents and Rebels*, 56–7.
[16] *Post van den Neder-Rhijn*, 8 (17 Sept. 1785), 377, 573.
[17] Schama, *Patriots and Liberators*, 91.

United Provinces were dangerously decayed and in urgent need of basic reform. But it was an appeal not to the regents, nobility, or Stadholder but to the people, 'worthy countrymen and fellow citizens'. Like Van der Capellen's tract, it insists on the crucial role to be played by the citizens' militias in forcing the necessary reforms through. But the essential principles of this restored, and purified, Republic were, just as in the past, the principles of the Revolt against Spain, the Union of Utrecht, and the subsequent historical development of the United Provinces. Here too the struggle between the party-factions in the aftermath of William III's death is seen as an attempt by the people—the guilds, militias, and sworn councils—to revert to the true essence of the Revolt, cutting back the corrupt power of the stadholderate and the regents. Arming the respectable citizenry in the manner of the American militias, in the eyes of the *Grondwettige Herstelling*, was the means to compel Stadholder and regents alike to respect the rights and interests of the middle strata of the population, the men of property and the professions, irrespective of religion, while simultaneously keeping the untutored and undisciplined mob at bay.[18] It contained a democratic element but was far from fully democratic in character, advocating the sovereignty of the people, in general terms, but government on the basis of existing, historically evolved institutions by the best qualified. And who were they? The most basic reform envisaged by the *Grondwettige Herstelling* was to replace the regents—as Pieter de la Court had proposed as long ago as the 1660s—with a new élite: those who by their ability, and conscientiousness, showed themselves worthy of being promoted from lower to higher offices.[19] Rule by such an 'enlightened' élite seemed to the authors of this compilation the true essence of republican government.

The Dutch Patriot Revolution was a product of the Enlightenment and age of Atlantic Democratic revolution. Its assumptions and outlook show many affinities with the thought-world of men throughout the western world eager for fundamental reform, and the sovereignty of the people, albeit in forms which would safeguard property and elevate the qualified above the masses. And yet, while a few contemporary English and French writers were drawn on, especially Price, Priestley, and Rousseau,[20] in the main, Patriot ideas grew out of the Dutch ideological debates of the mid-eighteenth century, including the exchanges between Wagenaar and Luzac, and were ultimately rooted in the seventeenth-century controversies about the nature

[18] Leeb, *Ideological Origins*, 189–92.
[19] Ibid. 192–3.
[20] Ibid. 193; Kossmann, *The Low Countries*, 44; Klein, 'Republikanisme', 191–3, 202.

of the Revolt against Spain and the works of Grotius, Graswinckel, De Witt, De la Court, Huber, Noodt, Van Slingelandt, and other seventeenth- and early eighteenth-century Dutch political writers. Towards Montesquieu there was a definite aversion, as his reverence for constitutional monarchs, and English examples, lent itself better to the Orangist than the Patriot message.[21]

The *Grondwettige Herstelling* abundantly demonstrates the appropriation of the 'people' by the Patriots. It scathingly attacks the tendency of Luzac and Van Goens to approve guardedly of the popular risings of 1672 and 1747–8. If sovereignty rests ultimately with the people, then the popular clamour for reform, now being directed against the Orangist regime, possessed equal, or greater legitimacy than those earlier eruptions, when the authentic efforts of popular leaders to restore liberty had been thwarted by the duplicity of the Orangists.

A key theorist among the Patriots was Rutger Jan Schimmelpenninck (1761–1825), later to become the last Grand Pensionary of the Batavian Republic (1805–6), who in 1784 published, in Latin, and the following year in Dutch, his *Verhandeling over eene wel ingerichte volksregeering* (Treatise Concerning a Well Constituted People's Regime), an eloquent plea for a democratic republic which serves the interests of its citizens. The work, which was widely noticed and discussed, and was reissued in 1794, was undoubtedly influenced by Rousseau, yet, at the same time, rooted in the traditions of classical republicanism, reaching back through the Golden Age, to the Revolt, and beyond to Roman republican writing.[22] One of his chief sources of inspiration was Cicero, whose stress on the moral basis of citizenship and good government, and the need to safeguard against corruption in high places, had long held appeal in the Dutch context.

Meanwhile Luzac, in his bulkiest publication, *Hollands Rijkdom* (4 vols.; Leiden, 1780–4), while still lambasting De Witt and the republicanism of Wagenaar, assured the public that he too cherished liberty and toleration, and detested oppression, but distanced himself from his earlier enthusiasm for the will of the 'people'. His contention now was that the stadholderate was simply the best and surest guarantee of both liberty and prosperity. Kluit, for his part, assailed Patriot ideology with a barrage of well-researched observations about the Revolt against Spain, contending that there was no truth in Patriot claims that the essence of the struggle against Philip II was the pursuit of liberty through popular sovereignty.[23]

[21] Velema, 'Elie Luzac and Two Dutch Revolutions', 143–4.
[22] Klein, 'Republikanisme', 191, 206.
[23] Leeb, *Ideological Origins*, 206–9.

A striking feature of the Patriot Revolution was that it simultaneously gained ground in the west and in the east. Two of the main centres of Patriot strength in the inland provinces were Deventer and Zwolle. Deventer, which had adhered to the States party-faction during the De Witt era and which had taken the lead in opposing the Orangists and the *reglement* of 1675, after William III's death, was also the first place in Overijssel where a Free Corps was set up, in the spring of 1783, its members swearing to defend the 'liberty, security, and tranquillity of the Fatherland in general', as well as in the city itself.[24] Deventer was also the first Overijssel town to reject the restored *reglement* of 1675 during the Patriot Revolution, transferring the power to choose the burgomasters from the Stadholder to the Sworn Council. Deventer and Zwolle both acquired a vigorous Free Corps and democratic movement. As in Utrecht and Holland, guild-members—shop-keepers, skilled artisans, and professionals—formed the backbone of the Patriot movement. In both towns (though it was weaker), there was also a substantial Orangist following. As far as occupational background was concerned, this consisted, to a greater extent than in Holland, of largely the same kind of people—shopkeepers and artisans. The main difference be-tween the popular blocs, other than their political ideology, was confes-sional, this too being reminiscent of the past. Ordinary Orangists were often motivated by Voetian attitudes and anti-Catholic feelings, viewing the Patriots as a movement friendly to Catholics.

Another striking feature of the Patriot movement was its success in surpassing the movements of 1702–7 and 1748 in co-ordinating revolution-ary activity in the various provinces and towns. At a mass assembly at Utrecht, attended by thousands of Free Corps militiamen from all over the Republic, in June 1785, an Act of Association was adopted, pledging the Free Corps to launch a co-ordinated drive to re-establish a 'true republican' constitution and restore the dispossessed rights of the citizenry. Some of the rhetoric was new and revolutionary in tone, and owed much to the American experience; but the reality of what was demanded, and being striven for, was only a slight extension of what was traditional in the eighteenth-century Dutch Republic and thus, the rhetoric aside, the Patriot Revolution was essentially a further development of the tendencies mani-fested in the movements of 1672, 1702–3, and 1747–8 rather than (as has often been supposed) a fundamentally new beginning linked to revolution-ary trends elsewhere in the late eighteenth-century western Atlantic world.[25]

---

[24] Te Brake, *Regents and Rebels*, 51.
[25] De Wit, *Strijd tussen aristocratie en democratie*, 43, Van Sas, 'The Patriot Revolution', 109–10; Prak, 'Citizen Radicalism', 93–6; Lademacher, *Die Niederlande*, 387–8.

At Leiden, a few weeks later, a gathering of Holland Free Corps delegates, among them the leading Patriot journalists Wybo Fijnje and Pieter Vreede, adopted the so-called Leiden Project, a high-sounding—if on closer inspection also rather backward-looking—platform proclaiming 'liberty' the foundation of the Republic and its citizens' rights, declaring the sovereignty of the people, and demanding a free, unhampered press, election of militia officers by the citizenry, and admission of all confessional groups to the Free Corps.[26] Huge demonstrations spread from Utrecht, to Dordrecht, Gouda, and Haarlem, mass petitions being presented to the *vroedschappen*, demanding an end to patrician oligarchy and election by the citizenry of civic office-holders.

The mass movement began at Utrecht, and it was there that the Patriots won their most resounding victories. Crowds of two to five thousand were regularly brought out, mostly in an orderly, non-violent manner but showing plenty of resolution. They countered the orange cockades of the Orangists by wearing black cockades and ribbons, the latter tied in a 'V' for *Vrijheid* (Freedom). Eventually the Utrecht city council caved in to the pressure. In the Holland towns, the revolutionary process was slower and somewhat less orderly. From 1784 onwards there were a series of street clashes between Patriot and Orangist crowds, especially in The Hague, Rotterdam, Haarlem, and Leiden. Orangist demonstrators, frequently from a slightly poorer, and less educated, spectrum of society than their adversaries and often women,[27] shouted 'Oranje boven! De patriotten onder!' (Up with Orange! Down with the patriots!). On 3 April 1784 a Free Corps company opened fire on an Orangist crowd in Rotterdam, killing four people and wounding others. In June 1784, the States of Holland published a placard blaming the Orangists for the disorder and forbidding Orangist demonstrations. In many towns the Free Corps began to suppress the display of Orangist banners, cockades, and ribbons, declaring 'orange' the colour of anti-patriotism and 'slavery'. After suppressing an Orangist riot in The Hague, on 4 September 1785, the States of Holland also transferred command over the army garrison at The Hague to the *Gecommitteerde Raden*. At this point the Stadholder and his Prussian consort, who had been feeling increasingly powerless and even imprisoned at the Binnenhof, left The Hague, retreating to a loyalist district of Gelderland.[28]

Everywhere the authorities were forced to yield, or depart, in the face of organized popular pressure. Increasingly, the Republic began to polarize

---

[26] Schama, *Patriots and Liberators*, 95; Prak, 'Citizen Radicalism', 89–93.
[27] Dekker, 'Revolutionaire en contrarevolutionaire vrouwen', 561–2.
[28] De Wit, *Nederlandse revolutie*, 37.

into pro- and anti-Patriot zones. The States of Utrecht abandoned the city in 1786, withdrawing to Amersfoort, where there was a regular army garrison. The purged Utrecht city council responded by convening a rival 'legal' assembly in the city which was boycotted by most of the *ridderschap* but attended by representatives from the pro-Patriot (predominantly Catholic) towns of Montfoort and Wijk-bij-Duurstede. The new 'burgher college' at Utrecht, the first democratically elected town council in the Republic, consisted of sixteen representatives of the people, mostly shopkeepers and petty tradesmen, among them an Arminian, a Mennonite, and two Catholics. The mass gathering of Free Corps at Utrecht, in August 1786, was attended by 13,517 militiamen, representing about half the total strength of the Patriot militias in the Republic. By the summer of 1786, the Patriots were triumphant, or so it seemed, in most of Utrecht, Holland, and Overijssel with significant centres of support also in Gelderland, north Brabant, and Groningen.[29] By contrast, in Zeeland, Friesland, and parts of Gelderland it was the Orangists who had the upper hand. Furthermore, in Holland itself, though for the moment the apparatus of civic government was mostly in Patriot hands, society was deeply divided. Much of the urban proletariat, and many farmers and fishermen, backed the Orangist side. This rift was widely reflected also in the countryside.[30] In some areas, such as in the Waterland district near Amsterdam, there were also networks of rural Patriot militia companies. In the villages, the local councils were mostly strongly Orangist, and the preachers more likely to be Voetian and Orangist than in the towns.[31] But there were some exceptions to this. A leading liberal Cocceian preacher who figured among the Patriot leadership was IJsbrand van Hamelsveld, who advocated separation of State and Church and who had spent the years 1766–76 in the Waterland village of Durgerdam, retaining a certain influence in the area.

The struggle entered its culminating phase in August 1786 when the *ridderschap* of Gelderland asked the Stadholder for States troops to restore two small towns of the Arnhem quarter, Elburg and Hattem, to obedience. The move was opposed by Patriot-dominated Arnhem and Zutphen. The troops duly appeared and occupied the two towns, provoking a furious outcry in the Patriot press throughout the United Provinces. The country was plunged in feverish tension, raising the spectre of civil war. Patriot clubs and Free Corps began establishing special defence zones in areas where they were strong, collecting money and stockpiling arms and supplies. The leader

---

[29] Geyl, *Studies*, 223; Te Brake, *Regents and Rebels*, 159, 162.
[30] Schutte, *Hollandse dorpssamenleving*, 132.
[31] Nieuwenhuis, *Keeshonden en Prinsmannen*, 157–8.

of the pro-Patriot party among the regents of the States of Holland, Cornelis de Gijselaar, Pensionary of Dordrecht, demanded in the States that Holland strip the 'new Alva'—meaning the Prince of Orange—of his office of captain-general and cease payments for the support of the States General's army.[32] The city of Utrecht was turned into a veritable armed camp. The situation was now decidedly explosive. A clash between regular troops and Patriot militia near Amersfoort, in May 1787, left eighty troops dead on the field.

A major impediment to the Patriots, as the crisis approached, was that the regent élites in the Holland towns, and not least Amsterdam, had mostly only gone along with the popular movement with an eye to reversing the Orangist gains of 1747–51 and pruning the Stadholder's power. Very few of them shared the democratic ideals of the journalists, lawyers, and other professionals who led the Patriot movement. Moreover, the more the Patriots drilled and prepared for armed conflict, the uneasier the States party-faction among the regents became.[33] This inner rift within the anti-Orangist front came out into the open, as soon as some of the Holland towns began to emulate the example of Utrecht and press for genuinely democratic civic government and election of *vroedschap* members by the citizenry. It was especially Dordrecht, Haarlem, and Leiden which sought to impose democratic systems on unwilling town councils. This of itself strengthened the position of those town councils, such as The Hague, Rotterdam, and Delft, where Orangists retained the upper hand. For increasingly it seemed the regents could preserve their power only in alliance with the Orangists.

In Amsterdam the split between Patriots and regent élite widened, in February 1787, when the Free Corps began organizing popular demonstrations to force the *vroedschap* to give up the traditional method of choosing its members, and accept democratic changes. Once the Patriot press and Free Corps turned against the town hall, a powerful Orangist reaction commenced. By April 1787, some of the Amsterdam regents were seeking a rapprochement with William V and organizing counter-pressure to that of the Free Corps by mobilizing the so-called *bijltjes*, the fiercely Orangist shipyard workers, carpenters, and bargemen from the industrial belt along the IJ, to the north of the city centre. The Patriot clubs had no alternative but to step up the popular pressure. On 21 April a huge demonstration filled Dam Square, in front of the Amsterdam Town Hall, and presented a petition demanding a purge of the *vroedschap*. With this support, the

---

[32] Schama, *Patriots and Liberators*, 109.   [33] Leeb, *Ideological Origins*, 214.

pro-Patriot regents were able to stage an internal coup and remove the anti-Patriots. Thus Amsterdam passed under Patriot control exercised through the burgher 'defence council' and the Patriot clubs. Many of the city's principal merchants and financiers departed for their rural villas or, in some cases, further afield. At the end of May the situation turned uglier when Free Corps units attacked the houses of several anti-Patriot regents. The wrecking of the bridges connecting the dockyard zone with the city proper prevented the *bijltjes* intervening.[34]

Despite the growing alienation of States party regents, the Patriot Revolution was still gaining ground. At Rotterdam in August 1787, the town hall was seized by the Patriot leader Pieter Paulus and his supporters. The Delft *vroedschap* was toppled and replaced by a Patriot burgher council which included two leading Patriot journalists, Wybo Fijnje and Gerrit Paape. Similar local coups took place at Leiden, Dordrecht, Alkmaar, and Hoorn. Under the leadership of Johan Valckenaer, a professor of law at Franeker, the Frisian Patriots, backed by the guilds and students of Franeker, as well as the citizenry of Dokkum and Sneek, denounced the States of Friesland meeting at Leeuwarden as illegal. Patriot militia seized the town of Harlingen, bringing the number of Frisian towns under Patriot control to four, and a rival Patriot States of Friesland was convened at Franeker.

On the other hand, the Orangist militias in Zeeland were increasingly well organized and confident. Often backed by crowds of seamen and fishermen, they were able to curb most Patriot activity in the province. A still more serious setback was the victory of the Orangists in Gelderland.[35] Here there were more regular army garrisons than in other parts of the country, and here, with British encouragement and money, a coup was organized which was mainly the work of the troops. Arnhem and Zutphen were seized in June 1787, the Free Corps suppressed. Both towns were covered in Orange banners and great quantities of ribbon, but the mass of orange seems to have been mainly supplied and pinned up by the garrison commanders, and the soldiery.[36] A number of burgher houses were plundered, especially in Arnhem. After securing the chief towns, garrison troops quickly disarmed the Free Corps in Harderwijk, Tiel, and Zaltbommel. By the end of June 1787, the Stadholder was again master of Gelderland.

During the summer of 1787 the tension in the United Provinces, political, social, and ideological, was acute. The national revival which the Patriots

---

[34] De Wit, *Nederlandse revolutie*, 82–3.
[35] Ibid. 110–13.
[36] Geyl, *Studies*, 218.

proclaimed was, like all true revolutionary programmes, intended to transform and revitalize every part of the people's life and life-style, a revival
which would be at once political, economic, military, cultural, and, by no
means least, moral. The 'Love of Fatherland', so deeply ingrained in Dutch
political discourse from the 1770s onwards, was inseparable from a tendency
to view the greatness and decay of peoples as essentially a moral phenomenon, rooted in the rise and fall of moral values and responsibility to society.
A deep preoccupation with checking the advance of irreligion and immorality permeated the pages of the Patriot newspapers and writings of Van der
Capellen, Paulus, Fijnje, Paape, and other leading Patriot publicists, and not
only their writings but no less those of Luzac, Kluit, and Rijklof Michael
van Goens, editor of the chief Orangist paper, the *Ouderwetse Nederlandsche
Patriot*, champion of the Enlightenment as well as of the Orangist cause.[37]

Orthodox Calvinist ministers of the Voetian tradition, and the Orangist
press, routinely denounced the Patriot clubs and Free Corps during the
1780s as nests of dissenters, heretics, atheists, and papists.[38] But, in reality,
most of the Patriot leadership and rank and file were drawn from a
Reformed background and the body of the Republic's preachers were as
much split as they had been, by the Voetian–Cocceian rift, over the past
century and more, and often along much the same lines. Under the Batavian
Republic, in 1800, there were around 1,570 Reformed preachers in the
Republic, as against 300 Mennonite and about fifty Remonstrant preachers
and a few hundred Catholic priests.[39] Of the Reformed preachers a significant minority inclined to Cocceian theology and radical politics.[40] In
Friesland, it was calculated that roughly a quarter of the Reformed
ministers were pro-Patriot. Of five Reformed preachers who took sides at
The Hague, during the 1780s, only two backed the Stadholder, three siding
with the Patriots.[41]

Orangist preachers were slightingly dismissed as 'precisians' and dogmat-
ists because of their stress on the confession of the faith and rigidity on
predestination and Grace. Pro-Patriot preachers, by contrast, were vilified
by the Orangists as 'Arminians' and friends of the Mennonites. The most
influential neo-Cocceian among the Patriot leadership was Van Hamelsveld,
who in his book *De zedelijke toestand der Nederlandsche Natie* (The Moral
State of the Dutch Nation), published after the defeat of the Patriot

[37] Van Sas, 'The Patriot Revolution', 102–3, 109.
[38] *Ouderwetse Nederlandsche Patriot*, ii. 358, 537 and iii. 88–92.
[39] Galdi, *Quadro politico*, ii. 72.
[40] Nieuwenhuis, *Keeshonden en Prinsmannen*, 159, 161.
[41] Schutte, 'Gereformeerden', 500–1.

Revolution, in 1791, proclaimed the Enlightenment to be Janus-headed, a force potentially for both good and evil. He extolled the Enlightenment not only for its spreading knowledge and love of reading, advancing education among the people, but for creating a sense of national awareness. But, no less ardently, he deplored its effect on life-style, its tendency to encourage irreligion and immorality. Van Hamelsveld's central idea was that a republic which is sound and stable must rest on a high level of public morality, which is not sustainable without high standards of private morality; this, in turn, cannot be maintained without a strong basis in religion. Thus for him the Reformed faith was the anchor of the state and the Revolution. Like all Patriot writers, steeped in a quest for 'republican virtue', Van Hamelsveld wished to promote the general welfare by infusing society with sterner moral ideals: 'a people which desires to be truly free, and to maintain its freedom, must be virtuous, industrious, fearless, thrifty, and frugal, not effeminate or sensual.'[42] Not the least attractive 'republican' trait of his hero Johan de Witt was the latter's simplicity of manners and dress, his going about like an ordinary member of the public, accompanied by only one servant.

To the extent that the Enlightenment was advancing irreligion and immorality in the United Provinces it was, in Van Hamelsveld's eyes, undermining republican freedom itself. He recognized that the Dutch were becoming a less religious nation and that the change was taking place with discomforting speed. There had been between three and four hundred theology candidates preparing for the Reformed ministry in the 1750s, when he himself had been a university student, he remarks, and whenever a living had become vacant, even in some isolated village, you could count on a good forty candidates hastening to apply. In 1790, he estimated, there were only between forty and fifty theology students preparing for the ministry in the whole of the Republic, about 10 per cent of the figure of a generation earlier.[43] The Enlightenment had done this, he acknowledged, but the bad Enlightenment of French ideas and sexual licentiousness which had progressed so far in Dutch society, he alleged, that it was now quite normal for supposedly respectable married women to conduct adulterous affairs.

For Enlightened Orangists, the United Provinces were already a model of 'civil freedom'; and the freedom of the press, which the Patriots so stridently demanded, already existed.[44] The central message of Van Goens's *Ouderwetse Nederlandsche Patriot* was that there is a difference between a free press and a licentious press and that what the Patriot papers were about was

---

[42] Van Hamelsveld, *Zedelijke toestand*, 404.
[43] Ibid. 457.
[44] Kluit, *De rechten van den Mensch*, 81, 103, 158.

to undermine the confessional, moral, and social pillars on which the stability and well-being of society rested, subverting respect for religion, and erasing the distinction between 'freedom' and 'licence', a licence which, if not suppressed, would destroy 'true Dutch freedom', the freedom to think, speak, and write 'in a free land and under a free people such as ours'.[45]

   The ideological gulf between Enlightened Orangists such as Van Goens, Luzac, and Kluit, and the Patriot ideologues, was, at least with respect to the terms they used, and style of thinking, a relatively narrow one.[46] Both sides built their ideology around 'freedom' and the idea of republican virtue, both stressed the dependence of political and economic well-being on religion and morality, both sets of intellectuals insisted on the need to spread love of the Fatherland among the people and fervently believed in the value of education, scholarship, and science. Yet, for all that, the ideological gap was unbridgeable given the fundamental differences between the two blocs on the nature of 'freedom' and especially press freedom, the place of the Church and its theology in society and politics, and, above all, the democratic dimension, the place of the people in politics. To many Orangists Patriot views seemed not just objectionable but godless, infamous, and destructive of society. In the tradition of the Orangists of the late seventeenth century, Van Goens's periodical repeatedly styled the Patriots a party of 'Remonstrants and other dissenters', meaning by this that much of their zeal derived from confessional hostility to the Dutch Reformed Church and that its aim was to undermine Church, society, and state.[47]

---

[45] *Ouderwetse Nederlandsche Patriot*, i. 141–2 and ii. 578–81, 602.
[46] Velema, 'Revolutie, contrarevolutie', 517–18.
[47] *Ouderwetse Nederlandsche Patriot*, iii. 88–92.

43

The Fall of the Republic

❖

THE ORANGIST COUNTER-REVOLUTION, 1787–1795

It by no means appeared, in the summer of 1787, that the Stadholder and his supporters, even though they had the regular army on their side, were strong enough to overwhelm the Patriot Revolution. In the end it was foreign intervention which proved decisive. British ministers, since the end of the Fourth Anglo-Dutch War, in 1784, had been continually active, distributing money and encouragement to Orangist leaders and proposing methods of undermining the Patriots. The Patriots regarded Britain as the principal enemy of the Republic, and of its commerce and colonial empire, and the British government was equally convinced that the Patriot Revolution constituted a serious threat to British interests—diplomatic, strategic, commercial, and maritime. Privately, it emerges from Van der Capellen's correspondence of the early 1780s, the Patriot leadership knew that Prussia was scarcely less antagonistic. But while it seemed prudent to do everything possible to avoid provoking the Prussian king, the prevailing anti-British rhetoric was fundamental to Patriot attitudes and ideology. Moreover, it was chiefly Britain which was encouraging Prussia to take measures against the Patriots. Consequently, whilst the anti-British rhetoric continued, there was remarkably little comment about Prussia. The death of Frederick the Great, in August 1786, and the succession to the Prussian throne and its possible consequences for the Republic, were scarcely discussed at all in the Dutch press. Prussia was referred to only in the politest terms.[1]

The Stadholder himself, weak and indecisive, did little to bring about the eventual intervention which crushed the Patriot Revolution.[2] The new king of Prussia, Friedrich Wilhelm II (1786–97), a disciplinarian and enemy of democratic ideas, as well as the brother of Wilhelmina, gave increasing attention to developments in the Republic. When Princess Wilhelmina was arrested by the Gouda Free Corps, near Schoonhoven, in June, he

---

[1] De Jongste, 'Beeldvorming', 526–9.   [2] Schutte, 'Willem IV en Willem V', 222.

proclaimed the actions of the Patriots a calculated insult to the House of Hohenzollern and, with strong British encouragement, began massing troops in the Prussian lands in, and adjoining, the Low Countries. Then, in September 1787, a Prussian army of 26,000 men crossed the frontier and marched in two columns towards the The Hague and Amsterdam. There was practically no resistance. Despite all the rhetoric about an armed citizenry, and the continual drilling of the Free Corps, the revolutionary fervour of the people's militias simply evaporated at the sight of Prussian bayonets. Utrecht capitulated without a fight. The Patriot Revolution disintegrated.

Backed by Prussian troops and British cash, William V returned to The Hague in triumph. His intention was to restore the Orangist regime on the same basis as before with only a minimum of retribution, but it was beyond his control to prevent a degree of stringency in the crack-down on Patriots, and the restricting of expression, that went rather further than he and some of his supporters would have wished. The press was muzzled, political meetings forbidden, and the Patriot clubs and Free Corps dissolved. The old-style militia companies, controlled by the town governments now purged of anti-Orangists, were restored, though not before Orangist mobs had taken to the streets and attacked the homes of leading Patriots, usually pillaging but not destroying them. In the best traditions of the Republic, hardly any Patriots were killed or grievously injured but large numbers were intimidated. Demoralized and fearful, several thousand prominent Patriots chose to flee rather than face further mob violence and official repression. Droves crossed into the Austrian Netherlands, many then moving on to find refuge in France, where Louis XVI made them welcome.

The man William V chose to steer the Orangist restoration was the Pensionary of Zeeland, Laurens Pieter van de Spiegel (1736–1800). Van de Spiegel, named Pensionary of Holland in December 1787, was an energetic and able regent politician—though not from an old regent family—somewhat in the tradition of Van Slingelandt. He too had carried out extensive historical research into the Republic's institutions—publishing a number of erudite historical works in the 1770s—and compiled political discourses. He had a deep knowledge of the Republic, and its past, and was no less convinced than Van Slingelandt of the need to reform the federal structure of the Republic and forge the provinces into a more integrated whole.

Also like Van Slingelandt, Van de Spiegel found his path impeded by a combination of inertia and vested interests. Nevertheless, he did achieve some reforms, most notably a long-needed revision of the provincial quotas, increasing Holland's share substantially, and Gelderland's slightly, while reducing those of Zeeland, Utrecht, and Friesland (see Table 8). He also began to reform the part of the colonial empire outside the sphere of the VOC. The Fourth Anglo-Dutch War had revealed that the WIC was not only effectively bankrupt but incapable of administering, or defending, its colonies.[3] Over the opposition of Zeeland, the Company was liquidated during 1791, the shareholders (whose shares were worth little and had received practically no dividends since 1780) were compensated with 30 per cent of the nominal value of their shares. As from January 1792, the former WIC territories in the Guyanas—Surinam, Essequebo, Demerary, and Pomeroon, the six Dutch Antilles, and the forts in West Africa—came under the direct sway of the States General. A new Generality college, the *Raad der Colonien in de West-Indien*, was set up. But the *Raad* achieved little in the way of reorganizing the colonies, and their defences in the few years remaining to the regime.

Van de Spiegel was far from being a nonentity. He battled to introduce reforms and increase support for the regime while, in the spirit of his master, avoiding drastic methods and showing considerable respect for the forms and procedures of the Republic. Arrests were few and the repression of which he was in charge remained moderate. But the avoidance of drastic methods meant that there was an early resurgence of the spirit of opposition and little prospect of sealing the Dutch populace off either from the Patriot émigré communities in France and the south Netherlands, or the revolutionary turmoil which erupted first in the Austrian Netherlands, in 1788, and then in France, in 1789.

THE CONSERVATIVE REVOLUTION IN THE 'SOUTH' AND THE NEW 'NETHERLANDS REPUBLIC'

For the Dutch Patriot exiles in France, the outbreak of the French Revolution, and universal ideology to which it gave rise, was an inspiring development. From 1789, the Patriot Revolution became inextricably linked, politically and ideologically, to the French Revolution. But, both before 1789 and subsequently, the Dutch revolutionary process contrasted sharply with (and remained largely detached from) that which erupted in the south Netherlands. There remained an unbridgeable gulf between the political, ideological, religious, and general cultural milieux in north and south which the march of Revolution only served to widen further. Assuredly, the Patriot movement was neither anti-Christian, nor unchristian.

---

[3] Emmer, 'Suiker, goud, en slaven', 470.

Nevertheless, it conspicuously lacked a confessional basis, rejecting confessional demands and premisses. No Church could claim any special status within the movement. Its intellectual world was shaped by the Enlightenment and the example of the American Revolution, but it also remained unshakeably convinced of the lasting validity of the Revolt against Spain, and the Republic's fundamental institutions, seeing these as the surest guides to a glorious future. The political and ideological upheaval in the south, by contrast, was essentially a reaction to 'Josephism', the enlightened absolutism of the Emperor Joseph II, as applied in the south Netherlands.[4]

Soon after succeeding his mother, Maria Theresa, as sole ruler of the Habsburg monarchy, in 1780, the Emperor resolved to visit his part of the Low Countries. His visit (May–July 1781) became the motor of a veritable 'revolution from above' no less far-reaching in its implications than the gathering Patriot movement, next door, to the north. Joseph curtailed the powers of the new regent in Brussels, his sister Maria Christina (1780–93) and her husband, bringing the south under the direct control of Vienna. He issued his Patent of Toleration (1781), enforcing toleration of Protestants and Jews on a land inured by two centuries of Counter-Reformation indoctrination to reject toleration. He suppressed superfluous monasteries and subjected the rest to Vienna, rather than Rome, restricted religious processions, reformed the guilds, began reforming the university of Leuven, curtailed ecclesiastical and noble privileges, and—more acceptably—ordered the reopening of the Scheldt to maritime traffic. In 1787 the Emperor embarked on plans for a radical reorganization of the entire judicial and administrative system, proposing to sweep away most existing jurisdictions and courts.

In the spring of 1787 a protest movement arose, especially in Brabant, headed by the Brussels lawyer Hendrik van der Noot (1731–1827). The States of Brabant reminded the Emperor that he ruled in the province under the terms of the same historic privileges as his Burgundian and Habsburg predecessors had sworn to uphold.[5] Scores of pamphlets appeared accusing the Emperor of trampling on the ancient constitutional rights of the southern provinces. In June 1787 Van der Noot and the Brussels guilds began organizing militia contingents not unlike those of the Patriots, in the north, except that they were more conservative in their political and ideological rhetoric. In September 1787 there was a popular rising in Brussels which led to the Austrians withdrawing their troops from the city.

---

[4] Hasquin, 'Le Joséphisme', 224–34.
[5] Polasky, 'Success of a Counter-Revolution', 414–15.

For two years the south simmered on the verge of a full-scale revolt. Matters came to a head in June 1789 when Joseph, whose limited patience had now run out, proclaimed all provincial privileges in the Austrian Netherlands 'abrogés, cassés et annulés'.[6] Meanwhile, the Belgian rebels were receiving assistance from the north. The Dutch and Belgian popular movements of the 1780s were so different, so contrasting in their attitudes to authority, religion, popular participation in government, traditional jurisdiction, and the House of Orange, that neither William V, nor his Prussian allies, were in the least inclined to discourage the agitation in the south. On the contrary, the authorities in The Hague, as in Berlin, were hostile to Joseph and his policies, and began encouraging a popular movement which was both conservative and anti-Austrian. Van der Noot established his counter-revolutionary committee in exile, at Breda, the town of William the Silent, where in the autumn of 1789 the rebels were allowed to concentrate their insurrectionary army. Remarkably, Van der Noot's political manifesto of 1789 was based, in places word for word, on the States General's Act of Abjuration, rejecting Philip II, of 1581, asserting the sacrosanctity of provincial privileges.[7]

In October 1789, the Belgian rebels stunned Europe by invading the south Netherlands from States Brabant and defeating the Austrians. The States General gathered in Brussels and proclaimed a new 'republic', with one eye on the American Revolution and the other on the Revolt against Spain.[8] The rebels called their new state the 'Republic of the United Netherlands States', the last word referring to 'States' in the traditional Low Countries sense. At this point the upheaval in the south divided into a conservative counter-revolutionary mainstream, headed by Van der Noot, and a liberal, democratic movement called the Vonckists after their leader J. F. Vonck (1743–92).[9] The conservatives held that, after deposition of the ruler, sovereignty reverted not to the people but the States. The Vonckists disagreed but found not only the nobility, clergy, and peasantry, but also the Brussels guilds arrayed against them. Massed rallies of armed guild-members and peasants denounced the Enlightenment, toleration, and the Vonckists, the press fuelling the popular loathing of the allegedly anti-religious 'philosophie de ce siècle'. By May 1790 most of the Vonckists had fled across the French frontier.

For several months this new republic in the Netherlands maintained itself with some vigour despite the shortcomings of its constitutional

---

[6] Ibid. 416.
[7] Kossmann, *The Low Countries*, 59.
[8] Dhondt, 'Conservatieve Brabantse ontwenteling', 435–6.
[9] Ibid. 439–41; Kossmann, *The Low Countries*, 60.

arrangements, and the States General's inability to obtain adequate co-operation and financial contributions from the provincial States. The United Netherlands States of the south issued their own propaganda medals in 1790, showing the Netherlands Lion holding the Liberty Hat aloft on a pole, the same symbol as figured on the propaganda medals of the Revolt against Spain in the 1570s. Ironically, many folk took to sporting Orange cockades, the symbol of reaction in the north, but, in the south, the emblem of allegiance to provincial privilege as defended by the Revolt led by Orange against Philip II.[10] Prussia, increasingly involved in the politics of the Low Countries, not only supported the new republic, hand in hand with the Orangist regime in the north, but sent in troops to assist.

For the moment, Prussia, even more than Britain, was the arbiter of the Low Countries. The Prussian monarch kept substantial forces in his territories in, and adjoining, the Netherlands. The new Emperor, Leopold II (1790–2), however, alarmed by the escalating Austro-Prussian rivalry in Hungary, Poland, and the Czech lands, as well as the Low Countries, and much less uncompromising than his deceased brother Joseph, energetically courted the Prussian regime at the Convention of Reichenach, which produced agreement in July 1790. Under this package, compromises were reached on east-central Europe and Prussia agreed that Austrian authority should be restored in the south Netherlands provided Joseph II's reforms were cancelled and there were no reprisals against those who had enjoyed Prussian backing. The new constitutional arrangements agreed for the south Netherlands were to be guaranteed by Prussia, the House of Orange, and Britain. Prussian troops were withdrawn from the fledgling state. In November 1790 an Austrian army of 30,000 men invaded the republic, entering Brussels in December. In the same month a further treaty of co-operation in the Low Countries between Austria, Prussia, Britain, and the House of Orange was signed in The Hague. Maria Christina returned to Brussels in June 1791.

The south Netherlands republic of 1789–90 was an ephemeral phenomenon, yet one which arose at a decisive moment in the history of Europe, and the Low Countries, and carried far-reaching implications. It demonstrated that the political, religious, and cultural gulf separating north and south in the Low Countries in the eighteenth century, and on the threshold of the nineteenth, could scarcely have been wider. The Brabant counter-revolutionaries of 1789 were the first political ideologues in the Low Countries to call the combined populace of the Dutch- and French-speaking south the

---

[10] Kossmann, *The Low Countries*, 62.

'Belgians' (de Belgen; les belges).[11] Their institutional conservatism, and Catholic devotion, amazed Europe. Their sense of distinctness from, and opposition to, the revolutionary movements in France, on the one side, and the north Netherlands, on the other, was unyielding. They rejected the Enlightenment and enlightened absolutism, though it is true that the Vonckists enjoyed somewhat more support in Flanders and the French-speaking provinces than they did in Brabant.

Yet, while it is right to insist on the different character of the popular movements in north and south, in the 1780s, the popular insurrection in the south was, nevertheless, an integral part of the wider Atlantic revolutionary upheaval engulfing the western world in the wake of the American Revolution, a process in which the Dutch Patriot movement was the first major European manifestation and the French Revolution the most dramatic. It is true that the Austrian Netherlands was the only segment of the west where there was a direct clash between enlightened absolutism and the call for popular participation inspired by the American and Dutch Patriot examples.[12] But a longing for a 'national' reawakening, constitutional renewal, arming the people, and the rhetoric of 'liberty' were likewise essential features of the republic of the southern Netherlands provinces and all these were unmistakable manifestations of the great crisis sweeping the Atlantic world.

THE END OF THE UNITED PROVINCES

The Dutch Patriots were inherently much more likely to join forces with the French Revolution than all but the most uncompromisingly Vonckist wing of the Belgian opposition, despite the Patriots' aversion to the more radical strains of French Enlightenment thought and revolutionary rhetoric. Geography, however, decreed that the south came under the control of revolutionary France first. The revolutionary cause gained ground in the south following the victory of the French armies at Jemappes, in November 1792, the south coming fully under French control with the crushing of the Austrian army at Fleurus, in June 1794. But the revolution imposed on the Austrian Netherlands, in 1792–4, was a revolution from outside. It displayed little continuity with the themes and preoccupations of the popular insurrection of the late 1780s and, as a result, enjoyed scant support among the populace. In October 1795, the southern Netherlands were formally annexed to France, an event followed by far-reaching institutional changes.

---

[11] Polasky, 'Success of a Counter-Revolution', 420.
[12] Dhondt, 'Conservatieve Brabantse omtwenteling', 427.

The former provincial administrations were swept away and replaced with nine French-style *départements*. The judicial system was replaced by the French revolutionary system. The religious orders were suppressed, in September 1796, and their buildings and property confiscated. A drive to reduce the influence of the secular clergy ensued in the years 1797–8 but this was entirely alien to most of the populace, its impetus deriving from France.

In the north Netherlands events followed a very different course. The French revolutionary armies were able to advance over the frozen great rivers, in January 1795. Their coming was preceded by a genuine build-up of revolutionary expectation and precipitated a wave of revolutionary agitation which swept ahead of the French troops. The numerous reading societies in the northern Netherlands had regained their former Patriot *élan* during 1793–4 and were again actively propagating anti-Orangist sentiment and radical ideas. By the summer of 1794, there were reported to be thirty-four reading societies, of between sixty and eighty members each, in Amsterdam alone, with numerous similar societies in all the large towns. Many of the membership were not only arming themselves with revolutionary ideas but also with guns, ready to resume the struggle which had broken off in 1787. At Utrecht there were twelve reading societies meeting in private homes, counting between them 1,000 Free Corps men armed with several hundred hidden firearms. By September 1794, Amsterdam was flooded with posters and pamphlets produced by the secret committee for the Revolution. There was an attempted rising, in October, which was promptly suppressed by an Orangist regime heavily bolstered by the British and Prussians.

When the advancing French reached Utrecht, in January 1795, they found a city enthusiastically awaiting them, festooned in tricolour pendants and the insignia of the Revolution. Seeing the advantage of legitimacy conferred on their invasion, by a carpet of risings unfolding ahead of them, the French paused before advancing on Amsterdam. Again the revolutionary committees went into action and, this time, took over the city, their example being rapidly emulated by revolutionary committees all over the country. The French invasion of 1795 was almost like a carnival, being 'happily conducted', as one British observer noted, the towns bedecked with tricolour flags and revolutionary posters as well as the black cockades of the Patriots. There was remarkably little violence against the persons, or property, of fleeing Orangist dignitaries.[13]

Particularly striking is the high degree of continuity between the revolutionary movement suppressed in 1787 and the Revolution resumed in 1795.

[13] Lademacher, *Geschichte der Niederlande*, 211.

Many of the same clubs, reading societies, printing presses, militia companies, and bookshops figured in 1795 as in the early and mid-1780s. And, indeed, the Dutch Revolution of 1795 was seen at the time as a continuation of the Patriot Revolution and, therefore, as being based on the principles which had supposedly inspired the Dutch Revolt and the creation of the Republic. It was a renewal, certainly, but not yet a sweeping away of the Republic. This sense of the Revolution being a genuine liberation, and sweeping away of tyranny, was heightened by the relatively disciplined, tactful conduct the French commanders imposed on their troops, which contrasted with the indiscipline of the retreating British and Prussians who, as English eyewitnesses themselves noted, took out their frustration on the populace, pillaging towns and villages as they went. The sense of the Revolution as a restoration expressed itself in innumerable victory parades, thanksgiving ceremonies, theatrical performances, and banquets in which there was much celebration of the Dutch past, and the Republic, as well as of the ideals of the French Revolution. There was also a return to 1787, and the past, in civic government. In Deventer's first democratic election for municipal office-holders, in March 1795, no fewer than seven of the ten most popular candidates had been members of the Patriot city council of 1787.[14]

The name of the Republic was changed to the 'Batavian Republic' in 1795. But it took time for the new leadership to organize and draw up the far-reaching reforms they had in mind. The Committee of Public Safety in Paris, and the French generals in the Netherlands, had given assurances to the Patriot leaders that they would not interfere in the setting up of a revolutionary Dutch Republic. So, for the moment, it was far from clear what form the imminent Batavian Republic would take. Democratic anti-Orangists were now in control of both civic and provincial as well as Generality institutions. But there had not yet been, and would not be for the next several years, any great change in institutions, procedures, or the administrative system as such. Indeed, it was still quite usual at the end of the 1790s to refer to the Batavian Republic as the 'United Provinces'.

---

[14] Te Brake, *Regents and Rebels*, 170.

44

Denouement

❖

The revolutionary government in Paris decided to acknowledge the Batavian Republic but, at the same time (yielding to pressure at home to extract compensation for the war the Republic had fought against France, since 1793), a 100 million guilder indemnity was imposed and States Flanders and Venlo, Roermond, and Maastricht annexed to France. Ceding States Flanders also meant that the Republic had to accept the permanent lifting of the Scheldt restrictions which had been in force since 1585.

For the rest, the Patriots now had a free hand to carry through their Revolution. But what, precisely, was this to involve? William V and his family had fled to England—much to Van de Spiegel's dismay—embarking at Scheveningen on 18 January 1795. The Pensionary was arrested on 4 February. His papers and conduct of affairs were thoroughly investigated by a Patriot commission, headed by Valckenaer, who had led the Patriot committee in exile, at Paris. But neither he nor other Orangist leaders who had remained were harshly treated. Matters followed a very different course than in France. After three years of rather mild imprisonment, Van de Spiegel was released. He fled to Germany in the last year of his life to join the Orangists in exile.

Purging Orangists, and replacing them with Patriots, proceeded at a brisk pace in all parts of the Republic. Revolutionary committees and militias took over the country. Quite quickly, democratic methods were introduced into civic government in many towns. The old regent oligarchy were by no means swept away, especially not at Amsterdam. But they had suffered a blow, both in principle and fact, from which they were never to recover. However, this was inherent in the Patriot Revolution of the 1780s and not incompatible with retaining the old, decentralized provincial structure of the Republic. The VOC was liquidated by decree, in December 1795, but the Generality committee which took over the administration of the East India trade and colonies, and South Africa, in March 1796, for the moment went no further than had the Generality college administering the former colonies of the WIC since 1792. For the time being, the Union of Utrecht of 1579 and most of the procedures of the old Republic remained largely in force.

Everywhere there was intense discussion in the clubs and revolutionary committees with a variety of pressures being brought to bear. In December 1795, the States General yielded to the widespread demand for the convening of a National Assembly to reform the constitution of the Republic, an assembly to consist of delegates not appointed by the provinces but elected by the people. In the elections of 1796, for the National Assembly, all male inhabitants over the age of 20, not in receipt of poor relief, were entitled to vote. The Assembly duly convened on 1 March 1796. Yet still the composition of the body of delegates showed only a partial break with the past. Some delegates were lawyers, journalists, and other professionals, but many were members of regent and noble families. More importantly, radicals who wished to sweep away the Union of Utrecht, and the old federal framework of the Republic, were by no means fully in the ascendant. The Assembly included a large bloc of anti-Orangist federalists who wished to avoid a sharp break on the institutional front, and retain much of the traditional structure.[1]

The outcome was a proposed new constitution which preserved the federal principle and many features of the United Provinces. This was eventually rejected by the electorate, in a plebiscite held in August 1797, but at the end of 1797 the situation was still one of deadlock, with the ruling establishment split between federalists and unitarists. In January 1798, the French backed a radical *coup d'état* which ejected the federalists from the National Assembly. As a result a fundamentally new, unitary constitution, sweeping away the entire structure of the past, was put to the electorate, and voted in, in April 1798. Yet the United Provinces were still not dead. The new constitution had been voted in by a drastically curtailed electorate from which both the Orangists and the federalists were debarred. Only some 30 per cent of the electorate voted at all. Furthermore, a large part of the support the new constitution received derived from the predominantly Catholic areas of what had been the Generality Lands. In June 1798 a second *coup d'état* took place, headed by a group of moderate Patriots who stressed the continuing validity of the traditions and institutions of the old Republic. They retained the new constitution but took no practical steps to implement it.

[1] De Wit, *Strijd tussen aristocratie en democratie*, 120–3.

The revolutionary *élan* of 1795 lasted only briefly. The crushing of the Dutch navy by the British at the battle of Camperdown, off Den Helder, in October 1797, definitively cooled the ardour of those who saw the Republic's salvation in waging a revolutionary war against Britain and marked the end of Dutch naval power as a significant force in global politics. The coup of June 1798, followed by the still more moderate coup of 1801, for the moment (until 1805) paralysed the effort to change fundamentally the institutional and administrative structures inherited from the past. Even where there were significant changes in form, between 1798 and 1805, the reality beneath the surface often showed a surprising degree of continuity with that of the old Republic.

Nothing was more fundamental to the pre-1795 United Provinces than provincial sovereignty and the organizing of administration, justice, taxation, and patronage on a provincial basis. Thus, one of the main tasks of the unitary constitution of 1798, and one that was essential to its objectives, was to dissolve these provincial structures. Sweeping plans were drawn up to subordinate the new 'departments', which were to replace the provinces, to central authority, render the departments purely administrative entities, and abolish old ways of thinking by breaking the links with the former provinces, changing their names, and redrawing their boundaries. Accordingly, Holland was now divided into three departments. Friesland merged with Groningen to form the new department of the Ems, States Brabant merged with slices of former Holland and Gelderland to create the new North Brabant, while Utrecht disappeared, being split between the new department of the Rhine (the rump of Gelderland) and that of Texel (North Holland).

But these arrangements failed to stick and, after 1801, the regime reverted in large part to the old provincial boundaries. Still more important, subordination to central authority was more in name than reality and much of the judicial and fiscal machinery for the moment remained in the hands of patricians and nobles who were not infrequently the same men who had run the provincial administrations before 1795. The 'turmoil of revolution has left Dutch society in a remarkably orderly state', noted an English visitor in 1800, amazed that the devices and legends on the coins and seals of the old Republic were still current, and not least that the Revolt against Spain, despite the two centuries that had elapsed in the mean time, was still so basic to the political outlook of the common people that its events were being 'related and dwelt on with all the minuteness and circumstantiality of recent events'.[2]

---

[2] Fell, *A Tour*, 190–1.

Another fundamental characteristic of the old Republic incompatible with the new was a high degree of civic autonomy. If the revolutionary ideology and centralizing aims of the Batavian Republic meant anything in practical terms, there had to be a sweeping away of the old-style, regent-dominated municipalities. Yet, for the time being, this did not happen. Until 1805–6 the city governments, not least the Amsterdam *vroedschap*, were largely successful in retaining control of the burghers' militias, taxation, justice, and much else. In Amsterdam the city council even readopted the old symbolic number of thirty-six seats.[3]

Yet another priority of the Batavian Revolution was to detach the Reformed Church from its special status and close links with the State, ending the exclusion of the non-Reformed from office-holding and civic government and their lower status in the militias, guilds, and universities. The Dutch Catholic population were indeed one of the mainsprings of the Batavian Revolution and no contrast between the revolutionary upheavals in north and south, in the 1790s, is more striking than the fact that while the Belgian populace largely shunned the Revolution imported from France, in the north, the Catholic population (despite the efforts of some Dutch priests to discourage revolutionary sentiment)[4] strongly supported the assault on the old regime. Following the radical coup early in 1798, a number of senior Catholic officials emerged. But here too the Revolution was largely frustrated by subsequent developments. Catholics tended to disappear again from the higher administration after 1798. There was little attempt to redistribute the country's large churches, church schools, and other properties, the bulk of which were in Reformed hands. The considerable leverage, and favoured position, of the Reformed, in the distribution of poor relief, remained largely intact. If Catholics, Mennonites, and Jews were now emancipated in theory, this was not yet the case in fact. Even central government's plan that in Amsterdam the Jews—who now formed about 11 per cent of the city's population—should serve alongside others in the citizens' militia was firmly blocked by the *vroedschap*.[5]

Given that the war was paralysing the Republic's commerce, shipping, and fisheries, that there was widespread resentment against the French troops and their requisitions, and that, more generally, the revolutionary war against the European monarchies appeared to be going badly in the late 1790s, orderly conditions held up remarkably well. The resurgence of Orangist sentiment remained limited. Encouraged by the successes of the

---

[3] Schama. *Patriots and Liberators*, 425.
[4] Kossmann, *The Low Countries*, 101.
[5] Michman, 'Emancipatie', 80–1.

coalition ranged against France, both the British government and the exiled Stadholder began actively planning the restoration of the old Republic, under the House of Orange, during 1798, and it was at that time that the scheme of merging Belgium with the north Netherlands to form a solid bulwark against both France, and revolutionary republican ideology, was first mooted in London.[6] An Anglo-Russian-Orangist invasion force was prepared. William V established his headquarters in Lingen, summoning the Dutch people to rise against their oppressors and restore the old Republic under the stadholderate. There were perfunctory attempts to rise in the east, effortlessly suppressed by the citizens' militias. However, when the British fleet landed 24,000 allied soldiers, mostly crack British troops, at the tip of the North Holland peninsula, the Republic was plunged in turmoil. Most of what remained of the Dutch navy mutinied, ran up the Orange flag, and surrendered. The invasion force, under Sir Ralph Abercromby, occupied Hoorn, Enkhuizen, and Alkmaar and began to advance towards Haarlem and Amsterdam. But there were few defections from the Batavian army and surprisingly restricted support among the population. Abercromby noted that even the best disposed 'will mount an Orange cockade and no more'.[7] The Franco-Dutch army, though no more numerous than the invaders, proved firmer than expected and, on 6 October 1799, defeated the British in a battle at Castricum, near Alkmaar. Abercromby fell back and, shortly after, the invasion was abandoned, the troops re-embarking for England.

The Batavian Republic was severely handicapped from the outset by the economic collapse and steep rise in poverty and distress. Yet the stability and resilience of Dutch society remained largely intact, as did much of the traditional fabric of social control, education, welfare, and church life. It is true that in both town and countryside there was a noticeable upsurge of crime and vagrancy and also of drunkenness—the gin distilleries were the only booming industry in the country apart from prostitution. Yet Amsterdam's prison population remained remarkably small by English standards, there were few executions for murder and armed robbery, and, for the most part, the streets remained both safe and clean. Assuredly, a British observer commented, in 1800, the form of the old Republic 'ought to be reverenced for its effects on the private and domestic institutions of life',[8] noting that the 'condition of servants in general throughout the United provinces is much superior to that of the same useful class of people in England'. A few years later, the Italian official Mattheo Galdi, who had acquired a detailed

---

[6] Kossmann, *The Low Countries*, 102.
[7] Haley, *British and the Dutch*, 220.
[8] Fell, *A Tour*, 200.

knowledge of the Batavian Republic, judged Dutch society a model of human progress and orderly conditions, a standard for the whole of Napoleonic Europe.[9]

ABOLISHED BY NAPOLEON

How and why then did the Batavian Republic collapse barely a decade after its birth? Essentially, it was crushed beneath the inexorable pressures of global war, caught between the irresistible force of Napoleon and the immovable object of British power.

At sea, and in the colonial sphere, Britain swept all before her. Shortly after his flight to Britain, William V had been persuaded to sign the so-called Circular Note of Kew (February 1795), ordering Dutch colonial governors not to resist the British and place their forts, harbours, and ships at Britain's disposal. Few colonial authorities obeyed, but many were confused and demoralized by the orders, creating a predicament heightened by the fact that in all the colonies, and especially Surinam and Curaçao, both official-dom and the colonists were bitterly divided into Patriot and Orangist factions. The governors of Malacca, Amboina, and west Sumatra, in compliance with Kew, capitulated without a fight. Cochin surrendered after a brief bombardment. The rest of the Dutch enclaves in southern India were quickly overrun. In February 1796, the British completed their conquest of Dutch Ceylon. By the end of the 1790s the Republic's East India empire and trade were crushed and paralysed.

British forces captured South Africa (which was largely pro-Patriot and anti-British) in September 1795. The colony was returned to the Republic under the treaty of Amiens (1802) but then re-annexed by Britain in 1806. Surinam and the west Guyana colonies were conquered in 1799, the latter being permanently absorbed, along with Ceylon, the Dutch enclaves in south India, and South Africa, into the British empire, Surinam being eventually returned to the new Kingdom of the Netherlands, in 1814. Curaçao, occupied by Britain in 1800, was also returned in 1814. The last act in the dismemberment of the Dutch empire was the British conquest of Java, in 1811.

Dutch shipping and the overseas trading system were devastated. The former dockyards and wharfs of the VOC at Middelburg, Rotterdam, Hoorn, and Enkhuizen were all shut down in 1803. The slump in Zeeland was so severe that by 1808 practically every shipyard, industrial mill, and

---

[9] Galdi, *Quadro politico*, ii. 69–70, 258, 273.

sizeable workshop in the province had been closed.[10] The population of Middelburg shrank from 20,000, in 1795, to only 13,000 by 1815. By 1797, the Enkhuizen herring fishery, in the seventeenth century the largest of all the herring fleets, had been reduced to one-fifth of its size in 1700 and, by 1810, had virtually ceased to exist. The long-term decline of the Republic's cities, in progress since 1688 and the onset of the Nine Years War, everywhere intensified. Leiden's population fell from about 31,000—roughly half the level of 1688—to only 28,500, Haarlem's from 21,000 to 17,500, Delft's from 9,500 to 7,500, and Amsterdam's—the only European metropolis to be shrinking—from about 200,000 to 180,000. Gin production expanded—the number of distilleries at Schiedam rose from 120 in 1775, to 220 by 1792 and 260 by 1798—but almost nothing else did. Even the manufacture of tobacco pipes at Gouda slumped disastrously, by some two-thirds, between 1790 and 1804.[11]

Yet it was ultimately the political, rather than the economic, realities of the situation which led to the aborting of the Republic. After Napoleon proclaimed himself Emperor of the French, in 1804, the regime in France no longer looked with favour on the persistence of republican forms and attitudes amongst the satellite states. As the dimensions, and cost, of the war against the European monarchies ranged against France grew, so the temptation to reduce the allies to pliable auxiliaries, under tight French control, increased. The end of the Batavian Republic, in all but name, came with the *coup d'état* of 1805, which sprang, essentially, from Napoleon's exasperation with what he regarded as the Republic's poor co-operation with France not only in the raising of men and money, for the war, but also in the enforcing of the continental economic blockade against Britain. (During these years, there was indeed a lively trade being carried in neutral bottoms, between the Republic and Britain.) The Emperor required closer collaboration, radical fiscal reform combined with a larger yield, and, as an inevitable prerequisite of both of these, a unified administration, and was determined to have his way. Over the winter of 1804–5, a new regime was installed at The Hague, headed by that veteran champion of the republican concept Rutger Jan Schimmelpenninck (see p. 1104 above). He now became the last Grand Pensionary of the Batavian Republic. The plebiscite held to approve the new unitarist constitution of 1805 elicited an astoundingly small turn-out—only 14,000 voters agreed; scarcely anyone bothered to oppose.

---

[10] Wintle, 'Economie van Zeeland', 116–17.
[11] Metelerkamp, *Tableau statistique*, 40–1, 70–3.

Yet, even now a thread of continuity with the past remained. Schimmelpenninck, who had by no means abandoned his earlier republican convictions, saw himself as in some way the champion of the traditions of the old Republic as well as of 1795. The reforms of 1805–6 marked a true watershed, however, sweeping away finally the structures of the past. This rapidly became evident in every sphere of national life. The Republic's tax system, under the skilful management of I. J. A. Gogel (1765–1821), another Patriot veteran and revolutionary, was thoroughly overhauled. The new general tax law ruled out provincial variations, and municipal taxes, except where provided for by national laws, abolished the excises on many foodstuffs, the basis of the old system, shifting the emphasis to progressive, direct taxation on the middling and richer strata of society, assessed on the basis of property and wealth.[12] Provincial and civic autonomy were liquidated, the 1805 law on local government depriving the municipalities of the power to introduce any economic or financial regulations on their own initiative. The power of the guilds was severely curtailed. At the same time, central government was strengthened and streamlined.

But the Schimmelpenninck regime of 1805–6 was not only a crucial watershed, it was living on borrowed time, a short but decisive transition phase which was, in many ways (apart from its republican rhetoric), a precursor of the monarchy of Louis Bonaparte imposed by the Emperor in March 1806. There had been rapid and fundamental change since 1804. But Napoleon wanted a Dutch regime which would respond fully to his requirements, strategic, naval, logistical, and economic, rather than one which put Dutch interests first, as had that of Schimmelpenninck and Gogel. And so the Republic was abolished and a monarchy put in its place. Yet the policies of the Schimmelpenninck regime had created a framework for a unitary state, suppressing most of the features of the old Republic; and these now became the policies of the monarchy of Louis Bonaparte. The further reform of local government, in 1807, finally reduced the 'departments' to the status of mere administrative organs, stripping local élites of all power and influence and eliminating what was left of civic and village autonomy. The legal code promulgated in 1809 had been in preparation since 1804; it swept away the departmental 'high courts', creating, for the first time in Dutch history, an integrated judicial system. The guilds were formally abolished in 1808. Indeed, in these years, practically every typical feature of the old Republic was finally erased, and consciously so. As a potent expression of his purpose, and the transformation he was resolved to carry through, Louis

---

[12] Schama, *Patriots and Liberators*, 501–14.

Bonaparte moved his royal court from The Hague, the political centre of the United Provinces, to Utrecht, in the autumn of 1807. Soon he moved it again, to Amsterdam. No less resonant with symbolic significance, the Amsterdam city council, obliged to make way for him, vacated its great and famous building, the epitome in architecture of the republican spirit of the pre-1795 regime. In 1808, the Amsterdam Town Hall, for so long the chief bastion of the Holland regents, became the royal palace. The Dutch Republic was no more.

BIBLIOGRAPHY

Published Primary Sources

AALSTIUS, JOHANNES, *Inleiding tot de Zeden-leer* (Dordrecht, 1705).

ACCARIAS DE SERIONNE, JACQUES, *La Richesse de la Hollande* (2 vols.; London, 1778).

AITZEMA, LIEUWE VAN, *Herstelde Leeuw, of Discours over 't gepasseerde in de Vereenigde Nederlanden in 't jaer 1650, ende 1651* (The Hague, 1652).

—— *Historie of verhael van saken van staet en oorlogh in, ende ontrent de Vereenigde Nederlanden* (14 vols.; The Hague, 1667–71).

—— *Verhael van de Nederlantsche Vreedehandeling* (2 vols.; The Hague, 1650).

ALTHUSIUS, JOHANNES, *The Politics of Johannes Althusius*, trans. F. S. Carney (London, 1965).

The Apologie of Prince William of Orange against the Proclamation of the King of Spaine, the English trans. of 1581, ed. H. Wansink (Leiden, 1969).

Archief voor de geschiedenis van het aartsbisdom Utrecht (75 vols.; Utrecht, 1875–1957).

Archives ou correspondance inédite de la Maison d'Orange-Nassau, ed. G. Groen van Prinsterer *et al.* (25 vols. in 5 series; Leiden and Utrecht, 1835–1915).

ARNOLDI, HENRICUS, *Vande Conscientie-dwangh* (Delft, 1629).

AUBÉRY DU MAURIER, B., 'Rapport van den ambassadeur Aubéry du Maurier (1624)', *BMHG* 2 (1879), 392–405.

AUBÉRY DU MAURIER, L., *Mémoires pour servir à l'histoire de Hollande et des autres Provinces Unies* (Paris, 1680).

BASNAGE, JACQUES, *Annales des Provinces-Unies depuis les négotiations pour la Paix de Munster* (The Hague, 1719).

—— *Histoire des Juifs depuis Jésus-Christ jusqu'à présent* (2nd edn.; 12 vols.; The Hague, 1716).

BAUDARTIUS, WILHELMUS, *Memoryen* (1620; 2nd edn. 14 books in 2 vols. Arnhem, 1624).

BAYLE, PIERRE, *Dictionnaire Historique et Critique* (4 vols; Rotterdam, 1720).

—— *Lettres* (3 vols.; Amsterdam, 1729).

—— *Het leven van B. de Spinoza, met eenige Aanteekeningen over zyn Bedryf, Schriften en Gevoelens*, trans. and annotated François Halma (Utrecht, 1698).

—— *Nouvelles de la République des Lettres* (12 vols.; Amsterdam, 1684–9).

BEAUFORT, LIEVEN DE, *Het leven van Willem den I, Prins van Oranje* (2nd edn.; 3 vols.; Leiden, 1732).

—— *Verhandeling van de vryheit in den Burgerstaet* (Leiden, 1737).

BEKKER, BALTHASAR, *De Betoverde Weereld* (Leeuwarden, 1691).

BEKKER, BALTHASAR, *De Friesche Godgeleerdheid* (Amsterdam, 1693).

—— *Kort Begryp der algemeine kerkelycke Historien* (Amsterdam, 1686).

—— *Kort Beright Aangaende alle de schriften welke over sijn Boek de Betoverde Weereld enen tijd lang heen en weder verwisseld zijn* (Franeker, 1692).

—— *Kort en Waarachtig Verhael van 't gebeurde . . . in den kerkenraad en classis van Amsterdam, en de synode van Noord-Holland* (Amsterdam, 1692).

—— *Nodige Bedenkingen op de Nieuwe Beweegingen onlangs verwekt . . . tegen den Auteur van 't Boek de Betoverde Weereld* (Amsterdam, 1692).

——*De Philosophia Cartesiana* (Wesel, 1668).

BENTHEM, HEINRICH LUDOLF, *Holländischer Kirch- und Schulen-Staat* (2 vols.; Frankfurt/Leipzig, 1698).

BENTINCK VAN RHOON, WILLEM, *Briefwisseling en aantekeningen*, ed. C. Gerretson and Pieter Geyl (Utrecht, 1934).

BENTIVOGLIO, GUIDO, *Relatione delle Province Vnite di Fiandra* (2 vols.; Liège, 1635).

BIENTJES, JULIA, *Holland und die Holländer im Urteil deutscher Reisender, 1400–1800* (Groningen, 1967).

Billyk verzoek der Amsterdamsche Burgery aan zyne Doorlugtige Hoogheyd (Amsterdam, 1748).

BLEYSWIJK, DIEDERIK VAN, *Memoiren* (Utrecht, 1887).

BOITET, R., *Beschryving van Delft* (Delft, 1729).

BOOMKAMP, GYSBERT, *Alkmaar en deszelfs geschiedenissen* (Rotterdam, 1747).

BOR, PIETER, *Oorspronck, begin ende vervolgh der Nederlantsche Oorlogen* (1595) (4 vols.; Leiden/Amsterdam, 1621).

BOYS, J. DU, *Korte Aenmerckingen op het Onbewesen bewys dat het gevoelen vander Sonne stillest andt ende des Aertryckx beweginghe niet strijdigh is met Godts-Woort* (The Hague, 1656).

—— *De Schadelickheyt van de Cartesiaensche Philosophie* (Utrecht, 1656).

BRANDT, GERARD, *Historie van de rechtspleging gehouden in den jaren 1618 ende 1619 ontrent de drie gevangenen heeren, Mr Johan van Oldenbarnevelt, Mr Rombout Hoogerbeets, Mr Hugo de Groot* (Rotterdam, 1723).

—— *Historie der Reformatie* (4 vols.; Amsterdam, 1677–1704).

—— *Historie der vermaerde zee- en koop-stadt Enkhuizen* (Enkhuizen, 1666).

—— *Het leven van Joost van den Vondel*, ed. P. Leendertz (The Hague, 1932).

Brief Narration of the Present Estate of the Bilbao Trade (n.p. n.d. [London, 1650]).

Briefwisseling tusschen de Gebroeders Van der Goes (1659–1673). ed. C. J. Gonnet (2 vols.; Amsterdam, 1899–1909).

Briefwisseling van Godard Adriaan van Reede van Amerongen en Everard van Weede van Dijkveld (1671–2), ed. M. van der Bijl and H. Quarles van Ufford, Nederlandse Historische Bronnen, 9 (The Hague, 1991).

Brieven geschreven ende gewisselt tusschen den Heer Johan de Witt, Raedt-pensionaris . . . ende de Gevolmaghtigden van den Staedt der Vereenighde Nederlanden (7 vols.; The Hague, 1723–7).

BROESMA, R., and BUSKEN HUET, G. (eds.), *Brieven over het Leycestersche tijdvak uit de papieren van Jean Hotman, BMHG* 34 (1913), 1–271.

BRUGMANS, H., *Correspondentie van Robert Dudley, graaf van Leycester en andere documenten betreffende zijn gouvernement-generaal in de Nederlande, 1585–1588*, WHG 3rd ser. 58 (3 vols.; Utrecht, 1931).

—— 'De Notulen en monumenten van het College van Commercie te Amsterdam, 1663–1665', *BMHG* 18 (1897), 181–330.

BRUN, JEAN, *Le Conseil d'extorsion* (Amsterdam, 1675).

—— *La Véritable Religion des Hollandois* (2 vols.; Amsterdam, 1675).

BURGER VAN SCOORL, DIRK, *Chronyk van Medenblik* (Hoorn, 1728).

BUZANVAL, PAUL CHOART, SEIGNEUR DE, *Lettres et négotiations*, ed. G. W. G. Vreede (Leiden, 1846).

CAPELLEN, ALEXANDER VAN DER, *Gedenkschriften* (2 vols.; Utrecht, 1777–8).

[CAPELLEN, JOAN DERK VAN DER], *Aan het Volk van Nederland* (Ostend, 1781).

Capita Selecta Veneto-Belgica (1629–31), ed. J. J. Poelhekke (The Hague, 1964).

CARLETON, SIR DUDLEY, *Letters from and to Sir Dudley Carleton, Knt. During his Embassy in Holland from January 1616 to Dec. 1620* (2nd edn.; London, 1775).

CARR, WILLIAM, *The Travellours Guide and Historian's Faithful Companion* (London, 1691).

CEYSSENS, LUCIEN, *La Fin de la première période du Jansénisme. Sources (1654–1660)* (2 vols.; Brussels/Rome, 1963).

—— *La Première Bulle contre Jansenius* (Brussels/Rome, 1961).

Le Chef des moqueurs démasqué (The Hague, 1707).

COCCEIUS, JOHANNES, *Indagatio naturae Sabbati et quietis Novi Testamenti* (Leiden, 1658).

—— *De Leer van het Verbond en het Testament van God* (1648), trans. W. J. van Asselt and H. G. Renger (Kampen, 1990).

Colección de documentos inéditos para la historia de España (CODOIN) (113 vols.; Madrid, 1842–95).

COMMELIN, CASPAR, *Beschryvinge van Amsterdam* (2nd edn.; 2 vols.; Amsterdam, 1726).

COORNHERT, DIRK VOLKERTSZ., *Spiegelken vande ongerechticheydt ofte menschelicheyt des vergodeden H. N. Vader vanden Huyse der Liefden* (n.p. 1581).

—— *Zedekunst dat is wellevenskunst* (1587; Leiden, 1942).

Correspondência diplomática de Francisco de Sousa Coutinho durante a sua embaixada em Holanda (3 vols.; Coimbra, 1920–55).

Correspondencia de la Infanta Archiduquesa Doña Isabel Clara Eugenia de Austria con el duque de Lerma y otros personajes, ed. A. Rodríguez Villa (Madrid, 1906).

De Correspondentie tussen Willem van Oranje en Jan van Nassau, 1578–1584, ed. J. H. Kluiver, *NHB* iv (1984).

Cort ende bondich verhael van de Arminiaensche Factie (n.p. [1628, Kn. 3960]) said to be by the Haarlem pensionary Gilles de Glarges.

COSTA, URIEL DA, *Examination of Pharisaic Traditions*, trans. H. P. Salomon and I. S. D. Sasson (Leiden, 1993).

COURT, PIETER DE LA, *Aanwysing der heilsame politike Gronden en Maximen van de Republike van Holland en West-Vriesland* (Leiden, 1669).

—— 'Brieven uit de correspondentie van Pieter de la Court en zijn verwanten (1661–1666)', ed. J. H. Kernkamp, *BMHG* 70 (1956), 82–165.

—— [V. D. H.], *Het Interest van Holland, ofte Grond van Hollands welvaren* (Amsterdam, 1662).

—— and COURT, JOHAN DE LA, *Politike Discoursen* (2 vols.; Amsterdam, 1662).

[C. P. T. R. DE], *Historie van het Leven en Sterven vande Heer Johan Olden-Barnevelt* (n.p. 1648).

CRISPEEL, J., *Politiecque Reflectien van Staat* (Utrecht, 1739).

'Een Dagboek uit het "Rampjaar" 1672', ed. J. F. Gebhard, *BMHG* 8 (1885), 45–116.

DAM, PIETER VAN, *Beschryvinge van de Oostindische Compagnie*, ed. F. W. Stapel (4 vols. in 7 parts; The Hague, 1927–54).

—— 'concept en consideratien' (1662), *Bijdragen tot de taal- land- en volkenkunde van Nederlandsch-Indië*, 74 (1918), 270–98.

DEFOE, DANIEL, *An Enquiry into the Danger and Consequences of a War with the Dutch* (London, 1712).

DEKKER, R. M., *Oproeren in Holland gezien door tijdgenoten* (Assen, 1979).

DESCARTES, RENÉ, *Correspondance*, ed. Ch. Adam and G. Milhaud (8 vols.; Paris, 1936–63).

—— *Œuvres*, ed. Ch. Adam and P. Tannery (12 vols.; Paris, 1897–1910).

—— *Correspondance of Descartes and Constantyn Huygens, 1635–1647*, ed. L. Roth (Oxford, 1926).

DEVENTER, M. L. VAN, *Gedenkstukken van Johan van Oldenbarnevelt en zijn tijd* (3 vols.; The Hague, 1862–5).

DIERICKX, M., *Documents inédits sur l'érection des nouveaux diocèses aux Pays-Bas (1521–1570)* (3 vols.; Brussels, 1960).

DILLEN, J. G. VAN, *Bronnen tot de geschiedenis van het bedrijfsleven en het gildewezen van Amsterdam* (3 vols.; The Hague, 1929–74).

—— *Amsterdam in 1585: het kohier der Capitale Impositie van 1585* (Amsterdam, 1941).

DUIJKERIUS, JOHANNES, *Het leven van Philopater. Vervolg van 't leven van Philopater (1691/1697)*, ed. G. Maréchal (Amsterdam, 1991).

DUMBAR, GERHARD, *Hedendaagsche Historie . . . en wel in 't Byzonder van Overyssel* (4 vols.; Amsterdam, 1781–1803).

—— *Verhandeling over het regt van overstemming ter staatsvergadering van de Provincie van Overyssel* (Deventer, 1783).

DUNGANUS, CORNELIUS, *Den Vreedsamen Christen* (Utrecht, 1628).

DUYCK, ANTHONIE, *Journaal van Anthonis Duyck, advokaat-fiskaal van den Raad van State (1591–1602)*, ed. L. Mulder (6 vols. in 3 parts; The Hague/Arnhem, 1862–6).

EMMIUS, UBBO, *De Agro Frisiae* (Groningen, 1646).

ENDEN, FRANCISCUS VAN DEN, *Vrye Politijke Stellingen en Consideratien van staat* (1665; Amsterdam, 1992).

[EPISCOPIUS, SIMON?], *Voorstant vande vryheyt der conscientie teghen den Conscientie-Dwangh van Henricus Arnoldi* (n.p. 1630).

[——] ,*Vrye Godes-dienst* (n.p. [1627, Kn. 3753]).

EPPENS, ABEL, *Kroniek van Groningen*, ed. J. A. Feith and H. Brugmans, WHG 3rd ser. 27 (Utrecht, 1911).

ERASMUS OF ROTTERDAM, *The Collected Works of Erasmus*, ed. R. J. Schoeck *et al.*, vols. i–x: *The Correspondence of Erasmus (1484–1534)*, trans. R. A. B. Mynors and D. F. S. Thomson (Toronto, 1974–92).

ESTRADES, GODEFROY D', *Lettres, mémoires et négociations de M. le Comte d'Estrades*, ed. Prosper Marchand (9 vols.; 'London' [The Hague], 1743).

FELL, R., *A Tour through the Batavian Republic during the Latter Part of the Year 1800* (London, 1801).

FIJNE, PASCHIER DE, *Eenige Tractaatjes* (2 parts; Amsterdam, 1735–6).

FOKKENS, MELCHIOR, *Beschryvingh der wijdt-vermaarde koop-stadt Amsterdam* (Amsterdam, 1664).

FRANCO MENDES, DAVID, *Memórias do estabelicimento e progresso dos judeus portuguezes e espanhões nesta famosa citade de Amsterdam*, *Studia Rosenthaliana*, 9 (1975).

FRUYTIER, JACOBUS, *Sions Worstelingen* (2nd edn.; Rotterdam, 1715).

GACHARD, L. P., *Actes des États-Généraux de 1632* (2 vols.; Brussels, 1853–66).

GALDI, MATTEO, *Quadro politico delle rivoluzioni delle Provincie-Unite e della Repubblica Batava* (2 vols.; Milan, 1809).

De gebannen Duyvel Weder In-geroepen (Hoorn, 1692) [Kn. 13865].

'Gedenkschrift van Joris de Bye', in *BMHG* 11 (1888), 400–59.

Genees-Middelen voor Holland (Antwerp, [1672, Kn. 10376]).

GELAZIUS MAJOR [pseudonym], *Overtuychde ontrouw* (n.p. 1676).

GOUTHOEVEN, W. VAN, *D'Oude Chronijcke ende Historien van Holland (met West-Vriesland) van Zeeland ende van Utrecht* (Dordrecht, 1620).

Grondigh Bericht, nopende den Intrest van desen Staet, vermidts de doodt van Sijn Hoogheyt (Rotterdam, 1651) [Kn. 7009]).

GROOT, PIETER DE, *Lettres de Pierre de Groot à Abraham de Wicquefort (1668–1674)*, ed. F. J. L. Krämer, WHG 3rd ser. 5 (The Hague, 1894).

—— *Vriende-Praetjen over het Eeuwig Edict* (n.p. [1672, (Kn. 10333]).

Groot Placaet-Boeck vervattende de placaten . . . van de . . . Staten Generael der Vereenigde Nederlanden ende van de . . . Staten van Hollandt en West-Vrieslandt (9 vols.; The Hague, 1658–1796).

GROTIUS, HUGO, *Briefwisseling*, ed. P. C. Molhuysen and B. L. Meulenbroek, the first 10 vols. covering the years 1597–1639 (The Hague, 1928–76).

—— *De Ivre Belli ac Pacis Libri Tres* (Paris, 1625).

—— *Meletius* (1611), ed. G. H. M. Posthumus Meyjes (Leiden, 1988).

—— *Oratie van . . . Hugo de Groot . . . ghedaen inde vergaderinghe der 36 raden der Stadt Amsterdam* (Enkhuizen, 1622).

—— *Pietas Ordinum Hollandiae ac Westfrisiae Vindicata* (Latin and Dutch versions, n.p. 1613).

—— *Remonstrantie nopende de ordre dije in de landen van Hollandt ende Westvrieslandt dijent gestelt op de joden*, ed. J. Meijer (Amsterdam, 1949).

—— *Verantwoordingh van de wettelijcke regieringh van Hollandt* ('Paris' [but Amsterdam], 1622).

HACKETT, SIR JOHN, *The Letters (1526–34)*, ed. E. Frances Rogers (Morgantown, W. Va., 1971).

HALLER, ALBRECHT VON, *Het Dagboek van zijn verblijf in Holland (1725–1727)*, ed. G. A. Lindeboom (Delft, 1958).

HALMA, FRANÇOIS, *Aanmerkingen op 't Vervolg van Philopater* (Utrecht, 1698).

HAMELSVELD, IJSBRAND VAN, *De Zedelijke toestand der Nederlandsche natie* (Amsterdam, 1791).

HARDENBROCK, GIJSBERT JAN VAN, *Gedenkschriften (1747–1787)*, ed. F. J. L. Krämer (Amsterdam, 1901).

HATTUM, BURCHARD JOAN VAN, *Geschiedenissen der stad Zwolle* (1767; new edn. 4 vols.; Zwolle, 1975).

HEERINGA, K. *Bronnen tot de geschiedenis van den Levantschen handel* (2 vols.; The Hague, 1930).

HELVÉTIUS, ADRIANUS ENGELHARD, 'Mémoire sur l'état présent du gouvernement des Provinces Unies' (1706), ed. M. van der Bijl, *BMHG* 80 (1966), 152–94.

Herstelden Barnevelt ofte 't Samenspraeck tusschen een Hollander, Seeu ende Vries (Leiden, [1663, Kn. 8799]).

HEURN, JOHAN HENDRIK VAN, *Historie der stad en Meyerye van 's Hertogenbosch*, (4 vols.; Utrecht, 1776–8).

HEUSSEN, H. F. VAN, *Historie ofte Beschryving van 't Utrechtsche bisdom* (3 vols.; Leiden, 1719).

HOEVEN, EMANUEL VAN DER, *Hollands aeloude vryheid, buyten het stadhouderschap* (3 vols.; Amsterdam, 1706).

—— *Leeven en Dood der doorlugtige Heeren Gebroeders Cornelis de Witt . . . en Johan de Witt, Raad Pensionaris van Holland* (Amsterdam, 1705).

Hollandse Vrijheid verdedigt tegen de Usurpatie der stadhouders (n.p. [1663, Kn. 8803]).

HOOFT, CORNELIS PIETERSZ, *Memorien en Adviezen*, ed. H. A. Enno van Gelder (Utrecht, 1925).

HOOGEWERFF, G. J. (ed.) *De twee reizen van Cosimo de' Medici Prins van Toscane door de Nederlanden (1667–69)* (Amsterdam, 1919).

HOOGHE, ROMEYN DE, *Spiegel van staat des Vereenigde Nederlanden* (2 vols.; Amsterdam, 1706–7).

HOOGSTRAETEN, SAMUEL VAN, *Inleyding tot de hooge schoole der schilderkonst* (Rotterdam, 1678).

HOUBRAKEN, ARNOLD, *De Groote Schouburgh der Nederlantsche konstschilders en schilderessen* (2nd edn.; 3 vols.; The Hague, 1753).

HUBER, ULRICUS, *Hedendaegse rechts-geleertheyt* (1686; Amsterdam, 1742).

—— *Spiegel van Doleancie en Reformatie na den tegenwoordigen toestant van het Vaderlandt* (1672), in Kalma and De Vries, *Friesland in het Rampjaar*, 120–36.

HUYGENS, CONSTANTIJN, *Briefwisseling (1608–1687)*, ed. J. A. Worp (6 vols.; The Hague, 1911–17).

—— *Gebruyck of ongebruyck van 't orgel in de kercken der Vereenighde Nederlanden* (1641), ed. F. L. Zwaan (Amsterdam, 1974).

It aade Friesche Terp, of Kronyk der geschiedenissen van de vrye Friesen (1677; Leeuwarden, 1834).

JAPIKSE, N., and RIJPERMAN, H. H. P. (eds.), *Resolutiën der Staten Generaal van 1576 tot 1609* (9 vols.; The Hague, 1917–71).

JEANNIN, PIERRE, *Les Négociations de Monsieur le Président Jeannin* (2 vols; Amsterdam, 1695).

[J. M.], *Histoire de la République des Provinces-Unies des Pais-Bas, depuis son établissement jusqu'à la mort de Guillaume III* (The Hague, 1704).

[JONCOURT, PIERRE DE], *Entretiens sur les différentes méthodes d'expliquer l'Écriture et de prêcher de ceux qu'on appelle Cocceiens et Voetiens dans les Provinces Unies* (Amsterdam, 1707).

JORIS, DAVID, *T Wonder-Boeck* (1542; 2nd edn.; 2 vols.; n.p. 1551).

Journaal van Mr Justinus van Beyer, heer van Hulzen, over de jaren 1743–1767, ed. H. D. J. van Schevichaven (Arnhem, 1906).

Journal Littéraire, vol. 1 (The Hague, 1715).

Journalen van den Stadhouder Willem II uit de jaren 1641–50, ed. F. J. L. Krämer, *BMHG* 27 (1906), 413–535.

JURIEU, PIERRE, *Le Philosophe de Rotterdam accusé, atteint et convaincu* (Amsterdam, 1706).

KATE, LAMBERT TEN, *Aenleiding tot de kennisse van het verhevene deel der Nederduitsche sprake* (Amsterdam, 1723).

—— *Gemeenschap tussen de Gottische Spraeke en de Nederduytsche vertoont* (Amsterdam, 1710).

KETTNER, FRIEDRICH ERNST, *De duobus Impostoribus Benedicto Spinosa et Balthasare Bekkero* (Leipzig, 1694).

Een Klare ende Korte Aenmerckinge op den tegenwoordigen staet, religie en politie onses lieven Vader-landts (n.p. [1637, Kn. 4545]).

KLUIT, ADRIAAN, *Historie der Hollandsche staatsregering tot aan het jaar 1795* (5 vols.; Amsterdam, 1802–5).

KLUIT, ADRIAAN, De Rechten van den Mensch in Vrankrijk geen gewaarde rechten in Nederland (Amsterdam, 1793).

KNUTTEL, W. P. C., Acta der Particuliere Synoden van Zuid-Holland, 1621–1700 (6 vols.; The Hague, 1908–16).

KOELMAN, JACOBUS, Wederlegging van B. Bekkers Betoverde Wereldt (Amsterdam, 1692).

Kort en Bondigh Verhael van 't geene in den Oorlogh tusschen den Koningh van Engelant . . . ende de H. M. Heeren Staten der Vrye Vereenigde Nederlanden . . . is voorgevallen (Amsterdam, 1667).

KOSSMANN, E. H., and MELLINK, A. F., Texts Concerning the Revolt of the Netherlands (Cambridge, 1974).

LAIRESSE, GERARD DE, Het Groot Schilderboek (1707; 2nd edn.; 2 vols.; Haarlem, 1740).

Lammerenkrijgh, anders Mennonisten kercken-twist (n.p. [1663, Kn. 8818]).

LE CLERC, JEAN, A Funeral Oration upon the Death of Mr Philip Limborch (London, 1713).

LE NOBLE, E. DE, La Pierre de touche politique (28 vols.; Paris, 1688–91).

LEE, M. (ed.), Dudley Carleton to John Chamberlain, 1603–1624: Jacobean Letters (New Brunswick, NJ, 1972).

LEENAERTSZ, CAREL, Copie vande Remonstrantie (Haarlem [1629, Kn. 3936]).

LEENHOF, FREDERICUS VAN, Zedig en Christelijk verandwoordschrift aan het bewaarde classis van Seven-Wolden (Amsterdam, 1684).

LEEUWEN, S. VAN, Batavia Illustrata (The Hague, 1665).

LETI, GREGORIO, Il ceremoniale historico e politico (6 vols.; Amsterdam, 1685).

—— Raguagli historici e politici (2 vols.; Amsterdam, 1700).

—— Teatro Belgico (2 vols.; Amsterdam, 1690).

LEYDECKER, JACOBUS, Dr Bekkers Philosophise Duyvel (Dordrecht, 1692).

Leydsche Proceduuren (n. p. [1664, Kn. 8978]).

LIMBORCH, PHILIPPUS VAN, Leven van Simon Episcopius, preface to Episcopius's Predicatien (Amsterdam, 1693).

—— 'Voor-reden' to John Hales and Walter Balcanquel, Korte Historie van het Synode van Dordrecht (The Hague, 1671).

LIPSIUS, JUSTUS, De Constantia Libri Duo (1584; Brussels, 1873).

LISTER, T. H., Life and Administration of Edward, First Earl of Clarendon, iii (documentary appendix) (London, 1838).

LOIS, S., Cronycke ofte korte Beschryvinge der stad Rotterdam (The Hague, 1746).

LOON, G. VAN, Beschryving der Nederlandsche Historipenningen (4 vols.; The Hague, 1726–31).

LUBBERTUS, SIBRANDUS, Brief D. Sibrandi Lvbberti . . . aenden Aertsbisschop van Cantelberch (Delft, 1613).

LUZAC, ELIE, Hollands Rijkdom (4 vols.; Leiden, 1780–3).

—— Het oordeel over de Heere Raadpensionaris Johan de Witt (Leiden, 1757).

—— De Zugt van den Heere Raadpensionaris Johan de Witt (Leiden, 1757).

MANDER, CAREL VAN, *Het Schilder-Boeck* (Haarlem, 1604).

MEERBEECK, ADRIAEN VAN, *Chroniecke vande Gantsche Werelt, ende sonder-linghe vande seventhien Nederlanden* (Antwerp, 1620).

MEIJER, LODEWIJK, *Philosophia S. Scripturae Interpres* (n.p. 1674).

Mémoires de Frédéric Henri Prince d'Orange (Amsterdam, 1733).

METELERKAMP, M. R., *Tableau statistique de la Hollande en 1804* (Paris, 1807).

METEREN, EMANUEL VAN, *Historie van de Oorlogen en Geschiedenissen der Nederlanden* (10 vols.; Gorcum, 1748–63).

MIERIS, FRANS VAN, *Beschryving der stad Leyden* (2 vols.; Leiden, 1742).

MOLHUYSEN, P. C., *Bronnen tot de geschiedenis der Leidsche universiteit*, vol. i (1574–1610) and vol. ii (1610–47) (The Hague, 1913–16).

MONTANUS, ARNOLDUS, *'t Vermeerderde Leven en Bedryf van Frederik Hendrik, Prince van Oranjen* (Amsterdam, 1653).

MORYSON, FYNES, *An Itinerary containing His Ten Yeares Travell through . . . Germany, Bohmerland, Switzerland, Netherland* (etc.) (London, 1617).

NAPJUS, EELCO, *Sneek. Historisch Chronyk* (1772; Leeuwarden, 1969).

Négociations de Monsieur le Comte d'Avaux en Hollande depuis 1679 jusqu'en 1688 (6 vols.; Paris, 1752–3).

NIEUWENTYT, BERNARD, *Gronden van Zekerheid of de regte betoogwyse der wiskundigen* (Amsterdam, 1720).

—— *Het Regt Gebruik der Werelt Beschouwingen ter overtuiginge van ongodisten en ongelovigen* (2nd edn.; Amsterdam, 1717).

NIJENHUIS, WILLEM, *Matthew Slade, 1569–1628: Letters to the English Ambassador* (Leiden, 1986).

NOODT, GERARD, *Du pouvoir des souverains et de la liberté de conscience en deux discours*, trans. Jean Barbeyrac (Amsterdam, 1714).

Nootwendighe ende vrypostighe Vermaninghe (n.p. [1620?, Kn. 3218]).

Notulen van de Staten van Zeeland (1588–1760) (c.170 vols.; Middelburg, n.d.).

Den Oprechten Patriot (n.p. [1672, Kn. 10497]).

ORLERS, JAN, *Beschryvinge der stadt Leyden* (Leiden, 1641).

Ouderwetse Nederlandsche Patriot, ed. R. M. C. van Goens (5 vols.; The Hague, 1781–3).

PARIVAL, JEAN DE, *Les Délices de la Hollande* (Leiden, 1662).

PAULUS, PIETER, *Discours du Représentant Pierre Paulus, Président de l'Assemblée Nationale* (The Hague, 1796).

—— *Verklaring der Unie van Utrecht* (3 vols.; Utrecht, 1775–6).

PENSO DE LA VEGA, JOSEPH, *Confusión de confusiones* (1688), ed. M. F. J. Smith (The Hague, 1939).

Perpetuel Edict en Eeuwigh-durende Wet tot voorstant vande Vryheyt (The Hague, 1667) [Kn. 9578].

PINTO, ISAAC DE, *Précis des arguments contre les matérialistes* (The Hague, 1774).

—— *Traité de la circulation et du crédit* (Amsterdam, 1771).

POLMAN, P., *Romeinse bescheiden voor de geschiedenis der rooms-katholieke kerk in Nederland, 1727–1853*, i. 1727–54 (The Hague, 1959).

POMPONNE, SIMON-NICHOLAS ARNAULD, MARQUIS DE, *Relation de mon ambassade en Hollande (1669–71)*, ed. H. H. Rowen (Utrecht, 1955).

PONTANUS, JOHANNES, *Historische Beschrijvinghe der seer wijt beroemde coopsstadt Amsterdam* (Amsterdam, 1614).

De Post van den Neder-Rhijn. ed. Pieter 't Hoen (12 vols.; Utrecht, 1781–7).

POSTHUMUS, N. W., *Bronnen tot de geschiedenis van de Leidsche textielnijverheid* (6 vols.; The Hague, 1910–22).

POTTLE, F. A., *Boswell in Holland, 1763–1764* (London, 1952).

PUTEANUS, ERYCIUS, *Des oorlogs ende Vredes Waeg-schale* (The Hague, 1633).

Het Recht der Souverainiteit van Hollandt (n.p. 1650 [Kn. 6741]).

Recueil des ordonnances des Pays-Bas. Règne d'Albert et Isabelle, ed. V. Brandts (2 vols.; Brussels, 1903–13).

REIGERSBERG, NICOLAES VAN, *Brieven van Nicolaes van Reigersberch aan Hugo de Groot*, ed. H. C. Rogge, WHG 3rd ser. 15 (Amsterdam, 1901).

'Relazione di Girolamo Trevisano. Anno 1620', in WHG 2nd ser. 37 (Utrecht, 1883), 387–472.

Relazioni veneziane. Venetiaanse berichten over de Vereenigde Nederlanden (1600–1795), ed. P. J. Blok (The Hague, 1909).

Request van de Borgerye (n.p. n.d. [Rotterdam, 1672, Kn. 10572]).

Resolutie bij de Heeren Raeden ende vroetschappen der stadt Haerlem ghenomen . . . nopende 't stuck van den Treves (Haarlem [1630, Kn. 4009]).

Resolutien van de Heeren Staten van Holland en West-Vriesland (276 vols.; The Hague, c.1750–98).

REYD, EVERHART VAN, *Historie der Nederlantsche Oorloghen, begin ende voortgangh tot den Jaere 1601* (Leeuwarden, 1650).

ROUSSET DE MISSY, JEAN, *Relation historique de la grande révolution arrivée dans la république des Provinces-Unies en 1747* (Amsterdam, 1747).

RUBENS, PIETER PAUL, *Letters*, trans. and ed. R. Saunders Magurn (Cambridge, Mass., 1955).

SAINTE-MARTHE, DENIS DE, *Entretiens touchant l'entreprise du Prince d'Orange sur l'Angleterre* (Paris, 1689).

SANDE, JOHAN VAN DEN, *Nederlandtsche Geschiedenissen* (n.p. 1650).

SARTRE, P., *Voyage en Hollande fait en 1719*, ed. V. Advielle (Paris, 1896).

SCALIGER, JOSEPH JUSTUS, *Autobiography*, ed. G. W. Robinson (Cambridge, 1927).

SCHOTANUS, CHRISTIANUS, *De geschiedenissen kerckelyck ende wereldtlyck van Friesland* (Franeker, 1658).

SCHREVELIUS, THEODORUS, *Harlemias, ofte de eerste Stichtinge der Stad Haarlem* (2nd edn.; Haarlem, 1754).

SCHRÖER, ALOIS, *Die Korrespondenz des Münsterer Fürstbischofs Christoph Bernhard von Galen mit dem heiligen Stuhl* (Münster, 1972).

SCHWAGER, JOHANN MORITZ, *Beytrag zur Geschichte der Intoleranz* (Leipzig, 1780).

Secreete Resolutien van de Ed. Groot Mog. Heeren Staaten van Hollandt en West-Vrieslandt (16 vols.; The Hague, 1791).

'S GRAVESANDE, WILLEM, *Œuvres philosophiques et mathématiques* (2 vols.; Amsterdam, 1774).

SIMONS, MENNO, *The Complete Writings of Menno Simons*, ed. J. Ch. Wenger (Scotdale, Pa., 1956).

SJOERDS, FOEKE, *Algemeene Beschryvinge van Oud en Nieuw Friesland* (2 parts in 4 vols.; Leeuwarden, 1765–8).

SLINGELANDT, SIMON VAN, *Staatkundige geschriften* (4 vols.; Amsterdam, 1784–5).

SMIT, J. G., 'Prins Maurits en de goede zaak. Brieven van Maurits uit de jaren 1617–1619', *NHB* i (1979), 43–173.

SPINOZA, BARUCH (BENEDICTUS) DE, *The Collected Works of Spinoza*, ed. and trans. E. Curley, i (Princeton, NJ, 1985).

—— *The Correspondence of Spinoza*, trans. A. Wolf (London, 1966).

—— *Tractatus Theologico-Politicus* (Gebhardt ed., 1925), trans. S. Shirley (Leiden, 1989).

—— *The Political Works*, ed. and trans. A. G. Wernham (Oxford, 1958).

STANYON, A., *An Account of Switzerland Written in the Year 1714* (London, 1714).

[STERMOND, JACOB], *Lauweren-krans gevlochten voor Syn Hoocheyt, Wilhelm, de Prince van Oranjen*, (n.p. [1650; Kn. 6851]).

STEVIN, SIMON, *Het Burgherlick Leven* (1590; Amsterdam, 1939).

STOUPPE, J. B., *La Religion des Hollandois* (Cologne, 1673).

TEELLINCK, MAXIMILIAN, *Vrijmoedige Aenspraeck aen sijn Hoogheyt de Heer Prince van Orangien* (Middelburg [1650, Kn. 6857]).

Tegenwoordige Staat der Vereenigde Nederlanden; behelzende eene Beschryving van Zeeland (2 vols.; Amsterdam, 1751–3).

TEMPLE, SIR WILLIAM, *Observations upon the United Provinces of the Netherlands* (Cambridge, 1932).

TEPELIUS, JOHANNES, *Historia Philosophiae Cartesianae* (Nuremberg, 1674).

THIEL-STROMAN, I. VAN, 'The Frans Hals Documents', in S. Slive (ed.), *Frans Hals* (London, 1989), 371–414.

THOMAS À KEMPIS, *Imitation of Christ*, trans. B. I. Knott (London, 1963).

THURLOE, JOHN, *A Collection of State Papers* (7 vols.; London, 1742).

TRIGLAND, JACOBUS, *Kerckelycke Geschiedenissen* (Leiden, 1650).

A Trip to Holland, being a Description of the Country, People and Manners: As also some select Observations on Amsterdam (n.p. [London], 1699).

USSELINCX, WILLEM, *Grondich Discours over desen aen-staenden Vrede-handel* (n.p. [1608, Kn, 1439]).

—— *Waerschouwinghe over den Treves met den Coninck van Spaengien* (Flushing, [1630, Kn. 4016]).

[UYTENHAGE DE MIST, J.], *Apologie ofte Verantwoordinge van den Ondienst der stadhouderlyke regeeringe* (Amsterdam, 1663).

—— *De Stadhouderlijcke regeeringe in Hollandt en West-Vrieslant* (Amsterdam, 1662).

UYTTENBOGAERT, JOHANNES, *Brieven en onuitgegeven stukken van Johannes Wtenbogaert*, ed. H. C. Rogge (7 vols.; Utrecht, 1868–75).

—— *Johannis Uytenbogaerts Leven* (2nd edn.; n.p. 1646).

—— *Ondersoek der Amsterdamsche Requesten* (n.p. 1628).

VALCKENIER, PETRUS, *'t Verwerd Europa* (1667; 2 vols.; Amsterdam, 1742).

[VELDE, ABRAHAM VAN DE] *Biddaghs-Meditatie en Na-trachtinge* (Utrecht, 1659).

—— *Oogen-salve, voor de blinde Hollanders* (Rotterdam, 1650).

VELIUS, THEODORUS, *Chronyk van Hoorn* (Hoorn, [1740; Kn. 6852]).

VELTHUYSEN, LAMBERT VAN, *Apologie voor het tractaet van de Afgoderye en Superstitie* (Utrecht, 1669).

—— *Bewys dat noch de Leere van de Sonne Stilstant en des aertryx bewegingh, noch de gronden vande philosophie van Renatus Des Cartes strydig sijn met Godts woort* (Utrecht, 1656).

VERBEEK, THEO, *René Descartes et Martin Schoock. La Querelle d'Utrecht* (Paris, 1988).

Den Ver-resenen Barnevelt betabbert met alle sijne politijcke maximen (n.p. [1663, Kn. 8797]).

VERVOU, FREDRICH VAN, *Enige Aenteekeningen van 't Gepasseerde in de vergadering van de Staten Generaal* (1616–20; Leeuwarden, 1874).

VERWER, WILLEM JANSZ., *Memoriaelbouck. Dagboek van gebeurtenissen te Haarlem van 1572–1581* (Haarlem, 1973).

VIVIEN, NICOLAAS, and HOP, CORNELIS, *Notulen gehouden ter Staten-Vergadering van Holland (1671–1675)*, ed. N. Japikse, WHG 3rd. ser. 19 (Amsterdam, 1903).

'Visitatie der kerken ten platten lande in het Sticht van Utrecht ten jare 1593', *BMHG* 7 (1884), 186–267.

VOETIUS, GISBERTUS, *Afscheydt Predicatie . . . Ghedaen in de Ghemeynte tot Heusden* (Utrecht, 1636).

—— *Politica Ecclesiastica* (4 vols.; Amsterdam, 1663–76).

VONDEL, JOOST VAN DEN, *Hekeldigten* (Amersfoort, 1707).

—— *Twee Zeevaart-gedichten*, ed. Marijke Spies (2 vols.; Amsterdam, 1987).

Vrede-Vaen voor Liefhebbers vant Vaderland (The Hague [1627, Kn. 3763]).

VROLIKHERT, G., *Vlissingsche kerkhemel* (Flushing, 1758).

WAEYEN, JOHANNES VAN DER, *De Betooverde Wereld ondersoght en weederlegt* (Franeker, 1693).

WAGENAAR, JAN, *Amsterdam in zijne opkomst, aanwas, geschiedenissen . . .* (3 vols.; Amsterdam, 1760).

—— *Historische verhandeling over de Natuur . . . der waardigheid van Stadhouder* (Amsterdam, 1787).

—— *Vaderlandsche Historie vervattende de geschiedenissen der nu Vereenigde Nederlanden* (21 vols.; Amsterdam, 1749–59).

—— *Vrymoedige aanmerckingen over . . . den Raadpensionaris Johan de Witt* (Amsterdam, 1757).

[WALTEN, ERICUS], *Aardige Duyvelary voorvallende in dese dagen* (Amsterdam, n.d. [1692?]).

—— *De Regtsinnige Policey* (The Hague, 1689).

WASSENAER, NICOLAAS VAN, *Historisch Verhael* (21 vols.; Amsterdam, 1622–32).

WATER, J. VAN DE, *Groot Placaat-Boeck vervattende alle plaecaten . . . der Staten 's lands van Utrecht* (3 vols.; Utrecht, 1729).

WATER, JOAN WILLEM TE, *Kort Verhael der Reformatie van Zeeland in de zestiende eeuw* (Middelburg, 1766).

WESTERMANN, J. C., 'Een memorie van 1751 over de tabaksindustrie en den tabakshandel in de Republiek', *EHJ* 22 (1943), 68–81.

WICQUEFORT, ABRAHAM DE, *Histoire des Provinces-Unies des Païs-Bas, depuis le parfait établissement de cet état par la paix de Munster* (4 vols.; Amsterdam, 1861–4).

—— 'Mémoire sur la guerre faite aux Provinces-Unies en l'année 1672', ed. J. A. Wijnne, *BMHG* 11 (1888), 70–344.

WIT, JOHAN DE, *Public Gebedt* (3 vols.; Amsterdam, 1663–4).

[——], *Den Schotschen Duyvel, betabbert in den Verresenen Barnevelt* (Utrecht, 1663 [Kn. 8801]).

WITT, JOHAN DE, *Deductie, ofte Declaratie van de Staten van Hollandt ende West-Vrieslandt* (1654; abridged English trans. in Rowen, *The Low Countries*, 191–7).

WITTICHIUS, CHRISTOFORUS, *Dissertationes duae quarum prior de S. Scripturae in rebus philosophicis abusu examinat* (Amsterdam, 1653).

Den Zeeuwsen Buatist, of Binnelandsen verrader ontdekt in een oproerige en landverdervend pasquil (Rotterdam, 1668 [Kn. 9622]).

ZOBELN, ENOCH, *Declaratio Apologetica . . . wider Bathasar Beekers . . . bezauberte Welt* (Leipzig, 1695).

Secondary Literature

AALBERS, J., *Rijcklof van Goens* (Groningen, 1916).

AALBERS, JOHAN, 'Factieuze tegenstellingen binnen het College van de ridderschap van Holland na de Vrede van Utrecht', *BMGN* 93 (1978), 412–45.

—— *De Republiek en de vrede van Europa* (Groningen, 1980).

AARKEL, J. A., VAN, *De houding van den raadpensionaris Simon van Slingelandt tegenover het huis van Oranje* (Amsterdam, 1925).

ABELS, P. H. A. M., 'Van Vlaamse broeders, slijkgeuzen en predestinateurs. De dolerende gemeente van Gouda, 1615–1619', in P. H. A. M. Abels *et al.* (eds.), *In en om de Sint Jan. Bijdragen tot de Goudse kerkgeschiedenis* (Delft, 1989).

—— and BOOMA, J. G. J. VAN, 'Tussen Rooms-katholiek en Utrechts-gereformeerd', in H. ten Boom *et al.* (eds.), *Utrechters entre-deux. Stad en Sticht in de eeuw van de Reformatie, 1520–1620* (Delft, 1992).

AERTS, E. and DELBEKE, J., 'Problemen bij de social-economische geschiedenis van het Vlaamse platteland, 1700–1850', *BMGN* 98 (1983), 583–96.

AKERMAN, S. *Queen Christina of Sweden and her Circle* (Leiden, 1991).

AKKERMAN, F., 'Agricola and Groningen', in F. Akkerman and A. J. Vanderjagt (eds.), *Rodolphus Agricola Phrisius, 1444–1485* (Leiden, 1988).

ALCALÁ-ZAMORA Y QUEIPO DE LLANO, JOSÉ, *España, Flandes y el Mar del Norte (1618–1639)* (Barcelona, 1975).

ALPERS, S., *The Art of Describing: Dutch Art in the Seventeenth Century* (Chicago, 1983).

—— *Rembrandt's Enterprise* (Chicago, 1988).

ALPHEN, G. VAN., *De stemming van de Engelschen tegen de Hollanders in Engeland tijdens de regering van den koning-stadhouder Willem III, 1688–1702* (Assen, 1938).

ANDRIESSEN, J., 'Jezuieten-auteurs over de oorzaken van den Nederlandschen opstand in de XVIe eeuw', *BGN* 1 (1946), 31–46.

—— *Jezuieten en het samenhorigheidsbesef der Nederlanden, 1585–1648* (Antwerp, 1957).

ANTHOLZ, H., *Politische Wirksamkeit des Johannes Althusius in Emden* (Aurich, 1955).

ARASARATNAM, S., *Dutch Power in Ceylon, 1658–1687* (Djambatan/The Hague, 1958).

—— 'The Dutch East India Company and its Coromandel Trade, 1700–1740', *Bijdragen tot de taal- land- en volkenkunde van Nederlandsch-Indië 123* (1967), 325–46.

ASSELT, W. J. VAN., 'Voetius en Cocceius over de rechtvaardiging', in J. van Oort *et al.* (eds.), *De onbekende Voetius* (Kampen, 1989), 32–47.

AUGUSTIJN, C., *Erasmus en de Reformatie* (Amsterdam, 1962).

—— 'The Ecclesiology of Erasmus', in J. Coppens (ed.), *Scrinium Erasmianum* (2 vols.; Leiden, 1969), ii. 135–55.

—— 'Gerard Geldenhouwer und die religiöse Toleranz', *Archiv für Reformationsgeschichte*, 69 (1978), 132–56.

—— 'Erasmus und die Juden', *NAK* 60 (1980), 22–38.

—— 'Anabaptisme in de Nederlanden', *Doopsgezinde Bijdragen*, 12–13 (1986–7), 13–28.

BAARS, C., 'Geschiedenis van het grondbezit van Gelderse en Utrechtse edelen in de Beijerlanden', AAG *Bijdragen*, 28 (1980), 109–44.

BAASCH, E., 'Hamburg und Holland im 17. und 18. Jahrhundert', *Hansische Geschichtsblätter*, 16 (1910), 45–102.

—— *Holländische Wirtschaftsgeschichte* (Jena, 1927).

BAELDE, M., *De Collaterale Raden onder Karel V en Filips II, 1531–1578* (Brussels, 1965).

—— 'Edellieden en juristen in het centrale bestuur der zestiende-eeuwse Nederlanden, 1531–1578', *TvG* 80 (1967), 39–51.

—— 'Het Gulden Vlies', *Spiegel Historiael*, 7 (1972), 220–7.

—— 'De Pacificatie van Gent in 1576', *BMGN* 91 (1976), 369–93.

—— 'De Nederlanden van de Spaanse erfopvolging tot beeldenstorm (1506–1566)', in I. Schöffer *et al.*, *De Lage Landen van 1500 tot 1780* (Brussels, 1978), 38–101.

BAETENS, R., *De nazomer van Antwerpens welvaart* (2 vols.; Brussels, 1976).

BAINTON, R. H., *David Joris. Wiedertäufer und Kämpfer für Toleranz im 16. Jahrhundert* (Leipzig, 1937).

BAKHUIZEN VAN DEN BRINK, R. C., 'Eerste vergadering der Staten van Holland (19 July 1572)', in R. C. Bakhuizen van den Brink, *Van Hollandsche Potaard. Studien en fragmenten* (Brussels, 1943), 201–28.

BANG, N. E., *Tabeller over skibsfart og varetransport gennem Oresund, 1497–1660* (3 vols.; Copenhagen, 1930–53).

—— and KORST, K., *Tabeller over skibsfart og varetransport gennem Oresund, 1661–1783* (3 vols.; Copenhagen, 1930–53).

BANGS, C. D., *Arminius: A Study in the Dutch Reformation* (Nashville, 1971).

—— 'Regents and Remonstrants in Amsterdam', in *In het spoor van Arminius . . . studies aangeboden aan Prof. G. J. Hoenderdaal* (Nieuwkoop, 1975), 15–29.

BÁNKI, Ö., 'De Utrechtse universiteit in de Hongaarsche beschavingsgeschiedenis', *Jaarboekje van 'Oud-Utrecht'* (1940), 87–117.

BANNATYNE, H., 'Utrecht in Crisis, 1586–1588', in *The Dutch in Crisis, 1585–1588: People and Problems in Leicester's Time*, publication of the Sir Thomas Browne Institute (Leiden, 1988), 35–52.

BANNIER, W. A. F., *De Landgrenzen van Nederland 1. Tot aan den Rijn* (Leiden, 1900).

BARBOUR, V., *Capitalism in Amsterdam in the 17th Century* (1950; 3rd imp.; Ann Arbor, Mich., 1976).

BARENDRECHT, S., *François van Aerssen* (Leiden, 1965).

BARNOUW, P. J., *Philippus van Limborch* (The Hague, 1963).

BARTSTRA, J. S., *Vlootherstel en legeraugmentatie, 1770–1780* (Assen, 1952).

BAUDOUIN, F., *Pietro Paulo Rubens* (1977; English edn. Antwerp, 1989).

BECKER, J., 'De "Rotterdamsche heyligh" . . . Zeventiende-eeuwse echo's op het standbeeld van Erasmus', in W. L. Rose (ed.), *Vondel bij gelegenheid* (Middelburg, 1979), 11–62.

BEENAKKER, A. J. M., *Breda in de eerste storm van de opstand* (Tilburg, 1971).

BELL, D., *Spinoza in Germany from 1670 to the Age of Goethe* (London, 1984).

BERCHET, G., *Cromwell e la Repubblica di Venezia* (Venice, 1864).

BERG, C. A. VAN DER, 'Zinzendorf en de Hernhutters te Amsterdam', *JGA* 46 (1954), 77–104.

BERG, J. VAN DEN, 'Willem Bentinck (1704–1774) en de theologische faculteit te Leiden', in S. Groenveld *et al.* (eds.), *Bestuurders en Geleerden* (Amsterdam, 1985), 169–77.

BERG, J. VAN DEN, 'Godsdienstig leven binnen het protestantisme in de 18e eeuw', in *NAGN* ix. 331–44.

—— *Dordt in de weegschaal. Kritische reacties op de synode van Dordrecht (1618–1619)* (Leiden, 1988).

BERGE, D. TEN, *Hooggeleerde en zoetvloeiende dichter Jacob Cats* (The Hague, 1979).

BERGH, G. C. J. J. VAN DEN, *The Life and Work of Gerard Noodt (1647–1725)* (Oxford, 1988).

BERGSMA, W., *Aggaeus van Albada* (c.*1525–1587*) (Meppel, 1983).

—— ' "Uyt christelijcken yver en ter eeren Godes". Wederdopers en verdraag-zaamheid', in M. Gijswijt-Hofstra (ed.), *Een schijn van verdraagzaamheid. Afwijking en tolerantie in Nederland van de zestiende eeuw tot heden* (Hilver-sum, 1989).

—— 'Calvinismus in Friesland um 1600 am Beispiel der Stadt Sneek', *Archiv für Reformationsgeschichte*, 80 (1989), 252–85.

—— 'Kalvinistysk krewearjen yn Molkwar yn de 17de ieu', *De Vrije Fries*, 69 (1989), 33–44.

BERGSTRÖM, I., *Dutch Still-Life Painting in the Seventeenth Century* (New York, 1956).

BERKEL, K. VAN, 'Intellectuals against Leeuwenhoek', in L. C. Palm and H. A. M. Snelders (eds.), *Antoni van Leeuwenhoek, 1632–1723* (Amsterdam, 1982).

—— *Isaac Beeckman (1588–1637) en de mechanisering van het wereldbeeld* (Amsterdam, 1983).

—— *In het voetspoor van Stevin. Geschiedenis van de natuurwetenschap in Nederland* (Amsterdam, 1985).

BERKELBACH VAN DER SPRENKEL, J. W., *Oranje en de vestiging van de Neder-landse staat* (Amsterdam, 1946).

BERKVENS-STEVELINCK, CH., 'La tolérance et l'héritage de Pierre Bayle (1647–1706) en Hollande dans la première moitié du XVIIIe siècle', *LIAS* 5 (1978), 257–72.

—— *Prosper Marchand. La Vie et l'œuvre (1678–1756)* (Leiden, 1987).

BERTI, S., ' "La Vie et l'esprit de Spinosa" (1719) e la prima traduzione francese dell' "Ethica" ', *Rivista Storica Italiana*, 98 (1986), 5–46.

—— 'Jan Vroesen, autore del "Traité des Trois Imposteurs" ', *Rivista Storica Italiana*, 103 (1991), 528–43.

—— 'Scepticism and the *Traité des trois imposteurs*', in R. H. Popkin and A. Vanderjagt (eds.), *Scepticism and Irreligion in the Seventeenth and Eight-eenth Centuries* (Leiden, 1993), 216–29.

BEUNINGEN, P. TH. VAN, *Wilhelmus Lindanus als Inquisiteur en sschop* (Assen, 1966).

BEUTIN, L., AND ENTHOLT, H., *Bremen und die Niederlande* (Weimar, 1939).

BIELEMAN, J., *Boeren op het Drentse zand, 1600–1910* (Wageningen, 1987).

—— 'Dutch Agriculture in the Golden Age, 1570–1660', in K. Davids and L. Noordegraaf (eds.), *The Dutch Economy in the Golden Age* (Amsterdam, 1993), 159–85.

BIETENHOLZ, P. G., 'Erasmus, Luther und die Stillen im Lande', *Bibliothèque d'Humanisme et Renaissance*, 47 (1985), 27–46.

BIJL, M. VAN DER, *Idee en interest. Voorgeschiedenis, verloop en achtergronden van de politieke twisten in Zeeland ... tussen 1702 en 1715* (Groningen, 1981).

—— 'Utrechts weerstand tegen de oorlogspolitiek tijdens de Spaanse Successie-oorlog', in *Van Standen tot Staten. Stichtse Historische Reeks 1.* (Utrecht, 1975), 135–99.

—— 'Pieter de la Court en de politieke werkelijkheid', in H. W. Blom and I. W. Wildenberg (eds.), *Pieter de la Court in zijn tijd* (Amsterdam, 1986), 65–91.

—— 'Willem III, Stadhouder-koning, pro religione et libertate', in W. F. de Gaay Fortma *et al.* (eds), *Achter den Tijd. Opstellen aangeboden aan Dr. G. Puchinger* (Haarlem, 1986), 155–82.

—— 'Kerk en politiek omstreeks 1700', in A. Wiggers *et al.* (eds.), *Rond de kerk in Zeeland. Derde verzameling bijdragen van de vereniging voor Nederlandse Kerkgeschiedenis* (Delft, 1991), 177–93.

BIJL, W., *Erasmus in het Nederlands tot 1617* (Nieuwkoop, 1978).

BISSCHOP, W. *Justus van Effen geschetst in zijn leven en werken* (Utrecht, 1859).

BLANKERT, A., *Kunst als regeringszaak in Amsterdam in de 17e eeuw* (Lochem, 1975).

—— *Vermeer of Delft* (1975; English edn. Oxford, 1978).

BLAUPOT TEN CATE, S., *Geschiedenis der doopsgezinden in Holland, Zeeland, Utrecht en Gelderland* (2 vols.; Amsterdam, 1847).

BLOCKMANS, W. P., 'Breuk of continuiteit? De Vlaamse privilegien van 1477 in het licht van het staatsvormingsproces', *Standen en Landen*, 80 (1985), 97–125.

—— 'Corruptie, patronage, makelaardij en venaliteit als symptomen van een ontluikende staatsvorming in de Bourgondisch-Habsburgse Nederlanden', *TvSG* 3 (1985), 231–47.

—— 'Alternatives to monarchical Centralisation: The Great Tradition of Revolt in Flanders and Brabant', in H. G. Koenigsberger (ed.), *Republiken und Republikanismus im Europa der frühen Neuzeit* (Munich, 1988), 145–54.

—— and HERWAARDEN, J. VAN, 'De Nederlanden van 1493 tot 1555', in *NAGN* v. 443–91.

—— and PETEGHEM, P. VAN, 'De Pacificatie van Gent als uiting van kontinuit in de politieke opvattingen van de standenvertegenwoordiging', *TvG* 89 (1976), 322–33.

—— and PREVENIER, W., 'Armoede in de Nederlanden van de 14e tot het midden van de 16e eeuw', *TvG* 88 (1975), 501–38.

—— —— *De Bourgondische Nederlanden* (Antwerp, 1983).

BLOK, P. J., *Frederik Hendrik, Prins van Oranje* (Amsterdam, 1924).

—— *Michiel Adriaanszoon de Ruyter* (The Hague, 1930).

BOER, M. G. DE, *De woelingen in Stad en Lande in het midden der 17e eeuw* (Groningen, 1893).

—— *Die Friedensunterhandlungen zwischen Spanien und den Niederlanden in den Jahren 1632 und 1633* (Groningen, 1898).

—— 'Hervatting der vijandelijkheden na het twaalfjarig bestand', *TvG* 35 (1920), 34–49.

—— *Tromp en de Duinkerkers* (Amsterdam, 1949).

BOER, M. G. L. DEN, 'De Unie van Utrecht, Duifhuis en de Utrechtse religievrede', *Jaarboek Oud-Utrecht* (1978), 71–88.

BOER-MEIBOOM, W. E. DE, *Archief van Pieter Steyn, 1749–1772* (The Hague, 1979).

BOGAERS, L., 'Een kwestie van macht?', *Volkskundig Bulletin*, 11 (1985), 102–26.

BOL, L. J. *Die holländische Marinemalerei des 17. Jahrhunderts* (Brunswick, 1973).

BONENFANT, P., *Philippe-le-Bon* (1943; 2nd edn. Brussels, 1955).

BONGER, H., *De Motivering van de godsdienstvrijheid bij . . . Coornhert* (Arnhem, 1954).

BOOGAART, ERNST VAN DEN (with P. Emmer, P. Klein, and K. Zandvliet), *La Expansión holandesa en el Atlántico, 1580–1800* (Madrid, 1992).

—— 'The Trade between Western Africa and the Atlantic World, 1600–90', *Journal of African History*, 33 (1992), 369–85.

BOOGMAN, J. C., 'De overgang van Gouda, Dordrecht, Leiden en Delft in de zomer van het jaar 1572', *TvG* 57 (1942), 81–109.

—— 'Die holländische Tradition in der niederländischen Geschichte', in G. A. M. Beekelaar *et al.* (eds.), *Vaderlands Verleden in Veelvoud* (The Hague, 1975), 89–104.

—— 'De *raison d'état* politicus Johan de Witt', *BMGN* 90 (1975), 379–407.

—— 'The Union of Utrecht: Its Genesis and Consequences', *BMGN* 94 (1979), 377–407.

BOOM, H. TEN, 'Het patriciaat te Rotterdam voor en na 1572', *Rotterdams Jaarboekje* (1990), 165–89.

BOONE, M., and BRAND, H., 'Ondermijning van het Groot Privilege van Holland, Zeeland en West-Friesland', *Holland*, 24 (1992), 2–21.

BOOY, E. P. DE, 'Het "basisonderwijs" in de zeventiende en achttiende eeuw—de Stichtse dorpsscholen', *BMGN* 92 (1977), 208–22.

BOT, P. N. M., *Humanisme en onderwijs in Nederland* (Utrecht/Antwerp, 1955).

BOTS, J., *Tussen Descartes en Darwin* (Assen, 1972).

BOTS, H., 'Tolerantie of gecultiveerde tweedracht', *BMGN* 107 (1992), 657–69.

—— 'Le Rôle des périodiques néerlandais pour la diffusion du livre (1684–1747)', in Ch. Berkvens-Stevelinck *et al.* (eds.), *Le Magasin de l'Univers: The Dutch Republic as the Centre of the European Book Trade* (Leiden, 1992), 49–70.

BOTS, J. A. H., and FRIJHOFF, W. TH. M., 'De studentenpopulatie van de Franeker academie', in G. Th. Jensma *et al.* (eds.), *Universiteit te Franeker, 1585–1811* (Leeuwarden, 1985), 56–72.

BOUTANT, CH., *L'Europe au grand tournant des années 1680* (Paris, 1985).

BOUWMAN, H., *Willem Teellinck en de practijk der Godzaligheid* (1928; Kampen, 1985).

BOUWMAN, M., *Voetius over het gezag der synoden* (Amsterdam, 1937).

BOVEN, M. VAN, and SEGAL, S., *Gerard en Cornelis van Spaendonck. Twee Brabantse bloemenschilders in Parijs* (1980; 2nd edn. Maarssen, 1988).

BOXER, C. R., *The Dutch Seaborne Empire, 1600–1800* (London, 1965).

—— *The Dutch in Brazil, 1624–54* (1957; new edn. Hamden, Conn., 1973).

—— *Jan Compagnie in War and Peace, 1602–1799* (London/Hong Kong, 1979).

—— *The Anglo-Dutch Wars of the 17th Century*, National Maritime Museum booklet (London, 1974).

BRAAM, A. VAN, 'Over de omvang van de Zaanse scheepsbouw', *Holland*, 24 (1992), 33–49.

BRAEKMAN, E. M., *Guy de Brès* (Brussels, 1960).

BRAKE, W. PH. TE, *Regents and Rebels* (Cambridge, Mass., 1989).

—— 'Provincial Histories and National Revolution in the Dutch Republic', in Jacob and Mijnhardt (eds.), *The Dutch Republic in the Eighteenth Century*, 60–90.

BRANDSMA, J. A., *Menno Simons van Witmarsum* (Drachten, 1960).

BRANTS, A., *Bijdrage tot de geschiedenis der Geldersche plooierijen* (Leiden, 1874).

BRANTS, V., *La Belgique au XVIIe siècle, Albert et Isabelle* (Louvain/Paris, 1910).

BREDIUS, A., *Johannes Torrentius. Schilder, 1589–1644* (The Hague, 1909).

—— 'Italiaansche schilderijen in 1672 door Haagsche en Delftsche schilders beoordeeld', *Oud-Holland*, 34 (1916), 88–93.

BREMMER, R. H., 'Het beleg en ontzet van Leiden (1574) een venster op de Opstand', *NAK* 47 (1965/6), 1666–94.

—— *Reformatie en rebellie* (Franeker, 1984).

BRIELS, J. G. C. A., *Zuid-Nederlanders in de Republiek, 1572–1630* (Sint-Niklaas, 1985).

—— 'De Zuidnederlandse immigratie, 1572–1630', *TvG* 100 (1987), 331–55.

BROEK ROELOFS, O. C., *Wilhelmus Baudartius* (Kampen, 1947).

BROKKEN, H. M., *Het ontstaan van de Hoekse en Kabeljauwse twisten* (Zutphen, 1982).

BROWN, CHRISTOPHER, *Carel Fabritius* (Oxford, 1981).

—— *Van Dyck* (Oxford, 1982).

—— *Dutch Landscape: The Early Years. Haarlem and Amsterdam 1590–1650*, National Gallery London exhibition catalogue (London, 1986).

BROWNING, R., *The War of the Austrian Succession* (Stroud, 1994).

BRUGMAN, J., 'Arabic Scholarship', in Th. H. Lunsingh Scheurleer and G. H. M. Posthumus Meyjes (eds.), *Leiden University in the Seventeenth Century* (Leiden, 1975), 203–16.

BRUGMANS, H., *Geschiedenis van Amsterdam* (2nd edn.; 6 vols.; Utrecht/Antwerp, 1972–3).

BRUGMANS, H. L., 'Autour de Diderot en Hollande', *Diderot Studies*, 3 (Geneva, 1961), 55–72.

BRUIJN, J. R., 'Dutch Privateering during the Second and Third Anglo-Dutch Wars', *Acta Historiae Neerlandicae*, 9 (1977), 79–93.

—— 'The Dutch Navy in its Political and Social Economic Setting of the Seventeenth Century', in Ch. Wilson and D. Proctor (eds.), *1688: The Seaborne Alliance and Diplomatic Revolution* (London, 1989), 45–58.

—— 'In een veranderend maritiem perspectief: het ontstaan van directies voor de vaart op de Oostzee, Noorwegen en Rusland', *Tijdschrift voor Zeegeschiedenis*, 9 (1990), 15–26.

—— *The Dutch Navy of the Seventeenth and Eighteenth Centuries* (Columbia, SC, 1993).

—— and LUCASSEN, L. (eds.), *Op de schepen der Oostindische Compagnie* (Groningen, 1980).

BRUIN, C. C. DE, 'Hinne Rode', *Jaarboek Oud-Utrecht* (1981), 191–208.

BRUIN, G. DE, *Geheimhouding en verraad. De geheimhouding van staatszaken ten tijde van de Republiek (1600–1750)* (The Hague, 1991).

BRULEZ, W., 'De zoutinvoer in de Nederlanden in de 16e eeuw', *TvG* 68 (1955), 181–92.

—— 'Scheepvaart in de Zuidelijke Nederlanden', in *NAGN* vi. 123–8.

BRUNEEL, C., 'L'Essor démographique', in *La Belgique autrichienne 1713–1794* (Europalia 87 Österreich) (Brussels, 1987), 163–200.

BUEREN, T. VAN, *Tot lof van Haarlem* (Hilversum, 1993).

BUIJNSTERS, P. J., 'Les Lumières hollandaises', *Studies on Voltaire and the Eighteenth Century*, 87 (1972), 197–215.

BUIJSSEN, E., *Between Fantasy and Reality: 17th Century Dutch Landscape Painting* (Baarn, 1993).

BUISMAN, J. F., *De ethische denkbeelden van Hendrik Laurensz Spiegel* (Wageningen, 1935).

BUNGE, W. VAN, 'De Rotterdamse collegiant Jacob Ostens', *De Zeventiende Eeuw*, 6 (1990), 65–82.

BUNING, E., OVERBEEK, P., and VERMEER, J., 'De huisgenoten des geloofs. De immigratie van de Huguenoten', *TvG* 100 (1987), 356–73.

BURCKHARDT, JACOB, *Recollections of Rubens* (1898; English edn. London, 1950).

BUSHKOVITCH, P. *The Merchants of Moscow, 1580–1650* (Cambridge, 1980).

BUSKEN HUET, C., *Het land van Rembrand* (1883; Amsterdam, 1987).

BUSSEMAKER, C. H., *Geschiedenis van Overijssel gedurende het eerste stadhouderlooze tijdperk* (2 vols; The Hague, 1888–9).

CARASSO-KOK, M., 'Schutters en stadsbestuur in Leiden, 1392–1421', in Marsilje *et al.* (eds.), *Uit Leidse bron geleverd*, 61–6.

—— 'De schutterijen in de Hollandse steden tot het einde der zestiende eeuw', in M. Carasso-Kok and J. Levy-van Helm (eds.), *Schutters in Holland. Kracht en zenuwen van de stad* (Haarlem, 1988), 16–35.

CARDOT, C. F., *Curazao hispánico. Antagonismo flamenco-español* (Caracas, 1973).

CARTER, A. C., *Neutrality or Commitment: The Evolution of Dutch Foreign Policy, 1667–1795* (London, 1975).

CERNY, G., *Theology, Politics and Letters at the Crossroads of European Civilization: Jacques Basnage and the Baylean Huguenot Refugees in the Dutch Republic* (Dordrecht, 1987).

CEYSSENS, L., *La Fin de la première période du Jansénisme. Sources des années 1654–60* (2 vols.; Brussels/Rome, 1963).

—— *La Première Bulle contre Jansenius* (Brussels/Rome, 1961).

Charles-Alexandre de Lorraine. Gouverneur général des Pays-Bas autrichiens, catalogue of the exhibition held in Brussels under the auspices of the Europalia 87 Österreich (Brussels, 1987).

CHARLIER, G., 'Diderot et la Hollande', *Revue de littérature comparée*, 22 (1947), 190–229.

CHÂTELET, A., *Early Dutch Painting: Painting in the Northern Netherlands in the Fifteenth Century* (1980; English edn. Oxford, 1981).

CHIJS, P. O. VAN DER, *De Munten der voormalige heeren en steden van Gelderland . . . tot aan de Pacificatie van Gent* (Haarlem, 1853).

CHORLEY, P., 'The Shift from Spanish to Central-European Merino Wools in the Verviers-Aachen Cloth Industry (1760–1815)', in E. Aerts and J. H. Munro (eds.), *Textiles of the Low Countries in European Economic History* (Leuven, 1990), 96–104.

CHRIST, M. P., *De Brabantsche Saecke* (Tilburg, 1984).

COHEN, G., *Écrivains français en Hollande dans la première moitié du XVIIe siècle* (Paris, 1920).

—— *Le Séjour de Saint-Évremond en Hollande et l'entrée de Spinoza dans le champ de la pensée française* (Paris, 1926).

COHEN, R., *Jews in another Environment: Surinam in the Second Half of the Eighteenth Century* (Leiden, 1991).

COLENBRANDER, H. T., 'De herkomst der Leidsche studenten', in *Pallas Leidensis* (Leiden, 1925), 275–91.

COOK, H. J., 'The New Philosophy in the Low Countries', in R. Porter and M. Teich (eds.), *The Scientific Revolution in National Context* (Cambridge, 1992), 115–49.

COOMBS, D., *The Conduct of the Dutch: British Opinion and the Dutch Alliance during the War of the Spanish Succession* (The Hague, 1958).

COONAN, J. S., 'Gelderland in the Sixteenth Century' (uncompleted St Andrews Ph.D. thesis, abandoned in 1984).

COORNAERT, E., *Un Centre industriel d'autrefois: la draperie-sayetterie d'Hondschoote* (Paris, 1930).

CORNELISSEN, J. D. M., *De eendracht van het land. Cultuurhistorische studies over Nederland in de zestiende en zeventiende eeuw* (Amsterdam, 1987).

A Corpus of Rembrandt Paintings, ed. J. Bruyn, B. Haak, S. H. Levie *et al.* (The Hague/Boston/London, 1982–).

COSSEE, G. H., 'Doopsgezinden en Remonstranten in de 18e eeuw', in *In het spoor van Arminius*, 61–74.

CRAEBECKX, J., 'Les Industries d'exportation dans les villes flamandes au XVIIe siècle', *Studi in onore di Amintore Fanfani* (6 vols; Milan, 1962), iv. 411–68.

—— 'Alva's Tiende Penning een mythe?' in G. A. M. Beekelaar *et al.* (eds.), *Vaderlands Verleden in Veelvoud* (The Hague, 1975), 182–208.

CRAMER, J. A., *Abraham Heidanus en zijn Cartesianisme* (Utrecht, 1889).

—— *De theologische faculteit te Utrecht ten tijde van Voetius* (Utrecht, 1932).

CREW, P. M., *Calvinist Preaching and Iconoclasm in the Netherlands, 1544–1569*, (Cambridge, 1978).

DAELEMANS, F., 'Pachten en welvaart op het platteland van Belgisch Brabant (15e–18e eeuw)', *AAG Bijdragen*, 28 (1986), 165–84.

DALEN, J. L. VAN, *Geschiedenis van Dordrecht* (2 vols.; Dordrecht, 1931–3).

DAMBRUYNE, J., 'De Gentse immobilienmarkt en de economische trend, 1590–1640', *BMGN* 104 (1989), 157–83.

—— 'Het versteningsproces en de bouwactiviteit te Gent in de zeventiende eeuw', *TvG* 102 (1989), 30–50.

DANKBAAR, W. F., *Martin Bucer's Beziehungen zu den Niederlanden* (The Hague, 1961).

DAVIDS, C. A., 'Migratie te Leiden in de achttiende eeuw', in H. A. Diederiks *et al.* (eds.), *Een stad in achteruitgang. Social-historische studies over Leiden in de achttiende eeuw* (Leiden, 1978).

—— 'Universiteiten, Illustre Scholen en de verspreiding van technische kennis in Nederland, eind 16e–begin 19e eeuw', *Batavia Academica*, 8 (1990), 3–34.

—— 'De technische ontwikkeling van Nederland in de vroeg-moderne tijd', *Jaarboek voor de geschiedenis van bedrijf en techniek*, 8 (1991), 9–37.

—— 'Technological Change and the economic Expansion of the Dutch Republic, 1580–1680', in K. Davids and L. Noordegraaf (eds.), *The Dutch Economy in the Golden Age* (Amsterdam, 1993), 79–104.

DECAVELE, J., *De dageraad van de Reformatie in Vlaanderen* (2 vols.; Brussels, 1975).

—— 'De mislukking van Oranje's "democratische politiek" in Vlaanderen', *BMGN* 99 (1984), 626–50.

—— 'Willem van Oranje, de "Vader" van een verscheurd Vaderland (1577–1584)', *Handelingen der Maatschappij voor Geschiedenis en Oudheidkunde te Gent*, 38 (1984), 69–80.

—— 'Brugse en Gentse mendicanten op de brandstapel in 1578', in H. Soly and R. Vermier (eds.), *Beleid en bestuur in de oude Nederlanden. Liber Amicorum Prof. Dr. M. Baelde* (Ghent, 1993), 73–94.

DEIJK, F., 'Elie Benoit (1640–1728), Historiographer and Politician after the Revocation of the Edict of Nantes', *NAK* 69 (1989), 54–92.

DEKKER, R., *Holland in beroering* (Baarn, 1982).

—— 'De staking van de Amsterdamse katoendrukkersknechts in 1744', *Textielhistorische Bijdragen*, 26 (1986), 24–38.

—— 'Revolutionaire en contrarevolutionaire vrouwen in Nederland, 1780–1800', *TvG* 102 (1989), 545–63.

—— 'Labour Conflicts and Working-Class Culture in Early Modern Holland', *International Review of Social History*, 35 (1990), 377–420.

—— ' "Private Vices, Public Virtues" revisited: The Dutch Background of Bernard Mandeville', *History of European Ideas*, 14 (1992), 481–98.

DELFOS, L., *Die Anfänge der Utrechter Union 1577–1587* (Berlin, 1941).

DEQUEKER, L., 'Heropleving van het Jodendom te Antwerpen in de zeventiende eeuw?', *De Zeventiende Eeuw*, 5 (1989), 154–61.

DESPRETZ-VAN DE CASTEELE, S., 'Het protectionisme in de Zuidelijke Nederlanden gedurende de tweede helft der 17e eeuw', *TvG* 78 (1965), 294–317.

DEURSEN, A. TH. VAN, 'De Raad van State en de Generaliteit (1590–1606)', *BGN* 19 (1964–5), 1–48.

—— *Honni soit qui mal y pense? De Republiek tussen de mogendheden (1610–1612)* (Amsterdam, 1965).

—— *De val van Wezel* (Kampen, 1967).

—— *Bavianen en slijkgeuzen* (Assen, 1974).

—— 'Staat van oorlog en generale petitie in de jonge Republiek', *BMGN* 91 (1976), 44–55.

—— *Het kopergeld van de Gouden Eeuw* (4 vols; Assen, 1978–80).

—— *Plain Lives in a Golden Age* (English trans. of above; by M. Ultee, Cambridge, 1991).

—— 'De Raadpensionaris Jacob Cats', *TvG* 92 (1979), 149–61.

—— 'Tussen eenheid en zelfstandigheid', in S. Groenveld and H. L. P. Leeuwenberg (eds.), *De Unie van Utrecht* (The Hague, 1979), 136–54.

—— 'Maurits', in Tamse (ed.), *Nassau en Oranje*, 83–109.

—— 'De Republiek der Zeven Verenigde Nederlanden (1588–1880)', in J. C. H. Blom and E. Lamberts (eds.), *Geschiedenis van de Nederlanden* (Rijswijk, 1993), 118–80.

DHONDT, L., 'De conservatieve Brabantse omtwenteling van 1789 en het proces van revolutie en contrarevolutie in de Zuidelijke Nederlanden tussen 1780 en 1830', *TvG* 102 (1989), 422–50.

DIBON, P. A. G., *L'Enseignement philosophique dans les universités néerlandaises à l'époque pré-cartésienne (1575–1650)* (Paris, 1954).

—— (ed.), *Pierre Bayle. Le philosophe de Rotterdam. Études et documents* (Amsterdam, 1959).

DIEDERIKS, H., *Een stad in verval. Amsterdam omstreeks 1800* (Amsterdam, 1982).

DIEDERIKS, H., 'Amsterdam 1600–1800. Demographische Entwicklung und Migration', in H. Schilling and W. Ehbrecht (eds.), *Niederlande und Nordwestdeutschland* (Cologne, 1983), 328–46.

DIERICKX, M., *L'Érection des nouveaux diocèses aux Pays-Bas, 1559–1570* (Brussels, 1967).

DIJK, H. VAN, and ROORDA, D. J., 'Sociale mobiliteit onder regenten van de Republiek', *TvG* 84 (1971), 306–28.

—— *Het patriciaat in Zierikzee tijdens de Republiek* (n.p. 1979).

DIJK, J. H. VAN, 'Bedreigd Delft', *BVGO* 6th ser. (1928), 177–98.

—— 'De geldelijke druk op de Delftse burgerij in de jaren 1572–76', *BVGO* 7th ser. 5 (1935), 169–86.

DIJKSTERHUIS, E. J., *Simon Stevin* (The Hague, 1943).

—— *The Mechanization of the World Picture* (1959; English edn. Princeton, NJ, 1986).

DILLEN, J. G. VAN, 'Amsterdam als wereldmarkt der edele metalen in de 17e en 18e eeuw', *De Economist* (1923), 538–50, 583–98, 717–30.

—— 'Effectenkoersen aan de Amsterdamsche beurs', *EHJ* 17 (1931), 1–46.

—— 'Summiere staat van de in 1622 in de provincie Holland gehouden volkstelling', *EHJ* 21 (1940), 167–89.

—— *Het oudste aandeelhoudersregister van de kamer Amsterdam der Oost-Indische Compagnie* (The Hague, 1958).

—— *Van Rijkdom en regenten* (The Hague, 1970).

DISNEY, A. R., *Twilight of the Pepper Empire* (Cambridge, Mass., 1978).

DIXON HUNT, J., 'Reckoning with Dutch Gardens', *Journal of Garden History*, 8 (1988), 41–60.

DOELEMAN, F., *De heerschappij van de Proost van Sint Jan in de Middeleeuwen, 1085–1595* (Zutphen, 1982).

DOLLINGER, P., *The German Hansa* (1964; English trans. London, 1970).

DOORNKAT KOOLMAN, J. TEN, *Dirk Philips, vriend en medewerker van Menno Simons* (Haarlem, 1964),

DORBAN, M., 'Les Débuts de la révolution industrielle', in *La Belgique autrichienne*, 121–62.

DORSTEN, J. A. VAN, *Poets, Patrons and Professors* (Leiden, 1962).

—— and STRONG, R. C., *Leicester's Triumph* (Leiden, 1964).

DROSSAERS, S. W. A., *Diplomatieke betrekkingen tusschen Spanje en de Republiek der Vereenigde Nederlanden, 1678–1684* (The Hague, 1915).

DUBBE, B., and VROOM, W. H., 'Mecenaat en kunstmarkt in de Nederlanden gedurende de zestiende eeuw', in *Kunst en Beeldenstorm*, catalogue of the Rijksmuseum Amsterdam (The Hague, 1986), 13–37.

DUDOK VAN HEEL, S. A. C., 'Waar waren de Amsterdamse katholieken in de zomer van 1585?', *JGA* 77 (1985), 13–53.

—— 'Een kooplieden-patriciaat kijkt ons aan', in *De smaak van de elite*, catalogue of the Amsterdam Historical Museum (The Hague, 1986), 19–39.

—— 'Amsterdamse schuil of huiskerken?', *Holland*, 25 (1993), 1–10.

DUITS, H., *Van Bartholomeusnacht tot Bataafse opstand* (Hilversum, 1990).

DUKE, A., *Reformation and Revolt in the Low Countries* (London, 1990).

DUKER, A. C., *Gisbertus Voetius* (3 vols.; Leiden, 1897–1914).

DUPLESSIS, R. S., *Lille and the Dutch Revolt* (Cambridge, 1991).

DURME, M. VAN, *Antoon Perrenot . . . Kardinaal van Granvelle* (Brussels, 1953).

ECHEVARRÍA BACIGALUPE, M. A., 'Un episodio en la guerra económica his-pano-holandesa', *Hispania*, 46 (1986), 57–70.

ECKBERG, C. J., *The Failure of Louis XIV's Dutch War* (Chapel Hill, NC, 1979).

ECKERT, W. P., *Erasmus von Rotterdam. Werk und Wirkung* (2 vols.; Cologne, 1967).

EDWARDS, E., 'The Amsterdam City Government 1672–1683/4', unpublished research paper delivered to the Low Countries History Seminar at the Institute of Historical Research, London.

EEKHOF, A., *De theologische faculteit te Leiden in de 17e eeuw* (Utrecht, 1921).

—— 'David Flud van Giffen en Johannes Braunius', *NAK* 20 (1927), 65–80.

ELIAS, J. E., *De vroedschap van Amsterdam* (2 vols.; Haarlem, 1903–8).

—— *Het voorspel van den eersten Engelschen Oorlog* (2 vols; The Hague, 1920).

ELLIOTT, J. H., *The Count-Duke of Olivares* (New Haven, Conn./London, 1986).

ELZINGA, S., *Het voorspel van den oorlog van 1672* (Haarlem, 1926).

—— 'Le Tarif de Colbert de 1664 et celui de 1667 et leur signification', *EHJ* 15 (1929), 221–73.

EMMANUEL, I. S, and EMMANUEL, S. A., *A History of the Jews of the Netherlands Antilles* (2 vols.; Cincinatti, 1970).

EMMER, P. C., 'The West India Company, 1621–1791', in L. Blussé and F. Gaastra (eds.), *Companies and Trade* (Leiden, 1981), 71–96.

—— 'Suiker, goud, en slaven; de Republiek in West Afrika en West-Indie, 1647–1800', in *Overzee; Nederlandse Koloniale Geschiedenis, 1590–1975* (Haarlem, 1982).

ENGELEN, T. L. M., *Nijmegen in de zeventiende eeuw*, Nijmeegse studiën 7 (Nijmegen, 1978).

ENSCHEDÉ, J. W., 'Papier en papierhandel in Noord-Nederland gedurende de zeventiende eeeuw', *Tijdschrift voor boek- en bibliotheekwezen*, 7 (1909), 97–188, 205–31.

—— 'Jean Nicolas de Parival en zijn *dialogues françois*', *BVGO* 5th ser. 2 (1915), 53–85.

EPKEMA, E., 'Pieter de Groot', *Tijdschrift voor Geschiedenis, Land- en Volkenkunde* 24 (1909), 173–87, 240–55.

EVANS, R. J. W., *The Making of the Habsburg Monarchy, 1550–1700* (Oxford, 1979).

EVENHUIS, R. B., *Ook dat was Amsterdam. De kerk der hervorming in de Gouden Eeuw*, vols. i–ii (Amsterdam, 1965–6).

EXALTO, K., 'Willem Teellinck (1579–1629)', in T. Brienen *et al.* (eds.), *De Nadere Reformatie* (The Hague, 1986), 17–48.

FABER, J. A., 'The Decline of the Baltic Grain Trade in the Second Half of the Seventeenth Century', *Acta Historiae Neerlandicae*, 1 (1966), 108–31.

—— *Drie eeuwen Friesland* (2 vols.; Leeuwarden, 1973).

—— 'De achttiende eeuw', in J. H. van Stuijvenberg (ed.), *De economische geschiedenis van Nederland* (Groningen, 1977), 119–56.

FABER, J. A., DIEDERIKS, H., and HART, S., 'Urbanisering, industrialisering en milieuaantasting in Nederland in de periode van 1500 tot 1800', AAG *Bijdragen*, 18 (1973), 251–71.

FARNELL, J. E., 'The Navigation Act of 1651', *Economic History Review*, 2nd ser. 16 (1964), 439–54.

FAULENBACH, H., *Weg und Ziel der Erkenntnis Christi. Eine Untersuchung zur Theologie des Johannes Coccejus* (Neukirchen, 1973).

FEDEROWICZ, J. K., *England's Baltic Trade in the Early Seventeenth Century* (Cambridge, 1980).

FEENSTRA, H., *Drentse edelen tijdens de Republiek* (n. p. 1985).

—— *Adel in de Ommelanden* (Groningen, 1988).

FEYS, E., 'De kerkelijke vertegenwoordiging in de Staten van Vlaanderen, (1596–1648)', *BMGN* 100 (1985), 405–26.

FLORIN, H., 'Simon Stevin (1548–1620)', in A. J. J. van de Velde *et al.* (eds.), *Simon Stevin, 1548–1948* (Brussels, 1948).

FOCKEMA ANDREAE, S. J., *De Nederlandse staat onder de Republiek* (Amsterdam, 1962).

—— *Album Studiosorum Academiae Franekerensis* (Franeker, 1968).

FONTAINE, P. F. M., *De Raad van State* (Groningen, 1954).

FONTAINE VERWEY, H., 'Le Rôle d'Henri de Brederode et la situation juridique de Vianen pendant l'insurrection des Pays-Bas', *Revue du Nord*, 40 (1958), 297–302.

FORMSMA, W. J., *De Ommelander strijd voor zelfstandigheid in de 16e eeuw (1536–1599)* (Assen, 1938).

—— 'De aanbieding van de landheerlijkheid over Groningen aan de hertog van Brunswijk in de jaren 1592–4', *BMGN* 90 (1975), 1–14.

—— *et al.* (eds.), *Historie van Groningen. Stad en Land* (Groningen, 1976).

FOUW, A. DE, *Onbekende raadpensionarissen* (The Hague, 1946).

FRANCÈS, M., *Spinoza dans les pays néerlandais de la seconde moitié du XVIIe siècle* (Paris, 1937).

FRANKEN, M. A. M., *Coenraad van Beuningen's politieke en diplomatieke aktiviteiten in de jaren 1667–1684* (Groningen, 1966).

FREDERIKS, J. G., 'Het Kabinet schilderijen van Petrus Scriverius', *Oud-Holland*, 12 (1894), 62–3.

FREEDBERG, D., *Dutch Landscape Prints* (London, 1980).

—— 'Art and Iconoclasm, 1525–1580: The Case of the Northern Netherlands', in *Kunst and Beeldenstorm*, Rijksmuseum exhibition catalogue (The Hague, 1986), 39–84.

—— 'Science, Commerce and Art', in D. Freedberg and J. de Vries (eds.), *Art in History, History in Art* (Santa Monica, Calif., 1991), 377–428.

FREMANTLE, K., *The Baroque Town Hall of Amsterdam* (Utrecht, 1959).

FRIJHOFF, W. TH. M., 'De Paniek van juni 1734', *AGKN* 19 (1977), 170–233.

—— 'Katholieke toekomstverwachting ten tijde van de Republiek', *BMGN* 98 (1983), 430–59.

—— 'Non satis dignitatis . . . Over de maatschappelijke status van geneeskundigen tijdens de Republiek', *TvG* 96 (1983), 379–406.

—— (ed.), *Geschiedenis van Zutphen* (Zutphen, 1989).

—— 'Verfransing? Franse taal en Nederlandse cultuur tot in de revolutietijd', *BMGN* 104 (1989), 592–609.

—— 'The Dutch Enlightenment and the Creation of Popular Culture', in Jacob and Mijnhardt, *The Dutch Republic in the Eighteenth Century*, 292–307.

FRITSCHY, J. M. F., *De Patriotten en de financien van de Bataafse Republiek* (The Hague, 1988).

FRUIN, R., *Verspreide geschriften*, ed. P. J. Blok *et al.* (10 vols.; The Hague, 1900–4).

—— *Geschiedenis der staatsinstellingen in Nederland tot den val der Republiek* (The Hague, 1901).

—— *Tien jaren uit den Tachtigjarigen Oorlog, 1588–1598* (The Hague, 1924).

GAASTRA, F., 'The Shifting Balance of Trade of the Dutch East India Company', in L. Blussé and F. Gaastra (eds.), *Companies and Trade* (Leiden, 1981), 47–70.

—— 'De VOC in Azië tot 1680', in *NAGN* vii. 174–219.

—— *Bewind en beleid bij de VOC, 1672–1702* (Zutphen, 1989).

—— *Geschiedenis van de VOC* (Zutphen, 1991).

GABRIËLS, A. J. C. M., *De heren als dienaren en de dienaar als heer. Het stadhouderlijk stelsel in de tweede helft van de achttiende eeuw* (The Hague, 1990).

GACHARD, L. P., *Histoire politique et diplomatique de Pierre-Paul Rubens* (Brussels, 1877).

GANS, M. H., *Memorboek* (Baarn, 1971).

GEBHARD, J. F., *Het leven van Mr Nicolaas Cornelisz. Witsen (1641–1717)* (2 vols.; Utrecht, 1881).

GEIKIE, R., and MONTGOMERY, I. A., *The Dutch Barrier, 1705–1719* (Cambridge, 1930).

GELDER, H. A. ENNO VAN, *De levensbeschouwing van Cornelis Pieterszoon Hooft* (Amsterdam, 1918).

—— *Revolutionnaire Reformatie* (Amsterdam, 1943).

GELDER, H. A. ENNO VAN, *Nederlandse dorpen in de 16e eeuw* (Amsterdam, 1953).

—— *Erasmus, schilders, en rederijkers* (Groningen, 1959).

—— *The Two Reformations of the Sixteenth Century* (The Hague, 1961).

—— *Van Beeldenstorm tot Pacificatie* (Amsterdam/Brussels, 1964).

—— 'Nederland geprotestantiseerd?', *TvG* 81 (1968), 445–64.

—— *Getemperde vrijheid* (Groningen, 1972).

GELDER, H. E. VAN, 'Hervorming en hervormden te Alkmaar', *Oud-Holland*, 40 (1922), 92–123.

GELDER, R. VAN, 'De Republiek als rariteitenkabinet', *TvG* 102 (1989), 213–19.

GELDEREN, M. VAN, 'The Machiavellian Moment and the Dutch Revolt: The Rise of Neostoicism and Dutch Republicanism', in G. Bock *et al.* (eds.), *Machiavelli and Republicanism* (Cambridge, 1990), 205–24.

—— *The Political Thought of the Dutch Revolt, 1555–1590* (Cambridge, 1992).

GEMERT, L. VAN, 'De Haagsche Broeder-Moord: Oranje ontmaskerd', *Literatuur*, 1 (1984), 268–76.

GERLACH, H., *Het proces tegen Oldenbarnevelt en de 'maximen in den staat'* (Haarlem, 1965).

Geschiedenis van Breda, ii. *Aspecten van de Stedelijk historie, 1568–1795* (no editor) (Schiedam, 1977).

GESELSCHAP, J. E. J. (ed.), *Gouda. Zeven eeuwen stad* (Gouda, 1972).

GEURTS, P. A. M., *De Nederlandse Opstand in de pamfletten* (Nijmegen, 1956).

—— *Het eerste grote conflict over de eigen rechtspraak der Leidse universiteit* (Utrecht, 1964).

—— *Voorgeschiedenis van het Statencollege te Leiden (1575–1593)* (Leiden, 1984).

GEYL, P., *Christoforo Suriano* (The Hague, 1913).

—— 'De agent Wolters over de woelingen van 1747 en 1748', *BMHG* 43 (1922), 45–128.

—— *Geschiedenis van de Nederlandse stam* (3 vols.; Amsterdam/Antwerp, 1948–9).

—— *The Revolt of the Netherlands, 1555–1609* (1932; 2nd edn. London, 1958).

—— *Studies en strijdschriften* (Groningen, 1958).

—— *Oranje en Stuart, 1641–1672* (1939; Zeist/Arnhem, 1963).

GIBBS., G. C., 'The Role of the Dutch Republic as the Intellectual Entrepot of Europe in the Seventeenth and Eighteenth Centuries', *BMGN* 86 (1971), 323–49.

—— 'Some Intellectual and Political Influences of the Huguenot Émigrés in the United Provinces, *c.*1680–1730', *BMGN* 90 (1975), 255–87.

GILTAIJ, J., *et al.*, *Perspectiven: Saenredam en de architectuurschilders van de 17e eeuw*, catalogue of the Museum Boymans-van Beuningen, Rotterdam (n.p. 1991).

GINDELY, A. *Geschichte des dreissigjährigen Krieges* (4 vols.; Prague, 1869–80).

GLASIUS, B., *Geschiedenis der Nationale Synode te Dordrecht* (2 vols.; Leiden, 1860–1).

GLAWISCHNIG, R., *Niederlande, Kalvinismus und Reichsgrafenstand, 1559–1584* (Marburg, 1973).

GOETERS, W., *Die Vorbereitung des Pietismus in der reformierten Kirche der Niederlande bis zur labadistischen Krisis 1670* (Leipzig, 1911).

GONNET, C. J., *Wallen en poorten van Haarlem* (Haarlem, 1881).

—— 'Oude schilderijen in en van de stad Haarlem', *Oud-Holland* (1933), 132–44.

GOONEWARDENA, K. W., *The Foundation of Dutch Power in Ceylon 1638–1658* (Djambatan, 1958).

GOSLINGA, A., *Slingelandt's Efforts towards European Peace* (The Hague, 1915).

GOSLINGA, C. CH., *The Dutch in the Caribbean and in the Guianas, 1680–1791* (Assen, 1985).

GOSSES, I. H., and JAPIKSE, N., *Handboek tot de staatkundige geschiedenis van Nederland* (The Hague, 1920).

GOTTSCHALK, M. K. E., *Historische geografie van westelijke Zeeuws-Vlaanderen* (Assen, 1955).

GRAFTON, A., *Joseph Scaliger: A Study in the History of Classical Scholarship* (2 vols; Oxford, 1983–93).

GRAPPERHAUS, F. H. M., *Alva en de Tiende Penning* (Zutphen, 1982).

GRAYSON, J. C., 'The Civic Militia in the County of Holland, 1560–81', *BMGN* 95 (1981), 35–63.

GREVER, J. H., 'Committees and Deputations in the Assemblies of the Dutch Republic 1666–68', *PER* 1 (1981), 13–33.

—— 'The Structure of Decision-Making in the States General of the Dutch Republic 1660–68', *PER* 2 (1982), 125–52.

—— 'The French Invasion of the Spanish Netherlands and the Provincial Assemblies in the Dutch Republic 1667–68', *PER* 4 (1984), 25–35.

—— 'The States of Friesland: Politics and Society during the 1660s', *PER* 9 (1989), 1–25.

GRIJZENHOUT, F., 'A Myth of Decline', in Jacob and Mijnhardt, *The Dutch Republic in the Eighteenth Century*, 324–37.

GRIMM, C., *Frans Hals: The Complete Work* (1989; English trans. New York, 1990).

GRISEBACH, L., *Willem Kalf, 1619–93* (Berlin, 1974).

GROENENDIJK, L. F., 'Petrus Wittewrongel', in T. Brienen *et al.* (eds.), *Figuren en thema's van de Nadere Reformatie* (Kampen, 1987), 64–70.

GROENHUIS, G., *De predikanten* (Groningen, 1977).

GROENVELD, S., *De Prins voor Amsterdam* (Bussum, 1967).

—— *Hooft als historieschrijver* (Weesp, 1981).

—— *Verlopend getij. De Nederlandse Republiek en de Engelse Burgeroorlog 1640–1646* (Dieren, 1984).

—— ' "Een enckel valsch ende lasterlijck verdichtsel". Een derde actie van Prins Willem II in Juli 1650', in Groenveld *et al.* (eds.), *Bestuurders en Geleerden*, 113–25.

1160   Bibliography

GROENVELD, S. 'The English Civil Wars as a Cause of the First Anglo-Dutch
   War, 1640–52', *Historical Journal*, 30 (1987), 541–66.
—— 'The Mecca of Authors? States Assemblies and Censorship in the Seven-
   teenth-Century Dutch Republic', *BN* 9 (1987), 63–86.
—— 'Willem II en de Stuarts, 1647–1650', *BMGN* 103 (1988), 157–81.
—— ' "Breda is den Bosch waerd". Politieke betekenis van het innemen van
   Breda in 1625 en 1637', *Jaarboek van de vereniging 'De Oranjeboom'*, 41
   (1988), 94–109.
—— ' "C'est le père, qui parle". Patronage bij Constantijn Huygens (1596–
   1687)', *Jaarboek Oranje-Nassau Museum* (1988), 53–106.
—— *Evidente factiën in den staet. Sociaal-politieke verhoudingen in de 17e-eeuwse
   Republiek der Verenigde Nederlanden* (Hilversum, 1990).
—— ' "J'equippe une flotte très considerable": The Dutch Side of the Glorious
   Revolution', in R. Beddard (ed.), *The Revolutions of 1688* (Oxford, 1991), 213–45.
—— *et al.* (eds.), *Bestuurders en Geleerden* (Amsterdam, 1985).
GROOT, A. H. DE, *The Ottoman Empire and the Dutch Republic 1610–1630*
   (Leiden/Istanbul, 1978).
GROOT, J. M. DE, 'Schilderijen van Aelbert Cuyp', in *Aelbert Cuyp en zijn familie.
   Schilders te Dordrecht*, catalogue of the Dordrechts Museum (n.p. 1978).
GROSHEIDE, D., 'Enige opmerkingen over de Reformatie en het humanisme in
   de Noordelijke Nederlanden', in *Serta Historica* (3 vols.; Kampen, 1967–72),
   ii. 72–93.
GUDLAUGSSON, S. J., *Geraert Ter Borch* (2 vols.; The Hague, 1959).
GUIBAL, C. J., *Democratie en oligarchie in Friesland tijdens de Republiek* (Assen,
   1934).
—— *Johan Willem Friso en zijn tijd* (Amsterdam, 1938).
GÜLDNER, G., *Das Toleranz-Problem in den Niederlanden im Ausgang des 16.
   Jahrhunderts* (Lübeck, 1968).
GUTMAN, M. P., *War and Rural Life in the Early Modern Low Countries*
   (Princeton, NJ, 1980).
HAAK, B., *The Golden Age: Dutch Painters of the Seventeenth Century* (London,
   1984).
HAAS, J. A. K., *De verdeling van de landen van Overmaas, 1644–62* (Assen, 1978).
HAENTJENS, A. H., *Simon Episcopius als apologeet van het Remonstrantisme*
   (Leiden, 1899).
HAGEDORN, B., *Ostfrieslands Handel und Schiffahrt vom Ausgang des 16.
   Jahrhunderts bis zum Westfälischen Frieden (1580–1648)* (Berlin, 1912).
HAITSMA MULIER, E. O. G., *The Myth of Venice and Dutch Republican Thought
   in the Seventeenth Century* (Assen, 1980).
—— *Het Nederlandse gezicht van Machiavelli* (Hilversum, 1989).
—— 'Between Humanism and Enlightenment: The Dutch Writing of History', in
   Jacob and Mijnhardt, *The Dutch Republic in the Eighteenth Century*, 170–87.
HAKS, D., *Huwelijk en gezin in Holland in de 17e en 18e eeuw* (Utrecht, 1985).

—— 'Libertinisme en Nederlands verhalend proza, 1650–1700', in G. Hekma and H. Roodenburg (eds.), *Soete minne en helsche boosheit. Seksuele voorstellingen in Nederland* (Nijmegen, 1988), 85–108.

HALEY, K. H. D., *An English Diplomat in the Low Countries: Sir William Temple and John de Witt, 1665–1672* (Oxford, 1986).

—— *The British and the Dutch* (London, 1988).

HALLEMA, A., *Hugo de Groot. Het Delftsch Orakel (1583–1645)* (The Hague, 1946).

HAMEL, J. A. VAN, *De eendracht van het land* (Amsterdam, 1945).

HAMILTON, A., *The Family of Love* (Cambridge, 1981).

HARKX, W. A. J. M., *Helmondse textielnijverheid in de loop der eeuwen* (Tilburg, 1967).

HARLINE, C. E., *Pamphlets, Printing and Political Culture in the Early Dutch Republic* (Dordrecht, 1987).

HART, M. C. 'T, *In Quest of Funds: Warfare and State Formation in the Netherlands, 1620–50* (Leiden, 1989).

—— *The Making of a Bourgeois State: War, Politics, and Finance during the Dutch Revolt* (Manchester, 1993).

—— 'Autonoom maar kwetsbaar. De Middelburgse regenten en de opstand van 1651', *De Zeventiende Eeuw*, 9 (1993), 51–62.

HART, S., *Geschrift en getal* (Dordrecht, 1976).

—— 'Rederij', in G. Asaert et al. (eds.), *Maritieme geschiedenis der Nederlanden* (4 vols.; Bussum, 1976), ii. 106–25.

HARTOG, M. W., 'Prins Willem III en de hertogshoed van Gelderland, 1673–5', *Gelre*, 69 (1976/7), 125–55.

HARVARD, H., *Michiel van Mierevelt et son gendre* (Paris, 1892).

HASQUIN, H., 'Le Joséphisme et ses racines', in *La Belgique autrichienne, 1713–1794,* (Europalia 87 Österreich) (Brussels, 1987), 201–38.

—— 'Le Temps des assainissements (1715–40)', ibid. 71–94.

HAZEWINCKEL, H. C., *Geschiedenis van Rotterdam* (3 vols.; Amsterdam, 1940–2).

HEERES, W. G., 'Annual Values of Amsterdam's Overseas Imports and Exports, 1697 to 1798', in W. G. Heeres et al. (eds.), *From Dunkirk to Danzig* (Hilversum, 1988), 263–80.

HEERINGA, T., *De Graafschap* (Zutphen, 1934).

HEININGEN, H. VAN, *Batenburg: eeuwenlang twistappel* (Wijchen, 1987).

HÉLIN, E., 'Demografische ontwikkeling van de Zuidelijke Nederlanden, 1500–1800', in *NAGN* v. 169–94.

HERINGA, J., *De eer en hoogheid van de staat* (Groningen, 1961).

—— (ed.), *Geschiedenis van Drenthe* (2 vols.; Meppel/Amsterdam, 1985).

HERMANS, J. M. M., 'Wat lazen Friezen aan het einde van de Middeleeuwen?', *De Vrije Fries*, 70 (1990), 7–38.

HERWAARDEN, J. VAN, 'Geloof en geloofsuitingen in de late middeleeuwen in de Nederlanden', *BMGN* 98 (1983), 400–29.

HIBBEN, C. C., *Gouda in Revolt* (Utrecht, 1983).

HIRSCHAUER, CH., *Les États d'Artois de leurs origines à l'occupation française, 1340–1640* (2 vols.; Paris/Brussels, 1923).

Hoeven, F. P. VAN DER, *Bijdrage tot de geschiedenis van den Sonttol* (Leiden, 1855).

HOFMAN, H. A., *Constantijn Huygens (1596–1687)* (Utrecht, 1983).

HOLT, M. P., *The Duke of Anjou and the Politique Struggle during the Wars of Religion* (Cambridge, 1986).

HOLTHUIS, P., 'Deventer in oorlog. Economische aspecten van de militaire conjunctuur, 1591–1609', *EHJ* 50 (1987), 32–50.

HOLTHUIZEN-SEEGERS, G. H. J., and NUSTELING, H. P. H., 'Arnhem tussen 1665 en 1744', *Gelre*, 78 (1987), 65–105.

HOOGEWERFF, G. J., *Jan van Scorel. Peintre de la Renaissance hollandaise* (The Hague, 1923).

—— *Geschiedenis van de St Lucasgilden in Nederland* (Amsterdam, 1947).

HOOP SCHEFFER, J. G. DE., *Geschiedenis der kerkhervorming in Nederland van haar ontstaan tot 1531* (2 vols.; Amsterdam, 1873).

HOUTMAN-DE SMEDT, H., 'De Zuidelijke Nederlanden, 1598–1780', in I. Schöffer *et al.* (eds.), *De Lage Landen van 1500 tot 1780* (1978; Amsterdam, 1991), 317–408.

—— 'Het prinsbisdom Luik, 1581–1787', ibid. 409–24.

HOUTTE, J. A. VAN, *Economische en sociale geschiedenis van de Lage Landen* (Zeist/Antwerp, 1964).

—— 'De zestiende eeuw', in J. A. van Stuijvenberg (ed.), *De economische geschiedenis van Nederland* (Groningen, 1977), 49–78.

HOUTZAGER, H. L., 'Gelukkig geneesheer tot Delft. Reinier de Graaf (1641–73)', *Holland*, 23 (1991), 163–72.

HOYNCK VAN PAPENDRECHT, A., *De Rotterdamsche plateel- en tegelbakkers en hun product, 1590–1851* (Rotterdam, 1920).

HSIA, R. PO-CHIA, *Society and Religion in Münster, 1535–1618* (New Haven, Conn., 1984).

HUBERT, E., *Les Pays-Bas espagnols et la République des Provinces-Unies depuis la paix de Munster jusqu'au traité d'Utrecht (1648–1713)* (Brussels, 1907).

HUGENHOLZ, F. W. N., 'The 1477 Crisis in the Burgundian duke's dominions', *BN* 2 (1962), 33–46.

HUISMAN, M., *La Belgique commerciale sous l'Empereur Charles VI* (Brussels, 1902).

HUIZINGA, J., *Erasmus of Rotterdam* (1924; London, 1952).

—— *The Waning of the Middle Ages* (1919; Harmondsworth, 1965).

—— *Verzamelde werken* (9 vols.; Haarlem, 1948–53).

HUUSSEN, A. H., 'Sodomy in the Dutch Republic during the Eighteenth Century', in R. P. Maccubbin (ed.), *Unauthorized Sexual Behaviour during the Enlightenment* (Williamsburg, Va., 1985), 169–78.

—— 'Doodstraf in Friesland', *De Vrije Fries*, 72 (1992), 65–74.

IJSSEWIJN, J., 'The Coming of Humanism in the Low Countries', in H. A. Oberman (ed.), *Itinerarium Italicum: Essays in Honour of P. O. Kristeller*, (Leiden, 1975), 193–304.

ISRAEL, J. I., *The Dutch Republic and the Hispanic World, 1606–1661* (Oxford, 1982).

—— 'Spanje en de Nederlandse Opstand', in F. Wieringa (ed.), *Republiek tussen vorsten. Oranje, Opstand, Vrijheid, Geloof* (Zutphen, 1984), 51–60.

—— *European Jewry in the Age of Mercantilism, 1550–1750* (Oxford, 1985).

—— *Dutch Primacy in World Trade, 1585–1740* (Oxford, 1989).

—— 'The Amsterdam Stock Exchange and the English Revolution of 1688', *TvG* 103 (1990), 412–40.

—— *Empires and Entrepots* (London, 1990).

—— (ed.), *The Anglo-Dutch Moment: Essays on the Glorious Revolution and its World Impact* (Cambridge, 1991).

—— 'The "New History" versus "Traditional History" in Interpreting Dutch World Trade Primacy', *BMGN* 106 (1991), 469–79.

—— 'William III and Toleration', in O. Grell *et al.*, *From Persecution to Toleration: The Glorious Revolution and Religion in England* (Oxford, 1991), 129–70.

—— 'Propaganda in the Making of the Glorious Revolution', in S. Roach (ed.), *Across the Narrow Seas* (London, 1991), 167–78.

—— 'England's Mercantilist Response to Dutch World Trade Primacy, 1647–1674', *BN* 10 (1992), 50–61.

ITTERSZON, G. P., *Franciscus Gomarus* (The Hague, 1929).

JAANUS, H. J., *Hervormd Delft ten tijde van Arend Cornelisz (1573–1605)* (Amsterdam, 1950)

JACOB, M. C., *The Radical Enlightenment: Pantheists, Freemasons and Republicans* (London, 1981).

—— 'Radicalism in the Dutch Enlightenment', in M. C. Jacob and W. Mijnhardt (eds.), *The Dutch Republic in the Eighteenth Century* (Ithaca, NY, 1992), 224–40.

JANSE, A., *Grenzen aan de macht* (The Hague, 1993).

JANSEN, J. C. G. M., 'Crisis en herstructurering in en rond Maastricht (1560–1640)', *Bijdragen tot de geschiedenis*, 73 (1990), 141–63.

JANSEN, H. P. H., *Hoekse en Kabeljauwse twisten* (Bussum, 1966).

—— 'De Bredase Nassaus', in Tamse (ed.), *Nassau en Oranje*, 13–44.

JANSMA, T. S., 'Philippe le Bon et la guerre hollando-wende (1438–1441)', *Revue du Nord*, 42 (1960), 5–18.

—— 'Hanze, Fugger, Amsterdam', *BMGN* 91 (1976), 1–22.

JAPIKSE, N., *De verwikkelingen tusschen de Republiek en Engeland van 1660–1665* (Leiden, 1900).

—— *Johan de Witt* (Amsterdam, 1915).

JAPIKSE, N., *Prins Willem III: De Stadhouder-koning* (2 vols.; Amsterdam, 1930–3).

JAPPE ALBERTS, W., *Geschiedenis van de beide Limburgen* (2 vols.; Assen, 1974).

—— and JANSEN, H. P. H., *Welvaart in wording. Sociaal-economische geschiedenis van Nederland van de vroegste tijden tot het einde van de middeleeuwen* (The Hague, 1964).

—— *et al.* (eds.), *Geschiedenis van Gelderland* (Zutphen, 1975).

JENNISKENS, A. H., *De magistraat van Nijmegen, 1619–1648* (Nijmegen, 1973).

JONES, J. R., *Marlborough* (Cambridge, 1993).

JONG, C. DE, 'De Walvisvaart', in G. Asaert *et al.*, *Maritieme geschiedenis der Nederlanden* (4 vols.; Bussum, 1976), ii. 309–14.

JONG, E. DE, ' "Netherlandish Hesperides": Garden Art in the Period of William and Mary, 1650–1702', *Journal of Garden History*, 2–3 (1988), 15–40.

JONG, J. DE, *Een deftig bestaan. Het dagelijks leven van regenten in de 17e en 18e eeuw* (Utrecht/Antwerp, 1987).

JONG, JAN DE, *De voorbereiding en constitueering van het kerkverband der Nederlandsche Gereformeerde kerken in de zestiende eeuw* (Groningen, 1911).

JONG, J. J. DE, *Met goed fatsoen. De elite in een Hollandse stad: Gouda, 1700–80* (The Hague, 1985).

JONG, O. J. DE, *De Reformatie in Culemborg* (Assen, 1957).

—— 'De eerste drie Noord-Hollandse synoden', *NAK* 58 (1977/8), 190–204.

—— 'Voetius en de tolerantie', in J. van Oort *et al.*, *De onbekende Voetius* (Kampen, 1989), 109–16.

JONGBLOET-VAN HOUTTE, G., 'De belegering en de val van Antwerpen belicht vanuit een koopmansarchief', *BMGN* 91 (1976), 23–43.

JONGE, H. J. DE, 'The Study of the New Testament', in Th. H. Lunsingh-Scheurleer *et al.* (eds.), *Leiden University* (Leiden, 1975), 65–110.

JONGSTE, J. A. F. DE., *Onrust aan het Spaarne. Haarlem in de jaren 1747–51* (The Hague, 1984).

—— 'Hollandse stadspensionarissen tijdens de Republiek' in Groenveld *et al.* (eds.), *Bestuurders en Geleerden*, 85–96.

—— ' "Een bewind op zijn smalst". Het politiek bedrijf in de jaren 1727–47', in *NAGN* ix. 44–59.

—— 'Beeldvorming rond Frederik II van Pruisen in de Republiek', *TvG* 104 (1991), 499–531.

—— 'The Restoration of the Orangist Regime in 1747', in Jacob and Mijnhard, *The Dutch Republic in the Eighteenth Century*, 32–59.

KAAJAN, H., *De groote synode van Dordrecht in 1618–19* (Amsterdam, 1918).

KALMA, J. J. and VRIES, K. DE (eds). *Friesland in het rampjaar 1672* (Leeuwarden, 1972).

—— *et al.* (eds.), *Geschiedenis van Friesland* (Drachten, 1968).

KALVEEN, C. A. VAN, 'De definitieve vestiging van de Reformatie te Amersfoort, 1579–81', *NAK* 62 (1982), 28–54.

KANNEGIETER, J. Z., *Geschiedenis van de vroegere Quakergemeenschap te Amsterdam* (Amsterdam/Haarlem, 1971).

KAPER, R., *Pamfletten over oorlog of vrede. Reakties van tijdgenoten op de vredesonderhandelingen van 1607–1609* (Amsterdam, 1980).

KAPLAN, B. J., 'Hubert Duifhuis and the Nature of Dutch Libertinism', *TvG* 105 (1992), 1–29.

KAPLAN, Y., *From Christianity to Judaism: The Story of Isaac Orobio de Castro* (Oxford, 1989).

KAPPELHOF, A. C. M., *De belastingheffing in de Meierij van Den Bosch gedurende de Generaliteitsperiode (1648–1730)* (Tilburg, 1986).

KATZEN, M. F., 'White Settlers and the Origin of a New Society, 1652–1778', in M. Wilson and L. Thompson (eds.), *The Oxford History of South Africa* (2 vols.; Oxford, 1969), i. 187–228.

KELLENBENZ, H., 'Der Pfeffermarkt um 1600 und die Hansestädte', *Hansische Geschichtsblätter*, 74 (1956), 28–49.

KEMP, C. M. VAN DER, *Maurits van Nassau* (4 vols.; Rotterdam, 1843).

KERKHOVEN, J. M., and BLOM, H. W., 'De la Court and Spinoza', in H. W. Blom and I. W. Wildenberg (eds.), *Pieter de la Court en zijn tijd* (Amsterdam, 1986).

KERNKAMP, G. W., *De sleutels van de Sont* (The Hague, 1890).

—— *De Utrechtsche Academie, 1636–1815* (2 vols.; Utrecht, 1936).

—— *Prins Willem II* (Amsterdam, 1943).

KERNKAMP, J. J., *Handel op den vijand, 1572–1609* (2 vols.; Utrecht, 1931–4).

KEUNING, J., *Petrus Plancius. Theoloog en geograaf 1552–1622* (Amsterdam, 1946).

KEYES, G. S., *Esaias van den Velde (1587–1630)* (Groningen, 1984).

KLAVEREN, G. VAN, 'Utrecht zonder regering, 1673–4', *Jaarboekje van 'Oud-Utrecht'* (1925), 93–109.

—— 'Nicolaas Chevalier en zijn "Chambre de Raretez" ', *Jaarboekje van 'Oud-Utrecht'* (1940), 141–57.

KLEIJNTJENS, J. C. J., and VAN CAMPEN, J. W. C., 'Bescheiden betreffende den Beeldenstorm van 1566 in de stad Utrecht', *BMHG* 53 (1932), 63–245.

KLEIN, P. W., 'De heffing van de 100e en 200e penning van het vermogen te Gouda', *EHJ* 3 (1965) 41–62.

—— 'De zeventiende eeuw', in J. H. Stuijvenberg (ed.), *De economische geschiedenis van Nederland* (Groningen, 1977), 79–118.

—— 'Nederlandse glasmakerijen in de zeventiende en àchttiende eeuw', *EHJ* 44 (1982), 31–43.

KLEIN, S. R. E., 'Republikanisme en patriottisme', *TvG* 106 (1993), 179–207.

KLEP, P. M. M., 'Het historisch moderniseringsproces van bevolking en arbeid: Belgisch Brabant 1700–1900', *EHJ* 42 (1979), 15–25.

—— 'Urban Decline in Brabant (1374–1806)', in H. van der Wee (ed.), *The Rise and Decline of Urban Industries in Italy and the Low Countries* (Leuven, 1988), 261–86.

KLERK, F. H. DE, 'Zestiende-eeuwse processies in Goes', in A. Wiggers *et al.*, *Rond de kerk in Zeeland* (Delft, 1991), 83–93.

KLEVER, W. N. A., 'Insignis opticus', *De Zeventiende Eeuw*, 6 (1990), 47–64.

—— 'Inleiding' to Franciscus van den Enden, *Vrije Politijke Stellingen* (Amsterdam, 1992), 13–119.

KLUIVER, J. H., 'Zeeuwse reacties op de Acte van Seclusie', *BMGN* 91 (1976), 406–28.

KLUYSKENS, J., 'Justus Lipsius' levenskeuze: het irenisme', *BMGN* 88 (1973), 19–37.

—— 'De klassieke oudheid, propaedeuse van het Christendom: het streven van Justus Lipsius', in F. de Nave (ed.), *Liber Amicorum Leon Voet* (Antwerp, 1985), 429–40.

KNAPPERT, L., *De opkomst van het protestantisme in een Noord-Nederlandsche stad* (Leiden, 1908).

KNEVEL, P., 'Onrust onder schutters', *Holland*, 20 (1988), 158–74.

KNUTTEL, W. P., *De toestand der Nederlandsche Katholieken ten tijde der Republiek* (2 vols.; The Hague, 1892–4).

—— 'Ericus Walten', *BVGO* 4th ser. 1 (1900), 345–455.

—— *Balthasar Bekker, de bestrijder van het bijgeloof* (1906; Groningen 1979).

—— *Verboden boeken in de Republiek der Vereenigde Nederlanden* (The Hague, 1914).

KOCH, A. C. F., 'The Reformation in Deventer in 1579–80', *Acta Historiae Neerlandicae*, 6 (1973), 27–66.

KOENIGSBERGER, H. G., 'Why did the States General of the Netherlands Become Revolutionary?', *PER* 2 (1982), 103–11.

—— 'Orange, Granvelle and Philip II', *BMGN* 99 (1984), 573–95.

—— 'Fürst und Generalstaaten. Maximilian I in den Niederlanden, 1477–93', *Historische Zeitschrift*, 242 (1986), 557–79.

KOHL, W., *Christoph Bernhard von Galen: Politische Geschichte des Fürstbistums Münster 1650–1678* (Münster, 1964).

KOK, J. A. DE, *Nederland op de breuklijn Rome-Reformatie* (Assen, 1964).

KOKKEN, H., *Steden en Staten* (The Hague, 1991).

KOLMAN, R. J., *De reductie van Nijmegen (1591) Voor en naspel* (Groningen, 1952).

KOOIJMANS, L., *Onder regenten. De elite in een Hollandse stad. Hoorn (1700–80)* (Dieren, 1985).

—— 'Een Hollandse visie op de Oostenrijkse Successieoorlog', *Holland*, 25 (1993), 11–23.

KOOPMANS, J. W., *De Staten van Holland en de Opstand* (The Hague, 1990).

KOSSMANN, E. H., *Politieke theorie in het zeventiende-eeuwse Nederland* (Amsterdam, 1960).

—— *The Low Countries, 1780–1940* (Oxford, 1978).

—— *Politieke theorie en geschiedenis. Verspreide opstellen en voordrachten* (Amsterdam, 1987).

KOTTE, W., *Van Gelderse bloem tot franse lelie. De franse bezetting van de stad Arnhem, 1672–1674* (Arnhem, 1972).

KRAMER, J. F., 'De Luthersche gemeente te Groningen in de 17e eeuw', *NAK* 16 (1921), 280–97.

KRIKKE-FRIJNS, A. J. M., 'Het ontstaan en de ontwikkeling van de R. K. armen-en wezenzorg in de 18e en 19e eeuw in Leiden', in Marsilje *et al.* (eds.), *Uit Leidse bron geleverd*, 295–302.

KRONENBERG, M. E., *Verboden boeken en opstandige drukkers in de hervormings-tijd* (Amsterdam, 1948).

—— 'Uitgaven van Luther in de Nederlanden verschenen tot 1541', *NAK* 40 (1953), 1–25.

KRULL, A. F., *Jacobus Koelman. Een kerkhistorische studie* (Sneek, 1901).

KÜHLER, G. H., *Geschiedenis der Nederlandsche doopsgezinden in de zestiende eeuw* (1932; Haarlem, 1961).

—— *Het socinianisme in Nederland* (1912; Leeuwarden, 1980).

KUILE, E. H. TER, 'De werkzaamheid van Lieven de Key in Haarlem', in *Oud-Holland* (1938), 245–52.

KUILE, G. J. TER, 'Het graafschap Lingen onder de Oranjes', *Verslagen . . . van de Vereeninging tot beoefening van Overijsselsch regt en geschiedenis*, 68 (1953), 13–31.

KURETSKY, S. D., *The Paintings of Jacob Ochtervelt (1634–1682)* (Montclair, NJ, 1979).

KURTZ, G. H., *Willem III en Amsterdam, 1683–1685* (Utrecht, 1928).

—— *Haarlem in het rampjaar 1672* (Haarlem, 1946).

KUYPER, W., *Dutch Classicist Architecture* (Delft, 1980).

LABROUSSE, E., *Pierre Bayle* (2 vols.; Dordrecht, 1985).

LADEMACHER, H., *Die Stellung des Prinzen von Oranien als Statthalter in den Niederlanden von 1572 bis 1584* (Bonn, 1958).

—— 'Wilhelm III von Oranien und Anthonie Heinsius', *Rheinische Viertel-jahresblätter* 34 (1970), 252–66.

—— *Geschichte der Niederlande* (Darmstadt, 1983).

LANCÉE, J. A. L., *Erasmus en het Hollands Humanisme* (Utrecht, 1979).

LAWRENCE, C., 'Hendrick de Keyser's Heemskerk Monument: The Origins of the Cult and Iconography of Dutch Naval Heroes', *Simiolus*, 28 (1993), 265–95.

LEEB, I. L., *The Ideological Origins of the Batavian Revolution* (The Hague, 1973).

LENTING, L. E., 'De benoeming van Graaf Johan van Nassau tot Stadhouder van Gelderland', *KHG* 4th ser. 5 (1864), 82–111.

—— 'Gelderland in betrekking tot de Unie van Utrecht', *BVGO* NS 4 (1866), 259–343.

LESGER, C., *Huur en conjunctuur. De woningmarkt in Amsterdam, 1550–1850* (Amsterdam, 1986).

LESGER, C., *Hoorn als stedelijk knooppunt* (Hilversum, 1990).

LEVY-VAN HELM, J., 'De Haarlemse schuttersstukken', in M. Carasso-Kok and J. Levy-van Helm (eds.), *Schutters in Holland. Kracht en zenuwen van de stad* (Haarlem, 1988), 104–23.

LIEBURG, F. A. VAN, *De Nadere Reformatie in Utrecht ten tijde van Voetius* (Rotterdam, 1989).

LIESKER, PH., *'Die Staatswissenschaftlichen Anschauungen Dirck Graswinckels* (Freiburg, 1901).

LIEVENSE-PELSER, E., 'De Remonstranten en hun kerk', *Jaarboek Amstelodamum*, 67 (1975), 121–36.

LIGTENBERG, C., *De armenzorg te Leiden tot het einde van de 16e eeuw* (The Hague, 1908).

LIJNDRAJER, P., *De ontwikkeling der stadhouderlijke macht onder Frederik Hendrik* (Amsterdam, 1859).

LINDE, J. M. VAN DER, *Surinaamse suikerheren en hun kerk* (Wageningen, 1966).

LINDE, S. VAN DER, *Jean Taffin* (Amsterdam, 1982).

LINDEBOOM, G. A., *Herman Boerhaave: The Man and his Work* (London, 1968).

LINDEBOOM, J., *Het Bijbelsche humanisme in Nederland* (Leiden, 1913).

——*Stiefkinderen van het Christendom* (The Hague, 1929).

LOENEN, J. VAN, *De Haarlemse brouwindustrie voor 1600* (Amsterdam, 1950).

LOGAN, A. M. S., *The 'Cabinet' of the Brothers Gerard and Jan Reynst* (Amsterdam, 1979).

LONCHAY, H., *La Rivalité de la France et de l'Espagne aux Pays-Bas (1635–1700)* (Brussels, 1896).

LOOSJES, J., *Geschiedenis der Luthersche kerk in de Nederlanden* (The Hague, 1921).

LOURDAUX, W., 'Les Dévots modernes, rénovateurs de la vie intellectuelle', *BMGN* 95 (1980), 279–97.

LUNSINGH SCHEURLEER, TH. H., and POSTHUMUS MEYJES, G. H. M. (eds.), *Leiden University in the Seventeenth Century: An Exchange of Learning* (Leiden, 1975).

MAANEN, I. J. VAN, and VERMEULEN, K., 'Het lagere volk van Amsterdam in de strijd tussen patriotten en oranjegezinden, 1780–1800', *TvSG* 20 (1980), 331–56.

MAANEN, R. C. J. VAN, 'De vermogensopbouw van de Leidse bevolking in het laatste kwart van den zestiende eeuw', *BMGN* 93 (1978), 1–42.

MAARSEVEEN, J. G. S. J., 'De Republiek en Frankrijk in het begin van de 17e eeuw', *Spiegel der Historie*, 4 (n.d.), 413–68.

MADDENS, N., *De beden in het graafschap Vlaanderen tijdens de regeering ven Keizer Karel V (1515–50)*, Standen en Landen, 72 (Kortrijk, 1978).

——'Invoering van de "Nieuwe Middelen" in het Graafschap Vlaanderen tijdens de regering van Keizer Karel', *Belgische Tijdschrift voor Filologie en Geschiedenis*, 62 (1979), 342–63, 861–98.

MALENGREAU, G., *L'Esprit particulariste et la révolution des Pays Bas au XVIe siècle* (Leuven, 1936).

MALSSEN, P. J. W. VAN, *Louis XIV d'après les pamphlets répandus en Hollande* (Paris, n.d.).

MALTBY, W. S., *Alba: A Biography of Fernando Alvarez de Toledo Third Duke of Alba, 1507–82* (Berkeley Los Angeles, 1983).

MANKE, I., *Emanuel de Witte 1617–1692* (Amsterdam, 1963).

MARÉCHAL, G. 'Inleiding' to Johannes Duijkerius, *Het leven van Philopater* (1691 and 1697; Amsterdam, 1991).

MARKISH, Sh., *Erasmus and the Jews* (Chicago, 1986).

MARNEF, G., *Het Calvinistisch bewind te Mechelen, 1580–1585* (Kortrijk, 1987).

——'Brabants Calvinisme in opmars', *Bijdragen tot de geschiedenis*, 70 (1987), 7–22.

——'Repressie en censuur in het Antwerps boekenbedrijf, 1567–76', *De Zeventiende eeuw*, 8 (1992), 221–31.

MARONIER, J. H., *Jacobus Arminius. Een biografie* (Amsterdam, 1905).

MARSILJE, J. W. *et al.* (eds.), *Uit Leidse bron geleverd* (Leiden, 1989).

MARTIN, W., *Het leven en werken van Gerrit Dou* (Leiden, 1901).

MARX, J., 'Un grand imprimeur au XVIIIe siècle: Elie Luzac fils (1723–96)', *Revue Belge de philologie et d'histoire*, 46 (1968), 779–86.

MEERE, J. M. M. DE, and NOORDEGRAAF, L., 'De sociale gelaagheid van Amsterdam in de Franse tijd', *JGA* 69 (1977), 156–75.

MEERTENS, P. J., *Letterkundig leven in Zeeland in de zestiende en de eerste helft der zeventiende eeuw* (Amsterdam, 1943).

MEESTER, B. DE, *Le Saint-Siège et les troubles des Pays-Bas (1566–1579)* (Leuven, 1934).

MEESTER, G. A. DE, *Geschiedenis van de Staten van Gelderland* (Harderwijk, 1864).

MEIHUIZEN, H. W., *Galenus Abrahamsz (1622–1706)* (Haarlem, 1954).

—— *Menno Simons* (Haarlem, 1961).

MEIJ, J. C. A. DE, *De watergeuzen en de Nederlanden, 1568–1572* (Amsterdam, 1972).

MEILINK-ROELOFSZ, M. A. P., *De vestiging der Nederlanders ter kuste Malabar* (The Hague, 1943).

MEINECKE, F., 'Petrus Valckeniers Lehre von den Interessen der Staaten', in *Aus Politik und Geschichte. Gedächtnisschrift für Georg von Below* (Berlin, 1928), 146–55.

MEINSMA, K. O., *Spinoza en zijn kring* (The Hague, 1896).

MELLES, J., *Joachim Oudaan. Heraut der verdraagzaamheid, 1628–1692* (Utrecht, 1958).

—— *Ministers aan de Maas* (The Hague, 1962).

MELLINK, A. F., *De wederdopers in de Noordelijke Nederlanden, 1531–44* (Groningen, 1953).

MENTINK, G. J., and VAN DER WOUDE, A. M., *Demografische ontwikkeling te Rotterdam en Cool in de 17e en 18e eeuw* (Rotterdam, 1965).

MENK, G., *Die Hohe Schule Herborn in ihrer Frühzeit (1584–1660)* (Wiesbaden, 1981).

MEULEN, P. VAN DER, *De comedies van Coornhert* (Assen, 1945).

MEYERE, J. A. L. DE, 'Utrechtse schilderkunst in de tweede helft van de 16de eeuw', *Jaarboek Oud-Utrecht* (1978), 106–41.

MICHMAN, J. 'De emancipatie van de Joden in Nederland', *BMGN* 96 (1981), 78–82.

MIEDEMA, H., 'The Appreciation of Paintings around 1600', in G. Luijten *et al.* (eds.), *Dawn of the Golden Age: Northern Netherlandish Art 1580–1620*, Rijksmuseum exhibition catalogue (Amsterdam, 1993), 122–35.

MIJNHARDT, W. W., 'De Nederlandse Verlichting. Een terreinverkenning', *Kleio*, 19 (1978), 245–63.

——*Tot Heil van 't Menschdom. Culturele genootschappen in Nederland, 1750–1815* (Amsterdam, 1987).

—— 'The Dutch Enlightenment: Humanism, Nationalism, and Decline', in Jacob and Mijnhardt, *The Dutch Republic in the Eighteenth Century*, 197–223.

MILLER, A., *Sir Joseph Yorke and Anglo-Dutch Relations, 1774–80* (The Hague, 1970).

MIMS, S. L., *Colbert's West India Policy* (New Haven, Conn., 1912).

MOLTKE, J. W. VON, *Govaert Flinck, 1615–1660* (Amsterdam, 1965).

MONTIAS, J. M., *Artists and Artisans in Delft* (Princeton, NJ, 1982).

—— *Vermeer and his Milieu* (Princeton, NJ, 1989).

—— 'Art Dealers in the Seventeenth-Century Netherlands', *Simiolus*, 18 (1988), 244–56.

—— 'Works of Art in Seventeenth-Century Amsterdam', in Freedberg and de Vries (eds.), *Art in History, History in Art*, 331–72.

MOORE, S. F. C., 'The Cathedral Chapter of St Maarten at Utrecht before the Revolt' (University of Southampton Ph.D. thesis, 1988).

MÖRKE, O., 'Konfessionalisierung als politisch-soziales Strukturprinzip. Das Verhältnis von Religion und Staatsbildung in der Republik der Vereinigten Niederlande im 16. und 17. Jahrhundert', *TvSG* 16 (1990), 31–60.

—— 'De hofcultuur van het huis Oranje-Nassau in de zeventiende eeuw', in P. te Boekhorst *et al.* (eds.), *Cultuur en maatschappij in Nederland, 1500–1800. Een historisch-antropologisch perspectief* (Meppel, 1992), 39–78.

MOUT, M. E. H. N., *Bohemen en de Nederlanden in de zestiende eeuw* (Leiden, 1975).

—— 'Het intellectuele milieu van Willem van Oranje', *BMGN* 99 (1984), 596–625.

—— 'In het schip: Justus Lipsius en de Nederlandse Opstand tot 1591', in Groenveld *et al.* (eds.), *Bestuurders en Geleerden*, 55–64.

MULLER, P. L., *De staat der Vereenigde Nederlanden in de jaren zijner wording, 1572–94* (Haarlem, 1872).

—— 'Spanje en de partijen in Nederland in 1650', *BVGO* NS 7 (1872), 136–83.

MULTHAUF, L. S., 'The Light of Lamp-Lanterns: Street Lighting in 17th-Century Amsterdam', *Technology and Culture*, 26 (1985), 236–52.

MUNCK, L. DE, *Heusden* (Heusden, 1970).

NAGTEGAAL, P., 'Stadsfinanciën en stedelijke economie', *EHJ* 52 (1989), 96–147.

NAUTA, D., *Samuel Maresius* (Amsterdam, 1935).

—— *Opera minora* (Kampen, 1961).

NAUWELAERTS, M. A., *Latijnse school en onderwijs te 's-Hertogenbosch tot 1629* (Tilburg, 1974).

NAVE, F. DE (ed.), *Antwerpen en de scheiding der Nederlanden (17 Augustus 1585)* (Antwerp, 1986).

NEALE, J. M., *A History of the So-Called Jansenist Church of Holland* (Oxford, 1858).

NÈVE, P. L., *Het Rijkskamergerecht en de Nederlanden* (Assen, 1972).

NIEROP, H. F. K. VAN, *Beeldenstorm en burgelijk verzet in Amsterdam, 1566–7* (Nijmegen, 1978).

—— *Van ridders tot regenten* (n.p. 1984; English trans.: *The Nobility of Holland* (Cambridge, 1993)).

NIEUWENHUIS, T., *Keeshonden en Prinsmannen* (Amsterdam, 1986).

NIJENHUIS, I. J. A., *Een joodse philosophe. Isaac de Pinto (1717–1787)* (Amsterdam, 1992).

NIJENHUIS, W., *Adrianus Saravia (c. 1532–1613)* (Leiden, 1980).

—— 'De publieke kerk veelkleurig en verdeeld bevoorrecht en onvrij', in *NAGN* i. 325–43.

NOBBS, D., *Theocracy and Toleration* (Cambridge, 1938).

NOORDAM, D. J., 'Prostitutie in Leiden in de 18e eeuw', in D. G. H. de Boer (ed.), *Leidse facetten. Tien studies over Leidse geschiedenis* (Zwolle, 1982), 65–102.

NOORDEGRAAF, L., *Daglonen in Alkmaar, 1500–1850* (Amsterdam, 1980).

—— 'Nijverheid in de Noordelijke Nederlanden', in *NAGN* vi. 12–26.

—— 'Levensstandaard en levensmiddelenpolitiek in Alkmaar vanaf het eind van de 16e tot in het begin van de 19e eeuw', *Alkmaarse Historische Reeks*, 4 (1980), 55–100.

—— and VALK, G., *De gave Gods. De Pest in Holland vanaf de late middeleeuwen* (Bergen, 1988).

NORTH, N., *Kunst und Kommerz im goldenen Zeitalter* (Cologne, 1992).

NOTTEN, M., *Rombout Verhulst, beeldhouwer (1624–98)* (The Hague, 1907).

NUSTELING, H. P. H., *Welvaart en werkgelegenheid in Amsterdam, 1540–1860* (Amsterdam, 1985).

—— 'The Netherlands and the Huguenot Émigrés', in J. A. H. Bots and G. H. M. Posthumus Meyjes (eds.), *La Révocation de l'Édit de Nantes et les Provinces-Unies 1685* (Amsterdam, 1986), 17–34.

NUSTELING, H. P. H., 'Periods and Caesurae in the Demographic and Economic History of the Netherlands, 1600–1900', *Economic and Social History in the Netherlands*, 1 (1989), 87–111.

—— 'Strijd om de commerciele suprematie in de zeventiende en achttiende eeuw', *Tijdschrift voor de Economische Geschiedenis in Nederland*, 6 (1992), 5–23.

OBERMAN, H. A., 'Wessel Gansfort: *Magister contradictionis*', in F. Akkerman, G. C. Huisman, and A. J. Vanderjagt (eds.), *Wessel Gansfort (1419–1489) and Northern Humanism* (Leiden, 1993), 97–121.

O'CONNOR, J. T., *Negotiator out of Season: The Career of Wilhelm Egon von Fürstenberg (1629–1704)* (Athens, Ga., 1978).

O'DONNELL, H., *La fuerza de desembarco de la Gran Armada contra Inglaterra (1588)* (Madrid, 1989).

OERLE, I. H. A. VAN, *Leiden binnen en buiten de stadsvesten* (2 vols.; Leiden, 1975).

OESTREICH, G., *Neostoicism and the Early Modern State* (Cambridge, 1982).

OLDEWELT, W. F. H., 'De scheepvaartsstatistiek van Amsterdam in de 17e en 18e eeuw', *Jaarboek Amstelodamum*, 45 (1953), 114–51.

—— 'De beroepsstructuur van de bevolking der Hollandse stemhebbende steden volgens de kohieren van de familiegelden van 1674, 1715 en 1742', *ESHJ* 25 (1989), 167–248.

OOSTERHOFF, F. G., *Leicester and the Netherlands, 1586–1587* (Utrecht, 1988).

OP 'T HOF, W. J., 'De Nadere Reformatie in Zeeland', in A. Wiggers *et al.* (eds.) *Rond de kerk in Zeeland* (Delft, 1991), 37–82.

—— 'De godsdienstige ligging van Johan de Brune', in P. J. Verkruijsse *et al.* (eds.), *Johan de Brune de Oude (1588–1658)* (Middelburg, 1990), 26–53.

OSTEN SACKEN, C. VON DER, *El Escorial. Estudio iconológico* (n.p. 1984).

OTTENHEYM, K. A., *Philips Vingboons (1607–1678), Architect* (Zutphen, 1989).

OUDENDIJK, J. K., *Johan de Witt en de zeemacht* (Amsterdam, 1944).

OUVRÉ, H., *Aubéry du Maurier. Étude sur l'histoire de la France et de la Hollande, 1566–1636* (Paris, 1853).

OVERDIEP, G., *De Groninger schansenkrijg (1589–94)* (Groningen, 1970).

OVERMEER, W. P. J., *De hervorming te Haarlem* (Haarlem, 1904).

OZINGA, M. D., *De Protestantsche kerkenbouw in Nederland van hervorming tot franschen tijd* (Amsterdam, 1929).

PALACIOS PRECIADO, J., *La trata de negros por Cartagena de Indias* (Tunja, 1973).

PANGE, J. DE, *Charnacé et l'alliance franco-hollandaise* (Paris, 1905).

PARAVACINI, W., 'Expansion et intégration. La noblesse des Pays-Bas à la cour de Philippe le Bon', *BMGN* 95 (1980), 298–314.

PARKER, G., *The Army of Flanders and the Spanish Road, 1567–1659* (Cambridge, 1972).

—— *The Dutch Revolt* (London, 1977).

—— *The Thirty Years' War* (London, 1984).

—— *The Military Revolution* (Cambridge, 1988).

PATER, J. C. H. DE, *Maurits en Oldenbarnevelt in den strijd om het Twaalfjarig Bestand* (Amsterdam, 1940).

—— 'Leicester en Overijssel', *TvG* 64 (1951), 245–76.

PATHUIS, A., 'Het handschrift "Ommelands eer" ', *AGKN* 7 (1965), 1–110.

PAUWELS, J. L., *Verzamelde opstellen* (Assen, 1965).

PEER, A. J. J. M. VAN, 'Drie collecties schilderijen van Jan Vermeer', *Oud-Holland*, 72 (1957), 92–103.

PERCIVAL-PRESCOTT, W., 'The Art of the Van de Veldes', in *The Art of the Van de Veldes* (National Maritime Museum, London, 1982), 23–32.

PETTEGREE, A., *Emden and the Dutch Revolt* (Oxford, 1992).

PHILIPS, J. F. R., 'Enige aanduidingen omtrent de bevolkingsontwikkeling . . . in het gebied van de huidige provincie Nederlands Limburg', *Jaarboek van het sociaal-historisch centrum voor Limburg*, 20 (1975), 1–47.

PIRENNE, L. P. L., *'s-Hertogenbosch tussen Atrecht en Utrecht (1576–79)* (Tongerlo, 1959).

PLAAT, G. VAN DER, 'Lieuwe van Aitzema's kijk op het stadhouderschap in de Republiek (1652–1669) en de crisis van 1650', *BMGN* 103 (1988), 341–72.

PLANTENGA, J. H., *L'Architecture religieuse dans l'ancien duché de Brabant (1598–1713)* (The Hague, 1926).

PLOOS, J. J. A., 'Adriaan Ploos van Amstel (1585–1639)', *Jaarboek Oud-Utrecht* (1980), 43–94.

POELHEKKE, J. J., *Geen blijder maer in tachtigh jaer. Verspreide studien* (Zutphen, 1973).

—— *Frederik Hendrik, Prins van Oranje* (Zutphen, 1978).

POL, F. VAN DER, *De Reformatie te Kampen* (Kampen, 1990).

POL, L. C. VAN DE, 'Beeld en werkelijkheid van de prostitutie in de zeventiende eeuw', in G. Hekma and H. Roodenburg (eds.), *Soete minne en helsche boosheit. Seksuele voorstellingen in Nederland, 1300–1850* (Nijmegen, 1988), 109–44.

POLASKY, J., 'The Success of a Counter-Revolution in Revolutionary Europe: The Brabant Revolution of 1789', *TvG* 102 (1989), 413–21.

POLISENSKY, J., *Tragic Triangle: The Netherlands, Spain and Bohemia, 1617–21* (Prague, 1991).

POLLENTIER, F., *De admiraliteit en de oorlog ter zee onder de Aartshertogen (1591–1609)* (Brussels, 1972).

POLMAN, P., *Katholiek Nederland in de achttiende eeuw* (3 vols.; Hilversum, 1968).

PONT, J. W., *Geschiedenis van het Lutheranisme in de Nederlanden tot 1618* (Haarlem, 1911).

POORT, M., 'English Garrisons in the United Provinces 1585–1616', in Bannatyne, *The Dutch in Crisis, 1585–1588*.

POPKIN, J. D., 'Print Culture in the Netherlands on the Eve of the Revolution', in Jacob and Mijnhardt, *The Dutch Republic in the Eighteenth Century*, 273–91.

POPKIN, R. H., *The History of Scepticism from Erasmus to Spinoza* (Berkeley/Los Angeles, 1979).

—— *Isaac La Peyrère (1596–1676)* (Leiden, 1987).

—— 'Some Aspects of Jewish–Christian Interchanges in Holland and England, 1640–1700', in J. van den Berg and E. G. E. van der Wall, *Jewish–Christian Relations in the Seventeenth Century* (Dordrecht, 1988), 3–32.

—— *The Third Force in Seventeenth-Century Thought* (Leiden, 1992).

PORTA, A., *Joan en Gerrit Corver. De politieke macht van Amsterdam, 1702–48* (Assen, 1975).

POST, R. R., *Kerkelijke verhoudingen in Nederland voor de Reformatie* (Utrecht, 1954).

—— *The Modern Devotion* (Leiden, 1968).

POSTHUMUS, N. W., *De geschiedenis van de Leidsche lakenindustrie* (3 vols.; The Hague, 1908–39).

—— *An Inquiry into the History of Prices in Holland* (2 vols.; Leiden, 1946–64).

POSTMA, F., 'Viglius van Aytta en Joachim Hopperus', *BMGN* 102 (1987), 29–43.

—— 'Nieuw licht op een oude zaak: de oprichting van de nieuwe bisdommen in 1559', *TvG* 103 (1990), 10–27.

POSTMA, J. M., *The Dutch in the Atlantic Slave Trade 1600–1815* (Cambridge, 1990).

POT, G. R. M., 'Tussen medelijden en spaarzaamheid. De regenten van het Leidse huiszittenhuis, 1700–95', *Holland*, 20 (1988), 65–85.

POT, J., *Het beleg van Zierikzee* (Leiden, 1925).

PRAK, M. R., *Gezeten burgers. De elite in een Hollandse stad, Leiden 1700–80* (n.p. 1985).

—— 'Burgers in beweging. Ideaal en werkelijkheid van de onlusten te Leiden in 1748', *BMGN* 106 (1991), 365–93.

—— 'Citizen Radicalism and Democracy in the Dutch Republic: The Patriot Movement of the 1780s', *Theory and Society*, 20 (1991), 73–102.

PRAKASH, O. *The Dutch East India Company and the Economy of Bengal, 1630–1720* (Princeton NJ, 1985).

PRICE, J. L., *Culture and Society in the Dutch Republic during the Seventeenth Century* (London, 1974).

—— 'William III, England and the Balance of Power in Europe', *Groniek*, 101 (1988), 67–78.

—— *Holland and the Dutch Republic in the Seventeenth Century* (Oxford, 1994).

PUT, E. ' "Het fundament van eene welgeregelde republique". De Antwerpse zondagsscholen in de 17e eeuw', *De Zeventiende Eeuw*, 5 (1989), 11–20.

RAA, F. J. G. TEN, and BAS, F. DE, *Het Staatsche leger, 1568–1795* (11 vols.; Breda/The Hague, 1911–50).

RACHFAHL, F., *Wilhelm von Oranien und der Niederländische Aufstand* (3 vols.; Halle, 1906–24).

RADEMAKER, C. S. M., 'Scriverius and Grotius', *Quaerendo*, 7 (1977), 46–57.

—— *Life and Work of Gerardus Joannes Vossius (1577–1649)* (Assen, 1981).

RAMSAY, G. D., *The Queen's Merchants and the Revolt of the Netherlands* (Manchester, 1986).

RATELBAND, K., 'Inleiding' to *Reizen naar West-Afrika van Pieter van den Broeke, 1605–14* (The Hague, 1950).

REES, O. VAN, *Verhandeling over de 'Aanwijsing der Politike Gronden'* . . . *van Pieter de la Court* (Utrecht, 1851).

REITSMA, R., *Centrifugal and Centripetal Forces in the Early Dutch Republic: The States of Overijssel, 1566–1600* (Amsterdam, 1982).

REX, W., *Essays on Pierre Bayle and Religious Controversy* (The Hague, 1965).

REIJNDERS, C., *Van 'Joodsche Natiën' tot joodse Nederlanders* (Amsterdam, 1970).

—— 'Joden en overheid in het 18-eeuwse Naarden', *Studia Rosenthaliana*, 6 (1972), 76–85.

RIDDER-SYMOENS, H. DE, 'Buitenlandse studenten aan de Franeker universiteit, 1585–1811', in G. Th. Jensma *et al.* (eds.), *Universiteit te Franeker, 1585–1811*, 73–89.

RIETBERGEN, P. J. A. N., *De eerste landvoogd Pieter Both (1568–1615, gouverneur-generaal van Nederlands-Indië)* (2 vols.; Zutphen, 1987).

—— ' 's-Werelds Schouwtoneel. Oorlog, Politiek en Economie in noord-west Europa ten tijde van Willem III', in A. G. H. Bachrach *et al.* (eds.), *Willem III De Stadhouder-koning en zijn tijd* (Amsterdam, 1988), 51–87.

—— 'A Fateful Alliance?', in Israel (ed.), *The Anglo-Dutch Moment*, 463–79.

RIJN, G. VAN, *Atlas van Stolk. Katalogus* (9 vols.; Amsterdam, 1895).

RODRÍGUEZ-SALGADO, M. J., *The Changing Face of Empire: Charles V, Philip II and Habsburg Authority, 1551–1559* (Cambridge, 1988).

RODRÍGUEZ VILLA, A., *Ambrosio Spínola, primer marqués de los Balbases* (Madrid, 1905).

ROEGIERS, J., 'De Jansenistische achtergronden van P. F. de Neny's streven naar een "Belgische Kerk" ', *BMGN* 91 (1976), 429–54.

ROESSINGH, H. K., 'Het Veluwse inwonertal, 1526–1947', AAG *Bijdragen*, 11 (1964), 126–50.

—— 'Tobacco Growing in Holland in the Seventeenth and Eighteenth Centuries', *Acta Historiae Neerlandicae*, 11 (1978), 18–54.

ROGGE, H. C., *Caspar Janszoon Coolhaes* (2 vols.; Amsterdam, 1856–8).

—— *Johannes Wttenbogaert en zijn tijd* (3 vols.; Amsterdam, 1874–6).

ROGIER, L. J., *Geschiedenis van het katholicisme in Noord-Nederland in de 16e en 17e eeuw* (3 vols.; Amsterdam, 1945–7).

—— *Paulus Buys en Leicester* (Nijmegen, 1948).

—— 'De Ware Vrijheid als oligarchie (1672–1747)', in G. A. M. Beekelaar *et al.* (eds.), *Vaderlands Verleden in Veelvoud* (The Hague, 1975), 292–311.

ROLDANUS, C. W., *Coenraad van Beuningen, staatsman en libertijn* (The Hague, 1931).

ROLDANUS, C. W., 'Adriaen Paets, een Republikein uit de nadagen', *TvG* 50 (1935), 134–66.

ROOD, W., *Comenius and the Low Countries* (Utrecht, 1970).

ROODEN, P. VAN, *Constantijn l'Empereur (1591–1648)* (Leiden, 1985).

—— and WESSELIUS, J. W., 'The Early Enlightenment and Judaism', *Studia Rosenthaliana*, 21 (1987), 140–53.

ROODENBURG, H., *Onder censuur. De kerkelijke tucht in de gereformeerde gemeente van Amsterdam, 1578–1700* (Hilversum, 1990).

ROORDA, D. J., 'Prins Willem III en het Utrechtse regeringsreglement', in *Van Standen tot Staten. 600 Jaar Staten van Utrecht* (Utrecht, 1975), 91–133.

—— *Partij en factie* (Groningen, 1978).

—— 'The Peace of Nijmegen', in J. A. H. Bots (ed.), *The Peace of Nijmegen, 1676–1679* (Amsterdam, 1980), 17–28.

—— 'Le secret du Prince. Monarchale tendenties in de Republiek, 1672–1702', in A. J. C. M. Gabriëls *et al.* (eds.), *Rond Prins en patriciaat. Verspreide opstellen* (Weesp, 1984), 172–92.

ROS, F. U., *Rennenberg en de Groningse Malcontenten* (Assen, 1964).

ROSENBERG, J., *Rembrandt: Life and Work* (London, 1964).

ROSENFELD, P., 'The Provincial Governors from the Minority of Charles V to the Revolt', *Standen en Landen*, 17 (1959), 1–63.

ROWEN, H. H., *The Low Countries in Early Modern Times* (London, 1972).

—— *John de Witt: Grand Pensionary of Holland* (Princeton, NJ, 1978).

—— *The Princes of Orange* (Cambridge, 1988).

—— *The Rhyme and Reason of Politics in Early Modern Europe: Collected Essays*, ed. G. E. Harline (Dordrecht, 1992).

ROYALTON-KISCH, M., *Adriaen van de Venne's Album* (London, 1988).

ROYEN, P. C. VAN, *Zeevarenden op de koopvaardijvloot omstreeks 1700* (Amsterdam, 1987).

RUMMEL, E., 'Nameless Critics in Erasmus' Annotations on the N.T.T', *Bibliothèque d'Humanisme et Renaissance*, 48 (1986), 41–57.

RUSSELL, M. A., 'Hendrik Vroom and the Origins of Dutch Marine Painting' (Ph.D. thesis, University of Maryland, 1983).

—— 'Seascape into Landscape', in Ch. Brown (ed.), *Dutch Landscape: The Early Years* (London, 1986), 63–71.

SALOMONS, A. F., 'De rol van de Amsterdamse burgerbeweging in de wetsverzetting van 1672', *BMGN* 106 (1991), 198–219.

SAS, N. C. F. VAN, 'Vaderlandsliefde, nationalisme en vaderlands gevoel in Nederland, 1770–1813', *TvG* 102 (1989), 471–95.

—— 'The Patriot Revolution: New Perspectives', in Jacob and Mijnhardt, *The Dutch Republic in the Eighteenth Century*, 91–122.

SASSEN, F., *Geschiedenis van de wijsbegeerte in Nederland* (Amsterdam, 1959).

—— *Het wijsgerig onderwijs aan de Illustre School te Breda, 1646–69* (Amsterdam, 1962).

—— *Het wijsgerig onderwijs aan de Illustre School te 's-Hertogenbosch (1636–1810)* (Amsterdam, 1963).

SCHAIK, A. H. M. VAN, 'Johan Christiaan van Erkel (1654–1734) en de vrijheid der Bataafse kerk', *AGKN* 17 (1975), 131–202.

SCHAMA, S., *Patriots and Liberators; Revolution in the Netherlands 1780–1813* (London, 1977).

—— 'The Enlightenment in the Netherlands', in R. Porter and M. Teich (eds.), *The Enlightenment in National Context* (Cambridge, 1981), 54–71.

—— *The Embarrassment of Riches* (London, 1987).

SCHEERDER, J., *De Beeldenstorm* (Bussum, 1974).

SCHENKEVELD-VAN DER DUSSEN, M. A., 'Inleiding' to A. Pels, *Gebruik en misbruik des toneels* (Culemborg, 1978).

SCHEPPER, H. DE, 'Vorstelijke ambtenarij en bureaukratisering in regering en en gewesten van 's konings Nederlanden (16e–17e eeuw)', *TvG* 90 (1977), 358–77.

—— 'De Grote Raad van Mechelen', *BMGN* 93 (1978), 389–411.

—— 'De burgelijke overheden en hun permanente kaders 1480–1579', in *NAGN*, v. 312–49.

—— *Belgium Nostrum, 1500–1650* (Antwerp, 1987).

SCHERFT, P., 'Philips Willem, een displaced person', *Oranje-Nassau Museum Jaarboek* (1980), 27–48.

SCHIERBEEK, A., *Jan Swammerdam (1637–80)* (Lochem, 1947).

—— *Antoni van Leeuwenhoek* (Lochem, 1950).

SCHILFGAARDE, A. P. VAN, *De graven van Limburg Stirum en de geschiedenis hunner bezittingen* (3 vols.; Assen, 1961).

SCHILLING, H., 'Bürgerkämpfe in Aachen zu Beginn des 17. Jahrhunderts', *Zeitschrift für historische Forschung*, 1 (1974), 175–231.

—— 'Die Politische Elite nordwestdeutscher Städte in den religiösen Auseinandersetzungen des 16. Jahrhunderts', in W. J. Mommsen (ed.), *Stadtbürgertum und Adel in der Reformation* (Stuttgart, 1979), 235–308.

—— 'Calvinismus und Freiheitsrechte', *BMGN* 102 (1987), 403–34.

—— 'Die Konfessionalisierung im Reich. Religiöser und gesellschaftlicher Wandel in Deutschland zwischen 1555 und 1620', *Historische Zeitschrift*, 246 (1988), 1–45.

SCHLOSS, CHR., 'Early Italianate Genre Paintings by Jan Weenix', *Oud-Holland*, 97 (1983), 69–97.

—— *Travel, Trade and Temptation: The Dutch Italianate Harbour Scene (1640–80)* (Ann Arbor, Mich., 1982).

SCHMAL, H., 'Patterns of De-Urbanization in the Netherlands between 1650 and 1850', in H. van der Wee (ed.), *The Rise and Decline of Urban Industries in Italy and the Low Countries* (Leuven, 1988), 287–306.

SCHNEIDER, A. VON, *Caravaggio und die Niederländer* (Amsterdam, 1967).

SCHNEPPEN, H., *Niederländische Universitäten und deutsche Geistesleben* (Münster, 1960).

SCHOEK, R. J., 'Agricola and Erasmus', in Akkerman and Vanderjagt (eds.), *Rodolphus Agricola Phrisius*, 181–8.

—— *Erasmus of Europe* (Edinburgh, 1990).

SCHÖFFER, I., 'The Batavian Myth during the sixteenth and seventeenth centuries', in I. Schöffer, *Veelvormig verleden* (Amsterdam, 1987).

SCHOLLIERS, E., 'De materiële verschijningsvorm van de armoede voor de industriële revolutie', *TvG* 88 (1975), 451–67.

—— 'De eerste schade van de scheiding', in J. Craebeckx *et al.* (eds.), *1585: op gescheiden wegen* (Leuven, 1988).

SCHREINER, J., 'Die Niederländer und die norwegische Holzausfuhr im 17. Jahrhundert', *TvG* 49 (1934), 303–28.

SCHRENK, G., *Gottesreich und Bund im älteren Protestantismus vornehmlich bei Johannes Coccejus* (Gütersloh, 1923).

SCHRYVER, R. DE, *Jan van Brouchoven, Graaf van Bergeyck, 1644–1725* (Brussels, 1965).

SCHULTE NORDHOLT, J. W., *The Dutch Republic and American Independence* (1979; Chapel Hill, NC, 1982).

SCHULTEN, C. M., and SCHULTEN, J. W. M., *Het leger in de zeventiende eeuw* (Bussum, 1969).

SCHUTTE, G. J., *De Nederlandse Patriotten en de koloniën* (Groningen, 1974).

—— 'De Republiek der Verenigde Nederlanden, 1702–1780', in I. Schöffer *et al.* (eds.), *De Lage Landen van 1500 tot 1780* (1978; Amsterdam, 1991), 269–316.

—— 'Willem IV en Willem V', in Tamse (ed.), *Nassau en Oranje*, 189–228.

—— *Een Hollandse dorpssamenleving in de late achttiende eeuw* (Franeker, 1989).

—— 'Gereformeerden en de Nederlandse revolutie in de achttiende eeuw', *TvG* 102 (1989), 496–516.

SCHWARTZ, G., *Rembrandt: His Life, his Paintings* (Harmondsworth, 1985).

—— *The Dutch World of Painting* (Maarssen, 1986).

SCOTT, H. M., 'Sir Joseph Yorke, Dutch Politics and the Origins of the Fourth Anglo-Dutch War', *Historical Journal*, 31 (1988), 571–89.

SCREECH, M. A., *Erasmus: Ecstasy and the Praise of Folly* (1980; 2nd edn. London, 1988).

SEELIGMANN, S., 'Het Marranen-probleem uit oekonomisch oogpunt', *Bijdragen . . . van het Genootschap voor Joodsche wetenschap in Nederland*, 3 (1925), 101–36.

SEGAL, S., *A Prosperous Past: The Sumptuous Still Life in the Netherlands, 1600–1700* (The Hague, 1989).

SELLIN, P. R., *Daniel Heinsius and Stuart England* (Leiden, 1968).

SICKENGA, J., *Het Hof van Friesland gedurende de zeventiende eeuw* (Leiden, 1869).

SIMON, I., 'Hendrik Niclaes und das "Huys der Liefde"', in D. Hofman (ed.), *Gedenkschrift für Wilhelm Foerste* (Cologne, 1970), 432–53.

SIMONI, A. E. C., '1598: An Exchange of Dutch Pamphlets and their Repercussions in England', in Th. Hermans and R. Salverda (eds.), *From Revolt to Riches* (London, 1993), 129–62.

SLEE, J. C. VAN, *De Rijnsburger Collegianten* (1895; Utrecht, 1980).

—— *De Illustre School te Deventer, 1630–1878* (The Hague, 1916).

SLICHER VAN BATH, B. H., *Een samenleving onder spanning* (Assen, 1957).

—— (ed.), *Geschiedenis van Overijssel* (Deventer, 1970).

SLIVE, S., *Jacob van Ruisdael* (New York, 1981).

SLOT, B. J., *Abel Tasman en de ontdekking van Nieuw Zeeland* (Amsterdam, 1992).

SLOTHOUWER, D. F., *De paleizen van Frederik Hendrik* (Leiden, 1945).

SLUIJTER, E. J., *De 'heydensche fabulen' in de Noordnederlandse schilderkunst, 1590–1670* (Leiden, 1986).

—— *Leidse fijnschilders* (Zwolle, n.d.).

SLUIS, J., VAN, *Herman Alexander Röell* (Leeuwarden, 1988).

SLUITER, E., 'Dutch–Spanish Rivalry in the Caribbean Area, 1594–1609', *Hispanic American Historical Review*, 28 (1948), 165–96.

SMID, M., *Ostfriesische Kirchengeschichte* (Pewsum, 1974).

SMIT, E. J. TH., 'Neercassel en Huissen (1675–79)', *AGKN* 17 (1975), 203–12.

SMIT, F. R. H., *Bestuursinstellingen en ambtenaren van de Landschap Drenthe (1600–1750)* (Assen, 1984).

SMIT, J., 'Hagepreeken en beeldenstorm te Delft 1566–7', *BMHG* 45 (1924), 206–50.

SMIT, J. G., 'De ambtenaren van de centrale overheidsorganen der Republiek in het begin van de zeventiende eeuw', *TvG* 90 (1977), 378–90.

SMIT, W. A. P., *Van Pascha tot Noah. Een verkenning van Vondels drama's* (3 vols.; Zwolle, 1956–62).

SMITH, G. L., *Religion and Trade in New Netherland* (Ithaca, NY, 1973).

SNELDERS, H. A. M., 'Antoni van Leeuwenhoek's Mechanistic View of the World', in L. C. Palm and H. A. M. Snelders (eds.), *Antoni van Leeuwenhoek, 1632–1723* (Amsterdam, 1982), 57–78.

SOLY, H., 'Economische ontwikkeling en sociale politiek in Europa tijdens de overgang van middeleeuwen naar nieuwe tijden', *TvG* 88 (1975), 584–97.

SONNINO, P., *Louis XIV and the Origins of the Dutch War* (Cambridge, 1988).

SPAANS, J., *Haarlem na de Reformatie* (The Hague, 1989).

SPIERENBURG, P., *Judicial Violence in the Dutch Republic* (Amsterdam, 1978).

SPIERTZ, M. P. G., 'De ontwikkelingsgang van de katholieke missie in Friesland, 1606–89', *AGKN* 21 (1979), 262–92.

—— 'Achtergronden van het Breve Memoriale een geruchtmakend anti-Jansenistisch geschrift uit 1697', *AGKN* 26 (1984), 180–207.

—— 'Priest and Layman in a Minority Church: The Roman Catholic Church in the North Netherlands, 1592–1686', *Studies in Church History*, 26 (1989), 287–301.

SPIERTZ, M. P. G., 'De kerkeraad van Zutphen in beraad (1591–1621)', in G. Ackermans *et al.* (eds.), *Kerk in beraad* (Nijmegen, 1991), 177–93.

—— 'Jansenisme in en rond de Nederlanden 1640–1690', *Trajecta*, 1 (1992), 114–67.

—— 'Anti-jansenisme en jansenisme in de Nederlanden in de achttiende en negentiende eeuw', *Trajecta*, 1 (1992), 233–51.

—— 'De katholieke geestelijke leiders en de wereldlijke overheid in de Republiek der Zeven Provincien', *Trajecta*, 2 (1993), 3–20.

—— *Reformatie en herleving van het katholicisme in Nijmegen (1591–1623)* (Nijmegen, 1993).

SPIJKER, W. VAN 'T, 'De acta van de Synode van Middelburg (1581)', in J. P. van Dooren (ed.), *De nationale Synode te Middelburg* (Middelburg, 1981), 64–127.

—— 'Voetius practicus', in J. van Oort *et al.* (eds.), *De onbekende Voetius* (Kampen, 1989), 242–56.

SPRUNGER, K. L., *Dutch Puritanism: A History of the English and Scottish Churches in the Netherlands* (Leiden, 1982).

SPRUNGER, M., 'Faillissementen. Een aspect van geestelijke tucht bij de Water-lands-doopsgezinde gemeente te Amsterdam in de zeventiende eeuw', *Doops-gezinde Bijdragen*, 17 (1991), 101–30.

SPRUYT, B. J., 'Humanisme, evangelisme en Reformatie in de Nederlanden, 1520–30', in W. de Graaf *et al.* (eds.), *Reformatie in meervoud* (Kampen, 1991), 26–54.

SPUFFORD, P., *Monetary Problems and Policies in the Burgundian Netherlands 1433–1496* (Leiden, 1970).

STECHOW, W., *Dutch Landscape Painting in the Seventeenth Century* (1966; Oxford, 1981).

STEEN, CH., *A Chronicle of Conflict: Tournai, 1559–1567* (Utrecht, 1985).

STEUR, A. G. VAN DER, 'Johan van Duivenvoirde en Woude (1547–1610), heer van Warmond, admiraal van Holland', *Hollandse Studien*, 7 (1975), 179–272.

STOLS, E., *De Spaanse Brabanders of de handelsbetrekkingen der Zuiderlijke Nederlanden met de Iberische wereld, 1598–1648* (Brussels, 1971).

—— 'Handel, geld- en bankwezen in de Zuidelijke Nederlanden, 1580–1650', in *NAGN* vii. 128–36.

STORK-PENNING, J. G., *Het grote werk* (Groningen, 1958).

STRAUB, E., *Pax et Imperium* (Paderborn, 1980).

STRIEN, C. D. VAN, *British Travellers in Holland during the Stuart Period* (Leiden, 1993).

STRUICK, J. E. A. L., *Gelre en Habsburg, 1492–1528* (Arnhem, 1960).

SUIJKERBUIJK, J. A. S. M., *Archief van Anthonie van der Heim, 1737–46* (The Hague, 1983).

SUTTON, P., *Pieter de Hooch* (Oxford, 1980).

SWART, K. W., *The Miracle of the Dutch Republic as Seen in the Seventeenth Century* (Inaugural lecture; London, 1969).

—— *William the Silent and the Revolt of the Netherlands* (London, 1978).

—— 'Wat bewoog Willem van Oranje de strijd tegen de Spaanse overheersing aan te binden', *BMGN* 99 (1984), 554–72.

—— 'Willem de Zwijger', in Tamse (ed.), *Nassau en Oranje*, 47–82.

—— *Willem van Oranje en de Nederlandse Opstand 1572–1584* (The Hague, 1994).

SWETSCHINSKI, D. M., 'The Portuguese Jewish Merchants of Seventeenth-Century Amsterdam: A Social Profile' (Brandeis University Ph.D. thesis, 1979).

SWILLENS, P. T. A., *Jacob van Campen. Schilder en bouwmeester, 1595–1657* (Assen, 1961).

SYMCOX, G., 'Louis XIV and the Outbreak of the Nine Years War', in R. Hatton (ed.), *Louis XIV and Europe* (London, 1976), 179–212.

SYPESTEYN, J. W. VAN, *Geschiedkundige bijdragen* (2 vols.; The Hague, 1864–5).

TAMSE, C. A. (ed.), *Nassau en Oranje* (Alphen aan de Rijn, 1979).

TAVERNE, E., *In 't land van belofte* (Maarssen, 1978).

TERWEN, J. J., 'De ontwerpgeschiedenis van de Marekerk te Leiden', *Opus Musivum* (Assen, 1964), 231–56.

—— and OTTENHEYM, K. A., *Pieter Post (1608–1669)* (Zutphen, 1993).

TEX, J. DEN, *Oldenbarnevelt* (5 vols.; Haarlem, 1960–72).

—— *Oldenbarnevelt* (English version, 2 vols.; Cambridge, 1973).

—— 'De Staten in Oldenbarnevelt's tijd', in *Van Standen tot Staten. 600 jaar Staten van Utrecht (1375–1975)* (Utrecht, 1975), 51–89.

THEISSEN, J. S., *Centraal gezag en Friesche vrijheid* (Groningen, 1907).

—— *De regering van Karel V in de Noordelijke Nederlanden* (Amsterdam, 1922).

THEUNISZ, J., *Carolus Clusius* (Amsterdam, 1939).

THIELEN, TH. A. M., *Geschiedenis van de enclave Groenlo-Lichtenvoorde* (Zutphen, 1966).

THIJS, A. K. L., 'De nijverheid te Antwerpen voor en na 1585', in f. de Nave (ed.), *Antwerpen en de scheiding der Nederlanden* (Antwerp, 1986), 79–83.

—— *Van Geuzenstad tot katholiek bolwerk* (n.p. 1990).

THIJSSEN-SCHOUTE, C. L., 'Le Cartésianisme aux Pays-Bays', in E. J. Dijksterhuis *et al.* (eds.), *Descartes et le cartésianisme hollandais* (Paris/Amsterdam, 1950), 183–260.

—— *Nederlands Cartesianisme* (1954; Utrecht, 1989).

—— *Uit de Republiek der letteren. Elf studien* (The Hague, 1967).

THOMAS, W., 'De mythe van de Spaanse Inquisitie in de Nederlanden van de zestiende eeuw', *BMGN* 105 (1990), 325–53.

TIDEMAN, J., *De Remonstrantsche broederschap* (Haarlem, 1847).

TILMANS, K., *Aurelius en de Divisiekroniek* (Hilversum, 1988).

—— 'Cornelius Aurelius (*c.*1460–1531) praeceptor Erasmi', in Akkerman and Vanderjagt, *Rodolphus Agricola Phrisius*, 200–10.

TOEBACK, P., 'Het kerkelijk-godsdienstige en culturele leven binnen het noordwestelijk deel van het hertogdom Brabant (1587–1609)', *Trajecta*, 1 (1992), 124–43.

TOPS, N. J., *Groll in de zeventiende en achttiende eeuw* (Groenlo, 1992).

TRACY, J. D., *A Financial Revolution in the Habsburg Netherlands* (Berkeley/Los Angeles, 1985).

—— *Holland under Habsburg Rule, 1506–1566* (Berkeley/Los Angeles, 1990).

TREVOR-ROPER, H. R., *The European Witch-Craze* (Harmondsworth, Middx., 1969).

TRIMP, J. C., *Jodocus van Lodensteyn. Predikant en dichter* (Kampen, 1987).

TROOST, W., 'William III, Brandenburg and the Construction of the Anti-French Coalition, 1672–88', in Israel (ed.), *The Anglo-Dutch Moment*, 299–344.

—— and WOLTJER, J. J., 'Brielle in hervormingstijd', BMGN (1972), 307–53.

TROOSTENBURG DE BRUYN, C. A. L. VAN, *Hervormde kerk in Nederlandsch Oost-Indië* (Arnhem, 1884).

TROSÉE, J. A. G. C., *Verraad van George van Lalaing, graaf van Rennenberg* ('s-Hertogenbosch, 1894).

TUCK, R., *Philosophy and Government, 1572–1651* (Cambridge, 1993).

TUKKER, C. A., *Classis van Dordrecht van 1573 tot 1609* (Leiden, 1965).

TÜMPEL, CHR., *Rembrandt. Kwadraat monografie* (Utrecht, 1992).

TURCK, M., 'Die Lakenhal in Leiden. Architektur als politisches Zeugnis', in Marsilje *et al.* (eds.), *Uit Leidse bron geleverd*, 401–6.

TURNBULL, G. H., *Hartlib, Dury and Comenius* (London, 1947).

UBACHS, J. H., *Twee heren, twee confessies. Maastricht, 1632–1673* (Assen, 1975).

UNGER, J. H. W., 'De standbeelden van Desiderius Erasmus', *Rotterdamsch Jaarboekje* (1890), 265–85.

UNGER, R. W., *Dutch Shipbuilding before 1800* (Assen, 1978).

—— 'Dutch Herring Technology and International Trade in the Seventeenth Century', *Journal of Economic History*, 40 (1980), 253–79.

—— 'Scheepvaart in de Noordelijke Nederlanden', in *NAGN* vi. 109–22.

UNGER, W. S., 'De publikatie der Sonttabellen voltooid', *TvG* 71 (1958), 147–205.

UYTVEN, R., VAN, 'Oudheid en middeleeuwen', in J. H. van Stuijvenberg (ed.), *De economische geschiedenis van Nederland* (Groningen, 1977), 1–48.

—— 'Crisis als cesuur, 1482–1494', in *NAGN* v. 420–35.

—— 'Splendour or Wealth? Art and Economy in the Burgundian Netherlands', *Transactions of the Cambridge Bibliographical Society*, 10 (1992), 101–24.

VALVEKENS, P. E., *De Inquisitie in de Nederlanden der zestiende eeuw* (Brussels, 1949).

VANDENBOSSCHE, H., *Adriaan Koerbagh en Spinoza*, Mededelingen vanwege het Spinozahuis, 38 (Leiden, 1978).

VANDENBROEKE, C. V., and VANDERPIJPEN, W., 'The Problem of the "Agricultural Revolution" in Flanders and in Belgium: Myth or Reality', in H. van der Wee and E. van Cauwenberghe (eds.), *Productivity of Land and Agricultural Innovation in the Low Countries (1250–1800)* (Leuven, 1978).

VANPAEMEL, G., 'Kerk en wetenschap: de strijd tegen het cartesianisme aan de Leuvense universiteit', *De zeventiende eeuw*, 5 (1989), 182–9.

VEEN, J. S. VAN, 'De overgang op kerkelijk gebied te Nijmegen in 1578 en 1579', *NAK* 16 (1921), 172–93.

VEENENDAAL, A. J., *Het Engels-Nederlands condominium in de Zuidelijke Nederlanden tijdens de Spaanse Successieoorlog, 1706–1716* (Utrecht, 1945).

—— (ed.), *Johan van Oldenbarnevelt. Bescheiden betreffende zijn staatkundig beleid en zijn familie* (2 vols.; The Hague, 1962–7).

VEEZE, B. J., *De raad van de Prinsen van Oranje tijdens de minderjarigheid van Willem III (1650–68)* (Assen, 1932).

VELDMAN, I. M., 'Maarten van Heemskerck's visie op het geloof', *Bulletin van het Rijksmuseum*, 35 (1987), 193–210.

VELEMA, W. R. E., 'Revolutie, contrarevolutie en het stadhouderschap, 1780–1795', *TvG* 102 (1989), 517–33.

—— 'Elie Luzac and Two Dutch Revolutions', in Jacob and Mijnhardt, *The Dutch Republic in the Eighteenth Century*, 123–46.

VERCRUYSSE, J., *Voltaire et la Hollande* (Geneva, 1966).

—— 'La Fortune de Bernard Nieuwentyt en France au XVIIIe siècle et les notes marginales de Voltaire', *Studies on Voltaire and the Eighteenth Century*, 30 (1964), 223–46.

VERHEES-VAN MEER, J. TH. H., *De zeeuwse kaapvaart tijdens de Spaanse Successieoorlog 1702–13* (Middelburg, 1986).

VERHEYDEN, A. L. E., *Le Conseil des troubles. Liste des condamnés (1567–73)* (Brussels, 1961).

VERHOFSTAD, K. J. W., *De regering der Nederlanden in de jaren 1555–9* (Nijmegen, 1937).

VERMASEREN, B. A., 'Sasbout Vosmeer en het voormalige kapitel van Sion in 1592', *AGKN* 23 (1981), 189–219.

VERMAUT, J., 'Structural Transformation in a Textile Centre: Bruges from the Sixteenth to the Nineteenth Century', in H. van der Wee (ed.), *The Rise and Decline of Urban Industries in Italy and the Low Countries* (Leuven, 1988), 187–20.

VERMIJ, R. H., 'De Staten van Holland en de adel in de periode van de Opstand', *Holland*, 18 (1986), 215–25.

—— 'Het copernicanisme in de Republiek', *TvG* 106 (1993), 349–67.

VERSTEGEN, S. W., *Gegoede ingezetenen. Jonkers en geerfden op de Veluwe, 1650–1830* (Arnhem, 1990).

VET, J. J. V. M. DE, *Pieter Rabus (1660–1702)* (Amsterdam, 1980).

VIJLBRIEF, I., *Van anti-aristocratie tot democratie* (Amsterdam, 1950).

VISSER, C. CH. G., *Luther's geschriften in de Nederlanden tot 1546* (Assen, 1969).

VISSER, H. B., *De geschiedenis van den sabbatsstrijd onder de gereformeerden in de zeventiende eeuw* (Utrecht, 1939).

VISSER, J. C., 'Dichtheid van de bevolking in de laat-middeleeuws stad', *Historisch Geografisch Tijdschrift*, 3 (1985), 10–22.

VOET, L. *Antwerp: The Golden Age* (Antwerp, 1973).

VOETEN, P., 'Antwerpens handel over Duinkerken tijdens het Twaalfjarig Bestand', *Bijdragen tot de geschiedenis inzonderheid van het oud hertogdom Brabant*, 39 (1956), 67–78.

VOOGT, N. J. J. DE, *De Doelistenbeweging te Amsterdam in 1748* (Utrecht, 1914).

VOOGT, W. I. DE, *Geschiedenis van het muntwezen der Vereenigde Nederlanden* (Amsterdam, 1874).

VOOYS, C. G. N. DE, *Geschiedenis van de Nederlandse taal* (Groningen, 1952).

VOS, P. H. D. DE, *De vroedschap van Zierikzee van de tweede helft der 16e eeuw tot 1795* (Middelburg, 1931).

VRANKRIJKER, A. C. J. DE, *De motiveering van onzen opstand* (Nijmegen, 1933).

—— *De staatsleer van Hugo de Groot en zijn Nederlandsche tijdgenoten* (Nijmegen, 1937).

VREEDE, G. W., *Inleiding tot eene geschiedenis der Nederlandsche diplomatie* (3 vols.; Utrecht, 1856–61).

VRIELINK, J. C., 'Harderwijk in de Gelderse Plooierijen 1702–17', *Herderewich-kroniek*, 8 (1981), 1–46.

VRIES, B. W., *From Pedlars to Textile Barons* (Amsterdam, 1989).

VRIES, J. DE, *The Dutch Rural Economy in the Golden Age, 1500–1700* (New Haven, Conn., 1974).

—— 'An Inquiry into the Behaviour of Wages in the Dutch Republic and the Southern Netherlands', *Acta Historiae Neerlandicae*, 10 (1978), 79–97.

—— *Barges and Capitalism*, AAG *Bijdragen*, 21 (Wageningen, 1978).

—— *European Urbanization, 1500–1800* (London, 1984).

—— 'The Dutch Rural Economy and the Landscape', in Christopher Brown (ed.), *Dutch Landscape: The Early Years* (London, 1986), 79–86.

—— 'Art History', in Freedberg and de Vries (eds.), *Art in History, History in Art*, 249–84.

—— 'The Labour Market', in K. Davids and L. Noordegraaf (eds.), *The Dutch Economy in the Golden Age* (Amsterdam, 1993), 55–78.

VRIES, PH. DE, 'Christiaan Huygens entre Descartes et le siècle des lumières, *Theoretische Geschiedenis*, 6 (1979), 3–19.

VRIES, R. J. DE, *Enkhuizen, 1650–1850* (Amsterdam, 1987).

VRIJER, M. J. A. DE, *Henricus Regius* (The Hague, 1917).

WAARDT, H. DE, *Toverij en samenleving. Holland 1500–1800* (The Hague, 1991).

WADDINGTON, A., *La République des Provinces-Unies, la France, et les Pays-Bas espagnols, 1630–50* (2 vols.; Lyons, 1895–7).

WADE, I. O., *The Clandestine Organization and Diffusion of Philosophic Ideas in France from 1700 to 1750* (Princeton, NJ, 1938).

WAGENAAR, L. H., *Hervormer van Gelderland. Levensbeschrijving van Johannes Fontanus* (Kampen, 1898).

WAITE, G. K., *David Joris and Dutch Anabaptism 1524-1543* (Ontario, 1990).

WALL, E. G. E. VAN DER. *De mystieke chiliast Petrus Serrarius (1600-69) en zijn wereld* (Leiden, 1987).

—— 'Profetie en providentie: de Coccejanen en de vroege verlichting', in P. Bange *et al.* (eds.), *Kerk en Verlichting* (Zwolle, 1990), 29-37.

—— 'Orthodoxy and Scepticism in the early Dutch Enlightenment', in Popkin and Vanderjagt (eds.), *Scepticism and Irreligion* (Leiden, 1993), 121-41.

WANSINK, H., 'Holland and Six Allies: The Republic of the Seven United Provinces', *BN* 4 (1971), 133-55.

—— *Politieke wetenschappen aan de Leidse Universiteit, 1575-1650* (Utrecht, 1981).

WARNSINCK, J. C. M., *De vloot van de koning-stadhouder, 1689-90* (Amsterdam, 1934).

WATERBOLK, E. H., *Rond Viglius van Aytta* (Leeuwarden, 1980).

—— *Vigliana* (Groningen, 1975).

WEE, H. VAN DER, *The Growth of the Antwerp Market and the European Economy* (3 vols.; The Hague, 1963).

—— 'Handel in de Zuidelijke Nederlanden', in *NAGN* vi. 58-74.

—— 'Antwoord op een industrieele uitdaging. De Nederlandse steden tijdens de late middeleeuwen en nieuwe tijd', *TvG* 100 (1987), 169-84.

—— 'De Overgang van middeleeuwen naar Nieuwe Tijd', in I. Schöffer *et al.* (eds.), *De Lage Landen van 1500 tot 1780,* (1978; Amsterdam, 1991), 11-37.

—— 'Industrial Dynamics and the Process of Urbanization and De-urbanization in the Low Countries', in H. van der Wee (ed.), *The Rise and Decline of Urban Industries in Italy and the Low Countries* (Lenven, 1988), 328-75.

WEEVERS, TH., *Poetry of the Netherlands in its European Context, 1170-1930* (London, 1960).

WEILER, A. G., 'De betekenis van de Moderne Devotie voor de Europese cultuur', *Trajecta,* 1 (1992), 33-48.

WELLENS, R., *Les États Généraux des Pays Bas des origines à la fin du règne de Philippe le Beau (1464-1506)* (Heule, 1974).

WELTEN, J. B. V., *Hervormers aan de Oosterschelde* (Amsterdam, 1991).

WERNHAM, R. B., 'The Mission of Thomas Wilkes to the United Provinces', in J. Conway Davies (ed.), *Studies Presented to Sir Hilary Jenkinson* (Oxford, 1957), 423-55.

—— 'English Policy and the Revolt of the Netherlands', *BN* 1 (1960), 29-40.

WERTHEIM-GIJSE WEENINK, A. H., *Democratische bewegingen in Gelderland 1672-1795* (Amsterdam, 1973).

WERTHEIM-GIJSE WEENINK, A. H., *Burgers in verzet tegen regentenheerschappij. Onrust in Sticht en Oversticht 1703–6* (Amsterdam, 1976).

—— 'Een kwarteeuw burgerverzet in de beide Nederlanden (1678–1719)', *BMGN* 99 (1984), 408–34.

WESSEL, J. H., *De leerstellige strijd tusschen Nederlandsche Gereformeerden en Doopsgezinden in de zestiende eeuw* (Assen, 1945).

WESSELS, H. D., 'Ketterij in de graafschap, 1520–43', *Gelre*, 71 (1980), 51–80.

WESTERGAARD, W., *The Danish West Indies under Company Rule (1671–1754)* (New York, 1917).

WESTRA, F., *Nederlandse ingenieurs en de fortificatiewerken in het eerste tijdperk van de Tachtigjarige Oorlog, 1573–1604* (Alphen aan den Rijn, 1992).

WHALEY, J., *Religious Toleration and Social Change in Hamburg, 1529–1819* (Cambridge, 1985).

WHEELOCK, A. K., *Perspective, Optics and Delft Artists around 1650* (New York, 1977).

WIECHMANN, A., 'Van Academia naar Akademie', in A. Wiechmann and L. C. Palm (eds.), *Een elektriserend geleerde. Martinus van Marum (1750–1837)* (Haarlem, 1987), 33–66.

WIELE, J. VAN DER, 'De Inquisitierechtbank van Pieter Titelmans in de zestiende eeuw in Vlaanderen', *BMGN* 97 (1982), 19–63.

WIERSUM, E., *De gedwongen vereeniging van Stad en Lande in 1594* (Groningen, 1898).

WIJMINGA, P. J., *Festus Hommius* (Leiden, 1899).

WIJN, J. W., *Het krijgswezen in den tijd van Prins Maurits* (Utrecht, 1934).

—— *Het beleg van Haarlem* (1943; The Hague, 1982).

WIJNNE, J. A., *De geschillen over de afdanking van 't krijgsvolk in de Verenigde Nederlanden in de jaren 1649 en 1650* (Utrecht, 1885).

WIJSENBEEK-OLTHUIS, TH. F., *Achter de gevels van Delft* (Hilversum, 1987).

WILLEMSEN, R., *Enkhuizen tijdens de Republiek* (Hilversum, 1988).

WILSON, CH., *Queen Elizabeth and the Revolt of the Netherlands* (London, 1970).

—— *Profit and Power: A Study of England and the Dutch Wars* (1957; The Hague, 1978).

WINTER, P. J. VAN, *Westerwolde. Generaliteitsland* (Groningen, 1948).

—— *De Zeven Provinciën* (Haarlemse Voordrachten, 13; Haarlem, 1954).

—— 'De Acte van Navigatie en de Vrede van Breda', *BGN* 4 (1949), 27–65.

WINTLE, M., 'De economie van Zeeland in 1808', *Archief Koninklijk Zeeuwsch Genootschap der Wetenschappen* (1985), 97–136.

WIT, C. H. E. DE, *De strijd tussen aristocratie en democratie in Nederland 1780–1848* (Heerlen, 1965).

—— *De Nederlandse revolutie van de achttiende eeuw* (Oirsbeek, 1974).

WIT, H. F. DE, *Gorcums heren. Regenten politiek 1650–1750* (Gorcum, 1981).

WOLTJER, J. J., *Friesland in hervormingstijd* (Leiden, 1962).

—— *De Leidse universiteit in verleden en heden* (Leiden, 1965).

—— 'De politieke betekenis van de Emdense synode', in D. Nauta *et al.* (eds.), *De Synode van Emden. Oktober 1571* (Kampen, 1971), 22–49.

—— 'Dutch Privileges, Real and Imaginary', *BN* 5 (1975), 19–35.

—— *Kleine oorzaken, grote gevolgen* (Leiden, 1975).

—— 'De Vrede-makers', *TvG* 89 (1976), 299–312.

—— 'Wisselende gestalten van de Unie', in S. Groenveld and H. L. P. Leeuwenberg (eds.), *De Unie van Utrecht* (The Hague, 1979), 88–101.

—— 'Willem III en Leiden', in Marsilje *et al.* (eds.), *Uit Leidse bron geleverd*, 417–31.

WORP, J. A., 'Dirk Rodenburg', *Oud-Holland*, 13 (1895), 65–89, 143–73, 209–37.

—— *Geschiedenis van het drama en van het toneel in Nederland* (2 vols.; Rotterdam, 1903).

WOUDE, A. M. VAN DER, *Het Noorderkwartier* (3 vols.; Wageningen, 1972).

—— 'Demografische ontwikkeling van de Noordelijke Nederlanden, 1500–1800', in *NAGN* 5, 102–68.

—— 'Onderwijs en opvoeding (1500–1800), in *NAGN* vii. 256–63.

—— 'De Schilderijproduktie in Holland tijdens de Republiek', in J. C. Dagevos *et al.* (eds.), *Kunst-zaken. Particulier initiatief en overheidsbeleid in de beeldende Kunst* (The Hague, 1991), 7–10.

WOUDE, C. VAN DER, *Hugo Grotius en zijn Pietas Ordinum Hollandiae ac Westfrisiae vindicata* (Kampen, 1961).

—— *Sibrandus Lubbertus* (Kampen, 1963).

YPEIJ, A., and DERMOUT, J. J., *Geschiedenis der Nederlandsche Hervormde Kerk* (6 vols; Breda, 1819–27).

YSSELSTEIN, G. T., *Van linnen en linnenkasten* (Amsterdam, 1946).

—— *Geschiedenis der tapijtweverijen in de Noordelijke Nederlanden* (2 vols.; Leiden, 1936).

ZANDEN, J. L. VAN, 'De economie van Holland: de periode 1650–1805: groei of achteruitgang?', *BMGN* 102 (1987), 562–609.

—— 'De prijs van de vooruitgang?', *EHJ* 51 (1988), 80–92.

—— 'Op zoek naar de "missing link" ', *TvSG* 51 (1988), 359–86.

—— *The Rise and Decline of Holland's Economy* (Manchester, 1993).

ZIJLSTRA, S., ' "Tgeloove is vrij". De tolerantiediscussie in de Noordelijke Nederlanden tussen 1620 and 1795', in M. Gijswijt-Hofstra (ed.), *Een schijn van verdraagzaamheid* (Hilversum, 1989), 41–68.

ZIJP, A., *De strijd tusschen de Staten van Gelderland en het Hof, 1543–1566* (Arnhem, 1913).

ZIJP, R. P., 'Spiritualisme in de 16e eeuw, een schets', in *Ketters en papen onder Filips II*, exhibition catalogue of the Rijksmuseum Het Catharijneconvent, Utrecht (The Hague, 1986), 75–93.

ZIJPP, N. VAN DER., *Geschiedenis der doopsgezinden in Nederland* (Arnhem, 1952).

ZILVERBERG, S. B. J., 'Lancelot van Brederode en zijn geschrift "Van de Apostatie" ', *NAK* 50 (1969/70), 230–43.

ZWITSER, H. L., 'Het quotenstelsel onder de Republiek der Verenigde Nederlanden', *Mededelingen van de Sectie Militaire Geschiedenis Landmachtstaf*, 5 (1982), 5–57.
—— '*De Militie van den staat*' (Amsterdam, 1991).

INDEX